FOURTH EDITION

Learning Java

Patrick Niemeyer and Daniel Leuck

O'REILLY®

Beijing • Cambridge • Farnham • Köln • Sebastopol • Tokyo

Learning Java, Fourth Edition

by Patrick Niemeyer and Daniel Leuck

Printed in the United States of America.

Published by O'Reilly Media, Inc., 1005 Gravenstein Highway North, Sebastopol, CA 95472.

O'Reilly books may be purchased for educational, business, or sales promotional use. Online editions are also available for most titles (*http://my.safaribooksonline.com*). For more information, contact our corporate/institutional sales department: 800-998-9938 or *corporate@oreilly.com*.

Editors: Mike Loukides and Meghan Blanchette
Production Editor: Rachel Steely
Copyeditor: Gillian McGarvey
Proofreader: Rachel Monaghan
Indexer: BIM Publishing Services, Inc.
Cover Designer: Randy Comer
Interior Designer: David Futato
Illustrators: Robert Romano and Rebecca Demarest

June 2013: Fourth Edition

Revision History for the Fourth Edition:

2013-06-06: First release

See *http://oreilly.com/catalog/errata.csp?isbn=9781449319243* for release details.

ISBN: 978-1-449-31924-3

[LSI]

Table of Contents

Preface

This book is about the Java programming language and environment. Whether you are a software developer or just someone who uses the Internet in your daily life, you've undoubtedly heard about Java. Its introduction was one of the most exciting developments in the history of the Web and Java applications have powered much of the growth of business on the Internet in the past 15 years. Java is, arguably, the most popular programming language in the world, used by millions of developers on almost every kind of computer imaginable. In the past decade, Java has surpassed languages such as C++ and Visual Basic in terms of developer demand and has become the de facto language for certain kinds of development—especially for web-based services. Most universities are now using Java in their introductory courses alongside the other important modern languages. Perhaps you are using this text in one of your classes right now!

This book gives you a thorough grounding in Java fundamentals and APIs. *Learning Java*, Fourth Edition, attempts to live up to its name by mapping out the Java language and its class libraries, programming techniques, and idioms. We'll dig deep into interesting areas and at least scratch the surface of the rest. Other titles from O'Reilly pick up where we leave off and provide more comprehensive information on specific areas and applications of Java.

Whenever possible, we provide compelling, realistic, and fun examples and avoid merely cataloging features. The examples are simple, but hint at what can be done. We won't be developing the next great "killer app" in these pages, but we hope to give you a starting point for many hours of experimentation and inspired tinkering that will lead you to develop one yourself.

Who Should Read This Book

This book is for computer professionals, students, technical people, and Finnish hackers. It's for everyone who has a need for hands-on experience with the Java language with an eye toward building real applications. This book could also be considered a crash course in object-oriented programming, networking, GUIs, and XML. As you learn about Java, you'll also learn a powerful and practical approach to software development, beginning with a deep understanding of the fundamentals of Java and its APIs.

Superficially, Java looks like C or C++, so you'll have a tiny head start in using this book if you have some experience with one of these languages. If you do not, don't worry. Don't make too much of the syntactic similarities between Java and C or C++. In many respects, Java acts like more dynamic languages such as Smalltalk and Lisp. Knowledge of another object-oriented programming language should certainly help, although you may have to change some ideas and unlearn a few habits. Java is considerably simpler than languages such as C++ and Smalltalk. If you learn well from concise examples and personal experimentation, we think you'll like this book.

The last part of this book branches out to discuss Java in the context of web applications, web services, and XML processing, so you should be familiar with the basic ideas behind web browsers, servers, and documents.

New Developments

This edition of *Learning Java* is actually the sixth edition—updated and retitled—of our original, popular *Exploring Java*. With each edition, we've taken great care not only to add new material covering additional features, but to thoroughly revise and update the existing content to synthesize the coverage and add years of real-world perspective and experience to these pages.

One noticeable change in recent editions is that we've deemphasized the use of applets, reflecting their diminished role in recent years in creating interactive web pages. In contrast, we've greatly expanded our coverage of Java web applications, web services, and XML, which are now mature technologies.

We cover all of the important features of the latest release of Java, officially called Java Standard Edition (SE) 7, JDK 1.7. Sun (Java's keeper before Oracle) has changed the naming scheme many times over the years. Sun coined the term *Java 2* to cover the major new features introduced in Java version 1.2 and dropped the term *JDK* in favor of *SDK*. With the sixth release, Sun skipped from Java version 1.4 to Java 5.0, but reprieved the term JDK and kept its numbering convention there. After that, we had Java 6 and now we reach Java 7.

This release of Java reflects a mature language with relatively few syntactic changes but significant updates to APIs and libraries. We've tried to capture these new features and update every example in this book to reflect not only the current Java practice, but style as well.

New in This Edition (Java 6 and 7)

This edition of the book has been significantly reworked to be as complete and up-to-date as possible. It incorporates changes from both the Java 6 and Java 7 releases that occurred since the last edition of this book. New topics in this edition include:

- New language features, including type inference in generics and improved exception handling and automatic resource management syntax
- New concurrency utilities including the Fork-Join framework
- The new NIO Files API, which allows new types of filesystem access to be implemented in Java
- New versions of the Java Servlets (3.0) and web services APIs, including use of the new annotations-based deployment and built-in web service container
- New version of JAXB (2.2) Java XML Binding, including use of the new annotations for binding Java to XML
- Improved Swing desktop integration and enhancements to key Swing components such as JTable
- Updated examples and analysis throughout the book

Using This Book

This book is organized roughly as follows:

- Chapters 1 and 2 provide a basic introduction to Java concepts and a tutorial to give you a jump start on Java programming.
- Chapter 3 discusses fundamental tools for developing with Java (the compiler, the interpreter, and the JAR file package).
- Chapters 4 through 7 describe the Java language itself, beginning with the basic syntax and then covering classes and objects, exceptions, arrays, enumerations, annotations, and much more.
- Chapter 8 covers generics and parameterized types in Java.
- Chapter 9 covers the language's built-in thread facilities and the Java Concurrency package, which should be of particular interest to advanced programmers.
- Chapter 10 covers text processing, formatting, scanning, string utilities, and the powerful regular expressions API.
- Chapter 11 covers much of the core API including utilities and collections.
- Chapter 12 covers Java I/O, streams, files, and the NIO package.

- Chapters 13 and 14 cover Java networking, including sockets and NIO, URLs, and RMI.
- Chapter 15 covers web applications using servlets, servlet filters, and WAR files, as well as web services.
- Chapters 16 through 21 cover GUI development with the Abstract Window Toolkit (AWT) and Swing, which provide graphical user interface (GUI) and image support.
- Chapter 22 covers the JavaBeans component architecture and introduces the NetBeans IDE.
- Chapter 23 covers applets.
- Chapter 24 covers the Java APIs for working with XML and XSLT, including XML Schema, validation, XPath, and XInclude, as well as XML binding with JAXB.
- Appendix A covers using the Eclipse IDE with the examples in this book.
- Appendix B describes BeanShell, a lightweight scripting language for Java developed by the authors of this book.

If you're like us, you don't read books from front to back. If you're really like us, you usually don't read the Preface at all. However, on the off chance that you will see this in time, here are a few suggestions:

- If you are an experienced programmer who has to learn Java in the next five minutes, you are probably looking for the examples. You might want to start by glancing at the tutorial in Chapter 2. If that doesn't float your boat, you should at least look at the information in Chapter 3, which explains how to use the compiler and interpreter, or Appendix A, which shows how to run the examples in the Eclipse IDE. This should get you started.
- Chapters 12 through 15 are essential if you are interested in writing advanced networked or web-based applications and services. This is one of the more interesting and important parts of Java.
- Chapters 16 through 22 discuss Java's graphics features and component architecture. You should read this if you are interested in writing graphical Java applications or applets.
- Chapter 24 covers the Java APIs for working with XML, including SAX, DOM, DTDs, XML Schema, and using XSL to render output for the Web. XML technology is becoming key to cross-platform development.

Online Resources

There are many online sources for information about Java. Oracle's official website for Java topics is *http://java.sun.com*; look here for the software, updates, and Java releases. This is where you'll find the JDK, which includes the compiler, the interpreter, and other tools.

You should also visit O'Reilly's Java site at *http://oreilly.com/java*. There you'll find information about other O'Reilly Java books, and a pointer to the home page for *Learning Java*, *http://oreil.ly/Java_4E*, where you'll find the source code examples for this book.

Conventions Used in This Book

The font conventions used in this book are quite simple.

Italic is used for:

- Unix pathnames, filenames, and program names
- Internet addresses, such as domain names and URLs
- New terms where they are defined
- Program names, compilers, interpreters, utilities, and commands
- Threads

`Constant width` is used for:

- Anything that might appear in a Java program, including method names, variable names, and class names
- Tags that might appear in an HTML or XML document
- Keywords, objects, and environment variables

`Constant width bold` is used for:

- Text that is typed by the user on the command line

`Constant width italic` is used for:

- Replaceable items in code

This icon designates a note, which is an important aside to the nearby text.

This icon designates a warning relating to the nearby text.

In the main body of text, we always use a pair of empty parentheses after a method name to distinguish methods from variables and other creatures.

In the Java source listings, we follow the coding conventions most frequently used in the Java community. Class names begin with capital letters; variable and method names begin with lowercase. All the letters in the names of constants are capitalized. We don't use underscores to separate words in a long name; following common practice, we capitalize individual words (after the first) and run the words together. For example: `thisIsAVariable`, `thisIsAMethod()`, `ThisIsAClass`, and `THISISACONSTANT`. Also, note that we differentiate between static and nonstatic methods when we refer to them. Unlike some books, we never write `Foo.bar()` to mean the `bar()` method of `Foo` unless `bar()` is a static method (paralleling the Java syntax in that case).

Using Code Examples

This book is here to help you get your job done. In general, if this book includes code examples, you may use the code in your programs and documentation. You do not need to contact us for permission unless you're reproducing a significant portion of the code. For example, writing a program that uses several chunks of code from this book does not require permission. Selling or distributing a CD-ROM of examples from O'Reilly books does require permission. Answering a question by citing this book and quoting example code does not require permission. Incorporating a significant amount of example code from this book into your product's documentation does require permission.

We appreciate, but do not require, attribution. An attribution usually includes the title, author, publisher, and ISBN. For example: "*Learning Java*, Fourth Edition, by Patrick Niemeyer and Daniel Leuck. Copyright 2013 Patrick Niemeyer and Daniel Leuck, 978-1-449-31924-3."

If you feel your use of code examples falls outside fair use or the permission given above, feel free to contact us at *permissions@oreilly.com*.

Safari® Books Online

Safari Books Online (*www.safaribooksonline.com*) is an on-demand digital library that delivers expert content in both book and video form from the world's leading authors in technology and business.

Technology professionals, software developers, web designers, and business and creative professionals use Safari Books Online as their primary resource for research, problem solving, learning, and certification training.

Safari Books Online offers a range of product mixes and pricing programs for organizations, government agencies, and individuals. Subscribers have access to thousands of books, training videos, and prepublication manuscripts in one fully searchable database from publishers like O'Reilly Media, Prentice Hall Professional, Addison-Wesley Professional, Microsoft Press, Sams, Que, Peachpit Press, Focal Press, Cisco Press, John Wiley & Sons, Syngress, Morgan Kaufmann, IBM Redbooks, Packt, Adobe Press, FT Press, Apress, Manning, New Riders, McGraw-Hill, Jones & Bartlett, Course Technology, and dozens more. For more information about Safari Books Online, please visit us online.

How to Contact Us

Please address comments and questions concerning this book to the publisher:

O'Reilly Media, Inc.
1005 Gravenstein Highway North
Sebastopol, CA 95472
800-998-9938 (in the United States or Canada)
707-829-0515 (international or local)
707-829-0104 (fax)

We have a web page for this book, where we list errata, examples, and any additional information. You can access this page at *http://oreil.ly/Java_4E*.

To comment or ask technical questions about this book, send email to *bookquestions@oreilly.com*.

For more information about our books, courses, conferences, and news, see our website at *http://www.oreilly.com*.

Find us on Facebook: *http://facebook.com/oreilly*

Follow us on Twitter: *http://twitter.com/oreillymedia*

Watch us on YouTube: *http://www.youtube.com/oreillymedia*

Acknowledgments

Many people have contributed to putting this book together, both in its *Exploring Java* incarnation and in its current form as *Learning Java*. Foremost, we would like to thank Tim O'Reilly for giving us the opportunity to write this book. Thanks to Mike Loukides, the series editor, whose patience and experience helped us get started on this journey. Thanks to Paula Ferguson and John Posner, who contributed their organizational and editing abilities at various times. And a special thanks to Deb Cameron, the tireless editor of this book, without whom the previous two editions might never have been finished and certainly wouldn't have resembled English. We could not have asked for a more skillful or responsive team of people with whom to work.

Speaking of borrowings, the original version of the glossary came from David Flanagan's book *Java in a Nutshell* (O'Reilly). We also borrowed several class hierarchy diagrams from David's book. These diagrams were based on similar diagrams by Charles L. Perkins.

Thanks also to Marc Wallace and Steven Burkett for reading the original work in progress and for the support of our friends at Washington University: Bryan O'Connor and Brian Gottlieb. Thanks also to Josh Peck, coauthor of the original book, *Exploring Java*. Thanks to all those who reviewed or answered questions: David Flanagan for generics; Henry Wong for the concurrency utilities; Jim Elliott, Marc Loy, and Brian Cole for Swing; Jack Shirazi for NIO; Tim Boudreau for NetBeans; Martin Aeschlimann, Jim Farley, and John Norman for Eclipse; Ed Howland for XML; and Ian Darwin for regular expressions. (Check out Ian's *Java Cookbook* [O'Reilly] for more examples.) Thanks also to Ray O'Leary, Mario Aquino, and Mark Volkmann for their reviews. And finally, thanks to my beautiful wife, Ellen Song, for putting up with me through all this work.

CHAPTER 1
A Modern Language

The greatest challenges and most exciting opportunities for software developers today lie in harnessing the power of networks. Applications created today, whatever their intended scope or audience, will almost certainly run on machines linked by a global network of computing resources. The increasing importance of networks is placing new demands on existing tools and fueling the demand for a rapidly growing list of completely new kinds of applications.

We want software that works—consistently, anywhere, on any platform—and that plays well with other applications. We want dynamic applications that take advantage of a connected world, capable of accessing disparate and distributed information sources. We want truly distributed software that can be extended and upgraded seamlessly. We want intelligent applications that can roam the Net for us, ferreting out information and serving as electronic emissaries. We have known for some time what kind of software we want, but it is really only in the past few years that we have begun to get it.

The problem, historically, has been that the tools for building these applications have fallen short. The requirements of speed and portability have been, for the most part, mutually exclusive, and security has been largely ignored or misunderstood. In the past, truly portable languages were bulky, interpreted, and slow. These languages were popular as much for their high-level functionality as for their portability. Fast languages usually provided speed by binding themselves to particular platforms, so they met the portability issue only halfway. There were even a few safe languages, but they were primarily offshoots of the portable languages and suffered from the same problems. Java is a modern language that addresses all three of these fronts: portability, speed, and security. This is why it has been a dominant language in the world of programming for more than a decade and a half.

Enter Java

The Java programming language, developed at Sun Microsystems under the guidance of Net luminaries James Gosling and Bill Joy, was designed to be a machine-independent programming language that is both safe enough to traverse networks and powerful enough to replace native executable code. Java addresses the issues raised here and played a starring role in the growth of the Internet, leading to where we are today.

Initially, most of the enthusiasm for Java centered on its capabilities for building embedded applications for the Web called *applets*. But in the early days, applets and other client-side GUI applications written in Java were limited. Today, Java has Swing, one of the most sophisticated toolkits for building graphical user interfaces (GUIs) in any language. This development has allowed Java to become a popular platform for developing traditional client-side application software.

Of even more importance, however, Java has become the premier platform for web-based applications and web services. These applications use technologies including the Java Servlet API, Java web services, and many popular open source and commercial Java application servers and frameworks. Java's portability and speed make it the platform of choice for modern business applications. Java servers running on open source Linux platforms are at the heart of the business and financial world today.

This book will show you how to use Java to accomplish real-world programming tasks. In the coming chapters we'll cover everything from text processing to networking, building rich client-side GUI applications with Swing and lightweight web-based applications and services.

Java's Origins

The seeds of Java were planted in 1990 by Sun Microsystems patriarch and chief researcher Bill Joy. At the time, Sun was competing in a relatively small workstation market while Microsoft was beginning its domination of the more mainstream, Intel-based PC world. When Sun missed the boat on the PC revolution, Joy retreated to Aspen, Colorado, to work on advanced research. He was committed to the idea of accomplishing complex tasks with simple software and founded the aptly named Sun Aspen Smallworks.

Of the original members of the small team of programmers assembled in Aspen, James Gosling will be remembered as the father of Java. Gosling first made a name for himself in the early 80s as the author of Gosling Emacs, the first version of the popular Emacs editor that was written in C and ran under Unix. Gosling Emacs became popular but was soon eclipsed by a free version, GNU Emacs, written by Emacs's original designer. By that time, Gosling had moved on to design Sun's NeWS, which briefly contended with the X Window System for control of the Unix GUI desktop in 1987. Although some people would argue that NeWS was superior to X, NeWS lost because Sun kept it proprietary and didn't publish source code while the primary developers of X formed the X Consortium and took the opposite approach.

Designing NeWS taught Gosling the power of integrating an expressive language with a network-aware windowing GUI. It also taught Sun that the Internet programming community will ultimately refuse to accept proprietary standards, no matter how good they may be. The seeds of Java's licensing scheme and open (if not quite "open source") code were sown by NeWS's failure. Gosling brought what he had learned to Bill Joy's nascent Aspen project. In 1992, work on the project led to the founding of the Sun subsidiary FirstPerson, Inc. Its mission was to lead Sun into the world of consumer electronics.

The FirstPerson team worked on developing software for information appliances, such as cellular phones and personal digital assistants (PDAs). The goal was to enable the transfer of information and real-time applications over cheap infrared and traditional packet-based networks. Memory and bandwidth limitations dictated small, efficient code. The nature of the applications also demanded they be safe and robust. Gosling and his teammates began programming in C++, but they soon found themselves confounded by a language that was too complex, unwieldy, and insecure for the task. They decided to start from scratch, and Gosling began working on something he dubbed "C++ minus minus."

With the foundering of the Apple Newton (Apple's earliest handheld computer), it became apparent that the PDA's ship had not yet come in, so Sun shifted FirstPerson's efforts to interactive TV (ITV). The programming language of choice for ITV set-top boxes was to be the near ancestor of Java, a language called Oak. Even with its elegance and ability to provide safe interactivity, Oak could not salvage the lost cause of ITV at that time. Customers didn't want it, and Sun soon abandoned the concept.

At that time, Joy and Gosling got together to decide on a new strategy for their innovative language. It was 1993, and the explosion of interest in the Web presented a new opportunity. Oak was small, safe, architecture-independent, and object-oriented. As it happens, these are also some of the requirements for a universal, Internet-savvy programming language. Sun quickly changed focus, and, with a little retooling, Oak became Java.

Growing Up

It would not be overstating it to say that Java caught on like wildfire. Even before its first official release when Java was still a nonproduct, nearly every major industry player had jumped on the Java bandwagon. Java licensees included Microsoft, Intel, IBM, and virtually all major hardware and software vendors. However, even with all this support Java took a lot of knocks and experienced some growing pains during its first few years.

A series of breach of contract and antitrust lawsuits between Sun and Microsoft over the distribution of Java and its use in Internet Explorer hampered its deployment on the world's most common desktop operating system—Windows. Microsoft's involvement with Java also become one focus of a larger federal lawsuit over serious anticompetitive practices at the company, with court testimony revealing concerted efforts by the software giant to undermine Java by introducing incompatibilities in its version of the language. Meanwhile, Microsoft introduced its own Java-derived language called C# (C-sharp) as part of its .NET initiative and dropped Java from inclusion in Windows. C# has gone on to become a very good language in its own right, enjoying more innovation in recent years than has Java.

But Java continues to spread on a wide variety of platforms. As we begin looking at the Java architecture, you'll see that much of what is exciting about Java comes from the self-contained, virtual machine environment in which Java applications run. Java was carefully designed so that this supporting architecture can be implemented either in software, for existing computer platforms, or in customized hardware. Hardware implementations of Java are used in some smart cards and other embedded systems. You can even buy "wearable" devices, such as rings and dog tags, that have Java interpreters embedded in them. Software implementations of Java are available for all modern computer platforms down to portable computing devices. Today, an offshoot of the Java platform is the basis for Google's Android operating system that powers billions of phones and other mobile devices.

In 2010, Oracle corporation bought Sun Microsystems and became the steward of the Java language. In a somewhat rocky start to its tenure, Oracle sued Google over its use of the Java language in Android and lost. In July of 2011, Oracle released Java SE 7, a significant Java release.

A Virtual Machine

Java is both a compiled and an interpreted language. Java source code is turned into simple binary instructions, much like ordinary microprocessor machine code. However, whereas C or C++ source is reduced to native instructions for a particular model of processor, Java source is compiled into a universal format—instructions for a *virtual machine.*

Compiled Java *bytecode* is executed by a Java runtime interpreter. The runtime system performs all the normal activities of a hardware processor, but it does so in a safe, virtual environment. It executes a stack-based instruction set and manages memory like an operating system. It creates and manipulates primitive data types and loads and invokes newly referenced blocks of code. Most importantly, it does all this in accordance with a strictly defined open specification that can be implemented by anyone who wants to produce a Java-compliant virtual machine. Together, the virtual machine and language definition provide a complete specification. There are no features of the base Java language left undefined or implementation-dependent. For example, Java specifies the sizes and mathematical properties of all its primitive data types rather than leaving it up to the platform implementation.

The Java interpreter is relatively lightweight and small; it can be implemented in whatever form is desirable for a particular platform. The interpreter may be run as a separate application or it can be embedded in another piece of software, such as a web browser. Put together, this means that Java code is implicitly portable. The same Java application bytecode can run on any platform that provides a Java runtime environment, as shown in Figure 1-1. You don't have to produce alternative versions of your application for different platforms, and you don't have to distribute source code to end users.

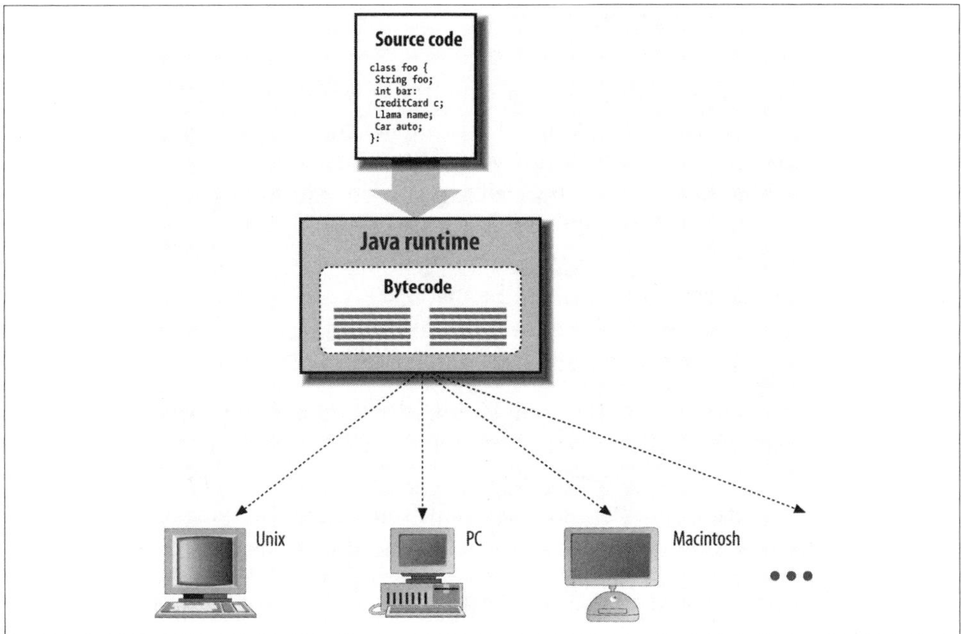

Figure 1-1. The Java runtime environment

The fundamental unit of Java code is the *class*. As in other object-oriented languages, classes are application components that hold executable code and data. Compiled Java classes are distributed in a universal binary format that contains Java bytecode and other class information. Classes can be maintained discretely and stored in files or archives locally or on a network server. Classes are located and loaded dynamically at runtime as they are needed by an application.

In addition to the platform-specific runtime system, Java has a number of fundamental classes that contain architecture-dependent methods. These *native methods* serve as the gateway between the Java virtual machine and the real world. They are implemented in a natively compiled language on the host platform and provide low-level access to resources such as the network, the windowing system, and the host filesystem. The vast majority of Java, however, is written in Java itself—bootstrapped from these basic primitives—and is therefore portable. This includes fundamental Java tools such as the Java compiler, networking, and GUI libraries, which are also written in Java and are therefore available on all Java platforms in exactly the same way without porting.

Historically, interpreters have been considered slow, but Java is not a traditional interpreted language. In addition to compiling source code down to portable bytecode, Java has also been carefully designed so that software implementations of the runtime system can further optimize their performance by compiling bytecode to native machine code on the fly. This is called just-in-time (JIT) or dynamic compilation. With JIT compilation, Java code can execute as fast as native code and maintain its transportability and security.

This is an often misunderstood point among those who want to compare language performance. There is only one intrinsic performance penalty that compiled Java code suffers at runtime for the sake of security and virtual machine design—array bounds checking. Everything else can be optimized to native code just as it can with a statically compiled language. Going beyond that, the Java language includes more structural information than many other languages, providing for more types of optimizations. Also remember that these optimizations can be made at runtime, taking into account the actual application behavior and characteristics. What can be done at compile time that can't be done better at runtime? Well, there is a tradeoff: time.

The problem with a traditional JIT compilation is that optimizing code takes time. So a JIT compiler can produce decent results, but may suffer a significant latency when the application starts up. This is generally not a problem for long-running server-side applications, but is a serious problem for client-side software and applications that run on smaller devices with limited capabilities. To address this, Java's compiler technology, called HotSpot, uses a trick called *adaptive compilation*. If you look at what programs actually spend their time doing, it turns out that they spend almost all their time executing a relatively small part of the code again and again. The chunk of code that is executed repeatedly may be only a small fraction of the total program, but its behavior determines the program's overall performance. Adaptive compilation also allows the Java runtime to take advantage of new kinds of optimizations that simply can't be done in a statically compiled language, hence the claim that Java code can run faster than C/C++ in some cases.

To take advantage of this fact, HotSpot starts out as a normal Java bytecode interpreter, but with a difference: it measures (profiles) the code as it is executing to see what parts are being executed repeatedly. Once it knows which parts of the code are crucial to performance, HotSpot compiles those sections into optimal native machine code. Since it compiles only a small portion of the program into machine code, it can afford to take the time necessary to optimize those portions. The rest of the program may not need to be compiled at all—just interpreted—saving memory and time. In fact, the Java VM can run in one of two modes: client and server, which determine whether it emphasizes quick startup time and memory conservation or flat out performance.

A natural question to ask at this point is, Why throw away all this good profiling information each time an application shuts down? Well, Sun partially broached this topic with the release of Java 5.0 through the use of shared, read-only classes that are stored persistently in an optimized form. This significantly reduced both the startup time and overhead of running many Java applications on a given machine. The technology for doing this is complex, but the idea is simple: optimize the parts of the program that need to go fast and don't worry about the rest.

Java Compared with Other Languages

Java draws on many years of programming experience with other languages in its choice of features. It is worth taking a moment to compare Java at a high level with some other languages, both for the benefit of those of you with other programming experience and for the newcomers who need to put things in context. We do not expect you to have a knowledge of any particular programming language in this book and when we refer to other languages by way of comparison, we hope that the comments are self-explanatory.

At least three pillars are necessary to support a universal programming language today: portability, speed, and security. Figure 1-2 shows how Java compares to a a few of the languages that were popular when it was created.

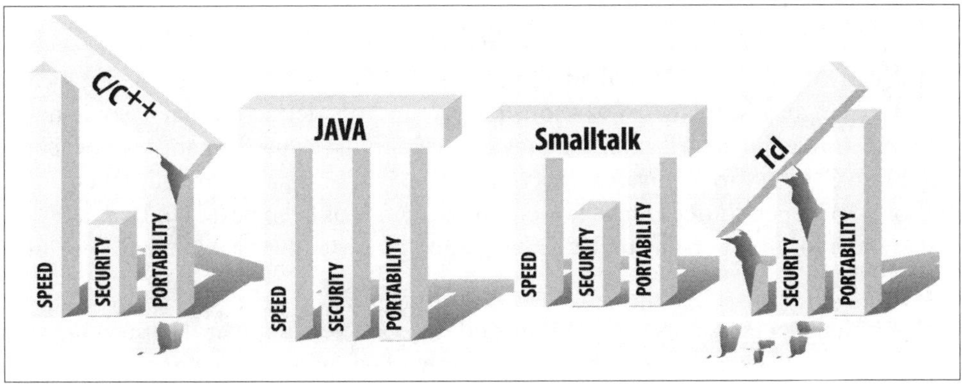

Figure 1-2. Programming languages compared

You may have heard that Java is a lot like C or C++, but that's really not true except at a superficial level. When you first look at Java code, you'll see that the basic syntax looks like C or C++. But that's where the similarities end. Java is by no means a direct descendant of C or a next-generation C++. If you compare language features, you'll see that Java actually has more in common with highly dynamic languages such as Smalltalk and Lisp. In fact, Java's implementation is about as far from native C as you can imagine.

If you are familiar with the current language landscape, you will notice that C#, a popular language, is missing from this comparison. C# is largely Microsoft's answer to Java, admittedly with a number of niceties layered on top. Given their common design goals and approach (e.g., use of a virtual machine, bytecode, sandbox, etc.), the platforms don't differ substantially in terms of their speed or security characteristics. C# is theoretically as portable as Java, but to date it is supported on far fewer platforms. Like Java, C# borrows heavily from C syntax but is really a closer relative of the dynamic languages. Most Java developers find it relatively easy to pick up C# and vice versa. The majority of time spent moving from one to the other is learning the standard library.

The surface-level similarities to these languages are worth noting, however. Java borrows heavily from C and C++ syntax, so you'll see terse language constructs, including an abundance of curly braces and semicolons. Java subscribes to the C philosophy that a good language should be compact; in other words, it should be sufficiently small and regular so a programmer can hold all the language's capabilities in his or her head at once. Just as C is extensible with libraries, packages of Java classes can be added to the core language components to extend its vocabulary.

C has been successful because it provides a reasonably feature-packed programming environment, with high performance and an acceptable degree of portability. Java also tries to balance functionality, speed, and portability, but it does so in a very different way. C trades functionality for portability; Java initially traded speed for portability. Java also addresses security issues that C does not (although in modern systems many of those concerns are now addressed in the operating system and hardware).

In the early days before JIT and adaptive compilation, Java was slower than statically compiled languages and there was a constant refrain from detractors that it would never catch up. But as we described in the previous section, Java's performance is now comparable to C or C++ for equivalent tasks and those criticisms have generally fallen quiet. ID Software's open source Quake2 video game engine has been ported to Java. If Java is fast enough for first-person combat video games, it's certainly fast enough for business applications.

Scripting languages such as Perl, Python, and Ruby are very popular. There's no reason a scripting language can't be suitable for safe, networked applications. But most scripting languages are not well suited for serious, large-scale programming. The attraction to scripting languages is that they are dynamic; they are powerful tools for rapid development. Some scripting languages such as Perl also provide powerful tools for text-processing tasks that more general-purpose languages find unwieldy. Scripting languages are also highly portable, albeit at the source code level.

Not to be confused with Java, JavaScript is an object-based scripting language originally developed by Netscape for the web browser. It serves as a web browser resident language for dynamic, interactive web-based applications. JavaScript takes its name from its integration with and similarities to Java, but the comparison really ends there. While there have been applications of JavaScript outside of the browser, it has not truly caught on as a general scripting language. For more information on JavaScript, check out *JavaScript: The Definitive Guide* by David Flanagan (O'Reilly).

The problem with scripting languages is that they are rather casual about program structure and data typing. Most scripting languages (with a hesitant exception for Python and later versions of Perl) are not object-oriented. They also have simplified type systems and generally don't provide for sophisticated scoping of variables and functions. These characteristics make them less suitable for building large, modular applications. Speed is another problem with scripting languages; the high-level, usually source-interpreted nature of these languages often makes them quite slow.

Advocates of individual scripting languages would take issue with some of these generalizations, and no doubt they'd be right in some cases. Scripting languages have improved in recent years—especially JavaScript, which has had an enormous amount of research poured into its performance. But the fundamental tradeoff is undeniable: scripting languages were born as loose, less structured alternatives to systems programming languages and are generally not ideal for large or complex projects for a variety of reasons, at least not today.

Java offers some of the essential advantages of a scripting language: it is highly dynamic, along with the added benefits of a lower-level language. Java has a powerful Regular Expression API that competes with Perl for working with text and language features that streamline coding with collections, variable argument lists, static imports of methods, and other syntactic sugar that make it more concise.

Incremental development with object-oriented components, combined with Java's simplicity, make it possible to develop applications rapidly and change them easily. Studies have found that development in Java is faster than in C or C++, strictly based on language features.[1] Java also comes with a large base of standard core classes for common tasks such as building GUIs and handling network communications. But along with these features, Java has the scalability and software-engineering advantages of more static languages. It provides a safe structure on which to build higher-level frameworks (and even other languages).

As we've already said, Java is similar in design to languages such as Smalltalk and Lisp. However, these languages were used mostly as research vehicles rather than for

1. See, for example, G. Phipps, "Comparing Observed Bug and Productivity Rates for Java and C++," (*http://bit.ly/10LPGOE*)*Software—Practice & Experience*, volume 29, 1999.

development of large-scale systems. One reason is that these languages never developed a standard portable binding to operating system services, such as the C standard library or the Java core classes. Smalltalk is compiled to an interpreted bytecode format, and it can be dynamically compiled to native code on the fly, just like Java. But Java improves on the design by using a bytecode verifier to ensure the correctness of compiled Java code. This verifier gives Java a performance advantage over Smalltalk because Java code requires fewer runtime checks. Java's bytecode verifier also helps with security issues, something that Smalltalk doesn't address.

Throughout the rest of this chapter, we'll present a bird's-eye view of the Java language. We'll explain what's new and what's not-so-new about Java and why.

Safety of Design

You have no doubt heard a lot about the fact that Java is designed to be a safe language. But what do we mean by safe? Safe from what or whom? The security features that attract the most attention for Java are those features that make possible new types of dynamically portable software. Java provides several layers of protection from dangerously flawed code as well as more mischievous things such as viruses and Trojan horses. In the next section, we'll take a look at how the Java virtual machine architecture assesses the safety of code before it's run and how the Java *class loader* (the bytecode loading mechanism of the Java interpreter) builds a wall around untrusted classes. These features provide the foundation for high-level security policies that can allow or disallow various kinds of activities on an application-by-application basis.

In this section, though, we'll look at some general features of the Java programming language. Perhaps more important than the specific security features, although often overlooked in the security din, is the safety that Java provides by addressing common design and programming problems. Java is intended to be as safe as possible from the simple mistakes we make ourselves as well as those we inherit from legacy software. The goal with Java has been to keep the language simple, provide tools that have demonstrated their usefulness, and let users build more complicated facilities on top of the language when needed.

Simplify, Simplify, Simplify...

With Java, simplicity rules. Since Java started with a clean slate, it was able to avoid features that proved to be messy or controversial in other languages. For example, Java doesn't allow programmer-defined operator overloading (which in some languages allows programmers to redefine the meaning of basic symbols like + and –). Java doesn't have a source code preprocessor, so it doesn't have things like macros, `#define` statements, or conditional source compilation. These constructs exist in other languages primarily to support platform dependencies, so in that sense, they should not be needed in Java. Conditional compilation is also commonly used for debugging, but Java's sophisticated runtime optimizations and features such as *assertions* solve the problem more elegantly (we'll cover these in Chapter 4).

Java provides a well-defined *package* structure for organizing class files. The package system allows the compiler to handle some of the functionality of the traditional *make* utility (a tool for building executables from source code). The compiler can also work with compiled Java classes directly because all type information is preserved; there is no need for extraneous source "header" files, as in C/C++. All this means that Java code requires less context to read. Indeed, you may sometimes find it faster to look at the Java source code than to refer to class documentation.

Java also takes a different approach to some structural features that have been troublesome in other languages. For example, Java supports only a single inheritance class hierarchy (each class may have only one "parent" class), but allows multiple inheritance of interfaces. An *interface*, like an abstract class in C++, specifies the behavior of an object without defining its implementation. It is a very powerful mechanism that allows the developer to define a "contract" for object behavior that can be used and referred to independently of any particular object implementation. Interfaces in Java eliminate the need for multiple inheritance of classes and the associated problems.

As you'll see in Chapter 4, Java is a fairly simple and elegant programming language and that is still a large part of its appeal.

Type Safety and Method Binding

One attribute of a language is the kind of *type checking* it uses. Generally, languages are categorized as *static* or *dynamic*, which refers to the amount of information about variables known at compile time versus what is known while the application is running.

In a strictly statically typed language such as C or C++, data types are etched in stone when the source code is compiled. The compiler benefits from this by having enough information to catch many kinds of errors before the code is executed. For example, the compiler would not allow you to store a floating-point value in an integer variable. The code then doesn't require runtime type checking, so it can be compiled to be small and fast. But statically typed languages are inflexible. They don't support collections as naturally as languages with dynamic type checking, and they make it impossible for an application to safely import new data types while it's running.

In contrast, a dynamic language such as Smalltalk or Lisp has a runtime system that manages the types of objects and performs necessary type checking while an application is executing. These kinds of languages allow for more complex behavior and are in many respects more powerful. However, they are also generally slower, less safe, and harder to debug.

The differences in languages have been likened to the differences among kinds of automobiles.[2] Statically typed languages such as C++ are analogous to a sports car: reasonably safe and fast, but useful only if you're driving on a nicely paved road. Highly dynamic languages such as Smalltalk are more like an off-road vehicle: they afford you more freedom but can be somewhat unwieldy. It can be fun (and sometimes faster) to go roaring through the backwoods, but you might also get stuck in a ditch or mauled by bears.

Another attribute of a language is the way it binds method calls to their definitions. In a static language such as C or C++, the definitions of methods are normally bound at compile time, unless the programmer specifies otherwise. Languages like Smalltalk, on the other hand, are called *late binding* because they locate the definitions of methods dynamically at runtime. Early binding is important for performance reasons; an application can run without the overhead incurred by searching for methods at runtime. But late binding is more flexible. It's also necessary in an object-oriented language where new types can be loaded dynamically and only the runtime system can determine which method to run.

Java provides some of the benefits of both C++ and Smalltalk; it's a statically typed, late-binding language. Every object in Java has a well-defined type that is known at compile time. This means the Java compiler can do the same kind of static type checking and usage analysis as C++. As a result, you can't assign an object to the wrong type of variable or call nonexistent methods on an object. The Java compiler goes even further and prevents you from using uninitialized variables and creating unreachable statements (see Chapter 4).

However, Java is fully runtime-typed as well. The Java runtime system keeps track of all objects and makes it possible to determine their types and relationships during execution. This means you can inspect an object at runtime to determine what it is. Unlike C or C++, casts from one type of object to another are checked by the runtime system, and it's possible to use new kinds of dynamically loaded objects with a degree of type safety. And because Java is a late binding language, it's always possible for a subclass to override methods in its superclass, even a subclass loaded at runtime.

Incremental Development

Java carries all data type and method signature information with it from its source code to its compiled bytecode form. This means that Java classes can be developed incrementally. Your own Java source code can also be compiled safely with classes from other sources your compiler has never seen. In other words, you can write new code that references binary class files without losing the type safety you gain from having the source code.

2. The credit for the car analogy goes to Marshall P. Cline, author of the C++ FAQ.

Java does not suffer from the "fragile base class" problem. In languages such as C++, the implementation of a base class can be effectively frozen because it has many derived classes; changing the base class may require recompilation of all of the derived classes. This is an especially difficult problem for developers of class libraries. Java avoids this problem by dynamically locating fields within classes. As long as a class maintains a valid form of its original structure, it can evolve without breaking other classes that are derived from it or that make use of it.

Dynamic Memory Management

Some of the most important differences between Java and lower-level languages such as C and C++ involve how Java manages memory. Java eliminates ad hoc "pointers" that can reference arbitrary areas of memory and adds object garbage collection and high-level arrays to the language. These features eliminate many otherwise insurmountable problems with safety, portability, and optimization.

Garbage collection alone has saved countless programmers from the single largest source of programming errors in C or C++: explicit memory allocation and deallocation. In addition to maintaining objects in memory, the Java runtime system keeps track of all references to those objects. When an object is no longer in use, Java automatically removes it from memory. You can, for the most part, simply ignore objects you no longer use, with confidence that the interpreter will clean them up at an appropriate time.

Java uses a sophisticated garbage collector that runs in the background, which means that most garbage collecting takes place during idle times, between I/O pauses, mouse clicks, or keyboard hits. Advanced runtime systems, such as HotSpot, have more advanced garbage collection that can differentiate the usage patterns of objects (such as short-lived versus long-lived) and optimize their collection. The Java runtime can now tune itself automatically for the optimal distribution of memory for different kinds of applications based on their behavior. With this kind of runtime profiling, automatic memory management can be much faster than the most diligently programmer-managed resources, something that some old-school programmers still find hard to believe.

We've said that Java doesn't have pointers. Strictly speaking, this statement is true, but it's also misleading. What Java provides are *references*—a safe kind of pointer. A reference is a strongly typed handle for an object. All objects in Java, with the exception of primitive numeric types, are accessed through references. You can use references to build all the normal kinds of data structures a C programmer would be accustomed to building with pointers, such as linked lists, trees, and so forth. The only difference is that with references, you have to do so in a typesafe way.

Another important difference between a reference and a pointer is that you can't play games (perform pointer arithmetic) with references to change their values; they can point only to specific objects or elements of an array. A reference is an atomic thing;

you can't manipulate the value of a reference except by assigning it to an object. References are passed by value, and you can't reference an object through more than a single level of indirection. The protection of references is one of the most fundamental aspects of Java security. It means that Java code has to play by the rules; it can't peek into places it shouldn't and circumvent the rules.

Java references can point only to class types. There are no pointers to methods. People sometimes complain about this missing feature, but you will find that most tasks that call for pointers to methods can be accomplished more cleanly using interfaces and adapter classes instead. We should also mention that Java has a sophisticated Reflection API that actually allows you to reference and invoke individual methods. However, this is not the normal way of doing things. We discuss reflection in Chapter 7.

Finally, we should mention that arrays in Java are true, first-class objects. They can be dynamically allocated and assigned like other objects. Arrays know their own size and type, and although you can't directly define or subclass array classes, they do have a well-defined inheritance relationship based on the relationship of their base types. Having true arrays in the language alleviates much of the need for pointer arithmetic, such as that used in C or C++.

Error Handling

Java's roots are in networked devices and embedded systems. For these applications, it's important to have robust and intelligent error management. Java has a powerful exception handling mechanism, somewhat like that in newer implementations of C++. Exceptions provide a more natural and elegant way to handle errors. Exceptions allow you to separate error handling code from normal code, which makes for cleaner, more readable applications.

When an exception occurs, it causes the flow of program execution to be transferred to a predesignated "catch" block of code. The exception carries with it an object that contains information about the situation that caused the exception. The Java compiler requires that a method either declare the exceptions it can generate or catch and deal with them itself. This promotes error information to the same level of importance as argument and return types for methods. As a Java programmer, you know precisely what exceptional conditions you must deal with, and you have help from the compiler in writing correct software that doesn't leave them unhandled.

Threads

Modern applications require a high degree of parallelism. Even a very single-minded application can have a complex user interface—which requires concurrent activities. As machines get faster, users become more sensitive to waiting for unrelated tasks that seize control of their time. Threads provide efficient multiprocessing and distribution of tasks for both client and server applications. Java makes threads easy to use because support for them is built into the language.

Concurrency is nice, but there's more to programming with threads than just performing multiple tasks simultaneously. In most cases, threads need to be *synchronized* (coordinated), which can be tricky without explicit language support. Java supports synchronization based on the *monitor* and *condition* model—a sort of lock and key system for accessing resources. The keyword `synchronized` designates methods and blocks of code for safe, serialized access within an object. There are also simple, primitive methods for explicit waiting and signaling between threads interested in the same object.

Java also has a high-level concurrency package that provides powerful utilities addressing common patterns in multithreaded programming, such as thread pools, coordination of tasks, and sophisticated locking. With the addition of the concurrency package and related utilities, Java provides some of the most advanced thread-related utilities of any language.

Although some developers may never have to write multithreaded code, learning to program with threads is an important part of mastering programming in Java and something all developers should grasp. See Chapter 9 for a discussion of this topic.

Scalability

At the lowest level, Java programs consist of *classes*. Classes are intended to be small, modular components. Over classes, Java provides *packages*, a layer of structure that groups classes into functional units. Packages provide a naming convention for organizing classes and a second tier of organizational control over the visibility of variables and methods in Java applications.

Within a package, a class is either publicly visible or protected from outside access. Packages form another type of scope that is closer to the application level. This lends itself to building reusable components that work together in a system. Packages also help in designing a scalable application that can grow without becoming a bird's nest of tightly coupled code.

Safety of Implementation

It's one thing to create a language that prevents you from shooting yourself in the foot; it's quite another to create one that prevents others from shooting you in the foot.

Encapsulation is the concept of hiding data and behavior within a class; it's an important part of object-oriented design. It helps you write clean, modular software. In most languages, however, the visibility of data items is simply part of the relationship between the programmer and the compiler. It's a matter of semantics, not an assertion about the actual security of the data in the context of the running program's environment.

When Bjarne Stroustrup chose the keyword `private` to designate hidden members of classes in C++, he was probably thinking about shielding a developer from the messy details of another developer's code, not the issues of shielding that developer's classes and objects from attack by someone else's viruses and Trojan horses. Arbitrary casting and pointer arithmetic in C or C++ make it trivial to violate access permissions on classes without breaking the rules of the language. Consider the following code:

```
// C++ code
class Finances {
    private:
        char creditCardNumber[16];
        ...
};

main() {
    Finances finances;

    // Forge a pointer to peek inside the class
    char *cardno = (char *)&finances;
    printf("Card Number = %.16s\n", cardno);
}
```

In this little C++ drama, we have written some code that violates the encapsulation of the `Finances` class and pulls out some secret information. This sort of shenanigan—abusing an untyped pointer—is not possible in Java. If this example seems unrealistic, consider how important it is to protect the foundation (system) classes of the runtime environment from similar kinds of attacks. If untrusted code can corrupt the components that provide access to real resources such as the filesystem, network, or windowing system, it certainly has a chance at stealing your credit card numbers.

If a Java application is to be able to dynamically download code from an untrusted source on the Internet and run it alongside applications that might contain confidential information, protection has to extend very deep. The Java security model wraps three layers of protection around imported classes, as shown in Figure 1-3.

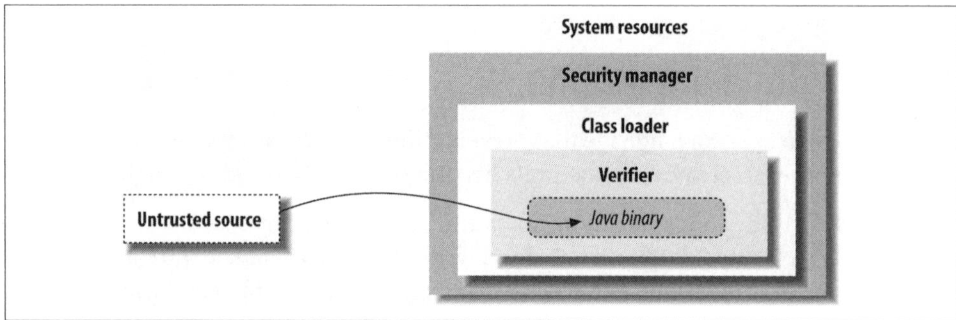

Figure 1-3. The Java security model

At the outside, application-level security decisions are made by a security manager in conjunction with a flexible security policy. A security manager controls access to system resources such as the filesystem, network ports, and windowing environment. A security manager relies on the ability of a class loader to protect basic system classes. A class loader handles loading classes from local storage or the network. At the innermost level, all system security ultimately rests on the Java verifier, which guarantees the integrity of incoming classes.

The Java bytecode verifier is a fixed part of the Java runtime system. Class loaders and security managers (or *security policies* to be more precise), however, are components that may be implemented differently by different applications, such as servers or web browsers. All three of these pieces need to be functioning properly to ensure security in the Java environment.

The Verifier

Java's first line of defense is the *bytecode verifier*. The verifier reads bytecode before it is run and makes sure it is well behaved and obeys the basic rules of the Java language. A trusted Java compiler won't produce code that does otherwise. However, it's possible for a mischievous person to deliberately assemble bad Java bytecode. It's the verifier's job to detect this.

Once code has been verified, it's considered safe from certain inadvertent or malicious errors. For example, verified code can't forge references or violate access permissions on objects (as in our credit card example). It can't perform illegal casts or use objects in unintended ways. It can't even cause certain types of internal errors, such as overflowing or underflowing the internal stack. These fundamental guarantees underlie all of Java's security.

You might be wondering, isn't this kind of safety implicit in lots of interpreted languages? Well, while it's true that you shouldn't be able to corrupt a BASIC interpreter with a bogus line of BASIC code, remember that the protection in most interpreted languages happens at a higher level. Those languages are likely to have heavyweight interpreters that do a great deal of runtime work, so they are necessarily slower and more cumbersome.

By comparison, Java bytecode is a relatively light, low-level instruction set. The ability to statically verify the Java bytecode before execution lets the Java interpreter run at full speed later with full safety, without expensive runtime checks. This was one of the fundamental innovations in Java.

The verifier is a type of mathematical "theorem prover." It steps through the Java bytecode and applies simple, inductive rules to determine certain aspects of how the bytecode will behave. This kind of analysis is possible because compiled Java bytecode contains a lot more type information than the object code of other languages of this kind. The bytecode also has to obey a few extra rules that simplify its behavior. First, most bytecode instructions operate only on individual data types. For example, with stack operations, there are separate instructions for object references and for each of the numeric types in Java. Similarly, there is a different instruction for moving each type of value into and out of a local variable.

Second, the type of object resulting from any operation is always known in advance. No bytecode operations consume values and produce more than one possible type of value as output. As a result, it's always possible to look at the next instruction and its operands and know the type of value that will result.

Because an operation always produces a known type, it's possible to determine the types of all items on the stack and in local variables at any point in the future by looking at the starting state. The collection of all this type information at any given time is called the *type state* of the stack; this is what Java tries to analyze before it runs an application. Java doesn't know anything about the actual values of stack and variable items at this time; it only knows what kind of items they are. However, this is enough information to enforce the security rules and to ensure that objects are not manipulated illegally.

To make it feasible to analyze the type state of the stack, Java places an additional restriction on how Java bytecode instructions are executed: all paths to the same point in the code must arrive with exactly the same type state.

Class Loaders

Java adds a second layer of security with a *class loader*. A class loader is responsible for bringing the bytecode for Java classes into the interpreter. Every application that loads classes from the network must use a class loader to handle this task.

After a class has been loaded and passed through the verifier, it remains associated with its class loader. As a result, classes are effectively partitioned into separate namespaces based on their origin. When a loaded class references another class name, the location of the new class is provided by the original class loader. This means that classes retrieved from a specific source can be restricted to interact only with other classes retrieved from that same location. For example, a Java-enabled web browser can use a class loader to build a separate space for all the classes loaded from a given URL. Sophisticated security based on cryptographically signed classes can also be implemented using class loaders.

The search for classes always begins with the built-in Java system classes. These classes are loaded from the locations specified by the Java interpreter's *classpath* (see Chapter 3). Classes in the classpath are loaded by the system only once and can't be replaced. This means that it's impossible for an application to replace fundamental system classes with its own versions that change their functionality.

Security Managers

A *security manager* is responsible for making application-level security decisions. A security manager is an object that can be installed by an application to restrict access to system resources. The security manager is consulted every time the application tries to access items such as the filesystem, network ports, external processes, and the windowing environment; the security manager can allow or deny the request.

Security managers are primarily of interest to applications that run untrusted code as part of their normal operation. For example, a Java-enabled web browser can run applets that may be retrieved from untrusted sources on the Net. Such a browser needs to install a security manager as one of its first actions. This security manager then restricts the kinds of access allowed after that point. This lets the application impose an effective level of trust before running an arbitrary piece of code. And once a security manager is installed, it can't be replaced.

The security manager works in conjunction with an access controller that lets you implement security policies at a high level by editing a declarative security policy file. Access policies can be as simple or complex as a particular application warrants. Sometimes it's sufficient simply to deny access to all resources or to general categories of services, such as the filesystem or network. But it's also possible to make sophisticated decisions based on high-level information. For example, a Java-enabled web browser could use an access policy that lets users specify how much an applet is to be trusted or that allows or denies access to specific resources on a case-by-case basis. Of course, this assumes that the browser can determine which applets it ought to trust. We'll discuss how this problem is addressed through code-signing shortly.

The integrity of a security manager is based on the protection afforded by the lower levels of the Java security model. Without the guarantees provided by the verifier and the class loader, high-level assertions about the safety of system resources are meaningless. The safety provided by the Java bytecode verifier means that the interpreter can't be corrupted or subverted and that Java code has to use components as they are intended. This, in turn, means that a class loader can guarantee that an application is using the core Java system classes and that these classes are the only way to access basic system resources. With these restrictions in place, it's possible to centralize control over those resources at a high level with a security manager and user-defined policy.

Application and User-Level Security

There's a fine line between having enough power to do something useful and having all the power to do anything you want. Java provides the foundation for a secure environment in which untrusted code can be quarantined, managed, and safely executed. However, unless you are content with keeping that code in a little black box and running it just for its own benefit, you will have to grant it access to at least some system resources so that it can be useful. Every kind of access carries with it certain risks and benefits. For example, in the web browser environment, the advantages of granting an untrusted (unknown) applet access to your windowing system are that it can display information and let you interact in a useful way. The associated risks are that the applet may instead display something worthless, annoying, or offensive.

At one extreme, the simple act of running an application gives it a resource—computation time—that it may put to good use or burn frivolously. It's difficult to prevent an untrusted application from wasting your time or even attempting a "denial of service" attack. At the other extreme, a powerful, trusted application may justifiably deserve access to all sorts of system resources (e.g., the filesystem, process creation, network interfaces); a malicious application could wreak havoc with these resources. The message here is that important and sometimes complex security issues have to be addressed.

In some situations, it may be acceptable to simply ask the user to "okay" requests. The Java language provides the tools to implement any security policies you want. However, what these policies will be ultimately depends on having confidence in the identity and integrity of the code in question. This is where digital signatures come into play.

Digital signatures, together with certificates, are techniques for verifying that data truly comes from the source it claims to have come from and hasn't been modified en route. If the Bank of Boofa signs its checkbook application, you can verify that the app actually came from the bank rather than an imposter and hasn't been modified. Therefore, you can tell your browser to trust applets that have the Bank of Boofa's signature.

A Java Road Map

With everything that's going on, it's hard to keep track of what's available now, what's promised, and what has been around for some time. The following sections constitute a road map that imposes some order on Java's past, present, and future.

The Past: Java 1.0–Java 1.6

Java 1.0 provided the basic framework for Java development: the language itself plus packages that let you write applets and simple applications. Although 1.0 is officially obsolete, there are still a lot of applets in existence that conform to its API.

Java 1.1 superseded 1.0, incorporating major improvements in the Abstract Window Toolkit (AWT) package (Java's original GUI facility), a new event pattern, new language facilities such as reflection and inner classes, and many other critical features. Java 1.1 is the version that was supported natively by most versions of Netscape and Microsoft Internet Explorer for many years. For various political reasons, the browser world was frozen in this condition for a long time. This version of Java is still considered a sort of baseline for applets, although even this will fall away as Microsoft drops support for Java in its platforms.

Java 1.2, dubbed "Java 2" by Sun, was a major release in December 1998. It provided many improvements and additions, mainly in terms of the set of APIs that were bundled into the standard distributions. The most notable additions were the inclusion of the Swing GUI package as a core API and a new, full-fledged 2D drawing API. Swing is Java's advanced user interface toolkit with capabilities far exceeding the old AWT's. (Swing, AWT, and some other packages have been variously called the JFC, or Java Foundation Classes.) Java 1.2 also added a proper Collections API to Java.

Java 1.3, released in early 2000, added minor features but was primarily focused on performance. With version 1.3, Java got significantly faster on many platforms and Swing received many bug fixes. In this timeframe, Java enterprise APIs such as Servlets and Enterprise JavaBeans also matured.

Java 1.4, released in 2002, integrated a major new set of APIs and many long-awaited features. This included language assertions, regular expressions, preferences and logging APIs, a new I/O system for high-volume applications, standard support for XML, fundamental improvements in AWT and Swing, and a greatly matured Java Servlets API for web applications.

Java 5, released in 2004, was a major release that introduced many long-awaited language syntax enhancements including generics, typesafe enumerations, the enhanced for-loop, variable argument lists, static imports, autoboxing and unboxing of primitives, as well as advanced metadata on classes. A new concurrency API provided powerful threading capabilities, and APIs for formatted printing and parsing similar to those in C were added. RMI has also been overhauled to eliminate the need for compiled stubs and skeletons. There were also major additions in the standard XML APIs.

Java 6, released in late 2006, was a relatively minor release that added no new syntactic features to the Java language, but bundled new extension APIs such as those for XML and web services.

The Present: Java 7

This book includes all the latest and greatest improvements through the final release of Java 7. This release adds some minor language syntax enhancements such as those to improve exception handling and resource management. It also includes some major API updates, such as a completely new filesystem API and additions to many others.

This edition of the book is the first since the Java 5 release and therefore has been completely overhauled to incorporate all of the changes from the Java 6 and Java 7 releases.

Here's a brief overview of the most important features of the current core Java API:

JDBC (Java Database Connectivity)
: A general facility for interacting with databases (introduced in Java 1.1).

RMI (Remote Method Invocation)
: Java's distributed objects system. RMI lets you call methods on objects hosted by a server running somewhere else on the network (introduced in Java 1.1).

Java Security
: A facility for controlling access to system resources, combined with a uniform interface to cryptography. Java Security is the basis for signed classes, which were discussed earlier.

JFC (Java Foundation Classes)
: A catch-all for a number of features, including the Swing user interface components; "pluggable look and feel," which means the ability of the user interface to adapt itself to the look and feel of the platform you're using; drag and drop; and accessibility, which means the ability to integrate with special software and hardware for people with disabilities.

Java 2D
: Part of JFC; enables high-quality graphics, font manipulation, and printing.

Internationalization
: The ability to write programs that adapt themselves to the language the user wants to use; the program automatically displays text in the appropriate language (introduced in Java 1.1).

JNDI (Java Naming and Directory Interface)
: A general service for looking up resources. JNDI unifies access to directory services, such as LDAP, Novell's NDS, and others.

The following are "standard extension" APIs. Some, such as those for working with XML and web services, are bundled with the standard edition of Java; some must be downloaded separately and deployed with your application or server.

JavaMail
: A uniform API for writing email software.

Java 3D
: A facility for developing applications with 3D graphics.

Java Media
: Another catch-all that includes Java 2D, Java 3D, the Java Media Framework (a framework for coordinating the display of many different kinds of media), Java Speech (for speech recognition and synthesis), Java Sound (high-quality audio), Java TV (for interactive television and similar applications), and others.

Java Servlets
: A facility that lets you write server-side web applications in Java.

Java Cryptography
: Actual implementations of cryptographic algorithms. (This package was separated from Java Security for legal reasons.)

JavaHelp
: A facility for writing help systems and incorporating them in Java programs.

Enterprise JavaBeans
: A component architecture for building distributed server-side applications.

Jini
: An interesting distributed component technology that is designed to enable distributed computing, discovery, and rendezvous of devices ranging from software tools to hardware and household appliances.

XML/XSL
: Tools for creating and manipulating XML documents, validating them, mapping them to and from Java objects, and transforming them with stylesheets.

Web services
: Tools for creating and deploying Java-based SOAP web services.

In this book, we'll try to give you a taste of as many features as possible; unfortunately for us (but fortunately for Java software developers), the Java environment has become so rich that it's impossible to cover everything in a single book.

The Future

Changes in Java have become less frequent as Java has matured over the years, but Java continues to be one of the most popular platforms for application development. This is especially true in the areas of web services, web application frameworks, and XML tools. While Java has not dominated mobile platforms in the way it seemed destined to, the Java language and core APIs are used to program for Google's Android mobile OS, which is used on billions of devices around the world. In the Microsoft camp, the Java-derived C# language has taken over much .NET development and brought the core Java syntax and patterns to those platforms.

Probably the most exciting areas of change in Java today are found in the trend toward lighter weight, simpler frameworks for business and the integration of the Java platform with dynamic languages for scripting web pages and extensions. There is much more interesting work to come.

Availability

You have several choices for Java development environments and runtime systems. Oracle's Java Development Kit (JDK) is available for Mac OS X, Windows, and Linux.

Visit Oracle's Java website (*http://java.sun.com*) at for more information about obtaining the latest JDK. This book's online content is available at *http://oreil.ly/Java_4E*.

There is also a whole array of popular Java Integrated Development Environments. We'll discuss two in this book: IBM's Eclipse (*http://eclipse.org*) and the Oracle NetBeans IDE (*http://netbeans.org*). These all-in-one development environments let you write, test, and package software with advanced tools at your fingertips. While Eclipse is unquestionably the most popular and is open source, this author's preferred IDE is Intellij IDEA by JetBrains, which now also has a free community edition.

CHAPTER 2

A First Application

Before diving into our full discussion of the Java language, let's get our feet wet by jumping into some working code and splashing around a bit. In this chapter, we'll build a friendly little application that illustrates many of the concepts used throughout the book. We'll take this opportunity to introduce general features of the Java language and applications.

This chapter also serves as a brief introduction to the object-oriented and multithreaded aspects of Java. If these concepts are new to you, we hope that encountering them here in Java for the first time will be a straightforward and pleasant experience. If you have worked with another object-oriented or multithreaded programming environment, you should especially appreciate Java's simplicity and elegance. This chapter is intended only to give you a bird's eye view of the Java language and a feel for how it is used. If you have trouble with any of the concepts introduced here, rest assured they will be covered in greater detail later in the book.

We can't stress enough the importance of experimentation as you learn new concepts here and throughout the book. Don't just read the examples—run them. The source code for these examples and all of the examples in this book can be found on our website (*http://oreil.ly/Learn_Java_4E*). Compile the programs and try them. Then, turn our examples into your examples: play with them, change their behavior, break them, fix them, and hopefully have some fun along the way.

Java Tools and Environment

Although it's possible to write, compile, and run Java applications with nothing more than Oracle's *Java Development Kit* (JDK) and a simple text editor (e.g., vi, Notepad, etc.), today the vast majority of Java code is written with the benefit of an *Integrated Development Environment* (IDE). The benefits of using an IDE include an all-in-one view of Java source code with syntax highlighting, navigation help, source control, integrated documentation, building, refactoring, and deployment all at your fingertips. Therefore, we are going to skip an academic command-line treatment and start with the most popular IDE, Eclipse. If you are adverse to using an IDE, feel free to use the command-line instructions `javac HelloJava.java` for compilation and `java HelloJava` to run the upcoming examples.

IBM originally spearheaded The Eclipse Project in 2001, leading a consortium of software vendors to create an open and extensible development environment to rival the then-legendary Visual Studio environment from Microsoft. Today, Eclipse has grown into a powerful open source platform supported by individuals and corporations alike, backed by a thriving ecosystem of plug-ins and frameworks. Although Java is the most popular language associated with Eclipse, the IDE supports dozens of languages. We will be doing a light introduction to Eclipse in this chapter. For a more comprehensive approach, see Appendix A.

Eclipse requires a *Java Runtime Environment* (JRE) to be installed. This book covers Java 7 language features, so although the examples in this chapter will work with older versions, it's best to have JDK 7 installed to ensure that all examples in the book compile. The JDK includes the JRE as well as developer tools. You can check to see which version, if any, you have installed by typing `java -version` at the command line. If Java isn't present, or if it's a version older than JDK 7 (confusingly also referred to as JDK 1.7), you will want to download the latest version from Oracle's download page (*http://www.oracle.com/technetwork/java/javase/downloads/index.html*). All that is required for the examples in this book is the basic JDK, which is the first option in the upper-left corner of the download page.

Eclipse is an open source IDE available at Eclipse.org (*http://www.eclipse.org/downloads/*). For the purposes of this book, and getting started with Java in general, the Eclipse Classic download is sufficient. Make sure the architecture of your JDK and Eclipse matches. In other words, don't use a 64-bit JDK with a 32-bit version of Eclipse or vice versa. The download is a compressed archive: *.zip* for Windows and *.tar.gz* on OS X and Linux. Double-click to expand and run the installer.

Configuring Eclipse and Creating a Project

The first time you run Eclipse, you'll be prompted to select a workspace. This is a root directory to hold new projects that you create within Eclipse. The default location is inside the application's folder itself, which is probably not what you want. Choose a location and click OK.

Eclipse greets you with the Welcome screen. Close this window by closing the Welcome tab within the application. If you want to come back later and go through the Eclipse tutorials and related help topics, you can return to this window by choosing Help → Welcome.

One last thing before we move on: Eclipse stores all of its configuration information in the *configuration* folder inside the Eclipse installation directory. If, at any point in this introduction, you feel that things are not right and you want to start from scratch, you can quit the application and remove this folder. You may also wish to remove your workspace items as they hold per-project state. Less drastically, if you wish to reset all of the application windows to their default locations, you can choose Window → Reset Perspective. We'll talk more about perspectives later.

We are going to create a project to hold all our examples. Select File → New → Java Project from the application menu and type **`Learning Java`** in the "Project name" field at the top of the dialog, as seen in Figure 2-1. Make sure the JRE version is set to JavaSE-1.7 as seen in the figure and click *Next* at the bottom.

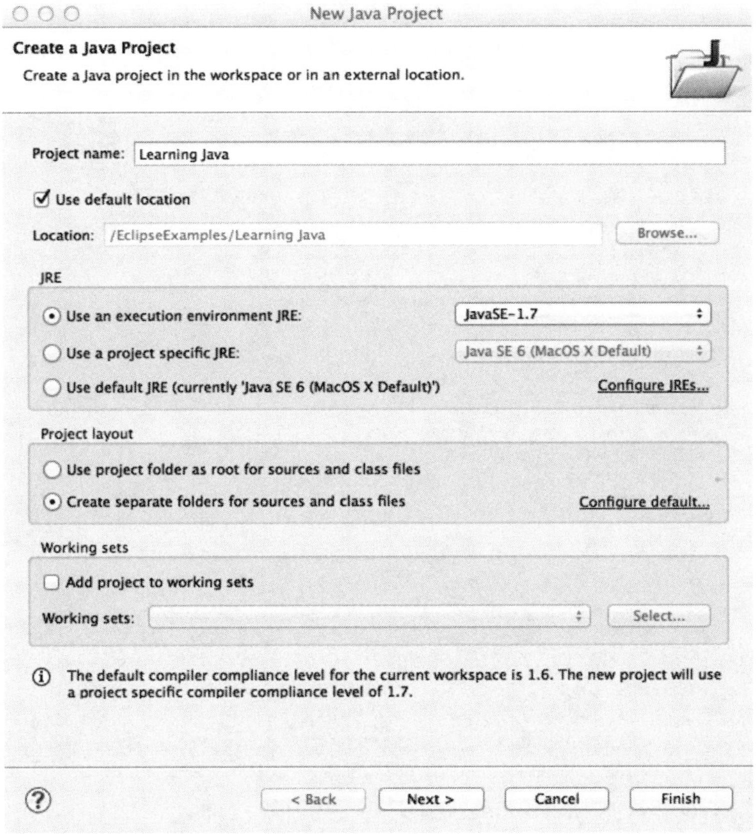

Figure 2-1. New Java Project dialog

Next, you will need to set your build path to the Java 7 system library. Select the *Libraries* tab and remove the Java 1.6 library. Click *Add Library* and select JavaSE-1.7. Eclipse is now configured to use Java 7. Click *Finish*.

Importing the Learning Java Examples

Let's load the examples from this book. You can find a ZIP file containing all of the examples from this book nicely packaged as an Eclipse project at *http://oreil.ly/Java_4E*. The Eclipse version of the examples is called *examples-eclipse.zip*. (The file *examples.zip* holds the same examples but packaged slightly differently and without the Eclipse project files.)

Next, we'll import the examples ZIP file. Choose File → Import to open the Import wizard. Select Archive File as the source and click *Next*. See Figure 2-2.

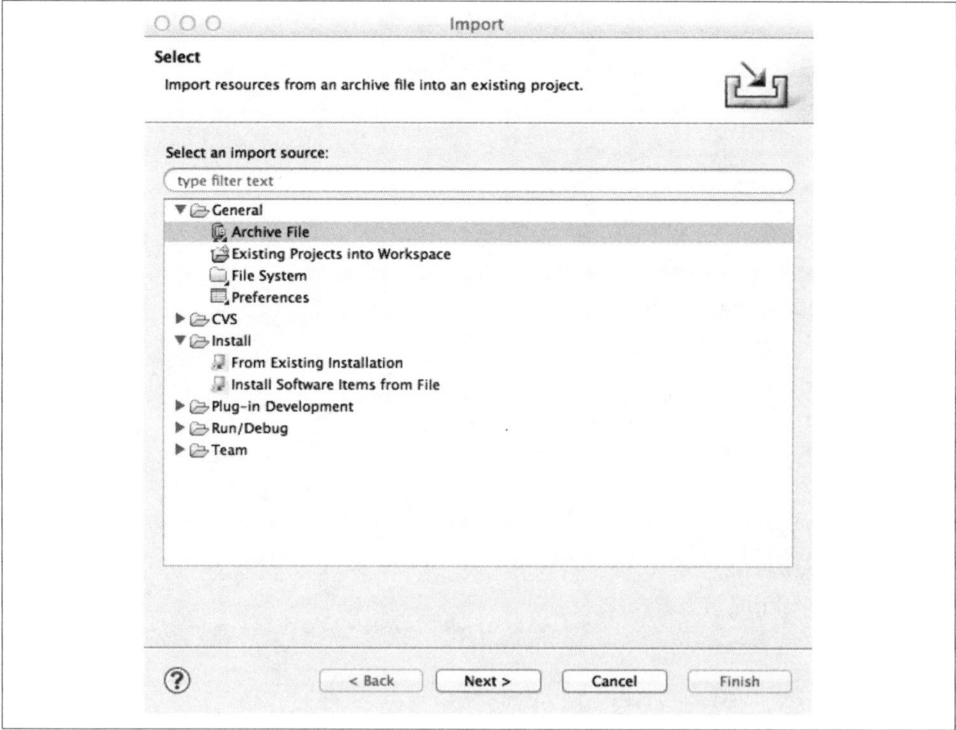

Figure 2-2. New Java Project dialog

Click the Browse button and choose the *examples-eclipse.zip* file as seen in Figure 2-3. Check the "Overwrite existing resources without warning" button so that our Eclipse-specific project file will overwrite the empty one in your new project. Click *Finish*.

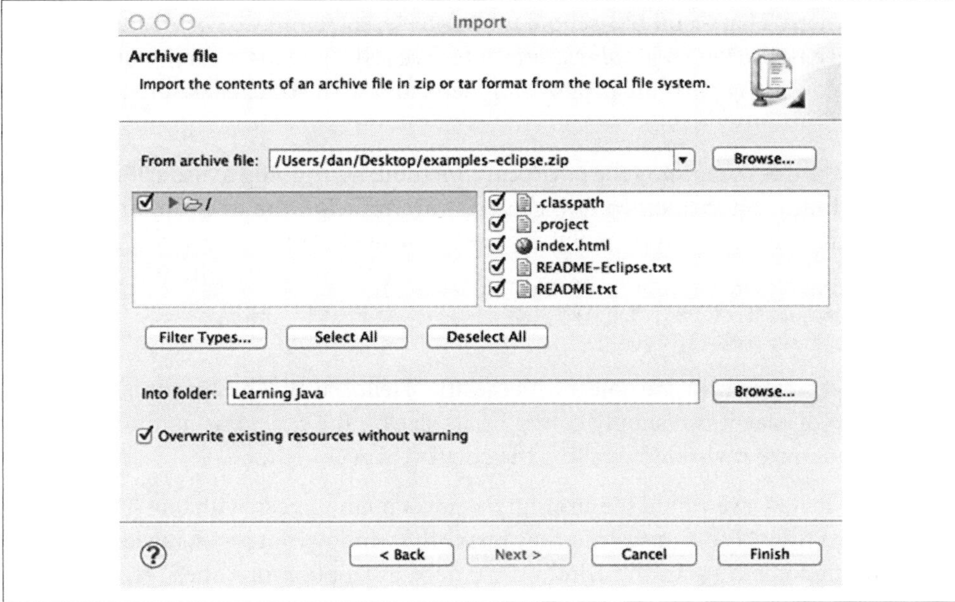

Figure 2-3. New Java Project dialog

Eclipse will now import all of the files from the archive and immediately begin building the source in the background (a small progress bar at the bottom of the screen will show this). On the left is the Package Explorer. It shows a tree view of the Java packages, libraries, and resources of our project. Click the folder handles to expand the tree and see source folders for each chapter in the book. Now we are ready to start coding!

HelloJava

In the tradition of introductory programming texts, we will begin with Java's equivalent of the archetypal "Hello World" application, `HelloJava`.

We'll end up taking four passes at this example before we're done (`HelloJava`, `HelloJava2`, etc.), adding features and introducing new concepts along the way. But let's start with the minimalist version:

```
public class HelloJava {
  public static void main( String[] args ) {
    System.out.println("Hello, Java!");
  }
}
```

This five-line program declares a class called `HelloJava` and a method called `main()`. It uses a predefined method called `println()` to write some text as output. This is a *command-line program*, which means that it runs in a shell or DOS window and prints its output there. That's a bit old-school for our taste, so before we go any further, we're going to give `HelloJava` a *graphical user interface* (GUI). Don't worry about the code yet; just follow along with the progression here, and we'll come back for explanations in a moment.

In place of the line containing the `println()` method, we're going to use a `JFrame` object to put a window on the screen. We can start by replacing the `println` line with the following three lines:

```
JFrame frame = new JFrame( "Hello, Java!" );
frame.setSize( 300, 300 );
frame.setVisible( true );
```

This snippet creates a `JFrame` object with the title "Hello, Java!" The `JFrame` is a graphical window. To display it, we simply configure its size on the screen using the `setSize()` method and make it visible by calling the `setVisible()` method.

If we stopped here, we would see an empty window on the screen with our "Hello, Java!" banner as its title. We'd like our message inside the window, not just scrawled at the top of it. To put something in the window, we need a couple more lines. The following complete example adds a `JLabel` object to display the text centered in our window. The additional `import` line at the top is necessary to tell Java where to find the `JFrame` and `JLabel` classes (the definitions of the `JFrame` and `JLabel` objects that we're using).

```
import javax.swing.*;

public class HelloJava {
  public static void main( String[] args ) {
    JFrame frame = new JFrame( "Hello, Java!" );
    JLabel label = new JLabel("Hello, Java!", JLabel.CENTER );
    frame.add(label);
    frame.setSize( 300, 300 );
    frame.setVisible( true );
  }
}
```

Now to compile and run this source, select the *ch02/HelloJava.java* class from the package explorer along the left and click the *Run* button in the toolbar along the top. The *Run* button is a green circle with a white arrow pointing to the right. See Figure 2-4.

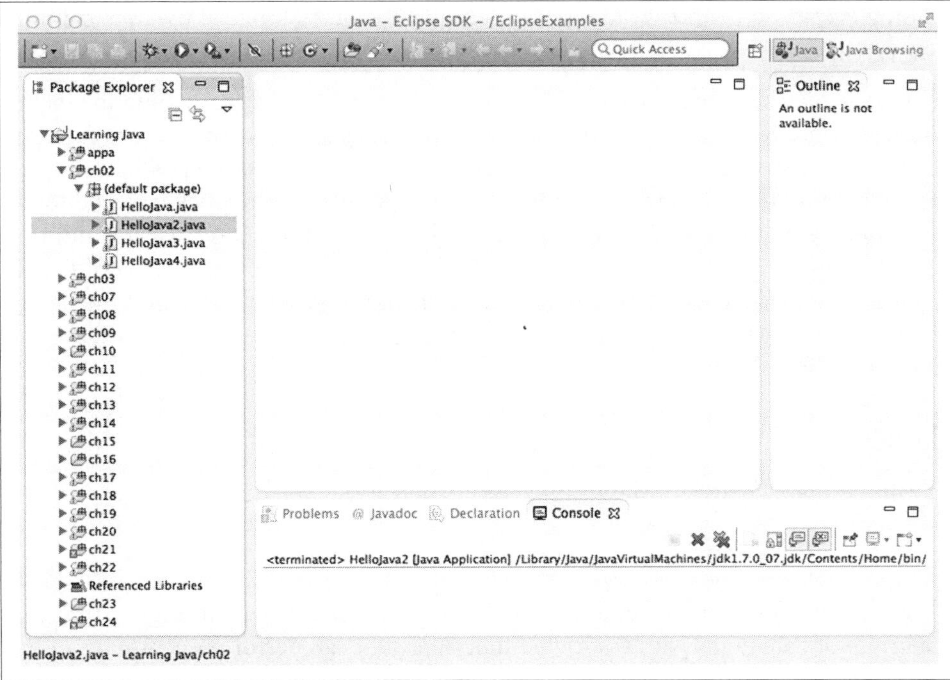

Figure 2-4. Running the HelloJava application

You should see the proclamation shown in Figure 2-5. Congratulations, you have run your first Java application! Take a moment to bask in the glow of your monitor.

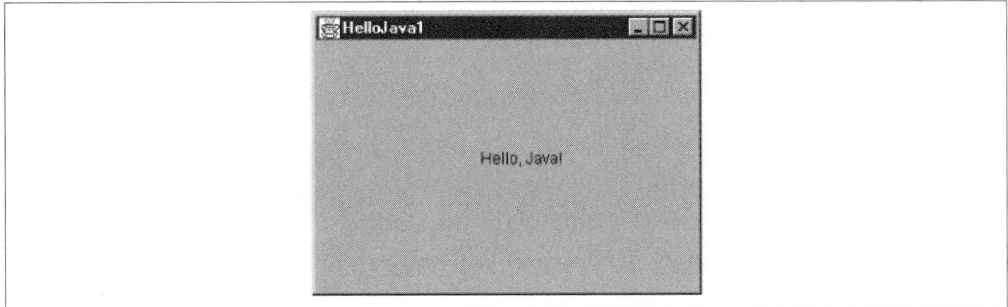

Figure 2-5. The output of the HelloJava application

Be aware that when you click on the window's close box, the window goes away, but your program is still running. (We'll fix this shutdown behavior in a later version of the example.) To stop the Java application in Eclipse, click the big red button in the console window. If you are running the example on the command line, type Ctrl-C. Note that nothing stops you from running more than one instance (copy) of the application at a time.

`HelloJava` may be a small program, but there is quite a bit going on behind the scenes. Those few lines represent the tip of an iceberg. What lies under the surface are the layers of functionality provided by the Java language and its foundation class libraries. Remember that in this chapter, we're going to cover a lot of ground quickly in an effort to show you the big picture. We'll try to offer enough detail for a good understanding of what is happening in each example, but will defer detailed explanations until the appropriate chapters. This holds for both elements of the Java language and the object-oriented concepts that apply to them. With that said, let's take a look now at what's going on in our first example.

Classes

The first example defines a class named `HelloJava`.

```
public class HelloJava {
...
```

Classes are the fundamental building blocks of most object-oriented languages. A *class* is a group of data items with associated functions that can perform operations on that data. The data items in a class are called *variables*, or sometimes *fields*; in Java, functions are called *methods*. The primary benefits of an object-oriented language are this association between data and functionality in class units and also the ability of classes to *encapsulate* or hide details, freeing the developer from worrying about low-level details.

In an application, a class might represent something concrete, such as a button on a screen or the information in a spreadsheet, or it could be something more abstract, such as a sorting algorithm or perhaps the sense of ennui in a video game character. A class representing a spreadsheet might, for example, have variables that represent the values of its individual cells and methods that perform operations on those cells, such as "clear a row" or "compute values."

Our `HelloJava` class is an entire Java application in a single class. It defines just one method, `main()` , which holds the body of our program:

```
public class HelloJava {
  public static void main( String[] args ) {
  ...
```

It is this `main()` method that is called first when the application is started. The bit labeled `String [] args` allows us to pass *command-line arguments* to the application. We'll walk through the `main()` method in the next section. Finally, we'll note that although this version of `HelloJava` does not define any variables as part of its class, it does use two variables, `frame` and `label`, inside its `main()` method. We'll have more to say about variables soon as well.

The main() Method

As we saw when we ran our example, running a Java application means picking a particular class and passing its name as an argument to the Java virtual machine. When we did this, the `java` command looked in our `HelloJava` class to see if it contained the special method named `main()` of just the right form. It did, and so it was executed. If it had not been there, we would have received an error message. The `main()` method is the entry point for applications. Every standalone Java application includes at least one class with a `main()` method that performs the necessary actions to start the rest of the program.

Our `main()` method sets up a window (a `JFrame`) to hold the visual output of the `HelloJava` class. Right now, it's doing all the work in the application. But in an object-oriented application, we normally delegate responsibilities to many different classes. In the next incarnation of our example, we're going to perform just such a split—creating a second class—and we'll see that as the example subsequently evolves, the `main()` method remains more or less the same, simply holding the startup procedure.

Let's quickly walk through our `main()` method, just so we know what it does. First, `main()` creates a `JFrame`, the window that will hold our example:

```
JFrame frame = new JFrame("Hello, Java!");
```

The word `new` in this line of code is very important. `JFrame` is the name of a class that represents a window on the screen, but the class itself is just a template, like a building plan. The `new` keyword tells Java to allocate memory and actually create a particular `JFrame` object. In this case, the argument inside the parentheses tells the `JFrame` what to display in its title bar. We could have left out the "Hello, Java" text and used empty parentheses to create a `JFrame` with no title, but only because the `JFrame` specifically allows us to do that.

When frame windows are first created, they are very small. Before we show the `JFrame`, we set its size to something reasonable:

```
frame.setSize( 300, 300 );
```

This is an example of invoking a method on a particular object. In this case, the `setSize()` method is defined by the `JFrame` class, and it affects the particular `JFrame` object we've placed in the variable `frame`. Like the frame, we also create an instance of `JLabel` to hold our text inside the window:

```
JLabel label = new JLabel("Hello, Java!", JLabel.CENTER );
```

`JLabel` is much like a physical label. It holds some text at a particular position—in this case, on our frame. This is a very object-oriented concept: using an object to hold some text, instead of simply invoking a method to "draw" the text and moving on. The rationale for this will become clearer later.

Next, we have to place the label into the frame we created:

```
frame.add( label );
```

Here, we're calling a method named `add()`to place our label inside the `JFrame`. The `JFrame` is a kind of container that can hold things. We'll talk more about that later. `main()`'s final task is to show the frame window and its contents, which otherwise would be invisible. An invisible window makes for a pretty boring application.

```
frame.setVisible( true );
```

That's the whole `main()` method. As we progress through the examples in this chapter, it will remain mostly unchanged as the `HelloJava` class evolves around it.

Classes and Objects

A class is a blueprint for a part of an application; it holds methods and variables that make up that component. Many individual working copies of a given class can exist while an application is active. These individual incarnations are called *instances* of the class, or *objects*. Two instances of a given class may contain different data, but they always have the same methods.

As an example, consider a `Button` class. There is only one `Button` class, but an application can create many different `Button` objects, each one an instance of the same class. Furthermore, two `Button` instances might contain different data, perhaps giving each a different appearance and performing a different action. In this sense, a class can be considered a mold for making the object it represents, something like a cookie cutter stamping out working instances of itself in the memory of the computer. As you'll see later, there's a bit more to it than that—a class can in fact share information among its instances—but this explanation suffices for now. Chapter 5 has the whole story on classes and objects.

The term *object* is very general and in some other contexts is used almost interchangeably with *class*. Objects are the abstract entities that all object-oriented languages refer to in one form or another. We will use *object* as a generic term for an instance of a class. We might, therefore, refer to an instance of the `Button` class as a button, a `Button` object, or, indiscriminately, as an object.

The `main()` method in the previous example creates a single instance of the `JLabel` class and shows it in an instance of the `JFrame` class. You could modify `main()` to create many instances of `JLabel`, perhaps each in a separate window.

Variables and Class Types

In Java, every class defines a new *type* (data type). A variable can be declared to be of this type and then hold instances of that class. A variable could, for example, be of type `Button` and hold an instance of the `Button` class, or of type `SpreadSheetCell` and hold a `SpreadSheetCell` object, just as it could be any of the simpler types, such as `int` or `float`, that represent numbers. The fact that variables have types and cannot simply hold any kind of object is another important feature of the language that ensures the safety and correctness of code.

Ignoring the variables used inside the `main()` method for the moment, only one other variable is declared in our simple `HelloJava` example. It's found in the declaration of the `main()` method itself:

```
public static void main( String [] args ) {
```

Just like functions in other languages, a method in Java declares a list of variables that it accepts as *arguments* or *parameters*, and it specifies the types of those variables. In this case, the main `method` is requiring that when it is invoked, it be passed a list of `String` objects in the variable named `args`. The `String` is the fundamental object representing text in Java. As we hinted earlier, Java uses the `args` parameter to pass any command-line arguments supplied to the Java virtual machine (VM) into your application. (We don't use them here.)

Up to this point, we have loosely referred to variables as holding objects. In reality, variables that have class types don't so much contain objects as point to them. Class-type variables are references to objects. A *reference* is a pointer to or a handle for an object. If you declare a class-type variable without assigning it an object, it doesn't point to anything. It's assigned the default value of `null`, meaning "no value." If you try to use a variable with a null value as if it were pointing to a real object, a runtime error, `NullPointerException`, occurs.

Of course, object references have to come from somewhere. In our example, we created two objects using the `new` operator. We'll examine object creation in more detail a little later in the chapter.

HelloComponent

Thus far, our `HelloJava` example has contained itself in a single class. In fact, because of its simple nature, it has really just served as a single, large method. Although we have used a couple of objects to display our GUI message, our own code does not illustrate any object-oriented structure. Well, we're going to correct that right now by adding a second class. To give us something to build on throughout this chapter, we're going to take over the job of the `JLabel` class (bye bye, `JLabel`!) and replace it with our own graphical class: `HelloComponent`. Our `HelloComponent` class will start simple, just displaying our "Hello, Java!" message at a fixed position. We'll add capabilities later.

The code for our new class is very simple; we added just a few more lines:

```
import java.awt.*;

class HelloComponent extends JComponent {
```

```
    public void paintComponent( Graphics g ) {
      g.drawString( "Hello, Java!", 125, 95 );
    }
  }
```

You can add this text to the *HelloJava.java* file, or you can place it in its own file called *HelloComponent.java*. If you put it in the same file, you must move the new `import` statement to the top of the file, along with the other one. To use our new class in place of the `JLabel`, simply replace the two lines referencing the label with:

```
frame.add( new HelloComponent() );
```

This time when you compile *HelloJava.java*, you will see two binary class files: *HelloJava.class* and *HelloComponent.class* (regardless of how you arranged the source). Running the code should look much like the `JLabel` version, but if you resize the window, you'll notice that our class does not automatically adjust to center the code.

So what have we done, and why have we gone to such lengths to insult the perfectly good `JLabel` component? We've created our new `HelloComponent` class, *extending* a generic graphical class called `JComponent`. To extend a class simply means to add functionality to an existing class, creating a new one. We'll get into that in the next section. Here we have created a new kind of `JComponent` that contains a method called `paintComponent()`, which is responsible for drawing our message. Our `paintComponent()` method takes one argument named (somewhat tersely) `g`, which is of type `Graphics`. When the `paintComponent()` method is invoked, a `Graphics` object is assigned to `g`, which we use in the body of the method. We'll say more about `paintComponent()` and the `Graphics` class in a moment. As for why, you'll understand when we add all sorts of new features to our new component later on.

Inheritance

Java classes are arranged in a parent-child hierarchy in which the parent and child are known as the *superclass* and *subclass*, respectively. We'll explore these concepts fully in Chapter 6. In Java, every class has exactly one superclass (a single parent), but possibly many subclasses. The only exception to this rule is the `Object` class, which sits atop the entire class hierarchy; it has no superclass.

The declaration of our class in the previous example uses the keyword `extends` to specify that `HelloComponent` is a subclass of the `JComponent` class:

```
public class HelloComponent extends JComponent { ... }
```

A subclass may inherit some or all the variables and methods of its superclass. Through inheritance, the subclass can use those variables and methods as if it has declared them itself. A subclass can add variables and methods of its own, and it can also *override* or change the meaning of inherited methods. When we use a subclass, overridden methods are hidden (replaced) by the subclass's own versions of them. In this way, inheritance provides a powerful mechanism whereby a subclass can refine or extend the functionality of its superclass.

For example, the hypothetical spreadsheet class might be subclassed to produce a new scientific spreadsheet class with extra mathematical functions and special built-in constants. In this case, the source code for the scientific spreadsheet might declare methods for the added mathematical functions and variables for the special constants, but the new class automatically has all the variables and methods that constitute the normal functionality of a spreadsheet; they are inherited from the parent spreadsheet class. This also means that the scientific spreadsheet maintains its identity as a spreadsheet, and we can use the extended version anywhere the simpler spreadsheet could be used. That last sentence has profound implications, which we'll explore throughout the book. It means that specialized objects can be used in place of more generic objects, customizing their behavior without changing the underlying application. This is called *polymorphism* and is one of the foundations of object-oriented programming.

Our `HelloComponent` class is a subclass of the `JComponent` class and inherits many variables and methods not explicitly declared in our source code. This is what allows our tiny class to serve as a component in a `JFrame`, with just a few customizations.

The JComponent Class

The `JComponent` class provides the framework for building all kinds of user interface components. Particular components—such as buttons, labels, and list boxes—are implemented as subclasses of `JComponent`.

We override methods in such a subclass to implement the behavior of our particular component. This may sound restrictive, as if we are limited to some predefined set of routines, but that is not the case at all. Keep in mind that the methods we are talking about are ways to interact with the windowing system. We don't have to squeeze our whole application in there. A realistic application might involve hundreds or thousands of classes, with legions of methods and variables and many threads of execution. The vast majority of these are related to the particulars of our job (these are called *domain* objects). The `JComponent` class and other predefined classes serve only as a framework on which to base code that handles certain types of user interface events and displays information to the user.

The `paintComponent()` method is an important method of the `JComponent` class; we override it to implement the way our particular component displays itself on the screen. The default behavior of `paintComponent()` doesn't do any drawing at all. If we hadn't overridden it in our subclass, our component would simply have been invisible. Here, we're overriding `paintComponent()` to do something only slightly more interesting. We don't override any of the other inherited members of `JComponent` because they provide basic functionality and reasonable defaults for this (trivial) example. As `HelloJava` grows, we'll delve deeper into the inherited members and use additional methods. We will also add some application-specific methods and variables specifically for the needs of `HelloComponent`.

`JComponent` is really the tip of another iceberg called Swing. Swing is Java's user interface toolkit, represented in our example by the `import` statement at the top; we'll discuss it in some detail in Chapters 16 through 18.

Relationships and Finger Pointing

We can correctly refer to `HelloComponent` as a `JComponent` because subclassing can be thought of as creating an "is a" relationship, in which the subclass "is a" kind of its superclass. `HelloComponent` is therefore a kind of `JComponent`. When we refer to a kind of object, we mean any instance of that object's class or any of its subclasses. Later, we will look more closely at the Java class hierarchy and see that `JComponent` is itself a subclass of the `Container` class, which is further derived from a class called `Component`, and so on, as shown in Figure 2-6.

In this sense, a `HelloComponent` object is a kind of `JComponent`, which is a kind of `Container`, and each of these can ultimately be considered to be a kind of `Component`. It's from these classes that `HelloComponent` inherits its basic GUI functionality and (as we'll discuss later) the ability to have other graphical components embedded within it as well.

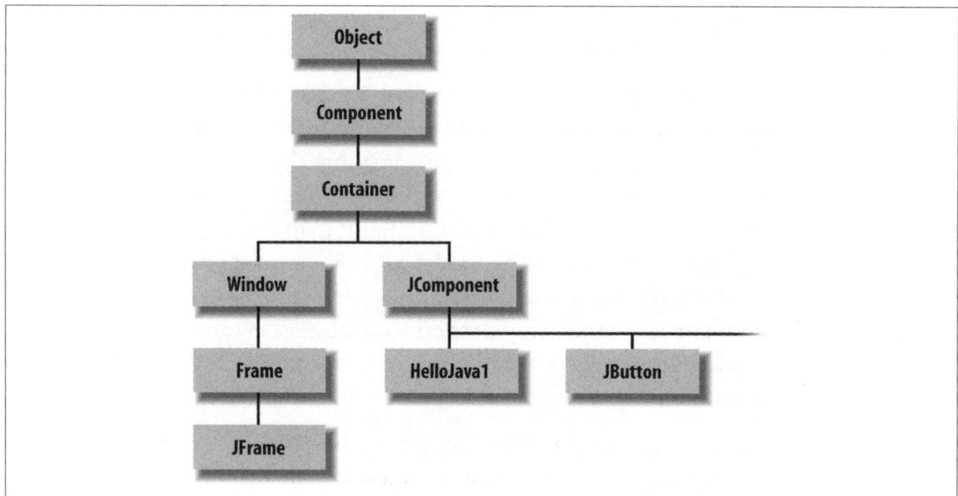

Figure 2-6. Part of the Java class hierarchy

`Component` is a subclass of the top-level `Object` class, so all these classes are types of `Object`. Every other class in the Java API inherits behavior from `Object`, which defines a few basic methods, as you'll see in Chapter 7. We'll continue to use the word *object* (lowercase *o*) in a generic way to refer to an instance of any class; we'll use `Object` to refer specifically to the type of that class.

Package and Imports

We mentioned earlier that the first line of our example tells Java where to find some of the classes that we've been using:

```
import javax.swing.*;
```

Specifically, it tells the compiler that we are going to be using classes from the Swing GUI toolkit (in this case, `JFrame`, `JLabel`, and `JComponent`). These classes are organized into a Java *package* called `javax.swing`. A Java package is a group of classes that are related by purpose or by application. Classes in the same package have special access privileges with respect to one another and may be designed to work together closely.

Packages are named in a hierarchical fashion with dot-separated components, such as `java.util` and `java.util.zip`. Classes in a package must follow conventions about where they are located in the classpath. They also take on the name of the package as part of their "full name" or, to use the proper terminology, their *fully qualified name*. For example, the fully qualified name of the `JComponent` class is `javax.swing.JComponent`. We could have referred to it by that name directly, in lieu of using the `import` statement:

```
public class HelloComponent extends javax.swing.JComponent {...}
```

The statement `import javax.swing.*` enables us to refer to all the classes in the `javax.swing` package by their simple names. So we don't have to use fully qualified names to refer to the `JComponent`, `JLabel`, and `JFrame` classes.

As we saw when we added our second example class, there may be one or more `import` statements in a given Java source file. The `imports` effectively create a "search path" that tells Java where to look for classes that we refer to by their simple, unqualified names. (It's not really a path, but it avoids ambiguous names that can create errors.) The `imports` we've seen use the dot star (`.*`) notation to indicate that the entire package should be imported. But you can also specify just a single class. For example, our current example uses only the `Graphics` class from the `java.awt` package. So we could have used `import java.awt.Graphics` instead of using the wildcard `*` to import all the Abstract Window Toolkit (AWT) package's classes. However, we are anticipating using several more classes from this package later.

The `java.` and `javax.` package hierarchies are special. Any package that begins with `java.` is part of the core Java API and is available on any platform that supports Java. The `javax.` package normally denotes a standard extension to the core platform, which may or may not be installed. However, in recent years, many standard extensions have been added to the core Java API without renaming them. The `javax.swing` package is an example; it is part of the core API in spite of its name. Figure 2-7 illustrates some of the core Java packages, showing a representative class or two from each.

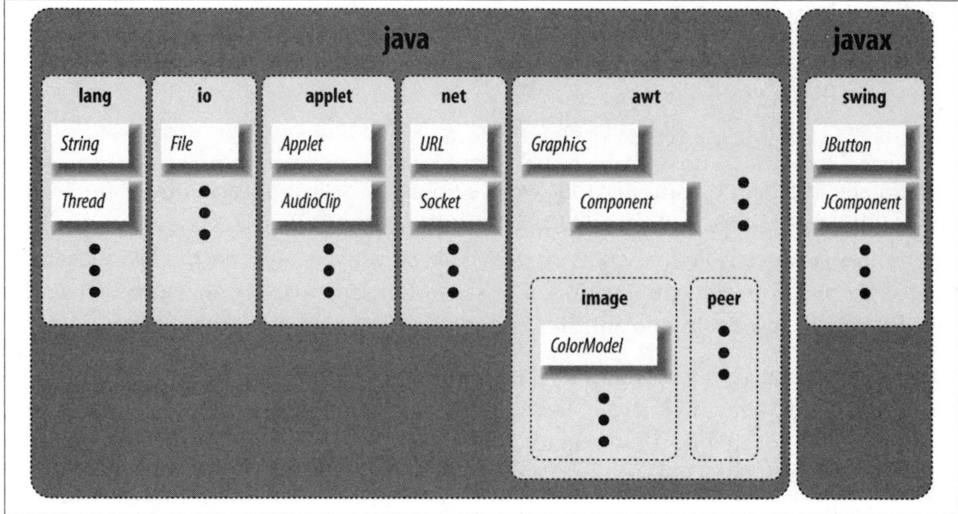

Figure 2-7. Some core Java packages

`java.lang` contains fundamental classes needed by the Java language itself; this package is imported automatically and that is why we didn't need an `import` statement to use class names such as `String` or `System` in our examples. The `java.awt` package contains classes of the older, graphical Abstract Window Toolkit; `java.net` contains the networking classes; and so on.

As you gain more experience with Java, you will come to realize that having a command of the packages available to you, what they do, when to use them, and how to use them is a critical part of becoming a successful Java developer.

The paintComponent() Method

The source for our `HelloComponent` class defines a method, `paintComponent()`, that overrides the `paintComponent()` method of the `JComponent` class:

```
public void paintComponent( Graphics g ) {
    g.drawString( "Hello, Java!", 125, 95 );
}
```

The `paintComponent()` method is called when it's time for our example to draw itself on the screen. It takes a single argument, a `Graphics` object, and doesn't return any type of value (`void`) to its caller.

Modifiers are keywords placed before classes, variables, and methods to alter their accessibility, behavior, or semantics. `paintComponent()` is declared as `public`, which means it can be invoked (called) by methods in classes other than `HelloComponent`. In this case, it's the Java windowing environment that is calling our `paintComponent()` method. A method or variable declared as `private` is accessible only from its own class.

The `Graphics` object, an instance of the `Graphics` class, represents a particular graphical drawing area. (It is also called a *graphics context*.) It contains methods that can be used to draw in this area, and variables that represent characteristics such as clipping or drawing modes. The particular `Graphics` object we are passed in the `paintComponent()` method corresponds to our `HelloComponent`'s area of the screen, inside our frame.

The `Graphics` class provides methods for rendering shapes, images, and text. In `HelloComponent`, we invoke the `drawString()` method of our `Graphics` object to scrawl our message at the specified coordinates. (For a description of the methods available in the `Graphics` class, see Chapter 20.)

As we've seen earlier, we access a method of an object by appending a dot (`.`) and its name to the object that holds it. We invoked the `drawString()` method of the `Graphics` object (referenced by our `g` variable) in this way:

```
g.drawString( "Hello, Java!", 125, 95 );
```

It may be difficult to get used to the idea that our application is drawn by a method that is called by an outside agent at arbitrary times. How can we do anything useful with this? How do we control what gets done and when? These answers are forthcoming. For now, just think about how you would begin to structure applications that respond on command instead of by their own initiative.

HelloJava2: The Sequel

Now that we've got some basics down, let's make our application a little more interactive. The following minor upgrade allows us to drag the message text around with the mouse.

We'll call this example `HelloJava2` rather than cause confusion by continuing to expand the old one, but the primary changes here and further on lie in adding capabilities to the `HelloComponent` class and simply making the corresponding changes to the names to keep them straight (e.g., `HelloComponent2`, `HelloComponent3`, and so on). Having just seen inheritance at work, you might wonder why we aren't creating a subclass of `HelloComponent` and exploiting inheritance to build upon our previous example and extend its functionality. Well, in this case, that would not provide much advantage, and for clarity we simply start over.

Here is `HelloJava2`:

```
//file: HelloJava2.java
import java.awt.*;
import java.awt.event.*;
import javax.swing.*;

public class HelloJava2
{
  public static void main( String[] args ) {
    JFrame frame = new JFrame( "HelloJava2" );
    frame.add( new HelloComponent2("Hello, Java!") );
    frame.setDefaultCloseOperation( JFrame.EXIT_ON_CLOSE );
    frame.setSize( 300, 300 );
    frame.setVisible( true );
  }
}

class HelloComponent2 extends JComponent
    implements MouseMotionListener
{
  String theMessage;
  int messageX = 125, messageY = 95; // Coordinates of the message

  public HelloComponent2( String message ) {
    theMessage = message;
    addMouseMotionListener(this);
  }

  public void paintComponent( Graphics g ) {
    g.drawString( theMessage, messageX, messageY );
  }

  public void mouseDragged(MouseEvent e) {
    // Save the mouse coordinates and paint the message.
    messageX = e.getX();

    messageY = e.getY();
    repaint();
  }

  public void mouseMoved(MouseEvent e) { }
}
```

Two slashes in a row indicate that the rest of the line is a comment. We've added a few comments to `HelloJava2` to help you keep track of everything.

Place the text of this example in a file called *HelloJava2.java* and compile it as before. You should get new class files, *HelloJava2.class* and *HelloComponent2.class*, as a result.

Run the example using the following command:

```
C:\> java HelloJava2
```

Or, if you are following in Eclipse, click the Run button. Feel free to substitute your own salacious comment for the "Hello, Java!" message and enjoy many hours of fun, dragging the text around with your mouse. Notice that now when you click the window's close button, the application exits; we'll explain that later when we talk about events. Now let's see what's changed.

Instance Variables

We have added some variables to the `HelloComponent2` class in our example:

```
int messageX = 125, messageY = 95;
String theMessage;
```

`messageX` and `messageY` are integers that hold the current coordinates of our movable message. We have crudely initialized them to default values that should place the message somewhere near the center of the window. Java integers are 32-bit signed numbers, so they can easily hold our coordinate values. The variable `theMessage` is of type `String` and can hold instances of the `String` class.

You should note that these three variables are declared inside the braces of the class definition, but not inside any particular method in that class. These variables are called *instance* variables, and they belong to the class as a whole. Specifically, copies of them appear in each separate instance of the class. Instance variables are always visible to (and usable by) all the methods inside their class. Depending on their modifiers, they may also be accessible from outside the class.

Unless otherwise initialized, instance variables are set to a default value of `0`, `false`, or `null`, depending on their type. Numeric types are set to `0`, Boolean variables are set to `false`, and class type variables always have their value set to `null`, which means "no value." Attempting to use an object with a `null` value results in a runtime error.

Instance variables differ from method arguments and other variables that are declared inside the scope of a particular method. The latter are called *local* variables. They are effectively private variables that can be seen only by code inside the method. Java doesn't initialize local variables, so you must assign values yourself. If you try to use a local variable that has not yet been assigned a value, your code generates a compile-time error. Local variables live only as long as the method is executing and then disappear, unless something else saves their value. Each time the method is invoked, its local variables are recreated and must be assigned values.

We have used the new variables to make our previously stodgy `paintComponent()` method more dynamic. Now all the arguments in the call to `drawString()` are determined by these variables.

Constructors

The `HelloComponent2` class includes a special kind of a method called a *constructor*. A constructor is called to set up a new instance of a class. When a new object is created, Java allocates storage for it, sets instance variables to their default values, and calls the constructor method for the class to do whatever application-level setup is required.

A constructor always has the same name as its class. For example, the constructor for the `HelloComponent2` class is called `HelloComponent2()`. Constructors don't have a return type, but you can think of them as creating an object of their class's type. Like other methods, constructors can take arguments. Their sole mission in life is to configure and initialize newly born class instances, possibly using information passed to them in these parameters.

An object is created with the `new` operator specifying the constructor for the class and any necessary arguments. The resulting object instance is returned as a value. In our example, a new `HelloComponent2` instance is created in the `main()` method by this line:

```
frame.add( new HelloComponent2("Hello, Java!") );
```

This line actually does two things. We could write them as two separate lines that are a little easier to understand:

```
HelloComponent2 newObject = new HelloComponent2("Hello, Java!");
frame.add( newObject );
```

The first line is the important one, where a new `HelloComponent2` object is created. The `HelloComponent2` constructor takes a `String` as an argument and, as we have arranged it, uses it to set the message that is displayed in the window. With a little magic from the Java compiler, quoted text in Java source code is turned into a `String` object. (See Chapter 10 for a complete discussion of the `String` class.) The second line simply adds our new component to the frame to make it visible, as we did in the previous examples.

While we're on the topic, if you'd like to make our message configurable, you can change the constructor line to the following:

```
HelloComponent2 newobj = new HelloComponent2( args[0] );
```

Now you can pass the text on the command line when you run the application using the following command:

```
C:\> java HelloJava2 "Hello, Java!"
```

`args[0]` refers to the first command-line parameter. Its meaning will become clearer when we discuss arrays later in the book. If you are using an IDE, such as Eclipse, you will need to configure it to accept your parameters before running it.

`HelloComponent2`'s constructor then does two things: it sets the text of `theMessage` instance variable and calls `addMouseMotionListener()`. This method is part of the event mechanism, which we discuss next. It tells the system, "Hey, I'm interested in anything that happens involving the mouse."

```
public HelloComponent2(String message) {
  theMessage = message;
  addMouseMotionListener( this );
}
```

The special, read-only variable called `this` is used to explicitly refer to our object (the "current" object context) in the call to `addMouseMotionListener()`. A method can use `this` to refer to the instance of the object that holds it. The following two statements are therefore equivalent ways of assigning the value to `theMessage` instance variable:

```
theMessage = message;
```

or:

```
this.theMessage = message;
```

We'll normally use the shorter, implicit form to refer to instance variables, but we'll need `this` when we have to explicitly pass a reference to our object to a method in another class. We often do this so that methods in other classes can invoke our public methods or use our public variables.

Events

The last two methods of `HelloComponent2`, `mouseDragged()` and `mouseMoved()`, let us get information from the mouse. Each time the user performs an action, such as pressing a key on the keyboard, moving the mouse, or perhaps banging his or her head against a touch screen, Java generates an *event*. An event represents an action that has occurred; it contains information about the action, such as its time and location. Most events are associated with a particular GUI component in an application. A keystroke, for instance, can correspond to a character being typed into a particular text entry field. Pressing a mouse button can activate a particular button on the screen. Even just moving the mouse within a certain area of the screen can trigger effects such as highlighting or changing the cursor's shape.

To work with these events, we've imported a new package, `java.awt.event`, which provides specific `Event` objects that we use to get information from the user. (Notice that importing `java.awt.*` doesn't automatically import the `event` package. Packages don't really contain other packages, even if the hierarchical naming scheme would imply that they do.)

There are many different event classes, including `MouseEvent`, `KeyEvent`, and `ActionEvent`. For the most part, the meaning of these events is fairly intuitive. A `MouseEvent` occurs when the user does something with the mouse, a `KeyEvent` occurs when the user presses a key, and so on. `ActionEvent` is a little special; we'll see it at work later in this chapter in our third version of HelloJava. For now, we'll focus on dealing with MouseEvents.

GUI components in Java generate events for specific kinds of user actions. For example, if you click the mouse inside a component, the component generates a mouse event. Objects can ask to receive the events from one or more components by registering a *listener* with the event source. For example, to declare that a listener wants to receive a component's mouse-motion events, you invoke that component's addMouseMotionListener() method, specifying the listener object as an argument. That's what our example is doing in its constructor. In this case, the component is calling its own addMouseMotionListener() method, with the argument this, meaning "I want to receive my own mouse-motion events."

That's how we register to receive events. But how do we actually get them? That's what the two mouse-related methods in our class are for. The mouseDragged() method is called automatically on a listener to receive the events generated when the user drags the mouse—that is, moves the mouse with any button pressed. The mouseMoved() method is called whenever the user moves the mouse over the area without pressing a button. In this case, we've placed these methods in our HelloComponent2 class and had it register itself as the listener. This is entirely appropriate for our new text-dragging component. More generally, good design usually dictates that event listeners be implemented as *adapter classes* that provide better separation of GUI and "business logic." We'll discuss that in detail later in the book.

Our mouseMoved() method is boring: it doesn't do anything. We ignore simple mouse motions and reserve our attention for dragging. mouseDragged() has a bit more meat to it. This method is called repeatedly by the windowing system to give us updates on the position of the mouse. Here it is:

```
public void mouseDragged( MouseEvent e ) {
  messageX = e.getX();
  messageY = e.getY();
  repaint();
}
```

The first argument to mouseDragged() is a MouseEvent object, e, that contains all the information we need to know about this event. We ask the MouseEvent to tell us the x and y coordinates of the mouse's current position by calling its getX() and getY() methods. We save these in the messageX and messageY instance variables for use elsewhere.

The beauty of the event model is that you have to handle only the kinds of events you want. If you don't care about keyboard events, you just don't register a listener for them; the user can type all she wants and you won't be bothered. If there are no listeners for a particular kind of event, Java won't even generate it. The result is that event handling is quite efficient.[1]

While we're discussing events, we should mention another small addition we slipped into `HelloJava2`:

```
frame.setDefaultCloseOperation( JFrame.EXIT_ON_CLOSE );
```

This line tells the frame to exit the application when its close button is pressed. It's called the "default" close operation because this operation, like almost every other GUI interaction, is governed by events. We could register a window listener to get notification of when the user pushes the close button and take whatever action we like, but this convenience method handles the common cases.

Finally, we've danced around a couple of questions here: how does the system know that our class contains the necessary `mouseDragged()` and `mouseMoved()` methods (where do these names come from)? And why do we have to supply a `mouseMoved()` method that doesn't do anything? The answer to these questions has to do with interfaces. We'll discuss interfaces after clearing up some unfinished business with `repaint()`.

The repaint() Method

Because we changed the coordinates for the message (when we dragged the mouse), we would like `HelloComponent2` to redraw itself. We do this by calling `repaint()`, which asks the system to redraw the screen at a later time. We can't call `paintComponent()` directly, even if we wanted to, because we don't have a graphics context to pass to it.

We can use the `repaint()` method of the `JComponent` class to request that our component be redrawn. `repaint()` causes the Java windowing system to schedule a call to our `paintComponent()` method at the next possible time; Java supplies the necessary `Graphics` object, as shown in Figure 2-8.

This mode of operation isn't just an inconvenience brought about by not having the right graphics context handy. The foremost advantage to this mode of operation is that the repainting behavior is handled by someone else while we are free to go about our business. The Java system has a separate, dedicated thread of execution that handles all `repaint()` requests. It can schedule and consolidate `repaint()` requests as necessary, which helps to prevent the windowing system from being overwhelmed during painting-intensive situations like scrolling. Another advantage is that all the painting functionality must be encapsulated through our `paintComponent()` method; we aren't tempted to spread it throughout the application.

1. Event handling in Java 1.0 was a very different story. Early on, Java did not have a notion of event listeners and all event handling happened by overriding methods in base GUI classes. This was both inefficient and led to poor design with a proliferation of highly specialized components.

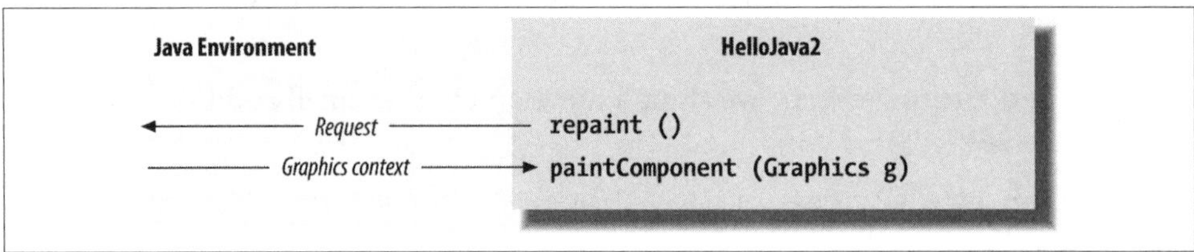

Figure 2-8. Invoking the repaint() method

Interfaces

Now it's time to face the question we avoided earlier: how does the system know to call `mouseDragged()` when a mouse event occurs? Is it simply a matter of knowing that `mouseDragged()` is some magic name that our event-handling method must have? Not quite; the answer to the question touches on the discussion of interfaces, which are one of the most important features of the Java language.

The first sign of an interface comes on the line of code that introduces the `HelloComponent2` class: we say that the class implements the `MouseMotionListener` interface.

```
class HelloComponent2 extends JComponent
    implements MouseMotionListener
{
```

Essentially, an interface is a list of methods that the class must have; this particular interface requires our class to have methods called `mouseDragged()` and `mouseMoved()`. The interface doesn't say what these methods have to do; indeed, `mouseMoved()` doesn't do anything. It does say that the methods must take a `MouseEvent` as an argument and return no value (that's what `void` means).

An interface is a contract between you, the code developer, and the compiler. By saying that your class implements the `MouseMotionListener` interface, you're saying that these methods will be available for other parts of the system to call. If you don't provide them, a compilation error will occur.

That's not the only way interfaces impact this program. An interface also acts like a class. For example, a method could return a `MouseMotionListener` or take a `MouseMotionListener` as an argument. When you refer to an object by an interface name in this way, it means that you don't care about the object's actual class; the only requirement is that the class implements that interface. `addMouseMotionListener()` is such a method: its argument must be an object that implements the `MouseMotionListener` interface. The argument we pass is `this`, the `HelloComponent2` object itself. The fact that it's an instance of `JComponent` is irrelevant; it could be a `Cookie`, an `Aardvark`, or any other class we dream up. What's important is that it implements `MouseMotionListener` and, thus, declares that it will have the two named methods. That's why we need a `mouseMoved()`

method, even though the one we supplied doesn't do anything: the `MouseMotionListener` interface says we must have one.

The Java distribution comes with many interfaces that define what classes have to do. This idea of a contract between the compiler and a class is very important. There are many situations like the one we just saw where you don't care what class something is, you just care that it has some capability, such as listening for mouse events. Interfaces give us a way of acting on objects based on their capabilities without knowing or caring about their actual type. They are a tremendously important concept in how we use Java as an object-oriented language, and we'll talk about them in detail in Chapter 4.

We'll also see shortly that interfaces provide a sort of escape clause to the Java rule that any new class can extend only a single class ("single inheritance"). A class in Java can extend only one class, but can implement as many interfaces as it wants; our next example implements two interfaces and the final example in this chapter implements three. In many ways, interfaces are almost like classes, but not quite. They can be used as data types, can extend other interfaces (but not classes), and can be inherited by classes (if class A implements interface B, subclasses of A also implement B). The crucial difference is that classes don't actually inherit methods from interfaces; the interfaces merely specify the methods the class must have.

HelloJava3: The Button Strikes!

Now we can move on to some fun stuff. `HelloJava3` brings us a new graphical interface component: `JButton`.[2] In this example, we add a `JButton` component to our application that changes the color of our text each time the button is pressed. The draggable-message capability is still there, too. Our new code looks like this:

```
//file: HelloJava3.java
import java.awt.*;
import java.awt.event.*;
import javax.swing.*;

public class HelloJava3
{

  public static void main( String[] args ) {
    JFrame frame = new JFrame( "HelloJava3" );
    frame.add( new HelloComponent3("Hello, Java!") );
    frame.setDefaultCloseOperation( JFrame.EXIT_ON_CLOSE );
    frame.setSize( 300, 300 );
```

2. Why isn't it just called a `Button`? `Button` is the name that was used in Java's original GUI toolkit, AWT. AWT had some significant shortcomings, so it was extended and essentially replaced by Swing in Java 1.2. Since AWT already took the reasonable names, such as `Button` and `MenuBar`, and mixing them in code could be confusing, Swing user interface component names start with J, such as `JButton` and `JMenuBar`.

```
    frame.setVisible( true );
  }
}

class HelloComponent3 extends JComponent
    implements MouseMotionListener, ActionListener
{
  String theMessage;
  int messageX = 125, messageY = 95;  // Coordinates of the message

  JButton theButton;

  int colorIndex;  // Current index into someColors
  static Color[] someColors = {
    Color.black, Color.red, Color.green, Color.blue, Color.magenta };

  public HelloComponent3( String message ) {
    theMessage = message;
    theButton = new JButton("Change Color");
    setLayout( new FlowLayout() );
    add( theButton );
    theButton.addActionListener( this );
    addMouseMotionListener( this );
  }

  public void paintComponent( Graphics g ) {
    g.drawString( theMessage, messageX, messageY );
  }

  public void mouseDragged( MouseEvent e ) {
    messageX = e.getX();
    messageY = e.getY();
    repaint();
  }

  public void mouseMoved( MouseEvent e ) {}

  public void actionPerformed( ActionEvent e ) {
    // Did somebody push our button?
    if (e.getSource() == theButton)
      changeColor();
  }

  synchronized private void changeColor() {
    // Change the index to the next color, awkwardly.
    if (++colorIndex == someColors.length)
      colorIndex = 0;
    setForeground( currentColor() ); // Use the new color.
    repaint();
  }
```

```
        synchronized private Color currentColor() {
          return someColors[colorIndex];
        }
      }
```

Compile HelloJava3 in the same way as the other applications. Run the example, and you should see the display shown in Figure 2-9. Drag the text. Each time you press the button, the color should change. Call your friends! Test yourself for color blindness!

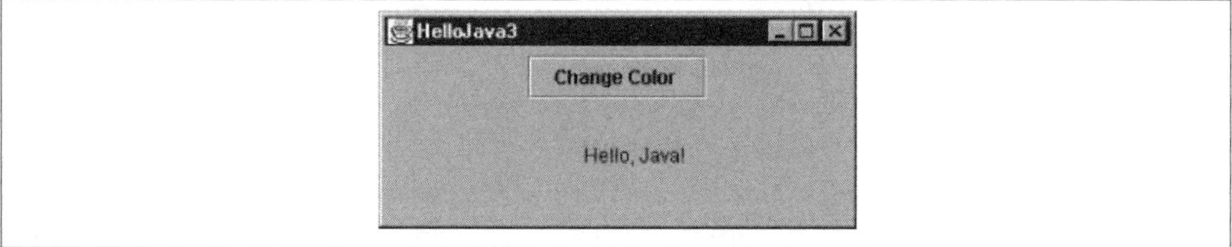

Figure 2-9. The HelloJava3 application

What have we added this time? Well, for starters, we have a new variable:

```
JButton theButton;
```

The theButton variable is of type JButton and is going to hold an instance of the javax.swing.JButton class. The JButton class, as you might expect, represents a graphical button, like other buttons in your windowing system.

Three additional lines in the constructor create the button and display it:

```
theButton = new JButton("Change Color");
setLayout( new FlowLayout() );
add( theButton );
```

In the first line, the new keyword creates an instance of the JButton class. The next line affects the way our component will be used as a container to hold the button. It tells HelloComponent3 how it should arrange components that are added to it for display—in this case, to use a scheme called a FlowLayout (more on that coming up). Finally, it adds the button to our component, just like we added HelloComponent3 to the content pane of the JFrame in the main() method.

Method Overloading

JButton has more than one constructor. A class can have multiple constructors, each taking different parameters and presumably using them to do different kinds of setup. When a class has multiple constructors, Java chooses the correct one based on the types of arguments used with them. We call the JButton constructor with a String argument, so Java locates the constructor method of the JButton class that takes a single String argument and uses it to set up the object. This is called *method overloading*. All methods in Java (not just constructors) can be overloaded; this is another aspect of the object-oriented programming principle of *polymorphism*.

Overloaded constructors generally provide a convenient way to initialize a new object. The `JButton` constructor we've used sets the text of the button as it is created:

```
theButton = new JButton("Change Color");
```

This is shorthand for creating the button and setting its label, like this:

```
theButton = new JButton();
theButton.setText("Change Color");
```

Components

We have used the terms *component* and *container* somewhat loosely to describe graphical elements of Java applications, but these terms are used in the names of actual classes in the `java.awt` package.

`Component` is a base class from which all of Java's GUI components are derived. It contains variables that represent the location, shape, general appearance, and status of the object as well as methods for basic painting and event handling. `javax.swing.JComponent` extends the base `Component` class and refines it for the Swing toolkit. The `paintComponent()` method we have been using in our example is inherited from the `JComponent` class. `HelloComponent` is a kind of `JComponent` and inherits all its public members, just as other GUI components do.

The `JButton` class is also derived from `JComponent` and therefore shares this functionality. This means that the developer of the `JButton` class had methods such as `paintComponent()` available with which to implement the behavior of the `JButton` object, just as we did when creating our example. What's exciting is that we are perfectly free to further subclass components such as `JButton` and override their behavior to create our own special types of user-interface components. `JButton` and `HelloComponent3` are, in this respect, equivalent types of things.

Containers

The `Container` class is an extended type of `Component` that maintains a list of child components and helps to group them. The `Container` causes its children to be displayed and arranges them on the screen according to a particular layout strategy.

Because a `Container` is also a `Component`, it can be placed alongside other `Component` objects in other `Containers` in a hierarchical fashion, as shown in Figure 2-10. Our `HelloComponent3` class is a kind of `Container` (by virtue of the `JComponent` class) and can therefore hold and manage other Java components and containers, such as buttons, sliders, text fields, and panels.

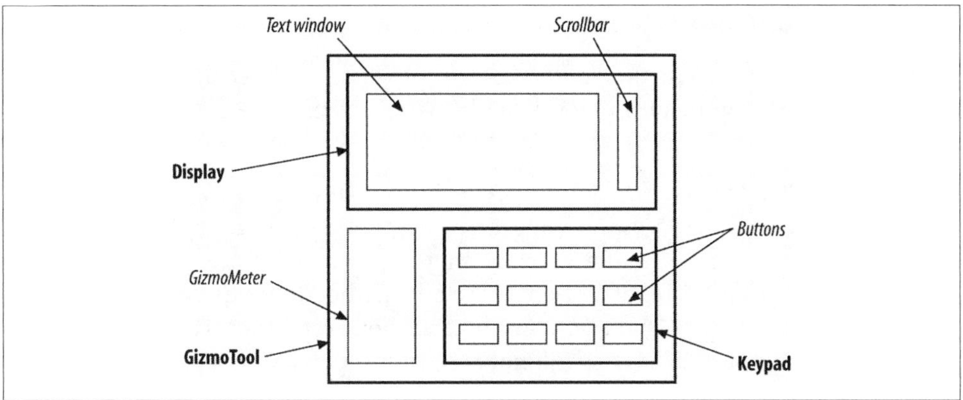

Figure 2-10. Layout of Java containers (in bold) and components (in italics)

In Figure 2-10, the italicized items are `Components`, and the bold items are `Containers`. The keypad is implemented as a container object that manages a number of keys. The keypad itself is contained in the `GizmoTool` container object.

Since `JComponent` descends from `Container`, it can be both a component and a container. In fact, we've already used it in this capacity in the `HelloComponent3` example. It does its own drawing and handles events, just like a component, but it also contains a button, just like a container.

Layout

Having created a `JButton` object, we need to place it in the container, but where? An object called a `LayoutManager` determines the location within the `HelloComponent3` container at which to display the `JButton`. A `LayoutManager` object embodies a particular scheme for arranging components on the screen and adjusting their sizes. There are several standard layout managers to choose from, and we can, of course, create new ones. In our case, we specify one of the standard managers, a `FlowLayout`. The net result is that the button is centered at the top of the `HelloComponent3` container. Our `JFrame` has another kind of layout, called `BorderLayout`. You'll learn more about layout managers in Chapter 19.

To add the button to the layout, we invoke the `add()` method that `HelloComponent3` inherits from `Container`, passing the `JButton` object as a parameter:

```
add( theButton );
```

`add()` is a method inherited by our class from the `Container` class. It appends our `JButton` to the list of components that the `HelloComponent3` container manages. Thereafter, `HelloComponent3` is responsible for the `JButton`: it causes the button to be displayed and it determines where in its window the button should be placed.

Subclassing and Subtypes

If you look up the `add()` method of the `Container` class, you'll see that it takes a `Component` object as an argument. In our example, we've given it a `JButton` object. What's going on?

As we've said, `JButton` is a subclass of the `Component` class. Because a subclass is a kind of its superclass and has, at minimum, the same public methods and variables, Java allows us to use an instance of a subclass anywhere we could use an instance of its superclass. `JButton` is a kind of `Component`, so any method that expects a `Component` as an argument will accept a `JButton`. The converse, however, is not true. A method signature expecting a particular class will not accept its superclass as a parameter.

More Events and Interfaces

Now that we have a `JButton`, we need some way to communicate with it—that is, to get the events it generates. We could just listen for mouse clicks within the button and act accordingly, but that would require customization, via subclassing of the `JButton`, and we would be giving up the advantages of using a pre-fab component. Instead, we have the `HelloComponent3` object listen for higher-level events, corresponding to button presses. A `JButton` generates a special kind of event called an `ActionEvent` when someone clicks on it with the mouse. To receive these events, we have added another method to the `HelloComponent3` class:

```
public void actionPerformed( ActionEvent e ) {
  if ( e.getSource() == theButton )
    changeColor();
}
```

If you followed the previous example, you shouldn't be surprised to see that `HelloComponent3` now declares that it implements the `ActionListener` interface in addition to `MouseMotionListener`. `ActionListener` requires us to implement an `actionPerformed()` method that is called whenever an `ActionEvent` occurs. You also shouldn't be surprised to see that we added a line to the `HelloComponent3` constructor, registering itself (`this`) as a listener for the button's action events:

```
theButton.addActionListener( this );
```

Note that this time, we're registering our component as a listener with a different object—the button—whereas previously we were asking for our own events.

The `actionPerformed()` method takes care of any action events that arise. First, it checks to make sure that the event's source (the component generating the event) is what we think it should be: `theButton`. This may seem superfluous; after all, there is only one button. What else could possibly generate an action event? In this application, nothing, but it's a good idea to check because another application may have many buttons, and you may need to figure out which one has been clicked. Or you may add a second button to this application later, and you don't want it to break something when you do. To check this, we call the `getSource()` method of the `ActionEvent` object, `e`. We then use the == operator to make sure the event source matches `theButton`.

In Java, == is a test for *identity*, not equality; it is `true` if the event source and `theButton` are the same object. The distinction between equality and identity is important. We would consider two `String` objects to be equal if they have the same characters in the same sequence. However, they might not be the same object. In Chapter 7, we'll look at the `equals()` method, which tests for equality.

Once we establish that event `e` comes from the right button, we call our `changeColor()` method, and we're finished.

You may wonder why we don't have to change `mouseDragged()` now that we have a `JButton` in our application. The rationale is that the coordinates of the event are all that matter for this method. We are not particularly concerned if the event falls within an area of the screen occupied by another component. This means you can drag the text right through the `JButton`: try it and see! In this case, the arrangement of containers means that the button is on top of our component, so the text is dragged beneath it.

Color Commentary

To support `HelloJava3`'s colorful side, we have added a couple of new variables and two helpful methods. We create and initialize an array of `Color` objects representing the colors through which we cycle when the button is pressed. We also declare an integer variable that serves as an index into this array, specifying the position of the current color:

```
int colorIndex;
static Color[] someColors = { Color.black, Color.red,
    Color.green, Color.blue, Color.magenta };
```

A number of things are going on here. First, let's look at the `Color` objects we are putting into the array. Instances of the `java.awt.Color` class represent colors; they are used by all classes in the `java.awt` package that deal with basic color graphics. Notice that we are referencing variables such as `Color.black` and `Color.red`. These look like examples of an object's instance variables, but `Color` is not an object, it's a class. What is the meaning of this? We'll discuss that next.

Static Members

A class can contain variables and methods that are shared among all instances of the class. These shared members are called *static variables* and *static methods*. The most common use of static variables in a class is to hold predefined constants or unchanging objects that all the instances can use.

This approach has two advantages. One advantage is that static values are shared by all instances of the class; the same value can be seen by all instances. More importantly, static members can be accessed even if no instances of the class exist. In this example, we use the static variable `Color.red` without having to create an instance of the `Color` class.

An instance of the `Color` class represents a visible color. For convenience, the `Color` class contains some static, predefined objects with friendly names such as `GREEN`, `RED`, and (the happy color) `MAGENTA`. The variable `GREEN`, for example, is a static member in the `Color` class. The data type of the variable `GREEN` is `Color`. Internally, in Java-land, it is initialized like this:

```
public final static Color GREEN = new Color(0, 255, 0);
```

The `GREEN` variable and the other static members of `Color` cannot be modified (after they've been initialized) so that they are effectively constants and can be optimized as such by the Java VM. The alternative to using these predefined colors is to create a color manually by specifying its red, green, and blue (RGB) components using a `Color` class constructor.

Arrays

Next, we turn our attention to the array. We have declared a variable called `someColors`, which is an array of `Color` objects. In Java, arrays are *first-class* objects. This means that an array itself is a type of object—one that knows how to hold an indexed list of some other type of object. An array is indexed by integers; when you index an array, the resulting value is an object reference—that is, a reference to the object that is located in the array's specified slot. Our code uses the `colorIndex` variable to index `someColors`. It's also possible to have an array of simple primitive types, such as `floats`, rather than objects.

When we declare an array, we can initialize it using the curly brace construct. Specifying a comma-separated list of elements inside curly braces is a convenience that instructs the compiler to create an instance of the array with those elements and assign it to our variable. Alternatively, we could have just declared our `someColors` variable and, later, allocated an array object for it and assigned individual elements to that array's slots. See Chapter 5 for a complete discussion of arrays.

Our Color Methods

Now we have an array of `Color` objects and a variable with which to index the array. Two private methods do the actual work for us. The `private` modifier on these methods specifies that they can be called only by other methods in the same instance of the class.

They cannot be accessed outside the object that contains them. We declare members to be `private` to hide the detailed inner workings of a class from the outside world. This is called *encapsulation* and is another tenet of object-oriented design as well as good programming practice. Private methods are created as helper functions for use solely in the class implementation.

The first method, `currentColor()`, is simply a convenience routine that returns the `Color` object representing the current text color. It returns the `Color` object in the `someColors` array at the index specified by our `colorIndex` variable:

```
synchronized private Color currentColor() {
  return someColors[colorIndex];
}
```

We could just as readily have used the expression `someColors[colorIndex]` everywhere we use `currentColor()`; however, creating methods to wrap common tasks is another way of shielding ourselves from the details of our class. In an alternative implementation, we might have shuffled off details of all color-related code into a separate class. We could have created a class that takes an array of colors in its constructor and then provides two methods: one to ask for the current color and one to cycle to the next color (just some food for thought).

The second method, `changeColor()`, is responsible for incrementing the `colorIndex` variable to point to the next `Color` in the array. `changeColor()` is called from our `actionPerformed()` method whenever the button is pressed:

```
synchronized private void changeColor() {
    // Change the index to the next color, awkwardly.
    if ( ++colorIndex == someColors.length )
      colorIndex = 0;
    setForeground( currentColor() ); // Use the new color.
    repaint();
}
```

Here we increment `colorIndex` and compare it to the length of the `someColors` array. All array objects have a variable called `length` that specifies the number of elements in the array. If we have reached the end of the array, we wrap around to the beginning by resetting the index to `0`. We've flagged this with a comment to indicate that we're doing something fishy here. But we'll come back to that in a moment. After changing the currently selected color, we do two things. First, we call the component's `setForeground()` method, which changes the color used to draw text in our component. Then we call `repaint()` to cause the component to be redrawn with the new color for the draggable message.

What is the `synchronized` keyword that appears in front of our `currentColor()` and `changeColor()` methods? Synchronization has to do with threads, which we'll examine in the next section. For now, all you need to know is that the `synchronized` keyword indicates that these two methods can never be running at the same time. They must always run in a mutually exclusive way.

The reason for this is related to the fishy way we increment our index. Notice that in `changeColor()`, we increment `colorIndex` before testing its value. Strictly speaking, this means that for some brief period of time while Java is running through our code, `colorIndex` can have a value that is past the end of our array. If our `currentColor()` method happened to run at that same moment, we would see a runtime "array out of bounds" error. Now, it would be easy for us to fix the problem in this case with some simple arithmetic before changing the value, but this simple example is representative of more general synchronization issues that we need to address. We'll use it to illustrate the use of the `synchronized` keyword. In the next section, you'll see that Java makes dealing with these problems relatively easy through language-level synchronization support.

HelloJava4: Netscape's Revenge

We have explored quite a few features of Java with the first three versions of the `Hello Java` application. But until now, our application has been rather passive; it has been completely *event-driven*, waiting patiently for events to come its way and responding to the whims of the user. Now our application is going to take some initiative—`Hello Java4` will blink![3] Here is the code for our latest version:

```
//file: HelloJava4.java
import java.awt.*;
import java.awt.event.*;
import javax.swing.*;

public class HelloJava4
{
  public static void main( String[] args ) {
    JFrame frame = new JFrame( "HelloJava4" );
    frame.add( new HelloComponent4("Hello, Java!") );
    frame.setDefaultCloseOperation( JFrame.EXIT_ON_CLOSE );
    frame.setSize( 300, 300 );
    frame.setVisible( true );
  }
}

class HelloComponent4 extends JComponent
    implements MouseMotionListener, ActionListener, Runnable
{
  String theMessage;
  int messageX = 125, messageY = 95; // Coordinates of the message
```

3. The title of this section, "Netscape's Revenge," refers to the infamous `<BLINK>` HTML tag introduced with an early version of the Netscape web browser.

```
JButton theButton;

int colorIndex; // Current index into someColors.
static Color[] someColors = {
  Color.black, Color.red, Color.green, Color.blue, Color.magenta };

boolean blinkState;


public HelloComponent4( String message ) {
  theMessage = message;
  theButton = new JButton("Change Color");
  setLayout( new FlowLayout() );
  add( theButton );
  theButton.addActionListener( this );
  addMouseMotionListener( this );
  Thread t = new Thread( this );
  t.start();
}

public void paintComponent( Graphics g ) {
  g.setColor(blinkState ? getBackground() : currentColor());
  g.drawString(theMessage, messageX, messageY);
}

public void mouseDragged(MouseEvent e) {
  messageX = e.getX();
  messageY = e.getY();
  repaint();
}

public void mouseMoved(MouseEvent e) { }

public void actionPerformed( ActionEvent e ) {
  if ( e.getSource() == theButton )
    changeColor();
}

synchronized private void changeColor() {
  if (++colorIndex == someColors.length)
    colorIndex = 0;
  setForeground( currentColor() );
  repaint();
}

synchronized private Color currentColor() {
  return someColors[colorIndex];
}

public void run() {
  try {
```

```
            while(true) {
              blinkState = !blinkState; // Toggle blinkState.
              repaint(); // Show the change.
              Thread.sleep(300);
            }
          } catch (InterruptedException ie) { }
        }
      }
```

Compile and run this version of HelloJava just like the others. You'll see that the text does, in fact, blink. Our apologies if you find this annoying—it's all in the name of education.

Threads

All the changes we've made in HelloJava4 have to do with setting up a separate thread of execution to make the text blink. Java is a *multithreaded* language, which means there can be many paths of execution effectively running at the same time. A *thread* is a separate flow of control within a program. Conceptually, threads are similar to processes. Unlike processes, multiple threads share the same program space, which means that they can share variables and methods (but also have their own local variables). Threads are also quite lightweight in comparison to processes, so it's conceivable for a single application to be running many (perhaps hundreds or thousands) of threads concurrently.

Multithreading provides a way for an application to handle many different tasks at the same time. It's easy to imagine multiple things going on at the same time in an application like a web browser. The user could be listening to an audio clip while scrolling an image; at the same time, the browser can be downloading another image. Multithreading is especially useful in GUI-based applications because it improves the interactive performance of these applications.

Unfortunately for us, programming with multiple threads can be quite a headache. The difficulty lies in making sure routines are implemented so they can be run concurrently by more than one thread at a time. If a routine changes the value of multiple state variables, for example, it may be important that those changes happen together, without overlapping changes affecting each other. Later in this section, we'll examine briefly the issue of coordinating multiple threads' access to shared data. In other languages, synchronization of threads can be extremely complex and error-prone. You'll see that Java gives you powerful tools that help you deal with many of these problems. See Chapter 9 for a detailed discussion of threads.

The Java runtime system creates and manages a number of threads. (Exactly how varies with the implementation.) We've already mentioned the repaint thread, which manages `repaint()` requests and event processing for GUI components that belong to the `java.awt` and `javax.swing` packages. Our example applications have done most of their work in one thread. Methods such as `mouseDragged()` and `actionPerformed()` are invoked by the windowing thread and run by its thread, on its time. Similarly, our `HelloComponent` constructor runs as part of the main application thread (the `main()` method). This means we are somewhat limited in the amount of processing we do within these methods. If we were, for instance, to go into an endless loop in our constructor, our application would never appear because it would never finish initializing. If we want an application to perform any extensive processing, such as animation, a lengthy calculation, or communication, we should create separate threads for these tasks.

The Thread Class

As you might have guessed, threads are created and controlled as `Thread` objects. An instance of the `java.lang.Thread` class corresponds to a single thread. It contains methods to start, control, and interrupt the thread's execution. Our plan here is to create a `Thread` object to handle our blinking code. We call the `Thread`'s `start()` method to begin execution. Once the thread starts, it continues to run until it completes its work, we interrupt it, or we stop the application.

So, how do we tell the thread which method to run? Well, the `Thread` object is rather picky; it always expects to execute a method called `run()` to perform the action of the thread. The `run()` method can, however, with a little persuasion, be located in any class we desire.

We specify the location of the `run()` method in one of two ways. First, the `Thread` class itself has a method called `run()`. One way to execute some Java code in a separate thread is to subclass `Thread` and override its `run()` method to do our bidding. Invoking the `start()` method of the subclass object causes its `run()` method to execute in a separate thread.

It's not usually desirable to create a subclass of `Thread` to contain our `run()` method. The `Thread` class has a constructor that takes an object as its argument. If we create a `Thread` object using this constructor and call its `start()` method, the `Thread` executes the `run()` method of the argument object rather than its own. In order to accomplish this, Java needs a guarantee that the object we are passing it does indeed contain a compatible `run()` method. We already know how to make such a guarantee: we use an interface. Java provides an interface named `Runnable` that must be implemented by any class that wants to become a `Thread`.

The Runnable Interface

We've implemented the `Runnable` interface in `HelloComponent4`. To create a thread, the `HelloComponent4` object passes itself (`this`) to the `Thread` constructor. This means that `HelloComponent4` must implement the `Runnable` interface by implementing the `run()`

method. This method is called automatically when the runtime system needs to start the thread.

We indicate that the class implements the interface in our class declaration:

```
public class HelloComponent4
    extends JComponent
    implements MouseMotionListener, ActionListener, Runnable {...}
```

At compile time, the Java compiler checks to make sure we abide by this statement. We have carried through by adding an appropriate `run()` method to `HelloComponent4`. It takes no arguments and returns no value. Our `run()` method accomplishes blinking by changing the color of our text a few times a second. It's a very short routine, but we're going to delay looking at it until we tie up some loose ends in dealing with the `Thread` itself.

Starting the Thread

We want the blinking to begin when the application starts, so we'll start the thread in the initialization code in `HelloComponent4`'s constructor. It takes only two lines:

```
Thread t = new Thread(this);
t.start();
```

First, the constructor creates a new instance of `Thread`, passing it the object that contains the `run()` method to the constructor. Since `HelloComponent4` itself contains our `run()` method, we pass the special variable `this` to the constructor. `this` always refers to our object. After creating the new `Thread`, we call its `start()` method to begin execution. This, in turn, invokes `HelloComponent4`'s `run()` method in the new thread.

Running Code in the Thread

Our `run()` method does its job by setting the value of the variable `blinkState`. We have added `blinkState`, a Boolean variable that can have the value `true` or `false`, to represent whether we are currently blinking on or off:

```
boolean blinkState;
```

A `setColor()` call has been added to our `paintComponent()` method to handle blinking. When `blinkState` is `true`, the call to `setColor()` draws the text in the background color, making it disappear:

```
g.setColor(blinkState ? getBackground() :
currentColor());
```

Here we are being very terse, using the C language-style ternary operator to return one of two alternative color values based on the value of `blinkState`. If `blinkState` is `true`, the value is the value returned by the `getBackground()` method. If it is `false`, the value is the value returned by `currentColor()`.

Finally, we come to the `run()` method itself:

```
public void run() {
  try {
    while( true ) {
      blinkState = !blinkState;
      repaint();
      Thread.sleep(300);
    }
  } catch (InterruptedException ie) {}
}
```

Basically, `run()` is an infinite `while` loop, which means the loop runs continuously until the thread is terminated by the application exiting (not a good idea in general, but it works for this simple example).

The body of the loop does three things on each pass:

- Flips the value of `blinkState` to its opposite value using the `not` operator (`!`)
- Calls `repaint()` to redraw the text
- Sleeps for 300 milliseconds (about a third of a second)

`sleep()` is a static method of the `Thread` class. The method can be invoked from anywhere and has the effect of putting the currently running thread to sleep for the specified number of milliseconds. The effect here is to give us approximately three blinks per second. The `try/catch` construct, described in the next section, traps any errors in the call to the `sleep()` method of the `Thread` class and, in this case, ignores them.

Exceptions

The `try/catch` statement in Java handles special conditions called *exceptions*. An exception is a message that is sent, normally in response to an error, during the execution of a statement or a method. When an exceptional condition arises, an object is created that contains information about the particular problem or condition. Exceptions act somewhat like events. Java stops execution at the place where the exception occurred, and the exception object is said to be *thrown* by that section of code. Like an event, an exception must be delivered somewhere and handled. The section of code that receives the exception object is said to *catch* the exception. An exception causes the execution of the instigating section of code to stop abruptly and transfers control to the code that receives the exception object.

The `try/catch` construct allows you to catch exceptions for a section of code. If an exception is caused by any statement inside a `try` clause, Java attempts to deliver the exception to the appropriate `catch` clause. A `catch` clause looks like a method declaration with one argument and no return type.

```
try {
    ...
} catch ( SomeExceptionType e ) {
    ...
}
```

If Java finds a `catch` clause with an argument type that matches the type of the exception, that `catch` clause is invoked. A `try` clause can have multiple `catch` clauses with different argument types; Java chooses the appropriate one in a way that is analogous to the selection of overloaded methods. You can catch multiple types of exceptions from a block of code. Depending on the type of exception thrown, the appropriate `catch` clause is executed.

If there is no `try/catch` clause surrounding the code, or a matching `catch` clause is not found, the exception is thrown up to the calling method. If the exception is not caught there, it's thrown up to another level, and so on until the exception is handled or the Java VM prints an error and exits. This provides a very flexible error-handling mechanism so that exceptions in deeply nested calls can bubble up to the surface of the call stack for handling. As a programmer, you need to know what exceptions a particular statement can generate. For this reason, methods in Java are required to declare the exceptions they can throw. If a method doesn't handle an exception itself, it must specify that it can throw that exception so that its calling method knows that it may have to handle it. See Chapter 4 for a complete discussion of exceptions and the `try/catch` clause.

Why do we need a `try/catch` clause in the `run()` method? What kind of exception can `Thread`'s `sleep()` method throw, and why do we care about it when we don't seem to check for exceptions anywhere else? Under some circumstances, `Thread`'s `sleep()` method can throw an `InterruptedException`, indicating that it was interrupted by another thread. Since the `run()` method specified in the `Runnable` interface doesn't declare that it can throw an `InterruptedException`, we must catch it ourselves, or else the compiler will complain. The `try/catch` statement in our example has an empty `catch` clause, which means that it handles the exception by ignoring it. In this case, our thread's functionality is so simple that it doesn't matter if it's interrupted (and it won't be anyway). All the other methods we have used either handle their own exceptions or throw only general-purpose exceptions called `RuntimeExceptions` that are assumed to be possible everywhere and don't need to be explicitly declared.

Synchronization

At any given time, we can have lots of threads running in an application. Unless we explicitly coordinate them, these threads will be executing methods without any regard for what the other threads are doing. Problems can arise when these methods share the same data. If one method is changing the value of some variables at the same time another method is reading these variables, it's possible that the reading thread might catch things in the middle and get some variables with old values and some with new. Depending on the application, this situation could cause a critical error.

In our `HelloJava` examples, both our `paintComponent()` and `mouseDragged()` methods access the `messageX` and `messageY` variables. Without knowing more about the implementation of the Java environment, we have to assume that these methods could conceivably be called by different threads and run concurrently. `paintComponent()` could be called while `mouseDragged()` is in the midst of updating `messageX` and `messageY`. At that point, the data is in an inconsistent state and if `paintComponent()` gets lucky, it could get the new `x` value with the old `y` value. Fortunately, Swing does not allow this to happen in this case because all event activity is handled by a single thread, and we probably would not even notice if it were to happen in this application anyway. We did, however, see another case in our `changeColor()` and `currentColor()` methods that is representative of the potential for a more serious "out of bounds" error.

The `synchronized` modifier tells Java to acquire a *lock* for the object that contains the method before executing that method. Only one method in the object can have the lock at any given time, which means that only one synchronized method in that object can be running at a time. This allows a method to alter data and leave it in a consistent state before a concurrently running method is allowed to access it. When the method is done, it releases the lock on the class.

Unlike synchronization in other languages, the `synchronized` keyword in Java provides locking at the language level. This means there is no way that you can forget to unlock a class. Even if the method throws an exception or the thread is terminated, Java will release the lock. This feature makes programming with threads in Java much easier than in other languages. See Chapter 9 for more details on coordinating threads and shared data.

Whew! Well, it's time to say goodbye to `HelloJava`. We hope that you have developed a feel for the major features of the Java language and that this will help you as you explore the details of programming with Java. If you are a bit bewildered by some of the material presented here, take heart. We'll be covering all the major topics presented here again in their own chapters throughout the book. This tutorial was meant to be something of a "trial by fire" to get the important concepts and terminology into your brain so that the next time you hear them you'll have a head start.

CHAPTER 3
Tools of the Trade

While you will almost certainly do the majority of your Java development in an IDE such as Eclipse, NetBeans, or (the author's favorite, Intellij IDEA), all of the core tools you need to build Java applications are included in the Java Development Kit (JDK) that you have likely already downloaded from Oracle for version 7. In this chapter, we'll discuss some of these command-line tools that you can use to compile, run, and package Java applications. There are many additional developer tools included in the JDK that we'll discuss throughout this book.

For an introduction to the Eclipse IDE and instructions for loading all of the examples in this book as an Eclipse project, see Appendix A. In Chapter 22, we introduce the NetBeans IDE with our discussion of the JavaBeans component architecture, so you will get additional GUI development environment experience there.

JDK Environment

After you install Java 7, the core *java* runtime command may appear in your path (available to run) automatically. However, many of the other commands provided with the JDK may not be available unless you add the Java *bin* directory to your execution path. The following commands show how to do this on Mac OS X and Windows. You will, of course, have to change the path to match the version of Java you have installed.

```
# Mac OS X
export JAVA_HOME=/Library/Java/JavaVirtualMachines/jdk1.7.0_09.jdk/Contents/Home
export PATH=$PATH:$JAVA_HOME/bin

# Windows
set JAVA_HOME=c:\Program Files\Java\jdk1.7.0_09
set PATH=%PATH%;%JAVA_HOME%\bin
```

On Mac OS X, the situation may be more confusing because recent versions ship with "stubs" for the Java commands installed. If you attempt to run one of these commands, the OS will prompt you to download Java at that time. As of the time of this writing, Mac OS X still ships with Java version 6, so you will need to download version 7 and set up your environment as just shown.

When in doubt, your go-to test for determining which version of the tools you are using is to use the `-version` flag on the *java* and *javac* commands:

```
java -version

# java version "1.7.0_07"
# Java(TM) SE Runtime Environment (build 1.7.0_07-b10)
# Java HotSpot(TM) 64-Bit Server VM (build 23.3-b01, mixed mode)

javac -version

# javac 1.7.0_07
```

The Java VM

A Java virtual machine (VM) is software that implements the Java runtime system and executes Java applications. It can be a standalone application like the *java* command that comes with the JDK or built into a larger application like a web browser. Usually the interpreter itself is a native application, supplied for each platform, which then bootstraps other tools written in the Java language. Tools such as Java compilers and IDEs are often implemented directly in Java to maximize their portability and extensibility. NetBeans, for example, is a pure-Java application.

The Java VM performs all the runtime activities of Java. It loads Java class files, verifies classes from untrusted sources, and executes the compiled bytecode. It manages memory and system resources. Good implementations also perform dynamic optimization, compiling Java bytecode into native machine instructions.

Running Java Applications

A standalone Java application must have at least one class containing a method called `main()`, which is the first code to be executed upon startup. To run the application, start the VM, specifying that class as an argument. You can also specify options to the interpreter as well as arguments to be passed to the application:

```
% java [interpreter options] class_name [program arguments]
```

The class should be specified as a fully qualified class name, including the package name, if any. Note, however, that you don't include the *.class* file extension. Here are a couple of examples:

```
%java animals.birds.BigBird
%java MyTest
```

The interpreter searches for the class in the *classpath*, a list of directories and archive files where classes are stored. We'll discuss the classpath in detail in the next section. The classpath can be specified either by an *environment variable* or with the command-line option `-classpath`. If both are present, the command-line option is used.

Alternately, the *java* command can be used to launch an "executable" Java archive (JAR) file:

```
% java -jar spaceblaster.jar
```

In this case, the JAR file includes metadata with the name of the startup class containing the `main()` method, and the classpath becomes the JAR file itself.

After loading the first class and executing its `main()` method, the application can reference other classes, start additional threads, and create its user interface or other structures, as shown in Figure 3-1.

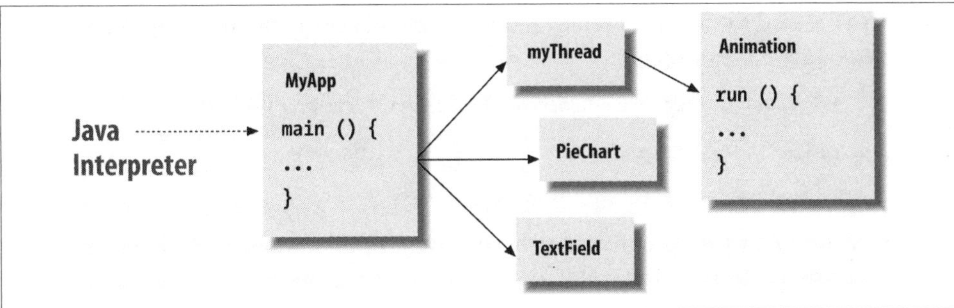

Figure 3-1. Starting a Java application

The `main()` method must have the right *method signature*. A method signature is the set of information that defines the method. It includes the method's name, arguments, and return type, as well as type and visibility modifiers. The `main()` method must be a `public`, `static` method that takes an array of `String` objects as its argument and does not return any value (`void`):

```
public static void main ( String [] myArgs )
```

The fact that `main()` is a `public` and `static` method simply means that it is globally accessible and that it can be called directly by name. We'll discuss the implications of visibility modifiers such as `public` and the meaning of `static` in Chapters 4 through 6.

The `main()` method's single argument, the array of `String` objects, holds the command-line arguments passed to the application. The name of the parameter doesn't matter; only the type is important. In Java, the content of `myArgs` is an array. In Java, arrays know how many elements they contain and can happily provide that information:

```
int numArgs = myArgs.length;
```

`myArgs[0]` is the first command-line argument, and so on.

The Java interpreter continues to run until the `main()` method of the initial class file returns and until any threads that it has started also exit. Special threads designated as *daemon* threads are automatically terminated when the rest of the application has completed.

System Properties

Although it is possible to read host environment variables from Java, it is discouraged for application configuration. Instead, Java allows any number of *system property* values to be passed to the application when the VM is started. System properties are simply name-value string pairs that are available to the application through the static `System.getProperty()` method. You can use these properties as a more structured and portable alternative to command-line arguments and environment variables for providing general configuration information to your application at startup. Each system property is passed to the interpreter on the command line using the *-D* option followed by *name=value*. For example:

```
% java -Dstreet=sesame -Dscene=alley animals.birds.BigBird
```

The value of the `street` property is then accessible this way:

```
String street = System.getProperty("street");
```

An application can get its configuration in myriad other ways, including via files or network configuration at runtime.

The Classpath

The concept of a *path* should be familiar to anyone who has worked on a DOS or Unix platform. It's an environment variable that provides an application with a list of places to look for some resource. The most common example is a path for executable programs. In a Unix shell, the `PATH` environment variable is a colon-separated list of directories that are searched, in order, when the user types the name of a command. The Java `CLASSPATH` environment variable, similarly, is a list of locations that are searched for Java class files. Both the Java interpreter and the Java compiler use the `CLASSPATH` when searching for packages and Java classes.

An element of the classpath can be a directory or a JAR file. Java also supports archives in the conventional ZIP format, but JAR and ZIP are really the same format. JARs are simple archives that include extra files (metadata) that describe each archive's contents. JAR files are created with the JDK's *jar* utility; many tools for creating ZIP archives are publicly available and can be used to inspect or create JAR files as well. The archive format enables large groups of classes and their resources to be distributed in a single file; the Java runtime automatically extracts individual class files from the archive as needed.

The precise means and format for setting the classpath vary from system to system. On a Unix system (including Mac OS X), you set the `CLASSPATH` environment variable with a colon-separated list of directories and class archive files:

```
%export CLASSPATH=/home/vicky/Java/classes:/home/josh/lib/foo.jar:.
```

This example specifies a classpath with three locations: a directory in the user's home, a JAR file in another user's directory, and the current directory, which is always specified with a dot (`.`). The last component of the classpath, the current directory, is useful when you are tinkering with classes.

On a Windows system, the `CLASSPATH` environment variable is set with a semicolon-separated list of directories and class archive files:

```
C:\> set CLASSPATH=C:\home\vicky\Java\classes;C:\home\josh\lib\foo.jar;.
```

The Java launcher and the other command-line tools know how to find the core classes, which are the classes included in every Java installation. The classes in the `java.lang`, `java.io`, `java.net`, and `javax.swing` packages, for example, are all core classes so you do not need to include these classes in your classpath.

The classpath may also include "*" wildcards that match all JAR files within a directory. For example:

```
export CLASSPATH=/home/pat/libs/*
```

To find other classes, the Java interpreter searches the elements of the classpath in order. The search combines the path location and the components of the fully qualified class name. For example, consider a search for the class `animals.birds.BigBird`. Searching the classpath directory */usr/lib/java* means the interpreter looks for an individual class file at */usr/lib/java/animals/birds/BigBird.class*. Searching a ZIP or JAR archive on the classpath, say */home/vicky/myutils.jar*, means that the interpreter looks for component file *animals/birds/BigBird.class* within that archive.

For the Java runtime, *java*, and the Java compiler, *javac*, the classpath can also be specified with the *-classpath* option:

```
% javac -classpath /home/pat/classes:/utils/utils.jar:. Foo.java
```

If you don't specify the `CLASSPATH` environment variable or command-line option, the classpath defaults to the current directory (`.`); this means that the files in your current directory are normally available. If you change the classpath and don't include the current directory, these files will no longer be accessible.

We suspect that about 80 percent of the problems that newcomers have when first learning Java are classpath-related. You may wish to pay particular attention to setting and checking the classpath when getting started. If you're working inside an IDE, it may remove some or all of the burden of managing the classpath. Ultimately, however, understanding the classpath and knowing exactly what is in it when your application runs is very important to your long-term sanity. The *javap* command, discussed next, can be useful in debugging classpath issues.

javap

A useful tool to know about is the *javap* command. With *javap*, you can print a description of a compiled class. You don't need the source code, and you don't even need to know exactly where it is, only that it is in your classpath. For example:

```
% javap java.util.Stack
```

prints the information about the `java.util.Stack` class:

```
Compiled from "Stack.java"
public class java.util.Stack<E> extends java.util.Vector<E> {
  public java.util.Stack();
  public E push(E);
  public synchronized E pop();
  public synchronized E peek();
  public boolean empty();
  public synchronized int search(java.lang.Object);
}
```

This is very useful if you don't have other documentation handy and can also be helpful in debugging classpath problems. Using *javap*, you can determine whether a class is in the classpath and possibly even which version you are looking at (many classpath issues involve duplicate classes in the classpath). If you are really curious, you can try *javap* with the *-c* option, which causes it to also print the JVM instructions for each method in the class!

The Java Compiler

In this section, we'll say a few words about *javac*, the Java compiler in the JDK. The *javac* compiler is written entirely in Java, so it's available for any platform that supports the Java runtime system. *javac* turns Java source code into a compiled class that contains Java bytecode. By convention, source files are named with a *.java* extension; the resulting class files have a *.class* extension. Each source code file is considered a single compilation unit. As you'll see in Chapter 6, classes in a given compilation unit share certain features, such as `package` and `import` statements.

javac allows one public class per file and insists that the file have the same name as the class. If the filename and class name don't match, *javac* issues a compilation error. A single file can contain multiple classes, as long as only one of the classes is public and is named for the file. Avoid packing too many classes into a single source file. Packing classes together in a *.java* file only superficially associates them. In Chapter 6, we'll talk about inner classes, classes that contain other classes and interfaces.

As an example, place the following source code in the file *BigBird.java*:

```
package animals.birds;

public class BigBird extends Bird {
    ...
}
```

Next, compile it with:

```
% javac BigBird.java
```

Unlike the Java interpreter, which takes just a class name as its argument, *javac* needs a filename (with the *.java* extension) to process. The previous command produces the class file *BigBird.class* in the same directory as the source file. While it's nice to see the class file in the same directory as the source for this example, for most real applications, you need to store the class file in an appropriate place in the classpath.

You can use the *-d* option with *javac* to specify an alternative directory for storing the class files *javac* generates. The specified directory is used as the root of the class hierarchy, so *.class* files are placed in this directory or in a subdirectory below it, depending on whether the class is contained in a package. (The compiler creates intermediate subdirectories automatically, if necessary.) For example, we can use the following command to create the *BigBird.class* file at */home/vicky/Java/classes/animals/birds/BigBird.class*:

```
% javac -d /home/vicky/Java/classes BigBird.java
```

You can specify multiple *.java* files in a single *javac* command; the compiler creates a class file for each source file. But you don't need to list the other classes your class references as long as they are in the classpath in either source or compiled form. During compilation, Java resolves all other class references using the classpath.

The Java compiler is more intelligent than your average compiler, replacing some of the functionality of a *make* utility. For example, *javac* compares the modification times of the source and class files for all classes and recompiles them as necessary. A compiled Java class remembers the source file from which it was compiled, and as long as the source file is available, *javac* can recompile it if necessary. If, in the previous example, class `BigBird` references another class, `animals.furry.Grover`, *javac* looks for the source file *Grover.java* in an `animals.furry` package and recompiles it if necessary to bring the *Grover.class* class file up-to-date.

By default, however, *javac* checks only source files that are referenced directly from other source files. This means that if you have an out-of-date class file that is referenced only by an up-to-date class file, it may not be noticed and recompiled. For that and many other reasons, most projects use a real build utility such as Apache's Ant to manage builds, packaging, and more. We discuss Ant in Chapter 15.

Finally, it's important to note that *javac* can compile an application even if only the compiled (binary) versions of some of the classes are available. You don't need source code for all your objects. Java class files contain all the data type and method signature information that source files contain, so compiling against binary class files is as typesafe (and exception safe) as compiling with Java source code.

JAR Files

Java Archive (JAR) files are Java's suitcases. They are the standard and portable way to pack up all the parts of your Java application into a compact bundle for distribution or installation. You can put whatever you want into a JAR file: Java class files, serialized objects, data files, images, audio, etc. A JAR file can also carry one or more digital signatures that attest to its integrity and authenticity. A signature can be attached to the file as a whole or to individual items in the file.

The Java runtime system can load class files directly from an archive in your `CLASSPATH`, as described earlier. Nonclass files (data, images, etc.) contained in your JAR file can also be retrieved from the classpath by your application using the `getResource()` method (described in Chapter 12). Using this facility, your code doesn't have to know whether any resource is in a plain file or a member of a JAR archive. Whether a given class or data file is an item in a JAR file or an individual file on the classpath, you can always refer to it in a standard way and let Java's class loader resolve the location.

File Compression

Items stored in JAR files are compressed with the standard ZIP file compression. Compression makes downloading classes over a network much faster. A quick survey of the standard Java distribution shows that a typical class file shrinks by about 40 percent when it is compressed. Text files such as HTML or ASCII containing English words often compress to one-tenth their original size or less. (On the other hand, image files don't normally get smaller when compressed as most common image formats are themselves a compression format.)

Java also has an archive format called *Pack200*, which is optimized specifically for Java class bytecode and can achieve over four times greater compression of Java classes than ZIP alone. We'll talk about Pack200 later in this chapter.

The jar Utility

The *jar* utility provided with the JDK is a simple tool for creating and reading JAR files. Its user interface isn't particularly friendly. It mimics the Unix *tar* (tape archive) command. If you're familiar with *tar*, you'll recognize the following incantations:

`jar -cvf jarFile path [ path ] [ ... ]`
: Create *jarFile* containing *path*(s).

`jar -tvf jarFile [ path ] [ ... ]`
: List the contents of *jarFile*, optionally showing just *path*(s).

`jar -xvf jarFile [ path ] [ ... ]`
: Extract the contents of *jarFile*, optionally extracting just *path*(s).

In these commands, the flag letters *c*, *t*, and *x* tell *jar* whether it is creating an archive, listing an archive's contents, or extracting files from an archive. The *f* means that the next argument is the name of the JAR file on which to operate. The optional *v* flag tells *jar* to be verbose when displaying information about files. In verbose mode, you get information about file sizes, modification times, and compression ratios.

Subsequent items on the command line (i.e., anything aside from the letters telling *jar* what to do and the file on which *jar* should operate) are taken as names of archive items. If you're creating an archive, the files and directories you list are placed in it. If you're extracting, only the filenames you list are extracted from the archive. (If you don't list any files, *jar* extracts everything in the archive.)

For example, let's say we have just completed our new game, *spaceblaster*. All the files associated with the game are in three directories. The Java classes themselves are in the *spaceblaster/game* directory, *spaceblaster/images* contains the game's images, and *spaceblaster/docs* contains associated game data. We can pack all this in an archive with this command:

```
% jar -cvf spaceblaster.jar spaceblaster
```

Because we requested verbose output, *jar* tells us what it is doing:

```
adding:spaceblaster/ (in=0) (out=0) (stored 0%)
adding:spaceblaster/game/ (in=0) (out=0) (stored 0%)
adding:spaceblaster/game/Game.class (in=8035) (out=3936) (deflated 51%)
adding:spaceblaster/game/Planetoid.class (in=6254) (out=3288) (deflated 47%)
adding:spaceblaster/game/SpaceShip.class (in=2295) (out=1280) (deflated 44%)
adding:spaceblaster/images/ (in=0) (out=0) (stored 0%)
adding:spaceblaster/images/spaceship.gif (in=6174) (out=5936) (deflated 3%)
adding:spaceblaster/images/planetoid.gif (in=23444) (out=23454) (deflated 0%)
adding:spaceblaster/docs/ (in=0) (out=0) (stored 0%)
adding:spaceblaster/docs/help1.html (in=3592) (out=1545) (deflated 56%)
adding:spaceblaster/docs/help2.html (in=3148) (out=1535) (deflated 51%)
```

jar creates the file *spaceblaster.jar* and adds the directory *spaceblaster*, adding the directories and files within *spaceblaster* to the archive. In verbose mode, *jar* reports the savings gained by compressing the files in the archive.

We can unpack the archive with this command:

```
% jar -xvf spaceblaster.jar
```

Likewise, we can extract an individual file or directory with:

```
% jar -xvf spaceblaster.jar filename
```

But, of course, you normally don't have to unpack a JAR file to use its contents; Java tools know how to extract files from archives automatically. We can list the contents of our JAR with the command:

```
% jar -tvf spaceblaster.jar
```

Here's the output; it lists all the files, their sizes, and their creation times:

```
0 Thu May 15 12:18:54 PDT 2003 META-INF/
  1074 Thu May 15 12:18:54 PDT 2003 META-INF/MANIFEST.MF
     0 Thu May 15 12:09:24 PDT 2003 spaceblaster/
     0 Thu May 15 11:59:32 PDT 2003 spaceblaster/game/
  8035 Thu May 15 12:14:08 PDT 2003 spaceblaster/game/Game.class
  6254 Thu May 15 12:15:18 PDT 2003 spaceblaster/game/Planetoid.class
  2295 Thu May 15 12:15:26 PDT 2003 spaceblaster/game/SpaceShip.class
     0 Thu May 15 12:17:00 PDT 2003 spaceblaster/images/
  6174 Thu May 15 12:16:54 PDT 2003 spaceblaster/images/spaceship.gif
 23444 Thu May 15 12:16:58 PDT 2003 spaceblaster/images/planetoid.gif
     0 Thu May 15 12:10:02 PDT 2003 spaceblaster/docs/
  3592 Thu May 15 12:10:16 PDT 2003 spaceblaster/docs/help1.html
  3148 Thu May 15 12:10:02 PDT 2003 spaceblaster/docs/help2.html
```

JAR manifests

Note that the *jar* command automatically adds a directory called *META-INF* to our archive. The *META-INF* directory holds files describing the contents of the JAR file. It always contains at least one file: *MANIFEST.MF*. The *MANIFEST.MF* file can contain a "packing list" naming the files in the archive along with a user-definable set of attributes for each entry.

The manifest is a text file containing a set of lines in the form *keyword: value*. The manifest is, by default, empty and contains only JAR file version information:

```
Manifest-Version: 1.0
Created-By: 1.7.0_07 (Oracle Corporation)
```

It is also possible to sign JAR files with a digital signature. When you do this, digest (checksum) information is added to the manifest for each archived item (as shown next) and the *META-INF* directory holds digital signature files for items in the archive.

```
Name: com/oreilly/Test.class
SHA1-Digest: dF2GZt8G11dXY2p4olzzIc5RjP3=
...
```

You can add your own information to the manifest descriptions by specifying your own supplemental, manifest file when you create the archive. This is one possible place to store other simple kinds of attribute information about the files in the archive, perhaps version or authorship information.

For example, we can create a file with the following *keyword: value* lines:

```
Name: spaceblaster/images/planetoid.gif
RevisionNumber: 42.7
Artist-Temperament: moody
```

To add this information to the manifest in our archive, place it in a file called *myManifest.mf* and give the following *jar* command:

```
% jar -cvmf myManifest.mf spaceblaster.jar spaceblaster
```

We included an additional option, `m`, which specifies that *jar* should read additional manifest information from the file given on the command line. How does *jar* know which file is which? Because `m` is before `f`, it expects to find the manifest information before the name of the JAR file it will create. If you think that's awkward, you're right; get the names in the wrong order, and *jar* does the wrong thing.

An application can get this manifest information from a JAR file using the `java.util.jar.Manifest` class.

We'll see more examples of adding information to the JAR manifest in Chapter 22. The JavaBeans APIs use manifest information to designate which classes are "beans" using a `Java-Bean` attribute. This information is used by IDEs that work with JavaBeans.

Making a JAR file runnable

Aside from attributes, you can put a few special values in the manifest file. One of these, `Main-Class`, allows you to specify the class containing the primary `main()` method for an application contained in the JAR:

```
Main-Class: com.oreilly.Game
```

If you add this to your JAR file manifest (using the `m` option described earlier), you can run the application directly from the JAR:

```
% java -jar spaceblaster.jar
```

More importantly, under Mac OS X, Windows, and other GUI environments, you can simply double-click on the JAR file to launch the application. The interpreter looks for the `Main-Class` value in the manifest, then loads the designated class as the application's startup class.

The pack200 Utility

Pack200 is an archive format that is optimized for storing compiled Java class files. Pack200 is not a new form of compression, but rather a super-efficient layout for class information that eliminates many types of waste and redundancy across related classes. It is effectively a bulk class-file format that deconstructs many classes and reassembles their parts efficiently into one catalog. This then allows a standard compression format like ZIP to work at maximum efficiency on the archive, achieving four or more times greater compression. The Java runtime does not understand the Pack200 format, so you cannot place archives of this type into the classpath. Instead, it is mainly an intermediate format that is very useful for transferring application JARs over the network for applets or other kinds of web-based applications.

You can convert a JAR to and from Pack200 format with the *pack200* and *unpack200* commands supplied with the JDK.

For example, to convert *foo.jar* to *foo.pack.gz*, use the *pack200* command:

```
% pack200 foo.pack.gz foo.jar
```

To convert *foo.pack.gz* to *foo.jar*:

```
% unpack200 foo.pack.gz foo.jar
```

Note that the Pack200 process completely tears down and reconstructs your classes at the class level, so the resulting *foo.jar* file will not be byte-for-byte the same as the original.

Policy Files

One of the truly novel things about Java is that security is built into the language. As described in Chapter 1, the Java VM can verify class files and Java's security manager can impose limits on what classes do. In early versions of Java, it was necessary to implement security policies *programmatically* by writing a Java security manager class and using it in your application. Later, a *declarative* security system was added. This system allows you to write *policy files*—text-based descriptions of permissions—which are much simpler and don't require code changes. These policy files tell the security manager what to allow and disallow and for whom.

In early versions of Java, much of the buzz had to do with the security of applets. Applets that were downloaded from untrusted locations could be run with security restrictions that prevented them from doing questionable things such as reading from or writing to the disk or contacting arbitrary computers on the network. With security policy files, it's easy to apply applet-style security to any application without modifying it. Furthermore, it's easy to fine-tune the access you grant. For example, you can allow an application to access only a specific directory on the disk, or you can allow network access to certain addresses.

Understanding security and security policies can be important, so we'll cover it here. However, in practice, you probably won't use this facility yourself, unless you are writing a framework for running applications from many unknown sources or need to restrict an application for some other reason.

The Default Security Manager

By default, no security manager is installed when you launch a Java application locally. You can turn on security using an option of the *java* interpreter to install a default security manager. The default security policy enforces many of the same rules as for applets. To see how this works, let's write a little program that does something questionable: it makes a network connection to some computer on the Internet. (We cover the specifics of network programming in Chapters 13 and 14.)

```
import java.net.*;

public class EvilEmpire {
  public static void main(String[] args) throws Exception{
    try {
      Socket s = new Socket("207.46.131.13", 80);
      System.out.println("Connected!");
    }
    catch (SecurityException e) {
      System.out.println("SecurityException: could not connect.");
    }
  }
}
```

If you run this program with the Java interpreter, it makes the network connection:

```
C:\> java EvilEmpire
Connected!
```

But because this program is "evil," let's install the default security manager, like this:

```
C:\> java -Djava.security.manager EvilEmpire
SecurityException: could not connect.
```

That's better, but suppose that the application actually has a legitimate reason to make its network connection. We'd like to leave the default security manager in place, just to be safe, but we'd like to grant this application permission to make a network connection.

The policytool Utility

To permit our `EvilEmpire` example to make a network connection, we need to create a *policy file* that contains the appropriate permission. A handy utility called *policytool*, included with the JDK, helps make policy files. Fire it up from a command line like this:

```
C:\> policytool
```

You may get an error message when *policytool* starts up about not finding a default policy file. Don't worry about this; just click *OK* to make the message go away.

We now add a network permission for the `EvilEmpire` application. The application is identified by its origin, also called a *codebase*, described by a URL. In this case, it is a `file:` URL that points to the location of the `EvilEmpire` application on your disk.

If you started up *policytool*, you should see its main window, shown in Figure 3-2. Click on *Add Policy Entry*. Another window pops up, like the one shown in Figure 3-3 (but with the fields empty).

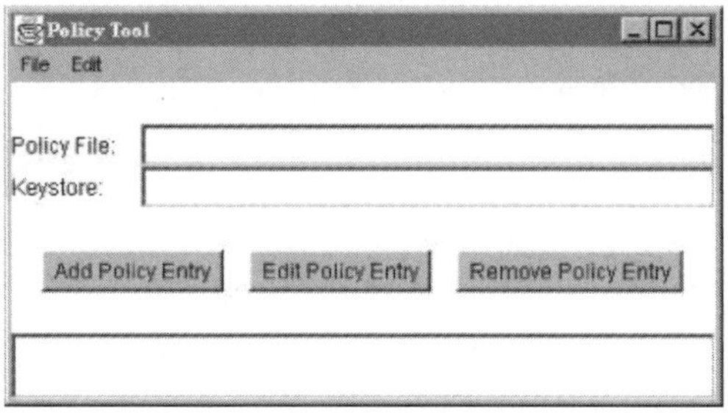

Figure 3-2. The Policy Tool window

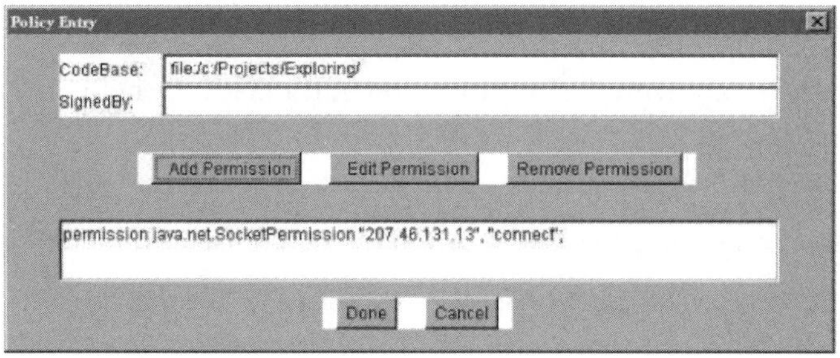

Figure 3-3. Adding a policy entry

First, fill in the codebase with the URL of the directory containing `EvilEmpire`. Then click on *Add Permission*. Yet another window pops up as shown in Figure 3-4.

Choose SocketPermission from the first combo box. Then fill out the second text field on the right side with the network address that `EvilEmpire` will connect to. Finally, choose Connect from the third combo box. Click on *OK*; you should see the new permission in the policy entry window, as shown in Figure 3-3.

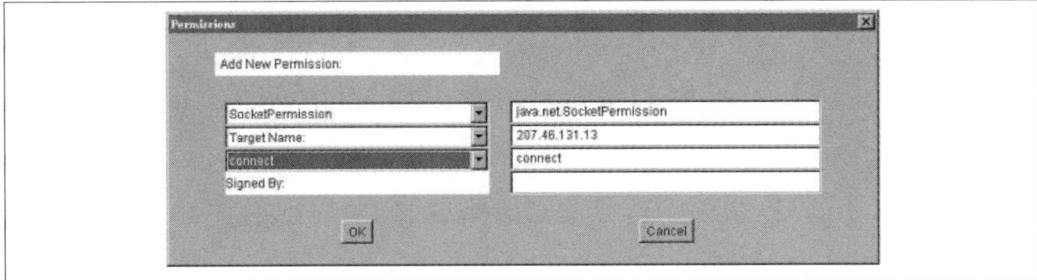

Figure 3-4. Creating a new permission

Click on *Done* to finish creating the policy. Then choose Save As from the File menu and save the policy file as something memorable, such as *EvilEmpire.policy*. You can quit *policytool* now; we're all done with it.

The policy file you just created is not complicated. Take a look at it with a text editor, which shows the simple syntax of the policy we created:

```
grant codeBase "file:/c:/Projects/Exploring/" {
  permission java.net.SocketPermission "207.46.131.13", "connect";
};
```

You can eschew *policytool* entirely and just create policy files with a text editor if you're more comfortable that way.

Using a Policy File with the Default Security Manager

Now that we've gone to the trouble of creating a policy file, let's use it. You can tell the default security manager to use the policy file with another command-line option to the `java` interpreter:

```
C:\> java -Djava.security.manager -Djava.security.policy=EvilEmpire.policy
      EvilEmpire
Connected!
```

`EvilEmpire` can now make its socket connection because we have explicitly granted it permission with a policy file. The default security manager still protects us in other ways, however. `EvilEmpire` cannot write or read files on the disk except in the directory it came from, and it cannot make connections to any other network addresses except the one we specified. Take a moment and bask in this warm fuzzy feeling.

CHAPTER 4

The Java Language

This chapter begins our introduction to the Java language syntax. Because readers come to this book with different levels of programming experience, it is difficult to set the right level for all audiences. We have tried to strike a balance between giving a thorough tour of the language syntax for beginners and providing enough background information so that a more experienced reader can quickly gauge the differences between Java and other languages. Since Java's syntax is derived from C, we make some comparisons to features of that language, but no prior knowledge of C is necessary. We spend more time on aspects of Java that are different from other languages and less on elemental programming concepts. For example, we'll take a close look at arrays in Java because they are significantly different from those in other languages. We won't, on the other hand, spend a lot of time explaining basic language constructs such as loops and control structures. Chapters 5 through 7 will build on this chapter by talking about Java's object-oriented side and complete the discussion of the core language. Chapter 8 discusses generics, a feature that enhances the way types work in the Java language, allowing you to write certain kinds of classes more flexibly and safely. After that, we dive into the Java APIs and see what we can do with the language. The rest of this book is filled with concise examples that do useful things and if you are left with any questions after these introductory chapters, we hope they'll be answered as you look at the code.

Text Encoding

Java is a language for the Internet. Since the citizens of the Net speak and write in many different human languages, Java must be able to handle a large number of languages as well. One of the ways in which Java supports internationalization is through the Unicode character set. Unicode is a worldwide standard that supports the scripts of most languages.[1] The latest version of Java bases its character and string data on the Unicode 6.0 standard, which uses at least two bytes to represent each symbol internally.

Java source code can be written using Unicode and stored in any number of character encodings, ranging from a full binary form to ASCII-encoded Unicode character values. This makes Java a friendly language for non-English-speaking programmers who can use their native language for class, method, and variable names just as they can for the text displayed by the application.

The Java `char` type and `String` class natively support Unicode values. Internally, the text is stored as multibyte characters using the UTF-16 encoding; however, the Java language and APIs make this transparent to you and you will not generally have to think about it. Unicode is also very ASCII-friendly (ASCII is the most common character encoding for English). The first 256 characters are defined to be identical to the first 256 characters in the ISO 8859-1 (Latin-1) character set, so Unicode is effectively backward-compatible with the most common English character sets. Furthermore, one of the most common file encodings for Unicode, called UTF-8, preserves ASCII values in their single byte form. This encoding is used by default in compiled Java class files, so storage remains compact for English text.

Most platforms can't display all currently defined Unicode characters. As a result, Java programs can be written with special Unicode escape sequences. A Unicode character can be represented with this escape sequence:

```
\uxxxx
```

`xxxx` is a sequence of one to four hexadecimal digits. The escape sequence indicates an ASCII-encoded Unicode character. This is also the form Java uses to output (print) Unicode characters in an environment that doesn't otherwise support them. Java also comes with classes to read and write Unicode character streams in specific encodings, including UTF-8.

Comments

Java supports both C-style *block comments* delimited by `/*` and `*/` and C++-style *line comments* indicated by `//`:

```
/*  This is a
        multiline
            comment.    */
```

1. For more information about Unicode, see *http://www.unicode.org*. Ironically, one of the scripts listed as "obsolete and archaic" and not currently supported by the Unicode standard is Javanese—a historical language of the people of the Island of Java.

```
// This is a single-line comment
// and so // is this
```

Block comments have both a beginning and end sequence and can cover large ranges of text. However, they cannot be "nested," meaning that you can't have a block comment inside of a block comment without the compiler getting confused. Single-line comments have only a start sequence and are delimited by the end of a line; extra // indicators inside a single line have no effect. Line comments are useful for short comments within methods; they don't conflict with block comments, so you can still comment out larger chunks of code in which they are nested.

Javadoc Comments

A block comment beginning with /** indicates a special *doccomment*. A doc comment is designed to be extracted by automated documentation generators, such as the JDK's *javadoc* program. A doc comment is terminated by the next */, just as with a regular block comment. Within the doc comment, lines beginning with @ are interpreted as special instructions for the documentation generator, giving it information about the source code. By convention, each line of a doc comment begins with a *, as shown in the following example, but this is optional. Any leading spacing and the * on each line are ignored:

```
/**
 * I think this class is possibly the most amazing thing you will
 * ever see. Let me tell you about my own personal vision and
 * motivation in creating it.
 * <p>
 * It all began when I was a small child, growing up on the
 * streets of Idaho. Potatoes were the rage, and life was good...
 *
 * @see PotatoPeeler
 * @see PotatoMasher
 * @author John 'Spuds' Smith
 * @version 1.00, 19 Dec 2006
 */
class Potato {
```

javadoc creates HTML documentation for classes by reading the source code and pulling out the embedded comments and @ tags. In this example, the tags cause author and version information to be presented in the class documentation. The @see tags produce hypertext links to the related class documentation.

The compiler also looks at the doc comments; in particular, it is interested in the @deprecated tag, which means that the method has been declared obsolete and should be avoided in new programs. The fact that a method is deprecated is noted in the compiled class file so a warning message can be generated whenever you use a deprecated feature in your code (even if the source isn't available).

Doc comments can appear above class, method, and variable definitions, but some tags may not be applicable to all of these. For example, the `@exception` tag can only be applied to methods. Table 4-1 summarizes the tags used in doc comments.

Table 4-1. Doc comment tags

Tag	Description	Applies to
`@see`	Associated class name	Class, method, or variable
`@author`	Author name	Class
`@version`	Version string	Class
`@param`	Parameter name and description	Method
`@return`	Description of return value	Method
`@exception`	Exception name and description	Method
`@deprecated`	Declares an item to be obsolete	Class, method, or variable
`@since`	Notes API version when item was added	Variable

Javadoc as metadata

Javadoc tags in doc comments represent *metadata* about the source code; that is, they add descriptive information about the structure or contents of the code that is not, strictly speaking, part of the application. Some additional tools extend the concept of Javadoc-style tags to include other kinds of metadata about Java programs that are carried with the compiled code and can more readily be used by the application to affect its compilation or runtime behavior. The Java *annotations* facility provides a more formal and extensible way to add metadata to Java classes, methods, and variables. We'll talk about annotations in Chapter 7. However, we should mention that there is a `@deprecated` annotation that has the same meaning as that of the Javadoc tag of the same name, and you may prefer to use that.

Types

The type system of a programming language describes how its data elements (variables and constants) are associated with storage in memory and how they are related to one another. In a statically typed language, such as C or C++, the type of a data element is a simple, unchanging attribute that often corresponds directly to some underlying hardware phenomenon, such as a register or a pointer value. In a more dynamic language such as Smalltalk or Lisp, variables can be assigned arbitrary elements and can effectively change their type throughout their lifetime. A considerable amount of overhead goes into validating what happens in these languages at runtime. Scripting languages such as Perl achieve ease of use by providing drastically simplified type systems in which only certain data elements can be stored in variables, and values are unified into a common representation, such as strings.

Java combines many of the best features of both statically and dynamically typed languages. As in a statically typed language, every variable and programming element in Java has a type that is known at compile time, so the runtime system doesn't normally have to check the validity of assignments between types while the code is executing. Unlike traditional C or C++, Java also maintains runtime information about objects and uses this to allow truly dynamic behavior. Java code may load new types at runtime and use them in fully object-oriented ways, allowing casting and full polymorphism (extending of types). Java code may also "reflect" upon or examine its own types at runtime, allowing advanced kinds of application behavior such as interpreters that can interact with compiled programs dynamically.

Java data types fall into two categories. *Primitive types* represent simple values that have built-in functionality in the language; they are fixed elements, such as literal constants and numbers. *Reference types* (or class types) include objects and arrays; they are called reference types because they "refer to" a large data type that is passed "by reference," as we'll explain shortly. *Generic types* are really just a kind of composition (combination) of class types and are therefore reference types as well.

Primitive Types

Numbers, characters, and Boolean values are fundamental elements in Java. Unlike some other (perhaps more pure) object-oriented languages, they are not objects. For those situations where it's desirable to treat a primitive value as an object, Java provides "wrapper" classes. The major advantage of treating primitive values as special is that the Java compiler and runtime can more readily optimize their implementation. Primitive values and computations can still be mapped down to hardware as they always have been in lower-level languages. Later we'll see how Java can automatically convert between primitive values and their object wrappers as needed to partially mask the difference between the two. We'll explain what that means in more detail in the next chapter when we discuss *boxing* and *unboxing* of primitive values.

An important portability feature of Java is that primitive types are precisely defined. For example, you never have to worry about the size of an `int` on a particular platform; it's always a 32-bit, signed, two's complement number. Table 4-2 summarizes Java's primitive types.

Table 4-2. Java primitive data types

Type	Definition
`boolean`	`true` or `false`
`char`	16-bit, Unicode character
`byte`	8-bit, signed, two's complement integer
`short`	16-bit, signed, two's complement integer
`int`	32-bit, signed, two's complement integer

Type	Definition
`long`	64-bit, signed, two's complement integer
`float`	32-bit, IEEE 754, floating-point value
`double`	64-bit, IEEE 754

Those of you with a C background may notice that the primitive types look like an idealization of C scalar types on a 32-bit machine, and you're absolutely right. That's how they're supposed to look. The 16-bit characters were forced by Unicode, and ad hoc pointers were deleted for other reasons. But overall, the syntax and semantics of Java primitive types derive from C.

Floating-point precision

Floating-point operations in Java follow the IEEE 754 international specification, which means that the result of floating-point calculations is normally the same on different Java platforms. However, Java allows for extended precision on platforms that support it. This can introduce extremely small-valued and arcane differences in the results of high-precision operations. Most applications would never notice this, but if you want to ensure that your application produces exactly the same results on different platforms, you can use the special keyword `strictfp` as a class modifier on the class containing the floating-point manipulation (we cover classes in the next chapter). The compiler then prohibits these platform-specific optimizations.

Variable declaration and initialization

Variables are declared inside of methods and classes with a type name followed by one or more comma-separated variable names. For example:

```
int foo;
double d1, d2;
boolean isFun;
```

Variables can optionally be initialized with an expression of the appropriate type when they are declared:

```
int foo = 42;
double d1 = 3.14, d2 = 2 * 3.14;
boolean isFun = true;
```

Variables that are declared as members of a class are set to default values if they aren't initialized (see Chapter 5). In this case, numeric types default to the appropriate flavor of zero, characters are set to the null character (`\0`), and Boolean variables have the value `false`. Local variables, which are declared inside a method and live only for the duration of a method call, on the other hand, must be explicitly initialized before they can be used. As we'll see, the compiler enforces this rule so there is no danger of forgetting.

Integer literals

Integer literals can be specified in octal (base 8), decimal (base 10), or hexadecimal (base 16). A decimal integer is specified by a sequence of digits beginning with one of the characters 1–9:

```
int i = 1230;
```

Octal numbers are distinguished from decimal numbers by a leading zero:

```
int i = 01230;             // i = 664 decimal
```

A hexadecimal number is denoted by the leading characters `0x` or `0X` (zero "x"), followed by a combination of digits and the characters a–f or A–F, which represent the decimal values 10–15:

```
int i = 0xFFFF;            // i = 65535 decimal
```

Integer literals are of type `int` unless they are suffixed with an `L`, denoting that they are to be produced as a `long` value:

```
long l = 13L;
long l = 13;       // equivalent: 13 is converted from type int
```

(The lowercase letter `l` is also acceptable but should be avoided because it often looks like the number `1`.)

When a numeric type is used in an assignment or an expression involving a "larger" type with a greater range, it can be *promoted* to the bigger type. In the second line of the previous example, the number `13` has the default type of `int`, but it's promoted to type `long` for assignment to the `long` variable. Certain other numeric and comparison operations also cause this kind of arithmetic promotion, as do mathematical expressions involving more than one type. For example, when multiplying a `byte` value by an `int` value, the compiler promotes the `byte` to an `int` first:

```
byte b = 42;
int i = 43;
int result = b * i;  // b is promoted to int before multiplication
```

A numeric value can never go the other way and be assigned to a type with a smaller range without an explicit cast, however:

```
int i = 13;
byte b = i;          // Compile-time error, explicit cast needed
byte b = (byte) i;   // OK
```

Conversions from floating-point to integer types always require an explicit cast because of the potential loss of precision.

Finally, we should note that if you are using Java 7 or later, you can add a bit of formatting to your numeric literals by utilizing the "_" underscore character between digits. So if you have particularly large strings of digits, you can break them up as in the following examples:

```
int RICHARD_NIXONS_SSN = 567_68_0515;
int for_no_reason = 1___2___3;
int JAVA_ID = 0xCAFE_BABE;
```

Underscores may only appear between digits, not at the beginning or end of a number or next to the "L" long integer signifier.

Floating-point literals

Floating-point values can be specified in decimal or scientific notation. Floating-point literals are of type `double` unless they are suffixed with an `f` or `F` denoting that they are to be produced as a `float` value. And just as with integer literals, in Java 7 you may use "_" underscore characters to format floating-point numbers—but only between digits, not at the beginning, end, or next to the decimal point or "F" signifier of the number.

```
double d = 8.31;
double e = 3.00e+8;
float f = 8.31F;
float g = 3.00e+8F;
float pi = 3.14_159_265_358;
```

Binary literals

A new feature of Java 7 is the introduction of binary literal values. This allows you to write out binary values directly by prefixing the number with a "0b" or "0B" (zero B).

```
byte one =     (byte)0b00000001;
byte two =     (byte)0b00000010;
byte four =    (byte)0b00000100;
byte sixteen = (byte)0b00001000;
int cafebabe = 0b11001010111111101011101010111110;
long lots_o_ones = (long)0b11111111111111111111111111111111111111111111111L;
```

Character literals

A literal character value can be specified either as a single-quoted character or as an escaped ASCII or Unicode sequence:

```
char a = 'a';
char newline = '\n';
char smiley = '\u263a';
```

Reference Types

In an object-oriented language like Java, you create new, complex data types from simple primitives by creating a `class`. Each class then serves as a new type in the language. For example, if we create a new class called `Foo` in Java, we are also implicitly creating a new type called `Foo`. The type of an item governs how it's used and where it can be assigned. As with primitives, an item of type `Foo` can, in general, be assigned to a variable of type `Foo` or passed as an argument to a method that accepts a `Foo` value.

A type is not just a simple attribute. Classes can have relationships with other classes and so do the types that they represent. All classes in Java exist in a parent-child hierarchy, where a child class or *subclass* is a specialized kind of its parent class. The corresponding types have the same relationship, where the type of the child class is considered a subtype of the parent class. Because child classes inherit all of the functionality of their parent classes, an object of the child's type is in some sense equivalent to or an extension of the parent type. An object of the child type can be used in place of an object of the parent's type. For example, if you create a new class, `Cat`, that extends `Animal`, the new type, `Cat`, is considered a subtype of `Animal`. Objects of type `Cat` can then be used anywhere an object of type `Animal` can be used; an object of type `Cat` is said to be assignable to a variable of type `Animal`. This is called *subtype polymorphism* and is one of the primary features of an object-oriented language. We'll look more closely at classes and objects in Chapter 5.

Primitive types in Java are used and passed "by value." In other words, when a primitive value like an `int` is assigned to a variable or passed as an argument to a method, it's simply copied. Reference types (class types), on the other hand, are always accessed "by reference." A *reference* is simply a handle or a name for an object. What a variable of a reference type holds is a "pointer" to an object of its type (or of a subtype, as described earlier). When the reference is assigned to a variable or passed to a method, only the reference is copied, not the object to which it's pointing. A reference is like a pointer in C or C++, except that its type is so strictly enforced. The reference value itself can't be explicitly created or changed. A variable acquires a reference value only through assignment to an appropriate object.

Let's run through an example. We declare a variable of type `Foo`, called `myFoo`, and assign it an appropriate object:[2]

```
Foo myFoo = new Foo();
Foo anotherFoo = myFoo;
```

2. The comparable code in C++ would be:

```
Foo& myFoo = *(new Foo());
Foo& anotherFoo = myFoo;
```

`myFoo` is a reference-type variable that holds a reference to the newly constructed `Foo` object. (For now, don't worry about the details of creating an object; we'll cover that in Chapter 5.) We declare a second `Foo` type variable, `anotherFoo`, and assign it to the same object. There are now two identical references : `myFoo` and `anotherFoo`, but only one actual `Foo` object instance. If we change things in the state of the `Foo` object itself, we see the same effect by looking at it with either reference.

Object references are passed to methods in the same way. In this case, either `myFoo` or `anotherFoo` would serve as equivalent arguments:

```
myMethod( myFoo );
```

An important, but sometimes confusing, distinction to make at this point is that the reference itself is a value and that value is copied when it is assigned to a variable or passed in a method call. Given our previous example, the argument passed to a method (a local variable from the method's point of view) is actually a third reference to the Foo object, in addition to `myFoo` and `anotherFoo`. The method can alter the state of the `Foo` object through that reference (calling its methods or altering its variables), but it can't change the caller's notion of the reference to `myFoo`: that is, the method can't change the caller's `myFoo` to point to a different `Foo` object; it can change only its own reference. This will be more obvious when we talk about methods later. Java differs from C++ in this respect. If you need to change a caller's reference to an object in Java, you need an additional level of indirection. The caller would have to wrap the reference in another object so that both could share the reference to it.

Reference types always point to objects, and objects are always defined by classes. However, two special kinds of reference types—arrays and interfaces—specify the type of object they point to in a slightly different way.

Arrays in Java have a special place in the type system. They are a special kind of object automatically created to hold a collection of some other type of object, known as the *base type*. Declaring an array type reference implicitly creates the new class type designed as a container for its base type, as you'll see in the next chapter.

Interfaces are a bit sneakier. An interface defines a set of methods and gives it a corresponding type. An object that implements the methods of the interface can be referred to by that interface type, as well as its own type. Variables and method arguments can be declared to be of interface types, just like other class types, and any object that implements the interface can be assigned to them. This adds flexibility in the type system and allows Java to cross the lines of the class hierarchy and make objects that effectively have many types. We'll cover interfaces in the next chapter as well.

Generic types or *parameterized types*, as we mentioned earlier, are an extension of the Java class syntax that allows for additional abstraction in the way classes work with other Java types. Generics allow for specialization of classes by the user without changing any of the original class's code. We cover generics in detail in Chapter 8.

A Word About Strings

Strings in Java are objects; they are therefore a reference type. `String` objects do, however, have some special help from the Java compiler that makes them look more like primitive types. Literal string values in Java source code are turned into `String` objects by the compiler. They can be used directly, passed as arguments to methods, or assigned to `String` type variables:

```
System.out.println( "Hello, World..." );
String s = "I am the walrus...";
String t = "John said: \"I am the walrus...\"";
```

The + symbol in Java is "overloaded" to perform string concatenation as well as regular numeric addition. Along with its sister +=, this is the only overloaded operator in Java:

```
String quote = "Four score and " + "seven years ago,";
String more = quote + " our" + " fathers" +  " brought...";
```

Java builds a single `String` object from the concatenated strings and provides it as the result of the expression. We discuss the `String` class and all things text-related in great detail in Chapter 10.

Statements and Expressions

Java *statements* appear inside methods and classes; they describe all activities of a Java program. Variable declarations and assignments, such as those in the previous section, are statements, as are basic language structures such as if/then conditionals and loops.

```
int size = 5;
if ( size > 10 )
    doSomething();
for( int x = 0; x < size; x++ ) { ... }
```

Expressions produce values; an expression is evaluated to produce a result that is to be used as part of another expression or in a statement. Method calls, object allocations, and, of course, mathematical expressions are examples of expressions. Technically, because variable assignments can be used as values for further assignments or operations (in somewhat questionable programming style), they can be considered to be both statements and expressions.

```
new Object();
Math.sin( 3.1415 );
42 * 64;
```

One of the tenets of Java is to keep things simple and consistent. To that end, when there are no other constraints, evaluations and initializations in Java always occur in the order in which they appear in the code—from left to right, top to bottom. We'll see this rule used in the evaluation of assignment expressions, method calls, and array indexes, to name a few cases. In some other languages, the order of evaluation is more complicated or even implementation-dependent. Java removes this element of danger by precisely and simply defining how the code is evaluated. This doesn't mean you should start writing obscure and convoluted statements, however. Relying on the order of evaluation of expressions in complex ways is a bad programming habit, even when it works. It produces code that is hard to read and harder to modify.

Statements

Statements and expressions in Java appear within a *code block*. A code block is syntactically a series of statements surrounded by an open curly brace ({) and a close curly brace (}). The statements in a code block can include variable declarations and most of the other sorts of statements and expressions we mentioned earlier:

```
{
    int size = 5;
    setName("Max");
    ...
}
```

Methods, which look like C functions, are in a sense just code blocks that take parameters and can be called by their names—for example, the method `setUpDog()`:

```
setUpDog( String name ) {
    int size = 5;
    setName( name );
    ...
}
```

Variable declarations are limited in scope to their enclosing code block—that is, they can't be seen outside of the nearest set of braces:

```
{
    int i = 5;
}

i = 6;           // Compile-time error, no such variable i
```

In this way, code blocks can be used to arbitrarily group other statements and variables. The most common use of code blocks, however, is to define a group of statements for use in a conditional or iterative statement.

if/else conditionals

We can define an `if/else` clause as follows:

```
if ( condition )
    statement;
[ else
    statement; ]
```

(The whole of the preceding example is itself a statement and could be nested within another if/else clause.) The if clause has the common functionality of taking two different forms: a "one-liner" or a block. The block form is as follows:

```
if ( condition ) {
    [ statement; ]
    [ statement; ]
    [ ... ]
} else {
    [ statement; ]
    [ statement; ]
    [ ... ]
}
```

The *condition* is a Boolean expression. A Boolean expression is a true or false value or an expression that evaluates to one of those. For example i == 0 is a Boolean expression that tests whether the integer i holds the value 0.

In the second form, the statements are in code blocks, and all their enclosed statements are executed if the corresponding (if or else) branch is taken. Any variables declared within each block are visible only to the statements within the block. Like the if/else conditional, most of the remaining Java statements are concerned with controlling the flow of execution. They act for the most part like their namesakes in other languages.

do/while loops

The do and while iterative statements have the familiar functionality; their conditional test is also a Boolean expression:

```
while ( condition )
    statement;
do
    statement;
while ( condition );
```

For example:

```
while( queue.isEmpty() )
    wait();
```

Unlike while or for loops (which we'll see next) that test their conditions first, a do-while loop always executes its statement body at least once.

The for loop

The most general form of the for loop is also a holdover from the C language:

```
for ( initialization; condition; incrementor )
    statement;
```

The variable initialization section can declare or initialize variables that are limited to the scope of the for statement. The for loop then begins a possible series of rounds in which the condition is first checked and, if true, the body statement (or block) is executed. Following each execution of the body, the incrementor expressions are evaluated to give them a chance to update variables before the next round begins:

```
for ( int i = 0; i < 100; i++ ) {
    System.out.println( i );
    int j = i;
    ...
}
```

This loop will execute 100 times, printing values from 0 to 99. Note that the variable `j` is local to the block (visible only to statements within it) and will not be accessible to the code "after" the `for` loop. If the condition of a `for` loop returns false on the first check, the body and incrementor section will never be executed.

You can use multiple comma-separated expressions in the initialization and incrementation sections of the `for` loop. For example:

```
for (int i = 0, j = 10; i < j; i++, j-- ) {
   ...
}
```

You can also initialize existing variables from outside the scope of the `for` loop within the initializer block. You might do this if you wanted to use the end value of the loop variable elsewhere:

```
int x;
for( x = 0; hasMoreValue(); x++ )
  getNextValue();
System.out.println( x );
```

The enhanced for loop

Java's auspiciously dubbed "enhanced `for` loop" acts like the "foreach" statement in some other languages, iterating over a series of values in an array or other type of collection:

```
for ( varDeclaration : iterable )
    statement;
```

The enhanced `for` loop can be used to loop over arrays of any type as well as any kind of Java object that implements the `java.lang.Iterable` interface. This includes most of the classes of the Java Collections API. We'll talk about arrays in this and the next chapter; Chapter 11 covers Java Collections. Here are a couple of examples:

```
int [] arrayOfInts = new int [] { 1, 2, 3, 4 };

for( int i  : arrayOfInts )
    System.out.println( i );

List<String> list = new ArrayList<String>();
list.add("foo");
list.add("bar");
```

```
for( String s : list )
    System.out.println( s );
```

Again, we haven't discussed arrays or the `List` class and special syntax in this example. What we're showing here is the enhanced `for` loop iterating over an array of integers and also a list of string values. In the second case, the `List` implements the `Iterable` interface and thus can be a target of the `for` loop.

switch statements

The most common form of the Java `switch` statement takes an integer (or a numeric type argument that can be automatically "promoted" to an integer type), a string type argument, or an "enum" type (discussed shortly) and selects among a number of alternative, constant `case` branches:[3]

```
switch ( expression )
{
    case constantExpression :
        statement;
    [ case constantExpression :statement;  ]
    ...
    [ default :
        statement;  ]
}
```

The case expression for each branch must evaluate to a different constant integer or string value at compile time. Strings are compared using the `String` `equals()` method, which we'll discuss in more detail in Chapter 10. An optional `default` case can be specified to catch unmatched conditions. When executed, the switch simply finds the branch matching its conditional expression (or the default branch) and executes the corresponding statement. But that's not the end of the story. Perhaps counterintuitively, the `switch` statement then continues executing branches after the matched branch until it hits the end of the switch or a special statement called `break`. Here are a couple of examples:

```
int value = 2;

switch( value ) {
    case 1:
        System.out.println( 1 );
    case 2:
        System.out.println( 2 );
    case 3:
        System.out.println( 3 );
}
```

3. Strings in `switch` statements were added in Java 7.

```
// prints 2, 3!
```

Using `break` to terminate each branch is more common:

```
int retValue = checkStatus();

switch ( retVal )
{
    case MyClass.GOOD :
        // something good
        break;
    case MyClass.BAD :
        // something bad
        break;
    default :
        // neither one
        break;
}
```

In this example, only one branch—`GOOD`, `BAD`, or the default—is executed. The "fall through" behavior of the switch is justified when you want to cover several possible case values with the same statement without resorting to a bunch of `if/else` statements:

```
int value = getSize();

switch( value ) {
    case MINISCULE:
    case TEENYWEENIE:
    case SMALL:
        System.out.println("Small" );
        break;
    case MEDIUM:
        System.out.println("Medium" );
        break;
    case LARGE:
    case EXTRALARGE:
        System.out.println("Large" );
        break;
}
```

This example effectively groups the six possible values into three cases.

Enumerations and switch statements

Enumerations are intended to replace much of the usage of integer constants for situations like the one just discussed with a typesafe alternative. Enumerations use objects as their values instead of integers but preserve the notion of ordering and comparability. We'll see in Chapter 5 that enumerations are declared much like classes and that the values can be "imported" into the code of your application to be used just like constants. For example:

```
enum Size { Small, Medium, Large }
```

You can use enumerations in switches in the same way that the previous switch examples used integer constants. In fact, it is much safer to do so because the enumerations have real types and the compiler does not let you mistakenly add cases that do not match any value or mix values from different enumerations.

```
// usage
Size size = ...;
switch ( size ) {
    case Small:
        ...
    case Medium:
        ...
    case Large:
        ...
}
```

Chapter 5 provides more details about enumerations.

break/continue

The Java `break` statement and its friend `continue` can also be used to cut short a loop or conditional statement by jumping out of it. A `break` causes Java to stop the current block statement and resume execution after it. In the following example, the `while` loop goes on endlessly until the `condition()` method returns true, triggering a `break` statement that stops the loop and proceeds at the point marked "after while."

```
while( true ) {
    if ( condition() )
        break;
}
// after while
```

A `continue` statement causes `for` and `while` loops to move on to their next iteration by returning to the point where they check their condition. The following example prints the numbers 0 through 99, skipping number 33.

```
for( int i=0; i < 100; i++ ) {
    if ( i == 33 )
        continue;
    System.out.println( i );
}
```

The `break` and `continue` statements look like those in the C language, but Java's forms have the additional ability to take a label as an argument and jump out multiple levels to the scope of the labeled point in the code. This usage is not very common in day-to-day Java coding, but may be important in special cases. Here is an outline:

```
labelOne:
    while ( condition ) {
        ...
```

```
            labelTwo:
                while ( condition ) {
                    ...

                    // break or continue point
                }
            // after labelTwo
        }
    // after labelOne
```

Enclosing statements, such as code blocks, conditionals, and loops, can be labeled with identifiers like `labelOne` and `labelTwo`. In this example, a `break` or `continue` without argument at the indicated position has the same effect as the earlier examples. A `break` causes processing to resume at the point labeled "after labelTwo"; a `continue` immediately causes the `labelTwo` loop to return to its condition test.

The statement `break labelTwo` at the indicated point has the same effect as an ordinary `break`, but `break labelOne` breaks both levels and resumes at the point labeled "after labelOne." Similarly, `continue labelTwo` serves as a normal `continue`, but `continue labelOne` returns to the test of the `labelOne` loop. Multilevel `break` and `continue` statements remove the main justification for the evil `goto` statement in C/C++.

There are a few Java statements we aren't going to discuss right now. The `try` , `catch`, and `finally` statements are used in exception handling, as we'll discuss later in this chapter. The `synchronized` statement in Java is used to coordinate access to statements among multiple threads of execution; see Chapter 9 for a discussion of thread synchronization.

Unreachable statements

On a final note, we should mention that the Java compiler flags "unreachable" statements as compile-time errors. An unreachable statement is one that the compiler determines won't be called at all. Of course, many methods may never actually be called in your code, but the compiler detects only those that it can "prove" are never called by simple checking at compile time. For example, a method with an unconditional return statement in the middle of it causes a compile-time error, as does a method with a conditional that the compiler can tell will never be fulfilled:

```
    if (1 < 2)
        return;
    // unreachable statements
```

Expressions

An expression produces a result, or value, when it is evaluated. The value of an expression can be a numeric type, as in an arithmetic expression; a reference type, as in an object allocation; or the special type, `void`, which is the declared type of a method that doesn't return a value. In the last case, the expression is evaluated only for its *side effects*; that is, the work it does aside from producing a value. The type of an expression is known at compile time. The value produced at runtime is either of this type or in the case of a reference type, a compatible (assignable) subtype.

Operators

Java supports almost all standard operators from the C language. These operators also have the same precedence in Java as they do in C, as shown in Table 4-3.

Table 4-3. Java operators

Precedence	Operator	Operand type	Description
1	++, —	Arithmetic	Increment and decrement
1	+, -	Arithmetic	Unary plus and minus
1	~	Integral	Bitwise complement
1	!	Boolean	Logical complement
1	(*type*)	Any	Cast
2	*, /, %	Arithmetic	Multiplication, division, remainder
3	+, -	Arithmetic	Addition and subtraction
3	+	String	String concatenation
4	<<	Integral	Left shift
4	>>	Integral	Right shift with sign extension
4	>>>	Integral	Right shift with no extension
5	<, <=, >, >=	Arithmetic	Numeric comparison
5	`instanceof`	Object	Type comparison
6	==, !=	Primitive	Equality and inequality of value
6	==, !=	Object	Equality and inequality of reference
7	&	Integral	Bitwise AND
7	&	Boolean	Boolean AND
8	^	Integral	Bitwise XOR
8	^	Boolean	Boolean XOR
9	|	Integral	Bitwise OR
9	|	Boolean	Boolean OR
10	&&	Boolean	Conditional AND
11	||	Boolean	Conditional OR
12	?:	N/A	Conditional ternary operator
13	=	Any	Assignment

We should also note that the percent (%) operator is not strictly a modulo, but a remainder, and can have a negative value.

Java also adds some new operators. As we've seen, the + operator can be used with String values to perform string concatenation. Because all integral types in Java are signed values, the >> operator can be used to perform a right-arithmetic-shift operation with sign extension. The >>> operator treats the operand as an unsigned number and performs a right-arithmetic-shift with no sign extension. The new operator is used to create objects; we will discuss it in detail shortly.

Assignment

While variable initialization (i.e., declaration and assignment together) is considered a statement with no resulting value, variable assignment alone is an expression:

```
int i, j;           // statement
i = 5;              // both expression and statement
```

Normally, we rely on assignment for its side effects alone, but an assignment can be used as a value in another part of an expression:

```
j = ( i = 5 );
```

Again, relying on order of evaluation extensively (in this case, using compound assignments in complex expressions) can make code obscure and hard to read.

The null value

The expression null can be assigned to any reference type. It means "no reference." A null reference can't be used to reference anything and attempting to do so generates a NullPointerException at runtime.

Variable access

The dot (.) operator is used to select members of a class or object instance. (We'll talk about those in detail in the following chapters.) It can retrieve the value of an instance variable (of an object) or a static variable (of a class). It can also specify a method to be invoked on an object or class:

```
int i = myObject.length;
String s = myObject.name;
myObject.someMethod();
```

A reference-type expression can be used in compound evaluations by selecting further variables or methods on the result:

```
int len = myObject.name.length();
int initialLen = myObject.name.substring(5, 10).length();
```

Here we have found the length of our name variable by invoking the length() method of the String object. In the second case, we took an intermediate step and asked for a substring of the name string. The substring method of the String class also returns a String reference, for which we ask the length. Compounding operations like this is also called *chaining* method calls, which we'll mention later. One chained selection operation that we've used a lot already is calling the `println()` method on the variable `out` of the `System` class:

```
System.out.println("calling println on out");
```

Method invocation

Methods are functions that live within a class and may be accessible through the class or its instances, depending on the kind of method. Invoking a method means to execute its body statements, passing in any required parameter variables and possibly getting a value in return. A method invocation is an expression that results in a value. The value's type is the *return type* of the method:

```
System.out.println( "Hello, World..." );
int myLength = myString.length();
```

Here, we invoked the methods `println()` and `length()` on different objects. The `length()` method returned an integer value; the return type of `println()` is `void` (no value).

This is all pretty simple, but in Chapter 5 we'll see that it gets a little more complex when there are methods with the same name but different parameter types in the same class or when a method is redefined in a child class, as described in Chapter 6.

Object creation

Objects in Java are allocated with the `new` operator:

```
Object o = new Object();
```

The argument to `new` is the constructor for the class. The *constructor* is a method that always has the same name as the class. The constructor specifies any required parameters to create an instance of the object. The value of the `new` expression is a reference of the type of the created object. Objects always have one or more constructors, though they may not always be accessible to you.

We look at object creation in detail in Chapter 5. For now, just note that object creation is a type of expression and that the result is an object reference. A minor oddity is that the binding of `new` is "tighter" than that of the dot (`.`) selector. So you can create a new object and invoke a method in it without assigning the object to a reference type variable if you have some reason to:

```
int hours = new Date().getHours();
```

The `Date` class is a utility class that represents the current time. Here we create a new instance of `Date` with the `new` operator and call its `getHours()` method to retrieve the current hour as an integer value. The `Date` object reference lives long enough to service the method call and is then cut loose and garbage-collected at some point in the future (see Chapter 5 for details about garbage collection).

Calling methods in object references in this way is, again, a matter of style. It would certainly be clearer to allocate an intermediate variable of type `Date` to hold the new object and then call its `getHours()` method. However, combining operations like this is common.

The instanceof operator

The `instanceof` operator can be used to determine the type of an object at runtime. It tests to see if an object is of the same type or a subtype of the target type. This is the same as asking if the object can be assigned to a variable of the target type. The target type may be a class, interface, or array type as we'll see later. `instanceof` returns a `boolean` value that indicates whether the object matches the type:

```
Boolean b;
String str = "foo";
b = ( str instanceof String ); // true, str is a String
b = ( str instanceof Object ); // also true, a String is an Object
//b = ( str instanceof Date ); // The compiler is smart enough to catch this!
```

`instanceof` also correctly reports whether the object is of the type of an array or a specified interface (as we'll discuss later):

```
if ( foo instanceof byte[] )
    ...
```

It is also important to note that the value `null` is not considered an instance of any object. The following test returns `false`, no matter what the declared type of the variable:

```
String s = null;
if ( s instanceof String )
    // false, null isn't an instance of anything
```

Exceptions

Java has its roots in embedded systems—software that runs inside specialized devices, such as handheld computers, cellular phones, and fancy toasters. In those kinds of applications, it's especially important that software errors be handled robustly. Most users would agree that it's unacceptable for their phone to simply crash or for their toast (and perhaps their house) to burn because their software failed. Given that we can't eliminate the possibility of software errors, it's a step in the right direction to recognize and deal with anticipated application-level errors methodically.

Dealing with errors in some languages is entirely the responsibility of the programmer. The language itself provides no help in identifying error types and no tools for dealing with them easily. In the C language, a routine generally indicates a failure by returning an "unreasonable" value (e.g., the idiomatic `-1` or `null`). As the programmer, you must know what constitutes a bad result and what it means. It's often awkward to work around the limitations of passing error values in the normal path of data flow.[4] An even worse problem is that certain types of errors can legitimately occur almost anywhere, and it's prohibitive and unreasonable to explicitly test for them at every point in the software.

Java offers an elegant solution to these problems through *exceptions*. (Java exception handling is similar to, but not quite the same as, exception handling in C++.) An *exception* indicates an unusual condition or an error condition. Program control becomes unconditionally transferred or "thrown" to a specially designated section of code where it's caught and handled. In this way, error handling is orthogonal to (or independent of) the normal flow of the program. We don't have to have special return values for all of our methods; errors are handled by a separate mechanism. Control can be passed a long distance from a deeply nested routine and handled in a single location when that is desirable, or an error can be handled immediately at its source. A few standard Java API methods still return `-1` as a special value, but these are generally limited to situations where we are expecting a special value and the situation is not really out of bounds.[5]

A Java method is required to specify the exceptions it can throw (i.e., the ones that it doesn't catch itself), and the compiler makes sure that callers of the method handle them. In this way, the information about what errors a method can produce is promoted to the same level of importance as its argument and return types. You may still decide to punt and ignore obvious errors, but in Java you must do so explicitly. (We'll discuss "runtime exceptions," which are not required to be declared or handled by the method, in a moment.)

Exceptions and Error Classes

Exceptions are represented by instances of the class `java.lang.Exception` and its subclasses. Subclasses of `Exception` can hold specialized information (and possibly behavior) for different kinds of exceptional conditions. However, more often they are simply "logical" subclasses that serve only to identify a new exception type. Figure 4-1 shows the subclasses of `Exception` in the `java.lang` package. It should give you a feel for how exceptions are organized. Most other packages define their own exception types, which usually are subclasses of `Exception` itself or of its important subclass `RuntimeException`, which we'll get to in a moment.

4. The somewhat obscure `setjmp()` and `longjmp()` statements in C can save a point in the execution of code and later return to it unconditionally from a deeply buried location. In a limited sense, this is the functionality of exceptions in Java.

5. For example, the `getHeight()` method of the `Image` class returns `-1` if the height isn't known yet. No error has occurred; the height will be available in the future. In this situation, throwing an exception would be inappropriate.

For example, an important exception class is `IOException` in the package `java.io`. The `IOException` class extends `Exception` and has many subclasses for typical I/O problems (such as a `FileNotFoundException`) and networking problems (such as a `MalformedURLException`). Network exceptions belong to the `java.net` package. Another important descendant of `IOException` is `RemoteException`, which belongs to the `java.rmi` package. It is used when problems arise during remote method invocation (RMI). Throughout this book, we mention exceptions you need to be aware of as we encounter them.

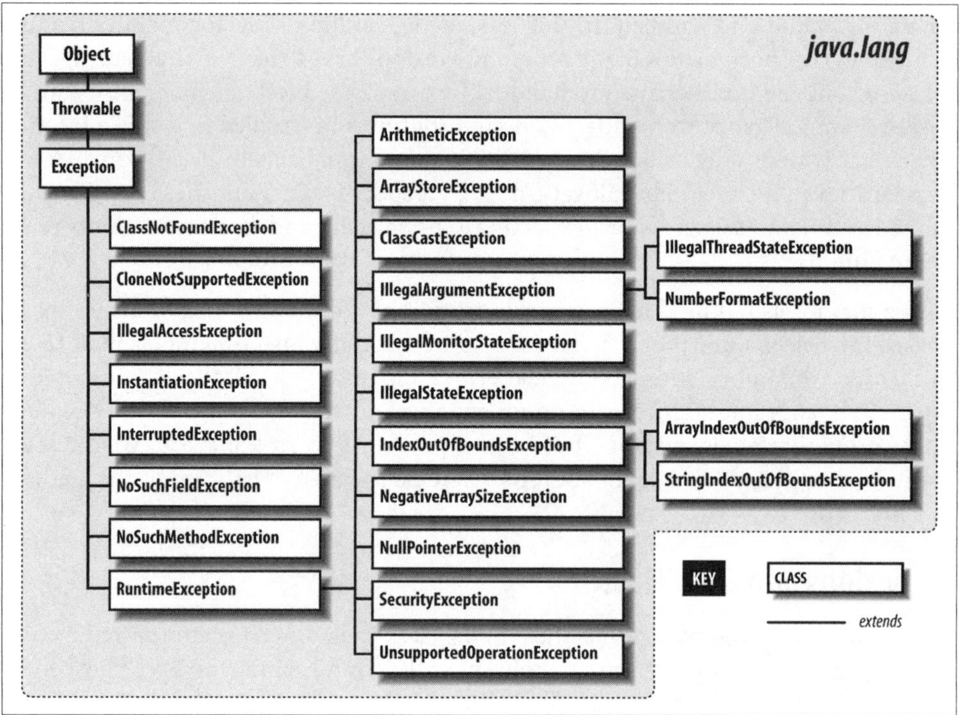

Figure 4-1. The java.lang.Exception subclasses

An `Exception` object is created by the code at the point where the error condition arises. It can be designed to hold any information that is necessary to describe the exceptional condition and also includes a full *stack trace* for debugging. (A stack trace is the list of all the methods called and the order in which they were called to reach the point where the exception was thrown.) The `Exception` object is passed as an argument to the handling block of code, along with the flow of control. This is where the terms *throw* and *catch* come from: the `Exception` object is thrown from one point in the code and caught by the other, where execution resumes.

The Java API also defines the `java.lang.Error` class for unrecoverable errors. The subclasses of `Error` in the `java.lang` package are shown in Figure 4-2. A notable `Error` type is `AssertionError`, which is used by the Java `assert` statement to indicate a failure (assertions are discussed later in this chapter). A few other packages define their own subclasses of `Error`, but subclasses of `Error` are much less common (and less useful) than subclasses of `Exception`. You generally needn't worry about these errors in your code (i.e., you do not have to catch them); they are intended to indicate fatal problems or virtual machine errors. An error of this kind usually causes the Java interpreter to display a message and exit. You are actively discouraged from trying to catch or recover from them because they are supposed to indicate a fatal program bug, not a routine condition.

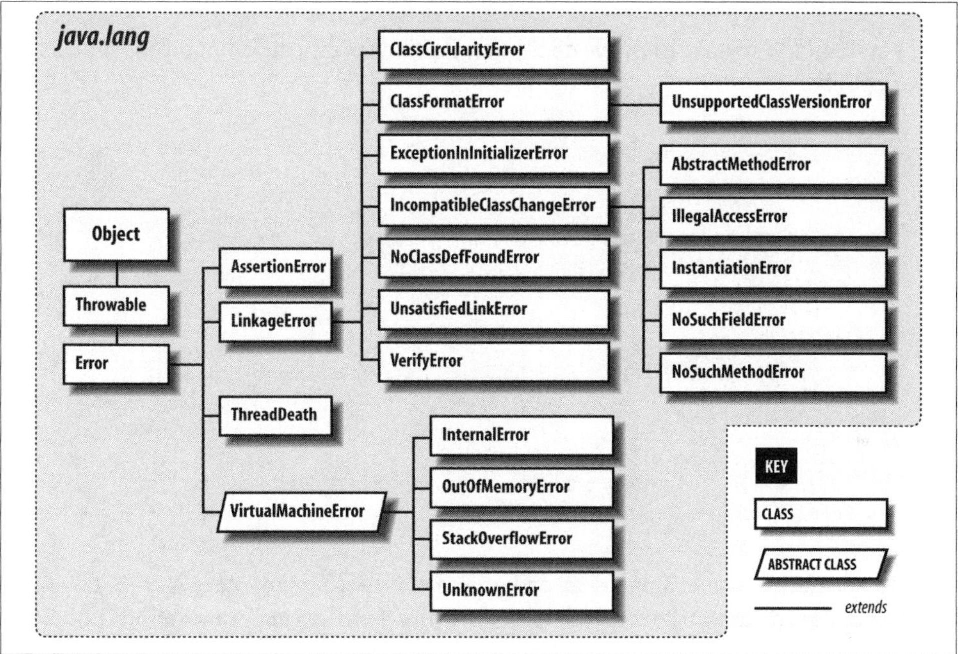

Figure 4-2. The java.lang.Error subclasses

Both `Exception` and `Error` are subclasses of `Throwable`. The `Throwable` class is the base class for objects that can be "thrown" with the `throw` statement. In general, you should extend only `Exception`, `Error`, or one of their subclasses.

Exception Handling

The `try`/`catch` guarding statements wrap a block of code and catch designated types of exceptions that occur within it:

```
try {
    readFromFile("foo");
    ...
}
catch ( Exception e ) {
    // Handle error
    System.out.println( "Exception while reading file: " + e );
    ...
}
```

In this example, exceptions that occur within the body of the `try` portion of the statement are directed to the `catch` clause for possible handling. The `catch` clause acts like a method; it specifies as an argument the type of exception it wants to handle and if it's invoked, it receives the `Exception` object as an argument. Here, we receive the object in the variable `e` and print it along with a message.

A `try` statement can have multiple `catch` clauses that specify different types (subclasses) of `Exception`:

```
try {
    readFromFile("foo");
    ...
}
catch ( FileNotFoundException e ) {
    // Handle file not found
    ...
}
catch ( IOException e ) {
    // Handle read error
    ...
}
catch ( Exception e ) {
    // Handle all other errors
    ...
}
```

The `catch` clauses are evaluated in order, and the first assignable match is taken. At most, one `catch` clause is executed, which means that the exceptions should be listed from most to least specific. In the previous example, we anticipate that the hypothetical `readFromFile()` can throw two different kinds of exceptions: one for a file not found and another for a more general read error. In the preceding example, `FileNotFoundException` is a subclass of `IOException`, so if the first `catch` clause were not there, the exception would be caught by the second in this case. Similarly, any subclass of `Exception` is assignable to the parent type `Exception`, so the third `catch` clause would catch anything passed by the first two. It acts here like the `default` clause in a `switch` statement and handles any remaining possibilities. We've shown it here for completeness, but in general you want to be as specific as possible in the exception types you catch.

One beauty of the `try/catch` scheme is that any statement in the `try` block can assume that all previous statements in the block succeeded. A problem won't arise suddenly because a programmer forgot to check the return value from a method. If an earlier statement fails, execution jumps immediately to the `catch` clause; later statements are never executed.

In Java 7, there is an alternative to using multiple `catch` clauses, and that is to handle multiple discrete exception types in a single `catch` clause using the "|" or syntax:

```
try {
    // read from network...
    // write to file..
catch ( ZipException | SSLException e ) {
    logException( e );
}
```

Using this "|" or syntax, we receive both types of exception in the same `catch` clause. So, what is the actual type of the `e` variable that we are passing to our log method? (What can we do with it?) In this case, it will be neither `ZipException` nor `SSLException` but `IOException`, which is the two exceptions' nearest common ancestor (the closest parent class type to which they are both assignable). In many cases, the nearest common type among the two or more argument exception types may simply be `Exception`, the parent of all exception types. The difference between catching these discrete exception types with a multiple-type `catch` clause and simply catching the common parent exception type is that we are limiting our `catch` to only these specifically enumerated exception types and we will not catch all the other `IOException` types, as would be the alternative in this case. The combination of multiple-type `catch` and ordering your `catch` clauses from most specific to most broad ("narrow" to "wide") types gives you great flexibility to structure your `catch` clauses to consolidate handling logic where it is appropriate and to not repeat code. There are more nuances to this feature, and we will return to it after we have discussed "throwing" and "rethrowing" exceptions.

Bubbling Up

What if we hadn't caught the exception? Where would it have gone? Well, if there is no enclosing `try/catch` statement, the exception pops up from the method in which it originated and is thrown from that method up to its caller. If that point in the calling method is within a `try` clause, control passes to the corresponding `catch` clause. Otherwise, the exception continues propagating up the call stack, from one method to its caller. In this way, the exception bubbles up until it's caught, or until it pops out of the top of the program, terminating it with a runtime error message. There's a bit more to it than that because in this case, the compiler might have forced us to deal with it along the way, but we'll get back to that in a moment.

Let's look at another example. In Figure 4-3, the method `getContent()` invokes the method `openConnection()` from within a `try/catch` statement. In turn, `openConnection()` invokes the method `sendRequest()`, which calls the method `write()` to send some data.

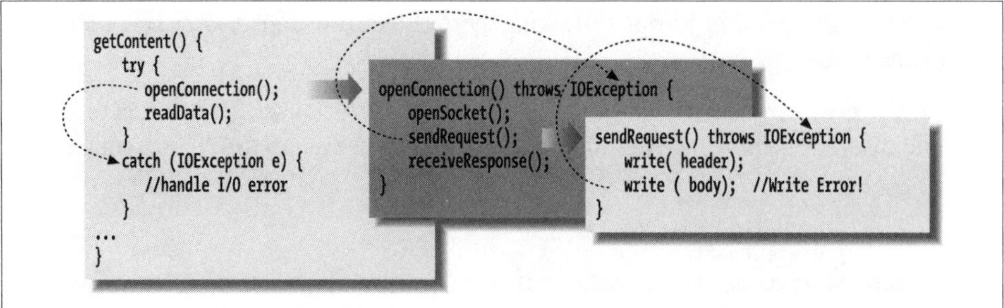

Figure 4-3. Exception propagation

In this figure, the second call to `write()` throws an `IOException`. Since `sendRequest()` doesn't contain a `try/catch` statement to handle the exception, it's thrown again from the point where it was called in the method `openConnection()`. Since `openConnection()` doesn't catch the exception either, it's thrown once more. Finally, it's caught by the `try` statement in `getContent()` and handled by its `catch` clause. Notice that each throwing method must declare with a "throws" clause that it can throw the particular type of exception. We'll discuss this shortly.

Stack Traces

Because an exception can bubble up quite a distance before it is caught and handled, we may need a way to determine exactly where it was thrown. It's also very important to know the context of how the point of the exception was reached; that is, which methods called which methods to get to that point. For these kinds of debugging and logging purposes, all exceptions can dump a stack trace that lists their method of origin and all the nested method calls it took to arrive there. Most commonly, the user sees a stack trace when it is printed using the `printStackTrace()` method.

```
try {
    // complex, deeply nested task
} catch ( Exception e ) {
    // dump information about exactly where the exception occurred
    e.printStackTrace( System.err );
    ...
}
```

For example, the stack trace for an exception might look like this:

```
java.io.FileNotFoundException: myfile.xml
      at java.io.FileInputStream.<init>(FileInputStream.java)
      at java.io.FileInputStream.<init>(FileInputStream.java)
      at MyApplication.loadFile(MyApplication.java:137)
      at MyApplication.main(MyApplication.java:5)
```

This stack trace indicates that the `main()` method of the class `MyApplication` called the method `loadFile()`. The `loadFile()` method then tried to construct a `FileInputStream`, which threw the `FileNotFoundException`. Note that once the stack trace reaches Java system classes (like `FileInputStream`), the line numbers may be lost. This can also happen when the code is optimized by some virtual machines. Usually, there is a way to disable the optimization temporarily to find the exact line numbers. However, in tricky situations, changing the timing of the application can affect the problem you're trying to debug, and other debugging techniques may be required.

Methods on the exception allow you to retrieve the stack trace information programmatically as well by using the `Throwable getStackTrace()` method. (`Throwable` is the base class of `Exception` and `Error`.) This method returns an array of `StackTraceElement` objects, each of which represents a method call on the stack. You can ask a `StackTraceElement` for details about that method's location using the methods `getFileName()`, `getClassName()`, `getMethodName()`, and `getLineNumber()`. Element zero of the array is the top of the stack, the final line of code that caused the exception; subsequent elements step back one method call each until the original `main()` method is reached.

Checked and Unchecked Exceptions

We mentioned earlier that Java forces us to be explicit about our error handling, but it's not necessary to require that every conceivable type of error be handled explicitly in every situation. Java exceptions are therefore divided into two categories: *checked* and *unchecked*. Most application-level exceptions are checked, which means that any method that throws one, either by generating it itself (as we'll discuss later) or by ignoring one that occurs within it, must declare that it can throw that type of exception in a special `throws` clause in its method declaration. We haven't yet talked in detail about declaring methods (see Chapter 5). For now, all you need to know is that methods have to declare the checked exceptions they can throw or allow to be thrown.

Again in Figure 4-3, notice that the methods `openConnection()` and `sendRequest()` both specify that they can throw an `IOException`. If we had to throw multiple types of exceptions, we could declare them separated by commas:

```
void readFile( String s ) throws IOException, InterruptedException {
    ...
}
```

The `throws` clause tells the compiler that a method is a possible source of that type of checked exception and that anyone calling that method must be prepared to deal with it. The caller must then either use a `try/catch` block to handle it, or it must, in turn, declare that it can throw the exception from itself.

In contrast, exceptions that are subclasses of either the class `java.lang.RuntimeException` or the class `java.lang.Error` are unchecked. See Figure 4-1 for the subclasses of

RuntimeException. (Subclasses of Error are generally reserved for serious class loading or runtime system problems.) It's not a compile-time error to ignore the possibility of these exceptions; methods also don't have to declare they can throw them. In all other respects, unchecked exceptions behave the same as other exceptions. We are free to catch them if we wish, but in this case we aren't required to.

Checked exceptions are intended to cover application-level problems, such as missing files and unavailable hosts. As good programmers (and upstanding citizens), we should design software to recover gracefully from these kinds of conditions. Unchecked exceptions are intended for system-level problems, such as "out of memory" and "array index out of bounds." While these may indicate application-level programming errors, they can occur almost anywhere and usually aren't possible to recover from. Fortunately, because they are unchecked exceptions, you don't have to wrap every one of your array-index operations in a try/catch statement (or declare all of the calling methods as a potential source of them).

To sum up, checked exceptions are problems that a reasonable application should try to handle gracefully; unchecked exceptions (runtime exceptions or errors) are problems from which we would not normally expect our software to recover. Error types are those explicitly intended to be conditions that we should not normally try to handle or recover from.

Throwing Exceptions

We can throw our own exceptions—either instances of Exception, one of its existing subclasses, or our own specialized exception classes. All we have to do is create an instance of the Exception and throw it with the throw statement:

```
throw new IOException();
```

Execution stops and is transferred to the nearest enclosing try/catch statement that can handle the exception type. (There is little point in keeping a reference to the Exception object we've created here.) An alternative constructor lets us specify a string with an error message:

```
throw new IOException("Sunspots!");
```

You can retrieve this string by using the Exception object's getMessage() method. Often, though, you can just print (or toString()) the exception object itself to get the message and stack trace.

By convention, all types of Exception have a String constructor like this. The preceding String message is not very useful. Normally, it will throw a more specific subclass Exception, which captures details or at least a more specific string explanation. Here's another example:

```
public void checkRead( String s ) {
    if ( new File(s).isAbsolute() || (s.indexOf("..") != -1) )
        throw new SecurityException(
           "Access to file : "+ s +" denied.");
}
```

In this code, we partially implement a method to check for an illegal path. If we find one, we throw a `SecurityException` with some information about the transgression.

Of course, we could include any other information that is useful in our own specialized subclasses of `Exception`. Often, though, just having a new type of exception is good enough because it's sufficient to help direct the flow of control. For example, if we are building a parser, we might want to make our own kind of exception to indicate a particular kind of failure:

```
class ParseException extends Exception {
    ParseException() {
        super();
    }
    ParseException( String desc ) {
        super( desc );
    }
}
```

See Chapter 5 for a full description of classes and class constructors. The body of our `Exception` class here simply allows a `ParseException` to be created in the conventional ways we've created exceptions previously (either generically or with a simple string description). Now that we have our new exception type, we can guard like this:

```
// Somewhere in our code
...
try {
    parseStream( input );
} catch ( ParseException pe ) {
    // Bad input...
} catch ( IOException ioe ) {
    // Low-level communications problem
}
```

As you can see, although our new exception doesn't currently hold any specialized information about the problem (it certainly could), it does let us distinguish a parse error from an arbitrary I/O error in the same chunk of code.

Chaining and rethrowing exceptions

Sometimes you'll want to take some action based on an exception and then turn around and throw a new exception in its place. This is common when building frameworks where low-level detailed exceptions are handled and represented by higher-level exceptions that can be managed more easily. For example, you might want to catch an `IOException` in a communications package, possibly perform some cleanup, and ultimately throw a higher-level exception of your own, maybe something like `LostServerConnection`.

You can do this in the obvious way by simply catching the exception and then throwing a new one, but then you lose important information, including the stack trace of the original "causal" exception. To deal with this, you can use the technique of *exception chaining*. This means that you include the causal exception in the new exception that you throw. Java has explicit support for exception chaining. The base `Exception` class can be constructed with an exception as an argument or the standard `String` message and an exception:

```
throw new Exception( "Here's the story...", causalException );
```

You can get access to the wrapped exception later with the `getCause()` method. More importantly, Java automatically prints both exceptions and their respective stack traces if you print the exception or if it is shown to the user.

You can add this kind of constructor to your own exception subclasses (delegating to the parent constructor) or you can take advantage of this pattern by using the `Throwable` method `initCause()` to set the causal exception explicitly after constructing your exception and before throwing it:

```
try {
  // ...
} catch ( IOException cause ) {
  Exception e =
    new IOException("What we have here is a failure to communicate...");
  e.initCause( cause );
  throw e;
}
```

Sometimes it's enough to simply do some logging or take some action and then rethrow the original exception:

```
try {
      // ...
    } catch ( IOException cause ) {
      log( e ); // Log it
      throw e;  // rethrow it
    }
```

But be aware that if you do that, the stack trace included in the exception will show the new throw location as the origin.

Narrowed rethrow

Prior to Java 7 if you wanted to handle a bunch of exception types in a single `catch` clause and then rethrow the original exception, you would inevitably end up widening the declared exception type to what was required to catch them all or having to do a lot of work to avoid that. In Java 7, the compiler has become smarter and can now do most of the work for us by allowing us to narrow the type of exceptions thrown back to the original types in most cases. This is best explained by example:

```
void myMethod() throws ZipException, SSLException
{
    try {
        // Possible cause of ZipException or SSLException
    } catch ( Exception e ) {
        log( e );
        throw e;
    }
}
```

In this example, we are exceedingly lazy and simply catch all exceptions with a broad catch `Exception` clause in order to log them prior to rethrowing. Prior to Java 7, the compiler would have insisted that the `throws` clause of our method declare that it throws the broad `Exception` type as well. However, the Java compiler is now smart enough in most cases to analyze the actual types of exceptions that may be thrown and allow us to prescribe the precise set of types. The same would be true if we had used the mutiple-type `catch` clause in this example, as you might have guessed. The preceding is a bit less intuitive, but very useful in shoring up the specificity of exception handling of code, including code written prior to Java 7, without requiring potentially tricky reworking of `catch` clauses.

try Creep

The `try` statement imposes a condition on the statements that it guards. It says that if an exception occurs within it, the remaining statements are abandoned. This has consequences for local variable initialization. If the compiler can't determine whether a local variable assignment placed inside a `try/catch` block will happen, it won't let us use the variable. For example:

```
void myMethod() {
    int foo;

    try {
        foo = getResults();
    }
    catch ( Exception e ) {
        ...
    }

    int bar = foo;  // Compile-time error: foo may not have been initialized
```

In this example, we can't use `foo` in the indicated place because there's a chance it was never assigned a value. One obvious option is to move the assignment inside the `try` statement:

```
try {
    foo = getResults();

    int bar = foo;  // Okay because we get here only
                    // if previous assignment succeeds
}
catch ( Exception e ) {
    ...
}
```

Sometimes this works just fine. However, now we have the same problem if we want to use bar later in myMethod(). If we're not careful, we might end up pulling everything into the try statement. The situation changes, however, if we transfer control out of the method in the catch clause:

```
try {
    foo = getResults();
}
catch ( Exception e ) {
    ...
    return;
}

int bar = foo;  // Okay because we get here only
                // if previous assignment succeeds
```

The compiler is smart enough to know that if an error had occurred in the try clause, we wouldn't have reached the bar assignment, so it allows us to refer to foo. Your code will dictate its own needs; you should just be aware of the options.

The finally Clause

What if we have something important to do before we exit our method from one of the catch clauses? To avoid duplicating the code in each catch branch and to make the cleanup more explicit, you can use the finally clause. A finally clause can be added after a try and any associated catch clauses. Any statements in the body of the finally clause are guaranteed to be executed no matter how control leaves the try body, whether an exception was thrown or not:

```
try {
    // Do something here

}
catch ( FileNotFoundException e ) {
    ...
}
catch ( IOException e ) {
    ...
}
catch ( Exception e ) {
    ...
```

```
}
finally {
    // Cleanup here is always executed
}
```

In this example, the statements at the cleanup point are executed eventually, no matter how control leaves the `try`. If control transfers to one of the `catch` clauses, the statements in `finally` are executed after the `catch` completes. If none of the `catch` clauses handles the exception, the `finally` statements are executed before the exception propagates to the next level.

If the statements in the `try` execute cleanly, or if we perform a `return` , `break`, or `continue`, the statements in the `finally` clause are still executed. To guarantee that some operations will run, we can even use `try` and `finally` without any `catch` clauses:

```
try {
    // Do something here
    return;
}
finally {
    System.out.println("Whoo-hoo!");
}
```

Exceptions that occur in a `catch` or `finally` clause are handled normally; the search for an enclosing `try/catch` begins outside the offending `try` statement, after the `finally` has been executed.

Try with Resources

A common use of the `finally` clause is to ensure that resources used in a `try` clause are cleaned up, no matter how the code exits the block.

```
try {
    // Socket sock = new Socket(...);
    // work with sock
} catch( IOException e ) {
    ...
}
finally {
    if ( sock != null ) { sock.close(); }
}
```

What we mean by "clean up" here is to deallocate expensive resources or close connections such as files, sockets, or database connections. In some cases, these resources might get cleaned up on their own eventually as Java reclaimed the garbage, but that would at best be at an unknown time in the future and at worst may never happen or may not happen before you run out of resources. So it is always best to guard against these situations. There are two problems with this venerable approach: first, it requires extra work to carry out this pattern in all of your code, including important things like null checks as shown in our example, and second, if you are juggling multiple resources in a single `finally` block, you have the possibility of your cleanup code throwing an exception (e.g., on `close()`) and leaving the job unfinished.

In Java 7, things have been greatly simplified via the new "`try` with resources" form of the `try` clause. In this form, you may place one or more resource initialization statements within parentheses after a `try` keyword and those resources will automatically be "closed" for you when control leaves the `try` block.

```
try (
    Socket sock = new Socket("128.252.120.1", 80);
    FileWriter file = new FileWriter("foo");
)
{
    // work with sock and file
} catch ( IOException e ) {
    ...
}
```

In this example, we initialize both a `Socket` object and a `FileWriter` object within the `try`-with-resources clause and use them within the body of the `try` statement. When control leaves the `try` statement, either after successful completion or via an exception, both resources are automatically closed by calling their `close()` method. Resources are closed in the *reverse of the order* in which they were constructed, so dependencies among them can be accommodated. This behavior is supported for any class that implements the `AutoCloseable` interface (which, at current count, over 100 different built-in classes do). The `close()` method of this interface is prescribed to release all resources associated with the object, and you can implement this easily in your own classes as well. When using `try` with resources, we don't have to add any code specifically to close the file or socket; it is done for us automatically.

Another problem that `try` with resources solves is the pesky situation we alluded to where an exception may be thrown during a close operation. Looking back to the prior example in which we used a `finally` clause to do our cleanup, if an exception had been raised by the `close()` method, it would have been thrown at that point, completely abandoning the original exception from the body of the `try` clause. But in using `try` with resources, we preserve the original exception. If an exception occurs while within the body of the `try` and one or more exceptions is raised during the subsequent autoclosing operations, it is the original exception from the body of the `try` that is bubbled up to the caller. Let's look at an example:

```
try (
    Socket sock = new Socket("128.252.120.1", 80); // potential exception #3
    FileWriter file = new FileWriter("foo"); // potential exception #2
)
{
    // work with sock and file // potential exception #1
}
```

Once the `try` has begun, if an exception occurs as exception point #1, Java will attempt to close both resources in reverse order, leading to potential exceptions at locations #2 and #3. In this case, the calling code will still receive exception #1. Exceptions #2 and #3 are not lost, however; they are merely "suppressed" and can be retrieved via the `Throwable getSuppressed()` method of the exception thrown to the caller. This returns an array of all of the supressed exceptions.

Performance Issues

Because of the way the Java virtual machine is implemented, guarding against an exception being thrown (using a `try`) is free. It doesn't add any overhead to the execution of your code. However, throwing an exception is not free. When an exception is thrown, Java has to locate the appropriate `try/catch` block and perform other time-consuming activities at runtime.

The result is that you should throw exceptions only in truly "exceptional" circumstances and avoid using them for expected conditions, especially when performance is an issue. For example, if you have a loop, it may be better to perform a small test on each pass and avoid throwing the exception rather than throwing it frequently. On the other hand, if the exception is thrown only once in a gazillion times, you may want to eliminate the overhead of the test code and not worry about the cost of throwing that exception. The general rule should be that exceptions are used for "out of bounds" or abnormal situations, not routine and expected conditions (such as the end of a file).

Assertions

An assertion is a simple pass/fail test of some condition, performed while your application is running. Assertions can be used to "sanity check" your code anywhere you believe certain conditions are guaranteed by correct program behavior. Assertions are distinct from other kinds of tests because they check conditions that should never be violated at a logical level: if the assertion fails, the application is to be considered broken and generally halts with an appropriate error message. Assertions are supported directly by the Java language and they can be turned on or off at runtime to remove any performance penalty of including them in your code.

Using assertions to test for the correct behavior of your application is a simple but powerful technique for ensuring software quality. It fills a gap between those aspects of software that can be checked automatically by the compiler and those more generally checked by "unit tests" and human testing. Assertions test assumptions about program behavior and make them guarantees (at least while they are activated).

If you have programmed before, you may have written something like the following:

```
if ( !condition )
    throw new AssertionError("fatal error: 42");
```

An assertion in Java is equivalent to this example, but is performed with the `assert` language keyword. It takes a Boolean condition and an optional expression value. If the assertion fails, an `AssertionError` is thrown, which usually causes Java to bail out of the application.

The optional expression may evaluate to either a primitive or object type. Either way, its sole purpose is to be turned into a string and shown to the user if the assertion fails; most often you'll use a string message explicitly. Here are some examples:

```
assert false;
assert ( array.length > min );
assert a > 0 : a  // shows value of a to the user
assert foo != null :  "foo is null!" // shows message "foo is null!" to user
```

In the event of failure, the first two assertions print only a generic message, whereas the third prints the value of `a` and the last prints the `foo is null!` message.

Again, the important thing about assertions is not just that they are more terse than the equivalent `if` condition, but that they can be enabled or disabled when you run the application. Disabling assertions means that their test conditions are not even evaluated, so there is no performance penalty for including them in your code (other than, perhaps, space in the class files when they are loaded).

Enabling and Disabling Assertions

Assertions are turned on or off at runtime. When disabled, assertions still exist in the class files but are not executed and consume no time. You can enable and disable assertions for an entire application or on a package-by-package or even class-by-class basis. By default, assertions are turned off in Java. To enable them for your code, use the `java` command flag `-ea` or `-enableassertions`:

```
% java -ea MyApplication
```

To turn on assertions for a particular class, append the class name:

```
% java -ea:com.oreilly.examples.Myclass  MyApplication
```

To turn on assertions just for particular packages, append the package name with trailing ellipses (. . .):

```
% java -ea:com.oreilly.examples...MyApplication
```

When you enable assertions for a package, Java also enables all subordinate package names (e.g., `com.oreilly.examples.text`). However, you can be more selective by using the corresponding `-da` or `-disableassertions` flag to negate individual packages or classes. You can combine all this to achieve arbitrary groupings like this:

```
% java -ea:com.oreilly.examples...
-da:com.oreilly.examples.text-ea:com.oreilly.examples.text.MonkeyTypewriters
MyApplication
```

This example enables assertions for the `com.oreilly.examples` package as a whole, excludes the package `com.oreilly.examples.text`, and then turns exceptions on for just one class, `MonkeyTypewriters`, in that package.

Using Assertions

An assertion enforces a rule about something that should be unchanging in your code and would otherwise go unchecked. You can use an assertion for added safety anywhere you want to verify your assumptions about program behavior that can't be checked by the compiler.

A common situation that cries out for an assertion is testing for multiple conditions or values where one should always be found. In this case, a failing assertion as the default or "fall through" behavior indicates the code is broken. For example, suppose we have a value called `direction` that should always contain either the constant value `LEFT` or `RIGHT`:

```
if ( direction == LEFT )
    doLeft();
else if ( direction == RIGHT )
    doRight()
else
    assert false : "bad direction";
```

The same applies to the default case of a switch:

```
switch ( direction ) {
    case LEFT:
        doLeft();
        break;
    case RIGHT:
        doRight();
        break;
    default:
        assert false;
}
```

In general, you should not use assertions for checking the validity of arguments to methods because you want that behavior to be part of your application, not just a test for quality control that can be turned off. The validity of input to a method is called its *preconditions*, and you should usually throw an exception if they are not met; this elevates the preconditions to part of the method's "contract" with the user. However, checking the correctness of results of your methods with assertions before returning them is a good idea; these are called *post-conditions*.

Sometimes determining what is or is not a precondition depends on your point of view. For example, when a method is used internally within a class, preconditions may already be guaranteed by the methods that call it. Public methods of the class should probably throw exceptions when their preconditions are violated, but a private method might use assertions because its callers are always closely related code that should obey the correct behavior.

Finally, note that assertions can not only test simple expressions but perform complex validation as well. Remember that anything you place in the condition expression of an `assert` statement is not evaluated when assertions are turned off. You can make helper methods for your assertions that may contain arbitrary amounts of code. And, although it suggests a dangerous programming style, you can even use assertions that have side effects to capture values for use by later assertions—all of which will be disabled when assertions are turned off. For example:

```
int savedValue;
assert ( savedValue = getValue()) != -1;
// Do work...
assert checkValue( savedValue );
```

Here, in the first `assert`, we use the helper method `getValue()` to retrieve some information and save it for later. Then, after doing some work, we check the saved value using another assertion, perhaps comparing results. When assertions are disabled, we'll no longer save or check the data. Note that it's necessary for us to be somewhat cute and make our first `assert` condition into a Boolean by checking for a known value. Again, using assertions with side effects is a bit dangerous because you have to be careful that those side effects are seen only by other assertions. Otherwise, you'll be changing your application behavior when you turn them off.

Arrays

An array is a special type of object that can hold an ordered collection of elements. The type of the elements of the array is called the *base type* of the array; the number of elements it holds is a fixed attribute called its *length*. Java supports arrays of all primitive and reference types.

The basic syntax of arrays looks much like that of C or C++. We create an array of a specified length and access the elements with the *index* operator, `[]`. Unlike other languages, however, arrays in Java are true, first-class objects. An array is an instance of a special Java `array` class and has a corresponding type in the type system. This means that to use an array, as with any other object, we first declare a variable of the appropriate type and then use the `new` operator to create an instance of it.

Array objects differ from other objects in Java in three respects:

- Java implicitly creates a special array class type for us whenever we declare a new type of array. It's not strictly necessary to know about this process in order to use arrays, but it helps in understanding their structure and their relationship to other objects in Java later.

- Java lets us use the [] operator to access array elements so that arrays look as we expect. We could implement our own classes that act like arrays, but we would have to settle for having methods such as `get()` and `set()` instead of using the special [] notation.
- Java provides a corresponding special form of the `new` operator that lets us construct an instance of an array with a specified length with the [] notation or initialize it directly from a structured list of values.

Array Types

An array type variable is denoted by a base type followed by the empty brackets, []. Alternatively, Java accepts a C-style declaration with the brackets placed after the array name.

The following are equivalent:

```
int [] arrayOfInts;  // preferred
int arrayOfInts [];  // C-style
```

In each case, `arrayOfInts` is declared as an array of integers. The size of the array is not yet an issue because we are declaring only the array type variable. We have not yet created an actual instance of the `array` class, with its associated storage. It's not even possible to specify the length of an array when declaring an array type variable. The size is strictly a function of the array object itself, not the reference to it.

An array of reference types can be created in the same way:

```
String [] someStrings;
Button [] someButtons;
```

Array Creation and Initialization

The `new` operator is used to create an instance of an array. After the `new` operator, we specify the base type of the array and its length with a bracketed integer expression:

```
arrayOfInts = new int [42];
someStrings = new String [ number + 2 ];
```

We can, of course, combine the steps of declaring and allocating the array:

```
double [] someNumbers = new double [20];
Component [] widgets = new Component [12];
```

Array indices start with zero. Thus, the first element of `someNumbers[]` is `0`, and the last element is `19`. After creation, the array elements are initialized to the default values for their type. For numeric types, this means the elements are initially zero:

```
int [] grades = new int [30];
grades[0] = 99;
```

```
grades[1] = 72;
// grades[2] == 0
```

The elements of an array of objects are references to the objects—just like individual variables they point to—but do not actually contain instances of the objects. The default value of each element is therefore `null` until we assign instances of appropriate objects:

```
String names [] = new String [4];
names [0] = new String();
names [1] = "Boofa";
names [2] = someObject.toString();
// names[3] == null
```

This is an important distinction that can cause confusion. In many other languages, the act of creating an array is the same as allocating storage for its elements. In Java, a newly allocated array of objects actually contains only reference variables, each with the value `null`.[6] That's not to say that there is no memory associated with an empty array; memory is needed to hold those references (the empty "slots" in the array). Figure 4-4 illustrates the `names` array of the previous example.

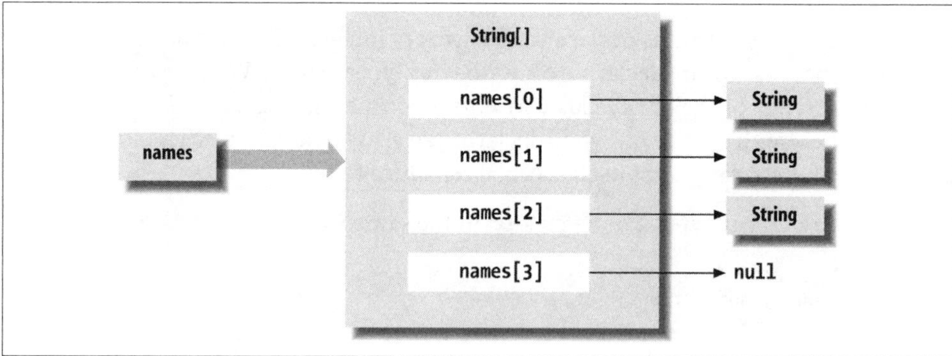

Figure 4-4. A Java array

`names` is a variable of type `String[]` (i.e., a string array). This particular `String[]` object contains four `String` type variables. We have assigned `String` objects to the first three array elements. The fourth has the default value `null`.

Java supports the C-style curly braces `{}` construct for creating an array and initializing its elements:

6. The analog in C or C++ is an array of pointers to objects. However, pointers in C or C++ are themselves two- or four-byte values. Allocating an array of pointers is, in actuality, allocating the storage for some number of those pointer objects. An array of references is conceptually similar, although references are not themselves objects. We can't manipulate references or parts of references other than by assignment, and their storage requirements (or lack thereof) are not part of the high-level Java language specification.

```
int [] primes = { 2, 3, 5, 7, 7+4 };     // e.g., primes[2] = 5
```

An array object of the proper type and length is implicitly created, and the values of the comma-separated list of expressions are assigned to its elements. Note that we did not use the new keyword or the array type here. The type of the array was inferred from the assignment.

We can use the {} syntax with an array of objects. In this case, each expression must evaluate to an object that can be assigned to a variable of the base type of the array or the value null. Here are some examples:

```
String [] verbs = { "run", "jump", someWord.toString() };
Button [] controls = { stopButton, new Button("Forwards"),
    new Button("Backwards") };
// All types are subtypes of Object
Object [] objects = { stopButton, "A word", null };
```

The following are equivalent:

```
Button [] threeButtons = new Button [3];
Button [] threeButtons = { null, null, null };
```

Using Arrays

The size of an array object is available in the public variable length:

```
char [] alphabet = new char [26];
int alphaLen = alphabet.length;                // alphaLen == 26

String [] musketeers = { "one", "two", "three" };
int num = musketeers.length;                   // num == 3
```

length is the only accessible field of an array; it is a variable, not a method. (Don't worry; the compiler tells you when you accidentally use parentheses as if it were a method, as everyone does now and then.)

Array access in Java is just like array access in other languages; you access an element by putting an integer-valued expression between brackets after the name of the array. The following example creates an array of Button objects called keyPad and then fills the array with Button objects:

```
Button [] keyPad = new Button [ 10 ];
for ( int i=0; i < keyPad.length; i++ )
   keyPad[ i ] = new Button( Integer.toString( i ) );
```

Remember that we can also use the enhanced for loop to iterate over array values. Here we'll use it to print all the values we just assigned:

```
for (Button b : keyPad)
    System.out.println(b);
```

Attempting to access an element that is outside the range of the array generates an `ArrayIndexOutOfBoundsException`. This is a type of `RuntimeException`, so you can either catch and handle it yourself if you really expect it, or ignore it, as we've already discussed:

```
String [] states = new String [50];

try {
    states[0] = "California";
    states[1] = "Oregon";
    ...
    states[50] = "McDonald's Land";  // Error: array out of bounds
}
catch ( ArrayIndexOutOfBoundsException err ) {
    System.out.println( "Handled error: " + err.getMessage() );
}
```

It's a common task to copy a range of elements from one array into another. One way to copy arrays is to use the low-level `arraycopy()` method of the `System` class:

```
System.arraycopy( source, sourceStart, destination, destStart, length );
```

The following example doubles the size of the `names` array from an earlier example:

```
String [] tmpVar = new String [ 2 * names.length ];
System.arraycopy( names, 0, tmpVar, 0, names.length );
names = tmpVar;
```

A new array, twice the size of `names`, is allocated and assigned to a temporary variable, `tmpVar`. The `arraycopy()` method is then used to copy the elements of `names` to the new array. Finally, the new array is assigned to `names`. If there are no remaining references to the old array object after `names` has been copied, it is garbage-collected on the next pass.

An easier way is to use the `java.util.ArrayscopyOf()` and `copyOfRange()` methods:

```
byte [] bar = new byte[] { 1, 2, 3, 4, 5 };

byte [] barCopy = Arrays.copyOf( bar, bar.length );
    // { 1, 2, 3, 4, 5 }
byte [] expanded = Arrays.copyOf( bar, bar.length+2 );
    // { 1, 2, 3, 4, 5, 0, 0 }

byte [] firstThree = Arrays.copyOfRange( bar, 0, 3 );
    // { 1, 2, 3 }
byte [] lastThree = Arrays.copyOfRange( bar, 2, bar.length );
    // { 3, 4, 5 }
byte [] lastThreePlusTwo = Arrays.copyOfRange( bar, 2, bar.length+2 );
    // { 3, 4, 5, 0, 0 }
```

The `copyOf()` method takes the original array and a target length. If the target length is larger than the original array length, then the new array is padded (with zeros or nulls) to the desired length. The `copyOfRange()` takes a starting index (inclusive) and an ending index (exclusive) and a desired length, which will also be padded if necessary.

Anonymous Arrays

Often it is convenient to create "throwaway" arrays, arrays that are used in one place and never referenced anywhere else. Such arrays don't need a name because you never need to refer to them again in that context. For example, you may want to create a collection of objects to pass as an argument to some method. It's easy enough to create a normal, named array, but if you don't actually work with the array (if you use the array only as a holder for some collection), you shouldn't need to do this. Java makes it easy to create "anonymous" (i.e., unnamed) arrays.

Let's say you need to call a method named `setPets()`, which takes an array of `Animal` objects as arguments. Provided `Cat` and `Dog` are subclasses of `Animal`, here's how to call `setPets()` using an anonymous array:

```
Dog pokey = new Dog ("gray");
Cat boojum = new Cat ("grey");
Cat simon = new Cat ("orange");
setPets ( new Animal [] { pokey, boojum, simon });
```

The syntax looks similar to the initialization of an array in a variable declaration. We implicitly define the size of the array and fill in its elements using the curly-brace notation. However, because this is not a variable declaration, we have to explicitly use the `new` operator and the array type to create the array object.

Anonymous arrays were sometimes used as a substitute for variable-length argument lists to methods, which are discussed in Chapter 5. With the introduction of variable-length argument lists in Java, the usefulness of anonymous arrays has diminished.

Multidimensional Arrays

Java supports multidimensional arrays in the form of arrays of array type objects. You create a multidimensional array with C-like syntax, using multiple bracket pairs, one for each dimension. You also use this syntax to access elements at various positions within the array. Here's an example of a multidimensional array that represents a chess board:

```
ChessPiece [][] chessBoard;
chessBoard = new ChessPiece [8][8];
chessBoard[0][0] = new ChessPiece.Rook;
chessBoard[1][0] = new ChessPiece.Pawn;
...
```

Here, `chessBoard` is declared as a variable of type `ChessPiece[][]` (i.e., an array of `ChessPiece` arrays). This declaration implicitly creates the type `ChessPiece[]` as well. The example illustrates the special form of the `new` operator used to create a multidimensional array. It creates an array of `ChessPiece[]` objects and then, in turn, makes each element into an array of `ChessPiece` objects. We then index `chessBoard` to specify values for particular `ChessPiece` elements. (We'll neglect the color of the pieces here.)

Of course, you can create arrays with more than two dimensions. Here's a slightly impractical example:

```
Color [][][] rgbCube = new Color [256][256][256];
rgbCube[0][0][0] = Color.black;
rgbCube[255][255][0] = Color.yellow;
...
```

We can specify a partial index of a multidimensional array to get a subarray of array type objects with fewer dimensions. In our example, the variable `chessBoard` is of type `ChessPiece[][]`. The expression `chessBoard[0]` is valid and refers to the first element of `chessBoard`, which, in Java, is of type `ChessPiece[]`. For example, we can populate our chess board one row at a time:

```
ChessPiece [] homeRow =  {
    new ChessPiece("Rook"), new ChessPiece("Knight"),
    new ChessPiece("Bishop"), new ChessPiece("King"),
    new ChessPiece("Queen"), new ChessPiece("Bishop"),
    new ChessPiece("Knight"), new ChessPiece("Rook")
};

chessBoard[0] = homeRow;
```

We don't necessarily have to specify the dimension sizes of a multidimensional array with a single `new` operation. The syntax of the `new` operator lets us leave the sizes of some dimensions unspecified. The size of at least the first dimension (the most significant dimension of the array) has to be specified, but the sizes of any number of trailing, less significant array dimensions may be left undefined. We can assign appropriate array-type values later.

We can create a checkerboard of Boolean values (which is not quite sufficient for a real game of checkers either) using this technique:

```
boolean [][] checkerBoard;
checkerBoard = new boolean [8][];
```

Here, `checkerBoard` is declared and created, but its elements, the eight `boolean[]` objects of the next level, are left empty. Thus, for example, `checkerBoard[0]` is `null` until we explicitly create an array and assign it, as follows:

```
checkerBoard[0] = new boolean [8];
checkerBoard[1] = new boolean [8];
...
checkerBoard[7] = new boolean [8];
```

The code of the previous two examples is equivalent to:

```
boolean [][] checkerBoard = new boolean [8][8];
```

One reason we might want to leave dimensions of an array unspecified is so that we can store arrays given to us by another method.

Note that because the length of the array is not part of its type, the arrays in the checkerboard do not necessarily have to be of the same length; that is, multidimensional arrays don't have to be rectangular. Here's a defective (but perfectly legal in Java) checkerboard:

```
checkerBoard[2] = new boolean [3];
checkerBoard[3] = new boolean [10];
```

And here's how you could create and initialize a triangular array:

```
int [][] triangle = new int [5][];
for (int i = 0; i < triangle.length; i++) {
    triangle[i] = new int [i + 1];
    for (int j = 0; j < i + 1; j++)
        triangle[i][j] = i + j;
}
```

Inside Arrays

We said earlier that arrays are instances of special array classes in the Java language. If arrays have classes, where do they fit into the class hierarchy and how are they related? These are good questions, but we need to talk more about the object-oriented aspects of Java before answering them. That's the subject of the next chapter. For now, take it on faith that arrays fit into the class hierarchy.

CHAPTER 5
Objects in Java

In this chapter, we get to the heart of Java and explore the object-oriented aspects of the language. The term *object-oriented design* refers to the art of decomposing an application into some number of objects, which are self-contained application components that work together. The goal is to break your problem down into a number of smaller problems that are simpler and easier to handle and maintain. Object-based designs have proven themselves over the years, and object-oriented languages such as Java provide a strong foundation for writing applications from the very small to the very large. Java was designed from the ground up to be an object-oriented language, and all of the Java APIs and libraries are built around solid object-based design patterns.

An object design "methodology" is a system or a set of rules created to help you break down your application into objects. Often this means mapping real-world entities and concepts (sometimes called the "problem domain") into application components. Various methodologies attempt to help you factor your application into a good set of reusable objects. This is good in principle, but the problem is that good object-oriented design is still more art than science. While you can learn from the various off-the-shelf design methodologies, none of them will help you in all situations. The truth is that there is no substitute for experience.

We won't try to push you into a particular methodology here; there are shelves full of books to do that.[1] Instead, we'll provide some common-sense hints to get you started. The following general design guidelines will hopefully make more sense after you've read this chapter and the next:

1. Once you have some experience with basic object-oriented concepts, you might want to look at *Design Patterns: Elements of Reusable Object-Oriented Software* by Gamma, Helm, Johnson, and Vlissides (Addison-Wesley). This book catalogs useful object-oriented designs that have been refined over the years by experience. Many appear in the design of the Java APIs.

- Hide as much of your implementation as possible. Never expose more of the internals of an object than you need to. This is key to building maintainable, reusable code. Avoid public variables in your objects, with the possible exception of constants. Instead define *accessor* methods to set and return values (even if they are simple types). Later, when you need to, you'll be able to modify and extend the behavior of your objects without breaking other classes that rely on them.
- Specialize objects only when you have to—use *composition* instead of *inheritance*. When you use an object in its existing form, as a piece of a new object, you are *composing* objects. When you change or refine the behavior of an object (by *subclassing*), you are using *inheritance*. You should try to reuse objects by composition rather than inheritance whenever possible because when you compose objects, you are taking full advantage of existing tools. Inheritance involves breaking down the encapsulation of an object and should be done only when there's a real advantage. Ask yourself if you really need to inherit the whole public interface of an object (do you want to be a "kind" of that object?) or whether you can just delegate certain jobs to the object and use it by composition.
- Minimize relationships between objects and try to organize related objects in packages. Classes that work closely together can be grouped using Java packages, which can hide those that are not of general interest. Only expose classes that you intend other people to use. The more loosely coupled your objects are, the easier it will be to reuse them later.

Classes

Classes are the building blocks of a Java application. A *class* can contain methods (functions), variables, initialization code, and, as we'll discuss later, other classes. It serves as a blueprint for making class *instances*, which are runtime objects (individual copies) that implement the class structure. You declare a class with the `class` keyword. Methods and variables of the class appear inside the braces of the class declaration:

```
class Pendulum {
    float mass;
    float length = 1.0f;
    int cycles;

    float getPosition ( float time ) {
        ...
    }
    ...
}
```

The `Pendulum` class contains three variables: `mass`, `length`, and `cycles`. It also defines a method called `getPosition()`, which takes a `float` value as an argument and returns a `float` value as a result. Variables and method declarations can appear in any order, but variable initializers can't make "forward references" to other variables that appear later. Once we've defined the `Pendulum` class, we can create a `Pendulum` object (an instance of that class) as follows:

```
Pendulum p;
p = new Pendulum();
```

Recall that our declaration of the variable `p` doesn't create a `Pendulum` object; it simply creates a variable that refers to an object of type `Pendulum`. We still had to create the object, using the `new` keyword, as shown in the second line of the preceding code snippet. Now that we've created a `Pendulum` object, we can access its variables and methods, as we've already seen many times:

```
p.mass = 5.0;
float pos = p.getPosition( 1.0 );
```

Two kinds of variables can be defined in a class: *instance variables* and *static variables*. Every object instance has its own set of instance variables; the values of these variables in one instance of an object can differ from the values in another object. We'll talk about static variables later, which, in contrast, are shared among all instances of an object. In either case, if you don't initialize a variable when you declare it, it's given a default value appropriate for its type (`null`, zero, or `false`).

Figure 5-1 shows a hypothetical `TextBook` application that uses two instances of `Pendulum` through the reference-type variables `bigPendulum` and `smallPendulum`. Each of these `Pendulum` objects has its own copy of `mass`, `length`, and `cycles`. As with variables, methods defined in a class may be *instance methods* or *static methods*. An instance method is associated with just one instance of the class, but the relationship isn't quite as simple as it is for variables. Instance methods are accessed through an object instance, but the object doesn't really have its own "copy" of the methods (there is no duplication of code). Instead, the association means that instance methods can "see" and operate on the values of the instance variables of the object. As you'll see in Chapter 6 when we talk about subclassing, there's more to learn about how methods see variables. In that chapter, we'll also discuss how instance methods can be "overridden" in child classes—a very important feature of object-oriented design. Both aspects differ from static methods, which we'll see are really more like global functions, as they are associated with a class by name only.

Accessing Fields and Methods

Inside a class, we can access variables and call methods of the class directly by name. Here's an example that expands on our `Pendulum`:

```
class Pendulum {
    ...
    void resetEverything() {
```

```
            mass = 1.0;
            length = 1.0;
            cycles = 0;
            ...
            float startingPosition = getPosition( 0.0 );
        }
        ...
    }
```

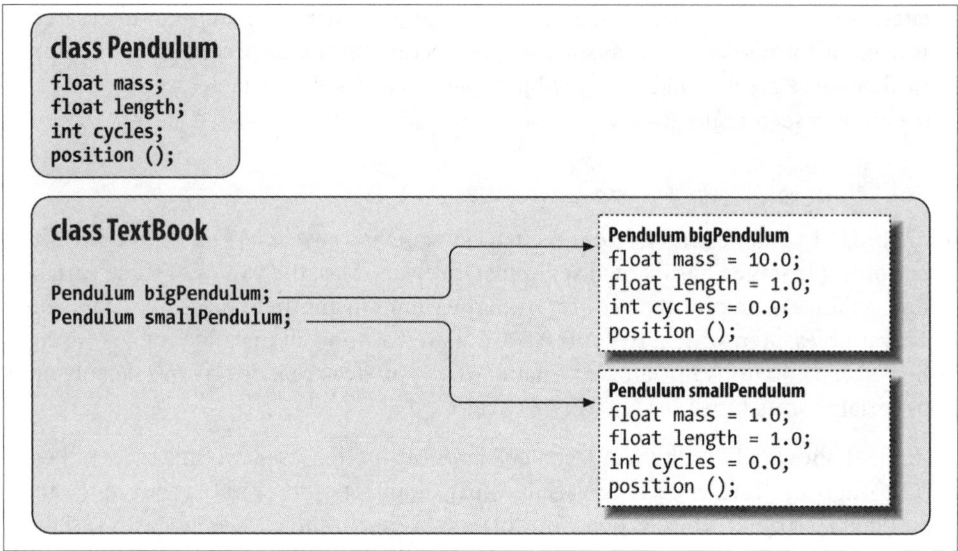

Figure 5-1. Instances of the Pendulum class

Other classes access members of an object through a reference, using the dot selector notation that we discussed in the last chapter:

```
    class TextBook {
        ...
        void showPendulum() {
            Pendulum bob = new Pendulum();
            ...
            int i = bob.cycles;
            bob.resetEverything();
            bob.mass = 1.01;
            ...
        }
        ...
    }
```

Here we have created a second class, `TextBook`, that uses a `Pendulum` object. It creates an instance in `showPendulum()` and then invokes methods and accesses variables of the object through the reference `bob`.

Several factors affect whether class members can be accessed from another class. You can use the visibility modifiers public, private, and protected to control access; classes can also be placed into a *package*, which affects their scope. The private modifier, for example, designates a variable or method for use only by other members of the class itself. In the previous example, we could change the declaration of our variable cycles to private:

```
class Pendulum {
    ...
    private int cycles;
    ...
```

Now we can't access cycles from TextBook:

```
class TextBook {
    ...
    void showPendulum() {
        ...
        int i = bob.cycles;  // Compile-time error
```

If we still need to access cycles in some capacity, we might add a public getCycles() method to the Pendulum class. (Creating accessor methods like this is a good design rule because it allows future flexibility in changing the type or behavior of the value.) We'll take a detailed look at packages, access modifiers, and how they affect the visibility of variables and methods in Chapter 6.

Static Members

As we've said, instance variables and methods are associated with and accessed through an instance of the class (i.e., through a particular object, like bob in the previous example). In contrast, members that are declared with the static modifier live in the class and are shared by all instances of the class. Variables declared with the static modifier are called *static variables* or *class variables*; similarly, these kinds of methods are called *static methods* or *class methods*. We can add a static variable to our Pendulum example:

```
class Pendulum {
    ...
    static float gravAccel = 9.80;
    ...
```

We have declared the new float variable gravAccel as static. That means that it is associated with the class, not with an individual instance and if we change its value (either directly or through any instance of a Pendulum), the value changes for all Pendulum objects, as shown in Figure 5-2.

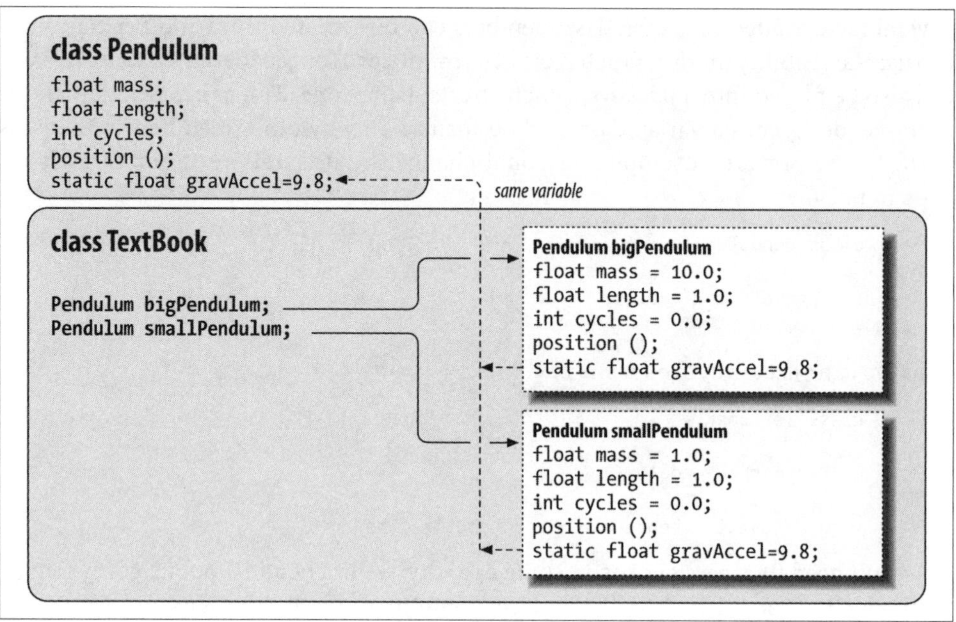

Figure 5-2. Static variables shared by all instances of a class

Static members can be accessed like instance members. Inside our `Pendulum` class, we can refer to `gravAccel` like any other variable:

```
class Pendulum {
    ...
    float getWeight () {
        return mass * gravAccel;
    }
    ...
}
```

However, since static members exist in the class itself, independent of any instance, we can also access them directly through the class. We don't need a `Pendulum` object to get or set the variable `gravAccel`; instead, we can use the class to select the variable:

```
Pendulum.gravAccel = 8.76;
```

This changes the value of `gravAccel` as seen by all instances. Why would we want to change the value of `gravAccel`? Well, perhaps we want to explore how pendulums would work on different planets. Static variables are also very useful for other kinds of data that is shared among classes at runtime. For instance, you can create methods to register your object instances so that they can communicate, or so that you can keep track of all of them. It's also common to use static variables to define constant values. In this case, we use the `static` modifier along with the `final` modifier. So, if we cared only about pendulums under the influence of the Earth's gravitational pull, we might change Pendulum as follows:

```
class Pendulum {
    ...
    static final float EARTH_G = 9.80;
    ...
```

We have followed a common convention here and named our constant with capital letters. The value of EARTH_G is a constant; it can be accessed through the class Pendulum or its instances, but its value can't be changed at runtime.

It's important to use the combination of `static` and `final` only for things that are really constant. That's because the compiler is allowed to "inline" such values within classes that reference them. This means that if you change a `static final` variable, you may have to recompile all code that uses that class (this is really the only case where you have to do that in Java). Static members are useful as flags and identifiers, which can be accessed from anywhere. They are also useful for values needed in the construction of an instance itself. In our example, we might declare a number of static values to represent various kinds of Pendulum objects:

```
class Pendulum {
    ...
    static int SIMPLE = 0, ONE_SPRING = 1, TWO_SPRING = 2;
    ...
```

We might then use these flags in a method that sets the type of a Pendulum or in a special constructor, as we'll discuss shortly:

```
Pendulum pendy = new Pendulum();
pendy.setType( Pendulum.ONE_SPRING );
```

Again, inside the Pendulum class, we can use static members directly by name, as well; there's no need for the `Pendulum.` prefix:

```
class Pendulum {
    ...
    void resetEverything() {
        setType ( SIMPLE );
        ...
    }
    ...
}
```

Constants versus enumerations

In the previous section, we saw two uses for static final variables (constants). The first was to create true constants; in that case, it was the numeric constant EARTH_G, but it could easily have been a `String` or `Date` value. The second usage was to create a fixed set of identifiers, `SIMPLE`, `ONE_SPRING`, etc., whose actual values were not as important as their uniqueness and, perhaps, their particular order.

Enumerations were added to the Java language to replace this identifier usage with a mechanism that is both safer and, in some cases, more efficient. We could have declared our pendulum types as an enumeration like so:

```
public enum PendulumTypes { Simple, OneSpring, TwoSpring }
```

This enumeration creates not only the values, but also a new type, `PendulumTypes`, whose value is limited to one of the three discrete identifiers. Calling code can refer to the values as it did through our class: `PendulumTypes.Simple`. We've changed our case convention here to diverge from the convention for integer constants, but you can stick with uppercase if you prefer.

Later, when we talk about importing classes and packages, we'll discuss the *static import* feature of Java, which allows us to import static identifiers and enumerations (which, as we've seen, are related) into a class so that we can use them by their simple names. For example:

```
new Pendulum(OneSpring );
```

We'll go into detail about enumerations later in this chapter after we've covered objects in more depth.

Methods

Methods appear inside class bodies. They contain local variable declarations and other Java statements that are executed when the method is invoked. Methods may return a value to the caller. They always specify a return type, which can be a primitive type, a reference type, or the type `void` , which indicates no returned value. Methods may take arguments, which are values supplied by the caller of the method.

Here's a simple example:

```
class Bird {
    int xPos, yPos;

    double fly ( int x, int y ) {
        double distance = Math.sqrt( x*x + y*y );
        flap( distance );
        xPos = x;
        yPos = y;
        return distance;
    }
    ...
}
```

In this example, the class `Bird` defines a method, `fly()`, that takes as arguments two integers: `x` and `y`. It returns a `double` type value as a result, using the `return` keyword.

Our method has a fixed number of arguments (two); however, methods can have *variable-length argument lists*, which allow the method to specify that it can take any number of arguments and sort them itself at runtime. We provide more details later in this chapter.

Local Variables

Our `fly()` method declares a local variable called `distance`, which it uses to compute the distance flown. A local variable is temporary; it exists only within the scope (the block) of its method. Local variables are allocated when a method is invoked; they are normally destroyed when the method returns. They can't be referenced from outside the method itself. If the method is executing concurrently in different threads, each thread has its own version of the method's local variables. A method's arguments also serve as local variables within the scope of the method; the only difference is that they are initialized by being passed in from the caller of the method.

An object created within a method and assigned to a local variable may or may not persist after the method has returned. As with all objects in Java, it depends on whether any references to the object remain. If an object is created, assigned to a local variable, and never used anywhere else, that object is no longer referenced when the local variable disappears from scope, so garbage collection removes the object. If, however, we assign the object to an instance variable of an object, pass it as an argument to another method, or pass it back as a return value, it may be saved by another variable holding its reference. We'll discuss object creation and garbage collection in more detail shortly.

Shadowing

If a local variable and an instance variable have the same name, the local variable *shadows* or hides the name of the instance variable within the scope of the method. In the following example, the local variables `xPos` and `yPos` hide the instance variables of the same name:

```
class Bird {
    int xPos, yPos;
    int xNest, yNest;
    ...
    double flyToNest() {
        int xPos = xNest;
        int yPos = yNest:
        return ( fly( xPos, yPos ) );
    }
    ...
}
```

When we set the values of the local variables in `flyToNest()`, it has no effect on the values of the instance variables.

The "this" reference

You can use the special reference this any time you need to refer explicitly to the current object or a member of the current object. Often you don't need to use this, because the reference to the current object is implicit; such is the case when using unambiguously named instance variables inside a class. But we can use this to refer explicitly to instance variables in our object, even if they are shadowed. The following example shows how we can use this to allow argument names that shadow instance variable names. This is a fairly common technique because it saves having to make up alternative names. Here's how we could implement our fly() method with shadowed variables:

```
class Bird {
    int xPos, yPos;

    double fly ( int xPos, int yPos ) {
        double distance = Math.sqrt( xPos*xPos + yPos*yPos );
        flap( distance );
        this.xPos = xPos;  // instance var = local vra
        this.yPos = yPos;
        return distance;
    }
    ...
}
```

In this example, the expression this.xPos refers to the instance variable xPos and assigns it the value of the local variable xPos, which would otherwise hide its name. The only reason we need to use this in the previous example is because we've used argument names that hide our instance variables, and we want to refer to the instance variables. You can also use the this reference any time you want to pass a reference to "the current" enclosing object to some other method; we'll show examples of that later.

Static Methods

Static methods (class methods), like static variables, belong to the class and not to individual instances of the class. What does this mean? Well, foremost, a static method lives outside of any particular class instance. It can be invoked by name, through the class name, without any objects around. Because it is not bound to a particular object instance, a static method can directly access only other static members (static variables and other static methods) of the class. It can't directly see any instance variables or call any instance methods, because to do so we'd have to ask, "on which instance?" Static methods can be called from instances, syntactically just like instance methods, but the important thing is that they can also be used independently.

Our fly() method uses a static method: Math.sqrt(), which is defined by the java.lang.Math class; we'll explore this class in detail in Chapter 11. For now, the important thing to note is that Math is the name of a class and not an instance of a Math object. (It so happens that you can't even make an instance of the Math class.) Because static methods can be invoked wherever the class name is available, class methods are closer to C-style functions. Static methods are particularly useful for utility methods that perform work that is useful either independently of instances or in working on instances. For example, in our `Bird` class, we could enumerate all of the available types of birds that can be created:

```
class Bird {
    ...
    static String [] getBirdTypes() { ... }

}
```

Here, we've defined a static method, `getBirdTypes()`, that returns an array of strings containing bird names. We can use `getBirdTypes()` from within an instance of `Bird`, just like an instance method. However, we can also call it from other classes, using the `Bird` class name:

```
String [] names = Bird.getBirdTypes();
```

Perhaps a special version of the `Bird` class constructor accepts the name of a bird type. We could use this list to decide what kind of bird to create.

Static methods also play an important role in various design patterns, where you limit the use of the `new` operator for a class to one method—a static method called a *factory method*. We'll talk more about object construction later, but suffice it to say that it's common to see usage like this:

```
Bird bird = Bird.createBird( "pigeon" );
```

Initializing Local Variables

In the `flyToNest()` example, we made a point of initializing the local variables `xPos` and `yPos`. Unlike instance variables, local variables must be initialized before they can be used. It's a compile-time error to try to access a local variable without first assigning it a value:

```
void myMethod() {
    int foo = 42;
    int bar;

    bar += 1;  // compile-time error, bar uninitialized

    bar = 99;
    bar += 1;  // would be OK here
}
```

Notice that this doesn't imply local variables have to be initialized when declared, just that the first time they are referenced must be in an assignment. More subtle possibilities arise when making assignments inside conditionals:

```
void myMethod {
  int foo;
  if ( someCondition ) {
    foo = 42;
    ...
  }
  foo += 1;   // Compile-time error, foo may not be initialized
}
```

In this example, foo is initialized only if someCondition is true. The compiler doesn't let you make this wager, so it flags the use of foo as an error. We could correct this situation in several ways. We could initialize the variable to a default value in advance or move the usage inside the conditional. We could also make sure the path of execution doesn't reach the uninitialized variable through some other means, depending on what makes sense for our particular application. For example, we could simply make sure that we assign foo a value in both the if and else branch. Or we could return from the method abruptly:

```
int foo;
...
if ( someCondition ) {
    foo = 42;
    ...
} else
    return;

foo += 1;
```

In this case, there's no chance of reaching foo in an uninitialized state, so the compiler allows the use of foo after the conditional.

Why is Java so picky about local variables? One of the most common (and insidious) sources of errors in C or C++ is forgetting to initialize local variables, so Java tries to help out. If it didn't, Java would suffer the same potential irregularities as C or C++.[2]

Argument Passing and References

In the beginning of Chapter 4, we described the distinction between primitive types, which are passed by value (by copying), and objects, which are passed by reference. Now that we've got a better handle on methods in Java, let's walk through an example:

```
void myMethod( int j, SomeKindOfObject o ) {
    ...
```

2. As with malloc'ed storage in C or C++, Java objects and their instance variables are allocated on a heap, which allows them default values once, when they are created. Local variables, however, are allocated on the Java virtual machine stack. As with the stack in C and C++, failing to initialize these could mean successive method calls could receive garbage values, and program execution might be inconsistent or implementation-dependent.

```
}

// use the method
int i = 0;
SomeKindOfObject obj = new SomeKindOfObject();
myMethod( i, obj );
```

The chunk of code calls `myMethod()`, passing it two arguments. The first argument, `i`, is passed by value; when the method is called, the value of `i` is copied into the method's parameter (a local variable to it) named `j`. If `myMethod()` changes the value of `j`, it's changing only its copy of the local variable.

In the same way, a copy of the reference to `obj` is placed into the reference variable `o` of `myMethod()`. Both references refer to the same object, so any changes made through either reference affect the actual (single) object instance. If we change the value of, say, `o.size`, the change is visible both as `o.size` (inside `myMethod()`) or as `obj.size` (in the calling method). However, if `myMethod()` changes the reference `o` itself—to point to another object—it's affecting only its local variable reference. It doesn't affect the caller's variable `obj`, which still refers to the original object. In this sense, passing the reference is like passing a pointer in C and unlike passing by reference in C++.

What if `myMethod()` needs to modify the calling method's notion of the `obj` reference as well (i.e., make `obj` point to a different object)? The easy way to do that is to wrap `obj` inside some kind of object. For example, we could wrap the object up as the lone element in an array:

```
SomeKindOfObject [] wrapper = new SomeKindOfObject [] { obj
};
```

All parties could then refer to the object as `wrapper[0]` and would have the ability to change the reference. This is not aesthetically pleasing, but it does illustrate that what is needed is the level of indirection.

Another possibility is to use `this` to pass a reference to the calling object. In that case, the calling object serves as the wrapper for the reference. Let's look at a piece of code that could be from an implementation of a linked list:

```
class Element {
    public Element nextElement;

    void addToList( List list ) {
        list.addToList( this );
    }
}

class List {
    void addToList( Element element ) {
        ...
        element.nextElement = getNextElement();
```

```
    }
}
```

Every element in a linked list contains a pointer to the next element in the list. In this code, the Element class represents one element; it includes a method for adding itself to the list. The List class itself contains a method for adding an arbitrary Element to the list. The method addToList() calls addToList() with the argument this (which is, of course, an Element). addToList() can use the this reference to modify the Element's nextElement instance variable. The same technique can be used in conjunction with interfaces to implement callbacks for arbitrary method invocations.

Wrappers for Primitive Types

As we described in Chapter 4, there is a schism in the Java world between class types (i.e., objects) and primitive types (i.e., numbers, characters, and Boolean values). Java accepts this tradeoff simply for efficiency reasons. When you're crunching numbers, you want your computations to be lightweight; having to use objects for primitive types complicates performance optimizations. For the times you want to treat values as objects, Java supplies a standard wrapper class for each of the primitive types, as shown in Table 5-1.

Table 5-1. Primitive type wrappers

Primitive	Wrapper
void	java.lang.Void
boolean	java.lang.Boolean
char	java.lang.Character
byte	java.lang.Byte
short	java.lang.Short
int	java.lang.Integer
long	java.lang.Long
float	java.lang.Float
double	java.lang.Double

An instance of a wrapper class encapsulates a single value of its corresponding type. It's an immutable object that serves as a container to hold the value and let us retrieve it later. You can construct a wrapper object from a primitive value or from a String representation of the value. The following statements are equivalent:

```
Float pi = new Float( 3.14 );
Float pi = new Float( "3.14" );
```

The wrapper constructors throw a NumberFormatException when there is an error in parsing a string.

Each of the numeric type wrappers implements the `java.lang.Number` interface, which provides "value" methods access to its value in all the primitive forms. You can retrieve scalar values with the methods `doubleValue()`, `floatValue()`, `longValue()`, `intValue()`, `shortValue()`, and `byteValue()`:

```
Double size = new Double ( 32.76 );

double d = size.doubleValue();      // 32.76
float f = size.floatValue();        // 32.76
long l = size.longValue();          // 32
int i = size.intValue();            // 32
```

This code is equivalent to casting the primitive `double` value to the various types.

The most common need for a wrapper is when you want to pass a primitive value to a method that requires an object. For example, in Chapter 11, we'll look at the Java Collections API, a sophisticated set of classes for dealing with object groups, such as lists, sets, and maps. All the Collections APIs work on object types, so primitives must be wrapped when stored in them. We'll see in the next section that Java makes this wrapping process automatic. For now, however, let's do it ourselves. As we'll see, a `List` is an extensible collection of `Objects`. We can use wrappers to hold numbers in a `List` (along with other objects):

```
// Simple Java code
List myNumbers = new ArrayList();
Integer thirtyThree = new Integer( 33 );
myNumbers.add( thirtyThree );
```

Here, we have created an `Integer` wrapper object so that we can insert the number into the `List`, using the `add()` method, which accepts an object. Later, when we are extracting elements from the `List`, we can recover the `int` value as follows:

```
// Simple Java code
Integer theNumber = (Integer)myNumbers.get(0);
int n = theNumber.intValue();           // 33
```

As we alluded to earlier, allowing Java to do this for us makes the code more concise and safer. The usage of the wrapper class is mostly hidden from us by the compiler, but it is still being used internally:

```
// Java code using autoboxing and generics
List<Integer> myNumbers = new ArrayList<Integer>();
myNumbers.add( 33 );
int n = myNumbers.get( 0 );
```

This example will make more sense as you read the next section on *autoboxing* and *unboxing* of primitive values.

Autoboxing and Unboxing of Primitives

The Java compiler automatically wraps primitives in their wrapper types and unwraps them where appropriate. This process is called autoboxing and unboxing the primitive. It happens when primitives are used as arguments and return values in methods and on simple assignment to variables. For example:

```
// Simple assignments
Integer integer = 5;
int i = new Integer(5);

// Method arguments and return types
Double multiply( Double a, Double b ) {
    return a.doubleValue() * b.doubleValue();
}

double d = multiply( 5.0, 5.0 );
```

In the first case, Java simply wrapped the value 5 into an `Integer` for us. In the second case, it unwrapped our `Integer` object to its primitive value. Next, we have a method that multiplies two `Double` wrapper objects and returns the result as a `Double` wrapper. This example actually has three cases of boxing and one case of unboxing. First, the two double primitive values are boxed to `Double` types in order to call the method. Next, the return statement of the method is actually being called on a primitive double value, which the compiler turns into a `Double` before it leaves the method. Finally, the compiler unboxes the return value on assignment to the primitive double variable `d`.

Performance implications of boxing

Gauging performance is tricky. For the vast majority of applications, the time it takes to perform tasks like creating a small object or calling a method is miniscule compared to other factors, such as I/O, user interaction, or the actual logic of the application. As a general rule, it's not wise to worry too much about these detailed performance issues until the application is mature (no premature optimization). However, we can anticipate that allowing Java to box and unbox primitives in performance-critical areas will not be as fast as using primitives directly. One aspect of this to consider is how many new objects are being created and reclaimed by the garbage collector. While in general Java may be forced to create a new object for each boxed primitive, there are optimizations for a small range of values. Java guarantees that the Boolean values `true` and `false`, as well as "small" valued numeric types ranging from 0 to 127 for bytes and chars and from −128 to 127 for shorts and integers, are *interned*. Saying that they are interned means that instead of creating a new object each time, Java reuses the same object on subsequent boxings. This is safe because primitive wrappers are immutable and cannot be changed.

```
Integer i = 4;
Integer j = 4;
System.out.println( i == j ); // This object equality is true only for small
                              // values.
```

The effect of this, as shown in this code snippet, is that for small identical values the boxed primitives are actually the same object. Java also attempts to intern string values in Java classes. We'll talk about that in Chapter 10.

Variable-Length Argument Lists

As we mentioned earlier, Java methods may have *variable-length argument lists* or "varargs" that allow them to take any number of arguments when invoked. The most common example usage of varargs is for the `printf()` style printing method, which allows any number of tags to be embedded in a string and takes an argument for each tag to be printed. For example:

```
System.out.printf("My name is %s and my age is %s\n", "Bob", 21 );
System.out.printf("Get the %s out of %s before I %s\n", item, place,
    action );
```

Varargs allow the `printf()` method to accept any number of items to print (from zero to dozens, as awkward as that would be).

A method accepting a variable argument list is equivalent to a method accepting an array of some type of object. The difference is that the compiler makes the method call accept individual, comma-separated values, and then packs them into the array for us. The syntax for declaring the varargs method uses ellipses (`...`) where the square brackets of an array might go. For example:

```
void printObjects( Object ... list ) {
    // list is an Object []
    for( Object o : list )
        System.out.println( o );
}
```

Inside the `printObjects()` method, the variable `list` is actually an `Object []` type. We could find out how many arguments were passed to us by asking the array for its length in the usual way:

```
System.out.println( "Number of arguments:" + list.length );
```

If the caller passed no arguments, the array will be empty.

In the case of our `printObjects()` method, we could pass a mix of primitive values as well as object types because the compiler would automatically box the primitives to their wrapper types for us before placing them into the `Object []`.

The variable argument list does not have to be of type `Object`. It can be of any type, including primitive types. For example:

```
printInts( int ... list ) {
    // list is an int []
}
// usage
```

```
printInts( 1, 2, 3, 4 );

printStrings( String ... list ) {
    // list is a String []
}
// usage
printStrings( "foo", "bar", "gee" );
```

The `printInts()` method receives an `int []` array of primitive `int` values. The `printStrings()` method receives a `String []` as its argument. The actual arguments must all be assignable (possibly after numeric promotion or boxing) to the type of the variable argument list. In other words, the `printInts()` method can only be called with numbers assignable to `int`, and the `printStrings()` method can only be called with `Strings`.

Varargs methods may also have any number of fixed arguments before the varargs declaration. This is how the `printf()` method guarantees that its first argument is the format string:

```
void printf( String format, Object ... args ) { ... }
```

Of course, a method can have only one varargs declaration, and it must come last in the method signature.

Method Overloading

Method overloading is the ability to define multiple methods with the same name in a class; when the method is invoked, the compiler picks the correct one based on the arguments passed to the method. This implies that overloaded methods must have different numbers or types of arguments. (In Chapter 6, we'll look at *method overriding*, which occurs when we declare methods with identical signatures in different classes.)

Method overloading (also called *ad-hoc polymorphism*) is a powerful and useful feature. The idea is to create methods that act in the same way on different types of arguments. This creates the illusion that a single method can operate on many types of arguments. The `print()` method in the standard `PrintStream` class is a good example of method overloading in action. As you've probably deduced by now, you can print a string representation of just about anything using this expression:

```
System.out.print( argument )
```

The variable `out` is a reference to an object (a `PrintStream`) that defines nine different, "overloaded" versions of the `print()` method. The versions take arguments of the following types: `Object`, `String`, `char[]`, `char`, `int`, `long`, `float`, `double`, and `boolean`.

```
class PrintStream {
    void print( Object arg ) { ... }
    void print( String arg ) { ... }
    void print( char [] arg ) { ... }
    ...
}
```

You can invoke the `print()` method with any of these types as an argument, and it's printed in an appropriate way. In a language without method overloading, this requires something more cumbersome, such as a uniquely named method for printing each type of object. In that case, it's your responsibility to figure out what method to use for each data type.

In the previous example, `print()` has been overloaded to support two reference types: `Object` and `String`. What if we try to call `print()` with some other reference type? Say, a `Date` object? When there's not an exact type match, the compiler searches for an acceptable, *assignable* match. Since `Date`, like all classes, is a subclass of `Object`, a `Date` object can be assigned to a variable of type `Object`. It's therefore an acceptable match, and the `Object` method is selected.

What if there's more than one possible match? For example, we try to print a subclass of `String` called `MyString`. (The `String` class is `final` so it can't really be subclassed, but let's use our imaginations.) `MyString` is assignable to either `String` or to `Object`. Here, the compiler makes a determination as to which match is "better" and selects that method. In this case, it's the `String` method.

The intuitive explanation for this is that the `String` class is "closer" to `MyString` in the inheritance hierarchy. It is a *more specific* match. A slightly more rigorous way of specifying it would be to say that a given method is more specific than another method if the argument types of the first method are all assignable to the argument types of the second method. In this case, the `String` method is more specific to a subclass of `String` than the `Object` method because type `String` is assignable to type `Object`. The reverse is not true.

If you're paying close attention, you may have noticed we said that the compiler resolves overloaded methods. Method overloading is not something that happens at runtime; this is an important distinction. It means that the selected method is chosen once, when the code is compiled. Once the overloaded method is selected, the choice is fixed until the code is recompiled, even if the class containing the called method is later revised and an even more specific overloaded method is added. This is in contrast to *overridden* methods, which are located at runtime and can be found even if they didn't exist when the calling class was compiled. In practice, this distinction will not usually be relevant to you, as you will likely recompile all of the necessary classes at the same time. We'll talk about method overriding later in the chapter.

Object Creation

Objects in Java are allocated on a system "heap" memory space. Unlike other languages, however, we needn't manage that memory ourselves. Java takes care of memory allocation and deallocation for you. Java explicitly allocates storage for an object when you create it with the new operator. More importantly, objects are removed by garbage collection when they're no longer referenced.

Constructors

Objects are allocated with the new operator using an *object constructor*. A constructor is a special method with the same name as its class and no return type. It's called when a new class instance is created, which gives the class an opportunity to set up the object for use. Constructors, like other methods, can accept arguments and can be overloaded (they are not, however, inherited like other methods; we'll discuss inheritance in Chapter 6).

```
class Date {
    long time;

    Date() {
        time = currentTime();
    }

    Date( String date ) {
        time = parseDate( date );
    }
    ...
}
```

In this example, the class Date has two constructors. The first takes no arguments; it's known as the *default constructor*. Default constructors play a special role: if we don't define any constructors for a class, an empty default constructor is supplied for us. The default constructor is what gets called whenever you create an object by calling its constructor with no arguments. Here we have implemented the default constructor so that it sets the instance variable time by calling a hypothetical method, currentTime(), which resembles the functionality of the real java.util.Date class. The second constructor takes a String argument. Presumably, this String contains a string representation of the time that can be parsed to set the time variable. Given the constructors in the previous example, we create a Date object in the following ways:

```
Date now = new Date();
Date christmas = new Date("Dec 25, 2006");
```

In each case, Java chooses the appropriate constructor at compile time based on the rules for overloaded method selection.

If we later remove all references to an allocated object, it'll be garbage-collected, as we'll discuss shortly:

```
christmas = null;          // fair game for the garbage collector
```

Setting this reference to null means it's no longer pointing to the "Dec 25, 2006" string object. Setting the variable christmas to any other value would have the same effect.

Unless the original string object is referenced by another variable, it's now inaccessible and can be garbage-collected. We're not suggesting that you have to set references to `null` to get the values garbage-collected. Often this just happens naturally when local variables fall out of scope, but items referenced by instance variables of objects live as long as the object itself lives (through references to it) and static variables live effectively forever.

A few more notes: constructors can't be declared `abstract`, `synchronized`, or `final` (we'll define the rest of those terms later). Constructors can, however, be declared with the visibility modifiers `public`, `private`, or `protected`, just like other methods, to control their accessibility. We'll talk in detail about visibility modifiers in the next chapter.

Working with Overloaded Constructors

A constructor can refer to another constructor in the same class or the immediate superclass using special forms of the `this` and `super` references. We'll discuss the first case here and return to that of the superclass constructor after we have talked more about subclassing and inheritance. A constructor can invoke another overloaded constructor in its class using the self-referential method call `this()` with appropriate arguments to select the desired constructor. If a constructor calls another constructor, *it must do so as its first statement*:

```
class Car {
    String model;
    int doors;

    Car( String model, int doors ) {
        this.model = model;
        this.doors = doors;
        // other, complicated setup
        ...
    }

    Car( String model ) {
        this( model, 4 /* doors */ );
    }
    ...
}
```

In this example, the class `Car` has two constructors. The first, more explicit, one accepts arguments specifying the car's model and its number of doors. The second constructor takes just the model as an argument and, in turn, calls the first constructor with a default value of four doors. The advantage of this approach is that you can have a single constructor do all the complicated setup work; other auxiliary constructors simply feed the appropriate arguments to that constructor.

The special call to `this()` must appear as the first statement in our delegating constructor. The syntax is restricted in this way because there's a need to identify a clear chain of command in the calling of constructors. At the end of the chain, Java invokes the constructor of the superclass (if we don't do it explicitly) to ensure that inherited members are initialized properly before we proceed.

There's also a point in the chain, just after invoking the constructor of the superclass, where the initializers of the current class's instance variables are evaluated. Before that point, we can't even reference the instance variables of our class. We'll explain this situation again in complete detail after we have talked about inheritance.

For now, all you need to know is that you can invoke a second constructor (delegate to it) only as the first statement of your constructor. For example, the following code is illegal and causes a compile-time error:

```
Car( String m ) {
    int doors = determineDoors();
    this( m, doors );    // Error: constructor call
                         // must be first statement
}
```

The simple model name constructor can't do any additional setup before calling the more explicit constructor. It can't even refer to an instance member for a constant value:

```
class Car {
    ...
    final int default_doors = 4;
    ...

    Car( String m ) {
        this( m, default_doors ); // Error: referencing
                                  // uninitialized variable
    }
    ...
}
```

The instance variable `defaultDoors` is not initialized until a later point in the chain of constructor calls setting up the object, so the compiler doesn't let us access it yet. Fortunately, we can solve this particular problem by using a static variable instead of an instance variable:

```
class Car {
    ...
    static final int DEFAULT_DOORS = 4;
    ...

    Car( String m ) {
        this( m, DEFAULT_DOORS );  // Okay!
    }
    ...
}
```

The static members of a class are initialized when the class is first loaded into the virtual machine, so it's safe to access them in a constructor.

Static and Nonstatic Initializer Blocks

It's possible to declare a block of code (some statements within curly braces) directly within the scope of a class. This code block doesn't belong to any method; instead, it's executed once, at the time the object is constructed, or, in the case of a code block marked `static`, at the time the class is loaded. These blocks can be used to do additional setup for the class or an object instance and are called *initializer blocks*.

Instance initializer blocks can be thought of as extensions of instance variable initialization. They're called at the time the instance variable's initializers are evaluated (after superclass construction, but before your constructor body), in the order in which they appear in the Java source:

```
class MyClass {
    Properties myProps = new Properties();
    // set up myProps
    {
        myProps.put("foo", "bar");
        myProps.put("boo", "gee");
    }
    int a = 5;
...
```

Normally, this kind of setup could be done just as well in the object's constructor. A notable exception is in the case of an anonymous inner class (see Chapter 6).

Similarly, you can use static initializer blocks to set up static class members. This more useful case allows the static members of a class to have complex initialization just like objects do with constructors:

```
class ColorWheel {
    static Hashtable colors = new Hashtable();

    // set up colors
    static {
        colors.put("Red", Color.red );
        colors.put("Green", Color.green );
        colors.put("Blue", Color.blue );
        ...
    }
    ...
}
```

The class `ColorWheel` provides a variable, `colors`, that maps the names of colors to `Color` objects in a `Hashtable`. The first time the class `ColorWheel` is referenced and loaded, the static components of `ColorWheel` are evaluated in the order they appear in the source. In this case, the static code block simply adds elements to the `colors` table.

Object Destruction

Now that we've seen how to create objects, it's time to talk about their destruction. If you're accustomed to programming in C or C++, you've probably spent time hunting down memory leaks in your code. Java takes care of object destruction for you; you don't have to worry about traditional memory leaks, and you can concentrate on more important programming tasks.[3]

Garbage Collection

Java uses a technique known as *garbage collection* to remove objects that are no longer needed. The garbage collector is Java's grim reaper. It lingers in the background, stalking objects and awaiting their demise. It finds and watches them, periodically counting references to them to see when their time has come. When all references to an object are gone and it's no longer accessible, the garbage-collection mechanism declares the object *unreachable* and reclaims its space back to the available pool of resources. An unreachable object is one that can no longer be found through any combination of "live" references in the running application.

Garbage collection uses a variety of algorithms; the Java virtual machine architecture doesn't require a particular scheme. It's worth noting, however, how some implementations of Java have accomplished this task. In the beginning, Java used a technique called "mark and sweep." In this scheme, Java first walks through the tree of all accessible object references and marks them as alive. Java then scans the heap, looking for identifiable objects that aren't marked. In this technique, Java is able to find objects on the heap because they are stored in a characteristic way and have a particular signature of bits in their handles unlikely to be reproduced naturally. This kind of algorithm doesn't become confused by the problem of cyclic references, in which objects can mutually reference each other and appear alive even when they are dead (Java handles this problem automatically). This scheme wasn't the fastest method, however, and caused pauses in the program. Since then, implementations have become much more sophisticated.

Modern Java garbage collectors effectively run continuously without forcing any lengthy delay in execution of the Java application. Because they are part of a runtime system, they can also accomplish some things that could not be done statically. Sun's Java implementation divides the memory heap into several areas for objects with different estimated lifespans. Short-lived objects are placed on a special part of the heap, which reduces the time to recycle them drastically. Objects that live longer can be moved to other, less volatile parts of the heap. In recent implementations, the garbage collector can even "tune" itself by adjusting the size of parts of the heap based on the actual

3. It's still possible in Java to write code that holds onto objects forever, consuming more and more memory. This isn't really a leak so much as it is hoarding memory. It is also usually much easier to track down with the correct tools and techniques.

application performance. The improvement in Java's garbage collection since the early releases has been remarkable and is one of the reasons that Java is now roughly equivalent in speed to traditional compiled languages.

In general, you do not have to concern yourself with the garbage-collection process. But one garbage-collection method can be useful for debugging. You can prompt the garbage collector to make a clean sweep explicitly by invoking the `System.gc()` method. This method is completely implementation-dependent and may do nothing, but it can be used if you want some guarantee that Java has cleaned up before you do an activity.

Finalization

Before an object is removed by garbage collection, its `finalize()` method is invoked to give it a last opportunity to clean up its act and free other kinds of resources it may be holding. While the garbage collector can reclaim memory resources, it may not take care of things such as closing files and terminating network connections as gracefully or efficiently as could your code. That's what the `finalize()` method is for. An object's `finalize()` method is called once and only once before the object is garbage-collected. However, there's no guarantee when that will happen. Garbage collection may, in theory, never run on a system that is not short of memory. It is also interesting to note that finalization and collection occur in two distinct phases of the garbage-collection process. First, items are finalized; then they are collected. It is, therefore, possible that finalization can (intentionally or unintentionally) create a lingering reference to the object in question, postponing its garbage collection. The object is, of course, subject to collection later if the reference goes away, but its `finalize()` method isn't called again.

The `finalize()` methods of superclasses are not invoked automatically for you. If you need to invoke the finalization routine of your parent classes, you should invoke the `finalize()` method of your superclass, using `super.finalize()`. We discuss inheritance and overridden methods in Chapter 6.

Weak and Soft References

In general, as we've described, Java's garbage collector reclaims objects when they are unreachable. An unreachable object, again, is one that is no longer referenced by any variables within your application and that is not reachable through any chain of references by any running thread. Such an object cannot be used by the application any longer and is, therefore, a clear case where the object should be removed.

In some situations, however, it is advantageous to have Java's garbage collector work with your application to decide when it is time to remove a particular object. For these cases, Java allows you to hold an object reference indirectly through a special wrapper object, a type of `java.lang.ref.Reference`. If Java then decides to remove the object, the reference the wrapper holds turns to `null` automatically. While the reference exists, you may continue to use it in the ordinary way and, if you wish, assign it elsewhere (using normal references), preventing its garbage collection.

There are two types of Reference wrappers that implement different schemes for deciding when to let their target references be garbage-collected. The first is called a WeakReference. *Weak references* are eligible for garbage collection immediately; they do not prevent garbage collection the way that ordinary "strong" references do. This means that if you have a combination of strong references and references contained in WeakReference wrappers in your application, the garbage collector waits until only WeakReferences remain and then collects the object. This is an essential feature that allows garbage collection to work with certain kinds of caching schemes. You'll often want to cache an object reference for performance (to avoid creating it or looking it up). But unless you take specific action to remove unneeded objects from your cache, the cache keeps those objects alive forever by maintaining live references to them. By using weak references, you can implement a cache that automatically throws away references when the object would normally be garbage-collected. In fact, an implementation of HashMap called WeakHashMap is provided that does just this (see Chapter 11 for details).

The second type of reference wrapper is called SoftReference. A *soft reference* is similar to a weak reference, but it tells the garbage collector to be less aggressive about reclaiming its contents. Soft-referenced objects are collected only when and if Java runs short of memory. This is useful for a slightly different kind of caching where you want to keep some content around unless there is a need to get rid of it. For example, a web browser can use soft references to cache images or HTML strings internally, thus keeping them around as long as possible until memory constraints come into play. (A more sophisticated application might also use its own scheme based on a "least recently used" marking of some kind.)

The java.lang.ref package contains the WeakReference and SoftReference wrappers, as well as a facility called ReferenceQueue that allows your application to receive a list of references that have been collected. It's important that your application use the queue or some other checking mechanism to remove the Reference objects themselves after their contents have been collected; otherwise, your cache will soon fill up with empty Reference object wrappers.

Enumerations

Now that we've covered the basics of classes, we can talk a bit more in depth about *enumerations*. As we've discussed, an enumeration is an object type in the Java language that is limited to an explicit set of values. The values have an order that is defined by their order of declaration in the code, and have a correspondence with a string name that is the same as their declared name in the source code.

We've already seen a couple of examples of enumerations used in place of static identifiers. For example:

```
enum Weekday { Sunday, Monday, Tuesday, Wednesday, Thursday, Friday,
    Saturday }

// usage
setDay( Weekday.Sunday );
```

Let's take a look at what the Java compiler is actually generating for the enum. It is a regular compiled Java class, in this case named `Weekday`, so we can display it with the `javap` command like so:

```
% javap Weekday

public final class Weekday extends java.lang.Enum {
    public static final Weekday Sunday;
    public static final Weekday Monday;
    public static final Weekday Tuesday;
    public static final Weekday Wednesday;
    public static final Weekday Thursday;
    public static final Weekday Friday;
    public static final Weekday Saturday;

    public static final Weekday[] values();
    public static Weekday valueOf(java.lang.String);
}
```

`Weekday` is a subclass of the `Enum` type with seven static, final, "constant" object references corresponding to our seven enumerated values. Each of the enumerated values is of type `Weekday`. The Java compiler does not let us extend this class or create any other instances of this type. The only instances of `Weekday` that will ever exist are the seven enumerated values. This is what gives enumerations their type safety. A method expecting a `Weekday` can be given one of only seven values. Unlike a numeric constant identifier, no value other than a `Weekday` will work. As we saw in Chapter 4, enumerations (unlike most objects) can also be used in `switch` statements with all the same benefits.

Because enumerations are static values, they can be imported with the Java *static import*, saving us some typing:

```
import static mypackage.Weekday.*;
...
setDay( Friday );
setDeadline( Sunday );
```

We should also mention that enumerations can be declared not only at the "top level" alongside classes, but within classes or interfaces as well. In this case, they act just like inner classes (see Chapter 6).

Enum Values

You can get the ordered list of enum values for a type with the static `values()` method.

```
Weekday [] weekdays = Weekday.values();
```

The `compareTo()` method of an enum compares an enum value to another value of the same enum type and returns an integer less than zero, zero, or greater than zero, indicating whether the target enum is "less than," "equal to," or "greater than" the order of the reference enum. This doesn't mean much for our `Weekdays`, but it might be useful for values that have a more numeric meaning or a (noncyclic) scale of some kind. For example:

```
Level level = Level.LOW;
Level anotherLevel = Level.HIGH;
if ( level.compareTo( anotherLevel ) > 0 ) // true
    doSomething();
```

We mentioned that enum values have a string correspondence for their names. You can get the string name of the value (which is exactly the same as it is declared in the source code) with the `name()` method. Going the other direction, you can "look up" any enum value by its class type and string name using the static `Enum.valueOf()` method:

```
String mondayString = Weekday.Monday.name(); // "Monday"
Weekday mondayWeekday = Enum.valueOf( Weekday.class, "Monday" );
```

The `name()` value is also used by the `toString()` method of the value, so printing an enum value does what you'd expect.

Customizing Enumerations

We said that the `java.lang.Enum` type cannot be directly extended and that you can't create new instances of enum types. However, you can add things to the generated enumeration class when it's declared. For example, the enumeration `java.util.concurrent.TimeUnit`, which has identifiers for time units such as SECONDS, MILLISECONDS, and MICROSECONDS, has a `sleep()` method that interprets its argument in the correct time scale:

```
import static java.util.concurrent.TimeUnit.*;

SECONDS.sleep( 5 ); // sleep 5 seconds
```

Enumerations can have values with constructors, methods, and fields just like other classes. For the most part, this is straightforward; you just add a semicolon after the enum values and then add your additional class members. Let's add a "fun" value and accessor method to our weekdays:

```
public enum Weekday
{
    Sunday(8), Monday(0), Tuesday(1), Wednesday(2), Thursday(4),
        Friday(6), Saturday(10) ;

    int fun;

    Weekday( int fun ) { this.fun = fun; }

    public int getFun() { return fun; }
}
```

Here, we've added an instance variable, `fun`, to the `Weekday` class, as well as a constructor and accessor method that work with the value. The declaration of our enum values each now accepts the constructor value, much like a constructor call without the `new` keyword. Note that the semicolon at the end of the values is mandatory. Each `Weekday` now has a `fun` attribute.

There is an odd special feature of enums that we didn't show. In addition to adding features to the enum class as a whole (as in our example), we can add methods and variables to individual values of the enumeration by giving them a body with curly braces (`{}`). This is best served by an example:

```
enum Cat {
    Himilayan, Siamese, Caleco,
    Persian {
        public void someMethod() { ... }
    }
}
```

Now, only the `Cat.Persian` enum value has the method. In this case, the compiler generates a subclass of `Cat` as an inner class of the `Persian` type to hold the extra member. (We'll talk about inner classes in Chapter 6.) You could use this to have the `Persian` member override a method in the base enum class.

CHAPTER 6
Relationships Among Classes

So far in our exploration of Java, we have seen how to create Java classes and objects, which are instances of those classes. By themselves, classes would be little more than a convention for organizing code. It is in the relationships between objects—their connections and privileges with respect to one another—that the power of an object-oriented language is really expressed.

That's what we'll cover in this chapter. In particular, we'll look at several kinds of relationships:

Inheritance relationships
: How a class inherits methods and variables from its parent class

Interfaces
: How to declare that a class implements certain behavior and define a type to refer to that behavior

Packaging
: How to organize objects into logical groups

Inner classes
: A generalization of classes that lets you nest a class definition inside another class definition

Subclassing and Inheritance

Classes in Java exist in a hierarchy. A class in Java can be declared as a *subclass* of another class using the `extends` keyword. A subclass *inherits* variables and methods from its *superclass* and can use them as if they were declared within the subclass itself:

```
class Animal {
    float weight;
    ...
```

```
    void eat() {
        ...
    }
    ...
}

class Mammal extends Animal {
    // inherits weight
    int heartRate;
    ...

    // inherits eat()
    void breathe() {
        ...
    }
}
```

In this example, an object of type `Mammal` has both the instance variable `weight` and the method `eat()`. They are inherited from `Animal`.

A class can *extend* only one other class. To use the proper terminology, Java allows *single inheritance* of class implementation. Later in this chapter, we'll talk about interfaces, which take the place of *multiple inheritance* as it's primarily used in other languages.

A subclass can be further subclassed. Normally, subclassing specializes or refines a class by adding variables and methods (you cannot remove or hide variables or methods by subclassing). For example:

```
class Cat extends Mammal {
    // inherits weight and heartRate
    boolean longHair;
    ...

    // inherits eat() and breathe()
    void purr() {
        ...
    }
}
```

The `Cat` class is a type of `Mammal` that is ultimately a type of `Animal`. `Cat` objects inherit all the characteristics of `Mammal` objects and, in turn, `Animal` objects. `Cat` also provides additional behavior in the form of the `purr()` method and the `longHair` variable. We can denote the class relationship in a diagram, as shown in Figure 6-1.

A subclass inherits all members of its superclass not designated as `private`. As we'll discuss shortly, other levels of visibility affect which inherited members of the class can be seen from outside of the class and its subclasses, but at a minimum, a subclass always has the same set of visible members as its parent. For this reason, the type of a subclass can be considered a *subtype* of its parent, and instances of the subtype can be used anywhere instances of the supertype are allowed. Consider the following example:

```
Cat simon = new Cat();
Animal creature = simon;
```

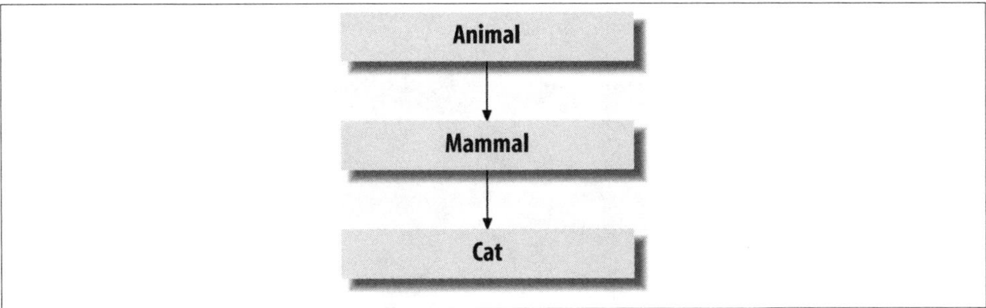

Figure 6-1. A class hierarchy

The `Cat` instance `simon` in this example can be assigned to the `Animal` type variable `creature` because `Cat` is a subtype of `Animal`. Similarly, any method accepting an `Animal` object would accept an instance of a `Cat` or any `Mammal` type as well. This is an important aspect of polymorphism in an object-oriented language such as Java. We'll see how it can be used to refine a class's behavior, as well as add new capabilities to it.

Shadowed Variables

In Chapter 5, we saw that a local variable of the same name as an instance variable *shadows* (hides) the instance variable. Similarly, an instance variable in a subclass can shadow an instance variable of the same name in its parent class, as shown in Figure 6-2. We're going to cover the details of this variable hiding now for completeness and in preparation for more advanced topics, but in practice you should almost never do this. It is much better in practice to structure your code to clearly differentiate variables using different names or naming conventions.

In Figure 6-2, the variable `weight` is declared in three places: as a local variable in the method `foodConsumption()` of the class `Mammal`, as an instance variable of the class `Mammal`, and as an instance variable of the class `Animal`. The actual variable selected when you reference it in the code would depend on the scope in which we are working and how you qualify the reference to it.

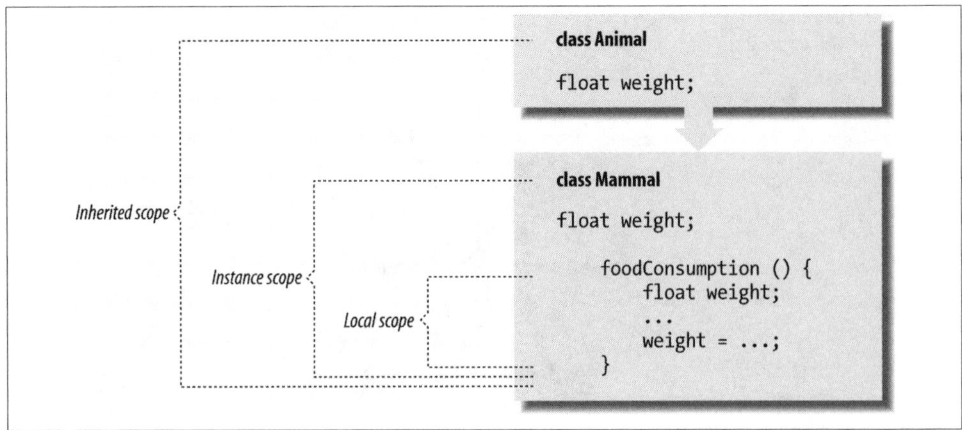

Figure 6-2. The scope of shadowed variables

In the previous example, all variables were of the same type. A slightly more plausible use of shadowed variables would involve changing their types. We could, for example, shadow an `int` variable with a `double` variable in a subclass that needs decimal values instead of integer values. We can do this without changing the existing code because, as its name suggests, when we shadow variables, we don't replace them but instead mask them. Both variables still exist; methods of the superclass see the original variable, and methods of the subclass see the new version. The determination of what variables the various methods see occurs at compile time.

Here's a simple example:

```
class IntegerCalculator {
    int sum;
    ...
}

class DecimalCalculator extends IntegerCalculator {
    double sum;
    ...
}
```

In this example, we shadow the instance variable `sum` to change its type from `int` to `double`.[1] Methods defined in the class `IntegerCalculator` see the integer variable `sum`, while methods defined in `DecimalCalculator` see the floating-point variable `sum`. However, both variables actually exist for a given instance of `DecimalCalculator`, and they can have independent values. In fact, any methods that `DecimalCalculator` inherits from `IntegerCalculator` actually see the integer variable `sum`.

1. Note that a better way to design our calculators would be to have an abstract `Calculator` class with two subclasses: `IntegerCalculator` and `DecimalCalculator`.

Because both variables exist in `DecimalCalculator`, we need a way to reference the variable inherited from `IntegerCalculator`. We do that using the `super` keyword as a qualifier on the reference:

```
int s = super.sum;
```

Inside of `DecimalCalculator`, the `super` keyword used in this manner selects the `sum` variable defined in the superclass. We'll explain the use of `super` more fully in a bit.

Another important point about shadowed variables has to do with how they work when we refer to an object by way of a less derived type (a parent type). For example, we can refer to a `DecimalCalculator` object as an `IntegerCalculator` by using it via a variable of type `IntegerCalculator`. If we do so and then access the variable `sum`, we get the integer variable, not the decimal one:

```
DecimalCalculator dc = new DecimalCalculator();
IntegerCalculator ic = dc;

int s = ic.sum;       // accesses IntegerCalculator sum
```

The same would be true if we accessed the object using an explicit cast to the `IntegerCalculator` type or when passing an instance into a method that accepts that parent type.

To reiterate, the usefulness of shadowed variables is limited. It's much better to abstract the use of variables like this in other ways than to use tricky scoping rules. However, it's important to understand the concepts here before we talk about doing the same thing with methods. We'll see a different and more dynamic type of behavior when methods shadow other methods, or to use the correct terminology, *override* other methods.

Overriding Methods

In Chapter 5, we saw that we could declare *overloaded methods* (i.e., methods with the same name but a different number or type of arguments) within a class. Overloaded method selection works in the way we described on all methods available to a class, including inherited ones. This means that a subclass can define additional overloaded methods that add to the overloaded methods provided by a superclass.

A subclass can do more than that; it can define a method that has exactly the *same* method signature (name and argument types) as a method in its superclass. In that case, the method in the subclass *overrides* the method in the superclass and effectively replaces its implementation, as shown in Figure 6-3. Overriding methods to change the behavior of objects is called *subtype polymorphism*. It's the usage most people think of when they talk about the power of object-oriented languages.

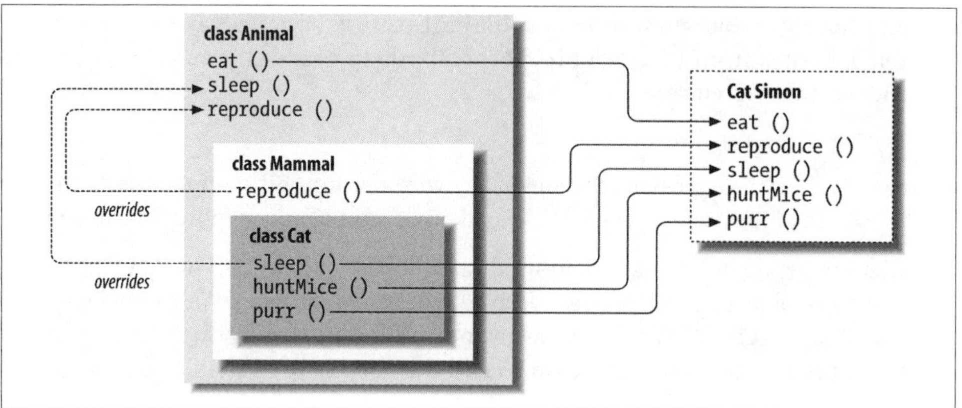

Figure 6-3. Method overriding

In Figure 6-3, `Mammal` overrides the `reproduce()` method of `Animal`, perhaps to specialize the method for the behavior of mammals giving birth to live young.[2] The `Cat` object's sleeping behavior is also overridden to be different from that of a general `Animal`, perhaps to accommodate cat naps. The `Cat` class also adds the more unique behaviors of purring and hunting mice.

From what you've seen so far, overridden methods probably look like they shadow methods in superclasses, just as variables do. But overridden methods are actually more powerful than that. When there are multiple implementations of a method in the inheritance hierarchy of an object, the one in the "most derived" class (the furthest down the hierarchy) always overrides the others, even if we refer to the object through a reference of one of the superclass types.[3]

For example, if we have a `Cat` instance assigned to a variable of the more general type `Animal`, and we call its `sleep()` method, we still get the `sleep()` method implemented in the `Cat` class, not the one in `Animal`:

```
Cat simon = new Cat();
Animal creature = simon;
  ...
creature.sleep();        // accesses Cat sleep();
```

In other words, for purposes of behavior (invoking methods), a `Cat` acts like a `Cat`, regardless of whether you refer to it as such. In other respects, the variable `creature` here may behave like an `Animal` reference. As we explained earlier, access to a shadowed variable through an `Animal` reference would find an implementation in the `Animal` class,

2. The `Platypus` is a highly unusual egg-laying `Mammal`. We could override the `reproduce()` behavior again for it in its own subclass of `Mammal`.

3. An overridden method in Java acts like a `virtual` method in C++.

not the `Cat` class. However, because methods are located *dynamically*, searching subclasses first, the appropriate method in the `Cat` class is invoked, even though we are treating it more generally as an `Animal` object. This means that the *behavior* of objects is dynamic. We can deal with specialized objects as if they were more general types and still take advantage of their specialized implementations of behavior.

@Override

A common programming error in Java is to accidentally overload a method when trying to override it. Any difference in the number or type of arguments (the method *signature*) produces two overloaded methods instead of a single, overridden method. The new annotations syntax in Java 5.0 provides a way to get the compiler to help with this problem. An annotation, as we'll describe in Chapter 7, allows us to add special markers or metadata to source code that can be read by the compiler or runtime tools. One of the standard annotations that Java defines is called `@Override` and it tells the compiler that the method it marks is intended to override a method in the superclass. The compiler then warns if the method doesn't match. For example, we could specify that the `sleep()` method of our `Cat` class overrides one in a superclass like so:

```
class Cat extends Mammal {
    ...
    @Override void sleep() { ... }
}
```

Overridden methods and dynamic binding

In a previous section, we mentioned that *overloaded* methods are selected by the compiler at compile time. *Overridden* methods, on the other hand, are selected dynamically at runtime. Even if we create an instance of a subclass our code has never seen before (perhaps a new class loaded over the network), any overriding methods that it contains are located and used at runtime, replacing those that existed when we last compiled our code.

In contrast, if we created a new class that implements an additional, more specific, overloaded method, and replace the compiled class in our classpath with it, our code would continue to use the implementation it discovered originally. This situation would persist until we recompiled our code along with the new class. Another effect of this is that casting (i.e., explicitly telling the compiler to treat an object as one of its assignable types) affects the selection of overloaded methods at compile time but not overridden methods.

In practice what we've just described is not something you need to worry about often, but it's important in understanding what the virtual machine does and does not do at runtime.

Static method binding

Static methods don't belong to any object instance; they are accessed directly through a class name, so they are not dynamically selected at runtime like instance methods. That is why static methods are called "static"; they are always bound at compile time.

A static method in a superclass can be shadowed by another static method in a subclass, as long as the original method was not declared final. However, both methods are always accessible directly via their respective class names. You can't "override" a static method with an instance method. In other words, you can't have a static method and instance method with the same signature in the same class hierarchy.

final methods and performance

In languages like C++, the default is for methods to act like shadowed variables, so you have to declare explicitly the methods you want to be dynamic (or, as C++ terms them, *virtual*). In Java, instance methods are, by default, dynamic. But you can use the `final` modifier to declare that an instance method can't be overridden in a subclass, and it won't be subject to dynamic binding.

We have seen `final` used with variables to effectively make them constants. When applied to a method, `final` means that its implementation is constant—no overriding allowed. `final` can also be applied to an entire class, which means the class can't be subclassed.

In the old days, dynamic method binding came with a significant performance penalty, and some people are still inclined to use the `final` modifier to guard against this. Modern Java runtime systems eliminate the need for this kind of tweaking. A profiling runtime can determine which methods are not being overridden and "optimistically" inline them, treating them as if they were final until it becomes necessary to do otherwise. As a rule, you should use the `final` keyword when it is correct for your program's structure, not for performance considerations.

Compiler optimizations

In some older versions of Java, the *javac* compiler can be run with a *-O* switch, which tells it to perform certain optimizations, like inlining, statically. Most of these optimizations are now done at runtime by smarter VMs, so switches like this are generally not necessary.

Another kind of optimization allows you to include debugging code in your Java source without incurring a size or performance penalty. Although Java doesn't have a preprocessor to explicitly control what source is included, you can get some of the same effects by making a block of code conditional on a constant (i.e., `static` and `final`) variable. The Java compiler is smart enough to remove this code when it determines that it won't be called. For example:

```
static final boolean DEBUG = false;
...
final void debug (String message) {
    if (DEBUG) {
        System.err.println(message);
        // do other stuff
        ...
    }
}
```

In this case, the compiler can recognize that the condition on the `DEBUG` variable is always `false`, and the body of the `debug()` method will be optimized away. With a modern compiler, the method call might even be optimized away entirely.

Note that this kind of debugging code is useful for purposes such as logging. In contrast to assertions, which we covered in Chapter 4, which are supposed to be yes/no tests that guarantee the correctness of your program logic, these conditional blocks of code might do expensive formatting or other output processing that is useful during develoment but you don't wish to have around in the final product.

Method selection revisited

By now you should have a good, intuitive feel for how methods are selected from the pool of potentially overloaded and overridden method names of a class. If, however, you are dying for more detail, we'll provide it now.

In a previous section, we offered an inductive rule for overloaded method resolution. It said that a method is considered more specific than another if its arguments are assignable to the arguments of the second method. We can now expand this rule to include the resolution of overridden methods by adding the following condition: to be more specific than another method, the type of the class containing the method must also be assignable to the type of the class holding the second method.

What does that mean? Well, the only classes whose types are assignable are classes in the same inheritance hierarchy, meaning that we're talking about the set of all methods of the same name in a class or any of its parent or child classes. Because subclass types are assignable to superclass types, but not vice versa, the resolution is pushed in the way that we expect down the chain toward the subclasses. This effectively adds a second dimension to the search, in which resolution is pushed down the inheritance tree toward more refined classes and, simultaneously, toward the most specific overloaded method within a given class.

Exceptions and overridden methods

An overriding method may change the behavior of an object, but in some ways, it must still fulfill the contract of the original method with the user. Specifically, an overriding method must adhere to the `throws` clause of the original method. The new method cannot throw new types of checked exceptions. It can only declare that it throws exception types assignable to those thrown by the method in the parent class; that is, it may declare that it throws the same types of exceptions or subtypes of those declared by the original method. If the new method does not throw any of the checked exceptions of the original, it does not have to declare them and callers of the method via the subclass do not have to guard against them. (In this way, you can override a method to "handle" exceptions for the user.)

So the new method may declare exactly the same checked exceptions as the original, or it has the option to refine those types by declaring that it throws more specific subtypes than the overridden method. This is not the same as just saying that the method can simply throw subtypes of its declared exceptions; any method can do that. The new method can actually redefine the `throws` clause of the method to be more specific. This technique is called *covariant* typing of the `throws` clause, which means that the exception types against which the user must guard change to become more refined with the subtype.

Let's quickly review what the `throws` clause really means. If a method declares that it can throw an `IOException`, it is really saying that it can throw exceptions of type `IOException` or its subtypes. For example, `FileNotFoundException` is a type of `IOException`. A method declaring that it can throw `IOException` could actually throw `FileNotFoundException` or any other subtype of `IOException` at runtime:

```
public void readFile() throws IOException {
    ...
    if ( error ) throw new FileNotFoundException( filename );
}
```

When we call this method, the compiler will ensure that we allow for the possibility of any kind of `IOException`, using either a `try/catch` block or by throwing the exception from our own method.

When we override a method in a subclass, we get an opportunity to rewrite the `throws` clause of the method a bit. The new method must still be backward-compatible with the original, so any checked exceptions it throws must be assignable to those thrown by the overridden method. But we can be more specific if we want, refining the type of exception to go along with the new method's behavior. For example:

```
class MeatInedibleException extends InedibleException { ... }

class Animal {
    void eat( Food f ) throws InedibleException {
        ...
    }
}
class Herbivore extends Animal {
    void eat( Food f ) throws MeatInedibleException {
        if ( f instanceof Meat )
```

```
                throw new MeatInedibleException();
            ...
        }
    }
```

In this code, `Animal` specifies that it can throw an `InedibleException` from its `eat()` method. `Herbivore` is a subclass of `Animal`, so its `eat()` method must also be able to throw an `InedibleException`. However, `Herbivore`'s `eat()` method actually declares that it throws a more specific exception: `MeatInedibleException`. It can do this because `MeatInedibleException` is a subtype of `InedibleException`. If we are working with an `Herbivore` type directly, the compiler will allow us to catch just the `MeatInedibleException` and not require us to guard against the more general `InedibleException`:

```
Herbivore creature = ...
try {
    creature.eat( food );
} catch ( MeatInedibleException ) {
    // creature can't eat this food because it's meat
}
```

On the other hand, if we don't care why the food is inedible, we're free to guard for the more general `InedibleException` alone and treat it as any other `Animal`.

To sum up, an overriding method can refine not only the behavior of the parent method, but also the type of checked exceptions it throws. Next, we'll talk about overridden methods that change their return type in exactly the same way.

Return types and overridden methods

For a method to qualify as an overridden method in a subclass, it must have exactly the same number and types of arguments. It must have the same "inputs," as it were. As we saw in the previous section, overriding methods may refine their "output" to some extent. Namely, they can narrow their `throws` clause by declaring that they throw subtypes of the original method's exception types. What about the main "output" of a method? Its return value? Can we change the return type of a method by overriding it? The answer is that Java gives us covariant return types on methods just as it does for exception types.

What this means is that when you override a method, you may change the return type to a subtype of the original method's return type. For example, if our `Animal` class has a factory method called `create()` that produces an instance of `Animal`, our `Mammal` class could refine the return type to `Mammal`:

```
class Animal {
    Animal create() { ... }
}
class Mammal extends Animal {
    Mammal create() { ... }
}
```

As we'll see later, this coding technique is very helpful because it eliminates some runtime casting of objects.

Special References: this and super

The special references `this` and `super` allow you to refer to the members of the current object instance or to members of the superclass, respectively. We have seen `this` used elsewhere to pass a reference to the current object and to refer to shadowed instance variables. The reference `super` does the same for the parents of a class. You can use it to refer to members of a superclass that have been shadowed or overridden. Being able to invoke the original method of the superclass allows us to use it as part of our new method, delegating to its behavior before or after we perform additional work:

```
class Animal {
    void eat( Food f ) throws InedibleException {
        // consume food
    }
}

class Herbivore extends Animal {
    void eat( Food f ) throws MeatInedibleException {
        // check if edible
        ...
        try {
            super.eat( f );
        } catch ( InedibleException e ) { ... }
    }
}
```

In this example, our `Herbivore` class overrides the `Animal eat()` method to first do some checking on the `food` object. After doing its job, it uses `super.eat()` to call the (otherwise overridden and inaccessible) implementation of `eat()` in its superclass.

`super` prompts a search for the method or variable to begin in the scope of the immediate superclass rather than the current class. The inherited method or variable found may reside in the immediate superclass or one further up the tree. The usage of the `super` reference when applied to overridden methods of a superclass is special; it tells the method resolution system to stop the dynamic method search at the superclass instead of at the most derived class (as it otherwise does). Without `super`, there would be no way to access overridden methods.

Casting

A *cast* explicitly tells the compiler to change the apparent type of an object reference. The main use for casts is when an object is temporarily assigned to a more general type. For example, if a `String` were assigned to a variable of type `Object`, to use it as a `String` again, we'd have to perform a cast to get it back. The compiler recognizes only the declared types of variables and doesn't know that we actually placed a `String` into it. In Java, casts are checked both at compile time and at runtime to make sure they are legal. At compile time the Java compiler will stop you from trying to perform a cast that cannot possibly work (such as turning a `Date` directly into a `String`). And at runtime, Java will check that casts that are plausible (such as our `Object` to `String`) are actually correct for the real objects involved.

Attempting to cast an object to an incompatible type at runtime results in a `ClassCastException`. Only casts between objects in the same inheritance hierarchy (and, as we'll see later, to appropriate interfaces) are legal in Java and pass the scrutiny of the compiler and the runtime system. Casts in Java affect only the treatment of references; they never change the form of the actual object. This is an important rule to keep in mind. You never change the object pointed to by a reference by casting it; you change only the compiler's (or runtime system's) notion of it.

A cast can be used to *narrow* or *downcast* the type of a reference—to make it more specific. Often, we'll do this when we have to retrieve an object from a more general type of collection or when it has been previously used as a less derived type. (The prototypical example is using an object in a collection, as we'll see in Chapter 11.) Continuing with our `Cat` example:

```
Animal creature;
Cat simon;
// ...

creature = simon;         // OK
// simon = creature;      // Compile-time error, incompatible type
simon = (Cat)creature;    // OK
```

We can't reassign the reference in `creature` to the variable `simon` even though we know it holds an instance of a `Cat` (Simon). We have to perform the indicated cast to narrow the reference. Note that an implicit cast was performed when we went the other way to *widen* the reference `simon` to type `Animal` during the first assignment. In this case, an explicit cast would have been legal but superfluous.

What all this means is that you can't lie or guess about what an object is. If you have a `Cat` object, you can use it as an `Animal` or even `Object` because all Java classes are a subclass of `Object`. But if you have an `Object` you think is a `Cat`, you have to perform a cast to get it back to an `Animal` or a `Cat`. If you aren't sure whether the `Object` is a `Cat` or a `Dog` at runtime, you can check it with `instanceof` before you perform the cast. If you do not check and you get the cast wrong, the runtime system throws a `ClassCastException`.

```
if ( creature instanceof Cat ) {
    Cat cat = (Cat)creature;
    cat.meow();
}
```

As we mentioned earlier, casting can affect the selection of compile-time items such as variables and overloaded methods, but not the selection of overridden methods. Figure 6-4 shows the difference. As shown in the top half of the diagram, casting the reference `simon` to type `Animal` (widening it) affects the selection of the shadowed variable `weight` within it. However, as the lower half of the diagram indicates, the cast doesn't affect the selection of the overridden method `sleep()`.

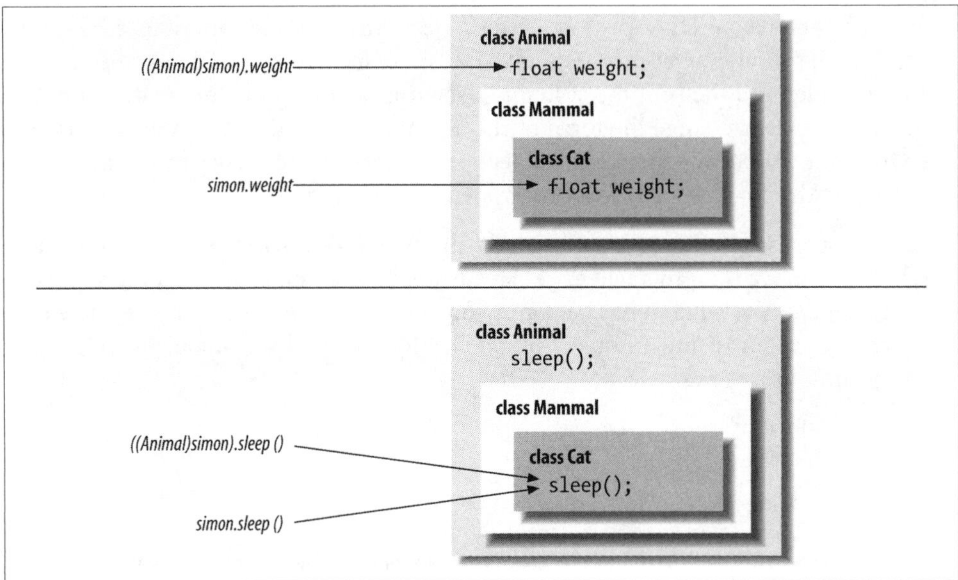

Figure 6-4. Casting and selection of methods and variables

Casting aspersions

Casting in Java is something that programmers strive to avoid. This is not only because it indicates a weakness in the static typing of the code, but because casts can also simply be tedious to use and make code less readable. Unfortunately, a great deal of code written in Java in the past has had no choice but to rely on casting so that it can work with any type of object the user requires. Java 5.0 introduced a major new language feature, generics, partly to address this issue. Generics allow Java code to be "typed" for a particular kind of object by the user, eliminating the need to cast in many situations. We'll cover generics in detail in Chapter 8 and see how they reduce the need for casts in most Java code.

Using Superclass Constructors

When we talked earlier about constructors, we discussed how the special statement `this()` invokes an overloaded constructor upon entry to another constructor. Similarly, the statement super() explicitly invokes the constructor of a superclass. Of course, we also talked about how Java makes a chain of constructor calls that includes the superclass's constructor, so why use super() explicitly? When Java makes an implicit call to the superclass constructor, it calls the default constructor. If we want to invoke a superclass constructor that takes arguments, we have to do so explicitly using super().

If we are going to call a superclass constructor with super(), it must be the first statement of our constructor, just as this() must be the first call we make in an overloaded constructor. Here's a simple example:

```
class Person {
    Person ( String name ) {
        //  setup based on name
        ...
    }
    ...
}

class Doctor extends Person {
    Doctor ( String name, String specialty ) {
        super( name );
        // setup based on specialty
        ...
    }
    ...
}
```

In this example, we use super() to take advantage of the implementation of the superclass constructor and avoid duplicating the code to set up the object based on its name. In fact, because the class Person doesn't define a default (no arguments) constructor, we have no choice but to call super() explicitly. Otherwise, the compiler would complain that it couldn't find an appropriate default constructor to call. In other words, if you subclass a class whose constructors all take arguments, you have to invoke one of the superclass's constructors explicitly from at least one of your subclass's constructors.

Instance variables of the class are initialized upon return from the superclass constructor, whether that's due to an explicit call to super() or an implicit call to the default superclass constructor.

Full Disclosure: Constructors and Initialization

We can now tell the full story of how constructors are chained together and when instance variable initialization occurs. The rule has three parts and is applied repeatedly for each successive constructor that is invoked:

- If the first statement of a constructor is an ordinary statement—that is, not a call to this() or super()—Java inserts an implicit call to super() to invoke the default constructor of the superclass. Upon returning from that call, Java initializes the instance variables of the current class and proceeds to execute the statements of the current constructor.

- If the first statement of a constructor is a call to a superclass constructor via `super()`, Java invokes the selected superclass constructor. Upon its return, Java initializes the current class's instance variables and proceeds with the statements of the current constructor.
- If the first statement of a constructor is a call to an overloaded constructor via `this()`, Java invokes the selected constructor, and upon its return, simply proceeds with the statements of the current constructor. The call to the superclass's constructor has happened within the overloaded constructor, either explicitly or implicitly, so the initialization of instance variables has already occurred.

Abstract Methods and Classes

A method in Java can be declared with the `abstract` modifier to indicate that it's just a prototype. An abstract method has no body; it's simply a signature declaration followed by a semicolon. You can't directly use a class that contains an abstract method; you must instead create a subclass that implements the abstract method's body:

```
abstract void vaporMethod( String name );
```

In Java, a class that contains one or more abstract methods must be explicitly declared as an abstract class, also using the `abstract` modifier:

```
abstract classVaporClass {
    ...
    abstract void vaporMethod( String name );
    ...
}
```

An abstract class can contain other nonabstract methods and ordinary variable declarations, but it can't be instantiated. To be used, it must be subclassed and its abstract methods must be "overridden" with methods that implement a body. Not all abstract methods have to be implemented in a single subclass, but a subclass that doesn't override all its superclass's abstract methods with actual, concrete implementations must also be declared `abstract`.

```
class MyVaporImplementation extends VaporClass {
    void vaporMethod( String name ) { ... }
}
```

Abstract classes provide a framework for classes that is to be "filled in" by the implementer. The `java.io.InputStream` class, for example, has a single abstract method called `read()`. Various subclasses of `InputStream` implement `read()` in their own ways to read from their own sources. The rest of the `InputStream` class, however, provides extended functionality built on the simple `read()` method. A subclass of `Input`

`Stream` inherits these nonabstract methods to provide functionality based on the simple `read()` method that the subclass implements.

Interfaces

Java expands on the concept of abstract methods with *interfaces*. It's often desirable to specify a group of abstract methods defining some behavior for an object without tying it to any implementation at all. In Java, this is called an interface. An interface defines a set of methods that a class must implement. A class in Java can declare that it *implements* an interface if it implements the required methods. Unlike extending an abstract class, a class implementing an interface doesn't have to inherit from any particular part of the inheritance hierarchy or use a particular implementation.

Interfaces are kind of like Boy Scout or Girl Scout merit badges. A scout who has learned to build a birdhouse can walk around wearing a little sleeve patch with a picture of one. This says to the world, "I know how to build a birdhouse." Similarly, an interface is a list of methods that define some set of behavior for an object. Any class that implements each method listed in the interface can declare at compile time that it implements the interface and wear, as its merit badge, an extra type—the interface's type.

Interface types act like class types. You can declare variables to be of an interface type, you can declare arguments of methods to accept interface types, and you can specify that the return type of a method is an interface type. In each case, what is meant is that any object that implements the interface (i.e., wears the right merit badge) can fill that role. In this sense, interfaces are orthogonal to the class hierarchy. They cut across the boundaries of what kind of object an item *is* and deal with it only in terms of what it can *do*. A class can implement as many interfaces as it desires. In this way, interfaces in Java replace much of the need for multiple inheritance in other languages (and all its messy complications).

An interface looks, essentially, like a purely `abstract` class (i.e., a class with only `abstract` methods). You define an interface with the `interface` keyword and list its methods with no bodies, just prototypes (signatures):

```
interface Driveable {
    boolean startEngine();
    void stopEngine();
    float accelerate( float acc );
    boolean turn( Direction dir );
}
```

The previous example defines an interface called `Driveable` with four methods. It's acceptable, but not necessary, to declare the methods in an interface with the `abstract` modifier; we haven't done that here. More importantly, the methods of an interface are always considered `public`, and you can optionally declare them as so. Why public? Well, the user of the interface wouldn't necessarily be able to see them otherwise, and interfaces are generally intended to describe the behavior of an object, not its implementation.

Interfaces define capabilities, so it's common to name interfaces after their capabilities. `Driveable`, `Runnable`, and `Updateable` are good interface names. Any class that implements all the methods can then declare that it implements the interface by using a special `implements` clause in its class definition. For example:

```
class Automobile implements Driveable {
    ...
    public boolean startEngine() {
        if ( notTooCold )
            engineRunning = true;
        ...
    }

    public void stopEngine() {
        engineRunning = false;
    }

    public float accelerate( float acc ) {
        ...
    }

    public boolean turn( Direction dir ) {
        ...
    }
    ...
}
```

Here, the class `Automobile` implements the methods of the `Driveable` interface and declares itself a type of `Driveable` using the `implements` keyword.

As shown in Figure 6-5, another class, such as `Lawnmower`, can also implement the `Driveable` interface. The figure illustrates the `Driveable` interface being implemented by two different classes. While it's possible that both `Automobile` and `Lawnmower` could derive from some primitive kind of vehicle, they don't have to in this scenario.

After declaring the interface, we have a new type, `Driveable`. We can declare variables of type `Driveable` and assign them any instance of a `Driveable` object:

```
Automobile auto = new Automobile();
Lawnmower mower = new Lawnmower();
Driveable vehicle;

vehicle = auto;
vehicle.startEngine();
vehicle.stopEngine();

vehicle = mower;
```

```
vehicle.startEngine();
vehicle.stopEngine();
```

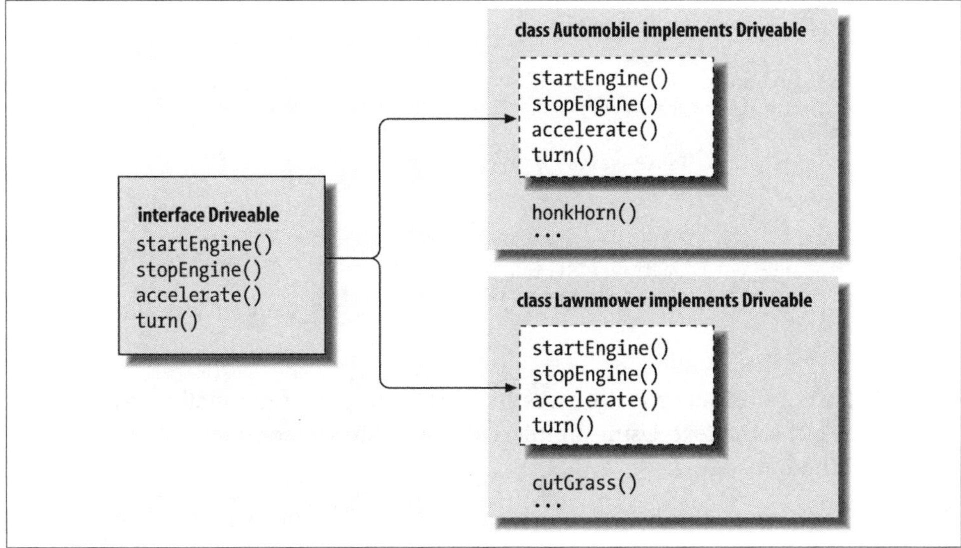

Figure 6-5. Implementing the Driveable interface

Both `Automobile` and `Lawnmower` implement `Driveable`, so they can be considered interchangeable objects of that type.

Interfaces as Callbacks

Interfaces can be used to implement "callbacks" in Java. This is when an object effectively passes a reference to one or more of its methods to another object. The callback occurs when the called object subsequently invokes one of the methods. In C or C++, this is prime territory for function pointers; Java uses interfaces instead. More generally, this concept is extended in Java to the concept of *events* in which listener objects register with event sources. We'll cover events in great detail in later chapters.

Consider two classes: a `TickerTape` class that displays data and a `TextSource` class that provides an information feed. We'd like our `TextSource` to send any new text data. We could have `TextSource` store a reference to a `TickerTape` object, but then we could never use our `TextSource` to send data to any other kind of object. Instead, we'd have to proliferate subclasses of `TextSource` that dealt with different types. A more elegant solution is to have `TextSource` store a reference to an interface type, `TextReceiver`:

```
interface TextReceiver {
    void receiveText( String text );
}
```

```
class TickerTape implements TextReceiver {
    public void receiveText( String text ) {
        System.out.println("TICKER:\n" + text + "\n");
    }
}

class TextSource {
    TextReceiver receiver;

    TextSource( TextReceiver r ) {
        receiver = r;
    }

    public void sendText( String s ) {
        receiver.receiveText( s );
    }
}
```

The only thing `TextSource` really cares about is finding the right method to invoke in order to output some text. Using an interface establishes a "contract," `receiveText()`, for that method.

When the `TextSource` is constructed, a reference to the `TickerTape` (which implements the interface) is stored in an instance variable. This "registers" the `TickerTape` as the `TextSource`'s "output device." Whenever it needs to output data, the `TextSource` calls the output device's `receiveText()` method. Later, we'll see that many APIs in Java use a model like this, but more often many "receivers" may register with the same source.

Interface Variables

Although interfaces mostly allow us to specify behavior without implementation, there's one exception. An interface can contain constants (`static final` variables), which can be referred to directly through the interface name, and which also appear in any class that implements the interface. This feature allows constants to be packaged for use with the methods of the interface:

```
interface Scaleable {
    static final int BIG = 0, MEDIUM = 1, SMALL = 2;
    void setScale( int size );
}
```

The `Scaleable` interface defines three integers: `BIG`, `MEDIUM`, and `SMALL`. All variables defined in interfaces are implicitly `final` and `static`; you don't need to use the modifiers, but for clarity, we recommend that you do. A class that implements `Scaleable` sees these constants:

```
class Box implements Scaleable {

    void setScale( int size ) {
        switch( size ) {
```

```
                case BIG:
                    ...
                case MEDIUM:
                    ...
                case SMALL:
                    ...
            }
        }
        ...
    }
```

While there is nothing technically wrong with using interfaces in this way, the main incentive for doing so disappeared when Java added enumerations and *static imports*. Using interfaces for this purpose is bad because all those public, static constants then appear in the public API of your class and can confuse those who use it. What's worse, you can't remove them later because other code may rely on the class that contains those values. It's better to use an enumeration or to put your constants in their own class and then use the new static import syntax to remove the hassle of referring to them. We'll discuss static import later in this chapter. This code snippet gives a glimpse of how it works:

```
enum SizeConstants { BIG, MEDIUM, SMALL }

// usage
static import mypackage.SizeConstants;
...
setSize( MEDIUM );
```

Flag interfaces

Sometimes completely empty interfaces serve as a marker that a class has a special property. The `java.io.Serializeable` interface is a good example. Classes that implement `Serializeable` don't have to add any methods or variables. Their additional type simply identifies them to Java as classes that want to be able to be serialized. This usage of interfaces is less important now that Java has annotations, described in Chapter 7.

Subinterfaces

An interface can extend another interface, just as a class can extend another class. Such an interface is called a *subinterface*. For example:

```
interface DynamicallyScaleable extends Scaleable {
    void changeScale( int size );
}
```

The interface `DynamicallyScaleable` extends our previous `Scaleable` interface and adds an additional method. A class that implements `DynamicallyScaleable` must implement all the methods of both interfaces.

Note here that we are using the term *extends* and not *implements* to subtype the interface. Interfaces can't implement anything! But an interface is allowed to extend as many interfaces as it wants. If you want to extend two or more interfaces, list them after the `extends` keyword, separated by commas:

```
interface DynamicallyScaleable extends Scaleable, SomethingElseable {
    ...
}
```

A class that implements this interface must also implement the other interfaces. Furthermore, interface subtypes are assignable to their supertypes in the same way that classes are, so an instance of `DynamicallyScaleable` can be assigned to a variable of type `Scaleable`, as you might expect.

Overlapping and conflicting methods

We should also note the possibility that when an interface extends two or more interfaces (or when a class implements two or more interfaces), there may be overlapping or conflicting methods in those interfaces. If two methods in different interfaces have exactly the same signature and return type, there is no problem and the implementation in the class satisfies both interfaces. If the methods differ in the way that overloaded methods do, the class must implement both method signatures. If the methods have the same name but differ in return or exception types, the class cannot implement both and compile-time errors occur.

Packages and Compilation Units

A *package* is a name for a group of related classes and interfaces. In Chapter 3, we discussed how Java uses package names to locate classes during compilation and at runtime. In this sense, packages are somewhat like libraries; they organize and manage sets of classes. Packages provide more than just source-code-level organization. They create an additional level of scope for their classes and the variables and methods within them. We'll talk about the visibility of classes later in this section. In the next section, we discuss the effect that packages have on access to variables and methods among classes.

Compilation Units

The source code for Java classes is organized into *compilation units*. A simple compilation unit contains a single class definition and is named for that class. The definition of a class named `MyClass`, for instance, could appear in a file named *MyClass.java*. For most of us, a compilation unit is just a file with a *.java* extension, but theoretically in an IDE, it could be an arbitrary entity. For brevity, we'll refer to a compilation unit simply as a file.

The division of classes into their own files is important because the Java compiler assumes much of the responsibility of a *make* or *build* utility. The compiler relies on the names of source files to find and compile dependent classes. It's possible to put more than one class definition into a single file, but there are some restrictions that we'll discuss shortly.

A class is declared to belong to a particular package with the `package` statement. The `package` statement must appear as the first statement in a file. There can be only one `package` statement, and it applies to the entire file:

```
package mytools.text;

class TextComponent {
    ...
}
```

In this example, the class `TextComponent` is placed in the package `mytools.text`.

Package Names

Package names are hierarchical in nature, using a dot-separated naming convention. By default, package name components correspond to directory names and serve as a unique path for the compiler and runtime systems to locate Java source files and classes. However, other than for locating files, package names in Java do not create real relationships between packages. There is really no such thing as a "subpackage." The package namespace is actually flat, not hierarchical. Packages under a particular part of a package hierarchy are related only by convention. For example, if we create another package called `mytools.text.poetry` (presumably for text classes that are specialized in some way to work with poetry), those classes won't be part of the `mytools.text` package; they won't have the access privileges of package members. In this sense, the package-naming convention can be misleading. One minor deviation from this notion is that assertions, which we described in Chapter 4, can be turned on or off for a package and all packages "under" it. But that is really just a convenience and not represented in the code structure.

Class Visibility

By default, a class is accessible only to other classes within its package. This means that our `TextComponent` class is available only to other classes in the `mytools.text` package. To be used outside of its package, a class must be declared as `public`:

```
package mytools.text;

public class TextEditor {
    ...
}
```

The class `TextEditor` can now be referenced anywhere. A Java source code file can have only a single `public` class defined within it and the file must be named for that class.

By hiding unimportant or extraneous classes, a package builds a *subsystem* that has a well-defined interface to the rest of the world. Public classes provide a *facade* for the operation of the system. The details of its inner workings can remain hidden, as shown in Figure 6-6. In this sense, packages can hide classes in the way classes hide private members. Nonpublic classes within a package are sometimes called *package private* for this reason.

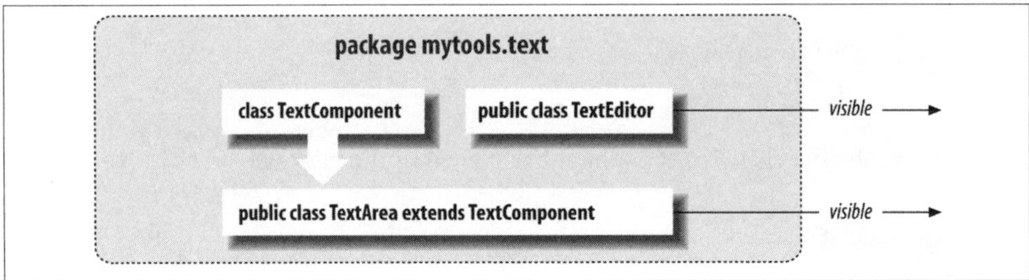

Figure 6-6. Packages and class visibility

Figure 6-6 shows part of the hypothetical `mytools.text` package. The classes `TextArea` and `TextEditor` are declared `public` so that they can be used elsewhere in an application. The class `TextComponent` is part of the implementation of `TextArea` and is not accessible from outside of the package.

Importing Classes

Classes within a package can refer to each other by their simple names. However, to locate a class in another package, we have to be more specific. Continuing with the previous example, an application can refer directly to our editor class by its *fully qualified name* of `mytools.text.TextEditor`. But we'd quickly grow tired of typing such long class names, so Java gives us the `import` statement. One or more `import` statements can appear at the top of a compilation unit, after the `package` statement. The `import` statements list the fully qualified names of classes and packages to be used within the file.

Like a `package` statement, an `import` statement applies to the entire compilation unit. Here's how you might use an `import` statement:

```
package somewhere.else;
import mytools.text.TextEditor;

class MyClass {
    TextEditor editBoy;
    ...
}
```

As shown in this example, once a class is imported, it can be referenced by its simple name throughout the code. It is also possible to import all the classes in a package using the * wildcard notation:

```
import mytools.text.*;
```

Now we can refer to all `public` classes in the `mytools.text` package by their simple names.

Obviously, there can be a problem with importing classes that have conflicting names. The compiler prevents you from explicitly importing two classes with the same name and gives you an error if you try to use an ambiguous class that could come from two packages imported with the package `import` notation. In this case, you just have to fall back to using fully qualified names to refer to those classes. You can either use the fully qualified name directly, or you can add an additional, single class `import` statement that disambiguates the class name. It doesn't matter whether this comes before or after the package import.

Other than the potential for naming conflicts, there's no penalty for importing many classes. Java doesn't carry extra baggage into the compiled class files. In other words, Java class files don't contain information about the imports; they only reference classes actually used in them.

> One note about conventions: in an effort to keep our examples short, we'll sometimes import entire packages (.*) even when we use only a class or two from it. In practice, it's usually better to be specific when possible and list individual, fully qualified class imports if there are only a few of them. Some people (especially those using IDEs that do it for them) avoid using package imports entirely, choosing to list every imported class individually. Usually, a compromise is your best bet. If you are going to use more than two or three classes from a package, consider the package import.

The unnamed package

A class that is defined in a compilation unit that doesn't specify a package falls into the large, amorphous unnamed package. Classes in this nameless package can refer to each other by their simple names. Their path at compile time and runtime is considered to be the current directory, so packageless classes are useful for experimentation and testing (and for brevity in examples in books about Java).

Static imports

A *static import* is a variation of the `import` statement that allows you to import static members of a class into the namespace of your file so that you don't have to qualify them when you use them. The best example of this is in working with the `java.lang.Math` class. With static import, we can get an illusion of built-in math "functions" and constants like so:

```
import static java.lang.Math.*;

// usage
double circumference = 2 * PI * radius;
double length = sin( theta ) * side;
int bigger = max( a, b );
int positive = abs( num );
```

This example imports all of the static members of the `java.lang.Math` class. We can also import individual members by name:

```
import static java.awt.Color.RED;
import static java.awt.Color.WHITE;
import static java.awt.Color.BLUE;

// usage
setField( BLUE );
setStripe( RED );
setStripe( WHITE );
```

To be precise, these static imports are importing a name, not a specific member, into the namespace of our file. For example, importing the name "foo" would bring in any constants named `foo` as well as any methods named `foo()` in the class.

Static imports are compelling and make code more succinct. Their usage, however, goes somewhat against the concepts of object-oriented programming. Static imports are best for utilities and other global convenience methods that do not require much context.

Visibility of Variables and Methods

One of the most important aspects of object-oriented design is *data hiding*, or *encapsulation*. By treating an object in some respects as a "black box" and ignoring the details of its implementation, we can write more resilient, simpler code with components that can be easily reused.

Basic Access Modifiers

By default, the variables and methods of a class are accessible to members of the class itself and to other classes in the same package. To borrow from C++ terminology, classes in the same package are *friendly*. We'll call this the default level of visibility. As you'll see as we go on, the default visibility lies in the middle of the range of restrictiveness that can be specified.

The modifiers `public` and `private`, on the other hand, define the extremes. As we mentioned earlier, methods and variables declared as `private` are accessible only within their class. At the other end of the spectrum, members declared as `public` are accessible from any class in any package, provided the class itself can be seen. (The class that contains the methods must also be `public` to be seen outside of its package, as we discussed previously.) The `public` members of a class should define its most general functionality—what the black box is supposed to do.

Figure 6-7 illustrates the four simplest levels of visibility, continuing the example from the previous section. Public members in `TextArea` are accessible from anywhere. Private members are not visible from outside the class. The default visibility allows access by other classes in the package.

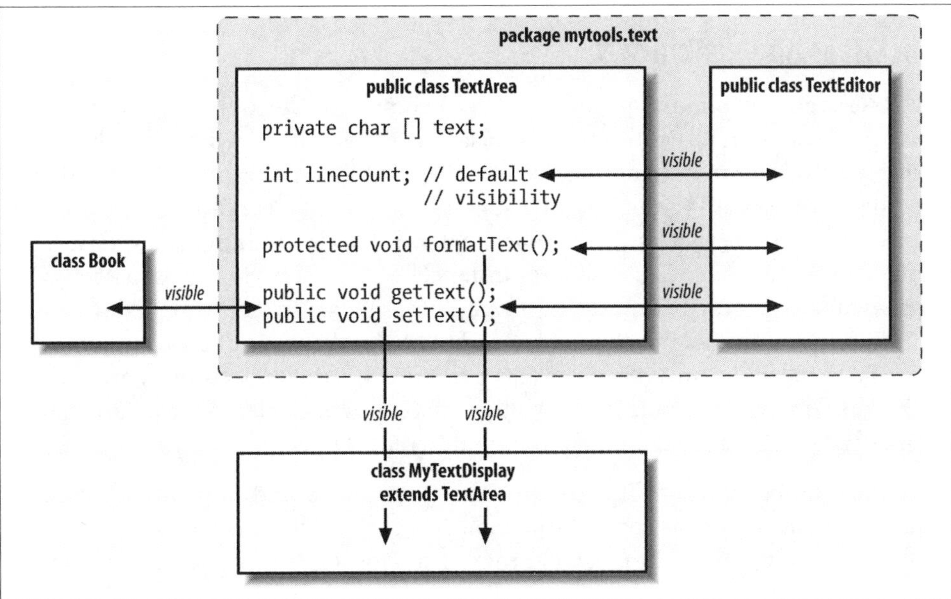

Figure 6-7. Private, default, protected, and public visibility

The `protected` modifier allows special access permissions for subclasses. Contrary to how it might sound, `protected` is slightly less restrictive than the default level of accessibility. In addition to the default access afforded classes in the same package, `protected` members are visible to subclasses of the class, even if they are defined in a different package. If you are a C++ programmer used to more restrictive meanings, this may rub you the wrong way.[4]

4. Early on, the Java language allowed for certain combinations of modifiers, one of which was `private protected`. The meaning of `private protected` was to limit visibility strictly to subclasses (and remove package access). This was later deemed confusing and overly complex. It is no longer supported.

Table 6-1 summarizes the levels of visibility available in Java; it runs generally from most to least restrictive. Methods and variables are always visible within a declaring class itself, so the table doesn't address that scope.

Table 6-1. Visibility modifiers

Modifier	Visibility outside the class
`private`	None
No modifier (default)	Classes in the package
`protected`	Classes in package and subclasses inside or outside the package
`public`	All classes

Subclasses and Visibility

Subclasses add two important (but unrelated) complications to the topic of visibility. First, when you override methods in a subclass, the overriding method must be at least as visible as the overridden method. While it is possible to take a `private` method and override it with a `public` method in a subclass, the reverse is not possible; you can't override a `public` method with a `private` method. This restriction makes sense if you recall that subtypes have to be usable as instances of their supertype (e.g., a `Mammal` is a subclass of `Animal` and, therefore, must be usable as an `Animal`). If we could override a method with a less visible method, we would have a problem: our `Mammal` might not be able to do all the things an `Animal` can. However, we can reduce the visibility of a variable. In this case, the variable acts like any other shadowed variable; the two variables are distinct and can have separate visibilities in different classes.

The next complication is a bit harder to follow: the `protected` variables of a class are visible to its subclasses, but only through objects of the subclass's type or its subtypes. In other words, a subclass can see a `protected` variable of its superclass as an inherited variable, but it can't access that same variable via a reference to the superclass itself. This statement could be confusing because it might not be obvious that visibility modifiers don't restrict access between instances of the same class in the same way that they restrict access between instances of different classes. Two instances of the same class can access all of each other's members, *including private ones*, as long as they refer to each other as the correct type. Said another way: two instances of `Cat` can access all of each other's variables and methods (including private ones), but a `Cat` can't access a protected member in an instance of `Animal` unless the compiler can prove that the `Animal` is a `Cat`. That is, `Cats` have the special privileges of being an `Animal` only with respect to other `Cats`, not just any `Animal`. If you find this hard to follow, don't worry too much. If you run into this as a problem in the real world, you are probably trying to do something trickier than you should.

Interfaces and Visibility

Interfaces behave like classes within packages. An interface can be declared `public` to make it visible outside its package. Under the default visibility, an interface is visible only inside its package. Like classes, only one `public` interface can be declared in a compilation unit (file).

Arrays and the Class Hierarchy

Now we're going to shift gears a bit and return to the topic of arrays, considering them from the object point of view. At the end of Chapter 4, we mentioned that arrays have a place in the Java class hierarchy, but we didn't give you any details. Now that we've discussed the object-oriented aspects of Java, we can give you the whole story.

Array classes live in a parallel Java class hierarchy under the `Object` class. If a class is a direct subclass of `Object`, an array class for that base type also exists as a direct subclass of `Object`. Arrays of more derived classes are subclasses of the corresponding array classes. For example, consider the following class types:

```
class Animal { ... }
class Bird extends Animal { ... }
class Penguin extends Bird { ... }
```

Figure 6-8 illustrates the class hierarchy for arrays of these classes. Arrays of the same dimension are related to one another in the same manner as their base type classes. In our example, `Bird` is a subclass of `Animal`, which means that the `Bird[]` type is a subtype of `Animal[]`. In the same way a `Bird` object can be used in place of an `Animal` object, a `Bird[]` array can be assigned to a variable of type `Animal[]`:

```
Animal [][] animals;
Bird [][] birds = new Bird [10][10];
birds[0][0] = new Bird();

// make animals and birds reference the same array object
animals = birds;
observe( animals[0][0] );               // processes Bird object
```

Because arrays are part of the class hierarchy, we can use `instanceof` to check the type of an array:

```
if ( birds instanceof Animal[][] )      // true
```

An array is a type of `Object` and thus can be assigned to `Object` type variables:

```
Object obj = animals;
```

Because Java knows the actual type of all objects, you can also cast back if appropriate:

```
animals = (Animal [][])something;
```

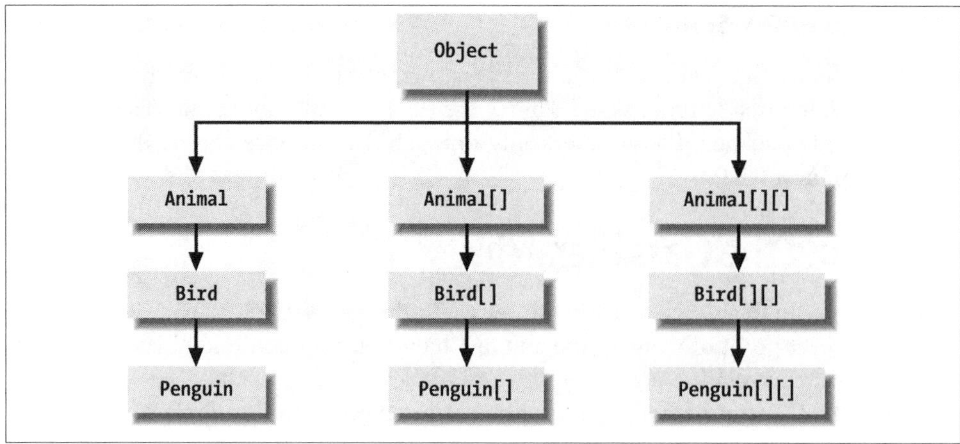

Figure 6-8. Arrays in the Java class hierarchy

ArrayStoreException

Because arrays have the property that an array of one type is assignable to an array of its supertype, it is possible to play games with the compiler and try to trick it into storing the wrong kind of object in an array. Java may not be able to check the types of all objects that you place into arrays at compile time. In those cases, it's possible to receive an `ArrayStoreException` at runtime if you try to assign the wrong type of object to an array element. For example:

```
String [] strings = new String [10];
Object [] objects = strings;  // alias String [] as Object []
objects[0] = new Date(); // Runtime ArrayStoreException!
```

Here, we have "aliased" a `String []` by assigning it to an `Object []`. By the third line, the compiler no longer knows the actual type of array stored in the object's variable and has no choice but to let us try whatever we want. Of course, at runtime the VM realizes that we are trying to put a `Date` object into an array of `Strings` and throws the `ArrayStoreException` for us. This type of problem shouldn't happen often for you in straightforward array use. We mention it here because the concept will come up again when we talk about generics in Chapter 8.

Inner Classes

All of the classes we've seen so far in this book have been *top-level*, "freestanding" classes declared at the file and package level. But classes in Java can actually be declared at any level of scope, within any set of curly braces (i.e., almost anywhere that you could put any other Java statement). These *inner classes* belong to another class or method as a variable would and may have their visibility limited to its scope in the same way. Inner classes are a useful and aesthetically pleasing facility for structuring code. Their cousins, *anonymous inner classes*, are an even more powerful shorthand that make it seem as if you can create new kinds of objects dynamically within Java's statically typed environment. In Java, anonymous inner classes play part of the role of *closures* in other languages, giving the effect of handling state and behavior independently of classes.

However, as we delve into their inner workings, we'll see that inner classes are not quite as aesthetically pleasing or dynamic as they seem. Inner classes are pure syntactic sugar; they are not supported by the VM and are instead mapped to regular Java classes by the compiler. As a programmer, you may never need be aware of this; you can simply rely on inner classes like any other language construct. However, you should know a little about how inner classes work to better understand the compiled code and a few potential side effects.

Inner classes are essentially nested classes, for example:

```
Class Animal {
    Class Brain {
        ...
    }
}
```

Here, the class `Brain` is an inner class: it is a class declared inside the scope of class `Animal`. Although the details of what that means require a bit of explanation, we'll start by saying that Java tries to make the meaning, as much as possible, the same as for the other members (methods and variables) living at that level of scope. For example, let's add a method to the `Animal` class:

```
Class Animal {
    Class Brain {
        ...
    }
    void performBehavior() { ... }
}
```

Both the inner class `Brain` and the method `performBehavior()` are within the scope of `Animal`. Therefore, anywhere within `Animal`, we can refer to `Brain` and `performBehavior()` directly, by name. Within `Animal`, we can call the constructor for `Brain` (`new Brain()`) to get a `Brain` object or invoke `performBehavior()` to carry out that method's function. But neither `Brain` nor `performBehavior()` are generally accessible outside of the class `Animal` without some additional qualification.

Within the body of the inner `Brain` class and the body of the `performBehavior()` method, we have direct access to all the other methods and variables of the `Animal` class. So, just as the `performBehavior()` method could work with the `Brain` class and create instances of `Brain`, methods within the `Brain` class can invoke the `performBehavior()` method of `Animal` as well as work with any other methods and variables declared in `Animal`. The `Brain` class "sees" all of the methods and variables of the `Animal` class directly in its scope.

That last bit has important consequences. From within `Brain`, we can invoke the method `performBehavior()`; that is, from within an instance of `Brain`, we can invoke the `performBehavior()` method of an instance of `Animal`. Well, which instance of `Animal`? If we have several `Animal` objects around (say, a few `Cats` and `Dogs`), we need to know whose `performBehavior()` method we are calling. What does it mean for a class definition to be "inside" another class definition? The answer is that a `Brain` object always lives within a single instance of `Animal`: the one that it was told about when it was created. We'll call the object that contains any instance of `Brain` its *enclosing instance*.

A `Brain` object cannot live outside of an enclosing instance of an `Animal` object. Anywhere you see an instance of `Brain`, it will be tethered to an instance of `Animal`. Although it is possible to construct a `Brain` object from elsewhere (i.e., another class), `Brain` always requires an enclosing instance of `Animal` to "hold" it. We'll also say now that if `Brain` is to be referred to from outside of `Animal`, it acts something like an `Animal.Brain` class. And just as with the `performBehavior()` method, modifiers can be applied to restrict its visibility. All of the usual visibility modifiers apply, and inner classes can also be declared `static`, as we'll discuss later.

We've said that within the `Animal` class, we can construct a `Brain` in the ordinary way, using `new Brain()`, for example. Although we'd probably never find a need to do it, we can also construct an instance of `Brain` from outside the class by referencing an instance of `Animal`. To do this requires that the inner class `Brain` be accessible and that we use a special form of the `new` operator designed just for inner classes:

```
Animal monkey = new Animal();
Animal.Brain monkeyBrain = monkey.new Brain();
```

Here, the `Animal` instance `monkey` is used to qualify the `new` operator on `Brain`. Again, this is not a very common thing to do and you can probably just forget that we said anything about it. Static inner classes are more useful. We'll talk about them a bit later.

Inner Classes as Adapters

A particularly important use of inner classes is to make *adapter classes*. An adapter class is a "helper" class that ties one class to another in a very specific way. Using adapter classes, you can write your classes more naturally, without having to anticipate every conceivable user's needs in advance. Instead, you provide adapter classes that marry your class to a particular interface. As an example, let's say that we have an `EmployeeList` object:

```
public class EmployeeList {
    private Employee [] employees = ... ;
    ...
}
```

`EmployeeList` holds information about a set of employees. Let's say that we would like to have `EmployeeList` provide its elements via an iterator. An iterator is a simple, standard interface to a sequence of objects. The `java.util.Iterator` interface has several methods:

```
public interface Iterator {
    boolean hasNext();
    Object next();
    void remove();
}
```

It lets us step through its elements, asking for the next one and testing to see if more remain. The iterator is a good candidate for an adapter class because it is an interface that our `EmployeeList` can't readily implement itself. Why can't the list implement the iterator directly? Because an iterator is a "one-way," disposable view of our data. It isn't intended to be reset and used again. It may also be necessary for there to be multiple iterators walking through the list at different points. We must, therefore, keep the iterator implementation separate from the `EmployeeList` itself. This is crying out for a simple class to provide the iterator capability. But what should that class look like?

Before we knew about inner classes, our only recourse would have been to make a new "top-level" class. We would probably feel obliged to call it `EmployeeListIterator`:

```
class EmployeeListIterator implements Iterator {
    // lots of knowledge about EmployeeList
    ...
}
```

Here we have a comment representing the machinery that the `EmployeeListIterator` requires. Think for just a second about what you'd have to do to implement that machinery. The resulting class would be completely coupled to the `EmployeeList` and unusable in other situations. Worse, in order to to function, it must have access to the inner workings of `EmployeeList`. We would have to allow `EmployeeListIterator` access to the private array in `EmployeeList`, exposing this data more widely than it should be. This is less than ideal.

This sounds like a job for inner classes. We already said that `EmployeeListIterator` was useless without an `EmployeeList`; this sounds a lot like the "lives inside" relationship we described earlier. Furthermore, an inner class lets us avoid the encapsulation problem because it can access all the members of its enclosing instance. Therefore, if we use an inner class to implement the iterator, the array `employees` can remain `private`, invisible outside the `EmployeeList`. So let's just shove that helper class inside the scope of our `EmployeeList`:

```
public class EmployeeList {
    private Employee [] employees = ... ;
    ...

    class Iterator implements java.util.Iterator {
        int element = 0;
```

```
            boolean hasNext() {
                return  element < employees.length ;
            }

            Object next() {
                if ( hasNext() )
                    return employees[ element++ ];
                else
                    throw new NoSuchElementException();
            }

            void remove() {
                 throw new UnsupportedOperationException();
            }
        }
    }
```

Now EmployeeList can provide a method like the following to let other classes work with the list:

```
    Iterator getIterator() {
            return new Iterator();
        }
```

One effect of the move is that we are free to be a little more familiar in the naming of our iterator class. Since it is no longer a top-level class, we can give it a name that is appropriate only within the EmployeeList. In this case, we've named it Iterator to emphasize what it does, but we don't need a name like EmployeeIterator that shows the relationship to the EmployeeList class because that's implicit. We've also filled in the guts of the Iterator class. As you can see, now that it is inside the scope of EmployeeList, Iterator has direct access to its private members, so it can directly access the employees array. This greatly simplifies the code and maintains compile-time safety.

Before we move on, we should note that inner classes can have constructors, variables, and initializers, even though we didn't need one in this example. They are, in all respects, real classes.

Inner Classes Within Methods

Inner classes may also be declared for "local" use within the body of a method. Returning to the Animal class, we can put Brain inside the performBehavior() method if we decide that the class is useful only inside that method:

```
    Class Animal {
        void performBehavior() {
            Class Brain {
                ...
            }
        }
    }
```

In this situation, the rules governing what `Brain` can see are the same as in our earlier example. The body of `Brain` can see anything in the scope of `performBehavior()` and above it (in the body of `Animal`). This includes local variables of `performBehavior()` and its arguments. But because of the fleeting nature of a method invocation, there are a few limitations and additional restrictions, as described in the following sections. If you are thinking that inner classes within methods sounds arcane, bear with us until we talk about anonymous inner classes, which are tremendously useful.

Limitations on inner classes in methods

`performBehavior()` is a method, and method invocations have limited lifetimes. When they exit, their local variables normally disappear into the abyss. However, an instance of `Brain` (like any object created in the method) lives on as long as it is referenced. Java must make sure that any local variables used by instances of `Brain` created within an invocation of `performBehavior()` also live on. Furthermore, all the instances of `Brain` that we make within a single invocation of `performBehavior()` must see the same local variables. To accomplish this, the compiler must be allowed to make copies of local variables. Thus, their values cannot change once an inner class has seen them. This means that any of the method's local variables or arguments that are referenced by the inner class must be declared `final`. The `final` modifier means that they are constant once assigned. This is a little confusing and easy to forget, but the compiler will graciously remind you. For example:

```
void performBehavior( final boolean nocturnal )
{
    class Brain {
        void sleep() {
            if ( nocturnal ) { ... }
        }
    }
}
```

In this code snippet, the argument `nocturnal` to the `performBehavior()` method must be marked `final` so that it can be referenced within the inner class `Brain`. This is just a technical limitation of how inner classes are implemented, ensuring that it's OK for the `Brain` class to keep a copy of the value.

Static inner classes

We mentioned earlier that the inner class `Brain` of the class `Animal` can, in some ways, be considered an `Animal.Brain` class—that is, it is possible to work with a `Brain` from outside the `Animal` class, using just such a qualified name: `Animal.Brain`. But as we described, given that our `Animal.Brain` class always requires an instance of an `Animal` as its enclosing instance, it's not as common to work with them directly in this way.

However, there is another situation in which we want to use inner classes by name. An inner class that lives within the body of a top-level class (not within a method or another inner class) can be declared `static`. For example:

```
class Animal  {
    static class MigrationPattern {
        ...
    }
    ...
}
```

A static inner class such as this acts just like a new top-level class called `Animal.MigrationPattern`. We can use it just like any other class, without regard to any enclosing instances. Although this may seem strange, it is not inconsistent because a static member never has an object instance associated with it. The requirement that the inner class be defined directly inside a top-level class ensures that an enclosing instance won't be needed. If we have permission, we can create an instance of the class using the qualified name:

```
Animal.MigrationPattern stlToSanFrancisco =
    new Animal.MigrationPattern();
```

As you see, the effect is that `Animal` acts something like a minipackage, holding the `MigrationPattern` class. Here, we have used the fully qualified name, but we could also import it like any other class:

```
import Animal.MigrationPattern;
```

This statement enables us to refer to the class simply as `MigrationPattern`. We can use all the standard visibility modifiers on inner classes, so a static inner class can have `private`, `protected`, `default`, or `public` visibility.

Here's another example. The Java 2D API uses static inner classes to implement specialized shape classes (i.e., the `java.awt.geom.Rectangle2D` class has two inner classes, `Float` and `Double`, that implement two different precisions). These shape classes are actually very simple subclasses; it would have been sad to have to multiply the number of top-level classes in that package by three to accommodate all of them. With inner classes, we can bundle them with their respective classes:

```
Rectangle2D.Float rect = new Rectangle2D.Float();
```

Anonymous inner classes

Now we get to the best part. As a general rule, the more deeply encapsulated and limited in scope our classes are, the more freedom we have in naming them. We saw this in our earlier iterator example. This is not just a purely aesthetic issue. Naming is an important part of writing readable, maintainable code. We generally want to use the most concise, meaningful names possible. A corollary to this is that we prefer to avoid doling out names for purely ephemeral objects that are going to be used only once.

Anonymous inner classes are an extension of the syntax of the new operation. When you create an anonymous inner class, you combine a class declaration with the allocation of an instance of that class, effectively creating a "one-time only" class and a class instance in one operation. After the new keyword, you specify either the name of a class or an interface, followed by a class body. The class body becomes an inner class, which either extends the specified class or, in the case of an interface, is expected to implement the interface. A single instance of the class is created and returned as the value.

For example, we could do away with the declaration of the Iterator class in the EmployeeList example by using an anonymous inner class in the getIterator() method:

```
Iterator getIterator()
{
    return new Iterator() {
        int element = 0;
        boolean hasNext() {
            return  element < employees.length ;
        }
        Object next() {
            if ( hasNext() )
                return employees[ element++ ];
            else
                throw new NoSuchElementException();
        }
        void remove() {
             throw new UnsupportedOperationException();
        }
    };
}
```

Here, we have simply moved the guts of Iterator into the body of an anonymous inner class. The call to new implicitly creates a class that implements the Iterator interface and returns an instance of the class as its result. Note the extent of the curly braces and the semicolon at the end. The getIterator() method contains a single statement, the return statement.

The previous example is a bit extreme and certainly does not improve readability. Inner classes are best used when you want to implement a few lines of code, but the verbiage and conspicuousness of declaring a separate class detracts from the task at hand. Here's a better example. Suppose that we want to start a new thread to execute the performBehavior() method of our Animal:

```
new Thread() {
    public void run() {  performBehavior();  }
}.start();
```

Here, we have gone over to the terse side. We've allocated and started a new Thread, using an anonymous inner class that extends the Thread class and invokes our performBehavior() method in its run() method. The effect is similar to using a method pointer in some other language. However, the inner class allows the compiler to check type consistency, which would be more difficult (or impossible) with a true method pointer. At the same time, our anonymous adapter class with its three lines of code is much more efficient and readable than creating a new, top-level adapter class named `AnimalBehaviorThreadAdapter`.

While we're getting a bit ahead of the story, anonymous adapter classes are a perfect fit for event handling (which we cover fully in Chapter 16). Skipping a lot of explanation, let's say you want the method `handleClicks()` to be called whenever the user clicks the mouse. You would write code such as:

```
addMouseListener( new MouseInputAdapter() {
    public void mouseClicked(MouseEvent e) { handleClicks(e); }
} );
```

In this case, the anonymous class extends the `MouseInputAdapter` class by overriding its `mouseClicked()` method to call our method. A lot is going on in a very small space, but the result is clean, readable code. You assign method names that are meaningful to you while allowing Java to do its job of type checking.

Scoping of the "this" reference

Sometimes an inner class may want to get a handle on its "parent" enclosing instance. It might want to pass a reference to its parent or to refer to one of the parent's variables or methods that has been hidden by one of its own. For example:

```
class Animal {
    int size;
    class Brain {
        int size;
    }
}
```

Here, as far as `Brain` is concerned, the variable `size` in `Animal` is shadowed by its own version.

Normally, an object refers to itself using the special `this` reference (implicitly or explicitly). But what is the meaning of `this` for an object with one or more enclosing instances? The answer is that an inner class has multiple `this` references. You can specify which `this` you want by prefixing it with the name of the class. For instance (no pun intended), we can get a reference to our `Animal` from within `Brain`, like so:

```
class Brain {
    Animal ourAnimal = Animal.this;
    ...
}
```

Similarly, we could refer to the `size` variable in `Animal`:

```
class Brain {
    int animalSize = Animal.this.size;
    ...
}
```

How do inner classes really work?

Finally, let's get our hands dirty and take a look at what's really going on when we use an inner class. We've said that the compiler is doing all the things that we had hoped to forget about. Let's see what's actually happening. Try compiling this trivial example:

```
class Animal {
    class Brain {
    }
}
```

What you'll find is that the compiler generates two *.class* files: *Animal.class* and *Animal $Brain.class.*

The second file is the class file for our inner class. Yes, as we feared, inner classes are really just compiler magic. The compiler has created the inner class for us as a normal, top-level class and named it by combining the class names with a dollar sign. The dollar sign is a valid character in class names, but is intended for use only by automated tools. (Please don't start naming your classes with dollar signs.) Had our class been more deeply nested, the intervening inner class names would have been attached in the same way to generate a unique top-level name.

Now take a look at the class with the JDK's `javap` utility. Starting in Java 5.0, you can refer to the inner class as `Animal.Brain`, but in earlier versions of Java, you may have to call the class by its real name, `Animal$Brain`:

```
% javap 'Animal$Brain'
class Animal$Brain extends java.lang.Object {
    Animal$Brain(Animal);
}
```

On a Windows system, it's not necessary to quote the argument, as we did on this Unix command line.

You'll see that the compiler has given our inner class a constructor that takes a reference to an `Animal` as an argument. This is how the real inner class gets the reference to its enclosing instance.

The worst thing about these additional class files is that you need to know they are there. Utilities such as *jar* don't automatically find them; when you're invoking such a utility, you need to specify these files explicitly or use a wildcard to find them:

```
% jar cvf animal.jar Animal*class
```

Security implications

Given what we just saw—that the inner class really does exist as an automatically generated top-level class—how does it get access to private variables? The answer, unfortunately, is that the compiler is forced to break the encapsulation of your object and insert accessor methods so that the inner class can reach them. The accessor methods are given package-level access, so your object is still safe within its package walls, but it is conceivable that this difference could be meaningful if people were allowed to create new classes within your package.

The visibility modifiers on inner classes also have some problems. Current implementations of the VM do not implement the notion of a `private` or `protected` class within a package, so giving your inner class anything other than `public` or default visibility is only a compile-time guarantee. It is difficult to conceive of how these security issues could be abused, but it is interesting to note that Java is straining a bit to stay within its original design.[5]

5. Inner classes were added to Java in version 1.1.

CHAPTER 7
Working with Objects and Classes

In the previous two chapters, we came to know Java objects and their interrelationships. We will now climb the scaffolding of the Java class hierarchy to the very top and finish our study of the core language at the summit. In this chapter, we'll talk about the `Object` class itself, which is the "grandmother" of all classes in Java. We'll also describe the even more fundamental `Class` class (the class named "Class") that represents Java classes in the Java virtual machine. We'll discuss what you can do with these components in their own right. This will lead us to a more general topic: the Java Reflection API, which lets a Java program inspect and interact with (possibly unknown) objects dynamically at runtime. Finally, we'll also talk about the Java Annotations API, which allows developers to add metadata to their source code for use by the compiler and runtime systems that look for it.

The Object Class

`java.lang.Object` is the ancestor of all objects; it's the primordial class from which all other classes are ultimately derived. Methods defined in `Object` are, therefore, very important because they appear in every instance of every class, throughout all of Java. At last count, there were nine public methods and two protected methods in `Object`. Five of these are versions of `wait()` and `notify()` that are used to synchronize threads on object instances, as we'll discuss in Chapter 9. The remaining four methods are used for basic comparison, conversion, and administration.

Every object has a `toString()` method that can be called when it's to be represented as a text value. `PrintStream` objects use `toString()` to print data, as discussed in Chapter 12. `toString()` is also used implicitly when an object is referenced in a string concatenation. Here are some examples:

```
MyObj myObject = new MyObj();
Answer theAnswer = new Answer();
```

```
System.out.println( myObject );
String s = "The answer is: " + theAnswer ;
```

To be friendly, a new kind of object can override `toString()` and implement its own version that provides appropriate information about itself. This is particularly helpful in debugging, where it is common to print the string value of an object to see what is going on. Two other methods, `equals()` and `hashCode()`, may also require specialization when you create a new class.

Equality and Equivalence

`equals()` determines whether two objects are equivalent. Precisely what that means for a particular class is something that you'll have to decide for yourself. Two `String` objects, for example, are considered equivalent if they hold precisely the same characters in the same sequence:

```
String userName = "Joe";
...
if ( userName.equals( suspectName ) )
    arrest( userName );
```

Using `equals()` is *not* the same as the "==" operator in Java:

```
if ( userName == suspectName )      // Wrong!
```

This statement tests whether the two reference variables, `userName` and `suspectName`, refer to the same object. It is a test for *identity*, not equality. Two variables that are identical (point to the same object) will necessarily be equal, but the converse is not always true. It is possible in Java to construct two `String` objects with the same contents that are, nonetheless, different instances of the `String` class—although, as we'll describe later, Java tries to help you avoid that when it can.

A class should override the `equals()` method if it needs to implement its own notion of equality. If you have no need to compare objects of a particular class, you don't necessarily need to override `equals()`.

Watch out for accidentally overloading `equals()` if you mean to override it. With overloading, the method signatures differ; with overriding, they must be the same. The `equals()` method signature specifies an `Object` argument so that an object can be compared to any other kind of object, not only those of its own class type. You'll probably want to consider only objects of the same type for equivalence. But in order to override (not overload) `equals()`, the method must specify its argument to be an `Object`.

Here's an example of correctly overriding an `equals()` method in class `Shoes` with an `equals()` method in subclass `Sneakers`. Using its own method, a `Sneakers` object can compare itself with any other object:

```
class Sneakers extends Shoes {
    public boolean equals( Object arg ) {
```

```
            if ( (arg != null) && (arg instanceof Sneakers) ) {
                // compare arg with this object to check equivalence
                // If comparison is okay...
                return true;
            }
            return false;
        }
        ...
    }
```

If we specified `public boolean equals(Sneakers arg) ...` in the `Sneakers` class, we'd overload the `equals()` method instead of overriding it. If the other object happens to be assigned to a non-`Sneakers` variable, the method signature won't match. The result: superclass `Shoes`'s implementation of `equals()` is called, which may or may not be what you intended.

Hashcodes

The `hashCode()` method returns an integer that is a hashcode for the object. A *hashcode* is like a signature or checksum for an object; it's a random-looking identifying number that is usually generated from the contents of the object. The hashcode should always be different for instances of the class that contain different data, but should be the same for instances that compare "equal" with the `equals()` method. Hashcodes are used in the process of storing objects in a `Hashtable` or a similar kind of collection. (A `Hashtable` is sometimes called a dictionary or associative array in other languages.) A random distribution of the hashcode values helps the `Hashtable` optimize its storage of objects by serving as an identifier for distributing them into storage evenly and quickly locating them later.

The default implementation of `hashCode()` in `Object` does not really implement this scheme. Instead it assigns each object instance a unique number. If you don't override this method when you create a subclass, each instance of your class will have a unique hashcode. This is sufficient for some objects. However, if your classes have a notion of equivalent objects (if you have overridden `equals()`) and you want equal objects to serve as equivalent keys in a `Hashtable`, you should override `hashCode()` so that your equivalent objects generate the same hashcode value. We'll return to the topic of hashcodes in more detail in Chapter 11 when we discuss the `Hashtable` and `HashMap` classes.

Cloning Objects

Objects can use the `clone()` method of the `Object` class to make copies of themselves. A copied object is a new object instance, separate from the original. It may or may not contain exactly the same state (the same instance variable values) as the original; that is controlled by the object being copied. Just as important, the decision as to whether the object allows itself to be cloned at all is up to the object.

The Java Object class provides the mechanism to make a simple copy of an object including all of its "shallow" state—a *bitwise* copy. But by default, this capability is turned off. (We'll show why in a moment.) To make itself cloneable, an object must implement the java.lang.Cloneable interface. This is a flag interface indicating to Java that the object wants to cooperate in being cloned (the interface does not actually contain any methods). If the object isn't cloneable, the clone() method throws a CloneNotSupportedException.

clone() is a protected method, so by default it can be called only by an object on itself, an object in the same package, or another object of the same type or a subtype. If we want to make an object cloneable by everyone, we have to override its clone() method and make it public.

Here is a simple, cloneable class—Sheep:

```
import java.util.HashMap;

public class Sheep implements Cloneable {
    HashMap flock = new HashMap();

    public Object clone() {
        try {
            return super.clone();
        } catch (CloneNotSupportedException e ) {
            throw new Error(
                "This should never happen because we implement Cloneable!");
        }
    }
}
```

Sheep has one instance variable, a HashMap called flock (which the sheep uses to keep track of its fellow sheep). Our class implements the Cloneable interface, indicating that it is OK to copy Sheep, and it has overridden the clone() method to make it public. Our clone() simply returns the object created by the superclass's clone() method—a copy of our Sheep. Unfortunately, the compiler is not smart enough to figure out that the object we're cloning will never throw the CloneNotSupportedException, so we have to guard against it anyway. Our sheep is now cloneable. We can make copies like so:

```
Sheep one = new Sheep();
Sheep anotherOne = (Sheep)one.clone();
```

The cast is necessary here because the return type of clone() is Object. We can do better by changing the return type of the overridden clone() method in the subclass and moving the cast into the clone() method itself, to make things a little easier on the users of the class:

```
public Sheep clone() {
    try {
        return (Sheep)super.clone();
    } catch (CloneNotSupportedException e ) {
```

```
            throw new Error("This should never happen!");
        }
    }

    // usage
    Sheep one = new Sheep();
    Sheep anotherOne = one.clone();
```

In either case, we now have two sheep instead of one. A properly implemented `equals()` method would tell us that the sheep are equivalent, but == tells us that they are, in fact, two distinct instances of `Sheep`. Java has made a *shallow copy* of our `Sheep`. What's so shallow about it? Java has simply copied the values of our variables. That means that the `flock` instance variable in each of our `Sheep` still holds the same information—that is, both sheep have a reference to the same `HashMap`. The situation looks like that shown in Figure 7-1.

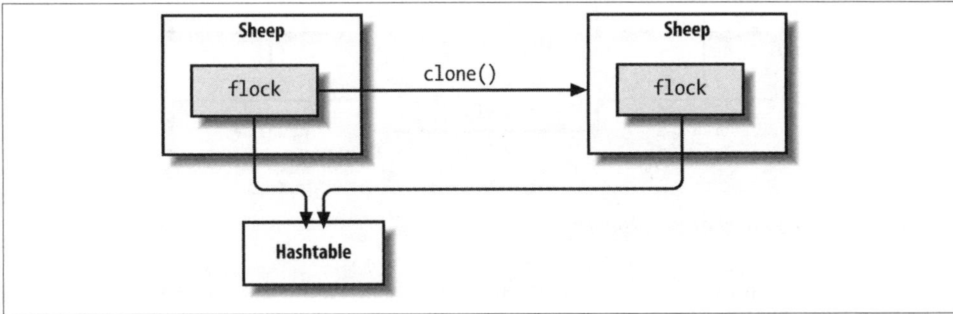

Figure 7-1. Shallow copy of an object

This may or may not be what you intended. If we instead want our `Sheep` to have separate copies of its full state (or something in between), we can take control ourselves. In the following example, `DeepSheep`, we implement a *deep copy*, duplicating our own `flock` variable:

```
    public class DeepSheep implements Cloneable {
        HashMap flock = new HashMap();

        public DeepSheep clone() {
            try {
                DeepSheep copy = (DeepSheep)super.clone();
                copy.flock = (HashMap)flock.clone();
                return copy;
            } catch (CloneNotSupportedException e ) {
                throw new Error("This should never happen!");
            }
        }
    }
```

Our `clone()` method now clones the `HashMap` as well. Now, when a `DeepSheep` is cloned, the situation looks more like that shown in Figure 7-2.

Each `DeepSheep` now has its own full copy of the map, which can contain different elements. You can see now why objects are not cloneable by default. It would make no sense to assume that all objects can be sensibly duplicated with a shallow copy. Likewise, it makes no sense to assume that a deep copy is necessary, or even correct. In this case, we probably don't need a deep copy; the flock contains the same members no matter which sheep you're looking at, so there's no need to copy the `HashMap`. But the decision depends on the object itself and its requirements.

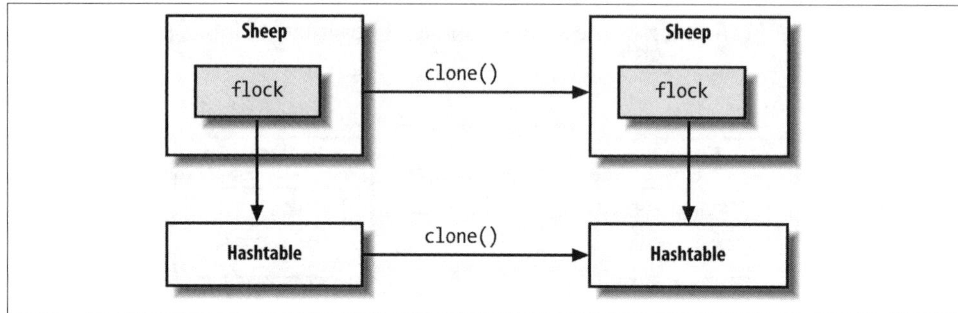

Figure 7-2. Deep copy of an object

The last method of `Object` we need to discuss is `getClass()`. This method returns a reference to the `Class` object that produced the `Object` instance. We'll talk about it next.

The Class Class

A good measure of the complexity of an object-oriented language is the degree of abstraction of its class structures. We know that every object in Java is an instance of a class, but what exactly is a class? In languages like traditional C++, objects are formulated by and instantiated from classes, but classes are really just artifacts of the compiler. In those languages, you see classes mentioned only in source code, not at runtime. By comparison, classes in Smalltalk are real, runtime entities in the language that are themselves described by "metaclasses" and "metaclass classes." Java strikes a happy medium between these two languages with what is effectively a two-tiered system that uses `Class` objects.

Classes in Java source code are represented at runtime by instances of the `java.lang.Class` class. There's a `Class` object for every object type you use; this `Class` object is responsible for producing instances of that type. But you don't generally have to worry about that unless you are interested in loading new kinds of classes dynamically at runtime or using a highly abstracted API that wants a "type" instead of an actual argument. The Class object is also the basis for "reflecting" on a class to find its methods and other properties, allowing you to find out about an object's structure or invoke its methods programmatically at runtime. We'll discuss reflection in the next section.

We get the Class associated with a particular object with the getClass() method:

```
String myString = "Foo!"
Class stringClass = myString.getClass();
```

We can also get the Class reference for a particular class statically, using the .class notation:

```
Class stringClass = String.class;
```

The .class reference looks like a static field that exists in every class. However, it is really resolved by the compiler.

One thing we can do with the Class object is ask for its full name:

```
String s = "Boofa!";
Class stringClass = s.getClass();
System.out.println( stringClass.getName() );   // "java.lang.String"
```

Another thing that we can do with a Class is to ask it to produce a new instance of its type of object. Continuing with the previous example:

```
try {
    String s2 = (String)stringClass.newInstance();
}
catch ( InstantiationException e ) { ... }
catch ( IllegalAccessException e ) { ... }
```

Here, newInstance() has a return type of Object, so we have to cast it to a reference of the appropriate type. This is fine, but we'll see in the next chapter that the Class class is a generic class, which means that we can parameterize it to be more specific about the Java type we're dealing with; that is, we can get the newInstance() method to return the correct type directly without the cast. We'll show this here, but don't worry if it doesn't make any sense yet:

```
Class<String> stringClass = String.class;
try {
    String s2 = stringClass.newInstance(); // no cast necessary
}
catch ( InstantiationException e ) { ... }
catch ( IllegalAccessException e ) { ... }
```

A couple of exceptions can be thrown here. An InstantiationException indicates that we're trying to instantiate an abstract class or an interface. IllegalAccessException is a more general exception that indicates that we can't access a constructor for the object. Note that newInstance() can create only an instance of a class that has an accessible default constructor. It doesn't allow us to pass any arguments to a constructor. (In the next section, we'll learn how to do just that using the Reflection API.)

All of this becomes more meaningful when we add the capability to look up a class by name. `forName()` is a `static` method of `Class` that returns a `Class` object given its name as a `String`:

```
try {
    Class sneakersClass = Class.forName("Sneakers");
} catch ( ClassNotFoundException e ) { ... }
```

A `ClassNotFoundException` is thrown if the class can't be located.

Combining these tools, we have the power to load new kinds of classes dynamically. When combined with the power of interfaces, we can use new data types loaded by a string name in our applications:

```
interface Typewriter {
    void typeLine( String s );
    ...
}

class Printer implements Typewriter {
    ...
}

class MyApplication {
    ...
    String outputDeviceName = "Printer";

    try {
        Class newClass = Class.forName( outputDeviceName );
        Typewriter device = (Typewriter)newClass.newInstance();
        ...
        device.typeLine("Hello...");
    }
    catch ( Exception e ) { ... }
}
```

Here, we have an application loading a class implementation (`Printer`, which implements the `Typewriter` interface) knowing only its name. Imagine the name was entered by the user or looked up from a configuration file. This kind of class loading is the basis for many kinds of configurable systems in Java.

Reflection

In this section, we'll take a look at the Java Reflection API, supported by the classes in the `java.lang.reflect` package. As its name suggests, reflection is the ability for a class or object to examine itself. Reflection lets Java code look at an object (more precisely, the class of the object) and determine its structure. Within the limits imposed by the security manager, you can find out what constructors, methods, and fields a class has, as well as their attributes. You can even change the value of fields, dynamically invoke methods, and construct new objects, much as if Java had primitive pointers to variables and methods. And you can do all this on objects that your code has never even seen before. The Annotations API also has the ability to preserve metadata about source code in the compiled classes and we can retrieve this information with the Reflection API.

We don't have room here to cover the Reflection API fully. As you might expect, the `reflect` package is complex and rich in details. But reflection has been designed so that you can do a lot with relatively little effort; 20% of the effort gives you 80% of the fun.

The Reflection API can be used to determine the capabilities of objects at runtime. It's used by object serialization to tear apart and build objects for transport over streams or into persistent storage. Obviously, the power to pick apart objects and see their internals must be zealously guarded by the security manager. The general rule is that your code is not allowed to do anything with the Reflection API that it couldn't do with static (ordinary, compiled) Java code. In short, reflection is a powerful tool, but it isn't an automatic loophole. By default, an object can't use it to work with fields or methods that it wouldn't normally be able to access (for example, another object's private fields), although those privileges can be granted, as we'll discuss later.

The three primary features of a class are its fields (variables), methods, and constructors. For purposes of describing and accessing an object, these three features are represented by separate classes in the Reflection API: `java.lang.reflect.Field`, `java.lang.reflect.Method`, and `java.lang.reflect.Constructor`. We can look up these members of a class through the `Class` object.

The `Class` class provides two pairs of methods for getting at each type of feature. One pair allows access to a class's public features (including those inherited from its superclasses) while the other pair allows access to any public or nonpublic item declared directly within the class (but not features that are inherited), subject to security considerations. Some examples:

- `getFields()` returns an array of `Field` objects representing all a class's public variables, including those it inherits.
- `getDeclaredFields()` returns an array representing all the variables declared in the class, regardless of their access modifiers, but not including inherited variables.
- For constructors, the distinction between "all constructors" and "declared constructors" is not meaningful (classes do not inherit constructors), so `getConstructors()` and `getDeclaredConstructors()` differ only in that the former returns public constructors while the latter returns all the class's constructors.

Each set of methods includes the methods for listing all the items at once (for example, `getFields()`) and an additional method for looking up a particular item by name and—for methods and constructors—by signature (for example, `getField()`, which takes the field name as an argument).

The following listing shows the methods in the `Class` class:

`Field [] getFields();`
: Get all public variables, including inherited ones.

`Field getField(String name);`
: Get the specified public variable, which may be inherited.

`Field [] getDeclaredFields();`
: Get all public and nonpublic variables declared in this class (not including those inherited from superclasses).

`Field getDeclaredField(String name);`
: Get the specified variable, public or nonpublic, declared in this class (inherited variables not considered).

`Method [] getMethods();`
: Get all public methods, including inherited ones.

`Method getMethod(String name, Class ... argumentTypes);`
: Get the specified public method that has arguments that match the types listed in `argumentTypes`. The method may be inherited.

`Method [] getDeclaredMethods();`
: Get all public and nonpublic methods declared in this class (not including those inherited from superclasses).

`Method getDeclaredMethod(String name, Class ... argumentTypes);`
: Get the specified method, public or nonpublic, that has arguments that match the types listed in `argumentTypes`, and which is declared in this class (inherited methods not considered).

`Constructor [] getConstructors();`
: Get all public constructors of this class.

`Constructor getConstructor(Class ... argumentTypes);`
: Get the specified public constructor of this class that has arguments that match the types listed in `argumentTypes`.

`Constructor [] getDeclaredConstructors();`
: Get all public and nonpublic constructors of this class.

`Constructor getDeclaredConstructor(Class ... argumentTypes);`
: Get the specified constructor, public or nonpublic, that has arguments that match the types listed in `argumentTypes`.

`Class [] getDeclaredClasses();`
: Get all public and nonpublic inner classes declared within this class.

`Constructor [] getInterfaces();`
: Get all interfaces implemented by this class, in the order in which they are declared.

As you can see, the four `getMethod()` and `getConstructor()` methods take advantage of the Java variable-length argument lists to allow you to pass in the argument types. In older versions of Java, you have to pass an array of `Class` types in their place. We'll show an example later.

As a quick example, we'll show how easy it is to list all the public methods of the `java.util.Calendar` class:

```
for ( Method method : Calendar.class.getMethods() )
    System.out.println( method );
```

Here, we've used the `.class` notation to get a reference to the `Class` of `Calendar`. Remember the discussion of the `Class` class; the reflection methods don't belong to a particular instance of `Calendar` itself; they belong to the `java.lang.Class` object that describes the `Calendar` class. If we wanted to start from an instance of `Calendar` (or, say, an unknown object), we could have used the `getClass()` method of the object instead:

```
Method [] methods = myUnknownObject.getClass().getMethods();
```

Modifiers and Security

All of the types of members of a Java class—fields, methods, constructors, and inner classes—have a method `getModifiers()` that returns a set of flags indicating whether the member is private, protected, default level, or publicly accessible. You can test for these with the `java.lang.reflect.Modifier` class, like so:

```
Method method = Object.class.getDeclaredMethod( "clone" ); // no arguments
int perms = method.getModifiers();
System.out.println( Modifier.isPublic( perms ) ); // false
System.out.println( Modifier.isProtected( perms ) ); // true
System.out.println( Modifier.isPrivate( perms ) ); // false
```

In this example, the `clone()` method in `Object` is protected.

Access to the Reflection API is governed by a security manager. A fully trusted application has access to all the previously discussed functionality; it can gain access to members of classes at the level of restriction normally granted code within its scope. It is, however, possible to grant special access to code so that it can use the Reflection API to gain access to private and protected members of other classes in a way that the Java language ordinarily disallows.

The `Field`, `Method`, and `Constructor` classes all extend from a base class called `AccessibleObject`. The `AccessibleObject` class has one important method called `setAccessible()`, which allows you to deactivate normal security when accessing that particular class member. That may sound too easy. It is indeed simple, but whether that method allows you to disable security or not is a function of the Java security manager and security policy. You can do this in a normal Java application running without any security policy, but not, for example, in an applet or other secure environment. For example, to be able to use the protected `clone()` method of the `Object` class, all we have to do (given no contravening security manager) is:

```
Method method = Object.class.getDeclaredMethod( "clone" );
method.setAccessible( true );
```

Accessing Fields

The class `java.lang.reflect.Field` represents static variables and instance variables. `Field` has a full set of overloaded accessor methods for all the base types (for example, `getInt()` and `setInt()`, `getBoolean()` and `setBoolean()`), and `get()` and `set()` methods for accessing fields that are reference types. Let's consider this class:

```
class BankAccount {
    public int balance;
}
```

With the Reflection API, we can read and modify the value of the public integer field `balance`:

```
BankAccount myBankAccount = ...;
...
try {
    Field balanceField = BankAccount.class.getField("balance");
    // read it
    int mybalance = balanceField.getInt( myBankAccount );
    // change it
    balanceField.setInt( myBankAccount, 42 );
} catch ( NoSuchFieldException e ) {
    ... // there is no "balance" field in this class
} catch ( IllegalAccessException e2) {
    ... // we don't have permission to access the field
}
```

In this example, we are assuming that we already know the structure of a `BankAccount` object. In general, we could gather that information from the object itself.

All the data access methods of `Field` take a reference to the particular object instance that we want to access. In this example, the `getField()` method returns a `Field` object that represents the `balance` of the `BankAccount` class; this object doesn't refer to any specific `BankAccount`. Therefore, to read or modify any specific `BankAccount`, we call `getInt()` and `setInt()` with a reference to `myBankAccount`, which is the particular object instance that contains the field with which we want to work. For a static field, we'd use the value `null` here. An exception occurs if we try to access a field that doesn't exist, or if we don't have the proper permission to read or write to the field. If we make balance a private field, we can still look up the Field object that describes it, but we won't be able to read or write its value.

Therefore, we aren't doing anything that we couldn't have done with static code at compile time; as long as balance is a public member of a class that we can access, we can write code to read and modify its value. What's important is that we're accessing balance at runtime, and we could just as easily use this technique to examine the balance field in a class that was dynamically loaded or that we just discovered by iterating through the class's fields with the getDeclaredFields() method.

Accessing Methods

The class java.lang.reflect.Method represents a static or instance method. Subject to the normal security rules, a Method object's invoke() method can be used to call the underlying object's method with specified arguments. Yes, Java does have something like a method pointer!

As an example, we'll write a Java application called Invoke that takes as command-line arguments the name of a Java class and the name of a method to invoke. For simplicity, we'll assume that the method is static and takes no arguments (quite a limitation):

```
//file: Invoke.java
import java.lang.reflect.*;

class Invoke {
  public static void main( String [] args ) {
    try {
      Class clas = Class.forName( args[0] );
      Method method = clas.getMethod( args[1] ); // Named method,
                                                 // no arguments
      Object ret =  method.invoke( null );  // Invoke a static method

      System.out.println(
          "Invoked static method: " + args[1]
          + " of class: " + args[0]
          + " with no args\nResults: " + ret );
    } catch ( ClassNotFoundException e ) {
      // Class.forName() can't find the class
    } catch ( NoSuchMethodException e2 ) {
      // that method doesn't exist
    } catch ( IllegalAccessException e3 ) {
      // we don't have permission to invoke that method
    } catch ( InvocationTargetException e4 ) {
      // an exception occurred while invoking that method
      System.out.println(
          "Method threw an: " + e4.getTargetException() );
    }
  }
}
```

We can run invoke to fetch the value of the system clock:

```
% java Invoke java.lang.System currentTimeMillis
Invoked static method: currentTimeMillis of class:
java.lang.System with no args
Results: 861129235818
```

Our first task is to look up the specified Class by name. To do so, we call the forName() method with the name of the desired class (the first command-line argument). We then ask for the specified method by its name. getMethod() has two arguments: the first is the method name (the second command-line argument), and the second is an array of Class objects that specifies the method's signature. (Remember that any method may be overloaded; you must specify the signature to make it clear which version you want.) Because our simple program calls only methods with no arguments, we create an anonymous empty array of Class objects. Had we wanted to invoke a method that takes arguments, we would have passed an array of the classes of their respective types, in the proper order. For primitive types, we would have used the standard wrappers (Integer, Float, Boolean, etc.) to hold the values. The classes of primitive types in Java are represented by special static TYPE fields of their respective wrappers; for example, use Integer.TYPE for the Class of an int. As shown in comments in the code, starting in Java 5.0, the getMethod() and invoke() methods accept variable-length argument lists, which means that we can omit the arguments entirely and Java will make the empty array for us.

Once we have the Method object, we call its invoke() method. This calls our target method and returns the result as an Object. To do anything nontrivial with this object, you must cast it to something more specific. Presumably, because we're calling the method, we know what kind of object to expect. But if we didn't, we could use the Method getReturnType() method to get the Class of the return type at runtime. If the returned value is a primitive type such as int or boolean, it will be wrapped in the standard wrapper class for its type. If the method returns void, invoke() returns a java.lang.Void object. This is the "wrapper" class that represents void return values.

The first argument to invoke() is the object on which we would like to invoke the method. If the method is static, there is no object, so we set the first argument to null. That's the case in our example. The second argument is an array of objects to be passed as arguments to the method. The types of these should match the types specified in the call to getMethod(). Because we're calling a method with no arguments, we can pass null for the second argument to invoke(). As with the return value, you must use wrapper classes for primitive argument types.

The exceptions shown in the previous code occur if we can't find or don't have permission to access the method. Additionally, an InvocationTargetException occurs if the method being invoked throws some kind of exception itself. You can find what it threw by calling the getTargetException() method of InvocationTargetException.

Accessing Constructors

The `java.lang.reflect.Constructor` class represents an object constructor in the same way that the `Method` class represents a method. You can use it, subject to the security manager, of course, to create a new instance of an object, even with constructors that require arguments. Recall that you can create instances of a class with `Class.newInstance()`, but you cannot specify arguments with that method. This is the solution to that problem, if you really need to do it.

Here, we'll create an instance of `java.util.Date`,[1] passing a string argument to the constructor:

```
try {
        Constructor<Date> cons =
            Date.class.getConstructor( String.class );
        Date date = cons.newInstance( "Jan 1, 2006" );
        System.out.println( date );
    } catch ( NoSuchMethodException e ) {
        // getConstructor() couldn't find the constructor we described
    } catch ( InstantiationException e2 ) {
        // the class is abstract
    } catch ( IllegalAccessException e3 ) {
        // we don't have permission to create an instance
    } catch ( InvocationTargetException e4 ) {
        // the construct threw an exception
    }
```

The story is much the same as with a method invocation; after all, a constructor is really no more than a method with some strange properties. We look up the appropriate constructor for our `Date` class—the one that takes a single `String` as its argument—by passing `getConstructor()` the `String.class` type. Here, we are using the Java 5.0 variable argument syntax. If the constructor required more arguments, we would pass additional `Class`es representing the class of each argument. We can then invoke `newInstance()`, passing it a corresponding argument object. Again, to pass primitive types, we would wrap them in their wrapper types first. Finally, we print the resulting object to a `Date`. Note that we've slipped in another strange construct using generics here. The `Constructor<Date>` type here simply allows us to specialize the `Constructor` for the `Date` type, alleviating the need to cast the result of the `newInstance()` method, as before.

The exceptions from the previous example apply here, too, along with `IllegalArgumentException` and `InstantiationException`. The latter is thrown if the class is `abstract` and, therefore, can't be instantiated.

1. This `Date` constructor is deprecated but will serve us for this example.

What About Arrays?

The Reflection API allows you to create and inspect arrays of base types using the `java.lang.reflect.Array` class. The process is very much the same as with the other classes, so we won't cover it in detail. The primary feature is a static method of `Array` called `newInstance()`, which creates an array that allows you to specify a base type and length. You can also use it to construct multidimensional array instances by specifying an array of lengths (one for each dimension). For more information, look in your favorite Java language reference.

Accessing Generic Type Information

In Chapter 8, we'll discuss generics, which first appeared in Java 5.0. Generics is a major addition that adds new dimensions (literally) to the concept of types in the Java language. With the addition of generics, types are no longer simply one-to-one with Java classes and interfaces but can be parameterized on one or more types to create a new, generic type. To make matters more complicated, these new types do not actually generate new classes, but instead are artifacts of the compiler. To keep the generic information, Java adds information to the compiled class files.

The Reflection API can accommodate all of this, mainly through the addition of the new `java.lang.reflect.Type` class, which is capable of representing generic types. Covering this in detail is a bit outside the scope of this book and because we won't even get to generics until Chapter 8, we won't devote much more space to this topic here. However, the following code snippets may guide you later if you return to the topic of accessing generic type information reflectively:

```
// public interface List<E> extends Collection<E> { ... }

TypeVariable [] tv = List.class.getTypeParameters();
System.out.println( tv[0].getName() ); // "E"
```

This snippet gets the type parameter of the `java.util.List` class and prints its name:

```
class StringList extends ArrayList<String> { }

Type type = StringList.class.getGenericSuperclass();

System.out.println( type );  //
// "java.util.ArrayList<java.lang.String>"


ParameterizedType pt = (ParameterizedType)type;
System.out.println( pt.getActualTypeArguments()[0] ); //
// "class java.lang.String"
```

This second snippet gets the `Type` for a class that extends a generic type and then prints the actual type on which it was parameterized.

Accessing Annotation Data

Later in this chapter, we discuss annotations, a feature that allows metadata to be added to Java classes, methods, and fields. Annotations can optionally be retained in the compiled Java classes and accessed through the Reflection API. This is one of several intended uses for annotations, allowing code at runtime to see the metadata and provide special services for the annotated code. For example, a property (field or setter method) on a Java object might be annotated to indicate that it is expecting a container application to set its value or export it in some way.

Covering this in detail is outside the scope of this book; however, getting annotation data through the Reflection API is easy. Java classes, as well as `Method` and `Field` objects, have the following pairs of methods (and some other related ones):

```
public <A extends Annotation> A getAnnotation(Class<A> annotationClass)
public Annotation[] getDeclaredAnnotations()
```

These methods (the first is a generic method, as covered in Chapter 8) return `java.lang.annotation.Annotation` type objects that represent the metadata.

Dynamic Interface Adapters

Ideally, Java reflection would allow us to do everything at runtime that we can do at compile time (without forcing us to generate and compile source into bytecode). But that is not entirely the case. Although we can dynamically load and create instances of objects at runtime using the `Class.forName()` method, there is no general way to create new types of objects—for which no class files preexist—on the fly.

The `java.lang.reflect.Proxy` class, however, takes a step toward solving this problem by allowing the creation of adapter objects that implement arbitrary Java interfaces at runtime. The `Proxy` class is a factory that can generate an adapter class, implementing any interface (or interfaces) you want. When methods are invoked on the adapter class, they are delegated to a single method in a designated `InvocationHandler` object. You can use this to create dynamic implementations of any kind of interface at runtime and handle the method calls anywhere you want. For example, using a `Proxy`, you could log all of the method calls on an interface, delegating them to a "real" implementation afterward. This kind of dynamic behavior is important for tools that work with Java beans, which must register event listeners. (We'll mention this again in Chapter 22.) It's also useful for a wide range of problems.

In the following snippet, we take an interface name and construct a proxy implementing the interface. It outputs a message whenever any of the interface's methods are invoked:

```
import java.lang.reflect.*;

InvocationHandler handler =
    new InvocationHandler() {
```

```
            Object invoke( Object proxy, Method method, Object[] args ) {
                System.out.println(
                    "Method: {[QUOTE-REPLACEMENT]}+ method.getName() +"()"
                    +" of interface: "+ interfaceName
                    + " invoked on proxy!"
                );
                return null;
            }
        };

    Class clas = Class.forName( MyInterface );

    MyInterface interfaceProxy =
        (MyInterface)Proxy.newProxyInstance(
            clas.getClassLoader(), new Class[] { class }, handler );

    // use MyInterface
    myInterface.anyMethod(); // Method: anyMethod() ... invoked on proxy!
```

The resulting object, `interfaceProxy`, is cast to the type of the interface we want. It will call our handler whenever any of its methods are invoked.

First, we make an implementation of `InvocationHandler`. This is an object with an `invoke()` method that takes as its argument the `Method` being called and an array of objects representing the arguments to the method call. We then fetch the class of the interface that we're going to implement using `Class.forName()`. Finally, we ask the proxy to create an adapter for us, specifying the types of interfaces (you can specify more than one) that we want implemented and the handler to use. `invoke()` is expected to return an object of the correct type for the method call. If it returns the wrong type, a special runtime exception is thrown. Any primitive types in the arguments or in the return value should be wrapped in the appropriate wrapper class. (The runtime system unwraps the return value, if necessary.)

What Is Reflection Good For?

Reflection, although in some sense a "back door" feature of the Java language, is finding more and more important uses. In this chapter, we mentioned that reflection is used to access runtime annotations. In Chapter 22, we'll see how reflection is used to dynamically discover capabilities and features of JavaBean objects. Those are pretty specialized applications—what can reflection do for us in everyday situations?

We could use reflection to go about acting as if Java had dynamic method invocation and other useful capabilities; in Chapter 22, we'll see a dynamic adapter class that uses reflection to make calls for us. As a general coding practice however, dynamic method invocation is a bad idea. One of the primary features of Java (and what distinguishes it from some similar languages) is its strong type safety. You abandon much of that when you take a dip in the reflecting pool. And although the performance of the Reflection API is very good, it is not precisely as fast as compiled method invocations in general.

More appropriately, you can use reflection in situations where you need to work with objects that you can't know about in advance. Reflection puts Java on a higher plane of programming languages, opening up possibilities for new kinds of applications. As we've mentioned, it makes possible one use of Java annotations at runtime, allowing us to inspect classes, methods, and fields for metadata. Another important and growing use for reflection is integrating Java with scripting languages. With reflection, you can write language interpreters in Java that can access the full Java APIs, create objects, invoke methods, modify variables, and do all the other things a Java program can do at compile time, while the program is running. In fact, you could go so far as to reimplement the Java language in Java, allowing completely dynamic programs that can do all sorts of things. Sound crazy? Well, someone has already done this—one of the authors of this book! We'll explain next.

The BeanShell Java scripting language

I (Pat) can't resist inserting a plug here for BeanShell—my free, open source, lightweight Java scripting language. BeanShell is just what we alluded to in the previous section—a Java application that uses the Reflection API to execute Java statements and expressions dynamically. You can use BeanShell interactively to quickly try out some of the examples in this book or take it further to start using Java syntax as a scripting language in your applications. BeanShell exercises the Java Reflection API to its fullest and serves as a demonstration of how dynamic the Java runtime environment really is.

You can find a copy of BeanShell at its own website (*http://www.beanshell.org*). See Appendix B for more information on getting started. We hope you find it both interesting and useful!

Annotations

As we mentioned in Chapter 4, Java for a long time has supported a limited kind of metadata in Java source code through the use of Javadoc comment tags. With Javadoc tags like `@deprecated` or `@author`, we can add some information to a class, method, or field by sticking it into comments above the item. In this case, the information is mainly useful to the Javadoc documentation generator, because comments exist only in Java source code. However, developers have long wanted a way to generalize metadata for other purposes. And in fact, some tools have been developed over the years that read extended Javadoc-style tags in comments and do all sorts of things with them, including code generation and documentation. In Java 5.0, a formal, extensible metadata system called annotations was added to the language that provides this kind of source-level functionality as well as new possibilities for using metadata at runtime.

Annotations allow you to add metadata to Java packages, classes, methods, and fields. This metadata can be utilized by tools at compile time and optionally retained in the compiled Java classes for use at runtime as well. The availability of annotation data to the running program opens up new uses for metadata. For example, annotations cannot only be used at compile time to generate auxiliary classes or resources, but also could be used by a server to provide special services to classes such as importing or exporting of values, security, or monitoring. Annotations will be used heavily in Java XML Binding (JAXB), the Java Servlets API, and Java Web Services (JAX-WS), as we'll see later in the book. In those cases, annotations are used to simplify configuration and deployment information.

Technically, according to the spec, annotations are not supposed to "directly affect the semantics of a program." However, that admonition is a little vague and there is some fear in the Java community that this facility will open a Pandora's box of possible abuses. Hopefully, developers will use them with restraint.

Only a handful of "built-in" annotations are commonly used in Java and we'll summarize them in this section. More built-in annotations are used with specialized packages such as those for web services and some are used in creating the annotations themselves. Creating your own annotations for use in your code is syntactically easy (essentially just like declaring an interface), but implementing the behavior for them via the compiler or a runtime system is a bit beyond the scope of this book, so we won't cover that here. The JDK provides a framework tool called *apt* that can be used to implement source-level annotations that generate and compile code or resource files at compile time. Accessing annotation data at runtime is done via the Reflection API as described briefly earlier in this chapter.

Using Annotations

Annotations are placed in the code preceding the annotated item using an `@` (at) symbol followed by the annotation class name. The `@Deprecated` annotation is an example of the simplest kind, a *marker* or *flag* annotation. A marker annotation indicates some semantics just by its presence. (In the case of `@Deprecated`, it means that the member is deprecated and the compiler should generate warnings if it is used.) To use the `@Deprecated` annotation, we place it before a Java class, method, or field like this:

```
@Deprecated
class OldClass { ... }

class AgingClass
{
    @Deprecated
    public someMethod() { ... }
    ...
}
```

More generally, annotations may take "arguments" in an extended method-like syntax. Table 7-1 summarizes the possible variations.

Table 7-1. Use of arguments in annotations

Example	Description
`@Deprecated`	Marker annotation (no "data")
`@WarningMessage("Something about...")`	Single argument
`@TestValues( { "one", "two" } )`	Array of arguments
`@Author( first="Pat", last="Niemeyer" )`	Named arguments

The first annotation in the table, `@Deprecated`, is a real annotation as described earlier; the remaining three are fictitious. To accept multiple values, an annotation may either use the curly brace ({}) array syntax or the more novel named argument syntax listed in the final example. The named syntax allows arguments to be passed in any order.

Package annotations

In the introduction, we mentioned that Java packages can be annotated. This raises the question of where one would place such an annotation, as there is ordinarily no location where we "declare" a Java package; we normally just use them implicitly. The answer is that by convention we can create a file named *package-info.java* and place it into the folder corresponding to the Java package. The file cannot contain Java classes, but should contain a package statement. Package annotations can be placed on this package statement. In the following example, we deprecate the whole package `learningjava.oldstuff` such that using any of its classes generates the deprecation warning.

```
// file: learningjava/service/package-info.java

/**
 * We can put package comments here too!
 */
@Deprecated
package learningjava.oldstuff;
```

Standard Annotations

Table 7-2 summarizes common annotations supplied with Java.

Table 7-2. Standard annotations

Annotation	Description
`@Deprecated`	Deprecation warning on member
`@Override`	Indicates that the annotated method must override a method in the parent class or else a compiler warning is issued
`@SuppressWarnings(value="` *type* `")`	Indicates that the specified warning types should be suppressed by the compiler for the annotated class or method

We have already discussed the `@Deprecated` and `@Override` annotations, the latter of which we covered in the section "Overriding Methods" on page 165. The `@SuppressWarnings` annotation is intended to have a compelling use in bridging legacy code with newer code using generics after Java 5.0, but some compilers may not implement it.

Additional annotations are supplied with Java as part of the `java.lang.annotations` package that are used to annotate only other annotations (they are really meta-annotations). For example, the `java.lang.annotation.Retention` annotation sets the retention policy for an annotation, specifying whether it is retained in the compiled class and loaded at runtime.

The apt Tool

The Java JDK ships with the command-line Annotation Processing Tool, *apt*, which is a sort of frontend to the *javac* compiler. *apt* uses pluggable annotation processors to process the annotations in source files before the code is compiled by *javac*. If you write your own source-level annotations, you can build a plug-in annotation processor for *apt* that will be invoked to process your annotations in the source code. Your annotation processor can be quite sophisticated, examining the structure of the source code (in a read-only fashion) through the supplied syntax tree (object model) and generating any additional files or actions that it wishes. If you generate new Java source files, they will be automatically compiled by *javac* for you. Running *apt* on a source file with no annotations simply falls through to *javac*.

CHAPTER 8
Generics

It's been over 15 years since the introduction of the Java programming language (and the first edition of this book). In that time, the Java language has matured and come into its own. But it wasn't until Java 5.0, the sixth major release of Java, that the core language itself changed in a significant way. Yes, there were subtle changes and drop-ins over the years. Inner classes, added very early on, were important. But no language improvements prior to that point affected all Java code or all Java developers in the way that generic types did in Java 5.0.

Generics are about abstraction. Generics let you create classes and methods that work in the same way on different types of objects. The term *generic* comes from the idea that we'd like to be able to write general algorithms that can be broadly reused for many types of objects rather than having to adapt our code to fit each circumstance. This concept is not new; it is the impetus behind object-oriented programming itself. Java generics do not so much add new capabilities to the language as they make reusable Java code easier to write and easier to read.

Generics take reuse to the next level by making the *type* of the objects with which we work into an explicit parameter of the generic code. For this reason, generics are also referred to as *parameterized types*. In the case of a generic class, the developer specifies a type as a parameter (an argument) whenever she uses the generic type. The class is parameterized by the supplied type to which the code adapts itself.

In other languages, generics are sometimes referred to as *templates*, which is more of an implementation term. Templates are like intermediate classes, waiting for their type parameters so that they can be used. Java takes a different path, which has both benefits and drawbacks that we'll describe in detail in this chapter.

There is much to say about Java generics. Some of the fine points may seem a bit obscure at first, but don't get discouraged. The vast majority of what you'll do with generics is easy and intuitive. The rest will come with a little patience and tinkering.

We begin our discussion with the most compelling case for generics: container classes and collections. Next, we take a step back and look at the good, bad, and ugly of how Java generics work before getting into the details of writing generic classes. We then introduce generic methods, which intelligently infer their parameter types based upon how they are invoked. We conclude by looking at a couple of real-world generic classes in the Java API.

Containers: Building a Better Mousetrap

In an object-oriented programming language like Java, polymorphism means that objects are always to some degree interchangeable. Any child of a type of object can serve in place of its parent type and, ultimately, every object is a child of `java.lang.Object`, the object-oriented "Eve," so to speak. It is natural, therefore, for the most general types of *containers* in Java to work with the type `Object` so that they can hold just about anything. By containers, we mean classes that hold instances of other classes in some way. The Java Collections Framework is the best example of containers. A `List`, for example, holds an ordered collection of elements of type `Object`. A `Map` holds an association of key-value pairs, with the keys and values also being of the most general type, `Object`. With a little help from wrappers for primitive types, this arrangement has served us well. But (not to get too Zen on you) in a sense, a "collection of any type" is also a "collection of no type," and working with `Objects` pushes a great deal of responsibility onto the user of the container.

It's kind of like a costume party for objects where everybody is wearing the same mask and disappears into the crowd of the collection. Once objects are dressed as the `Object` type, the compiler can no longer see the real types and loses track of them. It's up to the user to pierce the anonymity of the objects later by using a type cast. And like attempting to yank off a party-goer's fake beard, you'd better have the cast correct or you'll get an unwelcome surprise.

```
Date date = new Date();
List list = new ArrayList();
list.add( date );
...
Date firstElement = (Date)list.get(0); // Is the cast correct?  Maybe.
```

The `List` interface has an `add()` method that accepts any type of `Object`. Here, we assigned an instance of `ArrayList`, which is simply an implementation of the `List` interface, and added a `Date` object. Is the cast in this example correct? It depends on what happens in the elided "..." period of time.

Can Containers Be Fixed?

It's natural to ask if there is a way to make this situation better. What if we know that we are only going to put `Dates` into our list? Can't we just make our own list that only accepts

`Date` objects, get rid of the cast, and let the compiler help us again? The answer, surprisingly perhaps, is no. At least, not in a very satisfying way.

Our first instinct may be to try to "override" the methods of `ArrayList` in a subclass. But of course, rewriting the `add()` method in a subclass would not actually override anything; it would add a new *overloaded* method.

```
public void add( Object o ) { ... }
public void add( Date d ) { ... } // overloaded method
```

The resulting object still accepts any kind of object—it just invokes different methods to get there.

Moving along, we might take on a bigger task. For example, we might write our own `DateList` class that does not extend `ArrayList`, but rather delegates the guts of its methods to the `ArrayList` implementation. With a fair amount of tedious work, that would get us an object that does everything a `List` does but that works with `Dates`. However, we've now shot ourselves in the foot because our container is no longer an implementation of `List` and we can't use it interoperably with all of the utilities that deal with collections, such as `Collections.sort()`, or add it to another collection with the `Collection addAll()` method.

To generalize, the problem is that instead of refining the behavior of our objects, what we really want to do is to change their contract with the user. We want to adapt their API to a more specific type and polymorphism doesn't allow that. It would seem that we are stuck with `Objects` for our collections. And this is where generics come in.

Enter Generics

Generics are an enhancement to the syntax of classes that allow us to specialize the class for a given type or set of types. A generic class requires one or more *type parameters* wherever we refer to the class type and uses them to customize itself.

If you look at the source or Javadoc for the `List` class, for example, you'll see it defined something like this:

```
public class List< E > {
   ...
   public void add( E element ) { ... }
   public E get( int i ) { ... }
}
```

The identifier `E` between the angle brackets (<>) is a *type variable*. It indicates that the class `List` is generic and requires a Java type as an argument to make it complete. The name `E` is arbitrary, but there are conventions that we'll see as we go on. In this case, the type variable `E` represents the type of elements we want to store in the list. The `List` class refers to the type variable within its body and methods as if it were a real type, to be substituted later. The type variable may be used to declare instance variables, arguments to methods, and the return type of methods. In this case, `E` is used as the type for the elements we'll be adding via the `add()` method and the return type of the `get()` method. Let's see how to use it.

The same angle bracket syntax supplies the type parameter when we want to use the `List` type:

```
List<String> listOfStrings;
```

In this snippet, we declared a variable called `listOfStrings` using the generic type `List` with a type parameter of `String`. `String` refers to the `String` class, but we could have specialized `List` with any Java class type. For example:

```
List<Date> dates;
List<java.math.BigDecimal> decimals;
List<Foo> foos;
```

Completing the type by supplying its type parameter is called *instantiating the type*. It is also sometimes called *invoking the type*, by analogy with invoking a method and supplying its arguments. Whereas with a regular Java type, we simply refer to the type by name, a generic type must be instantiated with parameters wherever it is used.[1] Specifically, this means that we must instantiate the type everywhere types can appear as the declared type of a variable (as shown in this code snippet), as the type of a method argument, as the return type of a method, or in an object allocation expression using the `new` keyword.

Returning to our `listOfStrings`, what we have now is effectively a `List` in which the type `String` has been substituted for the type variable `E` in the class body:

```
public class List< String > {
   ...
   public void add( String element ) { ... }
   public String get( int i ) { ... }
}
```

We have specialized the `List` class to work with elements of type `String` and *only* elements of type `String`. This method signature is no longer capable of accepting an arbitrary `Object` type.

`List` is just an interface. To use the variable, we'll need to create an instance of some actual implementation of `List`. As we did in our introduction, we'll use `ArrayList`. As before, `ArrayList` is a class that implements the `List` interface, but in this case, both `List` and `ArrayList` are generic classes. As such, they require type parameters to instantiate them where they are used. Of course, we'll create our `ArrayList` to hold `String` elements to match our `List` of `Strings`:

1. That is, unless you want to use a generic type in a nongeneric way. We'll talk about "raw" types later in this chapter.

```
List<String> listOfStrings = new ArrayList<String>
List<String> listOfStrings = new ArrayList<>(); // Or shorthand in Java 7.0
                                                //  and later
```

As always, the `new` keyword takes a Java type and parentheses with possible arguments for the class's constructor. In this case, the type is `ArrayList<String>`—the generic `ArrayList` type instantiated with the `String` type.

Declaring variables as shown in the first line of the preceding example is a bit cumbersome because it requires us to type the generic parameter type twice (once on the left side in the variable type and once on the right in the initialing expression). And in complicated cases, the generic types can get very lengthy and nested within one another. In Java 7, the compiler is smart enough to infer the type of the initializing expression from the type of the variable to which you are assigning it. This is called *generic type inference* and boils down to the fact that you can shorthand the right side of your variable declarations by leaving out the contents of the <> notation, as shown in the example's second line.

We can now use our specialized `List` with strings. The compiler prevents us from even trying to put anything other than a `String` object (or a subtype of `String` if there were any) into the list and allows us to fetch them with the `get()` method without requiring any cast:

```
List<String> listOfStrings = new ArrayList<String>();
listOfStrings.add("eureka! ");
String s = listOfStrings.get(0); // "eureka! "

listOfStrings.add( new Date() ); // Compile-time Error!
```

Let's take another example from the Collections API. The `Map` interface provides a dictionary-like mapping that associates key objects with value objects. Keys and values do not have to be of the same type. The generic `Map` interface requires two type parameters: one for the key type and one for the value type. The Javadoc looks like this:

```
public class Map< K, V > {
    ...
    public V put( K key, V value ) { ... } // returns any old value
    public V get( K key ) { ... }
}
```

We can make a `Map` that stores `Employee` objects by `Integer` "employee ID" numbers like this:

```
Map< Integer, Employee > employees = new HashMap< Integer, Employee >();
Integer bobsId = ...;
Employee bob = ...;

employees.put( bobsId, bob );
Employee employee = employees.get( bobsId );
```

Here, we used `HashMap`, which is a generic class that implements the `Map` interface, and instantiated both types with the type parameters `Integer` and `Employee`. The `Map` now works only with keys of type `Integer` and holds values of type `Employee`.

The reason we used `Integer` here to hold our number is that the type parameters to a generic class must be class types. We can't parameterize a generic class with a primitive type, such as `int` or `boolean`. Fortunately, autoboxing of primitives in Java (see Chapter 5) makes it almost appear as if we can by allowing us to use primitive types as though they were wrapper types:

```
employees.put( 42, bob );
Employee bob = employees.get( 42 );
```

Here, autoboxing converted the integer `42` to an `Integer` wrapper for us twice.

In Chapter 11, we'll see that all of the Java collection classes and interfaces are generic. Furthermore, dozens of other APIs use generics to let you adapt them to specific types. We'll talk about them as they occur throughout the book.

Talking About Types

Before we move on to more important things, we should say a few words about the way we describe a particular parameterization of a generic class. Because the most common and compelling case for generics is for container-like objects, it's common to think in terms of a generic type "holding" a parameter type. In our example, we called our `List<String>` a "list of strings" because, sure enough, that's what it was. Similarly, we might have called our employee map a "Map of employee IDs to Employee objects." However, these descriptions focus a little more on what the classes *do* than on the type itself. Take instead a single object container called `Trap< E >` that could be instantiated on an object of type `Mouse` or of type `Bear`; that is, `Trap<Mouse>` or `Trap<Bear>`. Our instinct is to call the new type a "mouse trap" or "bear trap." Similarly, we could have thought of our list of strings as a new type: "string list" or our employee map as a new "integer employee object map" type. You may use whatever verbiage you prefer, but these latter descriptions focus more on the notion of the generic as a *type* and may help a little bit later when we discuss how generic types are related in the type system. There we'll see that the container terminology turns out to be a little counterintuitive.

In the following section, we'll continue our discussion of generic types in Java from a different perspective. We've seen a little of what they can do; now we need to talk about how they do it.

"There Is No Spoon"

In the movie *The Matrix*,[2] the hero Neo is offered a choice. Take the blue pill and remain in the world of fantasy, or take the red pill and see things as they really are. In dealing with generics in Java, we are faced with a similar ontological dilemma. We can go only so far in any discussion of generics before we are forced to confront the reality of how they are implemented. Our fantasy world is one created by the compiler to make our lives writing code easier to accept. Our reality (though not quite the dystopian nightmare in the movie) is a harsher place, filled with unseen dangers and questions. Why don't casts and tests work properly with generics? Why can't I implement what appear to be two different generic interfaces in one class? Why is it that I can declare an array of generic types, even though there is no way in Java to create such an array?!? We'll answer these questions and more in this chapter, and you won't even have to wait for the sequel. Let's get started.

The design goals for Java generics were formidable: add a radical new syntax to the language that safely introduces parameterized types with no impact on performance and, oh, by the way, make it backward-compatible with all existing Java code and don't change the compiled classes in any serious way. It's actually quite amazing that these conditions could be satisfied at all and no surprise that it took a while. But as always, compromises were required, which lead to some headaches.

To accomplish this feat, Java employs a technique called *erasure*, which relates to the idea that since most everything we do with generics applies statically at compile time, generic information does not need to be carried over into the compiled classes. The generic nature of the classes, enforced by the compiler can be "erased" in the compiled classes, which allows us to maintain compatibility with nongeneric code. While Java does retain information about the generic features of classes in the compiled form, this information is used mainly by the compiler. The Java runtime does not know anything about generics at all.

2. For those of you who might like some context for the title of this section, here is where it comes from:

   Boy: Do not try and bend the spoon. That's impossible. Instead, only try to realize the truth.

   Neo: What truth?

   Boy: There is no spoon.

   Neo: There is no spoon?

   Boy: Then you'll see that it is not the spoon that bends, it is only yourself.

   —Wachowski, Andy and Larry. *The Matrix*. 136 minutes. Warner Brothers, 1999.

Erasure

Let's take a look at a compiled generic class: our friend, `List`. We can do this easily with the *javap* command:

```
% javap java.util.List

public interface java.util.List extends java.util.Collection{
    ...
    public abstract boolean add(java.lang.Object);
    public abstract java.lang.Object get(int);
```

The result looks exactly like it did prior to Java generics, as you can confirm with any older version of the JDK. Notably, the type of elements used with the `add()` and `get()` methods is `Object`. Now, you might think that this is just a ruse and that when the actual type is instantiated, Java will create a new version of the class internally. But that's not the case. This is the one and only `List` class, and it is the actual runtime type used by all parameterizations of `List`; for example, `List<Date>` and `List<String>`, as we can confirm:

```
List<Date> dateList  = new ArrayList<Date>();
System.out.println( dateList instanceof List ); // true!
```

But our generic `dateList` clearly does not implement the `List` methods just discussed:

```
dateList.add( new Object() ); // Compile-time Error!
```

This illustrates the somewhat schizophrenic nature of Java generics. The compiler believes in them, but the runtime says they are an illusion. What if we try something a little more sane and simply check that our `dateList` is a `List<Date>`:

```
System.out.println( dateList instanceof List<Date> ); // Compile-time Error!
// Illegal, generic type for instanceof
```

This time the compiler simply puts its foot down and says, "No." You can't test for a generic type in an `instanceof` operation. Since there are no actual differentiable classes for different parameterizations of `List` at runtime, there is no way for the `instanceof` operator to tell the difference between one incarnation of `List` and another. All of the generic safety checking was done at compile time and now we're just dealing with a single actual `List` type.

What has really happened is that the compiler has erased all of the angle bracket syntax and replaced the type variables in our `List` class with a type that can work at runtime with any allowed type: in this case, `Object`. We would seem to be back where we started, except that the compiler still has the knowledge to enforce our usage of the generics in the code at compile time and can, therefore, handle the cast for us. If you decompile a class using a `List<Date>` (the *javap* command with the *-c* option shows you the bytecode, if you dare), you will see that the compiled code actually contains the cast to `Date`, even though we didn't write it ourselves.

We can now answer one of the questions we posed at the beginning of the section ("Why can't I implement what appear to be two different generic interfaces in one class?"). We can't have a class that implements two different generic `List` instantiations because they are really the same type at runtime and there is no way to tell them apart:

```
public abstract class DualList implements List<String>, List<Date> { }
// Error: java.util.List cannot be inherited with different arguments:
//    <java.lang.String> and <java.util.Date>
```

Raw Types

Although the compiler treats different parameterizations of a generic type as different types (with different APIs) at compile time, we have seen that only one real type exists at runtime. For example, the class of `List<Date>` and `List<String>` share the plain old Java class `List`. `List` is called the *raw type* of the generic class. Every generic has a raw type. It is the degenerate, "plain" Java form from which all of the generic type information has been removed and the type variables replaced by a general Java type like `Object`.[3]

It is still possible to use raw types in Java just as before generics were added to the language. The only difference is that the Java compiler generates a warning wherever they are used in an "unsafe" way. For example:

```
// nongeneric Java code using the raw type
List list = new ArrayList(); // assignment ok
list.add("foo"); // Compiler warning on usage of raw type
```

This snippet uses the raw `List` type just as old-fashioned Java code prior to Java 5 would have. The difference is that now the Java compiler issues an *unchecked warning* about the code if we attempt to insert an object into the list.

```
% javac MyClass.java
Note: MyClass.java uses unchecked or unsafe operations.
Note: Recompile with -Xlint:unchecked for details.
```

The compiler instructs us to use the `-Xlint:unchecked` option to get more specific information about the locations of unsafe operations:

```
% javac -Xlint:unchecked MyClass.java
warning: [unchecked] unchecked call to add(E) as a member of the raw type
         java.util.
List:   list.add("foo");
```

3. When generics were added in Java 5.0, things were carefully arranged such that the raw type of all of the generic classes worked out to be exactly the same as the earlier, nongeneric types. So the raw type of a `List` in Java 5.0 is the same as the old, nongeneric `List` type that had been around since JDK 1.2. Since the vast majority of current Java code at the time did not use generics, this type equivalency and compatibility was very important.

Note that creating and assigning the raw `ArrayList` does not generate a warning. It is only when we try to use an "unsafe" method (one that refers to a type variable) that we get the warning. This means that it's still OK to use older-style, nongeneric Java APIs that work with raw types. We only get warnings when we do something unsafe in our own code.

One more thing about erasure before we move on. In the previous examples, the type variables were replaced by the `Object` type, which could represent any type applicable to the type variable `E`. Later we'll see that this is not always the case. We can place limitations or *bounds* on the parameter types, and, when we do, the compiler can be more restrictive about the erasure of the type. We'll explain in more detail later after we discuss bounds, but, for example:

```
class Bounded< E extends Date > {
    public void addElement( E element ) { ... }
}
```

This parameter type declaration says that the element type `E` must be a subtype of the `Date` type. In this case, the erasure of the `addElement()` method is therefore more restrictive than `Object`, and the compiler uses `Date`:

```
public void addElement( Date element ) { ... }
```

`Date` is called the *upper bound* of this type, meaning that it is the top of the object hierarchy here and the type can be instantiated only on type `Date` or on "lower" (more derived) types.

Now that we have a handle on what generic types really are, we can go into a little more detail about how they behave.

Parameterized Type Relationships

We know now that parameterized types share a common, raw type. This is why our parameterized `List<Date>` is just a `List` at runtime. In fact, we can assign any instantiation of `List` to the raw type if we want:

```
List list = new ArrayList<Date>();
```

We can even go the other way and assign a raw type to a specific instantiation of the generic type:

```
List<Date> dates = new ArrayList(); // unchecked warning
```

This statement generates an unchecked warning on the assignment, but thereafter the compiler trusts that the list contained only `Dates` prior to the assignment. It is also permissible, albeit pointless, to perform a cast in this statement. We'll talk about casting to generic types a bit later.

Whatever the runtime types, the compiler is running the show and does not let us assign things that are clearly incompatible:

```
List<Date> dates = new ArrayList<String>(); // Compile-time Error!
```

Of course, the `ArrayList<String>` does not implement the methods of `List<Date>` conjured by the compiler, so these types are incompatible.

But what about more interesting type relationships? The `List` interface, for example, is a subtype of the more general `Collection` interface. Is a particular instantiation of the generic `List` also assignable to some instantiation of the generic `Collection`? Does it depend on the type parameters and their relationships? Clearly, a `List<Date>` is not a `Collection<String>`. But is a `List<Date>` a `Collection<Date>`? Can a `List<Date>` be a `Collection<Object>`?

We'll just blurt out the answer first, then walk through it and explain. The rule is that for the simple types of generic instantiations we've discussed so far, *inheritance applies only to the "base" generic type and not to the parameter types*. Furthermore, assignability applies only when the two generic types are instantiated on *exactly the same parameter type*. In other words, there is still one-dimensional inheritance, following the base generic class type, but with the additional restriction that the parameter types must be identical.

For example, recalling that a `List` is a type of `Collection`, we can assign instantiations of `List` to instantiations of `Collection` when the type parameter is exactly the same:

```
Collection<Date> cd;
List<Date> ld = new ArrayList<Date>();
cd = ld; // Ok!
```

This code snippet says that a `List<Date>` is a `Collection<Date>`—pretty intuitive. But trying the same logic on a variation in the parameter types fails:

```
List<Object> lo;
List<Date> ld = new ArrayList<Date>();
lo = ld; // Compile-time Error!  Incompatible types.
```

Although our intuition tells us that the `Dates` in that `List` could all live happily as `Objects` in a `List`, the assignment is an error. We'll explain precisely why in the next section, but for now just note that the type parameters are not exactly the same and that there is no inheritance relationship among parameter types in generics. This is a case where thinking of the instantiation in terms of types and not in terms of what they do helps. These are not really a "list of dates" and a "list of objects," but more like a `DateList` and an `ObjectList`, the relationship of which is not immediately obvious.

Try to pick out what's OK and what's not OK in the following example:

```
Collection<Number> cn;
List<Integer> li = new ArrayList<Integer>();
cn = li; // Compile-time Error!  Incompatible types.
```

It is possible for an instantiation of List to be an instantiation of Collection, but only if the parameter types are exactly the same. Inheritance doesn't follow the parameter types and this example fails.

One more thing: earlier we mentioned that this rule applies to the simple types of instantiations we've discussed so far in this chapter. What other types are there? Well, the kinds of instantiations we've seen so far where we plug in an actual Java type as a parameter are called *concrete type instantiations*. Later we'll talk about *wildcard instantiations*, which are akin to mathematical set operations on types. We'll see that it's possible to make more exotic instantiations of generics where the type relationships are actually two-dimensional, depending both on the base type and the parameterization. But don't worry: this doesn't come up very often and is not as scary as it sounds.

Why Isn't a List<Date> a List<Object>?

It's a reasonable question. Even with our brains thinking of arbitrary DateList and ObjectList types, we can still ask why they couldn't be assignable. Why shouldn't we be able to assign our List<Date> to a List<Object> and work with the Date elements as Object types?

The reason gets back to the heart of the rationale for generics that we discussed in the introduction: changing APIs. In the simplest case, supposing an ObjectList type extends a DateList type, the DateList would have all of the methods of ObjectList and we could still insert Objects into it. Now, you might object that generics let us change the APIs, so that doesn't apply anymore. That's true, but there is a bigger problem. If we could assign our DateList to an ObjectList variable, we would have to be able to use Object methods to insert elements of types other than Date into it. We could *alias* the DateList as an ObjectList and try to trick it into accepting some other type:

```
DateList dateList = new DateList();
ObjectList objectList = dateList; // Can't really do this
objectList.add( new Foo() ); // should be runtime error!
```

We'd expect to get a runtime error when the actual DateList implementation was presented with the wrong type of object. And therein lies the problem. Java generics have no runtime representation. Even if this functionality were useful, there is no way with the current scheme for Java to know what to do at runtime. Another way to look at it is that this feature is simply dangerous because it allows for an error at runtime that couldn't be caught at compile time. In general, we'd like to catch type errors at compile time. By disallowing these assignments, Java can guarantee that your code is typesafe if it compiles with no unchecked warnings.

Actually, that last sentence is not entirely true, but it doesn't have to do with generics; it has to do with arrays. If this all sounds familiar to you, it's because we mentioned it previously in relation to Java arrays. Array types have an inheritance relationship that allows this kind of aliasing to occur:

```
Date [] dates = new Date[10];
Object [] objects = dates;
objects[0] = "not a date"; // Runtime ArrayStoreException!
```

However, arrays have runtime representations as different classes and they check themselves at runtime, throwing an `ArrayStoreException` in just this case. So in theory, Java code is not guaranteed typesafe by the compiler if you use arrays in this way.

Casts

We've now talked about relationships between generic types and even between generic types and raw types. But we haven't brought up the concept of a cast yet. No cast was necessary when we interchanged generics with their raw types. Instead, we just crossed a line that triggers unchecked warnings from the compiler:

```
List list = new ArrayList<Date>();
List<Date> dl = list;  // unchecked warning
```

Normally, we use a cast in Java to work with two types that could be assignable. For example, we could attempt to cast an `Object` to a `Date` because it is plausible that the `Object` is a `Date` value. The cast then performs the check at runtime to see if we are correct. Casting between unrelated types is a compile-time error. For example, we can't even try to cast an `Integer` to a `String`. Those types have no inheritance relationship. What about casts between compatible generic types?

```
Collection<Date> cd = new ArrayList<Date>();
List<Date> ld = (List<Date>)cd; // Ok!
```

This code snippet shows a valid cast from a more general `Collection<Date>` to a `List<Date>`. The cast is plausible here because a `Collection<Date>` is assignable from and could actually be a `List<Date>`. Similarly, the following cast catches our mistake where we have aliased a `TreeSet<Date>` as a `Collection<Date>` and tried to cast it to a `List<Date>`:

```
Collection<Date> cd = new TreeSet<Date>();
List<Date> ld = (List<Date>)cd; // Runtime ClassCastException!
ld.add( new Date() );
```

There is one case where casts are not effective with generics, however, and that is when we are trying to differentiate the types based on their parameter types:

```
Object o = new ArrayList<String>();
List<Date> ld = (List<Date>)o; // unchecked warning, ineffective
Date d = ld.get(0); // unsafe at runtime, implicit cast may fail
```

Here, we aliased an `ArrayList<String>` as a plain `Object`. Next, we cast it to a `List<Date>`. Unfortunately, Java does not know the difference between a `List<String>` and a `List<Date>` at runtime, so the cast is fruitless. The compiler warns us of this by generating an unchecked warning at the location of the cast; we should be aware that when we try to use the cast object later, we might find out that it is incorrect. Casts on generic types are ineffective at runtime because of erasure and the lack of type information.

Writing Generic Classes

Now that we have (at least some of) the "end user" view of generics, let's try writing a few classes ourselves. In this section, we'll talk about how type variables are used in the definition of generic classes, where they may appear, and some of their limitations. We'll also talk about subclassing generic types.

The Type Variable

We've already seen the basics of how type variables are used in the declaration of a generic class. One or more type variables are declared in the angle bracket (<>) type declaration and used throughout the body and instance methods of the class. For example:

```
class Mouse { }
class Bear { }

class Trap< T >
{
    T trapped;

    public void snare( T trapped ) { this.trapped = trapped; }
    public T release() { return trapped; }
}

// usage
Trap<Mouse> mouseTrap = new Trap<Mouse>();
mouseTrap.snare( new Mouse() );
Mouse mouse = mouseTrap.release();
```

Here, we created a generic `Trap` class that can hold any type of object. We used the type variable `T` to declare an instance variable of the parameter type as well as in the argument type and return type of the two methods.

The scope of the type variable is the instance portion of the class, including methods and any instance initializer blocks. The static portion of the class is not affected by the generic parameterization, and type variables are not visible in static methods or static initializers. As you might guess, just as all instantiations of the generic type have only one actual class (the raw type), they have only one, shared static context as well. You cannot even invoke a static method through a parameterized type. You must use the raw type or an instance of the object.

The type variable can also be used in the type instantiation of other generic types used by the class. For example, if we wanted our `Trap` to hold more than one animal, we could create a `List` for them within our class by referencing the parameter type like so:

```
List<T> trappedList = new ArrayList<T>();
```

Just to cover all the bases, we should mention that instantiations of generic types on the type variable act just like any other type and can serve in all the places that other instantiations of a type can. For example, a method in our class can take a `List<T>` as an argument:

```
public void trapAll( List<T> list ) { ... }
```

The effective type of the `trapAll()` method in a `Trap<Mouse>` is then simply:

```
trapAll( List<Mouse> list ) { ... }
```

We should note that this is *not* what we mean by the term *generic method.* This is just a regular Java method that happens to take a generic type as an argument. We'll talk about real generic methods, which can *infer* their types from arguments, and assignment contexts later in this chapter. A type variable can also be used to parameterize a generic parent class, as we'll see in the next section.

Subclassing Generics

Generic types can be subclassed just like any other class by either generic or nongeneric child classes. A nongeneric subclass must extend a particular instantiation of the parent type, filling in the required parameters to make it concrete:

```
class DateList extends ArrayList<Date> { }

DateList dateList = new DateList();
dateList.add( new Date() );
List<Date> ld = dateList;
```

Here, we have created a nongeneric subclass, `DateList`, of the concrete generic instantiation `ArrayList<Date>`. The `DateList` is a type of `ArrayList<Date>` and inherits the particular instantiation of all of the methods, just as it would from any other parent. We can even assign it back to the parent type if we wish, as shown in this example.

A generic subtype of a generic class may extend either a concrete instantiation of the class, as in the previous example, or it may share a type variable that it "passes up" to the parent upon instantiation:

```
class AdjustableTrap< T > extends Trap< T > {
    public void setSize( int i ) { ... }
}
```

Here, the type variable T used to instantiate the AdjustableTrap class is passed along to instantiate the base class, Trap. When the user instantiates the AdjustableTrap on a particular parameter type, the parent class is instantiated on that type as well.

Exceptions and Generics

Types appear in the body of classes in another place—the throws clauses of methods. We can use type variables to define the type of exceptions thrown by methods, but to do so we need to introduce the concept of bounds. We cover bounds more in the next section. In this case, the usage is very simple. We just need to ensure that the type variable we want to use as our exception type is actually a type of Throwable. We can do that by adding an extends clause to the declaration of our type variable, like this:

```
< T extends Throwable >
```

Here is an example class, parameterized on a type that must be a kind of Throwable. Its test() method accepts an instance of that kind of object and throws it as a checked exception:

```
ExceptionTester< T extends Throwable >  {
    public void test( T exception ) throws T {// throw type is generic param
        throw exception;
    }
}

try {
    new ExceptionTester<ClassNotFoundException>().test(
        new ClassNotFoundException() );
} catch ( ClassNotFoundException e ) { ... }
```

The important part of this example is that the throws clause of our test method is defined to throw T, the generic parameter type of the class. This means that we can parameterize the type of exceptions thrown by a class.

The addition of the bound imposes the restriction that the parameter type used to instantiate the class T must be a type of Throwable. And we referenced the type T in the throws clause. So, an ExceptionTester<ClassNotFoundException> can throw a ClassNotFoundException from its test() method. Note that this is a checked exception and that fact has not been lost on the compiler. The compiler enforces the checked exception type that it just applied.

No generic throwables

We saw that a type variable can be used to specify the type of Throwable in the throws clause of a method. Perhaps ironically, however, we cannot use generics to create new types of exceptions. No generic subtypes of Throwable are allowed. If you think about this for a moment, you'll see that in order to be useful, generic Throwables would require `try/catch` blocks that can differentiate instantiations of `Throwable`. And because (once again) there is no runtime representation of generics, this isn't possible with erasure.

Parameter Type Limitations

We have seen the parameter types (type variables) of a generic class used to declare instance variables, method arguments, and return types as well as "passed along" to parameterize a generic superclass. One thing that we haven't talked about is the question of how or whether we can use the type variable of a generic class to construct instances of the parameter type or work with objects of the type in other concrete ways. We deliberately avoided this issue in our previous "exception tester" example by simply passing our exception object in as an argument. Could we have done away with this argument? The answer, unfortunately, is that due to the limitations of erasure, there really is no parameter type information to work with at runtime. In this section, we'll look at this problem and explore a workaround.

Because the type variable `T` has faithfully served as our parameter type everywhere else, you might imagine that we could use it to construct an instance of `T` using the `new` keyword. But we can't:

```
T element = new T(); // Error! Invalid syntax.
```

Remember that all type information is erased in the compiled class. The raw type does not have any way of knowing the type of object you want to construct at runtime. Nor is there any way to get at the `Class` of the parameter type through the type variable, for the same reason. So reflection won't help us here either. This means that, in general, generics are limited to working with parameter types in relatively hands-off ways (by reference only). This is one reason that generics are more useful for containers than in some other applications. This problem comes up often and there is a solution, although it's not quite as elegant as we'd like.

Using Class<T>

The only real way to get the type information that we need at runtime is to have the user explicitly pass in a `Class` reference, generally as one of the arguments to a method. Then we can explicitly refer to the class using reflection and create instances or do whatever else is necessary. This may sound like a really bad solution, without much type safety and placing a big burden on the developer to do the right thing. Fortunately, we can use a trick of generics to enforce this contract with the user and make it safe. Again, the basic idea is to have one of our methods accept the `Class` of the parameter type so that we can use it at runtime. Following our "exception tester" example:

```
public void test( Class type ) throws T { ... }
```

This isn't much better than it was before. Specifically, it doesn't guarantee that the Class type passed to the method will match the parameterized type of the class (used in the throws clause here).

Fortunately, the Class class is, itself, now a generic type. Specifically, all instances of the Class class created by the Java VM are instantiated with their own type as a parameter. The class of the String type, for example, is now Class<String>, not just some arbitrary instance of the raw Class type that happens to know about strings.

This has two ramifications. First, we can specify a particular instantiation of Class using the parameter type in our class. And second, since the Class class is now generic, all of the reflective and instance creation methods can be typed properly and no longer require casts, so we can write our test() method like this:

```
public void test( Class<T> type ) throws T {
    throw type.newInstance();
}
```

The only Class instance that can be passed to our test() method now is Class<T>, the Class for the parameter type T, on which we instantiated ExceptionTester. So, although the user still has the burden of passing in this seemingly extraneous Class argument, at least the compiler will ensure that we do it and do it correctly:

```
ExceptionTester<ArithmeticException> et =
    new ExceptionTester<ArithmeticException>();

et.test( ArithmeticException.class ); // no other .class will work
```

In this code snippet, attempting to pass any other Class argument to the test() method generates a compile-time error.

Bounds

In the process of discussing generics, we've already had to mention bounds a few times. A bound is a constraint on the type of a type parameter. Bounds use the extends keyword and some new syntax to limit the parameter types that may be applied to a generic type. In the case of a generic class, the bounds simply limit the type that may be supplied to instantiate it.

A type variable may extend a class or interface type, meaning that its instantiation must be of that type or a subtype:

```
class EmployeeList< T extends Employee > { ... }
```

Here, we made a generic EmployeeList type that can be instantiated only with Employee types. We could further require that the Employee type implement one or more interfaces using the special & syntax:

```
class EmployeeList< T extends Employee & Ranked & Printable > { ... }
```

The order of the & interface bounds is not significant, but only one class type can be specified and if there is one, it must come first. When a type has no specific bounds, the bound `extends Object` is implicit.

By applying bounds to our type, we not only limit the instantiations of the generic class, but we make the type arguments more useful. Now that we know that our type must extend some type or implement some set of interfaces, we can use variables and arguments declared with `T` by those other type names. Here is a somewhat contrived extension of our previous example:

```
class EmployeeList< T extends Employee & Ranked & Printable >
{
    Ranked ranking;
    List<Printable> printList = new ArrayList<Printable>();

    public void addEmployee( T employee ) {
        this.ranking = employee;  // T as Ranked
        printList.add( employee );  // T as Printable
    }
}
```

This example shows that by placing bounds on the generic parameter type we can require it to be of a particular class type or implement certain interface types. This allows us to use arguments of the parameter type passed to methods in more useful ways. In this example, we know that the `EmployeeList` will be instantiated with a generic type that is a `Printable` and so we can use the employee argument as a `Printable`.

Type variables can also refer to other type variables within the type declaration:

```
class Foo <A, B extends A> { ... }
```

We'll see a particularly vicious example of this later when we talk about the definition of the `Enum` class. We'll also see a more convenient technique for declaring how individual elements of a generic class relate to the parameter type when we cover wildcards in the next section.

Erasure and Bounds (Working with Legacy Code)

We mentioned earlier in our discussion of erasure that the resulting type used in place of the type parameter in the raw type for the generic class is the bound of the type variable. Specifically, we have seen many generics with no explicit bounds that defaulted to a bound of type `Object`. We also showed a quick example of a type that imposed a bound of `extends Date` and said that the type of its methods would be `Date` instead of `Object`. We can now be a little more specific.

The type after erasure used for the parameter type of a generic class is the *leftmost bound*; that is, the first bound specified after the `extends` keyword (literally the leftmost) becomes the type used in the erasure. This implies that if the type extends a class type, it is always the erased type because it must always come first. But if the type extends only interface types, the choice is up to us. This fine point is important for backward compatibility with nongeneric code. Often when creating generic versions of nongeneric APIs, we have the opportunity to "tighten up" the specification a bit. Being aware of the leftmost bound gives us a way to explicitly control the type of the erased class. For example, suppose we create a generic `List` class that we only want instantiated on `Listable` objects, but we'd prefer not to change the API of our old `List` class that accepted `Object` type elements. Our initial attempt:

```
class List< E extends Listable > { ... }
```

produces a raw type that accepts only `Listable`. However, we can insert a somewhat gratuitous additional type, `Object`, as the leftmost bound in order to get back our old API without changing the new generic bounds:

```
class List< E extends Object & Listable > { ... }
```

Inserting `Object` doesn't change the actual bounds of the generic class but does change the erased signature.

Wildcards

We mentioned earlier that the kinds of generic type instantiations discussed so far in this chapter have all been concrete type instantiations. We described this as meaning that all of the parameter arguments are real Java types. For example, `List<String>` and `List<Date>` are instantiations of the generic `List` class with the concrete types `String` and `Date`. Now we're going to look at another kind of generic type instantiation: *wildcard instantiation*.

As we'll see in this section, wildcards are Java's way of introducing polymorphism into the type parameter portion of the generic equation. A wildcard instantiation uses a question mark (`?`) in place of an actual type parameter at instantiation time and denotes that the type can be assigned any of a range of possible instantiations of the generic type. The `?` wildcard by itself is called the *unbounded wildcard* and denotes that any type instantiation is acceptable (assignable to the type).

```
List<?> anyInstantiationOfList = new ArrayList<Date>();
anyInstantiationOfList = new ArrayList<String>(); // another instantiation
```

In this snippet, we declared a variable `anyInstantiationOfList` whose type is the unbounded wildcard instantiation of the generic `List` type. (What a mouthful.) This means that the type we instantiated can be assigned any particular concrete instantiation of the `List` type, whether `Date`s, `String`s, or `Foo`s. Here, we assigned it a `List<Date>` first and, subsequently, a `List<String>`.

A Supertype of All Instantiations

The unbounded wildcard instantiation is a kind of `supertype` of all of these concrete instantiations. In contrast to the generic type relationships that we saw earlier, which followed only raw, "base" generic types, wildcards let us implement polymorphism on the parameter types. The unbounded wildcard is to generic type parameters what the `Object` type is to regular Java types: a supertype of everything.

```
// A List<Object> is not a List<Date>!
List<Object> objectList = new ArrayList<Date>() // Error!

// A List<?> can be a List<Date>
List<?> anyList = new ArrayList<Date>(); // Yes!
```

We are reminded in this example that `List<Object>` is not a `List<Date>`; polymorphism doesn't flow that way with generic instantiations of concrete types. But `List<?>`, the unbounded wildcard instantiation, can be assigned any instantiation of `List`. As we go on, we'll see that wildcards add a new dimension to the assignability of generic types.

Bounded Wildcards

A *bounded wildcard* is a wildcard that uses the `extends` keyword just as a type variable would to limit the range of assignable types. For example:

```
List<? extends Date> dateInstantiations = new ArrayList<Date>();
dateInstantiations = new ArrayList<MyDate>(); // another instantiation
```

Our `dateInstantiations` variable is limited to holding instantiations of `List` on parameter types of `Date` and its subclasses. So, we can assign it a `List<Date>` or a `List<MyDate>`. In the same way that the unbounded wildcard serves as a superclass for all instantiations of a generic type, bounded wildcards create more limited supertypes covering a narrower range of instantiations. In this case, our wildcard instantiation, `List<? extends Date>`, is the supertype of all instantiations of `List` on `Date` types. As with type parameter bounds, the bound `Date` is called the upper bound of the type.

Wildcard bounds may extend interfaces as well as use the `&` syntax to add interface requirements to the bound:

```
Trap< ? extends Catchable & Releaseable > trap;
```

In this case, the instantiation serves as a supertype of the set of instantiations on types implementing both the `Catchable` and `Releaseable` interfaces.

Thinking Outside the Container

Let's be clear about what the wildcard means in the context of a container type such as `List`. The unbounded wildcard instantiation may be assigned any type instantiation, but it does ultimately refer to *some particular type instantiation*. A wildcard instantiation serves as the type of a variable, and that variable eventually holds some actual concrete instantiation of the generic type:

```
List<?> someInstantiationOfList;
someInstantiationOfList = new ArrayList<Date>();
someInstantiationOfList = new ArrayList<String>();
```

In this example, our `List<?>` variable is either a `List<String>` or a `List<Date>`. It is *not* some new kind of `List` that can hold either `String` or `Date` elements.

In the same way, a wildcard with bounds ultimately holds one of the concrete instantiations assignable to its bounds. Imagine for a moment that we have a private class `Foo` with only one subclass `Bar` and no others. The expression `Collection<? extends Foo>` in this case means the set of two possibilities: either `Collection<Foo>` or `Collection<Bar>`—that is, either a `Collection` of elements with a common supertype of `Foo` or a collection of elements with a common supertype of `Bar`. Again, the wildcard instantiation matches either of those generic type instantiations. It does *not* create a new type of collection that can contain either `Foo`s or `Bar`s. (That is actually the job of `Collection<Foo>`, which can contain both `Foo` and `Bar` elements.)

For this reason, wildcard type instantiations are valid types for referencing an object, but they cannot be used as the type to create an instance of an object. In general, you cannot use a wildcard type with the `new` keyword to allocate an object instance because the wildcard denotes one or a possible set of objects. It doesn't make sense.

Lower Bounds

We saw the `extends` construct used to specify an upper bound for both type variables and wildcard instantiations. It implies a type that is "at the top" of the object hierarchy for the bound. Wildcard instantiations actually allow another type of bound called a *lower bound* as well. A lower bound is specified with the keyword `super` and, as you might guess, requires that instantiations be of a certain type or any of its supertypes, up to `Object`. For example:

```
List< ? super MyDate > listOfAssignableFromMyDate;
listOfAssignableFromMyDate = new ArrayList<MyDate>();
listOfAssignableFromMyDate = new ArrayList<Date>();
listOfAssignableFromMyDate = new ArrayList<Object>();
```

This wildcard instantiation creates a type that can hold any instantiation of `List` on the type `MyDate` or any of its supertypes. In our example world, that means the wildcard type can be assigned one of only three types: `List<MyDate>`, `List<Date>`, or `List<Object>`. Here, we have cut off the object inheritance hierarchy after three generations. No further subclasses of `MyDate` can be used.

As we hinted in the example, it may help to read `? super MyDate` as "Assignable from MyDate." Lower bounds are useful for cases where we want to be sure that a particular container instantiation can hold a particular element type, without limiting it to just the specific type of the element. We'll show a good example of this when we talk about generic methods later. For now, just try to digest this as complementary to upper bounds.

One last thing about lower bounds: only the wildcard instantiation syntax can use the `super` keyword to refer to lower bounds. Bounds of type variables in generic class declarations cannot have lower bounds. Erasure replaces all references to the type variables with their upper bounds, so runtime types have no way to enforce the contract.

Reading, Writing, and Arithmetic

We've glossed over an important issue so far in our discussion of wildcard types: namely, how can we use them? What kinds of types does the compiler enforce for variables and arguments that referred to the type variables in the generic class? For example, if we have a `List<?>` list of any instantiation type, what are the rules about putting objects into it and getting them back out? What is their type?

We have to take the two cases separately. Drawing on the analogy of a container, we'll call getting a return value from a method on an object as a specific type *reading the object as a type*. Conversely, we'll call passing arguments of a specific type to methods of the object *writing the object as a type*. So, for example, a `List<Date>` can be read and written as the `Date` type and a `Trap<Mouse>` has methods that can be read and written as the `Mouse` type.

To be more precise, though, we should say that `List<Date>` can be read as the `Date` type, but can be written as any subtype of `Date`. After all, we could add a `MyDate` to a `List<Date>`. Let's look now at the wildcard instantiation `List< ? extends Date >`. We know it holds an instantiation of the `List` type on some type of `Date`. What more can we say about the elements of such a `List`, which could hold *any* instantiation of the `Date` type? Well, the elements will always be subtypes of `Date`. This means that at a minimum, we should be able to read the object through our wildcard type as type `Date`:

```
List< ? extends Date > someDateList = new ArrayList<MyDate>();
...
Date date = someDateList.get( 0 ); // read as Date
```

The compiler lets us assign the value directly to a `Date` because it knows that whatever the instantiation of the `List`, the elements must be a subtype of `Date`. (Of course, we could have read the object as type `Object` or any supertype of `Date` if we'd wanted to as well.)

But what about going the other way and writing? If `someDatelist` could be an instantiation of `List` on any subclass of `Date`, how can we know what type of objects to write to it? (How can we safely call its `add()` method?) The answer is that we can't. Since we don't know the correct type, the compiler won't let us write anything to the `List` through our wildcard instantiation of the type:

```
List< ? extends Date > someDateList = new ArrayList<MyDate>();
someDatelist.add( new Date() ); // Compile-time Error!
someDatelist.add( new MyDate() ); // Compile-time Error!
```

Another way to put this is that because our wildcard instantiation has an upper bound of `Date`, we can only *read* the type as `Date`. We'll reiterate that in the form of a rule in a moment.

Recall that an unbounded wildcard is really just a wildcard with a bound of type `Object` `<? extends Object>`. Obviously, even an unbounded wildcard instantiation holds objects that can be assigned to `Object`, so it's OK to read an unbounded wildcard as the `Object` type:

```
List<?> someList = new ArrayList<String>();
...
Object object = someList.get( 0 ); // read as Object
```

But, of course, we cannot know the actual type of the elements, so we cannot write to the list through our unbounded wildcard type.

What about lower bounds? Well, the situation is neatly reversed with respect to reading and writing. Because we know that the elements of any instantiation matching our lower bounded wildcard must be a supertype of the lower bound, we can write to the object as the lower bound type through our wildcard:

```
List< ? super MyDate > listAssignableMyDate = new ArrayList<Date>();
listAssignableMyDate.add( new MyDate() );
listAssignableMyDate.add( new Date() ); // Compile-time Error!
```

But because we do not know what supertype of `MyDate` the elements are, we cannot read the list as any specific type. Of course, the `List` must still hold some type of `Object`, so we can always read the lower bounded list as type `Object` through the wildcard. The type `Object` is the default upper bound:

```
Object obj = listAssignableMyDate.get( 0 ); // read as Object
```

Whew. Well, having gone through that explanation, we can now sum it up concisely in an easy-to-remember rule:

> Wildcard instantiations of generic types can be read as their upper bound and written as their lower bound.

To elaborate: all wildcard instantiations have an upper bound of `Object` even if none other is specified, so all wildcard instantiations can at least be read as type `Object`. But not all wildcards have a lower bound. Only those using the `super` construct have a lower bound and so only those wildcard instantiations can be written as a type more specific than `Object`.

<?>, <Object>, and the Raw Type

We've covered a lot of ground and the semantics can be a bit hard to follow. Let's exercise our knowledge by reviewing a few cases that may or may not have similarities.

Natural questions to ask are, What good is the unbounded wildcard anyway? Why not just use the raw type? How do unbounded wildcard instantiation and raw types compare? The first difference is that the compiler will issue unchecked warnings when we use methods of the raw type. But that's superficial. Why is the compiler warning us? It's because it cannot stop us from abusing our raw type by foisting the wrong type of objects on it. Using an unbounded wildcard is like putting on boxing gloves and saying that we want to play by the rules. Doing so comes at a cost. The compiler guarantees that we are safe by allowing us only the operations that it knows are safe—namely, reading as type Object (the upper bound of everything). The compiler does not let us write to an unbounded wildcard at all. So why use the unbounded wildcard? To play by the rules of generics and guarantee that we don't do anything unsafe.

Next, we can knock down any notion that an unbounded wildcard instantiation is similar to an instantiation on the type Object. Remember that a List<?> holds *some* instantiation of List. It could be a List<Date> for all we know. But a List<Object> is actually a list that holds concrete Object types. The List<Object> can be read and written as Object. The List<?> can only be read (not written) and only read as Object in a degenerate sense. The elements of List<?> are actually all of some unknown type. The elements of the unknown type list all have a common supertype that could be Object or some other common type that is more restrictive than Object. The knowledge of what "could be" in the List<?> doesn't do much for us in practice, but means something completely different from List<Object>.

Finally, let's round out the comparisons by asking how List<Object> and the raw type compare. Now we're onto something. In fact, the raw type after erasure *is* effectively List<Object> as you'll recall. But in this case, we're telling the compiler that this is OK. Here, we are asking for a type with elements that can hold any type safely and the compiler obliges. The answer to the question of how List<Object> and the raw type List compare is that List<Object> is the "generic safe" version of the raw type of yesterday.

Wildcard Type Relationships

Before we leave our wild discussion of wildcard types, let's return one more time to the notion of wildcard type instantiations as types in the Java type system. Earlier in this chapter, we described how regular concrete instantiations of generic types are related by virtue of their "base" generic type inheritance, only with the proviso that their type parameters are exactly the same. Later, we tried to instill the idea that wildcard instantiations add an inheritance relationship to the type parameters, which is the other half of the generic instantiation. Now, we'll bring the two together. Things can get arcane pretty quickly, but the simple cases are easy to swallow.

The question is, if we have two different wildcard instantiations of a type or related types, how, if at all, are they related? For example, can an unbounded wildcard be assigned a value with a more restrictive bound because it can hold any instantiation?

```
List< ? extends Date > dateLists = ...;
List< ? >  anylists;
anyLists = dateLists; // Ok!
```

The answer is yes. For purposes of assignability, wildcard instantiations can be considered as types with possible supertype or subtype relationships determined by their bounds. Let's spell out the unbounded wildcard instantiation as it really is, an instantiation with an upper bound of `Object`:

```
List< ? extends Date > dateLists = ...;
List< ? extends Object >  objectLists;
objectLists = dateLists; // Ok!
```

The rule is that if the "base" generic, raw type is assignable and the bounds of the wildcard instantiation are also assignable, the overall types are assignable. Let's look at another example:

```
List< ? extends Integer > intLists = ...;
Collection< ? extends Number > numCollections;
numCollections = intLists; // Ok!
```

What this effectively says is that some `List` of `Integer` types can be treated as some `Collection` of `Number` types through the wildcard instantiation. If you think about it, you'll see that there is no conflict here. A `List` is certainly a `Collection`. And all we're doing is widening the type by which we can read the elements from `Integer` to `Number`. In neither case could we have written to the collection via the wildcard instantiation anyway.

What all this ultimately means is that with the introduction of wildcard instantiations, the type relationships of Java generic classes become two-dimensional. There is the raw type relationship to consider and then the wildcard parameter relationship. In fact, if you consider that generic classes may have more than one type parameter, the relationships can get even more complicated (*N*-dimensional). Fortunately, none of this comes up very often in the real world.

Generic Methods

Thus far in this chapter, we've talked about generic types and the implementation of generic classes. Now, we're going to look at a different kind of generic animal: *generic methods*. Generic methods essentially do for individual methods what type parameters do for generic classes. But as we'll see, generic methods are smarter and can figure out their parameter types from their usage context without having to be explicitly parameterized. (In reality, of course, it is the compiler that does this.) Generic methods can appear in any class (not just generic classes) and are very useful for a wide variety of applications.

First, let's quickly review the way that we've seen regular methods interact with generic types. We've seen that generic classes can contain methods that use type variables in their arguments and return types in order to adapt themselves to the parameterization of the class. We've also mentioned that generic types themselves can be used in most of the places that any other type can be used. So methods of generic or nongeneric classes can use generic types as argument and return types as well. Here are examples of those usages:

```
// Not generic methods

class GenericClass< T > {
     // method using generic class parameter type
    public void T cache( T entry ) { ... }
}
class RegularClass {
     // method using concrete generic type
    public List<Date> sortDates( List<Date> dates ) { ... }
    // method using wildcard generic type
    public List<?> reverse( List<?> dates ) { ... }
}
```

The `cache()` method in `GenericClass` accepts an argument of the parameter type `T` and also returns a value of type `T`. The `sortDates()` method, which appears in the nongeneric example class, works with a concrete generic type, and the `reverse()` method works with a wildcard instantiation of a generic type. These are examples of methods that work with generics, but they are not true generic methods.

Generic Methods Introduced

Like generic classes, generic methods have a parameter type declaration using the `<>` syntax. This syntax appears before the return type of the method:

```
// generic method
<T> T cache( T entry ) { ... }
```

This `cache()` method looks very much like our earlier example, except that it has its own parameter type declaration that defines the type variable `T`. This method is a generic method and can appear in either a generic or nongeneric class. The scope of `T` is limited to the method `cache()` and hides any definition of `T` in any enclosing generic class. As with generic classes, the type `T` can have bounds:

```
<T extends Entry & Cacheable > T cache( T entry ) { ... }
```

Unlike a generic class, it does not have to be instantiated with a specific parameter type for `T` before it is used. Instead, it *infers* the parameter type `T` from the type of its argument, `entry`. For example:

```
BlogEntry newBlogEntry = ...;
NewspaperEntry newNewspaperEntry = ...;

BlogEntry oldEntry = cache( newBlogEntry );
NewspaperEntry old = cache( newNewspaperEntry );
```

Here, our generic method `cache()` inferred the type `BlogEntry` (which we'll presume for the sake of the example is a type of `Entry` and `Cacheable`). `BlogEntry` became the type `T` of the return type and may have been used elsewhere internally by the method. In the next case, the `cache()` method was used on a different type of `Entry` and was able to return the new type in exactly the same way. That's what's powerful about generic methods: the ability to infer a parameter type from their usage context. We'll go into detail about that next.

Another difference with generic class components is that generic methods may be static:

```
class MathUtils {
    public static <T extends Number> T max( T x, T y ) { ... }
}
```

Constructors for classes are essentially methods, too, and follow the same rules as generic methods, minus the return type.

Type Inference from Arguments

In the previous section, we saw a method infer its type from an argument:

```
<T> T cache( T entry ) { ... }
```

But what if there is more than one argument? We saw just that situation in our last snippet, the static generic method `max( x, y )`. All looks well when we give it two identical types:

```
Integer max = MathUtils.max( new Integer(1), new Integer( 2 ) ) ;
```

But what does it make of the arguments in this invocation?

```
MathUtils.max( new Integer(1), new Float( 2 ) ) ;
```

In this case, the Java compiler does something really smart. It climbs up the argument type parent classes, looking for the *nearest common supertype*. Java also identifies the *nearest common interfaces* implemented by both of the types. It identifies that both the `Integer` and the `Float` types are subtypes of the `Number` type. It also recognizes that each of these implements (a certain generic instantiation of) the `Comparable` interface. Java then effectively makes this combination of types the parameter type of `T` for this method invocation. The resulting type is, to use the syntax of bounds, `Number &`

`Comparable`. What this means to us is that the result type `T` is assignable to anything matching that particular combination of types.

```
Number max = MathUtils.max( new Integer(1), new Float( 2 ) );
Comparable max = MathUtils.max( new Integer(1), new Float( 2 ) );
```

In English, this statement says that we can work with our `Integer` and our `Float` at the same time only if we think of them as `Numbers` or `Comparables`, which makes sense. The return type has become a new type, which is effectively a `Number` that also implements the `Comparable` interface.

This same inference logic works with any number of arguments. But to be useful, the arguments really have to share some important common supertype or interface. If they don't have anything in common, the result will be their de facto common ancestor, the `Object` type. For example, the nearest common supertype of a `String` and a `List` is `Object` along with the `Serializeable` interface. There's not much a method could do with a type lacking real bounds anyway.

Type Inference from Assignment Context

We've seen a generic method infer its parameter type from its argument types. But what if the type variable isn't used in any of the arguments or the method has no arguments? Suppose the method only has a parametric return type:

```
<T> T foo() { ... }
```

You might guess that this is an error because the compiler would appear to have no way of determining what type we want. But it's not! The Java compiler is smart enough to look at the context in which the method is called. Specifically, if the result of the method is assigned to a variable, the compiler tries to make the type of that variable the parameter type. Here's an example. We'll make a factory for our `Trap` objects:

```
<T> Trap<T> makeTrap() { return new Trap<T>(); }

// usage
Trap<Mouse> mouseTrap = makeTrap();
Trap<Bear> bearTrap = makeTrap();
```

The compiler has, as if by magic, determined what kind of instantiation of `Trap` we want based on the assignment context.

Before you get too excited about the possibilities, there's not much you can do with a plain type parameter in the body of that method. For example, we can't create instances of any particular concrete type `T`, so this limits the usefulness of factories. About all we can do is the sort of thing shown here, where we create instances of generics parameterized correctly for the context.

Furthermore, the inference only works on assignment to a variable. Java does not try to guess the parameter type based on the context if the method call is used in other ways, such as to produce an argument to a method or as the value of a return statement from a method. In those cases, the inferred type defaults to type `Object`. (See the section "Explicit Type Invocation" for a solution.)

Explicit Type Invocation

Although it should not be needed often, a syntax does exist for invoking a generic method with specific parameter types. The syntax is a bit awkward and involves a class or instance object prefix, followed by the familiar angle bracket type list, placed before the actual method invocation. Here are some examples:

```
Integer i = MathUtilities.<Integer>max( 42,  42 );
String s = fooObject.<String>foo( "foo" );
String s = this.<String>foo( "foo" );
```

The prefix must be a class or object instance containing the method. One situation where you'd need to use explicit type invocation is if you are calling a generic method that infers its type from the assignment context, but you are not assigning the value to a variable directly. For example, if you wanted to pass the result of our `makeTrap()` method as a parameter to another method, it would otherwise default to `Object`.

Wildcard Capture

Generic methods can do one more trick for us involving taming wildcard instantiations of generic types. The term *wildcard capture* refers to the fact that generic methods can work with arguments whose type is a wildcard instantiation of a type, just as if the type were known:

```
<T> Set<T> listToSet( List<T> list ) {
    Set<T> set = new HashSet<T>();
    set.addAll( list );
    return set;
}

// usage
List<?> list = new ArrayList<Date>();
Set<?> set = listToSet( list );
```

The result of these examples is that we converted an unknown instantiation of `List` to an unknown instantiation of `Set`. The type variable `T` represents the actual type of the argument, `list`, for purposes of the method body. The wildcard instantiation must match any bounds of the method parameter type. But because we can work with the type variable only through its bounds types, the compiler is free to refer to it by this new name, `T`, as if it were a known type. That may not seem very interesting, but it is useful because it allows methods that accept wildcard instantiations of types to delegate their work to other generic methods.

Another way to look at this is that generic methods are a more powerful alternative to methods using wildcard instantiations of types. We'll do a little comparison next.

Wildcard Types Versus Generic Methods

You'll recall that trying to work with an object through a wildcard instantiation of its generic type limits us to "reading" the object. We cannot "write" types to the object because its parameter type is unknown. In contrast, because generic methods can infer or "capture" an actual type for their arguments, they allow us to do a lot more with broad ranges of types than we could with wildcard instantiations alone.

For example, suppose we wanted to write a utility method that swaps the first two elements of a list. Using wildcards, we'd like to write something like this:

```
// Bad implementation
List<?> swap( List<?> list ) {
    Object tmp = list.get(0);
    list.set( 0, list.get(1) ); // error, can't write
    list.set( 1, tmp ); // error, can't write
    return list;
}
```

But we are not allowed to call the `set()` method of our list because we don't know what type it actually holds. We are really stuck and there isn't much we can do. But the corresponding generic method gives us a real type to hang our hat:

```
<T> List<T> swapGeneric( List<T> list ) {
    T tmp = list.get( 0 );
    list.set( 0, list.get(1) );
    list.set( 1, tmp );
    return list;
}
```

Here, we are able to declare a variable of the correct (inferred) type and write using the `set()` methods appropriately. It would seem that generic methods are the only way to go here. But there is a third path. Wildcard capture, as described in the previous section, allows us to delegate our wildcard version of the method to our actual generic method and use it as if the type were inferred, even though it's open-ended:

```
List<?> swap( List<?> list ) {
    return swapGeneric( list ); // delegate to generic form
}
```

Here, we delegated to the generic version.

Arrays of Parameterized Types

There is one place where we haven't yet considered how generic types affect the Java language: array types. After everything we've seen, it would seem natural to expect that arrays of generic types would come along for the ride. But as we'll see, Java has a schizophrenic relationship with arrays of parameterized types.

The first thing we need to do is recall how arrays work for regular Java types. An array is a kind of built-in collection of some base type of element. Furthermore, array types (including all multidimensional variations of the array) are true types in the Java language and are represented at runtime by unique class types. This is where the trouble begins. Although arrays in Java act a lot like generic collections (they change their APIs to adopt a particular type for "reading" and "writing"), they do not behave like Java generics with respect to their type relationships. As we saw in Chapter 6, arrays exist in the Java class hierarchy stemming from `Object` and extending down parallel branches with the plain Java objects.

Arrays are *covariant subtypes* of other types of arrays, which means that, unlike concrete generic types, although they change their method signatures, they are still related to their parents. This means that `Strings []` in Java is a subtype of `Object []`. This brings up the aliasing problem that we mentioned earlier. An array of `Strings` can be aliased as an array of `Objects` and we can attempt to put things into it illegally that won't be noticed until runtime:

```
String [] strings = new String[5];
Object [] objects = strings;
objects[0] = new Date(); // Runtime ArrayStoreException!
```

To prevent disaster, Java must check every array assignment for the correct type at runtime. But recall that generic types do not have real representations at runtime; there is only the raw type. So Java would have no way to know the difference between a `Trap<Mouse>` and a `Trap<Bear>` element in an array once the array was aliased as, say, an `Object []`. For this reason, Java does not allow you to create arrays of generic types—at least not concrete ones. (More on that later in this chapter.)

Using Array Types

Now, because we just said that Java won't let you make any of these arrays, you'd expect that would be pretty much the end of the story. But no! Even though we don't have real array implementations that perform the needed runtime behavior, Java allows us to declare the array type anyway. The catch is that you must break type safety in order to use them by using an array of the raw type as their implementation:

```
Trap<Mouse> [] tma = new Trap[10]; // unchecked warning
Trap<Mouse> tm = new Trap<Mouse>();
tma[0] = tm;
Trap<Mouse> again = tma[0];
```

Here, we declared an array of a generic type, `Trap<Mouse>`. Assigning any value (other than `null`) to this variable, `tma`, results in an unchecked warning from the compiler at the point of the assignment.

What we are effectively telling the compiler here is to trust us to make sure that the array contains only the correct generic types and asking it to allow us to use it thereafter as if it were checked. We do not get warnings at each usage as we would with a raw type, only at the point where we assign the array. The catch is that the compiler can't prevent us from abusing the array. The unchecked warning at the point where we assign the array is just a representative warning that reminds us that it's possible to abuse the array later.

What Good Are Arrays of Generic Types?

Why does Java even let us declare arrays of generic types? One important usage is that it allows generic types to be used in variable-length argument methods. For example:

```
void useLists( List<String> ... lists ) {
        List<String> ls0 = lists[0];
}
```

Another answer is that it's an escape hatch to preserve our ability to use arrays when necessary. You might want to do this for at least two reasons. First, arrays are faster than collections in many cases. The Java runtime is very good at optimizing array access, and sometimes it just might be worth it to you to eat the compiler warning to get the benefits. Second, there is the issue of interfacing generic code to legacy code in which only the Javadoc and your faith in the developer are your guarantees as to the contents. By assigning raw arrays to generic instantiations, we can at least ensure that in simple usage we don't abuse the types in the new code.

Wildcards in Array Types

In general, wildcard instantiations of generics can be used as the base type for arrays in the same way that concrete instantiations can. Let's look at an example:

```
ArrayList<?>[] arrayOfArrayLists = ...;
```

This type declaration is an array of unbounded wildcard instantiations of `ArrayList`. Each element of the array can hold an instance of the wildcard type, meaning in this case that each element of the array could hold a different instantiation of `ArrayList`. For example:

```
arrayOfArrayLists[0] = new ArrayList<Date>();
arrayOfArrayLists[1] = new ArrayList<String>();
```

There is also a secret surprise that we are going to spring on you relating to wildcard types in arrays. Although we said that Java won't let us create arrays of generic types, there is an exception to the rule. Java does allow us to create arrays of unbounded wildcard instantiations. Here are two examples:

```
ArrayList<?>[] arrayOfArrayLists = new ArrayList<?>[10];
arrayOfArrayLists[0] = new ArrayList<Date>();
```

```
Trap<?> [] arrayOfTraps = new Trap<?>[10];
arrayOfTraps[0] = new Trap<Mouse>();
```

Here, we not only declared two arrays of wildcard instantiations, but we allocated the arrays as well! The trick is that the arrays must be of the unbounded wildcard type. Why does this work? Because each element in the unbounded wildcard instantiation of the array can hold any instantiation, no runtime check of the generic portion of the type is necessary at runtime. Any instantiation of `ArrayList` is assignable to the element of type `ArrayList<?>`, so only the check of the raw type is required.

The term *reifiable type* is used to refer to any type that is unchanged by erasure. This includes plain Java concrete types, primitives, and unbounded wildcard instantiations. Reifiable types are kind of like the real people in *The Matrix*: they still exist when unplugged from the simulation.

Case Study: The Enum Class

If you take a look at the definition of the `java.lang.Enum` class in Java 5 or later, you'll see a rather bizarre-looking generic type declaration:

```
Enum< E extends Enum<E> > { ... }
```

In trying to parse this, you may be hampered by two thoughts, which we'll try to dispel right away. First, upon quick inspection this may appear to be recursive. The type variable `E` seems to be defined as something that's not yet finished being defined. But it's not really. We often have mathematical equations of the form `x = function( x )` and they are not recursive. What they really call for is a special value of `x` that satisfies the condition. Next, although it's pretty clear that `E` is a subtype of some formulation of the generic `Enum` type, you may jump to the conclusion that `E` itself must be a generic type. Remember that concrete types can extend generics just as well as generics can.

With these thoughts in mind, let's hunt for some arrangement that satisfies these bounds. Let's focus only on the bound for a moment:

```
E extends Enum<E>
```

`E` is a subclass of some parameterization of `Enum` and, in particular, the parameterization of `Enum` on the subclass type itself. To say this again, what it does is to require that any invocations of the `Enum` type are by subclasses of some parameterization of the `Enum` type. And specifically, the parameterizations of the `Enum` type supply their own type as the type parameter to their parent, `Enum`. What kind of class satisfies this condition?

```
class Foo extends Enum<Foo> { }
```

This Foo class does. The declaration of Foo, in fact, reads just as the bound does. Foo is a plain concrete type that extends Enum parameterized by its own type.[4]

What does this accomplish exactly? The first implication of this arrangement is that Enum can be instantiated only by subclasses of itself. Next, we have the condition that the Enum must be instantiated with the child type as its parameter type. This means that any methods of the parent Enum class that refer to the type variable E will now refer to the *child* type. This peculiar bound has guaranteed that child types customize their parent with their own type. In fact, this is exactly what the Enum class in Java needs in order to make enums work. The compareTo() method of a Java enum refers to the type variable and is intended to be applicable only to other instances of the specific child enum type:

```
public int compareTo( E e ) { ... }
```

For example, a Dog enum type should be able to compare only types of Dog and comparing a Dog with a Cat should produce a compile-time error. The bound accomplishes just that by adapting the compareTo() method to the Dog type:

```
class Dog extends Enum<Dog> { ... }
```

Normally, a nonfinal base class, having no way to know what children it may have in the future, could only refer to its own type as a general supertype for all of the children when it wants to work with others of its own kind. Methods of a nongeneric Enum class could only supply methods that work on any Enum. But through the magic of generics, we can effectively change the API of the class based on how it is invoked with parameters. In this case, we have arranged that all subclasses must supply themselves as the parameter for the base class, tailoring its methods to themselves and pushing the base type down a generation.

Case Study: The sort() Method

Poking around in the java.util.Collections class, we find all kinds of static utility methods for working with collections. Among them is this goody—the static generic method sort():

```
<T extends Comparable<? super T>> void sort( List<T> list ) { ... }
```

Another nut for us to crack. Let's focus on the last part of the bound:

```
Comparable<? super T>
```

This is a wildcard instantiation of the Comparable interface, so we can read the extends as implements if it helps. Comparable holds a compareTo() method for some

4. In real life, Java doesn't let us extend the Enum type; that's reserved for the enum keyword and the compiler. But the structure is as shown.

parameter type. A `Comparable<String>` means that the `compareTo()` method takes type `String`. Therefore, `Comparable<? super T>` is the set of instantiations of `Comparable` on `T` and all of its superclasses. A `Comparable<T>` suffices and, at the other end, so does a `Comparable<Object>`. What this means in English is that the elements must be comparable to their own type or some supertype of their own type. This is sufficient to ensure that the elements can all be compared to one another, but not as restrictive as saying that they must all implement the `compareTo()` method themselves. Some of the elements may inherit the `Comparable` interface from a parent class that knows how to compare only to a supertype of `T`, and that is exactly what is allowed here.

Conclusion

Java generics are a very powerful and useful addition to the language. Although some of the details we delved into later in this chapter may seem daunting, the common usage is very simple and compelling: generics make collections better. As you begin to write more code using generics, you will find that your code becomes more readable and more understandable. Generics make explicit what previously had to be inferred from usage.

CHAPTER 9
Threads

We take for granted that modern computer systems can manage many applications and operating system (OS) tasks running concurrently and make it appear that all the software is running simultaneously. While most systems today do have multiple processors and some processors can perform tricks to gain some degree of parallelism, for the most part a processor can only really handle one job at at time and what we are seeing is sleight of hand in the operating system, which juggles applications and turns its attention from one to the next so quickly that they appear to run at once.

In the old days, the unit of concurrency for such systems was the application or *process*. To the OS, a process was more or less a black box that decided what to do on its own. If an application required greater concurrency, it could get it only by running multiple processes and communicating between them, but this was a heavyweight approach and not very elegant. Later, the concept of *threads* was introduced. Threads provide fine-grained concurrency within a process under the application's own control. Threads have existed for a long time, but have historically been tricky to use. In Java, support for threading is built into the language, making it easier to work with threads. The Java concurrency utilities address common patterns and practices in multithreaded applications and raise them to the level of tangible Java APIs. Collectively, this means that Java is a language that supports threading both natively and at a high level. It also means that Java's APIs take full advantage of threading, so it's important that you gain some degree of familiarity with these concepts early in your exploration of Java. Not all developers will need to write applications that explicitly use threads or concurrency, but most will use some feature that is impacted by them.

Threads are integral to the design of many Java APIs, especially those involved in client-side applications, graphics, and sound. For example, when we look at GUI programming later in this book, you'll see that a component's `paint()` method isn't called directly by the application but rather by a separate drawing thread within the Java runtime system. At any given time, many such background threads may be performing activities in parallel with your application. On the server side, writing code that does explicit thread handling is less common and actively discouraged in the context of application servers and web applications. In those scenarios, the server environment should control the allocation of time. However, Java threads are there, servicing every request and running your application components. It's important to understand how your code fits into that environment.

In this chapter, we'll talk about writing applications that create and use their own threads explicitly. We'll talk about the low-level thread support built into the Java language first and then discuss the `java.util.concurrent` thread utilities package in detail at the end of this chapter.

Introducing Threads

Conceptually, a *thread* is a flow of control within a program. A thread is similar to the more familiar notion of a *process*, except that threads within the same application are much more closely related and share much of the same state. It's kind of like a golf course, which many golfers use at the same time. The threads cooperate to share a working area. They have access to the same objects, including static and instance variables, within their application. However, threads have their own copies of local variables, just as players share the golf course but do not share some personal items like clubs and balls.

Multiple threads in an application have the same problems as the golfers—in a word, synchronization. Just as you can't have two sets of players blindly playing the same green at the same time, you can't have several threads trying to access the same variables without some kind of coordination. Someone is bound to get hurt. A thread can reserve the right to use an object until it's finished with its task, just as a golf party gets exclusive rights to the green until it's done. And a thread that is more important can raise its priority, asserting its right to play through.

The devil is in the details, of course, and those details have historically made threads difficult to use. Fortunately, Java makes creating, controlling, and coordinating threads simpler by integrating some of these concepts directly into the language.

It is common to stumble over threads when you first work with them because creating a thread exercises many of your new Java skills all at once. You can avoid confusion by remembering that two players are always involved in running a thread: a Java language `Thread` object that represents the thread itself and an arbitrary target object that contains the method that the thread is to execute. Later, you will see that it is possible to play some sleight of hand and combine these two roles, but that special case just changes the packaging, not the relationship.

The Thread Class and the Runnable Interface

All execution in Java is associated with a `Thread` object, beginning with a "main" thread that is started by the Java VM to launch your application. A new thread is born when we create an instance of the `java.lang.Thread` class. The `Thread` object represents a real thread in the Java interpreter and serves as a handle for controlling and coordinating its execution. With it, we can start the thread, wait for it to complete, cause it to sleep for a time, or interrupt its activity. The constructor for the `Thread` class accepts information about where the thread should begin its execution. Conceptually, we would like to simply tell it what method to run, but because there are no pointers to methods in Java (not in this sense anyway), we can't specify one directly. Instead, we have to take a short detour and use the `java.lang.Runnable` interface to create or mark an object that contains a "runnable" method. `Runnable` defines a single, general-purpose `run()` method:

```
public interface Runnable {
     abstract public void run();
}
```

Every thread begins its life by executing the `run()` method in a `Runnable` object, which is the "target object" that was passed to the thread's constructor. The `run()` method can contain any code, but it must be public, take no arguments, have no return value, and throw no checked exceptions.

Any class that contains an appropriate `run()` method can declare that it implements the `Runnable` interface. An instance of this class is then a runnable object that can serve as the target of a new thread. If you don't want to put the `run()` method directly in your object (and very often you don't), you can always make an adapter class that serves as the `Runnable` for you. The adapter's `run()` method can then call any method it wants after the thread is started. We'll show examples of these options later.

Creating and starting threads

A newly born thread remains idle until we give it a figurative slap on the bottom by calling its `start()` method. The thread then wakes up and proceeds to execute the `run()` method of its target object. `start()` can be called only once in the lifetime of a thread. Once a thread starts, it continues running until the target object's `run()` method returns (or throws an unchecked exception of some kind). The `start()` method has a sort of evil twin method called `stop()`, which kills the thread permanently. However, this method is deprecated and should no longer be used. We'll explain why and give some examples of a better way to stop your threads later in this chapter. We will also look at some other methods you can use to control a thread's progress while it is running.

Let's look at an example. The following class, `Animation`, implements a `run()` method to drive its drawing loop:

```
class Animation implements Runnable {
    boolean animate = true;

    public void run() {
        while ( animate ) {
            // draw Frames
            ...
        }
    }
}
```

To use it, we create a Thread object, passing it an instance of Animation as its target object, and invoke its start() method. We can perform these steps explicitly:

```
Animation happy = new Animation("Mr. Happy");
Thread myThread = new Thread( happy );
myThread.start();
```

We created an instance of our Animation class and passed it as the argument to the constructor for myThread. When we call the start() method, myThread begins to execute Animation's run() method. Let the show begin!

This situation is not terribly object-oriented. More often, we want an object to handle its own threads, as shown in Figure 9-1, which depicts a Runnable object that creates and starts its own thread. We'll show our Animation class performing these actions in its constructor, although in practice it might be better to place them in a more explicit controller method (e.g., startAnimation()):

```
n
    class Animation implements Runnable {
        Thread myThread;
        Animation (String name) {
            myThread = new Thread( this );
            myThread.start();
        }
        ...
    }
```

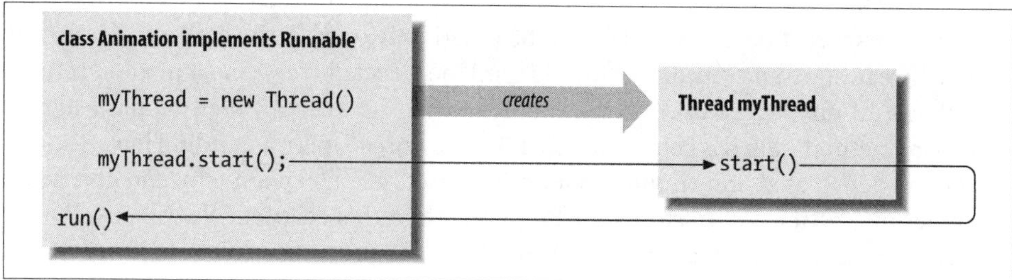

Figure 9-1. Interaction between Animation and its thread

In this case, the argument that we pass to the Thread constructor is this, the current object (which is a Runnable). We keep the Thread reference in the instance variable myThread in case we want to interrupt the show or exercise some other kind of control later.

A natural-born thread

The Runnable interface lets us make an arbitrary object the target of a thread, as we did in the previous example. This is the most important general usage of the Thread class. In most situations in which you need to use threads, you'll create a class (possibly a simple adapter class) that implements the Runnable interface.

However, we'd be remiss not to show you the other technique for creating a thread. Another design option is to make our target class a subclass of a type that is already runnable. As it turns out, the Thread class itself conveniently implements the Runnable interface; it has its own run() method, which we can override directly to do our bidding:

```
class Animation extends Thread {
    boolean animate = true;

    public void run() {
        while ( animate ) {
            // draw Frames
            ...
        }
    }
}
```

The skeleton of our Animation class looks much the same as before, except that our class is now a subclass of Thread. To go along with this scheme, the default constructor of the Thread class makes itself the default target—that is, by default, the Thread executes its own run() method when we call the start() method, as shown in Figure 9-2. Now our subclass can just override the run() method in the Thread class. (Thread itself defines an empty run() method.)

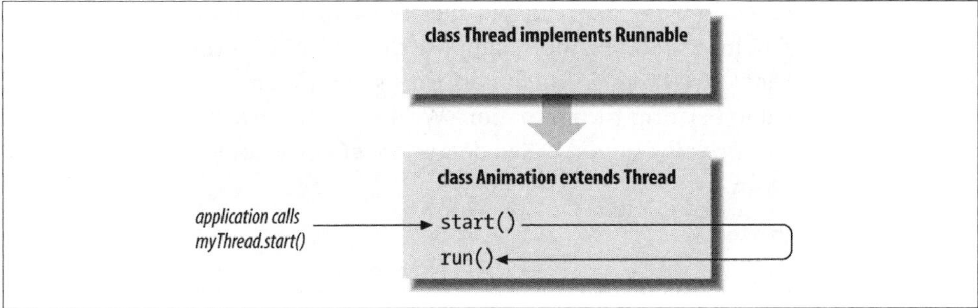

Figure 9-2. Animation as a subclass of Thread

Next, we create an instance of Animation and call its start() method (which it also inherited from Thread):

```
Animation bouncy = new Animation("Bouncy");
bouncy.start();
```

Alternatively, we can have the Animation object start its thread when it is created, as before:

```
class Animation extends Thread {

    Animation (String name) {
        start();
    }
    ...
}
```

Here, our Animation object just calls its own start() method when an instance is created. (It's probably better form to start and stop our objects explicitly after they're created rather than starting threads as a hidden side effect of object creation, but this serves the example well.)

Subclassing Thread may seem like a convenient way to bundle a thread and its target run() method. However, this approach often isn't the best design. If you subclass Thread to implement a thread, you are saying you need a new type of object that is a kind of Thread, which exposes all of the public API of the Thread class. While there is something satisfying about taking an object that's primarily concerned with performing a task and making it a Thread, the actual situations where you'll want to create a subclass of Thread should not be very common. In most cases, it is more natural to let the requirements of your program dictate the class structure and use Runnables to connect the execution and logic of your program.

Using an adapter

Finally, as we have suggested, we can build an adapter class to give us more control over how to structure the code. It is particularly convenient to create an anonymous inner class that implements Runnable and invokes an arbitrary method in our object. This almost gives the feel of starting a thread and specifying an arbitrary method to run, as if we had method pointers. For example, suppose that our Animation class provides a method called startAnimating(), which performs setup (loads the images, etc.) and then starts a thread to perform the animation. We'll say that the actual guts of the animation loop are in a private method called drawFrames(). We could use an adapter to run drawFrames() for us:

```
class Animation {

    public void startAnimating() {
        // do setup, load images, etc.
        ...
```

```
            // start a drawing thread
            Thread myThread = new Thread ( new Runnable() {
               public void run() { drawFrames(); }
            } );
            myThread.start();
        }

        private void drawFrames() {
            // do animation ...
        }
    }
```

In this code, the anonymous inner class implementing `Runnable` is generated for us by the compiler. We create a thread with this anonymous object as its target and have its `run()` method call our `drawFrames()` method. We have avoided implementing a generic `run()` method in our application code at the expense of generating an extra class.

Note that we could be even more terse in the previous example by simply having our anonymous inner class extend `Thread` rather than implement `Runnable`. We could also start the thread without saving a reference to it if we won't be using it later:

```
    new Thread() {
       public void run() { drawFrames(); }
    }.start();
```

Controlling Threads

We have seen the `start()` method used to begin execution of a new thread. Several other instance methods let us explicitly control a thread's execution:

- The static `Thread.sleep()` method causes the currently executing thread to wait for a designated period of time, without consuming much (or possibly any) CPU time.
- The methods `wait()` and `join()` coordinate the execution of two or more threads. We'll discuss them in detail when we talk about thread synchronization later in this chapter.
- The `interrupt()` method wakes up a thread that is sleeping in a `sleep()` or `wait()` operation or is otherwise blocked on a long I/O operation.[1]

Deprecated methods

We should also mention three deprecated thread control methods: `stop()`, `suspend()`, and `resume()`. The `stop()` method complements `start()`; it destroys the thread. `start()` and the deprecated `stop()` method can be called only once in the thread's

1. `interrupt()` has not worked consistently in all Java implementations historically.

lifecycle. By contrast, the deprecated `suspend()` and `resume()` methods were used to arbitrarily pause and then restart the execution of a thread.

Although these deprecated methods still exist in the latest version of Java (and will probably be there forever), they shouldn't be used in new code development. The problem with both `stop()` and `suspend()` is that they seize control of a thread's execution in an uncoordinated, harsh way. This makes programming difficult; it's not always easy for an application to anticipate and properly recover from being interrupted at an arbitrary point in its execution. Moreover, when a thread is seized using one of these methods, the Java runtime system must release all its internal locks used for thread synchronization. This can cause unexpected behavior and, in the case of `suspend()`, can easily lead to deadlock.

A better way to affect the execution of a thread—which requires just a bit more work on your part—is by creating some simple logic in your thread's code to use monitor variables (flags), possibly in conjunction with the `interrupt()` method, which allows you to wake up a sleeping thread. In other words, you should cause your thread to stop or resume what it is doing by asking it nicely rather than by pulling the rug out from under it unexpectedly. The thread examples in this book use this technique in one way or another.

The sleep() method

We often need to tell a thread to sit idle, or "sleep," for a fixed period of time. While a thread is asleep, or otherwise blocked from input of some kind, it doesn't consume CPU time or compete with other threads for processing. For this, we can call the static method `Thread.sleep()`, which affects the currently executing thread. The call causes the thread to go idle for a specified number of milliseconds:

```
try {
    // The current thread
    Thread.sleep( 1000 );
} catch ( InterruptedException e ) {
    // someone woke us up prematurely
}
```

The `sleep()` method may throw an `InterruptedException` if it is interrupted by another thread via the `interrupt()` method. As you see in the previous code, the thread can catch this exception and take the opportunity to perform some action—such as checking a variable to determine whether or not it should exit—or perhaps just perform some housekeeping and then go back to sleep.

The join() method

Finally, if you need to coordinate your activities with another thread by waiting for it to complete its task, you can use the `join()` method. Calling a thread's `join()` method causes the caller to block until the target thread completes. Alternatively, you can poll the thread by calling `join()` with a number of milliseconds to wait. This is a very coarse form of thread synchronization. Later in this chapter, we'll look at a much more general and powerful mechanism for coordinating thread activity: `wait()`, `notify()`, and even higher-level APIs in the `java.util.concurrent` package.

The interrupt() method

Earlier, we described the `interrupt()` method as a way to wake up a thread that is idle in a `sleep()`, `wait()`, or lengthy I/O operation. Any thread that is not running continuously (not a "hard loop") must enter one of these states periodically and so this is intended to be a point where the thread can be flagged to stop. When a thread is interrupted, its *interrupt status* flag is set. This can happen at any time, whether the thread is idle or not. The thread can test this status with the `isInterrupted()` method. `isInterrupted(boolean)`, another form, accepts a Boolean value indicating whether or not to clear the interrupt status. In this way, a thread can use the interrupt status as a flag and a signal.

This is indeed the prescribed functionality of the method. However, historically, this has been a weak spot, and Java implementations have had trouble getting it to work correctly in all cases. In early Java VMs (prior to version 1.1), `interrupt` did not work at all. More recent versions still have problems with interrupting I/O calls. By an I/O call, we mean when an application is blocked in a `read()` or `write()` method, moving bytes to or from a source such as a file or the network. In this case, Java is supposed to throw an `InterruptedIOException` when the `interrupt()` is performed. However, this has never been reliable across all Java implementations. To address this in Java 1.4, a new I/O framework (`java.nio`) was introduced with one of its goals being to specifically address these problems. When the thread associated with an NIO operation is interrupted, the thread wakes up and the I/O stream (called a "channel") is automatically closed. (See Chapter 12 for more about the NIO package.)

Death of a Thread

A thread continues to execute until one of the following happens:

- It explicitly returns from its target `run()` method.
- It encounters an uncaught runtime exception.
- The evil and nasty deprecated `stop()` method is called.

What happens if none of these things occurs, and the `run()` method for a thread never terminates? The answer is that the thread can live on, even after what is ostensibly the part of the application that created it has finished. This means we have to be aware of how our threads eventually terminate, or an application can end up leaving orphaned threads that unnecessarily consume resources or keep the application alive when it would otherwise quit.

In many cases, we really want to create background threads that do simple, periodic tasks in an application. The `setDaemon()` method can be used to mark a thread as a daemon thread that should be killed and discarded when no other nondaemon application threads remain. Normally, the Java interpreter continues to run until all threads have completed. But when daemon threads are the only threads still alive, the interpreter will exit.

Here's a devilish example using daemon threads:

```
class Devil extends Thread {
    Devil() {
        setDaemon( true );
        start();
    }
    public void run() {
        // perform evil tasks
    }
}
```

In this example, the `Devil` thread sets its daemon status when it is created. If any `Devil` threads remain when our application is otherwise complete, the runtime system kills them for us. We don't have to worry about cleaning them up.

Daemon threads are primarily useful in standalone Java applications and in the implementation of server frameworks, but not in component applications such as applets. Since an applet runs inside another Java application, any daemon threads it creates can continue to live until the controlling application exits—probably not the desired effect. A browser or any other application can use `ThreadGroups` to contain all the threads created by subsystems of an application and then clean them up if necessary.

One final note about killing threads gracefully. A very common problem new developers encounter the first time they create an application using an AWT or Swing component is that their application never exits; the Java VM seems to hang indefinitely after everything is finished. When working with graphics, Java has created an AWT thread to process input and painting events. The AWT thread is not a daemon thread, so it doesn't exit automatically when other application threads have completed, and the developer must call `System.exit()` explicitly. (If you think about it, this makes sense. Because most GUI applications are event-driven and simply wait for user input, they would otherwise simply exit after their startup code completed.)

Threading an Applet

Applets are embeddable Java applications that are expected to start and stop themselves on command, possibly many times in their lifetime. A Java-enabled web browser normally starts an applet when the applet is displayed and stops it when the user moves to another page or (in theory) when the user scrolls the applet out of view. To conform to this API, we would like an applet to cease its nonessential activity when it is stopped and resume it when started again. We'll talk about applets in Chapter 23, but it's not really essential to know about them here. We'll just use this as a more realistic example and as a transition to talk about our next topic, synchronization.

In this section, we will build `UpdateApplet`, a simple base class for an applet that maintains a thread to automatically update its display at regular intervals. `UpdateApplet` handles the basic creation and termination of the thread in the Applet's `start()` and `stop()` methods:

```
public class UpdateApplet extends java.applet.Applet
    implements Runnable
{
    Thread thread;
    boolean running;
    int updateInterval = 1000;

    public void run() {
        while ( running )
        {
            repaint();
            try {
                Thread.sleep( updateInterval );
            } catch ( InterruptedException e ) {
                System.out.println("interrupted...");
                return;
            }
        }
    }

    public void start() {
        System.out.println("starting...");
        if ( !running ) // naive approach
        {
            running = true;
            thread = new Thread(this);
            thread.start();
        }
    }

    public void stop() {
        System.out.println("stopping...");
        thread.interrupt();
        running = false;
    }
}
```

`UpdateApplet` is a `Runnable` object that alternately sleeps and calls its `repaint()` method. (There's nothing to paint, though, so running this applet is kind of boring. Later we'll subclass it to implement a digital clock.) It has two other public methods: `start()` and `stop()`. These are methods of the `Applet` class we are overriding; don't confuse them with the similarly named methods of the `Thread` class. These `start()` and `stop()` methods are called by the web browser or applet viewer to tell the applet when it should and should not be running.

`UpdateApplet` illustrates an environmentally friendly way to deal with threads in a simple applet. `UpdateApplet` simply dismisses its thread each time the applet is stopped and recreates it if the applet is restarted. When `UpdateApplet`'s `start()` method is called, we first check to make sure there is no currently running thread by checking the `running` flag. We then create one to begin our execution. When our applet is subsequently asked to stop, we set the flag indicating that it should stop and make sure the thread is awake by invoking its `interrupt()` method. In this way, we are sure to catch the thread either at the beginning of its next iteration or when it goes to sleep.

With `UpdateApplet` doing all the work for us, we can create the world's simplest clock applet with just a few lines of code. Figure 9-3 shows our `Clock`.

Figure 9-3. The Clock applet

Here's the code:

```
//file: Clock.java
public class Clock extends UpdateApplet {
    public void paint( java.awt.Graphics g ) {
        g.drawString( new java.util.Date().toString(), 10, 25 );
   }
}
```

The `java.util.Date().toString()` method creates a string that contains the current time.

Issues Lurking

Our applet seems pretty straightforward and, in fact, works as advertised. But some things in it should concern us when we're thinking about threads. Let's look at that quick check of the `running` flag before we start our new thread:

```
if ( !running ) // naive approach
{
    running = true;
    ... /* start thread */
```

Now, an Applet's start() and stop() methods are guaranteed to be called in sequence and probably by the same controlling thread. As a result, this check for the existence of the running thread in start() may not seem necessary here. The stop() method should always be called before the start() method is invoked again. But, in the style of defensive programming the test seems like a good thing to do, right? That may be so, but, in general, it's not enough to prevent bad things from happening. The test may prevent a simple case of misaligned stop() and start() calls, but the bigger question lurking here is, What happens if start() and stop() were called repeatedly or in very quick succession in a multithreaded environment? In the extreme case, it would be possible for two threads to enter the test at about the same time and there is the chance that we could end up with multiple threads started and out of our control. What is needed is a real way to gain exclusive access to a resource (our flag) for a period of time. That's what synchronization is all about, and we'll cover it in detail in the next section and throughout the rest of this chapter.

With synchronization, we might also consider more complex scenarios for our applet, such as keeping our thread alive but dormant while the applet is stopped. This would allow us to preserve expensive setup like network connections and clean them up later if necessary.

Synchronization

Every thread has a mind of its own. Normally, a thread goes about its business without any regard for what other threads in the application are doing. Threads may be time-sliced, which means they can run in arbitrary spurts and bursts as directed by the operating system. On a multiprocessor system, it is even possible for many different threads to be running simultaneously on different CPUs. This section is about coordinating the activities of two or more threads so that they can work together and not collide in their use of the same variables and methods (coordinating their play on the golf course).

Java provides a few simple structures for synchronizing the activities of threads. They are all based on the concept of monitors, a widely used synchronization scheme. You don't have to know the details about how monitors work to be able to use them, but it may help you to have a picture in mind.

A monitor is essentially a lock. The lock is attached to a resource that many threads may need to access, but that should be accessed by only one thread at a time. It's very much like a restroom with a lock on the door; if it's unlocked, you can enter and lock the door while you are using it. If the resource is not being used, the thread can acquire the lock and access the resource. When the thread is done, it relinquishes the lock, just as you unlock the restroom door and leave it open for the next person. However, if another thread already has the lock for the resource, all other threads must wait until the current thread is done and has released the lock. This is just like when the restroom is occupied when you arrive: you have to wait until the current user is done and unlocks the door.

Fortunately, Java makes the process of synchronizing access to resources fairly easy. The language handles setting up and acquiring locks; all you need to do is specify the resources that require synchronization.

Serializing Access to Methods

The most common need for synchronization among threads in Java is to serialize their access to some resource (an object)—in other words, to make sure that only one thread at a time can manipulate an object or variable.[2] In Java, every object has an associated lock. To be more specific, every class and every instance of a class has its own lock. The `synchronized` keyword marks places where a thread must acquire the lock before proceeding.

For example, suppose we implemented a `SpeechSynthesizer` class that contains a `say()` method. We don't want multiple threads calling `say()` at the same time because we wouldn't be able to understand anything being said. So we mark the `say()` method as `synchronized`, which means that a thread must acquire the lock on the `SpeechSynthesizer` object before it can speak:

```
class SpeechSynthesizer {
    synchronized void say( String words ) {
        // speak
    }
}
```

Because `say()` is an instance method, a thread must acquire the lock on the `SpeechSynthesizer` instance it's using before it can invoke the `say()` method. When `say()` has completed, it gives up the lock, which allows the next waiting thread to acquire the lock and run the method. It doesn't matter whether the thread is owned by the `SpeechSynthesizer` itself or some other object; every thread must acquire the same lock, that of the `SpeechSynthesizer` instance. If `say()` were a class (static) method instead of an instance method, we could still mark it as `synchronized`. In this case, because no instance object is involved, the lock is on the class object itself.

Often, you want to synchronize multiple methods of the same class so that only one method modifies or examines parts of the class at a time. All static synchronized methods in a class use the same class object lock. By the same token, all instance methods in a class use the same instance object lock. In this way, Java can guarantee that only one of a set of synchronized methods is running at a time. For example, a `SpreadSheet` class might contain a number of instance variables that represent cell values as well as some methods that manipulate the cells in a row:

2. Don't confuse the term *serialize* in this context with Java object *serialization*, which is a mechanism for making objects persistent. The underlying meaning (to place one thing after another) does apply to both, however. In the case of object serialization, the object's data is laid out, byte for byte, in a certain order.

```
class SpreadSheet {
    int cellA1, cellA2, cellA3;

    synchronized int sumRow() {
        return cellA1 + cellA2 + cellA3;
    }

    synchronized void setRow( int a1, int a2, int a3 ) {
        cellA1 = a1;
        cellA2 = a2;
        cellA3 = a3;
    }
    ...
}
```

In this example, methods `setRow()` and `sumRow()` both access the cell values. You can see that problems might arise if one thread were changing the values of the variables in `setRow()` at the same moment another thread was reading the values in `sumRow()`. To prevent this, we have marked both methods as `synchronized`. When threads are synchronized, only one runs at a time. If a thread is in the middle of executing `setRow()` when another thread calls `sumRow()`, the second thread waits until the first one finishes executing `setRow()` before it runs `sumRow()`. This synchronization allows us to preserve the consistency of the `SpreadSheet`. The best part is that all this locking and waiting is handled by Java; it's invisible to the programmer.

In addition to synchronizing entire methods, the `synchronized` keyword can be used in a special construct to guard arbitrary blocks of code. In this form, it also takes an explicit argument that specifies the object for which it is to acquire a lock:

```
synchronized ( myObject ) {
    // Functionality that needs exclusive access to resources
}
```

This code block can appear in any method. When it is reached, the thread has to acquire the lock on `myObject` before proceeding. In this way, we can synchronize methods (or parts of methods) in different classes in the same way as methods in the same class.

A synchronized instance method is, therefore, equivalent to a method with its statements synchronized on the current object. Thus:

```
synchronized void myMethod () {
    ...
}
```

is equivalent to:

```
void myMethod () {
    synchronized ( this ) {
        ...
    }
}
```

Accessing class and instance Variables from Multiple Threads

In the `SpreadSheet` example, we guarded access to a set of instance variables with a synchronized method in order to avoid changing one of the variables while someone was reading the others. We wanted to keep them coordinated. But what about individual variable types? Do they need to be synchronized? Normally, the answer is no. Almost all operations on primitives and object reference types in Java happen *atomically*: that is, they are handled by the VM in one step, with no opportunity for two threads to collide. This prevents threads from looking at references while they are in the process of being accessed by other threads.

But watch out—we did say *almost*. If you read the Java VM specification carefully, you will see that the `double` and `long` primitive types are not guaranteed to be handled atomically. Both of these types represent 64-bit values. The problem has to do with how the Java VM's stack handles them. It is possible that this specification will be beefed up in the future. But for now, to be strict, you should synchronize access to your `double` and `long` instance variables through accessor methods, or use the `volatile` keyword or an atomic wrapper class, which we'll describe next.

Another issue, independent of the atomicity of the values, is the notion of different threads in the VM caching values for periods of time—that is, even though one thread may have changed the value, the Java VM may not be obliged to make that value appear until the VM reaches a certain state known as a "memory barrier." While this should not be a problem in most real-world programming cases, you can address this by declaring the variable with the `volatile` keyword. This keyword indicates to the VM that the value may be changed by external threads and effectively synchronizes access to it automatically.

Finally, the `java.util.concurrent.atomic` package provides synchronized wrapper classes for all primitive types and references. These wrappers provide not only simple `set()` and `get()` operations on the values but also specialized "combo" operations, such as `compareAndSet()`, that work atomically and can be used to build higher-level synchronized application components. The classes in this package were designed specifically to map down to hardware-level functionality in many cases and can be very efficient. We'll talk more about them later in this chapter.

Reentrant locking

The locks acquired by Java upon entering a synchronized method or block of code are *reentrant*, meaning that the thread holding onto the lock may acquire the same lock again any number of times and never blocks waiting for itself. In most cases, this means that the code behaves as you'd expect; a thread can call a synchronized method recursively and can itself call upon other synchronized methods within the same object.

The wait() and notify() Methods

With the `synchronized` keyword, we can serialize the execution of methods and blocks of code so that only one thread at a time can execute a synchronized item. The `wait()` and `notify()` methods of the `Object` class extend this capability by allowing us to explicitly coordinate the waiting and running threads. Every object in Java is a subclass of `Object`, so every object inherits these methods. By using `wait()` and `notify()`, a thread can effectively give up its hold on a lock at an arbitrary point and then wait for another thread to give it back before continuing. All of the coordinated activity still happens inside synchronized blocks, and still only one thread is executing at a given time.

By executing `wait()` from a synchronized block, a thread gives up its hold on the lock and goes to sleep. A thread might do this if it needs to wait for something to happen in another part of the application, as we'll see shortly. Later, when the necessary event happens, the running thread calls `notify()` from a block synchronized on the same object. The first thread wakes up and begins trying to acquire the lock again. When the first thread manages to reacquire the lock, it continues from where it left off. However, the thread that was waiting may not get the lock immediately (or perhaps ever). It depends on when the second thread eventually releases the lock and which thread manages to snag it next. The first thread won't wake up from the `wait()` unless another thread calls `notify()`. An overloaded version of `wait()`, however, allows us to specify a timeout period. If another thread doesn't call `notify()` in the specified period, the waiting thread automatically wakes up.

Let's look at a simple scenario to see what's going on. In the following example, we'll assume there are three threads—one waiting to execute each of the three synchronized methods of the `MyThing` class. We'll call them the *waiter*, *notifier*, and *related* threads. Here's a code fragment to illustrate:

```
class MyThing {
    synchronized void waiterMethod() {
        // do some stuff
        wait();   // now wait for notifier to do something
        // continue where we left off
    }
    synchronized void notifierMethod() {
        // do some stuff
        notify();  // notify waiter that we've done it
        // continue doing stuff
    }
    synchronized void relatedMethod() {
        // do some related stuff
    }
    ...
}
```

Let's assume that a thread named *waiter* gets through the gate first and begins executing `waiterMethod()`. The two other threads are initially blocked when trying to acquire the lock for the `MyThing` object. When *waiter* executes the `wait()` method, it relinquishes its hold on the lock and goes to sleep. Now two viable threads are waiting for the lock. Which thread gets it depends on several factors, including chance and the priorities of the threads. (We'll discuss thread scheduling in the next section.)

Let's suppose that *notifier* is the next thread to acquire the lock, so it begins to run `notifierMethod()`. *waiter* continues to sleep, and *related* languishes, waiting for its turn. When *notifier* executes the call to `notify()`, the runtime system prods the *waiter* thread, effectively telling it something has changed. *waiter* wakes up and rejoins *related* in vying for the `MyThing` lock. It doesn't receive the lock automatically; it just changes its state from "Leave me alone" to "I want the lock."

At this point, *notifier* still owns the lock and continues to hold it until the synchronized `notifierMethod()` returns, or perhaps executes a `wait()` itself. At that point, the other two methods get to fight over the lock. *waiter* would like to continue executing `waiterMethod()` from the point where it left off, while *related*, which has been patient, would like to get started. We'll let you choose your own ending for the story.

For each call to `notify()`, the runtime system wakes up just one thread that is asleep in a `wait()` call. The group of threads waiting on a lock is called the *wait set*. If multiple threads are waiting, Java picks a thread on an arbitrary basis, which may be implementation-dependent. The `Object` class also provides a `notifyAll()` call to wake up all waiting threads. In most cases, you'll probably want to use `notifyAll()` rather than `notify()`. Keep in mind that `notify()` really means, "Hey, something related to this object has changed. The condition you are waiting for may have changed, so check it again." In general, there is no reason to assume only one thread at a time is interested in the change or able to act upon it. Different threads might look upon whatever has changed in different ways.

Wait conditions

In general, our *waiter* thread is waiting for a particular condition to change, and we will want it to sit in a loop like the following:

```
while ( condition != true )
    wait();
```

This test is called the *wait condition*. Other synchronized threads call `notify()` or `notifyAll()` when they have modified the environment so that the condition can be checked again. It's important to use a loop on the wait condition to be sure that the thread has been awakened for the right reason. Threads may also use a timed version of `wait()` to do periodic work while checking the condition in this way. Using wait conditions like this is also an alternative to polling and sleeping, as you'll see in the following section.

Passing Messages

We'll next illustrate a classic interaction between two threads: a `Producer` and a `Consumer`. A producer thread creates messages and places them into a queue while a consumer reads and displays them. To be realistic, we'll give the queue a maximum depth. And to make things really interesting, we'll have our consumer thread be lazy and run much more slowly than the producer. This means that `Producer` occasionally has to stop and wait for `Consumer` to catch up. The Java concurrency package has a `BlockingQueue` interface that provides exactly this kind of functionality, but we'll build it ourselves here using basic synchronization techniques first and then take a look at `Queues` and all of the collection classes in Chapter 11.

Here are the `Producer` and `Consumer` classes:

```
import java.util.*;

public class Consumer implements Runnable {
    Producer producer;

    Consumer( Producer producer ) {
        this.producer = producer;
    }

    public void run() {
        while ( true ) {
            String message = producer.getMessage();
            System.out.println("Got message: " + message);
            try {
                Thread.sleep( 2000 );
            } catch ( InterruptedException e ) { }
        }
    }

    public static void main(String args[]) {
        Producer producer = new Producer();
        new Thread( producer ).start();
        Consumer consumer = new Consumer( producer );
        new Thread( consumer ).start();
    }
}

public class Producer implements Runnable{
    static final int MAXQUEUE = 5;
    private List messages = new ArrayList();

    public void run() {
        while ( true ) {
            putMessage();
            try {
                Thread.sleep( 1000 );
            } catch ( InterruptedException e ) { }
```

```
        }
    }

    // called by Producer internally
    private synchronized void putMessage()
    {
        while ( messages.size() >= MAXQUEUE )
            try {
                wait();
            } catch( InterruptedException e ) { }

        messages.add( new java.util.Date().toString() );
        notify();
    }

    // called by Consumer externally
    public synchronized String getMessage()
    {
        while ( messages.size() == 0 )
            try {
                notify();
                wait();
            } catch( InterruptedException e ) { }
        String message = (String)messages.remove(0);
        notify();
        return message;
    }
}
```

For convenience, we have included a `main()` method in the `Consumer` class that runs the complete example. It creates a `Consumer` that is tied to a `Producer` and starts the two classes. You can run the example as follows:

```
% java Consumer
```

This produces the timestamp messages created by the `Producer`:

```
Got message: Sun Dec 19 03:35:55 CST 2006
Got message: Sun Dec 19 03:35:56 CST 2006
Got message: Sun Dec 19 03:35:57 CST 2006
...
```

The timestamps initially show a spacing of one second even though they appear every two seconds. Our `Producer` runs faster than our `Consumer`. `Producer` would like to generate a new message every second, while `Consumer` gets around to reading and displaying a message only every two seconds. Can you see how long it will take the message queue to fill up? What happens when it does?

Let's look at the code. We are using a few new tools here. `Producer` and `Consumer` implement the `Runnable` interface, and each has a thread associated with it. The `Producer` and `Consumer` classes pass messages through an instance of a `java.util.List` object. We haven't discussed the `List` class yet, but it is essentially a dynamic array of elements. We use this one as a queue by simply adding and removing elements in first-in, first-out order. The `List` has no maximum capacity of its own, but we impose one with our own check.

The important activity is in the synchronized methods: `putMessage()` and `getMessage()`. Although one of the methods is used by the `Producer` thread and the other by the `Consumer` thread, they both live in the `Producer` class so that we can coordinate them simply by declaring them `synchronized`. Here, they both implicitly use the `Producer` object's lock. If the queue is empty, the `Consumer` blocks in a call in the `Producer`, waiting for another message.

Another design option would implement the `getMessage()` method in the `Consumer` class and use a `synchronized` code block to synchronize explicitly on the `Producer` object. In either case, synchronizing on the `Producer` enables us to have multiple `Consumer` objects that feed from the same `Producer`. We'll do that later in this section.

`putMessage()`'s job is to add a new message to the queue. It can't do this if the queue is already full, so it first checks the number of elements in `messages`. If there is room, it stuffs in another timestamp message. If the queue is at its limit, however, `putMessage()` has to wait until there's space. In this situation, `putMessage()` executes a `wait()` and relies on the consumer to call `notify()` to wake it up after a message has been read. Here, we have `putMessage()` testing the condition in a loop. In this simple example, the test might not seem necessary; we could assume that when `putMessage()` wakes up, there is a free spot. However, it's important to always test our wait condition in a loop like this when we synchronize threads because there is no other way to be certain why our thread has been awakened. Before it finishes, `putMessage()` calls `notify()` itself to prod any `Consumer` that might be waiting on an empty queue.

`getMessage()` retrieves a message for the `Consumer`. It enters a loop like that of `putMessage()`, waiting for the queue to have at least one element before proceeding. If the queue is empty, it executes a `wait()` and expects the `Producer` to call `notify()` when more items are available. Notice that `getMessage()` makes its own calls to `notify()`. It does this any time the queue is empty, to prod a producer that might be sleeping and also after it consumes a message, to give the producer the go-ahead to fill the queue again. These scenarios are more plausible if there are more consumers, as we'll see next.

Let's add another consumer to the scenario, just to make things more interesting. Most of the necessary changes are in the `Consumer` class; here's the code for the modified class, now called `NamedConsumer`:

```
public class NamedConsumer implements Runnable
{
    Producer producer;
    String name;

    NamedConsumer(String name, Producer producer) {
        this.producer = producer;
```

```
            this.name = name;
        }

        public void run() {
            while ( true ) {
                String message = producer.getMessage();
                System.out.println(name + " got message: " + message);
                try {
                    Thread.sleep( 2000 );
                } catch ( InterruptedException e ) { }
            }
        }

        public static void main(String args[]) {
            Producer producer = new Producer();
            new Thread( producer ).start();

            NamedConsumer consumer = new NamedConsumer( "One", producer );
            new Thread( consumer ).start();
            consumer = new NamedConsumer( "Two", producer );
            new Thread( consumer ).start();
        }
    }
```

The `NamedConsumer` constructor takes a string name to identify each consumer. The `run()` method uses this name in the call to `println()` to identify which consumer received the message.

The only required modification to the `Producer` code is to change the `notify()` calls to `notifyAll()` calls in `putMessage()` and `getMessage()`. (We could have used `notifyAll()` in the first place.) Now, instead of the consumer and producer playing tag with the queue, we can have many players waiting for the condition of the queue to change. We might have a number of consumers waiting for a message, or we might have the producer waiting for a consumer to take a message. Any time the condition of the queue changes, we prod all of the waiting methods to reevaluate the situation by calling `notifyAll()`.

Here is some sample output when two `NamedConsumers` are running, as in the `main()` method shown previously:

```
One got message: Sat Mar 18 20:00:01 CST 2006
Two got message: Sat Mar 18 20:00:02 CST 2006
One got message: Sat Mar 18 20:00:03 CST 2006
Two got message: Sat Mar 18 20:00:04 CST 2006
One got message: Sat Mar 18 20:00:05 CST 2006
Two got message: Sat Mar 18 20:00:06 CST 2006
One got message: Sat Mar 18 20:00:07 CST 2006
Two got message: Sat Mar 18 20:00:08 CST 2006
...
```

We see nice, orderly alternation between the two consumers as a result of the calls to `sleep()` in the various methods. Interesting things would happen, however, if we were to remove all calls to `sleep()` and let things run at full speed. The threads would compete, and their behavior would depend on whether the system is using time-slicing. On a time-sliced system, there should be a fairly random distribution between the two consumers, while on a non-time-sliced system, a single consumer could monopolize the messages. We'll talk shortly about how threads compete for time when we discuss thread priority and scheduling.

Food for thought

Many things could be improved in this simple example. What we've tried to emphasize is a defensive style of programming with respect to notifications by threads. You need to rely on real-world conditions that you can test when synchronizing threads; it's not robust to simply assume that you'll get the right notifications in the right place at the right time. With that said, our example does generate extraneous notifications that wake up threads at times when there may not be work for them. For example, we generate notifications both when the queue is empty and when it's full. A better design might split these cases and use two different object locks. Fortunately, most programmers won't have to deal with issues at this level, especially because Java provides real `Queue`s and other high-level synchronization constructs.

ThreadLocal Objects

A common issue that arises is the need to maintain some information or state on a per-thread basis. For example, we might want to carry some context with the current thread as it executes our application. Or we might simply want to have a value that is different for different threads in the same way that each thread "sees" its own local variables in a method. Java supports this through the `ThreadLocal` class. A `ThreadLocal` is an object wrapper that automatically maintains a separate value for any thread calling it. For example:

```
ThreadLocal userID = new ThreadLocal();
userID.set("Pat");  // called by thread 1
userID.set("Bob"); // called by thread 2
userID.get(); // thread 1 gets "Pat"
userID.get(); // thread 2 gets "Bob"
```

You can use an instance of `ThreadLocal` anywhere you might use a static or instance variable to automatically maintain separate values for each thread. You can also extend `ThreadLocal` and override its `initialValue()` method. The `ThreadLocal` will then use this method to initialize its value once, the first time `get()` is called:

```
class MyThreadLocalFactory extends ThreadLocal<Factory> {
    protected Factory initialValue() { return new MyFactory(); }
}
```

`ThreadLocal`s are implemented using a `Map` attached to each `Thread` instance, so their values will disappear when the `Thread` is no longer used and garbage is collected.

A useful addition in Java 7 is the `ThreadLocalRandom` class, which is an extension of the `java.util.Random` class discussed in Chapter 11. The `ThreadLocalRandom` class eliminates contention (waiting due to synchronization) on the random-number generator when called from different threads.

Scheduling and Priority

Java makes few guarantees about how it schedules threads. Almost all of Java's thread scheduling is left up to the Java implementation and, to some degree, the application. Although it might have made sense (and would certainly have made many developers happier) if Java's developers had specified a scheduling algorithm, a single algorithm isn't necessarily suitable for all the roles that Java can play. Instead, Java's designers put the burden on you to write robust code that works no matter the scheduling algorithm, and let the implementation tune the algorithm for the best fit.[3]

The priority rules that we describe next are carefully worded in the Java language specification to be a general guideline for thread scheduling. You should be able to rely on this behavior overall (statistically), but it is not a good idea to write code that relies on very specific features of the scheduler to work properly. You should instead use the control and synchronization tools that we have described in this chapter to coordinate your threads.[4]

Every thread has a priority value. In general, any time a thread of a higher priority than the current thread becomes runnable (is started, stops sleeping, or is notified), it preempts the lower-priority thread and begins executing. By default, threads with the same priority are scheduled round-robin, which means once a thread starts to run, it continues until it does one of the following:

- Sleeps, by calling `Thread.sleep()` or `wait()`
- Waits for a lock, in order to run a `synchronized` method
- Blocks on I/O, for example, in a `read()` or `accept()` call
- Explicitly yields control, by calling `yield()`
- Terminates, by completing its target method or with a `stop()` call (deprecated)

3. A notable alternative to this is the real-time Java specification that defines specialized thread behavior for certain types of applications. It was developed under the Java community process and can be found at *https://rtsj.dev.java.net/*.

4. *Java Threads* by Scott Oaks and Henry Wong (O'Reilly) includes a detailed discussion of synchronization, scheduling, and other thread-related issues.

This situation looks something like Figure 9-4.

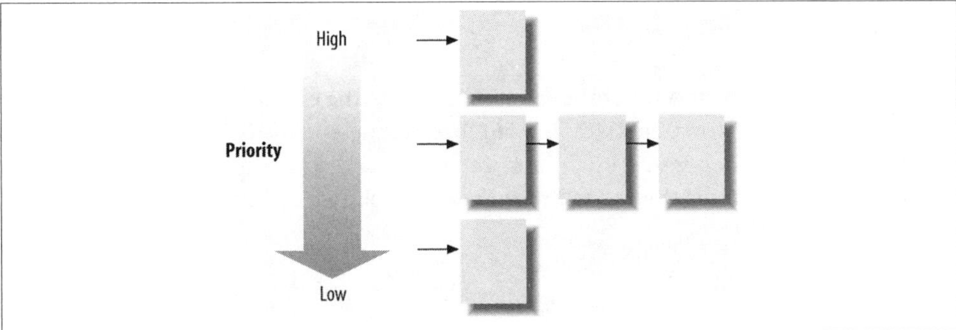

Figure 9-4. Priority preemptive, round-robin scheduling

Thread State

At any given time, a thread is in one of five general states that encompass its lifecycle and activities. These states are defined in the `Thread.State` enumeration and queried via the `getState()` method of the `Thread` class:

`NEW`
: The thread has been created but not yet started.

`RUNNABLE`
: The normal active state of a running thread, including the time when a thread is blocked in an I/O operation, like a read or write or network connection.

`BLOCKED`
: The thread is blocked, waiting to enter a synchronized method or code block. This includes the time when a thread has been awakened by a `notify()` and is attempting to reacquire its lock after a `wait()`.

`WAITING, TIMED_WAITING`
: The thread is waiting for another thread via a call to `wait()` or `join()`. In the case of `TIMED_WAITING`, the call has a timeout.

`TERMINATED`
: The thread has completed due to a return, an exception, or being stopped.

We can show the state of all threads in Java (in the current thread group) with the following snippet of code:

```
Thread [] threads = new Thread [ 64 ]; // max threads to show
int num = Thread.enumerate( threads );
for( int i = 0; i < num; i++ )
   System.out.println( threads[i] +":"+ threads[i].getState() );
```

You will probably not use this API in general programming, but it is interesting and useful for experimenting and learning about Java threads.

Time-Slicing

In addition to prioritization, all modern systems (with the exception of some embedded and "micro" Java environments) implement thread time-slicing. In a time-sliced system, thread processing is chopped up so that each thread runs for a short period of time before the context is switched to the next thread, as shown in Figure 9-5.

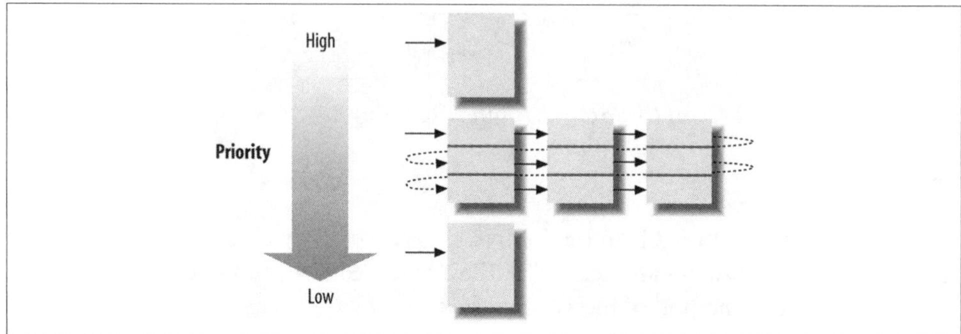

Figure 9-5. Priority preemptive, time-sliced scheduling

Higher-priority threads still preempt lower-priority threads in this scheme. The addition of time-slicing mixes up the processing among threads of the same priority; on a multiprocessor machine, threads may even be run simultaneously. This can introduce a difference in behavior for applications that don't use threads and synchronization properly.

Strictly speaking, because Java doesn't guarantee time-slicing, you shouldn't write code that relies on this type of scheduling; any software you write should function under round-robin scheduling. If you're wondering what your particular flavor of Java does, try the following experiment:

```
public class Thready {
    public static void main( String args [] ) {
        new ShowThread("Foo").start();
        new ShowThread("Bar").start();
    }

    static class ShowThread extends Thread {
        String message;

        ShowThread( String message ) {
            this.message = message;
        }
```

```
            public void run() {
                while ( true )
                    System.out.println( message );
            }
        }
    }
```

The Thready class starts up two ShowThread objects. ShowThread is a thread that goes into a hard loop (very bad form) and prints its message. Because we don't specify a priority for either thread, they both inherit the priority of their creator, so they have the same priority. When you run this example, you will see how your Java implementation does its scheduling. Under a round-robin scheme, only "Foo" should be printed; "Bar" never appears. In a time-slicing implementation, you should occasionally see the "Foo" and "Bar" messages alternate (which is most likely what you will see).

Priorities

As we said before, the priorities of threads exist as a general guideline for how the implementation should allocate time among competing threads. Unfortunately, with the complexity of how Java threads are mapped to native thread implementations, you cannot rely upon the exact meaning of priorities. Instead, you should only consider them a hint to the VM.

Let's play with the priority of our threads:

```
    class Thready {
        public static void main( String args [] ) {
            Thread foo = new ShowThread("Foo");
            foo.setPriority( Thread.MIN_PRIORITY );
            Thread bar = new ShowThread("Bar");
            bar.setPriority( Thread.MAX_PRIORITY );
            bar.start();
        }
    }
```

We would expect that with this change to our Thready class, the Bar thread would take over completely. If you run this code on the Solaris implementation of Java 5.0, that's what happens. The same is not true on Windows or with some older versions of Java. Similarly, if you change the priorities to values other than min and max, you may not see any difference at all. The subtleties relating to priority and performance relate to how Java threads and priorities are mapped to real threads in the OS. For this reason, thread priorities should be reserved for system and framework development.

Yielding

Whenever a thread sleeps, waits, or blocks on I/O, it gives up its time slot and another thread is scheduled. As long as you don't write methods that use hard loops, all threads should get their due. However, a thread can also signal that it is willing to give up its time voluntarily at any point with the `yield()` call. We can change our previous example to include a `yield()` on each iteration:

```
...
static class ShowThread extends Thread {
    ...
    public void run() {
        while ( true ) {
            System.out.println( message );
            yield();
        }
    }
}
```

You should see "Foo" and "Bar" messages strictly alternating. If you have threads that perform very intensive calculations or otherwise eat a lot of CPU time, you might want to find an appropriate place for them to yield control occasionally. Alternatively, you might want to drop the priority of your compute-intensive thread so that more important processing can proceed around it.

Unfortunately, the Java language specification is very weak with respect to `yield()`. It is another one of those things that you should consider an optimization hint rather than a guarantee. In the worst case, the runtime system may simply ignore calls to `yield()`.

Thread Groups

The `ThreadGroup` class allows us to deal with threads wholesale: we can use it to arrange threads in groups and deal with the groups as a whole. A thread group can contain other thread groups in addition to individual threads, so our arrangements can be hierarchical. Thread groups are particularly useful when we want to start a task that might create many threads of its own. By assigning the task a thread group, we can later identify and control all the task's threads. Thread groups are also the subject of restrictions that can be imposed by the Java Security Manager, so we can restrict a thread's behavior according to its thread group. For example, we can forbid threads in a particular group from interacting with threads in other groups. This is one way web browsers can prevent threads started by Java applets from stopping important system threads.

When we create a thread, it normally becomes part of the thread group to which the currently running thread belongs. To create a new thread group of our own, we can call the constructor:

```
ThreadGroup

myTaskGroup = new ThreadGroup("My Task Group");
```

The `ThreadGroup` constructor takes a name, which a debugger can use to help you identify the group. (You can also assign names to the threads themselves.) Once we have a group, we can put threads in the group by supplying the `ThreadGroup` object as an argument to the `Thread` constructor:

```
Thread myTask = new Thread( myTaskGroup, taskPerformer );
```

Here, `myTaskGroup` is the thread group, and `taskPerformer` is the target object (the `Runnable` object that performs the task). Any additional threads that `myTask` creates also belong to the `myTaskGroup` thread group.

Working with ThreadGroups

The `ThreadGroup` class exists so that you can control threads in batches. It has methods that parallel the basic `Thread` control methods—even the deprecated `stop()`, `suspend()`, and `resume()`. These methods operate on all the threads in a thread group. You can also mark a thread group as a "daemon"; a daemon thread group is automatically removed when all of its children are gone. If a thread group isn't a daemon, you have to call `destroy()` in order to remove it when it is empty.

We can set the maximum priority for threads created in a thread group by calling `setMaximumPriority()`. Thereafter, no threads can be created in the thread group with a priority to be higher than the maximum; threads that change their priority can't set their new priority to be higher than the maximum.

Finally, you can get a list of all threads in a group. The method `activeCount()` tells you how many threads are in the group; the method `enumerate()` gives you a list of them. We used the `enumerate()` method earlier when we showed the state of all threads in the default thread group using the static `Thread.enumerate()`method. The argument to `enumerate()` is an array of `Threads` that `enumerate()` fills in with the group's threads. Both `activeCount()` and `enumerate()` operate recursively on all thread groups that are contained in the group.

Uncaught Exceptions

In Java, unchecked exceptions that are not caught by any method eventually bubble up to the `run()` method of the running thread and are thrown from there. By default, Java deals with these by simply printing them to the system error stream or log and terminating the thread. However, you can specify your own "catchall" behavior for these exceptions by subclassing `ThreadGroup` and overriding the `uncaughtException()` method. When an uncaught exception is generated, it is handed to this method, which can take some action or throw it again before the thread terminates.

In Java 5.0, this pattern was extended by defining an interface, `Thread.UncaughtExceptionHandler`, and adding both per-thread and systemwide uncaught exception handlers in addition to the per-`ThreadGroup` exception handler. We can handle uncaught exceptions for a single thread like this:

```
Thread thread = new Thread();
thread.setUncaughtExceptionHandler(
    new Thread.UncaughtExceptionHandler() {
        public void uncaughtException( Thread t, Throwable e ) {
            System.err.println( t + " threw exception: " + e );
        }
} );
```

This example prints the exception before the thread dies. We could have set the same handler on the `ThreadGroup` in the same way or assigned it for all exceptions using the static `Thread.setDefaultUncaughtExceptionHandler()` method.

Thread Performance

The way that applications use threads and the associated costs and benefits have greatly impacted the design of many Java APIs. We will discuss some of the issues in detail in other chapters. But it is worth briefly mentioning some aspects of thread performance and how the use of threads has dictated the form and functionality of several recent Java packages.

The Cost of Synchronization

The act of acquiring locks to synchronize threads takes time, even when there is no contention. In older implementations of Java, this time could be significant. With newer VMs, it is almost negligible. However, unnecessary low-level synchronization can still slow applications by blocking threads where legitimate concurrent access otherwise could be allowed. Because of this, two important APIs, the Java Collections API and the Swing GUI API, were specifically crafted to avoid unnecessary synchronization by placing it under the developer's control.

The `java.util` Collections API replaces earlier, simple Java aggregate types—namely, `Vector` and `Hashtable`—with more fully featured and, notably, unsynchronized types (`List` and `Map`). The Collections API instead defers to application code to synchronize access to collections when necessary and provides special "fail fast" functionality to help detect concurrent access and throw an exception. It also provides synchronization "wrappers" that can provide safe access in the old style. Special concurrent-access-friendly implementations of the `Map` and `Queue` collections are included as part of the `java.util.concurrent` package. These implementations go even further in that they are written to allow a high degree of concurrent access without any user synchronization. We'll talk about these in Chapter 11.

The Java Swing GUI, which grew out of AWT, has taken a different approach to providing speed and safety. Swing dictates that modification of its components (with notable exceptions) must all be done by a single thread: the main event queue. Swing solves performance problems as well as nasty issues of determinism in event ordering by forcing a single super-thread to control the GUI. The application may access the event queue thread indirectly by pushing commands onto a queue through a simple interface.

Thread Resource Consumption

A fundamental pattern in Java, which will be illustrated in Chapters 12 and 13, is to start many threads to handle asynchronous external resources, such as socket connections. For maximum efficiency, a web server might be tempted to create a thread for each client connection it is servicing. With each client having its own thread, I/O operations may block and restart as needed. But as efficient as this may be in terms of throughput, it is a very inefficient use of server resources. Threads consume memory; each thread has its own "stack" for local variables, and switching between running threads (context switching) adds overhead to the CPU. While threads are relatively lightweight (in theory, it is possible to have hundreds or thousands running on a large server), at a certain point, the resources consumed by the threads themselves start defeating the purpose of starting more threads. Often, this point is reached with only a few dozen threads. Creating a thread per client is not always a scalable option.

An alternative approach is to create "thread pools" where a fixed number of threads pull tasks from a queue and return for more when they are finished. This recycling of threads makes for solid scalability, but it has historically been difficult to implement efficiently for servers in Java because stream I/O (for things like sockets) has not fully supported nonblocking operations. This changed with Java 1.4 and the introduction of the NIO (new I/O) package, `java.nio`. The NIO package introduced asynchronous I/O channels: nonblocking reads and writes plus the ability to "select" or test the readiness of streams for moving data. Channels can also be asynchronously closed, allowing threads to work with them gracefully. With the NIO package, it is possible to create servers with much more sophisticated, scalable thread patterns.

With Java 5.0, thread pools and job "executor" services were codified as utilities as part of the new `java.util.concurrent` package, meaning you don't have to write these yourself. We'll talk about them next when we discuss the concurrency utilities in Java.

Concurrency Utilities

So far in this chapter, we've demonstrated how to create and synchronize threads at a low level, using Java language primitives. The `java.util.concurrent` package and subpackages introduced with Java 5.0 build on this functionality, adding important threading utilities and codifying some common design patterns by supplying standard implementations. Roughly in order of generality, these areas include:

Thread-aware Collections implementations
: The `java.util.concurrent` package augments the Java Collections API with several implementations for specific threading models. These include timed wait and

blocking implementations of the `Queue` interface, as well as nonblocking, concurrent-access optimized implementations of the `Queue` and `Map` interfaces. The package also adds "copy on write" `List` and `Set` implementations for extremely efficient "almost always read" cases. These may sound complex, but actually cover some fairly simple cases very well. We'll cover the Collections API in Chapter 11.

Executors
: `Executors` run tasks, including `Runnables`, and abstract the concept of thread creation and pooling from the user. Executors are intended to be a high-level replacement for the idiom of creating new threads to service a series of jobs. Along with `Executors`, the `Callable` and `Future` interfaces are introduced, which expand upon `Runnable` to allow management, value return, and exception handling.

Low-level synchronization constructs
: The `java.util.concurrent.locks` package holds a set of classes, including `Lock` and `Condition`, that parallels the Java language-level synchronization primitives and promotes them to the level of a concrete API. The locks package also adds the concept of nonexclusive reader/writer locks, allowing for greater concurrency in synchronized data access.

High-level synchronization constructs
: This includes the classes `CyclicBarrier`, `CountDownLatch`, `Semaphore`, and `Exchanger`. These classes implement common synchronization patterns drawn from other languages and systems and can serve as the basis for new high-level tools.

Atomic operations (sounds very James Bond, doesn't it?)
: The `java.util.concurrent.atomic` package provides wrappers and utilities for atomic, "all-or-nothing" operations on primitive types and references. This includes simple combination atomic operations like testing a value before setting it and getting and incrementing a number in one operation.

With the possible exception of optimizations done by the Java VM for the `atomic` operations package, all of these utilities are implemented in pure Java, on top of the standard Java language synchronization constructs. This means that they are in a sense only convenience utilities and don't truly add new capabilities to the language. Their main role is to offer standard patterns and idioms in Java threading and make them safer and more efficient to use. A good example of this is the `Executor` utility, which allows a user to manage a set of tasks in a predefined threading model without having to delve into creating threads at all. Higher-level APIs like this both simplify coding and allow for greater optimization of the common cases.

We'll look at each of these areas in the remainder of this chapter, with the exception of the Collections implementations. We'll discuss those when we cover the Java Collections APIs in Chapter 11.

Before we dive in, we should give a shout-out to Doug Lea, the author of *Concurrent Programming in Java* (Addison-Wesley), who led the group that added these packages to Java and is largely responsible for creating them.

Executors

In this chapter, we've created a lot of `Threads` and hopefully shown how to use them effectively. But in the grand scheme of things, threads are a fairly low-level programming tool and, without care, can be error-prone. When we recognize certain common patterns that developers reproduce over and over again using threads, it's natural to want to elevate a pattern to the level of an API. One such related pair of patterns is the concept of an *executor* service that manages tasks and that of a *thread pool* that services tasks in an efficient way.

Thread pools have been implemented and reimplemented by vast numbers of developers in one way or another over the years and when you add in features like scheduling different threading models, they can get quite complex. To address these issues, the `java.util.concurrent` package includes interfaces for many default implementations of the executor pattern for common threading models. This includes sophisticated scheduling as well as asynchronous collection of results from the tasks, if they require it. In general, you can use an `Executor` as a replacement for creating one-off threads anywhere you need to execute `Runnable` objects. The advantage is that understanding and modifying the behavior of your code later is a lot easier when you work at this level.

For the simple case of running a number of tasks and watching for their completion, we can consider the base `Executor` interface, which executes `Runnable` objects for us. A convenient thing about `Executor` is that its companion utility class `Executors` is a factory for creating different kinds of `Executor` implementations. We'll talk about the various types it can produce in a bit, but for now let's use the method called `newFixedThreadPool()`, which, as its name suggests, returns an `Executor` that is implemented using a thread pool of a fixed size:

```
Executor executor = Executors.newFixedThreadPool( 3 ) ; // 3 threads

List<Runnable> runnables = ... ;
for( Runnable task : runnables )
    executor.execute( task );
```

Here, we are submitting a number of `Runnable` tasks to our `Executor`, which executes them using a pool with a maximum of three threads. If our list contains more than three tasks, then some of them will have to wait until a thread is free to service it. So, what happens when we submit the fourth item? The `Executor` interface doesn't really specify that. It's up to the particular implementation to decide. Without specifying more about its type, we don't know if an `Executor` is going to queue tasks, or if it will use a pool to service them. Some `Executor` implementations may block or even execute the `Runnable` right on the `execute()` call in the caller's thread. But in this case (and for all

Executor implementations created for us by the Executors factory methods), tasks are effectively put onto an unbounded queue. In the example, our loop submits all of the tasks immediately and they are queued by the executor until the three threads have serviced them.

With just a line or two of code in our example, we've been able to throttle the concurrency of our task list and avoid the details of constructing any threads ourselves. Later, if we decide we'd rather execute the tasks one at a time, the change is trivial (allocate just one thread!). Next, we'll take a step up and look at manageable tasks that produce values and executors that can schedule tasks for us.

Tasks with results: Callable and Future

Because the Runnable interface was created for Threads to consume, its API doesn't allow for direct feedback to the caller. The new Callable interface, which is effectively a replacement for Runnable, rectifies this situation by providing a call() method that both returns a result and can throw exceptions. Callable is a generic class that is parameterized by the type it returns. The following examples create a Callable that returns an integer:

```
class MyCallable implements Callable<Integer> {
    public Integer call() { return 2+2; }
}

// or anonymously
Callable<Integer> callable = new Callable<Integer>() {
    public Integer call() { return 2+2; }
};
```

There is also a convenience method for bridging Runnables to Callables in the Executors class. It takes a Runnable and a fixed value to return as a value when it completes:

```
Callable<Integer> callable = Executors.callable( runnable,
    42 /*return value*/ );
```

The new Future class is used with Callable and serves as a handle to wait for and retrieve the result of the task or cancel the task before it is executed. A Future is returned by the submit() methods of an ExecutorService, which is essentially a beefed-up Executor. We'll discuss ExecutorServices in the next section.

```
Future<Integer> result = executorService.submit( callable );
int val = result.get();  // blocks until ready
```

Future is also a generic interface, which is parameterized by its return type. This explains the somewhat cute name. For example, a Future<Integer> could be read as "a future integer." Future has both blocking and timed-wait get() methods to retrieve the result when it is ready, as well as an isDone() test method and a cancel() method to stop the task if it hasn't started yet. If the task has been cancelled, you get a CancellationException if you attempt to retrieve the result.

Enough said about these interfaces. Next, we'll look at the ExecutorService, which uses them.

ExecutorService

Our first Executor was little more than a sinkhole for Runnables and, as we described, required knowledge of the implementation to know how it would handle tasks. By contrast, an ExecutorService is intended to be an asynchronous task handler. Instead of an execute() method, it has submit() methods that accept a Callable (or Runnable) and return immediately with a Future object that can be used to manage the task and collect the result later. In addition to that, an ExecutorService has a lifecycle defined by its shutdown() method and related methods that can be used to stop the service gracefully after tasks are completed.

ExecutorService extends Executor. In fact, all of the implementations returned by the Executors factory methods are actually ExecutorServices—including the one we used in our first example. We'll look at these factory methods to see what kind of services are offered.

Executors offers three types of ExecutorService implementations:

newFixedThreadPool(int)
: This is the classic thread pool with a specified maximum pool size and an unbounded queue for task submission. If a thread dies for some reason while handling a task, a new one will be created to replace it. Threads are never removed from the pool until the service is shut down.

newCachedThreadPool()
: This pool uses an open-ended number of threads that grows and shrinks with demand. The main advantage of this service is that threads are cached for a period of time and reused, eliminating the overhead of creating new threads for short-lived tasks. Threads that are not used for one minute are removed. Tasks are submitted directly to threads; there is no real queuing.

newSingleThreadExecutor()
: This ExecutorService uses a single thread to execute tasks from an unbounded queue. In this sense, it is identical to a fixed thread pool with a pool size of 1.

Let's look at a more realistic usage of an ExecutorService, drawn from the TinyHttpd example in Chapter 13. In that chapter, we create a mini-web server to illustrate features of the networking APIs. Here, we won't show the networking details, but we'll implement the main request dispatching loop for the example using a thread pool executor service. (Flip to Chapter 13 to see the implementation of the Runnable client-connection handler class. That class works equally well with both examples.) Here we go:

```
public class ExecutorHttpd
{
```

```
  ExecutorService executor = Executors.newFixedThreadPool(3);

  public void start( int port ) throws IOException
  {
    final ServerSocket ss = new ServerSocket( port );
    while ( !executor.isShutdown() )
      executor.submit( new TinyHttpdConnection( ss.accept() ) );
  }

  public void shutdown() throws InterruptedException {
    executor.shutdown();
    executor.awaitTermination( 30, TimeUnit.SECONDS );
    executor.shutdownNow();
  }

  public static void main( String argv[] ) throws Exception
  {
    new ExecutorHttpd().start( Integer.parseInt(argv[0]) );
  }
}
```

The `ExecutorHttpd` class holds an instance of a fixed thread pool `ExecutorService` with three threads to service client connections. In the `start()` method of our class, we create a `ServerSocket` that accepts incoming network connections. We then enter a loop that runs as long as our service is not flagged to shut down. Inside the loop, we create a new connection handler (a `Runnable` instance of `TinyHttpdConnection`) for each connection and submit it to the executor. The `shutdown()` method of our class illustrates a graceful termination. First, we call `shutdown()` on the executor, which causes the service to stop accepting new tasks and allow the currently running ones to complete. Then we wait a reasonable period of time for all web requests to finish (30 seconds), using the `awaitTermination()` method before trying a less graceful ending with `shutdownNow()`. `shutdownNow()` attempts to interrupt or otherwise stop threads as quickly as possible. We leave things there, but the method actually returns a `List` of tasks that remain hung after the attempt. Finally, we have a `main()` method that exercises our example by creating an instance of `ExecutorHttpd` on a port specified as an argument to the program.

Collective tasks

In addition to its individual task `submit()` methods, `ExecutorService` also offers a set of collective `invokeAll()` and `invokeAny()` executor methods that submit multiple tasks as a group and return results either when they are all complete or when the first one completes, respectively. With this, we could reproduce our first example using a `List` of `Callables` like this:

```
List<Callable<Integer>> taskList = ...;
ExecutorService execService = Executors.newFixedThreadPool(3);
List<Future<Integer>> resultList = execService.invokeAll( taskList );
```

By contrast, the `invokeAny()` method returns just the first successfully completed task's result (cancelling all the remaining unexecuted tasks):

```
int result = execService.invokeAny( taskList );
```

Both methods also offer timed wait versions that time out after a specified period of time.

Scheduled tasks

For tasks that you'd like to run at a future time or on a periodic basis, use the `ScheduledExecutorService`. `ScheduledExecutorService` is an `ExecutorService` with additional "schedule" methods that take a delay for a `Runnable` or `Callable` or a period specification for a `Runnable`. Two additional factory methods of `Executors` produce scheduled executors:

```
Executors.newScheduledThreadPool(int);
Executors.newSingleThreadScheduledExecutor();
```

These are exactly like the similarly named methods for regular executor services, with the exception of returning a scheduled executor type.

To execute a task in the future, you specify a delay from the current time. For example:

```
ScheduledExecutorService exec = Executors.newScheduledThreadPool(3);

exec.schedule( runnable, 60, TimeUnit.SECONDS ); // run one minute in the
                                                 // future

// run at specified date and time
Calendar futureDate = ...; // convertfrom calendar
Date date = futureDate.getTime(); // to Date
long delay  = date.getTime() - System.currentTimeMillis(); // to relative
                                                           // millis
exec.schedule( runnable, delay, TimeUnit.MILLISECONDS ); // run at specified
                                                         // date
```

For periodic work, there are two kinds of recurring schedules—fixed delay and fixed rate. *Fixed delay* means that a fixed amount of time elapses between the end of the task's execution and the beginning of the next execution. *Fixed rate* means that the task should begin execution at fixed time intervals, regardless of how long the task takes. The difference comes into play when the time to execute the task is long relative to the interval. The following snippet schedules a logfile cleanup to occur in 12 hours and every 12 hours thereafter:

```
Runnable cleanup = new Runnable() {
    public void run() { cleanUpLogFiles(); }
};

long period = 12*60*60, delay = period; // seconds
```

```
Future<?> logService = executionService.scheduleAtFixedRate(
    cleanup, delay, period, TimeUnit.SECONDS );
```

Because the task for periodic schedules is a `Runnable`, the `Future` object does not return a useful value (it returns `null`) so we don't specify a parameter type in its generic type instantiation. The `Future` is still useful for cancelling the task at a later time if we wish:

```
logService.cancel();
```

We should mention that the `ScheduledExecutorService` bears a great deal of similarity to the `java.util.Timer` class that we'll discuss in Chapter 11, especially with regard to the periodic schedules. A `java.util.Timer` is always single-threaded, however.

CompletionService

A `CompletionService` is a lightweight queue-like frontend to an executor. The `CompletionService` provides `submit()` methods, which delegate their tasks to a particular instance of `Executor`, and then provides `take()` and `poll()` methods for retrieving `Future` results for completed tasks. Think of a `CompletionService` as a babysitter for the `Future`s, allowing you to easily gather up only completed results (as opposed to having to check each `Future` yourself to see which ones have finished and in what order). `ExecutorCompletionService` is a concrete implementation of `CompletionService` that takes an `Executor` in its constructor:

```
Executor executor = Executors.newFixedThreadPool(3);
CompletionService<Integer> completionService =
    new ExecutorCompletionService<Integer>( executor );

completionService.submit( callable );
completionService.submit( runnable, resultValue );

// poll for result
Future<Integer> result = completionService.poll();
if ( result != null )
    // use value...

// block, waiting for result
Future<Integer> result = completionService.take();
```

The ThreadPoolExecutor implementation

At various times in this chapter, we've referred to the different executor services produced by the `Executors` factory as different implementations of `ExecutorService`. But these implementations are just different configurations of a single, highly flexible implementation of `ExecutorService` called `ThreadPoolExecutorService`. You can use this implementation directly if you want; it offers some additional features. The primary constructor for `ThreadPoolExecutorService` allows you to specify both a "core" thread pool size and a maximum size, as well as a thread timeout value for removing idle threads. The core size is a minimum number of threads which, once created, are allowed to live indefinitely. The constructor also allows you to provide the task queue (an implementation of `BlockingQueue`) on which new tasks are placed. This last feature allows you to govern the queuing policy yourself. You could specify a queue with a limited capacity:

```
ExecutorService executorService = new ThreadPoolExecutor(
corePoolSize, maximumPoolSize, keepAliveTime, timeUnit, taskQueue );
```

The `ThreadPoolExecutor` implementation also has methods that allow you to change the core and maximum pool size while the service is active or to "prestart" the core threads before the service is used.

Actually, these last features bring up an interesting issue. If we know that our executor service is an implementation of `ThreadPoolExecutor`, we can cast it at runtime to get access to these extra methods and do things like change the pool size. This may not be what the designers of some services had in mind; in fact, it could be downright dangerous in the wrong hands. For this reason, `Executors` offers a number of "unconfigurable" wrapper methods that act something like the "unmodifiable" collection methods we'll see in the Java Collections API. These methods wrap an executor service in a delegator object that does not expose the implementation to the caller:

```
ExecutorService tweakable = Executors.newFixedThreadPool();
ExecutorService safe = Executors.unconfigurableExecutorService( tweakable );
```

An application server might, for example, wrap a service to protect itself from individual applications modifying (intentionally or accidentally) a global service used by many applications.

Thread production

We said that the `Executor` pattern is a general replacement for using `Threads` to run simple tasks. Although `Executors` shield us from `Thread` creation, there still may be cases where we want some control over how the threads used in our various thread pool implementations are constructed or set up. For this reason and to standardize `Thread` production in general, the concurrency package adds an explicit, factory API for thread creation.

The `ThreadFactory` interface provides a `newThread()` method. One of these factories is used by all service implementations that create threads. All of the factory methods of `Executors` have an additional form that accepts an explicit `ThreadFactory` as an argument. You can get the default thread factory used by these with the `Executors.defaultThreadFactory()` method. You could supply your own `ThreadFactory` to perform custom setup, such as `ThreadLocal` values or priorities.

The Fork/Join framework

So far we've seen how the Java concurrency utilities can be used to manage simple parallel programming scenarios. We've seen that we can submit many tasks to an `ExecutorService` and collect result values if needed through `Futures`. We've seen that we can schedule tasks to run at specified times and with specified frequencies. We've seen that we can delve into the details of the pooling and control the degree of parallelism (how many threads are used) if we wish. Later in this chapter, we'll look at APIs that help us coordinate threads so that we can do more complex jobs that require cooperation or explicit phases of operation in their data handling. In this section, we'll look at an API that helps you coordinate tasks in another way—by helping you take "scaleable" tasks and divide them up to match the processing power available at any given time.

Let's imagine that you have a task that performs a complex computation like rendering video or generating a complicated image. A natural place to start in parallizing it would be to divide the work for one frame or image into a fixed number of parts and feed them to an executor service. The executor service would be tuned to have as many threads as you wish to use (perhaps the same number as the number of CPUs or "cores" on your machine) and would assign each part to its own thread. If each task (each chunk of the image) requires about the same amount of work to complete and nothing else is competing for time on your computer, then this scenario is pretty optimal. We'd expect that each part of the image would be finished at about the same time and we'll be able to stitch them all together effectively. But what if some parts of the image are dramatically harder to render than other parts? What if one chunk takes ten or a hundred or a thousand times as much CPU power as another? (Imagine how much faster it may be to render a empty part of an image, for example.) Then we may find ourselves in a situation where many of the threads sit idle, while a few threads churn away doing all of the hard work. What can we do to address this?

Well, one approach would be to simply make our tasks more finely grained. We could make our individual jobs so small that no single one could possibly monopolize a thread for long. However, when tasks can vary in degree of difficulty by many orders of magnitude, this could lead to creating a very large number of tiny tasks and would probably be very inefficient, with threads switching jobs and, even worse, moving data around to accommodate the somewhat random order in which they would service the work requests. What is needed is a way for each task to keep itself busy, but allow other tasks to help when they get overloaded. Ideally, we'd also like to minimize discontinuities in the workflow and for data-intensive tasks, to avoid giving threads jobs that require completely new data to be loaded at each turn.

The *Fork/Join* framework is a new API added in Java 7 that provides just this—a way for you to structure your tasks so that they can be split up as needed to keep all of the available threads busy working on data with as much continuity as possible. Specifically, the Fork/Join framework relies on tasks that can be split up recursively (i.e., divided in two or more parts, with those parts then subdivided if needed, and so on). When a task is deemed too large to be completed quickly, the task is simply split up and the (now smaller) pieces are placed into a queue for the current thread. The framework then implements what is known as a "work stealing" algorithm, allowing threads that are free to grab unstarted tasks from their neighbors' queues. The combination of these techniques has some powerful advantages. First, it avoids unecessarily randomizing of the workload. Threads will tend to get to work on contiguous parts of their tasks as long as they stay busy. For data-intensive tasks, this may mean less loading of data across threads. However, when necessary, a thread can grab work from a neighbor. And therein comes the second advantage: by the nature of the recursive splitting of tasks, the largest/least-broken-up pieces of tasks will sit at the bottom of each thread's queue, which is exactly where a neighbor thread will look to steal work if needed. This means that when work is snatched, it will be redistributed in the largest possible chunks, further stabilizing the workload per thread, reducing stealing operations and context switching. It's a very clever algorithm that originated in the Cilk programming language.

To show off the Fork/Join framework, we will do some image rendering, which we'll use as an excuse to draw some fractals! Fractals are amazing mathematical shapes that arise from relatively simple iterative processes. The one that we'll be drawing is called the Mandelbrot set. Our Mandelbrot example code will do its drawing using the Fork/Join framework to break up the job of drawing the image to the available number of processors and keep them all busy (Figure 9-6). Before we start, a few caveats. First, we won't give a very good explanation of the drawing part that actually calculates the fractal. In the interest of keeping the example focused on the framework, we have compacted that code down to just a few lines that are very cryptic. Please see the footnotes for a link to a proper explanation of what it is doing. Next, our example will blindly break up the image chunks until they reach a fixed minimum size. While work stealing will indeed happen between threads in this case, a better algorithm might make the determination about when to split the job based on the actual rendering performance and reduce the overhead of unecessary splitting. (We won't have a large amount of data driving the rendering and so we're mainly focused on keeping the threads busy rather than minimizing splitting.)

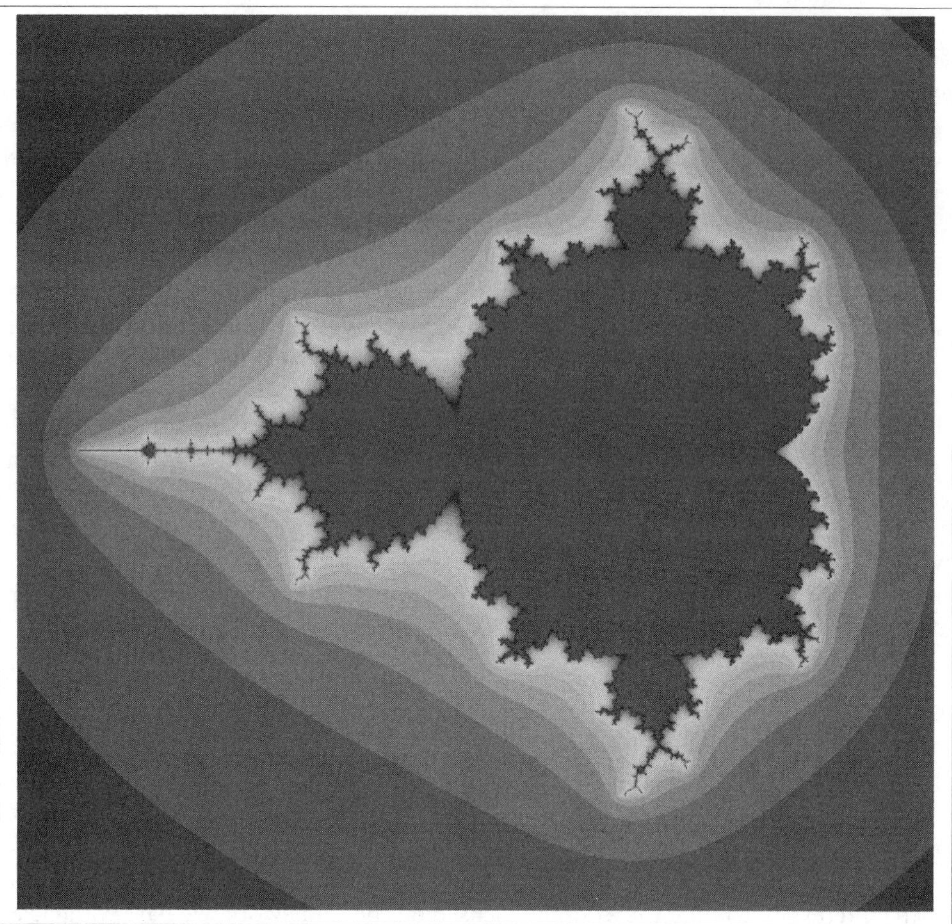

Figure 9-6. Mandelbrot Fork/Join

The Fork/Join framework API centers on a `ForkJoinPool` and various implementations of a kind of `Future` called a `ForkJoinTask`. The Fork/Join framework can be used in many different ways depending on how you wish to structure the tasks and make decisions about their division (forking) and collecting results (joining); however, we are only going to look at one common case. We will be using a kind of `ForkJoinTask` called `RecursiveAction`, which is just a `ForkJoinTask` that returns no value. We will subclass `RecursiveAction` with our `MandelbrotTask` and implement the one required abstract method: `compute()`. Within the `compute()` method, we will simply make a decision as to whether to split up the task or do the work immediately. Here is the code:

```
public class Mandelbrot extends JFrame
{
    @Override public void paint( Graphics g ) {
        BufferedImage image = new BufferedImage( getWidth(), getHeight(),
```

```
            BufferedImage.TYPE_INT_RGB );
        ForkJoinPool pool = new ForkJoinPool(); // defaults thread per processor
        pool.invoke( new MandelbrotTask( image, 0, image.getWidth()-1, 0,
            image.getHeight()-1 ) );
        g.drawImage( image, 0, 0, null );
    }

    public static void main( String[] args ) {
        Mandelbrot mandy = new Mandelbrot();
        mandy.setSize( 768, 768 );
        mandy.setVisible( true );
    }
}

class MandelbrotTask extends RecursiveAction
{
    private static double size = 3.0, offsetX = -0.7, thresholdSq = 100;
    private static int maxIterations = 30;
    private BufferedImage image;
    private int xStart, xEnd, yStart, yEnd;
    private static int taskSplitThreshold = 1024;

    MandelbrotTask( BufferedImage image, int xStart, int xEnd, int yStart,
        int yEnd ) {

        this.image = image;

        this.xStart = xStart;
        this.xEnd = xEnd;
        this.yStart = yStart;
        this.yEnd = yEnd;
    }

    public void render()
    {
        for ( int x = xStart; x <= xEnd; x++ ) {
            for ( int y = yStart; y <= yEnd; y++ )  {
                double r = x * size / image.getWidth() -size/2 + offsetX;
                double i = y * size / image.getHeight() -size/2;
                double zr=0, zi=0;
                int iter;
                for ( iter = 0; iter < maxIterations; iter++ ) {
                    double nzr = zr*zr - zi*zi + r;
                    double nzi = 2*zr*zi + i;
                    if ( nzr*nzr + nzi*nzi > thresholdSq ) { break; }
                    zr = nzr; zi=nzi;
                }
                image.setRGB( x, y, Color.HSBtoRGB( 0.5f * iter / maxIterations,
                    1.0f, 1.0f) );
            }
        }
    }
```

```
    @Override protected void compute()
    {
        int width = xEnd-xStart,  height = yEnd-yStart;
        if ( width*height < taskSplitThreshold ) {
            render();
        } else {
            invokeAll(
                new MandelbrotTask( image, xStart, xStart+width/2, yStart,
                    yStart+height/2 ),
                new MandelbrotTask( image, xStart+width/2+1, xEnd, yStart,
                    yStart+height/2 ),
                new MandelbrotTask( image, xStart, xStart+width/2,
                    yStart+height/2+1, yEnd ),
                new MandelbrotTask( image, xStart+width/2+1, xEnd,
                    yStart+height/2+1, yEnd )
            );
        }
    }
}
```

Try running the example and then dragging the window out to different sizes. Watch how it redraws as the window is dragged out to a large size. The fractal is generated by treating each point in the image as a complex number (a two-dimensional number) and applying a simple formula to it repeatedly: $Z=Z^2+C$, where Z is initially zero and C is related to the coordinate of the point. Then we color-code the point based on how fast that value grows. In some areas of the image, the values will grow quickly and we'll stop iterating on them; in other areas, we'll go on until we reach a number (`maxIterations`) of iterations. This means that some regions will take longer than others to generate and some threads will therefore steal work from others.

The `main()` method of the `Mandelbrot` class creates the main window, a `JFrame`, for us. (We saw some simple GUI programming in the introduction to the book and we'll return to it in Chapter 16 when we talk about `Swing`.) The main thing that we need to know here is that the JFrame's `paint()` method is displaying a buffered image and our various `MandelbrotTasks` are competing to render small rectangles of that image.

When the `paint()` method is invoked to redraw the screen, it creates a new `ForkJoinPool` and constructs a single `MandelbrotTask`. The `MandelbrotTask` encapsulates knowledge about a region of the image to draw—initially the entire image—and contains the method to render it. The initial `MandelbrotTask` is passed to the `ForkJoinPool`'s `invoke()`method, which is a blocking form of the `submit` method that will wait for the task to complete before returning. The `paint()` method will then draw the fully rendered image. As you can see, from the point of view of the `paint()` method, it has prescribed one task for the entire image and simply asked the `ForkJoinPool` to invoke it. All of the recursive division of labor is handled by the task in cooperation with the framework.

Within the MandelbrotTask's compute() method, we check to see how many pixels the task is being asked to render. If the number of pixels exceeds a specified threshold, we split the region into four quadrants and create a new MandelbrotTask for each of them. The four subtasks are then passed to the inherited invokeAll() method, which executes them and waits for all of them to complete before moving on (it effectively performs a join operation on them). If the number of pixels is under the threshold, the compute() method directly invokes the render() method to generate the fractal for that small portion of the image.

In our case, the division of tasks will proceed until the threshold has been reached and each of the threads in the pool is busy rendering regions of the screen. Then the tree of tasks will collapse back up, with each subdivided MandelbrotTask returning from its invokeAll() method invocation until the initial, top-level task is completed.

One last thing before we move on: an exercise for you if you are really interested in this topic. If you would like to visualize which threads are drawing which regions, you can do the following purely as an experiment: within the render() method, look up the name of the currently executing thread with the ThreadgetName() method. While this name will not be meaningful, it will be unique to a thread. Use a HashMap to assign that name a unique number and map it to that number each time you see it. Then use that number to determine the color of the rendered pixel instead of the fractal logic (or combine them to add a little tint or shade). This will allow you to see which threads are rendering which patches of the screen. On a fast system, this may not be very interesting, but if you stress the rendering by dragging the image to a very large size you should see some variations.

Locks

The java.util.concurrent.locks package holds classes that mimic and expand upon the built-in Java language synchronization primitives, adding "read/write" locks among other things. As we mentioned, these classes are utilities written in Java and don't strictly add anything new to the language semantics. However, they do provide more flexible usage at the expense of some of the built-in safety of Java language synchronization.

At the heart of the locks package are the Lock and Condition interfaces. Lock represents the same concept as a Java lock (monitor) that is associated with each object and class for use with synchronized methods and blocks. The Lock class provides for exclusive access by the owner of the lock by allowing only one party to hold the lock at a time through the lock() and unlock() methods. In Java language synchronization, this is accomplished implicitly with the synchronized keyword:

```
// synchronized method
synchronized void writeData() { ... }

// synchronized block
synchronized ( someObject ) {
```

```
    ...
}
```

Upon entry to the synchronized method or block, Java acquires the lock and automatically releases it upon exiting. Even if an exception is thrown or the thread dies unexpectedly, Java automatically releases all of the locks it acquired. Using the `Lock` class instead requires us (or allows us, depending on how you look at it) to explicitly lock when we want the resource and remember to unlock it when we are through. The locking is not tied to any particular scope, such as a single method or code block. To reproduce the effect of the synchronized method in the example, we'd use something like:

```
Lock lock = new ReentrantLock();

// method or block
lock.lock();
try {
     // body of method or block ...
} finally {
    lock.unlock()
}
```

The first caller to `lock()` acquires the lock and proceeds. Subsequent calls by other threads block until the lock is released. We perform the body of our locked operation in a `try/finally` block. This is generally important in order to ensure that we always unlock before we leave, but you are free to implement arbitrary protocols at your own risk.

The lock implementation in this example is called `ReentrantLock`. The name implies that this kind of lock acts like Java locks do in that the lock is associated with the caller's thread. The owner of a lock may reacquire ("relock") the lock as many times as it wishes. For example, a recursive method that locks a resource upon entry is fine.

In addition to the standard-looking `lock()` method, the `Lock` interface has `tryLock()` methods that do not block or that block for a specified period of time in order to acquire the lock. These conditional and timed wait locking forms are something that ordinary Java locks do not provide. The `ReentrantLock` implementation also has a notion of "fairness" that can be turned on or off when it is constructed. When fair is on, the lock attempts to hand out the lock to callers in the order in which they request it. Normal Java locks (and the default, unfair policy of `ReentrantLock`) do not make this guarantee.

Read and write locks

The `ReadWriteLock` interface is a gateway to two different locks, one for reading and one for writing. The idea behind read/write locks is that for most resources it is OK for many "readers" to be viewing data, as long as it is not changing. Conversely, a writer of the data generally requires exclusive access to it. This is just what read/write locks do. Any number of readers may acquire the read lock as long as no write lock is in place. Only one party may hold the write lock, and no readers may hold read locks while the write lock is out. A writer may have to wait for readers to finish before acquiring the write lock, and readers may have to wait for a writer to finish before they are allowed to acquire read locks:

```
ReadWriteLock rwLock = new ReentrantReadWriteLock( fair );

// reader thread 1
rwLock.readLock().lock();
// reader thread 2
rwLock.readLock().lock();

// writer thread
rwLock.writeLock().lock(); // blocks on threads 1 & 2
```

In this code snippet, two readers hold read locks while a writer blocks waiting on the write lock. When both readers have `unlock()`ed their read locks, the writer gains exclusive access to the lock and any subsequent readers block until the writer is finished.

The owner of a write lock can acquire a read lock, too, but not vice versa. Acquiring a read lock and then releasing the write lock is called *downgrading* the lock. Trying to acquire a write lock while holding a read lock (upgrading) is not allowed and causes a deadlock.

Conditions

To complete the picture of `Lock` as a parallel for Java language synchronization, we need an analog to the `wait()`, `notify()`, and `notifyAll()`mechanism. The `Condition` interface represents this functionality with its `await()`, `signal()`, and `signalAll()` methods. A `Condition` is associated with a `Lock` by the lock's `newCondition()` method. Unlike a normal Java lock, a `Lock` may have multiple `Condition` objects that represent multiple wait sets of threads.

The `Condition await()` method is used just like the `wait()` method of a Java object within a `synchronized` block:

```
Lock lock = ...
Condition condition = lock.newCondition();
lock.lock();
condition.await(); // block, waiting for signal()
lock.unlock();

// meanwhile, in another thread...
lock.lock();
condition.signal();
lock.unlock();
```

Like `wait()`, the `Condition await()` method can be called only when the thread is the owner of the lock associated with the condition and the `signal()` method may be called only by another thread that has acquired the lock. Interestingly, though, in this case, these restrictions are implementation details of the `java.util.concurrent` package;

some other implementation of these classes could conceivably change those restrictions in some way.

With the exception of the new reader/writer locks and some timed wait lock methods, it may not seem that the Locks package adds a great deal to Java. However, if you delve into it deeper, you'll find that it's also a toolkit for building new kinds of synchronization primitives and higher-level constructs. The locks package opens up a concrete implementation of Java's synchronization mechanism for all to tinker with and extend. A brief look at the implementation classes reveals nifty methods like `getOwner()` to tell you which thread owns a lock or `getReadLockCount()` to tell you how many readers are working on your data. Lots of things are possible with an open implementation like this, including specialized synchronization packages that do things like automatically detect deadlocks or tune themselves based on external information. There may also be cases where using the explicit lock API provided by this package performs better than language-level synchronization. But that probably doesn't justify the additional burden on developers except in special cases. Next, we'll move up a bit and look at some higher-level synchronization tools.

Synchronization Constructs

The `java.util.concurrent` package adds several higher-level synchronization utilities borrowed from other languages, including `CountDownLatch`, `Semaphore`, `CyclicBarrier`, and `Exchanger`.

CountDownLatch

The `CountDownLatch` is a very simple synchronization utility that allows any number of threads to block, waiting for a countdown value to reach `0` before being "released" to continue their activities. The `CountDownLatch` is initialized with the count when constructed. Thereafter, threads may block using the `await()` method or block for a limited period of time using the timed wait version of `await()`. Any running thread may decrement the counter at any time, whether threads are blocked or not. Once the counter reaches `0`, all waiting threads unblock and continue. Thereafter, any calls to `await()` do not block and the `await()` method returns `false`, indicating that the count has passed. The count cannot be reset.

```
CountDownLatch latch = new CountDownLatch( 2 ); // count from 2

// thread 1
latch.await(); // blocks thread 1

// thread 2
latch.countDown(); // count is 1
latch.countDown(); // count is 0, thread 1 proceeds
```

Countdown latches are used in a wide variety of synchronization schemes to coordinate a number of threads on one result or cause a thread to wait for a number of other threads to produce results. Later we'll talk about a related utility, `CyclicBarrier`, that explicitly waits for a number of threads to synchronize in order to coordinate an action.

Semaphore

Semaphores are a very old synchronization construct that has been used in many other languages. Conceptually, a semaphore is a pool of *permits*—intangible permission slips to perform some activity. The semaphore is initialized with a specified number of permits. Callers can then use the `acquire()` and `release()` methods to take and return these permits. Calling `acquire()` when no permits are available causes the caller to block until one is released. In this way, for example, a semaphore could be used to limit access to some resource to a specified number of threads:

```
int concurrentReaders = 5;
boolean fair = true;
Semaphore sem = new Semaphore( concurrentReaders, fair );

Data readData() throws InterruptedException {
    sem.acquire();
    // read data ...
    sem.release();

    return data;
}
```

In this code snippet, `readData()` effectively limits itself to five concurrent reading threads at any given time. Additional threads are blocked in the `acquire()` method until a permit is free. In this sense, a semaphore is vaguely like a lock with multiple owners. This is where the similarity ends, however.

In actuality, a semaphore differs from a lock in several ways. First, the "pool of permits" is really just a number. No actual value is returned by `acquire()` and no association is made with the acquirer of the lock. This means that any actual locking behavior is strictly cooperative (by convention in the application). It also means that "permits" can be acquired and released by different callers without respect to who actually "acquired" them. It's really just incrementing or decrementing the number. Also, because there is no real association with an "owner," semaphores are not reentrant in the way that real locks are. That is, if a thread calls `acquire()` multiple times, it simply decrements the counter multiple times. This behavior could be useful in some cases to count levels of recursion for security APIs, for example, but is not like a lock, in which one caller "owns" multiple permits. Finally, because the permits pool is really just a number, calling `acquire()` and `release()` out of sync can increase the permit pool beyond its starting point or decrement it below zero. It can even be initialized with a negative number if you wish to require releases before anyone acquires a permit.

In addition to acquire(), Semaphore has a tryAcquire() method that parallels the tryLock() method of Lock. It returns immediately, acquiring a permit if one was available and returning false otherwise. Another form of tryAcquire() accepts a timed wait period. Semaphores also have a notion of "fairness" in the ordering of acquire requests. By default, requests are not guaranteed to be ordered, but if the "fair" flag is set when the Semaphore is constructed, acquire() doles out permits in first-in-first-out (FIFO) order. The tradeoff is that ordering may impact performance a bit, depending on the implementation.

CyclicBarrier

The CyclicBarrier class is a synchronization point where a specified number of related threads meet after finishing their activities. When all of the threads have arrived, an optional, shared barrier action can be executed and then all of the threads are "released" to continue. The class is termed *cyclic* because it can then be used again in the case where the threads repeat their activities in this manner. CyclicBarrier is an alternative to using the join() method, which collects threads only after they have completed and returned from their run() method.

The following example, SiteTimer, accepts a number of URLs on the command line and times how long it takes to connect to each one, printing the results in sorted order. It performs the connections in parallel using a dedicated thread per site and uses a CyclicBarrier for the threads to rendezvous after each timing cycle. Then it prints the coordinated results before they begin again. This example also illustrates a number of Java features, including generics, collections, formatted printing, autoboxing, and an inner class. Although we haven't yet discussed collections or the network portion of the example, the usage is fairly simple, and you can return to the example after reading the relevant chapters later in this book.

```
import java.util.*;
import java.util.concurrent.*;
import java.net.*;
import java.io.IOException;

public class SiteTimer
{
   CyclicBarrier barrier;
   List<Result> results = new ArrayList<Result>();

   private class Result implements Comparable<Result>
   {
      Long time;
      String site;
      Result( Long time, String site ) {
         this.time = time;
         this.site = site;
      }
      public int compareTo( Result r ) { return time.compareTo( r.time ); }
```

```
    }

    static long timeConnect( String site ) {
        long start = System.currentTimeMillis();
        try {
            new URL( site ).openConnection().connect();
        } catch ( IOException e ) {
            return -1;
        }
        return System.currentTimeMillis() - start;
    }

    void showResults() {
        Collections.sort( results );
        for( Result result : results )
            System.out.printf( "%-30.30s : %d\n", result.site, result.time );
        System.out.println("-----------------");
    }

    public void start( String [] args )
    {
        Runnable showResultsAction = new Runnable() {
            public void run() {
                showResults();
                results.clear();
            } };
        barrier = new CyclicBarrier( args.length, showResultsAction );

        for ( final String site : args )
            new Thread() {
                public void run() {
                    while( true ) {
                        long time = timeConnect( site );
                        results.add( new Result( time, site ) );
                        try {
                            barrier.await();
                        } catch ( BrokenBarrierException e ) { return;
                        } catch ( InterruptedException e ) { return; }
                    }
                }
            }.start();
    }

    public static void main( String [] args ) throws IOException {
        new SiteTimer().start( args );
    }
}
```

The `start()` method constructs the barrier, specifying the number of threads that must be present before the group has fully arrived and the action to perform when all of the threads are ready. For each site, a thread is created that loops, timing the connection to the site and adding a result object to the list before blocking on the barrier's `await()`

method. When all of the threads reach the await() method, the barrier action fires, printing the results. All of the threads are then released to begin the next cycle.

If any of the waiting threads is interrupted or times out (using the timed wait version of the await() method) the barrier is said to be "broken" and all of the waiting threads receive a BrokenBarrierException. In theory, the barrier can be "fixed" by calling its reset() method, but this is complicated because only one thread from the group can reset the barrier properly. A reset() while any other thread is waiting causes the barrier to be broken and the waiting threads to receive the exception again, so it is probably best to start over at this point.

One more detail: the await() method returns an integer that indicates the order in which the threads arrived at the barrier. This can be used to divide up work for the next iteration of the threads. For example, if the threads' jobs are not identical, you could use the number to "elect" a leader thread or divide the threads into two or more groups.

Phaser

No *Star Trek* jokes here. Java 7 introduced a new concurrency utility called Phaser. Phaser is very similar to the CyclicBarrier except that it provides a bit more flexibility. Phaser draws its name in part from the fact that it assigns a number to each cycle of its threads (a phase number). Participating threads and bystanders can read this number to monitor activity in the barrier. In CyclicBarrier, the number of threads that are tracked by the barrier is fixed; new threads cannot join the party during its lifecycle. This differs from Phaser, where the number of participants can change over the life of the activity.

Exchanger

The Exchanger is a synchronization point for a pair of threads to exchange data items. An item of the same type is passed in each direction using the exchange() method. The first method to arrive at the Exchanger blocks, waiting for its mate. When the second method arrives, they each receive the other's argument to the exchange() method. Any number of actual threads may be using the Exchanger; they are simply paired in some order when they arrive. Exchanger is a generic class that is parameterized by the type of object to be passed:

```
Exchanger<ByteBuffer> xchange = new Exchanger<ByteBuffer>();

// thread 1
Buffer nextBuf = xchange.exchange( buffer1 ); // blocks

// thread 2
Buffer nextBuf = xchange.exchange( buffer2 );

// buffers exchanged, both threads continue...
```

The `Exchanger` pattern is primarily useful for reusing data objects or buffers between threads, as indicated in this code snippet. Say that you have a reader thread filling buffers with data and a writer thread writing the contents of the buffers somewhere. Using an `Exchanger`, the reader and writer can trade a pair of buffers back and forth without creating new ones. This may seem a bit arcane, but it has applications when using the NIO advanced I/O package, which we discuss in Chapters 12 and 13.

We should note that the `Exchanger` is similar to the `SynchronousQueue`, which we'll discuss in Chapter 11 when we cover the Collections API. The `Exchanger`, however, passes data in both directions, whereas `SynchronousQueue` simply passes elements in one direction.

Atomic Operations

The `java.util.concurrent.atomic` package holds an interesting set of wrapper classes for atomic, "all-or-nothing" operations on certain primitive types and reference values. An atomic operation is a kind of transaction where some sequence of events either completes or fails as a unit and there is no potential for any intermediate state to be seen. In this case, the transactions we're talking about are very simple operations that either set or get a value, possibly in combination with a simple test or mathematical operation. There are atomic wrapper classes for the following types: Booleans, integers, and long values as well as arrays of integers and longs and object references:

```
AtomicBoolean.java
AtomicInteger.java
AtomicIntegerArray.java
AtomicLong.java
AtomicLongArray.java
AtomicReference.java
AtomicReferenceArray.java
```

The `AtomicBoolean` class (which, by the way, has to compete with `java.awt.Robot` for coolest class name in Java) serves as a good example. At first glance, it seems like an oxymoron. After all, normal operations on Booleans in Java are atomic already. There is supposed to be no possible "in between" state for a Boolean to be misread by any fiesty multithreaded code (as there theoretically could be for long and double values). Instead, the usefulness of the `AtomicBoolean` wrapper is in its combination operations: `compareAndSet()` and `getAndSet()`:

```
AtomicBoolean bool = new AtomicBoolean( true );
bool.compareAndSet( expectedValue, newValue );
```

The `compareAndSet()` method first performs a comparison to an expected value (`true` or `false` in the case of a Boolean) and only if the value matches does it assign the new value. The interesting thing is that both of these operations happen "atomically," together. This means that there is no possibility of someone changing the value between the time that we checked it and assigned the new value. That may sound like a slim chance anyway, but it's very important for guaranteeing the semantics of flags. For example, suppose we have a master "shutdown" switch in our application and the thread that sets it wants to perform cleanup on the way out. Using `compareAndSet()` to test first, we can guarantee that only one thread can possibly set the flag and perform the procedure.

The `getAndSet()` method simply assigns the new value and returns the old value in the same, safe way. It's a little harder to see how this applies to a Boolean, so let's move on to `AtomicInteger` and `AtomicLong`. These numeric types have additional arithmetic combination operations:

```
int getAndIncrement()
int getAndDecrement()
int getAndAdd(int delta)
int incrementAndGet()
int decrementAndGet()
int addAndGet(int delta)
```

`getAndIncrement()` increments the value and then returns the previous value. `incrementAndGet()` does the converse, returning the new value. These operations are very useful for generating unique serial numbers. For example:

```
AtomicInteger serialNum = new AtomicInteger(0);

public int nextSerialNumber() {
    return serialNum.getAndIncrement();
}
```

We could have accomplished the same thing by synchronizing the method, but this is simpler and may be much faster.

Object-type references can also be wrapped for atomic operations, including `compareAndSet()` and `getAndSet()`. The `AtomicReference` class is generic and parameterized by the type of reference it wraps:

```
AtomicReference<Node> ref = new AtomicReference<Node>( node );
ref.compareAndSet( null, newNode );
```

Weak implementations

The `compareAndSet()` method has a strange twin named `weakCompareAndSet()`, which has the dubious distinction that it simply may not work when called. It is, however, nice enough to tell you when it doesn't work by returning `false`. What's the point of this? Well, by allowing this fuzziness, Java may be able to make the implementation of the weak method much faster than the "certain" one. You can loop and retry the weak method instead and it may improve performance on some architectures. This is all because the Java VM may be able to map these kinds of atomic operations all the way down to the hardware level for performance, but restrictions may apply that make it difficult to guarantee.

Field updaters

The `atomic` package also supplies a set of "field update" utilities for each of the types that it can wrap. These utilities use reflection (see Chapter 7) to perform the kinds of atomic operations we described previously on "naked" primitive types that are not already wrapped in their atomic wrapper classes. The field updaters work on variables in an object by name and type. The catch is that atomicity is guaranteed only with respect to other callers that use the field updaters or the regular atomic wrapper classes. No guarantees are made with respect to other threads that address the variables in arbitrary ways.

Conclusion

Java was one of the first mainstream languages to provide support for threading at the language level and is now one of the first languages to standardize high-level threading utilities and APIs as well. At this point, we've come to the end of our discussion of threads in Java and also, in a way, to the end of the first part of this book. In Chapters 1 through 9, we discussed the Java language: its syntax and "built-in" features. In the remainder of the book, we will focus mainly on the APIs and libraries that make up the rest of the Java platform. We will see that the real appeal of Java is the combination of this simple language married with powerful tools and standards.

CHAPTER 10
Working with Text

If you've been reading this book sequentially, you've read all about the core Java language constructs, including the object-oriented aspects of the language and the use of threads. Now it's time to shift gears and start talking about the Java Application Programming Interface (API), the collection of classes that compose the standard Java packages and come with every Java implementation. Java's core packages are one of its most distinguishing features. Many other object-oriented languages have similar features, but none has as extensive a set of standardized APIs and tools as Java does. This is both a reflection of and a reason for Java's success. Table 10-1 lists some of the important packages in the API and their corresponding chapters in this book.

Table 10-1. Java API packages

Package	Contents	Chapter
`java.lang`	Basic language classes	4–9
`java.lang.reflect`	Reflection	7
`java.util.concurrent`	Thread utilities	9
`java.text` `java.util.regex`	International text classes and regular expressions	10
`java.util`	Utilities and collections classes	10–12
`java.io` `java.nio`	Input and output Input and output	12 12
`java.net`	Networking and Remote Method Invocation classes	13–14
`java.rmi`	Remote Method Invocation classes	13
`javax.servlet`	Web applications	15
`javax.swing` `java.awt`	Swing GUI and 2D graphics	16–20

Package	Contents	Chapter

`java.awt.image`
`javax.imageio`
`javax.media`
	Images, sound, and video	21

`java.beans`	JavaBeans API	22
`java.applet`	The Applet API	23
`javax.xml`	The XML API	24

As you can see in Table 10-1, we have examined some classes in `java.lang` in earlier chapters while looking at the core language constructs. Starting with this chapter, we throw open the Java toolbox and begin examining the rest of the API classes, starting with text-related utilities, because they are fundamental to all kinds of applications.

Text-Related APIs

In this chapter, we cover most of the special-purpose, text-related APIs in Java, from simple classes for parsing words and numbers to advanced text formatting, internationalization, and regular expressions. But because so much of what we do with computers is oriented around text, classifying APIs as strictly text-related can be somewhat arbitrary. Some of the text-related packages we cover in the next chapter include the Java Calendar API, the Properties and User Preferences APIs, and the Logging API. But some of the most important tools in the text arena are those for working with the Extensible Markup Language, XML. In Chapter 24, we cover XML in detail, along with the XSL/XSLT stylesheet language. Together they provide a powerful framework for rendering documents.

Strings

We'll start by taking a closer look at the Java `String` class (or, more specifically, `java.lang.String`). Because working with `String`s is so fundamental, it's important to understand how they are implemented and what you can do with them. A `String` object encapsulates a sequence of Unicode characters. Internally, these characters are stored in a regular Java array, but the `String` object guards this array jealously and gives you access to it only through its own API. This is to support the idea that `String`s are *immutable*; once you create a `String` object, you can't change its value. Lots of operations on a `String` object appear to change the characters or length of a string, but what they really do is return a new `String` object that copies or internally references the needed characters of the original. Java implementations make an effort to consolidate identical strings used in the same class into a shared-string pool and to share parts of `String`s where possible.

The original motivation for all of this was performance. Immutable Strings can save memory and be optimized for speed by the Java VM. The flip side is that a programmer should have a basic understanding of the String class in order to avoid creating an excessive number of String objects in places where performance is an issue. That was especially true in the past, when VMs were slow and handled memory poorly. Nowadays, string usage is not usually an issue in the overall performance of a real application.[1]

Constructing Strings

Literal strings, defined in your source code, are declared with double quotes and can be assigned to a String variable:

```
String quote = "To be or not to be";
```

Java automatically converts the literal string into a String object and assigns it to the variable.

Strings keep track of their own length, so String objects in Java don't require special terminators. You can get the length of a String with the length() method. You can also test for a zero length string by using isEmpty():

```
int length = quote.length();
boolean empty = quote.isEmpty();
```

Strings can take advantage of the only overloaded operator in Java, the + operator, for string concatenation. The following code produces equivalent strings:

```
String name = "John " + "Smith";
String name = "John ".concat("Smith");
```

Literal strings can't span lines in Java source files, but we can concatenate lines to produce the same effect:

```
String poem =
    "'Twas brillig, and the slithy toves\n" +
    "   Did gyre and gimble in the wabe:\n" +
    "All mimsy were the borogoves,\n" +
    "   And the mome raths outgrabe.\n";
```

Embedding lengthy text in source code is not normally something you want to do. In this and the following chapter, we'll talk about ways to load Strings from files, special packages called resource bundles, and URLs. Technologies like Java Server Pages and template engines also provide a way to factor out large amounts of text from your code.

1. When in doubt, measure it! If your String-manipulating code is clean and easy to understand, don't rewrite it until someone proves to you that it is too slow. Chances are that they will be wrong. And don't be fooled by relative comparisons. A millisecond is 1,000 times slower than a microsecond, but it still may be negligible to your application's overall performance.

For example, in Chapter 14, we'll see how to load our poem from a web server by opening a URL like this:

```
InputStream poem = new URL(
    "http://myserver/~dodgson/jabberwocky.txt").openStream();
```

In addition to making strings from literal expressions, you can construct a `String` directly from an array of characters:

```
char [] data = new char [] { 'L', 'e', 'm', 'm', 'i', 'n', 'g' };
String lemming = new String( data );
```

You can also construct a `String` from an array of bytes:

```
byte [] data = new byte [] { (byte)97, (byte)98, (byte)99 };
String abc = new String(data, "ISO8859_1");
```

In this case, the second argument to the `String` constructor is the name of a character-encoding scheme. The `String` constructor uses it to convert the raw bytes in the specified encoding to the internally used standard 2-byte Unicode characters. If you don't specify a character encoding, the default encoding scheme on your system is used. We'll discuss character encodings more when we talk about the `Charset` class, IO, in Chapter 12.[2]

Conversely, the `charAt()` method of the `String` class lets you access the characters of a `String` in an array-like fashion:

```
String s = "Newton";
for ( int i = 0; i < s.length(); i++ )
    System.out.println( s.charAt( i ) );
```

This code prints the characters of the string one at a time. Alternately, we can get the characters all at once with `toCharArray()`. Here's a way to save typing a bunch of single quotes and get an array holding the alphabet:

```
char [] abcs = "abcdefghijklmnopqrstuvwxyz".toCharArray();
```

The notion that a `String` is a sequence of characters is also codified by the `String` class implementing the interface `java.lang.CharSequence`, which prescribes the methods `length()` and `charAt()` as well as a way to get a subset of the characters.

Strings from Things

Objects and primitive types in Java can be turned into a default textual representation as a `String`. For primitive types like numbers, the string should be fairly obvious; for object types, it is under the control of the object itself. We can get the string

2. On Mac OS X, the default encoding is MacRoman. In Windows, it is CP1252. On some Unix platforms it is ISO8859_1.

representation of an item with the static String.valueOf() method. Various overloaded versions of this method accept each of the primitive types:

```
String one = String.valueOf( 1 ); // integer, "1"
String two = String.valueOf( 2.384f );  // float, "2.384"
String notTrue = String.valueOf( false ); // boolean, "false"
```

All objects in Java have a toString() method that is inherited from the Object class. For many objects, this method returns a useful result that displays the contents of the object. For example, a java.util.Date object's toString() method returns the date it represents formatted as a string. For objects that do not provide a representation, the string result is just a unique identifier that can be used for debugging. The String.valueOf() method, when called for an object, invokes the object's toString() method and returns the result. The only real difference in using this method is that if you pass it a null object reference, it returns the String "null" for you, instead of producing a NullPointerException:

```
Date date = new Date();
// Equivalent, e.g., "Fri Dec 19 05:45:34 CST 1969"
String d1 = String.valueOf( date );
String d2 = date.toString();

date = null;
d1 = String.valueOf( date );  // "null"
d2 = date.toString();  // NullPointerException!
```

String concatenation uses the valueOf() method internally, so if you "add" an object or primitive using the plus operator (+), you get a String:

```
String today = "Today's date is :" + date;
```

You'll sometimes see people use the empty string and the plus operator (+) as shorthand to get the string value of an object. For example:

```
String two = "" + 2.384f;
String today = "" + new Date();
```

Comparing Strings

The standard equals() method can compare strings for *equality*; they contain exactly the same characters in the same order. You can use a different method, equalsIgnoreCase(), to check the equivalence of strings in a case-insensitive way:

```
String one = "FOO";
String two = "foo";

one.equals( two );             // false
one.equalsIgnoreCase( two );   // true
```

A common mistake for novice programmers in Java is to compare strings with the == operator when they intend to use the equals() method. Remember that strings are objects in Java, and == tests for object *identity*; that is, whether the two arguments being tested are the same object. In Java, it's easy to make two strings that have the same characters but are not the same string object. For example:

```
String foo1 = "foo";
String foo2 = String.valueOf( new char [] { 'f', 'o', 'o' } );

foo1 == foo2          // false!
foo1.equals( foo2 )  // true
```

This mistake is particularly dangerous because it often works for the common case in which you are comparing literal strings (strings declared with double quotes right in the code). The reason for this is that Java tries to manage strings efficiently by combining them. At compile time, Java finds all the identical strings within a given class and makes only one object for them. This is safe because strings are immutable and cannot change. You can coalesce strings yourself in this way at runtime using the `String intern()` method. Interning a string returns an equivalent string reference that is unique across the VM.

The `compareTo()` method compares the lexical value of the `String` to another `String`, determining whether it sorts alphabetically earlier than, the same as, or later than the target string. It returns an integer that is less than, equal to, or greater than zero:

```
String abc = "abc";
String def = "def";
String num = "123";

if ( abc.compareTo( def ) < 0 )          // true
if ( abc.compareTo( abc ) == 0 )         // true
if ( abc.compareTo( num ) > 0 )          // true
```

The `compareTo()` method compares strings strictly by their characters' positions in the Unicode specification. This works for simple text but does not handle all language variations well. The `Collator` class, discussed next, can be used for more sophisticated comparisons.

The Collator class

The `java.text` package provides a sophisticated set of classes for comparing strings in specific languages. German, for example, has vowels with umlauts and another character that resembles the Greek letter beta and represents a double "s." How should we sort these? Although the rules for sorting such characters are precisely defined, you can't assume that the lexical comparison we used earlier has the correct meaning for languages other than English. Fortunately, the `Collator` class takes care of these complex sorting problems.

In the following example, we use a `Collator` designed to compare German strings. You can obtain a default `Collator` by calling the `Collator.getInstance()` method with no arguments. Once you have an appropriate `Collator` instance, you can use its `compare()` method, which returns values just like `String`'s `compareTo()` method. The following code creates two strings for the German translations of "fun" and "later," using Unicode constants for these two special characters. It then compares them, using a `Collator` for the German locale. (`Locale`s help you deal with issues relevant to particular languages and cultures; we'll talk about them in detail later in this chapter.) The result in this case is that "fun" (Spaß) sorts before "later" (später):

```
String fun = "Spa\u00df";
String later = "sp\u00e4ter";

Collator german = Collator.getInstance(Locale.GERMAN);
if (german.compare(fun, later) < 0) // true
```

Using collators is essential if you're working with languages other than English. In Spanish, for example, "ll" and "ch" are treated as unique characters and alphabetized separately. A collator handles cases like these automatically.

Searching

The `String` class provides several simple methods for finding fixed substrings within a string. The `startsWith()` and `endsWith()` methods compare an argument string with the beginning and end of the `String`, respectively:

```
String url = "http://foo.bar.com/";
if ( url.startsWith("http:") )  // true
```

The `indexOf()` method searches for the first occurrence of a character or substring and returns the starting character position, or `-1` if the substring is not found:

```
String abcs = "abcdefghijklmnopqrstuvwxyz";
int i = abcs.indexOf( 'p' );     // 15
int i = abcs.indexOf( "def" );   // 3
int I = abcs.indexOf( "Fang" );  // -1
```

Similarly, `lastIndexOf()` searches backward through the string for the last occurrence of a character or substring.

The `contains()` method handles the very common task of checking to see whether a given substring is contained in the target string:

```
String log = "There is an emergency in sector 7!";
if  ( log.contains("emergency") ) pageSomeone();

// equivalent to
if ( log.indexOf("emergency") != -1 ) ...
```

For more complex searching, you can use the Regular Expression API, which allows you to look for and parse complex patterns. We'll talk about regular expressions later in this chapter.

Editing

A number of methods operate on the `String` and return a new `String` as a result. While this is useful, you should be aware that creating lots of strings in this manner can affect performance. If you need to modify a string often or build a complex string from components, you should use the `StringBuilder` class, as we'll discuss shortly.

`trim()` is a useful method that removes leading and trailing whitespace (i.e., carriage return, newline, and tab) from the `String`:

```
String str = "   abc   ";
str = str.trim();  // "abc"
```

In this example, we threw away the original `String` (with excess whitespace), and it will be garbage-collected.

The `toUpperCase()` and `toLowerCase()` methods return a new `String` of the appropriate case:

```
String down = "FOO".toLowerCase();       // "foo"
String up   = down.toUpperCase();        // "FOO"
```

`substring()` returns a specified range of characters. The starting index is *inclusive*; the ending is *exclusive*:

```
String abcs = "abcdefghijklmnopqrstuvwxyz";
String cde = abcs.substring( 2, 5 ); // "cde"
```

The `replace()` method provides simple, literal string substitution. One or more occurrences of the target string are replaced with the replacement string, moving from beginning to end. For example:

```
String message = "Hello NAME, how are you?".replace( "NAME", "Penny" );
// "Hello Penny, how are you?"
String xy = "xxooxxxoo".replace( "xx", "X" );
// "XooXxoo"
```

The `String` class also has two methods that allow you to do more complex pattern substitution: `replaceAll()` and `replaceFirst()`. Unlike the simple `replace()` method, these methods use regular expressions (a special syntax) to describe the replacement pattern, which we'll cover later in this chapter.

String Method Summary

Table 10-2 summarizes the methods provided by the `String` class.

Table 10-2. String methods

Method	Functionality
`charAt()`	Gets a particular character in the string
`compareTo()`	Compares the string with another string

Method	Functionality
concat()	Concatenates the string with another string
contains()	Checks whether the string contains another string
copyValueOf()	Returns a string equivalent to the specified character array
endsWith()	Checks whether the string ends with a specified suffix
equals()	Compares the string with another string
equalsIgnoreCase()	Compares the string with another string, ignoring case
getBytes()	Copies characters from the string into a byte array
getChars()	Copies characters from the string into a character array
hashCode()	Returns a hashcode for the string
indexOf()	Searches for the first occurrence of a character or substring in the string
intern()	Fetches a unique instance of the string from a global shared-string pool
isEmpty()	Returns true if the string is zero length
lastIndexOf()	Searches for the last occurrence of a character or substring in a string
length()	Returns the length of the string
matches()	Determines if the whole string matches a regular expression pattern
regionMatches()	Checks whether a region of the string matches the specified region of another string
replace()	Replaces all occurrences of a character in the string with another character
replaceAll()	Replaces all occurrences of a regular expression pattern with a pattern
replaceFirst()	Replaces the first occurrence of a regular expression pattern with a pattern
split()	Splits the string into an array of strings using a regular expression pattern as a delimiter
startsWith()	Checks whether the string starts with a specified prefix
substring()	Returns a substring from the string
toCharArray()	Returns the array of characters from the string
toLowerCase()	Converts the string to lowercase
toString()	Returns the string value of an object
toUpperCase()	Converts the string to uppercase
trim()	Removes leading and trailing whitespace from the string
valueOf()	Returns a string representation of a value

StringBuilder and StringBuffer

In contrast to the immutable string, the `java.lang.StringBuilder` class is a modifiable and expandable buffer for characters. You can use it to create a big string efficiently. `StringBuilder` and `StringBuffer` are twins; they have exactly the same API. `StringBuilder` was added in Java 5.0 as a drop-in, unsynchronized replacement for `StringBuffer`. We'll come back to that in a bit.

First, let's look at some examples of `String` construction:

```
// Could be better
String ball = "Hello";
ball = ball + " there.";
ball = ball + " How are you?";
```

This example creates an unnecessary `String` object each time we use the concatenation operator (+). Whether this is significant depends on how often this code is run and how big the string actually gets. Here's a more extreme example:

```
// Bad use of + ...
while( (line = readLine()) != EOF )
    text += line;
```

This example repeatedly produces new `String` objects. The character array must be copied over and over, which can adversely affect performance. The solution is to use a `StringBuilder` object and its `append()` method:

```
StringBuilder sb = new StringBuilder("Hello");
sb.append(" there.");
sb.append(" How are you?");

StringBuilder text = new StringBuilder();
while( (line = readline()) != EOF )
    text.append( line );
```

Here, the `StringBuilder` efficiently handles expanding the array as necessary. We can get a `String` back from the `StringBuilder` with its `toString()` method:

```
String message = sb.toString();
```

You can also retrieve part of a `StringBuilder` as a `String` by using one of the `substring()` methods.

You might be interested to know that when you write a long expression using string concatenation, the compiler generates code that uses a `StringBuilder` behind the scenes:

```
String foo = "To " + "be " + "or";
```

It is really equivalent to:

```
String foo = new
  StringBuilder().append("To ").append("be ").append("or").toString();
```

In this case, the compiler knows what you are trying to do and takes care of it for you.

The `StringBuilder` class provides a number of overloaded `append()` methods for adding any type of data to the buffer. `StringBuilder` also provides a number of overloaded `insert()` methods for inserting various types of data at a particular location in the string buffer. Furthermore, you can remove a single character or a range of characters with the `deleteCharAt()` and `delete()` methods. Finally, you can replace part of the

`StringBuilder` with the contents of a `String` using the `replace()` method. The `String` and `StringBuilder` classes cooperate so that, in some cases, no copy of the data has to be made; the string data is shared between the objects.

You should use a `StringBuilder` instead of a `String` any time you need to keep adding characters to a string; it's designed to handle such modifications efficiently. You can convert the `StringBuilder` to a `String` when you need it, or simply concatenate or print it anywhere you'd use a `String`.

As we said earlier, `StringBuilder` was added in Java 5.0 as a replacement for `StringBuffer`. The only real difference between the two is that the methods of `StringBuffer` are synchronized and the methods of `StringBuilder` are not. This means that if you wish to use `StringBuilder` from multiple threads concurrently, you must synchronize the access yourself (which is easily accomplished). The reason for the change is that most simple usage does not require any synchronization and shouldn't have to pay the associated penalty (slight as it is).

Internationalization

The Java VM lets us write code that executes in the same way on any Java platform. But in a global marketplace, that is only half the battle. A big question remains: will the application content and data be understandable to end users worldwide? Must users know English to use your application? The answer is that Java provides thorough support for *localizing* the text of your application for most modern languages and dialects. In this section, we'll talk about the concepts of internationalization (often abbreviated "I18N") and the classes that support them.

The java.util.Locale Class

Internationalization programming revolves around the `Locale` class. The class itself is very simple; it encapsulates a country code, a language code, and a rarely used variant code. Commonly used languages and countries are defined as constants in the `Locale` class. (Maybe it's ironic that these names are all in English.) You can retrieve the codes or readable names, as follows:

```
Locale l = Locale.ITALIAN;
System.out.println(l.getCountry());             // IT
System.out.println(l.getDisplayCountry());      // Italy
System.out.println(l.getLanguage());            // it
System.out.println(l.getDisplayLanguage());     // Italian
```

The country codes comply with ISO 3166. You will find a complete list of country codes at the RIPE Network Coordination Centre (*http://bit.ly/182iHGn*). The language codes comply with ISO 639. A complete list of language codes is online at the US government website (*http://1.usa.gov/14iSOkR*). There is no official set of variant codes; they are designated as vendor-specific or platform-specific. You can get an array of all supported

Locales with the static getAvailableLocales() method (which you might use to let your users choose). Or you can retrieve the default Locale for the location where your code is running with the static Locale.getDefault() method and let the system decide for you.

Many classes throughout the Java API use a Locale to decide how to represent text. We ran into one earlier when talking about sorting text with the Collator class. We'll see more later in this chapter used to format numbers and currency strings, and again in the next chapter with the DateFormat class, which uses Locales to determine how to format and parse dates and times. Without getting into the details yet, here is a quick example:

```
System.out.printf( Locale.ITALIAN, "%f\n", 3.14 ); // "3,14"
```

The preceding statement uses the Italian Locale to indicate that the decimal number 3.14 should be formatted as it would in Italian, using a comma instead of a decimal point. We'll talk more about formatting text later in this chapter.

Resource Bundles

Before we move on to the details of formatting messages and values, we might take a step back and ask a bigger question: what about the messages themselves? How can we write and manage applications that are truly multilingual in their user interfaces and in all the messages they display to the user? We can discover our locale, but how do we manage all of the application text in our code? The ResourceBundle class offers a clean, flexible solution for factoring out the text and resources of your application into language-specific classes or text files.

A ResourceBundle is a collection of objects that your application can access by name. It acts much like the Hashtable or Map collections we'll discuss in Chapter 11, looking up objects based on Strings that serve as keys. A ResourceBundle of a given name may be defined for many different Locales. To get a particular ResourceBundle, call the factory method ResourceBundle.getBundle(), which accepts the name of the ResourceBundle and a Locale. The following example gets the ResourceBundle named "Message" for two Locales; from each bundle, it retrieves the message whose key is "HelloMessage" and prints the message:

```
import java.util.*;

public class Hello {
  public static void main(String[] args) {
    ResourceBundle bun;
    bun = ResourceBundle.getBundle("Message", Locale.ITALY);
    System.out.println(bun.getString("HelloMessage"));
    bun = ResourceBundle.getBundle("Message", Locale.US);
    System.out.println(bun.getString("HelloMessage"));
```

```
    }
  }
```

The `getBundle()` method throws the runtime exception `MissingResourceException` if an appropriate `ResourceBundle` cannot be located.

You can provide `ResourceBundles` in two ways: either as compiled Java classes (hardcoded Java) or as simple property files. Resource bundles implemented as classes are either subclasses of `ListResourceBundle` or direct implementations of `ResourceBundle`. Resource bundles backed by a property file are represented at runtime by a `PropertyResourceBundle` object. `ResourceBundle.getBundle()` returns either a matching class or an instance of `PropertyResourceBundle` corresponding to a matching property file. The algorithm used by `getBundle()` is based on appending the country and language codes of the requested `Locale` to the name of the resource. Specifically, it searches for resources in this order:

```
name_language_country_variant
name_language_country
name_language
name
name_default-language_default-country_default-variant
name_default-language_default-country
name_default-language
```

In this example, when we try to get the `ResourceBundle` named `Message`, specific to `Locale.ITALY`, it searches for the following names (no variant codes are in the `Locales` we are using):

```
Message_it_IT
Message_it
Message
Message_en_US
Message_en
```

Let's define the `Message_it_IT ResourceBundle` as a hardcoded class, a subclass of `ListResourceBundle`:

```
import java.util.*;

public class Message_it_IT extends ListResourceBundle {
  public Object[][] getContents() {
    return contents;
  }

  static final Object[][] contents = {
    {"HelloMessage", "Buon giorno, world!"},
    {"OtherMessage", "Ciao."},
  };
}
```

ListResourceBundle makes it easy to define a ResourceBundle class; all we have to do is override the getContents() method. This method simply returns a two-dimensional array containing the names and values of its resources. In this example, contents[1][0] is the second key (OtherMessage), and contents [1][1] is the corresponding message (Ciao.).

Let's define a ResourceBundle for Locale.US. This time, we'll take the easy way and make a property file. Save the following data in a file called *Message_en_US.properties*:

```
HelloMessage=Hello, world!
OtherMessage=Bye.
```

So what happens if somebody runs your program in Locale.FRANCE and no ResourceBundle is defined for that Locale? To avoid a runtime MissingResourceException, it's a good idea to define a default ResourceBundle. In our example, you can change the name of the property file to *Message.properties*. That way, if a language- or country-specific ResourceBundle cannot be found, your application can still run (by falling back to this English representation).

Parsing and Formatting Text

Parsing and formatting text is a large, open-ended topic. So far in this chapter, we've looked at only primitive operations on strings—creation, basic editing, searching, and turning simple values into strings. Now we'd like to move on to more structured forms of text. Java has a rich set of APIs for parsing and printing formatted strings, including numbers, dates, times, and currency values. We'll cover most of these topics in this chapter, but we'll wait to discuss date and time formatting until Chapter 11.

We'll start with parsing—reading primitive numbers and values as strings and chopping long strings into tokens. Then we'll go the other way and look at formatting strings and the java.text package. We'll revisit the topic of internationalization to see how Java can localize parsing and formatting of text, numbers, and dates for particular locales. Finally, we'll take a detailed look at regular expressions, the most powerful text-parsing tool Java offers. Regular expressions let you define your own patterns of arbitrary complexity, search for them, and parse them from text.

We should mention that you're going to see a great deal of overlap between the new formatting and parsing APIs (printf and Scanner) introduced in Java 5.0 and the older APIs of the java.text package. The new APIs effectively replace much of the old ones and in some ways are easier to use. Nonetheless, it's good to know about both because so much existing code uses the older APIs.

Parsing Primitive Numbers

In Java, numbers and Booleans are primitive types—not objects. But for each primitive type, Java also defines a *primitive wrapper* class. Specifically, the `java.lang` package includes the following classes: `Byte`, `Short`, `Integer`, `Long`, `Float`, `Double`, and `Boolean`. We talked about these in Chapter 1, but we bring them up now because these classes hold static utility methods that know how to parse their respective types from strings. Each of these primitive wrapper classes has a static "parse" method that reads a `String` and returns the corresponding primitive type. For example:

```
byte b = Byte.parseByte("16");
int n = Integer.parseInt( "42" );
long l = Long.parseLong( "99999999999" );
float f = Float.parseFloat( "4.2" );
double d = Double.parseDouble( "99.99999999" );
boolean b = Boolean.parseBoolean("true");
// Prior to Java 5.0 use:
boolean b = new Boolean("true").booleanValue();
```

Alternately, the `java.util.Scanner` provides a single API for not only parsing individual primitive types from strings, but reading them from a stream of tokens. This example shows how to use it in place of the preceding wrapper classes:

```
byte b = new Scanner("16").nextByte();
int n = new Scanner("42").nextInt();
long l = new Scanner("99999999999").nextLong();
float f = new Scanner("4.2").nextFloat();
double d = new Scanner("99.99999999").nextDouble();
boolean b = new Scanner("true").nextBoolean();
```

We'll see `Scanner` used to parse multiple values from a `String` or stream when we discuss tokenizing text later in this chapter.

Working with alternate bases

It's easy to parse integer type numbers (`byte`, `short`, `int`, `long`) in alternate numeric bases. You can use the parse methods of the primitive wrapper classes by simply specifying the base as a second parameter:

```
long l = Long.parseLong( "CAFEBABE", 16 );  // l = 3405691582
byte b = Byte.parseByte ( "12", 8 ); // b = 10
```

All methods of the Java 5.0 `Scanner` class described earlier also accept a base as an optional argument:

```
long l = new Scanner( "CAFEBABE" ).nextLong( 16 );  // l = 3405691582
byte b = new Scanner( "12" ).nextByte( 8 ); // b = 10
```

You can go the other way and convert a `long` or integer value to a string value in a specified base using special static `toString()` methods of the `Integer` and `Long` classes:

```
String s = Long.toString( 3405691582L, 16 );  // s = "cafebabe"
```

For convenience, each class also has a static `toHexString()` method for working with base 16:

```
String s = Integer.toHexString( 255 ).toUpperCase();  // s = "FF";
```

Number formats

The preceding wrapper class parser methods handle the case of numbers formatted using only the simplest English conventions with no frills. If these parse methods do not understand the string, either because it's simply not a valid number or because the number is formatted in the convention of another language, they throw a `NumberFormatException`:

```
// Italian formatting
double d = Double.parseDouble("1.234,56");  // NumberFormatException
```

The `Scanner` API is smarter and can use `Locale`s to parse numbers in specific languages with more elaborate conventions. For example, the `Scanner` can handle comma-formatted numbers:

```
int n = new Scanner("99,999,999").nextInt();
```

You can specify a `Locale` other than the default with the `useLocale()` method. Let's parse that value in Italian now:

```
double d = new Scanner("1.234,56").useLocale( Locale.ITALIAN ).nextDouble();
```

If the `Scanner` cannot parse a string, it throws a runtime `InputMismatchException`:

```
double d = new Scanner("garbage").nextDouble(); // InputMismatchException
```

Prior to Java 5.0, this kind of parsing was accomplished using the `java.text` package with the `NumberFormat` class. The classes of the `java.text` package also allow you to parse additional types, such as dates, times, and localized currency values, that aren't handled by the `Scanner`. We'll look at these later in this chapter.

Tokenizing Text

A common programming task involves parsing a string of text into words or "tokens" that are separated by some set of delimiter characters, such as spaces or commas. The first example contains words separated by single spaces. The second, more realistic problem involves comma-delimited fields.

```
Now is the time for all good men (and women)...

Check Number, Description,       Amount
4231,         Java Programming, 1000.00
```

Java has several (unfortunately overlapping) APIs for handling situations like this. The most powerful and useful are the `String split()` and `Scanner` APIs. Both utilize regular expressions to allow you to break the string on arbitrary patterns. We haven't talked about regular expressions yet, but in order to show you how this works we'll just give you the necessary magic and explain in detail later in this chapter. We'll also mention a legacy utility, `java.util.StringTokenizer`, which uses simple character sets to split a string. `StringTokenizer` is not as powerful, but doesn't require an understanding of regular expressions.

The `String split()` method accepts a regular expression that describes a delimiter and uses it to chop the string into an array of `Strings`:

```
String text = "Now is the time for all good men";
String [] words = text.split("\\s");
// words = "Now", "is", "the", "time", ...

String text = "4231,         Java Programming, 1000.00";
String [] fields = text.split("\\s*,\\s*");
// fields = "4231", "Java Programming", "1000.00"
```

In the first example, we used the regular expression `\\s`, which matches a single whitespace character (space, tab, or carriage return). The `split()` method returned an array of eight strings. In the second example, we used a more complicated regular expression, `\\s*,\\s*`, which matches a comma surrounded by any number of contiguous spaces (possibly zero). This reduced our text to three nice, tidy fields.

With the new `Scanner` API, we could go a step further and parse the numbers of our second example as we extract them:

```
String text = "4231,         Java Programming, 1000.00";
Scanner scanner = new Scanner( text ).useDelimiter("\\s*,\\s*");
int checkNumber = scanner.nextInt(); // 4231
String description = scanner.next(); // "Java Programming"
float amount = scanner.nextFloat();  // 1000.00
```

Here, we've told the `Scanner` to use our regular expression as the delimiter and then called it repeatedly to parse each field as its corresponding type. The `Scanner` is convenient because it can read not only from `Strings` but directly from stream sources, such as `InputStreams`, `Files`, and `Channels`:

```
Scanner fileScanner = new Scanner( new File("spreadsheet.csv") );
fileScanner.useDelimiter( "\\s*,\\s* );
// ...
```

Another thing that you can do with the `Scanner` is to look ahead with the "hasNext" methods to see if another item is coming:

```
while( scanner.hasNextInt() ) {
  int n = scanner.nextInt();
  ...
}
```

StringTokenizer

Even though the StringTokenizer class that we mentioned is now a legacy item, it's good to know that it's there because it's been around since the beginning of Java and is used in a lot of code. StringTokenizer allows you to specify a delimiter as a set of characters and matches any number or combination of those characters as a delimiter between tokens. The following snippet reads the words of our first example:

```
String text = "Now is the time for all good men (and women)...";
StringTokenizer st = new StringTokenizer( text );

while ( st.hasMoreTokens() )  {
    String word = st.nextToken();
    ...
}
```

We invoke the hasMoreTokens() and nextToken() methods to loop over the words of the text. By default, the StringTokenizer class uses standard whitespace characters—carriage return, newline, and tab—as delimiters. You can also specify your own set of delimiter characters in the StringTokenizer constructor. Any contiguous combination of the specified characters that appears in the target string is skipped between tokens:

```
String text = "4231,     Java Programming, 1000.00";
StringTokenizer st = new StringTokenizer( text, "," );

while ( st.hasMoreTokens() )  {
   String word = st.nextToken();
   // word = "4231", "     Java Programming", "1000.00"
}
```

This isn't as clean as our regular expression example. Here we used a comma as the delimiter so we get extra leading whitespace in our description field. If we had added space to our delimiter string, the StringTokenizer would have broken our description into two words, "Java" and "Programming," which is not what we wanted. A solution here would be to use trim() to remove the leading and trailing space on each element.

Printf-Style Formatting

A standard feature that Java adopted from the C language is printf-style string formatting. printf-style formatting utilizes special format strings embedded into text to tell the formatting engine where to place arguments and give detailed specification about conversions, layout, and alignment. The printf formatting methods also make use of variable-length argument lists, which makes working with them much easier. Here is a quick example of printf-formatted output:

```
System.out.printf( "My name is %s and I am %d years old\n", name, age );
```

The printf formatting draws its name from the C language printf() function, so if you've done any C programming, this will look familiar. Java has extended the concept, adding some additional type safety and convenience features. Although Java has had some text formatting capabilities in the past (we'll discuss the `java.text` package and `MessageFormat` later), `printf` formatting was not really feasible until variable-length argument lists and autoboxing of primitive types were added in Java 5.0. (We mention this to explain why these similar APIs both exist in Java.)

Formatter

The primary new tool in our text formatting arsenal is the `java.util.Formatter` class and its `format()` method. Several convenience methods can hide the `Formatter` object from you and you may not need to create a `Formatter` directly. First, the static `String.format()` method can be used to format a `String` with arguments (like the C language `sprintf()` method):

```
String message =
    String.format("My name is %s and I am %d years old.", name, age );
```

Next, the `java.io.PrintStream` and `java.io.PrintWriter` classes, which are used for writing text to streams, have their own `format()` method. We discuss streams in Chapter 12, but this simply means that you can use this same `printf`-style formatting for writing strings to any kind of stream, whether it be to `System.out` standard console output, to a file, or to a network connection.

In addition to the `format()` method, `PrintStream` and `PrintWriter` also have a version of the format method that is actually called `printf()`. The `printf()` method is identical to and, in fact, simply delegates to the `format()` method. It's there solely as a shout-out to the C programmers and ex-C programmers in the audience.

The Format String

The syntax of the format string is compact and a bit cryptic at first, but not bad once you get used to it. The simplest format string is just a percent sign (%) followed by a conversion character. For example, the following text has two embedded format strings:

```
"My name is %s and I am %d years old."
```

The first conversion character is `s`, the most general format, which represents a string value; and the second is `d`, which represents an integer value. There are about a dozen basic conversion characters corresponding to different types and primitives and there are a couple of dozen more that are specifically used for formatting dates and times. We cover the basics here and return to date and time formatting in Chapter 11.

At first glance, some of the conversion characters may not seem to do much. For example, the `%s` general string conversion in our previous example would actually have handled the job of displaying the numeric age argument just as well as `%d`. However, these specialized conversion characters accomplish three things. First, they add a level of type safety. By specifying `%d`, we ensure that only an integer type is formatted at that location. If we make a mistake in the arguments, we get a runtime `IllegalFormatConversionException` instead of garbage in our string (and your IDE may flag it as well). Second, the format method is `Locale`-sensitive and capable of displaying numbers, percentages, dates, and times in many different languages just by specifying a `Locale` as an argument. By telling the `Formatter` the type of argument with type-specific conversion characters, `printf` can take into account language-specific localizations. Third, additional flags and fields can be used to govern layout with different meanings for different types of arguments. For example, with floating-point numbers, you can specify a precision in the format string.

The general layout of the embedded format string is as follows:

```
%[argument_index$][flags][width][.precision]conversion_type
```

Following the literal `%` are a number of optional items before the conversion type character. We'll discuss these as they come up, but here's the rundown. The `argument index` can be used to reorder or reuse individual arguments in the variable-length argument list by referring to them by number. The `flags` field holds one or more special flag characters governing the format. The `width` and `precision` fields control the size of the output for text and the number of digits displayed for floating-point numbers.

String Conversions

The conversion characters `s` represents the general string conversion type. Ultimately, all of the conversion types produce a `String`. What we mean is that the general string conversion takes the easy route to turning its argument into a string. Normally, this simply means calling `toString()` on the object. Since all of the arguments in the variable argument list are autoboxed, they are all `Objects`. Any primitives are represented by the results of calling `toString()` on their wrapper classes, which generally return the value as you'd expect. If the argument is null, the result is the `String` "null."

More interesting are objects that implement the `java.util.Formattable` interface. For these, the argument's `formatTo()` method is invoked, passing it the flags, width, and precision information and allowing it to return the string to be used. In this way, objects can control their own `printf` string representation, just as an object can do so using `toString()`.

Width, precision, and justification

For simple text arguments, you can think of the width and precision as a minimum and maximum number of characters to be output. As we'll see later, for floating-point numeric types, the precision changes meaning slightly and controls the number of digits displayed after the decimal point. We can see the effect on a simple string here:

```
System.out.printf("String is '%5s'\n", "A");
// String is '    A'
```

```
System.out.printf("String is '%.5s'\n", "Happy Birthday!");
// String is 'Happy'
```

In the first case, we specified a width of five characters, resulting in spaces being added to pad our argument. In the second example, we used the literal `.` followed by the precision value of 5 characters to limit the length of the string displayed, so our "Happy Birthday" string is truncated after the first five characters.

When our string was padded, it was right-justified (leading spaces added). You can control this with the flag character literal minus (`-`). Reversing our example:

```
System.out.printf("String is '%-5s'\n", "A");
// String is 'A    '
```

And, of course, we can combine all three, specifying a justification flag and a minimum and maximum width. Here is an example that prints words of varying lengths in two columns:

```
String [] words =
   new String [] { "abalone", "ape", "antidisestablishmentarianism" };
System.out.printf( "%-10s %s\n", "Word", "Length" );
for ( String word : words )
   System.out.printf( "%-10.10s %s\n", word, word.length() );

// output
Word       Length
abalone    7
ape        3
antidisest 28
```

Uppercase

The `s` conversion's big brother `S` indicates that the output of the conversion should be forced to uppercase. Several other primitive and numeric conversion characters follow this pattern, as we'll see later. For example:

```
String word = "abalone";
System.out.println(" The lucky word is: %S\n", word );
// The lucky word is: ABALONE
```

Numbered arguments

You can refer to an arbitrary argument by number from a format string using the `%n$` notation. For example, the following code snippet uses the single argument three times:

```
System.out.println( "A %1$s is a %1$s is a %1$S...", "rose" );
 // A rose is a rose is a ROSE...
```

Numbered arguments are useful for two reasons. The first, shown here, is simply for reusing the same argument in different places and with different conversions. The usefulness of this becomes more apparent when we look at `Date` and `Time` formatting in Chapter 11, where we may refer to the same item half a dozen times to get individual fields. The second advantage is that numbered arguments give the message the flexibility to reorder the arguments. This is important when you're using formatting strings to lay out a message for internationalization or customization purposes where convention may dictate a different ordering.

```
log.format("Error %d : %s\n", errNo, errMsg );
// Error 42 : Low Power
log.format("%2$s (Error %1$d)\n", errNo, errMsg );
// Low Power (Error 42)
```

Primitive and Numeric Conversions

Table 10-3 shows character and Boolean conversion characters.

Table 10-3. Character and Boolean conversion characters

Conversion	Type	Description	Example output
c	Character	Formats the result as a Unicode character	a
b, B	Boolean	Formats result as Boolean	true, FALSE

The c conversion character produces a Unicode character:

```
System.out.printf("The first letter is: %c\n", 'a' );
```

The b and B conversion characters output the Boolean value of their arguments. If the argument is null, the output is false. Strangely, if the argument is of a type other than Boolean, the output is true. B is identical to b except that it forces the output to uppercase.

```
System.out.printf( "The door is open: %b\n", ( door.status() == OPEN ) );
```

As for String types, a width value can be specified on c and b conversions to pad the result to a minimum length. Table 10-4 summarizes integer type conversion characters.

Table 10-4. Integer type conversion characters

Conversion	Type	Description	Example output
d	Integer	Formats the result as an integer.	999
x, X	Integer	Formats result as hexadecimal.	FF, 0xCAFE
o	Integer	Formats result as octal integer.	10, 010
h, H	Integer or object	Formats object as hexadecimal number. If object is not an integer, format its hashCode() value or "null" for null value.	7a71e498

The d, x, and o conversion characters handle the integer type values byte, short, int, and long. (The d apparently stands for decimal, which makes little sense in this context.) The h conversion is an oddity probably intended for debugging. Several important flags give additional control over the formatting of these numeric types. See the section "Flags" on page 337 for details.

A width value can be specified on these conversions to pad the result. Precision values are not allowed on integer conversions.

Table 10-5 lists floating-point type conversion characters.

Table 10-5. Floating-point type conversion characters

Conversion	Type	Description	Example output
`f`	Floating point	Formats result as decimal number.	`3.14`
`e`, `E`	Floating point	Formats result in scientific notation.	`3.000000e+08`
`g`, `G`	Floating point	Formats result in either decimal or scientific notation depending on value and precision.	`3.14`, `10.0e-15`
`a`, `A`	Floating point	Formats result as hexadecimal floating-point number with significand and exponent.	`0x1.fep7`

The `f` conversion character is the primary floating-point conversion character. `e` and `g` conversions allow for values to be formatted in scientific notation. `a` complements the ability in Java to assign floating-point values using hexadecimal significand and exponent notation, allowing bit-for-bit floating-point values to be displayed without ambiguity.

As always, a width value may be used to pad results to a minimum length. The precision value of the conversion, as its name suggests, controls the number of digits displayed after the decimal point for floating-point values. The value is rounded as necessary. If no precision value is specified, it defaults to six digits:

```
printf("float is %f\n",   1.23456789); // float is 1.234568
printf("float is %.3f\n", 1.23456789); // float is 1.235
printf("float is %.1f\n", 1.23456789); // float is 1.2
printf("float is %.0f\n", 1.23456789); // float is 1
```

The `g` conversion character determines whether to use decimal or scientific notation. First, the value is rounded to the specified precision. If the result is less than 10^{-4} (less than .0001) or if the result is greater than $10^{precision}$ (10 to the power of the precision value), it is displayed in scientific notation. Otherwise, decimal notation is displayed.

Flags

Table 10-6 summarizes supported flags to use in format strings.

Table 10-6. Flags for format strings

Flag	Arg types	Description	Example output
`-`	Any	Left-justifies result (pad space on the right)	`'foo '`
`+`	Numeric	Prefixes a + sign on positive results	`+1`
`' '`	Numeric	Prefixes a space on positive results (aligning them with negative values)	`' 1'`
`0`	Numeric	Pads number with leading zeros to accommodate width requirement	`000001`

Flag	Arg types	Description	Example output
,	Numeric	Formats numbers with commas or other `Locale`-specific grouping characters	`1,234,567`
(	Numeric	Encloses negative numbers in parentheses (a convention used to show credits)	`(42.50)`
#	x,X,o	Uses an alternate form for octal and hexadecimal output	`0xCAFE, 010`

As mentioned earlier, the - flag can be used to left-justify formatted output. The remaining flags affect the display of numeric types as described.

The # alternate form flag can be used to print octal and hexadecimal values with their standard prefixes—0x for hexadecimal or 0 for octal:

```
System.out.printf("%1$X, %1$#X", 0xCAFE, 0xCAFE ); // CAFE, 0xCAFE
System.out.printf("%1$o, %1$#o", 8, 8 ); // 10, 010
```

Miscellaneous

Table 10-7 lists the remaining formatting items.

Table 10-7. Miscellaneous formatting items

Conversion	Description
%	Produces a literal % character (Unicode `\u0025`)
n	Produces the platform-specific line separator (e.g., newline or carriage-return, newline)

Formatting with the java.text Package

The `java.text` package includes, among other things, a set of classes designed for generating and parsing string representations of objects. In this section, we'll talk about three classes: `NumberFormat`, `ChoiceFormat`, and `MessageFormat`. Chapter 11 describes the `DateFormat` class. As we said earlier, the classes of the `java.text` package overlap to a large degree with the capabilities of the `Scanner` and `printf`-style `Formatter`. Despite these new features, a number of areas in the parsing of currencies, dates, and times can only be handled with the `java.text` package.

The `NumberFormat` class can be used to format and parse currency, percentages, or plain old numbers. `NumberFormat` is an abstract class, but it has several useful factory methods that produce formatters for different types of numbers. For example, to format or parse currency strings, use `getCurrencyInstance()` :

```
double salary = 1234.56;
String here =     // $1,234.56
    NumberFormat.getCurrencyInstance().format(salary);
String italy =    // L 1.234,56
    NumberFormat.getCurrencyInstance(Locale.ITALY).format(salary);
```

The first statement generates an American salary, with a dollar sign, a comma to separate thousands, and a period as a decimal point. The second statement presents the same string in Italian, with a lire sign, a period to separate thousands, and a comma as a decimal point. Remember that `NumberFormat` worries about format only; it doesn't attempt to do currency conversion. We can go the other way and parse a formatted value using the `parse()` method, as we'll see in the next example.

Likewise, `getPercentInstance()` returns a formatter you can use for generating and parsing percentages. If you do not specify a `Locale` when calling a `getInstance()` method, the default `Locale` is used:

```
double progress = 0.44;
NumberFormat pf = NumberFormat.getPercentInstance();
System.out.println( pf.format(progress) );    // "44%"
try {
    System.out.println( pf.parse("77.2%") );  // "0.772"
}
catch (ParseException e) {}
```

And if you just want to generate and parse plain old numbers, use a `NumberFormat` returned by `getInstance()` or its equivalent, `getNumberInstance()` :

```
NumberFormat guiseppe = NumberFormat.getInstance(Locale.ITALY);

// defaults to Locale.US
NumberFormat joe = NumberFormat.getInstance();

try {
  double theValue = guiseppe.parse("34.663,252").doubleValue();
  System.out.println(joe.format(theValue));  // "34,663.252"
}
catch (ParseException e) {}
```

We use `guiseppe` to parse a number in Italian format (periods separate thousands, comma is the decimal point). The return type of `parse()` is `Number`, so we use the `doubleValue()` method to retrieve the value of the `Number` as a `double`. Then we use `joe` to format the number correctly for the default (U.S.) locale.

Here's a list of the factory methods for text formatters in the `java.text` package. Again, we'll look at the `DateFormat` methods in the next chapter.

```
NumberFormat.getCurrencyInstance()
NumberFormat.getCurrencyInstance(Locale inLocale)
NumberFormat.getInstance()
NumberFormat.getInstance(Locale inLocale)
NumberFormat.getNumberInstance()
NumberFormat.getNumberInstance(Locale inLocale)
NumberFormat.getPercentInstance()
NumberFormat.getPercentInstance(Locale inLocale)

DateFormat.getDateInstance()
DateFormat.getDateInstance(int style)
DateFormat.getDateInstance(int style, Locale aLocale)
DateFormat.getDateTimeInstance()
```

```
DateFormat.getDateTimeInstance(int dateStyle, int timeStyle)
DateFormat.getDateTimeInstance(int dateStyle, int timeStyle, Locale aLocale)
DateFormat.getInstance()
DateFormat.getTimeInstance()
DateFormat.getTimeInstance(int style)
DateFormat.getTimeInstance(int style, Locale aLocale)
```

Thus far, we've seen how to format numbers as text. Now, we'll take a look at a class, `ChoiceFormat`, that maps numerical ranges to text. `ChoiceFormat` is constructed by specifying the numerical ranges and the strings that correspond to them. One constructor accepts an array of `doubles` and an array of `Strings`, where each string corresponds to the range running from the matching number up to (but not including) the next number in the array:

```
double[] limits = new double [] {0, 20, 40};
String[] labels = new String [] {"young", "less young", "old"};
ChoiceFormat cf = new ChoiceFormat(limits, labels);
System.out.println(cf.format(12)); //"young"
System.out.println(cf.format(26)); // "less young"
```

You can specify both the limits and the labels using a special string in an alternative `ChoiceFormat` constructor:

```
ChoiceFormat cf = new ChoiceFormat("0#young|20#less young|40#old");
System.out.println(cf.format(40)); // old
System.out.println(cf.format(50)); // old
```

The limit and value pairs are separated by vertical bars (`|`); the number sign (`#`) separates each limit from its corresponding value.

`ChoiceFormat` is most useful for handling pluralization in messages, enabling you to avoid hideous constructions such as, "you have one file(s) open." You can create readable error messages by using `ChoiceFormat` along with the `MessageFormat` class.

MessageFormat

`MessageFormat` is a string formatter that uses a pattern string in the same way that `printf()` formatting does. `MessageFormat` has largely been replaced by `printf()`, which has more options and is more widely used outside of Java. Nonetheless, some may still prefer `MessageFormat`'s style, which is a bit less cryptic than that of `printf()`. `MessageFormat` has a static formatting method, `MessageFormat.format()`, paralleling the print-style formatting of `String.format()`.

Arguments in a `MessageFormat` format string are delineated by curly brackets and may include information about how they should be formatted. Each argument consists of a number, an optional type, and an optional style, as summarized in Table 10-8.

Table 10-8. MessageFormat arguments

Type	Styles
`Choice`	*`pattern`*
`Date`	`short`, `medium`, `long`, `full`, *`pattern`*
`Number`	`integer`, `percent`, `currency`, *`pattern`*
`Time`	`short`, `medium`, `long`, `full`, *`pattern`*

Let's use an example to clarify this:

```
//Equivalent to String.format("You have %s messages.", "no");
MessageFormat.format("You have {0} messages.", "no");
```

The special incantation `{0}` means "use element zero of the arguments supplied to the `format()` method." When we generate a message by calling `format()`, we pass in values to replace the placeholders (`{0}`, `{1}`, ...) in the template. In this case, we pass the string "no" as `arguments[0]`, yielding the result, `You have no messages.`

Let's try this example again, but this time, we'll format a number and a date instead of a string argument:

```
MessageFormat mf = new MessageFormat(
    "You have {0, number, integer} messages on {1, date, long}.");
    // "You have 93 messages on April 10, 2002."

System.out.println( mf.format( 93, new Date() ) );
```

In this example, we need to fill in two spaces in the template, so we need two arguments. The first must be a number and is formatted as an integer. The second must be a `Date` and is printed in the `long` format.

This is still sloppy. What if there is only one message? To make this grammatically correct, we can embed a `ChoiceFormat`-style pattern string in our `MessageFormat` pattern string:

```
MessageFormat mf = new MessageFormat(
  "You have {0, number, integer} message{0, choice, 0#s|1#|2#s}.");
// "You have 1 message."
System.out.println( mf.format( 1 ) );
```

In this case, we use the first argument twice: once to supply the number of messages and once to provide input to the `ChoiceFormat` pattern. The pattern says to add an `s` if the argument has the value `0` or is 2 or more.

When writing internationalized programs, you can use resource bundles to supply not only the text of messages, but also the format strings for your `MessageFormat` objects. In this way, you can automatically format messages that are in the appropriate language with dates and other language-dependent fields handled appropriately and in the appropriate order. Because arguments in the format string are numbered, you can refer to them in any location. For example, in English, you might say, "Disk C has 123 files"; in some other language, you might say, "123 files are on Disk C." You could implement both messages with the same set of arguments:

```
MessageFormat m1 = new MessageFormat(
    "Disk {0} has {1, number, integer} files.");
MessageFormat m2 = new MessageFormat(
    "{1, number, integer} files are on disk {0}.");
```

In real life, the code could be more compact; you'd use only a single `MessageFormat` object, initialized with a string taken from a resource bundle. Or you'd likely want to use the static `format` method or switch to `printf()` entirely.

Regular Expressions

Now it's time to take a brief detour on our trip through Java and enter the land of *regular expressions*. A regular expression, or regex for short, describes a text pattern. Regular expressions are used with many tools—including the `java.util.regex` package, text editors, and many scripting languages—to provide sophisticated text-searching and powerful string-manipulation capabilities.

If you are already familiar with the concept of regular expressions and how they are used with other languages, you may wish to skim through this section. At the very least, you'll need to look at the "The java.util.regex API" section later in this chapter, which covers the Java classes necessary to use them. On the other hand, if you've come to this point on your Java journey with a clean slate on this topic and you're wondering exactly what regular expressions are, then pop open your favorite beverage and get ready. You are about to learn about the most powerful tool in the arsenal of text manipulation and what is, in fact, a tiny language within a language, all in the span of a few pages.

Regex Notation

A regular expression describes a pattern in text. By pattern, we mean just about any feature you can imagine identifying in text from the literal characters alone, without actually understanding their meaning. This includes features, such as words, word groupings, lines and paragraphs, punctuation, case, and more generally, strings and numbers with a specific structure to them, such as phone numbers, email addresses, and quoted phrases. With regular expressions, you can search the dictionary for all the words that have the letter "q" without its pal "u" next to it, or words that start and end with the same letter. Once you have constructed a pattern, you can use simple tools to hunt for it in text or to determine if a given string matches it. A regex can also be arranged to help you dismember specific parts of the text it matched, which you could then use as elements of replacement text if you wish.

Write once, run away

Before moving on, we should say a few words about regular expression syntax in general. At the beginning of this section, we casually mentioned that we would be discussing a new language. Regular expressions do, in fact, constitute a simple form of programming language. If you think for a moment about the examples we cited earlier, you can see that something like a language is going to be needed to describe even simple patterns —such as email addresses—that have some variation in form.

A computer science textbook would classify regular expressions at the bottom of the hierarchy of computer languages, in terms of both what they can describe and what you can do with them. They are still capable of being quite sophisticated, however. As with most programming languages, the elements of regular expressions are simple, but they can be built up in combination to arbitrary complexity. And that is where things start to get sticky.

Since regexes work on strings, it is convenient to have a very compact notation that can be easily wedged between characters. But compact notation can be very cryptic, and experience shows that it is much easier to write a complex statement than to read it again later. Such is the curse of the regular expression. You may find that in a moment of late-night, caffeine-fueled inspiration, you can write a single glorious pattern to simplify the rest of your program down to one line. When you return to read that line the next day, however, it may look like Egyptian hieroglyphics to you. Simpler is generally better. If you can break your problem down and do it more clearly in several steps, maybe you should.

Escaped characters

Now that you're properly warned, we have to throw one more thing at you before we build you back up. Not only can the regex notation get a little hairy, but it is also somewhat ambiguous with ordinary Java strings. An important part of the notation is the escaped character, a character with a backslash in front of it. For example, the escaped `d` character, `\d`, (backslash 'd') is shorthand that matches any single digit character (0-9). However, you cannot simply write `\d` as part of a Java string, because Java uses the backslash for its own special characters and to specify Unicode character sequences (`\uxxxx`). Fortunately, Java gives us a replacement: an escaped backslash, which is two backslashes (\\), means a literal backslash. The rule is, when you want a backslash to appear in your regex, you must escape it with an extra one:

```
"\\d" // Java string that yields backslash "d"
```

And just to make things crazier, because regex notation itself uses backslash to denote special characters, it must provide the same "escape hatch" as well—allowing you to double up backslashes if you want a literal backslash. So if you want to specify a regular expression that includes a single literal backslash, it looks like this:

```
"\\\\"  // Java string yields two backslashes; regex yields one
```

Most of the "magic" operator characters you read about in this section operate on the character that precedes them, so these also must be escaped if you want their literal meaning. This includes such characters as `.`, `*`, `+`, braces `{}`, and parentheses `()`.

If you need to create part of an expression that has lots of literal characters in it, you can use the special delimiters `\Q` and `\E` to help you. Any text appearing between `\Q` and `\E` is automatically escaped. (You still need the Java `String` escapes—double backslashes for backslash, but not quadruple.) There is also a static method `Pattern.quote()`, which does the same thing, returning a properly escaped version of whatever string you give it.

Beyond that, my only suggestion to help maintain your sanity when working with these examples is to keep two copies—a comment line showing the naked regular expression and the real Java string, where you must double up all backslashes.

Characters and character classes

Now, let's dive into the actual regex syntax. The simplest form of a regular expression is plain, literal text, which has no special meaning and is matched directly (character for character) in the input. This can be a single character or more. For example, in the following string, the pattern "s" can match the character `s` in the words `rose` and `is`:

```
"A rose is $1.99."
```

The pattern "rose" can match only the literal word `rose`. But this isn't very interesting. Let's crank things up a notch by introducing some special characters and the notion of character "classes."

Any character: dot (`.`)

The special character dot (`.`) matches any single character. The pattern ".ose" matches rose, nose, _ose (space followed by ose) or any other character followed by the sequence ose. Two dots match any two characters, and so on. The dot operator is not discriminating; it normally stops only for an end-of-line character (and, optionally, you can tell it not to; we discuss that later).

We can consider "." to represent the group or class of all characters. And regexes define more interesting character classes as well.

Whitespace or nonwhitespace character: `\s`, `\S`

The special character `\s` matches a literal-space character or one of the following characters: `\t` (tab), `\r` (carriage return), `\n` (newline), `\f` (formfeed), and backspace. The corresponding special character `\S` does the inverse, matching any character except whitespace.

Digit or nondigit character: `\d`, `\D`

`\d` matches any of the digits 0-9. `\D` does the inverse, matching all characters except digits.

Word or nonword character: `\w`, `\W`

`\w` matches a "word" character, including upper- and lowercase letters A-Z, a-z, the digits 0-9, and the underscore character (_). `\W` matches everything except those characters.

Custom character classes

You can define your own character classes using the notation [...]. For example, the following class matches any of the characters a, b, c, x, y, or z:

```
[abcxyz]
```

The special x-y range notation can be used as shorthand for the alphabetic characters. The following example defines a character class containing all upper- and lowercase letters:

```
[A-Za-z]
```

Placing a caret (^) as the first character inside the brackets inverts the character class. This example matches any character except uppercase A-F:

```
[^A-F]    //  G, H, I, ..., a, b, c, ... etc.
```

Nesting character classes simply adds them:

```
[A-F[G-Z]]    // A-Z
```

The && logical AND notation can be used to take the intersection (characters in common):

```
[a-p&&[l-z]]  // l, m, n, o, p
[A-Z&&[^P]]  // A through Z except P
```

Position markers

The pattern "[Aa] rose" (including an upper- or lowercase A) matches three times in the following phrase:

```
"A rose is a rose is a rose"
```

Position characters allow you to designate the relative location of a match. The most important are ^ and `$`, which match the beginning and end of a line, respectively:

```
^[Aa] rose  // matches "A rose" at the beginning of line
[Aa] rose$  // matches "a rose" at end of line
```

By default, ^ and `$` match the beginning and end of "input," which is often a line. If you are working with multiple lines of text and wish to match the beginnings and endings of lines within a single large string, you can turn on "multiline" mode as described later in this chapter.

The position markers \b and \B match a word boundary or nonword boundary, respectively. For example, the following pattern matches rose and rosemary, but not primrose:

```
\brose
```

Iteration (multiplicity)

Simply matching fixed character patterns would not get us very far. Next, we look at operators that count the number of occurrences of a character (or more generally, of a pattern, as we'll see in "Capture groups" on page 347):

Any (zero or more iterations): asterisk (*)
: Placing an asterisk (*) after a character or character class means "allow any number of that type of character"—in other words, zero or more. For example, the following pattern matches a digit with any number of leading zeros (possibly none):

```
0*\d   // match a digit with any number of leading zeros
```

Some (one or more iterations): plus sign (+)
: The plus sign (+) means "one or more" iterations and is equivalent to XX* (pattern followed by pattern asterisk). For example, the following pattern matches a number with one or more digits, plus optional leading zeros:

```
0*\d+   // match a number (one or more digits) with optional leading
        // zeros
```

It may seem redundant to match the zeros at the beginning of an expression because zero is a digit and is thus matched by the \d+ portion of the expression anyway. However, we'll show later how you can pick apart the string using a regex and get at just the pieces you want. In this case, you might want to strip off the leading zeros and keep only the digits.

Optional (zero or one iteration): question mark (?)
: The question mark operator (?) allows exactly zero or one iteration. For example, the following pattern matches a credit-card expiration date, which may or may not have a slash in the middle:

```
\d\d/?\d\d  // match four digits with an optional slash in the middle
```

Range (between x and y iterations, inclusive): {x,y}
: The {x,y} curly-brace range operator is the most general iteration operator. It specifies a precise range to match. A range takes two arguments: a lower bound and an upper bound, separated by a comma. This regex matches any word with five to seven characters, inclusive:

```
\b\w{5,7}\b  // match words with at least 5 and at most 7 characters
```

At least x or more iterations (y is infinite): `{x,}`

If you omit the upper bound, simply leaving a dangling comma in the range, the upper bound becomes infinite. This is a way to specify a minimum of occurrences with no maximum.

Grouping

Just as in logical or mathematical operations, parentheses can be used in regular expressions to make subexpressions or to put boundaries on parts of expressions. This power lets us extend the operators we've talked about to work not only on characters, but also on words or other regular expressions. For example:

```
(yada)+
```

Here we are applying the + (one or more) operator to the whole pattern `yada`, not just one character. It matches yada, yadayada, yadayadayada, and so on.

Using grouping, we can start building more complex expressions. For example, while many email addresses have a three-part structure (e.g., *foo@bar.com*), the domain name portion can, in actuality, contain an arbitrary number of dot-separated components. To handle this properly, we can use an expression like this one:

```
\w+@\w+(\.\w)+   // Match an email address
```

This expression matches a word, followed by an `@` symbol, followed by another word and then one or more literal dot-separated words—e.g., *pat@pat.net*, *friend@foo.bar.com*, or *mate@foo.bar.co.uk*.

Capture groups

In addition to basic grouping of operations, parentheses have an important, additional role: the text matched by each parenthesized subexpression can be separately retrieved. That is, you can isolate the text that matched each subexpression. There is then a special syntax for referring to each capture group within the regular expression by number. This important feature has two uses.

First, you can construct a regular expression that refers to the text it has already matched and uses this text as a parameter for further matching. This allows you to express some very powerful things. For example, we can show the dictionary example we mentioned in the introduction. Let's find all the words that start and end with the same letter:

```
\b(\w)\w*\1\b  // match words beginning and ending with the same letter
```

See the `1` in this expression? It's a reference to the first capture group in the expression, `(\w)`. References to capture groups take the form `\`*n* where *n* is the number of the capture group, counting from left to right. In this example, the first capture group matches a word character on a word boundary. Then we allow any number of word characters up to the special reference `\1` (also followed by a word boundary). The `\1` means "the value matched in capture group one." Because these characters must be the same, this regex matches words that start and end with the same character.

The second use of capture groups is in referring to the matched portions of text while constructing replacement text. We'll show you how to do that a bit later when we talk about the Regular Expression API.

Capture groups can contain more than one character, of course, and you can have any number of groups. You can even nest capture groups. Next, we discuss exactly how they are numbered.

Numbering

Capture groups are numbered, starting at 1, and moving from left to right, by counting the number of open parentheses it takes to reach them. The special group number 0 always refers to the entire expression match. For example, consider the following string:

```
one ((two) (three (four)))
```

This string creates the following matches:

```
Group 0: one two three four
Group 1: two three four
Group 2: two
Group 3: three four
Group 4: four
```

Before going on, we should note one more thing. So far in this section we've glossed over the fact that parentheses are doing double duty: creating logical groupings for operations and defining capture groups. What if the two roles conflict? Suppose we have a complex regex that uses parentheses to group subexpressions and to create capture groups? In that case, you can use a special noncapturing group operator `(?:)` to do logical grouping instead of using parentheses. You probably won't need to do this often, but it's good to know.

Alternation

The vertical bar (|) operator denotes the logical OR operation, also called alternation or choice. The | operator does not operate on individual characters but instead applies to everything on either side of it. It splits the expression in two unless constrained by parentheses grouping. For example, a slightly naive approach to parsing dates might be the following:

```
\w+, \w+ \d+ \d+|\d\d/\d\d/\d\d\d\d  // pattern 1 or pattern 2
```

In this expression, the left matches patterns such as Fri, Oct 12, 2001, and the right matches 10/12/2001.

The following regex might be used to match email addresses with one of three domains (*net*, *edu*, and *gov*):

```
\w+@[\w\.]*\.(net|edu|gov)  // email address ending in .net, .edu, or .gov
```

Special options

There are several special options that affect the way the regex engine performs its matching. These options can be applied in two ways:

- You can pass in one or more flags during the `Pattern.compile()` step (discussed later in this chapter).
- You can include a special block of code in your regex.

We'll show the latter approach here. To do this, include one or more flags in a special block `(?x)`, where *x* is the flag for the option we want to turn on. Generally, you do this at the beginning of the regex. You can also turn off flags by adding a minus sign `(?-x)`, which allows you to apply flags to select parts of your pattern.

The following flags are available:

Case-insensitive: `(?i)`
: The `(?i)` flag tells the regex engine to ignore case while matching, for example:

```
(?i)yahoo   // match Yahoo, yahoo, yahOO, etc.
```

Dot all: `(?s)`
: The `(?s)` flag turns on "dot all" mode, allowing the dot character to match anything, including end-of-line characters. It is useful if you are matching patterns that span multiple lines. The `s` stands for "single-line mode," a somewhat confusing name derived from Perl.

Multiline: `(?m)`
: By default, `^` and `$` don't really match the beginning and end of lines (as defined by carriage return or newline combinations); they instead match the beginning or end of the entire input text. Turning on multiline mode with `(?m)` causes them to match the beginning and end of every line as well as the beginning and end of input. Specifically, this means the spot before the first character, the spot after the last character, and the spots just after and before line terminators inside the string.

Unix lines: `(?d)`
: The `(?d)` flag limits the definition of the line terminator for the `^`, `$`, and `.` special characters to Unix-style newline only (`\n`). By default, carriage return newline (`\r\n`) is also allowed.

Greediness

We've seen hints that regular expressions are capable of sorting some complex patterns. But there are cases where what should be matched is ambiguous (at least to us, though not to the regex engine). Probably the most important example has to do with the number of characters the iterator operators consume before stopping. The `.*` operation best illustrates this. Consider the following string:

```
"Now is the time for <bold>action</bold>, not words."
```

Suppose we want to search for all the HTML-style tags (the parts between the < and > characters), perhaps because we want to remove them.

We might naively start with this regex:

```
</?.*>  // match <, optional /, and then anything up to >
```

We then get the following match, which is much too long:

```
<bold>action</bold>
```

The problem is that the `.*` operation, like all the iteration operators, is by default "greedy," meaning that it consumes absolutely everything it can, up until the last match for the terminating character (in this case, >) in the file or line.

There are solutions for this problem. The first is to "say what it is"—that is, to be specific about what is allowed between the braces. The content of an HTML tag cannot actually include *anything*; for example, it cannot include a closing bracket (>). So we could rewrite our expression as:

```
</?\w*>  // match <, optional /, any number of word characters, then >
```

But suppose the content is not so easy to describe. For example, we might be looking for quoted strings in text, which could include just about any text. In that case, we can use a second approach and "say what it is not." We can invert our logic from the previous example and specify that anything *except* a closing bracket is allowed inside the brackets:

```
</?[^>]*>
```

This is probably the most efficient way to tell the regex engine what to do. It then knows exactly what to look for to stop reading. This approach has limitations, however. It is not obvious how to do this if the delimiter is more complex than a single character. It is also not very elegant.

Finally, we come to our general solution: the use of "reluctant" operators. For each of the iteration operators, there is an alternative, nongreedy form that consumes as few characters as possible, while still trying to get a match with what comes after it. This is exactly what we needed in our previous example.

Reluctant operators take the form of the standard operator with a "?" appended. (Yes, we know that's confusing.) We can now write our regex as:

```
</?.*?> // match <, optional /, minimum number of any chars, then >
```

We have appended ? to `.*` to cause `.*` to match as few characters as possible while still making the final match of >. The same technique (appending the ?) works with all the iteration operators, as in the two following examples:

```
.+?   // one or more, nongreedy
.{x,y}?  // between x and y, nongreedy
```

Lookaheads and lookbehinds

In order to understand our next topic, let's return for a moment to the position marking characters (`^`, `$`, `\b`, and `\B`) that we discussed earlier. Think about what exactly these special markers do for us. We say, for example, that the `\b` marker matches a word boundary. But the word "match" here may be a bit too strong. In reality, it "requires" a word boundary to appear at the specified point in the regex. Suppose we didn't have `\b`; how could we construct it? Well, we could try constructing a regex that matches the word boundary. It might seem easy, given the word and nonword character classes (`\w` and `\W`):

```
\w\W|\W\w  // match the start or end of a word
```

But now what? We could try inserting that pattern into our regular expressions wherever we would have used `\b`, but it's not really the same. We're actually matching those characters, not just requiring them. This regular expression matches the two characters composing the word *boundary* in addition to whatever else matches afterward, whereas the `\b` operator simply *requires* the word boundary but doesn't match any text. The distinction is that `\b` isn't a matching pattern but a kind of lookahead. A *lookahead* is a pattern that is required to match next in the string, but is not consumed by the regex engine. When a lookahead pattern succeeds, the pattern moves on, and the characters are left in the stream for the next part of the pattern to use. If the lookahead fails, the match fails (or it backtracks and tries a different approach).

We can make our own lookaheads with the lookahead operator `(?=)`. For example, to match the letter X at the end of a word, we could use:

```
(?=\w\W)X  // Find X at the end of a word
```

Here the regex engine requires the `\W\w` pattern to match but not consume the characters, leaving them for the next part of the pattern. This effectively allows us to write overlapping patterns (like the previous example). For instance, we can match the word "Pat" only when it's part of the word "Patrick," like so:

```
(?=Patrick)Pat  // Find Pat only in Patrick
```

Another operator, `(?!)`, the *negative lookahead*, requires that the pattern not match. We can find all the occurrences of Pat not inside of a Patrick with this:

```
(?!Patrick)Pat  // Find Pat never in Patrick
```

It's worth noting that we could have written all of these examples in other ways, by simply matching a larger amount of text. For instance, in the first example we could have matched the whole word "Patrick." But that is not as precise, and if we wanted to use capture groups to pull out the matched text or parts of it later, we'd have to play games to get what we want. For example, suppose we wanted to substitute something for Pat (say, change the font). We'd have to use an extra capture group and replace the text with itself. Using lookaheads is easier.

In addition to looking ahead in the stream, we can use the `(?<=)` and `(?<!)` *lookbehind* operators to look backward in the stream. For example, we can find my last name, but only when it refers to me:

```
(?<=Pat )Niemeyer   // Niemeyer, only when preceded by Pat
```

Or we can find the string "bean" when it is not part of the phrase "Java bean":

```
(?<!Java *)bean    // The word bean, not preceded by Java
```

In these cases, the lookbehind and the matched text didn't overlap because the lookbehind was before the matched text. But you can place a lookahead or lookbehind at either point—before or after the match—for example, we could also match Pat Niemeyer like this:

```
Niemeyer(?<=Pat Niemeyer)
```

The java.util.regex API

Now that we've covered the theory of how to construct regular expressions, the hard part is over. All that's left is to investigate the Java API for applying regexes: searching for them in strings, retrieving captured text, and replacing matches with substitution text.

Pattern

As we've said, the regex patterns that we write as strings are, in actuality, little programs describing how to match text. At runtime, the Java regex package compiles these little programs into a form that it can execute against some target text. Several simple convenience methods accept strings directly to use as patterns. More generally, however, Java allows you to explicitly compile your pattern and encapsulate it in an instance of a `Pattern` object. This is the most efficient way to handle patterns that are used more than once, because it eliminates needlessly recompiling the string. To compile a pattern, we use the static method `Pattern.compile()`:

```
Pattern urlPattern = Pattern.compile("\\w+://[\\w/]*");
```

Once you have a `Pattern`, you can ask it to create a `Matcher` object, which associates the pattern with a target string:

```
Matcher matcher = urlPattern.matcher( myText );
```

The matcher executes the matches. We'll talk about that next. But before we do, we'll just mention one convenience method of `Pattern`. The static method `Pattern.matches()` simply takes two strings—a regex and a target string—and determines if the target matches the regex. This is very convenient if you want to do a quick test once in your application. For example:

```
Boolean match = Pattern.matches( "\\d+\\.\\d+f?", myText );
```

This line of code can test if the string `myText` contains a Java-style floating-point number such as "42.0f." Note that the string must match completely in order to be considered a match.

The Matcher

A `Matcher` associates a pattern with a string and provides tools for testing, finding, and iterating over matches of the pattern against it. The `Matcher` is "stateful." For example, the `find()` method tries to find the next match each time it is called. But you can clear the `Matcher` and start over by calling its `reset()` method.

If you're just interested in "one big match"—that is, you're expecting your string to either match the pattern or not—you can use `matches()` or `lookingAt()`. These correspond roughly to the methods `equals()` and `startsWith()` of the `String` class. The `match es()` method asks if the string matches the pattern in its entirety (with no string characters left over) and returns `true` or `false`. The `lookingAt()` method does the same, except that it asks only whether the string starts with the pattern and doesn't care if the pattern uses up all the string's characters.

More generally, you'll want to be able to search through the string and find one or more matches. To do this, you can use the `find()` method. Each call to `find()` returns `true` or `false` for the next match of the pattern and internally notes the position of the matching text. You can get the starting and ending character positions with the `Matcher` `start()` and `end()` methods, or you can simply retrieve the matched text with the `group()` method. For example:

```
import java.util.regex.*;

String text="A horse is a horse, of course of course...";
String pattern="horse|course";

Matcher matcher = Pattern.compile( pattern ).matcher( text );
while ( matcher.find() )
  System.out.println(
    "Matched: '"+matcher.group()+"' at position "+matcher.start() );
```

The previous snippet prints the starting location of the words "horse" and "course" (four in all):

```
Matched: 'horse' at position 2
Matched: 'horse' at position 13
Matched: 'course' at position 23
Matched: 'course' at position 33
```

The method to retrieve the matched text is called `group()` because it refers to capture group zero (the entire match). You can also retrieve the text of other numbered capture groups by giving the `group()` method an integer argument. You can determine how many capture groups you have with the `groupCount()` method:

```
for (int i=1; i < matcher.groupCount(); i++)
System.out.println( matcher.group(i) );
```

Splitting and tokenizing strings

A very common need is to parse a string into a bunch of fields based on some delimiter, such as a comma. It's such a common problem that in Java 1.4, a method was added to the `String` class for doing just this. The `split()` method accepts a regular expression and returns an array of substrings broken around that pattern. For example:

```
String text = "Foo, bar ,   blah";
String [] fields = text.split( "\s*,\s*" );
```

yields a `String` array containing `Foo`, `bar`, and `blah`. You can control the maximum number of matches and also whether you get "empty" strings (for text that might have appeared between two adjacent delimiters) using an optional limit field.

If you are going to use an operation like this more than a few times in your code, you should probably compile the pattern and use its `split()` method, which is identical to the version in `String`. The `String split()` method is equivalent to:

```
Pattern.compile(pattern).split(string);
```

Another look at Scanner

As we mentioned when we introduced it, the `Scanner` class in Java 5.0 can use regular expressions to tokenize strings. You can specify a regular expression to use as the delimiter (instead of the default whitespace) either at construction time or with the `useDelimiter()` method. The `Scanner next()`, `hasNext()`, `skip()`, and `findInLine()` methods all take regular expressions as well. You can specify these either as strings or with a compiled `Pattern` object.

You can use the `findInLine()` method of `Scanner` as an improved `Matcher`. For example:

```
Scanner scanner = new Scanner( "Quantity: 42 items, Price $2.34" );
scanner.findInLine("[Qq]uantity[:\\s]*");
int quantity=scanner.nextInt();
scanner.findInLine("[Pp]rice.*\\$");
float price=scanner.nextFloat();
```

The previous snippet locates the quantity and price values, allowing for variations in capitalization and spacing before the numbers.

Before we move on, we'll also mention a "Stupid Scanner Trick" that, although we don't recommend it, you might find amusing. Using the `\A` boundary marker, which denotes the beginning of input, as a delimiter, we can tell the `Scanner` to return the whole input as a single string. This is an easy way to read the contents of any stream into one large string:

```
InputStream source  = new URL("http://www.oreilly.com/").openStream();
String text = new Scanner( source ).useDelimiter("\\A").next();
```

This is probably not the most efficient or understandable way to do it, but it may save you a little typing in your experimentation.

Replacing text

A common reason that you'll find yourself searching for a pattern in a string is to change it to something else. The regex package not only makes it easy to do this but also provides a simple notation to help you construct replacement text using bits of the matched text.

The most convenient form of this API is `Matcher`'s `replaceAll()` method, which substitutes a replacement string for each occurrence of the pattern and returns the result. For example:

```
String text = "Richard Nixon's social security number is: 567-68-0515.";
Matcher matcher =
Pattern.compile("\\d\\d\\d-\\d\\d\-\\d\\d\\d\\d").matcher( text );
String output = matcher.replaceAll("XXX-XX-XXXX");
```

This code replaces all occurrences of U.S. government Social Security numbers with "XXX-XX-XXXX" (perhaps for privacy considerations).

Using captured text in a replacement. . Literal substitution is nice, but we can make this more powerful by using capture groups in our substitution pattern. To do this, we use the simple convention of referring to numbered capture groups with the notation *$n*, where *n* is the group number. For example, suppose we wanted to show just a little of the Social Security number in the previous example, so that the user would know if we were talking about him. We could modify our regex to catch, for example, the last four digits like so:

```
\d\d\d-\d\d-(\d\d\d\d)
```

We can then use that in the substitution text:

```
String output = matcher.replaceAll("XXX-XX-$1");
```

The static method `Matcher.quoteReplacement()` can be used to escape a literal string (so that it ignores the $ notation) before using it as replacement text.

Controlling the substitution. The `replaceAll()` method is useful, but you may want more control over each substitution. You may want to change each match to something different or base the change on the match in some programmatic way.

To do this, you can use the `Matcher` `appendReplacement()` and `appendTail()` methods. These methods can be used in conjunction with the `find()` method as you iterate through matches to build a replacement string. `appendReplacement()` and `appendTail()` operate on a `StringBuffer` that you supply. The `appendReplacement()` method builds a replacement string by keeping track of where you are in the text and appending all *nonmatched* text to the buffer for you as well as the substitute text that you supply. Each call to `find()` appends the intervening text from the last call, followed by your replacement, then skips over all the matched characters to prepare for the next one. Finally, when you have reached the last match, you should call `appendTail()`, which appends any remaining text after the last match. We'll show an example of this next, as we build a simple "template engine."

Our simple template engine

Let's tie what we've discussed together in a nifty example. A common problem in Java applications is working with bulky, multiline text. In general, you don't want to store the text of messages in your application code because it makes them difficult to edit or internationalize. But when you move them to external files or resources, you need a way for your application to plug in information at runtime. The best example of this is in Java servlets; a generated HTML page is often 99% static text with only a few "variable" pieces plugged in. Technologies such as JSP and XSL were developed to address this. But these are big tools, and we have a simple problem. So let's create a simple solution —a template engine.

Our template engine reads text containing special template tags and substitutes values that we provide. And because generating HTML or XML is one of the most important applications of this, we'll be friendly to those formats by making our tags conform to the style of an XML comment. Specifically, our engine searches the text for tags that look like this:

```
<!--TEMPLATE:name  This is the template for the user name -->
```

XML-style comments start with `<!–` and can contain anything up to a closing –>. We'll add the convention of requiring a `TEMPLATE:name` field to specify the name of the value we want to use. Aside from that, we'll still allow any descriptive text the user wants to include. To be friendly (and consistent), we'll allow any amount of whitespace to appear in the tags, including multiline text in the comments. We'll also ignore the text case of the "TEMPLATE" identifier, just in case. Now, we could do this all with low-level `String` commands, looping over whitespace and taking many substrings. But using the power of regexes, we can do it much more cleanly and with only about seven lines of relevant code. (We've rounded out the example with a few more to make it more useful.)

```
import java.util.*;
import java.util.regex.*;


public class Template
{
    Properties values = new Properties();
    Pattern templateComment =
        Pattern.compile("(?si)<!--\\s*TEMPLATE:(\\w+).*?-->");

    public void set( String name, String value ) {
        values.setProperty( name, value );
    }

    public String fillIn( String text ) {
        Matcher matcher = templateComment.matcher( text );

        StringBuffer buffer = new StringBuffer();
        while( matcher.find() ) {
            String name = matcher.group(1);
            String value = values.getProperty( name );
            matcher.appendReplacement( buffer, value );
        }
        matcher.appendTail( buffer );
        return buffer.toString();
    }
}
```

You'd use the `Template` class like this:

```
String input = "<!-- TEMPLATE:name --> lives at "
   +"<!-- TEMPLATE:address -->";
Template template = new Template();
template.set("name", "Bob");
template.set("address", "1234 Main St.");
String output = template.fillIn( input );
```

In this code, `input` is a string containing tags for name and address. The `set()` method provides the values for those tags.

Let's start by picking apart the regex, `templatePattern`, in the example:

```
(?si)<!--\s*TEMPLATE:(\w+).*?-->
```

It looks scary, but it's actually very simple. Just start reading from left to right. First, we have the special flags declaration `(?si)` telling the regex engine that it should be in single-line mode, with `.*` matching all characters including newlines (`s`), and ignoring case (`i`). Next, there is the literal <!– followed by any amount of whitespace (`\s`) and the `TEMPLATE:` identifier. After the colon, we have a capture group (`\w+`), which reads our name identifier and saves it for us to retrieve later. We allow anything `(.*)` up to the –>, being careful to specify that `.*` should be nongreedy `(.*?)`. We don't want `.*` to consume other opening and closing comment tags all the way to the last one, but instead to find the smallest match (one tag).

Our `fillIn()` method does the work, accepting a template string, searching it, and "replacing" the tag values with the values from `set()`, which we have stored in a `Properties` table. Each time `fillIn()` is called, it creates a `Matcher` to wrap the input string and get ready to apply the pattern. It then creates a temporary `StringBuffer` to hold the output and loops, using the `Matcher find()` method to get each tag. For each match, it retrieves the value of the capture group (group one) that holds the tag name. It looks up the corresponding value and replaces the tag with this value in the output string buffer using the `appendReplacement()` method. (Remember that `appendReplacement()` fills in the intervening text on each call, so we don't have to.) All that remains is to call `appendTail()` at the end to get the remaining text after the last match and return the string value. That's it!

We hope this section has shown you some of the power provided by these tools and whetted your appetite for more. Regexes allow you to work in ways you may not have considered before. Especially now, when the software world is focused on textual representations of almost everything—from data to user interfaces—via XML and HTML, having powerful text-manipulation tools is fundamental. Just remember to keep those regexes simple so you can reuse them again and again.

CHAPTER 11
Core Utilities

In this chapter, we'll continue our look at the core Java APIs, covering more of the tools of the `java.util` package. The `java.util` package includes a wide range of utilities including tools for mathematical operations, fundamental data structures (collections), working with dates and times, storing user preference data, and logging.

Math Utilities

Java supports integer and floating-point arithmetic directly in the language. Higher-level math operations are supported through the `java.lang.Math` class. As you may have seen by now, wrapper classes for primitive data types allow you to treat them as objects. Wrapper classes also hold some methods for basic conversions.

First, a few words about built-in arithmetic in Java. Java handles errors in integer arithmetic by throwing an `ArithmeticException`:

```
int zero = 0;

try {
    int i = 72 / zero;
} catch ( ArithmeticException e ) {
    // division by zero
}
```

To generate the error in this example, we created the intermediate variable `zero`. The compiler is somewhat crafty and would have caught us if we had blatantly tried to perform division by a literal zero.

Floating-point arithmetic expressions, on the other hand, don't throw exceptions. Instead, they take on the special out-of-range values shown in Table 11-1.

Table 11-1. Special floating-point values

Value	Mathematical representation
`POSITIVE_INFINITY`	1.0/0.0
`NEGATIVE_INFINITY`	-1.0/0.0
`NaN`	0.0/0.0

The following example generates an infinite result:

```
double zero = 0.0;
double d = 1.0/zero;

if ( d == Double.POSITIVE_INFINITY )
    System.out.println( "Division by zero" );
```

The special value `NaN` (not a number) indicates the result of dividing zero by zero. This value has the special mathematical distinction of not being equal to itself (`NaN != NaN` evaluates to `true`). Use `Float.isNaN()` or `Double.isNaN()` to test for `NaN`.

The java.lang.Math Class

The `java.lang.Math` class is Java's math library. It holds a suite of static methods covering all of the usual mathematical operations like `sin()`, `cos()`, and `sqrt()`. The `Math` class isn't very object-oriented (you can't create an instance of `Math`). Instead, it's really just a convenient holder for static methods that are more like global functions. As we saw in Chapter 6, it's possible to use the static import functionality to import the names of static methods and constants like this directly into the scope of our class and use them by their simple, unqualified names.

Table 11-2 summarizes the methods in `java.lang.Math`.

Table 11-2. Methods in java.lang.Math

Method	Argument type(s)	Functionality
`Math.abs(a)`	`int`, `long`, `float`, `double`	Absolute value
`Math.acos(a)`	`double`	Arc cosine
`Math.asin(a)`	`double`	Arc sine
`Math.atan(a)`	`double`	Arc tangent
`Math.atan2(a,b)`	`double`	Angle part of rectangular-to-polar coordinate transform
`Math.ceil(a)`	`double`	Smallest whole number greater than or equal to a
`Math.cbrt(a)`	`double`	Cube root of a
`Math.cos(a)`	`double`	Cosine
`Math.cosh(a)`	`double`	Hyperbolic cosine
`Math.exp(a)`	`double`	`Math.E` to the power a
`Math.floor(a)`	`double`	Largest whole number less than or equal to a

Method	Argument type(s)	Functionality
Math.hypot(a,b)	double	Precision calculation of the sqrt() of a2 + b2
Math.log(a)	double	Natural logarithm of a
Math.log10(a)	double	Log base 10 of a
Math.max(a, b)	int, long, float, double	The value a or b closer to Long.MAX_VALUE
Math.min(a, b)	int, long, float, double	The value a or b closer to Long.MIN_VALUE
Math.pow(a, b)	double	a to the power b
Math.random()	None	Random-number generator
Math.rint(a)	double	Converts double value to integral value in double format
Math.round(a)	float, double	Rounds to whole number
Math.signum(a)	double, float	Get the sign of the number at 1.0, –1.0, or 0
Math.sin(a)	double	Sine
Math.sinh(a)	double	Hyperbolic sine
Math.sqrt(a)	double	Square root
Math.tan(a)	double	Tangent
Math.tanh(a)	double	Hyperbolic tangent
Math.toDegrees(a)	double	Convert radians to degrees
Math.toRadians(a)	double	Convert degrees to radians

log(), pow(), and sqrt() can throw a runtime ArithmeticException. abs(), max(), and min() are overloaded for all the scalar values, int, long, float, or double, and return the corresponding type. Versions of Math.round() accept either float or double and return int or long, respectively. The rest of the methods operate on and return double values:

```
double irrational = Math.sqrt( 2.0 ); // 1.414...
int bigger = Math.max( 3, 4 );  // 4
long one = Math.round( 1.125798 ); // 1
```

For convenience, Math also contains the static final double values E and PI:

```
double circumference = diameter  * Math.PI;
```

Big/Precise Numbers

If the long and double types are not large or precise enough for you, the java.math package provides two classes, BigInteger and BigDecimal, that support arbitrary-precision numbers. These full-featured classes have a bevy of methods for performing arbitrary-precision math and precisely controlling rounding of remainders. In the following example, we use BigDecimal to add two very large numbers and then create a fraction with a 100-digit result:

```
long l1 = 9223372036854775807L; // Long.MAX_VALUE
long l2 = 9223372036854775807L;
System.out.println( l1 + l2 ); // -2 ! Not good.

try {
    BigDecimal bd1 = new BigDecimal( "9223372036854775807" );
    BigDecimal bd2 = new BigDecimal( 9223372036854775807L );
    System.out.println( bd1.add( bd2 ) ); // 18446744073709551614

    BigDecimal numerator = new BigDecimal(1);
    BigDecimal denominator = new BigDecimal(3);
    BigDecimal fraction =
        numerator.divide( denominator, 100, BigDecimal.ROUND_UP );
    // 100 digit fraction = 0.333333 ... 3334
}
catch (NumberFormatException nfe) { }
catch (ArithmeticException ae) { }
```

If you implement cryptographic or scientific algorithms for fun, `BigInteger` is crucial. Other than that, you're not likely to need these classes.

Floating-Point Components

As we mentioned in Chapter 4, Java uses the IEEE 754 standard to represent floating-point numbers (float and double types) internally. Those of you familiar with how floating-point math works will already know that "decimal" numbers are represented in binary in this standard by separating the number into three components: a sign (positive or negative), an exponent representing the *magnitude* in powers of 2 of the number, and a *mantissa* using up most of the bits to represent the precise value irrespective of its magnitude. While for most applications the precision of float and double-type floating-point numbers is sufficient enough that we don't need to worry about running into limitations, there are times when specialized apps may wish to work with the floating-point values more directly.

By definition, floating-point numbers trade off precision and scale. Even the smallest Java floating-point type, `float`, can represent (literally) astronomical numbers ranging from negative 10^{-45} to positive 10^{38}. This is accomplished, put in decimal terms, by having the mantissa part of the floating-point value represent a fixed number of "digits" and the exponent tell us where to put the decimal point. As the numbers get larger in magnitude, the "precision" therefore gets shifted to the "left" as more digits appear to the left of the decimal point. What this means is that floating-point numbers can very precisly (with a large number of digits) represent small values like pi, but for bigger numbers (in the billions and trillions) those digits will be taken up with the more signifcant digits. Therefore, the gap between any two consecutive numbers that can be represented by a floating-point value grows larger as the numbers get bigger.

For some applications, knowing the limitations may be important. The `java.lang.Math` class therefore provides a few methods for interrogating floats and doubles about their precision. The `Math.ulp()` method retrieves the "unit of least precision" for a given floating-point number, which is the smallest value that bits in the mantissa represent at their current exponent. Another way to say this is that the `ulp()` is the approximate distance from the floating-point number to the next closest higher or lower floating-point number that can be represented. Adding positive values smaller than half the ULP to a float will not yield a new number. Adding values between half and the full ULP will result in the value plus the ULP. The `Math.nextUp()` method is a convenience that will take a float and tell you the next number that can be represented by adding the ULP.

```
float trillionish = (float)1e12; // trillionish ~= 999,999,995,904
float ulp = Math.ulp( f ); // ulp = 65536
float next = Math.nextUp( f ); // next ~= 1000000061440
trillionish += 32767; // trillionish still ~= 999,999,995,904. No change!
```

Additionally, the `java.lang.Math` class contains the method `getExponent()`, which retrieves the exponent part of a floating-point number (and from there one could determine the mantissa by division). It is also possible to get the raw bits of a float or double using their corresponding wrapper class methods `floatToIntBits()` and `doubleToRawLongBits()` and pick out the (IEEE standard) bits yourself.

Random Numbers

You can use the `java.util.Random` class to generate random values. It's a pseudorandom-number generator that is initialized with a 48-bit seed.[1] Because it's a pseudorandom algorithm, you'll get the same series of values every time you use the same seed value. The default constructor uses the current time to produce a seed, but you can specify your own value in the constructor:

```
long seed = mySeed;
Random rnums = new Random( seed );
```

After you have a generator, you can ask for one or more random values of various types using the methods listed in Table 11-3.

Table 11-3. Random-number methods

Method	Range
`nextBoolean()`	`true` or `false`
`nextInt()`	–2147483648 to 2147483647
`nextInt(int n)`	0 to (n – 1) inclusive
`nextLong()`	–9223372036854775808 to 9223372036854775807

1. The generator uses a linear congruential formula. See *The Art of Computer Programming, Volume 2: Seminumerical Algorithms* by Donald Knuth (Addison-Wesley).

Method	Range
`nextFloat()`	0.0 inclusive to 1.0 exclusive
`nextDouble()`	0.0 inclusive to 1.0 exclusive
`nextGaussian()`	Gaussian distributed double with mean 0.0 and standard deviation of 1.0

By default, the values are uniformly distributed. You can use the `nextGaussian()` method to create a Gaussian (bell curve) distribution of `double` values, with a mean of 0.0 and a standard deviation of 1.0. (Lots of natural phenomena follow a Gaussian distribution rather than a strictly uniform random one.)

The `static` method `Math.random()` retrieves a random `double` value. This method initializes a `private` random-number generator in the `Math` class the first time it's used, using the default `Random` constructor. Thus, every call to `Math.random()` corresponds to a call to `nextDouble()` on that random-number generator.

Dates and Times

Working with dates and times without the proper tools can be a chore. Fortunately, Java has three classes that handle most of the work for you. The `java.util.Date` class encapsulates a point in time. The `java.util.GregorianCalendar` class, which extends the abstract `java.util.Calendar`, translates between a point in time and calendar fields like month, day, and year. Finally, the `java.text.DateFormat` class knows how to generate and parse string representations of dates and times in many languages.[2]

The separation of the `Date` and `Calendar` classes is analogous to having a class representing temperature and a class that translates that temperature to Celsius units. A `Date` represents an absolute point in time as defined by a number of milliseconds from the reference point: midnight, Jan 1, 1970, GMT. This is the same frame of reference used by the `System.currentTimeMillis()` call. A `Calendar` encapsulates a point in time and maps it to higher-level (and messier) notions like years, months, weeks, and days, and deals with discontinuities like leap years. Conceivably, we could define subclasses of `Calendar` other than the default `GregorianCalendar`, say `JulianCalendar` or `LunarCalendar`, that map time using other sociological or cultural conventions.[3]

2. Prior to Java 1.1, the `Date` class handled some of the functions of a calendar as well. Most of these methods have now been deprecated. Today, the only purpose of the `Date` class is to represent a point in time.

3. Java's `GregorianCalendar` class is actually both a Julian and Gregorian calendar with a programmable cut-over date. For a wealth of information about time and world time-keeping conventions, see the U.S. Navy Directorate of Time (*http://tycho.usno.navy.mil*).

Working with Calendars

The default `GregorianCalendar` constructor creates a calendar initialized to the current time, in the current time zone:

```
GregorianCalendar now = new GregorianCalendar();
```

However, more generally we can just ask the `Calendar` class for an appropriate calendar instance without worrying about what type of calendar system the world is using this century:

```
Calendar now = Calendar.getInstance();
```

In either case, all the real work is done through the main `set()` and `get()` methods of `Calendar`. These methods use static identifiers to refer to calendar fields and values. For example:

```
Calendar birthday = Calendar.getInstance();
birthday.set( Calendar.YEAR, 1972 );
birthday.set( Calendar.MONTH, Calendar.MAY );
birthday.set( Calendar.DATE, 20 );
```

Here, we set the year, month, and day values on the calendar, altering the internal `Date` of the `Calendar` object. Any remaining fields that we did not set are left as they were initialized (to the current date and time when it was constructed). In this case, we did not really specify a full date and time; we simply overrode individual fields in the calendar.

The `Calendar` class contains identifiers for all of the standard date and time fields, as well as values such as days of the week and months of the year. The following are the most common identifiers:

- `YEAR`, `MONTH`
- `WEEK_OF_YEAR`, `WEEK_OF_MONTH`
- `DATE`, `DAY_OF_YEAR`, `DAY_OF_MONTH`, `DAY_OF_WEEK`
- `HOUR`, `HOUR_OF_DAY`, `AM_PM`
- `MINUTE`, `SECOND`, `MILLISECOND`
- `ZONE_OFFSET`, `DST_OFFSET`

`DATE` and `DAY_OF_MONTH` are synonymous. `HOUR` is a 12-hour clock that can be combined with `AM_PM`. The values are just what you would expect, as shown in the following:

- `SUNDAY`, `MONDAY`, `TUESDAY`...
- `JANUARY`, `FEBRUARY`, `MARCH`...
- `AM`, `PM`

In addition to the set() method for changing field values, the Calendar class has two additional methods for performing date math, add() and roll(). Using add(), you can move a calendar forward or backward in any unit of time easily, without having to calculate the other fields. For example, we can move our calendar forward four weeks:

```
Calendar cal = Calendar.getInstance();
System.out.println( cal.getTime() );
// Thu Nov 04 16:39:06 CST 2004

cal.add( Calendar.WEEK_OF_YEAR, 4 );
System.out.println( cal.getTime() );
// Thu Dec 02 16:39:06 CST 2004
```

The roll() method, by contrast, does not alter the other fields of the calendar, but arbitrarily adjusts individual fields. See the Spinner example in Chapter 17 for additional information about adding and subtracting time periods using the add() method.

Finally, you can always get the internal Date of the Calendar object or reinitialize the calendar to a specific Date using the getTime() and setTime() method:

```
// Get the absolute time the Calendar references
Date date = calendar.getTime();

// Reinitialize this calendar to the current date and time
Date now = new Date();
calendar.setTime( now );
```

Time Zones

An instance of the TimeZone class represents a time zone and the knowledge of daylight savings time at that location. You can construct a time zone from a string specifier in a number of ways. The most general approach is to use an offset from GMT, but many human-readable formats are included. (For a list, use TimeZone.getAvailableIDs().)

```
TimeZone.getTimeZone("US/Central");        // CST
TimeZone.getTimeZone("GMT-06");            // CST
TimeZone.getTimeZone("America/Chicago");   // CST
```

A Calendar inherits the default time zone from the platform on which it was created. You can set a different time zone with the setTimeZone() method:

```
GregorianCalendar smokey = new
GregorianCalendar();
smokey.setTimeZone( TimeZone.getTimeZone("US/Mountain") );
```

It's important to think about dates and time zones in the right way. Remember that a Date is an absolute point in time, while a Calendar translates that Date into localized fields that may depend on where you are. In a sense, it is meaningless to talk about the date "Nov 1, 2004," without specifying a time zone because at any given moment on earth, "now" could be one of two different calendar days. Even specifying a date and time such as “Nov 1, 2004, 9:01 pm” is ambiguous, because that particular combination of calendar and time fields occurs at 24 separate times over the span of a day as the world turns (see Figure 11-1). Only a complete date, time, and time zone specifies an absolute point in time, such as “Nov 1, 2004, 9:01 pm EST.” So it’s important to remember that the `Calendar` class defaults all of these fields for you even if you haven’t set them.

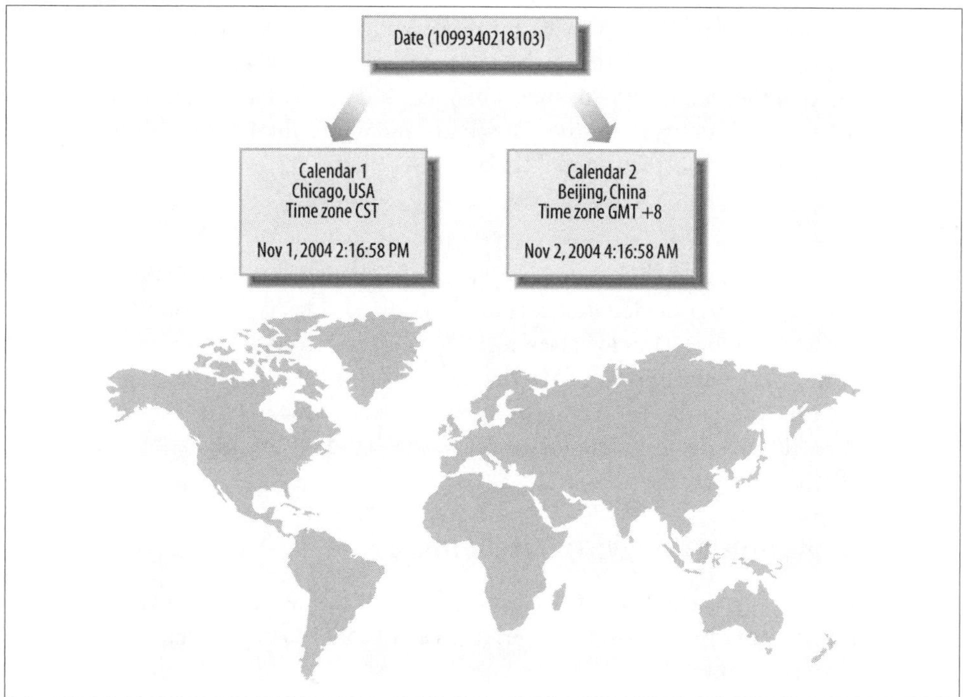

Figure 11-1. Calendars translate an absolute point in time to a localized data and time

The following example prints the day of the week for the same `Date` object in two different time zones:

```
Date date = new Date(); // point in time

TimeZone CST = TimeZone.getTimeZone( "America/Chicago" );
Calendar usa = Calendar.getInstance( CST );
usa.setTime( date );
System.out.println( usa.get( Calendar.DAY_OF_WEEK ) );  // 1

TimeZone GMT8 = TimeZone.getTimeZone( "GMT+08"); // Beijing
Calendar china = Calendar.getInstance( GMT8 );
china.setTime( date );
System.out.println( china.get( Calendar.DAY_OF_WEEK ) ); // 2
```

In this example, we could also have simply changed the time zone on the calendar usa using the setTimeZone() method. Unlike the field set() methods, setting the time zone does not change the underlying Date value of the calendar, only the interpretation of the fields.

The meaning of the Date object and its relationship to Calendar become particularly important when dealing with APIs for things such as databases that construct dates from incomplete date and time fields. If, as is entirely possible, you end up sending your Date object from a client application in one part of the world to a server in another, you may be surprised that the calendar fields have changed. In these situations, it's important to work with Calendars to translate the date fields and avoid the temptation to "fix" the problem by adding or subtracting real time from the date.

Locale

It should be clear now that Calendar is not just a fancy Date, but rather is something in between a time-keeping device and a time-formatting device. This point is brought home by the fact that the Calendar class is also locale-sensitive. In addition to the notion of a time zone, a Calendar has a Locale that governs conventions such as on which day the week begins and ends. You can specify an alternate locale with the setLocale() method. Most locale-specific details, however, are handled by the DateFormat class, which we'll discuss next.

Parsing and Formatting with DateFormat

As its name suggests, the DateFormat class formats Date objects and not Calendars, so the first step in formatting dates and times from a Calendar is to get back to a Date with the getTime() method:

```
Date birthDate = calendar.getTime();
```

To create string representations of dates and times, create a DateFormat object and apply its format() method to a Date object. Like the NumberFormat object we looked at in the previous chapter, DateFormat itself is abstract, but it has several static ("factory") methods that return useful DateFormat subclass instances. To get a default DateFormat, simply call getInstance():

```
DateFormat simple = DateFormat.getInstance();
String now = simple.format( new Date() );         // 4/12/06 6:06 AM
```

You can generate a date string or a time string, or both, using the getDateInstance(), getTimeInstance(), and getDateTimeInstance() factory methods. The argument to these methods describes what level of detail you'd like to see. DateFormat defines four constants representing detail levels: they are SHORT, MEDIUM, LONG, and FULL. There is also a DEFAULT, which is the same as MEDIUM. The following code creates three DateFormat instances: one to format a date, one to format a time, and one to format a date and time together. `getDateTimeInstance()` requires two arguments: the first specifies how to format the date, the second how to format the time:

```
// 12-Apr-06
DateFormat df  = DateFormat.getDateInstance(DateFormat.DEFAULT);

// 9:18:27 AM
DateFormat tf  = DateFormat.getTimeInstance(DateFormat.DEFAULT);

// Wednesday, April 12, 2006 9:18:27 o'clock AM EDT
DateFormat dtf =
  DateFormat.getDateTimeInstance( DateFormat.FULL, DateFormat.FULL );
```

We're showing only how to create the `DateFormat` objects here. In order to actually generate a `String` from a date, you'll need to call the `format()` method of these objects, passing a `Date` as an argument.

Formatting dates and times for other countries is just as easy. Overloaded factory methods accept a `Locale` argument:

```
// 12 avr. 06
DateFormat df =
  DateFormat.getDateInstance( DateFormat.DEFAULT, Locale.FRANCE );

// 9:27:49
DateFormat tf =
  DateFormat.getTimeInstance( DateFormat.DEFAULT, Locale.GERMANY );

// mercoledi 12 aprile 2006 9.27.49 GMT-04:00
DateFormat dtf =
    DateFormat.getDateTimeInstance(
        DateFormat.FULL, DateFormat.FULL, Locale.ITALY );
```

To parse a string representing a date, we use the `parse()` method of the `DateFormat` class. The result is a `Date` object. The parsing algorithms are finicky, so it's safest to parse dates and times that are in the same format produced by the `DateFormat`. The `parse()` method throws a `ParseException` if it doesn't understand the string you give it. All of the following calls to `parse()` succeed except the last; we don't supply a time zone, but the format for the time is `LONG`. Other exceptions are occasionally thrown from the `parse()` method. To cover all the bases, catch `NullPointerExceptions` and `StringIndexOutOfBoundsExceptions` also:

```
try {
  Date d;
  DateFormat df;

  df = DateFormat.getDateTimeInstance(
          DateFormat.FULL, DateFormat.FULL);
  d = df.parse("Wednesday, April 12, 2006 2:22:22 o'clock PM EDT");

  df = DateFormat.getDateTimeInstance(
```

```
            DateFormat.MEDIUM, DateFormat.MEDIUM);
    d = df.parse("12-Apr-06 2:22:22 PM");

    df = DateFormat.getDateTimeInstance(
            DateFormat.LONG, DateFormat.LONG);
    d = df.parse("April 12, 2006 2:22:22 PM EDT");

    // throws a ParseException; detail level mismatch
    d = df.parse("12-Apr-06 2:22:22 PM");
}
catch (Exception e) { ... }
```

Printf-Style Date and Time Formatting

The printf-style formatting covered in Chapter 10 can render dates and times to strings in completely arbitrary ways, without having to resort to `Calendar` methods to get components.

All date and time format strings use the same conversion character, `t` or `T`, followed by a suffix character that identifies the actual format or date/time component to be generated. For example, the format string `%tc` turns a `Date` argument into the string equivalent of what you get with the standard `Date toString()` method:

```
System.out.printf( "The date is %tc\n", new Date() );
// The date is Thu Nov 04 22:32:00 CST 2004
```

As with other conversion characters, the only difference between `t` and `T` is that the latter forces all of the output to uppercase. All time and date formatting is locale-sensitive, including the names of days and months and the A.M./P.M. identifier. To format a `Date` for another language, simply pass the `Locale` as the first argument:

```
System.out.printf( Locale.ITALIAN, "The date is %tc\n", new Date() );
// The date is gio nov 04 22:32:00 CST 2004
```

There are two additional composite, date-only formats and three composite time-only formats, as shown in the following table. The format string description in the third column of Table 11-4 refers to date and time component formats discussed in Tables 11-5 and 11-6.

Table 11-4. Composite date and time formats

Format suffix	Example	Components
c	Thu Nov 04 22:32:00 CST 2004	`%ta %tb %td %tT %tZ %tY`
D	11/04/04	`%tm/%td/%ty`
F	2004-11-04	`%tY-%tm-%td`
r	10:32:00 PM	`%tI:%tM:%tS %Tp`
R	22:32	`%tH:%tM`
T	22:32:00	`%tH:%tM:%tS`

Table 11-5 lists formats for accessing date components.

Table 11-5. Date component formats

Format suffix	Examples	Description
a	Sun, Mon, Tue...	Abbreviated day of week
A	Sunday, Monday...	Full day of week
b	Jan, Feb, Mar, ...	Abbreviated month
B	January, February, ...	Full month
Y	1999, 2004	Four-digit year
C	2004 = 20	High two digits of year
y	1999 = 99	Low two digits of year
j	001 ... 366	Day of year
m	01 ... 13	Month of year
d	01 ... 31	Day of month
e	1 ... 31	Day of month, no leading zeros

Table 11-6 lists formats for accessing time components.

Table 11-6. Time component formats

Format suffix	Examples	Description
H	00 ... 23	24-hour clock
k	0 ... 23	24-hour clock, no leading zeros
I	01 ... 12	12-hour clock
l	1 ... 12	12-hour clock, no leading zeros
M	00 ... 59	Minute
S	00 ... 60[a]	Second
L	000 ... 999	Millisecond
p	am, pm	Morning or afternoon designator
Z	CST, EST	Time zone name
z	-0600	Time zone GMT offset

[a] The second value (`60`) is a convention used to support leap seconds.

Timers

Java includes two handy classes for timed code execution. If you write a clock application, for example, you might want to update the display every second. You might want to play an alarm sound at some predetermined time. You could accomplish these tasks using multiple threads and calls to `Thread.sleep()`. But the `java.util.Timer` and `java.util.TimerTask` classes handle this for you.

The Timer class is a scheduler. Each instance of Timer has a single thread that runs in the background, watching the clock and executing one or more TimerTasks at appropriate times. You could, for example, schedule a task to run once at a specific time like this:

```
import java.util.*;

public class Y2K {
  public static void main(String[] args) {
    Timer timer = new Timer();

    TimerTask task = new TimerTask() {
      public void run() {
        System.out.println("Y2K!");
      }
    };

    Calendar cal = new GregorianCalendar( 2000, Calendar.JANUARY, 1 );
    timer.schedule( task, cal.getTime());
  }
}
```

TimerTask implements the Runnable interface. To create a task, you can simply subclass TimerTask and supply a run() method. Here, we've created a simple anonymous subclass of TimerTask that prints a message to System.out. Using the schedule() method of Timer, we've asked that the task be run on January 1, 2000. If the scheduled time has already passed (as in our example), the task is run immediately.

There are some other varieties of schedule(); you can run tasks once or at recurring intervals. There are two kinds of recurring tasks—fixed delay and fixed rate. *Fixed delay* means that a fixed amount of time elapses between the end of the task's execution and the beginning of the next execution. *Fixed rate* means that the task should begin execution at fixed time intervals. The difference comes into play when the time to execute the task is long relative to the interval. Keep in mind that tasks are executed by the Timer's single scheduler thread. If one task takes a very long time, other tasks may be delayed, in which case they run as soon as the thread becomes available.

You could, for example, update a clock display every second with code like this:

```
Timer timer = new Timer();

TimerTask task = new TimerTask() {
    public void run() {
        repaint(); // update the clock display
    }
};

timer.scheduleAtFixedRate( task, 0, 1000 );
```

A TimerTask can be canceled before its execution with its cancel() method.

Collections

Collections are data structures that are fundamental to all types of programming. Whenever we need to refer to a group of objects, we have some kind of collection. At the core language level, Java supports collections in the form of arrays. But arrays are static and because they have a fixed length, they are awkward for groups of things that grow and shrink over the lifetime of an application. Arrays also do not represent abstract relationships between objects well. In the early days, the Java platform had only two basic classes to address these needs: the `java.util.Vector` class, which represents a dynamic list of objects, and the `java.util.Hashtable` class, which holds a map of key/value pairs. Today, Java has a more comprehensive approach to collections called the Collections Framework. The older classes still exist, but they have been retrofitted into the framework (with some eccentricities) and are generally no longer used.

Though conceptually simple, collections are one of the most powerful parts of any programming language. Collections implement data structures that lie at the heart of managing complex problems. A great deal of basic computer science is devoted to describing the most efficient ways to implement certain types of algorithms over collections. Having these tools at your disposal and understanding how to use them can make your code both much smaller and faster. It can also save you from reinventing the wheel.

Prior to Java 5, the Collections Framework had two major drawbacks. The first was that —not having generic types to work with—collections were by necessity untyped and worked only with anonymous `Objects` instead of real types like `Dates` and `Strings`. This meant that you had to perform a type cast every time you took an object out of a collection. This flew in the face of Java's compile-time type safety. But in practice, this was less a problem than it was just plain cumbersome and tedious. The second issue was that, for practical reasons, collections could work only with objects and not with primitive types. This meant that any time you wanted to put a number or other primitive type into a collection, you had to store it in a wrapper class first and unpack it later upon retrieving it. The combination of these factors made code working with collections less readable and more dangerous to boot.

This all changed with the introduction of generic types and autoboxing of primitive values. First, the introduction of generic types, as we described in Chapter 8, has made it possible for truly typesafe collections to be under the control of the programmer. Second, the introduction of autoboxing and unboxing of primitive types means that you can generally treat objects and primitives as equals where collections are concerned. The combination of these new features can significantly reduce the amount of code you write and add safety as well. As we'll see, all of the collections classes now take advantage of these features.

The Collections Framework is based around a handful of interfaces in the `java.util` package. These interfaces are divided into two hierarchies. The first hierarchy descends from the `Collection` interface. This interface (and its descendants) represents a container that holds other objects. The second, separate hierarchy is based on the `Map` interface, which represents a group of key/value pairs where the key can be used to retrieve the value in an efficient way.

The Collection Interface

The mother of all collections is an interface appropriately named `Collection`. It serves as a container that holds other objects, its *elements*. It doesn't specify exactly how the objects are organized; it doesn't say, for example, whether duplicate objects are allowed or whether the objects are ordered in any way. These kinds of details are left to child interfaces. Nevertheless, the `Collection` interface defines some basic operations common to all collections:

`public boolean add(` *`element`* `)`
: This method adds the supplied object to this collection. If the operation succeeds, this method returns `true`. If the object already exists in this collection and the collection does not permit duplicates, `false` is returned. Furthermore, some collections are read-only. Those collections throw an `UnsupportedOperationException` if this method is called.

`public boolean remove(` *`element`* `)`
: This method removes the specified object from this collection. Like the `add()` method, this method returns `true` if the object is removed from the collection. If the object doesn't exist in this collection, `false` is returned. Read-only collections throw an `UnsupportedOperationException` if this method is called.

`public boolean contains(` *`element`* `)`
: This method returns `true` if the collection contains the specified object.

`public int size()`
: Use this method to find the number of elements in this collection.

`public boolean isEmpty()`
: This method returns `true` if this collection has no elements.

`public Iterator iterator()`
: Use this method to examine all the elements in this collection. This method returns an `Iterator`, which is an object you can use to step through the collection's elements. We'll talk more about iterators in the next section.

Additionally, the methods `addAll()`, `removeAll()`, and `containsAll()` accept another `Collection` and add, remove, or test for all of the elements of the supplied collection.

Generics and collections

When using generics, the `Collection` type is parameterized with a specific type of element that the collection will hold. This makes a generic collection of "anything" into a specific collection of some type of element. The parameter type becomes the compile-time type of the `element` arguments in all of the methods of `Collection` (in this case, the `add()`, `remove()`, and `contains()` methods listed earlier). For example, in the following code, we create a `Collection` that works with `Dates`:

```
Collection<Date> dates = new ArrayList<Date>(); // = new ArrayList<>() would
                                                 // also work.
dates.add( new Date() );
dates.add( "foo" ) // Error; string type where Date expected!!
```

`ArrayList` is just one implementation of `Collection`; we'll talk about it a bit later. The important thing is that we've declared the variable `dates` to be of the type `Collection<Date>`; that is, a collection of `Dates`, and we've allocated our `ArrayList` to match. Because our collection has been parameterized with the type `Date`, the `add()` method of the collection becomes `add( Date date )` and attempting to add any type of object other than a `Date` to the list would have caused a compile-time error.

If you are working with very old Java code that predates generics, you can simply drop the types and perform the appropriate casts. For example:

```
Collection dates = new ArrayList();
dates.add( new Date() );  // unchecked, compile-time warning
Date date = (Date)dates.get( 0 );
```

In this case, we'll get a compile time warning that we're using `ArrayList` in a potentially unsafe (nongeneric typesafe) way.

As we've described earlier in the book, this is essentially what the Java compiler is doing for us with generics. When using collections (or any generic classes) in this way under Java 5 or later, you will get compile-time warnings indicating that the usage is unchecked, meaning that it is possible to get an error at runtime if you have made a mistake. In this example, a mistake would not be caught until someone tried to retrieve the object from the collection and cast it to the expected type.

Legacy code and runtime type safety

If you are working with legacy Java code that predates Java 5 generics and you do not wish to introduce generics to it, you can still add a layer of type safety at runtime by switching to a runtime type-checked version of your collection types. Java supplies runtime-checked wrappers for all of the basic collection types. These wrappers enforce a specific Java element type at runtime by throwing `ClassCastException` if the wrong element is inserted. For example:

```
List list = new ArrayList();
list = Collections.checkedList( list, Date.class );
```

```
list.add( new Date() );
list.add( "foo" ); // Runtime ClassCastException!
```

Here, the static `Collections.checkedList()` method has wrapped our collection, `list`, in a wrapper that implements all of the methods of `List`, but checks that we are only holding `Dates`. The second argument to the method is the literal `Date.class` reference to the `Class` of `Date`. This serves to tell the wrapper what type we want to enforce. Corresponding "checked" collection methods exist for all of the basic collection interfaces that we'll see, including the base `Collection`, `List`, `Set`, and `Map`.

Converting between collections and arrays

Converting between collections and arrays is easy. For convenience, the elements of a collection can be retrieved as an array using the following methods:

```
public Object[] toArray()
public <E> E[] toArray( E[] a )
```

The first method returns a plain `Object` array. With the second form, we can be more specific and get back an array of the correct element type. If we supply an array of sufficient size, it will be filled in with the values. But if the array is too short (e.g., zero length), a new array of the *same type but the required length* will be created and returned to us. So you can just pass in an empty array of the correct type like this:

```
Collection<String> myCollection = ...;
String [] myStrings = myCollection.toArray( new String[0] );
```

(This trick is a little awkward and it would be nice if Java let us specify the type explicitly using a `Class` reference, but for some reason, this isn't the case.) Going the other way, you can convert an array of objects to a `List` collection with the static `asList()` method of the `java.util.Arrays` class:

```
String [] myStrings = ...;    List list = Arrays.asList( myStrings );
```

Iterator

An *iterator* is an object that lets you step through a sequence of values. This kind of operation comes up so often that it is given a standard interface: `java.util.Iterator`. The `Iterator` interface has only two primary methods:

`public E next()`
: This method returns the next element (an element of generic type E) of the associated collection.

`public boolean hasNext()`
: This method returns `true` if you have not yet stepped through all the `Collection`'s elements. In other words, it returns `true` if you can call `next()` to get the next element.

The following example shows how you could use an `Iterator` to print out every element of a collection:

```
public void printElements(Collection c, PrintStream out) {
    Iterator iterator = c.iterator();
    while ( iterator.hasNext() )
        out.println( iterator.next() );
}
```

In addition to the traversal methods, `Iterator` provides the ability to remove an element from a collection:

`public void remove()`
: This method removes the most recent object returned from `next()` from the associated `Collection`.

Not all iterators implement `remove()`. It doesn't make sense to be able to remove an element from a read-only collection, for example. If element removal is not allowed, an `UnsupportedOperationException` is thrown from this method. If you call `remove()` before first calling `next()`, or if you call `remove()` twice in a row, you'll get an `IllegalStateException`.

For loop over collections

A form of the `for` loop, described in Chapter 4, can operate over all types of `Collection` objects. For example, we can now step over all of the elements of a typed collection of `Date` objects like so:

```
Collection<Date> col = ...
for( Date date : col )
   System.out.println( date );
```

This feature of the Java built-in `for` loop is called the "enhanced" `for` loop (as opposed to the pregenerics, numeric-only `for` loop). The enhanced `for` loop applies only to `Collection` type collections, not `Map`s. `Map`s are another type of beast that really contain two distinct sets of objects (keys and values), so it's not obvious what your intentions would be in such a loop.

java.util.Enumeration

Prior to the introduction of the Collections API there was another iterator interface: `java.util.Enumeration`. It used the slightly more verbose names `nextElement()` and `hasMoreElements()`, but accomplished the same thing. Many older classes provide `Enumeration`s where they would now use `Iterator`. If you aren't worried about performance, you can just convert your `Enumeration` into a `List` with a static convenience method of the `java.util.Collections` class:

```
Enumeration myEnumeartion = ...;
List list = Collections.list( myEnumeration );
```

Collection Types

The `Collection` interface has three child interfaces. `Set` represents a collection in which duplicate elements are not allowed. `List` is a collection whose elements have a specific order. The `Queue` interface is a buffer for objects with a notion of a "head" element that's next in line for processing.

Set

`Set` has no methods besides the ones it inherits from `Collection`. It simply enforces its no-duplicates rule. If you try to add an element that already exists in a `Set`, the `add()` method simply returns `false`. `SortedSet` maintains elements in a prescribed order; like a sorted list that can contain no duplicates. It adds the methods `add()` and `remove()` to the `Set` interface. You can retrieve subsets (which are also sorted) using the `subSet()`, `headSet()`, and `tailSet()` methods. These methods accept one or a pair of elements that mark the boundaries. The `first()`, `last()`, and `comparator()` methods provide access to the first element, the last element, and the object used to compare elements (more on this later).

Java 7 adds `NavigableSet`, which extends `SortedSet` and adds methods for finding the closest match greater or lesser than a target value within the sort order of the `Set`. This interface can be implemented efficiently using techniques such as skip lists, which make finding ordered elements fast (Java 7 supplies such an implementation, which we'll note later).

List

The next child interface of `Collection` is `List`. The `List` is an ordered collection, similar to an array but with methods for manipulating the position of elements in the list:

`public boolean add( E` *`element`* `)`
: This method adds the specified element to the end of the list.

`public void add( int` *`index`* `, E` *`element`* `)`
: This method inserts the given object at the supplied position in the list. If the position is less than zero or greater than the list length, an `IndexOutOfBoundsException` will be thrown. The element that was previously at the supplied position, and all elements after it, are moved up one index position.

`public void remove( int` *`index`* `)`
: This method removes the element at the specified position. All subsequent elements move down one index position.

`public E get( int` *`index`* `)`
: This method returns the element at the given position.

`public Object set( int index , E element )`
: This method changes the element at the given position to the specified object. There must already be an object at the index or else an `IndexOutOfBoundsException` is thrown.

The type `E` in these methods refers to the parameterized element type of the `List` class. `Collection`, `Set`, and `List` are all interface types. We'll look at concrete implementations of these shortly.

Queue

A `Queue` is a collection that acts like a buffer for elements. The queue maintains the insertion order of items placed into it and has the notion of a "head" item. Queues may be first in, first out (FIFO) or last in, first out (LIFO) depending on the implementation:

`public boolean offer( E element )`
`public boolean add( E element )`
: The `offer()` method attempts to place the element into the queue, returning true if successful. Different `Queue` types may have different limits or restrictions on element types (including capacity). This method differs from the `add()` method inherited from `Collection` in that it returns a Boolean value instead of throwing an exception to indicate that the element cannot be accepted.

`public E poll()`
`public E remove()`
: The `poll()` method removes the element at the head of the queue and returns it. This method differs from the `Collection` method `remove()` in that if the queue is empty, `null` is returned instead of throwing an exception.

`public E peek()`
: This method returns the head element *without* removing it from the queue. If the queue is empty, `null` is returned.

Java 7 added `Deque`, which is a "double-ended" queue that supports adding, querying, and removing elements from either end of the queue (the head or the tail). `Dequeue` has versions of the queue methods—`offer`, `poll`, and `peek`—that operate on the first or last element: `offerFirst()`, `pollFirst()`, `peekFirst()`, `offerLast()`, `pollLast()`, `peekLast()`. Note that `Deque` extends `Queue` and so is still a type of `Queue`. If you use the plain `Queue` methods `offer()`, `poll()`, and `peek()` on a `Deque`, they operate as a FIFO queue. Specifically, calling `offer()` is equivalent to `offerLast()` and calling `poll()` or `peek()` is the same as calling `pollFirst()` or `peekFirst()`, respectively.

Finally, Java has a legacy `Stack` class that acts as a LIFO queue with "push" and "pop" operations, but `Deque` is generally better and should serve as a general replacement for `Stack`. Simply use `addFirst()` for "push" and `pollFirst()` for "pop."

BlockingQueue

`BlockingQueue` is part of the `java.util.concurrent` package. It extends the `Queue` interface for queues that may have a fixed capacity or other time-based limitations and allows the user to block, waiting for insertion of an item or for an available item to retrieve. It adds timed wait versions of `offer()` and `poll()` and additional, blocking `take()` and `put()` methods:

`public boolean offer( E element, long time, TimeUnit units )`
: This method attempts to place the element into the queue, just like the method of the base `Queue` interface, but blocks for up to the specified period of time as it waits for space to become available.

`public E poll( long time, timeUnit unit )`
: This method attempts to remove the element at the head of the queue, just like the method of the base `Queue` interface, but blocks for up to the specified period of time as it waits for an element to become available.

`public E take()`
: This method retrieves the element at the head of the queue, blocking if necessary until one becomes available.

`public void put( E element )`
: This method adds an element to the queue, blocking if necessary until space becomes available.

`public boolean add( E element )`
: This method attempts to add an element to the queue immediately. If successful, it returns `true`. If no space is available, it throws an `IllegalStateException`. This method is useful for cases where you are not expecting the queue to ever reject an item.

The Map Interface

The Collections Framework also includes the `java.util.Map`, which is a collection of key/value pairs. Other names for map are "dictionary" or "associative array." Maps store and retrieve elements with key values; they are very useful for things like caches or minimalist databases. When you store a value in a map, you associate a key object with a value. When you need to look up the value, the map retrieves it using the key.

With generics, a `Map` type is parameterized with two types: one for the keys and one for the values. The following snippet uses a `HashMap`, which is an efficient type of map implementation that we'll discuss later:

```
Map<String, Date> dateMap = new HashMap<String, Date>();
dateMap.put( "today", new Date() );
Date today = dateMap.get( "today" );
```

In legacy code, maps simply map `Object` types to `Object` types and require the appropriate cast to retrieve values.

The basic operations on `Map` are straightforward. In the following methods, the type `K` refers to the key parameter type and the type `V` refers to the value parameter type:

`public V put( K key , V value )`
: This method adds the specified key/value pair to the map. If the map already contains a value for the specified key, the old value is replaced and returned as the result.

`public V get( K key )`
: This method retrieves the value corresponding to `key` from the map.

`public V remove( K key )`
: This method removes the value corresponding to `key` from the map. The value removed is returned.

`public int size()`
: Use this method to find the number of key/value pairs in this map.

You can retrieve all the keys or values in the map:

`public Set keySet()`
: This method returns a `Set` that contains all the keys in this map.

`public Collection values()`
: Use this method to retrieve all the values in this map. The returned `Collection` can contain duplicate elements.

`Map` has one child interface, `SortedMap`. A `SortedMap` maintains its key/value pairs sorted in a particular order according to the key values. It provides the `subMap()`, `headMap()`, and `tailMap()` methods for retrieving sorted map subsets. Like `SortedSet`, it also provides a `comparator()` method, which returns an object that determines how the map keys are sorted. We'll talk more about that later. Java 7 adds a `NavigableMap` with functionality parallel to that of `NavigableSet`; namely, it adds methods to search the sorted elements for an element greater or lesser than a target value.

Finally, we should make it clear that although related, `Map` is not literally a type of `Collection` (`Map` does not extend the `Collection` interface). You might wonder why. All of the methods of the `Collection` interface would appear to make sense for `Map`, except for `iterator()`. A `Map`, again, has two sets of objects: keys and values, and separate iterators for each. This is why a `Map` does not implement `Collection`.

One more note about maps: some map implementations (including Java's standard `HashMap`) allow `null` to be used as a key or value, but others may not.

ConcurrentMap

The `ConcurrentMap` interface is part of the `java.util.concurrent` package. It extends the base `Map` interface and adds atomic put, remove, and replace functionality that is useful for concurrent programming:

`public V putIfAbsent( K key, V value )`
: This method associates the value with the key only if the key was not already in use. If the key exists, no action is taken. If the key does not exist, it is created. The resulting value (`existing` or `new`) is returned.

`public boolean remove( Object key, Object value )`
: This method removes the mapping (key and value) only if the current value associated with the key equals the supplied value. It returns `true` if the value was removed, `false` if not.

`public boolean replace( K key, V existingValue, V newValue)`
: This method replaces the value associated with the key only if the existing value equals the `existingValue` argument. It returns `true` if the value was replaced.

`public boolean replace( K key, V value )`
: This method replaces the value associated with the key only if a mapping already exists for the key (i.e., it already has some value).

Collection Implementations

Up until this point, we've talked only about interfaces. But you can't instantiate interfaces; you need concrete implementations. Of course, the Collections Framework includes useful implementations of all of the collections interfaces. In some cases, there are several alternatives from which to choose. To understand the tradeoffs between these implementations, it helps to have a basic understanding of a few of the most common data structures used in all programming: arrays, linked lists, trees, and hash maps. Many books have been written about these data structures, and we will not drag you into the mind-numbing details here. We'll hit the highlights briefly as a prelude to our discussion of the Java implementations. We should stress before we go on that the differences in the implementations of Java collections are only significant when working with very large numbers of elements or with extreme time sensitivity. For the most part, they all behave well enough to be interchangeable.

Arrays

It should be fairly obvious that plain old Java arrays, shown in Figure 11-2, would be good at holding an ordered collection of elements. As we mentioned earlier, however, one limitation of arrays is that they cannot grow. This means that to support a true `Collection`, arrays must be copied into larger arrays as capacity demands increase. Another problem with using arrays for lists is that inserting an element into the middle of an array or taking one out generally also involves copying large parts of the array to and fro, which is an expensive operation.

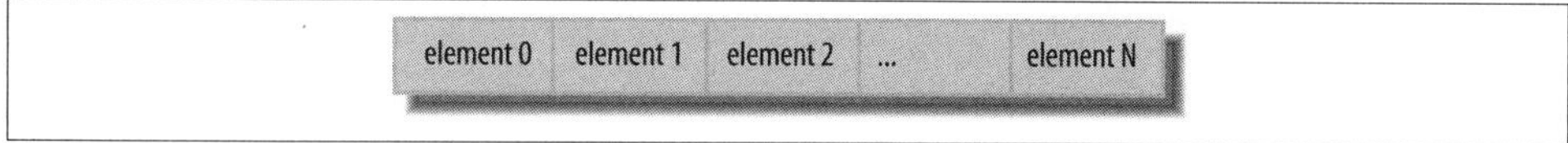

Figure 11-2. Array structure

Because of this, arrays are described as consuming *constant time* for retrieval, but *linear time* for insertion into or deletion from the body of the array. The term *constant time* here means that, in general, the time to retrieve an element stays roughly constant even as you add more elements to the array (this is due to the fact that arrays are fully indexed). Linear time means that the time to insert or delete an element takes longer and longer as the array adds elements; the time expense grows linearly with the number of elements. There are worse things too: exponential time, as you might imagine, means that an algorithm is useless for very large numbers of elements. Unless otherwise stated, all of the Java collection implementations work in linear time or better.

Arrays are useful when you are mostly reading or exclusively appending to the end of the collection.

Linked lists

A linked list, shown in Figure 11-3, holds its elements in a chain of *nodes*, each referencing the node before and after it (if any). In this way, the linked list forms an ordered collection that looks something like an array. Unlike the magic of an array, however, to retrieve an element from a linked list, you must traverse the list from either the head or tail to reach the correct spot. As you might have guessed, this is a linear-time operation that gets more expensive as the number of elements grows. The flip side is that once you're at the spot, inserting or deleting an element is a piece of cake: simply change the references and you're done. This means that insertions and deletions—at least near the head and tail of a linked list—are said to be in constant time.

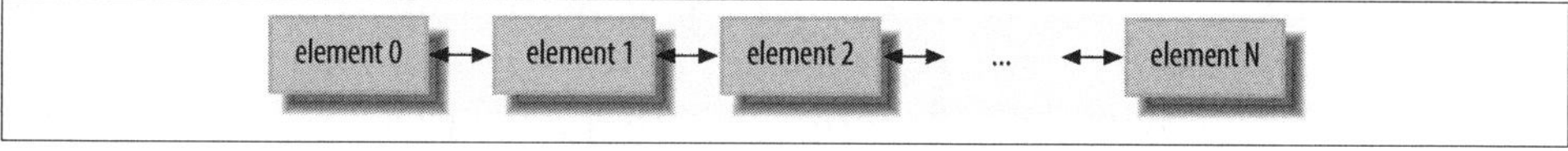

Figure 11-3. Linked list structure

Linked lists are useful when you are doing a lot of insertions or deletions on a collection. An interesting variation on the basic linked list is the "skip list," which is a kind of linked list that maintains a hierarchy of references spanning increasing ranges of elements instead of only pointing to the next element in the chain. The idea is that when you need to jump to the middle, you can use one of these "express lane" pointers to jump to the approximate location and then move forward or backward with finer granularity as needed by descending the pointer hierarchy. Java 7 adds skip list implementations of the `NavigableMap` and `NavigableSet` interfaces in the `java.util.concurrent` package for concurrent programming.

Trees

A tree is like a linked list in that it holds its elements in nodes that point to their neighbors. However, a tree, as its name suggests, does not have a linear structure, but instead arranges its elements in a cascade of branches like a family tree. The power of the tree structure is in sorting and searching elements that have a specified order. A *binary search tree*, as shown in Figure 11-4, arranges its elements such that the children divide up a range of values. One child holds values greater than the node and one child holds values lower. By applying this knowledge recursively on a properly "balanced" tree, we can rapidly find any value. The effort to search the tree is described as *log(n) time*, which means that it grows only with the logarithm of the number of elements, which is much better than the linear time it would take to check all of the elements by brute force.

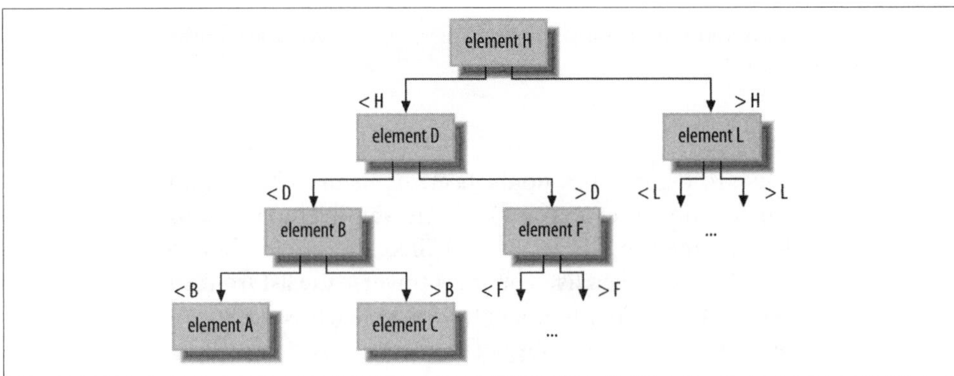

Figure 11-4. Tree structure

Trees are useful for maintaining and searching large collections of sorted elements. A similar concept that can be used for data that rarely requires updates is to use a plain sorted array with a binary search algorithm. In a binary search, you make (exponentially) decreasing size jumps into the sorted array to approximate locations for the element and then choose your next jump based on whether you have overshot or undershot the target. The Java `Arrays` class has several `binarySearch()` methods that operate on different types of arrays.

Hash maps

Hash maps are strange and magical beasts. A hash map (or hash table, as it is also called) uses a mathematical hash algorithm applied to its key value to distribute its element values into a series of "buckets." The algorithm relies on the hash algorithm to distribute the elements as uniformly (randomly) as possible. To retrieve an element by its key simply involves searching the correct bucket. Because the hash calculation is fast and can have a large number of buckets, there are few elements to search and retrieval is very fast. As we described in Chapter 7, all Java `Objects` have a hash value as determined by the `hashCode()` method. We'll say more about hash codes and key values for maps later in this chapter.

Hash map performance is governed by many factors, including the sophistication of the hash algorithm implemented by its elements (see Figure 11-5). In general, with a good hash function implementation, the Java `HashMap` operates in constant time for putting and retrieving elements. Hash maps are fast at mapping unsorted collections.

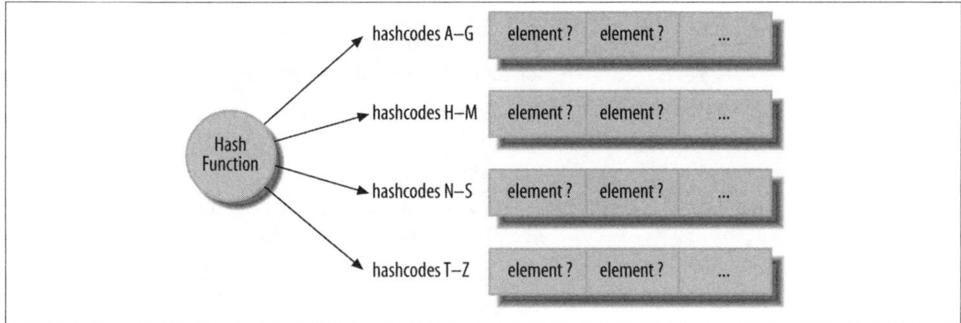

Figure 11-5. Hash map structure

Java Collections implementations

Table 11-7 lists the implementations of the Java Collections Framework by interface type.

Table 11-7. Collections Framework implementation classes

Interface	Implementation

`Set`	`HashSet`
	`LinkedHashSet`
	`CopyOnWriteArraySet`
	`EnumSet`
	`CopyOnWriteArraySet`

`SortedSet`	`TreeSet` `ConcurrentSkipListSet`

`List`	`ArrayList`
	`LinkedList`
	`Vector` [a]
	`Stack`
	`CopyOnWriteArrayList`

Interface	Implementation
Map	HashMap EnumMap LinkedHashMap IdentityHashMap Hashtable[a]
ConcurrentMap	ConcurrentHashMap ConcurrentSkipListMap
SortedMap	TreeMap
Queue / Dequeue	LinkedList ArrayDeque PriorityQueue DelayQueue SynchronousQueue ConcurrentLinkedQueue ConcurrentLinkedDequeue
BlockingQueue	ArrayBlockingQueue LinkedBlockingQueue PriorityBlockingQueue

[a] Vector and Hashtable are legacy classes and should generally be avoided in favor of ArrayList and HashMap, respectively.

ArrayList and LinkedList provide the array and linked list implementations of the List interface that was described earlier. ArrayList is satisfactory for most purposes, but you should use LinkedList when you plan to do a lot of insertions or deletions at various points in the list.

HashSet and HashMap provide a good hash map implementation of the Set and Map interfaces. The LinkedHashSet and LinkedHashMap implementations combine the hash algorithm with a linked list that maintains the *insertion order* of the elements. Note that these linked collections are ordered, but *not sorted* collections.

TreeSet and TreeMap maintain sorted collections using a tree data structure. In the case of TreeMap, it is the *key* values that are sorted. The sorting is accomplished by a comparator object. We'll discuss sorting later in this chapter.

Queue is implemented both by LinkedList (which implements List, Queue, and—as of Java 7, Deque) and PriorityQueue. A PriorityQueue's prioritization comes from a sorting order determined by a comparator supplied with its constructor. Elements that sort "least" or "lowest" have the highest priority. The various implementations of BlockingQueue mirror these for concurrency-aware queues.

Finally, IdentityHashMap is an alternate type of HashMap that uses object *identity* instead of object *equality* to determine which keys match which objects. Normally, any two objects that test equal with equals() operate as the same key in a Map. With Identity

HashMap, only the original object instance retrieves the element. We'll talk about hash codes and keys more in the next section.

We should also mention three specialized collections that we'll talk about later: EnumSet and EnumMap are specifically designed to work with Java enumerations. WeakHashMap uses weak references to cooperate with Java garbage collection.

Hash Codes and Key Values

The term *hash* in Hashtable and HashMap refers to the key hash value that these collections use to make their associations. Specifically, an element in a Hashtable or HashMap is not associated with a key strictly by the key object's identity but rather by a function of the key's contents. This allows keys that are equivalent to access the same object. By "equivalent," we mean those objects that compare true with equals(). If you store an object in a Hashtable using one object as a key, you can use any other object that equals() tells you is equivalent to retrieve the stored object.

It's easy to see why equivalence is important if you remember our discussion of strings. You may create two String objects that have the same characters in them but that are different objects in Java. In this case, the == operator tells you that the String objects are different, but the equals() method of the String class tells you that they are equivalent. Because they are equivalent, if we store an object in a HashMap using one of the String objects as a key, we can retrieve it using the other.

The hash code of an object makes this association based on content. As we mentioned in Chapter 7, the hash code is like a fingerprint of the object's data content. HashMap uses it to store the objects so that they can be retrieved efficiently. The hash code is nothing more than a number (an integer) that is a function of the data. The number is always the same for identical data, but the hashing function is intentionally designed to generate as different (random looking) a number as possible for different combinations of data. In other words, a very small change in the data should produce a big difference in the number. It should be unlikely that two nonidentical datasets, even very similar ones, would produce the same hash code.

As we described earlier, internally, HashMap really just keeps a number of lists of objects, but it puts objects into the lists based on their hash code. When it wants to find the object again, it can look at the hash code and know immediately how to get to the appropriate list. The HashMap still might end up with a number of objects to examine, but the list should be short. For each object in the short list it finds, it does the following comparison to see if the key matches:

```
if ((keyHashcode == storedKeyHashcode) && key.equals(storedKey))
    return object;
```

There is no prescribed way to generate hash codes. The only requirement is that they be somewhat randomly distributed and reproducible (based on the data). This means that two objects that are not the same could end up with the same hash code by accident. This is unlikely (there are 2^{32} possible integer values); moreover, it shouldn't cause a problem because as you can see in the preceding snippet, the HashMap ultimately checks the actual keys using equals(), as well as the hash codes, to find the match. Therefore, even if two key objects have the same hash code, they can still coexist in the HashMap as long as they don't test equal to one another as well. (To put it another way, if two keys' hashcodes are the same and the equals method says they are the same, then they will be considered the same key and retrieve the same value object.)

Hash codes are computed by an object's hashCode() method, which is inherited from the Object class if it isn't overridden. The default hashCode() method simply assigns each object instance a unique number to be used as a hash code. If a class does not override this method, each instance of the class will have a unique hash code. This goes along well with the default implementation of equals() in Object, which only compares objects for identity using ==; the effect being that these arbitrary objects serve as unique keys in maps.

You must override equals() in any classes for which equivalence of different objects is meaningful. Likewise, if you want equivalent objects to serve as equivalent keys, you must override the hashCode() method as well to return identical hash code values. To do this, you need to create some suitably randomizing, arbitrary function of the contents of your object. The only criterion for the function is that it should be almost certain to return different values for objects with different data, but the same value for objects with identical data.

Synchronized and Unsynchronized Collections

The java.util.Collections class contains important static utility methods for working with Sets and Maps. All the methods in Collections operate on interfaces, so they work regardless of the actual implementation classes you're using. The first methods we'll look at involve creating synchronized versions of our collections.

Most of the default collection implementations are not synchronized; that is, they are not safe for concurrent access by multiple threads. The reason for this is performance. In many applications, there is no need for synchronization, so the Collections API does not provide it by default. Instead, you can create a synchronized version of any collection using the following methods of the Collections class:

```
public static Collection synchronizedCollection(Collection c)
public static Set synchronizedSet(Set s)
public static List synchronizedList(List list)
public static Map synchronizedMap(Map m)
public static SortedSet synchronizedSortedSet(SortedSet s)
public static SortedMap synchronizedSortedMap(SortedMap m)
```

These methods return synchronized, threadsafe versions of the supplied collection, by wrapping them (in a new object that implements the same interface and delegates the calls to the underlying collection). For example, the following shows how to create a threadsafe `List`:

```
List list = new ArrayList();
List syncList = Collections.synchronizedList(list);
```

Multiple threads can call methods on this list safely and they will block as necessary to wait for the other threads to complete.

In contrast to the norm, the older `Hashtable` and `Vector` collections are synchronized by default (and, therefore, may be a bit slower when that's not needed). The "copy on write" collection implementations that we'll talk about later also do not require synchronization for their special applications. Finally, the `ConcurrentHashMap` and `ConcurrentLinkedQueue` implementations that we'll cover later are threadsafe and designed specifically to support a high degree of concurrent access *without* incurring a significant penalty for their internal synchronization.

Synchronizing iterators

This is important, so remember this! Although synchronized collections are threadsafe, the `Iterator`s returned from them are not. If you obtain an `Iterator` from a collection, you should do your own synchronization to ensure that the collection does not change as you're iterating through its elements. A convention does this by synchronizing on the collection itself with a `synchronized` block:

```
synchronized(syncList) {
    Iterator iterator = syncList.iterator();
    // do stuff with the iterator here
}
```

If you do not synchronize on the collection while iterating and the collection changes, Java attempts to throw a `ConcurrentModificationException`. However, this is not guaranteed.

ConcurrentHashMap and ConcurrentLinkedQueue

The `java.util.concurrent.ConcurrentHashMap` class is part of the concurrency utilities package and provides a `Map` that performs well under multithreaded access. A `ConcurrentHashMap` is safe for access from multiple threads, but it does not necessarily block threads during operations. Instead, some degree of overlapping operations, such as concurrent reads, are permitted safely. The `ConcurrentHashMap` can even allow a limited number of concurrent writes to happen while reads are being performed. These operations and iterators over the map do not throw a `ConcurrentModificationException`, but no guarantees are made as to exactly when one thread will see another thread's work. All views of the map are based upon the most recently committed writes.

Similarly, the ConcurrentLinkedQueue implementation provides the same sort of benefits for a linked queue, allowing some degree of overlapping writes and reads by concurrent users.

Read-Only and Read-Mostly Collections

You can use the Collections class to create read-only versions of any collection:

```
public static Collection unmodifiableCollection(Collection c)
public static Set unmodifiableSet(Set s)
public static List unmodifiableList(List list)
public static Map unmodifiableMap(Map m)
public static SortedSet unmodifiableSortedSet(SortedSet s)
public static SortedMap unmodifiableSortedMap(SortedMap m)
```

Making unmodifiable versions of collections is a useful way to ensure that a collection handed off to another part of your code is not modified intentionally or inadvertently. Attempting to modify a read-only collection results in an UnsupportedOperationException.

Copy-on-write ("read-mostly") collections

The java.util.concurrent package contains the CopyOnWriteArrayList and CopyOnWriteArraySet List and Set implementations. These classes are threadsafe and do not require explicit synchronization, but are heavily optimized for read operations. Any write operation causes the entire data structure to be copied internally in a blocking operation. The advantage is that if you are almost always reading, these implementations are extremely fast and no synchronization is required.

WeakHashMap

In Chapter 5, we introduced the idea of weak references—object references that don't prevent their objects from being removed by the garbage collector. WeakHashMap is an implementation of Map that makes use of weak references in its keys and values. This means that you don't have to remove key/value pairs from a Map when you're finished with them. Normally, if you removed all references to a key object from the rest of your application, the Map would still contain a reference and keep the object "alive," preventing garbage collection. WeakHashMap changes this; once you remove all references to a key object from the rest of the application, the WeakHashMap lets go of it, too and both the key and its corresponding value (if it is similarly unreferenced) are eligible for garbage collection.

EnumSet and EnumMap

EnumSet and EnumMap are collections designed to work specifically with the limited domain of objects defined by a Java enumerated type. (Enums are discussed in

Chapter 5.) Java enums are Java objects and there is no reason you can't use them as keys or values in collections otherwise. However, the EnumSet and EnumMap classes are highly optimized, taking advantage of the knowledge that the set or keys in the map, respectively, may be one of only a few individual objects. With this knowledge, storage can be compact and fast using bit fields internally. The idea is to make using collection operations on enumerations efficient enough to replace the general usage pattern of bit-flags and make binary logic operations unnecessary. Instead of using:

```
int flags = getFlags();
if ( flags & ( Constants.ERROR | Constants.WARNING ) != 0 )
```

we could use set operations:

```
EnumSet flags = getFlags();
if ( flags.contains( Constants.Error) ||
    flags.contains( Constants.Warning ) )
```

This code may not be as terse, but it is easier to understand and should be just as fast.

Sorting Collections

The Collections utilities include methods for performing common operations like sorting. Sorting comes in two varieties:

`public static void sort(List` *`list`* `)`
: This method sorts the given list. You can use this method only on lists whose elements implement the `java.lang.Comparable` interface. Luckily, many classes already implement this interface, including `String`, `Date`, `BigInteger`, and the wrapper classes for the primitive types (`Integer`, `Double`, etc.).

`public static void sort(List` *`list`*, `Comparatorc)`
: Use this method to sort a list whose elements don't implement the `Comparable` interface. The supplied `java.util.Comparator` does the work of comparing elements. You might, for example, write an `ImaginaryNumber` class and want to sort a list of them. You would then create a `Comparator` implementation that knew how to compare two imaginary numbers.

The sorted collections we discussed earlier, `SortedSet` and `SortedMap`, maintain their collections in a specified order using the `Comparable` interface of their elements. If the elements do not implement `Comparable`, you must supply a `Comparator` object yourself in the constructor of the implementation. For example:

```
Comparator myComparator = ...
SortedSet mySet = new TreeSet( myComparator );
```

Collections give you some other interesting capabilities, too. If you're interested in learning more, check out the `min()`, `max()`, `binarySearch()`, and `reverse()` methods.

A Thrilling Example

Collections is a bread-and-butter topic, which means it's hard to create exciting examples. The example in this section reads a text file, parses all its words, counts the number of occurrences, sorts them, and writes the results to another file. It gives you a good feel for how to use collections in your own programs. This example also shows features including generics, autoboxing, and the `Scanner` API.

```
import java.io.*;
import java.util.*;

public class WordSort
{
  public static void main(String[] args) throws IOException
  {
    if ( args.length < 2 ) {
      System.out.println("Usage: WordSort inputfile outputfile");
      return;
    }
    String inputfile = args[0];
    String outputfile = args[1];

    /*  Create the word map. Each key is a word and each value is an
        Integer that represents the number of times the word occurs
        in the input file.
    */
    Map<String,Integer> map = new TreeMap<>();

    Scanner scanner = new Scanner( new File(inputfile) );
    while ( scanner.hasNext() ) {
        String word = scanner.next();
        Integer count = map.get( word );
        count = ( count == null ? 1 : count +1 );
        map.put( word, count );
    }
    scanner.close();

    // get the map's keys
    List<String> keys = new ArrayList<>( map.keySet() );

    // write the results to the output file
    PrintWriter out = new PrintWriter( new FileWriter(outputfile) );
    for ( String key : keys )
      out.println( key + " : " + map.get(key) );
    out.close();
  }
}
```

Suppose, for example, that you have an input file named *Ian Moore.txt*:

```
Well it was my love that kept you going
Kept you strong enough to fall
```

```
And it was my heart you were breaking
When he hurt your pride

So how does it feel
How does it feel
How does it feel
How does it feel
```

You could run the example on this file using the following command:

```
% java WordSort "Ian Moore.txt" count.txt
```

The output file, *count.txt*, looks like this:

```
And : 1
How : 3
Kept : 1
So : 1
Well : 1
When : 1
breaking : 1
does : 4
enough : 1
...
```

The results are case-sensitive: "How" and "how" are recorded separately. You could modify this behavior by converting words to all lowercase after retrieving them from the `Scanner`.

Properties

The `java.util.Properties` class is a specialized hash table for strings. Properties are generally used to hold textual configuration data. Examples of this are the Java System properties, which are passed to a Java application on the command line. We'll cover those later in this section. More generally, you can use a `Properties` table to hold arbitrary configuration information for an application in an easily accessible format. The neat thing about a `Properties` object is that it can load and store its information in a plain text or XML text format using streams (see Chapter 12 for information on streams).

Any string values can be stored as key/value pairs in a `Properties` table. However, the convention is to use a dot-separated naming hierarchy to group property names into logical structures. (Unfortunately, this is just a convention, and you can't really work with groups of properties in a hierarchical way as this might imply.) For example, you can create an empty `Properties` object and add `String` key/value pairs just as you could with a `Map`:

```
Properties props = new Properties();
props.setProperty("myApp.xsize", "52");
props.setProperty("myApp.ysize", "79");
```

Thereafter, you can retrieve values with the `getProperty()` method:

```
String xsize = props.getProperty( "myApp.xsize" );
```

If the named property doesn't exist, `getProperty()` returns `null`. You can get an `Enumeration` of the property names with the `propertyNames()` method:

```
for ( Enumeration e = props.propertyNames(); e.hasMoreElements(); ) {
    String name = e.nextElement();
    ...
}
```

When you create a `Properties` object, you can specify a second object for default property values:

```
Properties defaults = ...
Properties props = new Properties( defaults );
```

Now, when you call `getProperty()`, the method searches the default table if it doesn't find the named property in the current table. An alternative version of `getProperty()` also accepts a default value; this value is returned instead of `null` if the property is not found in the current or default lists:

```
String xsize = props.getProperty( "myApp.xsize", "50" );
```

Loading and Storing

You can save a `Properties` table to an `OutputStream` using the `save()` method. The property information is output in a flat ASCII format. We'll talk about I/O in the next chapter, but bear with us for now. Continuing with the previous example, output the property information using the `System.out` stream as follows:

```
props.save( System.out, "Application Parameters" );
```

`System.out` is a standard output stream that prints to the console or command line of an application. We could also save the information to a file using a `FileOutputStream` as the first argument to `save()`. The second argument to `save()` is a `String` that is used as a header for the data. The previous code outputs something like the following to `System.out`:

```
#Application Parameters
#Mon Feb 12 09:24:23 CST 2001
myApp.ysize=79
myApp.xsize=52
```

The `load()` method reads the previously saved contents of a `Properties` object from an `InputStream`:

```
FileInputStream fin;
...
Properties props = new Properties()
props.load( fin );
```

The list() method is useful for debugging. It prints the contents to an OutputStream in a format that is more human-readable but not retrievable by load(). It truncates long lines with an ellipsis (...).

The Properties class also contains storeToXML() and loadFromXML() methods. These operate just like the save() and load() methods but write an XML file like the following:

```
<?xml version="1.0" encoding="UTF-8"?>
<!DOCTYPE properties SYSTEM "http://java.sun.com/dtd/properties.dtd"
>
<properties>
<comment>My Properties</comment>
<entry key="myApp.ysize">79</entry>
<entry key="myApp.xsize">52</entry>
</properties>
```

We'll cover XML in detail in Chapter 24.

System Properties

The java.lang.System class provides access to basic system environment information through the static System.getProperties() method. This method returns a Properties table that contains system properties. System properties take the place of environment variables in some programming environments. Table 11-8 summarizes system properties that are guaranteed to be defined in any Java environment.

Table 11-8. System properties

System property	Meaning
java.vendor	Vendor-specific string
java.vendor.url	URL of vendor
java.version	Java version
java.home	Java installation directory
java.class.version	Java class version
java.class.path	The classpath
os.name	Operating system name
os.arch	Operating system architecture
os.version	Operating system version
file.separator	File separator (such as / or \)
path.separator	Path separator (such as : or ;)
line.separator	Line separator (such as \n or \r\n)
user.name	User account name
user.home	User's home directory

Java applets and other Java applications that run with restrictions may be prevented from reading the following properties: `java.home`, `java.class.path`, `user.name`, `user.home`, and `user.dir`. As you'll see later, these restrictions are implemented by a `SecurityManager` object.

Your application can set system properties with the static method `System.setProperty()`. You can also set your own system properties when you run the Java interpreter, using the `-D` option:

```
% java -Dfoo=bar -Dcat=Boojum MyApp
```

Because it is common to use system properties to provide parameters such as numbers and colors, Java provides some convenience routines for retrieving property values and parsing them into their appropriate types. The classes `Boolean`, `Integer`, `Long`, and `Color` each come with a "get" method that looks up and parses a system property. For example, `Integer.getInteger("foo")` looks for a system property called `foo` and then returns it as an `Integer`.

The Preferences API

The Java Preferences API accommodates the need to store both system and per-user configuration data persistently across executions of the Java VM. The Preferences API is like a portable version of the Windows registry, a mini-database in which you can keep small amounts of information, accessible to all applications. Entries are stored as name/value pairs, where the values may be of several standard types including strings, numbers, Booleans, and even short byte arrays. We should stress that the Preferences API is not intended to be used as a true database and you can't store large amounts of data in it.

Preferences are stored logically in a tree. A preferences object is a node in the tree located by a unique path. You can think of preferences as files in a directory structure; within the file are stored one or more name/value pairs. To store or retrieve items, you ask for a preferences object for the correct path. Here is an example; we'll explain the node lookup shortly:

```
Preferences prefs = Preferences.userRoot().node("oreilly/learningjava");

prefs.put("author", "Niemeyer");
prefs.putInt("edition", 4);

String author = prefs.get("author", "unknown");
int edition = prefs.getInt("edition", -1);
```

In addition to the `String` and `int` type accessors, there are the following get methods for other types: `getLong()`, `getFloat()`, `getDouble()`, `getByteArray()`, and `getBoolean()`. Each of these get methods takes a key name and default value to be used if no value is defined. And, of course, for each get method, there is a corresponding "put" method that takes the name and a value of the corresponding type. Providing defaults in the get methods is mandatory. The intent is for applications to function even if there is no preference information or if the storage for it is not available, as we'll discuss later.

Preferences are stored in two separate trees: system preferences and user preferences. *System preferences* are shared by all users of the Java installation. But *user preferences* are maintained separately for each user; each user sees his or her own preference information. In our example, we used the static method `userRoot()` to fetch the root node (preference object) for the user preferences tree. We then asked that node to find the child node at the path *oreilly/learningjava*, using the `node()` method. The corresponding `systemRoot()` method provides the system root node.

The `node()` method accepts either a relative or an absolute path. A relative path asks the node to find the path relative to itself as a base. We also could have gotten our node this way:

```
Preferences prefs =
   Preferences.userRoot().node("oreilly").node("learningjava");
```

But `node()` also accepts an absolute path, in which case the base node serves only to designate the tree that the path is in. We could use the absolute path */oreilly/learningjava* as the argument to any `node()` method and reach our preferences object.

Preferences for Classes

Java is an object-oriented language, and so it's natural to wish to associate preference data with classes. In Chapter 12, we'll see that Java provides special facilities for loading resource files associated with class files. The Preferences API follows this pattern by associating a node with each Java package. Its convention is simple: the node path is just the package name with the dots (.) converted to slashes (/). All classes in the package share the same node.

You can get the preference object node for a class using the static `Preferences.userNodeForPackage()` or `Preferences.systemNodeForPackage()` methods, which take a `Class` as an argument and return the corresponding package node for the user and system trees, respectively. For example:

```
Preferences datePrefs = Preferences.systemNodeForPackage( Date.class );
Preferences myPrefs = Preferences.userNodeForPackage( MyClass.class );
Preferences morePrefs =
    Preferences.userNodeForPackage( myObject.getClass() );
```

Here, we've used the `.class` construct to refer to the `Class` object for the `Date` class in the system tree and to our own `MyClass` class in the user tree. The `Date` class is in the `java.util` package, so we'll get the node */java/util* in that case. You can get the `Class` for any object instance using the `getClass()` method.

Preferences Storage

There is no need to "create" nodes. When you ask for a node, you get a preferences object for that path in the tree. If you write something to it, that data is eventually placed in persistent storage, called the backing store. The *backing store* is the implementation-dependent storage mechanism used to hold the preference data. All the put methods return immediately, and no guarantees are made as to when the data is actually stored. You can force data to the backing store explicitly using the `flush()` method of the `Preferences` class. Conversely, you can use the `sync()` method to guarantee that a preferences object is up-to-date with respect to changes placed into the backing store by other applications or threads. Both `flush()` and `sync()` throw a `BackingStoreException` if data cannot be read or written for some reason.

You don't have to create nodes, but you can test for the existence of a data node with the `nodeExists()` method, and you can remove a node and all its children with the `removeNode()` method. To remove a data item from a node, use the `remove()` method, specifying the key; or you can remove all the data from a node with the `clear()` method (which is not the same as removing the node).

Although the details of the backing store are implementation-dependent, the Preferences API provides a simple import/export facility that can read and write parts of a preference tree to an XML file. (The format for the file is available at *http://java.sun.com/dtd/*.) A preference object can be written to an output stream with the `exportNode()` method. The `exportSubtree()` method writes the node and all its children. Going the other way, the static `Preferences.importPreferences()` method can read the XML file and populate the appropriate tree with its data. The XML file records whether it is user or system preferences, but user data is always placed into the current user's tree, regardless of who generated it.

It's interesting to note that because the import mechanism writes directly to the tree, you can't use this as a general data-to-XML storage mechanism (other APIs play that role). Also, although we said that the implementation details are not specified, it's interesting how things really work in the current implementation. On some systems, Java creates a directory hierarchy for each tree at *$JAVA_HOME/jre/.systemPrefs* and *$HOME/.java/.userPrefs*, respectively. In each directory, there is an XML file called *prefs.xml* corresponding to that node.

Change Notification

Often your application should be notified if changes are made to the preferences while it's running. You can get updates on preference changes using the `PreferenceChangeListener` and `NodeChangeListener` interfaces. These interfaces are examples of *event listener* interfaces, and we'll see many examples of these in Chapters 16 through 18. We'll also talk about the general pattern later in this chapter in the section "Observers and

Observables" on page 406. For now, we'll just say that by registering an object that implements `PreferenceChangeListener` with a node, you can receive updates on added, removed, and changed preference data for that node. The `NodeChangeListener` allows you to be told when child nodes are added to or removed from a specific node. Here is a snippet that prints all the data changes affecting our */oreilly/learningjava* node:

```
Preferences prefs =
    Preferences.userRoot().node("/oreilly/learningjava");

prefs.addPreferenceChangeListener( new PreferenceChangeListener() {
    public void preferenceChange(PreferenceChangeEvent e) {
        System.out.println("Value: " + e.getKey()
            + " changed to "+ e.getNewValue() );
    }
} );
```

In brief, this example listens for changes to preferences and prints them. If this example isn't immediately clear, it should be after you've read about events in Chapter 16 and beyond.

The Logging API

The `java.util.logging` package provides a highly flexible and easy-to-use logging framework for system information, error messages, and fine-grained tracing (debugging) output. With the logging package, you can apply filters to select log messages, direct their output to one or more destinations (including files and network services), and format the messages appropriately for their consumers.

Most importantly, much of this basic logging configuration can be set up externally at runtime through the use of a logging setup properties file or an external program. For example, by setting the right properties at runtime, you can specify that log messages are to be sent both to a designated file in XML format and also logged to the system console in a digested, human-readable form. Furthermore, for each of those destinations, you can specify the level or priority of messages to be logged, discarding those below a certain threshold of significance. By following the correct source conventions in your code, you can even make it possible to adjust the logging levels for specific parts of your application, allowing you to target individual packages and classes for detailed logging without being overwhelmed by too much output. The Logging API can even be controlled remotely via Java Management Extensions MBean APIs.

Overview

Any good logging API must have at least two guiding principles. First, performance should not inhibit the developer from using log messages freely. As with Java language assertions (discussed in Chapter 4), when log messages are turned off, they should not consume any significant amount of processing time. This means that there's no performance penalty for including logging statements as long as they're turned off. Second, although some users may want advanced features and configuration, a logging API must have some simple mode of usage that is convenient enough for time-starved developers to use in lieu of the old standby `System.out.println()`. Java's Logging API provides a simple model and many convenience methods that make it very tempting.

Loggers

The heart of the logging framework is the *logger*, an instance of `java.util.logging.Logger`. In most cases, this is the only class your code will ever have to deal with. A logger is constructed from the static `Logger.getLogger()` method, with a logger name as its argument. Logger names place loggers into a hierarchy with a global, root logger at the top and a tree and children below. This hierarchy allows the configuration to be inherited by parts of the tree so that logging can be automatically configured for different parts of your application. The convention is to use a separate logger instance in each major class or package and to use the dot-separated package and/or class name as the logger name. For example:

```
package com.oreilly.learnjava;
public class Book {
    static Logger log = Logger.getLogger("com.oreilly.learnjava.Book");
```

The logger provides a wide range of methods to log messages; some take very detailed information, and some convenience methods take only a string for ease of use. For example:

```
log.warning("Disk 90% full.");
log.info("New user joined chat room.");
```

We cover methods of the logger class in detail a bit later. The names `warning` and `info` are two examples of logging levels; there are seven levels ranging from SEVERE at the top to FINEST at the bottom. Distinguishing log messages in this way allows us to select the level of information that we want to see at runtime. Rather than simply logging everything and sorting through it later (with negative performance impact) we can tweak which messages are generated. We'll talk more about logging levels in the next section.

We should also mention that for convenience in very simple applications or experiments, a logger for the name "global" is provided in the static field `Logger.global`. You can use it as an alternative to the old standby `System.out.println()` for those cases where that is still a temptation:

```
Logger.global.info("Doing foo...")
```

Handlers

Loggers represent the client interface to the logging system, but the actual work of publishing messages to destinations (such as files or the console) is done by *handler* objects. Each logger may have one or more `Handler` objects associated with it, which includes several predefined handlers supplied with the Logging API: `ConsoleHandler`, `FileHandler`, `StreamHandler`, and `SocketHandler`. Each handler knows how to deliver messages to its respective destination. `ConsoleHandler` is used by the default configuration to print messages on the command line or system console. `FileHandler` can direct output to files using a supplied naming convention and automatically rotate the files as they become full. The others send messages to streams and sockets, respectively. There is one additional handler, `MemoryHandler`, that can hold a number of log messages in memory. `MemoryHandler` has a circular buffer, which maintains a certain number of messages until it is triggered to publish them to another designated handler.

As we said, loggers can be set to use one or more handlers. Loggers also send messages up the tree to each of their parent logger's handlers. In the simplest configuration, this means that all messages end up distributed by the root logger's handlers. We'll soon see how to set up output using the standard handlers for the console, files, etc.

Filters

Before a logger hands off a message to its handlers or its parent's handlers, it first checks whether the logging level is sufficient to proceed. If the message doesn't meet the required level, it is discarded at the source. In addition to level, you can implement arbitrary filtering of messages by creating `Filter` classes that examine the log message before it is processed. A `Filter` class can be applied to a logger externally at runtime in the same way that the logging level, handlers, and formatters, which are discussed next, can be. A `Filter` may also be attached to an individual `Handler` to filter records at the output stage (as opposed to the source).

Formatters

Internally, messages are carried in a neutral format, including all the source information provided. It is not until they are processed by a handler that they are formatted for output by an instance of a `Formatter` object. The logging package comes with two basic formatters: `SimpleFormatter` and `XMLFormatter`. The `SimpleFormatter` is the default used for console output. It produces short, human-readable summaries of log messages. `XMLFormatter` encodes all the log message details into an XML record format. The DTD for the format can be found at *http://java.sun.com/dtd/*.

Logging Levels

Table 11-9 lists the logging levels from most to least significant.

Table 11-9. Logging API logging levels

Level	Meaning
SEVERE	Application failure
WARNING	Notification of potential problem
INFO	Messages of general interest to end users
CONFIG	Detailed system configuration information for administrators
FINE, FINER, FINEST	Successively more detailed application tracing information for developers

These levels fall into three camps: end user, administrator, and developer. Applications often default to logging only messages of the `INFO` level and above (`INFO`, `WARNING`, and `SEVERE`). These levels are generally seen by end users and messages logged to them should be suitable for general consumption. In other words, they should be written clearly so they make sense to an average user of the application. Often these kinds of messages are presented to the end user on a system console or in a pop-up message dialog.

The `CONFIG` level should be used for relatively static but detailed system information that could assist an administrator or installer. This might include information about the installed software modules, host system characteristics, and configuration parameters. These details are important, but probably not as meaningful to an end user.

The `FINE`, `FINER`, and `FINEST` levels are for developers or others with knowledge of the internals of the application. These should be used for tracing the application at successive levels of detail. You can define your own meanings for these. We'll suggest a rough outline in our example, coming up next.

A Simple Example

In the following (admittedly very contrived) example, we use all the logging levels so that we can experiment with logging configuration. Although the sequence of messages is nonsensical, the text is representative of messages of that type.

```
import java.util.logging.*;

public class LogTest {
    public static void main(String argv[])
    {
        Logger logger = Logger.getLogger("com.oreilly.LogTest");

        logger.severe("Power lost - running on backup!");
        logger.warning("Database connection lost, retrying...");
        logger.info("Startup complete.");
        logger.config("Server configuration: standalone, JVM version 1.5");
        logger.fine("Loading graphing package.");
```

```
            logger.finer("Doing pie chart");
            logger.finest("Starting bubble sort: value ="+42);
        }
    }
```

There's not much to this example. We ask for a `logger` instance for our class using the static `Logger.getLogger()` method, specifying a class name. The convention is to use the fully qualified class name, so we'll pretend that our class is in a `com.oreilly` package.

Now, run `LogTest`. You should see output like the following on the system console:

```
Jan 6, 2002 3:24:36 PM LogTest main
SEVERE: Power lost - running on backup!
Jan 6, 2002 3:24:37 PM LogTest main
WARNING: Database connection lost, retrying...
Jan 6, 2002 3:24:37 PM LogTest main
INFO: Startup complete.
```

We see the `INFO`, `WARNING`, and `SEVERE` messages, each identified with a date and timestamp and the name of the class and method (`LogTest main`) from which they came. Notice that the lower-level messages did not appear. This is because the default logging level is normally set to `INFO`, meaning that only messages of severity `INFO` and above are logged. Also note that the output went to the system console and not to a logfile somewhere; that's also the default. Now we'll describe where these defaults are set and how to override them at runtime.

Logging Setup Properties

As we said in the introduction, probably the most important feature of the Logging API is the ability to configure so much of it at runtime through the use of external properties or applications. The default logging configuration is stored in the file *jre/lib/logging.properties* in the directory where Java is installed. It's a standard Java properties file (of the kind we described earlier in this chapter).

The format of this file is simple. You can make changes to it, but you don't have to. Instead, you can specify your own logging setup properties file on a case-by-case basis using a system property at runtime, as follows:

```
% java -Djava.util.logging.config.file=myfile.properties
```

In this command line, *myfile* is your properties file that contains the directive, which we'll describe next. If you want to make this file designation more permanent, you can do so by setting the filename in the corresponding entry using the Java Preferences API described earlier in this chapter. You can go even further and instead of specifying a setup file, supply a class that is responsible for setting up all logging configuration, but we won't get into that here.

A very simple logging properties file might look like this:

```
# Set the default logging level
.level = FINEST
# Direct output to the console
handlers = java.util.logging.ConsoleHandler
```

Here, we have set the default logging level for the entire application using the `.level` (that's dot-level) property. We have also used the `handlers` property to specify that an instance of the `ConsoleHandler` should be used (just like the default setup) to show messages on the console. If you run our application again, specifying this properties file as the logging setup, you will now see all our log messages.

But we're just getting warmed up. Next, let's look at a more complex configuration:

```
# Set the default logging level
.level = INFO

# Ouput to file and console
handlers = java.util.logging.FileHandler, java.util.logging.ConsoleHandler

# Configure the file output
java.util.logging.FileHandler.level = FINEST
java.util.logging.FileHandler.pattern = %h/Test.log
java.util.logging.FileHandler.limit = 25000
java.util.logging.FileHandler.count = 4
java.util.logging.FileHandler.formatter = java.util.logging.XMLFormatter

# Configure the console output
java.util.logging.ConsoleHandler.level = WARNING

# Levels for specific classes
com.oreilly.LogTest.level = FINEST
```

In this example, we have configured two log handlers: a `ConsoleHandler` with the logging level set to `WARNING` and also an instance of `FileHandler` that sends the output to an XML file. The file handler is configured to log messages at the `FINEST` level (all messages) and to rotate logfiles every 25,000 lines, keeping a maximum of four files.

The filename is controlled by the `pattern` property. Forward slashes in the filename are automatically localized to backslash (\) if necessary. The special symbol `%h` refers to the user home. You can use `%t` to refer to the system temporary directory. If filenames conflict, a number is appended automatically after a dot (starting at zero). Alternatively, you can use `%u` to indicate where a unique number should be inserted into the name. Similarly, when files rotate, a number is appended after a dot at the end. You can take control of where the rotation number is placed with the `%g` identifier.

In our example, we specified the `XMLFormatter` class. We could also have used the `SimpleFormatter` class to send the same kind of simple output to the console. The `ConsoleHandler` also allows us to specify any formatter we wish, using the `formatter` property.

Finally, we promised earlier that you could control logging levels for parts of your applications. To do this, set properties on your application loggers using their hierarchical names:

```
# Levels for specific logger (class) names
com.oreilly.LogTest.level = FINEST
```

Here, we've set the logging level for just our test logger, by name. The log properties follow the hierarchy, so we could set the logging level for all classes in the `oreilly` package with:

```
com.oreilly.level = FINEST
```

Logging levels are set in the order in which they are read in the properties file, so set the general ones first. Also note that the levels set on the handlers allow the file handler to filter only the messages being supplied by the loggers. So setting the file handler to `FINEST` won't revive messages squelched by a logger set to `SEVERE` (only the `SEVERE` messages will make it to the handler from that logger).

The Logger

In our example, we used the seven convenience methods named for the various logging levels. There are also three groups of general methods that can be used to provide more detailed information. The most general are:

```
log(Level level, String msg)
log(Level level, String msg, Object param1)
log(Level level, String msg, Object params[])
log(Level level, String msg, Throwable thrown)
```

These methods accept as their first argument a static logging level identifier from the `Level` class, followed by a parameter, array, or exception type. The level identifier is one of `Level.SEVERE`, `Level.WARNING`, `Level.INFO`, and so on.

In addition to these four methods, there are four corresponding methods named `logp()` that also take a source class and method name as the second and third arguments. In our example, we saw Java automatically determine that information, so why would we want to supply it? The answer is that Java may not always be able to determine the exact method name because of runtime dynamic optimization. The `p` in `logp` stands for "precise" and allows you to control this yourself.

There is yet another set of methods named `logrb()`—which probably should have been named `logprb()`—that take both the class and method names and a resource bundle name. The resource bundle localizes the messages (see the section "Resource Bundles" on page 326 in Chapter 10). More generally, a logger may have a resource bundle associated with it when it is created, using another form of the `getLogger` method:

```
Logger.getLogger("com.oreilly.LogTest", "logMessages");
```

In either case, the resource bundle name is passed along with the log message and can be used by the formatter. If a resource bundle is specified, the standard formatters treat the message text as a key and try to look up a localized message. Localized messages may include parameters using the standard message format notation and the form of `log()`, which accepts an argument array.

Finally, there are convenience methods called `entering()`, `exiting()`, and `throwing()` that developers can use to log detailed trace information.

Performance

In the introduction, we said that performance is a priority of the Logging API. To that end we've described that log messages are filtered at the source, using logging levels to cut off processing of messages early. This saves much of the expense of handling them. However, it cannot prevent certain kinds of setup work that you might do before the logging call. Specifically, because we're passing things into the log methods, it's common to construct detailed messages or render objects to strings as arguments. Often this kind of operation is costly. To avoid unnecessary string construction, you should wrap expensive log operations in a conditional test using the `Logger isLoggable()` method to test whether you should carry out the operation:

```
if ( log.isLoggable( Level.CONFIG ) ) {
    log.config("Configuration: "+ loadExpensiveConfigInfo() );
}
```

Observers and Observables

The `java.util.Observer` interface and `java.util.Observable` class are relatively small utilities, but they provide a glimpse of a fundamental design pattern in Java. Observers and observables are part of the MVC (Model-View-Controller) framework. It is an abstraction that lets a number of client objects (the *observers*) be notified whenever a certain object or resource (the *observable*) changes in some way. We will see this pattern used extensively in Java's event mechanism, which is covered in Chapters 16 through 19. Although these classes are not often used directly, it's worth looking at them in order to understand the pattern.

The `Observable` object has a method that an `Observer` calls to register its interest. When a change happens, the `Observable` sends a notification by calling a method in each of the `Observers`. The observers implement the `Observer` interface, which specifies that notification causes an `Observer` object's `update()` method to be called.

In the following example, we create a MessageBoard object that holds a String message. MessageBoard extends Observable, from which it inherits the mechanism for registering observers (addObserver()) and notifying observers (notifyObservers()). To observe the MessageBoard, we have Student objects that implement the Observer interface so that they can be notified when the message changes:

```
//file: MessageBoard.java
import java.util.*;

public class MessageBoard extends Observable {
    private String message;

    public String getMessage() {
        return message;
    }
    public void changeMessage( String message ) {
        this.message = message;
        setChanged();
        notifyObservers( message );
    }
    public static void main( String [] args ) {
        MessageBoard board = new MessageBoard();
        Student bob = new Student();
        Student joe = new Student();
        board.addObserver( bob );
        board.addObserver( joe );
        board.changeMessage("More Homework!");
    }
} // end of class MessageBoard

class Student implements Observer {
    public void update(Observable o, Object arg) {
        System.out.println( "Message board changed: " + arg );
    }
}
```

Our MessageBoard object extends Observable, which provides a method called addObserver(). Each Student object registers itself using this method and receives updates via its update() method. When a new message string is set using the MessageBoard's changeMessage() method, the Observable calls the setChanged() and notifyObservers() methods to notify the observers. notifyObservers() can take as an argument an Object to pass along as an indication of the change. This object—in this case, the String containing the new message—is passed to the observer's update() method as its second argument. The first argument to update() is the Observable object itself.

The main() method of MessageBoard creates a MessageBoard and registers two Student objects with it. Then it changes the message. When you run the code, you should see each Student object print the message as it is notified.

You can imagine how you could implement the observer/observable relationship yourself using a `List` to hold the list of observers. In Chapter 16 and beyond, we'll see that the Java AWT and Swing event model extends this design pattern to use strongly typed observables and observers, which are called events and event listeners. But for now, we turn our discussion of core utilities to another fundamental topic: I/O.

CHAPTER 12
Input/Output Facilities

In this chapter, we continue our exploration of the Java API by looking at many of the classes in the `java.io` and `java.nio` packages. These packages offer a rich set of tools for basic I/O and also provide the framework on which all file and network communication in Java is built.

Figure 12-1 shows the class hierarchy of these packages.

We'll start by looking at the stream classes in `java.io`, which are subclasses of the basic `InputStream`, `OutputStream`, `Reader`, and `Writer` classes. Then we'll examine the `File` class and discuss how you can read and write files using classes in `java.io`. We also take a quick look at data compression and serialization. Along the way, we'll also introduce the `java.nio` package. The NIO, or "new" I/O, package (introduced in Java 1.4) adds significant functionality tailored for building high-performance services and in some cases simply provides newer, better APIs that can be used in place of some `java.io` features.

Streams

Most fundamental I/O in Java is based on *streams*. A stream represents a flow of data with (at least conceptually) a *writer* at one end and a *reader* at the other. When you are working with the `java.io` package to perform terminal input and output, reading or writing files, or communicating through sockets in Java, you are using various types of streams. Later in this chapter, we'll look at the NIO package, which introduces a similar concept called a *channel*. One difference betwen the two is that streams are oriented around bytes or characters while channels are oriented around "buffers" containing those data types—yet they perform roughly the same job. Let's start by summarizing the available types of streams:

`InputStream`, `OutputStream`
: Abstract classes that define the basic functionality for reading or writing an unstructured sequence of bytes. All other byte streams in Java are built on top of the basic `InputStream` and `OutputStream`.

`Reader`, `Writer`
: Abstract classes that define the basic functionality for reading or writing a sequence of character data, with support for Unicode. All other character streams in Java are built on top of `Reader` and `Writer`.

`InputStreamReader`, `OutputStreamWriter`
: Classes that bridge byte and character streams by converting according to a specific character encoding scheme. (Remember: in Unicode, a character is not a byte!)

`DataInputStream`, `DataOutputStream`
: Specialized stream filters that add the ability to read and write multibyte data types, such as numeric primitives and `String` objects in a universal format.

`ObjectInputStream`, `ObjectOutputStream`
: Specialized stream filters that are capable of writing whole groups of serialized Java objects and reconstructing them.

`BufferedInputStream`, `BufferedOutputStream`, `BufferedReader`, `BufferedWriter`
: Specialized stream filters that add buffering for additional efficiency. For real-world I/O, a buffer is almost always used.

`PrintStream`, `PrintWriter`
: Specialized streams that simplify printing text.

`PipedInputStream`, `PipedOutputStream`, `PipedReader`, `PipedWriter`
: "Loopback" streams that can be used in pairs to move data within an application. Data written into a `PipedOutputStream` or `PipedWriter` is read from its corresponding `PipedInputStream` or `PipedReader`.

`FileInputStream`, `FileOutputStream`, `FileReader`, `FileWriter`
: Implementations of `InputStream`, `OutputStream`, `Reader`, and `Writer` that read from and write to files on the local filesystem.

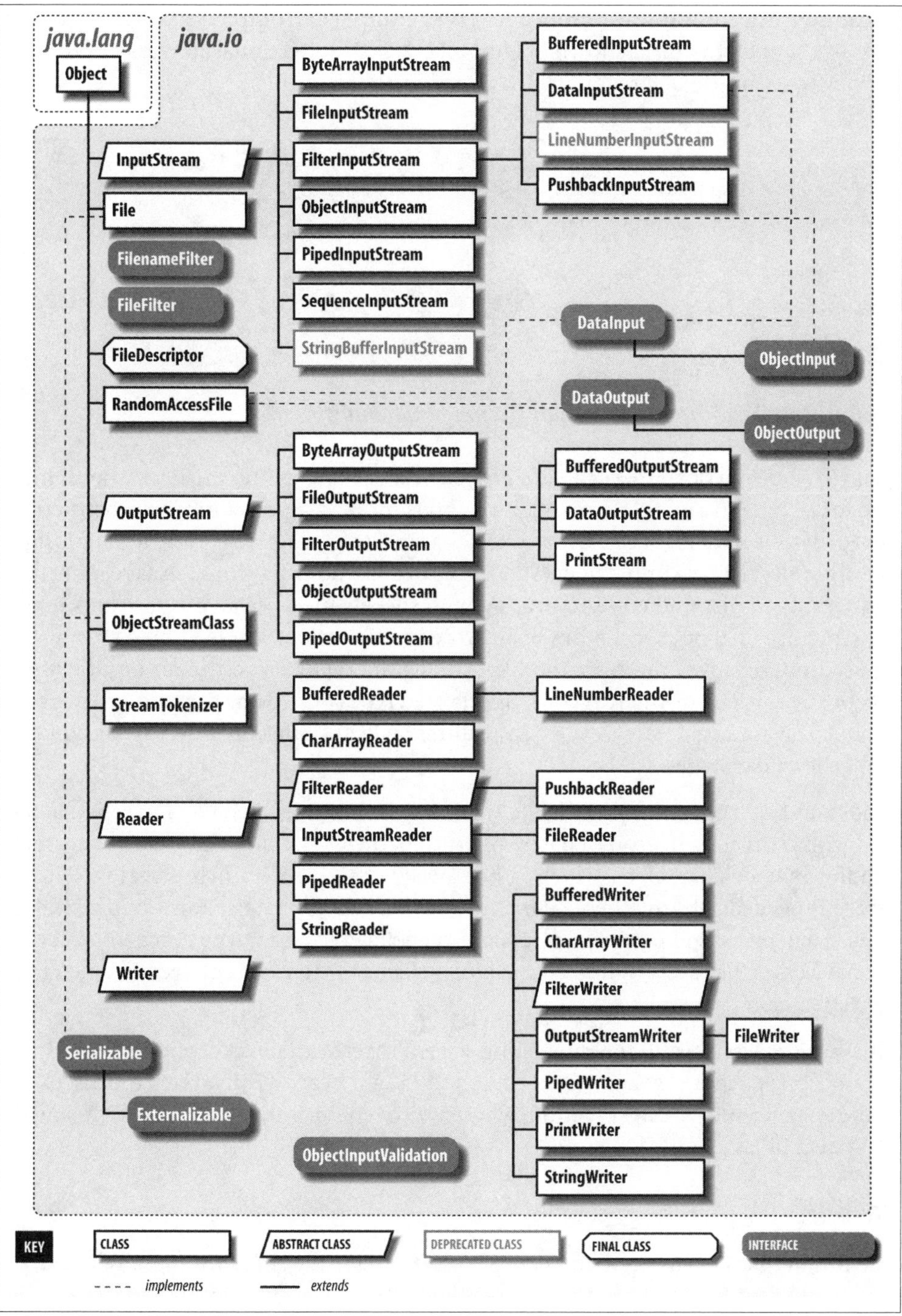

Figure 12-1. The java.io package

Streams in Java are one-way streets. The `java.io` input and output classes represent the ends of a simple stream, as shown in Figure 12-2. For bidirectional conversations, you'll use one of each type of stream.

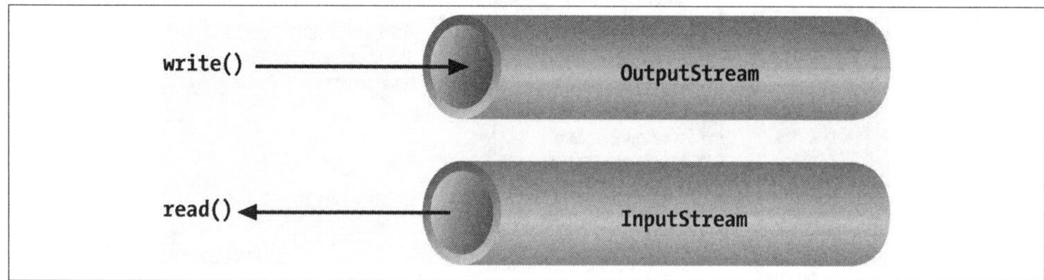

Figure 12-2. Basic input and output stream functionality

`InputStream` and `OutputStream` are *abstract* classes that define the lowest-level interface for all byte streams. They contain methods for reading or writing an unstructured flow of byte-level data. Because these classes are abstract, you can't create a generic input or output stream. Java implements subclasses of these for activities such as reading from and writing to files and communicating with sockets. Because all byte streams inherit the structure of `InputStream` or `OutputStream`, the various kinds of byte streams can be used interchangeably. A method specifying an `InputStream` as an argument can accept any subclass of `InputStream`. Specialized types of streams can also be layered or wrapped around basic streams to add features such as buffering, filtering, or handling higher-level data types.

`Reader` and `Writer` are very much like `InputStream` and `OutputStream`, except that they deal with characters instead of bytes. As true character streams, these classes correctly handle Unicode characters, which is not always the case with byte streams. Often, a bridge is needed between these character streams and the byte streams of physical devices, such as disks and networks. `InputStreamReader` and `OutputStreamWriter` are special classes that use a *character-encoding scheme* to translate between character and byte streams.

This section describes all the interesting stream types with the exception of `FileInputStream`, `FileOutputStream`, `FileReader`, and `FileWriter`. We postpone the discussion of file streams until the next section, where we cover issues involved with accessing the filesystem in Java.

Basic I/O

The prototypical example of an `InputStream` object is the *standard input* of a Java application. Like `stdin` in C or `cin` in C++, this is the source of input to a command-line (non-GUI) program. It is an input stream from the environment—usually a terminal window or possibly the output of another command. The `java.lang.System` class, a general repository for system-related resources, provides a reference to the standard input stream in the static variable `System.in`. It also provides a *standard output stream* and a *standard error stream* in the `out` and `err` variables, respectively.[1] The following example shows the correspondence:

```
InputStream stdin = System.in;
OutputStream stdout = System.out;
OutputStream stderr = System.err;
```

This snippet hides the fact that `System.out` and `System.err` aren't just `OutputStream` objects, but more specialized and useful `PrintStream` objects. We'll explain these later, but for now we can reference `out` and `err` as `OutputStream` objects because they are derived from `OutputStream`.

We can read a single byte at a time from standard input with the `InputStream`'s `read()` method. If you look closely at the API, you'll see that the `read()` method of the base `InputStream` class is an `abstract` method. What lies behind `System.in` is a particular implementation of `InputStream` that provides the real implementation of the `read()` method:

```
try {
    int val = System.in.read();
} catch ( IOException e ) {
    ...
}
```

Although we said that the `read()` method reads a byte value, the return type in the example is `int`, not `byte`. That's because the `read()` method of basic input streams in Java uses a convention carried over from the C language to indicate the end of a stream with a special value. Data byte values are returned as unsigned integers in the range 0 to 255 and the special value of `-1` is used to indicate that end of stream has been reached. You'll need to test for this condition when using the simple `read()` method. You can then cast the value to a byte if needed. The following example reads each byte from an input stream and prints its value:

```
try {
    int val;
    while( (val=System.in.read()) != -1 )
        System.out.println((byte)val);
} catch ( IOException e ) { ... }
```

As we've shown in the examples, the `read()` method can also throw an `IOException` if there is an error reading from the underlying stream source. Various subclasses of

1. Standard error is a stream that is usually reserved for error-related text messages that should be shown to the user of a command-line application. It is differentiated from the standard output, which often might be redirected to a file or another application and not seen by the user.

IOException may indicate that a source such as a file or network connection has had an error. Additionally, higher-level streams that read data types more complex than a single byte may throw EOFException ("end of file"), which indicates an unexpected or premature end of stream.

An overloaded form of read() fills a byte array with as much data as possible up to the capacity of the array and returns the number of bytes read:

```
byte [] buff = new byte [1024];
int got = System.in.read( buff );
```

In theory, we can also check the number of bytes available for reading at a given time on an InputStream using the available() method. With that information, we could create an array of exactly the right size:

```
int waiting = System.in.available();
if ( waiting > 0 ) {
    byte [] data = new byte [ waiting ];
    System.in.read( data );
    ...
}
```

However, the reliability of this technique depends on the ability of the underlying stream implementation to detect how much data can be retrieved. It generally works for files but should not be relied upon for all types of streams.

These read() methods block until at least some data is read (at least one byte). You must, in general, check the returned value to determine how much data you got and if you need to read more. (We look at nonblocking I/O later in this chapter.) The skip() method of InputStream provides a way of jumping over a number of bytes. Depending on the implementation of the stream, skipping bytes may be more efficient than reading them.

The close() method shuts down the stream and frees up any associated system resources. It's important for performance to remember to close most types of streams when you are finished using them. In some cases, streams may be closed automatically when objects are garbage-collected, but it is not a good idea to rely on this behavior. In Java 7, the *try-with-resources* language feature was added to make automatically closing streams and other closeable entities easier. We'll see some examples of that later in this chapter. The flag interface java.io.Closeable identifies all types of stream, channel, and related utility classes that can be closed.

Finally, we should mention that in addition to the System.in and System.out standard streams, Java provides the java.io.Console API through System.console(). You can use the Console to read passwords without echoing them to the screen.

Character Streams

In early versions of Java, some `InputStream` and `OutputStream` types included methods for reading and writing strings, but most of them operated by naively assuming that a 16-bit Unicode character was equivalent to an 8-bit byte in the stream. This works only for Latin-1 (ISO 8859-1) characters and not for the world of other encodings that are used with different languages. In Chapter 10, we saw that the `java.lang.String` class has a byte array constructor and a corresponding `getBytes()` method that each accept character encoding as an argument. In theory, we could use these as tools to transform arrays of bytes to and from Unicode characters so that we could work with byte streams that represent character data in any encoding format. Fortunately, however, we don't have to rely on this because Java has streams that handle this for us.

The `java.io Reader` and `Writer` character stream classes were introduced as streams that handle character data only. When you use these classes, you think only in terms of characters and string data and allow the underlying implementation to handle the conversion of bytes to a specific character encoding. As we'll see, some direct implementations of `Reader` and `Writer` exist, for example, for reading and writing files. But more generally, two special classes, `InputStreamReader` and `OutputStreamWriter`, bridge the gap between the world of character streams and the world of byte streams. These are, respectively, a `Reader` and a `Writer` that can be wrapped around any underlying byte stream to make it a character stream. An encoding scheme is used to convert between possible multibyte encoded values and Java Unicode characters. An encoding scheme can be specified by name in the constructor of `InputStreamReader` or `OutputStream Writer`. For convenience, the default constructor uses the system's default encoding scheme.

For example, let's parse a human-readable string from the standard input into an integer. We'll assume that the bytes coming from `System.in` use the system's default encoding scheme:

```
try {
    InputStream in = System.in;
    InputStreamReader charsIn = new InputStreamReader( in );
    BufferedReader bufferedCharsIn = new BufferedReader( inReader );

    String line = bufferedCharsIn.readLine();
    int i = NumberFormat.getInstance().parse( line ).intValue();
} catch ( IOException e ) {
} catch ( ParseException pe ) { }
```

First, we wrap an `InputStreamReader` around `System.in`. This reader converts the incoming bytes of `System.in` to characters using the default encoding scheme. Then, we wrap a `BufferedReader` around the `InputStreamReader`. `BufferedReader` adds the `readLine()` method, which we can use to grab a full line of text (up to a platform-specific, line-terminator character combination) into a String. The string is then parsed into an integer using the techniques described in Chapter 10.

The important thing to note is that we have taken a byte-oriented input stream, System.in, and safely converted it to a Reader for reading characters. If we wished to use an encoding other than the system default, we could have specified it in the InputStreamReader's constructor like so:

```
InputStreamReader reader = new InputStreamReader( System.in, "UTF-8" );
```

For each character that is read from the reader, the InputStreamReader reads one or more bytes and performs the necessary conversion to Unicode.

In Chapter 13, we use an InputStreamReader and a Writer in our simple web server example, where we must use a character encoding specified by the HTTP protocol. We also return to the topic of character encodings when we discuss the java.nio.charset API, which allows you to query for and use encoders and decoders explicitly on buffers of characters and bytes. Both InputStreamReader and OutputStreamWriter can accept a Charset codec object as well as a character encoding name.

Stream Wrappers

What if we want to do more than read and write a sequence of bytes or characters? We can use a "filter" stream, which is a type of InputStream, OutputStream, Reader, or Writer that wraps another stream and adds new features. A filter stream takes the target stream as an argument in its constructor and delegates calls to it after doing some additional processing of its own. For example, we can construct a BufferedInputStream to wrap the system standard input:

```
InputStream bufferedIn = new BufferedInputStream( System.in );
```

The BufferedInputStream is a type of filter stream that reads ahead and buffers a certain amount of data. (We'll talk more about it later in this chapter.) The BufferedInputStream wraps an additional layer of functionality around the underlying stream. Figure 12-3 shows this arrangement for a DataInputStream, which is a type of stream that can read higher-level data types, such as Java primitives and strings.

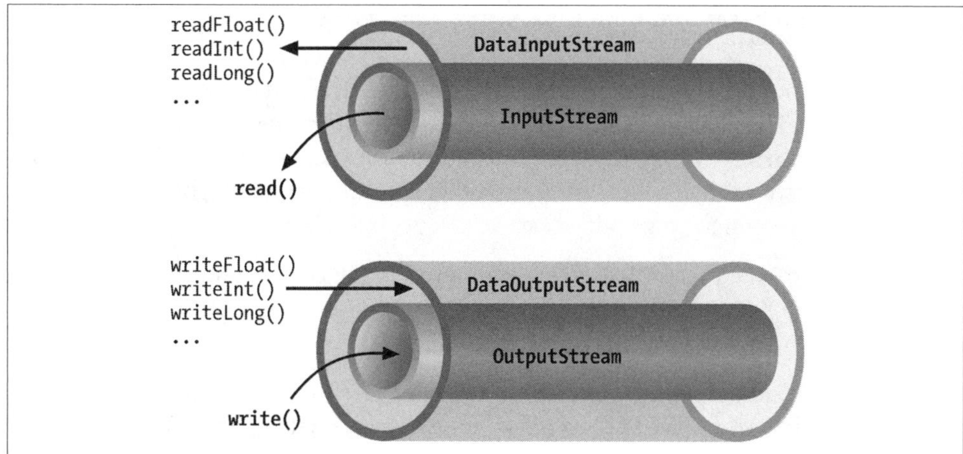

Figure 12-3. Layered streams

As you can see from the previous code snippet, the `BufferedInputStream` filter is a type of `InputStream`. Because filter streams are themselves subclasses of the basic stream types, they can be used as arguments to the construction of other filter streams. This allows filter streams to be layered on top of one another to provide different combinations of features. For example, we could first wrap our `System.in` with a `BufferedInputStream` and then wrap the `BufferedInputStream` with a `DataInputStream` for reading special data types with buffering.

Java provides base classes for creating new types of filter streams: `FilterInputStream`, `FilterOutputStream`, `FilterReader`, and `FilterWriter`. These superclasses provide the basic machinery for a "no op" filter (a filter that doesn't do anything) by delegating all their method calls to their underlying stream. Real filter streams subclass these and override various methods to add their additional processing. We'll make an example filter stream later in this chapter.

Data streams

`DataInputStream` and `DataOutputStream` are filter streams that let you read or write strings and primitive data types composed of more than a single byte. `DataInputStream` and `DataOutputStream` implement the `DataInput` and `DataOutput` interfaces, respectively. These interfaces define methods for reading or writing strings and all of the Java primitive types, including numbers and Boolean values. `DataOutputStream` encodes these values in a machine-independent manner and then writes them to its underlying byte stream. `DataInputStream` does the converse.

You can construct a `DataInputStream` from an `InputStream` and then use a method such as `readDouble()` to read a primitive data type:

```
DataInputStream dis = new DataInputStream( System.in );
double d = dis.readDouble();
```

This example wraps the standard input stream in a `DataInputStream` and uses it to read a `double` value. The `readDouble()` method reads bytes from the stream and constructs a `double` from them. The `DataInputStream` methods expect the bytes of numeric data types to be in *network byte order*, a standard that specifies that the high-order bytes are sent first (also known as "big endian," as we discuss later).

The `DataOutputStream` class provides write methods that correspond to the read methods in `DataInputStream`. For example, `writeInt()` writes an integer in binary format to the underlying output stream.

The `readUTF()` and `writeUTF()` methods of `DataInputStream` and `DataOutputStream` read and write a Java `String` of Unicode characters using the UTF-8 "transformation format" character encoding. UTF-8 is an ASCII-compatible encoding of Unicode characters that is very widely used. Not all encodings are guaranteed to preserve all Unicode characters, but UTF-8 does. You can also use UTF-8 with `Reader` and `Writer` streams by specifying it as the encoding name.

Buffered streams

The `BufferedInputStream`, `BufferedOutputStream`, `BufferedReader`, and `BufferedWriter` classes add a data buffer of a specified size to the stream path. A buffer can increase efficiency by reducing the number of physical read or write operations that correspond to `read()` or `write()` method calls. You create a buffered stream with an appropriate input or output stream and a buffer size. (You can also wrap another stream around a buffered stream so that it benefits from the buffering.) Here's a simple buffered input stream called `bis`:

```
BufferedInputStream bis = new BufferedInputStream(myInputStream, 32768);
...
bis.read();
```

In this example, we specify a buffer size of 32 KB. If we leave off the size of the buffer in the constructor, a reasonably sized one is chosen for us. (Currently the default is 8 KB.) On our first call to `read()`, `bis` tries to fill our entire 32 KB buffer with data, if it's available. Thereafter, calls to `read()` retrieve data from the buffer, which is refilled as necessary.

A `BufferedOutputStream` works in a similar way. Calls to `write()` store the data in a buffer; data is actually written only when the buffer fills up. You can also use the `flush()` method to wring out the contents of a `BufferedOutputStream` at any time. The `flush()` method is actually a method of the `OutputStream` class itself. It's important because it allows you to be sure that all data in any underlying streams and filter streams has been sent (before, for example, you wait for a response).

Some input streams such as BufferedInputStream support the ability to mark a location in the data and later reset the stream to that position. The mark() method sets the return point in the stream. It takes an integer value that specifies the number of bytes that can be read before the stream gives up and forgets about the mark. The reset() method returns the stream to the marked point; any data read after the call to mark() is read again.

This functionality could be useful when you are reading the stream in a parser. You may occasionally fail to parse a structure and so must try something else. In this situation, you can have your parser generate an error and then reset the stream to the point before it began parsing the structure:

```
BufferedInputStream input;
...
try {
    input.mark( MAX_DATA_STRUCTURE_SIZE );
    return( parseDataStructure( input ) );
}
catch ( ParseException e ) {
    input.reset();
    ...
}
```

The BufferedReader and BufferedWriter classes work just like their byte-based counterparts, except that they operate on characters instead of bytes.

PrintWriter and PrintStream

Another useful wrapper stream is java.io.PrintWriter. This class provides a suite of overloaded print() methods that turn their arguments into strings and push them out the stream. A complementary set of println() convenience methods appends a new line to the end of the strings. For formatted text output, printf() and the identical format() methods allow you to write printf-style formatted text to the stream.

PrintWriter is an unusual character stream because it can wrap either an OutputStream or another Writer. PrintWriter is the more capable big brother of the legacy PrintStream byte stream. The System.out and System.err streams are PrintStream objects; you have already seen such streams strewn throughout this book:

```
System.out.print("Hello, world...\n");
System.out.println("Hello, world...");
System.out.printf("The answer is %d", 17 );
System.out.println( 3.14 );
```

Early versions of Java did not have the Reader and Writer classes and used PrintStream, which convert bytes to characters by simply made assumptions about the character encoding. You should use a PrintWriter for all new development.

When you create a PrintWriter object, you can pass an additional Boolean value to the constructor, specifying whether it should "auto-flush." If this value is true, the PrintWriter automatically performs a flush() on the underlying OutputStream or Writer each time it sends a newline:

```
PrintWriter pw = new PrintWriter( myOutputStream, true /*autoFlush*/ );
    pw.println("Hello!"); // Stream is automatically flushed by the newline.
```

When this technique is used with a buffered output stream, it corresponds to the behavior of terminals that send data line by line.

The other big advantage that print streams have over regular character streams is that they shield you from exceptions thrown by the underlying streams. Unlike methods in other stream classes, the methods of PrintWriter and PrintStream do not throw IOExceptions. Instead, they provide a method to explicitly check for errors if required. This makes life a lot easier for printing text, which is a very common operation. You can check for errors with the checkError() method:

```
System.out.println( reallyLongString );
if ( System.out.checkError() ){ ...  // uh oh
```

Pipes

Normally, our applications are directly involved with one side of a given stream at a time. PipedInputStream and PipedOutputStream (or PipedReader and PipedWriter), however, let us create two sides of a stream and connect them, as shown in Figure 12-4. This can be used to provide a stream of communication between threads, for example, or as a "loopback" for testing. Often it's used as a crutch to interface a stream-oriented API to a non-stream-oriented API.

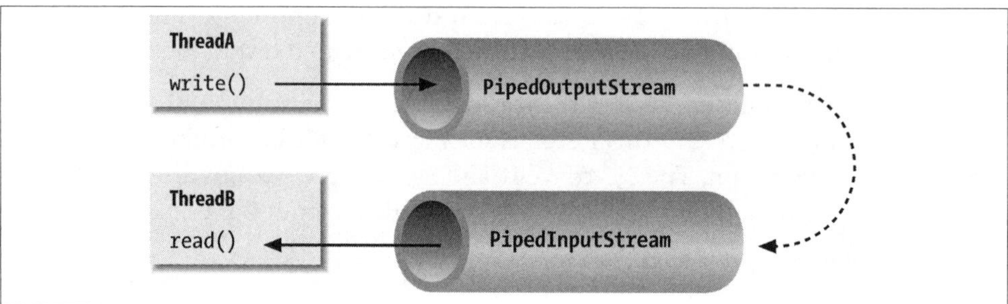

Figure 12-4. Piped streams

To create a bytestream pipe, we use both a PipedInputStream and a PipedOutputStream. We can simply choose a side and then construct the other side using the first as an argument:

```
PipedInputStream pin = new PipedInputStream();
PipedOutputStream pout = new PipedOutputStream( pin );
```

Alternatively:

```
PipedOutputStream pout = new PipedOutputStream();
PipedInputStream pin = new PipedInputStream( pout );
```

In each of these examples, the effect is to produce an input stream, `pin`, and an output stream, `pout`, that are connected. Data written to `pout` can then be read by `pin`. It is also possible to create the `PipedInputStream` and the `PipedOutputStream` separately and then connect them with the `connect()` method.

We can do exactly the same thing in the character-based world, using `PipedReader` and `PipedWriter` in place of `PipedInputStream` and `PipedOutputStream`.

After the two ends of the pipe are connected, use the two streams as you would other input and output streams. You can use `read()` to read data from the `PipedInputStream` (or `PipedReader`) and `write()` to write data to the `PipedOutputStream` (or `PipedWriter`). If the internal buffer of the pipe fills up, the writer blocks and waits until space is available. Conversely, if the pipe is empty, the reader blocks and waits until some data is available.

One advantage to using piped streams is that they provide stream functionality in our code without compelling us to build new, specialized streams. For example, we can use pipes to create a simple logging or "console" facility for our application. We can send messages to the logging facility through an ordinary `PrintWriter`, and then it can do whatever processing or buffering is required before sending the messages off to their ultimate destination. Because we are dealing with string messages, we use the character-based `PipedReader` and `PipedWriter` classes. The following example shows the skeleton of our logging facility:

```
class LoggerDaemon extends Thread
{
    PipedReader in = new PipedReader();

    LoggerDaemon() {
        start();
    }

    public void run() {
        BufferedReader bin = new BufferedReader( in );
        String s;
        try {
           while ( (s = bin.readLine()) != null ) {
                // process line of data
            }
        } catch (IOException e ) { }
    }
```

```
        PrintWriter getWriter() throws IOException {
            return new PrintWriter( new PipedWriter( in ) );
        }
    }

    class myApplication {
        public static void main ( String [] args ) throws IOException {
            PrintWriter out = new LoggerDaemon().getWriter();

            out.println("Application starting...");
            // ...
            out.println("Warning: does not compute!");
            // ...
        }
    }
```

LoggerDaemon reads strings from its end of the pipe, the PipedReader named in. LoggerDaemon also provides a method, getWriter(), which returns a PipedWriter that is connected to its input stream. To begin sending messages, we create a new LoggerDaemon and fetch the output stream. In order to read strings with the readLine() method, LoggerDaemon wraps a BufferedReader around its PipedReader. For convenience, it also presents its output pipe as a PrintWriter rather than a simple Writer.

One advantage of implementing LoggerDaemon with pipes is that we can log messages as easily as we write text to a terminal or any other stream. In other words, we can use all our normal tools and techniques, including printf(). Another advantage is that the processing happens in another thread, so we can go about our business while any processing takes place.

Streams from Strings and Back

StringReader is another useful stream class; it essentially wraps stream functionality around a String. Here's how to use a StringReader:

```
    String data = "There once was a man from Nantucket...";
    StringReader sr = new StringReader( data );

    char T = (char)sr.read();
    char h = (char)sr.read();
    char e = (char)sr.read();
```

Note that you will still have to catch IOExceptions that are thrown by some of the StringReader's methods.

The StringReader class is useful when you want to read data from a String as if it were coming from a stream, such as a file, pipe, or socket. Suppose you create a parser that expects to read from a stream, but you want to provide an alternative method that also parses a big string. You can easily add one using StringReader.

Turning things around, the `StringWriter` class lets us write to a character buffer via an output stream. The internal buffer grows as necessary to accommodate the data. When we are done, we can fetch the contents of the buffer as a `String`. In the following example, we create a `StringWriter` and wrap it in a `PrintWriter` for convenience:

```
StringWriter buffer = new StringWriter();
PrintWriter out = new PrintWriter( buffer );

out.println("A moose once bit my sister.");
out.println("No, really!");

String results = buffer.toString();
```

First, we print a few lines to the output stream to give it some data and then retrieve the results as a string with the `toString()` method. Alternately, we could get the results as a `StringBuffer` object using the `getBuffer()` method.

The `StringWriter` class is useful if you want to capture the output of something that normally sends output to a stream, such as a file or the console. A `PrintWriter` wrapped around a `StringWriter` is a viable alternative to using a `StringBuffer` to construct large strings piece by piece.

The `ByteArrayInputStream` and `ByteArrayOutputStream` work with bytes in the same way the previous examples worked with characters. You can write byte data to a `ByteArrayOutputStream` and retrieve it later with the `toByteArray()` method. Conversely, you can construct a `ByteArrayInputStream` from a byte array as `StringReader` does with a `String`. For example, if we want to see exactly what our `DataOutputStream` is writing when we tell it to encode a particular value, we could capture it with a byte array output stream:

```
ByteArrayOutputStream bao = new ByteArrayOutputStream();
DataOutputStream dao = new DataOutputStream( bao );
dao.writeInt( 16777216 );
dao.flush();

byte [] bytes = bao.toByteArray();
for( byte b : bytes )
    System.out.println( b );  // 1, 0, 0, 0
```

Implementing a Filter Stream

Before we leave streams, let's try making one of our own. We mentioned earlier that specialized stream wrappers are built on top of the `FilterInputStream` and `FilterOutputStream` classes. It's quite easy to create our own subclass of `FilterInputStream` that can be wrapped around other streams to add new functionality.

The following example, `rot13InputStream`, performs a *rot13* (rotate by 13 letters) operation on the bytes that it reads. *rot13* is a trivial obfuscation algorithm that shifts alphabetic characters to make them not quite human-readable (it simply passes over nonalphabetic characters without modifying them). rot13 *is* cute because it's symmetric: to "un-rot13" some text, you simply rot13 it again. Here's our `rot13InputStream` class:

```
public class rot13InputStream extends FilterInputStream
{
    public rot13InputStream ( InputStream i ) {
        super( i );
    }

    public int read() throws IOException {
        return rot13( in.read() );
    }

    // should override additional read() methods

    private int rot13 ( int c ) {
        if ( (c >= 'A') && (c <= 'Z') )
            c=(((c-'A')+13)%26)+'A';
        if ( (c >= 'a') && (c <= 'z') )
            c=(((c-'a')+13)%26)+'a';
        return c;
    }
}
```

The `FilterInputStream` needs to be initialized with an `InputStream`; this is the stream to be filtered. We provide an appropriate constructor for the `rot13InputStream` class and invoke the parent constructor with a call to `super()`. `FilterInputStream` contains a protected instance variable, `in`, in which it stores a reference to the specified `InputStream`, making it available to the rest of our class.

The primary feature of a `FilterInputStream` is that it delegates its input tasks to the underlying `InputStream`. For instance, a call to `FilterInputStream`'s `read()` method simply turns around and calls the `read()` method of the underlying `InputStream` to fetch a byte. The filtering happens when we do our extra work on the data as it passes through. In our example, the `read()` method fetches a byte from the underlying `InputStream`, `in`, and then performs the rot13 shift on the byte before returning it. The `rot13()` method shifts alphabetic characters while simply passing over all other values, including the end-of-stream value (`-1`). Our subclass is now a rot13 filter.

`read()` is the only `InputStream` method that `FilterInputStream` overrides. All other normal functionality of an `InputStream`, such as `skip()` and `available()`, is unmodified, so calls to these methods are answered by the underlying `InputStream`.

Strictly speaking, `rot13InputStream` works only on an ASCII byte stream because the underlying algorithm is based on the Roman alphabet. A more generalized character-scrambling algorithm would have to be based on `FilterReader` to handle 16-bit Unicode classes correctly. (Anyone want to try rot32768?) We should also note that we have not fully implemented our filter: we should also override the version of `read()` that takes a byte array and range specifiers, perhaps delegating it to our own `read`. Unless we do so, a reader using that method would get the raw stream.

File I/O

In this chapter, we're going to talk about the Java file I/O API. To be more precise, we are going to talk about two file APIs: first, there is the core `java.io` File I/O facility that has been part of Java since the beginning. Then there is the "new" `java.nio.file` API introduced in Java 7. In general the NIO packages, which we'll cover in detail later and which touch upon not only files but all types of network and channel I/O, were introduced to add advanced features that make Java more scaleable and higher performance. However, in the case of file NIO, the new package is also just somewhat of a "do-over" on the original API. In movie terms, you can think of the two APIs as the "classic" and the "reboot" of the series. The new API completely duplicates the functionality of the original, but because the core API is so fundamental (and in some cases simpler), it is likely that many people will prefer to keep using it. We'll start with the classic API centering on `java.io.File` and later we'll cover the new API, which centers on the analogous `java.nio.Path`.

Working with files in Java is easy, but poses some conceptual problems. Real-world filesystems can vary widely in architecture and implementation: think of the differences between Mac, PC, and Unix systems when it comes to filenames. Java tries to mask some of these differences and provide information to help an application tailor itself to the local environment, but it leaves a lot of the details of file access implementation dependent. We'll talk about techniques for dealing with this as we go.

Before we leave File I/O we'll also show you some tools for the special case of application "resource" files packaged with your app and loaded via the Java classpath.

The java.io.File Class

The `java.io.File` class encapsulates access to information about a file or directory. It can be used to get attribute information about a file, list the entries in a directory, and perform basic filesystem operations, such as removing a file or making a directory. While the `File` object handles these "meta" operations, it doesn't provide the API for reading and writing file data; there are file streams for that purpose.

File constructors

You can create an instance of `File` from a `String` pathname:

```
File fooFile = new File( "/tmp/foo.txt" );
File barDir = new File( "/tmp/bar" );
```

You can also create a file with a relative path:

```
File f = new File( "foo" );
```

In this case, Java works relative to the "current working directory" of the Java interpreter. You can determine the current working directory by reading the `user.dir` property in the `System Properties` list:

```
System.getProperty("user.dir"); // e.g.,"/Users/pat"
```

An overloaded version of the `File` constructor lets you specify the directory path and filename as separate `String` objects:

```
File fooFile = new File( "/tmp", "foo.txt" );
```

With yet another variation, you can specify the directory with a `File` object and the filename with a `String`:

```
File tmpDir = new File( "/tmp" ); // File for directory /tmp
File fooFile = new File ( tmpDir, "foo.txt" );
```

None of these `File` constructors actually creates a file or directory, and it is not an error to create a `File` object for a nonexistent file. The `File` object is just a handle for a file or directory whose properties you may wish to read, write, or test. For example, you can use the `exists()` instance method to learn whether the file or directory exists.

Path localization

One issue with working with files in Java is that pathnames are expected to follow the conventions of the local filesystem. Two differences are that the Windows filesystem uses "roots" or drive letters (for example, C:) and a backslash (\) instead of the forward slash (/) path separator that is used in other systems.

Java tries to compensate for the differences. For example, on Windows platforms, Java accepts paths with either forward slashes or backslashes. (On others, however, it only accepts forward slashes.)

Your best bet is to make sure you follow the filename conventions of the host filesystem. If your application has a GUI that is opening and saving files at the user's request, you should be able to handle that functionality with the Swing `JFileChooser` class. This class encapsulates a graphical file-selection dialog box. The methods of the `JFileChoos er` take care of system-dependent filename features for you.

If your application needs to deal with files on its own behalf, however, things get a little more complicated. The `File` class contains a few `static` variables to make this task possible. `File.separator` defines a `String` that specifies the file separator on the local host (e.g., / on Unix and Macintosh systems and \ on Windows systems); `File.sepa ratorChar` provides the same information as a `char`.

You can use this system-dependent information in several ways. Probably the simplest way to localize pathnames is to pick a convention that you use internally, such as the forward slash (/), and do a String replace to substitute for the localized separator character:

```
// we'll use forward slash as our standard
String path = "mail/2004/june/merle";
path = path.replace('/', File.separatorChar);
File mailbox = new File( path );
```

Alternatively, you could work with the components of a pathname and build the local pathname when you need it:

```
String [] path = { "mail", "2004", "june", "merle" };

   StringBuffer sb = new StringBuffer(path[0]);
for (int i=1; i< path.length; i++)
    sb.append( File.separator + path[i] );
File mailbox = new File( sb.toString() );
```

One thing to remember is that Java interprets a literal backslash character (\) in source code as an escape character when used in a String. To get a backslash in a String, you have to use \\.

To grapple with the issue of filesystems with multiple "roots" (for example, C:\ on Windows), the File class provides the static method listRoots(), which returns an array of File objects corresponding to the filesystem root directories. Again, in a GUI application, a graphical file chooser dialog shields you from this problem entirely.

File operations

Once we have a File object, we can use it to ask for information about and perform standard operations on the file or directory it represents. A number of methods let us ask questions about the File. For example, isFile() returns true if the File represents a regular file, while isDirectory() returns true if it's a directory. isAbsolute() indicates whether the File encapsulates an *absolute path* or *relative path* specification. An absolute path is a system-dependent notion that means that the path doesn't depend on the application's working directory or any concept of a working root or drive (e.g., in Windows, it is a full path including the drive letter: *c:\\Users\pat\foo.txt*).

Components of the File pathname are available through the following methods: getName(), getPath(), getAbsolutePath(), and getParent(). getName() returns a String for the filename without any directory information. If the File has an absolute path specification, getAbsolutePath() returns that path. Otherwise, it returns the relative path appended to the current working directory (attempting to make it an absolute path). getParent() returns the parent directory of the file or directory.

The string returned by getPath() or getAbsolutePath() may not follow the same case conventions as the underlying filesystem. You can retrieve the filesystem's own or "canonical" version of the file's path by using the method getCanonicalPath(). In Windows, for example, you can create a File object whose getAbsolutePath() is *C:\Autoexec.bat* but whose getCanonicalPath() is *C:\AUTOEXEC.BAT*; both actually point to the same file. This is useful for comparing filenames that may have been supplied with different case conventions or for showing them to the user.

You can get or set the modification time of a file or directory with lastModified() and setLastModified() methods. The value is a long that is the number of milliseconds since the *epoch* (Jan 1, 1970, 00:00:00 GMT). We can also get the size of the file in bytes with length().

Here's a fragment of code that prints some information about a file:

```
File fooFile = new File( "/tmp/boofa" );

String type = fooFile.isFile() ? "File " : "Directory ";
String name = fooFile.getName();
long len = fooFile.length();
System.out.println( type + name + ", " + len + " bytes " );
```

If the File object corresponds to a directory, we can list the files in the directory with the list() method or the listFiles() method:

```
File tmpDir = new File("/tmp" );
String [] fileNames = tmpDir.list();
File [] files = tmpDir.listFiles();
```

list() returns an array of String objects that contains filenames. listFiles() returns an array of File objects. Note that in neither case are the files guaranteed to be in any kind of order (alphabetical, for example). You can use the Collections API to sort strings alphabetically like so:

```
List list = Arrays.asList( sa );
Collections.sort(list);
```

If the File refers to a nonexistent directory, we can create the directory with mkdir() or mkdirs(). The mkdir() method creates at most a single directory level, so any intervening directories in the path must already exist. mkdirs() creates all directory levels necessary to create the full path of the File specification. In either case, if the directory cannot be created, the method returns false. Use renameTo() to rename a file or directory and delete() to delete a file or directory.

Although we can create a directory using the File object, this isn't the most common way to create a file; that's normally done implicitly when we intend to write data to it with a FileOutputStream or FileWriter, as we'll discuss in a moment. The exception is the createNewFile() method, which can be used to attempt to create a new zero-length file at the location pointed to by the File object. The useful thing about this method is that the operation is guaranteed to be "atomic" with respect to all other file creation in the filesystem. `createNewFile()` returns a Boolean value that tells you whether the file was created or not. This is sometimes used as a primitive locking feature—whoever creates the file first "wins." (The NIO package supports true file locks, as we'll see later.) This is useful in combination `deleteOnExit()`, which flags the file to be automatically removed when the Java VM exits. This combination allows you to guard resources or make an application that can only be run in a single instance at a time. Another file creation method that is related to the `File` class itself is the static method `createTempFile()`, which creates a file in a specified location using an automatically generated unique name. This, too, is useful in combination with `deleteOnExit()`.

The `toURL()` method converts a file path to a `file:` URL object. URLs are an abstraction that allows you to point to any kind of object anywhere on the Net. Converting a `File` reference to a URL may be useful for consistency with more general utilities that deal with URLs. See Chapter 14 for details. File URLs also come into greater use with the NIO File API where they can be used to reference new types of filesystems that are implemented directly in Java code.

Table 12-1 summarizes the methods provided by the `File` class.

Table 12-1. File methods

Method	Return type	Description
`canExecute()`	`Boolean`	Is the file executable?
`canRead()`	`Boolean`	Is the file (or directory) readable?
`canWrite()`	`Boolean`	Is the file (or directory) writable?
`createNewFile()`	`Boolean`	Creates a new file.
`createTempFile (String pfx, Stringsfx)`	`File`	Static method to create a new file, with the specified prefix and suffix, in the default temp file directory.
`delete()`	`Boolean`	Deletes the file (or directory).
`deleteOnExit()`	`Void`	When it exits, Java runtime system deletes the file.
`exists()`	`Boolean`	Does the file (or directory) exist?
`getAbsolutePath()`	`String`	Returns the absolute path of the file (or directory).
`getCanonicalPath()`	`String`	Returns the absolute, case-correct path of the file (or directory).
`getFreeSpace()`	`long`	Get the number of bytes of unallocated space on the partition holding this path or 0 if the path is invalid.
`getName()`	`String`	Returns the name of the file (or directory).
`getParent()`	`String`	Returns the name of the parent directory of the file (or directory).
`getPath()`	`String`	Returns the path of the file (or directory). (Not to be confused with `toPath()`).

Method	Return type	Description
getTotalSpace()	long	Get the size of the partition that contains the file path in bytes or 0 if the path is invalid.
getUseableSpace()	long	Get the number of bytes of user-accessible unallocated space on the partition holding this path or 0 if the path is invalid. This method attempts to take into account user write permissions.
isAbsolute()	boolean	Is the filename (or directory name) absolute?
isDirectory()	boolean	Is the item a directory?
isFile()	boolean	Is the item a file?
isHidden()	boolean	Is the item hidden? (System-dependent.)
lastModified()	long	Returns the last modification time of the file (or directory).
length()	long	Returns the length of the file.
list()	String []	Returns a list of files in the directory.
listFiles()	File[]	Returns the contents of the directory as an array of File objects.
listRoots()	File[]	Returns array of root filesystems if any (e.g., C:/, D:/).
mkdir()	boolean	Creates the directory.
mkdirs()	boolean	Creates all directories in the path.
renameTo(File *dest*)	boolean	Renames the file (or directory).
setExecutable()	boolean	Sets execute permissions for the file.
setLastModified()	boolean	Sets the last-modified time of the file (or directory).
setReadable()	boolean	Sets read permissions for the file.
setReadOnly()	boolean	Sets the file to read-only status.
setWriteable()	boolean	Sets the write permissions for the file.
toPath()	java.nio.file.Path	Convert the File to an NIO File Path (see the NIO File API). (Not to be confused with getPath().)
toURL()	java.net.URL	Generates a URL object for the file (or directory).

File Streams

OK, you're probably sick of hearing about files already and we haven't even written a byte yet! Well, now the fun begins. Java provides two fundamental streams for reading from and writing to files: FileInputStream and FileOutputStream. These streams provide the basic byte-oriented InputStream and OutputStream functionality that is applied to reading and writing files. They can be combined with the filter streams described earlier to work with files in the same way as other stream communications.

You can create a FileInputStream from a String pathname or a File object:

```
FileInputStream in = new FileInputStream( "/etc/passwd" );
```

When you create a `FileInputStream`, the Java runtime system attempts to open the specified file. Thus, the `FileInputStream` constructors can throw a `FileNotFoundException` if the specified file doesn't exist or an `IOException` if some other I/O error occurs. You must catch these exceptions in your code. Wherever possible, it's a good idea to get in the habit of using the new Java 7 `try`-with-resources construct to automatically close files for you when you are finished with them:

```
try ( FileInputStream fin = new FileInputStream( "/etc/passwd" ) ) {
    ....
    // Fin will be closed automatically if needed upon exiting the try clause.
}
```

When the stream is first created, its `available()` method and the `File` object's `length()` method should return the same value.

To read characters from a file as a `Reader`, you can wrap an `InputStreamReader` around a `FileInputStream`. If you want to use the default character-encoding scheme for the platform, you can use the `FileReader` class instead, which is provided as a convenience. `FileReader` is just a `FileInputStream` wrapped in an `InputStreamReader` with some defaults. For some crazy reason, you can't specify a character encoding for the `FileReader` to use, so it's probably best to ignore it and use `InputStreamReader` with `FileInputStream`.

The following class, `ListIt`, is a small utility that sends the contents of a file or directory to standard output:

```
//file: ListIt.java
import java.io.*;

class ListIt {
    public static void main ( String args[] ) throws Exception {
        File file =  new File( args[0] );

        if ( !file.exists() || !file.canRead() ) {
            System.out.println( "Can't read " + file );
            return;
        }

        if ( file.isDirectory() ) {
            String [] files = file.list();
            for ( String file : files )
                System.out.println( file );
        } else
            try {
                Reader ir = new InputStreamReader(
                    new FileInputStream( file ) );

                BufferedReader in = new BufferedReader( ir );
                String line;
                while ((line = in.readLine()) != null)
```

```
                    System.out.println(line);
                }
                catch ( FileNotFoundException e ) {
                    System.out.println( "File Disappeared" );
                }
            }
        }
```

ListIt constructs a File object from its first command-line argument and tests the File to see whether it exists and is readable. If the File is a directory, ListIt outputs the names of the files in the directory. Otherwise, ListIt reads and outputs the file, line by line.

For writing files, you can create a FileOutputStream from a String pathname or a File object. Unlike FileInputStream, however, the FileOutputStream constructors don't throw a FileNotFoundException. If the specified file doesn't exist, the FileOutputStream creates the file. The FileOutputStream constructors can throw an IOException if some other I/O error occurs, so you still need to handle this exception.

If the specified file does exist, the FileOutputStream opens it for writing. When you subsequently call the write() method, the new data overwrites the current contents of the file. If you need to append data to an existing file, you can use a form of the constructor that accepts a Boolean append flag:

```
    FileInputStream fooOut =
        new FileOutputStream( fooFile ); // overwrite fooFile
    FileInputStream pwdOut =
        new FileOutputStream( "/etc/passwd", true ); // append
```

Another way to append data to files is with RandomAccessFile, which we'll discuss shortly.

Just as with reading, to write characters (instead of bytes) to a file, you can wrap an OutputStreamWriter around a FileOutputStream. If you want to use the default character-encoding scheme, you can use the FileWriter class instead, which is provided as a convenience.

The following example reads a line of data from standard input and writes it to the file */tmp/foo.txt*:

```
    String s = new BufferedReader(
        new InputStreamReader( System.in ) ).readLine();
    File out = new File( "/tmp/foo.txt" );
    FileWriter fw = new FileWriter ( out );
    PrintWriter pw = new PrintWriter( fw )
    pw.println( s );pw.close();
```

Notice how we wrapped the FileWriter in a PrintWriter to facilitate writing the data. Also, to be a good filesystem citizen, we called the close() method when we're done with the FileWriter. Here, closing the PrintWriter closes the underlying Writer for us. We also could have used try-with-resources here.

RandomAccessFile

The java.io.RandomAccessFile class provides the ability to read and write data at a specified location in a file. RandomAccessFile implements both the DataInput and DataOutput interfaces, so you can use it to read and write strings and primitive types at locations in the file just as if it were a DataInputStream and DataOutputStream. However, because the class provides random, rather than sequential, access to file data, it's not a subclass of either InputStream or OutputStream.

You can create a RandomAccessFile from a String pathname or a File object. The constructor also takes a second String argument that specifies the mode of the file. Use the string r for a read-only file or rw for a read/write file.

```
try {
    RandomAccessFile users = new RandomAccessFile( "Users", "rw" )
 } catch (IOException e) { ... }
```

When you create a RandomAccessFile in read-only mode, Java tries to open the specified file. If the file doesn't exist, RandomAccessFile throws an IOException. If, however, you're creating a RandomAccessFile in read/write mode, the object creates the file if it doesn't exist. The constructor can still throw an IOException if another I/O error occurs, so you still need to handle this exception.

After you have created a RandomAccessFile, call any of the normal reading and writing methods, just as you would with a DataInputStream or DataOutputStream. If you try to write to a read-only file, the write method throws an IOException.

What makes a RandomAccessFile special is the seek() method. This method takes a long value and uses it to set the byte offset location for reading and writing in the file. You can use the getFilePointer() method to get the current location. If you need to append data to the end of the file, use length() to determine that location, then seek() to it. You can write or seek beyond the end of a file, but you can't read beyond the end of a file. The read() method throws an EOFException if you try to do this.

Here's an example of writing data for a simplistic database:

```
users.seek( userNum * RECORDSIZE );
users.writeUTF( userName );
users.writeInt( userID );
...
```

In this naive example, we assume that the String length for userName, along with any data that comes after it, fits within the specified record size.

Resource Paths

A big part of packaging and deploying an application is dealing with all of the resource files that must go with it, such as configuration files, graphics, and application data. Java provides several ways to access these resources. One way is to simply open files and read the bytes. Another is to construct a URL pointing to a well-known location in the filesystem or over the network. (We'll discuss working with URLs in detail in Chapter 14.) The problem with these methods is that they generally rely on knowledge of the application's location and packaging, which could change or break if it is moved. What is really needed is a universal way to access resources associated with our application, regardless of how it's installed. The `Class` class's `getResource()` method and the Java classpath provides just this. For example:

```
URL resource = MyApplication.class.getResource("/config/config.xml");
```

Instead of constructing a `File` reference to an absolute file path, or relying on composing information about an install directory, the `getResource()` method provides a standard way to get resources relative to the classpath of the application. A resource can be located either relative to a given class file or to the overall system classpath. `getResource()` uses the classloader that loads the application's class files to load the data. This means that no matter where the application classes reside—a web server, the local filesystem, or even inside a JAR file or other archive—we can load resources packaged with those classes consistently.

Although we haven't discussed URLs yet, we can tell you that many APIs for loading data (for example, images) accept a URL directly. If you're reading the data yourself, you can ask the URL for an `InputStream` with the URL `openStream()` method and treat it like any other stream. A convenience method called `getResourceAsStream()` skips this step for you and returns an `InputStream` directly.

`getResource()` takes as an argument a slash-separated *resource path* for the resource and returns a URL. There are two kinds of resource paths: absolute and relative. An absolute path begins with a slash (for example, */config/config.xml*). In this case, the search for the object begins at the "top" of the classpath. By the "top" of the classpath, we mean that Java looks within each element of the classpath (directory or JAR file) for the specified file. Given */config/config.xml*, it would check each directory or JAR file in the path for the file *config/config.xml*. In this case, the class on which `getResource()` is called doesn't matter as long as it's from a class loader that has the resource file in its classpath. For example:

```
URL data = AnyClass.getResource("/config/config.xml");
```

On the other hand, a relative URL does not begin with a slash (for example, *mydata.txt*). In this case, the search begins at the location of the class file on which `getResource()` is called. In other words, the path is relative to the package of the target class file. For example, if the class file *foo.bar.MyClass* is located at the path *foo/bar/*

MyClass.class in some directory or JAR of the classpath and the file *mydata.txt* is in the same directory (*foo/bar/mydata.txt*), we can request the file via *MyClass* with:

```
URL data = MyClass.getResource("mydata.txt");
```

In this case, the class and file come from the same logical directory. We say logical because the search is not limited to the classpath element from which the class was loaded. Instead, the same relative path is searched in each element of the classpath—just as with an absolute path—until it is found. Although we'd expect the file *mydata.txt* to be packaged physically with *MyClass.class*, it might be found in another JAR file or directory at the same relative and corresponding location.

For example, here's an application that looks up some resources:

```
package mypackage;
import java.net.URL;
import java.io.IOException;

public class FindResources {
  public static void main( String [] args ) throws IOException {
    // absolute from the classpath
    URL url = FindResources.class.getResource("/mypackage/foo.txt");
    // relative to the class location
    url = FindResources.class.getResource("foo.txt");
    // another relative document
    url = FindResources.class.getResource("docs/bar.txt");
  }
}
```

The `FindResources` class belongs to the `mypackage` package, so its class file will live in a *mypackage* directory somewhere on the classpath. `FindResources` locates the document *foo.txt* using an absolute and then a relative URL. At the end, `FindResources` uses a relative path to reach a document in the *mypackage/docs* directory. In each case, we refer to the `FindResources`'s `Class` object using the static `.class` notation. Alternatively, if we had an instance of the object, we could use its `getClass()` method to reach the `Class` object.

Again, `getResource()` returns a URL for whatever type of object you reference. This could be a text file or properties file that you want to read as a stream, or it might be an image or sound file or some other object. You can open a stream to the URL to parse the data yourself or hand the URL over to an API that deals with URLs. We discuss URLs in depth in Chapter 14. We should also emphasize that loading resources in this way completely shields your application from the details of how it is packaged or deployed. You may start with your application in loose files and then package it into a JAR file and the resources will still be loaded. Java applets (discussed in a later chapter) may even load files in this way over the network because the applet class loader treats the server as part of its classpath.

The NIO File API

We are now going to turn our attention from the original, "classic" Java File API to the new, NIO, File API introduced with Java 7. As we mentioned earlier, the NIO File API can be thought of as either a replacement for or a complement to the classic API. Included in the NIO package, the new API is nominally part of an effort to move Java toward a higher performance and more flexible style of I/O supporting *selectable* and asynchronously interruptable *channels*. However, in the context of working with files, the new API's strength is that it provides a fuller abstraction of the *filesystem* in Java.

In addition to better support for existing, real world, filesystem types—including for the first time the ability to copy and move files, manage links, and get detailed file attributes like owners and permissions—the new File API allows entirely new types of filesystems to be implemented directly in Java. The best example of this is the new ZIP filesystem provider that makes it possible to "mount" a ZIP archive file as a filesystem and work with the files within it directly using the standard APIs, just like any other filesystem. Additionally, the NIO File package provides some utilities that would have saved Java developers a lot of repeated code over the years, including directory tree change monitoring, filesystem traversal (a visitor pattern), filename "globbing," and convenience methods to read entire files directly into memory.

We'll cover the basic File API in this section and return to the NIO API again at the end of the chapter when we cover the full details of NIO buffers and channels. In particular, we'll talk about `ByteChannels` and `FileChannel`, which you can think of as alternate, buffer-oriented streams for reading and writing files and other types of data.

FileSystem and Path

The main players in the `java.nio.file` package are: the `FileSystem`, which represents an underlying storage mechanism and serves as a factory for `Path` objects; the `Path`, which represents a file or directory within the filesystem; and the `Files` utility, which contains a rich set of static methods for manipulating `Path` objects to perform all of the basic file operations analogous to the classic API.

The `FileSystems` (plural) class is our starting point. It is a factory for a `FileSystem` object:

```
// The default host computer filesystem
FileSystem fs = FileSystems.getDefault();

// A custom filesystem
URI zipURI = URI.create("jar:file:/Users/pat/tmp/MyArchive.zip");
FileSystem zipfs = FileSystems.newFileSystem( zipURI, env ) );
```

As shown in this snippet, often we'll simply ask for the default filesystem to manipulate files in the host computer's environment, as with the classic API. But the `FileSys` tems class can also construct a FileSystem by taking a URI (a special identifier) that references a custom filesystem type. We'll show an example of working with the ZIP filesystem provider later in this chapter when we discuss data compression.

FileSystem implements Closeable and when a FileSystem is closed, all open file channels and other streaming objects associated with it are closed as well. Attempting to read or write to those channels will throw an exception at that point. Note that the default filesystem (associated with the host computer) cannot be closed.

Once we have a FileSystem, we can use it as a factory for Path objects that represent files or directories. A Path can be constructed using a string representation just like the classic File, and subsequently used with methods of the Files utility to create, read, write, or delete the item.

```
Path fooPath = fs.getPath( "/tmp/foo.txt" );
OutputStream out = Files.newOutputStream( fooPath );
```

This example opens an OutputStream to write to the file *foo.txt*. By default, if the file does not exist, it will be created and if it does exist, it will be truncated (set to zero length) before new data is written—but you can change these results using options. We'll talk more about Files methods in the next section.

The Path object implements the java.lang.Iterable interface, which can be used to iterate through its literal path components (e.g., the slash separated "tmp" and "foo.txt" in the preceding snippet). Although if you want to traverse the path to find other files or directories, you might be more interested in the DirectoryStream and FileVisitor that we'll discuss later. Path also implements the java.nio.file.Watchable interface, which allows it to be monitored for changes. We'll also discuss watching file trees for changes in an upcoming section.

Path has convenience methods for resolving paths relative to a file or directory.

```
Path patPath =  fs.getPath( "/User/pat/" );

Path patTmp = patPath.resolve("tmp" ); // "/User/pat/tmp"

// Same as above, using a Path
Path tmpPath = fs.getPath( "tmp" );
Path patTmp = patPath.resolve( tmpPath ); // "/User/pat/tmp"

// Resolving a given absolute path against any path just yields given path
Path absPath = patPath.resolve( "/tmp" ); // "/tmp"

// Resolve sibling to Pat (same parent)
Path danPath = patPath.resolveSibling( "dan" ); // "/Users/dan"
```

In this snippet, we've shown the Pathresolve() and resolveSibling() methods used to find files or directories relative to a given Path object. The resolve() method is generally used to append a relative path to an existing Path representing a directory. If the argument provided to the `resolve()` method is an absolute path, it will just yield the absolute path (it acts kind of like the Unix or DOS "cd" command). The `resolveSibling()` method works the same way, but it is relative to the parent of the target `Path`; this method is useful for describing the target of a `move()` operation.

Path to classic file and back

To bridge the old and new APIs, corresponding `toPath()` and `toFile()` methods have been provided in `java.io.File` and `java.nio.file.Path`, respectively, to convert to the other form. Of course, the only types of `Paths` that can be produced from File are paths representing files and directories in the default host filesystem.

```
Path tmpPath = fs.getPath( "/tmp" );
File file = tmpPath.toFile();
File tmpFile = new File( "/tmp" );
Path path = tmpFile.toPath();
```

NIO File Operations

Once we have a `Path`, we can operate on it with static methods of the `Files` utility to create the path as a file or directory, read and write to it, and interrogate and set its properties. We'll list the bulk of them and then discuss some of the more important ones as we proceed.

The following table summarizes these methods of the `java.nio.file.Files` class. As you might expect, because the `Files` class handles all types of file operations, it contains a large number of methods. To make the table more readable, we have elided overloaded forms of the same method (those taking different kinds of arguments) and grouped corresponding and related types of methods together.

Table 12-2. NIO Files methods

Method	Return type	Description
`copy()`	long or `Path`	Copy a stream to a file path, file path to stream, or path to path. Returns the number of bytes copied or the target `Path`. A target file may optionally be replaced if it exists (the default is to fail if the target exists). Copying a directory results in an empty directory at the target (the contents are not copied). Copying a symbolic link copies the linked files data (producing a regular file copy).
`createDirectory()`, `createDirectories()`	`Path`	Create a single directory or all directories in a specified path. `createDirectory()` throws an exception if the directory already exists, whereas `createDirectories()` will ignore existing directories and only create as needed.

Method	Return type	Description
createFile()	Path	Creates an empty file. The operation is atomic and will only succeed if the file does not exist. (This property can be used to create flag files to guard resources, etc.)
createTempDirectory(), createTempFile()	Path	Create a temporary, guaranteed, uniquely named directory or file with the specified prefix. Optionally place it in the system default temp directory.
delete(), deleteIfExists()	void	Delete a file or an empty directory. deleteIfExists() will not throw an exception if the file does not exist.
exists(), notExists()	boolean	Determine whether the file exists (notExists() simply returns the opposite). Optionally specify whether links should be followed (by default they are).
exists(), isDirectory(), isExecutable(), isHidden(), isReadable(), isRegularFile(), isWriteable()	boolean	Tests basic file features: whether the path exists, is a directory, and other basic attributes.
createLink(), createSymbolicLink(), isSymbolicLink(), readSymbolicLink(), createLink()	boolean or Path	Create a hard or symbolic link, test to see if a file is a symbolic link, or read the target file pointed to by the symbolic link. Symbolic links are files that reference other files. Regular ("hard") links are low-level mirrors of a file where two filenames point to the same underlying data. If you don't know which to use, use a symbolic link.
getAttribute(), setAttribute(), getFileAttributeView(), readAttributes()	Object, Map, or FileAttributeView	Get or set filesystem-specific file attributes such as access and update times, detailed permissions, and owner information using implementation-specific names.
getFileStore()	FileStore	Get a FileStore object that represents the device, volume, or other type of partition of the filesystem on which the path resides.
getLastModifiedTime(), setLastModifiedTime()	FileTime or Path	Get or set the last modified time of a file or directory.
getOwner(), setOwner()	UserPrincipal	Get or set a UserPrincipal object representing the owner of the file. Use toString() or getName() to get a string representation of the user name.
getPosixFilePermissions(), setPosixFilePermissions()	Set or Path	Get or set the full POSIX user-group-other style read and write permissions for the path as a Set of PosixFilePermission enum values.

Method	Return type	Description
`isSameFile()`	boolean	Test to see whether the two paths reference the same file (which may potentially be true even if the paths are not identical).
`move()`	`Path`	Move a file or directory by renaming or copying it, optionally specifying whether to replace any existing target. Rename will be used unless a copy is required to move a file across file stores or filesystems. Directories can be moved using this method only if the simple rename is possible or if the directory is empty. If a directory move requires copying files across file stores or filesystems, the method throws an `IOException`. (In this case, you must copy the files yourself. See `walkFileTree()`.)
`newBufferedReader()`, `newBufferedWriter()`	`BufferedReader` or `BufferedWriter`	Open a file for reading via a `BufferedReader`, or create and open a file for writing via a `BufferedWriter`. In both cases, a character encoding is specified.
`newByteChannel()`	`SeekableByteChannel`	Create a new file or open an existing file as a seekable byte channel. (See the full discussion of NIO later in this chapter.) Consider using `FileChannelopen()` as an alternative.
`newDirectoryStream()`	`DirectoryStream`	Return a `DirectoryStream` for iterating over a directory hierarchy. Optionally, supply a glob pattern or filter object to match files.
`newInputStream()`, `newOutputStream()`	`InputStream` or `OutputStream`	Open a file for reading via an `InputStream` or create and open a file for writing via an `OuputStream`. Optionally, specify file truncation for the output stream; the default is to create a truncate on write.
`probeContentType()`	`String`	Returns the MIME type of the file if it can be determined by installed `FileTypeDetector` services or `null` if unknown.
`readAllBytes()`, `readAllLines()`	byte[] or `List<String>`	Read all data from the file as a byte [] or all characters as a list of strings using a specified character encoding.
`size()`	long	Get the size in bytes of the file at the specified path.
`walkFileTree()`	`Path`	Apply a `FileVisitor` to the specified directory tree, optionally specifying whether to follow links and a maximum depths of traversal.

Method	Return type	Description
write()	Path	Write an array of bytes or a collection of strings (with a specified character encoding) to the file at the specified path and close the file, optionally specifying append and truncation behavior. The default is to truncate and write the data.

With the preceding methods, we can fetch input or output streams or buffered readers and writers to a given file. We can also create paths as files and dirctories and iterate through file hierarchies. We'll discuss directory operations in the next section.

As a reminder, the `resolve()` and `resolveSibling()` methods of `Path` are useful for constructing targets for the `copy()` and `move()` operations.

```
// Move the file /tmp/foo.txt to /tmp/bar.txt
Path foo = fs.getPath("/tmp/foo.txt" );
Files.move( foo, foo.resolveSibling("bar.txt") );
```

For quickly reading and writing the contents of files without streaming, we can use the `read all` and `write` methods that move byte arrays or strings in and out of files in a single operation. These are very convenient for files that easily fit into memory.

```
// Read and write collection of String (e.g. lines of text)
Charset asciiCharset = Charset.forName("US-ASCII");
List<String> csvData = Files.readAllLines( csvPath, asciiCharset );
Files.write( newCSVPath, csvData, asciiCharset );

// Read and write bytes
byte [] data = Files.readAllBytes( dataPath );
Files.write( newDataPath, data );
```

Directory Operations

In addition to basic directory creation and manipulation methods of the `Files` class, there are methods for listing the files within a given directory and traversing all files and directories in a directory tree. To list the files in a single directory, we can use one of the `newDirectoryStream()` methods, which returns an iterable `DirectoryStream`.

```
// Print the files and directories in /tmp
try ( DirectoryStream<Path> paths = Files.newDirectoryStream(
    fs.getPath( "/tmp" ) ) ) {

    for ( Path path : paths ) { System.out.println( path ); }
}
```

The snippet lists the entries in "/tmp," iterating over the directory stream to print the results. Note that we open the `DirectoryStream` within a `try`-with-resources clause so that it is automatically closed for us. A `DirectoryStream` is implemented as a kind of one-way iterable that is analogous to a stream, and it must be closed to free up associated resources. The order in which the entries are returned is not defined by the API and you may need to store and sort them if ordering is required.

Another form of `newDirectoryStream()` takes a *glob pattern* to limit the files matched in the listing:

```
// Only files in /tmp matching "*.txt" (globbing)
try ( DirectoryStream<Path> paths = Files.newDirectoryStream(
    fs.getPath( "/tmp" ), "*.txt" ) ) {
    ...
```

File globbing filters filenames using the familiar "*" and a few other patterns to specify matching names. Table 12-3 provides some additional examples of file globbing patterns.

Table 12-3. File globbing pattern examples

Pattern	Example
*.txt	Filenames ending in ".txt"
*.{java,class}	Filenames ending in "java" or "class"
[a,b,c]*	Filenames starting with "a", "b", or "c"
[0-9]*	Filenames starting with the digits 0 through 9
[!0-9]*	Filenames starting with any character except 0 through 9
pass?.dat	Filenames starting with "pass" plus any character plus ".dat" (e.g., pass1.dat, passN.dat)

If globbing patterns are not sufficient, we can provide our own stream filter by implementing the `DirectoryStream.Filter` interface. The following snippet is the procedural (code) version of the "*.txt" glob pattern; matching filenames ending with ".txt". We've implemented the filter as an anonymous inner class here because it's short:

```
// Same as above using our own (anonymous) filter implementation
try ( DirectoryStream<Path> paths = Files.newDirectoryStream(
    fs.getPath( "/tmp" ),
    new DirectoryStream.Filter<Path>() {
        @Override
        public boolean accept( Path entry ) throws IOException {
            return entry.toString().endsWith( ".txt" );
        }
} ) ) {
    ...
```

Finally, if we need to iterate through a whole directory hierarchy instead of just a single directory, we can use a `FileVisitor`. The `FileswalkFileTree()` method takes a starting path and performs a depth-first traversal of the file hierarchy, giving the provided `FileVisitor` a chance to "visit" each path element in the tree. The following short snippet prints all file and directory names under the */Users/pat* path:

```
// Visit all of the files in a directory tree
Files.walkFileTree( fs.getPath( "/Users/pat"), new SimpleFileVisitor<Path>() {
```

```
        @Override
        public FileVisitResult visitFile( Path file, BasicFileAttributes attrs )
        {
            System.out.println( "path = " + file );
            return FileVisitResult.CONTINUE;
        }
    } );
```

For each entry in the file tree, our visitor's `visitFile()` method is invoked with the `Path` element and attributes as arguments. The visitor can perform any action it likes in relation to the file and then indicate whether or not the traversal should continue by returning one of a set of enumerated result types: `FileVisitResultCONTINUE` or `TERMINATE`. Here we have subclassed the `SimpleFileVisitor`, which is a convenience class that implements the methods of the `FileVisitor` interface for us with no-op (empty) bodies, allowing us to override only those of interest. Other methods available include `visitFileFailed()`, which is called if a file or directory cannot be visited (e.g., due to permissions), and the pair `preVisitDirectory()` and `postVisitDirectory()`, which can be used to perform actions before and after a new directory is visited. The `preVisitDirectory()` has additional usefulness in that it is allowed to return the value `SKIP_SUBTREE` to continue the traversal without descending into the target path and `SKIP_SIBLINGS` value, which indicates that traversal should continue, skipping the remaining entries at the same level as the target path.

As you can see, the file listing and traversal methods of the NIO File package are much more sophisticated than those of the classic `java.io` API and are a welcome addition.

Watching Paths

One of the nicest features of the NIO File API is the `WatchService`, which can monitor a `Path` for changes to any file or directory in the hierarchy. We can choose to receive events when files or directories are added, modified, or deleted. The following snippet watches for changes under the folder */Users/pat*:

```
    Path watchPath = fs.getPath("/Users/pat");
    WatchService watchService = fs.newWatchService();
    watchPath.register( watchService, ENTRY_CREATE, ENTRY_MODIFY, ENTRY_DELETE );

    while( true )
    {
        WatchKey changeKey = watchService.take();
        List<WatchEvent<?>> watchEvents = changeKey.pollEvents();
        for ( WatchEvent<?> watchEvent : watchEvents )
        {
            // Ours are all Path type events:
            WatchEvent<Path> pathEvent = (WatchEvent<Path>)watchEvent;

            Path path = pathEvent.context();
            WatchEvent.Kind<Path> eventKind = pathEvent.kind();
```

```
            System.out.println( eventKind + " for path: " + path );
        }

        changeKey.reset(); // Important!
    }
```

We construct a WatchService from a FileSystem using the newWatchService() call. Thereafter, we can register a Watchable object with the service (currently, Path is the only type of Watchable) and poll it for events. As shown, in actuality the API is the other way around and we call the watchable object's register() method, passing it the watch service and a variable length argument list of enumerated values representing the event types of interest: ENTRY_CREATE, ENTRY_MODIFY, or ENTRY_DELETE. One additonal type, OVERFLOW, can be registered in order to get events that indicate when the host implementation has been too slow to process all changes and some changes may have been lost.

After we are set up, we can poll for changes using the watch service take() method, which returns a WatchKey object. The take() method blocks until an event occurs; another form, poll(), is nonblocking. When we have a WatchKey containing events, we can retrieve them with the pollEvents() method. The API is, again, a bit awkward here as WatchEvent is a generic type parameterized on the kind of Watchable object. In our case, the only types possible are Path type events and so we cast as needed. The type of event (create, modify, delete) is indicated by the WatchEventkind() method and the changed path is indicated by the context() method. Finally, it's important that we call reset() on the WatchKey object in order to clear the events and be able to receive further updates.

Performance of the WatchService depends greatly on implementation. On many systems, filesystem monitoring is built into the operating system and we can get change events almost instantly. But in many cases, Java may fall back on its generic, background thread-based implementation of the watch service, which is very slow to detect changes. At the time of this writing, for example, Java 7 on Mac OS X does not take advantage of the OS-level file monitoring and instead uses the slow, generic polling service.

Serialization

Using a DataOutputStream, you could write an application that saves the data content of your objects one at a time as simple types. However, Java provides an even more powerful mechanism called object serialization that does almost all the work for you. In its simplest form, *object serialization* is an automatic way to save and load the state of an object. However, object serialization has greater depths that we cannot plumb within the scope of this book, including complete control over the serialization process and interesting twists such as class versioning.

Basically, an instance of any class that implements the `Serializable` interface can be saved to and restored from a stream. The stream subclasses, `ObjectInputStream` and `ObjectOutputStream`, are used to serialize primitive types and objects. Subclasses of `Serializable` classes are also serializable. The default serialization mechanism saves the value of all of the object's fields (public and private), except those that are static and those marked *transient*.

One of the most important (and tricky) things about serialization is that when an object is serialized, any object references it contains are also serialized. Serialization can capture entire "graphs" of interconnected objects and put them back together on the receiving end (we'll demonstrate this in an upcoming example). The implication is that any object we serialize must contain only references to other `Serializable` objects. We can prune the tree and limit the extent of what is serialized by marking nonserializable variables as `transient` or overriding the default serialization mechanisms. The `transient` modifier can be applied to any instance variable to indicate that its contents are not useful outside of the current context and should not be saved.

In the following example, we create a `Hashtable` and write it to a disk file called *hash.ser*. The `Hashtable` object is already serializable because it implements the `Serializable` interface.

```
import java.io.*;
import java.util.*;

public class Save {
  public static void main(String[] args) {
    Hashtable hash = new Hashtable();
    hash.put("string", "Gabriel Garcia Marquez");
    hash.put("int", new Integer(26));
    hash.put("double", new Double(Math.PI));

    try {
      FileOutputStream fileOut = new FileOutputStream( "hash.ser" );
      ObjectOutputStream out = new ObjectOutputStream( fileOut );
      out.writeObject( hash );
      out.close();
    }
    catch (Exception e) {
      System.out.println(e);
    }
  }
}
```

First, we construct a `Hashtable` with a few elements in it. Then, in the lines of code inside the `try` block, we write the `Hashtable` to a file called *hash.ser*, using the `writeObject()` method of `ObjectOutputStream`. The `ObjectOutputStream` class is a lot like the `DataOutputStream` class, except that it includes the powerful `writeObject()`method.

The Hashtable that we created has internal references to the items it contains. Thus, these components are automatically serialized along with the Hashtable. We'll see this in the next example when we deserialize the Hashtable.

```
import java.io.*;
import java.util.*;

public class Load {
  public static void main(String[] args) {
    try {
      FileInputStream fileIn = new FileInputStream("hash.ser");
      ObjectInputStream in = new ObjectInputStream(fileIn);
      Hashtable hash = (Hashtable)in.readObject();
      System.out.println( hash.toString() );
    }
    catch (Exception e) {
      System.out.println(e);
    }
  }
}
```

In this example, we read the Hashtable from the *hash.ser* file, using the readObject() method of ObjectInputStream. The ObjectInputStream class is a lot like DataInputStream, except that it includes the readObject() method. The return type of readObject() is Object, so we need to cast it to a Hashtable. Finally, we print the contents of the Hashtable using its toString() method.

Initialization with readObject()

Often, simple deserialization alone is not enough to reconstruct the full state of an object. For example, the object may have had transient fields representing state that could not be serialized, such as network connections, event registration, or decoded image data. Objects have an opportunity to do their own setup after deserialization by implementing a special method named readObject().

Not to be confused with the readObject() method of the ObjectInputStream, this method is implemented by the serializable object itself. To be recognized and used, the readObject() method must have a specific signature, and it must be private. The following snippet is taken from an animated JavaBean that we'll talk about in Chapter 22:

```
private void readObject(ObjectInputStream s)
    throws IOException, ClassNotFoundException
{
    s.defaultReadObject();
    initialize();
    if ( isRunning )
        start();
}
```

When the `readObject()` method with this signature exists in an object, it is called during the deserialization process. The argument to the method is the `ObjectInputStream` doing the object construction. We delegate to its `defaultReadObject()` method to do the normal deserialization from the stream and then do our custom setup. In this case, we call one of our methods named `initialize()` and, depending on our state, a method called `start()`.

Using a custom implementation of `readObject()` and a corresponding `writeObject()` method, we could take complete control of the serialized form of the object by reading and writing to the stream using lower-level write operations (bytes, strings, etc.) instead of delegating to the default implementation as we did before.

We'll talk a little more about serialization in Chapter 22 when we discuss JavaBeans.

SerialVersionUID

Java object serialization was designed to accommodate certain kinds of *compatible class changes* or evolution in the structure of classes. For example, changing the methods of a class does not necessarily mean that its serialized representation must change because only the data of variables is stored. Nor would simply adding a new field to a class necessarily prohibit us from loading an old serialized version of the class. We could simply allow the new variable to take its default value. By default, however, Java is very picky and errs on the side of caution. If you make any kind of change to the structure of your class, by default you'll get an `InvalidClassException` when trying to read previously serialized forms of the class.

Java detects these versions by performing a hash function on the structure of the class and storing a 64-bit value called the *Serial Version UID* (SUID), along with the serialized data. It can then compare the hash to the class when it is loaded.

Java allows us to take control of this process by looking for a special, magic field in our classes that looks like the following:

```
static final long serialVersionUID = -6849794470754667710L;
```

(The value is, of course, different for every class.) If it finds this static `serialVersionUID` `long` field in the class, it uses its value instead of performing the hash on the class. This value will be written out with serialized versions of the class and used for comparison when they are deserialized. This means that we are now in control of which versions of the class are compatible with which serialized representations. For example, we can create our serializable class from the beginning with our own SUID and then only increment it if we make a truly incompatible change and want to prevent older forms of the class from being loaded:

```
class MyDataObject implements Serializable {
    static final long serialVersionUID = 1; // Version 1
```

```
    ...
}
```

A utility called *serialver* that comes with the JDK allows you to calculate the hash that Java would otherwise use for the class. This is necessary if you did not plan ahead and already have serialized objects stored and need to modify the class afterward. Running the *serialver* command on the class displays the SUID that is necessary to match the value already stored:

```
% serialver SomeObject

static final long serialVersionUID = -6849794470754667710L;
```

By placing this value into your class, you can "freeze" the SUID at the specified value, allowing the class to change without affecting versioning.

Data Compression

The `java.util.zip` package contains classes you can use for data compression in streams or files. The classes in the `java.util.zip` package support two widespread compression formats: GZIP and ZIP. In this section, we'll talk about how to use these classes. We'll also present two useful example programs that build on what you have learned in this chapter. After that, we'll talk about a higher-level way to work with ZIP archives—as filesystems—introduced with Java 7.

Archives and Compressed Data

The `java.util.zip` package provides two filter streams for writing compressed data. The `GZIPOutputStream` is for writing data in GZIP compressed format. The `ZIPOutputStream` is for writing compressed ZIP archives, which can contain one or many files. To write compressed data in the GZIP format, simply wrap a `GZIPOutputStream` around an underlying stream and write to it. The following is a complete example that shows how to compress a file using the GZIP format, but the stream could just as well be sent over a network connection or to any other type of stream destination. Our `GZip` example is a command line utility that compresses a file.

```
import java.io.*;
import java.util.zip.*;

public class GZip {
  public static int sChunk = 8192;

  public static void main(String[] args) {
    if (args.length != 1) {
      System.out.println("Usage: GZip source");
      return;
    }
    // create output stream
```

```
      String zipname = args[0] + ".gz";
      GZIPOutputStream zipout;
      try {
        FileOutputStream out = new FileOutputStream(zipname);
        zipout = new GZIPOutputStream(out);
      }
      catch (IOException e) {
        System.out.println("Couldn't create " + zipname + ".");
        return;
      }
      byte[] buffer = new byte[sChunk];
      // compress the file
      try {
        FileInputStream in = new FileInputStream(args[0]);
        int length;
        while ((length = in.read(buffer, 0, sChunk)) != -1)
          zipout.write(buffer, 0, length);
        in.close();
      }
      catch (IOException e) {
        System.out.println("Couldn't compress " + args[0] + ".");
      }
      try { zipout.close(); }
      catch (IOException e) {}
    }
  }
```

First, we check to make sure we have a command-line argument representing a filename. We then construct a `GZIPOutputStream` wrapped around a `FileOutputStream` representing the given filename, with the *.gz* suffix appended. With this in place, we open the source file. We read chunks of data and write them into the `GZIPOutputStream`. Finally, we clean up by closing our open streams.

Zip archives

While GZIP is simple compression format for a stream or file, a ZIP archive is a file that is actually a collection of files, some (or all) of which may be compressed. Writing data to a ZIP archive file is a little more involved than simply wrapping a stream, but not difficult. Each item in the ZIP file is represented by a `ZipEntry` object. When writing to a `ZipOutputStream`, you'll need to call `putNextEntry()` before writing the data for each item. The following example shows how to create a `ZipOutputStream`. You'll notice that it starts out with a stream wrapper just like it did when creating a `GZIPOutputStream`:

```
  ZipOutputStream zipout;
  try {
    FileOutputStream out = new FileOutputStream("archive.zip");
    zipout = new ZipOutputStream(out);
  }
  catch (IOException e) {}
```

Let's say we have two files we want to write into this archive. Before we begin writing, we need to call `putNextEntry()` to set the name of the file within the archive and initialize the stream to the correct position for it. Here we create a simple ZipEntry with just a file name. You can set other ZIP format specific fields in `ZipEntry`, but most of the time, you won't need to bother with them.

```
try {
  ZipEntry entry = new ZipEntry("first.dat");
  zipout.putNextEntry(entry);
  zipout.write( ... ) // Write data for first file

  ZipEntry entry = new ZipEntry("second.dat");
  zipout.putNextEntry(entry);
  zipout.write( ... ) // Write data for second file
  . . .
  zipout.close();
}
catch (IOException e) {}
```

Decompressing Data

To decompress data in the GZIP format, simply wrap a `GZIPInputStream` around an underlying `FileInputStream` and read from it. The following example complements our earlier `GZip` example and shows how to decompress a GZIP file:

```
import java.io.*;
import java.util.zip.*;

public class GUnzip {
  public static int sChunk = 8192;
  public static void main(String[] args) {
    if (args.length != 1) {
      System.out.println("Usage: GUnzip source");
      return;
    }
    // create input stream
    String zipname, source;
    if (args[0].endsWith(".gz")) {
      zipname = args[0];
      source = args[0].substring(0, args[0].length() - 3);
    }
    else {
      zipname = args[0] + ".gz";
      source = args[0];
    }
    GZIPInputStream zipin;
    try {
      FileInputStream in = new FileInputStream(zipname);
      zipin = new GZIPInputStream(in);
    }
    catch (IOException e) {
```

```
        System.out.println("Couldn't open " + zipname + ".");
        return;
      }
      byte[] buffer = new byte[sChunk];
      // decompress the file
      try {
        FileOutputStream out = new FileOutputStream(source);
        int length;
        while ((length = zipin.read(buffer, 0, sChunk)) != -1)
          out.write(buffer, 0, length);
        out.close();
      }
      catch (IOException e) {
        System.out.println("Couldn't decompress " + args[0] + ".");
      }
      try { zipin.close(); }
      catch (IOException e) {}
    }
  }
```

First, we check to make sure we have a command-line argument representing a filename. If the argument ends with *.gz*, we figure out what the filename for the uncompressed file should be. Otherwise, we use the given argument and assume the compressed file has the *.gz* suffix. Then we construct a `GZIPInputStream` wrapped around a `FileInputStream` that represents the compressed file. With this in place, we open the target file. We read chunks of data from the `GZIPInputStream` and write them into the target file. Finally, we clean up by closing our open streams.

Reading a ZIP archive is also the mirror of writing. When reading from a `ZipInputStream`, you should call `getNextEntry()` before reading each item. When `getNextEntry()` returns `null`, there are no more items to read. The following example shows how to create a `ZipInputStream`:

```
ZipInputStream zipin;
try {
  FileInputStream in = new FileInputStream("archive.zip");
  zipin = new ZipInputStream(in);
}
catch (IOException e) {}
```

Suppose we want to read two files from this archive. Before we begin reading, we need to call `getNextEntry()`. At the very least, the entry gives us a name of the item we are reading from the archive:

```
try {
  ZipEntry first = zipin.getNextEntry();
  zipin.read( ... ) // Read the file data
} catch (IOException e) {}
```

Now, you can read the contents of the first item in the archive. When you come to the end of the item, the `read()` method returns `-1`. At this point, you can call getNextEntry() again to read the second item from the archive. If you call getNextEntry() and it returns null, there are no more items and you have reached the end of the archive.

Zip Archive As a Filesystem

One of the benefits of the new java.nio.file package introduce with Java 7 is the ability to implement custom filesystems in Java. (We talked about the File API for the NIO file package earlier in this chapter and we'll return to the more general NIO facilities in the next section.) Java 7 ships with one such custom filesystem implementation bundled within it: the Zip Filesystem Provider.[2] Using the Zip Filesystem Provider, we can open a ZIP archive and treat it like a filesystem: reading, writing, copying, and renaming files using all of the standard java.nio.file APIs, except that all of these operations happen inside the ZIP archive file instead of on the host computer filesystem (as you might otherwise expect).

The key to making this possible is that the NIO File API starts with a FileSystem abstraction that serves as a factory for Path objects. In our previous discussion of the NIO File API we always simply asked for the default filesystem using Filesystems.getDefault(). This time, we are going to target a particular custom filesystem type and destination by constructing a special URI for our ZIP archive. (As we'll discuss in the networking chapters, a URI is kind of like a URL except that it can be more abstract).

```
// Construct the URI pointing to the ZIP archive
URI zipURI = URI.create("jar:file:/Users/pat/tmp/MyArchive.zip");

// Open or create it and write a file
Map<String, String> env = new HashMap<>();
env.put("create", "true");
try ( FileSystem zipfs = FileSystems.newFileSystem( zipURI, env ) )
{
    Path path = zipfs.getPath("/README.txt");
    OutputStream out = Files.newOutputStream( path );
    try ( PrintWriter pw = new PrintWriter(
        new OutputStreamWriter( out ) ) ) {

        pw.println("Hello World!");
    }
}
```

In this snippet, we constructed a URI for our ZIP archive using the URIcreate() method and the special *jar:file:* prefix. (The Java JAR format is really just the ZIP format with some additional conventions.) We then used that URI with the Filesystems newFile

2. The Zip Filesystem Provider is also supplied as an example along with sample source code even though it's unclear if Oracle intends it to be a standard. But at the time of this writing, it is bundled with the JDK and JRE of Java 7 on all platforms.

`System()` method to create the right kind of filesystem reference for us. The `FileSystem` it returns will perform all of its operations on entries within the ZIP, but otherwise will behave just like we've seen previously. The other argument to the `newFileSystem()` method is a `Map` containing string properties that are specific to the provider. In this case, we pass in the value "create" as "true," indicating that we want the ZIP filesystem provider to create the archive if it does not already exist. In order to know what properties can be passed, you'll have to consult the documentation for the particular filesystem provider.

In our preceding snippet, we then create a `Path` for a file */README.txt* at the root folder of the filesystem and write a string to it. Because we are using `try`-with-resources clauses to encapsulate opening the filesystem and writing to the file, the resources will be automatically closed for us when the operation is complete.

Other operations proceed just as with "normal" files. For example, we can move a file by creating a path for the existing file and a path for the new location and then using the standard `Files move()` method.

```
// Move the file
try ( FileSystem zipfs = FileSystems.newFileSystem( fsURI, env ) )
{
    Path path = zipfs.getPath("/README.txt");
    Path toPath = zipfs.getPath("/README2.txt");
    Files.move( path, toPath );
}
```

The NIO Package

We are now going to complete our introduction to core Java I/O facilities by returning to the `java.nio` package. The name NIO stands for "New I/O" and, as we saw earlier in this chapter in our discussion of `java.nio.file`, one aspect of NIO is simply to update and enhance features of the legacy `java.io` package. Much of the general NIO functionality does indeed overlap with existing APIs. However, NIO was first introduced to address specific issues of scalability for large systems, especially in networked applications. The following section outlines the basic elements of NIO, which center on working with *buffers* and *channels*.

Asynchronous I/O

Most of the need for the NIO package was driven by the desire to add *nonblocking* and *selectable* I/O to Java. Prior to NIO, most read and write operations in Java were bound to threads and were forced to block for unpredictable amounts of time. Although certain APIs such as Sockets (which we'll see in Chapter 13) provided specific means to limit how long an I/O call could take, this was a workaround to compensate for the lack of a more general mechanism. In many languages, even those without threading, I/O could still be done efficiently by setting I/O streams to a nonblocking mode and testing them for their readiness to send or receive data. In a nonblocking mode, a read or write does only as much work as can be done immediately—filling or emptying a buffer and then returning. Combined with the ability to test for readiness, this allows a single-threaded application to continuously service many channels efficiently. The main thread "selects" a stream that is ready and works with it until it blocks and then moves on to another. On a single-processor system, this is fundamentally equivalent to using multiple threads. It turns out that this style of processing has scalability advantages even when using a pool of threads (rather than just one). We'll discuss this in detail in Chapter 13when we discuss networking and building servers that can handle many clients simultaneously.

In addition to nonblocking and selectable I/O, the NIO package enables closing and interrupting I/O operations asynchronously. As discussed in Chapter 9, prior to NIO there was no reliable way to stop or wake up a thread blocked in an I/O operation. With NIO, threads blocked in I/O operations always wake up when interrupted or when the channel is closed by anyone. Additionally, if you interrupt a thread while it is blocked in an NIO operation, its channel is automatically closed. (Closing the channel because the thread is interrupted might seem too strong, but usually it's the right thing to do.)

Performance

Channel I/O is designed around the concept of *buffers*, which are a sophisticated form of array, tailored to working with communications. The NIO package supports the concept of *direct buffers*—buffers that maintain their memory outside the Java VM in the host operating system. Because all real I/O operations ultimately have to work with the host OS by maintaining the buffer space there, some operations can be made much more efficient. Data moving between two external endpoints can be transferred without first copying it into Java and back out.

Mapped and Locked Files

NIO provides two general-purpose file-related features not found in `java.io`: memory-mapped files and file locking. We'll discuss memory-mapped files later, but suffice it to say that they allow you to work with file data as if it were all magically resident in memory. File locking supports the concept of shared and exclusive locks on regions of files—useful for concurrent access by multiple applications.

Channels

While `java.io` deals with streams, `java.nio` works with channels. A *channel* is an endpoint for communication. Although in practice channels are similar to streams, the underlying notion of a channel is more abstract and primitive. Whereas streams in `java.io` are defined in terms of input or output with methods to read and write bytes, the basic channel interface says nothing about how communications happen. It simply has the notion of being open or closed, supported via the methods `isOpen()` and `close()`. Implementations of channels for files, network sockets, or arbitrary devices then add their own methods for operations, such as reading, writing, or transferring data. The following channels are provided by NIO:

- `FileChannel`
- `Pipe.SinkChannel`, `Pipe.SourceChannel`
- `SocketChannel`, `ServerSocketChannel`, `DatagramChannel`

We'll cover `FileChannel` in this chapter. The `Pipe` channels are simply the channel equivalents of the `java.io Pipe` facilities. We'll talk about `Socket` and `Datagram` channels in Chapter 13. Additionally, in Java 7 there are now asynchronous versions of both the file and socket channels: `AsynchronousFileChannel`, `AsynchronousSocketChannel`, `AsynchronousServerSocketChannel`, and `AsynchronousDatagramChannel`. These asynchronous versions essentially buffer all of their operations through a thread pool and report results back through an asynchronous API. We'll talk about the asynchronous file channel later in this chapter.

All these basic channels implement the `ByteChannel` interface, designed for channels that have read and write methods like I/O streams. `ByteChannel`s read and write `ByteBuffer`s, however, as opposed to plain byte arrays.

In addition to these channel implementations, you can bridge channels with `java.io` I/O streams and readers and writers for interoperability. However, if you mix these features, you may not get the full benefits and performance offered by the NIO package.

Buffers

Most of the utilities of the `java.io` and `java.net` packages operate on byte arrays. The corresponding tools of the NIO package are built around `ByteBuffer`s (with character-based buffer `CharBuffer` for text). Byte arrays are simple, so why are buffers necessary? They serve several purposes:

- They formalize the usage patterns for buffered data, provide for things like read-only buffers, and keep track of read/write positions and limits within a large buffer space. They also provide a mark/reset facility like that of `java.io.BufferedInputStream`.
- They provide additional APIs for working with raw data representing primitive types. You can create buffers that "view" your byte data as a series of larger primitives, such as `short`s, `int`s, or `float`s. The most general type of data buffer, `ByteBuffer`, includes methods that let you read and write all primitive types just like `DataOutputStream` does for streams.

- They abstract the underlying storage of the data, allowing for special optimizations by Java. Specifically, buffers may be allocated as direct buffers that use native buffers of the host operating system instead of arrays in Java's memory. The NIO `Channel` facilities that work with buffers can recognize direct buffers automatically and try to optimize I/O to use them. For example, a read from a file channel into a Java byte array normally requires Java to copy the data for the read from the host operating system into Java's memory. With a direct buffer, the data can remain in the host operating system, outside Java's normal memory space until and unless it is needed.

Buffer operations

A buffer is a subclass of a `java.nio.Buffer` object. The base `Buffer` class is something like an array with state. It does not specify what type of elements it holds (that is for subtypes to decide), but it does define functionality that is common to all data buffers. A `Buffer` has a fixed size called its *capacity*. Although all the standard `Buffers` provide "random access" to their contents, a `Buffer` generally expects to be read and written sequentially, so `Buffers` maintain the notion of a *position* where the next element is read or written. In addition to position, a `Buffer` can maintain two other pieces of state information: a *limit*, which is a position that is a "soft" limit to the extent of a read or write, and a *mark*, which can be used to remember an earlier position for future recall.

Implementations of `Buffer` add specific, typed get and put methods that read and write the buffer contents. For example, `ByteBuffer` is a buffer of bytes and it has `get()` and `put()` methods that read and write bytes and arrays of bytes (along with many other useful methods we'll discuss later). Getting from and putting to the `Buffer` changes the position marker, so the `Buffer` keeps track of its contents somewhat like a stream. Attempting to read or write past the limit marker generates a `BufferUnderflowException` or `BufferOverflowException`, respectively.

The mark, position, limit, and capacity values always obey the following formula:

```
mark <= position <= limit <= capacity
```

The position for reading and writing the `Buffer` is always between the mark, which serves as a lower bound, and the limit, which serves as an upper bound. The capacity represents the physical extent of the buffer space.

You can set the position and limit markers explicitly with the `position()` and `limit()` methods. Several convenience methods are provided for common usage patterns. The `reset()` method sets the position back to the mark. If no mark has been set, an `InvalidMarkException` is thrown. The `clear()` method resets the position to `0` and makes the limit the capacity, readying the buffer for new data (the mark is discarded). Note that the `clear()` method does not actually do anything to the data in the buffer; it simply changes the position markers.

The `flip()` method is used for the common pattern of writing data into the buffer and then reading it back out. `flip` makes the current position the limit and then resets the current position to `0` (any mark is thrown away), which saves having to keep track of how much data was read. Another method, `rewind()`, simply resets the position to `0`, leaving the limit alone. You might use it to write the same size data again. Here is a snippet of code that uses these methods to read data from a channel and write it to two channels:

```
ByteBuffer buff = ...
while ( inChannel.read( buff ) > 0 ) { // position = ?
    buff.flip();    // limit = position; position = 0;
    outChannel.write( buff );
    buff.rewind();  // position = 0
    outChannel2.write( buff );
    buff.clear();   // position = 0; limit = capacity
}
```

This might be confusing the first time you look at it because here, the read from the `Channel` is actually a write to the `Buffer` and vice versa. Because this example writes all the available data up to the limit, either `flip()` or `rewind()` have the same effect in this case.

Buffer types

As stated earlier, various buffer types add get and put methods for reading and writing specific data types. Each of the Java primitive types has an associated buffer type: `ByteBuffer`, `CharBuffer`, `ShortBuffer`, `IntBuffer`, `LongBuffer`, `FloatBuffer`, and `DoubleBuffer`. Each provides get and put methods for reading and writing its type and arrays of its type. Of these, `ByteBuffer` is the most flexible. Because it has the "finest grain" of all the buffers, it has been given a full complement of get and put methods for reading and writing all the other data types as well as `byte`. Here are some `ByteBuffer` methods:

```
byte get()
char getChar()
short getShort()
int getInt()
long getLong()
float getFloat()
double getDouble()

void put(byte b)
void put(ByteBuffer src)
void put(byte[] src, int offset, int length)
void put(byte[] src)
void putChar(char value)
void putShort(short value)
void putInt(int value)
void putLong(long value)
```

```
void putFloat(float value)
void putDouble(double value)
```

As we said, all the standard buffers also support random access. For each of the aforementioned methods of `ByteBuffer`, an additional form takes an index; for example:

```
getLong( int index )
putLong( int index, long value )
```

But that's not all. `ByteBuffer` can also provide "views" of itself as any of the coarse-grained types. For example, you can fetch a `ShortBuffer` view of a `ByteBuffer` with the `asShortBuffer()` method. The `ShortBuffer` view is *backed* by the `ByteBuffer`, which means that they work on the same data, and changes to either one affect the other. The view buffer's extent starts at the `ByteBuffer`'s current position, and its capacity is a function of the remaining number of bytes, divided by the new type's size. (For example, `short`s consume two bytes each, `float`s four, and `long`s and `double`s take eight.) View buffers are convenient for reading and writing large blocks of a contiguous type within a `ByteBuffer`.

`CharBuffer`s are interesting as well, primarily because of their integration with `String`s. Both `CharBuffer`s and `String`s implement the `java.lang.CharSequence` interface. This is the interface that provides the standard `charAt()` and `length()` methods. Because of this, newer APIs (such as the `java.util.regex` package) allow you to use a `CharBuffer` or a `String` interchangeably. In this case, the `CharBuffer` acts like a modifiable `String` with user-configurable, logical start and end positions.

Byte order

Because we're talking about reading and writing types larger than a byte, the question arises: in what order do the bytes of multibyte values (e.g., `short`s and `int`s) get written? There are two camps in this world: "big endian" and "little endian."[3] Big endian means that the most significant bytes come first; little endian is the reverse. If you're writing binary data for consumption by some native application, this is important. Intel-compatible computers use little endian, and many workstations that run Unix use big endian. The `ByteOrder` class encapsulates the choice. You can specify the byte order to use with the `ByteBuffer order()` method, using the identifiers `ByteOrder.BIG_ENDIAN` and `ByteOrder.LITTLE_ENDIAN` like so:

```
byteArray.order( ByteOrder.BIG_ENDIAN );
```

You can retrieve the native ordering for your platform using the static `ByteOrder.nativeOrder()` method. (I know you're curious.)

3. The terms *big endian* and *little endian* come from Jonathan Swift's novel *Gulliver's Travels*, where it denoted two camps of Lilliputians: those who eat their eggs from the big end and those who eat them from the little end.

Allocating buffers

You can create a buffer either by allocating it explicitly using `allocate()` or by wrapping an existing plain Java array type. Each buffer type has a static `allocate()` method that takes a capacity (size) and also a `wrap()` method that takes an existing array:

```
CharBuffer cbuf = CharBuffer.allocate( 64*1024 );
```

A direct buffer is allocated in the same way, with the `allocateDirect()` method:

```
ByteBuffer bbuf = ByteBuffer.allocateDirect( 64*1024 );
ByteBuffer bbuf2 = ByteBuffer.wrap( someExistingArray );
```

As we described earlier, direct buffers can use operating system memory structures that are optimized for use with some kinds of I/O operations. The tradeoff is that allocating a direct buffer is a little slower and heavier weight operation than a plain buffer, so you should try to use them for longer-term buffers.

Character Encoders and Decoders

Character encoders and decoders turn characters into raw bytes and vice versa, mapping from the Unicode standard to particular encoding schemes. Encoders and decoders have long existed in Java for use by `Reader` and `Writer` streams and in the methods of the `String` class that work with byte arrays. However, early on there was no API for working with encoding explicitly; you simply referred to encoders and decoders wherever necessary by name as a `String`. The `java.nio.charset` package formalized the idea of a Unicode character set encoding with the `Charset` class.

The `Charset` class is a factory for `Charset` instances, which know how to encode character buffers to byte buffers and decode byte buffers to character buffers. You can look up a character set by name with the static `Charset.forName()` method and use it in conversions:

```
Charset charset = Charset.forName("US-ASCII");
CharBuffer charBuff = charset.decode( byteBuff );  // to ascii
ByteBuffer byteBuff = charset.encode( charBuff );  // and back
```

You can also test to see if an encoding is available with the static `Charset.isSupported()` method.

The following character sets are guaranteed to be supplied:

- US-ASCII
- ISO-8859-1
- UTF-8
- UTF-16BE
- UTF-16LE

- UTF-16

You can list all the encoders available on your platform using the static `availableCharsets()` method:

```
Map map = Charset.availableCharsets();
Iterator it = map.keySet().iterator();
while ( it.hasNext() )
    System.out.println( it.next() );
```

The result of `availableCharsets()` is a map because character sets may have "aliases" and appear under more than one name.

In addition to the buffer-oriented classes of the `java.nio` package, the `InputStreamReader` and `OutputStreamWriter` bridge classes of the `java.io` package have been updated to work with `Charset` as well. You can specify the encoding as a `Charset` object or by name.

CharsetEncoder and CharsetDecoder

You can get more control over the encoding and decoding process by creating an instance of `CharsetEncoder` or `CharsetDecoder` (a codec) with the `Charset newEncoder()` and `newDecoder()` methods. In the previous snippet, we assumed that all the data was available in a single buffer. More often, however, we might have to process data as it arrives in chunks. The encoder/decoder API allows for this by providing more general `encode()` and `decode()` methods that take a flag specifying whether more data is expected. The codec needs to know this because it might have been left hanging in the middle of a multibyte character conversion when the data ran out. If it knows that more data is coming, it does not throw an error on this incomplete conversion. In the following snippet, we use a decoder to read from a `ByteBuffer bbuff` and accumulate character data into a `CharBuffer cbuff`:

```
CharsetDecoder decoder = Charset.forName("US-ASCII").newDecoder();

boolean done = false;
while ( !done ) {
    bbuff.clear();
    done = ( in.read( bbuff ) == -1 );
    bbuff.flip();
    decoder.decode( bbuff, cbuff, done );
}
cbuff.flip();
// use cbuff. . .
```

Here, we look for the end of input condition on the `in` channel to set the flag `done`. Note that we take advantage of the `flip()` method on `ByteBuffer` to set the limit to the amount of data read and reset the position, setting us up for the decode operation in one step. The `encode()` and `decode()` methods also return a result object, `CoderResult`, that can determine the progress of encoding (we do not use it in the previous snippet). The methods `isError()`, `isUnderflow()`, and `isOverflow()` on the `CoderResult` specify why encoding stopped: for an error, a lack of bytes on the input buffer, or a full output buffer, respectively.

FileChannel

Now that we've covered the basics of channels and buffers, it's time to look at a real channel type. The `FileChannel` is the NIO equivalent of the `java.io.RandomAccessFile` , but it provides several core new features in addition to some performance optimizations. In particular, use a `FileChannel` in place of a plain `java.io` file stream if you wish to use file locking, memory-mapped file access, or highly optimized data transfer between files or between file and network channels.

A `FileChannel` can be created for a `Path` using the static `FileChannelopen()` method.

```
FileSystem fs = FileSystems.getDefault();
Path p = fs.getPath( "/tmp/foo.txt" );

// Open default for reading
try ( FileChannel channel = FileChannel.open(( p ) ) {
    ...
}

// Open with options for writing
import static java.nio.file.StandardOpenOption.*;

try ( FileChannel channel = FileChannel.open( p, WRITE, APPEND, ... ) ) {
    ...
}
```

By default, `open()` creates a read-only channel for the file. We can open a channel for writing or appending and control other more advanced features such as atomic create and data syncing by passing additional options as shown in the second part of the previous example. Table 12-4 summarizes these options.

Table 12-4. java.nio.file.StandardOpenOption

Option	Description
READ, WRITE	Open the file for read-only or write-only (default is read-only). Use both for read-write.
APPEND	Open the file for writing; all writes are positioned at the end of the file.
CREATE	Use with `WRITE` to open the file and create it if needed.
CREATE_NEW	Use with `WRITE` to create a file atomically; failing if the file already exists.
DELETE_ON_CLOSE	Attempt to delete the file when it is closed or, if open, when the VM exits.
SYNC, DSYNC	Wherever possible, guarantee that write operations block until all data is written to storage. SYNC does this for all file changes including data and metadata (attributes) whereas DSYNC only adds this requirement for the data content of the file.

Option	Description
SPARSE	Use when creating a new file, requests the file be sparse. On filesystems where this is supported, a sparse file handles very large, mostly empty files without allocating as much real storage for empty portions.
TRUNCATE_EXISTING	Use WRITE on an existing file, set the file length to zero upon opening it.

A FileChannel can also be constructed from a classic FileInputStream, FileOutputStream, or RandomAccessFile:

```
FileChannel readOnlyFc = new FileInputStream("file.txt").getChannel();
FileChannel readWriteFc = new RandomAccessFile("file.txt", "rw")
    .getChannel();
```

FileChannels created from these file input and output streams are read-only or write-only, respectively. To get a read/write FileChannel, you must construct a RandomAccessFile with read/write permissions, as in the previous example.

Using a FileChannel is just like a RandomAccessFile, but it works with ByteBuffer instead of byte arrays:

```
ByteBuffer bbuf = ByteBuffer.allocate( ... );
bbuf.clear();
readOnlyFc.position( index );
readOnlyFc.read( bbuf );
bbuf.flip();
readWriteFc.write( bbuf );
```

You can control how much data is read and written either by setting buffer position and limit markers or using another form of read/write that takes a buffer starting position and length. You can also read and write to a random position by supplying indexes with the read and write methods:

```
readWriteFc.read( bbuf, index )
readWriteFc.write( bbuf, index2 );
```

In each case, the actual number of bytes read or written depends on several factors. The operation tries to read or write to the limit of the buffer, and the vast majority of the time that is what happens with local file access. The operation is guaranteed to block only until at least one byte has been processed. Whatever happens, the number of bytes processed is returned, and the buffer position is updated accordingly, preparing you to repeat the operation until it is complete if needed. This is one of the conveniences of working with buffers; they can manage the count for you. Like standard streams, the channel read() method returns -1 upon reaching the end of input.

The size of the file is always available with the size() method. It can change if you write past the end of the file. Conversely, you can truncate the file to a specified length with the truncate() method.

Concurrent access

FileChannels are safe for use by multiple threads and guarantee that data "viewed" by them is consistent across channels in the same VM. Unless you specify the SYNC or DSYNC options, no guarantees are made about how quickly writes are propagated to the storage mechanism. If you only intermittently need to be sure that data is safe before moving on, you can use the force() method to flush changes to disk. The force() method takes a Boolean argument indicating whether or not file metadata, including timestamp and permissions, must be written (sync or dsync). Some systems keep track of reads on files as well as writes, so you can save a lot of updates if you set the flag to false, which indicates that you don't care about syncing that data immediately.

As with all Channels, a FileChannel may be closed by any thread. Once closed, all its read/write and position-related methods throw a ClosedChannelException.

File locking

FileChannels support exclusive and shared locks on regions of files through the lock() method:

```
FileLock fileLock = fileChannel.lock();
int start = 0, len = fileChannel2.size();
FileLock readLock = fileChannel2.lock( start, len, true );
```

Locks may be either shared or exclusive. An *exclusive* lock prevents others from acquiring a lock of any kind on the specified file or file region. A *shared* lock allows others to acquire overlapping shared locks but not exclusive locks. These are useful as write and read locks, respectively. When you are writing, you don't want others to be able to write until you're done, but when reading, you need only to block others from writing, not reading concurrently.

The no-args lock() method in the previous example attempts to acquire an exclusive lock for the whole file. The second form accepts a starting and length parameter as well as a flag indicating whether the lock should be shared (or exclusive). The FileLock object returned by the lock() method can be used to release the lock:

```
fileLock.release();
```

Note that file locks are only guaranteed be a *cooperative* API; they do not necessarily prevent anyone from reading or writing to the locked file contents. In general, the only way to guarantee that locks are obeyed is for both parties to attempt to acquire the lock and use it. Also, shared locks are not implemented on some systems, in which case all requested locks are exclusive. You can test whether a lock is shared with the isShared() method.

FileChannel locks are held until the channel is closed or interrupted, so performing locks within a try-with-resources statement will help ensure that locks are released more robustly.

```
try ( FileChannel channel = FileChannel.open( p, WRITE ) ) {
    channel.lock();
    ...
}
```

Memory-mapped files

One of the most interesting features offered through FileChannel is the ability to map a file into memory. When a file is *memory-mapped*, like magic it becomes accessible through a single ByteBuffer—as if the entire file was read into memory at once. The implementation of this is extremely efficient, generally among the fastest ways to access the data. For working with large files, memory mapping can save a lot of resources and time.

This may seem counterintuitive; we're getting a conceptually easier way to access our data and it's also faster and more efficient? What's the catch? There really is no catch. The reason for this is that all modern operating systems are based on the idea of virtual memory. In a nutshell, that means that the operating system makes disk space act like memory by continually paging (swapping 4KB blocks called "pages") between memory and disk, transparent to the applications. Operating systems are very good at this; they efficiently cache the data that the application is using and let go of what is not in use. Memory-mapping a file is really just taking advantage of what the OS is doing internally.

A good example of where a memory-mapped file would be useful is in a database. Imagine a 10 GB file containing records indexed at various positions. By mapping the file, we can work with a standard ByteBuffer, reading and writing data at arbitrary positions and letting the native operating system read and write the underlying data in fine-grained pages as necessary. We could emulate this behavior with RandomAccess File or FileChannel, but we would have to explicitly read and write data into buffers first, and the implementation would almost certainly not be as efficient.

A mapping is created with the FileChannel map() method. For example:

```
FileChannel fc =FileChannel.open( fs.getPath("index.db"), CREATE, READ,
    WRITE );
MappedByteBuffer mappedBuff =
    fc.map( FileChannel.MapMode.READ_WRITE, 0, fc.size() );
```

The map() method returns a MappedByteBuffer, which is simply the standard Byte Buffer with a few additional methods relating to the mapping. The most important is force(), which ensures that any data written to the buffer is flushed out to permanent storage on the disk. The READ_ONLY and READ_WRITE constant identifiers of the File Channel.MapMode static inner class specify the type of access. Read/write access is available only when mapping a read/write file channel. Data read through the buffer is always consistent within the same Java VM. It may also be consistent across applications on the same host machine, but this is not guaranteed.

Again, a MappedByteBuffer acts just like a ByteBuffer. Continuing with the previous example, we could decode the buffer with a character decoder and search for a pattern like so:

```
CharBuffer cbuff = Charset.forName("US-ASCII").decode( mappedBuff );
Matcher matcher = Pattern.compile("abc*").matcher( cbuff );
while ( matcher.find() )
    System.out.println( matcher.start()+": "+matcher.group(0) );
```

Here, we have implemented something like the Unix *grep* command by relying on the Regular Expression API working with our CharBuffer as a CharSequence. We've cheated a bit in this example since the CharBuffer allocated by the decode() method is as large as the mapped file and must be held in memory. To do this efficiently, we could use the CharsetDecoder discussed earlier in this chapter to iterate through the large mapped space without pulling everything into memory.

Direct transfer

The final feature of FileChannel that we'll examine is performance optimization. FileChannel supports two highly optimized data transfer methods: transferFrom() and transferTo(), which move data between the file channel and another channel. These methods can take advantage of direct buffers internally to move data between the channels as fast as possible, often without copying the bytes into Java's memory space at all. The following example should be the fastest way to implement a file copy in Java short of using the built-in Filescopy() method:

```
import java.nio.channels.*;
import java.nio.file.*;
import static java.nio.file.StandardOpenOption.*;

public class CopyFile
{
    public static void main( String [] args ) throws Exception
    {
        FileSystem fs = FileSystems.getDefault();
        Path fromFile = fs.getPath( args[0] );
        Path toFile = fs.getPath( args[1] );

        try (
            FileChannel in = FileChannel.open( fromFile );
            FileChannel out = FileChannel.open( toFile, CREATE, WRITE ); )
        {
            in.transferTo( 0, (int)in.size(), out );
        }
    }
}
```

AsynchronousFileChannel

When we return to NIO in the next chapter, we will see that network channels are types of `SelectableChannel`, which means that they can be managed with a *selector* to poll for when the channels are ready to be read or written and manage them efficiently without blocking threads. File channels are *not* selectable channels and most regular file operations simply block until they are completed. This is not to say that file operations always block until all the bytes we want are read from or written to disk. In general, read operations may return fewer bytes than requested and write operations may boh write fewer bytes and also may buffer data in memory unless we use the SYNC or DSYNC open options. But in a world where disk access can be many, many orders of magnitude slower than in-memory operations even these partial reads and writes may be slow enough that we do not wish to block waiting for them.

The obvious solution is to use multithreading and coordinate our reads and writes in a separate thread from our main logic. Java 7 has made this easier by introducing the `AysnchronousFileChannel`, which is a file channel that delegates all of its operations to a thread pool and can report results using a `Future` object or asynchronous callback. All read and write operations on asynchronous file channels must specify the byte offset for the operation (as there is no well-defined "current" offset into the file at any given time). The simplest example is to write a file update in the background without gathering results:

```
AsynchronousFileChannel channel = AsynchronousFileChannel.open( path,
    WRITE );

// Write logBuffer to the end of the file in the background, returning
// immediately
channel.write( logBuffer, channel.size() );
...
```

Here, we have constructed an `AsynchronousFileChannel` analogous to the way we'd open a regular file channel. Our write happens in the background and the `write()` method returns immediately. By default, the channel will use a system default thread pool to perform our write in the background. Alternately, we could have supplied our own `Executor` service for the thread pool as an argument to the `open()` call. If at some point we need to sync up and guarantee that all data is written, we can use the channel's `force()` method to block until all writes are complete.

A more interesting case is a read operation where we need the bytes returned from the operation. In this case we can supply a callback `CompletionHandler` object that will push the results to us when they are ready.

```
AsynchronousFileChannel channel = AsynchronousFileChannel.open( path );
ByteBuffer bbuff = ByteBuffer.allocate( 1024 );
Object attachment = ...;
channel.read( bbuff, offset, attachment,
    new CompletionHandler<Integer, Object>() {
```

```
        @Override
        public void completed( Integer result, Object attachment ) {
            System.out.println( "read bytes = " + result );
        }

        @Override
        public void failed( Throwable exc, Object attachment ){
            ...
        }
    } );
```

The additional argument `attachment` in the read call can be any object we like, and it is simply returned to us in the callback as a way for us to maintain any context needed to service the result. Here, we print the number of bytes ready, which as usual may be fewer than we requested, but at least didn't require us to wait for them. The other possibility illustrated here is that the read may fail, in which case our `failed()` method is invoked with the associated exception.

Scalable I/O with NIO

We've laid the groundwork for using the NIO package in this chapter, but left out some of the important pieces. In the next chapter, we'll see more of the real motivation for `java.nio` when we talk about nonblocking and selectable I/O. In addition to the performance optimizations that can be made through direct buffers, these capabilities make possible designs for network servers that use fewer threads and can scale well to large systems. In that chapter, we'll look at the other significant `Channel` types: `SocketChannel`, `ServerSocketChannel`, and `DatagramChannel`.

CHAPTER 13

Network Programming

The network is the soul of Java. Most of what is interesting about Java centers on the potential for dynamic, networked applications. As Java's networking APIs have matured, Java has also become the language of choice for implementing traditional client/server applications and services. In this chapter, we start our discussion of the `java.net` package, which contains the fundamental classes for communications and working with networked resources (we'll finish this discussion in Chapter 14). This chapter next discusses the `java.rmi` package, which provides Java's native, high-level, Remote Method Invocation (RMI) facilities. Finally, building on the material in Chapter 12, we complete our discussion of the `java.nio` package, which is highly efficient for implementing large servers.

The classes of `java.net` fall into two general categories: the Sockets API for working with low-level Internet protocols and higher-level, web-oriented APIs that work with uniform resource locators (URLs). Figure 13-1 shows the `java.net` package.

Java's Sockets API provides access to the standard network protocols used for communications between hosts on the Internet. Sockets are the mechanism underlying all other kinds of portable networked communications. Sockets are the lowest-level tool in the general networking toolbox—you can use sockets for any kind of communications between client and server or peer applications on the Net, but you have to implement your own application-level protocols for handling and interpreting the data. Higher-level networking tools, such as remote method invocation, HTTP, and web services are implemented on top of sockets.

Java RMI is a powerful tool that leverages Java object serialization, allowing you to transparently work with Java objects on remote machines almost as if they were local. With RMI, it is easy to write distributed applications in which clients and servers work with each other's data as full-fledged Java objects rather than raw streams or packets of data.

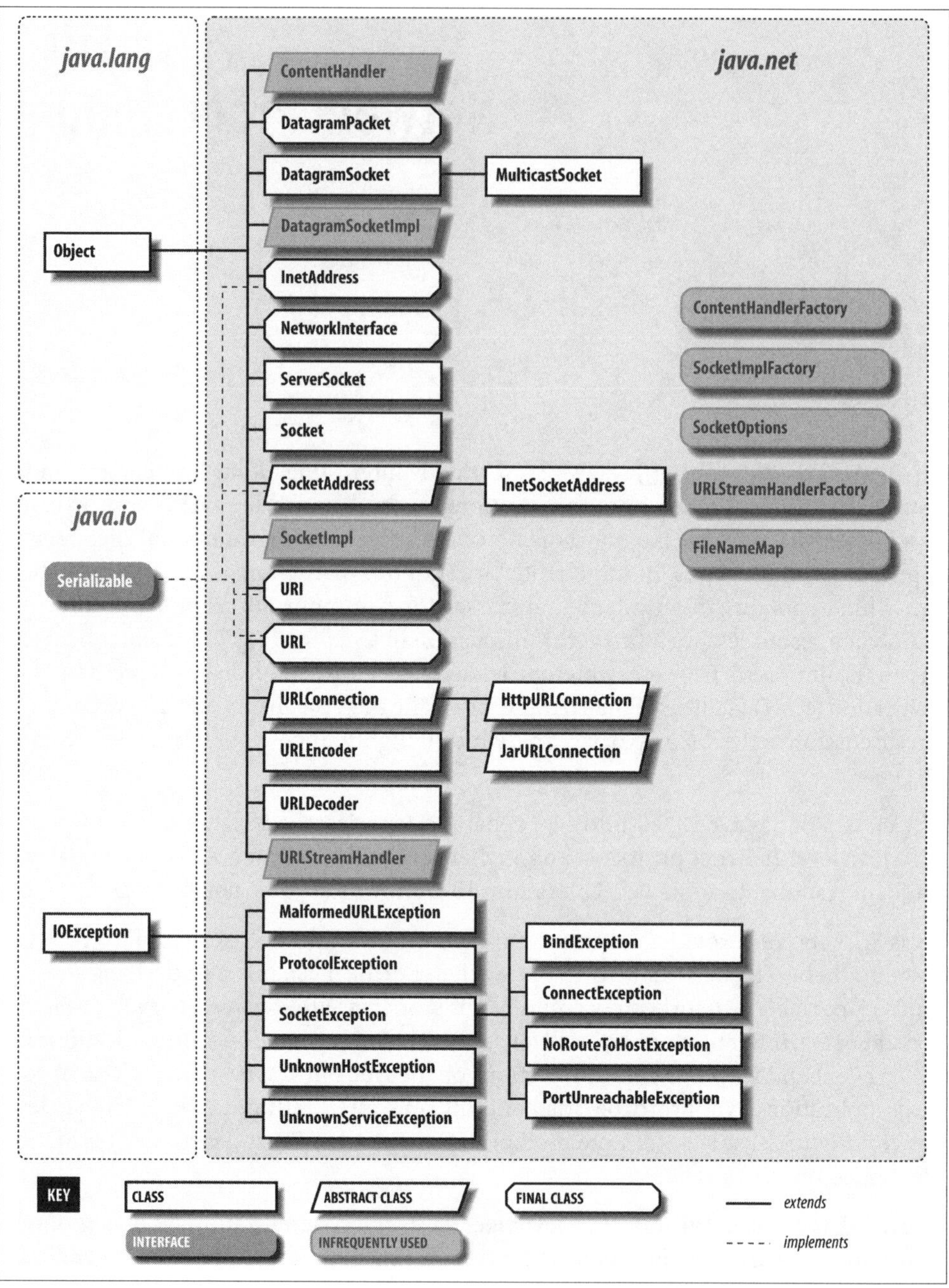

Figure 13-1. The java.net package

In contrast to RMI, which can only be used between two Java applications, *web services* is the term for the more general technology that provides platform-independent, loosely coupled invocation of services on remote servers using web standards such as HTTP and XML. We talk about web services in Chapters 14 and 15 when we discuss programming for the Web.

In this chapter, we'll provide some simple, practical examples of both high- and low-level Java network programming using sockets and RMI. In Chapter 14, we'll look at the other half of the `java.net` package, which lets clients work with web servers and services via URLs. Chapter 15 covers Java servlets and the tools that allow you to write web applications and services for web servers.

Sockets

Sockets are a low-level programming interface for networked communications. They send streams of data between applications that may or may not be on the same host. Sockets originated in BSD Unix and are, in some programming languages, hairy, complicated things with lots of small parts that can break off and endanger little children. The reason for this is that most socket APIs can be used with almost any kind of underlying network protocol. Since the protocols that transport data across the network can have radically different features, the socket interface can be quite complex.[1]

The `java.net` package supports a simplified, object-oriented socket interface that makes network communications considerably easier. If you've done network programming using sockets in other languages, you should be pleasantly surprised at how simple things can be when objects encapsulate the gory details. If this is the first time you've come across sockets, you'll find that talking to another application over the network can be as simple as reading a file or getting user input. Most forms of I/O in Java, including most network I/O, use the stream classes described in Chapter 12. Streams provide a unified I/O interface so that reading or writing across the Internet is similar to reading or writing on the local system. In addition to the stream-oriented interfaces, the Java networking APIs can work with the Java NIO buffer-oriented API for highly scalable applications. We'll see both in this chapter.

Java provides sockets to support three distinct classes of underlying protocols: `Sockets`, `DatagramSockets`, and `MulticastSockets`. In this first section, we look at Java's basic `Socket` class, which uses a *connection-oriented* and *reliable* protocol. A connection-oriented protocol provides the equivalent of a telephone conversation. After establishing a connection, two applications can send streams of data back and forth and the connection stays in place even when no one is talking. Because the protocol is reliable,

1. For a discussion of sockets in general, see *Unix Network Programming* by Richard Stevens (Prentice-Hall).

it also ensures that no data is lost (resending data as necessary) and that whatever you send always arrives in the order in which you sent it.

In the next section, we look at the `DatagramSocket` class, which uses a *connectionless, unreliable* protocol. A connectionless protocol is like the postal service. Applications can send short messages to each other, but no end-to-end connection is set up in advance and no attempt is made to keep the messages in order. It's not even guaranteed that the messages will arrive at all. A `MulticastSocket` is a variation of a `DatagramSocket` that performs multicasting—simultaneously sending data to multiple recipients. Working with multicast sockets is very much like working with datagram sockets. However, because multicasting is currently not widely supported across the Internet, we do not cover it here.

In theory, just about any protocol can be used underneath the socket layer (old-schoolers will remember things like Novell's IPX, Apple's AppleTalk, etc.). But in practice, there's only one important protocol family used on the Internet, and only one protocol family that Java supports: the Internet Protocol (IP). The `Socket` class speaks TCP, the connection-oriented flavor of IP, and the `DatagramSocket` class speaks UDP, the connectionless kind.

Clients and Servers

When writing network applications, it's common to talk about clients and servers. The distinction is increasingly vague, but the side that initiates the conversation is usually considered the *client*. The side that accepts the request is usually the *server*. In the case where two peer applications use sockets to talk, the distinction is less important, but for simplicity we'll use this definition.

For our purposes, the most important difference between a client and a server is that a client can create a socket to initiate a conversation with a server application at any time, while a server must be prepared in advance to listen for incoming conversations. The `java.net.Socket` class represents one side of an individual socket connection on both the client and server. In addition, the server uses the `java.net.ServerSocket` class to listen for new connections from clients. In most cases, an application acting as a server creates a `ServerSocket` object and waits, blocked in a call to its `accept()` method, until a connection arrives. When it arrives, the `accept()` method creates a `Socket` object that the server uses to communicate with the client. A server may carry on conversations with multiple clients at once; in this case, there is still only a single `ServerSocket`, but the server has multiple `Socket` objects—one associated with each client, as shown in Figure 13-2.

At the socket level, a client needs two pieces of information to locate and connect to a server on the Internet: a *hostname* (used to find the host computer's network address) and a *port number*. The port number is an identifier that differentiates between multiple clients or servers on the same host. A server application listens on a prearranged port while waiting for connections. Clients use the port number assigned to the service they want to access. If you think of the host computers as hotels and the applications as guests, the ports are like the guests' room numbers. For one person to call another, he or she must know the other party's hotel name and room number.

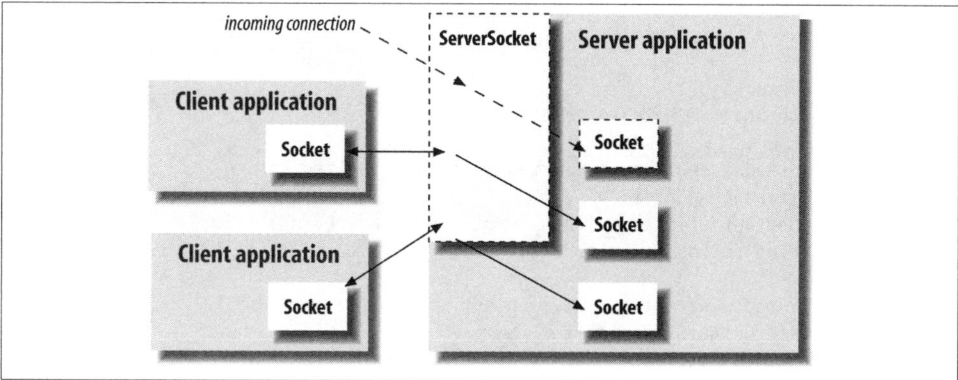

Figure 13-2. Clients and servers, Sockets and ServerSockets

Clients

A client application opens a connection to a server by constructing a `Socket` that specifies the hostname and port number of the desired server:

```
try {
    Socket sock = new Socket("wupost.wustl.edu", 25);
} catch ( UnknownHostException e ) {
    System.out.println("Can't find host.");
} catch ( IOException e ) {
    System.out.println("Error connecting to host.");
}
```

This code fragment attempts to connect a `Socket` to port 25 (the SMTP mail service) of the host *wupost.wustl.edu*. The client handles the possibility that the hostname can't be resolved (`UnknownHostException`) and that it might not be able to connect to it (`IOException`). In the preceding case, Java used DNS, the standard Domain Name Service, to resolve the hostname to an IP address for us. The constructor can also accept a string containing the host's raw IP address:

```
Socket sock = new Socket("22.66.89.167", 25);
```

After a connection is made, input and output streams can be retrieved with the `Socket` `getInputStream()` and `getOutputStream()` methods. The following (rather arbitrary) code sends and receives some data with the streams:

```
try {
    Socket server = new Socket("foo.bar.com", 1234);
    InputStream in = server.getInputStream();
```

```
        OutputStream out = server.getOutputStream();

        // write a byte
        out.write(42);

        // write a newline or carriage return delimited string
        PrintWriter pout = new PrintWriter( out, true );
        pout.println("Hello!");

        // read a byte
        byte back = (byte)in.read();

        // read a newline or carriage return delimited string
        BufferedReader bin =
          new BufferedReader( new InputStreamReader( in ) );
        String response = bin.readLine();

        // send a serialized Java object
        ObjectOutputStream oout = new
        ObjectOutputStream( out );
        oout.writeObject( new java.util.Date() );
        oout.flush();

        server.close();
    }
    catch (IOException e ) { ... }
```

In this exchange, the client first creates a `Socket` for communicating with the server. The `Socket` constructor specifies the server's hostname (*foo.bar.com*) and a prearranged port number (1234). Once the connection is established, the client writes a single byte to the server using the `OutputStream`'s `write()` method. To send a string of text more easily, it then wraps a `PrintWriter` around the `OutputStream`. Next, it performs the complementary operations: reading a byte back from the server using `InputStream`'s `read()` method and then creating a `BufferedReader` from which to get a full string of text. Finally, we do something really funky and send a serialized Java object to the server, using an `ObjectOutputStream`. (We'll talk in depth about sending serialized objects later in this chapter.) The client then terminates the connection with the `close()` method. All these operations have the potential to generate `IOException`s; our application will deal with these using the `catch` clause.

Servers

After a connection is established, a server application uses the same kind of `Socket` object for its side of the communications. However, to accept a connection from a client, it must first create a `ServerSocket`, bound to the correct port. Let's recreate the previous conversation from the server's point of view:

```
    // Meanwhile, on foo.bar.com...
    try {
```

```
        ServerSocket listener = new ServerSocket( 1234 );

        while ( !finished ) {
            Socket client = listener.accept();  // wait for connection

            InputStream in = client.getInputStream();
            OutputStream out = client.getOutputStream();

            // read a byte
            byte someByte = (byte)in.read();

            // read a newline or carriage-return-delimited string
            BufferedReader bin =
              new BufferedReader( new InputStreamReader( in ) );
            String someString = bin.readLine();

            // write a byte
            out.write(43);

            // say goodbye
            PrintWriter pout = new PrintWriter( out, true );
            pout.println("Goodbye!");

            // read a serialized Java object
            ObjectInputStream oin = new ObjectInputStream( in );
            Date date = (Date)oin.readObject();

            client.close();
        }

        listener.close();
    }
    catch (IOException e ) { ... }
    catch (ClassNotFoundException e2 ) { ... }
```

First, our server creates a `ServerSocket` attached to port 1234. On some systems, there are rules about which ports an application can use. Port numbers below 1024 are usually reserved for system processes and standard, *well-known* services, so we pick a port number outside of this range. The `ServerSocket` is created only once; thereafter, we can accept as many connections as arrive.

Next, we enter a loop, waiting for the `accept()` method of the `ServerSocket` to return an active `Socket` connection from a client. When a connection has been established, we perform the server side of our dialog, then close the connection and return to the top of the loop to wait for another connection. Finally, when the server application wants to stop listening for connections altogether, it calls the `close()` method of the `ServerSocket`.

This server is single-threaded; it handles one connection at a time, not calling `accept()` to listen for a new connection until it's finished with the current connection. A more realistic server would have a loop that accepts connections concurrently and passes them off to their own threads for processing. There is a lot to be said about implementing multithreaded servers. Later in this chapter, we'll create a tiny web server that starts a new thread for each connection and also a slightly more complex web server that uses the NIO package to handle many connections with a small number of threads.

Sockets and security

The previous examples presuppose that the client has permission to connect to the server and that the server is allowed to listen on the specified socket. If you're writing a general, standalone application, this is normally the case (and you can probably skip this section). However, untrusted applications (such as Java applets in a web browser) run under the auspices of a security policy that can impose arbitrary restrictions on what hosts they may or may not talk to and whether or not they can listen for connections.

For example, the security policy imposed on applets by most browsers allow untrusted applets to open socket connections only to the host that served them—that is, they can talk back only to the server from which their class files were retrieved. Untrusted applets are generally not allowed to open server sockets for incoming connections themselves. This doesn't mean that an untrusted applet can't cooperate with its server to communicate with anyone, anywhere. The applet's server could run a proxy that lets the applet communicate indirectly with anyone it likes. What this security policy prevents is malicious applets poking around inside corporate firewalls, making connections to trusted services. It places the burden of security on the originating server, not the client machine. Restricting access to the originating server limits the usefulness of Trojan applications that do annoying things from the client side. (You probably won't let your proxy spam people, because you'll be blamed.)

If you are going to run your own application under a security manager, you should be aware that the default security manager dissallows all network access. So in order to make network connections, you would have to modify your policy file to grant the appropriate permissions to your code (see Chapter 3 for details). The following policy file fragment sets the socket permissions to allow connections to or from any host on any nonprivileged port:

```
grant {
  permission java.net.SocketPermission
    "*:1024-", "listen,accept,connect";
};
```

When starting the Java interpreter, you can install the security manager and use this file (call it *mysecurity.policy*):

```
% java -Djava.security.manager ↵

\-Djava.security.policy=mysecurity.policy MyApplication
```

The DateAtHost Client

In the past, many networked computers ran a simple time service that dispensed their clock's local time on a well-known port. This was a precursor of NTP, the more general Network Time Protocol. The next example, `DateAtHost`, includes a subclass of `java.util.Date` that fetches the time from a remote host instead of initializing itself from the local clock. (See Chapter 11 for a complete discussion of the `Date` class.)

`DateAtHost` connects to the time service (port 37) and reads four bytes representing the time on the remote host. These four bytes have a peculiar specification that we decode to get the time. Here's the code:

```
//file: DateAtHost.java
import java.net.Socket;
import java.io.*;

public class DateAtHost extends java.util.Date {
    static int timePort = 37;
    // seconds from start of 20th century to Jan 1, 1970 00:00 GMT
    static final long offset = 2208988800L;

    public DateAtHost( String host ) throws IOException {
        this( host, timePort );
    }

    public DateAtHost( String host, int port ) throws IOException {
        Socket server = new Socket( host, port );
        DataInputStream din =
          new DataInputStream( server.getInputStream() );
        int time = din.readInt();
        server.close();

        setTime( (((1L << 32) + time) - offset) * 1000 );
    }
}
```

That's all there is to it. It's not very long, even with a few frills. We have supplied two possible constructors for `DateAtHost`. Normally we'd expect to use the first, which simply takes the name of the remote host as an argument. The second constructor specifies the hostname and the port number of the remote time service. (If the time service were running on a nonstandard port, we would use the second constructor to specify the alternate port number.) This second constructor does the work of making the connection and setting the time. The first constructor simply invokes the second (using the `this()` construct) with the default port as an argument. Supplying simplified constructors that invoke their siblings with default arguments is a common and useful pattern in Java; that is the main reason we've shown it here.

The second constructor opens a socket to the specified port on the remote host. It creates a `DataInputStream` to wrap the input stream and then reads a four-byte integer using the `readInt()` method. It's no coincidence that the bytes are in the right order. Java's `DataInputStream` and `DataOutputStream` classes work with the bytes of integer types in *network byte order* (most significant to least significant). The time protocol (and other standard network protocols that deal with binary data) also uses the network byte order, so we don't need to call any conversion routines. Explicit data conversions would probably be necessary if we were using a nonstandard protocol, especially when talking to a non-Java client or server. In that case, we'd have to read byte by byte and do some rearranging to get our four-byte value. After reading the data, we're finished with the socket, so we close it, terminating the connection to the server. Finally, the constructor initializes the rest of the object by calling `Date`'s `setTime()` method with the calculated time value.

The four bytes of the time value are interpreted as an integer representing the number of seconds since the beginning of the 20th century. `DateAtHost` converts this to Java's notion of absolute time—the count of milliseconds since January 1, 1970 (an arbitrary date standardized by C and Unix). The conversion first creates a `long` value, which is the unsigned equivalent of the integer `time`. It subtracts an offset to make the time relative to the epoch (January 1, 1970) rather than the century, and multiplies by 1,000 to convert to milliseconds. The converted time is used to initialize the object.

The `DateAtHost` class can work with a time retrieved from a remote host almost as easily as `Date` is used with the time on the local host. The only additional overhead is dealing with the possible `IOException` that can be thrown by the `DateAtHost` constructor:

```
try {
    Date d = new DateAtHost( "someserver.net" );
    System.out.println( "The time over there is: " + d );
}
catch ( IOException e ) { ... }
```

This example fetches the time at the host *someserver.net* and prints its value.

The TinyHttpd Server

Have you ever wanted to write your very own web server? Well, you're in luck. In this section, we're going to build `TinyHttpd`, a minimal but functional web server. `TinyHttpd` listens on a specified port and services simple HTTP `GET` requests. `GET` requests are simple text commands that look something like this:

```
GET /path/filename [ optional stuff ]
```

Your web browser sends one or more of these requests for each document it retrieves from a web server. Upon reading a request, our server attempts to open the specified file and send its contents. If that document contains references to images or other items to be displayed inline, the browser follows up with additional `GET` requests. For best performance, `TinyHttpd` services each request in its own thread. Therefore, `TinyHttpd` can service several requests concurrently.

This example works, but it's a bit oversimplified. First, it implements a very old subset of the HTTP protocol, so some browsers may turn their nose up at it. (I tested this in Safari on my Mac at the time of this writing and it worked well enough for this example's purposes.) Also remember that file pathnames are still somewhat architecture-dependent in Java. This example should work as it is on most systems, but would require some enhancement to be more robust. It's possible to write slightly more elaborate code that uses the environmental information provided by Java to tailor itself to the local system. (Chapter 12 gives some hints about how.)

Unless you have a firewall or other security in place, the next example serves files from your host without protection. Don't try this at work!

Now, without further ado, here's `TinyHttpd`:

```
//file: TinyHttpd.java
import java.net.*;
import java.io.*;
import java.util.regex.*;
import java.util.concurrent.*;

public class TinyHttpd {
  public static void main( String argv[] ) throws IOException {
    Executor executor = Executors.newFixedThreadPool(3);
    ServerSocket ss = new ServerSocket( Integer.parseInt(argv[0]) );
    while ( true )
      executor.execute( new TinyHttpdConnection( ss.accept() ) );
  }
}

class TinyHttpdConnection implements Runnable {
  Socket client;
  TinyHttpdConnection ( Socket client ) throws SocketException {
    this.client = client;
  }
  public void run() {
    try {
      BufferedReader in = new BufferedReader(
        new InputStreamReader(client.getInputStream(), "8859_1" ) );
      OutputStream out = client.getOutputStream();
      PrintWriter pout = new PrintWriter(
        new OutputStreamWriter(out, "8859_1"), true );
      String request = in.readLine();
      System.out.println( "Request: "+request);

      Matcher get = Pattern.compile("GET /?(\\S*).*").matcher( request );
      if ( get.matches() ) {
        request = get.group(1);
        if ( request.endsWith("/") || request.equals("") )
```

```
                request = request + "index.html";
              try {
                FileInputStream fis = new FileInputStream ( request );
                byte [] data = new byte [ 64*1024 ];
                for(int read; (read = fis.read( data )) > -1; )
                    out.write( data, 0, read );
                out.flush();
              } catch ( FileNotFoundException e ) {
                pout.println( "404 Object Not Found" ); }
            } else
              pout.println( "400 Bad Request" );
            client.close();
          } catch ( IOException e ) {
            System.out.println( "I/O error " + e ); }
        }
    }
```

Compile TinyHttpd and place it in your classpath, as described in Chapter 3. Go to a directory with some interesting documents and start the server, specifying an unused port number as an argument. For example:

```
% java TinyHttpd 1234
```

You should now be able to use your web browser to retrieve files from your host. You'll have to specify the port number you chose in the URL. For example, if your hostname is *foo.bar.com*, and you started the server as shown, you could reference a file as in:

```
http://foo.bar.com:1234/welcome.html
```

Or, more likely, if you're running both the server and your web browser on the same machine, you could reference a file as in:

```
http://localhost:1234/welcome.html
```

TinyHttpd looks for files relative to its current directory, so the pathnames you provide should be relative to that location. (Retrieved some files? Did you notice that when you retrieved an HTML file, your web browser automatically generated more requests for items like images that were contained within it?) Let's take a closer look.

The TinyHttpd application has two classes. The public TinyHttpd class contains the main() method of our standalone application. It begins by creating a ServerSocket, attached to the specified port. It then loops, waiting for client connections and creating instances of the second class, a TinyHttpdConnection, to service each request. The while loop waits for the ServerSocket accept() method to return a new Socket for each client connection. The Socket is passed as an argument to construct the TinyHttpdConnection that handles it. We use an Executor with a fixed pool size of three threads to service all of our connections.

TinyHttpdConnection is a Runnable object. For each connection we start a thread, which lives long enough to handle the single client connection and then dies. The body of TinyHttpdConnection's run() method is where all the magic happens. First, we fetch an OutputStream for talking back to our client. The second line reads the GET request from the InputStream into the variable request. This request is a single newline-terminated String that looks like the GET request we described earlier. For this, we use a BufferedInputStream wrapped around an InputStreamReader. (We'll say more about the InputStreamReader in a moment.)

We then parse the contents of request to extract a filename. Here, we are using the Regular Expression API (see Chapter 10 for a full discussion of regular expressions and the Regular Expression API). The pattern simply looks for the "GET" followed by an optional slash and then any string of nonwhitespace characters. We add the ".*" at the end to cause the pattern to match the whole input, so that we can use the Matcher match() method to test if the whole request made sense to us or not. The part that matches the filename is in a capture group: "(\\S*)". This allows us to retrieve that text with the Matcher group() method. Finally, we check to see if the requested filename looks like a directory name (i.e., ends in a slash) or is empty. In these cases, we append the familiar default filename *index.html* as a convenience.

Once we have the filename, we try to open the specified file and send its contents using a large byte array. Here we loop, reading one buffer at a time and writing to the client via the OutputStream. If we can't parse the request or the file doesn't exist, we use the PrintStream to send a textual message. Then we return a standard HTTP error message. Finally, we close the socket and return from run(), completing our task.

Do French web servers speak French?

In TinyHttpd, we explicitly created the InputStreamReader for our BufferedRead and the OutputStreamWriter for our PrintWriter. We do this so that we can specify the character encoding to use when converting to and from the byte representation of the HTTP protocol messages. (Note that we're not talking about the body of the file to be sent—that is simply a stream of raw bytes to us; rather we're talking about the GET and response messages.) If we didn't specify, we'd get the default character encoding for the local system. For many purposes that may be correct, but in this case, we are speaking of a well-defined international protocol and we should be specific. The RFC for HTTP specifies that web clients and servers should use the ISO8859-1 character encoding. We specify this encoding explicitly when we construct the InputStreamReader and OutputStreamWriter. As it turns out, ISO8859-1 is just plain ASCII and conversion to and from Unicode should always leave ASCII values unchanged, so again we would probably not be in any trouble if we did not specify an encoding. But it's important to think about these things at least once—and now you have.

Taming the daemon

An important problem with TinyHttpd is that there are no restrictions on the files it serves. With a little trickery, the daemon would happily send any file on your computer to the client. It would be nice if we could enforce the restriction that TinyHttpd serve only files that are in the current working directory or a subdirectory, as it normally does. An easy way to do this is to activate the Java Security Manager. Normally, a security manager is used to prevent Java code downloaded over the Net from doing anything suspicious. However, we can press the security manager into service to restrict file access in our application as well.

You can use a policy like the simple one that we provided earlier in this chapter; it allows the server to accept connections on a specified range of sockets. Fortuitously, the default file-access granted by the security policy does just what we'd like for this example: it allows an application access to files in its current working directory and subdirectories. So simply installing the security manager provides exactly the kind of file protection that we wanted in this case. (It would be easy to add additional permissions if you wish to extend the server's range to other well-defined areas.)

With the security manager in place, the daemon cannot access anything outside the current directory and its subdirectories. If it tries to, the security manager throws an exception and prevents access to the file. In that case, we should have `TinyHttpd` catch the `SecurityException` and return a proper message to the web browser. Add the following `catch` clause after the `FileNotFoundException`'s `catch` clause:

```
...
} catch ( Security Exception e ) {
    pout.println("403 Forbidden");
}
```

Room for improvement

`TinyHttpd` still has quite a bit of room for improvement. Technically, it implements only an obsolete subset of the HTTP protocol (version 0.9) in which the server expects only the `GET` request and returns just the content. All modern servers speak HTTP 1.1, which allows for additional metadata in both the HTTP request and response and requires certain data such as version number and content length. You could extend our simple server to add these extra bits of the header without a great deal of effort. HTTP 1.1 also has more sophisticated features such as allowing multiple client requests to be sent over one socket connection, which requires more elaborate code.

Of course, real web servers can do all sorts of other things. For example, you might consider adding a few lines of code to read directories and generate linked HTML listings as most web servers do. Have fun with this example, and you can learn quite a bit.

Socket Options

As we've said, the Java Sockets API is a somewhat simplified interface to the general socket mechanisms. In other environments, where all the gory details of the network are visible to you, a lot of complex and sometimes esoteric options can be set on sockets to govern the behavior of the underlying protocols. Java gives us access to a few important ones.

SO_TIMEOUT

The `SO_TIMEOUT` option sets a timer on all I/O methods of a socket that block so that you don't have to wait forever if they don't return. This works for operations such as `accept()` on server sockets and `read()` or `write()` on all sockets. If the timer expires before the operation would complete, an `InterruptedIOException` is thrown. You can catch the exception and continue to use the socket normally if it is appropriate, or you can take the opportunity to bail out of the operation. Multithreaded, blocking servers, such as `TinyHttpd`, can use this sort of technique for their shutdown logic:

```
serverSocket.setSoTimeout( 2000 ); // 2 seconds

while ( !shutdown ) {
    try {
        Socket client = serverSocket.accept();
        handleClient( client );
    } catch ( InterruptedIOException e ) {
        // ignore the exception
    }

    // exit
}
```

You set the timer by calling the `setSoTimeout()` method of the `Socket` class with the timeout period, in milliseconds, as an `int` argument. This works for regular `Socket`s, `ServerSocket`s (TCP), and `DatagramSocket`s (UDP), discussed later in this chapter. To find the current timeout value, call `getSoTimeout()` .

This feature is a workaround for the fact that stream-oriented I/O operations in Java are blocking, and there is no way to test or poll them for activity. Later in this chapter, we'll complete our discussion of the NIO package, which provides full nonblocking I/O for all types of operations, including sockets.

TCP_NODELAY

This option turns off a feature of TCP called Nagle's algorithm, which tries to prevent certain interactive applications from flooding the network with very tiny packets. For example, in our very first network example we sent a single byte to the network in one write. With this option on, under certain conditions, the TCP implementation might have decided to hold that byte for a very brief period, hoping for more data to fill the next packet. You can turn this "delay" off if you have a fast network and you want all packets sent as soon as possible. The `Socket setTcpNoDelay()` method takes a Boolean argument specifying whether the delay is on or off. To find out whether the `TCP_NODELAY` option is enabled, call `getTcpNoDelay()`, which returns a `boolean`.

SO_LINGER

This option controls what happens to any unsent data when you perform a `close()` on an active socket connection. Normally, the system blocks on the close and tries to deliver any network buffered data and close the connection gracefully. The `setSoLinger()` method of the `Socket` class takes two arguments: a `boolean` that enables or disables the option and an `int` that sets the time to wait (the *linger* value), in seconds. If you set the linger value to `0`, any unsent data is discarded and the TCP connection is aborted (terminated with a reset). To find the current linger value, call `getSoLinger()`.

TCP_KEEPALIVE

This option can be enabled with the `setKeepAlive()` method. It triggers a feature of TCP that polls the other side every two hours if there is no other activity. Normally, when no data is flowing on a TCP connection, no packets are sent. This can make it difficult to tell whether the other side is simply being quiet or has disappeared. If one side of the connection closes properly, this is detected. But if the other side simply disappears, we don't know unless and until we try to talk to it. For this reason, servers often use `TCP_KEEPALIVE` to detect lost client connections (where they might otherwise only respond to requests, rather than initiate them). `Keepalive` is not part of the TCP specification; it's an add-on that's not guaranteed to be implemented everywhere. If you can, the best way to detect lost clients is to implement the polling as part of your own protocol.

Half-close

In TCP, it is technically possible to close one direction of a stream but not the other. In other words, you can shut down sending but not receiving, or vice versa. A few protocols use this to indicate the end of a client request by closing the client side of the stream, allowing the end of stream to be detected by the server. You can shut down either half of a socket connection with `shutdownOutput()` or `shutdownInput()`.

Proxies and Firewalls

Most networks today are behind firewalls. Some firewalls not only prevent outsiders from getting in, but by default, prevent applications inside the firewall from opening direct socket-level connections to the outside network. Instead, firewalls that do this often provide a service called SOCKS (named for sockets) that acts as a proxy server for socket connections, giving the administrators more control over what connections are allowed. Firewalls may also be set up with direct proxies for higher-level protocols, such as HTTP and FTP, which allow even greater control and possibly screening of content. It's all about attempting to control who connects to whom and for what.

If your firewall does not allow any direct outside socket connections, even via SOCKS, your application may still be able to communicate with the outside world by using HTTP to send and receive data in this way. See Chapter 14 for an example of how to perform HTTP `POST` and `GET` operations to send and retrieve data through firewalls that allow web traffic.

Java has built-in support for SOCKS as well as HTTP and FTP protocol proxies. All you have to do is set some system properties in your application (in an applet, this should be already taken care of for you through your browser configuration, because you wouldn't have authority to set those properties). To configure Java to use a SOCKS (version 4 or 5) proxy server, set the following system properties:

`socksProxyHost`
: The SOCKS proxy server name.

`socksProxyPort`
: The SOCKS proxy port number.

If the SOCKS proxy requires a username and password, you can supply them in the additional properties `java.net.socks.username` and `java.net.socks.password`.

It's similar for HTTP and FTP proxies, which are set with separate properties:

`http.proxyHost`

`ftp.proxyHost`
: The proxy server name.

`http.proxyPort`
: The proxy port number.

`http.nonProxyHosts`
: A list of hosts for which direct connections should always be made. Hosts in the list are separated by vertical bars (|) and may include asterisks (*) as wildcards—for example, `myserver|*.mydomain`.

You can set these properties on the command line using the Java interpreter's `-D` option or by calling the `System.setProperty()` method. The following command runs `MyProgram` using the HTTP proxy server at *foo.bar.com* on port 1234:

```
% java -Dhttp.proxyServer=foo.bar.com -Dhttp.proxyPort=1234 MyProgram
```

ProxySelector

Java also has an API to allow programmatic control of Java's use of proxies. The `java.net.ProxySelector` class has a method that takes a uniform resource identifier (URI) object (a generalization of the URLs we use for web addresses; see Chapter 14) and returns a list of `java.net.Proxy` objects representing the proxies or direct connections to be used for the protocol specified. The default `ProxySelector` obeys the system properties we listed earlier. If required, you can create and install your own proxy selector to take control of the process and direct different destinations to different proxies. To see what decisions are being made, you can get the default selector with the static method `ProxySelector.getDefault()` and query it for various protocols with its `select()` method. The following example prints some string information about the preferred proxy (if any) for a specific HTTP URL:

```
ProxySelector ps = java.net.ProxySelector.getDefault();
List list = ps.select( new URI("http://java.sun.com/") );
System.out.println( list.get(0) );//e.g. HTTP@myserver:1234
```

Detailed information can be obtained from the proxy object, which contains a type identifier specifying `DIRECT`, `HTTP`, or `SOCKS` and a proxy address. To query for a SOCKS socket proxy for a given host and port, use a URI string of the form `socket://host:port`.

Datagram Sockets

`TinyHttpd` used a `Socket` to create a connection to the client using the TCP protocol. In that example, the TCP protocol took care of data integrity; we didn't have to worry about data arriving out of order or incorrect. Now, let's take a walk on the wild side, building an applet that uses a `java.net.DatagramSocket`, which uses the UDP protocol. A datagram is sort of like a letter sent via the postal service: it's a discrete chunk of data transmitted in one packet. Unlike the previous example, where we could get a convenient `OutputStream` from our `Socket` and write the data as if writing to a file with a `DatagramSocket`, we have to work one datagram at a time. (Of course, the TCP protocol was taking our `OutputStream` and slicing the data into packets, too, but we didn't have to worry about those details.)

UDP doesn't guarantee that the data is received. If the data packets are received, they may not arrive in the order in which they were sent; it's even possible for duplicate datagrams to arrive (under rare circumstances). Using UDP is something like cutting the pages out of the encyclopedia, putting them into separate envelopes, and mailing them to your friend. If your friend wants to read the encyclopedia, it's his or her job to put the pages in order. If some pages get lost in the mail, your friend has to send you a letter asking for replacements.

Obviously, you wouldn't use UDP to send a huge amount of data without error correction. However, it's significantly more efficient than TCP, particularly if you don't care about the order in which messages arrive or whether 100 percent of their arrival is guaranteed. For example, in a simple periodic database lookup, the client can send a query; the server's response itself constitutes an acknowledgment. If the response doesn't arrive within a certain time, the client can just send another query. It shouldn't be hard for the client to match responses to its original queries. Some important applications that use UDP are the Domain Name System (DNS) and Sun's Network File System (NFS).

The HeartBeat Applet

In this section, we build a simple applet, `HeartBeat`, that runs in a web browser and sends a datagram to its server each time it's started and stopped. We also build a simple standalone server application, `Pulse`, that receives these datagrams and prints them. Tracking the output could give you a crude measure of who is currently looking at your web page at any given time (assuming that firewalls do not block the UDP packets). This is the kind of thing UDP is good for: we don't want the overhead of a TCP socket, and if the datagrams get lost, it's no big deal.

First, the `HeartBeat` applet:

```
//file: HeartBeat.java
import java.net.*;
import java.io.*;

public class HeartBeat extends java.applet.Applet {
    String myHost;
    int myPort;

    public void init() {
        myHost = getCodeBase().getHost();
        myPort = Integer.parseInt( getParameter("myPort") );
    }

    private void sendMessage( String message ) {
        try {
            byte [] data = message.getBytes("UTF-8");
            InetAddress addr = InetAddress.getByName( myHost );
            DatagramPacket packet =
              new DatagramPacket( data, data.length, addr, myPort );
            DatagramSocket ds = new DatagramSocket();
            ds.send( packet );
            ds.close();
        } catch ( IOException e ) {
            System.out.println( e );  // Error creating socket
        }
    }

    public void start() {
        sendMessage("Arrived");
    }
    public void stop() {
        sendMessage("Departed");
    }
}
```

Compile the applet and include it in an HTML document with an `<applet>` tag:

```
<html><body>
    <h1>Heartbeat!</h1>
    <applet height="1 " width="1 " code="HeartBeat ">
```

```
    <param name="myPort" value="1234">
</applet>
</body></html>
```

Make sure to place the compiled *HeartBeat.class* file in the same directory as the HTML document (which we'll refer to as `heartbeat.html`). We talk more about embedding applets in HTML documents in Chapter 23.

The `myPort` parameter should specify the port number on which our server application listens for data ("1234" as just shown).

Next, the server-side application, `Pulse`:

```
//file: Pulse.java
import java.net.*;
import java.io.*;

public class Pulse {
    public static void main( String [] argv ) throws IOException {
        DatagramSocket s =
          new DatagramSocket( Integer.parseInt(argv[0]) );

        while ( true ) {
            DatagramPacket packet =
              new DatagramPacket( new byte [1024], 1024 );
            s.receive( packet );
            String message = new String(
                packet.getData(), 0, packet.getLength(),"UTF-8" );
            System.out.println( "Heartbeat from: "
              + packet.getAddress().getHostName()
              + " - " + message );
        }
    }
}
```

Compile `Pulse` and run it on your web server, specifying the port number as an argument:

```
% java Pulse 1234
```

The port number should be the same as the one you used in the `myPort` parameter of the `<applet>` tag for `HeartBeat`.

Now to run the example we're going to need a web server. Opening the file directly in your browser will not work here because, as we mentioned earlier, applets are only allowed to talk to the host that served them and when no web server is involved, the security manager doesn't allow any network communications at all. Fortunately, we wrote a satisfactory web server, `TinyHttpd`, earlier in this chapter! Just run `TinyHttpd` in the directory with your *heartbeat.html* file—being careful to specify a different port number than our `HeartBeat` client and `Pulse` server—and use it to serve up the page.

We tested this in Safari on a Mac at the time of this writing and it worked as expected. But if you have issues you can try a "real" web server and we won't be offended.

Now, pull up the web page in your browser. You won't see much there (a better application might do something visual as well), but you should get a blip from the `Pulse` application. Leave the page and return to it a few times. Each time the applet is started or stopped, it sends a message that `Pulse` reports:

```
Heartbeat from: foo.bar.com - Arrived
Heartbeat from: foo.bar.com - Departed
Heartbeat from: foo.bar.com - Arrived
Heartbeat from: foo.bar.com - Departed
...
```

Cool, eh? Just remember that the datagrams are not guaranteed to arrive (although it's highly unlikely you'll ever see them fail on a normal network), and it's possible that you could miss an arrival or a departure. Now let's look at the code.

The HeartBeat applet code

`HeartBeat` overrides the `init()`, `start()`, and `stop()` methods of the `Applet` class and implements one private method of its own, `sendMessage()`, which sends a datagram. (We haven't covered applets yet, so if you want more details, refer to Chapter 23.) `HeartBeat` begins its life in `init()`, where it determines the destination for its messages. It uses the `Applet getCodeBase()` and `getHost()` methods to find the name of its originating host and fetches the correct port number from the `myPort` parameter of the `<applet>` tag. After `init()` has finished, the `start()` and `stop()` methods are called whenever the applet is started or stopped. These methods merely call `sendMessage()` with the appropriate message.

`sendMessage()` is responsible for sending a `String` message to the server as a datagram. It takes the text as an argument, constructs a datagram packet containing the message, and then sends the datagram. All the datagram information is packed into a `java.net.DatagramPacket` object, including the destination and port number. The `DatagramPacket` is like an addressed envelope, stuffed with our bytes. After the `DatagramPacket` is created, `sendMessage()` simply has to open a `DatagramSocket` and send it.

The first five lines of `sendMessage()` build the `DatagramPacket`:

```
try {
    byte [] data = message.getBytes("UTF-8");
    InetAddress addr = InetAddress.getByName( myHost );
    DatagramPacket pack =
      new DatagramPacket(data, data.length, addr, myPort );
```

First, the contents of `message` are placed into an array of bytes called `data`. Next a `java.net.InetAddress` object is created by looking up the hostname `myHost`. An

`InetAddress` holds the network IP address for a host. This class also provides the static `getByName()` method for looking up an IP address by hostname using the system's *name service*. (We'll say more about `InetAddress` in the next section.) Finally, we call the `DatagramPacket` constructor with four arguments: the byte array containing our data, the length of the data, the destination address object, and the port number. We ask for the string to be encoded using the UTF-8 charset; we'll use the same character set to decode it.

The remaining lines construct a default client `DatagramSocket` and call its `send()` method to transmit the `DatagramPacket`. After sending the datagram, we close the socket:

```
DatagramSocket ds = new DatagramSocket();
ds.send( pack );
ds.close();
```

Two operations throw a type of `IOException`: the `InetAddress.getByName()` lookup and the `DatagramSocket send()` method. `InetAddress.getByName()` can throw an `UnknownHostException`, which is a type of `IOException` that indicates the hostname can't be resolved. If `send()` throws an `IOException`, it implies a serious client-side communication problem with the network. We need to catch these exceptions; our `catch` block simply prints a message telling us that something went wrong. If we get one of these exceptions, we can assume the datagram never arrived. However, we can't assume the inverse: even if we don't get an exception, we still don't know that the host is actually accessible or that the data actually arrived; with a `DatagramSocket`, we never find out from the API.

The Pulse server code

The `Pulse` server corresponds to the `HeartBeat` applet. First, it creates a `DatagramSock et` to listen on our prearranged port. This time, we specify a port number in the constructor; we get the port number from the command line as a string (`argv[0]`) and convert it to an integer with `Integer.parseInt()`. Note the difference between this call to the constructor and the call in `HeartBeat`. In the server, we need to listen for incoming datagrams on a prearranged port, so we need to specify the port when creating the `DatagramSocket`. The client just sends datagrams, so we don't have to specify the port in advance; we build the port number into the `DatagramPacket` itself.

Second, `Pulse` creates an empty `DatagramPacket` of a fixed maximum size to receive an incoming datagram. This form of the constructor for `DatagramPacket` takes a byte array and a length as arguments. As much data as possible is stored in the byte array when it's received. (A practical limit on the size of a UDP datagram that can be sent over the Internet is 8K, although datagrams can be larger for local network use—theoretically up to 64K.) Finally, `Pulse` calls the `DatagramSocket`'s `receive()` method to wait for a packet to arrive. When a packet arrives, its contents are printed by turning them to a string using UTF-8 encoding. We determine the actual number of received bytes from the packet's `getLength()` method.

As you can see, `DatagramSockets` are slightly more tedious than regular `Sockets`. With datagrams, it's harder to spackle over the messiness of the socket interface. The Java API rather slavishly follows the Unix interface, and that doesn't help. But all in all, it's not that hard to use datagrams for simple tasks.

InetAddress

The `java.net.InetAddress` class is the lowest-level Java API for working with IP addresses. Instances of `InetAddress` represent individual addresses and the `InetAddress` class provides the API for using the platform's name service to map a string hostname to a numeric IP address. Most of our networking examples showed the use of hostnames to identify remote servers, but under the covers, Java utilized the static `InetAddress.getByName()` method to map the name to a physical IP address. Java normally uses the DNS to perform this lookup (and it caches the results for efficiency). Most Java networking APIs (such as Sockets) will accept either a hostname or an `InetAddress` as a destination. The `InetAddress` class can also be used to perform reverse IP lookups (get a name for an IP address) as well as to find the primary address of the local host via the static `InetAddress.getLocalHost()` method.

A useful feature of `InetAddress` is the method `isReachable()`, which attempts to use the ICMP *ping* protocol to determine whether a remote address can be reached over the network. The ping protocol is the standard mechanism used to check reachability and latency on networks. It is a low-level IP protocol (along with TCP and UDP) and is not guaranteed to be supported everywhere. If `isReachable()` can't use ICMP, it attempts to use TCP to reach the echo service (port 7) on the remote host. For example:

```
InetAddress server = InetAddress.getByName("myserver");
If ( !server.isReachable( timeout ) ) // milliseconds
    pageSomeone();
```

Simple Serialized Object Protocols

Earlier in this chapter, we showed a hypothetical conversation in which a client and server exchanged some primitive data and a serialized Java object. Passing an object between two programs may not have seemed like a big deal at the time, but, in the context of Java as a portable bytecode language, it has big implications. In this section, we show how a protocol can be built using serialized Java objects.

Before we move on, it's worth considering network protocols. Most programmers would consider working with sockets to be tedious and complex. Even though Java makes sockets much easier to use than many other languages, sockets still provide only an unstructured flow of bytes between their endpoints. If you want to do serious communications using sockets, the first thing you have to do is come up with a protocol that defines the data you are sending and receiving. The most complex part of that protocol usually involves how to marshal (package) your data for transfer over the Net and unpack it on the other side.

As we've seen, Java's `DataInputStream` and `DataOuputStream` classes solve this problem for simple data types. We can read and write numbers, `Strings`, and Java primitives in a standard format that can be understood on any other Java platform. To do real work, however, we need to be able to put simple types together into larger structures. Java object serialization solves this problem elegantly by allowing us to send our data in the state in which we will use it—as Java objects. Serialization can even pack up entire graphs of interconnected objects and put them back together at a later time in another Java VM.

A Simple Object-Based Server

In the following example, a client sends a serialized object to the server, and the server responds in kind. The object sent by the client represents a request and the object returned by the server represents the response. The conversation ends when the client closes the connection. It's hard to imagine a simpler protocol. All the hairy details are taken care of by object serialization, which allows us to work with standard Java objects as we are used to doing.

To start, we define a class—`Request`—to serve as a base class for the various kinds of requests we make to the server. Using a common base class is a convenient way to identify the object as a type of request. In a real application, we might also use it to hold basic information, such as client names and passwords, timestamps, serial numbers, and so on. In our example, `Request` can be an empty class that exists so that others can extend it:

```
//file: Request.java
public class Request implements java.io.Serializable {}
```

`Request` implements `Serializable`, so all its subclasses are serializable by default. Next, we create some specific kinds of `Requests`. The first, `DateRequest`, is also a trivial class. We use it to ask the server to send us a `java.util.Date` object as a response:

```
//file: DateRequest.java
public class DateRequest extends Request {}
```

Next, we create a generic `WorkRequest` object. The client sends a `WorkRequest` to get the server to perform some computation. The server calls the `WorkRequest` object's `exe cute()` method to do the work on the server side and then returns the resulting object as a response:

```
//file: WorkRequest.java
public abstract class WorkRequest extends Request {
```

```
    public abstract Object execute();
}
```

For our application, we subclass `WorkRequest` to create `MyCalculation`, which adds code that performs a specific calculation; in this case, we just square a number:

```
//file: MyCalculation.java
public class MyCalculation extends WorkRequest {
    int n;

    public MyCalculation( int n ) {
        this.n = n;
    }
    public Object execute() {
        return new Integer( n * n );
    }
}
```

As far as data content is concerned, `MyCalculation` really doesn't do much; it only really transports an integer value for us. But keep in mind that a request object could hold lots of data, including references to many other objects in complex structures, such as arrays or linked lists. The only requirement is that all the objects to be sent must be serializable or must be able to be discarded by marking them as transient (see Chapter 12). Note that `MyCalculation` also contains behavior—the `execute()` operation. While Java object serialization sends only the data content of a class, in our discussion of RMI later in this chapter, we'll see how Java's ability to dynamically download bytecode for classes can make both the data content and behavior portable over the network.

It's also important to note that even without dynamically loading classes over the network (which is uncommon in practice), this design pattern, sometimes called the *command pattern*, is an important one. Using polymorphism to hide behavior details of tasks from the server allows the application to be easily extended. Polymorphism and Java object serialization are a powerful combination.

Now that we have our protocol, we need the server. The following `Server` class looks a lot like the `TinyHttpd` server we developed earlier in this chapter:

```
//file: Server.java
import java.net.*;
import java.io.*;

public class Server {
  public static void main( String argv[] ) throws IOException {
    ServerSocket ss = new ServerSocket( Integer.parseInt(argv[0]) );
    while ( true )
      new ServerConnection( ss.accept() ).start();
  }
} // end of class Server

class ServerConnection extends Thread {
  Socket client;
```

```
  ServerConnection ( Socket client ) throws SocketException {
    this.client = client;
  }

  public void run() {
    try {
      ObjectInputStream in =
        new ObjectInputStream( client.getInputStream() );
      ObjectOutputStream out =
        new ObjectOutputStream( client.getOutputStream() );
      while ( true ) {
        out.writeObject( processRequest( in.readObject() ) );
        out.flush();
      }
    } catch ( EOFException e3 ) { // Normal EOF
      try {
        client.close();
      } catch ( IOException e ) { }
    } catch ( IOException e ) {
      System.out.println( "I/O error " + e ); // I/O error
    } catch ( ClassNotFoundException e2 ) {
      System.out.println( e2 ); // unknown type of request object
    }
  }

  private Object processRequest( Object request ) {
    if ( request instanceof DateRequest )
      return new java.util.Date();
    else if ( request instanceof WorkRequest )
      return ((WorkRequest)request).execute();
    else
      return null;
  }
}
```

The `Server` handles each request in a separate thread. For each connection, the `run()` method creates an `ObjectInputStream` and an `ObjectOutputStream`, which the server uses to receive the request and send the response. The `processRequest()` method decides what the request means and comes up with the response. To figure out what kind of request we have, we use the `instanceof` operator to look at the object's type.

Finally, we get to our `Client`, which is even simpler:

```
//file: Client.java
import java.net.*;
import java.io.*;

public class Client {
  public static void main( String argv[] ) {
    try {
      Socket server =
        new Socket( argv[0], Integer.parseInt(argv[1]) );
```

```
            ObjectOutputStream out =
              new ObjectOutputStream( server.getOutputStream() );
            ObjectInputStream in =
              new ObjectInputStream( server.getInputStream() );

            out.writeObject( new DateRequest() );
            out.flush();
            System.out.println( in.readObject() );

            out.writeObject( new MyCalculation( 2 ) );
            out.flush();
            System.out.println( in.readObject() );

            server.close();
          } catch ( IOException e ) {
            System.out.println( "I/O error " + e ); // I/O error
          } catch ( ClassNotFoundException e2 ) {
            System.out.println( e2 ); // unknown type of response object
          }
        }
      }
```

Just like the server, `Client` creates the pair of object streams. It sends a `DateRequest` and prints the response; it then sends a `MyCalculation` object and prints the response. Finally, it closes the connection. On both the client and the server, we call the `flush()` method after each call to `writeObject()`. This method forces the system to send any buffered data, ensuring that the other side sees the entire request before we wait for a response. When the client closes the connection, our server catches the `EOFException` that is thrown and ends the session. Alternatively, our client could write a special object, perhaps `null`, to end the session; the server could watch for this item in its main loop.

The order in which we construct the object streams is important. We create the output streams first because the constructor of an `ObjectInputStream` tries to read a header from the stream to make sure that the `InputStream` really is an object stream. If we tried to create both of our input streams first, we would deadlock waiting for the other side to write the headers.

Finally, we run the example, giving it a port number as an argument:

```
% java Server 1234
```

Then we run the `Client`, telling it the server's hostname and port number:

```
% java Client flatland 1234
```

The result should look something like this:

```
Sun Mar 5 14:25:25 PDT 2006
4
```

All right, the result isn't that impressive, but it's easy to think of more substantial applications. Imagine that you need to perform a complex computation on many large datasets. Using serialized objects makes maintenance of the data objects natural and sending them over the wire trivial. There is no need to deal with byte-level protocols at all.

Limitations

As we mentioned earlier, there is one catch in this scenario: both the client and server need access to the necessary classes. That is, all the `Request` classes—including `MyCalculation`, which is really the property of the `Client`—must be deployed in the classpath on both the client and the server machines. In the next section, we'll see that it's possible to send the Java bytecode along with serialized objects to allow completely new kinds of objects to be transported dynamically over the network. We could create this solution on our own, adding to the earlier example using a network class loader to load the classes for us. But we don't have to: Java's RMI facility handles that for us. The ability to send both serialized data and class definitions over the network is not always needed, but it makes Java a powerful tool for prototyping and developing advanced distributed applications.

Remote Method Invocation

The most fundamental means of communication in Java is method invocation. Mechanisms such as the Java event model are built on simple method invocations between objects in the same virtual machine. Therefore, when we want to communicate between virtual machines on different hosts, it's natural to want a mechanism with similar capabilities and semantics—to run a method "over there." Java's RMI mechanism does just that. It lets us get a reference to an object on a remote host and use it almost as if it were in our own virtual machine. RMI lets us invoke methods on remote objects, passing real Java objects as arguments and getting real Java objects as returned values.

Remote invocation is nothing new. For many years, C programmers have used remote procedure calls (RPC) to execute a C function on a remote host and return the results. The primary difference between RPC in other languages and RMI is that RPC is usually primarily concerned with data structures. It's relatively easy to pack up data and ship it around, but RMI tries to do one better. In Java, we don't just work with data structures; we work with objects that contain both data and methods for operating on the data. Not only do we have to be able to ship the state of an object (the data) over the wire, but the recipient has to be able to interact with the object (use its methods) after receiving it. With Java RMI, you can work with network services in an object-oriented fashion, using real, extensible types and pass "live" references between client and server.

It should be no surprise that RMI uses object serialization, which allows us to send graphs of objects (objects and the tree of all the connected objects that they reference). When necessary, RMI can also use dynamic class loading and the security manager to transport Java classes safely. In addition to making remote method calls almost as easy to use as local calls, RMI makes it possible to ship both data and behavior (code) around the Net.

Real-World Usage

Now that the introduction has you all excited, we should put things in a little more context. While Java RMI has proven to be very powerful, it has never really caught on as a way to build general applications. Instead, RPC-like web services using XML and HTTP to transfer data using standardized network protocols have ruled for many years. The reason for this is primarily that they are cross-platform and can be easily consumed by JavaScript running within web browsers. Web services that run over HTTP are also generally immune to firewall issues since they use the same mechanism as all web pages. Since the tools to develop applications using web services have become mature and easy to use, developers tend to use them even when building applications purely in Java, where RMI might otherwise be more powerful. In this section we'll go ahead and show you what can be done with RMI; however, you will definitely want to check out the chapters on web services and web applications later in this book as well.

Remote and Nonremote Objects

Before an object can be used remotely through RMI, it must be serializable. But that's not sufficient. Remote objects in RMI are real distributed objects. As the name suggests, a remote object can be an object on a different machine or an object on the local host. The term *remote* means that the object is used through a special kind of object interface that can be passed over the network. Like normal Java objects, remote objects are passed by reference. Regardless of where the reference is used, the method invocation occurs on the original object, which still lives on its original host. If a remote host returns a reference to one of its remote objects to you, you can call the object's methods; the actual method invocations happen on the remote host where the underlying object resides.

Nonremote objects are simpler; they're just normal serializable objects. (You can pass these over the network as we did in the previous section.) The catch is that when you pass a nonremote object over the network, it is simply copied, so references to the object on one host are not the same as those on the remote host. Nonremote objects are passed by value (copying) as opposed to by reference. This may be acceptable for many kinds of data holder objects on your host, such as the client requests and server responses in our previous example. These types of objects are sometimes called value objects or *data transfer objects* (DTOs).

Remote interfaces

Remote objects implement a special *remote interface* that specifies which of the object's methods can be invoked remotely. The remote interface is part of the application that you create by extending the `java.rmi.Remote` interface. Your remote object then implements its remote interface as it would any other Java interface. In your client-side code, you should then refer to the remote object as an instance of the remote interface—not as an instance of its implementation class. Because both the real object and stub that the client receives implement the remote interface, they are equivalent as far as we are concerned (for method invocation); locally, we never have to worry about whether we have a reference to a stub or to an actual object. This *type equivalence* means that we can use normal language features such as casting with remote objects. Of course, public fields (variables) of the remote object are not accessible through an interface, so you must make accessor methods if you want to manipulate the remote object's fields.

One additional requirement for remote objects distinguishes them from local objects. All methods in the remote interface must declare that they can throw the exception `java.rmi.RemoteException`. This exception (or one of its subclasses) is thrown when any kind of networking error happens (for example, a server crash, network failure, or timeout). Some people see this as a limitation and try to paper over it in various ways. However, the `RemoteException` is there for a reason—remote objects can behave differently from local objects and your code needs to deal with that issue explicitly. There is no magic bullet (automatic retries, transactions) that truly makes the difference go away.

Here's a simple example of the remote interface that defines the behavior of `RemoteObject`; we give it two methods that can be invoked remotely, both of which return some kind of `Value` object:

```
import java.rmi.*;

public interface RemoteObject extends Remote {
    public Value doSomething() throws RemoteException;
    public Value doSomethingElse() throws RemoteException;
}
```

Exporting remote objects

You make a remote object available to the outside world by using the `java.rmi.server.UnicastRemoteObject` class. One way is simply to have the implementation of your remote object extend `UnicastRemoteObject`. When a subclass of `UnicastRemoteObject` is constructed, the RMI runtime system automatically "exports" it to start listening for network connections from clients. Like `java.lang.Object`, this superclass also provides implementations of `equals()`, `hashcode()`, and `toString()` that make sense for a remote object.

Here's a remote object class that implements the `RemoteObject` interface we showed earlier and extends `UnicastRemoteObject`; we haven't shown implementations for the two methods or the constructor:

```
public class MyRemoteObject implements RemoteObject
        extends java.rmi.UnicastRemoteObject
```

```
{
    public MyRemoteObject() throws RemoteException {...}
    public Value doSomething() throws RemoteException {...}
    public Value doSomethingElse() throws RemoteException {...}
    // nonremote methods
    private void doSomethingInternal() { ... }
}
```

Note that we have to supply a constructor that can throw a `RemoteException` (even if it does nothing) because `UnicastRemoteObject`'s default constructor throws `RemoteException` and, even if it's not shown, the Java language always delegates to the superclass constructor. This class can have as many additional methods as it needs (presumably most of them will be `private`, but that isn't strictly necessary), but these nonremote methods are not required to throw the remote exception.

Now, what if we can't or don't want to make our remote object implementation a subclass of `UnicastRemoteObject`? Suppose, for example, that it has to be a subclass of `BankAccount` or some other special base type for our system. Well, we can simply take over the job of exporting the object ourselves, using the static method `exportObject()` of `UnicastRemoteObject`. The `exportObject()` method takes as an argument a `Remote` interface and accomplishes what the `UnicastRemoteObject` constructor normally does for us. It returns as a value the remote object's client stub. However, you will normally not do anything with this directly. In the next section, we'll discuss how clients actually find your service, through the RMI registry (a lookup service).

Normally, exported objects listen on individual *ephemeral* (randomly assigned) port numbers by default. (This is implementation-dependent.) You can control the port number allocation explicitly by exporting your objects using another form of `UnicastRemoteObject.exportObject()`, which takes both a `Remote` interface and a port number as arguments.

Finally, the name `UnicastRemoteObject` begs the question, "What other kinds of remote objects are there?" Right now, few. There is another type of object called `Activatable` that is for RMI objects that require persistence over time. We'll say a few more words about RMI activation later in this chapter, but it's not something we will get into in detail.

The RMI registry

The registry is RMI's phone book. You use the registry to look up a reference to a registered remote object on another host, using an application-specified name. We've already described how remote references can be passed back and forth by remote method calls. The registry is needed to bootstrap the process by allowing the client to look up an initial object on the remote host.

The registry is implemented by a class called `Naming` and an application called `rmiregistry`. The `rmiregistry` application must be running on a host before you start a Java program that wants to advertise in the registry. You can then create instances of remote objects and bind them to particular names in the registry. A registry name can be anything you choose; it takes the form of a slash-separated path. When a client object wants to find your object, it constructs a special URL with the `rmi:` protocol, the hostname, and the object name. On the client, the RMI `Naming` class then talks to the registry and returns the remote object reference.

So, which objects need to register themselves with the registry? Initially, this can be any object that the client has no other way of finding. After that, a call to a remote method can return another remote object without using the registry. Likewise, a call to a remote method can have another remote object as its argument, without requiring the registry. You could design your system such that only one object registers itself and then serves as a factory for any other remote objects you need. In other words, it wouldn't be hard to build a simple object request factory that returns references to all the remote objects your application uses. Depending on how you structure your application, this may happen naturally anyway.

The RMI registry is just one implementation of a lookup mechanism for remote objects. It is not very sophisticated, and lookups tend to be slow. It is not intended to be a general-purpose directory service, but simply to bootstrap RMI communications. More generally, the Java Naming and Directory Interface (JNDI) is a Java API allowing access to other widely used name services that can provide this kind of functionality. JNDI is used with RMI as part of the Enterprise JavaBeans APIs.

An RMI Example

In our first example using RMI, we duplicate the simple serialized object protocol from the previous section. We make a remote RMI object called `MyServer` on which we can invoke methods to get a `Date` object or execute a `WorkRequest` object. First, we define our `Remote` interface:

```
//file: ServerRemote.java
import java.rmi.*;
import java.util.*;

public interface ServerRemote extends Remote {
    Date getDate() throws RemoteException;
    Object execute( WorkRequest work ) throws RemoteException;
}
```

The `ServerRemote` interface extends the `java.rmi.Remote` interface, which identifies objects that implement it as remote objects. We supply two methods that take the place of our old protocol: `getDate()` and `execute()`.

Next, we implement this interface in a class called `MyServer` that defines the bodies of these methods. (Another common convention for naming the implementation of remote interfaces is to append `Impl` to the class name. Using that convention, `MyServer` would instead be named something like `ServerImpl`.)

```
//file: MyServer.java
import java.rmi.*;
import java.util.*;

public class MyServer
    extends java.rmi.server.UnicastRemoteObject
    implements ServerRemote {

    public MyServer() throws RemoteException { }

    // implement the ServerRemote interface
    public Date getDate() throws RemoteException {
        return new Date();
    }

    public Object execute( WorkRequest work )
      throws RemoteException {
        return work.execute();
    }

    public static void main(String args[]) {
        try {
            ServerRemote server = new MyServer();
            Naming.rebind("NiftyServer", server);
        } catch (java.io.IOException e) {
            // problem registering server
        }
    }
}
```

MyServer extends UnicastRemoteObject so that when we create an instance of MyServ er, it is automatically exported and starts listening to the network. We start by providing a constructor that must throw RemoteException, which accommodates errors that might occur in exporting an instance. Next, MyServer implements the methods of the remote interface ServerRemote. These methods are straightforward.

The last method in this class is main(). This method lets the object set itself up as a server. main() creates an instance of the MyServer object and then calls the static method Naming.rebind() to place the object in the registry. The arguments to rebind() include the name of the remote object in the registry (NiftyServer)—which clients use to look up the object—and a reference to the server object itself. We could have called bind() instead, but rebind() handles the case where there's already a NiftyServer registered by replacing it.

We wouldn't need the main() method or this Naming business if we weren't expecting clients to use the registry to find the server—that is, we could omit main() and still use this object as a remote object. We would just be limited to passing the object in method invocations or returning it from method invocations—but that could be part of a factory pattern, as we discussed before.

Now we need our client:

```
//file: MyClient.java
import java.rmi.*;
import java.util.*;

public class MyClient {

    public static void main(String [] args)
      throws RemoteException {
        new MyClient( args[0] );
    }

    public MyClient(String host) {
        try {
            ServerRemote server = (ServerRemote)
                Naming.lookup("rmi://"+host+"/NiftyServer");
            System.out.println( server.getDate() );
            System.out.println(
              server.execute( new MyCalculation(2) ) );
        } catch (java.io.IOException e) {
              // I/O Error or bad URL
        } catch (NotBoundException e) {
              // NiftyServer isn't registered
        }
    }
}
```

When we run `MyClient`, we pass it the hostname of the server on which the registry is running. The `main()` method creates an instance of the `MyClient` object, passing the hostname from the command line as an argument to the constructor.

The constructor for `MyClient` uses the hostname to construct a URL for the object. The URL looks like this: *rmi://hostname/NiftyServer*. (Remember, `NiftyServer` is the name under which we registered our `ServerRemote`.) We pass the URL to the static `Naming.lookup()` method. If all goes well, we get back a reference to a `ServerRemote` (the remote interface). The registry has no idea what kind of object it will return; `lookup()` therefore returns an `Object`, which we must cast to `ServerRemote`, the remote interface type.

Running the example

You can run the client and server on the same machine or on different machines. First, make sure all the classes are in your classpath (or the current directory if there is no classpath) and then start the `rmiregistry` and `MyServer` on your server host:

```
% rmiregistry &(on Windows:start rmiregistry)
%java MyServer
```

Next, run the client, passing the name of the server host (or "localhost" for the local machine):

```
% java MyClientmyhost
```

The client should print the date and the number 4, which the server graciously calculated. Hooray! With just a few lines of code, you have created a powerful client/server application.

Dynamic class loading

Before running the example, we told you to distribute all of the class files to both the client and server machines. However, RMI was designed to ship classes in addition to data around the network; you shouldn't have to distribute all the classes in advance. Let's go a step further and have RMI load classes for us as needed. This involves a few extra steps.

First, we need to tell RMI where to find any other classes it needs. We can use the system property `java.rmi.server.codebase` to specify a URL on a web server (or FTP server) when we run our client or server. This URL specifies the location of a JAR file or a base directory where RMI begins its search for classes. When RMI sends a serialized object (i.e., an object's data) to a client, it also sends this URL. If the recipient needs the class file in addition to the data, it fetches the file at the specified URL. In addition to stub classes, other classes referenced by remote objects in the application can be loaded dynamically. Therefore, we don't have to distribute many class files to the client; we can let the client download them as necessary. In Figure 13-3, we see an example of `MyClient` going to the registry to get a reference to the `ServerRemote` object. Once there, `MyClient` dynamically downloads the stub class for `MyServer` from a web server running on the server object's host.

We can now split our class files more logically between the server and client machines. For example, we could withhold the `MyCalculation` class from the server because it really belongs to the client. Instead, we can make the `MyCalculation` class available via a web server on some machine (probably our client's) and specify the URL when we run `MyClient`:

```
% java -Djava.rmi.server.codebase='http://myserver/foo/'...
```

The trailing slash in the codebase URL is important: it says that the location is a base directory that contains the class files. In this case, we would expect that `MyCalculation` would be accessible at the URL *http://myserver/foo/MyCalculation.class.*

Next, we have to set up security. Since we are loading class files over the network and executing their methods, we must have a security manager in place to restrict the kinds of things those classes may do, at least when they are not coming from a trusted code source. RMI will not load any classes dynamically unless a security manager is installed. One easy way to meet this condition is to install the `RMISecurityManager` as the system security manager for your application. It is an example security manager that works with the default system policy and imposes some basic restrictions on what downloaded classes can do. To install the `RMISecurityManager`, simply add the following line to the beginning of the `main()` method of both the client and server applications (yes, we'll be sending code both ways in the next section):

```
main() {
    System.setSecurityManager( new RMISecurityManager() );
    ...
```

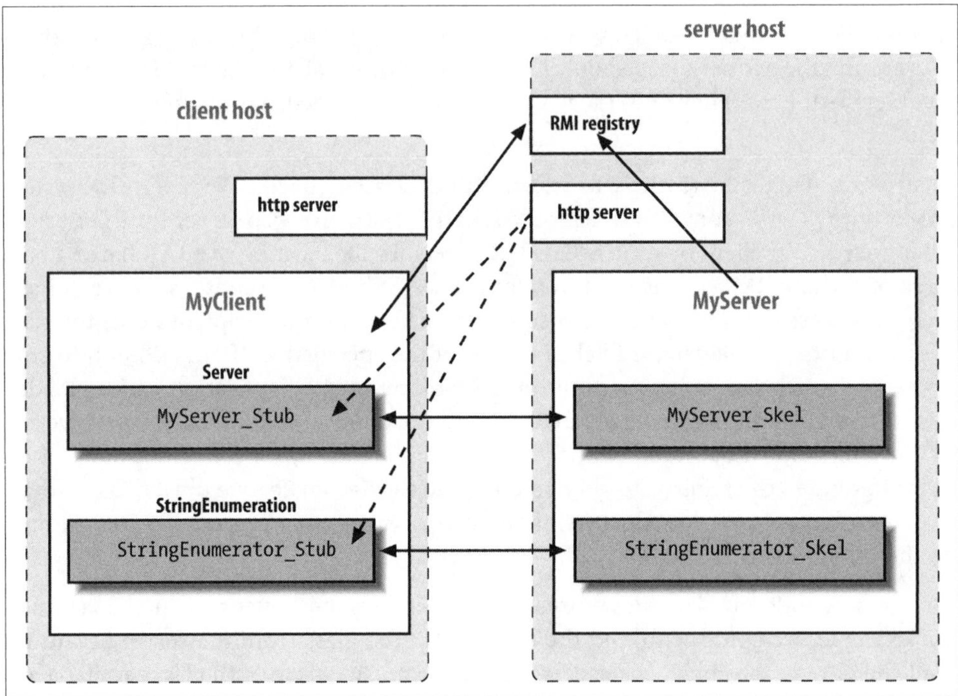

Figure 13-3. RMI applications and dynamic class loading

The `RMISecurityManager` works with the system security policy file to enforce restrictions. You have to provide a policy file that allows the client and server to do basic operations like make network connections. Unfortunately, allowing all the operations needed to load classes dynamically requires listing a lot of permission information and we don't want to get into that here. We suggest that for this example, you simply grant the code all permissions. Here is an example policy file—call it *mysecurity.policy*:

```
grant {
   permission java.security.AllPermission ;
};
```

(It's exceedingly lame, not to mention risky, to install a security manager and then tell it to enforce no real security, but we're more interested in looking at the networking code at the moment.)

To run our MyServer application, we would use a command such as:

```
% java -Djava.rmi.server.codebase='http://myserver/foo/' \
    -Djava.security.policy=mysecurity.policy MyServer
```

Finally, one last trick is required to enable dynamic class loading. As of the current implementation, the rmiregistry must be run without the classes that are to be loaded in its classpath. If the classes are in the classpath of rmiregistry, it does not annotate the serialized objects with the URLs of their class files, and no classes are dynamically loaded. This limitation is really annoying; all we can say is to heed the warning for now.

If you follow these directions, you should be able to run our client with only the MyClient class and the ServerRemote remote interface in its classpath. All the other classes are loaded dynamically from the specified server as needed.

Passing remote object references

So far, we haven't done anything that we couldn't have done with the simple object protocol. We used only one remote object, MyServer, and we got its reference from the RMI registry. Now we extend our example to pass some remote references between the client and server, allowing additional remote calls in both directions. We'll add two methods to our remote ServerRemoteinterface:

```
public interface ServerRemote extends Remote {
    ...
    StringIterator getList() throws RemoteException;
    void asyncExecute( WorkRequest work, WorkListener
    listener )
        throws RemoteException;
}
```

getList() retrieves a new kind of object from the server: a StringIterator. The StringIterator we've created is a simple list of strings with some methods for accessing the strings in order. We make it a remote object so that implementations of StringIterator stay on the server.

Next, we spice up our work request feature by adding an asyncExecute() method. asyncExecute() lets us hand off a WorkRequest object as before, but it does the calculation on its own time. The return type for asyncExecute() is void because it doesn't actually return a value; we get the result later. Along with the request, our client passes a reference to a WorkListener object that is to be notified when the WorkRequest is done. We'll have our client implement WorkListener itself.

Because this is to be a remote object, our interface must extend Remote and its methods must throw RemoteExceptions:

```
//file: StringIterator.java
import java.rmi.*;

public interface StringIterator extends Remote {
```

```
    public boolean hasNext() throws RemoteException;
    public String next() throws RemoteException;
}
```

Next, we provide a simple implementation of `StringIterator`, called `MyStringIterator`:

```
//file: MyStringIterator.java
import java.rmi.*;

public class MyStringIterator
  extends java.rmi.server.UnicastRemoteObject
  implements StringIterator {

    String [] list;
    int index = 0;

    public MyStringIterator( String [] list )
      throws RemoteException {
        this.list = list;
    }
    public boolean hasNext() throws RemoteException {
        return index < list.length;
    }
    public String next() throws RemoteException {
        return list[index++];
    }
}
```

`MyStringIterator` extends `UnicastRemoteObject`. Its methods are simple: it can give you the next string in the list, and it can tell you if there are any strings you haven't seen yet.

Next, we discuss the `WorkListener` remote interface that defines how an object should listen for a completed `WorkRequest`. It has one method, `workCompleted()`, which the server executing a `WorkRequest` calls when the job is done:

```
//file: WorkListener.java
import java.rmi.*;

public interface WorkListener extends Remote {
    public void workCompleted(WorkRequest request, Object result )
        throws RemoteException;
}
```

Let's add the new features to `MyServer`. We need to add implementations of the `getList()` and `asyncExecute()` methods, which we just added to the `ServerRemote` interface:

```
public class MyServer extends java.rmi.server.UnicastRemoteObject
                      implements ServerRemote {
  ...
  public StringIterator getList() throws RemoteException {
```

```
        return new MyStringIterator(
            new String [] { "Foo", "Bar", "Gee" } );
      }

      public void asyncExecute(
         final WorkRequest request, final WorkListener listener )
         throws java.rmi.RemoteException
      {
        new Thread() {
          public void run() {
            Object result = request.execute();
            try {
              listener.workCompleted( request, result );
            } catch ( RemoteException e ) {
              System.out.println( e ); // error calling client
            }
        }}.start();
      }
    }
```

getList() just returns a StringIterator with some stuff in it. asyncExecute() calls a WorkRequest's execute() method and notifies the listener when it's done. asyncExecute() runs the request in a separate thread, allowing the remote method call to return immediately. Later, when the work is done, the server uses the client's WorkListener interface to return the result.

We have to modify MyClient to implement the remote WorkListener interface. This turns MyClient into a remote object, so we will have it extend UnicastRemoteObject. We also add the workCompleted() method the WorkListener interface requires. Finally, we want MyClient to exercise the new features. We've put all of this in a new version of the client called MyClientAsync:

```
    //file: MyClientAsync.java
    import java.rmi.*;
    import java.util.*;

    public class MyClientAsync
        extends java.rmi.server.UnicastRemoteObject implements WorkListener
    {

        public MyClientAsync(String host) throws RemoteException
        {
            try {
                ServerRemote server = (ServerRemote)
                    Naming.lookup("rmi://"+host+"/NiftyServer");

                server.asyncExecute( new MyCalculation( 100 ), this );
                System.out.println("call done...");
            } catch (java.io.IOException e) {
                // I/O Error or bad URL
            } catch (NotBoundException e) {
```

```
                // NiftyServer isn't registered
            }
        }

        public void workCompleted( WorkRequest request, Object result )
            throws RemoteException
        {
            System.out.println("Async result: "+result );
        }

        public static void main(String [] args) throws RemoteException {
            new MyClientAsync( args[0] );
        }

    }
```

We use `getList()` to get the iterator from the server and then loop, printing the strings. We also call `asyncExecute()` to perform another calculation; this time, we square the number 100. The second argument to `asyncExecute()` is the `WorkListener` to notify when the data is ready; we pass a reference to ourselves (`this`).

Restart the RMI registry and `MyServer` on your server, and run the client somewhere. You should get the following:

```
Foo
Bar
Gee
Async result = 10000
```

We hope that this introduction has given you a feel for the tremendous power that RMI offers through object serialization and dynamic class loading. Java is one of the first programming languages to offer this kind of powerful framework for distributed applications. Although some of the advanced features are not used widely in business applications, RMI was the underpinning for the very widely used J2EE Enterprise JavaBeans architecture and is an important technology. For more information on RMI and J2EE, see *Java Enterprise in a Nutshell* (O'Reilly).

RMI and CORBA

Java supports an important alternative to RMI, called CORBA (Common Object Request Broker Architecture). We won't say much about CORBA here, but you should know that it exists. CORBA is an older distributed object standard developed by the Object Management Group (OMG), of which Sun Microsystems was one of the founding members. Its major advantage is that it works across languages: a Java program can use CORBA to talk to objects written in other languages, like C or C++. This may be a considerable advantage if you want to build a Java frontend for an older program that you can't afford to reimplement. CORBA also provides other services similar to those in the Java Enterprise APIs. CORBA's major disadvantages are that it's complex, inelegant, and somewhat arcane.

Scalable I/O with NIO

We'll now conclude the discussion of the NIO package we began in Chapter 12 by talking about nonblocking and selectable network communications. All our server examples in this chapter thus far have used a thread-bound pattern (one thread per I/O operation). In Java, this is very natural because of the ease with which we can create threads. It's also very efficient, within limits. Problems arise when you try to build very large-scale servers using this style of client handling. While on a large machine it's certainly possible to have hundreds or even thousands of threads (especially if they're mostly idle, waiting for I/O), this is a resource-hungry solution. Every thread you start in Java consumes memory for its internal stack, and the performance of managing this number of threads is highly system-dependent.

An alternate approach is to take a lesson from the old, dark days before threading was available and use nonblocking I/O operations to manage numerous communications from a single thread. Better yet, our server uses a configurable pool of threads, taking advantage of machines with many processors.

At the heart of this process is the concept of *selectable* I/O. It's not good enough to simply have nonblocking I/O operations if you have no way to efficiently poll for work to be done. The NIO package provides for efficient polling using selectable channels. A selectable channel allows for the registration of a special kind of listener called a *selector* that can check the readiness of the channel for operations, such as reading and writing or accepting or creating network connections.

The selector and the selection process are not typical Java listeners of the kind we'll see elsewhere in this book, but instead rather slavishly follow the conventions of C language systems. This is mainly for performance reasons; because this API is primarily intended for high-volume servers, it is bound very tightly to the traditional, underlying operating system facilities with less regard for ease of use. This, combined with the other details of using the NIO package, mean that this section is somewhat dense and the server we create here is one of the longer and more complex examples in the book. Don't be discouraged if you are a bit put off by this section. You can use the general techniques earlier in this chapter for most applications and reserve this knowledge for creating services that handle the very highest volumes of simultaneous client requests.

Selectable Channels

A selectable channel implements the `SelectableChannel` interface, which specifies that the channel can be set to a nonblocking mode and that it supports the select API that makes efficient polling possible. The primary implementations of selectable channels are those for working with the network: SocketChannel, ServerSocketChannel, and DatagramChannel. The only other selectable channel is the Pipe (which can be used in an analogous way for intra-VM communication).

At the heart of the process is the Selector object, which knows about a particular set of selectable channels and provides a select() method for determining their readiness for I/O operations. Conceptually, the process is simple; you register one or more channels with a selector and then poll it, asking it to tell you which set of channels is ready to go. In actuality, there are a few additional pieces involved.

First, the Selector does not work directly with channels but instead operates on SelectionKey objects. A SelectionKey object is created implicitly when the channel is registered with the Selector. It encapsulates the selectable channel as well as information about what types of operations (e.g., read, write) we are interested in waiting for. That information is held in the SelectionKey in a set of flags called the *interest set*, which can be changed by the application at any time. SelectionKeys are also used to return the results of a select operation. Each call to select() returns the number of SelectionKeys that are ready for some type of I/O. The keys are then retrieved with the selectedKeys() method. Each key also has a set of flags called the *ready set* that indicates which operation of interest is actually ready (possibly more than one). For example, a SelectionKey interest set might indicate that we want to know when its channel is ready for reading or writing. After a select operation, if that key is in the set returned by the selector, we know that it is ready for one or more of those operations, and we can check the key's ready set to find out which one.

Before we go on, we should say that although we have been saying that channels are registered with selectors, the API is (confusingly) the other way around. Selectors are actually registered with the one or more channels they manage, but it's better to mentally spackle over this and think of them the other way around.

Using Select

A Selector object is created using the Selector.open() method (Selector uses a factory pattern):

```
Selector selector = Selector.open();
```

To register one or more channels with the selector, set them to nonblocking mode:

```
SelectableChannel channelA = // ...
channelA.configureBlocking( false );
```

Next, register the channels:

```
int interestOps = SelectionKey.OP_READ | SelectionKey.OP_WRITE;
SelectionKey key = channelA.register( selector, interestOps );
```

When we register the channel, we have an opportunity to set the initial interest operations (or "interest ops"). These are defined by constant fields in the `SelectionKey` class:

`OP_READ`
: Ready to read

`OP_WRITE`
: Ready to write

`OP_CONNECT`
: Client-socket connection ready

`OP_ACCEPT`
: Server-socket connection ready

These fields are bit flags; you can logically OR them together as in this example to express interest in more than one type of operation.

The result of the `register()` method is a `SelectionKey` object. We can use the key to change the interest ops at any time with the `SelectionKey interestOps()` method or to unregister the channel from the `Selector` with the key's `cancel()` method.

This same key is also returned as the result of selection operations when its channel is ready. When the `SelectionKey` is returned, its ready set holds flags for the operations that do not block if called. We can retrieve the value of the flags with the `readySet()` method. Convenience methods are available to test for each operation in the ready set: `isReadable()`, `isWritable()`, `isConnectable()`, and `isAcceptable()`.

Depending on how you structure your application, it may not be necessary to save the `SelectionKey` at registration time. In our example, we let the `Selector` keep track of the keys for us, simply using them when they are ready. In fact, we go even further and put the `SelectionKey` to work by asking it to hold a reference for us! The `SelectionKey attach()` method is a convenience method that can attach an arbitrary object to the key for use by our application. We show how this can be useful in a bit.

After one or more channels are registered with the `Selector`, we can perform a `select` operation using one of its `select()` methods:

```
int readyCount = selector.select();
```

Without arguments, the method blocks until at least one channel is ready for some operation or until the `Selector`'s `wakeup()` method is called. Alternatively, you can use the form of `select()` that takes a timeout (in milliseconds) to wait for a ready channel before returning. There is also `selectNow()`, which always returns immediately. Both of these return methods count the number of ready channels.

You can use `select()` and `wakeup()` somewhat like `wait()` and `notify()`. The wakeup is necessary because once a selection is started, it will not see any changes to its key's interest ops until the next invocation. If another thread changes the interest ops, it must use wakeup() to prompt the selecting thread to select() again. The Selector is also heavily synchronized; for example, calls to register new channels block until the select is finished. Often it's much easier to simply use select with a short timeout and a loop, like this:

```
while ( selector.select( 50 ) == 0 );
```

However, if another thread is allowed to change the interest ops, you still need to use wakeup() to maximize throughput. Otherwise, in the worst case, you could end up waiting the full select wait period on every iteration, even when there is work to be done.

Next, we can get the set of ready channels from the Selector with the selected Keys() method and iterate through them, doing whatever our application dictates:

```
Set readySet = selector.selectedKeys();
for( Iterator it = readySet.iterator(); it.hasNext(); ) {
    SelectionKey key = (SelectionKey)it.next();
    it.remove();  // remove the key from the ready set
 // use the key
}
```

The ready set is returned to us as a java.util.Set, which we walk through with an Iterator (see Chapter 1). One important thing to note is that we've used the Itera tor's remove() method to remove the key from the ready set. The select() methods add keys only to the ready set or add flags to keys already in the set; they never remove them, so we must clear the keys when we handle them. You can get the full set of keys a Selector is managing with the keys() method, but you should not attempt to remove keys from that set; use the cancel() method on individual keys instead. Or you can close the entire Selector with its close() method, unregistering all its keys.

LargerHttpd

Let's put this information to use. In this section, we'll create the big brother of TinyHttpd (our minimalist web server) called LargerHttpd. The LargerHttpd server is a nonblocking web server that uses SocketChannels and a pool of threads to service requests. In this example, a single thread executes a main loop that accepts new connections and checks the readiness of existing client connections for reading or writing. Whenever a client needs attention, it places the job in a queue where a thread from our thread pool waits to service it. As we said, this example is a bit longer than we would like, but it is really the minimum that is necessary to show a realistic usage of the APIs:

```
import java.io.*;
import java.util.*;
import java.util.concurrent.*;
import java.net.*;
import java.nio.*;
import java.nio.channels.*;
```

```
import java.nio.charset.*;
import java.util.regex.*;

public class LargerHttpd
{
    Selector clientSelector;

    public void run( int port, int threads ) throws IOException
    {
        clientSelector = Selector.open();
        ServerSocketChannel ssc = ServerSocketChannel.open();
        ssc.configureBlocking(false);
        InetSocketAddress sa =  new InetSocketAddress( InetAddress
            .getLoopbackAddress(), port );
        ssc.socket().bind( sa );
        ssc.register( clientSelector, SelectionKey.OP_ACCEPT );

        Executor executor = Executors.newFixedThreadPool( threads );

        while ( true ) {
            try {
                while ( clientSelector.select(100) == 0 );
                Set<SelectionKey> readySet = clientSelector.selectedKeys();
                for(Iterator<SelectionKey> it=readySet.iterator();
                    it.hasNext();)
                {
                    final SelectionKey key = it.next();
                    it.remove();
                    if ( key.isAcceptable() ) {
                        acceptClient( ssc );
                    } else {
                        key.interestOps( 0 );
                        executor.execute( new Runnable() {
                          public void run() {
                            try {
                                handleClient( key );
                            } catch ( IOException e) {
                              System.out.println(e);
                            }
                          }
                        } );
                    }
                }
            } catch ( IOException e ) { System.out.println(e); }
        }
    }

    void acceptClient( ServerSocketChannel ssc ) throws IOException
    {
        SocketChannel clientSocket = ssc.accept();
        clientSocket.configureBlocking(false);
```

```
        SelectionKey key =  clientSocket.register( clientSelector,
            SelectionKey.OP_READ );
        HttpdConnection client = new HttpdConnection( clientSocket );
        key.attach( client );
    }

    void handleClient( SelectionKey key ) throws IOException
    {
        HttpdConnection client = (HttpdConnection)key.attachment();
        if ( key.isReadable() ) {
            client.read( key );
        } else {
            client.write( key );
        }
        clientSelector.wakeup();
    }

    public static void main( String argv[] ) throws IOException {
        //new LargerHttpd().run( Integer.parseInt(argv[0]), 3/*threads*/ );
        new LargerHttpd().run( 1235, 3/*threads*/ );
    }
}

class HttpdConnection
{
    static Charset charset = Charset.forName("8859_1");
    static Pattern httpGetPattern = Pattern.compile("(?s)GET /?(\\S*).*");
    SocketChannel clientSocket;
    ByteBuffer buff = ByteBuffer.allocateDirect( 64*1024 );
    String request;
    String response;
    FileChannel file;
    int filePosition;

    HttpdConnection ( SocketChannel clientSocket ) {
        this.clientSocket = clientSocket;
    }

    void read( SelectionKey key ) throws IOException {
        if ( request == null && (clientSocket.read( buff ) == -1
                || buff.get( buff.position()-1 ) == '\n' ) )
            processRequest( key );
        else
            key.interestOps( SelectionKey.OP_READ );
    }

    void processRequest( SelectionKey key ) {
        buff.flip();
        request = charset.decode( buff ).toString();
        Matcher get = httpGetPattern.matcher( request );
        if ( get.matches() ) {
            request = get.group(1);
```

```
            if ( request.endsWith("/") || request.equals("") )
                request = request + "index.html";
            System.out.println( "Request: "+request);
            try {
                file = new FileInputStream ( request ).getChannel();
            } catch ( FileNotFoundException e ) {
                response = "404 Object Not Found";
            }
        } else
            response = "400 Bad Request" ;

        if ( response != null ) {
            buff.clear();
            charset.newEncoder().encode(
                CharBuffer.wrap( response ), buff, true );
            buff.flip();
        }
        key.interestOps( SelectionKey.OP_WRITE );
    }

    void write( SelectionKey key ) throws IOException {
        if ( response != null ) {
            clientSocket.write( buff );
            if ( buff.remaining() == 0 )
                response = null;
        } else if ( file != null ) {
            int remaining = (int)file.size()-filePosition;
            long sent = file.transferTo( filePosition, remaining,
                clientSocket);
            if ( sent >= remaining || remaining <= 0 ) {
                file.close();
                file = null;
            } else
                filePosition += sent;
        }
        if ( response == null && file == null ) {
            clientSocket.close();
            key.cancel();
        } else
            key.interestOps( SelectionKey.OP_WRITE );
    }
}
```

From a bird's-eye view, the structure of `LargerHttpd` is the same as `TinyHttpd`. The main class, `LargerHttpd`, accepts connections, and a connection class, `HttpdConnection`, encapsulates a socket and handles the conversation with the client. However, this time, instead of each connection object being a `Runnable` serviced in its own thread, its functionality is broken into two primary methods called `read()` and `write()`. The job of our `LargerHttpd` is to accept new client socket connections, wrap them in an instance of `HttpdConnection`, and then watch the client's status with a `Selector`. Whenever we detect that a client is ready to send or receive data, we hand off a `Runnable` task to our

Executor. The task calls read() or write() on the corresponding client, based on the operation that is is ready.

The HttpConnection object encapsulates the state of the conversation with the client. Because its interface is rather coarse, it must keep track of whether it is waiting to read more input, generate a response, or write file output. The HttpdConnection also manages the interest set of its key so that it can effectively schedule itself to be woken up when it's ready for reading or writing. The association between the HttpdConnection and the key is made by using the key's attach() and attachment() methods.

LargerHttpd's acceptClient() method does several things. First, it accepts the new socket connection. Next, it configures and registers it with the selector with an initial interest set for reading. Finally, it creates the HttpdConnection for the socket, and attaches the HttpdConnection object to the key for later retrieval.

The main loop of LargerHttpd is fairly straightforward. First, we set up the ServerSocketChannel. This is similar to setting up a plain ServerSocket, except that we must first create an InetSocketAddress object to hold the local loopback address and port combination of our server socket and then explicitly bind our socket to that address with the ServerSocketChannel bind() method. We also configure the server socket to nonblocking mode and register it with our main Selector so that we can select for client connections in the same loop that we use to select for client read and write readiness.

In the main select loop, we check to see whether the key is ready for an accept operation and if so, we call acceptClient(); if not, we set the key's interest set to zero with the interestOps() method and dispatch the key to our handleClient() method via a Runnable task. It's important that we change the interest set to zero to clear it before the next loop; otherwise, we'd be in a race to see whether the thread pool performed its maximum work before we detected another ready condition. Setting the interest ops to 0 and resetting it in the HttpdConnection object upon completion ensures that only one thread is handling a given client at a time.

For each operation that is ready, we dispatch a task to our Executor. The task calls handleClient(), passing it the selection key. From the key, we retrieve the associated HttpdConnection object and call the appropriate service method based on whether the key is ready for reading or writing. After that, it's up to the connection object to do its job. Each call to the read() method simply does what would be one iteration of a read loop in a thread-bound application. Each read gets as much data as available and checks to see whether we've reached the end of a line (a \n newline character). Upon reaching the end of a line, we dispatch the call to the processRequest() method, which turns the byte buffer into text and uses the same techniques as our TinyHttpd to parse the request into a file pathname. On each incomplete call to read(), we set the interest ops of our key back to OP_READ. Upon completing the read and processing the request, we switch to using OP_WRITE because we are now ready to send a response.

The `write()` method keeps track of whether it's sending a text response (error message) or a file by using the `response` and `file` instance variables. When sending a file, we use the `FileChannel`'s `transferTo()` method to transfer bytes from the file directly to the network socket without copying them into Java's memory space. (This is indeed an efficient little web server.) And that's about it. When we're done, we close the client socket and cancel our key, which causes it to be removed from the `Selector`'s key set during the next `select` operation (discarding our `HttpdConnection` object with it).

Nonblocking Client-Side Operations

Our example showed `SocketChannel` used for nonblocking, selectable I/O in a typical server application. It's less common to need nonblocking I/O from a client, but there is certainly no reason you can't do it. Perhaps you're writing a peer-to-peer (P2P) application that manages many connections from both sides.

For the client side of communications, one additional tool is provided: a nonblocking socket-connect operation. The process of creating a TCP connection from the client side involves contacting the remote host in a two-phase acknowledgment. This process normally blocks until the connection is established. However, the NIO package provides an alternative that allows you to initiate the connection and then poll for its status. When set to nonblocking mode, a call to a `SocketChannel`'s `connect()` method returns immediately. The connection is then attempted (and possibly succeeds or fails) in the background. Later, a `Selector` can be used, checking for the `OP_CONNECT` flag to see when the socket is ready to "finish connecting." The connection is finished by invoking the `SocketChannel`'s `finishConnect()` method, which either returns or throws an `IOException` indicating the failure. The process of finishing the connection is really more about collecting the results of the asynchronous connection—acknowledging its success or failure—than about doing work.

CHAPTER 14

Programming for the Web

When you think about the Web, you probably think of web-based applications and services. If you are asked to go deeper, you may consider tools such as web browsers and web servers that support those applications and move data around the network. But it's important to note that standards and protocols, not the applications and tools themselves, have enabled the Web's growth. Since the earliest days of the Internet, there have been ways to move files from here to there, and document formats that were just as powerful as HTML, but there was not a unifying model for how to identify, retrieve, and display information, nor was there a universal way for applications to interact with that data over the network. Since the web explosion began, HTML has reigned supreme as a common format for documents, and most developers have at least some familiarity with it. In this chapter, we're going to talk a bit about its cousin, HTTP, the protocol that handles communications between web clients and servers, and URLs, which provide a standard for naming and addressing objects on the Web. Java provides a very simple API for working with URLs to address objects on the Web. In this chapter, we'll discuss how to write web clients that can interact with the servers using the HTTP `GET` and `POST` methods and also say a bit about web services, which are the next step up the evolutionary chain. In Chapter 15, we'll jump over to the server side and take a look at servlets and web services, which are Java programs that run on web servers and implement the other side of these conversations.

Uniform Resource Locators (URLs)

A URL points to an object on the Internet. It's a text string that identifies an item, tells you where to find it, and specifies a method for communicating with it or retrieving it from its source. A URL can refer to any kind of information source. It might point to static data, such as a file on a local filesystem, a web server, or an FTP site; or it can point to a more dynamic object such as an RSS news feed or a record in a database. URLs can even refer to more dynamic resources such as communication sessions and email addresses.

Because there are many different ways to locate an item on the Net and different mediums and transports require different kinds of information, URLs can have many forms. The most common form has four components: a network host or server, the name of the item, its location on that host, and a protocol by which the host should communicate:

```
protocol://hostname/path/item-name
```

`protocol` (also called the "scheme") is an identifier such as `http` or `ftp`; *`hostname`* is usually an Internet host and domain name; and the *`path`* and *`item`* components form a unique path that identifies the object on that host. Variants of this form allow extra information to be packed into the URL, specifying, for example, port numbers for the communications protocol and fragment identifiers that reference sections inside documents. Other, more specialized types of URLs such as "mailto" URLs for email addresses or URLs for addressing things like database components may not follow this format precisely, but do conform to the general notion of a protocol followed by a unique identifier. (Some of these would more properly be called URIs, which we'll discuss later.)

Because most URLs have the notion of a hierarchy or path, we sometimes speak of a URL that is relative to another URL, called a *base URL*. In that case, we are using the base URL as a starting point and supplying additional information to target an object relative to that URL. For example, the base URL might point to a directory on a web server and a relative URL might name a particular file in that directory or in a subdirectory.

The URL Class

Bringing this down to a more concrete level is the Java URL class. The URL class represents a URL address and provides a simple API for accessing web resources, such as documents and applications on servers. It can use an extensible set of protocol and content handlers to perform the necessary communication and in theory even data conversion. With the URL class, an application can open a connection to a server on the network and retrieve content with just a few lines of code. As new types of servers and new formats for content evolve, additional URL handlers can be supplied to retrieve and interpret the data without modifying your applications.

A URL is represented by an instance of the `java.net.URL` class. A `URL` object manages all the component information within a URL string and provides methods for retrieving the object it identifies. We can construct a `URL` object from a URL string or from its component parts:

```
try {
    URL aDoc =
      new URL( "http://foo.bar.com/documents/homepage.html" );
    URL sameDoc =
      new URL("http","foo.bar.com","documents/homepage.html");
} catch ( MalformedURLException e ) { ... }
```

These two URL objects point to the same network resource, the *homepage.html* document on the server *foo.bar.com*. Whether the resource actually exists and is available isn't known until we try to access it. When initially constructed, the URL object contains only data about the object's location and how to access it. No connection to the server has been made. We can examine the various parts of the URL with the getProtocol(), getHost(), and getFile() methods. We can also compare it to another URL with the sameFile() method (which has an unfortunate name for something that may not point to a file). sameFile() determines whether two URLs point to the same resource. It can be fooled, but sameFile() does more than compare the URL strings for equality; it takes into account the possibility that one server may have several names as well as other factors. (It doesn't go as far as to fetch the resources and compare them, however.)

When a URL is created, its specification is parsed to identify just the protocol component. If the protocol doesn't make sense, or if Java can't find a protocol handler for it, the URL constructor throws a MalformedURLException. A *protocol handler* is a Java class that implements the communications protocol for accessing the URL resource. For example, given an http URL, Java prepares to use the HTTP protocol handler to retrieve documents from the specified web server.

As of Java 7, URL protocol handlers are guaranteed to be provided for http, https (secure HTTP), and ftp, as well as local file URLs and jar URLs that refer to files inside JAR archives. Outside of that, it gets a little dicey. We'll talk more about the issues surrounding content and protocol handlers a bit later in this chapter.

Stream Data

The lowest-level and most general way to get data back from a URL is to ask for an InputStream from the URL by calling openStream(). Getting the data as a stream may also be useful if you want to receive continuous updates from a dynamic information source. The drawback is that you have to parse the contents of the byte stream yourself. Working in this mode is basically the same as working with a byte stream from socket communications, but the URL protocol handler has already dealt with all of the server communications and is providing you with just the content portion of the transaction. Not all types of URLs support the openStream() method because not all types of URLs refer to concrete data; you'll get an UnknownServiceException if the URL doesn't.

The following code prints the contents of an HTML file on a web server:

```
try {
    URL url = new URL("http://server/index.html");
```

```
        BufferedReader bin = new BufferedReader (
            new InputStreamReader( url.openStream() ));

        String line;
        while ( (line = bin.readLine()) != null ) {
            System.out.println( line );
        }
        bin.close();
    } catch (Exception e) { }
```

We ask for an `InputStream` with `openStream()` and wrap it in a `BufferedReader` to read the lines of text. Because we specify the `http` protocol in the URL, we enlist the services of an HTTP protocol handler. Note that we haven't talked about content handlers yet. In this case, because we're reading directly from the input stream, no content handler (no transformation of the content data) is involved.

Getting the Content as an Object

As we said previously, reading raw content from a stream is the most general mechanism for accessing data over the Web. `openStream()` leaves the parsing of data up to you. The URL class, however, was intended to support a more sophisticated, pluggable, content-handling mechanism. We'll discuss this now, but be aware that it is not widely used because of lack of standardization and limitations in how you can deploy new handlers. Although the Java community made some progress in recent years in standardizing a small set of protocol handlers, no such effort was made to standardize content handlers. This means that although this part of the discussion is interesting, its usefulness is limited.

The way it's supposed to work is that when Java knows the type of content being retrieved from a URL and a proper content handler is available, you can retrieve the `URL` content as an appropriate Java object by calling the `URL`'s `getContent()` method. In this mode of operation, `getContent()` initiates a connection to the host, fetches the data for you, determines the type of data, and then invokes a content handler to turn the bytes into a Java object. It acts sort of as if you had read a serialized Java object, as in Chapter 13. Java will try to determine the type of the content by looking at its MIME type, its file extension, or even by examining the bytes directly.

For example, given the URL *http://foo.bar.com/index.html*, a call to `getContent()` uses the HTTP protocol handler to retrieve data and might use an HTML content handler to turn the data into an appropriate document object. Similarly, a GIF file might be turned into an AWT `ImageProducer` object using a GIF content handler. If we access the GIF file using an FTP URL, Java would use the same content handler but a different protocol handler to receive the data.

Since the content handler must be able to return any type of object, the return type of `getContent()` is `Object`. This might leave us wondering what kind of object we got. In a moment, we'll describe how we could ask the protocol handler about the object's MIME type. Based on this, and whatever other knowledge we have about the kind of object we are expecting, we can cast the `Object` to its appropriate, more specific type. For example, if we expect an image, we might cast the result of `getContent()` to `ImageProducer`:

```
try {
    ImageProducer ip = (ImageProducer)myURL.getContent();
} catch ( ClassCastException e ) { ... }
```

Various kinds of errors can occur when trying to retrieve the data. For example, `getContent()` can throw an `IOException` if there is a communications error. Other kinds of errors can occur at the application level: some knowledge of how the application-specific content and protocol handlers deal with errors is necessary. One problem that could arise is that a content handler for the data's MIME type wouldn't be available. In this case, `getContent()` invokes a special "unknown type" handler that returns the data as a raw `InputStream` (back to square one).

In some situations, we may also need knowledge of the protocol handler. For example, consider a `URL` that refers to a nonexistent file on an HTTP server. When requested, the server returns the familiar "404 Not Found" message. To deal with protocol-specific operations like this, we may need to talk to the protocol handler, which we'll discuss next.

Managing Connections

Upon calling `openStream()` or `getContent()` on a `URL`, the protocol handler is consulted and a connection is made to the remote server or location. Connections are represented by a `URLConnection` object, subtypes of which manage different protocol-specific communications and offer additional metadata about the source. The `HttpURLConnection` class, for example, handles basic web requests and also adds some HTTP-specific capabilities such as interpreting "404 Not Found" messages and other web server errors. We'll talk more about `HttpURLConnection` later in this chapter.

We can get a `URLConnection` from our `URL` directly with the `openConnection()` method. One of the things we can do with the `URLConnection` is ask for the object's content type before reading data. For example:

```
URLConnection connection = myURL.openConnection();
String mimeType = connection.getContentType();
InputStream in = connection.getInputStream();
```

Despite its name, a `URLConnection` object is initially created in a raw, unconnected state. In this example, the network connection was not actually initiated until we called the `getContentType()` method. The `URLConnection` does not talk to the source until data is requested or its `connect()` method is explicitly invoked. Prior to connection, network parameters and protocol-specific features can be set up. For example, we can set timeouts on the initial connection to the server and on reads:

```
URLConnection connection = myURL.openConnection();
connection.setConnectTimeout( 10000 ); // milliseconds
connection.setReadTimeout( 10000 ); // milliseconds
InputStream in = connection.getInputStream();
```

As we'll see in the section "Using the POST Method," we can get at the protocol-specific information by casting the `URLConnection` to its specific subtype.

Handlers in Practice

The content- and protocol-handler mechanisms we've described are very flexible; to handle new types of URLs, you need only add the appropriate handler classes. One interesting application of this would be Java-based web browsers that could handle new and specialized kinds of URLs by downloading them over the Net. The idea for this was touted in the earliest days of Java. Unfortunately, it never came to fruition. There is no API for dynamically downloading new content and protocol handlers. In fact, there is no standard API for determining what content and protocol handlers exist on a given platform.

Java currently mandates protocol handlers for HTTP, HTTPS, FTP, FILE, and JAR. While in practice you will generally find these basic protocol handlers with all versions of Java, that's not entirely comforting, and the story for content handlers is even less clear. The standard Java classes don't, for example, include content handlers for HTML, GIF, JPEG, or other common data types. Furthermore, although content and protocol handlers are part of the Java API and an intrinsic part of the mechanism for working with URLs, specific content and protocol handlers aren't defined. Even those protocol handlers that have been bundled in Java are still packaged as part of the Sun implementation classes and are not truly part of the core API for all to see.

In summary, the Java content- and protocol-handler mechanism was a forward-thinking approach that never quite materialized. The promise of web browsers that dynamically extend themselves for new types of protocols and new content is, like flying cars, always just a few years away. Although the basic mechanics of the protocol-handler mechanism are useful (especially now with some standardization) for decoding content in your own applications, you should probably turn to other, newer frameworks that have a bit more specificity.

Useful Handler Frameworks

The idea of dynamically downloadable handlers could also be applied to other kinds of handler-like components. For example, the Java XML community is fond of referring to XML as a way to apply semantics (meaning) to documents and to Java as a portable way to supply the behavior that goes along with those semantics. It's possible that an XML viewer could be built with downloadable handlers for displaying XML tags.

The JavaBeans APIs touch upon this subject with the Java Activation Framework (JAF), which provides a way to detect the data stream type and "encapsulate access to it" in a Java bean. If this sounds suspiciously like the content handler's job, it is. Unfortunately, it looks like these APIs will not be merged and, outside of the Java Mail API, the JAF has not been widely used.

Fortunately, for working with URL streams of images, music, and video, very mature APIs are available. The Java Advanced Imaging API (JAI) includes a well-defined, extensible set of handlers for most image types, and the Java Media Framework (JMF) can play most common music and video types found online.

Talking to Web Applications

Web browsers are the universal clients for web applications. They retrieve documents for display and serve as a user interface, primarily through the use of HTML, JavaScript, and linked documents. In this section, we'll show how to write client-side Java code that uses HTTP through the `URL` class to work with web applications directly using `GET` and `POST` operations to retrieve and send data. Later in this chapter, we'll begin a discussion of web services, which marry HTTP with XML to enable cross-platform application-to-application communications using web standards.

There are many reasons an application might want to communicate via HTTP. For example, compatibility with another browser-based application might be important, or you might need to gain access to a server through a firewall where direct socket connections (and RMI) are problematic. HTTP is the lingua franca of the Net, and despite its limitations (or more likely because of its simplicity), it has rapidly become one of the most widely supported protocols in the world. As for using Java on the client side, all the other reasons you would write a client-side GUI or non-GUI application (as opposed to a pure web/HTML-based application) also present themselves. A client-side GUI can perform sophisticated presentation and validation while, with the techniques presented here, still using web-enabled services over the network.

The primary task we discuss here is sending data to the server, specifically HTML form-encoded data. In a web browser, the name/value pairs of HTML form fields are encoded in a special format and sent to the server using one of two methods. The first method, using the HTTP `GET` command, encodes the user's input into the URL and requests the corresponding document. The server recognizes that the first part of the URL refers to a program and invokes it, passing along the information encoded in the URL as a parameter. The second method uses the HTTP `POST` command to ask the server to accept the encoded data and pass it to a web application as a stream. In Java, we can create a URL that refers to a server-side program and request or send it data using the `GET` and

POST methods. (In Chapter 15, we'll see how to build web applications that implement the other side of this conversation.)

Using the GET Method

Using the GET method of encoding data in a URL is pretty easy. All we have to do is create a URL pointing to a server program and use a simple convention to tack on the encoded name/value pairs that make up our data. For example, the following code snippet opens a URL to an old-school CGI program called *login.cgi* on the server *myhost* and passes it two name/value pairs. It then prints whatever text the CGI sends back:

```
URL url = new URL(
    // this string should be URL-encoded
    "http://myhost/cgi-bin/login.cgi?Name=Pat&Password=foobar");

BufferedReader bin = new BufferedReader (
  new InputStreamReader( url.openStream() ));

String line;
while ( (line = bin.readLine()) != null ) {
    System.out.println( line );
}
```

To form the URL with parameters, we start with the base URL of *login.cgi*; we add a question mark (?), which marks the beginning of the parameter data, followed by the first name/value pair. We can add as many pairs as we want, separated by ampersand (&) characters. The rest of our code simply opens the stream and reads back the response from the server. Remember that creating a URL doesn't actually open the connection. In this case, the URL connection was made implicitly when we called openStream(). Although we are assuming here that our server sends back text, it could send anything.

It's important to point out that we have skipped a step here. This example works because our name/value pairs happen to be simple text. If any "nonprintable" or special characters (including ? or &) are in the pairs, they must be encoded first. The java.net.URLEncoder class provides a utility for encoding the data. We'll show how to use it in the next example.

Another important thing is that although this small example sends a password field, you should never send sensitive data using this simplistic approach. The data in this example is sent in clear text across the network (it is not encrypted). And in this case, the password field would appear anywhere the URL is printed as well (e.g., server logs and bookmarks). We'll talk about secure web communications later in this chapter and when we discuss writing web applications using servlets in Chapter 15.

Using the POST Method

Here's a small application that acts like an HTML form. It gathers data from two text fields—`name` and `password`—and posts the data to a specified URL using the HTTP `POST` method. This Swing-based client application works with a server-side web-based application, just like a web browser.

Here's the code:

```
//file: Post.java
import java.net.*;
import java.io.*;
import java.awt.*;
import java.awt.event.*;
import javax.swing.*;

public class Post extends JPanel implements ActionListener {
  JTextField nameField, passwordField;
  String postURL;

  GridBagConstraints constraints = new GridBagConstraints(  );

  void addGB( Component component, int x, int y ) {
    constraints.gridx = x;  constraints.gridy = y;
    add ( component, constraints );
  }

  public Post( String postURL ) {

    this.postURL = postURL;

    setBorder(BorderFactory.createEmptyBorder(5, 10, 5, 5));
    JButton postButton = new JButton("Post");
    postButton.addActionListener( this );
    setLayout( new GridBagLayout(  ) );
    constraints.fill = GridBagConstraints.HORIZONTAL;
    addGB( new JLabel("Name ", JLabel.TRAILING), 0, 0 );
    addGB( nameField = new JTextField(20), 1, 0 );
    addGB( new JLabel("Password ", JLabel.TRAILING), 0, 1 );
    addGB( passwordField = new JPasswordField(20), 1, 1 );
    constraints.fill = GridBagConstraints.NONE;
    constraints.gridwidth = 2;
    constraints.anchor = GridBagConstraints.EAST;
    addGB( postButton, 1, 2 );
  }

  public void actionPerformed(ActionEvent e) {
    postData(  );
  }

  protected void postData(  ) {
    StringBuffer sb = new StringBuffer(  );
```

```
    sb.append( URLEncoder.encode("Name") + "=" );
    sb.append( URLEncoder.encode(nameField.getText(  )) );
    sb.append( "&" + URLEncoder.encode("Password") + "=" );
    sb.append( URLEncoder.encode(passwordField.getText(  )) );
    String formData = sb.toString(  );

    try {
      URL url = new URL( postURL );
      HttpURLConnection urlcon =
          (HttpURLConnection) url.openConnection(  );
      urlcon.setRequestMethod("POST");
      urlcon.setRequestProperty("Content-type",
          "application/x-www-form-urlencoded");
      urlcon.setDoOutput(true);
      urlcon.setDoInput(true);
      PrintWriter pout = new PrintWriter( new OutputStreamWriter(
          urlcon.getOutputStream(  ), "8859_1"), true );
      pout.print( formData );
      pout.flush(  );

      // read results...
      if ( urlcon.getResponseCode(  ) != HttpURLConnection.HTTP_OK )
        System.out.println("Posted ok!");
      else {
        System.out.println("Bad post...");
        return;
      }
      //InputStream in = urlcon.getInputStream(  );
      // ...

    } catch (MalformedURLException e) {
      System.out.println(e);     // bad postURL
    } catch (IOException e2) {
      System.out.println(e2);    // I/O error
    }
  }

  public static void main( String [] args ) {
    JFrame frame = new JFrame("SimplePost");
    frame.add( new Post( args[0] ), "Center" );
    frame.pack(  );
    frame.setVisible(true);
  }
}
```

When you run this application, you must specify the URL of the server program on the command line. For example:

```
% java Post http://www.myserver.example/cgi-bin/login.cgi
```

The beginning of the application creates the form; there's nothing here that won't be obvious after you've read Chapters 16 through 18, which cover the AWT and Swing

GUI toolkits. All the magic happens in the protected `postData()` method. First, we create a `StringBuffer` and load it with name/value pairs, separated by ampersands. (We don't need the initial question mark when we're using the `POST` method because we're not appending to a URL string.) Each pair is first encoded using the static `URLEncoder.encode()` method. We run the name fields through the encoder as well as the value fields, even though we know that in this case they contain no special characters.

Next, we set up the connection to the server program. In our previous example, we weren't required to do anything special to send the data because the request was made by the simple act of opening the URL on the server. Here, we have to carry some of the weight of talking to the remote web server. Fortunately, the `HttpURLConnection` object does most of the work for us; we just have to tell it that we want to do a `POST` to the URL and the type of data we are sending. We ask for the `URLConnection` object that is using the URL's `openConnection()` method. We know that we are using the HTTP protocol so we should be able to cast it to an `HttpURLConnection` type, which has the support we need. Because HTTP is one of the guaranteed protocols, we can safely make this assumption.

We then use `setRequestMethod()` to tell the connection we want to do a `POST` operation. We also use `setRequestProperty()` to set the `Content-Type` field of our HTTP request to the appropriate type—in this case, the proper MIME type for encoded form data. (This is necessary to tell the server what kind of data we're sending.) Finally, we use the `setDoOutput()` and `setDoInput()` methods to tell the connection that we want to both send and receive stream data. The URL connection infers from this combination that we are going to do a `POST` operation and expects a response. Next, we get an output stream from the connection with `getOutputStream()` and create a `PrintWriter` so that we can easily write our encoded data.

After we post the data, our application calls `getResponseCode()` to see whether the HTTP response code from the server indicates that the `POST` was successful. Other response codes (defined as constants in `HttpURLConnection`) indicate various failures. At the end of our example, we indicate where we could have read back the text of the response. For this application, we'll assume that simply knowing that the post was successful is sufficient.

Although form-encoded data (as indicated by the MIME type we specified for the `Content-Type` field) is the most common, other types of communications are possible. We could have used the input and output streams to exchange arbitrary data types with the server program. The `POST` operation could send any kind of data; the server application simply has to know how to handle it. One final note: if you are writing an application that needs to decode form data, you can use the `java.net.URLDecoder` to undo the operation of the `URLEncoder`. If you use the Servlet API, this happens automatically, as you'll see in Chapter 15.

The HttpURLConnection

Other information from the request is available from the `HttpURLConnection` as well. We could use `getContentType()` and `getContentEncoding()` to determine the MIME type and encoding of the response. We could also interrogate the HTTP response headers by using `getHeaderField()`. (HTTP response headers are metadata name/value pairs carried with the response.) Convenience methods can fetch integer and date-formatted header fields, `getHeaderFieldInt()` and `getHeaderFieldDate()`, which return an `int` and a `long` type, respectively. The content length and last modification date are provided through `getContentLength()` and `getLastModified()`.

SSL and Secure Web Communications

The previous examples sent a field called `Password` to the server. However, standard HTTP doesn't provide encryption to hide our data. Fortunately, adding security for `GET` and `POST` operations like this is easy (trivial in fact, for the client-side developer). Where available, you simply have to use a secure form of the HTTP protocol—HTTPS:

```
https://www.myserver.example/cgi-bin/login.cgi
```

HTTPS is a version of the standard HTTP protocol run over Secure Sockets Layer (SSL), which uses public-key encryption techniques to encrypt the browser-to-server communications. Most web browsers and servers currently come with built-in support for HTTPS (or raw SSL sockets). Therefore, if your web server supports HTTPS and has it configured, you can use a browser to send and receive secure data simply by specifying the `https` protocol in your URLs. There is much more to learn about SSL and related aspects of security such as authenticating whom you are actually talking to, but as far as basic data encryption goes, this is all you have to do. It is not something your code has to deal with directly. The Java JRE standard edition ships with SSL and HTTPS support, and beginning with Java 5.0, all Java implementations must support HTTPS as well as HTTP for URL connections. We'll discuss writing secure web applications in more detail in Chapter 15.

URLs, URNs, and URIs

Earlier, we discussed URLs and distinguished them from the concept of URNs. Whereas a URL points to a specific location on the Net and specifies a protocol or *scheme* for accessing its contents, a URN is simply a globally unique name. A URL is analogous to giving someone your phone number. But a URN is more like giving them your social security number. Your phone number may change, but your social security number is supposed to uniquely identify you forever.

While it's possible that some mechanism might be able to look at a given URN and tie it to a location (a URL), it is not necessarily so. URNs are intended only to be permanent, unique, abstract identifiers for an item, whereas a URL is a mechanism you can use to get in touch with a resource right now. You can use a phone number to contact me today, but you can use my social security number to uniquely identify me anytime.

An example of a URN is *http://www.w3.org/1999/XSL/Transform*, which is the identifier for a version of the Extensible Stylesheet Language, standardized by the W3C. Now, it also happens that this is a URL (you can go to that address and find information about the standard), but that is for convenience only. This URN's primary mission is to uniquely label the version of the programming language in a way that never changes.

Collectively, URLs and URNs are called Uniform Resource Identifiers or URIs. A URI is simply a URL or URN. So, URLs and URNs are kinds of URIs. The reason for this abstraction is that URLs and URNs, by definition, have some things in common. All URIs are supposed to be human-readable and "transcribable" (it should be possible to write them on the back of a napkin). They always have a hierarchical structure, and they are always unique. Both URLs and URNs also share some common syntax, which is described by RFC 2396.

The `java.net.URI` class formalizes these distinctions. The difference between the URI and URL classes is that the URI class does not try to parse the contents of the identifier and apply any "meaning." Whereas the URL class immediately attempts to parse the scheme portion of the URL and locate a protocol handler, the URI class doesn't interpret its content. It serves only to allow us to work with the identifier as structured text, according to the general rules of URI syntax. With the URI class, you can construct the string, resolve relative paths, and perform equality or comparison operations, but no hostname or protocol resolution is done.

Web Services

Web services is a big, fast-moving topic and the subject of many other fine O'Reilly books. However, because we have already covered so many of the basic networking concepts (and we'll cover XML in detail in Chapter 24), we would be shirking our duties if we didn't provide an introduction to this important area of application development. We conclude this chapter on client-side web communications with a small example of invoking a web service.

In contrast to regular web applications intended to be visited by web browsers, web services are application-level APIs intended to be invoked by other application components. The primary distinction from other types of interapplication communications mechanisms is that they use web standards and XML to maximize cross-platform interoperability. We will leave the analysis of when exactly this is important and the cost versus benefits tradeoffs out of our discussion here. But the value in this idea should be evident from the explosion of web-based business applications in the past few years. Web services allow web-based applications to provide well-defined, cross-platform interfaces for other web-based applications.

XML-RPC

The term *web services* means different things to different people and has spawned many (too many) new standards in recent years. In fact, there are so many web service standards named with the prefix "WS" now that they are collectively known as "WS-*" (affectionately referred to as WS "splat" or WS "death star"). However, the original concept is simple: web services take the ubiquitous, universally understood, and easily implemented HTTP transaction and marry it with XML to define a standard for invoking application services over the Web. The process is a type of *remote procedure call* in which HTTP plays its traditional role as the basic communication provider and XML adds a "business envelope" in which structured data is passed. This RPC-style web service interaction defines both the basic structure of an invocation request and also a set of XML encodings for marshaling the primitive data types, allowing data parameters and results to be exchanged in a truly cross-platform way. In contrast, another form of web services—termed "document style"—places more emphasis on the exchange of application-specific XML documents than on RPC-style data marshaling and unmarshaling. We will concentrate on RPC-style web services because they currently provide the tightest coupling to Java.

WSDL

A key component of web services technology is the Web Services Description Language (WSDL). Using this standard, a structured XML document describes a web service, the individual functions (methods) it offers, and the XML data types for their respective arguments and return values. WSDL is a type of interface definition language (IDL) and plays that role for web services. However, a WSDL document can also specify the service location and other features that are not traditionally part of the service definitely.

For the client-side web services developer, the WSDL document describing a service contains all of the information needed to generate the client-side code used to invoke the service from Java or any other language. As we'll see in our example, it is not even necessary to have an understanding of WSDL to use the service. One can simply generate the client-side interfaces and use them from a Java language viewpoint. We'll see in Chapter 15 that we can generate the WSDL document for a new service directly from our own Java code as well.

The Tools

The Java JAX-WS Java API for XML Web Services comes bundled with Java 6 and later and contains all of the tools necessary to use, create, and work with web services in Java. It's even possible to deploy web services for testing in simple scenarios using out-of-the-box tools. As you might imagine, Java web services make extensive use of the JAXP APIs for working with XML. JAX-WS adds the classes necessary for remote calls, as well as the development-time *wsimport* and *wsgen* tools. The *wsimport* tool reads a WSDL description file and generates the required Java interface and implementation classes to invoke it. The *wsgen* tool reads Java code containing web service annotations and can generate WSDL and other deployment-related files.

There are many application servers that provide their own mechanisms for deploying web services and generating client-side code. The Apache CXF project is another popular Java web services alternative that can work with JAX-WS and other standards.

The Weather Service Client

This example shows just how easy it is to use a web service from client-side code. We're going to create a client for a web-based weather lookup service. The service accepts a U.S. zip code as an argument and returns the city, state, and weather conditions as a result. Please note that the server-side component of this example is hosted by a company called *cdyne.com*, which is a professional web services provider. Because this is a third-party site, we cannot guarantee that it will remain active. If for any reason this service disappears, don't fret—we'll build our own example in Chapter 15, where we implement a simple web service ourselves.

All that we need to get started is the web service WSDL description file. You can view the weather service at the WSDL website (*http://bit.ly/13moiTh*). It's an XML file that defines a set of operations and data types for arguments and results. The file is not intended to be human readable, and should make more sense after we discuss XML in Chapter 24.

To generate the client code needed to interact with the service, we run the `wsimport` utility that is found in the JDK bin and pass it the WSDL location like so:

```
% wsimport http://wsf.cdyne.com/WeatherWS/Weather.asmx?WSDL
```

When *wsimport* completes, you should find a new directory tree named *com/cdyne/ws/weatherws* that contains compiled Java classes for the temperature service client interface and an implementation. The wsimport command has many useful options: you may wish to use the `-keep` option to retain the generated source code for the client classes so that you can store the source with your application. There is also a `-p` option that lets you override the generated Java package name.

The generated code contains a class called `Weather` that represents the overall service and an interface called `WeatherSoap` that represents various *ports* or groups of methods on the service, among other implementation classes. (The "port" is WSDL terminology for a group of functions on a web service.) If you retain the soure code (with `-keep`) and take a look at it, you'll see that the generated classes use Java annotations to identify the service elements. The `Weather` class is marked with `@WebServiceClient` and the `WeatherSoap` interface is marked as `@WebService`. Furthermore, the methods of the `WeatherSoap` interface are marked with `@WebMethod`. These annotations add metadata to the code to identify the service and capture the information needed from the WSDL to map to the service XML. We'll discuss web service annotations more when we build and deploy the server side of a web service in the next chapter. We'll also see annotations used in analogous ways when we discuss XML binding with JAXB in Chapter 24.

Our client application can now use these classes to invoke the service. The following code looks up the current weather in the 63132 zip code:

```
import com.cdyne.ws.weatherws.*;

public class WSTest {
    public static void main( String[] args )
    {
        WeatherSoap weatherService = new Weather().getWeatherSoap();
        WeatherReturn weather = weatherService.getCityWeatherByZIP( "63132" );
        System.out.format("%s, %s : %s : Temperature: %s, Wind: %s",
            weather.getCity(), weather.getState(), weather.getDescription(),
            weather.getTemperature(), weather.getWind() );
    }
}
```

Remember that you need to either add the compiled service classes to your classpath or compile the generated source files along with the example code. If you run it, you should see output like the following. Note that although this service has returned the values as strings, in general, web service bindings to Java would allow elements like the temperature to be returned as numeric types.

```
Saint Louis, MO : Partly Cloudy : Temperature: 25, Wind: CALM
```

We'll return to the topic of web services and implement our own web service in the next chapter, where we hop over to the server side of things and start building web applications.

CHAPTER 15
Web Applications and Web Services

We're now going to take a leap from the client side to the server side to learn how to write web-based Java applications and services. What distinguishes a web-based application from a regular Java program is that much of the code, logic, or data resides on the server, at least initally, and the user utilizes a web browser or a lightweight client to access it. This is a very appealing model of software deployment facilitated by the increased standardization and power of HTML and JavaScript in web browsers as well as higher-speed Internet connectivity and better application-to-application web service standards.

Most of this chapter is about the mechanics of the Servlet API, which is a Java framework for writing application components for servers. The Servlet API is used in both Java web applications and often in the implementation of application-to-application web services. We'll deal with servlets directly in the first part of this chapter, when writing examples used from a web browser. Later, we'll look at application-level web services that are designed to provide data and services to all types of client applications in a more behind-the-scenes fashion. The two types of server-side applications have some things in common, including how they can be deployed to an application server using a Web Archive (WAR) file and the fact that they are often combined in advanced applications that both render pages on the server and use JavaScript to pull data from web services on the client side.

The Servlet API lives in the `javax.servlet` package, which is a standard Java API extension. Deploying and running servlets requires an *application server* or *servlet container*—a Java-based server that acts like a web server and handles requests bound for servlet components—and so the Servlet API is not bundled with the standard edition of Java. We will recommend that you download Apache Tomcat to run the examples in this chapter and at that time, you can grab the Servlet API JAR file from that distribution in order to compile the example classes. Many Java IDEs can also install the necessary JAR file for you automatically.

The APIs used for building and deploying application-to-application web services are part of the `javax.jws` package. Although the JWS API is also technically a standard extension, it is bundled with the standard edition of Java and so you can write Java web service clients out-of-the-box, with no additional components. You can even deploy web services directly using a minimal built-in server functionality bundled with the standard edition of Java with no additional application server required. However, this feature is mostly useful for testing, as the built-in server does not perform as well as the various other application servers such as Tomcat. This chapter covers Java Servlet API 3.0 and JWS (JAX-WS) version 2.2.

Servers that support the full set of Java Enterprise APIs including servlets, web services, JSPs, and older technology like Enterprise JavaBeans are called *application servers*. JBoss is a free, open source Java application server (*http://www.jboss.org*), and BEA's WebLogic is a popular commercial application server. The free Apache Tomcat server that we'll use in this chapter started out primarily as a servlet container, but now runs web services and everything needed for serious application development. Tomcat can be used by itself or in conjunction with another web server such as Apache. Tomcat is easy to configure and is a pure Java application, so you can use it on any platform that has a Java VM. You can download it from *http://jakarta.apache.org/tomcat/*.

Web Application Technologies

Many different ways of writing server-side software for web applications have evolved over the years. Early on, the standard was CGI, which provided a way to service web browser requests with scripting language such as Perl. Various web servers also offered native-language APIs, such as modules for the Apache web server written in C and C++. The Java Servlet API, however, rapidly became the most popular architecture for building web-based applications because it offered portability, security, and high performance. Today, Java-based web services compete with similar services offered by Microsoft .NET and alternatives such as Ruby on Rails for building web application components. However, the overriding trend in web applications today is to focus less on the server technology and more on client-side technologies such as JavaScript and HTML5 in communication with server-side components and web services regardless of the implementation language. We'll try to offer some perspective on this throughout this chapter.

Page-Oriented Versus "Single Page" Applications

For most of the lifetime of Java, web-based applications followed the same basic paradigm: the browser makes a request to a particular URL; the server generates a page of HTML in response; and actions by the user drive the browser to the next page. In this exchange, most or all of the work is done on the server side, which is seemingly logical given that that's where data and services often reside. The problem with this application model is that it is inherently limited by the loss of responsiveness, continuity, and state experienced by the user when loading new "pages" in the browser. It's difficult to make a web-based application as seamless as a desktop application when the user must jump through a series of discrete pages and it is technically more challenging to maintain application data across those pages. After all, web browsers were not designed to host applications, they were designed to host documents.

But a lot has changed in web application development in recent years. Standards for HTML and JavaScript have matured to the point where it is practical to write applications in which most of the user interface and logic reside on the client side and background calls are made to the server for data and services. In this paradigm, the server effectively returns just a single "page" of HTML that references the bulk of the JavaScript, CSS, and other resources used to render the application interface. JavaScript then takes over, manipulating elements on the page or creating new ones dynamically using advanced HTML DOM features to produce the UI. JavaScript also makes asynchronous (background) calls to the server to fetch data and invoke services. In many cases, the results are returned as XML, leading to the term *Asynchronous JavaScript and XML* (AJAX) for this style of interaction.

This new model simplifies and empowers web development in many ways. No longer must the client work in a single-page, request-response regime where views and requests are ping-ponged back and forth. The client is now more equivalent to a desktop application in that it can respond to user input fluidly and manage remote data and services without interrupting the user.

Before we move on to our discussion of the Servlet API, we will briefly describe Java's relationship to some related web technologies, old and new.

JSPs

JSPs are a document-centric (page-oriented) way to write server-side applications. They consist of HTML source utilizing custom tag libraries along with a Java-like syntax embedded within the pages. JSPs are compiled dynamically by the web server into Java servlets and can work with Java APIs directly and indirectly in order to generate dynamic content for the pages. Although all of the work still occurs on the server side, JSPs allow the developer to work as if code was running directly in the page, which has both benefits and drawbacks. The benefit of this sort of "immediate mode" programming style is that it is easy to grasp and quick to crank out. The drawback is that it can lead to an unmanageable mix of business logic and presentation logic in the pages. The more code that appears mixed in with the static content, the greater the maintenance headache.

Most large-scale JSP projects utilize custom tag libraries to minimize ad hoc code in the pages. JSPs are also used in combination with *controller* servlets that can do the heavy lifting and business logic for them. In this case, the term *controller* refers to the Model-View-Controller (MVC) separation of concerns that we introduced earlier when talking about Swing GUIs. Maintaining this separation leverages the advantages of JSP while avoiding its pitfalls.

XML and XSL

XML is a set of standards for working with structured information in text form. The Extensible Stylesheet Language (XSL) is a language for transforming XML documents into other kinds of documents, including HTML. The combination of servlets that can generate XML content and XSL stylesheets that can transform content for presentation is a very powerful combination, covered in detail in Chapter 24. As we'll discuss later, web services also use XML as their native data format, making them completely portable across platforms and languages. And, of course, XML is the basis for returning data to JavaScript applications in the original AJAX style of web development.

Web Application Frameworks

If we think about web applications in terms of the classic MVC model, then a traditional page-oriented application generally has "view" components rendered in the browser, while the model (data) and controllers (logic) reside on the server side. We've mentioned some reasons why this style of web application is fading in favor of "single page" applications where more of these components move into the browser; however, over the years many frameworks have been developed to support this classic web app arrangement. Generally these frameworks work at a higher level than servlets, providing a convenient way to write controller components, connect them, and configure page views for the results.

One of the most popular frameworks for building page-oriented web applications has been the Apache Foundation's Struts Web Application Framework. Struts implements the MVC paradigm by providing both a modular controller component architecture and an extensive tag library for JSP page view development. Struts abstracts some of the mapping and navigation aspects required to glue together a web application through the use of an XML-based configuration file and also adds the ability to do declarative mapping of HTML forms to Java objects as well as automated validation of form fields.

JSF was Sun's response to Struts. Developed through the Java Community Process (including some of the original Struts people) it was intended to become the "official" Java-sanctioned web-application framework. JSF built upon lessons learned with Struts and refined the MVC model with server-side application components and more fine-grained navigation and event management. JSF met mixed reviews and never really surpassed Struts in popularity.

Spring Web Flow is another popular web application MVC system that is based on the Spring application framework. There are many, many examples of Java web application frameworks.

Google Web Toolkit

Google Web Toolkit, or GWT, is a free framework produced by Google that allows developers to write web applications using the Java programming language. GWT compiles Java components to JavaScript that runs in a web browser and communicates with the server via a custom RPC mechanism that acts something like Java RMI. The GWT environment provides its own set of Java GUI classes and a substantial subset of the standard Java libraries. GWT is a very powerful framework that makes it possible to write large and complex applications with most of the benefits of the Java programming language while running in a web browser. However, GWT has a somewhat steeper learning curve than some other web frameworks (especially for those unfamiliar with both Java and JavaScript).

HTML5, AJAX, and More...

Java lives on the server side of web applications. To build the client pieces of applications that run in browsers, we must cooperate with Java's namesake, JavaScript. As we've mentioned, in recent years efforts to standardize advanced features of HTML and JavaScript have paid off in a real revolution in the capabilities of web applications and the way in which they are built. Much of this began with adding more dynamic behavior to clients via AJAX calls. More recently, the explosion of mobile browsers has fueled the adoption of the HTML5 standard, bringing web browsers a richer feature set including a more complete DOM, native video and audio media support, general canvas drawing and vector graphics support, and offline data storage. Even more exciting technologies can be used today while working their way through the standards process. One to keep an eye on is WebSockets, which provides for low-latency messaging between the browser and server and should enable many new types of applications.

Java Web Applications

So far we've used the term *web application* generically, referring to any kind of browser-based application that is located on a web server. Now we are going to be more precise with that term. In the context of the Java Servlet API, a web application is a collection of servlets and Java web services that support Java classes, content such as HTML or JSP pages and images, and configuration information. For deployment (installation on a web server), a web application is bundled into a WAR file. We'll discuss WAR files in detail later, but suffice it to say that they are really just JAR archives that contain all the application files along with some deployment information. The important thing is that the standardization of WAR files means not only that the Java code is portable, but also that the process of deploying the application to a server is standardized.

Most WAR archives have at their core a *web.xml* file. This is an XML configuration file that describes which servlets are to be deployed, their names and URL paths, their initialization parameters, and a host of other information, including security and authentication requirements. In recent years, however, the *web.xml* file has become optional for many applications due to the introduction of Java annotations that take the place of the XML configuration. In most cases, you can now deploy your servlets and Java web services simply by annotating the classes with the necessary information and packaging them into the WAR file, or using a combination of the two. We'll discuss this in detail later in the chapter.

Web applications, or web apps, also have a well-defined runtime environment. Each web app has its own "root" path on the web server, meaning that all the URLs addressing its servlets and files start with a common unique prefix (e.g., *http://www.oreilly.com/someapplication/*). The web app's servlets are also isolated from those of other web applications. Web apps cannot directly access each other's files (although they may be allowed to do so through the web server, of course). Each web app also has its own *servlet context*. We'll discuss the servlet context in more detail, but in brief, it is a common area for servlets within an application to share information and get resources from the environment. The high degree of isolation between web applications is intended to support the dynamic deployment and updating of applications required by modern business systems and to address security and reliability concerns. Web apps are intended to be coarse-grained, relatively complete applications—not to be tightly coupled with other web apps. Although there's no reason you can't make web apps cooperate at a high level, for sharing logic across applications you might want to consider web services, which we'll discuss later in this chapter.

The Servlet Lifecycle

Let's jump now to the Servlet API and get started building servlets. We'll fill in the gaps later when we discuss various parts of the APIs and WAR file structure in more detail. The Servlet API is very simple (reminiscent of the old Applet API). The base `Servlet` class has three lifecycle methods—`init()`, `service()`, and `destroy()`—along with some methods for getting configuration parameters and servlet resources. However, these methods are not often used directly by developers. Generally developers will implement the `doGet()` and `doPost()` methods of the `HttpServlet` subclass and access shared resources through the servlet context, as we'll discuss shortly.

Generally, only one instance of each deployed servlet class is instantiated per container. More precisely, it is one instance per servlet entry in the *web.xml* file, but we'll talk more about servlet deployment later. In the past, there was an exception to that rule when using the special `SingleThreadModel` type of servlet. As of Servlet API 2.4, single-threaded servlets have been deprecated.

By default, servlets are expected to handle requests in a multithreaded way; that is, the servlet's service methods may be invoked by many threads at the same time. This means that you should not store per-request or per-client data in instance variables of your servlet object. (Of course, you can store general data related to the servlet's operation, as long as it does not change on a per-request basis.) Per-client state information can be stored in a client *session* object on the server or in a client-side cookie, which persists across client requests. We'll talk about client state later as well.

The `service()` method of a servlet accepts two parameters: a servlet "request" object and a servlet "response" object. These provide tools for reading the client request and generating output; we'll talk about them (or rather their `HttpServlet` versions) in detail in the examples.

Servlets

The package of primary interest to us here is `javax.servlet.http`, which contains APIs specific to servlets that handle HTTP requests for web servers. In theory, you can write servlets for other protocols, but nobody really does that and we are going to discuss servlets as if all servlets were HTTP-related.

The primary tool provided by the `javax.servlet.http` package is the `HttpServlet` base class. This is an abstract servlet that provides some basic implementation details related to handling an HTTP request. In particular, it overrides the generic servlet `service()` request and breaks it out into several HTTP-related methods, including `doGet()`, `doPost()`, `doPut()`, and `doDelete()`. The default `service()` method examines the request to determine what kind it is and dispatches it to one of these methods, so you can override one or more of them to implement the specific protocol behavior you need.

`doGet()` and `doPost()` correspond to the standard HTTP `GET` and `POST` operations. `GET` is the standard request for retrieving a file or document at a specified URL. `POST` is the method by which a client sends an arbitrary amount of data to the server. HTML forms utilize `POST` to send data as do most web services.

To round these out, `HttpServlet` provides the `doPut()` and `doDelete()` methods. These methods correspond to a less widely used part of the HTTP protocol, which is meant to provide a way to upload and remove files or file-like entities. `doPut()` is supposed to be like `POST` but with slightly different semantics (a `PUT` is supposed to logically replace the item identified by the URL, whereas `POST` presents data to it); `doDelete()` would be its opposite.

`HttpServlet` also implements three other HTTP-related methods for you: `doHead()`, `doTrace()`, and `doOptions()`. You don't normally need to override these methods. `doHead()` implements the HTTP `HEAD` request, which asks for the headers of a `GET` request without the body. `HttpServlet` implements this by default in the trivial way, by performing the `GET` method and then sending only the headers. You may wish to override `doHead()` with a more efficient implementation if you can provide one as an optimization. `doTrace()` and `doOptions()` implement other features of HTTP that allow for debugging and simple client/server capabilities negotiation. You shouldn't normally need to override these.

Along with `HttpServlet`, `javax.servlet.http` also includes subclasses of the objects `ServletRequest` and `ServletResponse`, `HttpServletRequest` and `HttpServletResponse`. These subclasses provide, respectively, the input and output streams needed to read and write client data. They also provide the APIs for getting or setting HTTP header information and, as we'll see, client session information. Rather than document these dryly, we'll show them in the context of some examples. As usual, we'll start with the simplest possible example.

The HelloClient Servlet

Here's our servlet version of "Hello, World," `HelloClient`:

```
@WebServlet(urlPatterns={"/hello"})
public class HelloClient extends HttpServlet
{
    public void doGet(HttpServletRequest request, HttpServletResponse response)
        throws ServletException, IOException
    {
        response.setContentType("text/html"); // must come first
        PrintWriter out = response.getWriter();
        out.println(
            "<html><head><title>Hello Client!</title></head><body>"
            + "<h1>Hello Client!</h1>"
            + "</body></html>" );
    }
}
```

If you want to try this servlet right away, skip ahead to "WAR Files and Deployment" on page 559, where we walk through the process of deploying this servlet. Because we've included the `WebServlet` annotation in our class, this servlet does not need a *web.xml* file for deployment. All you have to do is bundle the class file into a particular folder within a WAR archive (a fancy ZIP file) and drop it into a directory monitored by the Tomcat server. For now, we're going to focus on just the servlet example code itself, which is pretty simple in this case.

Let's have a look at the example. `HelloClient` extends the base `HttpServlet` class and overrides the `doGet()` method to handle simple requests. In this case, we want to respond to any `GET` request by sending back a one-line HTML document that says "Hello Client!" First, we tell the container what kind of response we are going to generate, using the `setContentType()` method of the `HttpServletResponse` object. We specify the MIME type "text/html" for our HTML response. Then, we get the output stream using the `getWriter()` method and print the message to it. It is not necessary for us to explicitly close the stream. We'll talk more about managing the output stream throughout this chapter.

ServletExceptions

The doGet() method of our example servlet declares that it can throw a ServletException. All of the service methods of the Servlet API may throw a ServletException to indicate that a request has failed. A ServletException can be constructed with a string message and an optional Throwable parameter that can carry any corresponding exception representing the root cause of the problem:

```
throw new ServletException("utter failure", someException );
```

By default, the web server determines exactly what is shown to the user whenever a ServletException is thrown; often there is a "development mode" where the exception and its stack trace are displayed. Using the *web.xml* file, you can designate custom error pages. (See the section "Error and Index Pages" on page 564 for details.)

Alternatively, a servlet may throw an UnavailableException, a subclass of ServletException, to indicate that it cannot handle requests. This exception can be thrown to indicate that the condition is permanent or that it should last for a specified period of seconds.

Content type

Before fetching the output stream and writing to it, we must specify the kind of output we are sending by calling the response parameter's setContentType() method. In this case, we set the content type to text/html, which is the proper MIME type for an HTML document. In general, though, it's possible for a servlet to generate any kind of data, including audio, video, or some other kind of text or binary document. If we were writing a generic FileServlet to serve files like a regular web server, we might inspect the filename extension and determine the MIME type from that or from direct inspection of the data. (This is a good use for the java.nio.file.Files probeConentType() method!) For writing binary data, you can use the getOutputStream() method to get an OutputStream as opposed to a Writer.

The content type is used in the Content-Type: header of the server's HTTP response, which tells the client what to expect even before it starts reading the result. This allows your web browser to prompt you with the "Save File" dialog when you click on a ZIP archive or executable program. When the content-type string is used in its full form to specify the character encoding (for example, text/html; charset=ISO-8859-1), the information is also used by the servlet engine to set the character encoding of the PrintWriter output stream. As a result, you should always call the setContentType() method before fetching the writer with the getWriter() method. The character encoding can also be set separately via the servlet response setCharacterEncoding() method.

The Servlet Response

In addition to providing the output stream for writing content to the client, the `HttpServletResponse` object provides methods for controlling other aspects of the HTTP response, including headers, error result codes, redirects, and servlet container buffering.

HTTP headers are metadata name/value pairs sent with the response. You can add headers (standard or custom) to the response with the `setHeader()` and `addHeader()` methods (headers may have multiple values). There are also convenience methods for setting headers with integer and date values:

```
response.setIntHeader("MagicNumber", 42);
response.setDateHeader("CurrentTime", System.currentTimeMillis() );
```

When you write data to the client, the servlet container automatically sets the HTTP response code to a value of 200, which means OK. Using the `sendError()` method, you can generate other HTTP response codes. `HttpServletResponse` contains predefined constants for all of the standard codes. Here are a few common ones:

```
HttpServletResponse.SC_OK
HttpServletResponse.SC_BAD_REQUEST
HttpServletResponse.SC_FORBIDDEN
HttpServletResponse.SC_NOT_FOUND
HttpServletResponse.SC_INTERNAL_SERVER_ERROR
HttpServletResponse.SC_NOT_IMPLEMENTED
HttpServletResponse.SC_SERVICE_UNAVAILABLE
```

When you generate an error with `sendError()`, the response is over and you can't write any actual content to the client. You can specify a short error message, however, which may be shown to the client. (See the section "A Simple Filter" on page 572.)

An HTTP redirect is a special kind of response that tells the client web browser to go to a different URL. Normally this happens quickly and without any interaction from the user. You can send a redirect with the `sendRedirect()` method:

```
response.sendRedirect("http://www.oreilly.com/");
```

While we're talking about the response, we should say a few words about buffering. Most responses are buffered internally by the servlet container until the servlet service method has exited or a preset maximum size has been reached. This allows the container to set the HTTP content-length header automatically, telling the client how much data to expect. You can control the size of this buffer with the `setBufferSize()` method, specifying a size in bytes. You can even clear it and start over if no data has been written to the client. To clear the buffer, use `isCommitted()` to test whether any data has been set, then use `resetBuffer()` to dump the data if none has been sent. If you are sending a lot of data, you may wish to set the content length explicitly with the `setContentLength()` method.

Servlet Parameters

Our first example showed how to accept a basic request. Of course, to do anything really useful, we'll need to get some information from the client. Fortunately, the servlet engine handles this for us, interpreting both `GET` and `POST` form-encoded data from the client and providing it to us through the simple `getParameter()` method of the servlet request.

GET, POST, and "extra path"

There are two common ways to pass information from your web browser to a servlet or CGI program. The most general is to "post" it, meaning that your client encodes the information and sends it as a stream to the program, which decodes it. Posting can be used to upload large amounts of form data or other data, including files. The other way to pass information is to somehow encode the information in the URL of your client's request. The primary way to do this is to use `GET`-style encoding of parameters in the URL string. In this case, the web browser encodes the parameters and appends them to the end of the URL string. The server decodes them and passes them to the application.

As we described in Chapter 14, `GET`-style encoding takes the parameters and appends them to the URL in a name/value fashion, with the first parameter preceded by a question mark (?) and the rest separated by ampersands (&). The entire string is expected to be *URL-encoded*: any special characters (such as spaces, ?, and & in the string) are specially encoded.

Another way to pass data in the URL is called *extra path*. This simply means that when the server has located your servlet or CGI program as the target of a URL, it takes any remaining path components of the URL string and hands them over as an extra part of the URL. For example, consider these URLs:

```
http://www.myserver.example/servlets/MyServlet
http://www.myserver.example/servlets/MyServlet/foo/bar
```

Suppose the server maps the first URL to the servlet called `MyServlet`. When given the second URL, the server also invokes `MyServlet`, but considers `/foo/bar` to be "extra path" that can be retrieved through the servlet request `getExtraPath()` method. This technique is useful for making more human-readable and meaningful URL pathnames, especially for document-centric content.

Both `GET` and `POST` encoding can be used with HTML forms on the client by specifying `get` or `post` in the `action` attribute of the form tag. The browser handles the encoding; on the server side, the servlet engine handles the decoding.

The content type used by a client to post form data to a servlet is: "application/x-www-form-urlencoded." The Servlet API automatically parses this kind of data and makes it available through the `getParameter()` method. However, if you do not call the `getParameter()` method, the data remains available, unparsed, in the input stream and can be read by the servlet directly.

GET or POST: Which one to use?

To users, the primary difference between GET and POST is that they can see the GET information in the encoded URL shown in their web browser. This can be useful because the user can cut and paste that URL (the result of a search, for example) and mail it to a friend or bookmark it for future reference. POST information is not visible to the user and ceases to exist after it's sent to the server. This behavior goes along with the protocol's intent that GET and POST are to have different semantics. By definition, the result of a GET operation is not supposed to have any side effects; that is, it's not supposed to cause the server to perform any persistent operations (such as making a purchase in a shopping cart). In theory, that's the job of POST. That's why your web browser warns you about reposting form data again if you hit reload on a page that was the result of a form posting.

The extra path style would be useful for a servlet that retrieves files or handles a range of URLs in a human-readable way. Extra path information is often useful for URLs that the user must see or remember, because it looks like any other path.

The ShowParameters Servlet

Our first example didn't do much. This next example prints the values of any parameters that were received. We'll start by handling GET requests and then make some trivial modifications to handle POST as well. Here's the code:

```
import java.io.*;
import javax.servlet.http.*;
import java.util.*;

public class ShowParameters extends HttpServlet
{
    public void doGet(HttpServletRequest request, HttpServletResponse response)
      throws IOException
    {
        showRequestParameters( request, response );
    }

    void showRequestParameters(HttpServletRequest request,
        HttpServletResponse response)
        throws IOException
    {
        response.setContentType("text/html");
        PrintWriter out = response.getWriter();

        out.println(
          "<html><head><title>Show Parameters</title></head><body>"
          + "<h1>Parameters</h1><ul>");

        Map<String, String[]> params = request.getParameterMap();
        for ( String name : params.keySet() )
        {
```

```
                String [] values = params.get( name );
                out.println("<li>"+ name +" = "+ Arrays.asList(values) );
            }

            out.close(  );
        }
    }
```

As in the first example, we override the `doGet()` method. We delegate the request to a helper method that we've created, called `showRequestParameters()`, a method that enumerates the parameters using the request object's `getParameterMap()` method, which returns a map of parameter name to values, and prints the names and values. Note that a parameter may have multiple values if it is repeated in the request from the client, hence the map contains `String []`. To make thing pretty, we listed each parameter in HTML with `<li>` tag.

As it stands, our servlet would respond to any URL that contains a `GET` request. Let's round it out by adding our own form to the output and also accommodating `POST` method requests. To accept posts, we override the `doPost()` method. The implementation of `doPost()` could simply call our `showRequestParameters()` method, but we can make it simpler still. The API lets us treat `GET` and `POST` requests interchangeably because the servlet engine handles the decoding of request parameters. So we simply delegate the `doPost()` operation to `doGet()`.

Add the following method to the example:

```
public void doPost( HttpServletRequest request, HttpServletResponse response)
  throws ServletException, IOException
{
    doGet( request, response );
}
```

Now, let's add an HTML form to the output. The form lets the user fill in some parameters and submit them to the servlet. Add this line to the `showRequestParameters()` method before the call to `out.close()`:

```
out.println("</ul><p><form method=\"POST\" action=\""
        + request.getRequestURI() + "\">"
  + "Field 1 <input name=\"Field 1\" size=20><br>"
  + "Field 2 <input name=\"Field 2\" size=20><br>"
  + "<br><input type=\"submit\" value=\"Submit\"></form>"
);
```

The form's `action` attribute is the URL of our servlet so that our servlet will get the data back. We use the `getRequestURI()` method to get the location of our servlet. For the `method` attribute, we've specified a `POST` operation, but you can try changing the operation to `GET` to see both styles.

So far, we haven't done anything terribly exciting. In the next example, we'll add some power by introducing a user session to store client data between requests. But before we go on, we should mention a useful standard servlet, `SnoopServlet`, that is akin to our previous example.

User Session Management

One of the nicest features of the Servlet API is its simple mechanism for managing a user session. By a session, we mean that the servlet can maintain information over multiple pages and through multiple transactions as navigated by the user; this is also called maintaining state. Providing continuity through a series of web pages is important in many kinds of applications, such as handling a login process or tracking purchases in a shopping cart. In a sense, session data takes the place of instance data in your servlet object. It lets you store data between invocations of your service methods.

Session tracking is supported by the servlet container; you normally don't have to worry about the details of how it's accomplished. It's done in one of two ways: using client-side cookies or URL rewriting. *Client-side cookies* are a standard HTTP mechanism for getting the client web browser to cooperate in storing state information for you. A cookie is basically just a name/value attribute that is issued by the server, stored on the client, and returned by the client whenever it is accessing a certain group of URLs on a specified server. Cookies can track a single session or multiple user visits.

URL rewriting appends session-tracking information to the URL, using `GET`-style encoding or extra path information. The term *rewriting* applies because the server rewrites the URL before it is seen by the client and absorbs the extra information before it is passed back to the servlet. In order to support URL rewriting, a servlet must take the extra step to encode any URLs it generates in content (e.g., HTML links that may return to the page) using a special method of the `HttpServletResponse` object. We'll describe this later. You need to allow for URL rewriting by the server if you want your application to work with browsers that do not support cookies or have them disabled. Many sites simply choose not to work without cookies.

To the servlet programmer, state information is made available through an `HttpSession` object, which acts like a hashtable for storing any objects you would like to carry through the session. The objects stay on the server side; a special identifier is sent to the client through a cookie or URL rewriting. On the way back, the identifier is mapped to a session, and the session is associated with the servlet again.

The ShowSession Servlet

Here's a simple servlet that shows how to store some string information to track a session:

```
import java.io.*;
import javax.servlet.ServletException;
import javax.servlet.http.*;
import java.util.Enumeration;
```

```
public class ShowSession extends HttpServlet {

    public void doPost(
        HttpServletRequest request, HttpServletResponse response)
        throws ServletException, IOException
    {
        doGet( request, response );
    }

    public void doGet(
        HttpServletRequest request, HttpServletResponse response)
        throws ServletException, IOException
    {
        HttpSession session = request.getSession();
        boolean clear = request.getParameter("clear") != null;
        if ( clear )
            session.invalidate();
        else {
            String name = request.getParameter("Name");
            String value = request.getParameter("Value");
            if ( name != null && value != null )
                session.setAttribute( name, value );
        }

        response.setContentType("text/html");
        PrintWriter out = response.getWriter();
        out.println(
          "<html><head><title>Show Session</title></head><body>");

        if ( clear )
            out.println("<h1>Session Cleared:</h1>");
        else {
            out.println("<h1>In this session:</h1><ul>");
            Enumeration names = session.getAttributeNames();
            while ( names.hasMoreElements() ) {
                String name = (String)names.nextElement();
                out.println( "<li>"+name+" = " +session.getAttribute(
                    name ) );
            }
        }

        out.println(
          "</ul><p><hr><h1>Add String</h1>"
          + "<form method=\"POST\" action=\""
          + request.getRequestURI() +"\">"
          + "Name: <input name=\"Name\" size=20><br>"
          + "Value: <input name=\"Value\" size=20><br>"
          + "<br><input type=\"submit\" value=\"Submit\">"
          + "<input type=\"submit\" name=\"clear\" value=\"Clear\"></form>"
        );
    }
}
```

When you invoke the servlet, you are presented with a form that prompts you to enter a name and a value. The value string is stored in a session object under the name provided. Each time the servlet is called, it outputs the list of all data items associated with the session. You will see the session grow as each item is added (in this case, until you restart your web browser or the server).

The basic mechanics are much like our `ShowParameters` servlet. Our `doGet()` method generates the form, which points back to our servlet via a `POST` method. We override `doPost()` to delegate back to our `doGet()` method, allowing it to handle everything. Once in `doGet()`, we attempt to fetch the user session object from the `request` object using `getSession()`. The `HttpSession` object supplied by the request functions like a hashtable. There is a `setAttribute()` method, which takes a string name and an `Object` argument, and a corresponding `getAttribute()` method. In our example, we use the `getAttributeNames()` method to enumerate the values currently stored in the session and to print them.

By default, `getSession()` creates a session if one does not exist. If you want to test for a session or explicitly control when one is created, you can call the overloaded version `getSession(false)`, which does not automatically create a new session and returns `null` if there is no session. Alternately, you can check to see if a session was just created with the `isNew()` method. To clear a session immediately, we can use the `invalidate()` method. After calling `invalidate()` on a session, we are not allowed to access it again, so we set a flag in our example and show the "Session Cleared" message. Sessions may also become invalid on their own by timing out. You can control session timeout in the application server or through the *web.xml* file (via the "session-timeout" value of the "session config" section). It is possible, through an interface we'll talk about later in this chapter, to find out when a session times out. In general, this appears to the application as either no session or a new session on the next request. User sessions are private to each web application and are not shared across applications.

We mentioned earlier that an extra step is required to support URL rewriting for web browsers that don't support cookies. To do this, we must make sure that any URLs we generate in content are first passed through the `HttpServletResponse encodeURL()` method. This method takes a string URL and returns a modified string only if URL rewriting is necessary. Normally, when cookies are available, it returns the same string. In our previous example, we could have encoded the server form URL that was retrieved from `getRequestURI()` before passing it to the client if we wanted to allow for users without cookies.

The ShoppingCart Servlet

Now we build on the previous example to make a servlet that could be used as part of an online store. `ShoppingCart` lets users choose items and add them to their basket until checkout time. The page generated is not that pretty, but you can have your web designer guy clean that up with some CSS (smiley). Here we are just concentrating on the Servlet API:

```
import java.io.*;
import javax.servlet.ServletException;
import javax.servlet.http.*;
import java.util.Enumeration;

public class ShoppingCart extends HttpServlet
{
    String [] items = new String [] {
        "Chocolate Covered Crickets", "Raspberry Roaches",
        "Buttery Butterflies", "Chicken Flavored Chicklets(tm)" };

    public void doPost(
        HttpServletRequest request, HttpServletResponse response)
        throws IOException, ServletException
    {
        doGet( request, response );
    }

    public void doGet(
        HttpServletRequest request, HttpServletResponse response)
        throws ServletException, IOException
    {
        response.setContentType("text/html");
        PrintWriter out = response.getWriter();

        // get or create the session information
        HttpSession session = request.getSession();
        int [] purchases = (int [])session.getAttribute("purchases");
        if ( purchases == null ) {
            purchases = new int [ items.length ];
            session.setAttribute( "purchases", purchases );
        }

        out.println( "<html><head><title>Shopping Cart</title>"
                     + "</title></head><body><p>" );

        if ( request.getParameter("checkout") != null )
            out.println("<h1>Thanks for ordering!</h1>");
        else  {
            if ( request.getParameter("add") != null ) {
                addPurchases( request, purchases );
                out.println(
                    "<h1>Purchase added.  Please continue</h1>");
            } else {
                if ( request.getParameter("clear") != null )
                    for (int i=0; i<purchases.length; i++)
                         purchases[i] = 0;
                out.println("<h1>Please Select Your Items!</h1>");
            }
```

```
            doForm( out, request.getRequestURI() );
        }
        showPurchases( out, purchases );
        out.close();
    }

    void addPurchases( HttpServletRequest request, int [] purchases ) {
        for (int i=0; i<items.length; i++) {
            String added = request.getParameter( items[i] );
            if ( added !=null && !added.equals("") )
                purchases[i] += Integer.parseInt( added );
        }
    }

    void doForm( PrintWriter out, String requestURI ) {
        out.println( "<form method=POST action="+ requestURI +">" );

        for(int i=0; i< items.length; i++)
            out.println( "Quantity <input name=\"" + items[i]
              + "\" value=0 size=3> of: " + items[i] + "<br>");
        out.println(
          "<p><input type=submit name=add value=\"Add To Cart\">"
          + "<input type=submit name=checkout value=\"Check Out\">"
          + "<input type=submit name=clear value=\"Clear Cart\">"
          + "</form>" );
    }

    void showPurchases( PrintWriter out, int [] purchases )
        throws IOException {

        out.println("<hr><h2>Your Shopping Basket</h2>");
        for (int i=0; i<items.length; i++)
            if ( purchases[i] != 0 )
                out.println( purchases[i] +"  "+ items[i] +"<br>" );
    }
}
```

Note that `ShoppingCart` has some instance data: a `String` array that holds a list of products. We're making the assumption that the product selection is the same for all customers. If it's not, we'd have to generate the product list on the fly or put it in the session for the user. We cannot store any per-request or per-user data in instance variables.

We see the same basic pattern as in our previous servlets, with `doPost()` delegating to `doGet()`, and `doGet()` generating the body of the output and a form for gathering new data. We've broken down the work using a few helper methods: `doForm()`, `addPurchases()`, and `showPurchases()`. Our shopping cart form has three submit buttons: one for adding items to the cart, one for checkout, and one for clearing the cart. In each case, we display the contents of the cart. Depending on the button pressed (indicated by the name of the parameter), we add new purchases, clear the list, or show the results as a checkout window.

The form is generated by our `doForm()` method, using the list of items for sale. As in the other examples, we supply our servlet's address as the target of the form. Next, we placed an integer array called `purchases` into the user session. Each element in `purchases` holds a count of the number of each item the user wants to buy. We create the array after retrieving the session simply by asking the session for it. If this is a new session, and the array hasn't been created, `getAttribute()` gives us a null value and we create an empty array to populate. Because we generate the form using the names from the `items` array, it's easy for `addPurchases()` to check for each name using `getParameter()` and increment the `purchases` array for the number of items requested. We also test for the value being equal to the empty string, because some web browsers send empty strings for unused field values. Finally, `showPurchases()` loops over the purchases array and prints the name and quantity for each item that the user has purchased.

Cookies

In our previous examples, a session lived only until you shut down your web browser or the server. You can do more long-term user tracking or identification that lasts beyond a single browser session by managing cookies explicitly. You can send a cookie to the client by creating a `javax.servlet.http.Cookie` object and adding it to the servlet response using the `addCookie()` method. Later, you can retrieve the cookie information from the servlet request and use it to look up persistent information in a database. The following servlet sends a "Learning Java" cookie to your web browser and displays it when you return to the page:

```
import java.io.*;
import javax.servlet.*;
import javax.servlet.http.*;

public class CookieCutter extends HttpServlet
{
    public void doGet(HttpServletRequest request, HttpServletResponse response)
      throws IOException, ServletException
    {
        response.setContentType("text/html");
        PrintWriter out = response.getWriter(  );

        if ( request.getParameter("setcookie") != null ) {
            Cookie cookie = new Cookie("Learningjava", "Cookies!");
            cookie.setMaxAge(3600);
            response.addCookie(cookie);
            out.println("<html><body><h1>Cookie Set...</h1>");
        } else {
            out.println("<html><body>");
            Cookie[] cookies = request.getCookies(  );
            if ( cookies.length == 0 ) {
```

```
                out.println("<h1>No cookies found...</h1>");
            } else {
                for (int i = 0; i < cookies.length; i++)
                    out.print("<h1>Name: "+ cookies[i].getName() + "<br>"
                             + "Value: " + cookies[i].getValue() + "</h1>" );
            }
            out.println("<p><a href=\""+ request.getRequestURI()
              +"?setcookie=true\">"
              +"Reset the Learning Java cookie.</a>");
        }
        out.println("</body></html>");
    }
}
```

This example simply enumerates the cookies supplied by the request object using the `getCookies()` method and prints their names and values. We provide a `GET`-style link that points back to our servlet with a parameter `setcookie`, indicating that we should set the cookie. In that case, we create a `Cookie` object using the specified name and value and add it to the response with the `addCookie()` method. We set the maximum age of the cookie to 3,600 seconds, so it remains in the browser for an hour before being discarded (we'll talk about tracking a cookie across multiple sessions later). Specifying a negative time period indicates that the cookie should not be stored persistently and should be erased when the browser exits. A time period of `0` deletes any existing cookie immediately.

Two other `Cookie` methods are of interest: `setDomain()` and `setPath()`. These methods allow you to specify the domain name and path component that determines where the client will send the cookie. If you're writing some kind of purchase applet for L.L. Bean, you don't want clients sending your cookies over to Eddie Bauer. In practice, however, this cannot happen. The default domain is the domain of the server sending the cookie. (You cannot in general specify other domains for security reasons.) The `path` parameter defaults to the base URL of the servlet, but you can specify a wider (or narrower) range of URLs on the host server by manually setting this parameter.

The ServletContext API

Web applications have access to the server environment through the `ServletContext` API, a reference to which can be obtained from the `HttpServlet getServletContext()` method:

```
ServletContext context = getServletContext();
```

Each web app has its own `ServletContext`. The context provides a shared space in which a web app's servlets may rendezvous and share objects. Objects may be placed into the context with the `setAttribute()` method and retrieved by name with the `getAttribute()` method:

```
context.setAttribute("myapp.statistics", myObject);
Object stats = context.getAttribute("myapp.statistics");
```

Attribute names beginning with "java." and "javax." are reserved for use by Java. You can opt to use the standard package-naming conventions for your attributes to avoid conflicts.

The `ServletContext` provides a listener API that can be used to add items to the servlet context when the application server starts up and to tear them down when it shuts down. This is a good way to initiate shared services. We'll show an example of this in the next section when we talk about asynchronous servlets.

One standard attribute that can be accessed through the servlet context is a reference to a private working directory represented by a `java.io.File` object. This temp directory is guaranteed unique to the web app. No guarantees are made about it being cleared upon exit, however, so you should use the temporary file API to create files here (unless you wish to try to keep them beyond the server exit). For example:

```
File tmpDir = (File)context.getAttribute("javax.servlet.context.tempdir");
File tmpFile = File.createTempFile( "appprefix", "appsuffix", tmpDir );
```

The servlet context also provides direct access to the web app's files from its root directory. The `getResource()` method is similar to the `Class getResource()` method (see Chapter 12). It takes a pathname and returns a special local URL for accessing that resource. In this case, it takes a path rooted in the servlet base directory (WAR file). The servlet may obtain references to files, including those in the *WEB-INF* directory, using this method. For example, a servlet could fetch an input stream for its own *web.xml* file:

```
InputStream in = context.getResourceAsStream("/WEB-INF/web.xml");
```

It could also use a URL reference to get one of its images:

```
URL bunnyURL = context.getResource("/images/happybunny.gif");
```

The method `getResourcePaths()` may be used to fetch a directory-style listing of all the resource files available matching a specified path. The return value is a `java.util.Set` collection of strings naming the resources available under the specified path. For example, the path */* lists all files in the WAR; the path */WEB-INF/* lists at least the *web.xml* file and *classes* directory.

The `ServletContext` is also a factory for `RequestDispatcher` objects, which we won't cover here, but which allow for servlets to forward to or include the results of other servlets in their responses.

Asynchronous Servlets

The following is a somewhat advanced topic, but we'll cover it now to round out our discussion of the Servlet API. Servlets may run in an asynchronous mode, where the servlet service method is allowed to exit, but the response to the user is held open until it can be completed efficiently. While the response is held open, it does not actively consume resources or block threads in the servlet container. This is intended to support nonblocking, NIO-style services as discussed in Chapters 13 and 14.

Asynchronous servlets are an excellent way to handle very slow servlet processes, as long as there is a way to efficiently poll for or receive some truly asynchronous notification of their completion. As we discussed when talking about NIO, one of the limiting factors in the scalability of web services is thread consumption. Threads hold a lot of resources and so simply allowing them to block and wait for completion of a task is inefficient. As we saw earlier, NIO supports a style of programming where one thread can manage a large number of network connections. Asynchronous servlets allow servlets to participate in this model. The basic idea is that you pass a job to a background service and put the servlet request on the shelf until it can be completed. As long as the background processor is implemented in such a way that it can manage the jobs without waiting (via polling or receiving updates asynchronously), then there is no point where threads must block.

Later in this chapter, we'll utilize a simple test servlet called `WaitServlet` that simply goes to sleep for a specified period of time before returning a result. This is a prime example of an *inefficient* use of threads. Our dumb `WaitServlet` blocks a thread (by sleeping) until it is "ready" to complete the transaction. In the following example, we'll get ahead of ourselves a bit and create a more efficient version of this tool, `BackgroundWaitServlet`, that will not block any threads in the servlet container while it waits.

Before we start, let's check our preconditions for whether an asynchronous servlet will be useful: do we have an efficient way to poll or receive notification when our "task" is complete without blocking a thread? (It's important to ask this to avoid simply moving thread blocking from the servlet to another location.) Yes, in our case, we can use a timer to notify us when the time has passed. An efficient timer implementation like `java.util.Timer` will use only one thread to manage many timed requests. We'll choose to use a `ScheduledExecutorService` from the `java.util.concurrent` package for this. It will execute any `Runnable` for us after a specified delay and makes a perfect shared background service for our asynchronous servlet.

The following example servlet returns a generic response after a delay of five seconds. The difference between this servlet and the naive one we use elsewhere in this chapter would become apparent if we flooded our server with requests. We should find that the asynchronous version would be limited primarily by TCP/IP resources in the host OS and not by more valuable memory on the server.

```
import javax.servlet.*;
import javax.servlet.annotation.*;
import javax.servlet.http.*;
import java.io.*;
import java.util.concurrent.*;
```

```
@WebServlet(
    urlPatterns={"/bgwait"},
    asyncSupported = true
)
public class BackgroundWaitServlet extends HttpServlet
{
    public void doGet( HttpServletRequest request, HttpServletResponse response)
        throws ServletException, IOException
    {
        final AsyncContext asyncContext = request.startAsync();
        ScheduledExecutorService executor =
            (ScheduledExecutorService)request.getServletContext().getAttribute(
            "BackgroundWaitExecutor");
        executor.schedule( new RespondLaterJob( asyncContext ), 5,
            TimeUnit.SECONDS );
    }
}

class RespondLaterJob implements Runnable
{
    private AsyncContext asyncContext;

    RespondLaterJob( AsyncContext asyncContext ) {
        this.asyncContext = asyncContext;
    }

    @Override
    public void run()
    {
        try {
            ServletResponse response = asyncContext.getResponse();
            response.setContentType("text/html");
            PrintWriter out = response.getWriter();
            out.println(
                "<html><body><h1>WaitServlet Response</h1></body></html>"
            );
        } catch ( IOException e ) { throw new RuntimeException( e ); }

        asyncContext.complete();
    }
}
```

We've included the `WebServlet` annotation in this example in order to show the `asyn cSupported` attribute. This attribute must be set on any servlets and servlet filters (discussed later) that will be involved in the request.

The implementation of our `doGet()` method is straightforward: we initiate the asynchronous behavior by calling the `startAsync()` method on the servlet request. That method returns to us an `AsyncContext` object that represents the caller context and includes the servlet request and response objects. At this point, we are free to arrange to service the request using any means we wish; the only requirement is that we must keep the AsyncContext object with our task so that it can be used later to send the results and close the transaction.

In our example, we look up our shared ScheduledExcecutorService from the servlet context by name ("BackgroundWaitExecutor") and pass it a custom Runnable object. (We'll talk about how the service got there in a bit.) We've created a RespondLaterJob that implements Runnable and holds onto the AsyncContext for later use. When the job runs in the future, we simply get the servlet response from the AsyncContext and send our response as usual. The final step is to call the complete() method on AsyncContext in order to close the call and return to the client.

The final step raises a couple of interesting issues: first, we do not necessarily have to call complete() immediately after writing to the response. Instead, we could write part of the result and go back to sleep, waiting for our service to wake us up when there is more data. Indeed, this is how we might work with an NIO data source. Second, instead of calling complete() to finalize the results for the client, we could use an alternate method, dispatch(), to forward the servlet request to another servlet, perhaps in a chain of servlets. The next servlet could write additional content or perhaps simply use resources put into the servlet context by the first servlet to handle the request. The dispatch() method accepts a URL string for the target servlet or, when called with no arguments, sends the request back to the original servlet.

OK, so how did our ScheduledExecutorService get into the servlet context? The best way to manage shared services and resources in the servlet context is via a ServletContextListener. A context listener has two lifecycle methods that can be used to set up and tear down services when the servlet container starts up and shuts down, respectively. We can deploy our listener simply by marking the class with a WebListener annotation and placing it in the WAR file as usual.

```
import javax.servlet.*;
import javax.servlet.annotation.*;
import java.util.concurrent.*;

@WebListener
public class BackgroundWaitService implements ServletContextListener
{
    ScheduledExecutorService executor;

    public void contextInitialized( ServletContextEvent sce )
    {
        this.executor = Executors.newScheduledThreadPool( 3 );
        sce.getServletContext().setAttribute( "BackgroundWaitExecutor",
            executor );
    }

    public void contextDestroyed(ServletContextEvent sce)
    {
        ScheduledExecutorService executor =
```

```
            Executors.newScheduledThreadPool( 3 );
        executor.shutdownNow();
    }
}
```

WAR Files and Deployment

As we described in the introduction to this chapter, a WAR file is an archive that contains all the parts of a web application: Java class files for servlets and web services, JSPs, HTML pages, images, and other resources. The WAR file is simply a JAR file (which is itself a fancy ZIP file) with specified directories for the Java code and one designated configuration file: the *web.xml* file, which tells the application server what to run and how to run it. WAR files always have the extension *.war*, but they can be created and read with the standard *jar* tool.

The contents of a typical WAR might look like this, as revealed by the *jar* tool:

```
$ jar tvf shoppingcart.war

    index.html
    purchase.html
    receipt.html
    images/happybunny.gif
    WEB-INF/web.xml
    WEB-INF/classes/com/mycompany/PurchaseServlet.class
    WEB-INF/classes/com/mycompany/ReturnServlet.class
    WEB-INF/lib/thirdparty.jar
```

When deployed, the name of the WAR becomes, by default, the root path of the web application—in this case, *shoppingcart*. Thus, the base URL for this web app, if deployed on *http://www.oreilly.com*, is *http://www.oreilly.com/shoppingcart/*, and all references to its documents, images, and servlets start with that path. The top level of the WAR file becomes the document root (base directory) for serving files. Our *index.html* file appears at the base URL we just mentioned, and our *happybunny.gif* image is referenced as *http://www.oreilly.com/shoppingcart/images/happybunny.gif*.

The *WEB-INF* directory (all caps, hyphenated) is a special directory that contains all deployment information and application code. This directory is protected by the web server, and its contents are not visible to outside users of the application, even if you add *WEB-INF* to the base URL. Your application classes can load additional files from this area using `getResource()` on the servlet context, however, so it is a safe place to store application resources. The *WEB-INF* directory also contains the *web.xml* file, which we'll talk more about in the next section.

The *WEB-INF/classes* and *WEB-INF/lib* directories contain Java class files and JAR libraries, respectively. The *WEB-INF/classes* directory is automatically added to the classpath of the web application, so any class files placed here (using the normal Java package conventions) are available to the application. After that, any JAR files located in

WEB-INF/lib are appended to the web app's classpath (the order in which they are appended is, unfortunately, not specified). You can place your classes in either location. During development, it is often easier to work with the "loose" *classes* directory and use the *lib* directory for supporting classes and third-party tools. It's also possible to install JAR files directly in the servlet container to make them available to all web apps running on that server. This is often done for common libraries that will be used by many web apps. The location for placing the libraries, however, is not standard and any classes that are deployed in this way cannot be automatically reloaded if changed—a feature of WAR files that we'll discuss later. Servlet API requires that each server provide a directory for these extension JARs and that the classes there will be loaded by a single classloader and made visible to the web application.

Configuration with web.xml and Annotations

The *web.xml* file is an XML configuration file that lists servlets and related entities to be deployed, the relative names (URL paths) under which to deploy them, their initialization parameters, and their deployment details, including security and authorization. For most of the history of Java web applications, this was the only deployment configuration mechanism. However, as of the Servlet 3.0 API, there are additional options. Most configuration can now be done using Java annotations. We saw the WebServlet annotation used in the first example, `HelloClient`, to declare the servlet and specify its deployment URL path. Using the annotation, we could deploy the servlet to the Tomcat server without any *web.xml* file. Another option with the Servlet 3.0 API is to deploy servlet procedurally—using Java code at runtime.

In this section we will describe both the XML and annotation style of configuration. For most purposes, you will find it easier to use the annotations, but there are a couple of reasons to understand the XML configuration as well. First, the *web.xml* can be used to override or extend the hardcoded annotation configuration. Using the XML, you can change configuration at deployment time without recompiling the classes. In general, configuration in the XML will take precedence over the annotations. It is also possible to tell the server to ignore the annotations completely, using an attribute called `metadata-complete` in the *web.xml*. Next, there may be some residual configuration, especially relating to options of the servlet container, which can only be done through XML.

We will assume that you have at least a passing familiarity with XML, but you can simply copy these examples in a cut-and-paste fashion. (For details about working with Java and XML, see Chapter 24.) Let's start with a simple *web.xml* file for our `HelloClient` servlet example. It looks like this:

```
<web-app>
    <servlet>
        <servlet-name>helloclient1</servlet-name>
        <servlet-class>HelloClient</servlet-class>
```

```
    </servlet>
    <servlet-mapping>
        <servlet-name>helloclient1</servlet-name>
        <url-pattern>/hello</url-pattern>
    </servlet-mapping>
</web-app>
```

The top-level element of the document is called `<web-app>`. Many types of entries may appear inside the `<web-app>`, but the most basic are `<servlet>` declarations and `<servlet-mapping>` deployment mappings. The `<servlet>` declaration tag is used to declare an instance of a servlet and, optionally, to give it initialization and other parameters. One instance of the servlet class is instantiated for each `<servlet>` tag appearing in the *web.xml* file.

At minimum, the `<servlet>` declaration requires two pieces of information: a `<servlet-name>`, which serves as a handle to reference the servlet elsewhere in the *web.xml* file, and the `<servlet-class>` tag, which specifies the Java class name of the servlet. Here, we named the servlet `helloclient1`. We named it like this to emphasize that we could declare other instances of the same servlet if we wanted to, possibly giving them different initialization parameters, etc. The class name for our servlet is, of course, `HelloClient`. In a real application, the servlet class would likely have a full package name, such as `com.oreilly.servlets.HelloClient`.

A servlet declaration may also include one or more initialization parameters, which are made available to the servlet through the `ServletConfig` object's `getInitParameter()` method:

```
<servlet>
    <servlet-name>helloclient1</servlet-name>
    <servlet-class>HelloClient</servlet-class>
    <init-param>
        <param-name>foo</param-name>
        <param-value>bar</param-value>
    </init-param>
</servlet>
```

Next, we have our `<servlet-mapping>`, which associates the servlet instance with a path on the web server:

```
<servlet-mapping>
    <servlet-name>helloclient1</servlet-name>
    <url-pattern>/hello</url-pattern>
</servlet-mapping>
```

Here we mapped our servlet to the path */hello*. (We could include additional url-patterns in the mapping if desired.) If we later name our WAR *learningjava.war* and deploy it on *www.oreilly.com*, the full path to this servlet would be *http://www.oreilly.com/learningjava/hello*. Just as we could declare more than one servlet instance with the `<servlet>` tag, we could declare more than one `<servlet-mapping>` for a given servlet instance. We could, for example, redundantly map the same `helloclient1` instance to the paths */hello* and */hola*. The `<url-pattern>` tag provides some very flexible ways to specify the URLs that should match a servlet. We'll talk about this in detail in the next section.

Finally, we should mention that although the *web.xml* example listed earlier will work on some application servers, it is technically incomplete because it is missing formal information that specifies the version of XML it is using and the version of the *web.xml* file standard with which it complies. To make it fully compliant with the standards, add a line such as:

```
<?xml version="1.0" encoding="ISO-8859-1"?>
```

As of Servlet API 2.5, the *web.xml* version information takes advantage of XML Schemas. (We'll talk about XML DTDs and XML Schemas in Chapter 24.) The additional information is inserted into the `<web-app>` element:

```
<web-app
    xmlns="http://java.sun.com/xml/ns/j2ee"
    xmlns:xsi="http://www.w3.org/2001/XMLSchema-instance"
    xsi:schemaLocation="http://java.sun.com/xml/ns/j2ee
    http://java.sun.com/xml/ns/j2ee/web-app_2_5.xsd”
    version=”2.5”>
```

If you leave them out, the application may still run, but it will be harder for the servlet container to detect errors in your configuration and give you clear error messages.

The equivalent of the preceding servlet declaration and mapping is, as we saw earlier, our one line annotation:

```
@WebServlet(urlPatterns={"/hello", "/hola"})
public class HelloClient extends HttpServlet {
   ...
}
```

Here the `WebServlet` attribute `urlPatterns` allows us to specify one or more URL patterns that are the equivalent to the `url-pattern` declaration in the *web.xml*.

URL Pattern Mappings

The `<url-pattern>` specified in the previous example was a simple string, `/hello`. For this pattern, only an exact match of the base URL followed by `/hello` would invoke our servlet. The `<url-pattern>` tag is capable of more powerful patterns, however, including wildcards. For example, specifying a `<url-pattern>` of `/hello*` allows our servlet to be invoked by URLs such as *http://www.oreilly.com/learningjava/helloworld* or `.../hellobaby`. You can even specify wildcards with extensions (e.g., `*.html` or `*.foo`, meaning that the servlet is invoked for any path that ends with those characters).

Using wildcards can result in more than one match. Consider URLs ending in /scooby* and /scoobydoo*. Which should be matched for a URL ending in .../scoobydoobiedoo? What if we have a third possible match because of a wildcard suffix extension mapping? The rules for resolving these are as follows.

First, any exact match is taken. For example, /hello matches the /hello URL pattern in our example regardless of any additional /hello*. Failing that, the container looks for the longest prefix match. So /scoobydoobiedoo matches the second pattern, /scoobydoo*, because it is longer and presumably more specific. Failing any matches there, the container looks at wildcard suffix mappings. A request ending in .foo matches a *.foo mapping at this point in the process. Finally, failing any matches there, the container looks for a default, catchall mapping named /*. A servlet mapped to /* picks up anything unmatched by this point. If there is no default servlet mapping, the request fails with a "404 not found" message.

Deploying HelloClient

Once you've deployed the HelloClient servlet, it should be easy to add examples to the WAR as you work with them in this chapter. In this section, we'll show you how to build a WAR by hand. In "Building WAR Files with Ant" later in this chapter, we'll show a more realistic way to manage your applications using the popular build tool, Ant. You can also grab the full set of examples, along with their source code, in the *learningjava.war* file from this book's website at *http://oreil.ly/Java_4E.*

To create the WAR by hand, we first create the *WEB-INF* and *WEB-INF/classes* directories. If you are using a *web.xml* file, place it into *WEB-INF.* Put the *HelloClient.class* into *WEB-INF/classes.* Use the *jar* command to create *learningjava.war* (WEB-INF at the "top" level of the archive):

```
$ jar cvf learningjava.war WEB-INF
```

You can also include documents and other resources in the WAR by adding their names after the *WEB-INF* directory. This command produces the file *learningjava.war*. You can verify the contents using the *jar* command:

```
$ jar tvf learningjava.war
document1.html
WEB-INF/web.xml
WEB-INF/classes/HelloClient.class
```

Now all that is necessary is to drop the WAR into the correct location for your server. If you have not already, you should download and install Apache Tomcat. The location for WAR files is the *webapps* directory within your Tomcat installation directory. Place your WAR here, and start the server. If Tomcat is configured with the default port number, you should be able to point to the HelloClient servlet with one of two URLs: *http://localhost:8080/learningjava/hello* or *http://<yourserver>:8080/learningjava/*

hello, where `<yourserver>` is the name or IP address of your server. If you have trouble, look in the *logs* directory of the Tomcat folder for errors.

Reloading web apps

All servlet containers are supposed to provide a facility for reloading WAR files; many support reloading of individual servlet classes after they have been modified. Reloading WARs is part of the servlet specification and is especially useful during development. Support for reloading web apps varies from server to server. Normally, all that you have to do is drop a new WAR in place of the old one in the proper location (e.g., the *webapps* directory for Tomcat) and the container shuts down the old application and deploys the new version. This works in Tomcat when the "autoDeploy" attribute is set (it is on by default) and also in BEA's WebLogic application server when it is configured in development mode.

Some servers, including Tomcat, "explode" WARs by unpacking them into a directory under the *webapps* directory, or they allow you explicitly to configure a root directory (or "context") for your unpacked web app through their own configuration files. In this mode, they may allow you to replace individual files, which can be especially useful for tweaking HTML or JSPs. Tomcat automatically reloads WAR files when they change them (unless configured not to), so all you have to do is drop an updated WAR over the old one and it will redeploy it as necessary. In some cases, it may be necessary to restart the server to make all changes take effect. When in doubt, shut down and restart.

Tomcat also provides a client-side "deployer" package that integrates with Ant to automate building, deploying, and redeploying applications. We'll discuss Ant later in this chapter.

Error and Index Pages

One of the finer points of writing a professional-looking web application is taking care to handle errors well. Nothing annoys a user more than getting a funny-looking page with some technical mumbo-jumbo error information on it when he expected the receipt for his Christmas present. Through the *web.xml* file, it is possible to specify documents or servlets to handle error pages that are shown for various conditions, as well as the special case of *welcome files* (index files) that are invoked for paths corresponding to directories. At this time, there is no corresponding way to declare error pages or welcome files using annotations.

You can designate a page or servlet that can handle various HTTP error status codes, such as "404 Not Found" and "403 Forbidden," using one or more `<error-page>`declarations:

```
<web-app>
...
    <error-page>
```

```
        <error-code>404</error-code>
        <location>/notfound.html</location>
    </error-page>
    <error-page>
        <error-code>403</error-code>
        <location>/secret.html</location>
    </error-page>
```

Additionally, you can designate error pages based on Java exception types that may be thrown from the servlet. For example:

```
<error-page>
    <exception-type>java.lang.IOException</exception-type>
    <location>/ioexception.html</location>
</error-page>
```

This declaration catches any `IOExceptions` generated from servlets in the web app and displays the *ioexception.html* page. If no matching exceptions are found in the `<error-page>` declarations, and the exception is of type `ServletException` (or a subclass), the container makes a second try to find the correct handler. It looks for a wrapped exception (the "cause" exception) contained in the `ServletException` and attempts to match it to an error page declaration.

In the Servlet 3.0 API, you can also designate a catchall error page that will handle any unhandled error codes and exception types as follows:

```
<error-page>
    <location>/anyerror.html</location>
</error-page>
```

As we've mentioned, you can use a servlet to handle your error pages, just as you can use a static document. In fact, the container supplies several helpful pieces of information to an error-handling servlet, which the servlet can use in generating a response. The information is made available in the form of servlet request attributes through the method `getAttribute()`:

```
Object requestAttribute = servletRequest.getAttribute("name");
```

Attributes are like servlet parameters, except that they can be arbitrary objects. We have seen attributes of the `ServletContext` in "The ServletContext API" on page 554 section. In this case, we are talking about attributes of the request. When a servlet (or JSP or filter) is invoked to handle an error condition, the following string attributes are set in the request:

```
javax.servlet.error.servlet_name
javax.servlet.error.request_uri
javax.servlet.error.message
```

Depending on whether the `<error-page>` declaration was based on an `<error-code>` or `<exception-type>` condition, the request also contains one of the following two attributes:

```
// status code Integer or Exception object
javax.servlet.error.status_code
javax.servlet.error.exception
```

In the case of a status code, the attribute is an `Integer` representing the code. In the case of the exception type, the object is the actual instigating exception.

Indexes for directory paths can be designated in a similar way. Normally, when a user specifies a directory URL path, the web server searches for a default file in that directory to be displayed. The most common example of this is the ubiquitous *index.html* file. You can designate your own ordered list of files to look for by adding a `<welcome-file-list>` entry to your *web.xml* file. For example:

```
<welcome-file-list>
    <welcome-file>index.html</welcome-file>
    <welcome-file>index.htm</welcome-file>
</welcome-file-list>
```

`<welcome-file-list>` specifies that when a partial request (directory path) is received, the server should search first for a file named *index.html* and, if that is not found, a file called *index.htm*. If none of the specified welcome files is found, it is left up to the server to decide what kind of page to display. Servers are generally configured to display a directory-like listing or to produce an error message.

Security and Authentication

One of the most powerful features of web app deployment with the Servlet API is the ability to define *declarative security* constraints, meaning that you can spell out in the *web.xml* file exactly which areas of your web app (URL paths to documents, directories, servlets, etc.) are login-protected, the types of users allowed access to them, and the class of security protocol required for communications. It is not necessary to write code in your servlets to implement these basic security procedures.

There are two types of entries in the *web.xml* file that control security and authentication. First are the `<security-constraint>` entries, which provide authorization based on user roles and secure transport of data, if desired. Second is the `<login-config>` entry, which determines the kind of authentication used for the web application.

Protecting Resources with Roles

Let's take a look at a simple example. The following *web.xml* excerpt defines an area called "Secret documents" with a URL pattern of */secret/** and designates that only users with the role "secretagent" may access them. It specifies the simplest form of login process: the BASIC authentication model, which causes the browser to prompt the user with a simple pop-up username and password dialog box:

```
<web-app>
...
```

```
<security-constraint>
    <web-resource-collection>
        <web-resource-name>Secret documents</web-resource-name>
        <url-pattern>/secret/*</url-pattern>
    </web-resource-collection>
    <auth-constraint>
        <role-name>secretagent</role-name>
    </auth-constraint>
</security-constraint>

<login-config>
    <auth-method>BASIC</auth-method>
</login-config>
```

Each `<security-constraint>` block has one `<web-resource-collection>` section that designates a named list of URL patterns for areas of the web app, followed by an `<auth-constraint>` section listing user roles that are allowed to access those areas.

We can do the equivalent configuration for a given servlet using the SecurityServlet annotation with an `HttpConstraint` annotation element as follows:

```
@ServletSecurity(
    @HttpConstraint(rolesAllowed = "secretagent")
)
public class SecureHelloClient extends HttpServlet
{ ...
```

You can add this annotation to our test servlet or add the XML example setup to the *web.xml* file for the *learningjava.war* file and prepare to try it out. However, there is one additional step that you'll have to take to get this working: create the user role "secretagent" and an actual user with this role in our application server environment.

Access to protected areas is granted to user roles, not individual users. A user role is effectively just a group of users; instead of granting access to individual users by name, you grant access to roles, and users are assigned one or more roles. A user role is an abstraction from users. Actual user information (name and password, etc.) is handled outside the scope of the web app, in the application server environment (possibly integrated with the host platform operating system). Generally, application servers have their own tools for creating users and assigning individuals (or actual groups of users) their roles. A given username may have many roles associated with it.

When attempting to access a login-protected area, the user's valid login will be assessed to see if she has the correct role for access. For the Tomcat server, adding test users and assigning them roles is easy; simply edit the file *conf/tomcat-users.xml*. To add a user named "bond" with the "secretagent" role, you'd add an entry such as:

```
<user username="bond" password="007" roles="secretagent"/>
```

For other servers, you'll have to refer to the documentation to determine how to add users and assign security roles.

Secure Data Transport

Before we move on, there is one more piece of the security constraint to discuss: the transport guarantee. Each `<security-constraint>` block may end with a `<user-data-constraint>` entry, which designates one of three levels of transport security for the protocol used to transfer data to and from the protected area over the Internet. For example:

```
<security-constraint>
...
    <user-data-constraint>
        <transport-guarantee>CONFIDENTIAL</transport-guarantee>
    </user-data-constraint>
</security-constraint>
```

The three levels are NONE, INTEGRAL, and CONFIDENTIAL. NONE is equivalent to leaving out the section, which indicates that no special transport is required. This is the standard for normal web traffic, which is generally sent in plain text over the network. The INTEGRAL level of security specifies that any transport protocol used must guarantee the data sent is not modified in transit. This implies the use of digital signatures or some other method of validating the data at the receiving end, but it does not require that the data be encrypted and hidden while it is transported. Finally, CONFIDENTIAL implies both INTEGRAL and encrypted. In practice, the only widely used secure transport in web browsers is SSL. Requiring a transport guarantee other than NONE typically forces the use of SSL by the client browser.

We can configure the equivalent transport security for a servlet using the `ServletSecurity` annotation along with the `HttpMethodConstraint` annotation, as follows:

```
@ServletSecurity(
    httpMethodConstraints = @HttpMethodConstraint( value="GET",
        transportGuarantee = ServletSecurity.TransportGuarantee.CONFIDENTIAL)
)
public class SecureHelloClient extends HttpServlet { ... }

@ServletSecurity(
    value = @HttpConstraint(rolesAllowed = "secretagent"),
    httpMethodConstraints = @HttpMethodConstraint( value="GET",
        transportGuarantee = ServletSecurity.TransportGuarantee.CONFIDENTIAL)
)
public class SecureHelloClient extends HttpServlet { ... }
```

Here we use the `httpMethodConstraints` attribute with an `HttpMethodConstraint` annotation to designate that the servlet may only be accessed using the HTTP GET method and only with `CONFIDENTIAL` level security. Combining the transport security with a `rolesAllowed` annotation can be done as shown in the preceding example.

Authenticating Users

This section shows how to declare a custom login form to perform user login. First, we'll show the *web.xml* style and then discuss the Servlet 3.0 alternative, which gives us more flexibility.

The `<login-conf>` section determines exactly how a user authenticates herself (logs in) to the protected area. The `<auth-method>` tag allows four types of login authentication to be specified: BASIC, DIGEST, FORM, and CLIENT-CERT. In our example, we showed the BASIC method, which uses the standard web browser login and password dialog. BASIC authentication sends the user's name and password in plain text over the Internet unless a transport guarantee has been used separately to start SSL and encrypt the data stream. DIGEST is a variation on BASIC that obscures the text of the password but adds little real security; it is not widely used. FORM is equivalent to BASIC, but instead of using the browser's dialog, we can use our own HTML form to post the username and password data to the container. The form data can come from a static HTML page or from one generated by a servlet. Again, form data is sent in plain text unless otherwise protected by a transport guarantee (SSL). CLIENT-CERT is an interesting option. It specifies that the client must be identified using a client-side public key certificate. This implies the use of a protocol like SSL, which allows for secure exchange and mutual authentication using digital certificates. The exact method of setting up a client-side certificate is browser-dependent.

The FORM method is most useful because it allows us to customize the look of the login page (we recommend using SSL to secure the data stream). We can also specify an error page to use if the authentication fails. Here is a sample `<login-config>` using the form method:

```
<login-config>
    <auth-method>FORM</auth-method>
    <form-login-config>
        <form-login-page>/login.html</form-login-page>
        <form-error-page>/login_error.html</form-error-page>
    </form-login-config>
</login-config>
```

The login page must contain an HTML form with a specially named pair of fields for the name and password. Here is a simple *login.html* file:

```
<html>
<head><title>Login</title></head>
<body>
    <form method="POST" action="j_security_check">
        Username: <input type="text" name="j_username"><br>
        Password: <input type="password" name="j_password"><br>
        <input type="submit" value="submit">
    </form>
```

```
</body>
</html>
```

The username field is called `j_username`, the password field is called `j_password`, and the URL used for the form action attribute is `j_security_check`. There are no special requirements for the error page, but normally you will want to provide a "try again" message and repeat the login form.

In the Servlet 3.0 API, the HttpServletRequest API contains methods for explicitly logging in and logging out a user. However, it is also specified that a user's login is no longer valid after the user session times out or is invalidated. Therefore, you can effectively log out the user by calling `invalidate()` on the session:

```
request.logout();    request.getSession().invalidate();
```

With Servlet 3.0, we can also take control of the login process ourselves by utilizing the `ServletRequest login()` method to perform our own login operation. All we have to do is arrange our own login servlet that accepts a username and password (securely) and then calls the login method. This gives you great flexibility over how and when the user login occurs. And, of course, you can log the user out with the corresponding `logout()` method.

```
@ServletSecurity(
    httpMethodConstraints = @HttpMethodConstraint( value="POST",
        transportGuarantee = ServletSecurity.TransportGuarantee.CONFIDENTIAL)
)
@WebServlet( urlPatterns={"/mylogin"} )
public class MyLogin extends HttpServlet
{
    public void doGet(HttpServletRequest request, HttpServletResponse response)
        throws ServletException, IOException
    {
       String user = request.getParameter("user");
       String password = request.getParameter("pass");
       request.login( user, password );
       // Dispatch or redirect to the next page...
    }
```

Procedural Authorization

We should mention that in addition to the declarative security offered by the *web.xml* file, servlets may perform their own active procedural (or programmatic) security using all the authentication information available to the container. We won't cover this in detail, but here are the basics.

The name of the authenticated user is available through the method `HttpServletRequest getRemoteUser()`, and the type of authentication provided can be determined with the `getAuthType()` method. Servlets can work with security roles using the `isUserInRole()` method. (Doing this requires adding some additional mappings in the *web.xml* file, which allows the servlet to refer to the security roles by reference names.)

For advanced applications, a `java.security.Principal` object for the user can be retrieved with the `getUserPrincipal()` method of the request. In the case where a secure transport like SSL was used, the method `isSecure()` returns `true`, and detailed information about how the principal was authenticated—the cipher type, key size, and certificate chain—is made available through request attributes. It is useful to note that the notion of being "logged in" to a web application, from the servlet container's point of view, is defined as there being a valid (non-`null`) value returned by the `getUserPrincipal()` method.

Servlet Filters

The servlet Filter API generalizes the Java Servlet API to allow modular component "filters" to operate on the servlet request and responses in a sort of pipeline. Filters are *chained*, meaning that when more than one filter is applied, the servlet request is passed through each filter in succession, with each having an opportunity to act upon or modify the request before passing it to the next filter. Similarly, upon completion, the servlet result is effectively passed back through the chain on its return trip to the browser. Servlet filters may operate on any requests to a web application, not just those handled by the servlets; they may filter static content, as well. You can also control whether filters are applied to error and welcome pages as well as pages forwarded or included using the request dispatcher (from servlet to servlet).

Filters can be declared and mapped to servlets in the *web.xml* file or using annotations. There are two ways to map a filter: using a URL pattern like those used for servlets or by specifying a servlet by its servlet name as defined in its servlet config. Filters obey the same basic rules as servlets when it comes to URL matching, but when multiple filters match a path, they are each invoked.

When using *web.xml*, the order of the chain is determined by the order in which matching filter mappings appear in the *web.xml* file, with `<url-pattern>` matches taking precedence over `<servlet-name>` matches. This is contrary to the way in which servlet URL matching is done, with specific matches taking the highest priority. Filter chains are constructed as follows. First, each filter with a matching URL pattern is called in the order in which it appears in the *web.xml* file; next, each filter with a matching servlet name is called, also in order of appearance. URL patterns take a higher priority than filters specifically associated with a servlet, so in this case, patterns such as `/*` have first crack at an incoming request.

Servlet filters may be declared and mapped using the `WebFilter` annotation. There is no corresponding way to control filter ordering using annotations; however, as always you can mix annotations and *web.xml* to minimize the XML configuration by only declaring the filter mappings in the XML. (We'll discuss configuration more later in this chapter.)

The Filter API is very simple and mimics the Servlet API. A servlet filter implements the `javax.servlet.Filter` interface and implements three methods: `init()`, `doFilter()`, and `destroy()`. The `doFilter()` method is where the work is performed. For each incoming request, the `ServletRequest` and `ServletResponse` objects are passed to `doFilter()`. Here, we have a chance to examine and modify these objects—or even substitute our own objects for them—before passing them to the next filter and, ultimately, the servlet (or user) on the other side. Our link to the rest of the filter chain is another parameter of `doFilter()`, the `FilterChain` object. With `FilterChain`, we can invoke the next element in the pipeline. The following section presents an example.

A Simple Filter

For our first filter, we'll do something easy but practical: create a filter that limits the number of concurrent connections to its URLs. We'll simply have our filter keep a counter of the active connections passing through it and turn away new requests when they exceed a specified limit:

```
import java.io.*;
import javax.servlet.*;
import javax.servlet.annotation.*;
import javax.servlet.http.*;

public class ConLimitFilter implements Filter
{
    int limit;
    volatile int count;

    public void init( FilterConfig filterConfig )
        throws ServletException
    {
        String s = filterConfig.getInitParameter("limit");
        if ( s == null )
            throw new ServletException("Missing init parameter: "+limit);
        limit = Integer.parseInt( s );
    }

    public void doFilter (
        ServletRequest req, ServletResponse res, FilterChain chain )
            throws IOException, ServletException
    {
        if ( count > limit ) {
            HttpServletResponse httpRes = (HttpServletResponse)res;
            httpRes.sendError( httpRes.SC_SERVICE_UNAVAILABLE, "Too Busy.");
        } else {
            ++count;
            chain.doFilter( req, res );
```

```
            --count;
        }
    }

    public void destroy() { }
}
```

ConLimitFilter implements the three lifecycle methods of the Filter interface: init(), doFilter(), and destroy(). In our init() method, we use the FilterConfig object to look for an initialization parameter named "limit" and turn it into an integer. Users can set this value in the section of the *web.xml* file where the instance of our filter is declared or in the annotation as shown. The doFilter() method implements all our logic. First, it receives ServletRequest and ServletResponse object pairs for incoming requests. Depending on the counter, it then either passes them down the chain by invoking the next doFilter() method on the FilterChain object, or rejects them by generating its own response. We use the standard HTTP message "504 Service Unavailable" when we deny new connections.

Calling doFilter() on the FilterChain object continues processing by invoking the next filter in the chain or by invoking the servlet if ours is the last filter. Alternatively, when we choose to reject the call, we use the ServletResponse to generate our own response and then simply allow doFilter() to exit. This stops the processing chain at our filter, although any filters called before us still have an opportunity to intervene as the request effectively traverses back to the client.

Notice that ConLimitFilter increments the count before calling doFilter() and decrements it after. Prior to calling doFilter(), we can work on the request before it reaches the rest of the chain and the servlet. After the call to doFilter(), the chain to the servlet has completed, and the request is sent back to the client. This is our opportunity to do any post-processing of the response.

Finally, we should mention that although we've been talking about the servlet request and response as if they were HttpServletRequest and HttpServletResponse, the doFilter() method actually takes the more generic ServletRequest and ServletResponse objects as parameters. As filter implementers, we are expected to determine when it is safe to treat them as HTTP traffic and perform the cast as necessary (which we do here in order to use the sendError() HTTP response method).

A Test Servlet

Before we go on, here is a simple test servlet you can use to try out this filter and the other filters we'll develop in this section. It's called WaitServlet and, as its name implies, it simply waits. You can specify how long it waits as a number of seconds with the servlet parameter time. (This is the "dumb" version of the BackgroundWaitServlet that we created earlier in this chapter when discussing asynchronous servlets.)

```
import java.io.*;
import javax.servlet.*;
import javax.servlet.http.*;

public class WaitServlet extends HttpServlet
{
    public void doGet( HttpServletRequest request,
        HttpServletResponse response )
        throws ServletException, IOException
    {
        String waitStr = request.getParameter("time");
        if ( waitStr == null )
            throw new ServletException("Missing parameter: time");
        int wait = Integer.parseInt(waitStr);

        try {
            Thread.sleep( wait * 1000 );
        } catch( InterruptedException e ) {
            throw new ServletException(e);
        }

        response.setContentType("text/html");
        PrintWriter out = response.getWriter();
        out.println(
            "<html><body><h1>WaitServlet Response</h1></body></html>");
        out.close();
    }
}
```

By making multiple simultaneous requests to the `WaitServlet`, you can try out the `ConLimitFilter`. Note that some web browsers won't open multiple requests to the same URL or may delay opening multiple tabs. You may have to add extraneous parameters to trick the web browser. Alternately, you may wish to use the *curl* command-line utility to make the requests if you have it.

Declaring and Mapping Filters

In the *web.xml* file filters are declared and mapped much as servlets are. Like servlets, one instance of a filter class is created for each filter declaration in the *web.xml* file. A filter declaration looks like this:

```
<filter>
    <filter-name>defaultsfilter1</filter-name>
    <filter-class>RequestDefaultsFilter</filter-class>
</filter>
```

It specifies a filter handle name to be used for reference within the *web.xml* file and the filter's Java class name. Filter declarations may also contain `<init-param>` parameter sections, just like servlet declarations.

Filters are mapped to resources with `<filter-mapping>` declarations that specify the filter handle name and either the specific servlet handle name or a URL pattern, as we discussed earlier:

```
<filter-mapping>
    <filter-name>conlimitfilter1</filter-name>
    <servlet-name>waitservlet1</servlet-name>
 </filter-mapping>

<filter-mapping>
    <filter-name>conlimitfilter1</filter-name>
    <url-pattern>/*</url-pattern>
 </filter-mapping>
```

The corresponding `WebFilter` annotation can declare and map filters as well as supply filter parameters. The annotation will accept either a `urlPatterns` or a `servletNames` attribute for the mapping.

```
@WebFilter(
    urlPatterns = "/*",
    initParams = {
        @WebInitParam(name="limit", value="3")
    }
)
```

Filtering the Servlet Request

Our first filter example was not very exciting because it did not actually modify any information going to or coming from the servlet. Next, let's do some actual "filtering" by modifying the incoming request before it reaches a servlet. In this example, we'll create a request "defaulting" filter that automatically supplies default values for specified servlet parameters when they are not provided in the incoming request. Here is the `RequestDefaultsFilter`:

```
import java.io.*;
import javax.servlet.*;
import javax.servlet.http.*;

public class RequestDefaultsFilter implements Filter
{
    FilterConfig filterConfig;

    public void init( FilterConfig filterConfig ) throws ServletException
    {
        this.filterConfig = filterConfig;
    }

    public void doFilter (
        ServletRequest req, ServletResponse res, FilterChain chain )
            throws IOException, ServletException
    {
```

```
            WrappedRequest wrappedRequest =
                new WrappedRequest( (HttpServletRequest)req );
            chain.doFilter( wrappedRequest, res );
        }

        public void destroy() { }

        class WrappedRequest extends HttpServletRequestWrapper
        {
            WrappedRequest( HttpServletRequest req ) {
                super( req );
            }

            public String getParameter( String name ) {
                String value = super.getParameter( name );
                if ( value == null )
                    value = filterConfig.getInitParameter( name );
                return value;
            }
        }
    }
```

To interpose ourselves in the data flow, we must do something drastic. We kidnap the incoming `HttpServletRequest` object and replace it with an imposter that does our bidding. The technique, which we'll use here for modifying the request object and later for modifying the response, is to wrap the real request with an adapter, allowing us to override some of its methods. Here, we will take control of the `HttpServletRequest`'s `getParameter()` method, modifying it to look for default values where it would otherwise return `null`.

Again, we implement the three lifecycle methods of `Filter`, but this time, before invoking `doFilter()` on the filter chain to continue processing, we wrap the incoming `HttpServletRequest` in our own class, `WrappedRequest`. `WrappedRequest` extends a special adapter called `HttpServletRequestWrapper`. This wrapper class is a convenience utility that extends `HttpServletRequest`. It accepts a reference to a target `HttpServletRequest` object and, by default, delegates all of its methods to that target. This makes it very convenient for us to simply override one or more methods of interest to us. All we have to do is override `getParameter()` in our `WrappedRequest` class and add our functionality. Here, we simply call our parent's `getParameter()`, and in the case where the value is `null`, we try to substitute a filter initialization parameter of the same name.

Try this example using the `WaitServlet` with a filter declaration and mapping or annotation as follows:

```
<filter>
    <filter-name>defaultsfilter1</filter-name>
    <filter-class>RequestDefaultsFilter</filter-class>
    <init-param>
```

```
        <param-name>time</param-name>
        <param-value>3</param-value>
    </init-param>
</filter>
<filter-mapping>
    <filter-name>defaultsfilter1</filter-name>
    <servlet-name>waitservlet1</servlet-name>
</filter-mapping>

@WebFilter(
    servletNames = "waitservlet1",
    initParams = {
        @WebInitParam(name="time", value="3")
    }
)
```

Now the `WaitServlet` receives a default time value of three seconds even when you don't specify one.

Filtering the Servlet Response

Filtering the request was fairly easy, and we can do something similar with the response object using exactly the same technique. There is a corresponding `HttpServletResponseWrapper` that we can use to wrap the response before the servlet uses it to communicate back to the client. By wrapping the response, we can intercept methods that the servlet uses to write the response, just as we intercepted the `getParameter()` method that the servlet used in reading the incoming data. For example, we could override the `sendError()` method of the `HttpServletResponse` object and modify it to redirect to a specified page. In this way, we could create a servlet filter that emulates the programmable error page control offered in the *web.xml* file. But the most interesting technique available to us, and the one we'll show here, involves actually modifying the data written by the servlet before it reaches the client. In order to do this, we have to pull a double "switcheroo." We wrap the servlet response to override the `getWriter()` method and then create our own wrapper for the client's `PrintWriter` object supplied by this method, one that buffers the data written and allows us to modify it. This is a useful and powerful technique, but it can be tricky.

Our example, `LinkResponseFilter`, is an automatic hyperlink-generating filter that reads HTML responses and searches them for patterns supplied as regular expressions. When it matches a pattern, it turns it into an HTML link. The pattern and links are specified in the filter initialization parameters. You could extend this example with access to a database or XML file and add more rules to make it into a useful site-management helper. Here it is:

```
import java.io.*;
import java.util.*;
import javax.servlet.*;
import javax.servlet.http.*;
```

```
public class LinkResponseFilter implements Filter
{
    FilterConfig filterConfig;

    public void init( FilterConfig filterConfig )
        throws ServletException
    {
        this.filterConfig = filterConfig;
    }

    public void doFilter (
        ServletRequest req, ServletResponse res, FilterChain chain )
            throws IOException, ServletException
    {
        WrappedResponse wrappedResponse =
            new WrappedResponse( (HttpServletResponse)res );
        chain.doFilter( req, wrappedResponse );
        wrappedResponse.close();
    }

    public void destroy() { }

    class WrappedResponse extends HttpServletResponseWrapper
    {
        boolean linkText;
        PrintWriter client;

        WrappedResponse( HttpServletResponse res ) {
            super( res );
        }

        public void setContentType( String mime ) {
            super.setContentType( mime );
            if ( mime.startsWith("text/html") )
                linkText = true;
        }

        public PrintWriter getWriter() throws
        IOException {
            if ( client == null )
                if ( linkText )
                    client = new LinkWriter(
                        super.getWriter(), new ByteArrayOutputStream() );
                else
                    client = super.getWriter();
            return client;
        }

        void close() {
            if ( client != null )
                client.close();
```

```
        }
    }

    class LinkWriter extends PrintWriter
    {
        ByteArrayOutputStream buffer;
        Writer client;

        LinkWriter( Writer client, ByteArrayOutputStream buffer ) {
            super( buffer );
            this.buffer = buffer;
            this.client = client;
        }

        public void close() {
            try {
                flush();
                client.write( linkText( buffer.toString() ) );
                client.close();
            } catch ( IOException e ) {
                setError();
            }
        }

        String linkText( String text ) {
            Enumeration en = filterConfig.getInitParameterNames();
            while ( en.hasMoreElements() ) {
                String pattern = (String)en.nextElement();
                String value = filterConfig.getInitParameter( pattern );
                text = text.replaceAll(
                    pattern, "<a href="+value+">$0</a>" );
            }
            return text;
        }
    }
}
```

That was a bit longer than our previous examples, but the basics are the same. We wrapped the `HttpServletResponse` object with our own `WrappedResponse` class using the `HttpServletResponseWrapper` helper class. Our `WrappedResponse` overrides two methods: `getWriter()` and `setContentType()`. We override `setContentType()` in order to set a flag that indicates whether the output is of type "text/html" (an HTML document). We don't want to be performing regular-expression replacements on binary data such as images, for example, should they happen to match our filter. We also override `getWriter()` to provide our substitute writer stream, `LinkWriter`. Our `LinkWriter` class is a `PrintStream` that takes as arguments the client `PrintWriter` and a `ByteArrayOutputStream` that serves as a buffer for storing output data before it is written. We are careful to substitute our `LinkWriter` only if the `linkText` Boolean set by `setContent()` is `true`. When we do use our `LinkWriter`, we cache the stream so that any subsequent calls to `getWriter()` return the same object. Finally, we have added one method to the response object: `close()`. A normal `HttpServletResponse` does not have a `close()` method. We use ours on the return trip to the client to indicate that the `LinkWriter` should complete its processing and write the actual data to the client. We do this in case the client does not explicitly close the output stream before exiting the servlet service methods.

This explains the important parts of our filter-writing example. Let's wrap up by looking at the `LinkWriter`, which does the magic in this example. `LinkWriter` is a `PrintStream` that holds references to two other `Writers`: the true client `PrintWriter` and a `ByteArrayOutputStream`. The `LinkWriter` calls its superclass constructor, passing the `ByteArrayOutputStream` as the target stream, so all of its default functionality (its `print()` methods) writes to the byte array. Our only real job is to intercept the `close()` method of the `PrintStream` and add our text linking before sending the data. When `LinkWriter` is closed, it flushes itself to force any data buffered in its superclass out to the `ByteArrayOutputStream`. It then retrieves the buffered data (with the `ByteArrayOutputStream toString()` method) and invokes its `linkText()` method to create the hyperlinks before writing the linked data to the client. The `linkText()` method simply loops over all the filter initialization parameters, treating them as patterns, and uses the `StringreplaceAll()` method to turn them into hyperlinks. (See Chapter 1 for more about `replaceAll()`.)

This example works, but it has limitations. First, we cannot buffer an infinite amount of data. A better implementation would make a decision about when to start writing data to the client, potentially based on the client-specified buffer size of the `HttpServletResponse` API. Next, our implementation of `linkText()` could probably be speeded up by constructing one large regular expression using alternation. You will undoubtedly find other ways in which it can be improved.

Building WAR Files with Ant

Thus far in this book, we have not become too preoccupied with special tools to help you construct Java applications. Partly, this is because it's outside the scope of this text, and partly it reflects a small bias of the authors against getting too entangled with particular development environments. There is, however, one universal tool that should be in the arsenal of every Java developer: the Jakarta Project's Ant. Ant is a project builder for Java, a pure Java application that fills the role that *make* does for C applications. Ant has many advantages over *make* when building Java code, not the least of which is that it comes with a wealth of special "targets" (declarative commands) to perform common Java-related operations such as building WAR files. Ant is fast, portable, and easy to install and use. Make it your friend.

We won't cover the usage of Ant in detail here. You can learn more and download it from its home page (*http://jakarta.apache.org/ant/*). To get you started, we give you a sample build file here. The Ant build file supplied with the examples for this chapter will compile the source and build the completed WAR file for you. You can find it with the example source.

A Development-Oriented Directory Layout

At the beginning of this chapter, we described the layout of a WAR, including the standard files and directories that must appear inside the archive. While this file organization is necessary for deployment inside the archive, it may not be the best way to organize your project during development. Maintaining *web.xml* and libraries inside a directory named *WEB-INF* under all of your content may be convenient for running the *jar* command, but it doesn't line up well with how those areas are created or maintained from a development perspective. Fortunately, with a simple Ant build file, we can create our WAR from an arbitrary project layout.

Let's choose a directory structure that is a little more oriented toward project development. For example:

```
myapplication
|
|-- src
|-- lib
|-- docs
|-- web.xml
```

We place our source code tree under *src*, our required library JAR files under *lib*, and our content under *docs*. We leave *web.xml* at the top where it's easy to tweak parameters, etc.

Here is a simple Ant *build.xml* file for constructing a WAR from the new directory structure:

```
<project name="myapplication" default="compile" basedir=".">

    <property name="war-file" value="${ant.project.name}.war"/>
    <property name="src-dir" value="src" />
    <property name="build-dir" value="classes" />
    <property name="docs-dir" value="docs" />
    <property name="webxml-file" value="web.xml" />
    <property name="lib-dir" value="lib" />

    <target name="compile" depends="">
        <mkdir dir="${build-dir}"/>
        <javac srcdir="${src-dir}" destdir="${build-dir}"/>
    </target>

    <target name="war" depends="compile">
        <war warfile="${war-file}" webxml="${webxml-file}">
            <classes dir="${build-dir}"/>
            <fileset dir="${docs-dir}"/>
            <lib dir="${lib-dir}"/>
```

```
        </war>
    </target>

    <target name="clean">
        <delete dir="${build-dir}"/>
        <delete file="${war-file}"/>
    </target>

</project>
```

A *build.xml* file such as this comes with the source code for the examples from this chapter. You can use it to compile your code (the default target) simply by running `ant`, or you can compile and build the WAR by specifying the `war` target like this:

```
% ant war
```

Our *build.xml* file tells Ant to find all the Java files under the *src* tree that need building and compile them into a "build" directory named *classes*. Running *ant war* creates the file *myapplication.war*, placing all of the docs and the *web.xml* file in the correct locations. You can clean up everything and remove the generated *classes* directory and WAR by typing **`antclean`** on the command line.

There is nothing really project-specific in this sample build file except the project name attribute in the first line, which you replace with your application's name. And we reference that name only to specify the name of the WAR to generate. You can customize the names of any of the files or directories for your own layout by changing the Ant `<property>` declarations. The *learningjava.war* file example for this chapter comes with a version of this Ant *build.xml* file.

Deploying and Redeploying WARs with Ant

With Tomcat, you can download a client-side "deployer" package, which provides Ant targets for deploying, redeploying, starting, stopping, and undeploying a web app on a running Tomcat server. The deployer package utilizes the Tomcat manager. Similar Ant tasks exist for other servers, such as WebLogic. Making these tasks part of your Ant build script can save a great deal of time and effort. The deployer package can be found along with the main Tomcat download (*http://jakarta.apache.org/tomcat/*).

Implementing Web Services

Now that we've covered servlets and web applications in detail, we'd like to return to the topic of web services. In the previous chapter, we introduced the concept of a web service as an extension of the basic HTTP web transaction, using XML content for application-to-application communication instead of consumption by a web browser client. In that chapter, we showed how easy it is to invoke an RPC-style web service, by using client-side classes generated from a WSDL description file. In this section, we'll show the other side of that equation and demonstrate how to implement and deploy a web service.

The world of web services has evolved quickly, as have the APIs, buzzwords, and hype. The appeal of this style of interapplication communication using simple web protocols has, to some extent, been tarnished by the design-by-committee approach of many standards bodies and competitors adding features and layers to the web services concept. The truth is that web services were originally simple and elegant when compared to more elaborate protocols, largely because they did not support all of the same semantics—state management, callbacks, transactions, authentication, and security. As these features are added, the complexity returned. We will not cover all aspects of web services in detail but instead focus on the basic RPC style that is appealing for a wide variety of simple applications.

In Chapter 14, we walked through generating and running the client side of a web service (the weather service). In this chapter, we'll build and deploy our own web service, a simple one that echoes parameters back to the client: `EchoService`. We'll be using the built in JAX-WS APIs tools and services container to run this example, although you could deploy the service to Tomcat as well with some additional configuration and packaging into a WAR file.

Defining the Service

To build our client-side API in Chapter 14, we began by downloading the WSDL description file for the (existing) weather service. The WSDL, again, is an XML file that describes the functions of the service and the types of arguments and return values they use. From this description, the *wsimport* command was able to generate the client-side classes that we needed to invoke the service remotely from Java.

In creating our own web service, we have (at least) two choices. We could follow an analogous process, writing a WSDL document describing our service and using it to generate the necessary server-side framework. The *wsimport* class that we used before can be used to generate the necessary, annotated service interface for us and we could implement it with our code. However, there is a much easier way: going code-first.

The *wsgen* command complements *wsimport* by adding the capability to read annotated Java classes and generate WSDL and related service classes for us. Even better, if we deploy our class using the built-in JAX-WS endpoint publisher, it will take care of generating all of this for us. This means that to test a simple web service, all we really have to do is write a service class that marks the class and service methods with the correct annotations and invoke the publisher. It really couldn't get much easier.

Our Echo Service

We'll create a simple service that echoes a few different kinds of values: an `int`, a `String`, and one of our own object types (a data holder object), `MyObject`. In the next section, we'll examine the data types and how they are handled in more detail. Here is the code:

```
package learningjava.service;

import javax.jws.*;
import javax.xml.ws.Endpoint;

@WebService
public class Echo
{
    @WebMethod
    public int echoInt( int value ) { return value; }

    @WebMethod
    public String echoString( String value ) { return value; }

    @WebMethod
    public MyObject echoMyObject( MyObject value ) { return value; }

    public static void main( String[] args )
    {
        Endpoint endpoint = Endpoint.publish( "http://localhost:8080/echo",
            new Echo() );
    }
}

public class MyObject
{
    int intValue;
    String stringValue;

    public MyObject() { }

    public MyObject( int i, String s ) {
        this.intValue = i;
        this.stringValue = s;
    }

    public int getIntValue() { return intValue; }
    public void setIntValue( int intValue ) { this.intValue = intValue; }

    public String getStringValue() {
        return stringValue;
    }
    public void setStringValue( String stringValue ) {
        this.stringValue = stringValue;
```

```
        }
    }
```

We've named our {[QUOTE-REPLACEMENT]}echo" methods individually to differentiate them because WSDL doesn't really handle overloaded methods. (If we'd had a name collision, JAX-WS would give us a runtime warning and choose one for us.) We've placed these into a `learningjava.service` package because it will be easier to work with the tools that way. This package name will be used in the default *namespace* and package name for generated client code. We could override the default using the `targetNamespace` attribute of the WebService annotation (and it would probably be wise to do so in order to keep your interface stable).

To deploy our web service, we use the JAX-WS `Endpoint` class `publish()` method. This method takes a URI string that indicates the desired host, port, and service path as well as an instance of our class. Obviously, the only host that will work in this arrangement is our local computer, which can normally be accessed by the name: "localhost." Here, we ran the service on port 8080 under the path "/echo".

Using the Service

After running the service, drive your web browser to the service URL to get a test page. If you are running the server on the same machine, the URL should be the same as the URI you passed to the `publish()` method. However, under some circumstances you may have to substitute "127.0.0.1" for "localhost."

```
http://localhost:8080/echo
http://127.0.0.1:8080/echo
```

You should see a description of the service similar to the one shown in Figure 15-1. This tells you that the service is active and gives you its configuration information. You can click on the WSDL link to view the WSDL description file that was generated for our service. The WSDL URL should be your base service URL with "?wsdl" appended.

We can use the WSDL to generate a client and test our service, just as we did in Chapter 14. In the following command, we've specified that the generated classes should go into a separate package, `learningjava.client.impl`, to avoid confusion between the generated classes and our original. We've also used the `-keep` option to retain the source code instead of just the compiled class files (you may want to look at them). The final argument is the URL for our generated WSDL, which you can copy from the test page as shown previously.

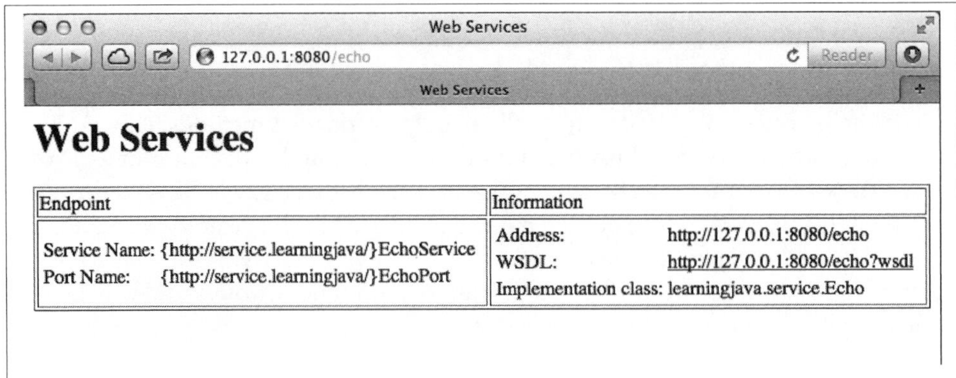

Figure 15-1. Web services description

```
% wsimport -p learningjava.client.impl -keep http://localhost:8080/echo?wsdl
```

Next, we'll create a small client that uses these generated classes to test the service:

```
package learningjava.client;

import learningjava.client.impl.*;

public class EchoClient
{
    public static void main( String [] args ) throws java.rmi.RemoteException
    {
        Echo service = new EchoService().getEchoPort();
        int i = service.echoInt( 42 );
        System.out.println( i );
        String s = service.echoString( "Hello!" );
        System.out.println( s );
        MyObject myObject = new MyObject();
        myObject.setIntValue( 42 );
        myObject.setStringValue( "Foo!" );
        MyObject myObj = service.echoMyObject( myObject );
        System.out.println( myObj.getStringValue() );
    }
}
```

As you can infer from our code, *wsimport* has generated an `EchoService` class that represents our service. Service classes may contain multiple service groups, so in order to get our `Echo` interface, we ask for the Echo "port" with `getEchoPort()`. (*Port* is WSDL terminology for a service interface.)

Run the client, and it should bounce the values between the client and server and display them. And there we are! As we said in the introduction, the actual code required to implement and invoke our service is quite minimal and the fact that Java now bundles a simple web service container with the standard edition makes Java an ideal platform for working with web services.

Data Types

As you might guess, because the data for our service has to be expressed as XML in a standard way, there are some limitations to the type of objects that can be transferred. JAX-WS and WSDL support most of the common Java data types and many standard classes directly. Actually, it would be more appropriate to say that JAXB—the Java XML binding API—supports these Java types, as JAX-WS uses JAXB for this aspect. We'll talk more about Java XML data binding and XML Schemas in Chapter 24.

JAX-WS and JAXB can also decompose JavaBeans-compliant data classes composed of these standard types so that you can use your own classes, as we saw with the `MyObject` argument in our `Echo` service.

Standard types

Table 15-1 summarizes the directly supported types (those types that map directly to W3C Schema types; see Chapter 24 for more on XML mapping of Java types.

Table 15-1. Standard types

Category	Types
Primitives and their wrappers	`boolean`, `Boolean`, `byte`, `Byte`, `short`, `Short`, `float`, `Float`, `int`, `Integer`, `long`, `Long`, `double`, `Double`
Class types	`java.lang.String`, `java.math.BigDecimal`, `java.math.BigInteger`, `java.util.Calendar`, `java.util.Date`, `java.util.UUID`, `java.net.URI`, `java.awt.Image` (as byte [])
Collections	Array types, List types, Set types

Maps and other complex collection types are not currently supported. To maintain the widest compatability for cross-platform web services, it's best to stick with objects composed of simple data types and arrays or lists of those types.

Value data objects

As we said, JAX-WS can also work with our own object types, although there are several requirements and a caveat to mention. First, to be able to be marshaled, our objects must contain only fields that are supported data types (or further compositions of those). Next, our objects must follow two JavaBeans design patterns. It must have a public, no-args constructor and, if it contains any nonpublic fields, they must have "getter" and "setter" accessor methods. Chapter 22 provides more details about these issues.

Finally, unlike Java RMI, web services do not support the "behavior" or the real identity of our domain objects from end to end. When a Java client uses our WSDL document to generate implementation classes, they will be getting simple data-holder replicas of the classes we specify. These "value objects" will pass along all of the data content of our objects, but are not related to the originals in any other way. Our server-side implementation will, of course, receive the data in the form of our own "real" domain objects. That is why they need to have available constructors so that the server-side framework can create and populate them for us to consume.

Conclusion

This chapter, covering Java web applications and Java web services, is one of the fastest-changing topics that we cover in this book. It is a big topic, and we could only really address it here in the context of the Java APIs that support it. We recommend that you supplement what you have learned here with additional reading, especially on the techniques for building applications using HTML5 and JavaScript that communicate with Java using servlets or web services.

CHAPTER 16
Swing

Swing is Java's graphical user interface toolkit. The `javax.swing` package (and its numerous subpackages) contain classes representing interface items such as windows, buttons, combo boxes, trees, tables, and menus—everything you need to build a modern, rich client-side application.

Swing is part of a larger collection of software called the Java Foundation Classes (JFC), which includes the following APIs:

- The Abstract Window Toolkit (AWT), the original user interface toolkit and base graphics classes
- Swing, the pure Java user interface toolkit
- Accessibility, which provides tools for integrating nonstandard input and output devices into your user interfaces
- The 2D API, a comprehensive set of classes for high-quality drawing
- Drag and Drop, an API that supports the drag-and-drop metaphor

JFC is one of the largest and most complex parts of the standard Java platform, so it shouldn't be any surprise that we'll take several chapters to discuss it. In fact, we won't even get to talk about all of it, just the most important parts—Swing and the 2D API. Here's the lay of the land:

- This chapter covers the basic concepts you need to understand how to build user interfaces with Swing.
- Chapter 17 discusses the basic components from which user interfaces are built: buttons, lists, text fields, checkboxes, and so on.
- Chapter 18 dives further into the Swing toolkit, describing text components, trees, tables, and other advanced components.

- Chapter 19 discusses layout managers, which are responsible for arranging components within a window.
- Chapter 20 discusses the fundamentals of drawing, including simple image display.
- Chapter 21 covers the image generation and processing tools of the `java.awt.image` package. We'll throw in audio and video for good measure.

We can't cover the full functionality of Swing in this book; if you want the whole story, see *Java Swing* by Marc Loy, Robert Eckstein, Dave Wood, Brian Cole, and James Elliott (O'Reilly). Instead, we'll cover the basic tools you are most likely to use and show some examples of what can be done with some of the more advanced features. Figure 16-1 shows the user interface component classes of the `javax.swing` package.

To understand Swing, it helps to understand its predecessor, AWT. As its name suggests, AWT is an abstraction. Like the rest of Java, it was designed to be portable; its functionality is the same for all Java implementations. However, people generally expect their applications to have a consistent look and feel and that is usually different on different platforms. So AWT was designed to provide the same functionality on all platforms, yet have the appearance of a native application. The idea is that you could choose to write your code under Windows, then run it on an X Window System or a Macintosh and get more or less the native look and feel on each platform for free.To achieve platform binding, AWT uses interchangeable *toolkits* that interact with the host windowing system to display user interface components. This shields the Java application from the details of its environment in which it's running and keeps the APIs pure. Let's say you ask AWT to create a button. When your application or applet runs, a toolkit appropriate to the host environment renders the button appropriately: on Windows, you can get a button that looks like other Windows buttons; on a Macintosh, you can get a Mac button; and so on.

AWT had some serious shortcomings, however. The worst was that the use of platform-specific toolkits meant that AWT applications might be subtly incompatible on different platforms. Furthermore, AWT lacked advanced user interface components, such as trees and grids, which were not common to all environments. AWT provided the desired look and feel, but limited the features and true portability of Java GUI applications.

Swing takes a fundamentally different approach. Instead of using native toolkits to supply interface items, such as buttons and combo boxes, components in Swing are implemented in Java itself. This means that, whatever platform you're using, by default a Swing button (for example) looks the same. However, Swing also provides a powerful, pluggable look-and-feel API that allows the native operating system appearance to be rendered at the Java level. Working purely in Java makes Swing much less prone to platform-specific bugs, which were a problem for AWT. It also means that Swing components are much more flexible and can be extended and modified in your applications in ways that native components could never be.

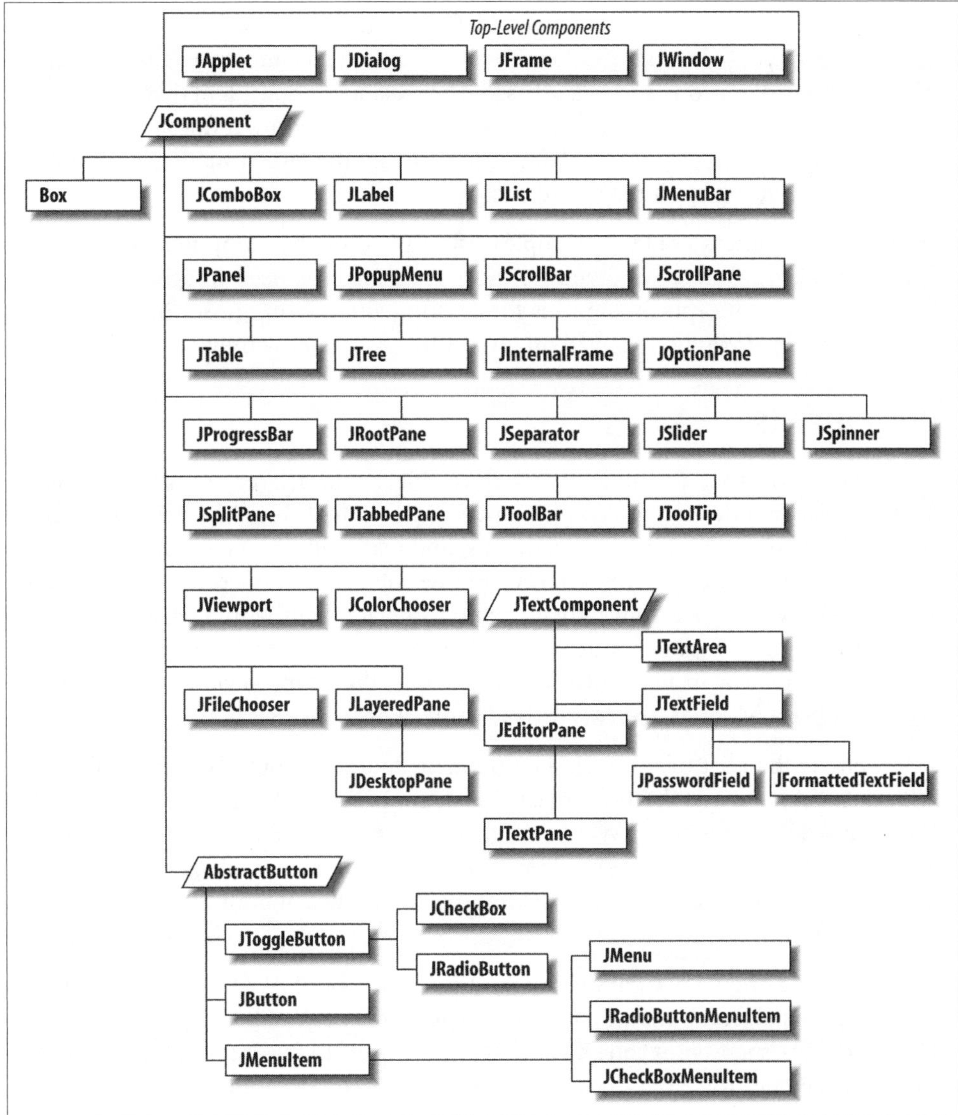

Figure 16-1. User interface components in the javax.swing package

Working with user interface components in Swing is meant to be easy. When building a user interface for your application, you'll be working with a large set of prefabricated components. It's easy to assemble a collection of user interface components (buttons, text areas, etc.) and arrange them inside containers to build complex layouts. However, when necessary, you can build upon these simple components to make entirely new kinds of interface gadgets that are completely portable and reusable.

Swing uses *layout managers* to arrange *components* inside *containers* and control their sizing and positioning. Layout managers define a strategy for arranging components instead of specifying absolute positions. For example, you can define a user interface with a collection of buttons and text areas and be reasonably confident that it will always display correctly, even if the user resizes the application window. It doesn't matter what platform or user interface look-and-feel you're using; the layout manager should still position them sensibly with respect to each other.

The next two chapters contain examples using most of the components in the `javax.swing` package. Before we dive into those examples, we need to spend some time talking about the concepts Swing uses for creating and handling user interfaces. This material should get you up to speed on GUI concepts and how they are used in Java.

Components

A *component* is the fundamental user interface object in Java. Everything you see on the display in a Java application is a component. This includes things like windows, panels, buttons, checkboxes, scrollbars, lists, menus, and text fields. To be used, a component usually must be placed in a *container*. Container objects group components, arrange them for display using a layout manager, and associate them with a particular display device. All Swing components are derived from the abstract `javax.swing.JComponent` class, as you saw in Figure 16-1. For example, the `JButton` class is a subclass of `AbstractButton`, which is itself a subclass of the `JComponent` class.

`JComponent` is the root of the Swing component hierarchy, but it descends from the AWT `Container` class. At this bottom level, Swing is based on AWT, so our conversation occasionally delves into the AWT package. `Container`'s superclass is `Component`, the root of all AWT components, and `Component`'s superclass is, finally, `Object`. Because `JComponent` inherits from `Container`, it has the capabilities of both a component and a container.

AWT and Swing, then, have parallel hierarchies. The root of AWT's hierarchy is `Component`, while Swing's components are based on `JComponent`. You'll find similar classes in both hierarchies, such as `Button` and `JButton`, `List`, and `JList`. But Swing is much more than a replacement for AWT—it contains sophisticated components as well as a real implementation of the Model-View-Controller (MVC) paradigm, which we'll discuss later.

For the sake of simplicity, we can split the functionality of the `JComponent` class into two categories: appearance and behavior. The `JComponent` class contains methods and variables that control an object's general appearance. This includes basic attributes, such as its visibility, its current size and location, and certain common graphical defaults, such as font and background color, used by different subclasses in different ways. The

`JComponent` class also contains graphics and event-handling methods, which are overridden by subclasses to produce all of the different kinds of widgets that we will see.

When a component is first displayed, it's associated with a particular display device. The `JComponent` class encapsulates access to its display area on that device. It includes tools for rendering graphics, for working with off-screen resources, and for receiving user input. Under the covers, `JComponent` makes heavy use of the Java 2D API to handle things like font smoothing, rendering optimizations, and rendering hints. With recent versions of Java (6 and later), rendering speed and quality are often indistinguishable from native applications on popular operating systems.

When we talk about a component's behavior, we mean the way it responds to user-driven events. When the user performs an action (such as pressing the mouse button) within a component's display area, a Swing thread delivers an event object that describes what happened. The event is delivered to objects that have registered themselves as listeners for that type of event from that component. For example, when the user clicks on a button, the button generates an `ActionEvent` object. To receive those events, an object registers with the button as an `ActionListener`.

Events are delivered by invoking designated event handler methods within the receiving object (the "listener"). A listener object receives specific types of events through methods of its listener interfaces (for example, through the `actionPerformed()` method of the `ActionListener` interface) for the types of events in which it is interested. Specific types of events cover different categories of component user interaction. For example, `MouseEvents` describe activities of the mouse within a component's area, `KeyEvents` describe keypresses, and higher-level events (such as `ActionEvents`) indicate that a user interface component has done its job.

We will describe events thoroughly in this chapter because they are so fundamental to the way in which user interfaces function in Java. But they aren't limited to building user interfaces; they are an important interobject communications mechanism, which may be used by completely nongraphical parts of an application, as well. They are particularly important in the context of JavaBeans, which uses events as a generalized change-notification mechanism.

Swing's event architecture is very flexible. Instead of requiring every component to listen for and handle events for its own bit of the user interface, an application may register arbitrary event "handler" objects to receive the events for one or more components and "glue" those events to the correct application logic. A container might, for example, process some of the events relating to its child components.

In the graphical realm, the primary responsibility of a container is to lay out the components it contains visually, within its borders. A component informs its container when it does something that might affect other components in the container, such as changing its size or visibility. The container then tells its layout manager that it is time to rearrange the child components.

As we mentioned, Swing components are all fundamentally derived from `Container`. This doesn't mean that all Swing components can meaningfully contain arbitrary GUI elements within themselves. It does mean that the container-component relationship is built in at a low level. Containers can manage and arrange `JComponent` objects without knowing what they are or what they are doing. Components can be swapped and replaced with new versions easily and combined into composite user interface objects that can be treated as individual components themselves. This lends itself well to building larger, reusable user interface items.

Peers and Look-and-Feel

Swing components are sometimes referred to as *peerless*, or *lightweight*. These terms refer to the relationship that AWT has (and Swing does not have, respectively) with the native toolkits for rendering components on each platform. To get native components on the screen, AWT utilizes a set of peer objects that bridge the gap from pure Java to the host operating system.

At some level, of course, all our components have to talk to objects that contain native methods to interact with the host operating environment; the difference is at what level this occurs. AWT uses a set of peer interfaces. The peer interface makes it possible for a pure Java-language graphic component to use a corresponding real component—the peer object—in the native environment. With AWT, you don't generally deal directly with peer interfaces or the objects behind them; peer handling is encapsulated within the `Component` class.

AWT relies heavily on peers. For example, if you create a window and add eight buttons to it, AWT creates nine peers for you—one for the window and one for each of the buttons. As an application programmer, you don't have to worry about the peers, but they are always lurking under the surface, doing the real work of interacting with the operating system's windowing toolkit.

In Swing, by contrast, most components are *peerless*, or *lightweight*. This means that Swing components don't have any direct interaction with the underlying windowing system. They draw themselves in their parent container and respond to user events in pure Java, with no native code involved. In Swing, only the top-level (lowest API level) windows interact with the windowing system. These Swing containers descend from AWT counterparts, and, thus, still have peers. In Swing, if you create a window and add eight buttons to it, only one peer is created—for the window. Because it has fewer interactions with the underlying windowing system than AWT, Swing is less vulnerable to the peculiarities of any particular platform.

With lightweight components, it is easy to change their appearance. Because each component draws itself instead of relying on a peer, it can decide at runtime how to render itself. Accordingly, Swing supports different *look-and-feel* schemes, which can be changed at runtime. (A look-and-feel is the collected appearance of components in an application.) Look-and-feels based on Windows, Macintosh, and Motif are available (though licensing issues may encumber their use on various platforms), as well as several entirely original Java creations, including Metal, Synth and Nimbus. Metal is the default cross-platform look-and-feel. It has a flat minimalist aesthetic and is very functional but, at this point, appears dated when compared to current versions of popular desktop environments. Synth makes Java applications "skinnable" at a high level using an XML descriptor file and images as resources. Java SE 6 update 10 introduced Nimbus, the first Java look-and-feel that is aesthetically on par with modern desktop operating systems such as OS X and Windows. Nimbus is vector-based, which allows components to be smoothly scaled for use on the new generation of high-density displays. If you want a consistent cross-platform look-and-feel, Nimbus is the best option.

The MVC Framework

Before continuing our discussion of GUI concepts, we want to make a brief aside and talk about the MVC framework. As we've discussed, MVC is a method of building reusable components that logically separates the structure, presentation, and behavior of a component into separate pieces. MVC is primarily concerned with building user interface components, but the basic ideas can be applied to many design issues; its principles can be seen throughout Java.

The fundamental idea behind MVC is the separation of the data model for an item from its presentation. For example, we can draw different representations of the data in a spreadsheet (e.g., bar graphs, pie charts). The data is the *model*; the particular representation is the *view*. A single model can have many views that present the data differently. A user interface component's *controller* defines and governs its behavior. Typically, this includes changes to the model, which, in turn, cause the view(s) to change. For a checkbox component, the data model could be a single Boolean variable, indicating whether it's checked or not. The behavior for handling mouse-click events would alter the model, and the view would examine that data when it draws the on-screen representation.

The way in which Swing objects communicate, by passing events from sources to listeners, is part of this MVC concept of separation. Event listeners are "observers" (controllers) and event sources are "observables" (models).[1] When an observable changes or performs a function, it notifies all its observers of the activity.

Swing components explicitly support MVC. Each component is actually composed of two pieces. One piece, called the UI-delegate, is responsible for the "view" and "controller" roles. It takes care of drawing the component and responding to user events. The second piece is the data model itself. This separation makes it possible for multiple Swing components to share a single data model. For example, a read-only text box and a drop-down list box could use the same list of strings as a data model.

Painting

In an event-driven environment such as Swing, components can be asked to draw themselves at any time. In a more procedural programming environment, you might expect a component to be involved in drawing only when first created or when it changes its appearance. In Java, however, components act in a way that is closely tied to the underlying behavior of the display environment. For example, when you obscure a component with another window and then reexpose it, a Swing thread may ask the component to redraw itself.

Swing asks a component to draw itself by calling its `paint()` method. `paint()` may be called at any time, but in practice, it's called when the object is first made visible, whenever it changes its appearance, or whenever some tragedy in the display system messes up its area. Because `paint()` can't generally make any assumptions about why it was called, it must redraw the component's entire display. The system may limit the drawing if only part of the component needs to be redrawn, but you don't have to worry about this. Swing is fairly smart and will do everything it can to avoid asking components to redraw themselves (including using "backing store" where applicable).

A component never calls its `paint()` method directly. Instead, if a component requires redrawing, it requests a call to `paint()` by invoking `repaint()`. The `repaint()` method asks Swing to schedule the component for repainting. At some point after that, a call to `paint()` occurs. Swing is allowed to manage these requests in whatever way is most efficient. If there are too many requests to handle, or if there are multiple requests for the same component, the thread can collapse a number of repaint requests into a single call to `paint()`. This means that you don't normally know exactly when `paint()` is called in response to a `repaint()`; all you can expect is that it happens at least once, after you request it.

1. In Chapter 11, we described the `Observer` class and `Observable` interface of the `java.util` package. Swing doesn't use these classes directly, but it does use exactly the same design pattern for handling event sources and listeners.

Calling repaint() is normally an implicit request to be updated as soon as possible. Another form of repaint() allows you to specify a time period within which you would like an update, giving the system more flexibility in scheduling the request. The system tries to repaint the component within the time you specify, but if you happen to make more than one repaint request within that time period, the system may simply condense them to carry out a single update within the time you specified. An application performing simple animation could use this method to govern its refresh rate (by specifying a period that is the inverse of the desired frame rate).

As we've mentioned, Swing components can act as containers holding other components. Because every Swing component does its own drawing, Swing components are responsible for telling any contained components to draw themselves. Fortunately, this is all taken care of for you by a component's default paint() method. If you override this method, however, you have to make sure to call the superclass's implementation like this:

```
public void paint(Graphics g) {
    super.paint(g);
    ...
}
```

There's a cleaner way around this problem. All Swing components have a method called paintComponent(). While paint() is responsible for drawing the component as well as its contained components, paintComponent()'s sole responsibility is drawing the component itself. If you override paintComponent() instead of paint(), you won't have to worry about drawing contained components.

Both paint() and paintComponent() receive a single argument: a Graphics object. The Graphics object represents the component's graphics context. It corresponds to the area of the screen on which the component can draw and provides the methods for performing primitive drawing and image manipulation. (We'll look at the Graphics class in detail in Chapter 18.)

Enabling and Disabling Components

Standard Swing components can be turned on and off by calling the setEnabled() method. When a component such as a JButton or JTextField is disabled, it becomes "ghosted" or "greyed out" and doesn't respond to user input.

For example, let's see how to create a component that can be used only once. This requires getting ahead of the story; we won't explain some aspects of this example until later. Earlier, we said that a JButton generates an ActionEvent when it is pressed. This event is delivered to the listeners' actionPerformed() method. The following code disables the component that generated the event:

```
public boolean void actionPerformed(ActionEvent e ) {
    ((JComponent)e.getSource()).setEnabled(false);
}
```

This code calls `getSource()` to find out which component generated the event. We cast the result to `JComponent` because we don't necessarily know what kind of component we're dealing with; it might not be a button, because other kinds of components can generate action events. Once we know which component generated the event, we disable it.

You can also disable an entire container. Disabling a `JPanel`, for instance, disables all the components it contains.

Focus, Please

In order to receive keyboard events, a component has to have keyboard *focus*. The component with the focus is the currently *selected* component on the screen and is usually highlighted visually. It receives all keyboard event information until the focus changes to a new component. Typically, a component receives focus when the user clicks on it with the mouse or navigates to it using the keyboard. A component can ask for focus with the `JComponent` 's `requestFocus()` method. You can configure whether a given component is eligible to receive focus with the `setFocusable()` method. By default, most components, including things such as buttons and checkboxes, are "focusable." To make an entire window and its components nonfocusable, use the `Window` `setFocusableWindowState()` method.

The control of focus is often at the heart of the user's experience with an application. Especially with text entry fields and forms, users are accustomed to a smooth transfer of focus with the use of keyboard navigation cues (e.g., Tab and Shift-Tab for forward and backward field navigation). The management of focus in a large GUI with many components could be complex. Fortunately, in Java 1.4 and later, Swing handles almost all this behavior for you, so, in general, you don't have to implement code to specify how focus is transferred. Java 1.4 introduced an entirely new focus subsystem. The flexible `KeyboardFocusManager` API provides the expected common behavior by default and allows customization via `FocusTraversalPolicy` objects. We'll discuss focus-related events later in this chapter and focus navigation more in Chapter 18.

Other Component Methods

The `JComponent` class is very large; it has to provide the base-level functionality for all the various kinds of Java GUI objects. It inherits a lot of functionality from its parent `Container` and `Component` classes. We don't have room to document every method of the `JComponent` class here, but we'll flesh out our discussion by covering some of the more important ones:

`Container getParent()`
`String getName()`
`void setName(String name)`

Get or assign the `String` name of this component. Naming a component is useful for debugging. The name is returned by `toString()`.

`void setVisible(boolean visible)`

Make the component visible or invisible within its container. If you change the component's visibility, the container's layout manager automatically lays out its visible components.

`Color getForeground()`
`void setForeground(Color c)`
`void setBackground(Color c)`
`Color getBackground()`

Get and set the foreground and background colors for this component. The foreground color of any component is the default color used for drawing. For example, it is the color used for text in a text field as well as the default drawing color for the `Graphics` object passed to the component's `paint()` and `paintComponent()` methods. The background color is used to fill the component's area when it is cleared by the default implementation of `update()`.

`Dimension getSize()`
`void setSize(int width, int height)`

Get and set the current size of the component. Note that a layout manager may change the size of a component even after you've set its size yourself. To change the size a component "wants" to be, use `setPreferredSize()`. There are other methods in `JComponent` to set its location, but this is normally the job of a layout manager.

`Dimension getPreferredSize()`
`void setPreferredSize(Dimension preferredSize)`

Use these methods to examine or set the preferred size of a component. Layout managers attempt to set components to their preferred sizes. If you change a component's preferred size, you must call the method `revalidate()` on the component to get it laid out again.

`Cursor getCursor()`
`void setCursor(Cursor cursor)`

Get or set the type of cursor (mouse pointer) used when the mouse is over this component's area. For example:

```
JComponent myComponent = ...;
Cursor crossHairs =
    Cursor.getPredefinedCursor( Cursor.CROSSHAIR_CURSOR );
myComponent.setCursor( crossHairs );
```

Containers

A container is a kind of component that holds and manages other components. Three of the most useful general container types are `JFrame`, `JPanel`, and `JApplet`. A `JFrame` is a top-level window on your display. `JFrame` is derived from `java.awt.Window`, which is pretty much the same but lacks a border (`JWindow` is the swing version of `Window`). A `JPanel` is a generic container element that groups components inside `JFrame`s and other `JPanel`s. The `JApplet` class is a kind of container that provides the foundation for applets that run inside web browsers. Like other containers, a `JApplet` can hold other user-interface components. You can also use the `JComponent` class directly, like a `JPanel`, to hold components inside another container. With the exception of `JFrame`, `JWindow`, `JApplet`, and `JDialog` (another window-like container), which are derived from AWT components, all the components and containers in Swing are lightweight.

A container maintains the list of "child" components it manages and has methods for dealing with those components. Note that this child relationship refers to a visual hierarchy, not a subclass/superclass hierarchy. By themselves, most components aren't very useful until they are added to a container and displayed. The `add()` method of the `Container` class adds a component to the container. Thereafter, this component can be displayed in the container's display area and positioned by its layout manager. You can remove a component from a container with the `remove()` method.

Layout Managers

A *layout manager* is an object that controls the placement and sizing of components within the display area of a container. A layout manager is like a window manager in a display system; it controls where the components go and how big they are. Every container has a default layout manager, but you can install a new one by calling the container's `setLayout()` method.

Swing comes with a few layout managers that implement common layout schemes. The default layout manager for a `JPanel` is a `FlowLayout`, which tries to place objects at their preferred size from left to right and top to bottom in the container. The default for a `JFrame` is a `BorderLayout`, which places objects at specific locations within the window, such as `NORTH`, `SOUTH`, and `CENTER`. Another layout manager, `GridLayout`, arranges components in a rectangular grid. The most general (and difficult to use) layout manager is `GridBagLayout`, which lets you do the kinds of things you can do with HTML tables. (We'll get into the details of all these layout managers in Chapter 19.)

When you add a component to a container using a simple layout manager, you'll often use the version of `add()` that takes a single `Component` as an argument. However, if you're using a layout manager that uses "constraints," such as `BorderLayout` or `GridBagLayout`, you must specify additional information about where to put the new component. For that, you can use the version that takes a constraint object. Here's how to place a component at the top edge of a container that uses a `BorderLayout` manager:

```
myContainer.add(myComponent, BorderLayout.NORTH);
```

In this case, the constraint object is the static member variable `NORTH`. `GridBagLayout` uses a much more complex constraint object to specify positioning.

Insets

Insets specify a container's margins; the space specified by the container's insets won't be used by a layout manager. Insets are described by an `Insets` object, which has four public `int` fields: `top`, `bottom`, `left`, and `right`. You normally don't need to worry about the insets; the container sets them automatically, taking into account extras like the menu bar that may appear at the top of a frame. To find the insets, call the component's `getInsets()` method, which returns an `Insets` object.

Z-Ordering (Stacking Components)

With the standard layout managers, components are not allowed to overlap. However, if you use custom-built layout managers or absolute positioning, components within a container may overlap. If they do, the order in which components were added to a container matters. When components overlap, they are "stacked" in the order in which they were added: the first component added to the container is on top, and the last is on the bottom. To give you more control over stacking, two additional forms of the `add()` method take an extra integer argument that lets you specify the component's exact position in the container's stacking order. Again, you don't normally need to think about this, but it's nice to know for the sake of completeness that it's there.

The revalidate() and doLayout() Methods

A layout manager arranges the components in a container only when it is asked to do so. Several things can mess up a container after it's initially laid out:

- Changing its size
- Resizing or moving one of its child components
- Adding, showing, removing, or hiding a child component

Any of these actions cause the container to be marked *invalid*. This means that it needs to have its child components readjusted by its layout manager. In most cases, Swing readjusts the layout automatically. All components, not just containers, maintain a notion of when they are valid or invalid. If the size, location, or internal layout of a Swing component changes, its `revalidate()` method is automatically called. Internally, the `revalidate()` method first calls the method `invalidate()` to mark the component and all its enclosing containers as invalid. It then validates the tree. Validation descends the hierarchy, starting at the nearest *validation root* container, recursively validating each child. Validating a child `Container` means invoking its `doLayout()` method, which asks the layout manager to do its job and then notes that the `Container` has been reorganized by setting its state to valid again. A validation root is a container that can accommodate children of any size such as `JScrollPane` (and, hence, can accommodate any possible changes in its child hierarchy without upsetting its own parents).

There are a few cases in which you may need to tell Swing to fix things manually. One example is when you change the preferred size of a component (as opposed to its actual onscreen size). To clean up the layout, call the `revalidate()` method. For example, if you have a small `JPanel`—say, a keypad holding some buttons—and you change the preferred size of the `JPanel` by calling its `setPreferredSize()` method, you should also call `revalidate()` on the panel or its immediate container. The layout manager of the panel then rearranges its buttons to fit inside its new area.

Managing Components

There are a few additional tools of the `Container` class we should mention:

`Component[] getComponents()`
: Returns the container's components in an array.

`void list(PrintWriter out, int indent)`
: Generates a list of the components in this container and writes them to the specified `PrintWriter`.

`Component getComponentAt(int x, int y)`
: Tells you what component is at the specified coordinates in the container's coordinate system.

Listening for Components

You can use the `ContainerListener` interface to automate setting up a container's new components. A container that implements this interface can receive an event whenever it gains or loses a component. This facility makes it easy for a container to micromanage its components.

Windows, Frames and Splash Screens

Windows and frames are the top-level containers for Java components. A `JWindow` is simply a plain, graphical screen that displays in your windowing system. Windows have no frills; they are mainly suitable for pop-up windows and in situations where drop-down components such as menus and combo boxes extend outside their parent frame. `JFrame`, on the other hand, is a subclass of `JWindow` that has a titlebar, window-managed buttons (close, minimize, etc.), and border. You can drag a frame around on the screen and resize it, using the ordinary controls for your windowing environment. Figure 16-2 shows a `JFrame` on the left and a `JWindow` on the right.

All other Swing components and containers must be held, at some level, inside a `JWindow` or `JFrame`. Applets are a kind of `Container`. Even applets must be housed in a frame or window, though normally you don't see an applet's parent frame because it is part of (or simply is) the browser or `appletviewer` displaying the applet.

Figure 16-2. A frame and a window

`JFrame`s and `JWindow`s are the only components that can be displayed without being added or attached to another `Container`. After creating a `JFrame` or `JWindow`, you can call the `setVisible()` method to display it. The following short application creates a `JFrame` and a `JWindow` and displays them side by side, just as in Figure 16-2.

```
//file: TopLevelWindows.java
import javax.swing.*;

public class TopLevelWindows {
  public static void main(String[] args) {
    JFrame frame = new JFrame("The Frame");
    frame.setSize(300, 300);
    frame.setLocation(100, 100);

    JWindow window = new JWindow();
    window.setSize(300, 300);
    window.setLocation(500, 100);

    frame.setVisible(true);
    window.setVisible(true);
  }
}
```

The `JFrame` constructor can take a `String` argument that supplies a title, displayed in the `JFrame`'s titlebar. (Or you can create the `JFrame` with no title and call `setTitle()` to supply the title later.) The `JFrame`'s size and location on your desktop are determined by the calls to `setSize()` and `setLocation()`. After creating the `JFrame`, we create a

JWindow in almost exactly the same way. The JWindow doesn't have a titlebar, so there are no arguments to the JWindow constructor.

Once the JFrame and JWindow are set up, we call setVisible(true) to get them on the screen. The setVisible() method returns immediately, without blocking. Fortunately, our application does not exit, even though we've reached the end of the main() method, because the windows are still visible. You can close the JFrame by clicking on the close button in the titlebar. JFrame's default behavior is to hide itself when you click on the box by calling setVisible(false). You can alter this behavior by calling the setDefaultCloseOperation() method or by adding an event listener, which we'll cover later. Because we haven't arranged any other means here, you will need to hit Ctrl-C or whatever keystroke kills a process on your machine in order to stop execution of the TopLevelWindows application.

Use of a SplashScreen, which is an AWT class used to control a specialized container, is the preferred way to display a start-up screen for Swing applications. Prior to Java 1.6, applications were forced to use Window or JWindow for this purpose, but these are suboptimal solutions for a splash screen because they are only displayed after the JVM, AWT, and Swing libraries are initialized. The new splash screen object allows you to specify an image file in your application jar's manifest (see Chapter 3) that will be displayed immediately after launch without having to wait for the JVM to initialize. Specifying a splash screen image in your jar manifest is trivial.

```
Manifest-Version: 1.0
Main-Class: MangoMango1
SplashScreen-Image: ripe_mango.png
```

No code is required to display a splash screen. The *ripe_mango.png* image will appear centered on the screen until the first AWT or Swing window is shown by the MangoMango1 application. Supported image types are GIF, JPEG, and PNG.

Other Methods for Controlling Frames

The setLocation() method of the Component class can be used on a JFrame or JWindow to set its position on the screen. The x and y coordinates are relative to the screen's origin (the top-left corner).

You can use the toFront() and toBack() methods to place a JFrame or JWindow in front of, or behind, other windows. By default, a user is allowed to resize a JFrame, but you can prevent resizing by calling setResizable(false) before showing the JFrame.

On most systems, frames can be "iconified"—that is, they can be shrunk down and represented by a little icon image. You can get and set a frame's icon image by calling getIconImage() and setIconImage(). As you can with all components, you can set the cursor by calling the setCursor() method.

Content Panes

Windows and frames have a little more structure than simple containers. Specifically, to support some of the fancier GUI features that require overlaying graphics (such as pop ups and menus), windows and frames actually consist of a number of separate overlapping container "panes" (as in glass) with names such as the root pane, layered pane, and glass pane. The primary pane of interest is usually the *content pane*. The content pane is just a `Container` that covers the visible area of the `JFrame` or `JWindow`; it is the container to which we want to add child components.

For convenience, `JFrame` and `JWindow` delegate methods such as `add()` and `setLayout()` to their `ContentPane`. In other words, calling `myFrame.add(component)` is equivalent to calling `myFrame.getContentPane().add(component)`.

```
//file: MangoMango1.java
import java.awt.*;
import javax.swing.*;

public class MangoMango1 {
  public static void main(String[] args) {
    JFrame frame = new JFrame("The Frame");
 // The three methods below are delegated to the frame's ContentPane.
    frame.setLayout(new FlowLayout());
    frame.add(new JLabel("Mango"));
    frame.add(new JButton("Mango"));

    frame.setLocation(100, 100);
    frame.pack();
    frame.setVisible(true);
  }
}
```

The call to `JFrame`'s `pack()` method tells the frame window to resize itself to the minimum size required to hold all its components. Instead of having to determine the size of the `JFrame`, `pack` tells it to be "just big enough." If you do want to set the absolute size of the `JFrame` yourself, call `setSize()` instead.

We'll cover labels and buttons in Chapter 17 and layouts in Chapter 19.

Desktop Integration

One of the focuses of Java 6 was improving desktop integration so that Swing apps can stand toe-to-toe with native apps. The new desktop features provide access to the system tray, browser, email client and file/application associations.

The `Desktop` class in `java.awt` provides the ability to:

- Navigate to a URI with the default browser
- Launch the default mail client and populate the "To:" field

- Open, edit, or print a file utilizing its associated application

The Desktop class has a very simple API. The following example opens the default browser and navigates to the Duke Lemur Center's home page.

```
//file: DisplayLemur.java
import java.awt.*;
import java.io.*;
import java.net.*;

public class DisplayLemur {
    public static void main(String[] args) {
        URI uri = null;
        try {
            uri = new URI("http://lemur.duke.edu");
            Desktop.getDesktop().browse(uri);
        } catch(IOException ioe) {
            System.out.println("Cannot browse to " + uri);
        } catch(URISyntaxException use) {
            System.out.println("The URI " + uri + " is malformed");
        }
    }
}
```

All the aforementioned desktop features are similarly available as single method calls on the Desktop singleton: open(File file), edit(File file), print(File file), and mail(URI mailtoURI).

The SystemTray class, also found in java.awt, provides access to the area of the desktop that allows menu items to perform actions on currently running programs. On Windows, this is the Taskbar Status Area. On OS X, it's the Menu Extras area on the right of the system menu. On GNOME, it's the Notification Area.

The following example creates a TrayIcon, places it in the SystemTray, and attaches a single menu item. Selecting the menu item will cause a greeting dialog to appear.

```
import java.awt.*;
import java.awt.event.*;
import java.awt.image.*;
import javax.swing.*;

public class AlohaTray {

    public static void main(String[] args) throws AWTException {
        MenuItem greetItem = new MenuItem("Greet me");

        // Listen for a menu selection and display a greeting dialog
        greetItem.addActionListener(new ActionListener() {
            public void actionPerformed(ActionEvent e) {
                JOptionPane.showMessageDialog(null, "Aloha!");
                System.exit(0);
            }
```

```
            });

            // Create the TrayIcon's PopupMenu and add the MenuItem
            PopupMenu popup = new PopupMenu();
            popup.add(greetItem);

            // Create the TrayIcon and add it to the SystemTray
            TrayIcon trayIcon = new TrayIcon(getIconImage(),
                "A friendly greeting", popup);
            SystemTray.getSystemTray().add(trayIcon);
        }

        // Grabbing a default Swing icon for the SystemTray
        private static Image getIconImage() {
            Icon icon = UIManager.getIcon("OptionPane.informationIcon");
            BufferedImage image = new BufferedImage(icon.getIconWidth(),
                icon.getIconHeight(), BufferedImage.TYPE_INT_ARGB);
            icon.paintIcon(null, image.getGraphics(), 0, 0);
            return image;
        }
    }
```

Events

We've spent a lot of time discussing the different kinds of objects in Swing—components, containers, and special containers such as frames and windows. Now it's time to discuss interobject communication in detail.

Swing objects communicate by sending events. The way we talk about events—"firing" them and "handling" them—makes it sound as if they are part of some special Java language feature. But they aren't. An event is simply an ordinary Java object that is delivered to its receiver by invoking an ordinary Java method. Everything else, however interesting, is purely convention. The entire Java event mechanism is really just a set of conventions for the kinds of descriptive objects that should be delivered; these conventions prescribe when, how, and to whom events should be delivered.

Events are sent from a single source object to one or more listeners. A listener implements prescribed event-handling methods that enable it to receive a type of event. It then registers itself with a source of that kind of event. Sometimes an adapter object may be interposed between the event source and the listener, but in any case, registration of a listener is always established before any events are delivered.

An event object is an instance of a subclass of `java.util.EventObject`; it holds information about something that's happened to its source. The `EventObject` parent class itself serves mainly to identify event objects; the only information it contains is a reference to the event source (the object that sent the event). Components don't normally send or receive `EventObjects` as such; they work with subclasses that provide more specific information.

AWTEvent is a subclass of java.awt.EventObject; further subclasses of AWTEvent provide information about specific event types. Swing has events of its own that descend directly from EventObject. For the most part, you'll just be working with specific event subclasses from the AWT or Swing packages.

ActionEvents correspond to a decisive "action" that a user has taken with the component, such as clicking a button or pressing Enter. An ActionEvent carries the name of an action to be performed (the *action command*) by the program. MouseEvents are generated when a user uses the mouse within a component's area. They describe the state of the mouse and therefore carry such information as the x and y coordinates and the state of your mouse buttons at the time the MouseEvent was created.

ActionEvent operates at a higher semantic level than MouseEvent: an ActionEvent lets us know that a component has performed its job; a MouseEvent simply confers a lot of information about the mouse at a given time. You could figure out that somebody clicked on a JButton by examining mouse events, but it is simpler to work with action events. The precise meaning of an event can also depend on the context in which it is received.

Event Receivers and Listener Interfaces

An event is delivered by passing it as an argument to the receiving object's event handler method. ActionEvents, for example, are always delivered to a method called actionPerformed() in the receiver:

```
public void actionPerformed( ActionEvent e ) {
    ...
}
```

For each type of event, a corresponding listener interface prescribes the method(s) it must provide to receive those events. In this case, any object that receives ActionEvents must implement the ActionListener interface:

```
public interface ActionListener extends
java.util.EventListener {
    public void actionPerformed( ActionEvent e );
}
```

All listener interfaces are subinterfaces of java.util.EventListener, which is an empty interface. It exists only to help Java-based tools such as IDEs identify listener interfaces.

Listener interfaces are required for a number of reasons. First, they help to identify objects that can receive a given type of event—they make event hookups "strongly typed." Event listener interfaces allow us to give the event handler methods friendly, descriptive names and still make it easy for documentation, tools, and humans to recognize them in a class. Next, listener interfaces are useful because several methods can be specified for an event receiver. For example, the FocusListener interface contains two methods:

```
abstract void focusGained( FocusEvent e );
abstract void focusLost( FocusEvent e );
```

Although these methods each take a `FocusEvent` as an argument, they correspond to different reasons (contexts) for firing the event—in this case, whether the `FocusEvent` means that focus was received or lost. In this case, you could also figure out what happened by inspecting the event; all `AWTEvents` contain a constant specifying the event's type. But by using two methods, the `FocusListener` interface saves you the effort: if `focusGained()` is called, you know the event type was `FOCUS_GAINED`.

Similarly, the `MouseListener` interface defines five methods for receiving mouse events (and `MouseMotionListener` defines two more), each of which gives you some additional information about why the event occurred. In general, the listener interfaces group sets of related event handler methods; the method called in any given situation provides a context for the information in the event object.

There can be more than one listener interface for dealing with a particular kind of event. For example, the `MouseListener` interface describes methods for receiving `MouseEvents` when the mouse enters or exits an area or a mouse button is pressed or released. `MouseMotionListener` is an entirely separate interface that describes methods to get mouse events when the mouse is moved (no buttons pressed) or dragged (buttons pressed). By separating mouse events into these two categories, Java lets you be a little more selective about the circumstances under which you want to receive `MouseEvents`. You can register as a listener for mouse events without receiving mouse motion events; because mouse motion events are extremely common, you don't want to handle them if you don't need to.

Two simple patterns govern the naming of Swing event listener interfaces and handler methods:

- Event handler methods are public methods that return type `void` and take a single event object (a subclass of `java.util.EventObject`) as an argument.[2]
- Listener interfaces are subclasses of `java.util.EventListener` that are named with the suffix "Listener"—for example, `MouseListener` and `ActionListener`.

These may seem obvious, but they are nonetheless important because they are our first hint of a design pattern governing how to build components that work with events.

2. This rule is not complete. The JavaBeans conventions (see Chapter 22) allows event handler methods to take additional arguments when absolutely necessary and also to throw checked exceptions.

Event Sources

The previous section described the machinery an event receiver uses to listen for events. In this section, we'll describe how a receiver tells an event source to send it events as they occur.

To receive events, an eligible listener must register itself with an event source. It does this by calling an "add listener" method in the event source and passing a reference to itself. (Thus, this scheme implements a *callback* facility.) For example, the Swing `JButton` class is a source of `ActionEvent`s. Here's how a `TheReceiver` object might register to receive these events:

```
// receiver of ActionEvents
class TheReceiver implements ActionListener
{
   // source of ActionEvents
   JButton theButton = new JButton("Belly");

   TheReceiver() {
      ...
      theButton.addActionListener( this );
   }

   public void actionPerformed( ActionEvent e ) {
      // Belly Button pushed...
   }
```

`TheReciever` makes a call to the button's `addActionListener()` to receive `ActionEvent`s from the button when they occur. It passes the reference `this` to register itself as an `ActionListener`.

To manage its listeners, an `ActionEvent` source (like the `JButton`) always implements two methods:

```
// ActionEvent source
public void addActionListener(ActionListener listener) {
    ...
}
public void removeActionListener(ActionListener listener) {
    ...
}
```

The `removeActionListener()` method removes the listener from the list so that it will not receive future events of that kind. Swing components supply implementations of both methods; normally, you won't need to implement them yourself. It's important to pay attention to how your application uses event sources and listeners. It's OK to throw away an event source without removing its listeners, but it isn't necessarily OK to throw away listeners without removing them from the source first because the event source might maintain references to them, preventing them from being garbage-collected.

You may be expecting some kind of "event source" interface listing these two methods and identifying an object as a source of this event type, but there isn't one. There are no event source interfaces in the current conventions. If you are analyzing a class and trying to determine what events it generates, you have to look for the paired add and remove methods. For example, the presence of the `addActionListener()` and `removeActionListener()` methods define the object as a source of `ActionEvents`. If you happen to be a human being, you can simply look at the documentation, but if the documentation isn't available, or if you're writing a program that needs to analyze a class (a process called *reflection*), you can look for this design pattern. (The `java.beans.Introspector` utility class can do this for you.)

A source of `FooEvent` events for the `FooListener` interface must implement a pair of add/remove methods:

- `addFooListener(FooListener` *`listener`* `)`
- `removeFooListener(FooListener` *`listener`* `)`

If an event source can support only one event listener (unicast delivery), the add listener method can throw the `java.util.TooManyListenersException`.

What do all the naming patterns up to this point accomplish? For one thing, they make it possible for automated tools and integrated development environments to divine sources of particular events. Tools that work with JavaBeans will use the Java reflection and introspection APIs to search for these kinds of design patterns and identify the events that can be fired by a component.

At a more concrete level, it also means that event hookups are strongly typed, just like the rest of Java. So it's impossible to accidentally hook up the wrong kind of components; for example, you can't register to receive `ItemEvents` from a `JButton` because a button doesn't have an `addItemListener()` method. Java knows at compile time what types of events can be delivered to whom.

Event Delivery

Swing and AWT events are multicast; every event is associated with a single source but can be delivered to any number of receivers. When an event is fired, it is delivered individually to each listener on the list (see Figure 16-3).

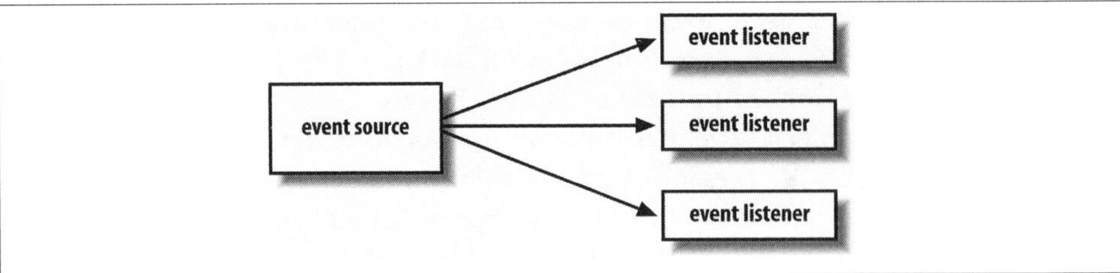

Figure 16-3. Event delivery

There are no guarantees about the order in which events are delivered. Nor are there any guarantees about what happens if you register yourself more than once with an event source; you may or may not get the event more than once. Similarly, you should assume that every listener receives the same event data. In general, events are immutable; they can't be changed by their listeners.

To be complete, we could say that event delivery is synchronous with respect to the event source, but that is because the event delivery is really just the invocation of a normal Java method. The source of the event calls the handler method of each listener. However, listeners shouldn't assume that all the events will be sent in the same thread unless they are AWT/Swing events, which are always sent serially by a global event dispatcher thread.

Event Types

All the events used by Swing GUI components are subclasses of `java.util.EventObject`. You can use or subclass any of the `EventObject` types for use in your own components. We describe the important event types here.

The events and listeners that are used by Swing fall into two packages: `java.awt.event` and `javax.swing.event`. As we've discussed, the structure of components has changed significantly between AWT and Swing. The event mechanism, however, is fundamentally the same, so the events and listeners in `java.awt.event` are used by Swing components. In addition, Swing has added event types and listeners in the package `javax.swing.event`.

`java.awt.event.ComponentEvent` is the base class for events that can be fired by any component. This includes events that provide notification when a component changes its dimensions or visibility, as well as the other event types for mouse operations and keypresses. `ContainerEvents` are fired by containers when components are added or removed.

The java.awt.event.InputEvent Class

MouseEvents, which track the state of the mouse, and KeyEvents, which are fired when the user uses the keyboard, are kinds of java.awt.event.InputEvents. When the user presses a key or moves the mouse within a component's area, the events are generated with that component identified as the source.

Input events and GUI events are processed in a special event queue that is managed by Swing. This gives Swing control over how all its events are delivered. First, under some circumstances, a sequence of the same type of event may be compressed into a single event. This is done to make some event types more efficient—in particular, mouse events and some special internal events used to control repainting. Perhaps more important to us, input events are delivered with extra information that lets listeners decide if the component itself should act on the event.

Mouse and Key Modifiers on InputEvents

InputEvents come with a set of flags for special modifiers. These let you detect whether the Shift, Control, or Alt keys were held down during a mouse button or keypress, and, in the case of a mouse button press, distinguish which mouse button was involved. The following are the flag values contained in java.awt.event.InputEvent:

SHIFT_MASK
: Shift key with event

CTRL_MASK
: Control key with event

ALT_MASK
: Windows Alt key or Mac Option/Alt with event; equivalent to BUTTON2_MASK

META_MASK
: Mac Command key with event; equivalent to BUTTON3_MASK

BUTTON1_MASK
: Mouse Button 1

BUTTON2_MASK
: Mouse Button 2; equivalent to ALT_MASK

BUTTON3_MASK
: Mouse Button 3; equivalent to META_MASK

To check for one or more flags, evaluate the bitwise AND of the complete set of modifiers and the flag or flags you're interested in. The complete set of modifiers involved in the event is returned by the InputEvent's getModifiers() method:

```
public void mousePressed (MouseEvent e) {
    int mods = e.getModifiers();
```

```
        if ((mods & InputEvent.SHIFT_MASK) != 0) {
            // shifted Mouse Button press
        }
    }
```

The three BUTTON flags can determine which mouse button was pressed on a two- or three-button mouse. BUTTON2_MASK is equivalent to ALT_MASK, and BUTTON3_MASK is equivalent to META_MASK. This means that pushing the second mouse button is equivalent to pressing the first (or only) button with the Alt key depressed, and the third button is equivalent to the first with the "Meta" key depressed. These provide some minimal portability even for systems that don't provide multibutton mice. However, for the most common uses of these buttons—pop-up menus—you don't have to write explicit code; Swing provides special support that automatically maps to the correct gesture in each environment (see the PopupMenu class in Chapter 17).

Mouse-wheel events

Java 1.4 added support for the mouse wheel, which is a scrolling device in place of a middle mouse button. By default, Swing handles mouse-wheel movement for scrollable components, so you should not have to write explicit code to handle this. Mouse-wheel events are handled a little differently from other events because the conventions for using the mouse wheel don't always require the mouse to be over a scrolling component. If the immediate target component of a mouse-wheel event is not registered to receive it, a search is made for the first enclosing container that wants to consume the event. This allows components enclosed in ScrollPanes to operate as expected.

If you wish to explicitly handle mouse-wheel events, you can register to receive them using the MouseWheelListener interface shown in Table 16-1 in the next section. Mouse-wheel events encapsulate information about the amount of scrolling and the type of scroll unit, which on most systems may be configured externally to be fine-grained scroll units or large blocks. If you want a physical measure of how far the wheel was turned, you can get that with the getWheelRotation() method, which returns a number of clicks.

Focus Events

As we mentioned earlier, focus handling is largely done automatically in Swing applications and we'll discuss it further in Chapter 18. However, understanding how focus events are handled will help you understand and customize components.

As we described, a component can make itself eligible to receive focus using the JComponent setFocusable() method (Windows may use setFocusableWindowState()). A component normally receives focus when the user clicks on it with the mouse. It can also programmatically request focus using the requestFocus() or requestFocusInWindow() methods. The requestFocusInWindow() method acts just like requestFocus() except that it does not ask for transfer across windows. (There are currently limitations on some platforms that prevent focus transfer from native applications to Java applications, so using `requestFocusInWindow()` guarantees portability by adding this restriction.)

Although a component can request focus explicitly, the only way to verify when a component has received or lost focus is by using the `FocusListener` interface (see Tables 16-1 and 16-2). You can use this interface to customize the behavior of your component when it is ready for input (e.g., the `TextField`'s blinking cursor). Also, input components often respond to the loss of focus by committing their changes. For example, `JTextFields` and other components can be arranged to validate themselves when the user attempts to move to a new field and to prevent the focus change until the field is valid (as we'll see in Chapter 18).

Assuming that there is currently no focus, the following sequence of events happens when a component receives focus:

```
WINDOW_ACTIVATED
WINDOW_GAINED_FOCUS
FOCUS_GAINED
```

The first two are `WindowEvents` delivered to the component's containing `Window`, and the third is a `FocusEvent` that is sent to the component itself. If a component in another window subsequently receives focus, the following complementary sequence will occur:

```
FOCUS_LOST
WINDOW_FOCUS_LOST
WINDOW_DEACTIVATED
```

These events carry a certain amount of context with them. The receiving component can determine the component and window from which the focus is being transferred. The yielding component and window are called "opposites" and are available with the `FocusEventgetOppositeComponent()` and `WindowEvent getOppositeWindow()` methods. If the opposite is part of a native non-Java application, then these values may be `null`.

Focus gained and lost events may also be marked as "temporary," as determined by the `FocusEvent isTemporary()` method. The concept of a temporary focus change is used for components such as pop-up menus, scrollbars, and window manipulation where control is expected to return to the primary component later. The distinction is made for components to "commit" or validate data upon losing focus. No commit should happen on a temporary loss of focus.

Event Summary

Tables 16-1 and 16-2 summarize commonly used Swing events, which Swing components fire them, and the methods of the listener interfaces that receive them. The events and listeners are divided between the packages `java.awt.event` and `javax.swing.event`.

Table 16-1. Swing component and container events

Event	Fired by	Listener interface	Handler methods

`java.awt.event.ComponentEvent`	All components	`ComponentListener`	`componentResized()`
			`componentMoved()`
			`componentShown()`
			`componentHidden()`

`java.awt.event.FocusEvent`	All components	`FocusListener`	`focusGained()` `focusLost()`

`java.awt.event.KeyEvent`	All components	`KeyListener`	`keyTyped()`
			`keyPressed()`
			`keyReleased()`

`java.awt.event.MouseEvent`	All components	`MouseListener`	`mouseClicked()`
			`mousePressed()`
			`mouseReleased()`
			`mouseEntered()`
			`mouseExited()`

		`MouseMotionListener`	`mouseDragged()` `mouseMoved()`
`java.awt.event.ContainerEvent`	All containers	`ContainerListener`	`componentAdded()` `componentRemoved()`

Table 16-2. Component-specific swing events

Event	Fired by	Listener interface	Handler method

`java.awt.event.ActionEvent`	`JButton`
	`JCheckBoxMenuItem`
	`JComboBox`
	`JFileChooser`
	`JList`
	`JRadioButtonMenuItem`
	`JTextField`
	`JToggleButton`
		`ActionListener`	`actionPerformed()`

`java.awt.event.AdjustmentEvent`	`JScrollBar`	`AdjustmentListener`	`adjustmentValueChanged()`
`javax.swing.event.CaretEvent`	`JTextComponent`	`CaretListener`	`caretUpdate()`

Event	Fired by	Listener interface	Handler method
javax.swing.event. HyperlinkEvent	JEditorPane JTextPane	Hyperlink- Listener	hyperlinkUpdate()
java.awt.event.Internal FrameEvent	JInternalFrame	InternalFrame- Listener	internalFrame- Activated() internalFrame- Closed() internalFrame- Closing() internalFrame- Deactivated() internalFrame- Deiconified() internalFrame- Iconified() internalFrame- Opened()
java.awt.event.ItemEvent	JCheckBoxMenuItem JComboBox JRadioButtonMenuI tem JToggleButton	ItemListener	itemStateChanged()
javax.swing.event.List DataEvent	ListModel	ListDataListen er	contentsChanged() intervalAdded() intervalRemoved()
javax.swing.event.List SelectionEvent	JList ListSelectionModel	ListSelection- Listener	valueChanged()
javax.swing.event.MenuEvent	JMenu	MenuListener	menuCanceled() menuDeselected() menuSelected()
javax.swing.event.PopupMenuE vent	JPopupMenu	PopupMenu- Listener	popupMenuCanceled() popupMenuWill- BecomeInvisible() popupMenuWill- BecomeVisible()
javax.swing.event.MenuKeyEvent	JMenuItem	MenuKeyListener	menuKeyPressed() menuKeyReleased() menuKeyTyped()

Event	Fired by	Listener interface	Handler method
javax.swing.event.MenuDrag MouseEvent	JMenuItem	MenuDragMouse-Listener	menuDragMouse-Dragged() menuDragMouse-Entered() menuDragMouse-Exited() menuDragMouse-Released()
javax.swing.event.TableColumn ModelEvent	TableColumnModel [a]	TableColumn-ModelListener	columnAdded() columnMargin-Changed() columnMoved() columnRemoved() columnSelection-Changed()
javax.swing.event.TableModelE vent	TableModel	TableModel-Listener	tableChanged()
javax.swing.event.Tree ExpansionEvent	Jtree	TreeExpansion-Listener	treeCollapsed() treeExpanded()
javax.swing.event.TreeModelE vent	TreeModel	TreeModel-Listener	treeNodesChanged() treeNodesInserted() treeNodesRemoved() treeStructure-Changed()
javax.swing.event.Tree SelectionEvent	JTree TreeSelectionModel	TreeSelection-Listener	valueChanged()
javax.swing.event.Undoable EditEvent	jav ax.swing.text.Docu ment	UndoableEdit-Listener	undoableEdit-Happened()
java.awt.event.WindowEvent	JDialog JFrame JWindow	WindowListener	windowOpened() windowClosing() windowClosed() windowIconified() windowDeiconified() windowActivated() windowDeactivated()

[a] The TableColumnModel class breaks with convention in the names of the methods that add listeners. They are addColumnModelListener() and removeColumnModelListener().

In Swing, a component's model and view are distinct. Strictly speaking, components don't fire events; models do. When you press a JButton, for example, it's actually the button's data model that fires an ActionEvent, not the button itself. But JButton has a convenience method for registering ActionListeners; this method passes its argument through to register the listener with the button model. In many cases (as with `JButtons`), you don't have to deal with the data model separately from the view, so we can speak loosely of the component itself firing the events. `InputEvents` are, of course, generated by the native input system and fired for the appropriate component, although the listener responds as though they're generated by the component.

Adapter Classes

It's not ideal to have your application components implement a bunch of listener interfaces and receive events directly. Sometimes it's not even possible. Being an event receiver forces you to modify or subclass your objects to implement the appropriate event listener interfaces and add the code necessary to handle the events. And because we are talking about Swing events here, a more subtle issue is that you would be, of necessity, building GUI logic into parts of your application that shouldn't have to know anything about the GUI. Let's look at an example.

In Figure 16-4, we drew the plans for our Vegomatic food processor. We made our `Vegomatic` object implement the `ActionListener` interface so that it can receive events directly from the three `JButton` components: `Chop`, `Puree`, and `Frappe`. The problem is that our `Vegomatic` object now has to know more than how to mangle food. It also has to be aware that it is driven by three controls—specifically, buttons that send action commands—and be aware of which methods it should invoke for those commands. Our boxes labeling the GUI and application code overlap in an unwholesome way. If the marketing people should later want to add or remove buttons or perhaps just change the names, we have to be careful. We may have to modify the logic in our `Vegomatic` object. All is not well.

An alternative is to place an adapter class between our event source and receiver. An *adapter* is a simple object whose sole purpose is to map an incoming event to an outgoing method.

Figure 16-5 shows a better design that uses three adapter classes, one for each button. The implementation of the first adapter might look like:

```
class VegomaticAdapter1 implements ActionListener {
    Vegomatic vegomatic;
    VegomaticAdapter1 ( Vegomatic vegomatic ) {
        this.vegomatic = vegomatic;
    }
    public void actionPerformed( ActionEvent e ) {
        vegomatic.chopFood();
    }
}
```

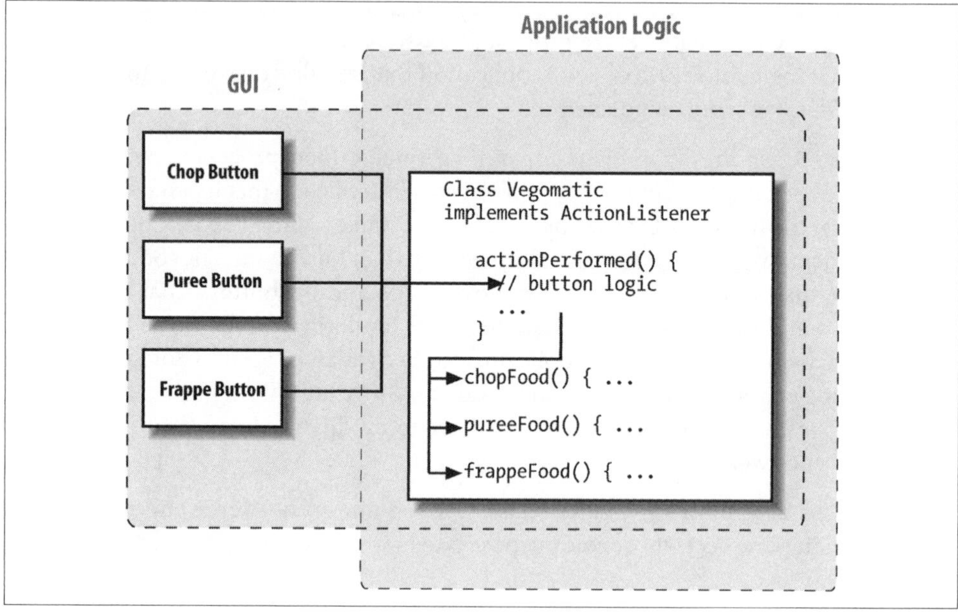

Figure 16-4. Implementing the ActionListener interface directly

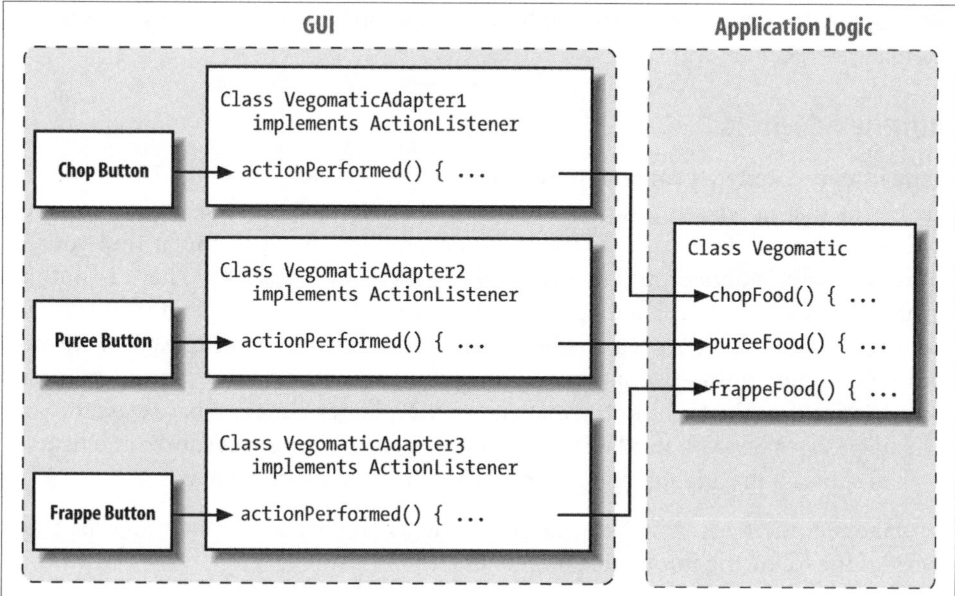

Figure 16-5. Implementing the ActionListener interface using adapter classes

So somewhere in the code where we build our GUI, we could register our listener like this:

```
Vegomatic theVegomatic = ...;
Button chopButton = ...;

// make the hookup
chopButton.addActionListener( new VegomaticAdapter1(theVegomatic) );
```

Instead of registering itself (`this`) as the `Button`'s listener, the adapter registers the `Vegomatic` object (`theVegomatic`). In this way, the adapter acts as an intermediary, hooking up an event source (the button) with an event receiver (the virtual chopper).

We have completely separated the messiness of our GUI from the application code. However, we have added three new classes to our application, none of which does very much. Is that good? It depends on your vantage point.

Under different circumstances, our buttons may have been able to share a common adapter class that was simply instantiated with different parameters. Various tradeoffs can be made between size, efficiency, and elegance of code. Adapter classes will often be generated automatically by development tools. The way we've named our adapter classes `VegomaticAdapter1`, `VegomaticAdapter2`, and `VegomaticAdapter3` hints at this. More often, when handcoding, you'll use an anonymous inner class, as we'll see in the next section. At the other extreme, we can forsake Java's strong typing and use the

Reflection API to create a completely dynamic hookup between an event source and its listener.

Dummy Adapters

Many listener interfaces contain more than one event handler method. Unfortunately, this means that to register yourself as interested in any one of those events, you must implement the whole listener interface. To accomplish this, you might find yourself typing dummy "stubbed-out" methods to complete the interface. There is nothing wrong with this, but it is a bit tedious. To save you some trouble, AWT and Swing provide some helper classes that implement these dummy methods for you. For each of the most common listener interfaces containing more than one method, there is an adapter class containing the stubbed methods. You can use the adapter class as a base class for your own adapters. When you need a class to patch together your event source and listener, you can subclass the adapter and override only the methods you want.

For example, the `MouseAdapter` class implements the `MouseListener` interface and provides the following minimalist implementation:

```
public void mouseClicked(MouseEvent e) {};
public void mousePressed(MouseEvent e) {};
public void mouseReleased(MouseEvent e) {};
public void mouseEntered(MouseEvent e) {};
public void mouseExited(MouseEvent e) {};
```

This isn't a tremendous time saver; it's simply a bit of sugar. The primary advantage comes into play when we use the `MouseAdapter` as the base for our own adapter in an anonymous inner class. For example, suppose we want to catch a `mousePressed()` event in some component and blow up a building. We can use the following to make the hookup:

```
someComponent.addMouseListener( new MouseAdapter() {
    public void MousePressed(MouseEvent e) {
        building.blowUp();
    }
} );
```

We've taken artistic liberties with the formatting, but it's pretty readable. Moreover, we've avoided creating stub methods for the four unused event handler methods. Writing adapters is common enough that it's nice to avoid typing those extra few lines and perhaps stave off the onset of carpal tunnel syndrome for a few more hours. Remember that any time you use an inner class, the compiler is generating a class for you, so the messiness you've saved in your source still exists in the output classes.

The AWT Robot!

This topic may not be of immediate use to everyone, but sometimes an API is just interesting enough that it deserves mentioning. In Java 1.3, a class with the intriguing name `java.awt.Robot` was added. The AWT robot provides an API for generating input events such as keystrokes and mouse gestures programmatically. It could be used to build automated GUI testing tools and the like. The following example uses the `Robot` class to move the mouse to the upper-left area of the screen and perform a series of events corresponding to a double-click. On most Windows systems, this opens up the *My Computer* folder that lives in that region of the screen.

```
public class RobotExample
{
    public static void main( String [] args ) throws Exception
    {
        Robot r = new Robot();
        r.mouseMove(35,35);
        r.mousePress( InputEvent.BUTTON1_MASK );
        r.mouseRelease( InputEvent.BUTTON1_MASK );
        Thread.sleep(50);
        r.mousePress( InputEvent.BUTTON1_MASK );
        r.mouseRelease( InputEvent.BUTTON1_MASK );
    }
}
```

In addition to its magic fingers, the AWT robot also has eyes! You can use the `Robot` class to capture an image of the screen or a rectangular portion of it by using the `createScreenCapture()` method. (Note that you can get the exact dimensions of the screen from the AWT's `getScreenSize()` method.)

Java 5.0 added a correspondingly useful API, `java.awt.MouseInfo`, which allows the gathering of mouse movement information from anywhere on the screen (not restricted to the area within the Java application's windows). The combination of `Robot` and `MouseInfo` should make it easier to record and play back events occurring anywhere on the screen from within Java.

Multithreading in Swing

An important compromise was made early in the design of Swing relating to speed, GUI consistency, and thread safety. To provide maximum performance and simplicity in the common case, Swing does not explicitly synchronize access to most Swing component methods. This means that most Swing components are, technically, not threadsafe for multithreaded applications. Now don't panic: it's not as bad as it sounds because there is a plan. All event processing in AWT/Swing is handled by a single system thread using a single system event queue. The queue serves two purposes. First, it eliminates thread safety issues by making all GUI modifications happen in a single thread. Second, the queue imposes a strict ordering of all activity in Swing. Because painting is handled in Swing using events, all screen updating is also ordered with respect to all event handling.

What this means for you is that multithreaded programs need to be careful about how they update Swing components after they are *realized* (added to a visible container). If you make arbitrary modifications to Swing components from your own threads, you run the risk of malformed rendering on the screen and inconsistent behavior.

There are several conditions under which it is always safe to modify a Swing component. First, Swing components can be modified before they are realized. The term *realized* originates from the days when the component would have created its peer object. It is the point when it is added to a visible container or when it is made visible in the case of a window. Most of our examples in this book set up GUI components in their `main()` method, add them to a `JFrame`, and then, as their final action, cause the `JFrame` to be displayed using `setVisible()`. This setup style is safe because components are not realized until the container is made visible. Actually, that last sentence is not entirely true. Technically, components can also be realized by the `JFrame()` `pack()` method. However, because no GUI is shown until the container is made visible, it is unlikely that any GUI activity can be mishandled.

Second, it's safe to modify Swing components from code that is already running from the system event handler's thread. Because all events are processed by the event queue, the methods of all Swing event listeners are normally invoked by the system event-handling thread. This means that event handler methods and, transitively, any methods called from those methods during the lifetime of that call, can freely modify Swing GUI components because they are already running in the system event-dispatching thread. If unsure of whether some bit of code will ever be called outside the normal event thread, you can use the static method `SwingUtilities.isEventDispatchThread()` to test the identity of the current thread. You can then perform your activity using the event-queue mechanism we'll talk about next.

Finally, Swing components can be safely modified when the API documentation explicitly says that the method is threadsafe. Many important methods of Swing components are explicitly documented as threadsafe. These include the `JComponent` `repaint()` and `revalidate()` methods, many methods of Swing text components, and all listener add and remove methods.

If you can't meet any of the requirements for thread safety listed previously, you can use a simple API to get the system event queue to perform arbitrary activities for you on the event-handling thread. This is accomplished using the `invokeAndWait()` or `invokeLater()` static methods of the `javax.swing.SwingUtilities` class:

`public static void invokeLater(Runnable doRun)`
: Use this method to ask Swing to execute the `run()` method of the specified `Runnable`.

`public static void invokeAndWait(Runnable doRun)throwsInterruptedException,InvocationTargetException`

This method is just like `invokeLater()` except that it waits until the `run()` method has completed before returning.

You can put any activities you want inside a `Runnable` object and cause the event dispatcher to perform them using these methods. Often you'll use an inner class; for example:

```
SwingUtilities.invokeLater( new Runnable() {
    public void run() {
        MyComponent.setVisible(false);
    }
} );
```

Java 7 introduced the `SwingWorker` class to assist in situations where you have a background process that needs to update a Swing UI after the process is complete or incrementally as it's running. In the former case, it's a simple matter of subclassing `SwingWorker`, and putting your long-running code in `doInBackground()` and your UI update code in `done()`.

```
package learning;

import java.awt.BorderLayout;
import java.awt.event.ActionEvent;
import java.awt.event.ActionListener;

import javax.swing.*;

public class MysteryOfTheUniverse extends JFrame {

    JTextArea textArea;
    JButton solveButton;

    public MysteryOfTheUniverse() {
        super("Mystery of the Universe Solver");

        setDefaultCloseOperation( JFrame.EXIT_ON_CLOSE );
        setSize(300, 300);

        textArea = new JTextArea();

        solveButton = new JButton("Solve Mystery");
        solveButton.addActionListener(new ActionListener() {
            public void actionPerformed(ActionEvent ae) {
                solveButton.setEnabled(false);
                solveMysteryOfTheUniverse();
            }
        });

        add(solveButton, BorderLayout.NORTH);
```

```
        add(new JScrollPane(textArea));
        add(new JButton("Click me! I'm not blocking."),
            BorderLayout.SOUTH);
    }

    public void solveMysteryOfTheUniverse() {
        (new MysteryWorker()).execute();
    }

    class MysteryWorker extends SwingWorker<String, Object> {

        @Override
        public String doInBackground() {

            // Thinking for 4 seconds, but not blocking the UI
            try {
                Thread.currentThread().sleep(4000);
            } catch (InterruptedException ignore) {}

            solveButton.setEnabled(true);

            return "Egg salad";
        }

        @Override
        protected void done() {
            try {
                textArea.setText(get());
            } catch (Exception ignore) {}
        }
    }

    public static void main(String[] args) {
        new MysteryOfTheUniverse().setVisible(true);
    }
}
```

When you click the Solve button, the application spends four seconds solving the mystery of the universe. If we weren't using `SwingWorker`, the event dispatch thread would block, making the Click Me button at the bottom of the screen unclickable. Thanks to `SwingWorker`, the UI remains usable during the time the background task is executing. Don't trust us. Try it!

`SwingWorker` can be used in more complex situations such as incremental updates of a progress bar. See `SwingWorker`'s JavaDoc introduction for an example of this usage.

You may find that you won't have to use the event dispatcher or `SwingWorker` in simple GUI applications because most activity happens in response to user interface events where it is safe to modify components. However, consider these caveats when you create threads to perform long-running tasks such as loading data or communicating over the network.

CHAPTER 17

Using Swing Components

In the previous chapter, we discussed a number of concepts, including how Java's user interface facility is put together and how the fundamental pieces work. You should understand components and containers and how they work together to create a display, events and how components use them to communicate with the rest of your application, and layout managers.

Now that we're done reviewing general concepts and background, we'll get to the fun stuff: how to do things with Swing. We will cover most of the components that the Swing package supplies, how to use these components in applets and applications, and how to build your own components. We will have lots of code and lots of pretty examples to look at.

There's more material on this topic than fits in a single chapter. In this chapter, we'll cover all the basic user interface components. In the next chapter, we'll cover some of the more involved topics: text components, trees, tables, and creating your own components.

Buttons and Labels

We'll start with the simplest components: buttons and labels. Frankly, there isn't much to say about them. If you've seen one button, you've seen them all, and you've already seen buttons in the applications in Chapter 2 (`HelloJava3` and `HelloJava4`). A button generates an `ActionEvent` when the user presses it. To receive these events, your program registers an `ActionListener`, which must implement the `actionPerformed()` method. The argument passed to `actionPerformed()` is the event itself.

There's one more thing worth saying about buttons, which applies to any component that generates an action event. Java lets us specify an "action command" string for buttons (and other components, like menu items, that can generate action events). The action command is less interesting than it sounds. It is just a `String` that serves to identify the component that sent the event. By default, the action command of a `JButton` is the same as its label; it is included in action events so that you could use it to figure out which button an event came from. However, you'll often know this from the context of your event listener.

To get the action command from an action event, call the event's `getActionCommand()` method. The following code checks whether the user pressed the button labeled *Yes*:

```
public void actionPerformed(ActionEvent e){
    if (e.getActionCommand().equals("Yes") {
        //the user pressed "Yes"; do something
        ...
    }
}
```

Yes is a string, not a command per se. You can change the action command by calling the button's `setActionCommand()` method. The following code changes button `myButton`'s action command to "confirm:"

```
myButton.setActionCommand("confirm");
```

It's a good idea to get used to setting action commands explicitly; this helps to prevent your code from breaking when you or some other developer internationalizes it or otherwise changes the button's label. If you rely on the button's label, your code stops working as soon as that label changes; a French user might see the label `Oui` rather than `Yes`.

Swing buttons can have an image in addition to a label. The `JButton` class includes constructors that accept an `Icon` object, which knows how to draw itself. You can create buttons with captions, images, or both. A handy class called `ImageIcon` takes care of loading an image for you and can be used to add an image to a button. The following example shows how this works:

```
//file: PictureButton.java
import java.awt.*;
import java.awt.event.*;
import javax.swing.*;

public class PictureButton {
  public static void main(String[] args)
  {
    JFrame frame = new JFrame();
    Icon icon = new ImageIcon("rhino.gif");
    JButton button = new JButton(icon);

    button.addActionListener( new ActionListener() {
      public void actionPerformed(ActionEvent ae) {
        System.out.println("Urp!");
      }
```

```
        });

        frame.getContentPane().add( button );
        frame.pack();
        frame.setDefaultCloseOperation( JFrame.EXIT_ON_CLOSE );
        frame.setVisible(true);
    }
}
```

The example creates an `ImageIcon` from the *rhino.gif* file. Then, a `JButton` is created from the `ImageIcon`. The whole thing is displayed in a `JFrame`. This example also shows the idiom of using an anonymous inner class as an `ActionListener`.

There's even less to be said about `JLabel` components. They're just text strings or images housed in a component. There aren't any special events associated with labels; about all you can do is specify the text's alignment, which controls the position of the text within the label's display area. As with buttons, `JLabels` can be created with `Icons` if you want to create a picture label. The following code creates some labels with different options:

```
// default alignment (CENTER)
JLabel label1 = new JLabel("Lions");

// left aligned
JLabel label2 = new JLabel("Tigers", SwingConstants.LEFT);

//label with no text, default alignment
JLabel label3 = new JLabel();

// create image icon
Icon icon = new ImageIcon("rhino.gif");

// create image label
JLabel label4 = new JLabel(icon);

// assigning text to label3
label3.setText("and Bears");

// set alignment
label3.setHorizontalAlignment(SwingConstants.RIGHT);
```

The alignment constants are defined in the `SwingConstants` interface.

We've built several labels using a variety of constructors and several of the class's methods. To display the labels, just add them to a container by calling the container's `add()` method.

You can set other label characteristics, such as changing their font or color, using the methods of the `Component` class, `JLabel`'s distant ancestor. For example, you can call `setFont()` and `setBackground()` on a label, as with any other component.

Given that labels are so simple, why do we need them at all? Why not find a way to draw a text string directly on the container object? Remember that a `JLabel` is a `JComponent`. That means that labels have the normal complement of methods for setting fonts and colors that we mentioned earlier as well as the ability to be persistently and sensibly managed by a layout manager. Therefore, they're much more flexible than a text string drawn procedurally at an arbitrary location within a container. Speaking of layouts—if you use the `setText()` method to change the text of your label, the label's preferred size may change. But the label's container automatically lays out its components when this happens so you don't have to worry about it.

HTML Text in Buttons and Labels

A neat feature of Swing is that it can interpret HTML-formatted text in `JLabel` and `JButton` labels. The following example shows how to create a button with some HTML-formatted text:

```
JButton button = new JButton(
  "<html>"
  + "S<font size=-1>MALL<font size=+0> "
  + "C<font size=-1>APITALS");
```

Older versions of Java may not render complex HTML very well. But as of JDK 1.4, most basic HTML features are supported, including crazy things such as images and tables.

Figure 17-1 uses an HTML table to arrange its text.

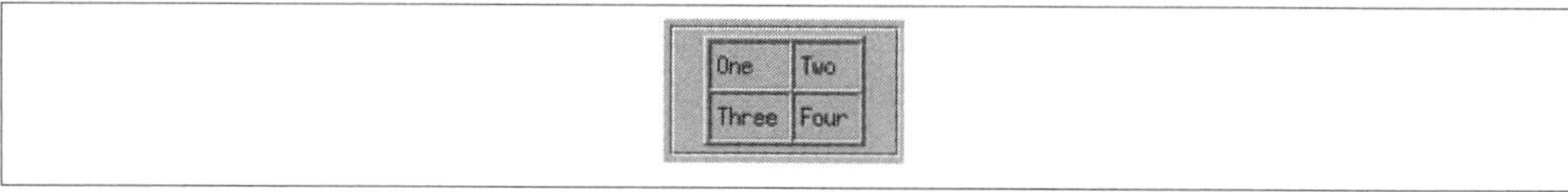

Figure 17-1. Button using HTML table

Figure 17-2 uses an HTML image tag to display an image.

Figure 17-2. Button using HTML img tag

The code for the two figures looks like this:

```
String html=
    "<html><table border=1>"
    +"<tr><td>One</td><td>Two</td></tr>"
    +"<tr><td>Three</td><td>Four</td></tr>"
    +"</table>";
JButton button = new JButton(html);

String html2=
    "<html><h3>Learning Java</h3>"
    +"<img src=\"http://www.oreilly.com/catalog/covers/learnjava3.s.gif\">";
Jbutton button2 = new JButton(html2);
```

Checkboxes and Radio Buttons

A checkbox is a labeled toggle switch. Each time the user clicks it, its state toggles between checked and unchecked. Swing implements the checkbox as a special kind of button. Radio buttons are similar to checkboxes, but they are normally used in groups. Clicking on one radio button in the group automatically turns the others off. They are named for the mechanical preset buttons on old car radios (like some of us had in high school).

Checkboxes and radio buttons are represented by instances of `JCheckBox` and `JRadioButton`, respectively. Radio buttons can be tethered together using an instance of another class called `ButtonGroup` . By now you're probably well into the swing of things (no pun intended) and could easily master these classes on your own. We'll use an example to illustrate a different way of dealing with the state of components and to show off a few more things about containers.

A `JCheckBox` sends `ItemEvents` when it's pushed. Because a checkbox is a kind of button, it also fires `ActionEvents` when checked. For something like a checkbox, we might want to be lazy and check on the state of the buttons only at some later time, such as when the user commits an action. For example, when filling out a form you may only care about the user's choices when the submit button is finally pressed.

The next application, `DriveThrough`, lets us check off selections on a fast food menu, as shown in Figure 17-3.

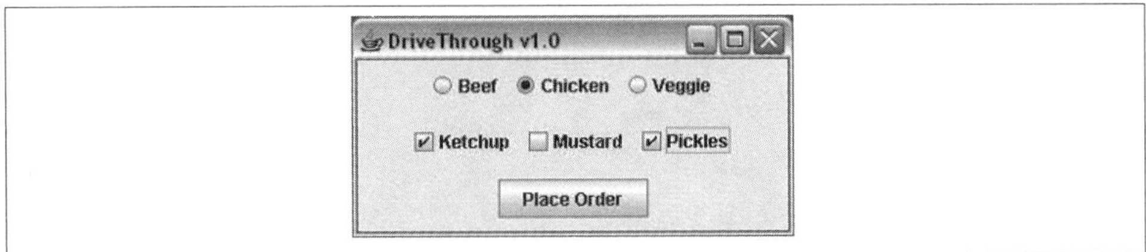

Figure 17-3. The DriveThrough application

`DriveThrough` prints the results when you press the Place Order button. Therefore, we can ignore all the events generated by our checkboxes and radio buttons and listen only for the action events generated by the submit button:

```
//file: DriveThrough.java
import java.awt.*;
import java.awt.event.*;
import javax.swing.*;

public class DriveThrough
{
  public static void main(String[] args) {
    JFrame frame = new JFrame("Lister v1.0");

    JPanel entreePanel = new JPanel();
    final ButtonGroup entreeGroup = new ButtonGroup();
    JRadioButton radioButton;
    entreePanel.add(radioButton = new JRadioButton("Beef"));
    radioButton.setActionCommand("Beef");
    entreeGroup.add(radioButton);
    entreePanel.add(radioButton = new JRadioButton("Chicken"));
    radioButton.setActionCommand("Chicken");
    entreeGroup.add(radioButton);
    entreePanel.add(radioButton = new JRadioButton("Veggie", true));
    radioButton.setActionCommand("Veggie");
    entreeGroup.add(radioButton);

    final JPanel condimentsPanel = new JPanel();
    condimentsPanel.add(new JCheckBox("Ketchup"));
    condimentsPanel.add(new JCheckBox("Mustard"));
    condimentsPanel.add(new JCheckBox("Pickles"));

    JPanel orderPanel = new JPanel();
    JButton orderButton = new JButton("Place Order");
```

```
        orderPanel.add(orderButton);

        Container content = frame.getContentPane(); // unnecessary in 5.0+
        content.setLayout(new GridLayout(3, 1));
        content.add(entreePanel);
        content.add(condimentsPanel);
        content.add(orderPanel);

        orderButton.addActionListener(new ActionListener() {
          public void actionPerformed(ActionEvent ae) {
            String entree =
              entreeGroup.getSelection().getActionCommand();
            System.out.println(entree + " sandwich");
            Component[] components = condimentsPanel.getComponents();
            for ( Component c : components ) {
              JCheckBox cb = (JCheckBox)c;
              if (cb.isSelected())
                System.out.println("With " + cb.getText());
            }
          }
        });

        frame.setDefaultCloseOperation( JFrame.EXIT_ON_CLOSE );
        frame.setSize(300, 150);
        frame.setVisible(true);
      }
    }
```

`DriveThrough` lays out three panels. The radio buttons in the `entreePanel` are tied together through a `ButtonGroup` object. We `add()` the buttons to a `ButtonGroup` to make them mutually exclusive. The `ButtonGroup` object is an odd animal. One might expect it to be a container or a component, but it isn't; it's simply a helper object that allows only one `RadioButton` to be selected at a time.

In this example, the button group forces you to choose a beef, chicken, or veggie entree, but not more than one. The condiment choices, which are `JCheckBoxes`, aren't in a button group, so you can request any combination of ketchup, mustard, and pickles on your sandwich.

When the *Place Order* button is pushed, we receive an `ActionEvent` in the `actionPerformed()` method of our inner `ActionListener`. At this point, we gather the information in the radio buttons and checkboxes and print it. `actionPerformed()` simply reads the state of the various buttons. We could have saved references to the buttons in a number of ways; this example demonstrates two. First, we find out which entree was selected. To do so, we call the `ButtonGroup`'s `getSelection()` method. This returns a `ButtonModel`, upon which we immediately call `getActionCommand()`. This returns the action command as we set it when we created the radio buttons. The action commands for the buttons are the entrée names, which is exactly what we need.

To find which condiments were selected, we use a more complicated procedure. The problem is that condiments aren't mutually exclusive, so we don't have the convenience of a `ButtonGroup`. Instead, we ask the condiments `JPanel` for a list of its components. The `getComponents()` method returns an array of references to the container's child components. We'll use this to loop over the components and print the results. We cast each element of the array back to `JCheckBox` and call its `isSelected()` method to see if the checkbox is on or off. If we were dealing with different types of components in the array, we could determine each component's type with the `instanceof` operator. Or, more generally, we could maintain references to the elements of our form in some explicit way (a map by name, perhaps).

Lists and Combo Boxes

`JLists` and `JComboBoxes` are a step up on the evolutionary chain from `JButtons` and `JLabels`. Lists let the user choose from a group of alternatives. They can be configured to force a single selection or allow multiple choices. Usually, only a small group of choices is displayed at a time; a scrollbar lets the user move to the choices that aren't visible. The user can select an item by clicking on it. She can expand the selection to a range of items by holding down Shift and clicking on another item. To make discontinuous selections, the user can hold down the Control key instead of the Shift key (on a Mac, this is the Command key).

A combo box is a crossbreed between a text field and a list. It displays a single line of text (possibly with an image) and a downward-pointing arrow on one side. If you click on the arrow, the combo box opens up and displays a list of choices. You can select a single choice by clicking on it. After a selection is made, the combo box closes up; the list disappears, and the new selection is shown in the text field.

Like other components in Swing, lists and combo boxes have data models that are distinct from visual components. The list also has a selection model that controls how selections can be made on the list data.

Lists and combo boxes are similar because they have similar data models. Each is simply an array of acceptable choices. This similarity is reflected in Swing, of course: the type of a `JComboBox`'s data model is a subclass of the type used for a `JList`'s data model. The next example demonstrates this relationship.

The following example creates a window with a combo box, a list, and a button. The combo box and the list use the same data model. When you press the button, the program writes out the current set of selected items in the list (see Figure 17-4).

Figure 17-4. A combo box and a list using the same data model

Here's the code for the example:

```
//file: Lister.java
import java.awt.*;
import java.awt.event.*;
import javax.swing.*;

public class Lister {
  public static void main(String[] args) {
    JFrame frame = new JFrame("Lister v1.0");

    // create a combo box
    String [] items = { "uno", "due", "tre", "quattro", "cinque",
                        "sei", "sette", "otto", "nove", "deici",
                        "undici", "dodici" };
    JComboBox comboBox = new JComboBox(items);
    comboBox.setEditable(true);

    // create a list with the same data model
    final JList list = new JList(comboBox.getModel());

    // create a button; when it's pressed, print out
    // the selection in the list
    JButton button = new JButton("Per favore");
    button.addActionListener(new ActionListener() {
      public void actionPerformed(ActionEvent ae) {
        Object[] selection = list.getSelectedValues();
        System.out.println("-----");
        for ( Object o : selection )
          System.out.println( o );
      }
    });

    // put the controls the content pane
    Container c = frame.getContentPane();  // unnecessary  in 5.0+
    JPanel comboPanel = new JPanel();
    comboPanel.add(comboBox);
    c.add(comboPanel, BorderLayout.NORTH);
    c.add(new JScrollPane(list), BorderLayout.CENTER);
```

```
            c.add(button, BorderLayout.SOUTH);

            frame.setSize(200, 200);
            frame.setDefaultCloseOperation( JFrame.EXIT_ON_CLOSE );
            frame.setVisible(true);
        }
    }
```

The combo box is created from an array of strings. This is a convenience—behind the scenes, the `JComboBox` constructor creates a data model from the strings you supply and sets the `JComboBox` to use that data model. Our list is then created using the data model of the combo box. This works because `JList` expects to use a `ListModel` for its data model, and the `ComboBoxModel` used by the `JComboBox` is a subclass of `ListModel`.

The button's action event handler simply prints out the selected items in the list, which are retrieved with a call to `getSelectedValues()`. This method actually returns an object array, not a string array. List and combo box items, like many other things in Swing, are not limited to text. You can use images, drawings, or some combination of text and images. We simply print the result as a string.

You might expect that selecting one item in the combo box would select the same item in the list. In Swing components, selection is controlled by a selection model. The combo box and the list have distinct selection models; after all, you can select only one item from the combo box, while it's possible to select multiple items from the list. Thus, while the two components share a data model, they have separate selection models.

We've made the combo box editable. By default, it would not be editable: the user could choose only one item in the drop-down list. With an editable combo box, the user can type in a selection, as if it were a text field. Noneditable combo boxes are useful if you just want to offer a limited set of choices; editable combo boxes are handy when you want to accept any input but offer some common choices.

There's a great class tucked away in the last example that deserves some recognition. It's `JScrollPane`. In `Lister`, you'll notice that we created one when we added the `List` to the main window. `JScrollPane` simply wraps itself around another `Component` and provides scrollbars as necessary. The scrollbars show up if the contained `Component`'s preferred size (as returned by `getPreferredSize()`) is greater than the size of the `JScrollPane` itself. In the previous example, the scrollbars show up whenever the size of the `List` exceeds the available space.

You can use `JScrollPane` to wrap any `Component`, including components with drawings, images, or complex user interface panels. We'll discuss `JScrollPane` in more detail later in this chapter, and we'll use it frequently with the text components in Chapter 18.

The Spinner

JList and JComboBox are two ways to let the user choose from a set of values. A JComboBox has added flexibility when it is made editable, but, in general, both of these components are limited in that they can only prompt the user from a fixed set of choices. In Java 1.4, Swing added a component called JSpinner that is useful for large or open-ended sequences of values such as numbers or dates. The JSpinner is a cousin of the JComboBox; it displays a value in a field, but instead of providing a drop-down list of choices, it gives the user a small pair of up and down arrows for moving over a range of values (see Figure 17-5). Like the combo box, a JSpinner can also be made editable, allowing the user to type a valid value directly into the field.

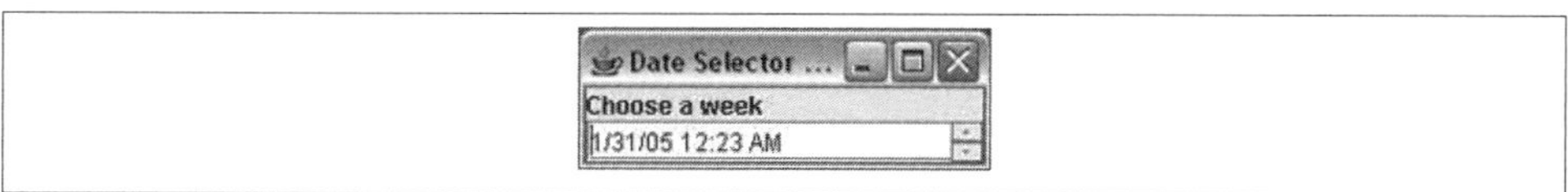

Figure 17-5. Image of DateSelector application

Swing provides three basic types of Spinners, represented by three different data models for the JSpinner component: SpinnerListModel, SpinnerNumberModel, and SpinnerDateModel.

The SpinnerListModel acts like a combo box, specifying a fixed set of objects:

```
String [] options = new String [] { "small", "medium", "large", "huge" };
SpinnerListModel model = new SpinnerListModel( options );
JSpinner spinner = new JSpinner( model );
```

You can retrieve the current value from the model at any time:

```
String value = (String)model.getValue();
```

Alternatively, you can register a ChangeListener to receive updates as the user changes values. With a SpinnerListModel, if the spinner is editable and the user enters a value directly, it is validated against the set of choices before being accepted. This behavior is a little different from the other types of SpinnerModels which, when editable, accept any valid value of the correct type (e.g., a number or date).

The SpinnerNumberModel displays numeric values. It can be configured with initial, minimum, and maximum values:

```
double initial=5.0, min=0.0, max=10.0, increment=0.1;
SpinnerNumberModel model =
    new SpinnerNumberModel( initial, min, max, increment );
JSpinner spinner = new JSpinner(model);
```

Here we have constructed a spinner with an initial value of 5.0 that allows the user to change the value to between 0 and 10.0 in increments of 0.1. The SpinnerNumberModel getNumber() method retrieves the current value.

Perhaps the most interesting feature of the JSpinner is the SpinnerDateModel, which allows the user to choose calendar dates by moving in specified increments of time. The SpinnerDateModel accepts a range, such as the SpinnerNumberModel, but the values are Date objects and the increment is a java.util.Calendar constant field such as Calendar.DAY, Calendar.WEEK, and so on. The following example, DateSelector, creates a JSpinner showing the current date and time. It allows the user to change the date in increments of one week, over a range of one year (six months forward or back). A ChangeListener is registered with the model to display the values as they are modified:

```
import java.awt.*;
import java.awt.event.*;
import javax.swing.*;
import javax.swing.event.*;
import java.util.*;

public class DateSelector {
  public static void main(String[] args)
  {
    JFrame frame = new JFrame("DateSelector v1.0");

    Calendar now = Calendar.getInstance();
    Calendar earliest = (Calendar)now.clone();
    earliest.add( Calendar.MONTH, -6 );
    Calendar latest = (Calendar)now.clone();
    latest.add( Calendar.MONTH, 6 );
    SpinnerModel model = new SpinnerDateModel(
        now.getTime(), earliest.getTime(), latest.getTime(),
        Calendar.WEEK_OF_YEAR);
    final JSpinner spinner = new JSpinner(model);
    // Disable the built-in date editor
    spinner.setEditor(new JSpinner.DefaultEditor(spinner) );

    model.addChangeListener( new ChangeListener() {
        public void stateChanged(ChangeEvent e) {
            System.out.println( ((SpinnerDateModel)e.getSource())
                .getDate() );
        }
    } );

    frame.getContentPane().add( "North", new JLabel("Choose a week") );
    frame.getContentPane().add( "Center", spinner );
    frame.pack();
    frame.setDefaultCloseOperation( JFrame.EXIT_ON_CLOSE );
    frame.setVisible(true);
  }
}
```

As we said, the SpinnerCalendarModel acts just like the SpinnerNumberModel, except that it works with Date objects and uses the special Calendar constants as increments. To create dates, we construct a Calendar object for the correct time and use its getTime() method. In this example, we used the Calendar's add() method to set the minimum and maximum values six months in each direction. Table 17-1 shows values for increments in the Calendar.

Table 17-1. Calendar field values

Field value	Increment
Calendar.MILLISECOND	One millisecond
Calendar.SECOND	One second
Calendar.MINUTE	One minute
Calendar.HOUR Calendar.HOUR_OF_DAY	One hour
Calendar.AM_PM	A.M. or P.M.
Calendar.DAY_OF_WEEK Calendar.DAY_OF_MONTH Calendar.DAY_OF_YEAR	One day
Calendar.MONTH	One month
Calendar.YEAR	One year
Calendar.ERA	B.C. or A.D. in the Gregorian calendar

The SpinnerDateModel uses the Calendar add() method with a value of 1 or -1 and the corresponding constant value to increment or decrement the value. Increments of one have the same effect on several of the constants, as indicated in Table 17-1.

Borders

Any Swing component can have a decorative border. JComponent includes a method called setBorder(); all you have to do is call it, passing it an appropriate implementation of the Border interface.

Swing provides many useful Border implementations in the javax.swing.border package. You could create an instance of one of these classes and pass it to a component's setBorder() method, but there's an even simpler technique.

The BorderFactory class creates any kind of border for you using static "factory" methods. Creating and setting a component's border, then, is simple:

```
JLabel labelTwo = new JLabel("I have an etched border.");
labelTwo.setBorder(BorderFactory.createEtchedBorder());
```

Every component has a setBorder() method, from simple labels and buttons right up to the fancy text and table components that we cover in Chapter 18.

BorderFactory is convenient, but it does not offer every option of every border type. For example, if you want to create a raised EtchedBorder instead of the default lowered border, you'll need to use EtchedBorder's constructor, like this:

```
JLabel labelTwo = new JLabel("I have a raised etched border.");
labelTwo.setBorder( new EtchedBorder(EtchedBorder.RAISED) );
```

The Border implementation classes are listed and briefly described here:

BevelBorder
: This border draws raised or lowered beveled edges, giving an illusion of depth.

SoftBevelBorder
: This border is similar to BevelBorder, but thinner.

EmptyBorder
: Doesn't do any drawing, but does take up space. You can use it to give a component a little breathing room in a crowded user interface.

EtchedBorder
: A lowered etched border gives the appearance of a rectangle that has been chiseled into a piece of stone. A raised etched border looks like it is standing out from the surface of the screen.

LineBorder
: Draws a simple rectangle around a component. You can specify the color and width of the line in LineBorder's constructor.

MatteBorder
: A souped-up version of LineBorder. You can create a MatteBorder with a certain color and specify the size of the border on the left, top, right, and bottom of the component. MatteBorder also allows you to pass in an Icon that will be used to draw the border. This could be an image (ImageIcon) or any other implementation of the Icon interface.

TitledBorder
: A regular border with a title. TitledBorder doesn't actually draw a border; it just draws a title in conjunction with another border object. You can specify the locations of the title, its justification, and its font. This border type is particularly useful for grouping different sets of controls in a complicated interface.

CompoundBorder
: A border that contains two other borders. This is especially handy if you want to enclose a component in an EmptyBorder and then put something decorative around it, such as an EtchedBorder or a MatteBorder.

The following example shows off some different border types. It's only a sampler, though; many more border types are available. Furthermore, the example only encloses labels with borders. You can put a border around any component in Swing. The example is shown in Figure 17-6.

Figure 17-6. A bevy of borders

Here is the source code:

```
//file: Borders.java
import java.awt.*;
import java.awt.event.*;
import javax.swing.*;
import javax.swing.border.*;

public class Borders {
  public static void main(String[] args) {
    // create a JFrame to hold everything
    JFrame frame = new JFrame("Borders");

    // Create labels with borders.
    int center = SwingConstants.CENTER;
    JLabel labelOne = new JLabel("raised BevelBorder", center);
    labelOne.setBorder(
        BorderFactory.createBevelBorder(BevelBorder.RAISED));
    JLabel labelTwo = new JLabel("EtchedBorder", center);
    labelTwo.setBorder(BorderFactory.createEtchedBorder());
    JLabel labelThree = new JLabel("MatteBorder", center);
    labelThree.setBorder(
        BorderFactory.createMatteBorder(10, 10, 10, 10, Color.pink));
    JLabel labelFour = new JLabel("TitledBorder", center);
    Border etch = BorderFactory.createEtchedBorder();
    labelFour.setBorder(
        BorderFactory.createTitledBorder(etch, "Title"));
    JLabel labelFive = new JLabel("TitledBorder", center);
    Border low = BorderFactory.createLoweredBevelBorder();
    labelFive.setBorder(
        BorderFactory.createTitledBorder(low, "Title",
        TitledBorder.RIGHT, TitledBorder.BOTTOM));
```

```
        JLabel labelSix = new JLabel("CompoundBorder", center);
        Border one = BorderFactory.createEtchedBorder();
        Border two =
            BorderFactory.createMatteBorder(4, 4, 4, 4, Color.blue);
        labelSix.setBorder(BorderFactory.createCompoundBorder(one, two));

        // add components to the content pane
        Container c = f.getContentPane();  // unnecessary  in 5.0+
        c.setLayout(new GridLayout(3, 2));
        c.add(labelOne);
        c.add(labelTwo);
        c.add(labelThree);
        c.add(labelFour);
        c.add(labelFive);
        c.add(labelSix);

        frame.setDefaultCloseOperation( JFrame.EXIT_ON_CLOSE );
        frame.pack();
        frame.setVisible(true);
    }
}
```

Menus

A `JMenu` is a standard pull-down menu with a fixed name. Menus can hold other menus as submenu items, enabling you to implement complex menu structures. In Swing, menus are first-class components, just like everything else. You can place them any place a component would go. Another class, `JMenuBar`, holds menus in the conventional horizontal bar. Menu bars are real components, too, so you can place them any place you want in a container: top, bottom, or middle. But in the middle of a container, it usually makes more sense to use a `JComboBox` rather than some kind of menu.

Menu items may have associated images and shortcut keys; there are even menu items that look like checkboxes and radio buttons. Menu items are really a kind of button. Like buttons, menu items fire action events when they are selected. You can respond to menu items by registering action listeners with them.

There are two ways to use the keyboard with menus. The first is called *mnemonics*. A mnemonic is one character in the menu name. If you hold down the Alt key and type a menu's mnemonic, the menu drops down, just as if you had clicked on it with the mouse. Menu items may also have mnemonics. Once a menu is dropped down, you can select individual items in the same way.

Menu items may also have accelerators. An *accelerator* is a key combination that selects the menu item, whether or not the menu that contains it is showing. A common example is the accelerator Ctrl-C, which is frequently used as a shortcut for the Copy item in the Edit menu.

The next example demonstrates several different features of menus. It creates a menu bar with three different menus. The first, Utensils, contains several menu items, a submenu, a separator, and a Quit item that includes both a mnemonic and an accelerator. The second menu, Spices, contains menu items that look and act like checkboxes. Finally, the Cheese menu demonstrates radio button menu items.

The application is shown in Figure 17-7 with one of its menus dropped down. Choosing Quit from the Utensils menu (or pressing Ctrl-Q) removes the window.

```
//file: DinnerMenu.java
import java.awt.*;
import java.awt.event.*;
import javax.swing.*;

public class DinnerMenu
{
  public static void main(String[] args) {
    JFrame frame = new JFrame("Dinner Menu");

    // create the Utensils menu
    JMenu utensils = new JMenu("Utensils");
    utensils.setMnemonic(KeyEvent.VK_U);
    utensils.add(new JMenuItem("Fork"));
    utensils.add(new JMenuItem("Knife"));
    utensils.add(new JMenuItem("Spoon"));
    JMenu hybrid = new JMenu("Hybrid");
    hybrid.add(new JMenuItem("Spork"));
    hybrid.add(new JMenuItem("Spife"));
    hybrid.add(new JMenuItem("Knork"));
    utensils.add(hybrid);
    utensils.addSeparator();

    // do some fancy stuff with the Quit item
    JMenuItem quitItem = new JMenuItem("Quit");
    quitItem.setMnemonic(KeyEvent.VK_Q);
    quitItem.setAccelerator(
        KeyStroke.getKeyStroke(KeyEvent.VK_Q, Event.CTRL_MASK));
    quitItem.addActionListener(new ActionListener() {
      public void actionPerformed(ActionEvent e) { System.exit(0); }
    });
    utensils.add(quitItem);

    // create the Spices menu
    JMenu spices = new JMenu("Spices");
    spices.setMnemonic(KeyEvent.VK_S);
    spices.add(new JCheckBoxMenuItem("Thyme"));
    spices.add(new JCheckBoxMenuItem("Rosemary"));
    spices.add(new JCheckBoxMenuItem("Oregano", true));
    spices.add(new JCheckBoxMenuItem("Fennel"));

    // create the Cheese menu
    JMenu cheese = new JMenu("Cheese");
```

```
        cheese.setMnemonic(KeyEvent.VK_C);
        ButtonGroup group = new ButtonGroup();
        JRadioButtonMenuItem rbmi;
        rbmi = new JRadioButtonMenuItem("Regular", true);
        group.add(rbmi);
        cheese.add(rbmi);
        rbmi = new JRadioButtonMenuItem("Extra");
        group.add(rbmi);
        cheese.add(rbmi);
        rbmi = new JRadioButtonMenuItem("Blue");
        group.add(rbmi);
        cheese.add(rbmi);

        // create a menu bar and use it in this JFrame
        JMenuBar menuBar = new JMenuBar();
        menuBar.add(utensils);
        menuBar.add(spices);
        menuBar.add(cheese);
        frame.setJMenuBar(menuBar);

        frame.setDefaultCloseOperation( JFrame.EXIT_ON_CLOSE );
        frame.setSize(200,200);
        frame.setVisible(true);
      }
    }
```

Yes, we know. Quit doesn't belong in the Utensils menu. If it's driving you crazy, you can go back and add a File menu as an exercise when we're through.

Creating menus is pretty simple work. You create a `JMenu` object, specifying the menu's title. Like the text of `JButton`s and `JLabel`s, menu labels can contain simple HTML. Then you just add `JMenuItem`s to the `JMenu`. You can also add `JMenu`s to a `JMenu`; they show up as submenus. This is shown in the creation of the Utensils menu:

```
    JMenu utensils = new JMenu("Utensils");
    utensils.setMnemonic(KeyEvent.VK_U);
    utensils.add(new JMenuItem("Fork"));
    utensils.add(new JMenuItem("Knife"));
    utensils.add(new JMenuItem("Spoon"));
    JMenu hybrid = new JMenu("Hybrid");
    hybrid.add(new JMenuItem("Spork"));
    hybrid.add(new JMenuItem("Spife"));
    hybrid.add(new JMenuItem("Knork"));
    utensils.add(hybrid);
```

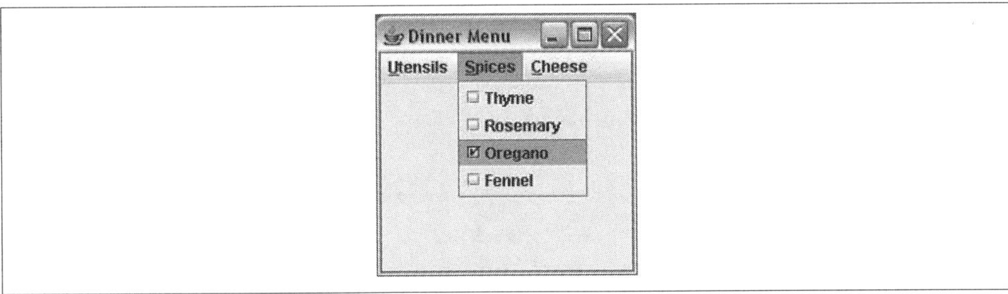

Figure 17-7. The DinnerMenu application

In the second line, we set the mnemonic for this menu using a constant defined in the `KeyEvent` class, which has static identifiers for all keys on the keyboard.

You can add those pretty separator lines with a single call:

```
utensils.addSeparator();
```

The Quit menu item has some bells and whistles we should explain. First, we create the menu item and set its mnemonic, just as we did before for the Utensils menu:

```
JMenuItem quitItem = new JMenuItem("Quit");
quitItem.setMnemonic(KeyEvent.VK_Q);
```

Now we want to create an accelerator for the menu item. We do this with the help of a class called `KeyStroke` :

```
quitItem.setAccelerator(
    KeyStroke.getKeyStroke(KeyEvent.VK_Q, Event.CTRL_MASK));
```

Finally, to actually do something in response to the menu item, we register an action listener:

```
quitItem.addActionListener(new ActionListener() {
    public void actionPerformed(ActionEvent e) { System.exit(0); }
});
```

Our action listener exits the application when the Quit item is selected.

Creating the Spices menu is just as easy, except that we use `JCheckBoxMenuItems` instead of regular `JMenuItems`. The result is a menu full of items that behave like checkboxes.

The next menu, Cheese, is a little more tricky. We want the items to be radio buttons, but we need to place them in a `ButtonGroup` to ensure they are mutually exclusive. Each item, then, is created, added to the button group, and added to the menu itself.

The final step is to place the menus we've just created in a `JMenuBar`. This is simply a component that lays out menus in a horizontal bar. We have two options for adding it to our `JFrame`. Because the `JMenuBar` is a real component, we could add it to the content pane of the `JFrame`. Instead, we use a convenience method called `setJMenuBar()`, which automatically places the JMenuBar at the top of the frame's content pane. This saves us the trouble of altering the layout or size of the content pane; it is adjusted to coexist peacefully with the menu bar.

Pop-Up Menus

One of Swing's nifty components is JPopupMenu, a context menu that appears at the mouse location when you press the appropriate mouse button or keystroke. (On a two-button mouse, clicking the right mouse button invokes a pop-up menu. On a single-button Mac, you Command-click.) Which button you press depends on the platform you're using; fortunately, from the code's point of view you don't have to care—Swing figures it out for you.

The care and feeding of JPopupMenu is basically the same as any other menu. You use a different constructor—JPopupMenu()—to create it, but otherwise, you build a menu and add elements to it the same way. The big difference is that you don't attach it to a JMenuBar. Instead, just pop up the menu whenever and wherever you need it. Prior to Java 5.0, this process is a little cumbersome; you have to register to receive the appropriate mouse events, check them to see if they are the pop-up trigger and then pop the menu manually. With Java 5.0, the process is simplified by having components manage their own pop-up menus.

First, we'll show an example of explicit pop-up handling. The following example, PopupColorMenu, contains three buttons. You can use a JPopupMenu to set the color of each button or the background frame itself, depending on where you click the mouse.

```
//file: PopUpColorMenu.java
import java.awt.*;
import java.awt.event.*;
import javax.swing.*;

public class PopUpColorMenu implements ActionListener
{
  Component selectedComponent;

  public PopUpColorMenu() {
    JFrame frame = new JFrame("PopUpColorMenu v1.0");

    final JPopupMenu colorMenu = new JPopupMenu("Color");
    colorMenu.add(makeMenuItem("Red"));
    colorMenu.add(makeMenuItem("Green"));
    colorMenu.add(makeMenuItem("Blue"));

    MouseListener mouseListener = new MouseAdapter() {
      public void mousePressed(MouseEvent e) { checkPopup(e); }
      public void mouseClicked(MouseEvent e) { checkPopup(e); }
      public void mouseReleased(MouseEvent e) { checkPopup(e); }
      private void checkPopup(MouseEvent e) {
```

```
        if (e.isPopupTrigger()) {
          selectedComponent = e.getComponent();
          colorMenu.show(e.getComponent(), e.getX(), e.getY());
        }
      }
    };

    Container content = frame.getContentPane(); // unnecessary  in 5.0+
    content.setLayout(new FlowLayout());
    JButton button = new JButton("Uno");
    button.addMouseListener(mouseListener);
    content.add(button);
    button = new JButton("Due");
    button.addMouseListener(mouseListener);
    content.add(button);
    button = new JButton("Tre");
    button.addMouseListener(mouseListener);
    content.add(button);

    frame.getContentPane().addMouseListener(mouseListener);

    frame.setSize(200,50);
    frame.setDefaultCloseOperation( JFrame.EXIT_ON_CLOSE );
    frame.setVisible(true);
  }

  public void actionPerformed(ActionEvent e) {
    String color = e.getActionCommand();
    if (color.equals("Red"))
      selectedComponent.setBackground(Color.red);
    else if (color.equals("Green"))
      selectedComponent.setBackground(Color.green);
    else if (color.equals("Blue"))
      selectedComponent.setBackground(Color.blue);
  }

  private JMenuItem makeMenuItem(String label) {
    JMenuItem item = new JMenuItem(label);
    item.addActionListener( this );
    return item;
  }

  public static void main(String[] args) {
     new PopUpColorMenu();
  }
}
```

Figure 17-8 shows the example in action; the user is preparing to change the color of the bottom button.

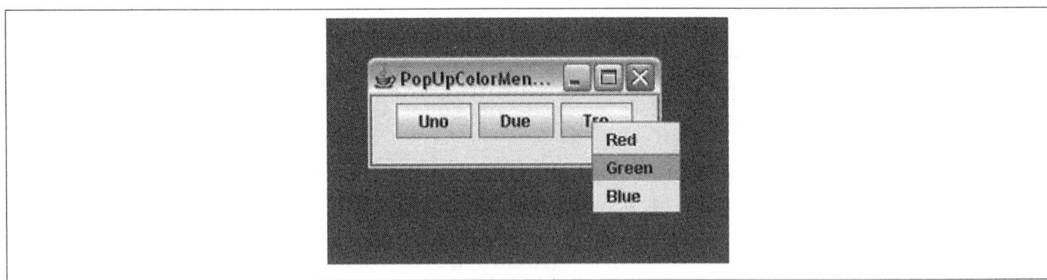

Figure 17-8. The PopupColorMenu application

Because the pop-up menu is triggered by mouse events (in this example), we need to register a `MouseListener` for any of the components to which it applies. In this example, all three buttons and the content pane of the frame are eligible for the color pop-up menu. Therefore, we add a mouse event listener for all these components explicitly. The same instance of an anonymous inner `MouseAdapter` subclass is used in each case. In this class, we override the `mousePressed()`, `mouseReleased()`, and `mouseClicked()` methods to display the pop-up menu when we get an appropriate event. How do we know what an "appropriate event" is? Fortunately, we don't need to worry about the specifics of our user's platform; we just need to call the event's `isPopupTrigger()` method. If this method returns `true`, we know the user has done whatever normally displays a pop-up menu on his system.

Once we know that the user wants to raise a pop-up menu, we display it by calling its `show()` method with the mouse event coordinates as arguments.

If we want to provide different menus for different types of components or the background, we create different mouse listeners for each different kind of component. The mouse listeners invoke different kinds of pop-up menus as appropriate.

The only thing left is to handle the action events from the pop-up menu items. We use a helper method called `makeMenuItem()` to register the `PopUpColorMenu` window as an action listener for every item we add. The example implements `ActionListener` and has the required `actionPerformed()` method. This method reads the action command from the event, which is equal to the selected menu item's label by default. It then sets the background color of the selected component appropriately.

Component-Managed Pop Ups

Things get a bit easier in Java 5.0, using the new pop-up menu API for components. In Java 5.0, any `JComponent` can manage a `JPopupMenu` directly with the `setComponentPopupMenu()` method. `JComponents` can also be told to simply inherit their parent container's pop-up menu via the `setInheritsPopupMenu()` method. This combination makes it very simple to implement a context menu that should appear in many components within a container.

Unfortunately, this doesn't lend itself well to our previous example (PopupColorMenu) for two reasons. First, we need to know which component the mouse was in when the pop up was triggered and we don't get that information using this API. The pop-up handling is actually delegated to the container, not inherited. Second, not all types of components are registered to receive mouse events by default.[1] As a result, we'll create a new example that is more appropriate for a "one context menu to rule them all" application. The following example, ContextMenu, shows a TextArea and TextField that both inherit the same JPopupMenu from their JPanel container. When you select a menu item, the action is displayed in the text area.

```
import java.awt.*;
import java.awt.event.*;
import javax.swing.*;

public class ContextMenu implements ActionListener
{
  JTextArea textArea = new JTextArea();

  public ContextMenu()
  {
    final JPopupMenu contextMenu = new JPopupMenu("Edit");
    contextMenu.add(makeMenuItem("Save"));
    contextMenu.add(makeMenuItem("Save As"));
    contextMenu.add(makeMenuItem("Close"));

    JFrame frame = new JFrame("ContextMenu v1.0");
    JPanel panel = new JPanel();
    panel.setLayout( new BorderLayout() );
    frame.getContentPane( ).add( panel );
    panel.setComponentPopupMenu( contextMenu );

    textArea.setInheritsPopupMenu( true );
    panel.add( BorderLayout.CENTER, textArea );

    JTextField textField = new JTextField();
    textField.setInheritsPopupMenu( true );
    panel.add( BorderLayout.SOUTH, textField );

    frame.setDefaultCloseOperation( JFrame.EXIT_ON_CLOSE );
    frame.setSize(400,200);
    frame.setVisible(true);
  }
```

1. Components such as JPanel and JLabel by default do not expect to handle mouse events. When you register a listener such as MouseListener, it registers itself internally to begin processing these events. Unfortunately, at the time of this writing, using setInheritsPopupMenu() does not trigger this functionality. As a workaround, you could register a dummy mouse listener with these components to prompt them to expect mouse events and properly trigger context menus if you want them.

```
    public void actionPerformed( ActionEvent e ) {
      textArea.append( e.getActionCommand() +"\n" );
    }

    private JMenuItem makeMenuItem(String label) {
      JMenuItem item = new JMenuItem(label);
      item.addActionListener( this );
      return item;
    }

    public static void main(String[] args) {
       new ContextMenu();
    }
  }
```

We've constructed our `JPopupMenu` as before, but this time we are not responsible for listening for mouse clicks or triggering the pop up explicitly. Instead, we use the `setComponentPopupMenu()` method to ask the `JPanel` to handle it for us. We use `setInheritsPopupMenu()` on both the `JTextArea` and `JTextField` so that they will both delegate pop-up trigger mouse clicks to the `JPanel` automatically.

The JScrollPane Class

We used `JScrollPane` earlier in this chapter without explaining much about it. In this section, we'll remedy the situation.

A `JScrollPane` is a container that can hold one component. Said another way, a `JScrollPane`*wraps* another component. By default, if the wrapped component is larger than the `JScrollPane` itself, the `JScrollPane` supplies scrollbars. `JScrollPane` handles the events from the scrollbars and displays the appropriate portion of the contained component.

Technically, `JScrollPane` is a `Container`, but it's a funny one. It has its own layout manager, which can't be changed, and it accommodates only one component at a time. This isn't really a limitation. If you want to put a lot of stuff in a `JScrollPane`, just collect your components in a `JPanel`, with whatever layout manager you like, and put that panel into the `JScrollPane`.

When you create a `JScrollPane`, you specify the conditions under which its scrollbars are displayed. This is called the *scrollbar display policy*; a separate policy is used for the horizontal and vertical scrollbars. The following constants can be used to specify the policy for each of the scrollbars:

`HORIZONTAL_SCROLLBAR_AS_NEEDED`
`VERTICAL_SCROLLBAR_AS_NEEDED`
: Displays a scrollbar only if the wrapped component doesn't fit.

HORIZONTAL_SCROLLBAR_ALWAYS
VERTICAL_SCROLLBAR_ALWAYS
: Always shows a scrollbar, regardless of the contained component's size.

HORIZONTAL_SCROLLBAR_NEVER
VERTICAL_SCROLLBAR_NEVER
: Never shows a scrollbar, even if the contained component won't fit. If you use this policy, you should provide some other way to manipulate the `JScrollPane`.

By default, the policies are `HORIZONTAL_SCROLLBAR_AS_NEEDED` and `VERTICAL_SCROLLBAR_AS_NEEDED`.

Support for scrolling with mouse wheels is automatic as of Java 1.4. You do not have to do anything explicit in your application to get this to work.

The following example uses a `JScrollPane` to display a large image (see Figure 17-9). The application itself is very simple; all we do is place the image in a `JLabel`, wrap a `JScrollPane` around it, and put the `JScrollPane` in a `JFrame`'s content pane.

Figure 17-9. The ScrollPaneFrame application

Here's the code:

```
//file: ScrollPaneFrame.java
import java.awt.*;
import java.awt.event.*;
import javax.swing.*;

public class ScrollPaneFrame
{
  public static void main(String[] args) {
    String filename = "Piazza di Spagna.jpg";
    if (args.length > 0)
      filename = args[0];
```

```
        JFrame frame = new JFrame("ScrollPaneFrame v1.0");
        JLabel image = new JLabel( new ImageIcon(filename) );
        frame.getContentPane().add( new JScrollPane(image) );

        frame.setSize(300, 300);
        frame.setDefaultCloseOperation( JFrame.EXIT_ON_CLOSE );
        frame.setVisible(true);
    }
}
```

To hold the image, we have used a `JLabel` and `ImageIcon`. The `ImageIcon` class preloads the image using a `MediaTracker` and determines its dimensions. It's also possible to have the `ImageIcon` show the image as it loads or to ask it for information on the status of loading the image. We'll discuss image management in Chapter 21.

The JSplitPane Class

A *split pane* is a special container that holds two components, each in its own subpane. A *splitter bar* adjusts the sizes of the two subpanes. In a document viewer, for example, you might use a split pane to show a table of contents next to a page of text.

The following example uses two `JLabel`s containing `ImageIcon`s, like the previous example. It displays the two labels, wrapped in `JScrollPane`s, on either side of a `JSplitPane` (see Figure 17-10). You can drag the splitter bar back and forth to adjust the sizes of the two contained components.

```
//file: SplitPaneFrame.java
import java.awt.*;
import java.awt.event.*;
import javax.swing.*;
import javax.swing.border.*;

public class SplitPaneFrame {
  public static void main(String[] args) {
    String fileOne = "Piazza di Spagna.jpg";
    String fileTwo = "L1-Light.jpg";
    if (args.length > 0) fileOne = args[0];
    if (args.length > 1) fileTwo = args[1];

    JFrame frame = new JFrame("SplitPaneFrame");

    JLabel leftImage = new JLabel( new ImageIcon( fileOne ) );
    Component left = new JScrollPane(leftImage);
    JLabel rightImage = new JLabel( new ImageIcon( fileTwo ) );
    Component right = new JScrollPane(rightImage);

    JSplitPane split =
      new JSplitPane(JSplitPane.HORIZONTAL_SPLIT, left, right);
    split.setDividerLocation(100);
    frame.getContentPane().add(split);
```

```
        frame.setDefaultCloseOperation( JFrame.EXIT_ON_CLOSE );
        frame.setSize(300, 200);
        frame.setVisible(true);
    }
}
```

Figure 17-10. Using a split pane

The JTabbedPane Class

If you've ever right-clicked on the desktop to set your Display Properties in Windows, you already know what a `JTabbedPane` is. It's a container with labeled tabs (e.g., Themes, Screen Saver, Appearance). When you click on a tab, a new set of controls is shown in the body of the `JTabbedPane`. In Swing, `JTabbedPane` is simply a specialized container.

Each tab has a name. To add a tab to the `JTabbedPane`, simply call `addTab()`. You'll need to specify the name of the tab as well as a component that supplies the tab's contents. Typically, it's a container holding other components.

Even though the `JTabbedPane` only shows one set of components at a time, be aware that all the components on all the pages are alive and in memory at one time. If you have components that hog processor time or memory, try to put them into a "sleep" state when they are not showing.

The following example shows how to create a `JTabbedPane`. It adds standard Swing components to a tab named Controls. The second tab is filled with a scrollable image, which was presented in the previous examples.

```
//file: TabbedPaneFrame.java
import java.awt.*;
import java.awt.event.*;
import javax.swing.*;
import javax.swing.border.*;

public class TabbedPaneFrame {
  public static void main(String[] args)
```

```
    {
      JFrame frame = new JFrame("TabbedPaneFrame");
      JTabbedPane tabby = new JTabbedPane();

      // create the controls pane
      JPanel controls = new JPanel();
      controls.add(new JLabel("Service:"));
      JList list = new JList(
          new String[] { "Web server", "FTP server" });
      list.setBorder(BorderFactory.createEtchedBorder());
      controls.add(list);
      controls.add(new JButton("Start"));

      // create an image pane
      String filename = "Piazza di Spagna.jpg";
      JLabel image = new JLabel( new ImageIcon(filename) );
      JComponent picture = new JScrollPane(image);
      tabby.addTab("Controls", controls);
      tabby.addTab("Picture", picture);

      frame.getContentPane().add(tabby);

      frame.setSize(200, 200);
      frame.setDefaultCloseOperation( JFrame.EXIT_ON_CLOSE );
      frame.setVisible(true);
    }
  }
```

The code isn't especially fancy, but the result is an impressive-looking user interface. The first tab is a `JPanel` that contains some other components, including a `JList` with an etched border. The second tab simply contains the `JLabel` with `ImageIcon` wrapped in a `JScrollPane`. The running example is shown in Figure 17-11.

Our example has only two tabs and they fit quite easily, but in a realistic application it is easy to run out of room. By default, when there are too many tabs to display in a single row, `JTabbedPane` automatically wraps them into additional rows. This behavior fits with the tab notion quite well, giving the appearance of a filing cabinet, but it also necessitates that when you select a tab from the back row, the tabs must be rearranged to bring the selected tab to the foreground. Many users find this confusing, and it violates a principal of user interface design that says that controls should remain in the same location. Alternatively, you can configure the tabbed pane to use a single, scrolling row of tabs by specifying a scrolling tab layout policy like this:

```
setTabLayoutPolicy( JTabbedPane.SCROLL_TAB_LAYOUT );
```

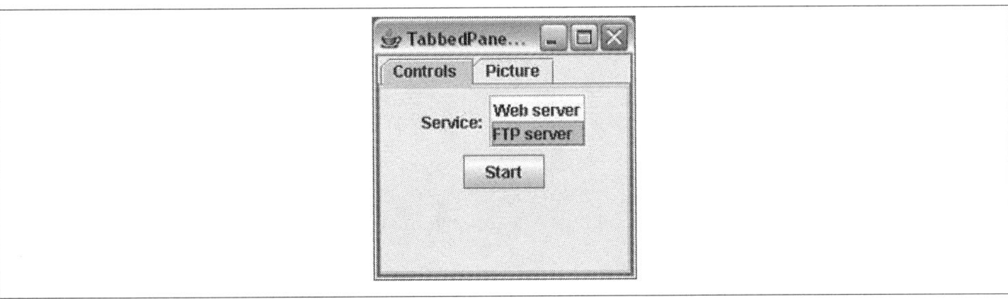

Figure 17-11. Using a tabbed pane

Java 6 introduced the ability to add custom components to tabs. The most common use of this capability is the addition of buttons on tabs for functions such as close, info, tear away, etc. The following example demonstrates how to use the new `setTabComponentAt(int index, Component component)` method to add a close button on each tab.

```
//file: ClosableTabs.java
import javax.swing.*;
import java.awt.*;
import java.awt.event.*;

public class ClosableTabs extends JTabbedPane {

    public void addTab(String title, Color color) {
        JPanel pane = new JPanel();
        pane.setBackground(color);
        int loc = getTabCount();
        insertTab(title, null, pane, null, loc);
        setTabComponentAt(loc, new Tab(title));
    }

    public static void main(String[] args) {
        SwingUtilities.invokeLater(new Runnable(){
            public void run(){
                JFrame frame = new JFrame("Closable Tabs");

                ClosableTabs tabs = new ClosableTabs();
                tabs.addTab("Blue", Color.BLUE);
                tabs.addTab("Green", Color.GREEN);
                tabs.addTab("Red", Color.RED);
                frame.add(tabs);

                frame.setDefaultCloseOperation(
                    JFrame.EXIT_ON_CLOSE);
                frame.setSize(new Dimension(300, 150));
                frame.setLocationRelativeTo(null);
                frame.setVisible(true);
            }});
    }
```

```
/**
 * The component used as a tab (i.e., the tab itself as opposed
 * to the content)
 */
private class Tab extends JPanel {

    public Tab(String title) {
        super(new FlowLayout(FlowLayout.LEFT, 0, 0));
        setOpaque(false);

        // The tab's title
        JLabel label = new JLabel(title);

        // Creating a space to the right of the close button
        label.setBorder(BorderFactory.createEmptyBorder(0, 0,
            0, 2));

        add(label);

        // The tab's close button
        JButton button = new CloseButton();
        add(button);

        // This is necessary for vertical alignment of the
        // tab's content
        setBorder(BorderFactory.createEmptyBorder(2, 0, 0, 0));
    }

    private class CloseButton extends JButton
        implements ActionListener {

        public CloseButton() {
            setPreferredSize(new Dimension(17, 17));
            setOpaque(false);
            setContentAreaFilled(false);
            setBorderPainted(false);
            setRolloverEnabled(true);
            setFocusable(false);
            addActionListener(this);
        }

        public void actionPerformed(ActionEvent e) {
            int i = ClosableTabs.this.indexOfTabComponent(
                Tab.this);
            if (i != -1) {
                ClosableTabs.this.remove(i);
            }
        }

        protected void paintComponent(Graphics g) {
            Graphics2D g2 = (Graphics2D)g;
            g2.setStroke(new BasicStroke(2));
```

```
                    // Show red on roll-over
                    g2.setColor(Color.BLACK);
                    if (getModel().isRollover()) {
                        g2.setColor(Color.RED);
                    }

                    // Paint the "X"
                    int offset = 5;
                    g2.drawLine(offset, offset, getWidth() -
                        offset - 1, getHeight() - offset - 1);
                    g2.drawLine(getWidth() - offset - 1, offset,
                        offset, getHeight() - offset - 1);
                    g2.dispose();
                }
            }
        }
    }
```

Scrollbars and Sliders

`JScrollPane` is such a handy component that you may not ever need to use scrollbars by themselves. In fact, if you ever do find yourself using a scrollbar by itself, chances are that you really want to use another component called a *slider*.

There's not much point in describing the appearance and functionality of scrollbars and sliders. Instead, let's jump right in with an example that includes both components. Figure 17-12 shows a simple example with both a scrollbar and a slider.

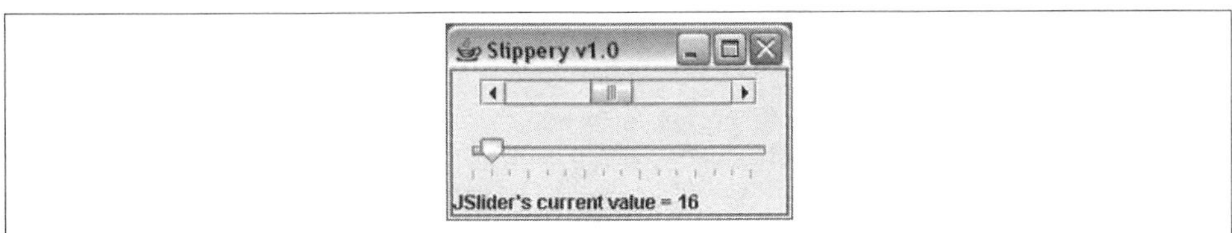

Figure 17-12. Using a scrollbar and a slider

Here is the source code for this example:

```
//file: Slippery.java
import java.awt.*;
import java.awt.event.*;
import javax.swing.*;
import javax.swing.event.*;

public class Slippery {
  public static void main(String[] args)
  {
    JFrame frame = new JFrame("Slippery v1.0");
```

```
        Container content = frame.getContentPane();  // unnecessary  in 5.0+

        JPanel main = new JPanel(new GridLayout(2, 1));
        JPanel scrollBarPanel = new JPanel();
        final JScrollBar scrollBar =
            new JScrollBar(JScrollBar.HORIZONTAL, 0, 48, 0, 255);
        int height = scrollBar.getPreferredSize().height;
        scrollBar.setPreferredSize(new Dimension(175, height));
        scrollBarPanel.add(scrollBar);
        main.add(scrollBarPanel);

        JPanel sliderPanel = new JPanel();
        final JSlider slider =
            new JSlider(JSlider.HORIZONTAL, 0, 255, 128);
        slider.setMajorTickSpacing(48);
        slider.setMinorTickSpacing(16);
        slider.setPaintTicks(true);
        sliderPanel.add(slider);
        main.add(sliderPanel);

        content.add(main, BorderLayout.CENTER);

        final JLabel statusLabel =
            new JLabel("Welcome to Slippery v1.0");
        content.add(statusLabel, BorderLayout.SOUTH);

        // wire up the event handlers
        scrollBar.addAdjustmentListener(new AdjustmentListener() {
          public void adjustmentValueChanged(AdjustmentEvent e) {
            statusLabel.setText("JScrollBar's current value = "
                                + scrollBar.getValue());
          }
        });

        slider.addChangeListener(new ChangeListener() {
          public void stateChanged(ChangeEvent e) {
            statusLabel.setText("JSlider's current value = "
                                + slider.getValue());
          }
        });

        frame.pack();
        frame.setDefaultCloseOperation( JFrame.EXIT_ON_CLOSE );
        frame.setVisible(true);
    }
}
```

All we've really done here is added a JScrollBar and a JSlider to our main window. If the user adjusts either of these components, the current value of the component is displayed in a JLabel at the bottom of the window.

You create both the `JScrollBar` and `JSlider` by specifying an orientation, either `HORIZONTAL` or `VERTICAL`. You can also specify the minimum and maximum values for the components, as well as the initial value. The `JScrollBar` supports one additional parameter, the *extent*. The extent simply refers to what range of values is represented by the slider within the scroll bar. For example, in a scrollbar that runs from 0 to 255, an extent of 128 means that the slider will be half the width of the scrollable area of the scrollbar.

`JSlider` supports the idea of *tick marks*, lines drawn at certain values along the slider's length. *Major tick marks* are slightly larger than *minor tick marks*. To draw tick marks, just specify an interval for major and minor tick marks, and then paint the tick marks:

```
slider.setMajorTickSpacing(48);
slider.setMinorTickSpacing(16);
slider.setPaintTicks(true);
```

`JSlider` also supports labeling the ticks with text strings, using the `setLabelTable()` method.

Responding to events from the two components is straightforward. The `JScrollBar` sends out `AdjustmentEvents` every time something happens; the `JSlider` fires off `ChangeEvents` when its value changes. In our simple example, we display the new value of the changed component in the `JLabel` at the bottom of the window.

Dialogs

A dialog is another standard feature of user interfaces. Dialogs are frequently used to present information to the user ("Your fruit salad is ready.") or to ask a question ("Shall I bring the car around?"). Dialogs are used so commonly in GUI applications that Swing includes a handy set of prebuilt dialogs. These are accessible from static methods in the `JOptionPane` class. Many variations are possible; `JOptionPane` groups them into four basic types:

Message dialog
: Displays a message to the user, usually accompanied by an OK button.

Confirmation dialog
: Ask a question and displays answer buttons—usually Yes, No, and Cancel.

Input dialog
: Asks the user to type in a string.

Option dialogs
: The most general type. You pass it your own components, which are displayed in the dialog.

A confirmation dialog is shown in Figure 17-13.

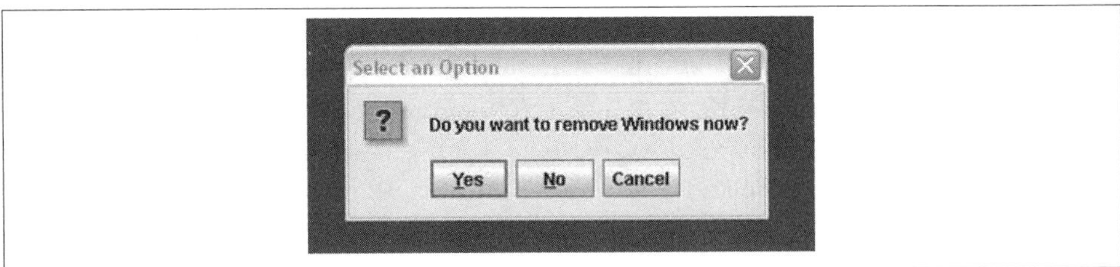

Figure 17-13. Using a confirmation dialog

Let's look at examples of each kind of dialog. The following code produces a message dialog:

```
JOptionPane.showMessageDialog(frame, "You have mail.");
```

The first parameter to `showMessageDialog()` is the parent component (in this case, `frame`, an existing `JFrame`). The dialog will be centered on the parent component. If you pass `null` for the parent component, the dialog is centered in your screen. The dialogs that `JOptionPane` displays are *modal*, which means they block other input to your application while they are showing.

Here's a slightly fancier message dialog. We've specified a title for the dialog and a message type, which affects the icon that is displayed:

```
JOptionPane.showMessageDialog(frame, "You are low on memory.",
        "Apocalyptic message", JOptionPane.WARNING_MESSAGE);
```

Here's how to display the confirmation dialog shown in Figure 17-13:

```
int result = JOptionPane.showConfirmDialog(null,
        "Do you want to remove Windows now?");
```

In this case, we've passed `null` for the parent component and it will be displayed centered on the screen. Special values are returned from `showConfirmDialog()` to indicate which button was pressed. A full example later in this section shows how to use this return value.

Sometimes you need to ask the user to type some input. The following code puts up a dialog requesting the user's name:

```
String name = JOptionPane.showInputDialog(null,
        "Please enter your name.");
```

Whatever the user types is returned as a `String` or `null` if the user presses the Cancel button.

The most general type of dialog is the option dialog. You supply an array of objects you wish to be displayed; `JOptionPane` takes care of formatting them and displaying the dialog. The following example displays a text label, a `JTextField`, and a `JPasswordField`. (Text components are described in the next chapter.)

```
JTextField userField = new JTextField();
JPasswordField passField = new JPasswordField();
String message = "Please enter your user name and password.";
result = JOptionPane.showOptionDialog(frame,
    new Object[] { message, userField, passField },
    "Login", JOptionPane.OK_CANCEL_OPTION,
    JOptionPane.QUESTION_MESSAGE,
    null, null, null);
```

We've also specified a dialog title ("Login") in the call to `showOptionDialog()`. We want OK and Cancel buttons, so we pass `OK_CANCEL_OPTION` as the dialog type. The `QUESTION_MESSAGE` argument indicates we'd like to see the question mark icon. The last three items are optional: an `Icon`, an array of different choices, and a current selection. Because the icon parameter is `null`, a default is used. If the array of choices and the current selection parameters were not `null`, `JOptionPane` might try to display the choices in a list or combo box.

The following application includes all the examples we've covered:

```
import javax.swing.*;

public class ExerciseOptions {
  public static void main(String[] args) {
    JFrame frame = new JFrame("ExerciseOptions v1.0");
    frame.setSize(200, 200);
    frame.setVisible(true);

    JOptionPane.showMessageDialog(frame, "You have mail.");
    JOptionPane.showMessageDialog(frame, "You are low on memory.",
        "Apocalyptic message", JOptionPane.WARNING_MESSAGE);

    int result = JOptionPane.showConfirmDialog(null,
        "Do you want to remove Windows now?");
    switch (result) {
      case JOptionPane.YES_OPTION:
        System.out.println("Yes"); break;
      case JOptionPane.NO_OPTION:
        System.out.println("No"); break;
      case JOptionPane.CANCEL_OPTION:
        System.out.println("Cancel"); break;
      case JOptionPane.CLOSED_OPTION:
        System.out.println("Closed"); break;
    }

    String name = JOptionPane.showInputDialog(null,
        "Please enter your name.");
    System.out.println(name);

    JTextField userField = new JTextField();
```

```
        JPasswordField passField = new JPasswordField();
        String message = "Please enter your user name and password.";
        result = JOptionPane.showOptionDialog(frame,
            new Object[] { message, userField, passField },
            "Login", JOptionPane.OK_CANCEL_OPTION,
            JOptionPane.QUESTION_MESSAGE,
            null, null, null);
        if (result == JOptionPane.OK_OPTION)
          System.out.println(userField.getText() +
              " " +  new String(passField.getPassword()));

        System.exit(0);
      }
    }
```

File Selection Dialog

A JFileChooser is a standard file selection box. As with other Swing components, JFileChooser is implemented in pure Java, so it can look and act the same on different platforms or take on the native appearance of the operating system, depending on what look and feel is in effect.

Selecting files all day can be pretty boring without a greater purpose, so we'll exercise the JFileChooser in a mini-editor application. Editor provides a text area in which we can load and work with files. (The JFileChooser created by Editor is shown in Figure 17-14.) We'll stop just shy of the capability to save and let you fill in the blanks (with a few caveats).

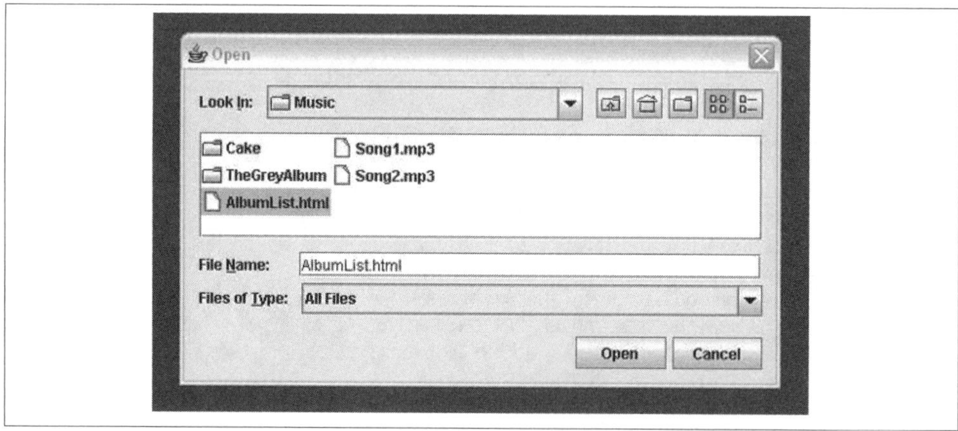

Figure 17-14. Using a JFileChooser

Here's the code:

```
import java.awt.*;
import java.awt.event.*;
import java.io.*;
import javax.swing.*;

public class Editor extends JFrame implements ActionListener
{
  private JEditorPane textPane = new JEditorPane();

  public Editor() {
    super("Editor v1.0");
    Container content = getContentPane();  // unnecessary  in 5.0+
    content.add(new JScrollPane(textPane), BorderLayout.CENTER);
    JMenu menu = new JMenu("File");
    menu.add(makeMenuItem("Open"));
    menu.add(makeMenuItem("Save"));
    menu.add(makeMenuItem("Quit"));
    JMenuBar menuBar = new JMenuBar();
    menuBar.add(menu);
    setJMenuBar(menuBar);
    setSize(300, 300);
setDefaultCloseOperation( JFrame.EXIT_ON_CLOSE );
  }

  public void actionPerformed(ActionEvent e) {
    String command = e.getActionCommand();
    if (command.equals("Quit")) System.exit(0);
    else if (command.equals("Open")) loadFile();
    else if (command.equals("Save")) saveFile();
  }

  private void loadFile () {
    JFileChooser chooser = new JFileChooser();
    int result = chooser.showOpenDialog(this);
    if (result == JFileChooser.CANCEL_OPTION) return;
    try {
      File file = chooser.getSelectedFile();
      java.net.URL url = file.toURL();
      textPane.setPage(url);
    }
    catch (Exception e) {
      textPane.setText("Could not load file: " + e);
    }
  }

  private void saveFile() {
    JFileChooser chooser = new JFileChooser();
    chooser.showSaveDialog(this);
    // Save file data...
  }

  private JMenuItem makeMenuItem( String name ) {
```

```
      JMenuItem m = new JMenuItem( name );
      m.addActionListener( this );
      return m;
    }

    public static void main(String[] s) {
  new Editor().setVisible(true);
    }
  }
```

Editor is a JFrame that lays itself out with a JEditorPane (which is covered in Chapter 18) and a pull-down menu. From the pull-down File menu, we can Open, Save, or Quit. The actionPerformed() method catches the events associated with these menu selections and takes the appropriate action.

The interesting parts of Editor are the private methods loadFile() and saveFile(). The loadFile() method creates a new JFileChooser and calls its showOpenDialog() method.

A JFileChooser does its work when the showOpenDialog() method is called. This method blocks the caller until the dialog completes its job, at which time the file chooser disappears. After that, we can retrieve the designated file with the getFile() method. In loadFile(), we convert the selected File to a URL and pass it to the JEditorPane, which displays the selected file. As you'll learn in the next chapter, JEditorPane can display HTML and RTF files.

You can fill out the unfinished saveFile() method if you wish, but it would be prudent to add the standard safety precautions. For example, you could use one of the confirmation dialogs we just looked at to prompt the user before overwriting an existing file.

The Color Chooser

Swing is chock full of goodies. JColorChooser is yet another ready-made dialog supplied with Swing; it allows your users to choose colors. The following brief example shows how easy it is to use JColorChooser:

```
import java.awt.*;
import java.awt.event.*;
import javax.swing.*;

public class LocalColor {
  public static void main(String[] args) {
    final JFrame frame = new JFrame("LocalColor v1.0");
    final Container content = frame.getContentPane();  // unnecessary in 5.0+
    content.setLayout(new GridBagLayout());
    JButton button = new JButton("Change color...");
    content.add(button);

    button.addActionListener(new ActionListener() {
      public void actionPerformed(ActionEvent e) {
```

```
            Color c = JColorChooser.showDialog(frame,
                "Choose a color", content.getBackground());
            if (c != null) content.setBackground(c);
          }
        });

        frame.setSize(200, 200);
        frame.setDefaultCloseOperation( JFrame.EXIT_ON_CLOSE );
        frame.setVisible(true);
      }
    }
```

This example shows a frame window with a single button. When you click on the button, a color chooser pops up. After you select a color, it becomes the background color of the frame window.

Basically, all we have to do is call `JColorChooser`'s static method `showDialog()`. In this example, we specified a parent component, a dialog title, and an initial color value. But you can get away with just specifying a parent component. Whatever color the user chooses is returned; if the user presses the Cancel button, `null` is returned.

CHAPTER 18

More Swing Components

In the previous chapter, we described most of the components that Swing offers for building user interfaces. In this chapter, you'll find out about the rest. These include Swing's text components, trees, and tables. These types of components have considerable depth but are quite easy to use if you accept their default options. We'll show you the easy way to use these components and start to describe the more advanced features of each. Later in this chapter, we'll also give an example of how to implement your own, custom components in Swing.

Text Components

Swing offers sophisticated text components, from plain-text entry boxes to HTML renderers. For full coverage of Swing's text capabilities, see O'Reilly's *Java Swing*. In that encyclopedic book, several meaty chapters are devoted to text. It's a huge subject; we'll just scratch the surface here.

Let's begin by examining the simpler text components. `JTextField` is a single-line text editor and `JTextArea` is a simple, multiline text editor. Both `JTextField` and `JTextArea` derive from the `JTextComponent` class, which provides the functionality they have in common. This includes methods for setting and retrieving the displayed text, specifying whether the text is "editable" or read-only, manipulating the cursor position within the text, and manipulating text selections.

Observing changes in text components requires an understanding of how the components implement the Model-View-Controller (MVC) architecture. You may recall from the last chapter that Swing components implement a true MVC architecture. It's in the text components that you first get an inkling of a clear separation between the M and VC parts of the MVC architecture. The model for text components is an object called a `Document`. When you add or remove text from a `JTextField` or a `JTextArea`, the corresponding `Document` is changed. It's the document itself, not the visual components, that generates text-related events when something changes. To receive notification of JTextArea changes, therefore, you register with the underlying Document, not with the JTextArea component itself:

```
JTextArea textArea = new JTextArea();
Document doc = textArea.getDocument();
doc.addDocumentListener(someListener);
```

As you'll see in an upcoming example, you can easily have more than one visual text component use the same underlying Document data model.

In addition, JTextField components generate ActionEvents whenever the user presses the Return key within the field. To get these events, just implement the ActionListener interface and register your listener using the addActionListener() method.

The next sections contain a couple of simple applications that show you how to work with text areas and fields.

The TextEntryBox Application

Our first example, TextEntryBox, creates a JTextArea and ties it to a JTextField, as you can see in Figure 18-1.

Figure 18-1. The TextEntryBox application

When the user hits Return in the JTextField, we receive an ActionEvent and add the line to the JTextArea's display. Try it out. You may have to click your mouse in the JTextField to give it focus before typing in it. If you fill up the display with lines, you can test-drive the scroll bar:

```
//file: TextEntryBox.java
import java.awt.*;
import java.awt.event.*;
import javax.swing.*;

public class TextEntryBox {

  public static void main(String[] args) {
    JFrame frame = new JFrame("Text Entry Box");
```

```
        final JTextArea area = new JTextArea();
        area.setFont(new Font("Serif", Font.BOLD, 18));
        area.setText("Howdy!\n");
        final JTextField field = new JTextField();

        frame.add(new JScrollPane(area), BorderLayout.CENTER);
        frame.add(field, BorderLayout.SOUTH);
        field.requestFocus();

        field.addActionListener(new ActionListener() {
          public void actionPerformed(ActionEvent ae) {
            area.append(field.getText() + '\n');
            field.setText("");
          }
        });

        frame.setDefaultCloseOperation( JFrame.EXIT_ON_CLOSE );
        frame.setSize(200, 300);
        frame.setVisible(true);
      }
    }
```

`TextEntryBox` is exceedingly simple; we've done a few things to make it more interesting. We give the text area a bigger font using `Component`'s `setFont()` method; fonts are discussed in Chapter 20. Finally, we want to be notified whenever the user presses Return in the text field, so we register an anonymous inner class as a listener for action events.

Pressing Return in the `JTextField` generates an action event, and that's where the fun begins. We handle the event in the `actionPerformed()` method of our inner `ActionListener` implementation. Then, we use the `getText()` and `setText()` methods to manipulate the text that the user has typed. These methods can be used for `JTextField` and `JTextArea`, as these components are both derived from the `JTextComponent` class and, therefore, have some common functionality.

The event handler, `actionPerformed()`, calls `field.getText()` to read the text that the user typed into our `JTextField`. It then adds this text to the `JTextArea` by calling `area.append()`. Finally, we clear the text field by calling the method `field.setText("")`, preparing it for more input.

Remember, the text components really are distinct from the text data model, the `Document`. When you call `setText()`, `getText()`, or `append()`, these methods are shorthand for operations on an underlying `Document`.

By default, `JTextField` and `JTextArea` are editable; you can type and edit in both text components. They can be changed to output-only areas by calling `setEditable(false)`. Both text components also support *selections*. A selection is a range of text that is highlighted for copying, cutting, or pasting in your windowing system. You select text by dragging the mouse over it; you can then cut, copy, and paste it into other text windows using the default keyboard gestures. On most systems, these are Ctrl-C for copy, Ctrl-V for paste, and Ctrl-X for cut (on the Mac it's Command-C, Command-V, and Command-X). You can also programmatically manage these operations using the JTextComponent's cut(), copy(), and paste() methods. You could, for example, create a pop-up menu with the standard cut, copy, and paste options using these methods. The current text selection is returned by getSelectedText(), and you can set the selection using selectText(), which takes an index range or selectAll().

Notice how JTextArea fits neatly inside a JScrollPane. The scroll pane gives us the expected scrollbars and scrolling behavior if the text in the JTextArea becomes too large for the available space.

Formatted Text

The JFormattedTextField component provides explicit support for editing complex formatted values such as numbers and dates. JFormattedTextField acts somewhat like a JTextField, except that it accepts a format-specifying object in its constructor and manages a complex object type (such as Date or Integer) through its setValue() and getValue() methods. The following example shows the construction of a simple form with different types of formatted fields:

```
import java.text.*;
import javax.swing.*;
import javax.swing.text.*;
import java.util.Date;

public class

FormattedFields
{
    public static void main( String[] args ) throws Exception {
        Box form = Box.createVerticalBox();
        form.add( new JLabel("Name:") );
        form.add( new JTextField("Joe User") );

        form.add( new JLabel("Birthday:") );
        JFormattedTextField birthdayField =
            new JFormattedTextField(new SimpleDateFormat("MM/dd/yy"));
        birthdayField.setValue( new Date() );
        form.add( birthdayField );

        form.add( new JLabel("Age:") );
        form.add(new JFormattedTextField(new Integer(32)));

        form.add( new JLabel("Hairs on Body:") );
        JFormattedTextField hairsField
            = new JFormattedTextField( new DecimalFormat("###,###") );
        hairsField.setValue(new Integer(100000));
        form.add( hairsField );
```

```
            form.add( new JLabel("Phone Number:") );
            JFormattedTextField phoneField =
                new JFormattedTextField( new MaskFormatter("(###)###-####") );
            phoneField.setValue("(314)555-1212");
            form.add( phoneField );

            JFrame frame = new JFrame("User Information");
            frame.getContentPane().add(form);
            frame.pack();
            frame.setDefaultCloseOperation( JFrame.EXIT_ON_CLOSE );
            frame.setVisible(true);
        }
    }
```

`JFormattedTextField` can be constructed in a variety of ways. You can use a plain instance of `java.lang.Number` (e.g., `Integer` and `Float`) as a prototype or set the layout explicitly using a formatting object from the `java.text` package: `java.text.NumberFormat`, `java.text.DateFormat`, or the more arbitrary `java.text.MaskFormatter`. The `NumberFormat` and `DateFormat` classes of the `java.text` package are discussed in Chapters 10 and 11. `MaskFormatter` allows you to construct arbitrary physical layout conventions. In a moment, we'll discuss input filtering and component validation, which also allow you to restrict the kinds of characters that could fill the fields or perform arbitrary checks on the data. Finally, we should mention that in this example, we've used a `Box` container. A `Box` is just a Swing container that uses a `BoxLayout`, which we'll discuss more in Chapter 19.

After construction, you can set a valid value using `setValue()` and retrieve the last valid value with `getValue()`. To do this, you'll have to cast the value back to the correct type based on the format you are using. For example, this statement retrieves the date from our birthday field:

```
    Date bday = (Date)birthdayField.getValue();
```

`JFormattedTextField` validates its text when the user attempts to shift focus to a new field (either by clicking with the mouse outside of the field or using keyboard navigation). By default, `JFormattedTextField` handles invalid input by simply reverting to the last valid value. If you wish to allow invalid input to remain in the field for further editing, you can set the `setFocusLostBehavior()` method with the value `JFormattedTextField.COMMIT` (the default is `COMMIT_OR_REVERT`). In any case, invalid input does not change the value property retrieved by `getValue()`.

Filtering Input

`JFormattedTextField` does not know about all format types itself; instead, it uses `AbstractFormatter` objects that know about particular format types. The `AbstractFormatters`, in turn, provide implementations of two interfaces: `DocumentFilter` and `NavigationFilter`. A `DocumentFilter` attaches to implementations of `Document` and allows you to intercept editing commands, modifying them as you wish. A NavigationFilter can be attached to JTextComponents to control the movement of the cursor (as in a mask-formatted field). You can implement your own AbstractFormatters for use with JFormattedTextField, and, more generally, you can use the DocumentFilter interface to control how documents are edited in any type of text component. For example, you could create a DocumentFilter that maps characters to uppercase or strange symbols. DocumentFilter provides a low-level, edit-by-edit means of controlling or mapping user input. We will show an example of this now. In the following section, we discuss how to implement higher-level field *validation* that ensures the correctness of data after it is entered, in the same way that the formatted text field did for us earlier.

DocumentFilter

The following example, DocFilter, applies a document filter to a JTextField. Our DocumentFilter simply maps any input to uppercase. Here is the code:

```
import java.text.*;
import javax.swing.*;
import javax.swing.text.*;

public class DocFilter
{
   public static void main( String[] args ) throws Exception
   {
      JTextField field = new JTextField(30);

      ((AbstractDocument)(field.getDocument())).setDocumentFilter(
         new DocumentFilter()
      {
         public void insertString(
            FilterBypass fb, int offset, String string, AttributeSet attr)
               throws BadLocationException
            {
               fb.insertString( offset, string.toUpperCase(), attr );
            }

         public void replace(
            FilterBypass fb, int offset, int length, String string,
            AttributeSet attr) throws BadLocationException
            {
               fb.replace( offset, length, string.toUpperCase(), attr );
            }
      } );

      JFrame frame = new JFrame("User Information");
      frame.add( field );
      frame.pack();
      frame.setDefaultCloseOperation( JFrame.EXIT_ON_CLOSE );
      frame.setVisible(true);
```

```
        }
    }
```

The methods `insertString()` and `replace()` of the `DocumentFilter` are called when text is added to the document or modified. Within them, we have an opportunity to filter the text before passing it on. When we are ready to apply the text, we use the `FilterBypass` reference to pass it along. `FilterBypass` has the same set of methods, which apply the changes directly to the document. The `DocumentFilter remove()` method can also be used to intercept edits to the document that remove characters. One thing to note in our example is that not all `Documents` have a `setDocumentFilter()` method. Instead, we have to cast our document to an `AbstractDocument`. Only document implementations that extend `AbstractDocument` accept filters (unless you implement your own). This sad state of affairs is because the Document Filter API was added in Java 1.4, and it was decided that changes could not be made to the original `Document` interface.

Validating Data

Low-level input filtering prevents you from doing such things as entering a number where a character should be. In this section, we're going to talk about high-level validation, which accounts for things like February having only 28 days or a credit card number being for a Visa or MasterCard. Whereas character filtering prevents you from entering incorrect data, field validation happens after data has been entered. Normally, validation occurs when the user tries to change focus and leave the field, either by clicking the mouse or through keyboard navigation. Java 1.4 added the `InputVerifier` API, which allows you to validate the contents of a component before focus is transferred. Although we are going to talk about this in the context of text fields, an `InputVerifier` can actually be attached to any `JComponent` to validate its state in this way.

The following example creates a pair of text fields. The first allows any value to be entered, while the second accepts only numbers between 0 and 100. When both fields are happy, you can freely move between them. However, when you enter an invalid value in the second field and try to leave, the program just beeps and selects the text. The focus remains trapped until you correct the problem.

```
import javax.swing.*;

public class Validator
{
    public static void main( String[] args ) throws Exception {
        Box form = Box.createVerticalBox();
        form.add( new JLabel("Any Value") );
        form.add( new JTextField("5000") );

        form.add( new JLabel("Only 0-100") );
        JTextField rangeField = new JTextField("50");
        rangeField.setInputVerifier( new InputVerifier() {
```

```
            public boolean verify( JComponent comp ) {
                JTextField field = (JTextField)comp;
                boolean passed = false;
                try {
                    int n = Integer.parseInt(field.getText());
                    passed = ( 0 <= n && n <= 100 );
                } catch (NumberFormatException e) { }
                if ( !passed ) {
                    comp.getToolkit().beep();
                    field.selectAll();
                }
                return passed;
            }
        } );
        form.add( rangeField );

        JFrame frame = new JFrame("User Information");
        frame.add(form);
        frame.setDefaultCloseOperation( JFrame.EXIT_ON_CLOSE );
        frame.pack();
        frame.setVisible(true);
    }
}
```

We've created an anonymous inner class extending `InputVerifier` with this code. The API is very simple; at validation time, our `verify()` method is called, and we are passed a reference to the component needing checking. Here we cast to the correct type (we know what we are verifying, of course) and parse the number. If it is out of range, we beep and select the text. We then return `true` or `false` indicating whether the value passes validation.

You can use an `InputVerifier` in combination with a `JFormattedTextField` to both guide user input into the correct format and validate the semantics of what the user entered.

Say the Magic Word

Before we move on from our discussion of formatted text, we should mention that Swing includes a class just for typing passwords, called `JPasswordField`. A `JPasswordField` behaves just like a `JTextField` (it's a subclass), except every character typed is echoed as the same, obfuscating character, typically an asterisk. Figure 18-2 shows the option dialog example that was presented in Chapter 17. The example includes a `JTextField` and a `JPasswordField`.

The creation and use of `JPasswordField` is basically the same as for `JTextField`. If you find asterisks distasteful, you can tell the `JPasswordField` to use a different character using the `setEchoChar()` method.

Normally, you would use `getText()` to retrieve the text typed into the `JPasswordField`. This method, however, is deprecated; you should use `getPassword()` instead. The `getPassword()` method returns a character array rather than a `String` object. This is done because character arrays are a little less vulnerable than `Strings` to discover by memory-snooping password sniffer programs and they can be erased directly and easily. If you're not that concerned, you can simply create a new `String` from the character array. Note that methods in the Java cryptographic classes accept passwords as character arrays, not strings, so you can pass the results of a `getPassword()` call directly to methods in the cryptographic classes without ever creating a `String`.

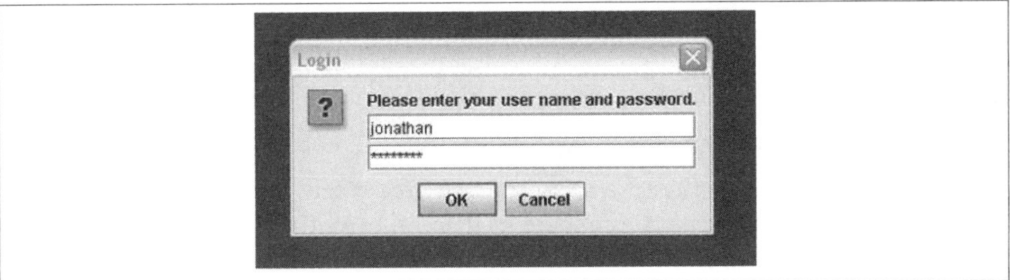

Figure 18-2. Using a JPasswordField in a dialog

Sharing a Data Model

Our next example shows how easy it is to make two or more text components share the same `Document`; Figure 18-3 shows what the application looks like.

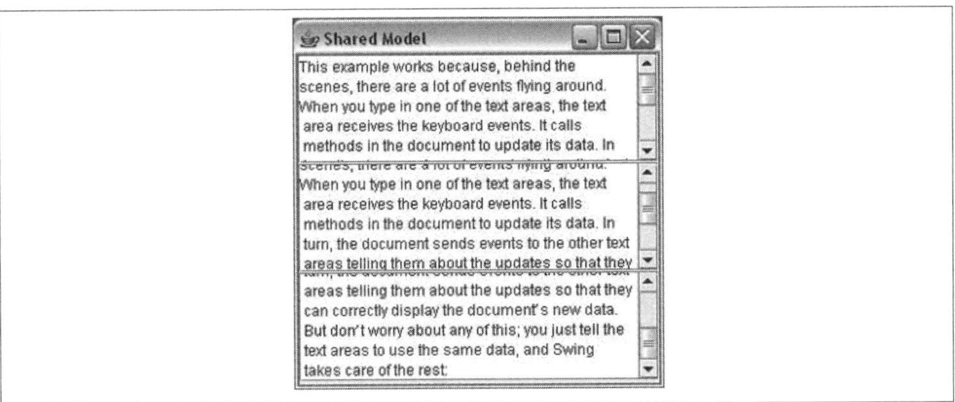

Figure 18-3. Three views of the same data model

Anything the user types into any text area is reflected in all of them. All we had to do is make all the text areas use the same data model, like this:

```
JTextArea areaFiftyOne = new JTextArea();
JTextArea areaFiftyTwo = new JTextArea();
areaFiftyTwo.setDocument(areaFiftyOne.getDocument());
JTextArea areaFiftyThree = new JTextArea();
areaFiftyThree.setDocument(areaFiftyOne.getDocument());
```

We could just as easily make seven text areas sharing the same document—or seventy. While this example may not look very useful, keep in mind that you can scroll different text areas to different places in the same document. That's one of the beauties of putting multiple views on the same data; you get to examine different parts of it. Another useful technique is viewing the same data in different ways. You could, for example, view some tabular numerical data as both a spreadsheet and a pie chart. The MVC architecture that Swing uses means that it's possible to do this in an intelligent way so that if numbers in a spreadsheet are updated, a pie chart that uses the same data is automatically updated, too.

This example works because, behind the scenes, there are a lot of events flying around. When you type in one of the text areas, the text area receives the keyboard events. It calls methods in the document to update its data. In turn, the document sends events to the other text areas telling them about the updates so that they can correctly display the document's new data. But don't worry about any of this; you just tell the text areas to use the same data, and Swing takes care of the rest:

```
//file: SharedModel.java
import java.awt.*;
import java.awt.event.*;
import javax.swing.*;

public class SharedModel {
    public static void main(String[] args) {
    JFrame frame = new JFrame("Shared Model");

    JTextArea areaFiftyOne = new JTextArea();
    JTextArea areaFiftyTwo = new JTextArea();
    areaFiftyTwo.setDocument(areaFiftyOne.getDocument());
    JTextArea areaFiftyThree = new JTextArea();
    areaFiftyThree.setDocument(areaFiftyOne.getDocument());

    frame.setLayout(new GridLayout(3, 1));
    frame.add(new JScrollPane(areaFiftyOne));
    frame.add(new JScrollPane(areaFiftyTwo));
    frame.add(new JScrollPane(areaFiftyThree));

    frame.setDefaultCloseOperation( JFrame.EXIT_ON_CLOSE );
    frame.setSize(300, 300);
    frame.setVisible(true);
  }
}
```

Setting up the display is simple. We use a `GridLayout` (discussed in the next chapter) and add three text areas to the layout. Then, all we have to do is tell the text areas to use the same `Document`.

HTML and RTF for Free

Most user interfaces will use only two subclasses of `JTextComponent`. These are the simple `JTextField` and `JTextArea` classes that we just covered. That's just the tip of the iceberg, however. Swing offers sophisticated text capabilities through two other subclasses of `JTextComponent`: `JEditorPane` and `JTextPane`.

The first of these, `JEditorPane`, can display HTML and Rich Text Format (RTF) documents out of the box and provides a plug-in framework for support of other content types. It fires one more type of event, a `HyperlinkEvent`. Subtypes of this event are fired off when the mouse enters, exits, or clicks on a hyperlink. Combined with `JEditorPane`'s HTML display capabilities, it's easy to build a simple browser. The following browser, as shown in Figure 18-4, has only about 70 lines of code.

```
//file: CanisMinor.java
import java.awt.*;
import java.awt.event.*;
import java.net.*;
import javax.swing.*;
import javax.swing.event.*;

public class CanisMinor extends JFrame {
  protected JEditorPane mEditorPane;
  protected JTextField mURLField;

  public CanisMinor(String urlString) {
    super("CanisMinor v1.0");
    createGUI(urlString);
  }

  protected void createGUI( String urlString ) {
    setLayout(new BorderLayout());

    JToolBar urlToolBar = new JToolBar();
    mURLField = new JTextField(urlString, 40);
    urlToolBar.add(new JLabel("Location "));
    urlToolBar.add(mURLField);
    add(urlToolBar, BorderLayout.NORTH);
```

```
    mEditorPane = new JEditorPane();
    mEditorPane.setEditable(false);
    add(new JScrollPane(mEditorPane), BorderLayout.CENTER);

    openURL(urlString);

    mURLField.addActionListener(new ActionListener() {
      public void actionPerformed(ActionEvent ae) {
        openURL(ae.getActionCommand());
      }
    });

    mEditorPane.addHyperlinkListener(new LinkActivator());

    setSize(500, 600);
    setDefaultCloseOperation( JFrame.EXIT_ON_CLOSE );
  }

  protected void openURL(String urlString) {
    try {
      URL url = new URL(urlString);
      mEditorPane.setPage(url);
      mURLField.setText(url.toExternalForm());
    }
    catch (Exception e) {
      System.out.println("Couldn't open " + urlString + ":" + e);
    }
  }

  class LinkActivator implements HyperlinkListener {
    public void hyperlinkUpdate(HyperlinkEvent he) {
      HyperlinkEvent.EventType type = he.getEventType();
      if (type == HyperlinkEvent.EventType.ACTIVATED)
        openURL(he.getURL().toExternalForm());
    }
  }

  public static void main(String[] args) {
    String urlString = "http://en.wikinews.org/wiki/Special:Random";
    if (args.length > 0)
       urlString = args[0];
    new CanisMinor( urlString ).setVisible( true );
  }
}
```

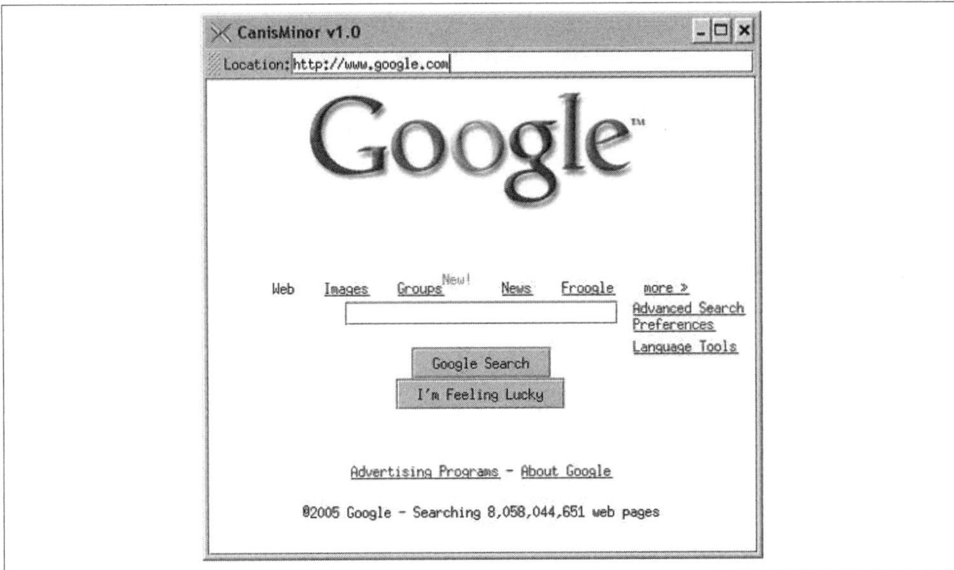

Figure 18-4. The CanisMinor application, a simple web browser

`JEditorPane` is the center of this little application. Passing a URL to `setPage()` causes the `JEditorPane` to load a new page, either from a local file or from somewhere across the Internet. To go to a new page, enter it in the text field at the top of the window and press Return. This fires an `ActionEvent` that sets the new page location of the `JEditorPane`. It can display RTF files, too (RTF is the text or nonbinary storage format for Microsoft Word documents).

Responding to hyperlinks correctly is simply a matter of responding to the `HyperlinkEvents` thrown by the `JEditorPane`. This behavior is encapsulated in the `LinkActivator` inner class. In this case, the only activity we are interested in is when the user "activates" the hyperlink by clicking on it. We respond by setting the location of the `JEditorPane` to the location given under the hyperlink. Surf away!

Behind the scenes, something called an `EditorKit` handles displaying documents for the `JEditorPane`. Different kinds of `EditorKits` can display different kinds of documents. For HTML, the `HTMLEditorKit` class (in the `javax.swing.text.html` package) handles the display. Currently, this class supports HTML 3.2. Sun says that future enhancements will move the `HTMLEditorKit` toward the HTML 4.0 standard, but even with Java 7 this area hasn't seen much progress. The `HTMLEditorKit` handles other features of HTML, including HTML forms, in the expected way—automatically submitting results when a submit button is pushed. A `FormSubmitEvent` enables programmatic involvement in form submission.

If you browse around with this example browser, you will quickly find that most modern web pages can't be rendered well by the current `HTMLEditorKit`. In their current state, `JEditorPane` and `HTMLEditorKit` are best suited for simple uses such as an HTML help system. There is an excellent commercial Java browser component from JadeLiquid called WebRenderer (*http://www.webrenderer.com*).

There's another component here that we haven't covered before—the `JToolBar`. This nifty container houses our URL text field. Initially, the `JToolBar` starts out at the top of the window. But you can pick it up by clicking on the little dotted box near its left edge, then drag it around to different parts of the window. You can place this toolbar at the top, left, right, or bottom of the window, or you can drag it outside the window entirely, where it will inhabit a window of its own. This behavior comes for free from the `JToolBar` class. We only had to create a `JToolBar` and add some components to it. The `JToolBar` is just a container, so we add it to the content pane of our window to give it an initial location.

Managing Text Yourself

Swing offers one last subclass of `JTextComponent` that can do just about anything you want: `JTextPane`. The basic text components, `JTextField` and `JTextArea`, are limited to a single font in a single style. But `JTextPane`, a subclass of `JEditorPane`, can display multiple fonts and multiple styles in the same component. It also includes support for highlighting, image embedding, and other advanced features.

We'll take a peek at `JTextPane` by creating a text pane with some styled text. Remember, the text itself is stored in an underlying data model, the `Document`. To create styled text, we simply associate a set of text attributes with different parts of the document's text. Swing includes classes and methods for manipulating sets of attributes, like specifying a bold font or a different color for the text. Attributes themselves are contained in a class called `SimpleAttributeSet`; these attribute sets are manipulated with static methods in the `StyleConstants` class. For example, to create a set of attributes that specifies the color red, you could do this:

```
SimpleAttributeSet redstyle = new SimpleAttributeSet();
StyleConstants.setForeground(redstyle, Color.red);
```

To add some red text to a document, you would just pass the text and the attributes to the document's `insertString()` method, like this:

```
document.insertString(6, "Some red text", redstyle);
```

The first argument to `insertString()` is an offset into the text. An exception is thrown if you pass in an offset that's greater than the current length of the document. If you pass `null` for the attribute set, the text is added in the `JTextPane`'s default font and style.

Our simple example creates several attribute sets and uses them to add plain and styled text to a `JTextPane`, as shown in Figure 18-5:

```
//file: Styling.java
import java.awt.*;
import java.awt.event.*;
import javax.swing.*;
import javax.swing.text.*;

public class Styling extends JFrame {
  private JTextPane textPane;

  public Styling() {
    super("Stylin' v1.0");
    setSize(300, 200);

    textPane = new JTextPane();
    textPane.setFont(new Font("Serif", Font.PLAIN, 24));

    // create some handy attribute sets
    SimpleAttributeSet red = new SimpleAttributeSet();
    StyleConstants.setForeground(red, Color.red);
    StyleConstants.setBold(red, true);
    SimpleAttributeSet blue = new SimpleAttributeSet();
    StyleConstants.setForeground(blue, Color.blue);
    SimpleAttributeSet italic = new SimpleAttributeSet();
    StyleConstants.setItalic(italic, true);
    StyleConstants.setForeground(italic, Color.orange);

    // add the text
    append("In a ", null);
    append("sky", blue);
    append(" full of people\nOnly some want to ", null);
    append("fly", italic);
    append("\nIsn't that ", null);
    append("crazy", red);
    append("?", null);

    add(new JScrollPane(textPane), BorderLayout.CENTER);
    setDefaultCloseOperation( JFrame.EXIT_ON_CLOSE );
  }

  protected void append(String s, AttributeSet attributes) {
    Document d = textPane.getDocument();
    try { d.insertString(d.getLength(), s, attributes); }
    catch (BadLocationException ble) {}
  }

  public static void main(String[] args) {
    new Styling().setVisible(true);
  }
}
```

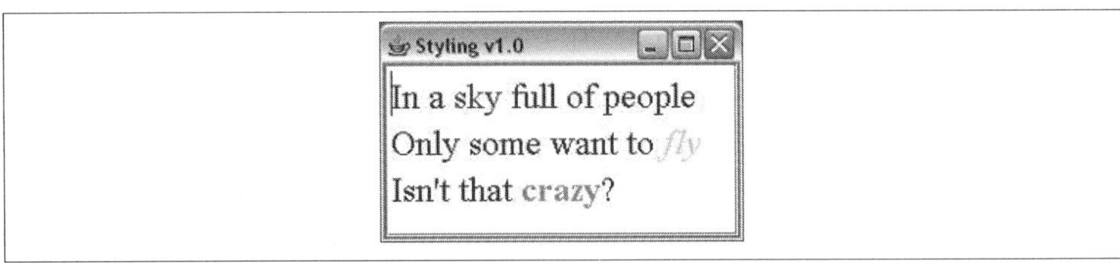

Figure 18-5. Using styled text in a JTextPane

This example creates a `JTextPane`, which is saved in a member variable. Three different attribute sets are created using combinations of text styles and foreground colors. Then, using a helper method called `append()`, text is added to the `JTextPane`.

The `append()` method tacks a text `String` on the end of the `JTextPane`'s document, using the supplied attributes. Remember that if the attributes are `null`, the text is displayed with the `JTextPane`'s default font and style.

You can go ahead and add your own text if you wish. If you place the caret inside one of the differently styled words and type, the new text comes out in the appropriate style. Pretty cool, eh? You'll also notice that `JTextPane` gives us word-wrapping behavior for free. And because we've wrapped the `JTextPane` in a `JScrollPane`, we get scrolling for free, too. Swing allows you to do some really cool stuff without breaking a sweat. Just wait—there's plenty more to come.

This simple example should give you some idea of what `JTextPane` can do. It's reasonably easy to build a simple word processor with `JTextPane`, and complex commercial-grade word processors are definitely possible.

If `JTextPane` still isn't good enough for you, or you need some finer control over character, word, and paragraph layout, you can actually draw text, carets, and highlight shapes yourself. A class in the 2D API called `TextLayout` simplifies much of this work, but it's outside the scope of this book. For coverage of `TextLayout` and other advanced text drawing topics, see *Java 2D Graphics* by Jonathan Knudsen (O'Reilly).

Focus Navigation

We've brought up the topic of focus many times in our discussion so far, and we've told you that the handling and user navigation of focus is mostly done automatically. The focus system is very powerful and can be heavily customized through the use of "focus traversal policy" objects that control keyboard navigation. For typical application behavior, you won't have to deal with this directly, but we'll explain a few features you should know about.

Swing handles keyboard focus navigation through the `KeyboardFocusManager` class. This class uses `FocusTraversalPolicy` "strategy" objects that implement the actual schemes for locating the next component to receive focus. There are two primary `FocusTraversalPolicy` types supplied with Java. The first, `DefaultFocusTraversalPolicy`, is part of the AWT package. It emulates the legacy AWT-style focus management that navigated components in the order in which they were added to their container. The next, `LayoutFocusTraversalPolicy`, is the default for all Swing applications. It examines the layout and attempts to provide the more typical navigation from left to right and top to bottom, based on component position and size.

The focus traversal policy is inherited from containers and oriented around groups of components known as "root cycles." By default, each individual window and `JInternalFrame` is its own root cycle. In other words, focus traverses all of its child components repeatedly (jumping from the last component back to the first), and won't, by default, leave the container through keyboard navigation.

The default Swing policy uses the following keys for keyboard navigation:

Forward
: Tab or Ctrl-Tab (Ctrl-Tab also works inside text areas)

Back
: Shift-Tab or Ctrl-Shift-Tab (Ctrl-Shift-Tab also works inside text areas)

You can define your own focus traversal keys for forward and back navigation, as well as for navigation across root cycles using the `setFocusTraversalKeys()` method of a container. Here is an example that adds the keystroke Ctrl-N to the list of forward key navigation for components in a Frame:

```
frame.getFocusTraversalKeys(
    KeyboardFocusManager.FORWARD_TRAVERSAL_KEYS );
AWTKeyStroke ks = AWTKeyStroke.getAWTKeyStroke(
    KeyEvent.VK_N, InputEvent.CTRL_DOWN_MASK );
Set new = new HashSet( old );
set.add( ks );
frame.setFocusTraversalKeys(
    KeyboardFocusManager.FORWARD_TRAVERSAL_KEYS,set);
```

Keys are defined by the `AWTKeyStroke` class, which encapsulates the key and input modifiers—in this case, the Control key. Constants in the `KeyboardFocusManager` specify forward, back, and up or down root cycle transfer across windows.

Finally, you can also move focus programmatically using the following methods of `KeyboardFocusManager`:

```
focusNextComponent()
focusPreviousComponent()
upFocusCycle()
downFocusCycle()
```

Trees

One of Swing's advanced components is `JTree`. Trees are good for representing hierarchical information, like the contents of a disk drive or a company's organizational chart. As with all Swing components, the data model is distinct from the visual representation. This means you can do things such as update the data model and trust that the visual component will be updated properly.

`JTree` is powerful and complex. It's big enough, in fact, that like the text tools, the classes that support `JTree` have their own package, `javax.swing.tree`. However, if you accept the default options for almost everything, `JTree` is very easy to use. Figure 18-6 shows a `JTree` running in a Swing application that we'll describe later.

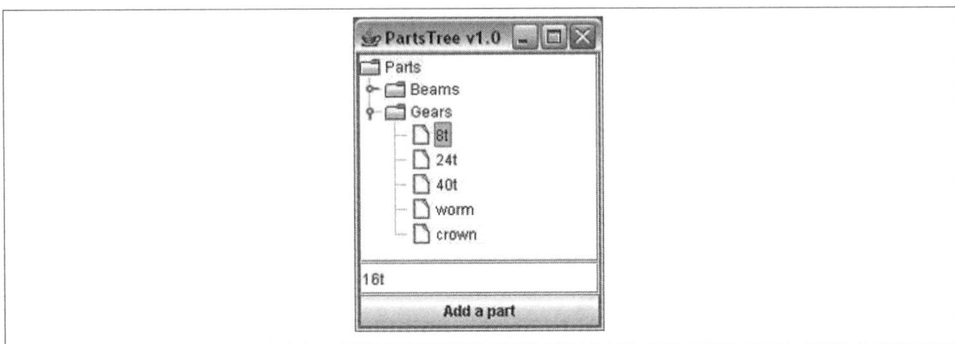

Figure 18-6. The JTree class in action

Nodes and Models

A tree's data model is made up of interconnected nodes. A node has a name—typically, a parent—and some number of children (possibly 0). In Swing, a node is represented by the `TreeNode` interface. Nodes that can be modified are represented by `MutableTreeNode`. A concrete implementation of this interface is `DefaultMutableTreeNode`. One node, called the *root* node, usually resides at the top of the hierarchy.

A tree's data model is represented by the `TreeModel` interface. Swing provides an implementation of this interface called `DefaultTreeModel`. You can create a `DefaultTreeModel` by passing a root `TreeNode` to its constructor.

You could create a `TreeModel` with just one node like this:

```
TreeNode root = new DefaultMutableTreeNode("Root node");
TreeModel model = new DefaultTreeModel(root);
```

Here's another example with a real hierarchy. The root node contains two nodes, Node 1 and Group. The Group node contains Node 2 and Node 3 as subnodes.

```
MutableTreeNode root = new DefaultMutableTreeNode("Root node");
MutableTreeNode group = new DefaultMutableTreeNode("Group");
root.insert(group, 0);
root.insert(new DefaultMutableTreeNode("Node 1"), 1);
group.insert(new DefaultMutableTreeNode("Node 2"), 0);
group.insert(new DefaultMutableTreeNode("Node 3"), 1);
```

The second parameter to the `insert()` method is the index of the node in the parent. After you organize your nodes, you can create a `TreeModel` in the same way as before:

```
TreeModel model = new DefaultTreeModel(root);
```

Save a Tree

Once you have a tree model, creating a `JTree` is simple:

```
JTree tree = new JTree(model);
```

The `JTree` behaves like a souped-up `JList`. As Figure 18-6 shows, the `JTree` automatically shows nodes with no children as a sheet of paper, while nodes that contain other nodes are shown as folders. You can expand and collapse nodes by clicking on the little knobs to the left of the folder icons. You can also expand and collapse nodes by double-clicking on them. You can select nodes; multiple selections are possible using the Shift and Control keys. And, as with a `JList`, you should put a `JTree` in a `JScrollPane` if you want it to scroll.

Tree Events

A tree fires off several flavors of events. You can find out when nodes have been expanded and collapsed, when nodes are about to be expanded or collapsed (because the user has clicked on them), and when selections occur. Three distinct event listener interfaces handle this information.

```
TreeExpansionListener
TreeWillExpandListener
TreeSelectionListener
```

Tree selections are a tricky business. You can select any combination of nodes by using the Control key and clicking on nodes. Tree selections are described by a `TreePath`, which describes how to get from the root node to the selected nodes.

The following example registers an event listener that prints out the last selected node:

```
tree.addTreeSelectionListener(new TreeSelectionListener() {
  public void valueChanged(TreeSelectionEvent e) {
    TreePath tp = e.getNewLeadSelectionPath();
    System.out.println(tp.getLastPathComponent());
  }
});
```

A Complete Example

This section contains an example that showcases the following tree techniques:

- Construction of a tree model, using `DefaultMutableTreeNode`
- Creation and display of a `JTree`
- Listening for tree selection events
- Modifying the tree's data model while the `JTree` is showing

Here's the source code for the example:

```
//file: PartsTree.java
import java.awt.*;
import java.awt.event.*;
import javax.swing.*;
import javax.swing.event.*;
import javax.swing.tree.*;

public class PartsTree {
  public static void main(String[] args) {
    // create a hierarchy of nodes
    MutableTreeNode root = new DefaultMutableTreeNode("Parts");
    MutableTreeNode beams = new DefaultMutableTreeNode("Beams");
    MutableTreeNode gears = new DefaultMutableTreeNode("Gears");
    root.insert(beams, 0);
    root.insert(gears, 1);
    beams.insert(new DefaultMutableTreeNode("1x4 black"), 0);
    beams.insert(new DefaultMutableTreeNode("1x6 black"), 1);
    beams.insert(new DefaultMutableTreeNode("1x8 black"), 2);
    beams.insert(new DefaultMutableTreeNode("1x12 black"), 3);
    gears.insert(new DefaultMutableTreeNode("8t"), 0);
    gears.insert(new DefaultMutableTreeNode("24t"), 1);
    gears.insert(new DefaultMutableTreeNode("40t"), 2);
    gears.insert(new DefaultMutableTreeNode("worm"), 3);
    gears.insert(new DefaultMutableTreeNode("crown"), 4);

    // create the JTree
    final DefaultTreeModel model = new DefaultTreeModel(root);
    final JTree tree = new JTree(model);

    // create a text field and button to modify the data model
    final JTextField nameField = new JTextField("16t");
    final JButton button = new JButton("Add a part");
    button.setEnabled(false);
    button.addActionListener(new ActionListener() {
      public void actionPerformed(ActionEvent e) {
        TreePath tp = tree.getSelectionPath();
        MutableTreeNode insertNode =
            (MutableTreeNode)tp.getLastPathComponent();
        int insertIndex = 0;
```

```
            if (insertNode.getParent() != null) {
              MutableTreeNode parent =
                  (MutableTreeNode)insertNode.getParent();
              insertIndex = parent.getIndex(insertNode) + 1;
              insertNode = parent;
            }
            MutableTreeNode node =
                new DefaultMutableTreeNode(nameField.getText());
            model.insertNodeInto(node, insertNode, insertIndex);
          }
        });
        JPanel addPanel = new JPanel(new GridLayout(2, 1));
        addPanel.add(nameField);
        addPanel.add(button);

        // listen for selections
        tree.addTreeSelectionListener(new TreeSelectionListener() {
          public void valueChanged(TreeSelectionEvent e) {
            TreePath tp = e.getNewLeadSelectionPath();
            button.setEnabled(tp != null);
          }
        });

        // create a JFrame to hold the tree
        JFrame frame = new JFrame("PartsTree v1.0");

        frame.setDefaultCloseOperation( JFrame.EXIT_ON_CLOSE );
        frame.setSize(200, 200);
        frame.add(new JScrollPane(tree));
        frame.add(addPanel, BorderLayout.SOUTH);
        frame.setVisible(true);
      }
    }
```

The example begins by creating a node hierarchy. The root node is called `Parts`. It contains two subnodes named `Beams` and `Gears`, as shown:

```
MutableTreeNode root = new DefaultMutableTreeNode("Parts");
MutableTreeNode beams = new DefaultMutableTreeNode("Beams");
MutableTreeNode gears = new DefaultMutableTreeNode("Gears");
root.insert(beams, 0);
root.insert(gears, 1);
```

The `Beams` and `Gears` nodes contain a handful of items each.

The "Add a part" button inserts a new item into the tree at the level of the current node, and just after it. You can specify the name of the new node by typing it in the text field above the button. To determine where the node should be added, the current selection is first obtained in the anonymous inner class `ActionListener`:

```
TreePath tp = tree.getSelectionPath();
MutableTreeNode insertNode =
  (MutableTreeNode)tp.getLastPathComponent();
```

The new node should be added to the parent node of the current node, so it ends up being a sibling of the current node. The only hitch here is that if the current node is the root node, it won't have a parent. If a parent does exist, we determine the index of the currently selected node, and then add the new node at the next index:

```
int insertIndex = 0;
if (insertNode.getParent() != null) {
  MutableTreeNode parent =
      (MutableTreeNode)insertNode.getParent();
  insertIndex = parent.getIndex(insertNode) + 1;
  insertNode = parent;
}
MutableTreeNode node =
    new DefaultMutableTreeNode(nameField.getText());
model.insertNodeInto(node, insertNode, insertIndex);
```

You must add the new node to the tree's data model using `insertNodeInto()`—not to the `MutableTableNode` itself. The model notifies the `JTree` that it needs to update itself.

We have another event handler in this example, one that listens for tree selection events. Basically, we want to enable our "Add a part" button only if a current selection exists:

```
tree.addTreeSelectionListener(new TreeSelectionListener() {
  public void valueChanged(TreeSelectionEvent e) {
    TreePath tp = e.getNewLeadSelectionPath();
    button.setEnabled(tp != null);
  }
});
```

When you first start this application, the button is disabled. As soon as you select something, it is enabled, and you can add nodes to the tree with abandon. If you want to see the button disabled again, you can unselect everything by holding the Control key and clicking on the current selection.

Tables

Tables present information in orderly rows and columns. This is useful for presenting financial figures or representing data from a relational database. Like trees, tables in Swing are incredibly powerful and customizable. If you go with the default options, they're also pretty easy to use.

The `JTable` class represents a visual table component. A `JTable` is based on a `TableModel`, one of a dozen or so supporting interfaces and classes in the `javax.swing.table` package.

A First Stab: Freeloading

`JTable` has one constructor that creates a default table model for you from arrays of data. You just need to supply it with the names of your column headers and a 2D array of `Objects` representing the table's data. The first index selects the table's row; the second index selects the column. The following example shows how easy it is to get going with tables using this constructor:

```
//file: DullShipTable.java
import java.awt.*;
import java.awt.event.*;
import javax.swing.*;
import javax.swing.table.*;

public class DullShipTable {
  public static void main(String[] args) {
    // create some tabular data
    String[] headings =
      new String[] {"Number", "Hot?", "Origin",
                    "Destination", "Ship Date", "Weight" };
    Object[][] data = new Object[][] {
      { "100420", Boolean.FALSE, "Des Moines IA", "Spokane WA",
          "02/06/2000", new Float(450) },
      { "202174", Boolean.TRUE, "Basking Ridge NJ", "Princeton NJ",
          "05/20/2000", new Float(1250) },
      { "450877", Boolean.TRUE, "St. Paul MN", "Austin TX",
          "03/20/2000", new Float(1745) },
      { "101891", Boolean.FALSE, "Boston MA", "Albany NY",
          "04/04/2000", new Float(88) }
    };

    // create the data model and the JTable
    JTable table = new JTable(data, headings);

    JFrame frame = new JFrame("DullShipTable v1.0");
    frame.add(new JScrollPane(table));

    frame.setDefaultCloseOperation( JFrame.EXIT_ON_CLOSE );
    frame.setSize(500, 200);
    frame.setVisible(true);
  }
}
```

This small application produces the display shown in Figure 18-7.

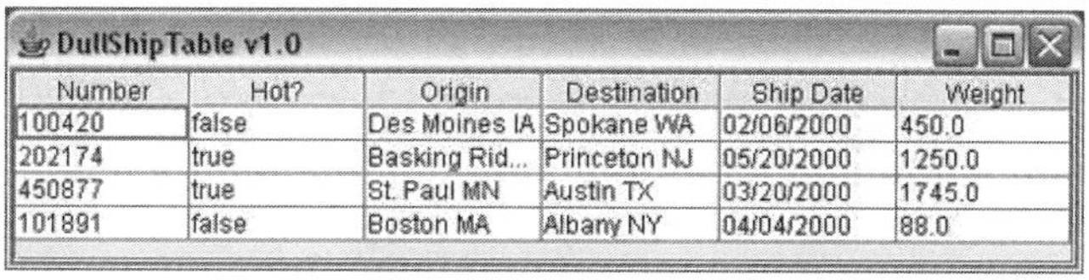

DullShipTable v1.0

Number	Hot?	Origin	Destination	Ship Date	Weight
100420	false	Des Moines IA	Spokane WA	02/06/2000	450.0
202174	true	Basking Rid...	Princeton NJ	05/20/2000	1250.0
450877	true	St. Paul MN	Austin TX	03/20/2000	1745.0
101891	false	Boston MA	Albany NY	04/04/2000	88.0

Figure 18-7. A rudimentary JTable

For very little typing, we've gotten some pretty impressive stuff. Here are a few things that come for free:

Column headings
: The `JTable` has automatically formatted the column headings differently than the table cells. It's clear that they are not part of the table's data area.

Cell overflow
: If a cell's data is too long to fit in the cell, it is automatically truncated and shown with an ellipsis (...). This is shown in the Origin cell in the second row in Figure 18-7.

Row selection
: You can click on any cell in the table to select its entire row. This behavior is controllable; you can select single cells, entire rows, entire columns, or some combination of these. To configure the `JTable`'s selection behavior, use the `setCellSelectionEnabled()`, `setColumnSelectionAllowed()`, and `setRowSelectionAllowed()` methods.

Cell editing
: Double-clicking on a cell opens it for editing; you'll get a little cursor in the cell. You can type directly into the cell to change the cell's data.

Column sizing
: If you position the mouse cursor between two column headings, you'll get a little left-right arrow cursor. Click and drag to change the size of the column to the left. Depending on how the `JTable` is configured, the other columns may also change size. The resizing behavior is controlled with the `setAutoResizeMode()` method.

Column reordering
: If you click and drag on a column heading, you can move the entire column to another part of the table.

Play with this for a while. It's fun!

Round Two: Creating a Table Model

`JTable` is a very powerful component. You get a lot of very nice behavior for free. However, the default settings are not quite what we wanted for this simple example. In particular, we intended the table entries to be read-only; they should not be editable. Also, we'd like entries in the Hot? column to be checkboxes instead of words. Finally, it would be nice if the Weight column were formatted appropriately for numbers rather than for text.

To achieve more flexibility with `JTable`, we'll write our own data model by implementing the `TableModel` interface. Fortunately, Swing makes this easy by supplying a class that does most of the work, `AbstractTableModel`. To create a table model, we'll just subclass `AbstractTableModel` and override whatever behavior we want to change.

At a minimum, all `AbstractTableModel` subclasses have to define the following three methods:

`public int getRowCount()`, `public int getColumnCount()`
: Returns the number of rows and columns in this data model

`public Object getValueAt(int` *`row`* `, int` *`column`* `)`
: Returns the value for the given cell

When the `JTable` needs data values, it calls the `getValueAt()` method in the table model. To get an idea of the total size of the table, `JTable` calls the `getRowCount()` and `getColumnCount()` methods in the table model.

A very simple table model looks like this:

```
public static class ShipTableModel extends AbstractTableModel {
  private Object[][] data = new Object[][] {
    { "100420", Boolean.FALSE, "Des Moines IA", "Spokane WA",
        "02/06/2000", new Float(450) },
    { "202174", Boolean.TRUE, "Basking Ridge NJ", "Princeton NJ",
        "05/20/2000", new Float(1250) },
    { "450877", Boolean.TRUE, "St. Paul MN", "Austin TX",
        "03/20/2000", new Float(1745) },
    { "101891", Boolean.FALSE, "Boston MA", "Albany NY",
        "04/04/2000", new Float(88) }
  };

  public int getRowCount() { return data.length; }
  public int getColumnCount() { return data[0].length; }

  public Object getValueAt(int row, int column) {
    return data[row][column];
  }
}
```

We'd like to use the same column headings that we used in the previous example. The table model supplies these through a method called `getColumnName()`. We could add column headings to our simple table model like this:

```
private String[] headings = new String[] {
  "Number", "Hot?", "Origin", "Destination", "Ship Date", "Weight"
};

public String getColumnName(int column) {
  return headings[column];
}
```

By default, `AbstractTableModel` makes all its cells noneditable, which is what we wanted. No changes need to be made for this.

The final modification is to have the Hot? column and the Weight column formatted specially. To do this, we give our table model some knowledge about the column types.

JTable automatically generates checkbox cells for Boolean column types and specially formatted number cells for Number types. To give the table model some intelligence about its column types, we override the getColumnClass() method. The JTable calls this method to determine the data type of each column. It may then represent the data in a special way. This table model returns the class of the item in the first row of its data:

```
public Class getColumnClass(int column) {
  return data[0][column].getClass();
}
```

That's really all there is to do. The following complete example illustrates how you can use your own table model to create a JTable using the techniques just described:

```
//file: ShipTable.java
import java.awt.*;
import java.awt.event.*;
import javax.swing.*;
import javax.swing.table.*;

public class ShipTable {
  public static class ShipTableModel extends AbstractTableModel {
    private String[] headings = new String[] {
      "Number", "Hot?", "Origin", "Destination", "Ship Date", "Weight"
    };
    private Object[][] data = new Object[][] {
      { "100420", Boolean.FALSE, "Des Moines IA", "Spokane WA",
          "02/06/2000", new Float(450) },
      { "202174", Boolean.TRUE, "Basking Ridge NJ", "Princeton NJ",
          "05/20/2000", new Float(1250) },
      { "450877", Boolean.TRUE, "St. Paul MN", "Austin TX",
          "03/20/2000", new Float(1745) },
      { "101891", Boolean.FALSE, "Boston MA", "Albany NY",
          "04/04/2000", new Float(88) }
    };

    public int getRowCount() { return data.length; }
    public int getColumnCount() { return data[0].length; }

    public Object getValueAt(int row, int column) {
      return data[row][column];
    }

    public String getColumnName(int column) {
      return headings[column];
    }

    public Class getColumnClass(int column) {
      return data[0][column].getClass();
    }
  }

  public static void main(String[] args)
```

```
    {
      // create the data model and the JTable
      TableModel model = new ShipTableModel();
      JTable table = new JTable(model);

      table.setAutoResizeMode(JTable.AUTO_RESIZE_OFF);

      JFrame frame = new JFrame("ShipTable v1.0");
      frame.getContentPane().add(new JScrollPane(table));
      frame.setDefaultCloseOperation( JFrame.EXIT_ON_CLOSE );
      frame.setSize(500, 200);
      frame.setVisible(true);
    }
  }
```

The running application is shown in Figure 18-8.

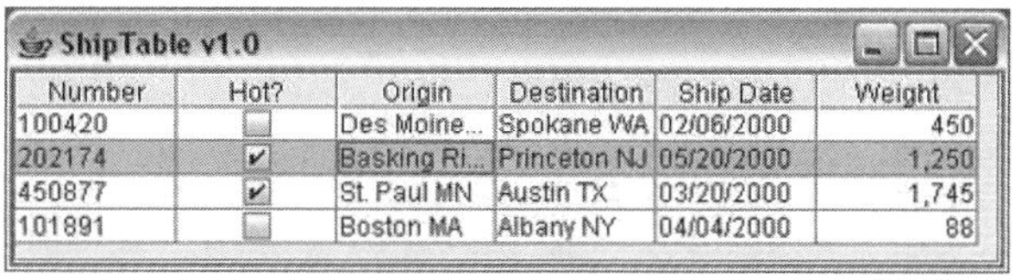

Number	Hot?	Origin	Destination	Ship Date	Weight
100420	☐	Des Moine...	Spokane WA	02/06/2000	450
202174	☑	Basking Ri...	Princeton NJ	05/20/2000	1,250
450877	☑	St. Paul MN	Austin TX	03/20/2000	1,745
101891	☐	Boston MA	Albany NY	04/04/2000	88

Figure 18-8. Customizing a table

Round Three: A Simple Spreadsheet

To illustrate just how powerful and flexible the separation of the data model from the GUI can be, we'll show a more complex model. In the following example, we'll implement a very slim but functional spreadsheet (see Figure 18-9) using almost no customization of the `JTable`. All of the data processing is in a `TableModel` called `SpreadSheetModel`.

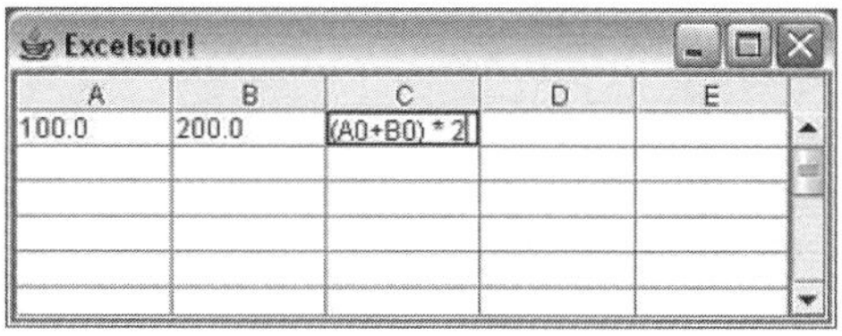

A	B	C	D	E
100.0	200.0	(A0+B0) * 2		

Figure 18-9. A simple spreadsheet

Our spreadsheet does the expected stuff—allowing you to enter numbers or mathematical expressions such as `(A1*B2)+C3` into each cell.[1] All cell editing and updating is driven by the standard `JTable`. We implement the methods necessary to set and retrieve cell data. Of course, we don't do any real validation here, so it's easy to break our table. (For example, there is no check for circular dependencies, which may be undesirable.)

As you will see, the bulk of the code in this example is in the inner class used to parse the value of the equations in the cells. If you don't find this part interesting, you might want to skip ahead. But if you have never seen an example of this kind of parsing before, we think you will find it to be very cool. Through the magic of recursion and Java's powerful `String` manipulation, it takes us only about 50 lines of code to implement a parser capable of handling basic arithmetic with arbitrarily nested parentheses.

Here's the code:

```
//file: SpreadsheetModel.java
import java.util.StringTokenizer;
import javax.swing.*;
import javax.swing.table.AbstractTableModel;
import java.awt.event.*;

public class SpreadsheetModel extends AbstractTableModel {
  Expression [][] data;

  public SpreadsheetModel( int rows, int cols ) {
    data = new Expression [rows][cols];
  }

  public void setValueAt(Object value, int row, int col) {
    data[row][col] = new Expression( (String)value );
    fireTableDataChanged();
  }

  public Object getValueAt( int row, int col ) {
    if ( data[row][col] != null )
      try { return data[row][col].eval() + ""; }
      catch ( BadExpression e ) { return "Error"; }
    return "";
  }
  public int getRowCount() { return data.length; }
  public int getColumnCount() { return data[0].length; }
  public boolean isCellEditable(int row, int col) { return true; }

  class Expression {
    String text;
    StringTokenizer tokens;
    String token;
```

1. You may need to double-click on a cell to edit it.

```
  Expression( String text ) { this.text = text.trim(); }

  float eval() throws BadExpression {
    tokens = new StringTokenizer( text, " */+-()", true );
    try { return sum(); }
    catch ( Exception e ) { throw new BadExpression(); }
  }

  private float sum() {
    float value = term();
    while( more() && match("+-") )
      if ( match("+") ) { consume(); value = value + term(); }
      else { consume(); value = value - term(); }
    return value;
  }
  private float term() {
    float value = element();
    while( more() && match( "*/") )
      if ( match("*") ) { consume(); value = value * element(); }
      else { consume(); value = value / element(); }
    return value;
  }
  private float element() {
    float value;
    if ( match( "(") ) { consume(); value = sum(); }
    else {
      String svalue;
      if ( Character.isLetter( token().charAt(0) ) ) {
      int col = findColumn( token().charAt(0) + "" );
      int row = Character.digit( token().charAt(1), 10 );
      svalue = (String)getValueAt( row, col );
    } else
      svalue = token();
      value = Float.parseFloat( svalue );
    }
    consume(); // ")" or value token
    return value;
  }
  private String token() {
    if ( token == null )
      while ( (token=tokens.nextToken()).equals(" ") );
    return token;
  }
  private void consume() { token = null; }
  private boolean match( String s ) { return s.indexOf( token() )!=-1; }
  private boolean more() { return tokens.hasMoreTokens(); }
}

class BadExpression extends Exception { }

public static void main( String [] args ) {
```

```
            JFrame frame = new JFrame("Excelsior!");
            JTable table = new JTable( new SpreadsheetModel(15, 5) );
            table.setPreferredScrollableViewportSize( table.getPreferredSize() );
            table.setCellSelectionEnabled(true);
            frame.getContentPane().add( new JScrollPane( table ) );
            frame.setDefaultCloseOperation( JFrame.EXIT_ON_CLOSE );
            frame.pack();
            frame.show();
        }
    }
```

Our model extends AbstractTableModel and overrides just a few methods. As you can see, our data is stored in a 2D array of Expression objects. The setValueAt() method of our model creates Expression objects from the strings typed by the user and stores them in the array. The getValueAt() method returns a value for a cell by calling the expression's eval() method. If the user enters some invalid text in a cell, a BadExpression exception is thrown, and the word *error* is placed in the cell as a value. The only other methods of TableModel we must override are getRowCount(), getColumnCount(), and isCellEditable() in order to determine the dimensions of the spreadsheet and to allow the user to edit the fields. That's it! The helper method findColumn() is inherited from the AbstractTableModel.

Now on to the good stuff. We'll employ our old friend StringTokenizer to read the expression string as separate values and the mathematical symbols (+-*/()) one by one. These tokens are then processed by the three parser methods: sum(), term(), and element(). The methods call one another generally from the top down, but it might be easier to read them in reverse to see what's happening.

At the bottom level, element() reads individual numeric values or cell names (e.g., 5.0 or B2). Above that, the term() method operates on the values supplied by element() and applies any multiplication or division operations. And at the top, sum() operates on the values that are returned by term() and applies addition or subtraction to them. If the element() method encounters parentheses, it makes a call to sum() to handle the nested expression. Eventually, the nested sum returns (possibly after further recursion), and the parenthesized expression is reduced to a single value, which is returned by element(). The magic of recursion has untangled the nesting for us. The other small piece of magic here is in the ordering of the three parser methods. Having sum() call term() and term() call element() imposes the precedence of operators; that is, "atomic" values are parsed first (at the bottom), then multiplication, and finally, addition or subtraction.

The grammar parsing relies on four simple helper methods that make the code more manageable: token(), consume(), match(), and more(). token() calls the string tokenizer to get the next value, and match() compares it with a specified value. consume() is used to move to the next token, and more() indicates when the final token has been processed.

Sorting and Filtering

Java 6 introduced easy-to-use sorting and filtering for `JTables`. The following example demonstrates use of the default `TableRowSorter` and a simple regular expression filter.

```
//file: SortFilterTable.java
import javax.swing.*;
import javax.swing.table.*;
import javax.swing.event.*;

import java.awt.BorderLayout;
import java.util.regex.PatternSyntaxException;

public class SortFilterTable extends JFrame {

    private JTable table;
    private JTextField filterField;

    public SortFilterTable() {

        super("Table Sorting & Filtering");
        setSize(500, 200);
        setDefaultCloseOperation( JFrame.EXIT_ON_CLOSE );

        // Create a simple table model
        TableModel model = new AbstractTableModel() {
            private String[] columns = {"Name", "Pet", "Children"};

            private Object[][] people = {
                    {"Dan Leuck", "chameleon", 1},
                    {"Pat Niemeyer", "sugar glider", 2},
                    {"John Doe", "dog", 3},
                    {"Jane Doe", "panda", 2}
                    };

            public int getColumnCount() { return columns.length; }

            public int getRowCount() { return people.length; }

            public Object getValueAt(int row, int col) {
                return people[row][col];
            }

            public Class getColumnClass(int col) {
                return getValueAt(0, col).getClass();
            }

        };

        table = new JTable(model);
        table.setAutoCreateRowSorter(true);
        table.setFillsViewportHeight(true);
```

```
        // Create the filter area
        JPanel filterPanel = new JPanel(new BorderLayout());
        JLabel filterLabel = new JLabel("Filter ",
            SwingConstants.TRAILING);
        filterPanel.add(filterLabel, BorderLayout.WEST);
        filterField = new JTextField();
        filterLabel.setLabelFor(filterField);
        filterPanel.add(filterField);

        // Apply the filter when the filter text field changes
        filterField.getDocument().addDocumentListener(
            new DocumentListener() {
                public void changedUpdate(DocumentEvent e) {
                    filter();
                }
                public void insertUpdate(DocumentEvent e) {
                    filter();
                }
                public void removeUpdate(DocumentEvent e) {
                    filter();
                }
            });

        filterPanel.setBorder(BorderFactory.createEmptyBorder(2,
            2, 2, 2));

        add(filterPanel, BorderLayout.NORTH);

        add(new JScrollPane(table));
    }

    // Filter on the first column
    private void filter() {
        RowFilter<TableModel, Object> filter = null;

        // Update if the filter expression is valid
        try {
            // Apply the regular expression to columns 0 and 1
            filter = RowFilter.regexFilter(filterField.getText(),
                0, 1);
        } catch (PatternSyntaxException e) {
            return;
        }
        ((TableRowSorter)table.getRowSorter()).setRowFilter(
            filter);
    }

    public static void main(String[] args) {
        new SortFilterTable().setVisible(true);
    }
}
```

Try clicking on the column headers to sort. We are using the default sorting behavior, which utilizes the natural sort order of cell values (i.e., alphabetical for strings, value for numbers, etc.). You can easily override the sorting behavior by implementing your own comparator and setting it on the `TableRowSorter`:

```
TableRowSorter<TableModel> reverseSorter
    = new TableRowSorter<TableModel>(table.getModel());
reverseSorter.setComparator(0, new Comparator<String>() {
    public int compare(String a, String b) {
        return -a.compareTo(b);
    }
});
table.setRowSorter(reverseSorter);
```

If you require more advanced sorting, you can subclass `TableRowSorter` or its superclass, `DefaultRowSorter`.

Entering text in the field above the table will apply a filter using the text as a regular expression over the values in the first two columns (indices 0 and 1). For example, try entering "Doe". The table will now display only John Doe and Jane Doe.

Printing JTables

Swing makes the printing of JTables a snap. Think we're kidding? If you accept the basic default behavior, all that is required to pop up a print dialog box is the following:

```
myJTable.print();
```

That's it. The default behavior scales the printed table to the width of the page. This is called "fit width" mode. You can control that setting using the `PrintMode` enumeration of `JTable`, which has values of `NORMAL` and `FIT_WIDTH`:

```
table.print( JTable.PrintMode.NORMAL );
```

The "normal" (ironically, nondefault) mode will allow the table to split across multiple pages horizontally to print without sizing down. In both cases, the table rows may span multiple pages vertically.

Other forms of the `JTable print()` method allow you to add header and footer text to the page and to take greater control of the printing process and attributes. We'll talk a little more about printing when we cover 2D drawing in Chapter 20.

Desktops

At this point, you might be thinking that there's nothing more that Swing could possibly do, but it just keeps getting better. If you've ever wished that you could have windows within windows in Java, Swing makes it possible with `JDesktopPane` and `JInternalFrame`. Figure 18-10 shows how this appears.

You get a lot of behavior for free from `JInternalFrame`. Internal frames can be moved by clicking and dragging the titlebar. They can be resized by clicking and dragging on the window's borders. Internal frames can be iconified, which means reducing them to a small icon representation on the desktop. Internal frames may also be made to fit the entire size of the desktop (maximized). To you, the programmer, the internal frame is just a kind of special container. You can put your application's data inside an internal frame just as with any other type of container.

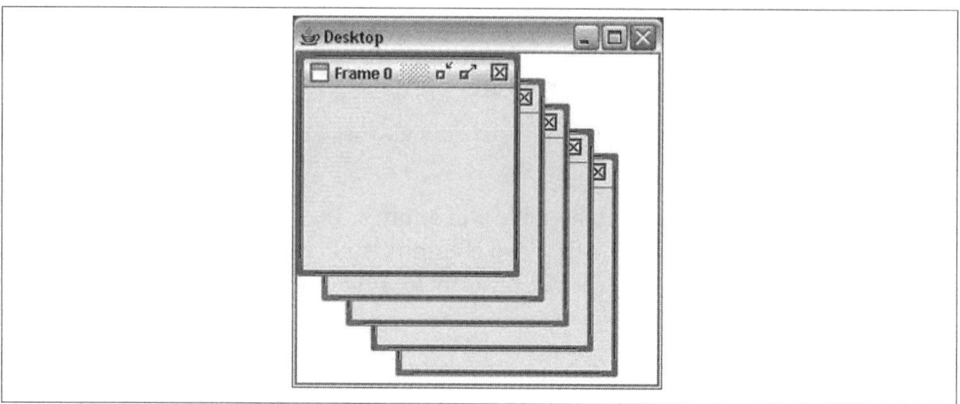

Figure 18-10. Using internal frames on a JDesktopPane

The following brief example shows how to create the windows shown in Figure 18-10:

```
//file: Desktop.java
import java.awt.*;
import java.awt.event.*;
import javax.swing.*;
import javax.swing.border.*;

public class Desktop {
  public static void main(String[] args) {
    JFrame frame = new JFrame("Desktop");

    JDesktopPane desktop = new JDesktopPane();
    for (int i = 0; i < 5; i++) {
      JInternalFrame internal =
          new JInternalFrame("Frame " + i, true, true, true, true);
      internal.setSize(180, 180);
      internal.setLocation(i * 20, i * 20);
      internal.setVisible(true);
      desktop.add(internal);
    }

    frame.setSize(300, 300);
    frame.setDefaultCloseOperation( JFrame.EXIT_ON_CLOSE );
    frame.setContentPane(desktop);
```

```
        frame.setVisible(true);
      }
    }
```

All we've done here is to create a `JDesktopPane` and add internal frames to it. When each `JInternalFrame` is constructed, we specify a window title. The four `true` values passed in the constructor specify that the new window should be resizable, closable, maximizable, and iconifiable.

`JInternalFrames` fire off their own set of events. However, `InternalFrameEvent` and `InternalFrameListener` are just like `WindowEvent` and `WindowListener` with the names changed. If you want to hear about a `JInternalFrame` closing, just register an `InternalFrameListener` and define the `internalFrameClosing()` method. This is just like defining the `windowClosing()` method for a `JFrame`.

Pluggable Look-and-Feel

We mentioned before that Swing components can easily change their appearance, like master spies or thespians. Generally, different kinds of components within an application have coordinated appearances that are similar in some way. For example, they probably use the same font and the same basic color scheme. The collection of appearances and common behavior of GUI components is called a *look-and-feel* (L&F).

Part of the job of designing a GUI for an operating system is designing the L&F. Mac OS, therefore, has its own distinctive L&F, as does Windows. Java offers several different L&F schemes for Swing components. If you're adept at graphic design, you can write your own L&F schemes and easily convince Swing to use them. This chameleon-like ability to change appearance is called *pluggable look-and-feel*, sometimes abbreviated PLAF (don't pronounce that out loud if others are eating).

Seeing is believing. Here's an example that creates a handful of Swing components. Menu items allow you to change the L&F dynamically while the application is running:

```
//file: QuickChange.java
import java.awt.*;
import java.awt.event.*;
import javax.swing.*;

public class QuickChange extends JFrame {

  public QuickChange() {
    super("QuickChange v1.0");
    createGUI();
  }

  protected void createGUI() {
    setSize(300, 200);
```

```
    // create a simple File menu
    JMenu file = new JMenu("File", true);
    JMenuItem quit = new JMenuItem("Quit");
    file.add(quit);
    quit.addActionListener(new ActionListener() {
      public void actionPerformed(ActionEvent e) { System.exit(0); }
    });

    // create the Look & Feel menu
    JMenu lnf = new JMenu("Look & Feel", true);
    ButtonGroup buttonGroup = new ButtonGroup();
    final UIManager.LookAndFeelInfo[] info =
        UIManager.getInstalledLookAndFeels();
    for (int i = 0; i < info.length; i++) {
      JRadioButtonMenuItem item = new
          JRadioButtonMenuItem(info[i].getName(), i == 0);
      final String className = info[i].getClassName();
      item.addActionListener(new ActionListener() {
        public void actionPerformed(ActionEvent ae) {
          try { UIManager.setLookAndFeel(className); }
          catch (Exception e) { System.out.println(e); }
          SwingUtilities.updateComponentTreeUI(QuickChange.this);
        }
      });
      buttonGroup.add(item);
      lnf.add(item);
    }

    // add the menu bar
    JMenuBar mb = new JMenuBar();
    mb.add(file);
    mb.add(lnf);
    setJMenuBar(mb);

    // add some components
    JPanel jp = new JPanel();
    jp.add(new JCheckBox("JCheckBox"));
    String[] names =
      new String[] { "Tosca", "Cavaradossi", "Scarpia",
                     "Angelotti", "Spoletta", "Sciarrone",
                     "Carceriere", "Il sagrestano", "Un pastore" };
    jp.add(new JComboBox(names));
    jp.add(new JButton("JButton"));
    jp.add(new JLabel("JLabel"));
    jp.add(new JTextField("JTextField"));
    JPanel main = new JPanel(new GridLayout(1, 2));
    main.add(jp);
    main.add(new JScrollPane(new JList(names)));
    setContentPane(main);
    setDefaultCloseOperation( JFrame.EXIT_ON_CLOSE );
  }
```

```
    public static void main(String[] args) {
      new QuickChange().setVisible(true);
    }
  }
```

The interesting part of this application is creating a menu of the available L&Fs. First, we ask a class called `UIManager` to tell us all about the available L&Fs on our computer:

```
final UIManager.LookAndFeelInfo[] info =
        UIManager.getInstalledLookAndFeels();
```

Information about L&Fs is returned as instances of `UIManager.LookAndFeelInfo`. Despite the long name, there's not much to this class; it just associates a name, such as Metal, and the name of the class that implements the L&F, such as `javax.swing.plaf.metal.MetalLookAndFeel`. In the `QuickChange` example, we create a menu item from each L&F name. If the menu item is selected, we tell the `UIManager` to use the selected L&F class. To make sure all the components are redrawn with the new L&F, we call `updateComponentTreeUI()`, a static method in the `SwingUtilities` class.

The JDK includes several L&Fs: Windows, OS X, Motif, the original Metal L&F, the highly customizable Synth, and the newest edition, Nimbus. Windows, OS X, and Motif are recreations of their corresponding native desktop environments. If you're running Swing on Mac OS X, the default L&F is an implementation of Aqua, the UI design for all new Mac applications. Unfortunately, you cannot use this L&F on any other platforms because of licensing issues (the Windows L&F has similar restrictions).

The Metal L&F and its Ocean theme are the default on some platforms, but at this point they appear dated compared to modern windowing systems. The newest edition, Nimbus, is a far superior alternative. Its aethetics are on par with modern windowing systems and its use of scaleable vector graphics allows it to shine on high-density displays at various sizes. Nimbus is actually a highly evolved subclass of the Synth L&F.

Synth accommodates the new trend in skinnable user interfaces. Many applications now allow users to customize the L&F very easily, using only images and simple preferences files to create new appearances. Skinnability is not the same as a full-blown pluggable L&F, but it lets you do a lot without any programming required. Synth acts like an ordinary L&F, but can be customized through the use of images and XML description files to create new looks. For example, the borders of components (such as the shiny metal look of the Metal L&F) can be described by providing an example image and then specifying the offsets of the interior "corners" as well as the method to use (stretch or tile) to cover larger areas. Synth then uses the image to paint the borders of whatever components you specify. Synth can do quite a lot and even allows you to specify Java objects to be involved in painting, so you can resort to programming again if your L&F gets too complex.

Creating Custom Components

In this chapter and the previous one, we've worked with different user interface objects. We've used Swing's impressive repertoire of components as building blocks and extended their functionality, but we haven't actually created any new components. In this section, we create an entirely new component from scratch, a *dial*.

Until now, our examples have been fairly self-contained; they generally know everything about what to do and don't rely on additional parts to do processing. Our menu example created a `DinnerFrame` class that had a menu of dinner options, but it included all the processing needed to handle the user's selections. If we wanted to process the selections differently, we'd have to modify the class. A true component separates the detection of user input from the handling of those choices. It lets the user take some action and then informs other interested parties by emitting events.

Generating Events

Because we want our new classes to be components, they should communicate the way components communicate: by generating event objects and sending those events to listeners. So far, we've written a lot of code that listened for events but haven't seen an example that generated its own custom events.

Generating events sounds like it might be difficult, but it isn't. You can either create new kinds of events by subclassing `java.util.EventObject`, or use one of the standard event types. In either case, you just need to allow registration of listeners for your events and provide a means to deliver events to those listeners. Swing's `JComponent` class provides a protected member variable called `listenerList`, which you can use to keep track of event listeners. It's an instance of `EventListenerList`; basically it acts like the maître d' at a restaurant, keeping track of all event listeners, sorted by type.

Often, you won't need to worry about creating a custom event type. `JComponent` has methods that support firing of generic `PropertyChangeEvents` whenever one of a component's properties changes. The example we'll look at next uses this infrastructure to fire `PropertyChangeEvents` whenever a value changes.

A Dial Component

The standard Swing classes don't have a component that's similar to an old-fashioned dial—for example, the volume control on your radio. (The `JSlider` fills this role, of course.) In this section, we implement a `Dial` class. The dial has a value that can be adjusted by clicking and dragging to "twist" the dial (see Figure 18-11). As the value of the dial changes, `DialEvents` are fired off by the component. The dial can be used just like any other Java component. We even have a custom `DialListener` interface that matches the `DialEvent` class.

Figure 18-11. The Dial component

Here's the `Dial` code:

```
//file: Dial.java
import java.awt.*;
import java.awt.event.*;
import java.util.*;
import javax.swing.*;

public class Dial extends JComponent {
  int minValue, nvalue, maxValue, radius;

  public Dial() { this(0, 100, 0); }

  public Dial(int minValue, int maxValue, int value) {
    setMinimum( minValue );
    setMaximum( maxValue );
    setValue( value );
    setForeground( Color.lightGray );

    addMouseListener(new MouseAdapter() {
      public void mousePressed(MouseEvent e) { spin(e); }
    });
    addMouseMotionListener(new MouseMotionAdapter() {
      public void mouseDragged(MouseEvent e) { spin(e); }
    });
  }

  protected void spin( MouseEvent e ) {
    int y = e.getY();
    int x = e.getX();
    double th = Math.atan((1.0 * y - radius) / (x - radius));
    int value=(int)(th / (2 * Math.PI) * (maxValue - minValue));
    if (x < radius)
      setValue( value + (maxValue-minValue) / 2 + minValue);
    else if (y < radius)
      setValue( value + maxValue );
    else
      setValue( value + minValue);
  }
```

```
public void paintComponent(Graphics g) {
  Graphics2D g2 = (Graphics2D)g;
  int tick = 10;
  radius = Math.min( getSize().width,getSize().height )/2 - tick;
  g2.setPaint( getForeground().darker() );
  g2.drawLine( radius * 2 + tick / 2, radius,
     radius * 2 + tick, radius);
  g2.setStroke( new BasicStroke(2) );
  draw3DCircle( g2, 0, 0, radius, true );
  int knobRadius = radius / 7;
  double th = nvalue * (2 * Math.PI) / (maxValue - minValue);
  int x = (int)(Math.cos(th) * (radius - knobRadius * 3)),
  y = (int)(Math.sin(th) * (radius - knobRadius * 3));
  g2.setStroke(new BasicStroke(1));
  draw3DCircle(g2, x + radius - knobRadius,
     y + radius - knobRadius, knobRadius, false );
}

private void draw3DCircle(
    Graphics g, int x, int y, int radius, boolean raised)
{
  Color foreground = getForeground();
  Color light = foreground.brighter();
  Color dark = foreground.darker();
  g.setColor(foreground);
  g.fillOval(x, y, radius * 2, radius * 2);
  g.setColor(raised ? light : dark);
  g.drawArc(x, y, radius * 2, radius * 2, 45, 180);
  g.setColor(raised ? dark : light);
  g.drawArc(x, y, radius * 2, radius * 2, 225, 180);
}

public Dimension getPreferredSize() {
  return new Dimension(100, 100);
}

public void setValue( int value ) {
  this.nvalue = value - minValue;
  repaint();
  fireEvent();
}
public int getValue()  { return nvalue+minValue; }
public void setMinimum(int minValue)  { this.minValue = minValue; }
public int getMinimum()  { return minValue; }
public void setMaximum(int maxValue)  { this.maxValue = maxValue; }
public int getMaximum()  { return maxValue; }

public void addDialListener(DialListener listener) {
  listenerList.add( DialListener.class, listener );
}
public void removeDialListener(DialListener listener) {
  listenerList.remove( DialListener.class, listener );
```

```
    }

    void fireEvent() {
      Object[] listeners = listenerList.getListenerList();
      for ( int i = 0; i < listeners.length; i += 2 )
        if ( listeners[i] == DialListener.class )
          ((DialListener)listeners[i + 1]).dialAdjusted(
            new DialEvent(this, getValue()) );
    }

    public static void main(String[] args) {
      JFrame frame = new JFrame("Dial v1.0");
      final JLabel statusLabel = new JLabel("Welcome to Dial v1.0");
      final Dial dial = new Dial();
      frame.add(dial, BorderLayout.CENTER);
      frame.add(statusLabel, BorderLayout.SOUTH);

      dial.addDialListener(new DialListener() {
        public void dialAdjusted(DialEvent e) {
          statusLabel.setText("Value is " + e.getValue());
        }
      });

      frame.setDefaultCloseOperation( JFrame.EXIT_ON_CLOSE );
      frame.setSize( 150, 150 );
      frame.setVisible( true );
    }
  }
```

Here's `DialEvent`, a simple subclass of `java.util.EventObject`:

```
//file: DialEvent.java
import java.awt.*;

public class DialEvent extends java.util.EventObject {
    int value;

    DialEvent( Dial source, int value ) {
        super( source );
        this.value = value;
    }

    public int getValue() {
        return value;
    }
}
```

Finally, here's the code for `DialListener`:

```
//file: DialListener.java
public interface DialListener extends java.util.EventListener {
    void dialAdjusted( DialEvent e );
}
```

Let's start from the top of the `Dial` class. We'll focus on the structure and leave you to figure out the trigonometry on your own.

`Dial`'s `main()` method demonstrates how to use the dial to build a user interface. It creates a `Dial` and adds it to a `JFrame`. Then `main()` registers a dial listener on the dial. Whenever a `DialEvent` is received, the value of the dial is examined and displayed in a `JLabel` at the bottom of the frame window.

The constructor for the `Dial` class stores the dial's minimum, maximum, and current values; a default constructor provides a minimum of `0`, a maximum of `100`, and a current value of `0`. The constructor sets the foreground color of the dial and registers listeners for mouse events. If the mouse is pressed or dragged, `Dial`'s `spin()` method is called to update the dial's value. `spin()` performs some basic trigonometry to figure out what the new value of the dial should be.

`paintComponent()` and `draw3DCircle()` do a lot of trigonometry to figure out how to display the dial. `draw3DCircle()` is a private helper method that draws a circle that appears either raised or depressed; we use this to make the dial look three-dimensional.

The next group of methods provides ways to retrieve or change the dial's current setting and the minimum and maximum values. The important thing to notice here is the pattern of get and set methods for all of the important values used by the `Dial`. We will talk more about this in Chapter 22. Also, notice that the `setValue()` method does two important things: it repaints the component to reflect the new value and fires the `DialEvent` signifying the change.

The final group of methods in the `Dial` class provides the plumbing necessary for our event firing. `addDialListener()` and `removeDialListener()` take care of maintaining the listener list. Using the `listenerList` member variable we inherited from `JComponent` makes this an easy task. The `fireEvent()` method retrieves the registered listeners for this component. It sends a `DialEvent` to any registered `DialListeners`.

Model and View Separation

The `Dial` example is overly simplified. All Swing components, as we've discussed, keep their data model and view separate. In the `Dial` component, we've combined these elements in a single class, which limits its reusability. To have `Dial` implement the MVC paradigm, we would have developed a dial data model and something called a UI-delegate that handled displaying the component and responding to user events. For a full treatment of this subject, see the `JogShuttle` example in O'Reilly's *Java Swing*.

In Chapter 19, we'll take what we know about components and containers and put them together using layout managers to create complex GUIs.

CHAPTER 19
Layout Managers

A *layout manager* arranges the child components of a container, as shown in Figure 19-1. It positions and sets the size of components within the container's display area according to a particular layout scheme. The layout manager's job is to fit the components into the available area while maintaining some spatial relationships among them. AWT and Swing come with several standard layout managers that will collectively handle most situations; you can also make your own layout managers if you have special requirements.

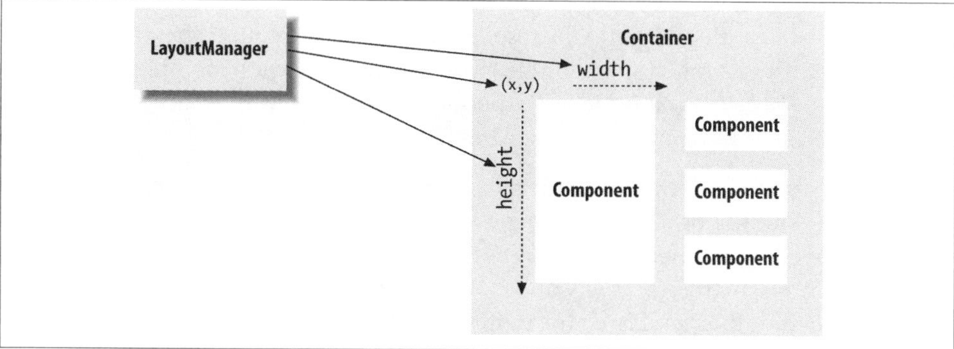

Figure 19-1. A layout manager at work

Every container has a default layout manager. When you make a new container, it comes with a `LayoutManager` object of the appropriate type. You can install a new layout manager at any time by using the `setLayout()` method. For example, we can set the layout manager of a Swing container to a type called `BorderLayout` like so:

```
myContainer.setLayout( new BorderLayout() );
```

Notice that although we have created a `BorderLayout`, we haven't bothered to save a reference to it. This is typical; after installing a layout manager, it usually does its work behind the scenes by interacting with the container. You rarely call the layout manager's methods directly, so you don't usually need a reference (a notable exception is `CardLayout`). However, you do need to know what the layout manager is going to do with your components as you work with them.

The `LayoutManager` is consulted whenever a container's `doLayout()` method is called to reorganize the contents. It does its job by calling the `setLocation()` or `setBounds()` methods of the individual child components to arrange them in the container's display area. A container is laid out the first time it is displayed and thereafter whenever the container's `revalidate()` method is called. Containers that are a subclass of the `Window` class (`Frame`, `JFrame`, and `JWindow`) are automatically validated whenever they are packed or resized. Calling `pack()` sets the window's size as small as possible while granting all its components their preferred sizes.

Every component provides three important pieces of information used by the layout manager in placing and sizing it: a minimum size, a maximum size, and a preferred size. These sizes are reported by the `getMinimumSize()`, `getMaximumSize()`, and `getPreferredSize()` methods of `Component`, respectively. For example, a plain `JButton` object can normally be changed to any size. However, the button's designer can provide a preferred size for a good-looking button. The layout manager might use this size when there are no other constraints, or it might ignore it, depending on its scheme. If we give the button a label, the button may need a new minimum size to display itself properly. The layout manager should generally respect the button's minimum size and guarantee that it has at least that much space. Similarly, a particular component might not be able to display itself properly if it is too large (perhaps it has to scale up an image); it can use `getMaximumSize()` to report the largest size it considers acceptable.

The preferred size of a `Container` object has the same meaning as for any other type of component. However, because a `Container` may hold its own components and want to arrange them in its own layout, its preferred size is a function of its layout manager. The layout manager is, therefore, involved in both sides of the issue. It asks the components in its container for their preferred (or minimum) sizes in order to arrange them. Based on those values, it calculates the preferred size for its own container (which can then be communicated to the container's parent and so on).

When a layout manager is called to arrange its components, it is working within a fixed area. It usually begins by looking at its container's dimensions and the preferred or minimum sizes of the child components. It then doles out screen area and sets the sizes of components according to its scheme and specific constraints.

You can set the minimum, preferred, and maximum sizes for a component with the `setMinimumSize()`, `setMaximumSize()`, and `setPreferredSize()` methods. Take care when setting these properties because generally those values should be calculated based on the real conditions of the component, not just fixed at a static value that looks good in one particular case. You can override the `getMinimumSize()`, `getMaximumSize()`, and `getPreferredSize()` methods of your own components to allow them to calculate those values, but you should do this only if you are specializing the component and it has new needs. In general, if you find yourself fighting with a layout manager because it's changing the size of one of your components, you are probably using the wrong kind of layout manager or not composing your user interface properly. Often it's easier to use a number of `JPanel` objects in a given display, each one with its own `LayoutManager`. Try breaking down the problem: place related components in their own `JPanel` and then arrange the panels in the container. When that becomes unwieldy, use a constraint-based layout manager such as `GridBagLayout` or `SpringLayout`, which we'll discuss later in this chapter.

FlowLayout

`FlowLayout` is a simple layout manager that tries to arrange components at their preferred sizes, from left to right and top to bottom in the container. A `FlowLayout` can have a specified row justification of `LEFT`, `CENTER`, or `RIGHT` and a fixed horizontal and vertical padding. By default, a flow layout uses `CENTER` justification, meaning that all components are centered within the area allotted to them. `FlowLayout` is the default for `JPanel`s.

The following example adds five buttons to the content pane of a `JFrame` using the default `FlowLayout`:

```
//file: Flow.java
import java.awt.*;
import java.awt.event.*;
import javax.swing.*;

public class Flow extends JPanel {

  public Flow() {
    // FlowLayout is default layout manager for a JPanel
    add(new JButton("One"));
    add(new JButton("Two"));
    add(new JButton("Three"));
    add(new JButton("Four"));
    add(new JButton("Five"));
  }

  public static void main(String[] args) {
    JFrame frame = new JFrame("Flow");
    frame.setDefaultCloseOperation( JFrame.EXIT_ON_CLOSE );

    frame.setSize(400, 75);
    frame.setLocation(200, 200);
    Flow flow = new Flow();
```

```
        frame.setContentPane(flow);
        frame.setVisible(true);
    }
}
```

The result is shown in Figure 19-2.

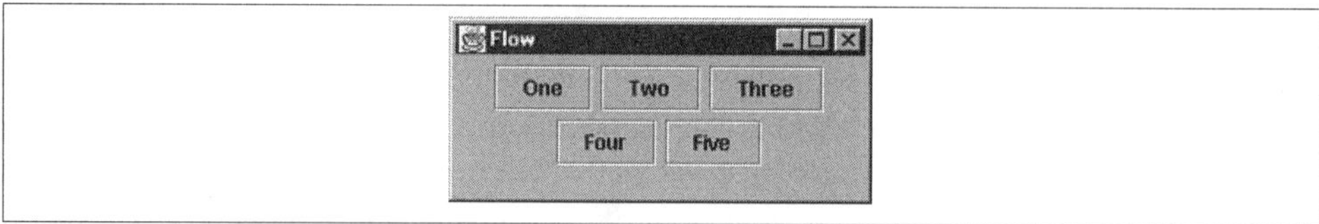

Figure 19-2. A flow layout

Try resizing the window. If it is made narrow enough, some of the buttons will spill over to a second or third row.

GridLayout

`GridLayout` arranges components into regularly spaced rows and columns. The components are arbitrarily resized to fit the grid; their minimum and preferred sizes are consequently ignored. `GridLayout` is most useful for arranging identically sized objects—perhaps a set of `JPanels`, each using a different layout manager.

`GridLayout` takes the number of rows and columns in its constructor. If you subsequently give it too many objects to manage, it adds extra columns to make the objects fit. You can also set the number of rows or columns to `0`, which means that you don't care how many elements the layout manager packs in that dimension. For example, `GridLayout(2,0)` requests a layout with two rows and an unlimited number of columns; if you put 10 components into this layout, you'll get 2 rows of 5 columns each.[1]

The following example sets a `GridLayout` with three rows and two columns as its layout manager:

```
//file: Grid.java
import java.awt.*;
import java.awt.event.*;
import javax.swing.*;

public class Grid extends JPanel {

  public Grid() {
    setLayout(new GridLayout(3, 2));
```

1. Calling `new GridLayout(0, 0)` causes a runtime exception; either the rows or columns parameter must be greater than zero.

```
      add(new JButton("One"));
      add(new JButton("Two"));
      add(new JButton("Three"));
      add(new JButton("Four"));
      add(new JButton("Five"));
    }

    public static void main(String[] args) {
      JFrame frame = new JFrame("Grid");
      frame.setDefaultCloseOperation( JFrame.EXIT_ON_CLOSE );
      frame.setSize(200, 200);
      frame.setLocation(200, 200);
      frame.setContentPane(new Grid());
      frame.setVisible(true);
    }
  }
```

The results are shown in Figure 19-3.

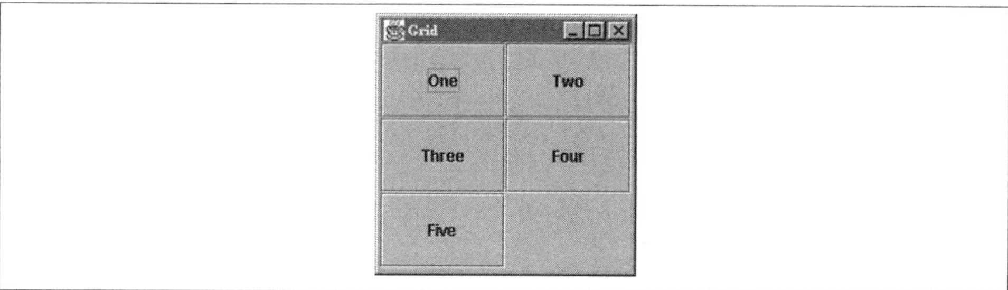

Figure 19-3. A grid layout

The five buttons are laid out in order from left to right, top to bottom, with one empty spot.

BorderLayout

`BorderLayout` is a little more interesting. It tries to arrange objects in one of five geographical locations, represented by constants in the `BorderLayout` class: `NORTH`, `SOUTH`, `EAST`, `WEST`, and `CENTER`, optionally with some padding between. `BorderLayout` is the default layout for the content panes of `JWindow` and `JFrame` objects. Because each component is associated with a direction, `BorderLayout` can manage at most five components; it squashes or stretches those components to fit its constraints. As we'll see in the second example, this means that you often want to have `BorderLayout` manage sets of components in their own panels.

When we add a component to a container with a border layout, we need to specify both the component and the position at which to add it. To do so, we use an overloaded version of the container's `add()` method that takes an additional argument as a *constraint*. The constraint specifies the name of a position within the `BorderLayout`.

The following application sets a `BorderLayout` and adds our five buttons again, named for their locations:

```
//file: Border1.java
import java.awt.*;
import java.awt.event.*;
import javax.swing.*;

public class Border1 extends JPanel {

  public Border1() {
    setLayout(new BorderLayout());
    add(new JButton("North"), BorderLayout.NORTH );
    add(new JButton("South"), BorderLayout.SOUTH );
    add(new JButton("East"), BorderLayout.EAST );
    add(new JButton("West"), BorderLayout.WEST );
    add(new JButton("Center"), BorderLayout.CENTER );
  }

  public static void main(String[] args) {
    JFrame frame = new JFrame("Border1");
    frame.setDefaultCloseOperation( JFrame.EXIT_ON_CLOSE );
    frame.setSize(300, 300);
    frame.setLocation(200, 200);
    frame.setContentPane(new Border1());
    frame.setVisible(true);
  }
}
```

The result is shown in Figure 19-4.

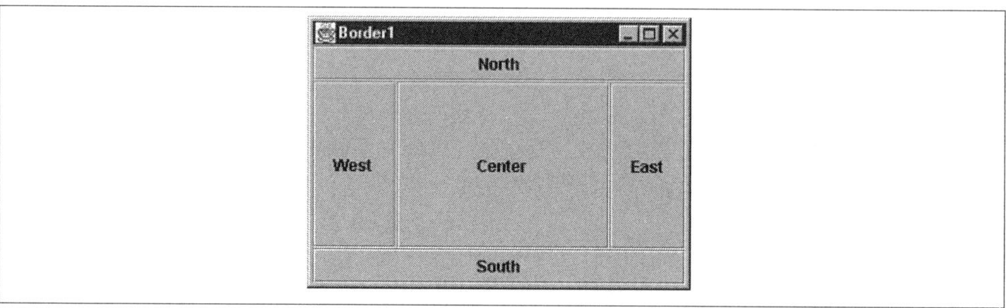

Figure 19-4. A border layout

So, how exactly is the area divided up? Well, the objects at `NORTH` and `SOUTH` get their preferred height and fill the display area horizontally. `EAST` and `WEST` components, on the other hand, get their preferred width and fill the remaining area between `NORTH` and

SOUTH vertically. Finally, the CENTER object takes all the rest of the space. As you can see in Figure 19-4, our buttons get distorted into interesting shapes.

What if we don't want BorderLayout messing with the sizes of our components? One option would be to put each button in its own JPanel. The default layout for a JPanel is FlowLayout, which respects the preferred size of components. The preferred sizes of the panels are effectively the preferred sizes of the buttons, but if the panels are stretched, they won't pull their buttons with them. The following application illustrates this approach:

```
//file: Border2.java
import java.awt.*;
import java.awt.event.*;
import javax.swing.*;

public class Border2 extends JPanel {

  public Border2() {
    setLayout(new BorderLayout());
    JPanel p = new JPanel();
    p.add(new JButton("North"));
    add(p, BorderLayout.NORTH);
    p = new JPanel();
    p.add(new JButton("South"));
    add(p, BorderLayout.SOUTH);
    p = new JPanel();
    p.add(new JButton("East"));
    add(p, BorderLayout.EAST);
    p = new JPanel();
    p.add(new JButton("West"));
    add(p, BorderLayout.WEST);
    p = new JPanel();
    p.add(new JButton("Center"));
    add(p, BorderLayout.CENTER);
  }

  public static void main(String[] args) {
    JFrame frame = new JFrame("Border2");
    frame.setDefaultCloseOperation( JFrame.EXIT_ON_CLOSE );
    frame.setSize(225, 150);
    frame.setLocation(200, 200);
    frame.setContentPane(new Border2());
    frame.setVisible(true);
  }
}
```

The result is shown in Figure 19-5.

In the example, we create a number of panels, put our buttons inside the panels, and put the panels into the frame window, which has the BorderLayout manager. Now, the JPanel for the CENTER button soaks up the extra space that comes from the

BorderLayout. Each JPanel's FlowLayout centers the button in the panel and uses the button's preferred size. In this case, it's all a bit awkward. We'll see how we could accomplish this more directly using GridBagLayout shortly.

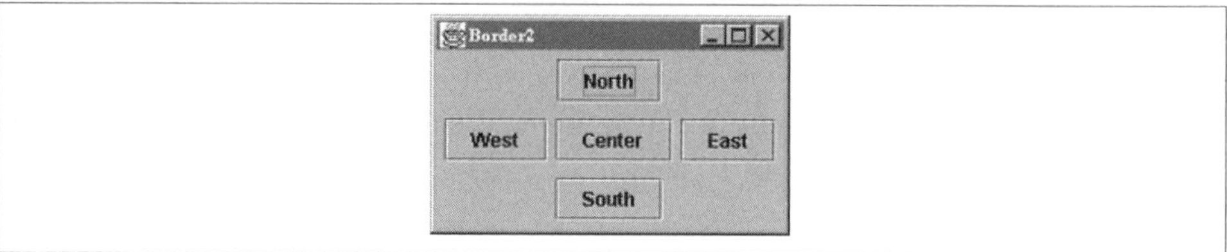

Figure 19-5. Another border layout

BoxLayout

Most layout managers are part of the java.awt package and were defined back when Java was first released. Swing adds a couple of new general-purpose layout managers in the javax.swing package; one is BoxLayout. This layout manager is useful for creating simple toolbars or vertical button bars. It lays out components in a single row or column. It is similar to FlowLayout except that it does not wrap components into new rows.

Although you can use BoxLayout directly, Swing includes a handy container called Box that takes care of the details for you. Every Box uses BoxLayout, but you don't really have to worry about it; the Box class includes some very useful methods for laying out components.

You can create a horizontal or vertical box using Box's static methods.

```
Container horizontalBox = Box.createHorizontalBox();
Container verticalBox = Box.createVerticalBox();
```

Once the Box is created, you can add() components as usual:

```
Container box = Box.createHorizontalBox();
box.add(new JButton("In the"));
```

Box includes several other static methods that create special invisible components that can be used to guide the BoxLayout. The first of these is *glue*; glue is really space between components in the Box. When the Box is resized, glue expands or contracts as more or less space is available. The other special invisible component type is a *strut*. Like glue, a strut represents space between components, but it doesn't resize.

The following example creates a horizontal Box (shown in Figure 19-6) that includes both glue and struts. Play around by resizing the window to see the effect of the glue and the struts.

```
//file: Boxer.java
import java.awt.*;
```

```
import java.awt.event.*;
import javax.swing.*;

public class Boxer extends JPanel {
  public static void main(String[] args) {
    JFrame frame = new JFrame("Boxer");
    frame.setDefaultCloseOperation( JFrame.EXIT_ON_CLOSE );
    frame.setSize(250, 250);
    frame.setLocation(200, 200);
    Container box = Box.createHorizontalBox();
    box.add(Box.createHorizontalGlue());
    box.add(new JButton("In the"));
    box.add(Box.createHorizontalGlue());
    box.add(new JButton("clearing"));
    box.add(Box.createHorizontalStrut(10));
    box.add(new JButton("stands"));
    box.add(Box.createHorizontalStrut(10));
    box.add(new JButton("a"));
    box.add(Box.createHorizontalGlue());
    box.add(new JButton("boxer"));
    box.add(Box.createHorizontalGlue());
    frame.getContentPane().add(box, BorderLayout.CENTER);
    frame.pack();
    frame.setVisible(true);
  }
}
```

Figure 19-6. Using the Box class

Components are added sequentially for display from left to right or top to bottom with optional glue or strut constraints placed between them. By default, components simply line up one after another with no space between them. Glue acts like a spring, allowing its adjacent components to move to occupy the space evenly. A strut imposes a fixed space between adjacent components.

CardLayout

`CardLayout` is a special layout manager for creating the effect of a "stack" of components. Instead of arranging all of the container's components, it displays only one at a time. You might use this kind of layout to implement a custom-tabbed panel of some kind. In fact, there's probably little reason to use this layout given the Swing `JTabbedPane` component described in Chapter 17. We include it here mainly for completeness.

To add a component to a CardLayout, use a two-argument version of the container's add() method; the extra argument is an arbitrary string that serves as the card's name:

```
add("netconfigscreen", myComponent);
```

To bring a particular card to the top of the stack, call the CardLayout's show() method with two arguments: the parent Container and the name of the card you want to show. There are also methods—first(), last(), next(), and previous()—for working with the stack of cards. These are all CardLayout instance methods. To invoke them, you need a reference to the CardLayout object itself, not to the container it manages. Each method takes a single argument: the parent Container. Here's an example:

```
//file: Card.java
import java.awt.*;
import java.awt.event.*;
import javax.swing.*;

public class Card extends JPanel {
  CardLayout cards = new CardLayout();

  public Card() {
    setLayout(cards);
    ActionListener listener = new ActionListener() {
      public void actionPerformed(ActionEvent e) {
        cards.next(Card.this);
      }
    };
    JButton button;
    button = new JButton("one");
    button.addActionListener(listener);
    add(button, "one");
    button = new JButton("two");
    button.addActionListener(listener);
    add(button, "two");
    button = new JButton("three");
    button.addActionListener(listener);
    add(button, "three");
  }

  public static void main(String[] args) {
    JFrame frame = new JFrame("Card");
    frame.setDefaultCloseOperation( JFrame.EXIT_ON_CLOSE );
    frame.setSize(200, 200);
    frame.setLocation(200, 200);
    frame.setContentPane(new Card());
    frame.setVisible(true);
  }
}
```

We add three buttons to the layout and cycle through them as they are pressed. An anonymous inner class serves as an action listener for each button; it simply calls

CardLayout's next() method whenever a button is pressed. Card.this refers to the Card object, which is the container in this case. In a more realistic example, we would build a group of panels, each of which might implement some part of a complex user interface and add those panels to the layout. Each panel would have its own layout manager. The panels would be resized to fill the entire area available (i.e., the area of the Container they are in), and their individual layout managers would arrange their internal components.

GridBagLayout

GridBagLayout is a very flexible layout manager that allows you to position components relative to one another using constraints. With GridBagLayout (and a fair amount of effort), you can create almost any imaginable layout. Components are arranged at logical coordinates on an abstract grid. We call them "logical" coordinates because they designate positions in the space of rows and columns formed by the set of components. Rows and columns of the grid stretch to different sizes, based on the sizes and constraints of the components they hold.

A row or column in a GridBagLayout expands to accommodate the dimensions and constraints of the largest component it contains. Individual components may also be told to span more than one row or column. Components that aren't as large as their grid cell can be anchored (positioned to one side) within their cell. They can also be set to fill or expand their size in either dimension. Extra area in the grid rows and columns can be parceled out according to the weight constraints of the components. In this way, you can control how various components will grow and stretch when a window is resized.

GridBagLayout is much easier to use in a graphical WYSIWYG GUI builder environment. That's because working with GridBag is kind of like messing with the old rabbit-ears antennae on your television. It's not particularly difficult to get the results that you want through trial and error, but writing out hard and fast rules for how to go about it is difficult. In short, GridBagLayout is complex and has some quirks. It is also simply a bit ugly both in model and implementation. Remember that you can do a lot with nested panels and by composing simpler layout managers within one another. If you look back through this chapter, you'll see some examples of composite layouts; it's up to you to determine how far you should go before making the break from simpler layout managers to a more complex all-in-one layout manager like GridBagLayout.

The GridBagConstraints Class

Having stated that GridBagLayout is complex and a bit ugly, we're going to contradict ourselves a little and say that its API is surprisingly simple. There is only one constructor with no arguments—GridBagLayout()—and there aren't a lot of fancy methods to control how the display works.

The appearance of a grid bag layout is controlled by sets of `GridBagConstraints`, and that's where things get hairy. Each component that is managed by a `GridBagLayout` is associated with a `GridBagConstraints` object. `GridBagConstraints` holds the following variables, which we'll describe in detail shortly:

`int gridx`
`int gridy`
: Controls the position of the component on the layout's grid

`int weightx`
`int weighty`
: Controls how additional space in the row or column is allotted to the component

`int fill`
: Controls whether the component expands to fill the allotted space

`int gridheight`
`int gridwidth`
: Controls the number of rows or columns the component spans

`int anchor`
: Controls the position of the component if there is extra room within the allotted space

`int ipadx`
`int ipady`
: Controls padding between the component and the borders of its area

`Insets insets`
: Controls padding between the component and neighboring components

To make a set of constraints for a component or components, create a new instance of `GridBagConstraints` and set these public variables to the appropriate values. (There is also a large constructor that takes all 11 arguments.)

The easiest way to associate a set of constraints with a component is to use the version of `add()` that takes both a component object and a layout object as arguments. This puts the component in the container and associates the `GridBagConstraints` object with it:

```
Container content = getContentPane();
JComponent component = new JLabel("constrain me, please...");
GridBagConstraints constraints = new GridBagConstraints();
constraints.gridx = x;
constraints.gridy = y;
...
content.add(component, constraints);
```

You can also add a component to a GridBagLayout using the single argument add() method and then calling the layout's setConstraints() method directly to pass it the GridBagConstraints object for that component:

```
add(component);
...
myGridBagLayout.setConstraints(component, constraints);
```

In either case, the set of constraints is copied when it is applied to the component. It's the individual constraints that apply to the component, not the GridBagConstraints object. Therefore, you're free to create a single set of GridBagConstraints, modify it as needed, and apply it as needed to different objects. You might want to create a helper method that sets the constraints appropriately, then adds the component with its constraints to the layout. That's the approach we'll take in our examples; our helper method is called addGB(), and it takes a component plus a pair of coordinates as arguments. These coordinates become the gridx and gridy values for the constraints. We could expand upon this later and overload addGB() to take more parameters for other constraints that we often change from component to component.

Grid Coordinates

One of the biggest surprises in the GridBagLayout is that there's no way to specify the size of the grid. There doesn't have to be. The grid size is determined implicitly by the constraints of all the objects; the layout manager picks dimensions large enough so that everything fits. Thus, if you put one component in a layout and set its gridx and gridy constraints each to 25, the layout manager creates a virtual 25 × 25 grid, with rows and columns numbered from 0 to 24. If you then add a second component with a gridx of 30 and a gridy of 13, the virtual grid's dimensions change to 30 × 25. You don't have to worry about setting up an appropriate number of rows and columns. The layout manager does it automatically as you add components.

With this knowledge, we're ready to create some simple displays. We'll start by arranging a group of components in a cross shape. We maintain explicit x and y local variables, setting them as we add the components to our grid. This is partly for clarity, but it can be a handy technique when you want to add a number of components in a row or column. You can simply increment gridx or gridy before adding each component. This is a simple and problem-free way to achieve relative placement. (Later, we'll describe GridBagConstraints's RELATIVE constant, which performs relative placement automatically.) The following code shows the first layout (see Figure 19-7):

```
//file: GridBag1.java
import java.awt.*;
import java.awt.event.*;
import javax.swing.*;

public class GridBag1 extends JPanel {
  GridBagConstraints constraints = new GridBagConstraints();
```

```
  public GridBag1() {
    setLayout(new GridBagLayout());
    int x, y;  // for clarity
    addGB(new JButton("North"),  x = 1, y = 0);
    addGB(new JButton("West"),   x = 0, y = 1);
    addGB(new JButton("Center"), x = 1, y = 1);
    addGB(new JButton("East"),   x = 2, y = 1);
    addGB(new JButton("South"),  x = 1, y = 2);
  }

  void addGB(Component component, int x, int y) {
    constraints.gridx = x;
    constraints.gridy = y;
    add(component, constraints);
  }

  public static void main(String[] args) {
    JFrame frame = new JFrame("GridBag1");
    frame.setDefaultCloseOperation( JFrame.EXIT_ON_CLOSE );
    frame.setSize(225, 150);
    frame.setLocation(200, 200);
    frame.setContentPane(new GridBag1());
    frame.setVisible(true);
  }
}
```

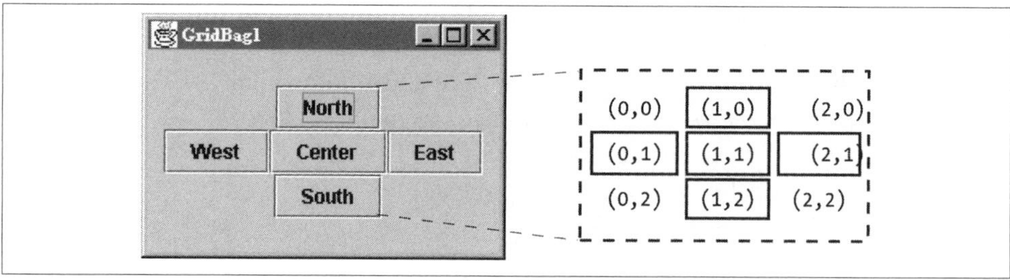

Figure 19-7. A simple GridBagLayout

The buttons in this example are "clumped" together in the center of their display area. Each button is displayed at its preferred size, without stretching to fill the available space. This is how the layout manager behaves when the "weight" constraints are left unset. We'll talk more about weights in the next two sections.

The fill Constraint

Let's make the buttons expand to fill the entire `JFrame` window. To do so, we must take two steps: we must set the `fill` constraint for each button to the value `BOTH`, and we must set the `weightx` and `weighty` to nonzero values, as shown in this example:

```
//file: GridBag2.java
import java.awt.*;
import java.awt.event.*;
import javax.swing.*;

public class GridBag2 extends JPanel {
  GridBagConstraints constraints = new GridBagConstraints();

  public GridBag2() {
    setLayout(new GridBagLayout());
    constraints.weightx = 1.0;
    constraints.weighty = 1.0;
    constraints.fill = GridBagConstraints.BOTH;
    int x, y;  // for clarity
    addGB(new JButton("North"),  x = 1, y = 0);
    addGB(new JButton("West"),   x = 0, y = 1);
    addGB(new JButton("Center"), x = 1, y = 1);
    addGB(new JButton("East"),   x = 2, y = 1);
    addGB(new JButton("South"),  x = 1, y = 2);
  }

  void addGB(Component component, int x, int y) {
    constraints.gridx = x;
    constraints.gridy = y;
    add(component, constraints);
  }

  public static void main(String[] args) {
    JFrame frame = new JFrame("GridBag2");
    frame.setDefaultCloseOperation( JFrame.EXIT_ON_CLOSE );
    frame.setSize(225, 150);
    frame.setLocation(200, 200);
    frame.setContentPane(new GridBag2());
    frame.setVisible(true);
  }
}
```

Figure 19-8 shows the resulting layout.

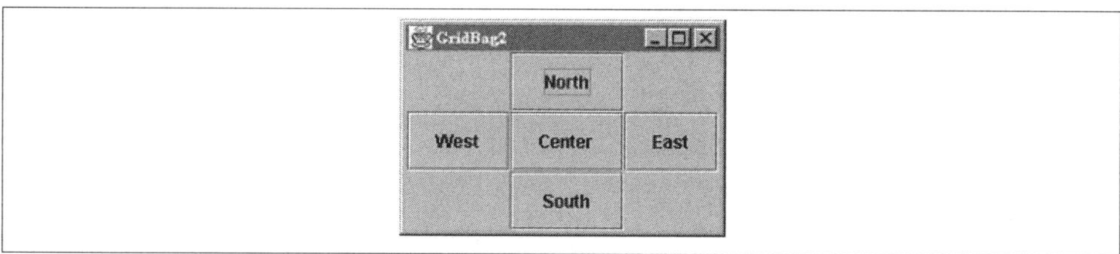

Figure 19-8. Making buttons fill the available space

BOTH is one of the constants of the GridBagConstraints class; it tells the component to fill the available space in both directions. Here are the constants you can use to set the fill field:

HORIZONTAL
: Fill the available horizontal space.

VERTICAL
: Fill the available vertical space.

BOTH
: Fill the available space in both directions.

NONE
: Don't fill the available space; display the component at its preferred size.

We set the weight constraints to 1.0; in this example, it doesn't matter what they are, provided each component has the same nonzero weight. Filling doesn't occur if the component's weight in the direction you're filling is 0, which is the default value.

Spanning Rows and Columns

One of the most important features of GridBaglayout is that it lets you create arrangements in which components span two or more rows or columns. To do so, set the gridwidth and gridheight variables of the GridBagConstraints. The following example creates such a display; button one spans two columns vertically and button four spans two horizontally. Figure 19-9 shows the resulting layout.

```
//file: GridBag3.java
import java.awt.*;
import java.awt.event.*;
import javax.swing.*;

public class GridBag3 extends JPanel {
  GridBagConstraints constraints = new GridBagConstraints();

  public GridBag3() {
    setLayout(new GridBagLayout());
    constraints.weightx = 1.0;
    constraints.weighty = 1.0;
    constraints.fill = GridBagConstraints.BOTH;
    int x, y;  // for clarity
    constraints.gridheight = 2; // span two rows
    addGB(new JButton("one"),   x = 0, y = 0);
    constraints.gridheight = 1; // set it back
    addGB(new JButton("two"),   x = 1, y = 0);
    addGB(new JButton("three"), x = 2, y = 0);
    constraints.gridwidth = 2; // span two columns
    addGB(new JButton("four"),  x = 1, y = 1);
    constraints.gridwidth = 1; // set it back
```

```
  }

  void addGB(Component component, int x, int y) {
    constraints.gridx = x;
    constraints.gridy = y;
    add(component, constraints);
  }

  public static void main(String[] args) {
    JFrame frame = new JFrame("GridBag3");
    frame.setDefaultCloseOperation( JFrame.EXIT_ON_CLOSE );
    frame.setSize(200, 200);
    frame.setLocation(200, 200);
    frame.setContentPane(new GridBag3());
    frame.setVisible(true);
  }
}
```

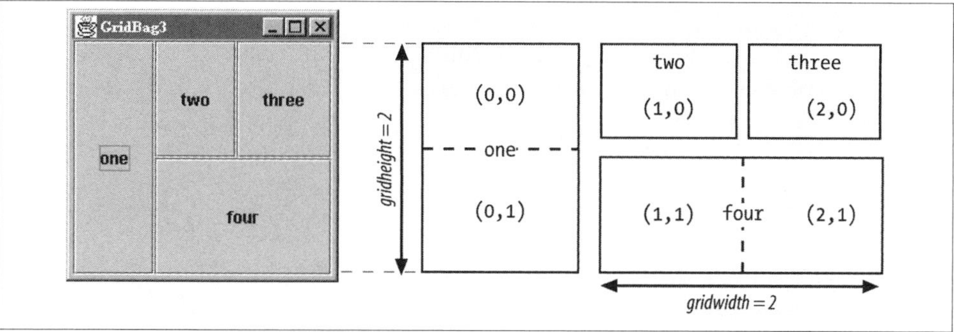

Figure 19-9. Making components span rows and columns

The size of each element is controlled by the `gridwidth` and `gridheight` values of its constraints. For button one, we set `gridheight` to 2; therefore, it is two cells high. Its `gridx` and `gridy` positions are both `0`, so it occupies cell (0,0) and the cell directly below it, (0,1). Likewise, button four has a `gridwidth` of 2 and a `gridheight` of `1`, so it occupies two cells horizontally. We place this button in cell (1,1), so it occupies that cell and its neighbor, (2,1).

In this example, we set the `fill` to `BOTH` and `weightx` and `weighty` to `1` for all components. By doing so, we tell each button to occupy all the space available and give them all equal weighting. Strictly speaking, this isn't necessary. However, it makes it easier to see exactly how much space each button occupies.

Weighting

The `weightx` and `weighty` variables of a `GridBagConstraints` object determine how "extra" space in the container is distributed among the columns or rows in the layout.

As long as you keep things simple, the effect these variables have is fairly intuitive: the larger the weight, the greater the amount of space allocated to the component, relative to its peers. Figure 19-10 shows what happens if we vary the `weightx` constraint from `0.1` to `1.0` as we place three buttons in a row.

Here's the code:

```
//file: GridBag4.java
import java.awt.*;
import java.awt.event.*;
import javax.swing.*;

public class GridBag4 extends JPanel {
  GridBagConstraints constraints = new GridBagConstraints();

  public GridBag4() {
    setLayout(new GridBagLayout());
    constraints.fill = GridBagConstraints.BOTH;
    constraints.weighty = 1.0;
    int x, y; // for clarity
    constraints.weightx = 0.1;
    addGB(new JButton("one"),   x = 0, y = 0);
    constraints.weightx = 0.5;
    addGB(new JButton("two"),   ++x,   y);
    constraints.weightx = 1.0;
    addGB(new JButton("three"), ++x,   y);
  }

  void addGB(Component component, int x, int y) {
    constraints.gridx = x;
    constraints.gridy = y;
    add(component, constraints);
  }

  public static void main(String[] args) {
    JFrame frame = new JFrame("GridBag4");
    frame.setDefaultCloseOperation( JFrame.EXIT_ON_CLOSE );
    frame.setSize(300, 100);
    frame.setLocation(200, 200);
    frame.setContentPane(new GridBag4());
    frame.setVisible(true);
  }
}
```

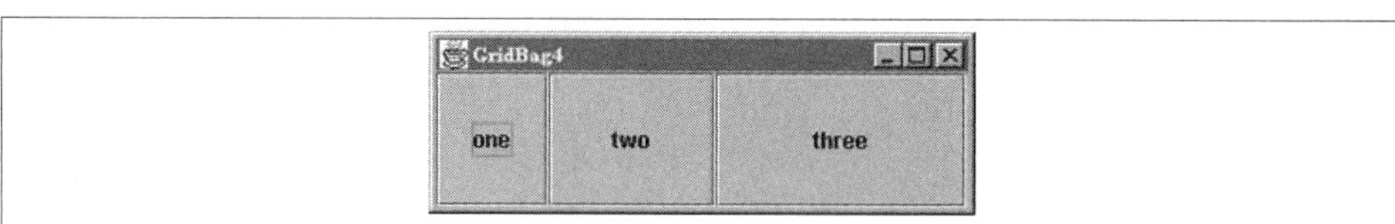

Figure 19-10. Using weight to control component size

The specific values of the weights are not meaningful; it is only their relative proportions that matter. After the preferred sizes of the components (including padding and insets—see the next section) are determined, any extra space is doled out in proportion to the component's weights. For example, if each of our three components had the same weight, each would receive a third of the extra space. To make this more obvious, you may prefer to express the weights for a row or column as fractions totaling 1.0—for example: 0.25, 0.25, 0.50. Components with a weight of `0` receive no extra space.

The situation is a bit more complicated when there are multiple rows or columns and when there is even the possibility of components spanning more than one cell. In the general case, `GridBagLayout` calculates an effective overall weight for each row and column and then distributes the extra space to them proportionally. Note that the previous single-row example is just a special case where the columns each have one component. The gory details of the calculations follow.

Calculating the weights of rows and columns

For a given row or column ("rank"), `GridBagLayout` first considers the weights of all the components contained strictly within that rank—ignoring those that span more than one cell. The greatest individual weight becomes the overall weight of the row or column. Intuitively, this means that `GridBagLayout` is trying to accommodate the needs of the weightiest component in that rank.

Next, `GridBagLayout` considers the components that occupy more than one cell and things get a little weird. `GridbagLayout` wants to evaluate them to see whether they affect the determination of the largest weight in a row or column. However, because these components occupy more than one cell, `GridBagLayout` divides their weight among the ranks (rows or columns) that they span.

`GridBagLayout` tries to calculate an effective weight for the portion of the component that occupies each row or column. It does this by trying to divide the weight of the component among the ranks in the same proportions that the length (or height) of the component will be shared by the ranks. But how does it know what the proportions will be before the whole grid is determined? That's what it's trying to calculate, after all. It simply guesses based on the row or column weights already determined. `GridBagLayout` uses the weights determined by the first round of calculations to split up the weight of the component over the ranks that it occupies. For each row or column, it then considers that fraction of the weight to be the component's weight for that rank. That weight then contends for the "heaviest weight" in the row or column, possibly changing the overall weight of that row or column, as we described earlier.

Anchoring

If a component is smaller than the space available for it, it is centered by default. But centering isn't the only possibility. The `anchor` constraint tells a grid bag layout how to position a component within its cell in the grid. Possible values are `GridBagConstraints.CENTER`, `NORTH`, `NORTHEAST`, `EAST`, `SOUTHEAST`, `SOUTH`, `SOUTHWEST`, `WEST`, and `NORTHWEST`. For example, an anchor of `GridBagConstraints.NORTH` centers a component at the top of its display area; `SOUTHEAST` places a component at the bottom-right corner of its area.

Padding and Insets

Another way to control the behavior of a component in a grid bag layout is to use padding and insets. Padding is determined by the `ipadx` and `ipady` fields of `GridBagConstraints`. They specify horizontal and vertical "growth factors" for the component. In Figure 19-11, the West button is larger because we have set the `ipadx` and `ipady` values of its constraints to `25`. Therefore, the layout manager gets the button's preferred size and adds 25 pixels in each direction to determine the button's actual size. The sizes of the other buttons are unchanged because their padding is set to `0` (the default), but their spacing is different. The West button is unnaturally tall, which means that the middle row of the layout must be taller than the others.

```
//file: GridBag5.java
import java.awt.*;
import java.awt.event.*;
import javax.swing.*;

public class GridBag5 extends JPanel {
  GridBagConstraints constraints = new GridBagConstraints();

  public GridBag5() {
    setLayout(new GridBagLayout
           ());
    int x, y;  // for clarity
    addGB(new JButton("North"),  x = 1, y = 0);
    constraints.ipadx = 25;  // add padding
    constraints.ipady = 25;
    addGB(new JButton("West"),   x = 0, y = 1);
    constraints.ipadx = 0;   // remove padding
    constraints.ipady = 0;
    addGB(new JButton("Center"), x = 1, y = 1);
    addGB(new JButton("East"),   x = 2, y = 1);
    addGB(new JButton("South"),  x = 1, y = 2);
  }

  void addGB(Component component, int x, int y) {
    constraints.gridx = x;
```

```
      constraints.gridy = y;
      add(component, constraints);
    }

    public static void main(String[] args) {
      JFrame frame = new JFrame("GridBag5");
      frame.setDefaultCloseOperation( JFrame.EXIT_ON_CLOSE );

      frame.setSize(250, 250);
      frame.setLocation(200, 200);
      frame.setContentPane(new GridBag5());
      frame.setVisible(true);
    }
  }
```

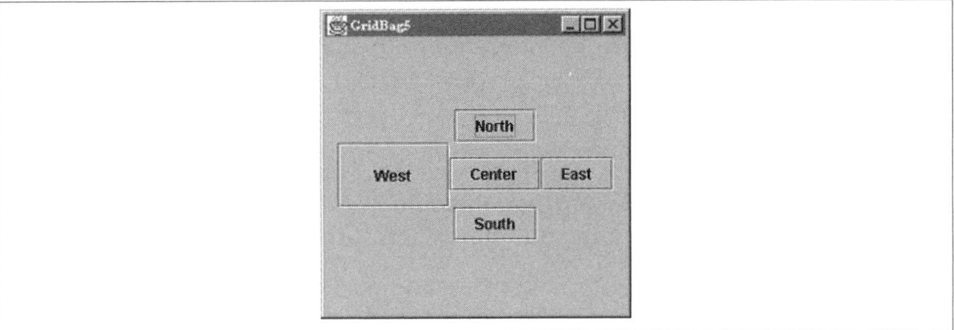

Figure 19-11. Using padding and insets in a layout

Notice that the horizontal padding, `ipadx`, is added on both the left and right sides of the button. Therefore, the button grows horizontally by twice the value of `ipadx`. Likewise, the vertical padding, `ipady`, is added on both the top and the bottom.

Insets add space between the edges of the component and its cell. They are stored in the `insets` field of `GridBagConstraints`, which is an `Insets` object. An `Insets` object has four fields to specify the margins on the component's `top`, `bottom`, `left`, and `right`. The relationship between insets and padding can be confusing. As shown in Figure 19-12, padding is added to the component itself, increasing its size. Insets are external to the component and represent the margin between the component and its cell.

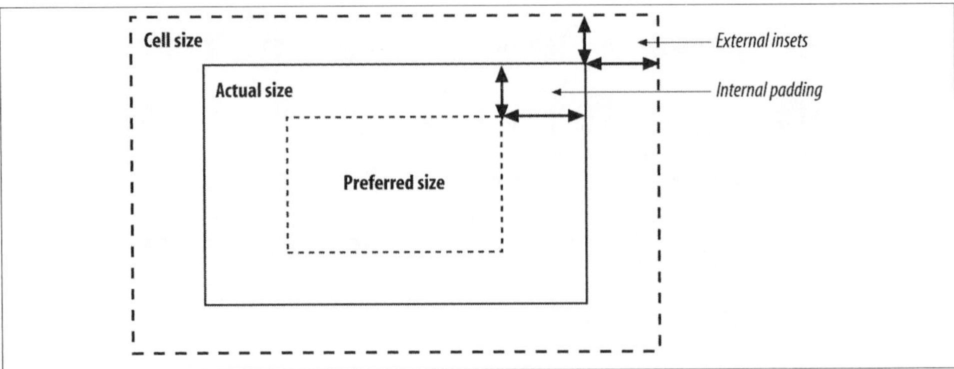

Figure 19-12. The relationship between padding and insets

Padding and weighting have an odd interaction with each other. If you use padding, it's best to use the default `weightx` and `weighty` values for each component.

Relative Positioning

In all our grid bag layouts so far, we have specified the `gridx` and `gridy` coordinates of each component explicitly using its constraints. Another alternative is relative positioning.

Conceptually, *relative positioning* is simple: we just say, "put this component to the right of (or below) the previous component." To do so, you can set `gridx` or `gridy` to the constant `GridBagConstraints.RELATIVE`. Unfortunately, it's not as simple as this. Here are a couple of warnings:

- To place a component to the right of the previous one, set `gridx` to `RELATIVE`*and* use the same value for `gridy` that you used for the previous component.
- Similarly, to place a component below the previous one, set `gridy` to `RELATIVE`*and* leave `gridx` unchanged.
- Setting both `gridx` and `gridy` to `RELATIVE` places all the components in one row, not in a diagonal line, as you might expect. (This is the default.)

In other words, if `gridx` or `gridy` is `RELATIVE`, you had better leave the other value unchanged. `RELATIVE` makes it easy to arrange a lot of components in a row or a column. That's what it was intended for; if you try to do something else, you're fighting against the layout manager, not working with it.

`GridBagLayout` allows another kind of relative positioning in which you specify where, in a row or a column, the component should be placed overall using the `gridwidth` and `gridheight` fields of `GridBagConstraints`. Setting either of these to the constant `REMAINDER` says that the component should be the last item in its row or column and, therefore, should occupy all the remaining space. Setting either `gridwidth` or `gridheight` to `RELATIVE` says that it should be the second to the last item in its row or column. Unfortunately, you can use these constants to create constraints that can't possibly be met; for example, you can say that two components must be the last component in a row. In these cases, the layout manager tries to do something reasonable, but it will almost certainly be something you don't want done.

Composite Layouts

Sometimes things don't fall neatly into little boxes. This is true of layouts as well as life. For example, if you want to use some of `GridBagLayout`'s weighting features for part of your GUI, you could create separate layouts for different parts of the GUI and combine them with yet another layout. That's how we'll build the pocket calculator interface in Figure 19-13. We will use three grid bag layouts: one for the first row of buttons (C, %, +), one for the last (0, ., =) and one for the window itself. The master layout (the window's) manages the text field we use for the display, the panels containing the first and last rows of buttons, and the 12 buttons in the middle.[2]

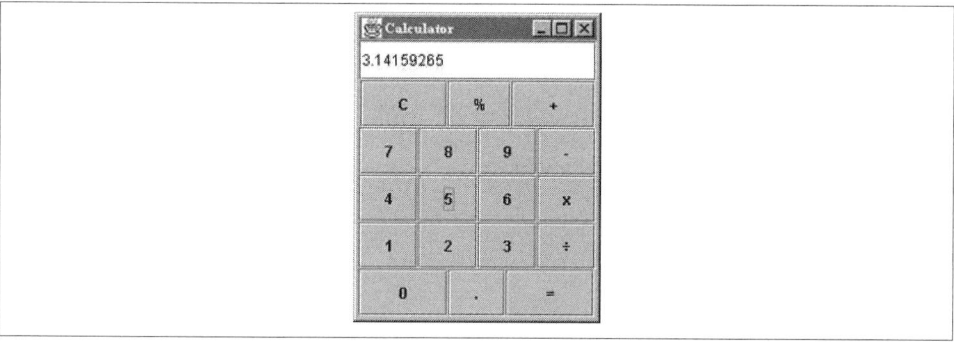

Figure 19-13. The Calculator application

Here's the code for the `Calculator` example. It implements only the user interface (i.e., the keyboard); it collects everything you type in the display field until you press C (clear). Figuring out how to connect the GUI to some other code that would perform the operations is up to you. One strategy would be to send an event to the object that does the computation whenever the user presses the equals sign. That object could read the contents of the text field, parse it, do the computation, and display the results.

```
//file: Calculator.java
import java.awt.*;
import java.awt.event.*;
```

2. If you're curious, this calculator is based on the ELORG-801, encountered in an online "calculator museum" (*http://bit.ly/14pwEvS*).

```
import javax.swing.*;

public class Calculator extends JPanel implements ActionListener {
  GridBagConstraints gbc = new GridBagConstraints();
  JTextField theDisplay = new JTextField();

  public Calculator() {
    gbc.weightx = 1.0;  gbc.weighty = 1.0;
    gbc.fill = GridBagConstraints.BOTH;
    ContainerListener listener = new ContainerAdapter() {
      public void componentAdded(ContainerEvent e) {
        Component comp = e.getChild();
        if (comp instanceof JButton)
          ((JButton)comp).addActionListener(Calculator.this);
      }
    };
    addContainerListener(listener);
    gbc.gridwidth = 4;
    addGB(this, theDisplay, 0, 0);
    // make the top row
    JPanel topRow = new JPanel();
    topRow.addContainerListener(listener);
    gbc.gridwidth = 1;
    gbc.weightx = 1.0;
    addGB(topRow, new JButton("C"), 0, 0);
    gbc.weightx = 0.33;
    addGB(topRow, new JButton("%"), 1, 0);
    gbc.weightx = 1.0;
    addGB(topRow, new JButton("+"), 2, 0 );
    gbc.gridwidth = 4;
    addGB(this, topRow, 0, 1);
    gbc.weightx = 1.0;  gbc.gridwidth = 1;
    // make the digits
    for(int j=0; j<3; j++)
        for(int i=0; i<3; i++)
            addGB(this, new JButton("" + ((2-j)*3+i+1) ), i, j+2);
    // -, x, and divide
    addGB(this, new JButton("-"), 3, 2);
    addGB(this, new JButton("x"), 3, 3);
    addGB(this, new JButton("\u00F7"), 3, 4);
    // make the bottom row
    JPanel bottomRow = new JPanel();
    bottomRow.addContainerListener(listener);
    gbc.weightx = 1.0;
    addGB(bottomRow, new JButton("0"), 0, 0);
    gbc.weightx = 0.33;
    addGB(bottomRow, new JButton("."), 1, 0);
    gbc.weightx = 1.0;
    addGB(bottomRow, new JButton("="), 2, 0);
    gbc.gridwidth = 4;
    addGB(this, bottomRow, 0, 5);
  }
```

```
  void addGB(Container cont, Component comp, int x, int y) {
    if ((cont.getLayout() instanceof GridBagLayout) == false)
      cont.setLayout(new GridBagLayout());
    gbc.gridx = x; gbc.gridy = y;
    cont.add(comp, gbc);
  }

  public void actionPerformed(ActionEvent e) {
    if (e.getActionCommand().equals("C"))
      theDisplay.setText("");
    else
      theDisplay.setText(theDisplay.getText()
                         + e.getActionCommand());
  }

  public static void main(String[] args) {
    JFrame frame = new JFrame("Calculator");
    frame.setDefaultCloseOperation( JFrame.EXIT_ON_CLOSE );
    frame.setSize(200, 250);
    frame.setLocation(200, 200);
    frame.setContentPane(new Calculator());
    frame.setVisible(true);
  }
}
```

Once again, we use an `addGB()` helper method to add components with their constraints to the layout. Before discussing how to build the layout, let's take a look at `addGB()`. We said earlier that three layout managers are in our user interface: one for the application panel itself, one for the panel containing the first row of buttons (`topRow`), and one for the panel containing the bottom row of buttons (`bottomRow`). We use `addGB()` for all three layouts; its first argument specifies the container to which to add the component. Thus, when the first argument is `this`, we're adding an object to the content pane of the `JFrame`. When the first argument is `topRow`, we're adding a button to the first row of buttons. `addGB()` first checks the container's layout manager and sets it to `GridBagLayout` if it isn't already set properly. It sets the object's position by modifying a set of constraints, `gbc`, and then uses these constraints to add the object to the container.

We use a single set of constraints throughout the example, modifying fields as we see fit. The constraints are initialized in `Calculator`'s constructor. Before calling `addGB()`, we set any fields of `gbc` for which the defaults are inappropriate. Thus, for the answer display, we set the grid width to 4 and add the answer display directly to the application panel (`this`). The `add()` method, which is called by `addGB()`, makes a copy of the constraints, so we're free to reuse `gbc` throughout the application.

The first and last rows of buttons motivate the use of multiple `GridBagLayout` containers, each with its own grid. These buttons appear to straddle grid lines, but you really can't accomplish this using a single grid. Therefore, `topRow` has its own layout manager, with three horizontal cells, allowing each button in the row to have a grid width of 1.

To control the size of the buttons, we set the `weightx` variables so that the clear and plus buttons take up more space than the percent button. We then add the `topRow` as a whole to the application, with a grid width of 4. The bottom row is built similarly.

To build the buttons for the digits 1–9, we use a doubly nested loop. There's nothing particularly interesting about this loop, except that it's probably a bit too cute. The minus, multiply, and divide buttons are also simple: we create a button with the appropriate label and use `addGB()` to place it in the application. It's worth noting that we used a Unicode constant to request a real division sign rather than wimping out and using a slash.

That's it for the user interface; what's left is event handling. Each button generates action events; we need to register listeners for these events. We'll make the application panel, the `Calculator`, the listener for all the buttons. To register the `Calculator` as a listener, we'll be clever. Whenever a component is added to a container, the container generates a `ContainerEvent`. We use an anonymous inner class `ContainerListener` to register listeners for our buttons. This means that the `Calculator` must register as a `ContainerListener` for itself and for the two panels, `topRow` and `bottomRow`. The `componentAdded()` method is very simple. It calls `getChild()` to find out what component caused the event (i.e., what component was added). If that component is a button, it registers the `Calculator` as an `ActionListener` for that button.

`actionPerformed()` is called whenever the user presses any button. It clears the display if the user pressed the C button; otherwise, it appends the button's action command (in this case, its label) to the display.

Combining layout managers is an extremely useful trick. Granted, this example verges on overkill. You won't often need to create a composite layout using multiple grid bags. Composite layouts are common, however, with `BorderLayout`; you'll frequently use different layout managers for each of a border layout's regions. For example, the `CENTER` region might be a `ScrollPane`, which has its own special-purpose layout manager; the `EAST` and `SOUTH` regions might be panels managed by grid layouts or flow layouts, as appropriate.

Other Layout Managers

We've covered the most commonly used layout managers; with them, you should be able to create just about any user interface you like. There are two other layout managers in the `javax.swing` package, `SpringLayout` and `GroupLayout`. They are designed primarily for use with visual GUI builders but can be handcoded. O'Reilly's *Java Swing* covers these layout managers in detail. Additionally, there are many useful third-party LayoutManagers, including MigLayout (*http://www.miglayout.com/*) and JGoodies FormLayout (*http://www.jgoodies.com/*).

Absolute Positioning

It's possible to set the layout manager to `null`: no layout control. You might do this to position an object on the display at absolute coordinates. This is usually not the right approach. Components might have different minimum sizes on different platforms, so your interface would not be very portable.

The following example doesn't use a layout manager and works with absolute coordinates instead:

```
//file: MoveButton.java
import java.awt.*;
import java.awt.event.*;
import javax.swing.*;

public class MoveButton extends JPanel {
  JButton button = new JButton("I Move");

  public MoveButton() {
    setLayout(null);
    add(button);
    button.setSize(button.getPreferredSize());
    button.setLocation(20, 20);
    addMouseListener(new MouseAdapter() {
      public void mousePressed(MouseEvent e) {
      button.setLocation(e.getX(), e.getY());
      }
    });
  }

  public static void main(String[] args) {
    JFrame frame = new JFrame("MoveButton");
    frame.setDefaultCloseOperation( JFrame.EXIT_ON_CLOSE );
    frame.setSize(250, 200);
    frame.setLocation(200, 200);
    frame.setContentPane(new MoveButton());
    frame.setVisible(true);
  }
}
```

Click in the window area outside of the button to move the button to a new location. Try resizing the window and note that the button stays at a fixed position relative to the window's upper-left corner.

CHAPTER 20

Drawing with the 2D API

In previous chapters, we looked at the components and component architecture of graphical user interfaces (GUIs) using Java's Swing and AWT packages. Now, we're going to drop down a level and look at the procedural APIs for rendering graphics in Java applications. These APIs are used by components to paint themselves on the screen and to display icons and graphics. As of Java 7, Java2D is hardware-accelerated on all major platforms, so well-constructed Java clients should enjoy performance similar to native applications.

This chapter goes into some detail about Java's sophisticated 2D, resolution-independent drawing API and the core tools for loading and displaying images. In the next chapter, we'll explore dynamic image-processing tools in more detail and look at the classes that allow you to generate and modify image data, pixel by pixel.

The Big Picture

The classes you'll use for drawing come from six packages: `java.awt`, `java.awt.color`, `java.awt.font`, `java.awt.geom`, `java.awt.image`, and `java.awt.print`. Collectively, these classes make up most of the 2D API and cover the drawing of shapes, text, and images. Figure 20-1 shows a bird's-eye view of these classes. There's much more in the 2D API than we can cover in two chapters. For a full treatment, see Jonathan Knudsen's *Java 2D Graphics* (O'Reilly).

An instance of `java.awt.Graphics2D` is called a *graphics context*. It represents a drawing surface—such as a component's display area, a page on a printer, or an offscreen image buffer. A graphics context provides methods for drawing three kinds of graphics objects: shapes, text, and images. `Graphics2D` is called a graphics context because it also holds contextual information about the drawing area. This information includes the drawing area's clipping region, painting color, transfer mode, text font, and geometric transformation. If you consider the drawing area to be a painter's canvas, you might think of a graphics context as an easel that holds a set of tools and marks off the work area.

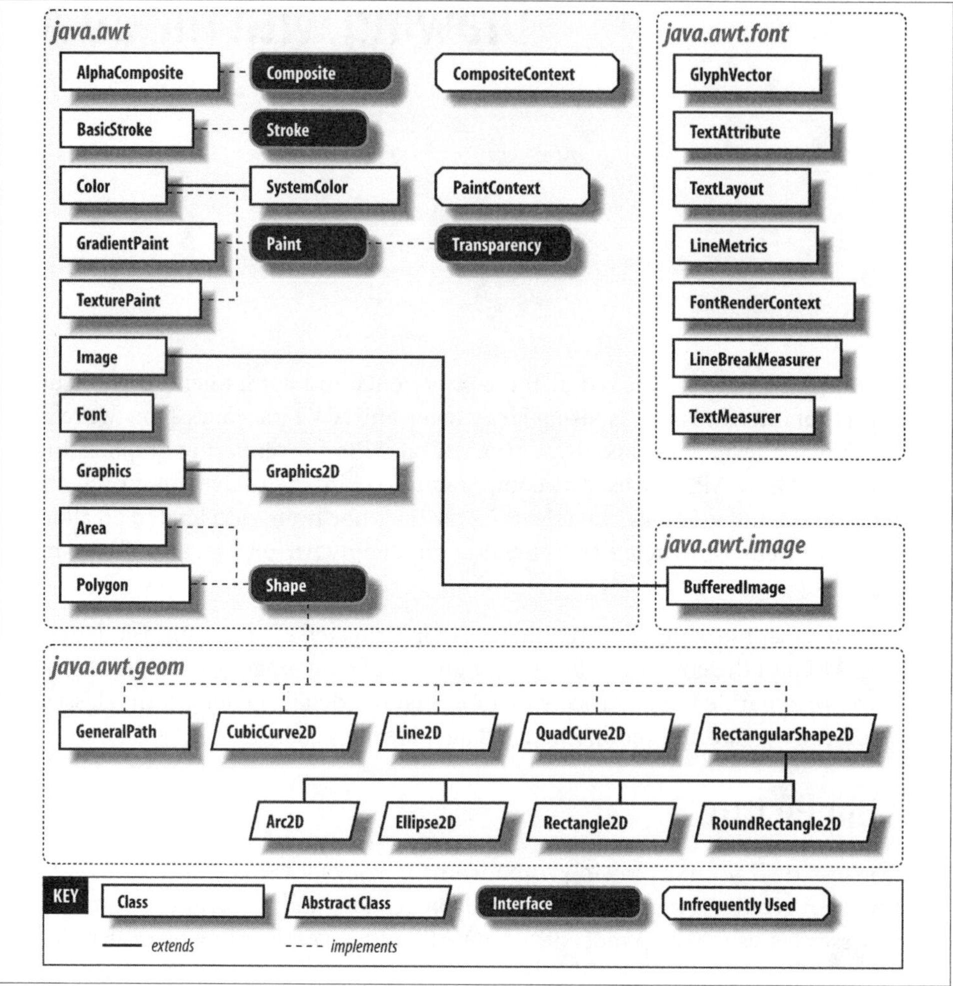

Figure 20-1. Graphics classes of the 2D API

There are four ways to acquire a `Graphics2D` object. The following list describes them in order from the most common to the least:

From AWT or Swing as the result of a painting request on a component
: In this case, a new graphics context for the appropriate area is created and passed to your component's `paint()` or `update()` method. (The `update()` method really applies only to AWT components, not the newer Swing components.)

Directly from an offscreen image buffer
: In this case, we ask the image buffer for a graphics context directly. We'll use this when we discuss techniques such as double buffering.

By copying an existing `Graphics2D` *object*
: Duplicating a graphics object can be useful for more elaborate drawing operations; different copies of a `Graphics2D` object can draw on the same area, but with different attributes and clipping regions. A `Graphics2D` object can be copied by calling the `create()` method.

Directly from an onscreen component
: It's possible to ask a component to give you a `Graphics2D` object for its display area. However, this is almost always a mistake; if you feel tempted to do this, think about why you're trying to circumvent the normal `paint()`/`repaint()` mechanism.

Each time a component's `paint()` method is called, the windowing system provides the component with a new `Graphics2D` object for drawing in the display area. This means that attributes set during one painting session, such as the drawing color or clipping region, are reset the next time `paint()` is called. (Each call to `paint()` starts with a tidy new easel.) For the most common attributes, such as foreground color, background color, and font, we can set defaults in the component itself. Thereafter, the graphics contexts for painting in that component come with those properties initialized appropriately.

The `paint()` method can make no assumptions about what is already drawn on the screen. It is responsible for rendering its entire work area. Higher-level APIs are normally responsible for buffering output and limiting the number of times `paint()` is invoked for a component. AWT components may use an additional method called `update()`, which allows them to update their appearance under the assumption that their previous artwork is still on the screen. However, this method is not used by Swing components.

For backward compatibility, a graphics context is always passed to the `paint()` method as an object of type `Graphics`. If you want to take advantage of the nifty features in the 2D API (as you almost undoubtedly will), you need to cast this reference to a `Graphics2D` object. You'll see how this works in the upcoming examples.

The Rendering Pipeline

One of the strengths of the 2D API is that shapes, text, and images are manipulated in many of the same ways. In this section, we'll describe what happens to shapes, text, and images after you give them to a `Graphics2D` object. *Rendering* is the process of taking some collection of shapes, text, and images and figuring out how to represent them by coloring pixels on a screen or printer. `Graphics2D` supports four rendering operations:

- Draw a shape's outline with the `draw()` method.
- Fill a shape's interior with the `fill()` method.
- Draw some text with the `drawString()` method.
- Draw an image with any of the many forms of the `drawImage()` method.

The graphics context represented by a `Graphics2D` object holds the following properties, whose values are controlled by corresponding accessor methods—for example, `getFont()` and `setFont()`:

Paint
: The current *paint* (an object of type `java.awt.Paint`) determines what color or pattern will be used to fill a shape. This affects the drawing of shape outlines and text as well. You can change the current paint using `Graphics2D`'s `setPaint()` method. Note that the `Color` class implements the `Paint` interface, so you can pass `Color`s to `setPaint()` if you want to use solid colors.

Stroke
: `Graphics2D` uses the *stroke* to determine how to draw the outline of shapes that are passed to its `draw()` method. In graphics terminology, to "stroke" a shape means to take a path defined by the shape and effectively trace it with a pen or brush of a certain size and characteristics. For example, drawing the shape of a circle using a stroke that acts like a solid line would yield a washer or ring shape. The `stroke` object in the `Graphics2D` API is a little more abstract than that. It accepts the input shape to be stroked and returns an enclosed shape representing the outline, which `Graphics2D` then fills. You can set the current stroke by using `setStroke()`. The 2D API comes with a handy class, `java.awt.BasicStroke`, that implements different line widths, end styles, join styles, and dashing.

Font
: Text is rendered by creating a shape that represents the characters to be drawn. The current *font* determines the shapes that are created for a given set of characters. The resulting text shape is then filled. The current font is set using `setFont()`. The 2D API gives applications access to all the TrueType and PostScript Type 1 fonts that are installed. As of Java 7, OpenType/CFF fonts are also supported.

Transformation
: Shapes, text, and images can be geometrically *transformed* before they are rendered. This means that they may be moved, rotated, and stretched. `Graphics2D`'s transformation converts coordinates from "user space" to "device space." By default, `Graphics2D` uses a transformation that maps 72 units in user space to one inch on the output device. If you draw a line from point (0, 0) to point (72, 0) using the default transformation, it will be one inch long, regardless of whether it is drawn

on your monitor or your printer. The current transformation can be modified using the `translate()`, `rotate()`, `scale()`, and `shear()` methods.

Compositing rule
: A *compositing rule* determines how the colors of a new drawing operation are combined with existing colors on the `Graphics2D`'s drawing surface. This attribute is set using `setComposite()`, which accepts an instance of `java.awt.AlphaComposite`. Compositing allows you to make parts of a drawing or image completely or partially transparent, or to combine them in other interesting ways.

Clipping shape
: All rendering operations are limited to the interior of the *clipping shape*. No pixels outside this shape are modified. By default, the clipping shape allows rendering on the entire drawing surface (usually, the rectangular area of a `Component`). However, you can further limit this using any simple or complex shape (for example, text shapes).

Rendering hints
: There are different techniques that can be used to render graphics primitives. Usually these represent a tradeoff between rendering speed and visual quality or vice versa. Rendering hints (constants defined in the `RenderingHints` class) specify which techniques to use.

Graphics primitives (shapes, text, and images) pass through the rendering engine in a series of operations called the *rendering pipeline*. Let's walk through the pipeline. It can be reduced to four steps; the first step depends on the rendering operation:

1. Transform the shape. For shapes that will be filled, the shape is simply transformed using the `Graphics2D`'s current transformation. For shapes whose outlines are drawn using `draw()`, the current stroke is used to stroke the shape's outline. Then the stroked outline is transformed like any other filled shape. Text is displayed by mapping characters to shapes using the current font. The resulting text shapes are transformed like any other filled shape. Images are also transformed using the current transformation.
2. Determine the colors to be used. For a filled shape, the current *paint* object determines the colors that should be used to fill the shape. For drawing an image, the colors are taken from the image itself.
3. Combine the colors with the existing drawing surface using the current *compositing rule*.
4. Clip the results using the current *clipping shape*.

The *rendering hints* are used throughout to control the rendering quality.

A Quick Tour of Java 2D

Next we'll embark on a quick tour of Java 2D, including working with shapes and text. We'll finish with an example of Java 2D in action.

Filling Shapes

The simplest path through the rendering pipeline is filling shapes. For example, the following code creates an ellipse and fills it with a solid color. (This code would live inside a paint() method somewhere. We'll present a complete, ready-to-run example a little later.)

```
Shape c = new Ellipse2D.Float(50, 25, 150, 150); // x,y,width,height
g2.setPaint(Color.blue);
g2.fill(c);
```

Here, g2 is our Graphics2D object. The Ellipse2D shape class is abstract, but is implemented by concrete inner subclasses called Float and Double that work with float or double precision, respectively. The Rectangle2D class, similarly, has concrete subclasses Rectangle2D.Float and Rectangle2D.Double.

In the call to setPaint(), we tell Graphics2D to use a solid color, blue, for all subsequent filling operations. Next, the call to fill() tells Graphics2D to fill the given shape.

All geometric shapes in the 2D API are represented by implementations of the java.awt.geom.Shape interface. This interface defines methods that are common to all shapes, like returning a rectangle bounding box or testing if a point is inside the shape. The java.awt.geom package is a smorgasbord of useful shape classes, including Rectangle2D, RoundRectangle2D (a rectangle with rounded corners), Arc2D, Ellipse2D, and others. In addition, a few more basic classes in java.awt are Shapes: Rectangle, Polygon, and Area.

Drawing Shape Outlines

Drawing a shape's outline is only a little bit more complicated. Consider the following example:

```
Shape r = new Rectangle2D.Float(100, 75, 100, 100);
g2.setStroke(new BasicStroke(4));
g2.setPaint(Color.yellow);
g2.draw(r);
```

Here, we tell Graphics2D to use a stroke that is four units wide and a solid color, yellow, for filling the stroke. When we call draw(), Graphics2D uses the stroke to create a new shape, the outline, from the given rectangle. The outline shape is then filled just as before; this effectively draws the rectangle's outline. The rectangle itself is not filled.

Convenience Methods

Graphics2D includes quite a few convenience methods for drawing and filling common shapes; these methods are actually inherited from the Graphics class. Table 20-1 summarizes these methods. It's a little easier to call fillRect() rather than instantiating a rectangle shape and passing it to fill().

Table 20-1. Shape-drawing methods in the graphics class

Method	Description
draw3DRect()	Draws a highlighted, 3D rectangle
drawArc()	Draws an arc
drawLine()	Draws a line
drawOval()	Draws an oval
drawPolygon()	Draws a polygon, closing it by connecting the endpoints
drawPolyline()	Draws a line connecting a series of points, without closing it
drawRect()	Draws a rectangle
drawRoundRect()	Draws a rounded-corner rectangle
fill3DRect()	Draws a filled, highlighted, 3D rectangle
fillArc()	Draws a filled arc
fillOval()	Draws a filled oval
fillPolygon()	Draws a filled polygon
fillRect()	Draws a filled rectangle
FillRoundRect()	Draws a filled, rounded-corner rectangle

As you can see, for each of the fill() methods in the table, there is a corresponding draw() method that renders the shape as an unfilled line drawing. With the exception of fillArc() and fillPolygon(), each method takes a simple x, y specification for the top-left corner of the shape and a width and height for its size.

The most flexible convenience method draws a polygon, which is specified by two arrays that contain the x and y coordinates of the vertices. Methods in the Graphics class take two such arrays and draw the polygon's outline or fill the polygon.

The methods listed in Table 20-1 are shortcuts for more general methods in Graphics2D. The more general procedure is to first create a java.awt.geom.Shape object and then pass it to the draw() or fill() method of Graphics2D. For example, you could create a Polygon object from coordinate arrays. Since a Polygon implements the Shape interface, you can pass it to Graphics2D's general draw() or fill() method.

The fillArc() method requires six integer arguments. The first four specify the bounding box for an oval—just like the fillOval() method. The final two arguments specify what portion of the oval we want to draw, as a starting angular position and an offset, both of which are specified in degrees. The zero-degree mark is at three o'clock; a positive angle is clockwise. For example, to draw the right half of a circle, you might call:

```
g.fillArc(0, 0, radius * 2, radius * 2, -90, 180);
```

`draw3DRect()` automatically chooses shading colors by "darkening" the current color. So you should set the color to something other than black, which is the default (maybe gray or white); if you don't, you'll just get a black rectangle with a thick outline.

Drawing Text

Like drawing a shape's outline, drawing text is just a simple variation on filling a shape. When you ask `Graphics2D` to draw text, it determines the shapes that need to be drawn and fills them. The shapes that represent characters are called *glyphs*. A font is a collection of glyphs. Here's an example of drawing text:

```
g2.setFont(new Font("Times New Roman", Font.PLAIN, 64));
g2.setPaint(Color.red);
g2.drawString("Hello, 2D!", 50, 150);
```

When we call `drawString()`, `Graphics2D` uses the current font to retrieve the glyphs that correspond to the characters in the string. Then the glyphs (which are really just `Shape`s) are filled using the current `Paint`.

Drawing Images

Images are treated a little differently than shapes. In particular, the current `Paint` is not used to render an image because the image contains its own color information for each pixel (it *is* the paint, effectively). The following example loads an image from a file and displays it:

```
Image i = Toolkit.getDefaultToolkit().getImage("camel.gif");
g2.drawImage(i, 75, 50, this);
```

In this case, the call to `drawImage()` tells `Graphics2D` to place the image at the given location. We'll explain the fourth argument, which is used for monitoring image loading later.

Transformations and rendering

Four parts of the pipeline affect every graphics operation. In particular, all rendering is subject to being transformed, composited, and clipped. Rendering hints are used to affect all of `Graphics2D`'s rendering.

This example shows how to modify the current transformation with a translation and a rotation:

```
g2.translate(50, 0);
g2.rotate(Math.PI / 6);
```

Every graphics primitive drawn by g2 will now have this transformation applied to it (a shift of 50 units right and a rotation of 30 degrees clockwise). We can have a similarly global effect on compositing:

```
AlphaComposite ac = AlphaComposite.getInstance(
    AlphaComposite.SRC_OVER, (float).5);
g2.setComposite(ac);
```

Now, every graphics primitive we draw will be half transparent; we'll explain more about this later.

All drawing operations are clipped by the current clipping shape, which is any object implementing the Shape interface. In the following example, the clipping shape is set to an ellipse:

```
Shape e = new Ellipse2D.Float(50, 25, 250, 150);
g2.clip(e);
```

You can obtain the current clipping shape using getClip(); this is handy if you want to restore it later using the setClip() method.

Finally, the rendering hints influence all drawing operations. In the following example, we tell Graphics2D to use anti-aliasing, a technique that smoothes out the rough pixel edges of shapes and text:

```
g2.setRenderingHint(RenderingHints.KEY_ANTIALIASING,
    RenderingHints.VALUE_ANTIALIAS_ON);
```

The RenderingHints class contains other keys and values that represent other rendering hints. If you really like to fiddle with knobs and dials, this is a good class to check out.

The Whole Iguana

Let's put everything together now, just to show how graphics primitives travel through the rendering pipeline. The following example demonstrates the use of Graphics2D from the beginning to the end of the rendering pipeline. With very few lines of code, we are able to draw some pretty complicated stuff (see Figure 20-2).

Here's the code:

```
//file: Iguana.java
import java.awt.*;
import java.awt.event.*;
import java.awt.geom.*;
import javax.swing.*;

public class Iguana extends JComponent {
  private Image image;
  private int theta;
```

```
public Iguana() {
  image = Toolkit.getDefaultToolkit().getImage(
      "Piazza di Spagna.small.jpg");
  theta = 0;
  addMouseListener(new MouseAdapter() {
    public void mousePressed(MouseEvent me) {
      theta = (theta + 15) % 360;
      repaint();
    }
  });
}

public void paint(Graphics g) {
  Graphics2D g2 = (Graphics2D)g;

  g2.setRenderingHint(RenderingHints.KEY_ANTIALIASING,
      RenderingHints.VALUE_ANTIALIAS_ON);

  int cx = getSize().width / 2;
  int cy = getSize().height / 2;

  g2.translate(cx, cy);
  g2.rotate(theta * Math.PI / 180);

  Shape oldClip = g2.getClip();
  Shape e = new Ellipse2D.Float(-cx, -cy, cx * 2, cy * 2);
  g2.clip(e);

  Shape c = new Ellipse2D.Float(-cx, -cy, cx * 3 / 4, cy * 2);
  g2.setPaint(new GradientPaint(40, 40, Color.blue,
      60, 50, Color.white, true));
  g2.fill(c);

  g2.setPaint(Color.yellow);
  g2.fillOval(cx / 4, 0, cx, cy);

  g2.setClip(oldClip);

  g2.setFont(new Font("Times New Roman", Font.PLAIN, 64));
  g2.setPaint(new GradientPaint(-cx, 0, Color.red,
      cx, 0, Color.black, false));
  g2.drawString("Hello, 2D!", -cx * 3 / 4, cy / 4);

  AlphaComposite ac = AlphaComposite.getInstance(
      AlphaComposite.SRC_OVER, (float).75);
  g2.setComposite(ac);

  Shape r = new RoundRectangle2D.Float(0, -cy * 3 / 4,
      cx * 3 / 4, cy * 3 / 4, 20, 20);
  g2.setStroke(new BasicStroke(4));
  g2.setPaint(Color.magenta);
```

```
    g2.fill(r);
    g2.setPaint(Color.green);
    g2.draw(r);

    g2.drawImage(image, -cx / 2, -cy / 2, this);
  }

  public static void main(String[] args) {
    JFrame frame = new JFrame("Iguana");
    frame.setLayout(new BorderLayout());
    frame.add(new Iguana(), BorderLayout.CENTER);
    frame.setSize(300, 300);
    frame.setDefaultCloseOperation( JFrame.EXIT_ON_CLOSE );
    frame.setVisible(true);
  }
}
```

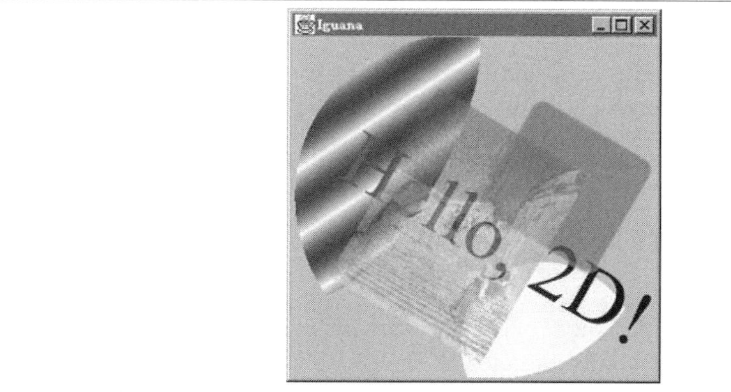

Figure 20-2. Exercising the 2D API

The `Iguana` class is a subclass of `JComponent` with a very fancy `paint()` method. The `main()` method takes care of creating a `JFrame` that holds the `Iguana` component.

`Iguana`'s constructor loads a small image (we'll talk more about this later) and sets up a mouse event handler. This handler changes a member variable, `theta`, and repaints the component. Each time you click, the entire drawing is rotated by 15 degrees.

`Iguana`'s `paint()` method does some pretty interesting stuff, but none of it is very difficult. First, user space is transformed so that the origin is at the center of the component. The user space is then rotated by `theta`:

```
g2.translate(cx, cy);
g2.rotate(theta * Math.PI / 180);
```

`Iguana` saves the current (default) clipping shape before setting it to a large ellipse. Then, `Iguana` draws two filled ellipses. The first is drawn by instantiating an `Ellipse2D` and filling it; the second is drawn using the fillOval() convenience method. (We'll talk about the color gradient in the first ellipse in the next section.) As you can see in Figure 20-2, both ellipses are clipped by the elliptical clipping shape. After filling the two ellipses, Iguana restores the old clipping shape.

Next, Iguana draws some text (see the section "Using Fonts" on page 751). The next action is to modify the compositing rule as follows:

```
AlphaComposite ac = AlphaComposite.getInstance(
    AlphaComposite.SRC_OVER, (float).75);
g2.setComposite(ac);
```

The only thing this means is that we want everything to be drawn with transparency. The AlphaComposite class defines constants that represent different compositing rules, much the way the Color class contains constants that represent different predefined colors. In this case, we're asking for the *source over destination* rule (SRC_OVER), but with an additional alpha multiplier of 0.75. Source over destination means that whatever we're drawing (the source) should be placed on top of whatever's already there (the destination). The alpha multiplier means that everything we draw will be treated at 0.75, or three quarters, of its normal opacity, allowing the existing drawing to "show through."

You can see the effect of the new compositing rule in the rounded rectangle and the image, which both allow previously drawn elements to show through.

Filling Shapes

Iguana fills its shapes with a number of colors, using the setPaint() method of Graphics2D. This method sets the current color in the graphics context, so we set it to a different color before each drawing operation. setPaint() accepts any object that implements the Paint interface. The 2D API includes three implementations of this interface, representing solid colors, color gradients, and textures.

Solid Colors

The java.awt.Color class represents color in Java. A Color object describes a single color and implements the Paint interface for filling an area with it. You can create an arbitrary Color by specifying the red, green, and blue values, either as integers between 0 and 255 or as floating-point values between 0.0 and 1.0. The (somewhat strange) getColor() method can be used to look up a named color in the system properties table, as described in Chapter 11.

The Color class also defines a number of static final color values; we used these in the Iguana example. These constants, such as Color.black and Color.red, provide a convenient set of basic color objects for your drawings.

Excessive creation of redundant color instances is a common cause of memory bloat in Java clients. Consider using a factory pattern to ensure you don't have 200 instances of periwinkle.

Color Gradients

A *color gradient* is a smooth blend between two or more colors. The `GradientPaint` class encapsulates this idea in a handy implementation of the `Paint` interface. All you need to do is specify two points and the color at each point. `GradientPaint` takes care of the details so that the color fades smoothly from one point to the other. In the previous example, the ellipse is filled with a gradient this way:

```
g2.setPaint(new GradientPaint(40, 40, Color.blue,
    60, 50, Color.white, true));
```

The last parameter in `GradientPaint`'s constructor determines whether the gradient is *cyclic*. In a cyclic gradient, the colors keep fluctuating beyond the two points that you've specified. Otherwise, the gradient just draws a single blend from one point to the other. Beyond each endpoint, the color is solid.

Java 6 added multistop gradient capabilities to `LinearGradientPaint` and `RadialGradientPaint`. A multistop gradient can, for example, smoothly fade from green to blue to red.

Textures

A *texture* is simply an image repeated over and over like a floor tile. This concept is represented in the 2D API with the `TexturePaint` class. To create a texture, just specify the image to be used and the rectangle that will be used to reproduce it. To do this, you also need to know how to create and use images, which we'll get to a little later.

Desktop Colors

The `Color` class makes it easy to construct a particular color; however, that's not always what you want to do. Sometimes you want to match a preexisting color scheme. This is particularly important when you are designing a user interface; you might want your components to have the same colors as other components on that platform and to change automatically if the user redefines his or her color scheme.

That's where the `SystemColor` class comes in. A system color represents the color used by the local windowing system in a certain context. The `SystemColor` class holds lots of predefined system colors, just like the `Color` class holds some predefined basic colors. For example, the field `activeCaption` represents the color used for the background of the titlebar of an active window; `activeCaptionText` represents the color used for the title itself. `menu` represents the background color of menu selections; `menuText` represents the color of a menu item's text when it is not selected; `textHighlightText` is the color used when the menu item is selected; and so on. You could use the `window` value to set the color of a `Window` to match the other windows on the user's screen—whether or not they're generated by Java programs.

```
myWindow.setBackground( SystemColor.window );
```

Because the `SystemColor` class is a subclass of `Color`, you can use it wherever you would use a `Color`. However, the `SystemColor` constants are tricky. They are constant, immutable objects as far as you, the programmer, are concerned (your code is not allowed to modify them), but they can be modified at runtime by the system. If the user changes his color scheme, the system colors are automatically updated to follow suit; as a result, anything displayed with system colors will automatically change color the next time it is redrawn. For example, the window `myWindow` would automatically change its background color to the new background color.

The `SystemColor` class has one noticeable shortcoming. You can't compare a system color to a `Color` directly; the `Color.equals()` method doesn't return reliable results. For example, if you want to find out whether the window background color is red, you can't call:

```
Color.red.equals(SystemColor.window);
```

Instead, you should use `getRGB()` to find the color components of both objects and compare them, rather than comparing the objects themselves.

Stroking Shape Outlines

Just as a `Graphics2D` object's current paint determines how its shapes are filled, its current stroke determines how its shapes are outlined. The current stroke determines such drawing features as line thickness, line dashing, and end styles. In the old days, lines were one pixel wide and that was that. With Java 2D, line thickness can be set with floating-point accuracy and the results, like everything else, are subject to the rendering pipeline's transformations and scaling.

To set the current stroke in `Graphics2D`, call `setStroke()` with any implementation of the `Stroke` interface. Fortunately, the 2D API includes a `BasicStroke` class that probably does everything you need. Using `BasicStroke`, you can create dashed lines, control the decoration that is added to line ends, and decide how the corners in an outline should be drawn.

By default, `Graphics2D` uses a solid stroke with a width of 1. In the previous `Iguana` example, the line width is changed just before the outline of the rounded rectangle is drawn, like so:

```
g2.setStroke(new BasicStroke(4));
```

Using Fonts

Text fonts in Java are represented by instances of the `java.awt.Font` class. A `Font` object is constructed from a name, style identifier, and a point size. We can create a `Font` object at any time, but it's meaningful only when applied to a particular component on a given display device. Here are a couple of fonts:

```
Font smallFont = new Font("Monospaced", Font.PLAIN, 10);
Font bigFont = new Font("Serif", Font.BOLD, 18);
```

Font names come in three varieties: *family* names, *face* names (also called font names), and *logical* names. Family and font names are closely related. For example, Garamond Italic is a font name for a font whose family name is Garamond.

A *logical name* is a generic name for the font family. The following logical font names should be available on all platforms:

- `Serif` (generic name for `TimesRoman`)
- `SansSerif` (generic name for `Helvetica`)
- `Monospaced` (generic name for `Courier`)
- `Dialog`
- `DialogInput`

The logical font name is mapped to an actual font on the local platform. Java's *fonts.properties* file maps the font names to the available fonts, covering as much of the Unicode character set as possible. If you request a font that doesn't exist, you get the default font.

One of the big wins in the 2D API is that it can use most of the fonts you have installed on your computer. The following program prints out a full list of the fonts that are available to the 2D API:

```
//file: ShowFonts.java
import java.awt.*;

public class ShowFonts {
  public static void main(String[] args) {
    Font[] fonts;
    fonts =
     GraphicsEnvironment.getLocalGraphicsEnvironment().getAllFonts();
    for (int i = 0; i < fonts.length; i++) {
      System.out.print(fonts[i].getFontName() + " : ");
      System.out.print(fonts[i].getFamily() + " : ");
      System.out.print(fonts[i].getName());
      System.out.println();
    }
  }
}
```

Note, however, that the fonts installed on your system may not match the fonts installed on someone else's system. For true portability, you can use one of the logical names (although your application won't look exactly the same on all platforms) or go with the defaults. Alternatively, you can test for the existence of your preferred font and fall back on a logical font, or you can allow your users to configure the application by choosing fonts themselves.

The `static` method `Font.getFont()` looks up a font by name in the system properties list just like `Color.getColor()`. And as with `Color.getColor()`, this is interesting but useless. Normally, you'll either choose a `Font` from one that is available in the environment (as in the `ShowFonts` example) or use identifiers to describe the font you want in the `Font` constructor.

The `Font` class defines three `static` style identifiers: `PLAIN`, `BOLD`, and `ITALIC`. You can use these values on all fonts, although some fonts may not provide bold or italic versions. The point size determines the size of the font on a display. If a given point size isn't available, `Font` substitutes a default size.

You can retrieve information about an existing `Font` with a number of routines. The `getName()`, `getSize()`, and `getStyle()` methods retrieve the logical name, point size, and style, respectively. You can use the `getFamily()` method to find out the family name, while `getFontName()` returns the face name of the font.

Finally, to actually use a `Font` object, you can simply specify it as an argument to the `setFont()` method of a `Component` or `Graphics2D` object. Subsequent text drawing commands such as `drawString()` for that component or in that graphics context use the specified font.

Font Metrics

To get detailed size and spacing information for text rendered in a font, we can ask for a `java.awt.font.LineMetrics` object. Different systems have different real fonts available; the available fonts may not match the font you request. Furthermore, the measurements of different characters within a single font may be different, especially in multilingual text. Thus, a `LineMetrics` object presents information about a particular set of text in a particular font on a particular system, not general information about a font. For example, if you ask for the metrics of a nine-point `Monospaced` font, what you get isn't some abstract truth about `Monospaced` fonts; you get the metrics of the font that the particular system uses for nine-point `Monospaced`—which may not be exactly nine points or even fixed width.

Use the `getLineMetrics()` method for a `Font` to retrieve the metrics for text as it would appear for that component. This method also needs to know some information about how you plan to render the text—if you're planning to use anti-aliasing, for instance, which affects the text measurements. This extra information is encapsulated in the

`FontRenderContext` class. Fortunately, you can just ask `Graphics2D` for its current `FontRenderContext` rather than having to create one yourself:

```
public void paint(Graphics g) {
  Graphics2D g2 = (Graphics2D)g;
  ...
  FontRenderContext frc = g2.getFontRenderContext();
  LineMetrics metrics = font.getLineMetrics("Monkey", frc);
  ...
}
```

The `Font` class also has a `getStringBounds()` method that returns the bounding box of a piece of text:

```
public void paint(Graphics g) {
  Graphics2D g2 = (Graphics2D)g;
  ...
  FontRenderContext frc = g2.getFontRenderContext();
  float messageWidth =
      (float)font.getStringBounds("Monkey", frc).getWidth();
  ...
}
```

The following application, `FontShow`, displays a word and draws reference lines showing certain characteristics of its font, as shown in Figure 20-3. Clicking in the application window toggles the point size between a small and a large value.

```
//file: FontShow.java
import java.awt.*;
import java.awt.event.*;
import java.awt.font.*;
import javax.swing.*;

public class FontShow extends JComponent
{
  private static final int PAD = 25;   // frilly line padding
  private boolean bigFont = true;
  private String message;

  public FontShow(String message) {
    this.message = message;
    addMouseListener(new MouseAdapter() {
      public void mouseClicked(MouseEvent e) {
        bigFont = !bigFont;
        repaint();
      }
    });
  }

  public void paint(Graphics g)
  {
    Graphics2D g2 = (Graphics2D)g;
```

```
    g2.setRenderingHint(RenderingHints.KEY_ANTIALIASING,
        RenderingHints.VALUE_ANTIALIAS_ON);

    int size = bigFont ? 96 : 64;
    Font font = new Font("Dialog", Font.PLAIN, size);
    g2.setFont(font);
    int width = getSize().width;
    int height = getSize().height;

    FontRenderContext frc = g2.getFontRenderContext();
    LineMetrics metrics = font.getLineMetrics(message, frc);
    float messageWidth =
        (float)font.getStringBounds(message, frc).getWidth();

    // center text
    float ascent = metrics.getAscent();
    float descent = metrics.getDescent();
    float x = (width - messageWidth) / 2;
    float y = (height + metrics.getHeight()) / 2 - descent;

    g2.setPaint(getBackground());
    g2.fillRect(0, 0, width, height);

    g2.setPaint(getForeground());
    g2.drawString(message, x, y);

    g2.setPaint(Color.white);  // Base lines
    drawLine(g2, x - PAD, y, x + messageWidth + PAD, y);
    drawLine(g2, x, y + PAD, x, y - ascent - PAD);
    g2.setPaint(Color.green);  // Ascent line
    drawLine(g2, x - PAD, y - ascent,
             x + messageWidth + PAD, y - ascent);
    g2.setPaint(Color.red);    // Descent line
    drawLine(g2, x - PAD, y + descent,
             x + messageWidth + PAD, y + descent);
  }

  private void drawLine(Graphics2D g2,
      double x0, double y0, double x1, double y1) {
    Shape line = new java.awt.geom.Line2D.Double(x0, y0, x1, y1);
    g2.draw(line);
  }

  public static void main(String args[]) {
    String message = "Lemming";
    if (args.length > 0) message = args[0];

    JFrame frame = new JFrame("FontShow");
    frame.setSize(420, 300);
    frame.setDefaultCloseOperation( JFrame.EXIT_ON_CLOSE );
    frame.getContentPane().add(new FontShow(message));
    frame.setVisible(true);
```

```
    }
}
```

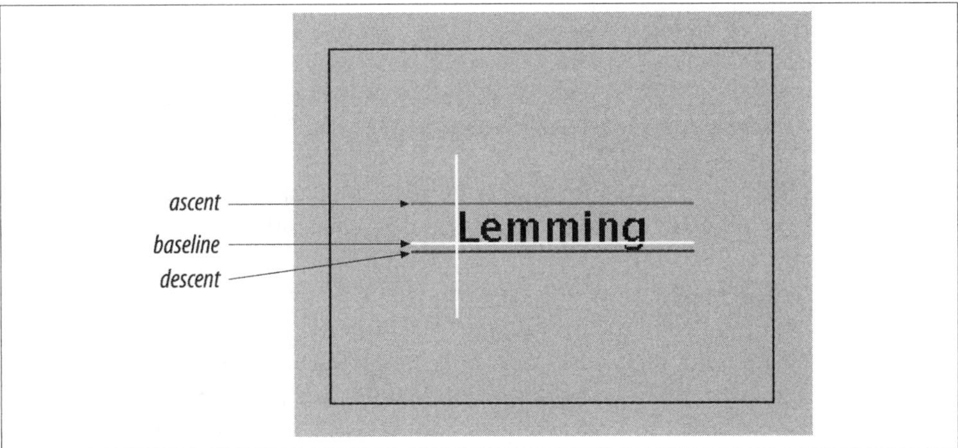

Figure 20-3. The FontShow application

You can specify the text to be displayed as a command-line argument:

```
% java FontShow "When in the course of human events ..."
```

`FontShow` may look a bit complicated, but there's really not much to it. The bulk of the code is in `paint()`, which sets the font, draws the text, and adds a few lines to illustrate some of the font's characteristics (metrics). For fun, we also catch mouse clicks (using an event handler defined in the constructor) and alternate the font size by setting the `bigFont` toggle variable and repainting.

By default, text is rendered above and to the right of the coordinates specified in the `drawString()` method. Think of that starting point as the origin of a coordinate system; the axes are the *baselines* of the font. `FontShow` draws these lines in white. The greatest height the characters stretch above the baseline is called the *ascent* and is shown by a green line. Some fonts also have parts of letters that fall below the baseline. The farthest distance any character reaches below the baseline is called the *descent*, which is illustrated with a red line.

We ask for the ascent and descent of our font with the `LineMetrics` class's `getAscent()` and `getDescent()` methods. We also ask for the width of our string (when rendered in this font) with `Font`'s `getStringBounds()` method. This information is used to center the word in the display area. To center the word vertically, we use the height and adjust with the descent to calculate the baseline location. Table 20-2 provides a short list of methods that return useful font metrics.

Table 20-2. LineMetrics methods

Method	Description
`getAscent()`	Height above baseline
`getDescent()`	Depth below baseline
`getLeading()`	Standard vertical spacing between lines
`getHeight()`	Total line height (ascent + descent + leading)

Leading space is the padding between lines of text. The `getHeight()` method reports the total height of a line of text, including the leading space.

Displaying Images

So far, we've worked with methods for drawing simple shapes and displaying text. For more complex graphics, we'll be working with images. In a typical Swing application, the simplest way to display an image in your application is to use an `ImageIcon` with a `JLabel` component. Here, we are talking about working with image data at a lower level, for painting. The 2D API has a powerful set of tools for generating and displaying image data. We'll start with the basics of the `java.awt.Image` class and see how to load an image into an application and draw it where you want it. The Java AWT toolkit will handle most of the details for us. In the next chapter, we'll go further to discuss how to manage image loading manually as well as how to create and manipulate raw pixel data, allowing you to create any kind of graphics you can dream up.

The core AWT supports images encoded in JPEG, PNG, and GIF. (This includes GIF89a animations so that you can work with simple animations as easily as static images.) If you need to work with other types of images, you can turn to the Java Advanced Imaging `javax.imageio` framework. We'll mention it briefly here and again in the next chapter when we discuss the `BufferedImage` class.

In many ways, the ImageIO framework supercedes and replaces the older image handling functionality of the core AWT just as Swing extends and replaces the old AWT components. The ImageIO framework is easily extensible for new image types through plug-ins. However, out of the box, all that it adds in terms of image type support is the ability to read bitmap (BMP) and wireless bitmap (WBMP) images. Since most Java code can and does use the original AWT functionality, that is where we'll focus.

The Image Class

The `java.awt.Image` class represents a view of an image. The view is created from an image source that produces pixel data. Images can be from a static source, such as a JPEG file, or a dynamic one, such as a video stream or a graphics engine.

AWT Images are created with the `getImage()` and `createImage()` methods of the `java.awt.Toolkit` class. There are two forms of each method, which accept a URL or plain filename, respectively. `createImage()` can also accept a byte array of image data directly.

When bundling images with your application, you should use the `Class` class's `getResource()` method (discussed in Chapter 1) to construct a URL reference to the file from the application classpath. `getResource()` allows you to bundle images along with your application, inside JAR files or anywhere else in the classpath. The following code fragment shows some examples of loading images with the `getImage()` method:

```
Toolkit toolkit = Toolkit.getDefaultToolkit();

// Application resource URL - Best method
URL daffyURL = getClass().getResource("/cartoons/images/daffy.gif");
Image daffyDuckImage = toolkit.getImage( daffyURL );

// Absolute URL -
URL monaURL = new URL( "http://myserver/images/mona_lisa.png");
Image monaImage = toolkit.getImage( monaURL );

// Local file -
Image elvisImage = toolkit.getImage("c:/elvis/lateryears/fatelvis1.jpg" );
```

The `createImage()` method looks just like `getImage()`; the difference is that `getImage()` "interns" images and shares them when it receives multiple requests for the same data. The `createImage()` method does not do this (it creates a new `Image` object every time) and relies on you to cache and share the image. `getImage()` is convenient in an application that uses a limited number of images for the life of the application, but it may not ever release the image data. You should use `createImage()` and cache the `Image` objects yourself when it's an issue.

The `javax.imageio.ImageIO` class similarly provides several static `read()` methods that can load images from a `File`, `URL`, or `InputStream`:

```
URL daffyURL = getClass().getResource("/cartoons/images/daffy.gif");
Image daffyDuckImage = ImageIO.read( daffyURL );
```

We'll discuss image loading with AWT and the ImageIO framework in more detail in Chapter 21.

Once we have an `Image` object, we can draw it into a graphics context with the `drawImage()` method of the `Graphics` class. The simplest form of the `drawImage()` method takes four parameters: the `Image` object, the `x`, `y` coordinates at which to draw it, and a reference to a special *image observer* object. We'll show an example involving `drawImage()` soon, but first let's say a word about image observers.

Image Observers

Images are processed asynchronously, which means that Java performs image operations, such as loading and scaling in the background (allowing the user code to continue). In a typical client application, this might not be important; images may be small for things like buttons, and are probably bundled with the application for almost instant retrieval. However, Java was designed to work with image data over the Web as well as locally, and you will see this expressed in the APIs for working with image data.

For example, the `getImage()` method always returns immediately, even if the image data has to be retrieved over the network from Mars and isn't available yet. In fact, if it's a new image, Java won't even begin to fetch the data until we try to display or manipulate it. The advantage of this technique is that Java can do the work of a powerful, multithreaded image processing environment for us. However, it also introduces several problems. If Java is loading an image for us, how do we know when it's completely loaded? What if we want to work with the image as it arrives? What if we need to know properties of the image (like its dimensions) before we can start working with it? What if there's an error in loading the image?

These issues are handled by *image observers*, objects that implement the `ImageObserver` interface. All operations that draw or examine `Image` objects are asynchronous and take an image observer object as a parameter. The `ImageObserver` monitors the image operation's status and can make that information available to the rest of the application. When image data is loaded from its source by the graphics system, your image observer is notified of its progress, including when new pixels are available, when a complete frame of the image is ready, and if there is an error during loading. The image observer also receives attribute information about the image, such as its dimensions and properties, as soon as they are known.

The `drawImage()` method, like other image operations, takes a reference to an `ImageObserver` object as a parameter. `drawImage()` returns a `boolean` value specifying whether or not the image was painted in its entirety. If the image data has not yet been loaded or is only partially available, `drawImage()` paints whatever fraction of the image it can and returns. In the background, the graphics system starts (or continues) loading the image data. The image observer object is registered as interested in information about the image. The observer is then called repeatedly as more pixel information is available and again when the entire image is complete. The image observer can do whatever it wants with this information. Most often the information is used to call `repaint()` to prompt the application to draw the image again with the updated data. In this way, an application or applet can draw the image as it arrives for a progressive loading effect. Alternatively, it could wait until the entire image is loaded before displaying it.

Image observers are covered in Chapter 21. For now, let's avoid the issue by using a prefabricated image observer. The `Component` class implements the `ImageObserver` interface and provides some simple repainting behavior, which means every component can serve as its own default image observer. We can simply pass a reference to whatever component is doing the painting as the image observer parameter of a `drawImage()` call:

```
public void paint( Graphics g ) {
    g.drawImage( monaImage, x, y, this );
    ...
```

Our component serves as the image observer and calls `repaint()` for us to redraw the image as necessary. If the image arrives slowly, our component is notified repeatedly as new chunks become available. As a result, the image appears gradually as it's loaded.[1]

Preloading images

We'll discuss image loading in more detail in the next chapter when we look at the `MediaTracker` utility, which monitors the load progress of one or more images. However, we'll skip ahead a bit here and show you the easy shortcut for loading a single image and making sure it's complete and ready to draw. You can use the `javax.swing.ImageIcon` class to do the dirty work for you:

```
ImageIcon icon = new ImageIcon("myimage.jpg");
Image image = icon.getImage();
```

Images loaded by the `ImageIO read()` methods are returned fully loaded. `ImageIO` provides its own API for monitoring image loading progress. That API follows a more standard event source/listener pattern, but we won't get into it here.

Scaling and Size

Another version of `drawImage()` renders a scaled version of the image:

```
g.drawImage( monaImage, x, y, x2, y2, this );
```

This draws the entire image within the rectangle formed by the points `x`, `y` and `x2`, `y2`, scaling as necessary. `drawImage()` behaves the same as before; the image is processed by the component as it arrives, and the image observer is notified as more pixel data and the completed image are available. Several other overloaded versions of `drawImage()` provide more complex options: you can scale, crop, and perform some simple transpositions.

Normally, however, for performance you want to make a scaled copy of an image (as opposed to simply painting one at draw time); you can use `getScaledInstance()` for this purpose. Here's how:

1. The `awt.image.incrementaldraw` and `awt.image.redrawrate` system properties control this behavior. `redrawrate` limits how often `repaint()` is called; the default value is every 100 milliseconds. `incrementaldraw`'s default value, `true`, enables this behavior. Setting it to `false` delays drawing until the entire image has arrived.

```
Image scaledDaffy =
  daffyImage.getScaledInstance( 100, 200, Image.SCALE_AREA_AVERAGING );
```

This method scales the original image to the given size—in this case, 100 by 200 pixels. It returns a new Image that you can draw like any other image. SCALE_AREA_AVERAGING is a constant that tells getScaledImage() what scaling algorithm to use. The algorithm used here tries to do a decent job of scaling at the expense of time. Some alternatives that take less time are SCALE_REPLICATE, which scales by replicating scan lines and columns (which is fast, but probably not pretty). You can also specify either SCALE_FAST or SCALE_SMOOTH and let the implementation choose an appropriate algorithm that optimizes for time or quality. If you don't have specific requirements, you should use SCALE_DEFAULT, which ideally would be set by a preference in the user's environment.

If you are going to draw the image more than once (which you almost always will), creating a scaled copy of the image can improve performance dramatically. Otherwise, repeated calls to drawImage() with scaling requirements cause the image to be scaled every time, which wastes processing time.

The Image getHeight() and getWidth() methods retrieve the dimensions of an image. Because this information may not be available until the image data is completely loaded, both methods also take an ImageObserver object as a parameter. If the dimensions aren't yet available, they return values of -1 and notify the observer when the actual value is known. We'll see how to deal with these and other problems a bit later. For now, we'll continue to use our Component as the image observer and move on to some general painting techniques.

Drawing Techniques

Now that we've learned about the basic tools, let's put a few of them together. In this section, we'll look at some techniques for doing fast and flicker-free drawing and painting. If you're interested in animation, this is for you. Drawing operations take time, and time spent drawing leads to delays and imperfect results. Our goals are to minimize the amount of drawing work we do and, as much as possible, to do that work away from the eyes of the user. To do this, we use two techniques: clipping and double buffering. Fortunately, Swing now handles double buffering by default. You won't have to implement this logic on your own, but it's useful to understand it.

Our first example, DragImage, illustrates some of the issues in updating a display. Like many animations, it has two parts: a constant background and a changing object in the foreground. In this case, the background is a checkerboard pattern, and the object is a small, scaled that image we can drag around on top of it, as shown in Figure 20-4:

```
import java.awt.*;
import java.awt.event.*;
import javax.swing.*;
```

```
public class DragImage extends JComponent
    implements MouseMotionListener
{
  static int imageWidth=60, imageHeight=60;
  int grid = 10;
  int imageX, imageY;
  Image image;

  public DragImage(Image i) {
    image = i;
    addMouseMotionListener(this);
  }

  public void mouseDragged(MouseEvent e) {
    imageX = e.getX();
    imageY = e.getY();
    repaint();
  }
  public void mouseMoved(MouseEvent e) {}

  public void paint(Graphics g) {
    Graphics2D g2 = (Graphics2D)g;

    int w = getSize().width / grid;
    int h = getSize().height / grid;
    boolean black = false;
    for (int y = 0; y <= grid; y++)
      for (int x = 0; x <= grid; x++) {
        g2.setPaint(black ? Color.black : Color.white);
        black = !black;
        g2.fillRect(x * w, y * h, w, h);
      }
    g2.drawImage(image, imageX, imageY, this);
  }

  public static void main(String[] args) {
    String imageFile = "L1-Light.jpg";
    if (args.length > 0)
      imageFile = args[0];

    // Turn off double buffering
    //RepaintManager.currentManager(null).setDoubleBufferingEnabled(false);

    Image image = Toolkit.getDefaultToolkit().getImage(
        DragImage.class.getResource(imageFile));
    image = image.getScaledInstance(
        imageWidth,imageHeight,Image.SCALE_DEFAULT);
    JFrame frame = new JFrame("DragImage");
    frame.add( new DragImage(image) );
    frame.setSize(300, 300);
    frame.setDefaultCloseOperation( JFrame.EXIT_ON_CLOSE );
```

```
        frame.setVisible(true);
    }
}
```

Figure 20-4. The DragImage application

Run the application, optionally specifying an image file as a command-line argument. Then try dragging the image around on the pattern.

`DragImage` is a custom component that overrides the `JComponent paint()` method to do its drawing. In the `main()` method, we load the image and prescale it to improve performance. We then create the `DragImage` component and place it in the content pane. As the mouse is dragged, `DragImage` keeps track of its most recent position in two instance variables, `imageX` and `imageY`. On each call to `mouseDragged()`, the coordinates are updated, and `repaint()` is called to ask that the display be updated. When `paint()` is called, it looks at some parameters, draws the checkerboard pattern to fill the applet's area and finally paints the small version of the image at the latest coordinates.

Now for a few arcane details about differences between `JComponent` and a plain AWT `Component`. First, the default `JComponent update()` method simply calls our `paint()` method. Prior to Java 1.4, the AWT `Component` class's default `update()` method first cleared the screen area using a `clearRect()` call before calling `paint`. Remember that the difference between `paint()` and `update()` is that `paint()` draws the entire area and `update()` assumes the screen region is intact from the last draw. In AWT, `update()` was overly conservative; in Swing, it's more optimistic. This is noteworthy if you are working with an older AWT-based application. In that case, you can simply override `update()` to call `paint()`.

A more important difference between AWT and Swing is that Swing components by default perform *double buffering* of the output of their `paint()` method.

Double Buffering

Double buffering means that instead of drawing directly on the screen, Swing first performs drawing operations in an offscreen buffer and then copies the completed work to the display in a single painting operation, as shown in Figure 20-5. It takes the same amount of time to do the drawing work, but once it's done, double buffering instantaneously updates our display so that the user does not perceive any flickering or progressively rendered output.

You'll see how to implement this technique yourself when we use an offscreen buffer later in this chapter. However, Swing does this kind of double buffering for you whenever you use a Swing component in a Swing container. AWT components do not have automatic double buffering capability.

It is interesting to take our example and turn off double buffering to see the effect. Each Swing `JComponent` has a method called `setDoubleBuffered()` that can be set to `false` in order to disable the technique. Or you can disable it for all components using a call to the Swing `RepaintManager`, as we've indicated in comments in the example. Try uncommenting that line of `DragImage` and observe the difference in appearance.

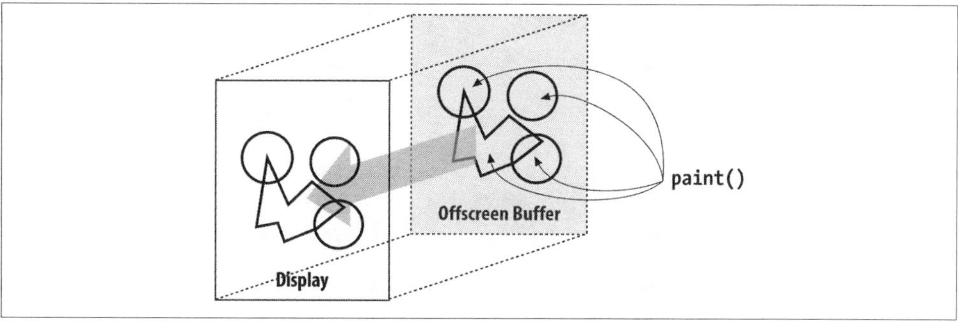

Figure 20-5. Double buffering

The difference is most dramatic when you are using a slow system or performing complex drawing operations. Double buffering eliminates all of the flickering. However, on a slow system, it can decrease performance noticeably. In extreme cases (such as a game), it may be beneficial to provide an option to disable double buffering.

Our example is pretty fast, but we're still doing some wasted drawing. Most of the background stays the same each time it's painted. You might try to make `paint()` smarter, so that it wouldn't redraw these areas, but remember that `paint()` has to be able to draw the entire scene because it might be called in situations when the display isn't intact. The solution is to draw only part of the picture whenever the mouse moves. Next, we'll talk about clipping.

Limiting Drawing with Clipping

Whenever the mouse is dragged, `DragImage` responds by updating its coordinates and calling `repaint()`. But `repaint()` by default causes the entire component to be redrawn. Most of this drawing is unnecessary. It turns out that there's another version of `repaint()` that lets you specify a rectangular area that should be drawn—in essence, a clipping region.

Why does it help to restrict the drawing area? Foremost, drawing operations that fall outside the clipping region are not displayed. If a drawing operation overlaps the clipping region, we see only the part that's inside. A second effect is that, in a good implementation, the graphics context can recognize drawing operations that fall completely outside the clipping region and ignore them altogether. Eliminating unnecessary operations can save time if we're doing something complex, such as filling a bunch of polygons. This doesn't save the time our application spends calling the drawing methods, but the overhead of calling these kinds of drawing methods is usually negligible compared to the time it takes to execute them. (If we were generating an image pixel by pixel, this would not be the case, as the calculations would be the major time sink, not the drawing.)

So we can save some time in our application by redrawing only the affected portion of the display. We can pick the smallest rectangular area that includes both the old image position and the new image position, as shown in Figure 20-6. This is the only portion of the display that really needs to change; everything else stays the same.

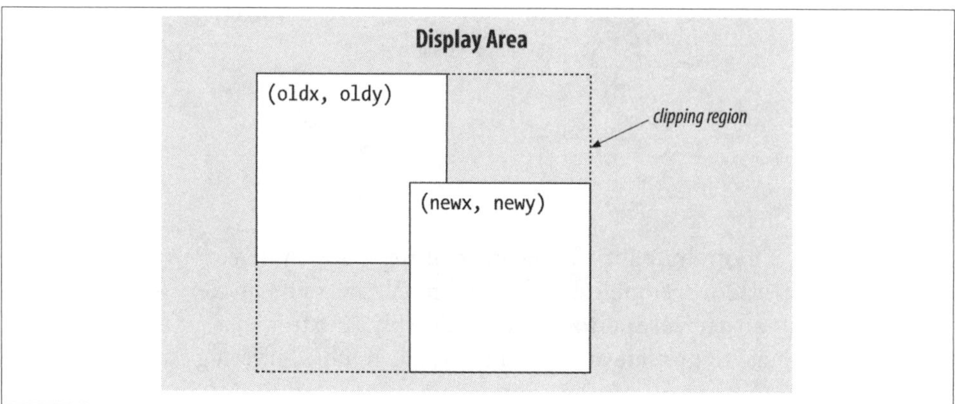

Figure 20-6. Determining the clipping region

A smarter algorithm could save even more time by redrawing only those regions that have changed. However, the simple clipping strategy we've implemented here can be applied to many kinds of drawing and gives good performance, particularly if the area being changed is small.

One important thing to note is that, in addition to looking at the new position, our updating operation now has to remember the last position at which the image was drawn. Let's fix our application so it will use a specified clipping region. To keep this short and emphasize the changes, we'll take some liberties with design and make our next example a subclass of `DragImage`. Let's call it `ClippedDragImage`.

```
import java.awt.*;
import java.awt.event.*;
import javax.swing.*;

public class ClippedDragImage extends DragImage {
  int oldX, oldY;

  public ClippedDragImage( Image i ) { super(i); }

  public void mouseDragged(MouseEvent e) {
    imageX = e.getX();
    imageY = e.getY();
    Rectangle r = getAffectedArea(
        oldX, oldY, imageX, imageY, imageWidth, imageHeight);
    repaint(r);  // repaint just the affected part of the component
    oldX = imageX;
    oldY = imageY;
  }

  private Rectangle getAffectedArea(
    int oldx, int oldy, int newx, int newy, int width, int height)
  {
    int x = Math.min(oldx, newx);
    int y = Math.min(oldy, newy);
    int w = (Math.max(oldx, newx) + width) - x;
    int h = (Math.max(oldy, newy) + height) - y;
    return new Rectangle(x, y, w, h);
  }

  public static void main(String[] args) {
    String imageFile = "L1-Light.jpg";
    if (args.length > 0)
      imageFile = args[0];

    // Turn off double buffering
    //RepaintManager.currentManager(null).setDoubleBufferingEnabled(false);

    Image image = Toolkit.getDefaultToolkit().getImage(
        ClippedDragImage.class.getResource(imageFile));
    image = image.getScaledInstance(
        imageWidth,imageHeight,Image.SCALE_DEFAULT);
    JFrame frame = new JFrame("ClippedDragImage");
    frame.add( new ClippedDragImage(image) );
    frame.setSize(300, 300);
    frame.setDefaultCloseOperation( JFrame.EXIT_ON_CLOSE );
    frame.setVisible(true);
```

```
    }
}
```

You may or may not find that `ClippedDragImage` is significantly faster. Modern desktop computers are so fast that this kind of operation is child's play for them. However, the fundamental technique is important and applicable to more sophisticated applications.

What have we changed? First, we've overridden `mouseDragged()` so that instead of setting the current coordinates of the image, it figures out the area that has changed by using a new `private` method. `getAffectedArea()` takes the new and old coordinates and the width and height of the image as arguments. It determines the bounding rectangle as shown in Figure 20-6, then calls `repaint()` to draw only the affected area of the screen. `mouseDragged()` also saves the current position by setting the `oldX` and `oldY` variables.

Try turning off double buffering on this example and compare it to the unbuffered previous example to see how much less work is being done. You probably won't see the difference; computers are just too fast nowadays. If you were using the 2D API to do some fancy rendering, it might help a lot.

Offscreen Drawing

In addition to serving as buffers for double buffering, offscreen images are useful for saving complex, hard-to-produce, background information. We'll look at a fun, simple example: the doodle pad. `DoodlePad` is a simple drawing tool that lets us scribble by dragging the mouse, as shown in Figure 20-7. It draws into an offscreen image; its `paint()` method simply copies the image to the display area.

```
//file: DoodlePad.java
import java.awt.*;
import java.awt.event.*;
import javax.swing.*;

public class DoodlePad
{
  public static void main(String[] args)
  {
    JFrame frame = new JFrame("DoodlePad");
    frame.setLayout(new BorderLayout());
    final DrawPad drawPad = new DrawPad();
    frame.add(drawPad, BorderLayout.CENTER);
    JPanel panel = new JPanel();
    JButton clearButton = new JButton("Clear");
    clearButton.addActionListener(new ActionListener() {
      public void actionPerformed(ActionEvent e) {
        drawPad.clear();
      }
    });
    panel.add(clearButton);
```

```
    frame.add(panel, BorderLayout.SOUTH);
    frame.setSize(280, 300);
    frame.setDefaultCloseOperation( JFrame.EXIT_ON_CLOSE );
    frame.setVisible(true);
  }

} // end of class DoodlePad

class DrawPad extends JComponent
{
  Image image;
  Graphics2D graphics2D;
  int currentX, currentY, oldX, oldY;

  public DrawPad() {
    setDoubleBuffered(false);
    addMouseListener(new MouseAdapter() {
      public void mousePressed(MouseEvent e) {
        oldX = e.getX();
        oldY = e.getY();
      }
    });
    addMouseMotionListener(new MouseMotionAdapter() {
      public void mouseDragged(MouseEvent e) {
        currentX = e.getX();
        currentY = e.getY();
        if (graphics2D != null)
          graphics2D.drawLine(oldX, oldY, currentX, currentY);
        repaint();
        oldX = currentX;
        oldY = currentY;
      }
    });
  }

  public void paintComponent(Graphics g) {
    if (image == null) {
      image = createImage(getSize().width, getSize().height);
      graphics2D = (Graphics2D)image.getGraphics();
      graphics2D.setRenderingHint(RenderingHints.KEY_ANTIALIASING,
          RenderingHints.VALUE_ANTIALIAS_ON);
      clear();
    }
    g.drawImage(image, 0, 0, null);
  }

  public void clear() {
    graphics2D.setPaint(Color.white);
    graphics2D.fillRect(0, 0, getSize().width, getSize().height);
    graphics2D.setPaint(Color.black);
    repaint();
```

```
        }
    }
```

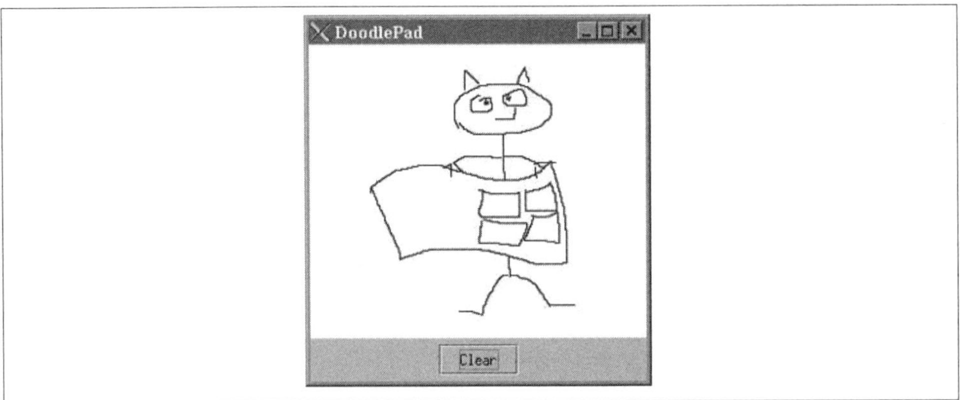

Figure 20-7. The DoodlePad application

Give it a try. Draw a nice moose or a sunset. We just drew a lovely cartoon of Bill Gates. If you make a mistake, hit the Clear button and start over.

The parts should be familiar by now. We made a type of `JComponent` called `DrawPad`. The new `DrawPad` component uses inner classes to supply handlers for the `MouseListener` and `MouseMotionListener` interfaces. We used the `JComponent createImage()` method to create an empty offscreen image buffer to hold our scribble. Mouse-dragging events trigger us to draw lines into the offscreen image and call `repaint()` to update the display. `DrawPad`'s `paint()` method does a `drawImage()` to copy the offscreen drawing area to the display. In this way, `DrawPad` saves our sketch information.

What is unusual about `DrawPad` is that it does some drawing outside of `paint()`. In this example, we want to let the user scribble with the mouse, so we should respond to every mouse movement. Therefore, we do our work, drawing to the offscreen buffer in `mouseDragged()` itself. As a rule, we should be careful about doing heavy work in event-handling methods because we don't want to interfere with other tasks that the windowing system's painting thread is performing. In this case, our line drawing option should not be a burden, and our primary concern is getting as close a coupling as possible between the mouse movement events and the sketch on the screen. A more elaborate example might push coordinates into a queue for some other drawing thread to consume, thus freeing up the event handler thread.

In addition to drawing a line as the user drags the mouse, the `mouseDragged()` handler maintains a pair of previous coordinates to be used as a starting point for the next line segment. The `mousePressed()` handler resets the previous coordinates to the current mouse position whenever the user moves the mouse. Finally, `DrawPad` provides a `clear()` method that clears the offscreen buffer and calls `repaint()` to update the display. The DoodlePad application ties the clear() method to an appropriately labeled button through another anonymous inner class.

What if we wanted to do something with the image after the user has finished scribbling on it? As we'll see in the next chapter, we could get the pixel data for the image and work with that. It wouldn't be hard to create a save facility that stores the pixel data and reproduces it later. Think about how you might go about creating a networked "bathroom wall," where people could scribble on your web pages.

Printing

Earlier in this chapter, we hinted at the possibility that you could draw the same stuff on the screen and the printer. It's true; all you really need to do is get a Graphics2D object that represents a printer rather than an area of the screen. Java's printing API provides the necessary plumbing. There isn't room here to describe the whole Printing API, but we will provide you with a short example that will let you get your feet wet (and your paper flowing).

The printing classes are tucked away in the java.awt.print package. You can print anything that implements the Printable interface. This interface has only one method—you guessed it, print()—which is like the paint() methods we've already worked with. It accepts a Graphics object that represents the drawing surface of the printer's page. It also accepts a PageFormat object that encapsulates information about the paper on which you're printing. Finally, print() is passed the number of the page that is being rendered. All Swing components implement a print() method, which you can use or override to customize their printed appearance.

Your print() implementation should either render the requested page or state that it doesn't exist. You can do this by returning special values from print(), either Printable.PAGE_EXISTS or Printable.NO_SUCH_PAGE.

You can control a print job, including showing print and page setup dialogs, using the PrinterJob class. The following class enables you to get something on paper. In this example, we work both sides of the printing equation: implementing a simple Printable interface to generate our data and printing it with the PrinterJob API.

```
//file: UnbelievablySimplePrint.java
import java.awt.*;
import java.awt.print.*;

public class UnbelievablySimplePrint implements Printable
{
  private static Font sFont = new Font("Serif", Font.PLAIN , 64);

  public int print(Graphics g, PageFormat Pf, int pageIndex)
      throws PrinterException
  {
```

```
    if (pageIndex > 0) return NO_SUCH_PAGE;
    Graphics2D g2 = (Graphics2D)g;
    g2.setFont(sFont);
    g2.setPaint(Color.black);
    g2.drawString("Save a tree!", 96, 144);
    return PAGE_EXISTS;
  }

  public static void main(String[] args) {
    PrinterJob job = PrinterJob.getPrinterJob();
    job.setPrintable(new UnbelievablySimplePrint());
    if (job.printDialog()) {
      try {
        job.print();
      }
      catch (PrinterException e) {}
    }
    System.exit(0);
  }
}
```

There's not much to this example. We've created an implementation of `Printable`, called `UnbelievablySimplePrint`. It has a very simple `print()` method that draws some text.

The rest of the work, in the `main()` method, has to do with setting up the print job. First, we create a new `PrinterJob` and tell it what we want to print:

```
PrinterJob job = PrinterJob.getPrinterJob();
job.setPrintable(new UnbelievablySimplePrint());
```

Then, we use the `printDialog()` method to show the standard print dialog. If the user presses the OK button, `printDialog()` returns `true` and `main()` goes ahead with the printing.

Notice that in the `print()` method, we perform the familiar cast from `Graphics` to `Graphics2D`. The full power of the 2D API is available for printing. In a real application, you'd probably have some subclass of `Component` that was also a `Printable`. The `print()` method could simply call the component's `paint()` method to create a component that performs the same rendering to both the screen and the printer.

CHAPTER 21

Working with Images and Other Media

Until this point, we've confined ourselves to working with the high-level drawing commands of the `Graphics2D` class, using images in a hands-off mode. In this section, we'll clear up some of the mystery surrounding images and see how they can be created and transformed. The classes in the `java.awt.image` package handle images and their internals; Figure 21-1 shows the important classes in this package.

First, we'll return to our discussion of image loading and see how we can get more control over image data using an `ImageObserver` to watch as it's processed asynchronously by GUI components. We'll also see how to use the `MediaTracker` utility to handle the details for us. Then, we'll move on to the good stuff and have a look at `BufferedImage`, which is an image whose pixel data is exposed to you through a memory buffer. If you're interested in creating sophisticated graphics, rendered images, or video, this will teach you about the foundations of image construction in Java.

Looking in the other directions, we will also be referring occasionally to the `javax.imageio` package, which is part of the Java Advanced Imaging API (JAI). If you need even more advanced capabilities such as image tiling, loading scaled versions of images over the network, and deferred execution of image data processing for working with really large images, you'll want to look at JAI.

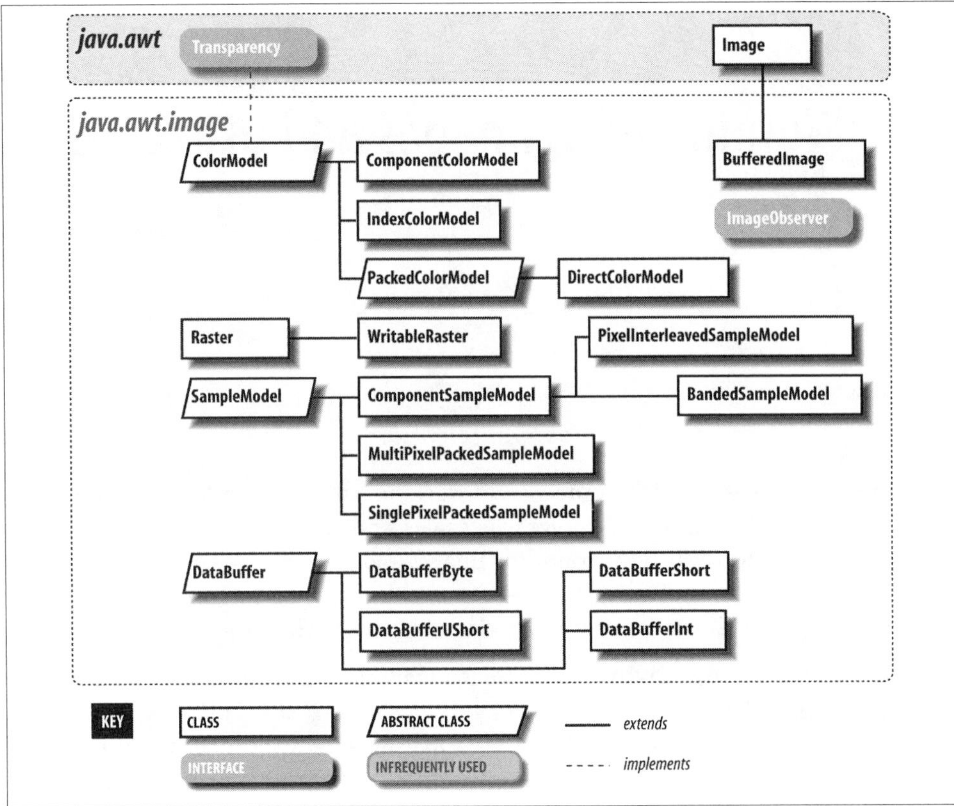

Figure 21-1. The java.awt.image package

Loading Images

One of the challenges in building software for networked applications is that data is not always instantly available. Since some of Java's roots are in Internet applications such as web browsers, its image handling APIs were designed specifically to accommodate the fact that images might take some time to load over a slow network, providing for detailed information about image-loading progress. While many client applications do not require handling of image data in this way, it's still useful to understand this mechanism if for no other reason than it appears in the most basic image-related APIs. The Swing toolkit adds its own layer of image handling over this with components such as `ImageIcon`, which encapsulates an image source for you. After reading this chapter, you'll have an understanding of how the layers fit together.

ImageObserver

In the previous chapter, we mentioned that all operations on image data (e.g., loading, drawing, scaling) allow you to specify an "image observer" object as a participant. An image observer implements the `ImageObserver` interface, allowing it to receive notification as information about the image becomes available. The image observer is essentially a callback that is notified progressively as the image is loaded. For a static image, such as a GIF or JPEG data file, the observer is notified as chunks of image data arrive and also when the entire image is complete. For a video source or animation (e.g., GIF89), the image observer is notified at the end of each frame as the continuous stream of pixel data is generated.

The image observer can do whatever it wants with this information. For example, in the last chapter we used the image observer built into the base `Component` class. Although you probably didn't see it happen in our examples, the `Component` image observer invoked `repaint()` for us each time a new section of the image became available so that the picture, if it had taken a long time to load, would have displayed progressively. A different kind of image observer might have waited for the entire image before telling the application to display it; yet another use for an observer might be to update a loading meter showing how far the image loading had progressed.

To be an image observer, implement the `imageUpdate()` method, which is defined by the `java.awt.image.ImageObserver` interface:

```
public boolean imageUpdate(Image image, int flags, int x, int y,
                           int width, int height)
```

`imageUpdate()` is called by the graphics system, as needed, to pass the observer information about the construction of its view of the image. The `image` parameter holds a reference to the `Image` object in question. `flags` is an integer whose bits specify what information about the image is now available. The flag values are defined as `static` variables in the `ImageObserver` interface, as illustrated in this example:

```
//file: ObserveImageLoad.java
import java.awt.*;
import java.awt.image.*;

public class ObserveImageLoad {

  public static void main( String [] args)
  {
   ImageObserver myObserver = new ImageObserver() {
      public boolean imageUpdate(
         Image image, int flags, int x, int y, int width, int height)
      {
         if ( (flags & HEIGHT) !=0 )
           System.out.println("Image height = " + height );
         if ( (flags & WIDTH ) !=0 )
           System.out.println("Image width = " + width );
```

```
            if ( (flags & FRAMEBITS) != 0 )
              System.out.println("Another frame finished.");
            if ( (flags & SOMEBITS) != 0 )
               System.out.println("Image section :"
                   + new Rectangle( x, y, width, height ) );
            if ( (flags & ALLBITS) != 0 )
              System.out.println("Image finished!");
            if ( (flags & ABORT) != 0 )
              System.out.println("Image load aborted...");
            return true;
        }
    };

      Toolkit toolkit = Toolkit.getDefaultToolkit();
      Image img = toolkit.getImage( args[0] );
      toolkit.prepareImage( img, -1, -1, myObserver );
    }
  }
```

Run the example, supplying an image file as the command-line argument and observe the output. You'll see a number of incremental messages about loading the image.

The `flags` integer determines which of the other parameters—`x`, `y`, `width`, and `height` —hold valid data and what that data means. To test whether a particular flag in the `flags` integer is set, we have to resort to some binary shenanigans—using the `&` (`AND`) operator). The `width` and `height` parameters play a dual role. If `SOMEBITS` is set, they represent the size of the chunk of the image that has just been delivered. If `HEIGHT` or `WIDTH` is set, however, they represent the overall image dimensions. Finally, `imageUpdate()` returns a `boolean` value indicating whether or not it's interested in future updates.

In this example, after requesting the `Image` object with `getImage()`, we kick-start the loading process with the Toolkit's `prepareImage()` method, which takes our image observer as an argument. Using an Image API method such as `drawImage()`, `scaleImage()`, or asking for image dimensions with `getWidth()` or `getHeight()` will also suffice to start the operation. Remember that although the `getImage()` method created the image object, it doesn't begin loading the data until one of the image operations requires it.

The example shows the lowest-level general mechanism for starting and monitoring the process of loading image data. You should be able to see how we could implement all sorts of sophisticated image loading and tracking schemes with this. The two most important strategies (to draw an image progressively, as it's constructed, or to wait until it's complete and draw it in its entirety) are handled for us. We have already seen that the `Component` class implements the first scheme. Another class, `java.awt.MediaTracker`, is a general utility that tracks the loading of a number of images or other media types for us. We'll look at it in the next section.

MediaTracker

java.awt.MediaTracker is a utility class that simplifies life if we have to wait for one or more images to be loaded completely before they're displayed. A MediaTracker monitors the loading of an image or a group of images and lets us check on them periodically or wait until they are finished. MediaTracker implements the ImageObserver interface that we just discussed, allowing it to receive image updates.

The following code snippet illustrates how to use a MediaTracker to wait while an image is prepared:

```
//file: StatusImage.java
import java.awt.*;
import javax.swing.*;

public class StatusImage extends JComponent
{
  boolean loaded = false;
  String message = "Loading...";
  Image image;

  public StatusImage( Image image ) { this.image = image; }

  public void paint(Graphics g) {
    if (loaded)
        g.drawImage(image, 0, 0, this);
    else {
      g.drawRect(0, 0, getSize().width - 1, getSize().height - 1);
      g.drawString(message, 20, 20);
    }
  }
  public void loaded() {
    loaded = true;
    repaint();
  }
  public void setMessage( String msg ) {
    message = msg;
    repaint();
  }

  public static void main( String [] args ) {
    JFrame frame = new JFrame("TrackImage");
    Image image = Toolkit.getDefaultToolkit().getImage( args[0] );
    StatusImage statusImage = new StatusImage( image );
    frame.add( statusImage );
    frame.setSize(300,300);
    frame.setVisible(true);

    MediaTracker tracker = new MediaTracker( statusImage );
    int MAIN_IMAGE = 0;
    tracker.addImage( image, MAIN_IMAGE );
```

```
            try {
                tracker.waitForID( MAIN_IMAGE ); }
            catch (InterruptedException e) {}
            if ( tracker.isErrorID( MAIN_IMAGE ) )
                statusImage.setMessage( "Error" );
            else
                statusImage.loaded();
        }
    }
```

In this example, we created a trivial component called StatusImage that accepts an image and draws a text status message until it is told that the image is loaded. It then displays the image. The only interesting part here is that we use a MediaTracker to load the image data for us, simplifying our logic.

First, we create a MediaTracker to manage the image. The MediaTracker constructor takes a Component as an argument; this is supposed to be the component onto which the image is later drawn. This argument is somewhat of a holdover from earlier Java days with AWT. If you don't have the component reference handy, you can simply substitute a generic component reference like so:

```
    Component comp = new Component();
```

After creating the MediaTracker, we assign it images to manage. Each image is associated with an integer that identifier we can use later for checking on its status or to wait for its completion. Multiple images can be associated with the same identifier, letting us manage them as a group. The value of the identifier is also meant to prioritize loading when waiting on multiple sets of images; lower IDs have higher priority. In this case, we want to manage only a single image, so we created one identifier called MAIN_IMAGE and passed it as the ID for our image in the call to addImage().

Next, we call the MediaTracker waitforID() routine, which blocks on the image, waiting for it to finish loading. If successful, we tell our example component to use the image and repaint. Another MediaTracker method, waitForAll(), waits for all images to complete, not just a single ID. It's possible to be interrupted here by an InterruptedException. We should also test for errors during image preparation with isErrorID(). In our example, we change the status message if we find one.

The MediaTracker checkID() and checkAll() methods may be used to poll periodically the status of images loading, returning true or false to indicate whether loading is finished. The checkAll() method does this for the union of all images being loaded. Additionally, the statusID() and statusAll() methods return a constant indicating the status or final condition of an image load. The value is one of the MediaTracker constant values: LOADING, ABORTED, ERROR, or COMPLETE. For statusAll(), the value is the bitwise OR value of all of the various statuses.

This may seem like a lot of work to go through just to put up a status message while loading a single image. MediaTracker is more valuable when you are working with many raw images that have to be available before you can begin parts of an application. It saves implementing a custom ImageObserver for every application. For general Swing application work, you can use yet another simplification by employing the ImageIcon component to use a MediaTracker. This is covered next.

ImageIcon

In Chapter 17, we discussed Swing components that can work with images using the Icon interface. In particular, the ImageIcon class accepts an image filename or URL and can render it into a component. Internally, ImageIcon uses a MediaTracker to fully load the image in the call to its constructor. It can also provide the Image reference back. So, a shortcut to what we did in the last few sections—getting an image loaded fully before using it—would be:

```
ImageIcon icon = new ImageIcon("myimage.jpg");
Image image = icon.getImage();
```

This quirky approach saves a few lines of typing, but uses an icon in an odd way and is not very clear. ImageIcon also gives you direct access to the MediaTracker it's using through the getMediaTracker() method or tells you the MediaTracker load status through the getImageLoadStatus() method. This returns one of the MediaTracker constants: ABORTED, ERROR, or COMPLETE.

ImageIO

As we mentioned in the introduction to Chapter 1, the javax.imageio package is a standard extension that deals with reading and writing many image formats. It is a part of the larger Java Advanced Imaging (JAI) API. This API supports advanced manipulation and display of images. While the AWT has a relatively fixed set of functionality, JAI is an extensible framework that accepts plug-ins for new image formats and features. The imageio portion of JAI is bundled with Java 1.4 and later, so we can take advantage of it on all current Java releases. ImageIO effectively supercedes the APIs we've talked about here with new ones for loading and monitoring image data, and although we won't cover it in detail, we will discuss it briefly here for several reasons. First, it is fairly easy to use. Second, ImageIO natively works with BufferedImages and not just plain AWT Images. As we'll discuss throughout the rest of this chapter, buffered images can expose their pixel data for you to read or manipulate. Finally, using ImageIO allows you both to load and save BufferedImages to files. The core AWT has no tools for encoding image data for saving to files.

Previously, we showed how easy it is to load an image with the static read() methods of the ImageIO class, which accept either a File, URL, or InputStream:

```
File file = new File("/Users/pat/images/boojum.gif");
BufferedImage bi = ImageIO.read( file );
```

In this example, we revealed that the type returned is actually a `BufferedImage`, which is a subtype of `Image`. The `ImageIO.read()` method, like the AWT `getImage()` method, automatically detects the image type and decodes it properly. Because `ImageIO` is extensible, it's useful to be able to list the types of images it can decode. You get this information with the `ImageIO.getReaderFormatNames()` method, which returns an array of strings corresponding roughly to file extensions for the image types it understands. (`ImageIO` does not rely on file extensions to detect image types; rather, it looks at the content of the file.)

Images loaded by the `ImageIO.read()` methods are fully loaded before they are returned, so the method blocks until they are done. If you want more fine-grained information on the progress of image loading, you can use the `IIOReadProgressListener` interface of the `javax.imageio.event` package, which roughly corresponds to the AWT `ImageObserver`. To use it, you must delve a little deeper into the ImageIO API by first looking up an appropriate `ImageReader` object with which to register the listener:

```
import javax.imageio.*;
import javax.imageio.stream.*;
import javax.imageio.event.*;

File file = new File("image.jpg");
ImageInputStream iis = ImageIO.createImageInputStream( file );

Iterator readers = ImageIO.getImageReaders( iis );
ImageReader reader = (ImageReader)readers.next(); // choose first one

reader.addIIOReadProgressListener( readProgressListener );
reader.setInput( iis, true );
BufferedImage bi = reader.read( 0/*index*/ );
```

This code is fairly straightforward. The `ReadProgressListener` is used like any of the AWT or Swing event interfaces we've seen before. You can refer to the Javadoc for the exact methods you must implement.

Finally, in addition to the progress listener, two other listener APIs, `IIOReadUpdateListener` and `IIOReadWarningListener`, offer information on pixel changes (e.g., for progressive loading) and loading errors. There are also, of course, "write" versions of all of these tools that handle the flip side, saving image data. We'll return to that topic later in this chapter.

Producing Image Data

There are two approaches to generating image data. The high-level method is to treat the image as a drawing surface and use the methods of `Graphics2D` to render things into the image. The second way is to twiddle the bits that represent the pixels of the image data yourself. This is harder, but gives you arbitrary control for handling specific formats or mathematically analyzing or creating image data.

Drawing Animations

Let's begin with the simpler approach, rendering an image through drawing. We'll throw in a twist to make things interesting: we'll build an animation. Each frame will be rendered as we go along. This is very similar to the double buffering we examined in the last chapter, except that this time we'll use a timer instead of mouse events as the signal to generate new frames.

Swing performs double buffering automatically, so we don't even need to worry about the animation flickering. Although it looks like we're drawing directly to the screen, we're really drawing into an image that Swing uses for double buffering. All we need to do is draw the right thing at the right time.

Let's look at an example, `Hypnosis`, that illustrates the technique. This example shows a constantly shifting shape that bounces around the inside of a component. When screen savers first came of age, this kind of thing was pretty hot stuff. `Hypnosis` is shown in Figure 21-2.

Figure 21-2. A simple animation

Here is its source code:

```
//file: Hypnosis.java
import java.awt.*;
import java.awt.event.*;
import java.awt.geom.GeneralPath;
import javax.swing.*;

public class Hypnosis extends JComponent implements Runnable {
  private int[] coordinates;
  private int[] deltas;
  private Paint paint;

  public Hypnosis(int numberOfSegments) {
```

```
    int numberOfCoordinates = numberOfSegments * 4 + 2;
    coordinates = new int[numberOfCoordinates];
    deltas = new int[numberOfCoordinates];
    for (int i = 0 ; i < numberOfCoordinates; i++) {
      coordinates[i] = (int)(Math.random() * 300);
      deltas[i] = (int)(Math.random() * 4 + 3);
      if (deltas[i] > 4) deltas[i] = -(deltas[i] - 3);
    }
    paint = new GradientPaint(0, 0, Color.BLUE,
        20, 10, Color.RED, true);

    Thread t = new Thread(this);
    t.start();
  }

  public void run() {
    try {
      while (true) {
        timeStep();
        repaint();
        Thread.sleep(1000 / 24);
      }
    }
    catch (InterruptedException ie) {}
  }

  public void paint(Graphics g) {
    Graphics2D g2 = (Graphics2D)g;
    g2.setRenderingHint(RenderingHints.KEY_ANTIALIASING,
        RenderingHints.VALUE_ANTIALIAS_ON);
    Shape s = createShape();
    g2.setPaint(paint);
    g2.fill(s);
    g2.setPaint(Color.WHITE);
    g2.draw(s);
  }

  private void timeStep() {
    Dimension d = getSize();
    if (d.width == 0 || d.height == 0) return;
    for (int i = 0; i < coordinates.length; i++) {
      coordinates[i] += deltas[i];
      int limit = (i % 2 == 0) ? d.width : d.height;
      if (coordinates[i] < 0) {
        coordinates[i] = 0;
        deltas[i] = -deltas[i];
      }
      else if (coordinates[i] > limit) {
        coordinates[i] = limit - 1;
        deltas[i] = -deltas[i];
      }
    }
```

```
    }

    private Shape createShape() {
      GeneralPath path = new GeneralPath();
      path.moveTo(coordinates[0], coordinates[1]);
      for (int i = 2; i < coordinates.length; i += 4)
        path.quadTo(coordinates[i], coordinates[i + 1],
            coordinates[i + 2], coordinates[i + 3]);
      path.closePath();
      return path;
    }

    public static void main(String[] args) {
      JFrame frame = new JFrame("Hypnosis");
      frame.add( new Hypnosis(4) );
      frame.setSize(300, 300);
      frame.setDefaultCloseOperation( JFrame.EXIT_ON_CLOSE );
      frame.setVisible(true);
    }
  }
```

The `main()` method does the usual grunt work of setting up the `JFrame` that holds our animation component.

The `Hypnosis` component has a very basic strategy for animation. It holds some number of coordinate pairs in its coordinates member variable. A corresponding array, `deltas`, holds "delta" amounts that are added to the coordinates every time the figure is supposed to change. To render the complex shape you see in Figure 21-2, `Hypnosis` creates a special `Shape` object from the coordinate array every time the component is drawn.

`Hypnosis`'s constructor has two important tasks. First, it fills up the coordinate and delta arrays with random values. The number of array elements is determined by an argument to the constructor. The constructor's second task is to start up a new thread that drives the animation.

The animation is done in the `run()` method. This method calls `timeStep()`, which repaints the component and waits for a short time (details to follow). Every time `timeStep()` is called, the coordinates array is updated and `repaint()` is called. This results in a call to `paint()`, which creates a shape from the coordinate array and draws it.

The `paint()` method is relatively simple. It uses a helper method, called `createShape()`, to create a shape from the coordinate array. The shape is then filled, using a `Paint` stored as a member variable. The shape's outline is also drawn in white.

The `timeStep()` method updates all the elements of the coordinate array by adding the corresponding element of deltas. If any coordinates are now out of the component's bounds, they are adjusted and the corresponding delta is negated. This produces the effect of bouncing off the sides of the component.

createShape() creates a shape from the coordinate array. It uses the GeneralPath class, a useful Shape implementation that allows you to build shapes using straight and curved line segments. In this case, we create a shape from a series of quadratic curves, close it to create an area, and fill it.

BufferedImage Anatomy

So far, we've talked about java.awt.Images and how they can be loaded and drawn. What if you really want to get inside the image to examine and update its data? Image doesn't give you access to its data. You'll need to use a more sophisticated kind of image: java.awt.image.BufferedImage. The classes are closely related—BufferedImage, in fact, is a subclass of Image. BufferedImage gives you all sorts of control over the actual data that makes up the image and provides many capabilities beyond the basic Image class. Because it's a subclass of Image, you can still pass a BufferedImage to any of Graphics2D's methods that accept an Image. Why aren't all Images BufferedImages? Because BufferedImages are memory intensive.

To create an image from raw data, you need to understand exactly how a Buffered Image is put together. The full details can get quite complex—the BufferedImage class was designed to support images in nearly any storage format you can imagine. But, for common operations, it's not that difficult to use. Figure 21-3 shows the elements of a BufferedImage.

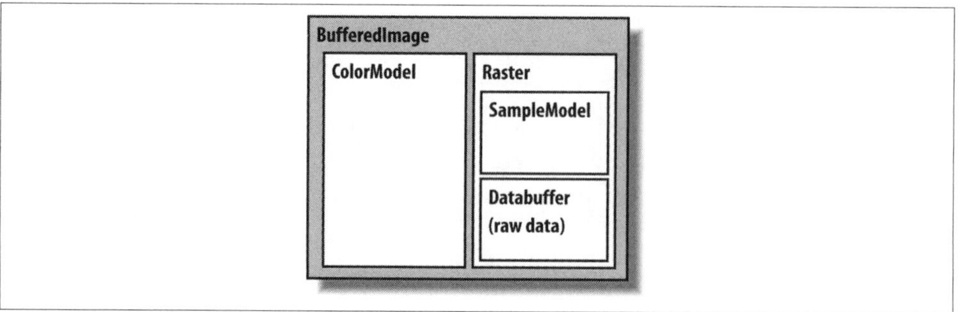

Figure 21-3. Inside a BufferedImage

An image is simply a rectangle of colored pixels, which is a simple enough concept. There's a lot of complexity underneath the BufferedImage class because there are a lot of different ways to represent the colors of pixels. For example, you might have an image with RGB data in which each pixel's red, green, and blue values were stored as the elements of byte arrays. Or you might have an RGB image where each pixel was represented by an integer that contained red, green, and blue component values. Or you could have a 16-level grayscale image with eight pixels stored in each element of an integer array. You get the idea; there are many different ways to store image data, and `BufferedImage` is designed to support all of them.

A `BufferedImage` consists of two pieces, a `Raster` and a `ColorModel`. The `Raster` contains the actual image data. You can think of it as an array of pixel values. It can answer the question, "What are the color data values for the pixel at 51, 17?" The `Raster` for an RGB image would return three values, while a `Raster` for a grayscale image would return a single value. `WritableRaster`, a subclass of `Raster`, also supports modifying pixel data values.

The `ColorModel`'s job is to interpret the image data as colors. The `ColorModel` can translate the data values that come from the `Raster` into `Color` objects. An RGB color model, for example, would know how to interpret three data values as red, green, and blue. A grayscale color model could interpret a single data value as a gray level. Conceptually, at least, this is how an image is displayed on the screen. The graphics system retrieves the data for each pixel of the image from the `Raster`. Then the `ColorModel` tells what color each pixel should be, and the graphics system is able to set the color of each pixel.

The `Raster` itself is made up of two pieces: a `DataBuffer` and a `SampleModel`. A `DataBuffer` is a wrapper for the raw data arrays, which are `byte`, `short`, or `int` arrays. `DataBuffer` has handy subclasses—`DataBufferByte`, `DataBufferShort`, and `DataBufferInt`—that allow you to create a `DataBuffer` from raw data arrays. You'll see an example of this technique later in the `StaticGenerator` example.

The `SampleModel` knows how to extract the data values for a particular pixel from the `DataBuffer`. It knows the layout of the arrays in the `DataBuffer` and is ultimately responsible for answering the question, "What are the data values for pixel x, y?" `SampleModels` are a little tricky to work with, but fortunately you'll probably never need to create or use one directly. As we'll see, the `Raster` class has many static ("factory") methods that create preconfigured `Rasters` for you, including their component `DataBuffers` and `SampleModels`.

As Figure 21-1 shows, the 2D API comes with various flavors of `ColorModels`, `SampleModels`, and `DataBuffers`. These serve as handy building blocks that cover most common image storage formats. You'll rarely need to subclass any of these classes to create a `BufferedImage`.

Color Models

As we've said, there are many different ways to encode color information: red, green, blue (RGB) values; hue, saturation, value (HSV); hue, lightness, saturation (HLS); and more. In addition, you can provide full-color information for each pixel, or you can just specify an index into a color table (palette) for each pixel. The way you represent a color is called a *color model*. The 2D API provides tools to support any color model you could imagine. Here, we'll just cover two broad groups of color models: *direct* and *indexed*.

As you might expect, you must specify a color model in order to generate pixel data; the `abstract` class `java.awt.image.ColorModel` represents a color model. By default, Java 2D uses a direct color model called ARGB. The A stands for "alpha," which is the historical name for transparency. RGB refers to the red, green, and blue color components that are combined to produce a single, composite color. In the default ARGB model, each pixel is represented by a 32-bit integer that is interpreted as four 8-bit fields; in order, the fields represent the alpha (transparency), red, green, and blue components of the color, as shown in Figure 21-4.

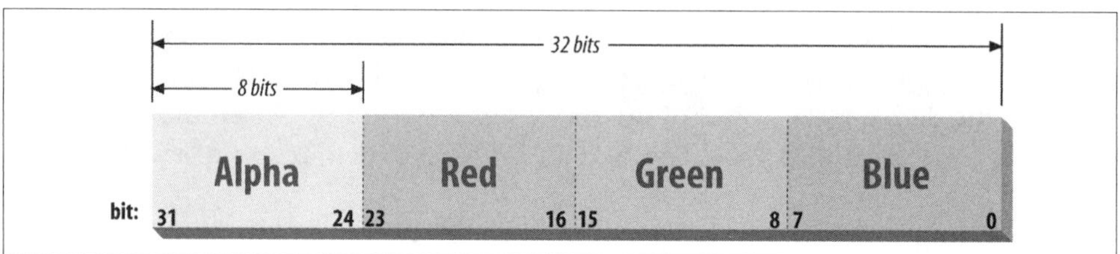

Figure 21-4. ARGB color encoding

To create an instance of the default ARGB model, call the `static getRGBdefault()` method in `ColorModel`. This method returns a `DirectColorModel` object; `DirectColorModel` is a subclass of `ColorModel`. You can also create other direct color models by calling a `DirectColorModel` constructor, but you shouldn't need to do this unless you have a fairly exotic application.

In an indexed color model, each pixel is represented by a smaller piece of information: an index into a table of real color values. Several common image formats, including GIF, use an indexed color model. For some applications, generating data with an indexed model may be more convenient. If you are writing an application for an 8-bit display or smaller, using an indexed model may be more efficient, because your hardware is internally using an indexed color model of some form.

Creating an Image

Let's take a look at producing some image data. A picture is worth a thousand words, and, fortunately, we can generate a pretty picture in significantly fewer than a thousand words of Java. If we just want to render image frames byte by byte, you can put together a `BufferedImage` pretty easily.

The following application, `ColorPan`, creates an image from an array of integers holding RGB pixel values:

```
//file: ColorPan.java
import java.awt.*;
import java.awt.image.*;
import javax.swing.*;

public class ColorPan extends JComponent {
  BufferedImage image;

  public void initialize() {
    int width = getSize().width;
    int height = getSize().height;
    int[] data = new int [width * height];
    int i = 0;
    for (int y = 0; y < height; y++) {
      int red = (y * 255) / (height - 1);
      for (int x = 0; x < width; x++) {
        int green = (x * 255) / (width - 1);
        int blue = 128;
        data[i++] = (red << 16) | (green << 8 ) | blue;
      }
    }
    image = new BufferedImage(width, height,
        BufferedImage.TYPE_INT_RGB);
    image.setRGB(0, 0, width, height, data, 0, width);
  }

  public void paint(Graphics g) {
    if (image == null)
        initialize();
    g.drawImage(image, 0, 0, this);
  }

  public void setBounds(int x, int y, int width, int height) {
    super.setBounds(x,y,width,height);
    initialize();
  }

  public static void main(String[] args) {
    JFrame frame = new JFrame("ColorPan");
    frame.add(new ColorPan());
    frame.setSize(300, 300);
    frame.setDefaultCloseOperation( JFrame.EXIT_ON_CLOSE );
    frame.setVisible(true);
  }
}
```

Give it a try. The size of the image is determined by the size of the application window. You should get a very colorful box that pans from deep blue at the upper-left corner to bright yellow at the bottom right, with green and red at the other extremes.

We create a BufferedImage in the initialize() method and then display the image in paint(). The variable data is a 1D array of integers that holds 32-bit RGB pixel values. In initialize(), we loop over every pixel in the image and assign it an RGB value. The blue component is always 128, half its maximum intensity. The red component varies from 0 to 255 along the y-axis; likewise, the green component varies from 0 to 255 along the x-axis. This statement combines these components into an RGB value:

```
data[i++] = (red << 16) | (green << 8 ) | blue;
```

The bitwise left-shift operator (<<) should be familiar to anyone who has programmed in C. It simply shoves the bits over by the specified number of positions in our 32-bit value.

When we create the BufferedImage, all its data is zeroed out. All we specify in the constructor is the width and height of the image and its type. BufferedImage includes quite a few constants representing image storage types. We've chosen TYPE_INT_RGB here, which indicates that we want to store the image as RGB data packed into integers. The constructor takes care of creating an appropriate ColorModel, Raster, SampleModel, and DataBuffer for us. Then we simply use the setRGB() method to assign our data to the image. In this way, we've side-stepped the messy innards of BufferedImage. In the next example, we'll take a closer look at the details.

Once we have the image, we can draw it on the display with the standard drawImage() method. We also override the Component setBounds() method in order to determine when the frame is resized and reinitialize the image to the new size.

Updating a BufferedImage

BufferedImage can also be used to update an image dynamically. Because the image's data arrays are directly accessible, you can simply change the data and redraw the picture whenever you want. This is probably the easiest way to build your own low-level animation software. The following example simulates the static on an old black-and-white television screen. It generates successive frames of random black and white pixels and displays each frame when it is complete. Figure 21-5 shows one frame of random static.

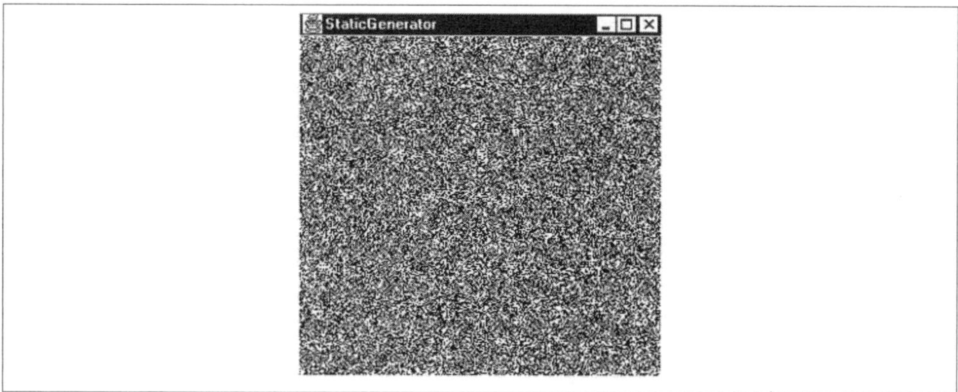

Figure 21-5. A frame of random static

Here's the code:

```
//file: StaticGenerator.java
import java.awt.*;
import java.awt.event.*;
import java.awt.image.*;
import java.util.Random;
import javax.swing.*;

public class StaticGenerator extends JComponent implements Runnable {
  byte[] data;
  BufferedImage image;
  Random random;

  public void initialize() {
    int w = getSize().width, h = getSize().height;
    int length = ((w + 7) * h) / 8;
    data = new byte[length];
    DataBuffer db = new DataBufferByte(data, length);
    WritableRaster wr = Raster.createPackedRaster(db, w, h, 1, null);
    ColorModel cm = new IndexColorModel(1, 2,
        new byte[] { (byte)0, (byte)255 },
        new byte[] { (byte)0, (byte)255 },
        new byte[] { (byte)0, (byte)255 });
    image = new BufferedImage(cm, wr, false, null);
    random = new Random();
  }

  public void run() {
    if ( random == null )
        initialize();
    while (true) {
      random.nextBytes(data);
      repaint();
      try { Thread.sleep(1000 / 24); }
```

```
        catch( InterruptedException e ) { /* die */ }
      }
    }

    public void paint(Graphics g) {
      if (image == null) initialize();
      g.drawImage(image, 0, 0, this);
    }

    public void setBounds(int x, int y, int width, int height) {
      super.setBounds(x,y,width,height);
      initialize();
    }

    public static void main(String[] args) {
      //RepaintManager.currentManager(null).setDoubleBufferingEnabled(false);
      JFrame frame = new JFrame("StaticGenerator");
      StaticGenerator staticGen = new StaticGenerator();
      frame.add( staticGen );
      frame.setSize(300, 300);
      frame.setDefaultCloseOperation( JFrame.EXIT_ON_CLOSE );
      frame.setVisible(true);
      new Thread( staticGen ).start();
    }
  }
```

The `initialize()` method sets up the `BufferedImage` that produces the sequence of images. We build this image from the bottom up, starting with the raw data array. Since we're only displaying two colors here, black and white, we need only one bit per pixel. We want a 0 bit to represent black and a 1 bit to represent white. This calls for an indexed color model, which we'll create a little later.

We'll store our image data as a byte array, where each array element holds eight pixels from our black-and-white image. The array length, then, is calculated by multiplying the width and height of the image and dividing by eight. To keep things simple, we'll arrange for each image row to start on a byte boundary. For example, an image 13 pixels wide actually uses 2 bytes (16 bits) for each row:

```
int length = (w + 7)/8 * h;
```

This calculation rounds upward the number of bytes required to fill a row and then multiplies by the number of rows. Next, the actual byte array is created. The member variable `data` holds a reference to this array. Later, we'll use `data` to change the image data dynamically. Once we have the image data array, it's easy to create a `DataBuffer` from it:

```
data = new byte[length];
DataBuffer db = new DataBufferByte(data, length);
```

`DataBuffer` has several subclasses, such as `DataBufferByte`, that make it easy to create a data buffer from raw arrays.

Logically, the next step is to create a SampleModel. We could then create a Raster from the SampleModel and the DataBuffer. Lucky for us, though, the Raster class contains a bevy of useful static methods that create common types of Rasters. One of these methods creates a Raster from data that contains multiple pixels packed into array elements. We simply use this method, supplying the data buffer, the width and height, and indicating that each pixel uses one bit:

```
WritableRaster wr = Raster.createPackedRaster(db, w, h, 1, null/*ul corner*/);
```

The last argument to this method is a java.awt.Point that indicates where the upper-left corner of the Raster should be. By passing null, we use the default of 0, 0.

The last piece of the puzzle is the ColorModel. Each pixel is either 0 or 1, but how should that be interpreted as color? In this case, we use an IndexColorModel with a very small palette. The palette has only two entries, one each for black and white:

```
ColorModel cm = new IndexColorModel(1, 2,
        new byte[] { (byte)0, (byte)255 },
        new byte[] { (byte)0, (byte)255 },
        new byte[] { (byte)0, (byte)255 });
```

The IndexColorModel constructor that we've used here accepts the number of bits per pixel (one), the number of entries in the palette (two), and three byte arrays that are the red, green, and blue components of the palette colors. Our palette consists of two colors: black (0, 0, 0) and white (255, 255, 255).

Now that we've got all the pieces, we just need to create a BufferedImage. This image is also stored in a member variable so we can draw it later. To create the BufferedImage, we pass the color model and writable raster we just created:

```
image = new BufferedImage(cm, wr, false, null);
```

All the hard work is done now. Our paint() method just draws the image, using drawImage().

The init() method starts a thread that generates the pixel data. The run() method takes care of generating the pixel data. It uses a java.util.Random object to fill the data image byte array with random values. Because the data array is the actual image data for our image, changing the data values changes the appearance of the image. After we fill the array with random data, a call to repaint() shows the new image on the screen.

You can also try turning off double buffering by uncommenting the line involving the RepaintManager. Now it will look even more like an old TV screen, flickering and all!

That's about all there is. It's worth noting how simple it is to create this animation. Once we have the BufferedImage, we treat it like any other image. The code that generates the image sequence can be arbitrarily complex. But that complexity never infects the simple task of getting the image on the screen and updating it.

Filtering Image Data

An *image filter* is an object that performs transformations on image data. The Java 2D API supports image filtering through the `BufferedImageOp` interface. An image filter takes a `BufferedImage` as input (the *source image*) and performs some processing on the image data, producing another `BufferedImage` (the *destination image*).

The 2D API comes with a handy toolbox of `BufferedImageOp` implementations, as summarized in Table 21-1.

Table 21-1. Image operators in the 2D API

Name	Description
`AffineTransformOp`	Transforms an image geometrically
`ColorConvertOp`	Converts from one color space to another
`ConvolveOp`	Performs a convolution, a mathematical operation that can be used to blur, sharpen, or otherwise process an image
`LookupOp`	Uses one or more lookup tables to process image values
`RescaleOp`	Uses multiplication to process image values

Let's take a look at two of the simpler image operators. First, try the following application. It loads an image (the first command-line argument is the filename) and processes it in different ways as you select items from the combo box. The application is shown in Figure 21-6.

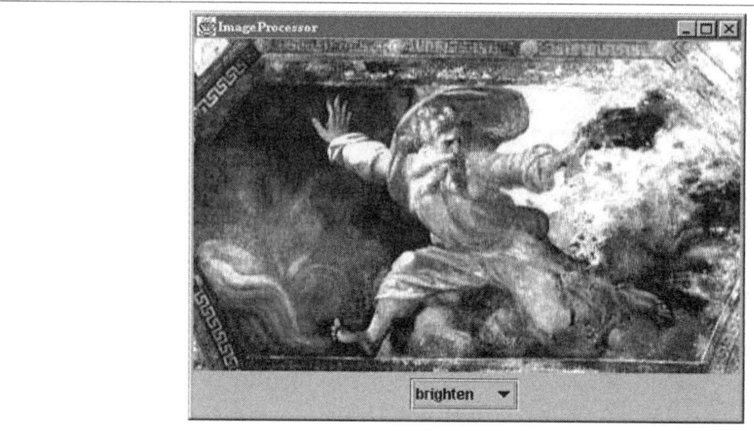

Figure 21-6. The ImageProcessor application

Here's the source code:

```
//file: ImageProcessor.java
import java.awt.*;
```

```
import java.awt.event.*;
import java.awt.geom.*;
import java.awt.image.*;
import javax.swing.*;

public class ImageProcessor extends JComponent {
  private BufferedImage source, destination;
  private JComboBox options;

  public ImageProcessor( BufferedImage image ) {
    source = destination = image;
    setBackground(Color.white);
    setLayout(new BorderLayout());
    // create a panel to hold the combo box
    JPanel controls = new JPanel();
    // create the combo box with the names of the area operators
    options = new JComboBox(
      new String[] { "[source]", "brighten", "darken", "rotate", "scale" }
    );
    // perform some processing when the selection changes
    options.addItemListener(new ItemListener() {
      public void itemStateChanged(ItemEvent ie) {
        // retrieve the selection option from the combo box
        String option = (String)options.getSelectedItem();
        // process the image according to the selected option
        BufferedImageOp op = null;
        if (option.equals("[source]"))
          destination = source;
        else if (option.equals("brighten"))
          op = new RescaleOp(1.5f, 0, null);
        else if (option.equals("darken"))
          op = new RescaleOp(.5f, 0, null);
        else if (option.equals("rotate"))
          op = new AffineTransformOp(
              AffineTransform.getRotateInstance(Math.PI / 6), null);
        else if (option.equals("scale"))
          op = new AffineTransformOp(
              AffineTransform.getScaleInstance(.5, .5), null);
        if (op != null) destination = op.filter(source, null);
        repaint();
      }
    });
    controls.add(options);
    add(controls, BorderLayout.SOUTH);
  }

  public void paintComponent(Graphics g) {
    int imageWidth = destination.getWidth();
    int imageHeight = destination.getHeight();
    int width = getSize().width;
    int height = getSize().height;
    g.drawImage(destination,
```

```
            (width - imageWidth) / 2, (height - imageHeight) / 2, null);
    }

    public static void main(String[] args) {
      String filename = args[0];

      ImageIcon icon = new ImageIcon(filename);
      Image i = icon.getImage();

      // draw the Image into a BufferedImage
      int w = i.getWidth(null), h = i.getHeight(null);
      BufferedImage buffImage = new BufferedImage(w, h,
          BufferedImage.TYPE_INT_RGB);
      Graphics2D imageGraphics = buffImage.createGraphics();
      imageGraphics.drawImage(i, 0, 0, null);

      JFrame frame = new JFrame("ImageProcessor");
      frame.add(new ImageProcessor(buffImage));
      frame.setSize(buffImage.getWidth(), buffImage.getHeight());
      frame.setDefaultCloseOperation( JFrame.EXIT_ON_CLOSE );
      frame.setVisible(true);
    }
  }
```

There's quite a bit packed into the `ImageProcessor` application. After you've played around with it, come back and read about the details.

How ImageProcessor Works

The basic operation of `ImageProcessor` is very straightforward. It loads a source image, specified with a command-line argument in its `main()` method. The image is displayed along with a combo box. When you select different items from the combo box, `Image Processor` performs some image-processing operation on the source image and displays the result (the destination image). Most of this work occurs in the `ItemListen er` event handler that is created in `ImageProcessor`'s constructor (a dubious design because we don't want to tie up event-handling threads for too long, but we'll let it slide here). Depending on the option that is selected, a `BufferedImageOp` (called `op`) is instantiated and used to process the source image, like this:

```
destination = op.filter(source, null);
```

The destination image is returned from the `filter()` method. If we already had a destination image of the right size to hold the output, we could have passed it as the second argument to `filter()`, which would improve the performance of the application a bit. If you just pass `null`, as we have here, an appropriate destination image is created and returned to you. Once the destination image is created, `paint()`'s job is very simple; it just draws the destination image, centered on the component.

Converting an Image to a BufferedImage

Image processing can be performed only on `BufferedImage`s, not `Image`s. Remember that the core AWT tools all work with `Image` and that only if you are loading images using the `ImageIO` package will you get `BufferedImage`s. Our `ImageProcessor` example demonstrates an important technique: how to convert a plain AWT `Image` to a `BufferedImage`. You do it by painting into the buffer, effectively copying the data. The `main()` method loads an `Image` from a file using `Toolkit`'s `getImage()` method:

```
Image i = Toolkit.getDefaultToolkit().getImage(filename);
```

Next, `main()` uses a `MediaTracker` to make sure the image data is fully loaded.

Finally, the trick of converting an `Image` to a `BufferedImage` is to draw the `Image` into the drawing surface of the `BufferedImage`. Because we know the `Image` is fully loaded, we just need to create a `BufferedImage`, get its graphics context, and draw the `Image` into it:

```
BufferedImage bi = new BufferedImage(w, h,
        BufferedImage.TYPE_INT_RGB);
Graphics2D imageGraphics = bi.createGraphics();
imageGraphics.drawImage(i, 0, 0, null);
```

Using the RescaleOp Class

Rescaling is an image operation that multiplies all the pixel values in the image by some constant. It doesn't affect the size of the image in any way (in case you thought *rescaling* meant *scaling*), but it does affect the brightness of its pixel's colors. In an RGB image, for example, each of the red, green, and blue values for each pixel would be multiplied by the rescaling multiplier. If you want, you can also adjust the results by adding an offset. In the 2D API, rescaling is performed by the `java.awt.image.RescaleOp` class. To create such an operator, specify the multiplier, offset, and a set of hints that control the quality of the conversion. In this case, we'll use a zero offset and not bother with the hints (by passing `null`):

```
op = new RescaleOp(1.5f, 0, null);
```

Here, we've specified a multiplier of 1.5 and an offset of 0. All values in the destination image will be 1.5 times the values in the source image, which has the net result of making the image brighter. To perform the operation, we call the `filter()` method from the `BufferedImageOp` interface.

Using the AffineTransformOp Class

An affine transformation is a kind of 2D transformation that preserves parallel lines; this includes operations like scaling, rotating, and shearing. The `java.awt.image.AffineTransformOp` image operator geometrically transforms a source image to produce the destination image. To create an `AffineTransformOp`, specify the transformation you want in the form of an `java.awt.geom.AffineTransform`. The `ImageProcessor` application includes two examples of this operator, one for rotation and one for scaling. As before, the `AffineTransformOp` constructor accepts a set of hints; we'll just pass `null` to keep things simple:

```
else if (option.equals("rotate"))
  op = new AffineTransformOp(
      AffineTransform.getRotateInstance(Math.PI / 6), null);
else if (option.equals("scale"))
  op = new AffineTransformOp(
      AffineTransform.getScaleInstance(.5, .5), null);
```

In both cases, we obtain an `AffineTransform` by calling one of its static methods. In the first case, we get a rotational transformation by supplying an angle. This transformation is wrapped in an `AffineTransformOp`. This operator has the effect of rotating the source image around its origin to create the destination image. In the second case, a scaling transformation is wrapped in an `AffineTransformOp`. The two scaling values, .5 and .5, specify that the image should be reduced to half its original size in both the x and y axes.

When using an `AffineTransformOp` to scale images, it's important to note two things. Scaling an image up will always result in poor quality. When scaling an image down, and more generally with any affine transform, you can choose between speed and quality. Using `AffineTransformOp.TYPE_NEAREST_NEIGHBOR` as the second argument in your `AffineTransformOp` constructor will give you speed. For the best quality use `AffineTransformOp.TYPE_BICUBIC`. `AffineTransformOp.TYPE_BILINEAR` balances speed and quality.

One interesting aspect of `AffineTransformOp` is that you may "lose" part of your image when it's transformed. For example, when using the rotate image operator in the `ImageProcessor` application, the destination image will have clipped some of the original image out. Both the source and destination images have the same origin, so if any part of the image gets transformed into negative x or y space, it is lost. To work around this problem, you can structure your transformations such that the entire destination image is in positive coordinate space.

Saving Image Data

We've spent a lot of time talking about loading images from files and generating and transforming image data, but nothing about saving it. First, let's remember that saving an image to a file such as a JPG or GIF really implies doing two things: encoding it (highly compressing the data in a way optimized for the type of image) and then writing it to a file, possibly with various metadata. As we mentioned earlier, the core AWT does not provide tools for encoding image data, only decoding it. By contrast, the ImageIO framework has the capability of writing images in any format that it can read.

Writing a `BufferedImage` is simply a matter of calling the static `ImageIO write()` method:

```
File outFile = new File("/tmp/myImage.png");
ImageIO.write( bufferedImage , "png", outFile );
```

The second argument is a string identifier that names the image type. You can get the list of supported formats by calling `ImageIO.getWriterFormatNames()`. We should note that the actual type of the image argument is something called `RenderedImage`, but `BufferedImage` implements that interface.

You can get more control over the encoding (for example, JPG quality settings) by getting an `ImageWriter` for the output format and using `ImageWriteParams`. The process is similar to that in the reader progress listener snippet from the section "ImageIO" on page 777.

Simple Audio

Now we'll turn from images and open our ears to audio. Java Sound API provides fine-grained support for the creation and manipulation of both sampled audio and MIDI music, as well as control over MIDI devices. There's space here only to scratch the surface by examining how to play simple sampled sound and MIDI music files. With the standard Java Sound support bundled with Java, you can play a wide range of file formats including AIFF, AU, Windows WAV, standard MIDI files, and Rich Music Format (RMF) files. We'll discuss other formats (such as MP3) along with video media in the next section.

`java.applet.AudioClip` defines the simplest interface for objects that can play sound. An object that implements `AudioClip` can be told to `play()` its sound data, `stop()` playing the sound, or `loop()` continuously.

The `Applet` class provides a handy static method, `newAudioClip()`, that retrieves sounds from files or over the network. (And there is no reason we can't use it in a non-applet application.) The method takes an absolute or relative URL to specify where the audio file is located and returns an `AudioClip`. The following application, `NoisyButton`, gives a simple example:

```
//file: NoisyButton.java
import java.applet.*;
import java.awt.*;
import java.awt.event.*;
import javax.swing.*;

public class NoisyButton {

  public static void main(String[] args) throws Exception {
    JFrame frame = new JFrame("NoisyButton");
    java.io.File file = new java.io.File( args[0] );
```

```
        final AudioClip sound = Applet.newAudioClip(file.toURL());

        JButton button = new JButton("Woof!");
        button.addActionListener(new ActionListener() {
          public void actionPerformed(ActionEvent e) { sound.play(); }
        });

        Container content = frame.getContentPane();
        content.setBackground(Color.pink);
        content.setLayout(new GridBagLayout());
        content.add(button);
        frame.setVisible(true);
        frame.setSize(200, 200);
        frame.setDefaultCloseOperation( JFrame.EXIT_ON_CLOSE );
        frame.setVisible(true);
    }
}
```

Run `NoisyButton`, passing the name of the audio file you wish to use as the argument. (We've supplied one called *bark.aiff*.)

`NoisyButton` retrieves the `AudioClip` using a `File` and the `toURL()`method to reference it as a URL. When the button is pushed, we call the `play()` method of the `AudioClip` to start things. After that, it plays to completion unless we call the `stop()` method to interrupt it.

This interface is simple, but there is a lot of machinery behind the scenes. Next, we'll look at the Java Media Framework, which supports a wider range of media types.

Java Media Framework

Get some popcorn—Java can play movies! To do this, though, we'll need one of Java's standard extension APIs, the Java Media Framework (JMF). The JMF defines a set of interfaces and classes in the `javax.media` and `javax.media.protocol` packages. You can download the latest JMF from Oracle's website (*http://bit.ly/YWPAUk*). To use the JMF, add *jmf.jar* to your classpath. Or, depending on what version of the JMF you download, a friendly installation program may do this for you.

We'll only scratch the surface of JMF here, by working with an important interface called `Player`. Specific implementations of `Player` deal with different media "container" types, such as Apple QuickTime (*.mov*) and Windows Video (*.avi*). For a full list of supported media types and codecs, consult the latest JMF documentation. There are also players for audio types, including MP3. `Player`s are handed out by a high-level class in the JMF called `Manager`. One way to obtain a `Player` is to specify the URL of a movie.

What about Windows media player format as well as MP3?

```
Player player = Manager.createPlayer(url);
```

Because video files are so large and playing them requires significant system resources, `Players` have a multistep lifecycle from the time they're created to the time they actually play something. We'll look at only one step, *realizing*. In this step, the `Player` determines (by looking at the media file) the system resources that it needs to play the media file.

```
player.realize();
```

The `realize()` method returns right away; it kicks off the realizing process in a separate thread. When the `Player` is finished realizing, it sends out an event. Once you receive this event, you can obtain one of two `Components` from the `Player`. The first is a visual component that, for visual media types, shows the media. The second is a control component that provides a prefab user interface for controlling the media presentation. The control normally includes start, stop, and pause buttons, along with volume controls and attendant goodies.

The `Player` has to be realized before you ask for these components so that it has important information, like how big the component should be. After that, getting the component is easy. Here's an example:

```
Component c = player.getVisualComponent();
```

Now, we just need to add the component to the screen somewhere. We can play the media right away (although this actually moves the `Player` through several other internal states):

```
player.start();
```

The following example, `MediaPlayer`, uses the JMF to load and display a movie or audio file from a specified URL:

```
//file: MediaPlayer.java
import java.awt.*;
import java.net.URL;
import javax.swing.*;
import javax.media.*;

public class MediaPlayer
{
   public static void main( String[] args ) throws Exception {
      final JFrame frame = new JFrame("MediaPlayer");
      frame.setDefaultCloseOperation( JFrame.EXIT_ON_CLOSE );
      URL url = new URL( args[0] );
      final Player player = Manager.createPlayer( url );

      player.addControllerListener( new ControllerListener() {
         public void controllerUpdate( ControllerEvent ce ) {
            if ( ce instanceof RealizeCompleteEvent )
            {
               Component visual = player.getVisualComponent();
               Component control = player.getControlPanelComponent();
               if ( visual != null )
```

```
                frame.add( visual, BorderLayout.CENTER );
              frame.add( control, BorderLayout.SOUTH );
              frame.pack();
              frame.setVisible( true );
              player.start();
            }
          }
        });

        player.realize();
      }
    }
```

This class creates a `JFrame` that holds the media. Then, it creates a `Player` from the URL specified on the command line and tells the `Player` to `realize()`. There's nothing else we can do until the `Player` is realized, so the rest of the code operates inside a `ControllerListener` after the `RealizeCompleteEvent` is received.

In the event handler, we get the `Player`'s visual and controller components and add them to the `JFrame`. We display the `JFrame` and, finally, we play the movie. It's very simple!

To use the `MediaPlayer`, pass it the URL of a movie or audio file on the command line. Here are a couple of examples:

```
% java MediaPlayer file:dancing_baby.avi
% java MediaPlayerhttp://myserver/mp3s/TheCure/KissMe/catch.mp3
```

Figure 21-7 shows the "dancing baby" AVI running in the MediaPlayer. Feel free to dance along if you want.

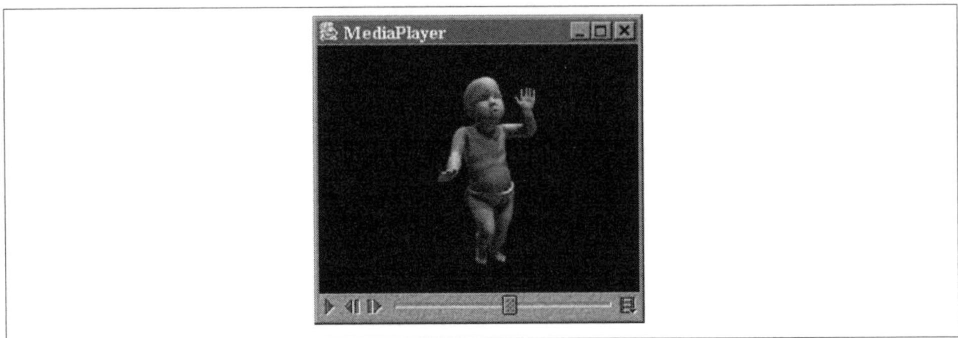

Figure 21-7. Image of the dancing baby AVI

CHAPTER 22
JavaBeans

JavaBeans is a design pattern and a component architecture for Java. It is a set of rules for writing highly reusable software elements that can be understood by both developers and development tools. Writing components to the JavaBeans specification means your code will be easier to read and you won't have to write as much custom code to glue components together. It also allows you to leverage JavaBean-aware development environments that can recognize the features of these components automatically and connect them in a plug-and-play fashion to build parts of applications.

In this chapter, we'll use the NetBeans IDE to create simple applications by connecting Java beans visually. We will also create our own reusable beans to add to the palette of components in the IDE. Although this type of visual application design has never quite reached the level it was expected to (we'll talk about some of the reasons why later), it is still very useful in GUI development. Perhaps more important though, the fundamental JavaBeans patterns are firmly entrenched in all aspects of the core Java APIs, so understanding them is important. We will cover all of these aspects in this chapter, including hand-coding with Java beans and some related APIs.

What's a Bean?

What exactly is or are JavaBeans? *JavaBeans* (the architecture) defines a set of rules; *Java beans* are ordinary Java objects that play by these rules. That is, Java beans are Java objects that conform to the JavaBeans API and design patterns. By doing so, they can be recognized and manipulated by tools (especially visual application builder environments) as well as by hand coding. Beans live and work in the Java runtime system, as do all Java objects. They communicate with their neighbors using events and other normal method invocations.

For examples of Java beans, we need look no further than the `javax.swing` packages. All the familiar components, such as `JButton`, `JTextArea`, and `JScrollpane`, follow the

JavaBeans design patterns and are beans. Much of what you learned in Chapter 16 about Swing components prepared you for understanding beans. Although most of the Swing components aren't very useful in isolation, in general, beans can also be large and complex application components, such as spreadsheets or document editors. We'll talk more about exactly what makes a bean a bean in a moment. For now, we want to give you a better sense of how they are used.

One of the goals of JavaBeans is to allow components to be manipulated visually within a graphical application builder. Beans can be chosen from a palette of tools and manipulated graphically by an application designer. The Swing components we mentioned earlier are obvious candidates for this kind of usage. But Java beans can be not only simple UI components, such as buttons and sliders, but also more complex and abstract components. It is easy to get the impression that beans are, themselves, always graphical objects, but Java beans can implement any part of an application, including "invisible" parts that perform calculations, storage, and communications. Three characteristics of the JavaBeans architecture aim to make it possible to work with application components in this way:

Design patterns
: The most important characteristic of a Java bean is simply a layer of standardization. Design patterns (i.e., coding conventions) let tools and humans recognize the basic features of a bean and manipulate it without knowing how it is implemented. We might say that beans are "self-documenting." By examining a bean, we can tell what events it can fire and receive; we can also learn about its properties (the equivalent of its public variables) and methods. Beans can also provide explicit ("bean info") information about their features tailored specifically for IDEs.

Reflection
: Reflection is an important feature of the Java language. (It's discussed in Chapter 7.) Reflection makes it possible for Java code to inspect and manipulate new Java objects at runtime. In the context of JavaBeans, reflection lets a development tool analyze a bean's capabilities, examine the values of its fields, and invoke its methods. Essentially, reflection allows Java objects that hook up at runtime to do all the things that could be done if the objects had been put together at compile time. Even if a bean doesn't come bundled with any "built-in" documentation, we can still gather information about its capabilities and properties by directly inspecting the class using reflection.

Object serialization
: Finally, the Java Serialization API allows us to "freeze-dry" a live application or application component and revive it later. This is an important capability that makes it possible to piece together applications without extensive code generation. Rather than customizing and compiling large amounts of Java code to build our application on startup, we can simply configure beans, tweak their appearance, and save them.

Later, the beans can be restored with all their state and interconnections intact. This makes possible a fundamentally different way of thinking about the design process. It is easy to use serialized objects from handwritten Java code as well, so we can freely mix serialized beans with plain-old bean classes and other Java code. There is also a "long-term" object serialization mechanism that saves Java beans in an XML format that is very resilient to changes in classes.

What Constitutes a Bean?

The bean examples we mentioned have ranged from simple buttons to spreadsheets. Obviously, a button bean would be much less complex than a spreadsheet and would be used at a different level of the application's design. At what level are beans intended to be used? The JavaBeans architecture is supposed to scale well from small to large; simple beans can be used to build larger beans. A small bean may consist of a single class; a large bean may have many. Beans can also work together through their container to provide services to other beans.

Simple beans are little more than ordinary Java objects. In fact, any Java class that has a default (empty) constructor could be considered a bean. A bean should also be serializable, although the JavaBeans specification doesn't strictly require that. These two criteria ensure that we can create an instance of the bean dynamically and that we can later save the bean as part of a group or composition of beans. There are no other requirements. Beans are not required to inherit from a base bean class, and they don't have to implement any special interface.

A useful bean should send and receive events and expose its properties to the world. To do so, it follows the appropriate design patterns for naming the relevant methods so that these features can be automatically discovered. Most nontrivial beans intended for use in a visual application builder IDE also provide information about themselves in the form of a `BeanInfo` class. A `BeanInfo` class implements the `BeanInfo` interface, which holds methods that describe a bean's features in more detail, along with extra packaging, such as icons for display to the user. Normally, this "bean info" is supplied by a separate class that is named for and supplied with the bean.

The NetBeans IDE

We can't have a full discussion of beans without spending a little time talking about the builder environments in which they are used. In this chapter, we use the NetBeans IDE version 7.2 to demonstrate our beans. NetBeans is a popular, pure Java development environment. In this case, the *integrated* in *integrated development environment* means that NetBeans offers powerful source and visual editor capabilities, templates that aid in the creation of various types of Java classes, and the ability to compile, run, and debug applications, all in one tool. In particular, we'll be using the visual development environment of NetBeans to glue together our Java beans and try them out. Other IDEs offer similar capabilities. See Appendix A for a brief comparison of NetBeans and the Eclipse IDE. We've chosen NetBeans to use in this chapter because its mature GUI builder environment makes it easy to illustrate the concepts here.

Because NetBeans is a full-blown production development environment, it has many features we don't use in these examples. For that reason, we can't really provide a full introduction to it here. We will provide only bare-bones directions here for demonstrating the Java beans in this chapter. Most of the techniques you see here will apply in some form in other IDEs as well.

Installing and Running NetBeans

You should install Java 7.0 before you install NetBeans. If you installed the JDK from Sun's website, you may have downloaded a combined JDK and NetBeans bundle, so you may already have it installed. The standalone installation of NetBeans can be found at *http://www.netbeans.org*. Follow the simple installation instructions for those packages (you may have to reboot if you just installed Java). When you're all set, launch NetBeans. When you first start NetBeans, a welcome screen appears. Close it for now by clicking the small x on its tab. (If you want to return to this welcome screen later to take the NetBeans tutorials, choose Help → Welcome Screen.)

Installing our example beans

Before we get started, we'll have to add the example beans used in this chapter to the NetBeans palette. NetBeans installs Java beans in a central location that can be used by multiple projects in the editor.

1. To install our beans, grab our demonstration beans JAR file, *magicbeans.jar*, from this book's website (*http://oreil.ly/Learn_Java_4E*).
2. Save the file locally and then select Tools → Palette → Swing/AWT Components to add the beans.
3. Click "Add from Jar," then navigate to and select the *magicbeans.jar* file and click Next. The wizard then shows you a list of beans that our JAR contains (there should be eight altogether).
4. Select all of them (click the first and shift-click the last), then click Next.
5. NetBeans prompts you for the palette category under which you wish to file these; select Beans (which would otherwise be empty), then click Finish and Close.

We'll see these beans soon when we start editing an application.

Creating a project and file

Now, we must create a new project to hold our work. To create a new project, select New Project from the File menu. In the Categories pane of the wizard, select General and in the Projects pane, select Java Application, and then click Next. Give your project a name, such as LearningJava, and specify a location or leave the defaults. Uncheck the box labeled Create Main Class because we will create our own, then click Finish to create our empty project. If this is the first time you've created a project in NetBeans, you may see a message that says that NetBeans is scanning project classpaths; this may take a few minutes.

Next, we need to create a class file to put into our project. Select New File from the File menu. NetBeans prompts you with a wizard. In the Categories pane, select Java GUI Forms and in the File Types pane, select JFrame Form. Choosing JFrame Form gives us a Java class file extending `JFrame` with the basic structure of a GUI application already set up for us. Click Next, then give the file a name, such as LearningJava1. You may leave the package set to the default package if you wish. Now click Finish; the screen looks like Figure 22-1.

The NetBeans workspace

Figure 22-1 shows the NetBeans application. The screen has three main areas with a toolbar at the top. The left area is the explorer window. Tabs in the explorer window can show a Java package and class-oriented view of our project, a filesystem view, or a runtime environment view. The explorer is shown with our *LearningJava1.java* class selected. The bottom left is the Navigator area, which shows the methods and properties of the class, and in the case of a GUI component the child component layout within it. In the center area is our workspace with tabs for each open file (currently one). Because we selected a GUI-type file, NetBeans has placed us into GUI "design" mode and shows us an empty box where we will place our beans. Click alternately on the Source and Design buttons to switch between the Java source code and this view (try it out).

On the right side are a Palette pane and a Properties pane, which is currently showing some properties of the currently selected file, but will show the properties of the currently selected bean component when we add one to the design area. The Palette has groupings for different types of beans. The Swing group includes all the standard Swing components. AWT holds older AWT components. Layouts holds Java layout managers.

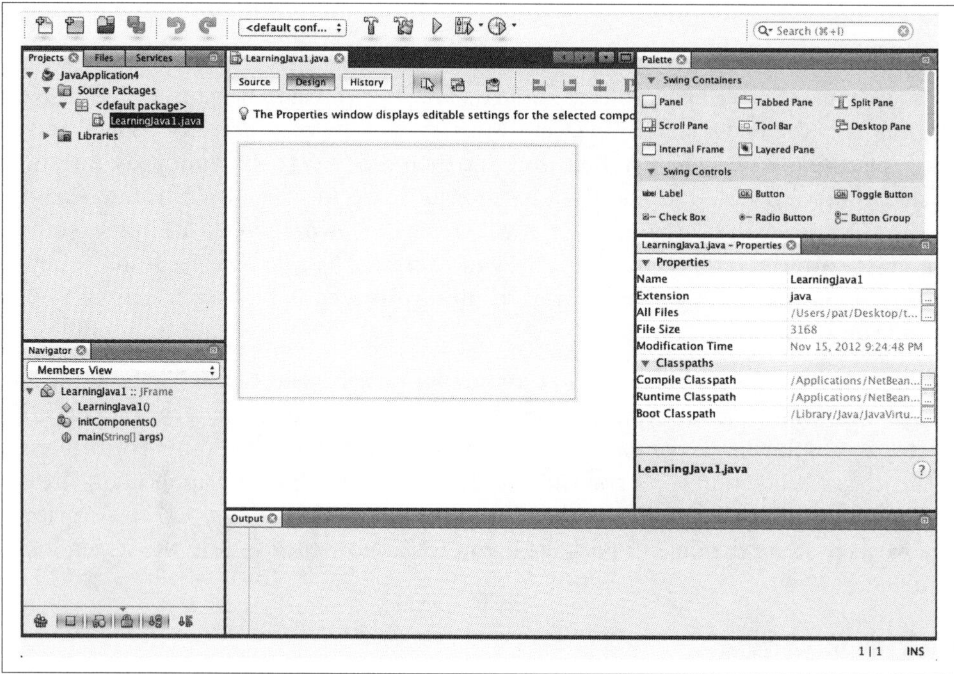

Figure 22-1. The NetBeans workspace

Under Palette, select Swing (it may be selected by default) to see some of the available Swing components (they appear as icons at the top of the window). Now scroll down and select Beans to see the beans we imported earlier. You should see the friendly `Dial` component bean from Chapter 18, along with a tiny person bean. The rest of our beans lack pretty icons because these example beans aren't packaged with them. (We'll talk about packaging later in the chapter.) Figure 22-2 shows the bean palette.

To place a bean into the workspace, click on it and then click in the workspace. Before you do that, though, you may want to set an appropriate layout manager. The Inspector holds a tree that shows all the components (visible and invisible) in the project. By right-clicking on the `JFrame` (our top-level container) in either the workspace or the tree, you can select Set Layout to specify the layout manager for the frame. For now, try using AbsoluteLayout, provided by NetBeans. This allows you to arbitrarily place and move beans within the container. You wouldn't want to do this in general, but for our examples it will make life a bit easier. The other layout managers are easy enough to use, but we'll refer you to NetBeans tutorials for the details.

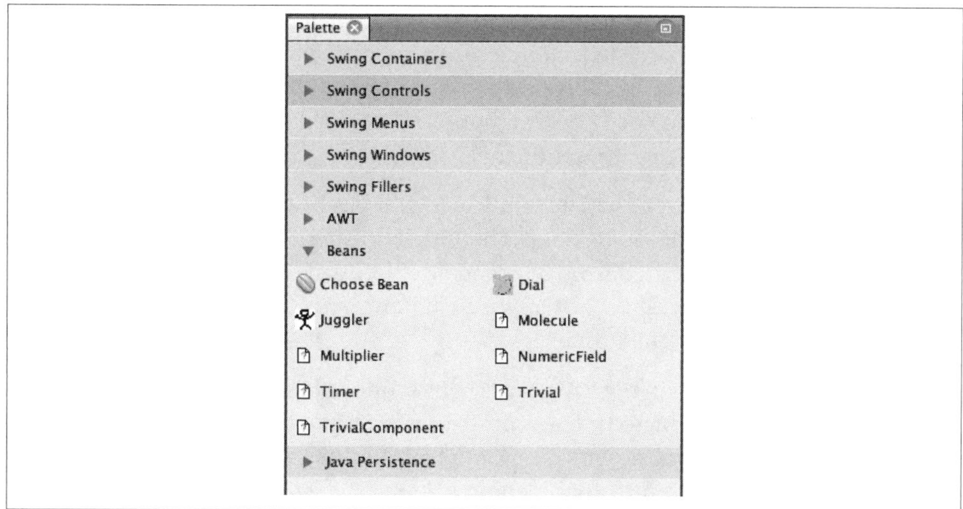

Figure 22-2. The bean palette

Properties and Customizers

Properties represent the "state" or "data" content of a bean. These features can be manipulated externally to configure the bean. For a bean that's a GUI component, you might expect its properties to include its size, colors, and other features of its basic appearance. Properties are similar in concept to an object's public variables. Like a variable, a property can be a primitive type (such as a number or Boolean), or it can be a complex object type (such as a `String` or a collection of spreadsheet data). Unlike variables, properties are always manipulated using methods to set and get the value; this enables a bean to take action whenever a property changes. By sending an event when a property changes, a bean can notify other interested beans of the change (which we will discuss later in this chapter).

Let's pull a couple of beans into NetBeans and take a look at their properties. Click on a button (this will be a `JButton`) from the Swing Controls group of the palette, and then click in the workspace. When the `JButton` was first loaded by NetBeans, it was inspected to discover its properties. When we select an instance of the button, NetBeans displays these properties in the Properties pane and allows us to modify them.

The button has about eight basic properties, followed by a few additional groupings. The list called Other Properties adds more detail. There is also a Layout properties section (these are in actuality not properties of the `JButton`, but are here for convenience) as well as an Accessibility properties list (for components that have accessibility-related properties). The `foreground` and `background` properties are colors; their current values are displayed in the corresponding box. `font` is the font for the label text; an example of the font is shown. `text` is the text of the button's label. You can also set an image icon for the button, the tooltip text that appears when the mouse hovers over the item, and a keyboard shortcut identifier, called a *mnemonic*. Try typing something new for the value of the `text` property and hit return to see the button label change. Click on the background color to enter a numeric color value, or, better yet, press the "..." button to pop up a color-chooser dialog.

Most of these basic properties will be familiar to you because many GUI beans inherit them from the base `JComponent` class. The Other Properties section lists almost 50 additional properties inherited from `JComponent`. NetBeans is making an effort to categorize these for us. As we'll see when we create our own beans, we can limit which properties are included in the Properties pane.

Now place a `Juggler` bean in the workspace (this is one of Sun's original demonstration Java beans that we have updated). The animation starts, and the juggler begins juggling some roughly drawn beans, as shown in Figure 22-3. If he gets annoying, don't worry; we'll have him under our control soon enough.

You can see that this bean has a different set of properties, including an interesting one called `animationRate`. It is an integer property that controls the delay in milliseconds between displays of the juggler's frames. Try changing its value. The juggler changes speed as you type each value. Good beans give you immediate feedback when you change their properties. Uncheck the checkbox next to the Boolean `juggling` property to stop the show if you want.

Notice that the Properties pane provides a way to display and edit each of the different property types. For the `foreground` and `background` properties of the `JButton`, the pane displays the color; if you click on them, a color selection dialog pops up. Similarly, if you click on the `font` property, you get a font selection dialog. For `integer` and `string` values, you can type a new value into the field. NetBeans understands and can edit the most useful basic Java types.

Since the property types are open-ended, beans with more complex property types can supply their own *property editor*. The `Molecule` bean that we'll play with in the next section, for example, uses a custom property editor that lets us choose the type of molecule. If it needs even more control over how its properties are displayed, a bean can provide a *customizer*, which allows a bean to provide its own GUI for editing its properties. (For example, a customizer could let you draw an icon for a button.)

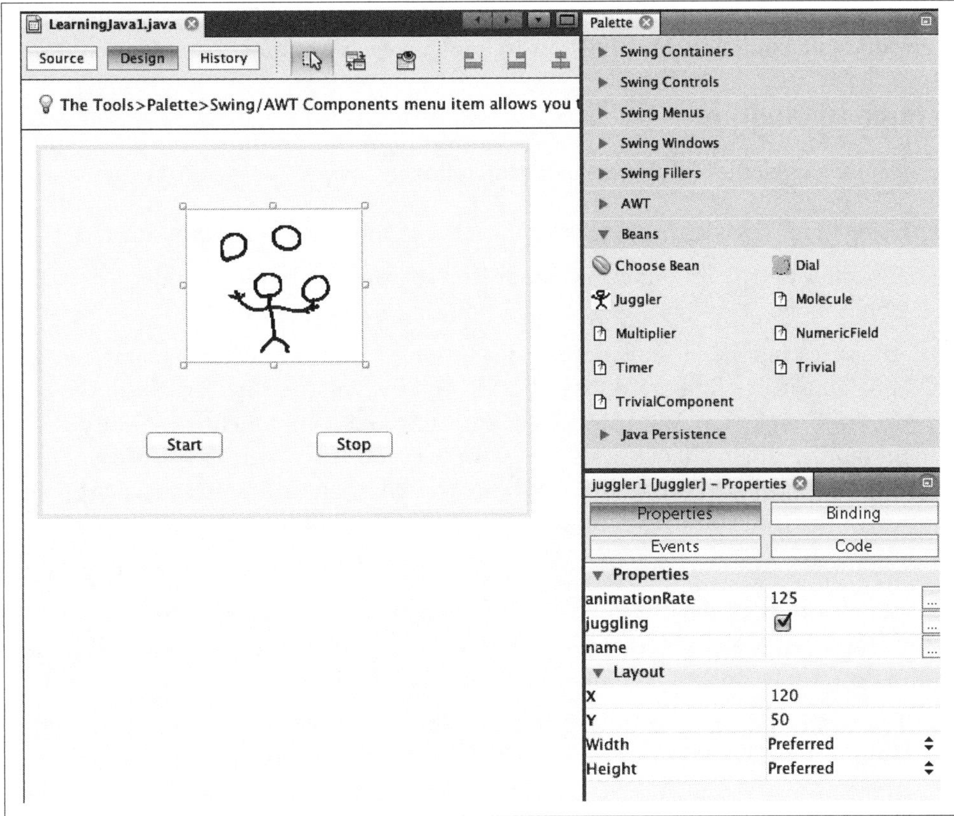

Figure 22-3. Juggling beans

Event Hookups and Adapters

Beans use events to communicate. As we mentioned in Chapter 16, events are not limited to GUI components but can be used for signaling and passing information in more general applications. An event is simply a notification; information describing the event and other data are wrapped up in a subclass of `EventObject` and passed to the receiving object by a method invocation. Event sources register listeners that want to receive the events when they occur. Event receivers implement the appropriate listener interface containing the method needed to receive the events. This is Java's general event mechanism in a nutshell.

It's often useful to place an adapter between an event source and a listener. An adapter can be used when an object doesn't know how to receive a particular event; it enables the object to handle the event anyway. The adapter can translate the event into some other action, such as a call to a different method or an update of some data. One of the jobs of NetBeans is to help us hook up event sources to event listeners. Another job is to produce adapter code that allows us to hook up events in more complex ways.

Taming the Juggler

Let's get our juggler under control with the following steps:

1. Using the Properties pane, change the label of your button to read "Start."
2. Now click the small Connection Mode icon at the top of the GUI builder (the second icon, showing two items with arrows pointing at one another).
3. After pressing the button, NetBeans is waiting for us to select two components to "hook up." Click first on the Start button and then on the `Juggler`. NetBeans pops up the Connection Wizard, indicating the source component (the button) and prompting you to choose from a large list of events (see Figure 22-4). Most of them are standard Swing events that can be generated by any kind of `JComponent`. What we're after is the button's action event.
4. Expand the folder named *action*, and select `actionPerformed` as the source event.
5. At the bottom of the dialog box NetBeans indicates the name of an event handler method that it will generate for us. Leave the method name as is. Click Next to go to the Specify Target Operation screen for the `Juggler`.
6. The wizard prompts us to choose a property to set on the `Juggler`, as shown in Figure 22-5. The display shows three of the `Juggler`'s properties. Choose the `juggling` property as the target and click Next.
7. Enter **`true`** in the Value field and click Finish. NetBeans takes you to the source view and shows you the method it has generated to respond to the button action.

We have completed a hookup between the button and the `Juggler`. When the button fires an action event, the `juggling` property of the `Juggler` is set to `true`.

Scroll around the source view and take a look at the code that NetBeans has generated to make this connection for us. Specifically, in the `initComponents()` method of our class, it has created an anonymous inner class to serve as the `ActionListener` for `ActionEvents` from our button (which it has named `jButton1`):

```
jButton1.addActionListener(new java.awt.event.ActionListener() {
    public void actionPerformed(java.awt.event.ActionEvent evt) {
        jButton1ActionPerformed(evt);
    }
});
```

The adapter calls a private method that sets the property on our `Juggler`:

```
private void jButton1ActionPerformed(java.awt.event.ActionEvent evt) {
    juggler1.setJuggling(true);
}
```

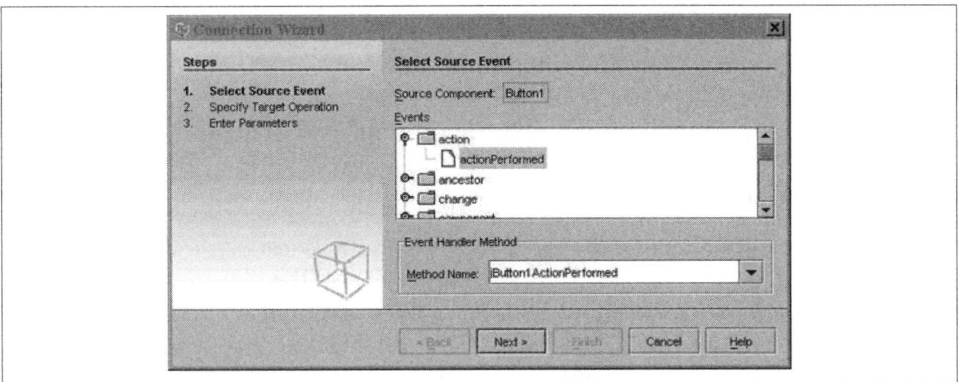

Figure 22-4. Selecting a source event in the Connection Wizard

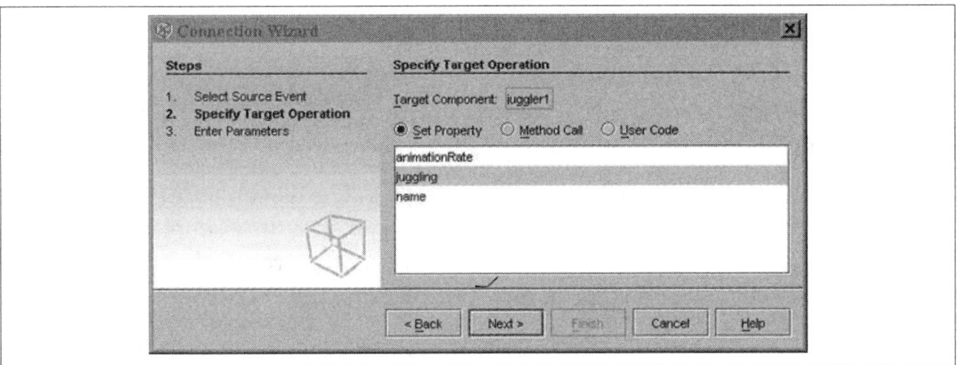

Figure 22-5. Specifying a target operation in the Connection Wizard

You'll notice that most of the code that was written for us is shaded grey to indicate that it is autogenerated code and can't be directly modified. The body of the private method is open, however, and we could modify it to perform arbitrary activities when the button is pushed. In NetBeans, the hookup is just a starting point.

This may all seem a little obtuse. After all, if we had made the `Juggler` an `ActionListener` in the first place, we would expect to hook it directly to the button. The use of adapters provides a great deal of flexibility, however, as we'll see next.

To complete our example, click the Design button, then repeat the process, adding a second `JButton` labeled "Stop." We could implement the Stop button in the same way that we did the Start button, by passing a specific value to the juggling method, but we're going to try an alternative here. Click the Connection Wizard icon; select the Stop button and the `Juggler` as its target. Again, choose the `actionPerformed` method as the source, but this time, instead of selecting a property on the `Juggler`, click the Method Call radio button to see a list of available methods on the `Juggler` bean. Scroll all the way down and select the `stopJuggling()` method. Click Finish to complete the hookup, and look at the generated code if you wish. With this, we have seen an example of hooking up a source of action events to generate an arbitrary method call on a bean. (Of course, there is a `startJuggling()` method as well, which we could have used for the first button.)

Running the example

Now, the `Juggler` will do our bidding. Right-click on the *LearningJava1.java* file in the Projects tab of the Explorer pane (or in the source view of the file) and select Run File. Watch as NetBeans compiles and runs our example. You should be able to start and stop the juggler using the buttons! When you are done, quit the juggler application and return to the GUI editor. Close this example by closing its tab in the workspace, and let's move on. (There is no need to save the file explicitly; NetBeans saves automatically as you edit.)

Molecular Motion

Let's look at one more interesting example, shown in Figure 22-6. Create a new file in our project as before, choosing Java GUI Forms from the Categories pane and JFrame Form in the File Types pane. Call this file *LearningJava2*.

Grab a `Molecule` bean and place it in the workspace. (The default `BorderLayout` maximizes its area if you place the bean in the center.) If you run the example now, you will see that by dragging the mouse within the image, you can rotate the model in three dimensions. Try changing the type of molecule by using the Properties pane: ethane is fun.[1]

Let's see what we can do with our molecule. Grab a `Timer` bean from the palette. `Timer` is a clock.[2] Every so many milliseconds, `Timer` fires an event. The timer is controlled by an `long` property called `delay`, which determines the number of milliseconds between events. `Timer` is an "invisible" bean; it is not derived from a `JComponent` and doesn't have a graphical appearance, just as an internal timer in an application doesn't normally have a presence on the screen. NetBeans shows these invisible beans just like any other bean in the Navigator pane on the left. When you wish to select the `Timer`, click on it in the tree in the Navigator pane.

1. As of this writing, Sun's Molecule example has some problems when used in NetBeans. Selecting a molecule type other than the default causes a compile-time error. You can use the Preview Design button on the NetBeans form editor to try the other molecule types.

2. A `Timer` bean used to come with the NetBeans distribution but disappeared in version 4.0, so we've added our own replacement. We won't discuss it here, but the source code is with the other bean examples and there is nothing special that isn't covered elsewhere.

Let's hook the `Timer` to our `Molecule`. Start the Connection Wizard and select the `Timer` (from the tree) and then the `Molecule`. Choose the `Timer`'s `timerFired()` event from the list (expand the folder to display it). Click Next and select the Method Call radio button. Find and select the `rotateOnX()` method and click Finish. Run the example. Now the `Molecule` should turn on its own every time it receives an event from the timer. Try changing the timer's `delay` property. You can also hook the `Timer` to the `Molecule`'s `rotateOnY()` method. Use a different instance of `Timer` and, by setting different delay values, make it turn at different rates in each dimension. Fun!

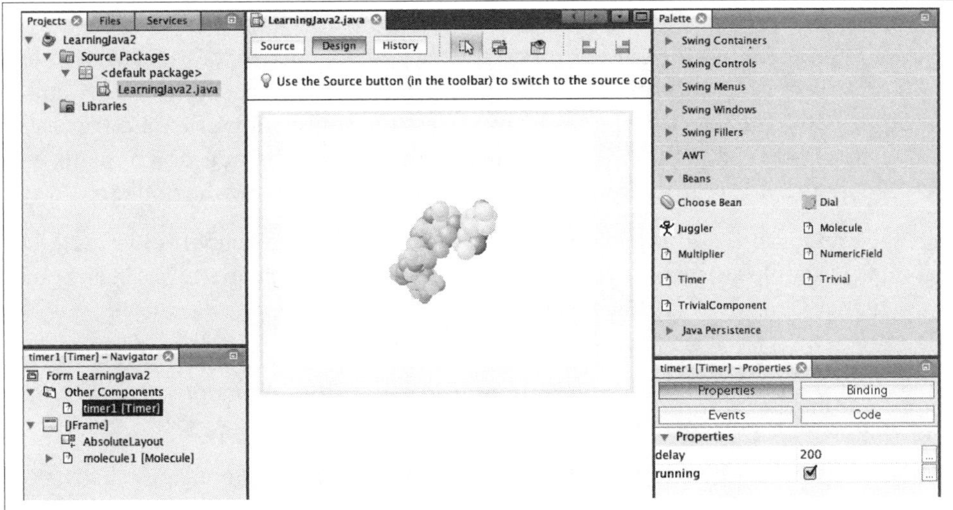

Figure 22-6. The Molecule bean and the Timer

Binding Properties

By using a combination of events and adapters, we can connect beans in many interesting ways. We can even "bind" two beans together so that if a property changes in the first bean, the corresponding property is automatically changed in the second bean. In this scenario, the beans don't necessarily have to be of the same type, but in order to make sense, the properties do.

Close the `Molecule` file and start a new one. Grab two `NumericField` beans from the palette, drop them in the workspace, and select one of them. You'll probably want to set the AbsoluteLayout again. You can also adjust the width of the fields by dragging them at the sides. You'll notice that a `NumericField` has many of the standard properties of a Swing component. If you look in the Other Properties section of the Properties pane, you can find an integer property called `value` that represents the numeric value of the field. You can set it there or enter a number directly into the field when you run the program. `NumericField` rejects nonnumeric text.

Let's bind the value property of one of the fields to the other. Activate the Connection Wizard to create a connection between the two fields. Click first on numericField1 and then on numericField2 so that numericField1 is the source. In the wizard, choose the propertyChange() event of the source field. This is the listener method for PropertyChangeEvent, a generic event sent by beans when one of their properties changes. When a bean fires property change events in response to changes in a particular property, that property is said to be "bound." This means that it is possible to bind the property to another bean through the generic mechanism. In this case, the value property of our NumericField beans is a bound property, so whenever it changes, a PropertyChangeEvent is fired.

Choose Next, and select the value property as the target for numericField2. Click Next again, and select the Property radio button on the Parameters screen. Click the "..." editor button to pop up a Select Property dialog. Select the source numeric field (probably named numericField1, if that is your source button) from the pull-down menu, and then choose the value property. Click OK and Finish to complete the hookup.

Run the application, and try entering values in the first field (numericField1). The second field should change each time. The second bean's value property has been bound to the first.

Try binding the value property in the other direction as well so that you can change the value in either bean, and the changes are propagated in both directions. (Some simple logic in the beans prevents infinite loops from happening here.)

NetBeans has again generated an adapter for us. This time, the adapter listens for PropertyChangeEvents and invokes the setValue() method of our target field. We haven't done anything earth shattering. The PropertyChangeEvent does carry some extra information—the old and new values of the property—but we're not using them here. And with the Connection Wizard, you can use any event source as the impetus to set a property on your target bean. Finally, as we've seen, the property can derive its value from any other bean in the layout. The flexibility of the Connection Wizard is, to some extent, masking the purpose of the events, but that's OK. If we are interested in the specific property that changed, or if we want to apply logic about the value, we can fill in the generated method with our own code.

Many Swing components have bound properties, which are usually documented in the Javadoc for the class.

Constraining Properties

In the previous section, we discussed how beans fire PropertyChangeEvents to notify other beans (and adapters) that a property has changed. In that scenario, the object that receives the event is simply a passive listener as far as the event's source is concerned. JavaBeans also supports *constrained properties*, in which the event listener gets to say whether it will allow a bean to change the property's value. If the new value is rejected, the change is cancelled; the event source keeps its old value.

The concept of constrained properties has not been heavily used in the normal operation of Swing, so we won't cover it in detail here. But it goes something like this. Normally, `PropertyChangeEvents` are delivered to a `propertyChange()` method in the listener. Constrained properties are implemented by delivering `PropertyChangeEvents` to a separate listener method called `vetoableChange()`. The `vetoableChange()` method throws a `PropertyVetoException` if it doesn't like a proposed change. In this way, components can govern the acceptable values set by other components.

Building Beans

Now that you have a feel for how beans look from the user's perspective, let's build some. In this section, we will become the Magic Beans Company. We will create some beans, package them for distribution, and use them in NetBeans to build a very simple application. (The complete JAR file, along with all the example code for this chapter, is online at *http://oreil.ly/Learn_Java_4E*.)

The first thing we'll remind you of is that absolutely anything can be a bean. Even the following class is a bean, albeit an invisible one:

```
public class Trivial implements java.io.Serializable {}
```

Of course, this bean isn't very useful: it doesn't have any properties, and it doesn't do anything. But it's a bean nonetheless, and we can drag it into NetBeans as long as we package it correctly. If we modify this class to extend `JComponent`, we suddenly have a graphical bean that be seen in the layout, with lots of standard Swing properties, such as size and color information:

```
public class TrivialComponent extends JComponent {}
```

Next, let's look at a bean that's a bit more useful.

The Dial Bean

We created a nifty `Dial` component in Chapter 18. What would it take to turn it into a bean? Surprise: it is already a bean! The `Dial` has a number of properties that it exposes in the way prescribed by JavaBeans. A get method retrieves the value of a property; for example, `getValue()` retrieves the dial's current value. Likewise, a set method, `setValue()`, modifies the dial's value. The dial has two other properties, which also have get and set methods: `minimum` and `maximum`. This is all the `Dial` needs to inform a tool such as NetBeans what properties it has and how to work with them. Because `Dial` is a `JComponent`, it also has all the standard Swing properties, such as color and size. The `JComponent` provides the set and get methods for all its properties.

To use our `Dial`, we'll put it in a Java package named `magicbeans` and store it in a JAR file that can be loaded by NetBeans. The source code (*http://examples.oreilly.com/0636920023463/*), which can be found online, includes an Ant build file (see Chapter 15) that compiles the code and creates the final JAR file.

If you were starting from scratch, it would go like this: first, create a directory called *magicbeans* to hold our beans, add a `package` statement to the source files *Dial.java*, *DialEvent.java*, and *DialListener.java* (from Chapter 18), put the source files into the *magicbeans* directory, and compile them (using the command *javac magicBeans/Dial.java*) to create class files.

Next, we need to create a manifest file that tells NetBeans which of the classes in the JAR file are beans and which are support files or unrelated. At this point, we have only one bean, *Dial.class*, so create the following file, called *magicBeans.manifest*:

```
Name: magicbeans/Dial.class
Java-Bean: True
```

The `Name:` label identifies the class file as it will appear in the JAR: `magicbeans/Dial.class`. Specifications appearing after an item's `Name:` line and before an empty line apply to that item. (See Chapter 3 for more details.) We have added the attribute `Java-Bean: True`, which flags this class as a bean to tools that read the manifest. We will add an entry like this for each bean in our package. We don't need to flag support classes (such as `DialEvent` and `DialListener`) as beans because we won't want to manipulate them directly with NetBeans; in fact, we don't need to mention them in the manifest at all.

To create the JAR file, including our manifest information, enter this command:

```
% jar -cvmf magicbeans.manifest magicbeans.jar magicbeans/*.class
```

If you loaded the precompiled examples as instructed earlier, then you already have the `Dial` bean loaded into NetBeans. The version supplied in the precompiled *magicbeans.jar* file has additional packaging that allows it to appear with a spiffy icon in the palette, as we'll discuss a bit later. (If you haven't loaded the example JAR, you can import the one we just created by selecting Palette → Swing/AWT Components dialog from the Tools menu, as described earlier in this chapter.) If you want to replace the `Dial` bean on your palette, you can remove it by right-clicking on the icon and selecting Delete before importing the new JAR. (Actually, NetBeans 7.2 should reload the JAR automatically if you overwrite it.)

You should now have an entry for `Dial` in the bean palette. Drop an instance of the `Dial` bean into a new JFrame Form file in NetBeans.

As Figure 22-7 shows, the `Dial`'s properties—maximum, minimum, and value—appear in the Properties pane and can be modified by NetBeans. If you just created the `Dial` JAR following our minimal instructions, you'll see these properties along with all the

Swing properties inherited from the `JComponent` class. The figure shows the `Dial` bean as it appears later in this chapter (with the supplied packaging), after we've learned about the `BeanInfo` class. We're almost there.

Now we're ready to put the `Dial` to use. Reopen the `Juggler` file that we created in the first section of this chapter. Add an instance of our new magic `Dial` bean to the scenario, as shown in Figure 22-8.

Bind the `value` property of the `Dial` to the `animationRate` of the `Juggler`. Use the Connection Wizard, as before, selecting the `Dial` and then the `Juggler`. Select the `DialEvent` source and bind the `animationRate` property, selecting the `Dial`'s value as the property source. When you complete the hookup, you should be able to vary the speed of the juggler by turning the dial. Try changing the maximum and minimum values of the dial to change the range.

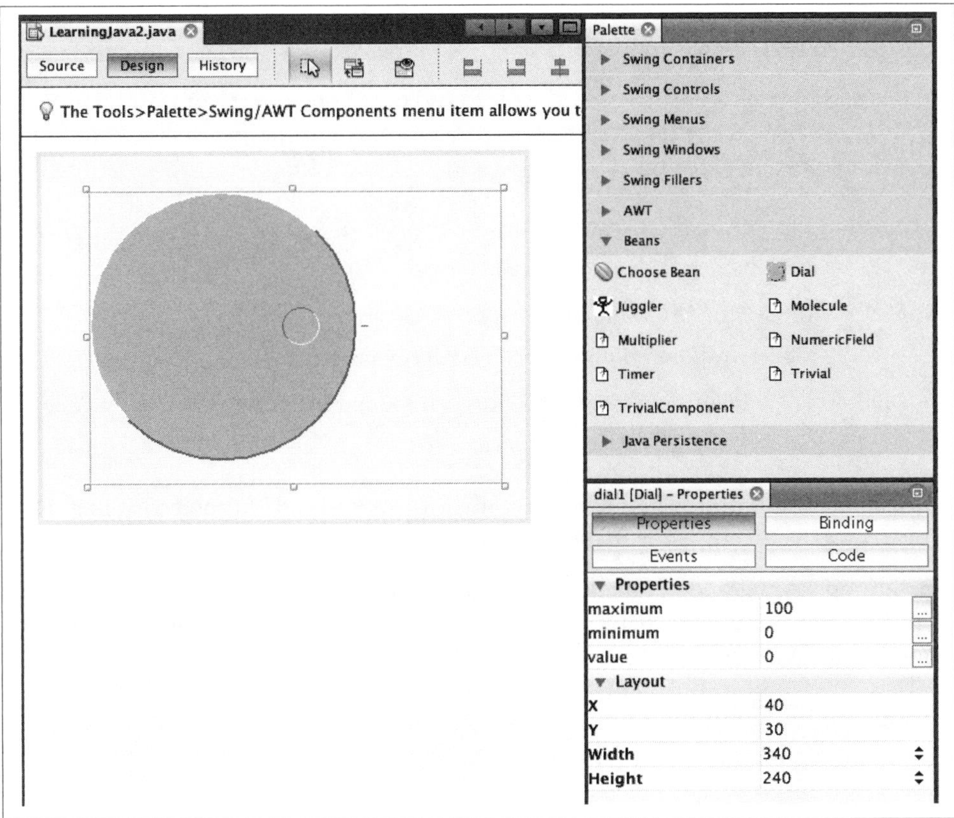

Figure 22-7. The Dial component as a bean

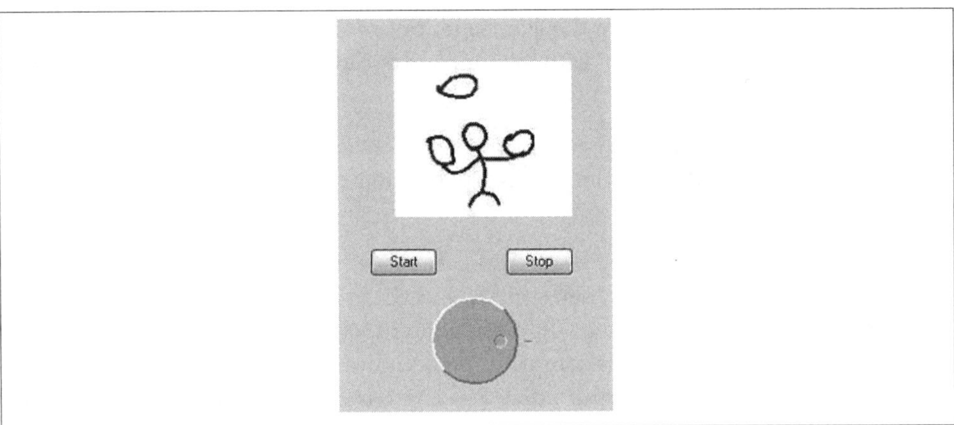

Figure 22-8. The Juggler with a dialable animation rate

Design Patterns for Properties

We said earlier that tools such as NetBeans found out about a bean's properties by looking at its get and set methods. The easiest way to make properties visible is to follow these simple design patterns:

- Method for getting the current value of a property:

```
public PropertyType getPropertyName()
```

- Method for setting the value of a property:

```
public void setPropertyName( PropertyType arg )
```

- Method for determining whether a Boolean-valued property is currently `true`:

```
public boolean isPropertyName()
```

The last method is optional and is used only for properties with Boolean values. (You could use the get method for Boolean values as well.)

The appropriate set and get methods for these features of our bean are already in the `Dial` class, either methods that we added or methods inherited from the `java.awt.Component` and `javax.swing.JComponent` classes:

```
// inherited from Component
public Color getForeground()
public void setForeground(Color c)

public Color getBackground()
public void setBackground(Color c)

public Font getFont()
public void setFont(Font f)
```

```
// many others from Component and JComponent

// part of the Dial itself
public int getValue()
public void setValue(int v)

public int getMinimum()
public void setMinimum(int m)

public int getMaximum()
public void setMaximum(int m)
```

JavaBeans allows read and write-only properties, which are implemented simply by leaving out the get or set method.

NetBeans uses the Reflection API to find out about the `Dial` bean's methods; it then uses these naming conventions to learn what properties are available. When we use the properties editor to change a value, NetBeans dynamically invokes the correct set method to change the value.

If you look further at the `JComponent` class, you'll notice that other methods match the design pattern. For example, what about the `setCursor()` and `getCursor()` pair? NetBeans doesn't know how to display or edit a cursor, and we didn't supply an editor, so it ignores those properties in the properties sheet.

NetBeans automatically pulls the property's name from the name of its accessor methods; it then lowercases the name for display on the properties sheet. For example, the `font` property is derived from `getFont`. Later, we'll show how to provide a `BeanInfo` class that overrides the way these properties are displayed, which allows you to provide your own friendly property names. Again, if you used the `Dial` bean from our precompiled example JAR, you'll see only our three `Dial` properties. The `JComponent` properties are hidden by our packaging a `BeanInfo` class that determines the properties we wish to show.

Generating bean patterns in NetBeans

NetBeans automatically recognizes JavaBeans getter and setter method patterns in classes. In the source code view, select the Source menu Insert Code option and choose Getter and Setter to automatically generate getter and setter methods for fields in your class. This can save you a bit of typing if you need to add a lot of properties.

Limitations of Visual Design

These examples have pointed to the idea that we can create at least a trivial application by hooking beans together in a mostly visual way. In other development environments, this kind of bean hookup has been pushed even further. For example, Sun's original

"BeanBox" experimental Java bean container took a different approach than NetBeans. It allowed the developer to work with "live" Java bean instances, dynamically generating adapter code at runtime and relying solely on object serialization to save the resulting work. This kind of design is, in a sense, the real goal of the JavaBeans architecture. It is true "what you see is what you get" (WYSIWYG) programming. However, pure visual design without the ability to integrate handwritten code, as we can do in NetBeans, has not yet proven to scale beyond these kinds of simple applications, and pure visual programming environments beyond just GUI screen layout have thus far failed to catch on.

Serialization Versus Code Generation

If you've been keeping an eye on the NetBeans source window while we've been working, you may have noticed the code that is being generated when you modify properties of beans. By default, NetBeans generates method calls to set values on beans in the `initComponents()` method. For example, if you set the value of one of your `NumericField` beans to 42 in the Properties pane, this value gets hardcoded into the application as an initial value of the bean by a call to `setValue()` on the bean object at initialization time. But if you click on the Code button in the Properties pane, you'll see that we have another option. This area holds properties that govern how NetBeans generates the application code. By changing the Code Generation property from Generate Code to Serialize, you change NetBeans' behavior. Instead of generating method calls in the source code, it saves your fully configured bean as a serialized object and then generates the appropriate code to load the freeze-dried bean into the application from a file.

Try changing the code generation property for a `Juggler` bean to Serialize. Switching to the source code view and looking at the `initComponents()` method, you'll see a line for that bean that uses the static `Beans.instantiate()` method to load a serialized copy of the bean.

NetBeans treats the serialized bean file as part of the source code and will regenerate it whenever it saves the source file. In order to run this example, we must first perform a manual build. Select Build → Build Main Project, then you can run the file as before with the Run File context menu. The reason for the explicit build is to prompt NetBeans to copy the serialized bean file from the source folder of your source file over to the compiled classes directory (it should be smart enough to do this itself). You should see the serialized bean file, named something like: *LearnJava1_juggler1.ser* alongside your source file (and deployed to the *classes* directory). You can run the example and confirm that it behaves exactly like the code-generated version. (This is pretty neat if you think about it.)

We'll discuss working with serialized beans in more detail later in this chapter and ask you to refer to this stored bean file.

Customizing with BeanInfo

So far, everything NetBeans has known about our beans has been determined by low-level reflection—that is, by looking at the methods of our classes. The java.Beans.Introspector class gathers information on a bean using reflection, then analyzes and describes a bean to any tool that wants to know about it. The introspection process works only if the class follows the JavaBeans naming conventions for its methods; furthermore, it gives us little control over exactly what properties and events appear in NetBeans menus. For example, we've seen that NetBeans by default shows all the stuff we inherit from the base Swing component. We can change that by creating BeanInfo classes for our beans. A BeanInfo class provides the JavaBeans introspector with explicit information about the properties, methods, and events of a bean; we can even use it to customize the text that appears in menus in NetBeans (and in other IDEs).

A BeanInfo class implements the BeanInfo interface. That's a complicated proposition; in most situations, the introspector's default behavior is reasonable. Instead of implementing the BeanInfo interface, we extend the SimpleBeanInfo class, which implements all of BeanInfo's methods. We can override specific methods to provide the information we want; when we don't override a method, we'll get the introspector's default behavior.

In the next few sections, we'll develop the DialBeanInfo class that provides explicit information about our Dial bean.

Getting Properties Information

We'll start out by describing the Dial's properties. To do so, we must implement the getPropertyDescriptors() method. This method simply returns an array of PropertyDescriptor objects—one for each property we want to publicize.

To create a PropertyDescriptor, call its constructor with two arguments: the property's name and the class. In the following code, we create descriptors for the Dial's value, minimum, and maximum properties. We next call a few methods of the PropertyDescriptor class to provide additional information about each property. If our methods were bound (generated PropertyChangeEvents when modified), we'd call the setBound() method of their PropertyDescriptors. Our code is prepared to catch an IntrospectionException, which can occur if something goes wrong while creating the property descriptors, such as encountering a nonexistent method:

```
//file: DialBeanInfo.java
package magicbeans;
import java.beans.*;

public class DialBeanInfo extends SimpleBeanInfo {

  public PropertyDescriptor[] getPropertyDescriptors() {
```

```
        try {
          PropertyDescriptor value =
            new PropertyDescriptor("value", Dial.class);
          PropertyDescriptor minimum =
            new PropertyDescriptor("minimum", Dial.class);
          PropertyDescriptor maximum =
            new PropertyDescriptor("maximum", Dial.class);

          return new PropertyDescriptor [] { value, minimum, maximum };
        }
        catch (IntrospectionException e) {
          return null;
        }
      }
    }
```

Perhaps the most useful thing about `DialBeanInfo` is that by providing explicit information for our properties, we automatically hide other properties that introspection might find. After compiling `DialBeanInfo` and packaging it with the `Dial`, you'll see that its `JComponent` properties no longer appear in the NetBeans properties editor. (This has been the case all along if you started with the precompiled example JAR.)

A `PropertyDescriptor` can provide a lot of other information about a property: the names of the accessor methods (if you decide not to use the standard naming convention), information about whether the property is constrained, and a class to use as a property editor (if the standard property editors aren't sufficient).

Getting events information

The `Dial` bean defines its own event: the `DialEvent`. We'd like to tell development tools about this event so that we can build applications using it. The process for telling the world about our event is similar to what we did previously: we add a method to the `DialBeanInfo` class called `getEventSetDescriptors()`, which returns an array of `EventSetDescriptors`.

Events are described in terms of their listener interfaces, not in terms of the event classes themselves, so our `getEventSetDescriptors()` method creates a descriptor for the `DialListener` interface. Here's the code to add to the `DialBeanInfo` class:

```
    public EventSetDescriptor[] getEventSetDescriptors() {
      try {
        EventSetDescriptor dial = new EventSetDescriptor(
          Dial.class, "dialAdjusted",
          DialListener.class, "dialAdjusted");
        dial.setDisplayName("Dial Adjusted");

        return new EventSetDescriptor [] { dial };
      }
      catch (IntrospectionException e) {
        return null;
```

```
    }
  }
```

In this method, we create an `EventSetDescriptor` object: `dial`. The constructor for an `EventSetDescriptor` takes four arguments: the class that generates the event, the name of the event (the name that is displayed, by default, by a development tool), the listener class, and the name of the method to which the event can be delivered. (Other constructors let you deal with listener interfaces that have several methods.) After creating the descriptor, we call the `setDisplayName()` method to provide a friendly name to be displayed by development tools such as NetBeans. (This overrides the default name specified in the constructor.)

Just as the property descriptors we supply hide the properties that were discovered by reflection, the `EventSetDescriptors` can hide the other events that are inherited from the base component classes. In theory, when you recompile `DialBeanInfo`, package it in a JAR, and load it into NetBeans, you should see only the two events that we have explicitly described: our own `DialEvent` and `PropertyChangeEvent` (displayed as "Dial Adjusted" and "Bound property change"). Unfortunately, the current version of NetBeans ignores this information.

Once we have an `EventSetDescriptor`, we can provide other kinds of information about the event. For example, we can state that the event is *unicast*, which means that it can have only one listener.

Supplying icons

Some of the beans that come with NetBeans are displayed on the palette with a cute icon. This makes life more pleasant for everyone. To supply an icon for the `BeanInfo` object we have been developing, we have it implement the `getIcon()` method. You can supply up to four icons, with sizes of 16 × 16 or 32 × 32, in color or monochrome. Here's the `getIcon()` method for `DialBeanInfo`:

```
public class DialBeanInfo extends SimpleBeanInfo {
  ...
  public java.awt.Image getIcon(int iconKind) {

    if (iconKind == BeanInfo.ICON_COLOR_16x16) {
      return loadImage("DialIconColor16.gif");
    } else
    if (iconKind == BeanInfo.ICON_COLOR_32x32) {
      return loadImage("DialIconColor32.gif");
    } else
    if (iconKind == BeanInfo.ICON_MONO_16x16) {
      return loadImage("DialIconMono16.gif");
    } else
    if (iconKind == BeanInfo.ICON_MONO_32x32) {
      return loadImage("DialIconMono32.gif");
    }
```

```
        return null;
    }
```

This method is called with a constant, indicating what kind of icon is being requested; for example, BeanInfo.ICON_COLOR_16x16 requests a 16 × 16 color image. If an appropriate icon is available, it loads the image and returns an Image object. If the icon isn't available, it returns null. For convenience, you can package the images in the same JAR file as the bean and its BeanInfo class.

Though we haven't used them here, you can also use a BeanInfo object to provide information about other public methods of your bean (for example, array-valued properties) and other features.

Creating customizers and property editors

JavaBeans lets you provide a *customizer* for your beans. Customizers are objects that do advanced customization for a bean as a whole; they let you provide your own GUI for tweaking your bean. We won't show you how to write a customizer; it's not too difficult, but it's beyond the scope of this chapter. Suffice it to say that a customizer must implement the java.beans.Customizer interface and should extend Component (or JComponent) so that it can be displayed.

Property editors are a way of giving the properties sheet additional capabilities. For example, you could supply a property editor to let you edit a property type that is specific to your bean. You could provide a property editor that would let you edit an object's price in dollars and cents. We've already seen a couple of property editors: the editor used for Color-valued properties is fundamentally the same as a property editor you might write yourself. In addition, the Molecule bean uses a property editor to specify its moleculeName property. A *property editor* isn't quite as fancy as a customizer, but describing it fully is also beyond the scope of this chapter.

Again, describing how to write a property editor is also beyond the scope of this chapter. However, it might help you to know that a property editor must implement the PropertyEditor interface; it usually does so by extending the PropertyEditorSupport class, which provides default implementations for most of the methods.

Handcoding with Beans

So far, we've seen how to create and use beans within a bean application builder environment. That is the primary motivation for JavaBeans, at least in GUI development. But beans are not limited to being used by automated tools. There's no reason we can't use beans in handwritten code. You could use a builder to assemble beans for the user interface of your application and then load that serialized bean or a collection of beans in your own code, just as NetBeans does when told to use object serialization. We'll give an example of that in a moment.

Bean Instantiation and Type Management

Beans are an abstraction over simple Java classes. They add, by convention, features that are not part of the Java language. To enable certain additional capabilities of JavaBeans, we use special tools that take the place of basic language operations. Specifically, when working with beans, we are provided with replacements for three basic Java operations: creating an object with `new`, checking the type of an object with the `instanceof` operator, and casting a type with a `cast` expression. In place of these, use the corresponding static methods of the `java.beans.Beans` class, shown in Table 22-1.

Table 22-1. Methods of the java.beans.Beans class

Operator	Equivalent
`New`	`Beans.instantiate(classloader, name)`
`Instanceof`	`Beans.isInstanceOf(object, class)`

`Beans.instantiate()` is the `new` operation for beans. It takes a class loader and the name of a bean class or serialized bean as arguments. Its advantage over the plain `new` operator is that it can also load beans from a serialized form. If you use `instantiate()`, you don't have to specify in advance whether you will provide the bean as a class or as a serialized object. The `instantiate()` method first tries to load a resource file based on the name bean, by turning package-style names (with dots) into a path-style name with slashes and then appending the suffix *.ser*. For example, `magicbeans.NumericField` becomes *magicbeans/NumericField.ser*. If the serialized form of the bean is not found, the `instantiate()` method attempts to create an instance of the class by name.[3]

`Beans.isInstanceOf()` and `Beans.getInstanceOf()` do the jobs of checking a bean's type and casting it to a new type. These methods were intended to allow one or more beans to work together to implement "virtual" or dynamic types. They are supposed to allow beans to take control of this behavior, providing different "views" of themselves. However, they currently don't add any functionality and aren't widely used.

Working with Serialized Beans

Remember the `Juggler` we serialized a while back? Well, it's time to revive him, just like Han Solo from his "Carbonite" tomb in *Star Wars*. We'll assume that you saved the `Juggler` by flipping on the Serialization property while working with the `LearnJava1` class and that NetBeans, therefore, saved him in the file *LearnJava1_juggler1.ser*. If you didn't do this, you can use the following snippet of code to serialize the bean to a file of your choice:

3. This feature would seemingly be applicable to XML-serialized Java beans using the `XMLOutputStream` as well, but it is not currently implemented for them. This is another sign that the JavaBeans APIs have stagnated.

```
// Serialize a Juggler instance to a file...
import magicbeans.sunw.demo.juggler.Juggler;
import java.io.*;

public class SerializeJuggler {
   public static void main( String [] args ) throws Exception
   {
      Juggler duke = new Juggler();
      ObjectOutputStream oout = new ObjectOutputStream(
         new FileOutputStream("juggler.ser") );
      oout.writeObject( duke );
      oout.close();
   }
}
```

Once you have the frozen *Juggler*, compile the following small application:

```
//file: BackFromTheDead.java
import java.awt.Component;
import javax.swing.*;
import java.beans.*;

public class BackFromTheDead extends JFrame {

  public BackFromTheDead( String name ) {
    super("Revived Beans!");
    try {
      Object bean = Beans.instantiate(
        getClass().getClassLoader(), name );

      if ( Beans.isInstanceOf( bean, JComponent.class) ) {
        JComponent comp = (JComponent)
          Beans.getInstanceOf(bean, JComponent.class);
        getContentPane().add("Center", comp);
      } else {
          System.out.println("Bean is not a JComponent...");
      }
    } catch ( java.io.IOException e1 ) {
      System.out.println("Error loading the serialized object");
    } catch ( ClassNotFoundException e2 ) {
      System.out.println(
         "Can't find the class that goes with the object");
    }
  }

  public static void main(String [] args) {
    JFrame frame = new BackFromTheDead( args[0] );
    frame.pack();
    frame.setVisible(true);
  }
}
```

Run this program, passing the name of your serialized object as an argument and making sure that our *magicbeans.jar* file is in your classpath. The name should *not* include the *.ser* extension in the name; the `Beans.instantiate()` method adds this automatically in its search for the serialized or class version. The juggler should spring back to life, juggling once again as shown in Figure 22-9.

Figure 22-9. The restored Juggler

In `BackFromTheDead`, we use `Beans.instantiate()` to load our serialized bean by name. We then check to see whether it is a GUI component using `Beans.isInstanceOf()`. (It is, because the `Juggler` is a subclass of `java.awt.Component`.) Finally, we cast the instantiated object to a `Component` with `Beans.getInstanceOf()` and add it to our application's `JFrame`. Notice that we still need a static Java cast to turn the `Object` returned by `getInstanceOf()` into a `JComponent`. This cast may seem gratuitous, but it is the bridge between the dynamic beans lookup of the type and the static, compile-time view of the type.

Everything we've done here could be done using the plain `java.io.ObjectInputStream` discussed in Chapter 12. But these bean management methods are intended to shield the user from details of how the beans are implemented and stored.

One more thing before we move on. We blithely noted that when the `Juggler` was restored, the bean began juggling again. This implies that threads were started when the bean was deserialized. Serialization doesn't automatically manage transient resources such as threads or even loaded images, but it's easy to take control of the process to finish reconstructing the bean's state when it is deserialized. Have a look at the `Juggler` source code (provided with the examples) and refer to Chapter 12 for a discussion of object deserialization using the `readObject()` method.

Runtime Event Hookups with Reflection

We've discussed reflection largely in terms of how design tools use it to analyze classes. Today, reflection is frequently finding its way into applications to perform dynamic activities that wouldn't be possible otherwise. In this section, we'll look at a dynamic event adapter that can be configured at runtime.

In Chapter 16, we saw how adapter classes could be built to connect event firings to arbitrary methods in our code, allowing us to cleanly separate GUI and logic in our applications. In this chapter, we have seen how NetBeans interposes this adapter code between beans to do this for us.

The AWT/Swing event model reduces the need to subclass components to perform simple hookups. If we start relying heavily on special adapter classes, we can quickly end up with as many adapters as components. Anonymous inner classes let us hide these classes, but they're still there. A potential solution for large or specialized applications is to create *generic* event adapters that serve a number of event sources and targets simultaneously.

The `java.beans.EventHandler` is a dynamic event dispatcher that simply calls methods in response to events. What makes the `EventHandler` unusual in Java is that it is the first standard utility to use reflection to allow us to specify the method by *name*. In other words, you ask the `EventHandler` to direct events to a handler by specifying the handler object and the string name of the method to invoke on that object.

We can use the `create()` method of `EventHandler` to get an adapter for a specified type of event listener, specifying a target object and method name to call when that event occurs. The target object doesn't have to be a listener for the particular event type or any other particular kind of object. The following application, `DynamicHookup`, uses the `EventHandler` to connect a button to a `launchTheMissiles()` method in our class:

```
//file: DynamicHookup.java
import javax.swing.*;
import java.awt.event.*;
import java.beans.EventHandler;

public class DynamicHookup extends JFrame {
  JLabel label = new JLabel( "Ready...", JLabel.CENTER );
  int count;

  public DynamicHookup() {
    JButton launchButton = new JButton("Launch!");
    getContentPane().add( launchButton, "South" );
    getContentPane().add( label, "Center" );
        launchButton.addActionListener(
                (ActionListener)EventHandler.create(
                        ActionListener.class, this, "launchTheMissiles"));
  }
  public void launchTheMissiles() {
    label.setText("Launched: "+ count++ );
  }

  public static void main(String[] args) {
    JFrame frame = new DynamicHookup();
        frame.setDefaultCloseOperation( JFrame.EXIT_ON_CLOSE );
    frame.setSize(150, 150);
```

```
        frame.setVisible( true );
    }
}
```

Here, we call the EventHandler's create() method, passing it the ActionListener class, the target object (this), and a string with the name of the method to invoke on the target when the event arrives. EventHandler internally creates a listener of the appropriate type and registers our target information. Not only do we eliminate an inner class, but the implementation of EventHandler may allow it to share adapters internally, producing very few objects.

This example shows how we would call a method that takes no arguments—but the EventHandler can actually do more, setting JavaBeans properties in response to events. The following form of create() tells EventHandler to call the launchTheMissiles() method, passing the source property of the ActionEvent as an argument:

```
EventHandler.create(
   ActionListener.class, target, "launchTheMissiles", "source")
```

All events have a source property (via the getSource() method), but we can go further, specifying a chain of property "gets" separated by dots, which are applied before the value is passed to the method. For example:

```
EventHandler.create(
   ActionListener.class, target, "launchTheMissiles", "source.text")
```

The source.text parameter causes the value getSource().getText() to be passed as an argument to launchTheMissiles(). In our case, that would be the label of our button. Other forms of create() allow more flexibility in selecting which methods of a multimethod listener interface are used as well as other options. We won't cover every detail of the tool here.

How it works

The EventHandler uses the java.lang.reflect.Proxy, which is a factory that can generate adapters implementing any type of interface at runtime. By specifying one or more event listener interfaces (e.g., ActionListener), we get an adapter that implements those listener interfaces generated for us on the fly. The adapter is a specially created class that delegates all the method calls on its interfaces to a designated InvocationHandler object. See Chapter 1 for more information about proxy classes.

BeanContext and BeanContextServices

So far we've talked about some sophisticated mechanisms for connecting Java beans together at design time and runtime. However, we haven't talked at all about the environment in which Java beans live. To build advanced, extensible applications, we'd like a way for Java beans to find each other or "rendezvous" at runtime. The java.beans.beancontext package provides this kind of container environment. It also provides a generic "services" lookup mechanism for beans that wish to advertise their capabilities. These mechanisms have existed for some time, but they haven't found much use in the standard Java packages. Still, they are interesting and important facilities that you can use in your own applications.

You can find a full explanation and example of how to use the bean context to find beans and listen for services in the expanded material on this book's website.

The Java Activation Framework

The Java Activation Framework (JAF) can be used by beans that work with many external data types, such as media retrieved from files and streams. It is essentially a generalized content/protocol handler mechanism for JavaBeans. The javax.activation package contains an extensible set of classes that wrap arbitrary, raw data sources to provide access to their data as streams or objects, identify the MIME type of the data, and enumerate a registered set of "commands" for operating on the data.

The JAF provides two primary interfaces: DataSource and DataHandler. The DataSource acts like the protocol handlers we discussed in Chapter 14. It wraps the data source and determines a MIME type for the data stream. The DataHandler acts like a content handler, except it provides a great deal more than access to the data. A DataHandler is constructed to wrap a DataSource and interpret the data in different forms. It also provides a list of command operations that can be used to access the data. DataHandler also implements the java.awt.datatransfer.Transferable interface, allowing data to be passed among application components in a well-defined way.

Enterprise JavaBeans and POJO-Based Enterprise Frameworks

Enterprise JavaBeans (EJB) is a very big topic, and we can't do more than provide a few paragraphs of insight here. If you want more information, see *Enterprise JavaBeans* by Richard Monson-Haefel (O'Reilly). The thrust of EJB takes the JavaBeans philosophy of portable, pluggable components and extends it to the server side to accommodate the sorts of things that multitiered, networked, and database-centric applications require. Although EJB pays homage to the basic JavaBeans concepts, it is much larger and more specialized. It doesn't have a lot in common with the kinds of things we've been talking about in this chapter. EJBs are server-side components for networked applications. EJBs and plain Java beans are both reusable, portable components that can be deployed and configured for specific environments. But in the case of EJBs, the components encapsulate access to business logic and database tables instead of GUI and program elements.

EJB ties together a number of other Java enterprise-oriented APIs—including database access, transactions, and name services—into a single component model for server applications. EJB imposes a lot more structure on how you write code than plain-old Java beans. It does so to allow the server-side *EJB container* to take on a lot of responsibility and optimize your application's activities without your having to write a lot of code.

The first two major releases of *Java Enterprise Edition*, which include EJBs, were considered by many to be overly complicated. Many classes, interfaces, and configuration files were required to support EJBs. As a result, a number of popular open source frameworks that make use of Plain Old Java Objects (POJOs) to accomplish the same tasks quickly rose to prominence. POJOs are Java objects that are not required to follow any convention, implement any interface, or inherit from any base class, although in practice they are often JavaBeans. The most notable of the POJO-based frameworks are Hibernate, a framework for mapping Java object state to a database, and Spring, a general-purpose enterprise application development framework.

CHAPTER 23
Applets

One of the original promises of Java was that applications could be delivered over the network to your computer as needed. Instead of the old days of buying a shrink-wrapped box containing a word processor, installing it, and upgrading it every few years, it would now be possible to obtain and use software directly from the Internet, safely and on any platform. Today, we take networked distribution of software for granted. Mobile devices have driven the advent of app stores for installed software, and many (if not the majority) of the most highly used applications are now purely browser-based. Unfortunately for Java fans, these advances took different paths, arguably less elegant, than the Java platform offered and took longer to arrive than they likely could have.

This chapter is about the *applet* API, which was Java's earliest mechanism for delivering applications to the web browser. Applets are not widely used today, but they are part of the vernacular and are still doing well in some niches. While you may not wish to write applets going forward, it is useful to understand their basic functionality. As we review applets, we will also touch on general areas of interest along the way, such as the Java security model.

An applet is a Java program that runs within the context of a web page. Like an image or hyperlink, it "owns" some rectangular area of the user's screen. When the web browser loads a page that contains a Java applet, it knows how to load the classes of the applet and run them. This chapter describes how applets work and how they are incorporated into web pages. We'll also talk about the Java Plug-in and related technologies such as Java Web Start briefly.

The Politics of Browser-Based Applications

First, a bit of history. The potential for applets to add dynamic content to web pages was one of the driving forces behind the spread of the Java programming language. Prior to Java's introduction in 1994, there was really no standard way to do this; even the now-ubiquitous animated GIF images were not yet widely supported. Sun's HotJava Java-based web browser was the first to support applets. It was Java's original "killer application." Later, in 1995, Netscape announced that it would support the Applet API in its browsers, and soon after that Microsoft jumped on the bandwagon. For a while, it seemed that Java would power the future of the Web, but there were many bumps in the road to come.

Many problems, both technical and political, plagued the early years of Java's use in browsers and client-side applications. Performance issues were to be expected in such a young platform. But what really crippled Java early on was the nonportable and buggy AWT, Java's original GUI toolkit. Many people overlook the fact that Java's success as a portable language is in large part a result of just how much of the Java API is implemented *in* Java. You might be surprised to learn just how many Java internals involve no native code—everything from cryptography to DNS is done in Java—requiring no porting for new platforms. Similarly, the renaissance of Java GUI applications seen in later years was due almost entirely to the introduction of the pure Java Swing GUI toolkit. In contrast, the original AWT system was based on native code, which had to be ported to each new system, taking into account subtle and tricky platform dependencies. AWT was effectively a large, graphical C program that Java talked to through a set of interfaces and Java was, to some extent, unfairly painted as nonportable and buggy by association.

Java faced other, less technical obstacles as well. Netscape foisted the original AWT upon the world when it insisted that Java be released with "native look and feel" in lieu of a less capable, but truly portable, graphical toolkit. It later introduced a pure Java GUI toolkit called IFC (an ancestor of Swing), but it struggled to gain traction. Later, Microsoft effectively stuck us with AWT by freezing the level of the Applet API in its browsers at Java 1.1. Applets languished with poor GUIs while lawsuits between Sun and Microsoft dragged on in the 1990s. The result was that support for applets in web browsers remained a mess.

Sun made an attempt to insulate Java from the browser battles with the introduction of the Java Plug-in. The Plug-in allowed applets to run in an up-to-date Java VM, but by this point lacked the critical mass and near-universal adoption necessary to make such a plug-in useful. The weaker but more prevalent Adobe Flash plug-in flourished, as developers desperately wanted a way to deploy richer applications to the browser. In the 2000s, JavaScript and HTML matured greatly and made the browser itself more of a viable platform for deploying software, leading to the great irony that JavaScript, the slower and less capable namesake of Java, became the de facto programming language of the Web.

Find it a bit depressing? Well, take heart; JavaScript has evolved into a worthy platform for the client side, Flash is fading, and Java has dominated server-side development and made possible portable libraries that have fueled much of the Internet revolution. We cannot say what the future holds, but Java in some form will likely be a player in it for many decades to come.

Applet Support and the Java Plug-in

As we mentioned earlier, the state of support for Java in web browsers has always been a mess. The most reliable way to run Java in a web browser has always been the Java Plug-in. The Plug-in is a free, user-installed component (implemented differently for each browser) that supports Java itself. Using the Plug-in makes an end-run around the poor support built into the browser by using a separate software package that can be installed and updated independently of the browser releases.

Recently, some platforms—notably Mac OS X—have dropped the built-in support for Java in the browser entirely and rely on users to install the Java Plug-in if they wish to run applets. This is not ideal, but does simplify things by eliminating some of the ambiguity. If you have installed Java 7 on OS X or Windows, then you should already have the Java Plug-in needed to run the applets discussed in this chapter. In some cases, the first time you attempt to view a page containing an applet, you may be prompted to enable Java in the browser. You may also want to consult the Java "control panel" in Windows or "preference pane" in Mac OS X for additional preferences related to Java after installing Java 7.

The JApplet Class

A `JApplet` is a Swing `JPanel` with a mission. It is a GUI container that has some extra structure to allow it to be used in the "alien" environment of a web browser. Applets also have a lifecycle that lets them act more like an application than a static component. Although applets tend to be relatively simple, there's no inherent restriction on their complexity other than the issues of downloading and caching their content. Historically, applets have tended to be small "widgets."

The `javax.swing.JApplet` class defines the core functionality of an applet. (`java.awt.Applet` is the older, AWT-based form.)

Structurally, an applet is a wrapper for your Java code. In contrast to a standalone graphical Java application, which starts up from a `main()` method and creates a GUI, an applet itself is a component that expects to be dropped into someone else's GUI. Thus, an applet can't run by itself; it runs in the context of a web browser or a special appletviewer program (which we'll talk about later). Instead of having your application create a `JFrame` to hold your GUI, you stuff your application inside a `JApplet` (which itself extends `Container`) and let the browser add your applet to the page.

Applets are placed on web pages with the <applet> HTML tag, which we'll cover later in this chapter. At its simplest, you just specify the name of the applet class and a size in pixels for the applet:

```
<applet code="AnalogClock" width="100" height="100"></applet>
```

Pragmatically, an applet is an intruder into someone else's environment and therefore has to be treated with suspicion. The web browsers that run applets impose restrictions on what the applet is allowed to do. The restrictions are enforced by an applet security manager. The browser provides everything the applet needs through an applet context—the API the applet uses to interact with its environment.

A JApplet expects to be embedded in a page and used in a viewing environment that provides it with resources. In all other respects, however, applets are just ordinary Panel objects. As Figure 23-1 shows, an applet is a kind of Panel. Like any other Panel, a JApplet can contain user interface components and use all the basic drawing and event-handling capabilities of the Component class. You can draw on a JApplet by overriding its paint() method and respond to events in the JApplet's display area by providing the appropriate event listeners. Applets also have additional structure that helps them interact with the browser environment.

Aside from the top-level structure and the security restrictions, there is no difference between an applet and an application. If your application can live within the limits imposed by a browser's security manager, you can structure it to function as both an applet and a standalone application. Normally, you'll use your applet class itself only as a thin wrapper to manage the lifecycle and appearance of your application—create the GUI, start, and stop. So, the bulk of your code should be easily adaptable to either a standalone or applet deployment.

Applet Lifecycle

The Applet class contains four methods that can be overridden to guide it through its lifecycle. The init(), start(), stop(), and destroy() methods are called by the appletviewer or web browser to direct the applet's behavior. init() is called once, after the applet is created. The init() method is where you perform basic setup such as parsing parameters, building a user interface, and loading resources.

By convention, applets don't provide an explicit constructor to do any setup. The reason for this is that the constructor is meant to be called by the applet's environment, for simple creation of the applet. This might happen before the applet has access to certain resources, such as information about its environment. Therefore, an applet doesn't normally do any work there; instead it should rely on the default constructor for the JApplet class and do its initialization in the init() method.

The start() method is called whenever the applet becomes visible; it shouldn't be a surprise then that the stop() method is called whenever the applet becomes invisible.

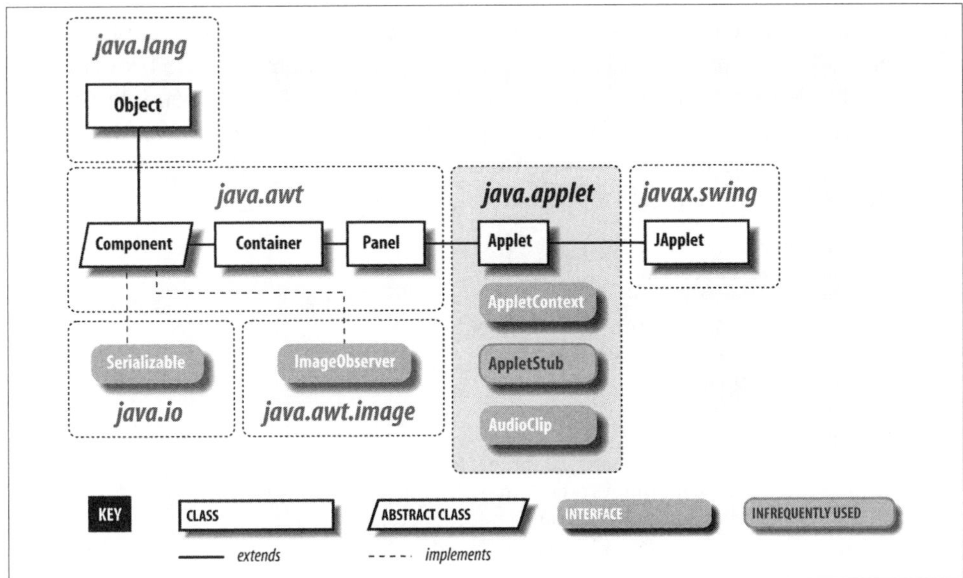

Figure 23-1. The java.applet package

`init()` is called only once in the life of an applet, but `start()` and `stop()` can be called any number of times (although always in the logical sequence). The `start()` method is called when the applet is displayed, such as when it scrolls onto the screen; `stop()` will be called if the applet scrolls off the screen, or the viewer leaves the document. `start()` tells the applet it should be active. The applet may want to create threads, animate, or otherwise perform useful (or annoying) activity. `stop()` is called to let the applet know it should go dormant. Applets should cease CPU-intensive or wasteful activity when they are stopped and resume when (and if) they are restarted. However, there's no requirement that an invisible applet stop computing; in some applications, it may be useful for the applet to continue running in the background. Just be considerate of your user, who doesn't want an invisible applet dragging down system performance.

Finally, the `destroy()` method gives the applet a last chance to clean up before it's removed—some time after the last call to `stop()`. For example, an applet might want to gracefully close down suspended communications channels at this time. Exactly when `destroy()` is called depends on the browser; Netscape calls `destroy()` just prior to deleting the applet from its cache. This means that although an applet can cling to life after being told to `stop()`, how long it can go on is unpredictable. If you want to maintain an applet as the user progresses through other pages of activities, you may have to put it in an HTML frame, so that it remains visible and won't be told to `stop()` (see "Applet persistence and navigation" on page 841).

If you've read this entire book up until now, you've already seen a couple of applets that snuck in among other topics. In Chapter 9, we created a simple clock applet, and in Chapter 13, we used an applet to send packets of information from a web browser. Now let's try a simple Swing-based example using `JApplet`. The following example, `ShowApplet`, shown in Figure 23-2, does nothing special, but you can use it to test the version of Java that's running in your browser (and see if the Plug-in is installed) and to see when the applet is started and stopped. It's a good reference.

```
import javax.swing.*;
import java.awt.event.*;

public class ShowApplet extends JApplet {
   JTextArea text = new JTextArea();
   int startCount;

   public void init() {
      JButton button = new JButton("Press Me");
      button.addActionListener( new ActionListener() {
         public void actionPerformed( ActionEvent e ) {
            text.append("Button Pressed!\n");
         }
      } );
      getContentPane().add( "Center", new JScrollPane( text ) );
      JPanel panel = new JPanel();
      panel.add( button );
      getContentPane().add( "South", panel );
      text.append( "Java Version: "
         +System.getProperty("java.version")+"\n" );
      text.append( "Applet init()\n" );
   }
   public void start() {
      text.append( "Applet started: "+ startCount++ +"\n" );
   }
   public void stop() {
      text.append( "Applet stopped.\n" );
   }
}
```

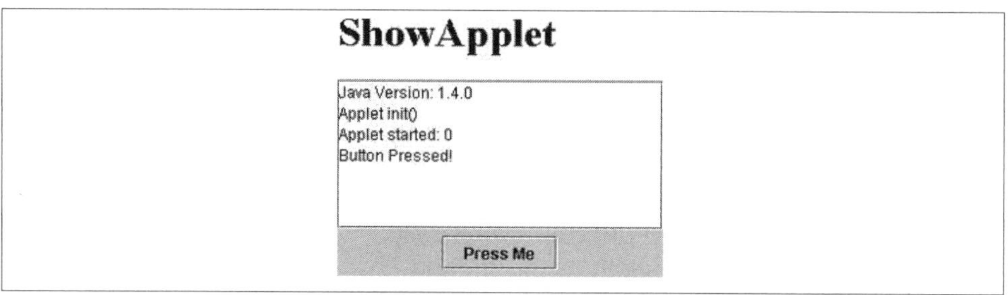

Figure 23-2. ShowApplet

After compiling the applet, we have to create an HTML page in which to embed it. The following will do:

```
<html><head><title>ShowApplet</title></head>
<body>
<applet code="ShowApplet" width="300" height="300">
   Your browser does not understand Java.</applet>
</body>
</html>
```

We'll discuss the `applet` tag and other issues related to embedding applets in documents in detail later in this chapter. For now, just save this in a file called *showapplet.html*. Load the file with your favorite web browser and see what happens. (We're assuming you have installed Java on your computer by this point; you may have to enable Java in your browser to see the applet if it is disabled by default.) If you have access to a web server, you can use it. Otherwise, you can open the file locally using either the browser's Open File menu option or a URL such as:

```
file:///Users/somedir/showapplet.html
```

The applet shows the version of Java running it and prints messages when its button is pressed. If you have installed the latest Java Plug-in you should see "Java version: 1.7" in the box, regardless of which browser you are using (including Microsoft Internet Explorer). The applet prints messages when its `start()` and `stop()` methods are called, along with a count. You can use this to experiment with different browsers and page-layout configurations to see when your applet is reloaded or restarted. If your browser fails to display the applet with the correct version of Java, don't worry. Later in this chapter, we'll talk about how to convert the HTML to force the browser to use the Java Plug-in explicitly.

The Applet Security Sandbox

Applets are quarantined within the browser by an applet `SecurityManager`. The `SecurityManager` is part of the web browser or `appletviewer` application. It is installed before the browser loads any applets and implements the basic restrictions that let the user run untrusted applets (loaded over the Internet) safely. Remember, there are no inherent security restrictions on a standalone Java application. It is the browser that limits what applets are allowed to do using a security policy.

Most browsers impose the following restrictions on untrusted applets:

- Untrusted applets can't read or write files on the local host.
- Untrusted applets can open network connections (sockets) only to the server from which they originated.
- Untrusted applets can't start other processes on the local host.

- Untrusted applets can't have native methods.

The motivation for these restrictions should be fairly obvious: you clearly wouldn't want a program coming from some random Internet site to access your files or run arbitrary programs. Although untrusted applets can't directly read and write files on the client side or talk to arbitrary hosts on the network, applets can work with servers to store data and communicate. For example, an applet can use Java's RMI facility to do processing on its server. An applet can communicate with other applets on the Net by proxy through its server.

Trusted applets

We've been using the term *untrusted applet*, so it should come as no surprise that it is also possible to have such a thing as a *trusted applet*. Applets become trusted through the use of digital signatures, by *signing* the JAR file containing your applet code. Because a signature identifies the applet's origin unambiguously, the user can distinguish between trusted applets (i.e., applets that come from a site or person you trust not to do anything harmful) and run-of-the-mill untrusted applets. In browser environments that support signing, trusted applets can be granted permission to "go outside" of the applet security sandbox. Trusted applets can be allowed to do all of the things that standalone Java applications can do: read and write files, open network connections to arbitrary machines, and interact with the local operating system by starting processes. Trusted applets still can't have native methods, but including native methods in an applet would destroy its portability anyway.

Because signed applets are now a fairly niche topic, we no longer cover them in this chapter. If you need more details on them, please visit the "extras" page (*http://oreil.ly/Java_4E*) for this book, where we post additional material not included in the book as well as the example source code.

Getting Applet Resources

An applet must communicate with its browser or applet viewer. For example, it may need configuration parameters from the HTML document in which it appears. An applet may also need to load images, audio clips, and other items. It may also want to ask the viewer about other applets on the same HTML page in order to communicate with them. To get resources from the environment, applets use the `AppletStub` and `AppletContext` interfaces, provided by the browser.

Applet parameters

An applet can get configuration parameters from `<param>` tags placed inside the `<applet>` tag in the HTML document, as we'll describe later. You can retrieve these parameters using `Applet`'s `getParameter()` method. For example, the following code reads parameters called `imageName` and `sheep` from its HTML page:

```
String imageName = getParameter( "imageName" );
try  {
    int numberOfSheep = Integer.parseInt( getParameter( "sheep" ) );
} catch ( NumberFormatException e ) { /* use default */ }
```

There is an API that allows an applet to provide information (help) about the parameters it accepts. The applet's `getParameterInfo()` can return an array of string arrays, listing and describing the applet's parameters. However, it's unclear that anyone uses this API.

Applet resources

An applet can find out where it lives using the `getDocumentBase()` and `getCodeBase()` methods. `getDocumentBase()` returns the base URL of the document in which the applet appears; `getCodeBase()` returns the base URL of the `Applet`'s class files (these two are often the same). An applet can use these methods to construct relative URLs from which to load other resources from its server, such as images, sounds, and other data. The `getImage()` method takes a URL and asks for an image from the viewer environment. The image may be cached or loaded when later used. The `getAudioClip()` method, similarly, retrieves sound clips.

The following example uses `getCodeBase()` to construct a URL and load a properties configuration file, located in the same remote directory on the web server as the applet's class file:

```
Properties props = new Properties();
try {
  URL url = new URL( getCodeBase(), "appletConfig.props" );
  props.load( url.openStream() );
} catch ( IOException e ) { /* failed */ }
```

A better way to load resources is by calling the `getResource()` and `getResourceAsStream()` methods of the `Class` class, which search the applet's JAR files (if any) as well as its codebase, which is an extension of the classpath for applets. The following code loads the same properties file in a more portable way:

```
Properties props = new Properties();
try {
  props.load( getClass().getResourceAsStream( "appletConfig.props") );
} catch ( IOException e ) { /* failed */ }
```

An applet can ask its viewer to retrieve an image by calling the `getImage()` method. The location of the image to be retrieved is given as a URL, either absolute or fetched from an applet's resources:

```
public class MyApplet extends javax.swing.JApplet {
  public void init() {
    try {
      // absolute URL
      URL monaURL =
          new URL( "http://myserver/images/mona_lisa.gif");
```

```
            Image monaImage = getImage( monaURL );
            // applet resource URL
            URL daffyURL =
                getClass().getResource("cartoons/images/daffy.gif");
            Image daffyDuckImage = getImage( daffyURL );
          }
          catch ( MalformedURLException e ) {
              // unintelligable url
          }
        }
        // ...
    }
```

Again, using `getResource()` is preferred; it looks for the image in the applet's JAR file (if there is one), before looking elsewhere in the applet's classpath on the server. (We'll talk more later about how classes are located for applets.)

Driving the browser

The *status line* is a blurb of text that usually appears somewhere in the web browser's display, indicating a current activity. An applet can request that some text be placed in the status line with the `showStatus()` method. (The browser isn't required to do anything in response to this call, but most browsers will oblige you.)

An applet can also ask the browser to show a new document. To do this, the applet makes a call to the `showDocument(url)` method of the `AppletContext`. You can get a reference to the `AppletContext` with the applet's `getAppletContext()` method. Calling `showDocument(url)` replaces the currently showing document, which means that your currently running applet will be stopped.

Another version of `showDocument()` takes an additional `String` argument to tell the browser where to display the new URL:

```
getAppletContext().showDocument( url, name );
```

The `name` argument can be the name of an existing labeled HTML frame; the document referenced by the URL is displayed in that frame. You can use this method to create an applet that "drives" the browser to new locations dynamically but keeps itself active on the screen in a separate frame. This is common for applets that act like navigation controls or menus. If the named frame doesn't exist, the browser creates a new top-level window to hold it. Alternatively, `name` can have one of the following special values:

`self`
: Show in the current frame

`_parent`
: Show in the parent of our frame

`_top`
: Show in outermost (top-level) frame

`_blank`
: Show in a new top-level browser window

Both `showStatus()` and `showDocument()` requests may be ignored by a cold-hearted viewer or web browser. Nothing in browser-land is ever certain.

Inter-applet communication

Although it's not very common, applets that are embedded in documents loaded from the same location on a website can use a simple mechanism to locate one another and coordinate their activities on a page. Once an applet has a reference to another applet, it can communicate with it just as with any other object, by invoking methods and sending events. The `getApplet()` method of the applet context looks for an applet by name:

```
Applet clock = getAppletContext().getApplet("theClock");
```

Give an applet a name within your HTML document using the `name` attribute of the `<applet>` tag. Alternatively, you can use the `getApplets()` method to enumerate all the available applets in the pages.

The tricky thing with applet communications is that applets run inside the security sandbox. An untrusted applet can "see" and communicate only with objects that were loaded by the same class loader. Currently, the only reliable criterion for when applets share a class loader is when they share a common base URL. For example, all the applets contained in web pages loaded from the base URL of *http://foo.bar.com/mypages/* should share a class loader and should be able to see each other. This includes documents such as *mypages/foo.html* and *mypages/bar.html*, but not *mypages/morestuff/foo.html.*

When applets do share a class loader, other techniques are possible, too. As with any other class, you can call static methods in applets by name. So you could use static methods in one of your applets as a "registry" to coordinate your activities.

Applet persistence and navigation

One of the biggest shortcomings of the Applet API is the lack of a real context for coordinating their activities during navigation across a multipage document or web application. The Applet API simply wasn't designed for this. Although an applet's life cycle is well defined in terms of its API, it is not well defined in terms of management by the browser or scope of visibility. As we described in the previous section, applets loaded from the same codebase can rendezvous at runtime using their name attributes. But there are no guarantees about how long an applet will live—or whether it will be stopped as opposed to being destroyed—once it is out of view. If you experiment with our `ShowApplet` in various browsers and in the Java Plug-in (which we'll discuss later), you'll see that, in some cases, the applet is stopped and restarted when the user leaves the page, but more often the applet is reinitialized from scratch. This makes designing multipage applications that work in all browsers difficult.

One solution has been to use static methods as a shared "registry," as mentioned earlier. However, the details governing how classes loaded by applets are managed are even less well-defined than the management of the applets themselves. In Java 1.4, a pair of methods was added to the `AppletContext` to support short-term applet persistence: `setStream()` and `getStream()`. With these methods, an applet can ask the context to save a stream of byte data by a key value and return it later. The notion of providing the state to the context as a stream is a little odd, but easy enough to accommodate. Here is an example:

```
getAppletContext.setStream("myStream",
    new ByteArrayInputStream( "This is some test data...".getBytes() ) );
```

Later, the stream data can be retrieved:

```
InputStream in = getAppletContext.getStream( "myStream" );
```

Currently, the data is retained only as long as the browser is running. If you need more complex state and navigation capabilities, you might consider using a signed applet to write to a file or taking advantage of the Java Web Start API to install your application locally.

The <applet> Tag

Applets are embedded in HTML documents with the `<applet>` tag. The `<applet>` tag resembles the HTML `<img>` image tag. It contains attributes that identify the applet to be displayed and, optionally, give the web browser hints about how it should be shown.[1]

The standard image tag sizing and alignment attributes, such as `height` and `width`, can be used inside the applet tag. However, unlike images, applets have both an opening `<applet>` and a closing `</applet>` tag. Sandwiched between these can be any number of `<param>` tags that contain configuration data to be passed to the applet:

```
<applet attributeattribute ... >
    <param parameter >
    <param parameter >
    ...
</applet>
```

1. If you aren't familiar with HTML or other markup languages, you may want to refer to *HTML & XHTML: The Definitive Guide* by Chuck Musciano and Bill Kennedy (O'Reilly) for a complete reference on HTML and structured web documents.

Attributes

Attributes are name/value pairs that are interpreted by a web browser or applet viewer. Attributes of the <applet> tag specify general features that apply to any applet, such as size and alignment. The definition of the <applet> tag lists a fixed set of recognized attributes; specifying an incorrect or nonexistent attribute should be considered an HTML error.

Three attributes are required in the <applet> tag. Two of these attributes, width and height, specify the space that the applet occupies on the screen. The third required attribute must be either code or object; you must supply one of these attributes, and you can't specify both. The code attribute specifies the class file from which the applet is loaded; the object attribute specifies a serialized representation of an applet. Most often, you'll use the code attribute.

The following is an HTML fragment for a simple clock applet that takes no parameters and requires no special HTML layout:

```
<applet code="AnalogClock" width="100" height="100"></applet>
```

The HTML file that contains this <applet> tag must be stored in the same directory as the *AnalogClock.class* class file. The applet tag is not sensitive to spacing in the HTML, so the previous tag could be also be formatted a little more readably like so:

```
<applet
    code="AnalogClock"
    width="100"
    height="100">
</applet>
```

Parameters

Parameters are analogous to command-line arguments; they provide a way to pass information to an applet. Each <param> tag contains a name and a value that are passed as string values to the applet:

```
<param name = "parameter_name" value = "parameter_value">
```

Parameters provide a means of embedding application-specific data and configuration information within an HTML document. Our AnalogClock applet, for example, might accept a parameter that selects between local and universal time:

```
<applet code="AnalogClock" width="100" height="100">
    <param name="zone" value="GMT">
</applet>
```

Presumably, this AnalogClock applet is designed to look for a parameter named zone with a possible value of GMT.

Parameter names and values should be quoted and can contain spaces and other white-space characters. The parameters a given applet expects are, of course, determined by the developer of that applet. There is no standard set of parameter names or values; it's up to the applet to interpret the parameter name/value pairs that are passed to it. Any number of parameters can be specified, and the applet may choose to use or ignore them as it sees fit.

¿Habla Applet?

Web browsers are supposed to ignore tags they don't understand; if the web browser doesn't know about the `<applet>` or `<param>` tags, we would expect them to disappear, and any HTML between the `<applet>` and `</applet>` tags to appear normally. By convention, Java-enabled web browsers ignore any extra HTML between the `<applet>` and `</applet>` tags. Combined, this means we can place some alternative HTML inside the `<applet>` tag, which is displayed only by web browsers that can't run the applet.

For our `AnalogClock` example, we could display a small text explanation and an image of the clock applet as a teaser:

```
<applet code="AnalogClock" width="100" height="100">
    <param name="zone" value="GMT">
    <strong>If you see this, you don't have a Java-enabled Web
    browser. Here's a picture of what you are missing.</strong>
    <img src="clockface.gif">
</applet>
```

The Complete <applet> Tag

We'll now spell out the complete syntax for the `<applet>` tag:

```
<applet
    code = class_name
```

or:

```
    object = serialized_applet_name

    width = pixels_high
    height = pixels_wide

    [ codebase = location_URL ]
    [ archive = comma_separated_list_of_archive_files ]
    [ name = applet_instance_name ]
    [ alt = alternate_text ]
    [ align = style ]
    [ vspace = vertical pad pixels ]
    [ hspace = horizontal pad pixels ]
>
    [ <param name = parameter_name value = parameter_value> ]
    [ <param ...  ]
```

```
    [ HTML code for non-Java-aware browsers ]
</applet>
```

Either the `code` attribute or the `object` attribute must be present to specify the applet to run. The `code` attribute specifies the applet's class file; you'll see this most frequently. The `object` attribute specifies a serialized representation of an applet. When you use the `object` attribute to load an applet, the applet's `init()` method is not called. However, the serialized applet's `start()` method is called.

The `width`, `height`, `align`, `vspace`, and `hspace` attributes determine the preferred size, alignment, and padding, respectively. The `width` and `height` attributes are required.

The `codebase` attribute specifies the base URL to be searched for the applet's class files. If this attribute isn't present, the browser looks in the same location as the HTML file. The `archive` attribute specifies a list of JAR or ZIP files in which the applet's class files are located. To put two or more files in the list, separate the filenames with commas; for example, the following attribute tells the browser to load and search three archives for the applet's classes:

```
archive="Part1.jar,Part2.jar,Utilities.jar"
```

The archive files listed by the `archive` tag are loaded from the codebase URL. When searching for classes, a browser checks the archives before searching any other locations on the server.

The `alt` attribute specifies alternate text that is displayed by browsers that understand the `<applet>` tag and its attributes but have Java disabled or don't run applets. This attribute can also describe the applet because in this case, any alternate HTML between `<applet>` and `</applet>` is, by convention, ignored by Java-enabled browsers.

The `name` attribute specifies an instance name for the executing applet. This is a name specified as a unique label for each copy of an applet on a particular HTML page. For example, if we include our clock twice on the same page (using two applet tags), we should give each instance a unique name to differentiate them:

```
<applet code="AnalogClock" name="bigClock" width="300" height="300">
</applet>
<applet code="AnalogClock" name="smallClock" width="50" height="50">
</applet>
```

Applets can use instance names to recognize and communicate with other applets on the same page. We could, for instance, create a "clock setter" applet that knows how to set the time on an `AnalogClock` applet and pass it the instance name of a particular target clock on this page as a parameter. This might look something like:

```
<applet code="ClockSetter">
    <param name="clockToSet" value="bigClock">
</applet>
```

Loading Class Files

The code attribute of the <applet> tag should specify the name of an applet. This is either a simple class name or a package path and class name. For now, let's look at simple class names; we'll discuss packages in a moment. By default, the Java runtime system looks for the class file in the same location as the HTML document that contains it. This location is known as the *base URL* for the document.

Consider an HTML document, *clock.html*, that contains our clock applet example:

```
<applet code="AnalogClock" width="100" height="100"></applet>
```

Let's say we retrieve the document at the following URL:

```
http://www.time.ch/documents/clock.html
```

Java tries to retrieve the applet class file from the same base location:

```
http://www.time.ch/documents/AnalogClock.class
```

The codebase attribute of the <applet> tag specifies an alternative base URL for the class file search. Let's say our HTML document now specifies codebase, as in the following example:

```
<applet
    codebase="http://www.joes.ch/stuff/"
    code="AnalogClock"
    width="100"
    height="100">
</applet>
```

Java now looks for the applet class file at:

```
http://www.joes.ch/stuff/AnalogClock.class
```

Packages

For "loose" applet class files that are not packaged into archives, Java uses the standard package name to directory path mapping to locate files on the server. The only difference is that the requests are not local file lookups, but instead are requests to the web server at the applet's codebase URL. Before a class file is retrieved from a server, its package name component is translated by the client into a relative pathname under the applet's codebase.

Let's suppose that our AnalogClock has been placed into a package called time.clock (a subordinate package for clock-related classes, within a package for time-related classes). The fully qualified name of our class is time.clock.AnalogClock. Our simple <applet> tag would now look like:

```
<applet code="time.clock.AnalogClock" width="100" height="100"></applet>
```

Let's say the *clock.html* document is once again retrieved from:

```
http://www.time.ch/documents/clock.html
```

Java now looks for the class file in the following location:

```
http://www.time.ch/documents/time/clock/AnalogClock.class
```

The same is true when specifying an alternative `codebase`:

```
<applet
    codebase="http://www.joes.ch/stuff/"
    code="time.clock.AnalogClock"
    width="100"
    height="100">
</applet>
```

Java now tries to find the class in the corresponding path under this base URL:

```
http://www.joes.ch/stuff/time/clock/AnalogClock.class
```

appletviewer

The Java SDK comes with an applet viewer program, aptly called *appletviewer*. To use *appletviewer*, specify the URL of the document on the command line. For example, to view our (still only theoretical) `AnalogClock` at the URL shown earlier, use the following command:

```
% appletviewer http://www.time.ch/documents/clock.html
```

appletviewer retrieves all applets in the specified document and displays each one in a separate window. *appletviewer* isn't a web browser; it doesn't attempt to display HTML. It was primarily useful before the Java Plug-in as a way to test an applet in a specific version of the Java runtime.

Java Web Start

The Java Web Start API is an alternative to using applets. Java Web Start uses the Java Network Launching Protocol (JNLP) to transparently download and install Java applications locally. The only thing the user has to do is to click on the install link on a web page. The installed applications can then be launched just like any installed application, by clicking on an icon on the desktop or through the Start menu, but they continue to be managed by the Java security policy unless otherwise authorized by the user. Web Start applications also automatically check for upgrades and update themselves over the Net. Java Web Start is a form of *zero administration* client installation, which implies that the client doesn't have to do any work to install or maintain the application. JNLP applications may be signed (allowing the user to grant them fine-grained privileges), or unsigned. But even unsigned JNLP applications can take advantage of standard APIs that prompt the user for permission to perform basic operations, such as opening files and printing.

Packaging your application to use JNLP is relatively easy, but we won't get into it here. The process mainly involves creating a JNLP deployment file that lists your JARs and specifies any special permission they require. You must then include an appropriate link in your web page that uses Web Start. The first time a user tries to install a JNLP application, he will have to install the Java Plug-in. Thereafter, the Java Web Start component manages all JNLP installs. See Oracle's website (*http://bit.ly/13xLt0s*) for more information.

Conclusion

In this chapter, we covered some of the events that led to the current, fractured world of Java in the web browser and set the scene as it is. The Java Plug-in is currently your only real option for running Java in the browser. New technologies such as Java Web Start provide alternative directions for client-side deployment that may also be appealing. Finally, there are a variety of third-party products that produce clickable installers for Java applications that you may wish to consider.

CHAPTER 24
XML

Every now and then, an idea comes along that in retrospect seems just so simple and obvious that everyone wonders why it hadn't been seen all along. Often when that happens, it turns out that the idea isn't really all that new after all. The Java revolution began by drawing on ideas from generations of programming languages that came before it. XML—the Extensible Markup Language—does for content what Java did for programming: draws on some old ideas and uses them to provide a portable way to describe data.

XML is a simple, common format for representing structured information as text. The concept of XML follows the success of HTML as a universal document presentation format and generalizes it to handle any kind of data. In the process, XML has not only recast HTML, but has transformed the way many businesses think about their information. In the context of a world driven more and more by documents and data exchange, XML is an important foundation technology.

The Butler Did It

This chapter is one of the longest in this book and deals with many APIs and concepts. Part of the reason for this is that there has been a great deal of evolution of XML tools over time in order to support working with XML at different levels of abstraction. We're going to introduce you to the APIs that we think remain important and useful in this chapter and to some extent we'll do this by starting at the bottom level and working our way up. First we'll cover basic XML concepts and low-level APIs such as the event-driven SAX (Simple API for Java) and model-building DOM (Document Object Model). We'll also discuss related technologies such as XML Schema validation, XPath queries, and XSL (Extensible Style Sheet) transformation. Later in this chapter, we'll discuss the higher-level JAXB, Java XML Binding API, for mapping plain Java objects directly to XML and back.

This means that for some of you, the most useful material may be toward the end of this chapter where we cover the high-level tools. So we want to reassure you that things get more interesting as the chapter progresses. When we reach the section on JAXB we'll see that we can take plain old Java objects (POJOs) and write them to XML by adding (in the simplest case) a one-line annotation. The following snippet shows a Java `Person` and `Address` class and the corresponding XML that they would map to by default.

```
@XmlRootElement
public class Person {
    public String name;
    public Address address;
    public int age;
}
public class Address {
    public String city, street;
    public int number, zip;
}

<person>
    <name>Pat Niemeyer</name>
    <address>
        <city>St. Louis</city>
        <street>Java St.</street>
        <number>1234</number>
        <zip>54321</zip>
    </address>
    <age>42</age>
</person>
```

But before we go there, let's take a step back and talk about the motivation and "rules" of XML documents and some of the ways we can parse and generate them.

A Bit of Background

XML and HTML are called *markup languages* because of the way they add structure to plain-text documents—by surrounding parts of the text with tags that indicate structure or meaning, much as someone with a pen might highlight a sentence and add a note. While HTML predefines a set of tags and their structure, XML is a blank slate in which the author gets to define the tags, the rules, and their meanings.

Both XML and HTML owe their lineage to Standard Generalized Markup Language (SGML)—the mother of all markup languages. SGML has been used in the publishing industry for decades (including at O'Reilly). But it wasn't until the Web captured the world that it came into the mainstream through HTML. HTML started as a very small application of SGML, and if HTML has done anything at all, it has proven that simplicity reigns.

Text Versus Binary

When Tim Berners-Lee began postulating the Web back at CERN in the late 1980s, he wanted to organize project information using hypertext with links embedded in plain text.[1] When the Web needed a protocol, HTTP—a simple, text-based client-server protocol—was invented. So, what exactly is so enchanting about the idea of plain text? Why, for example, didn't Tim turn to the Microsoft Word format as the basis for web documents? Surely a binary, non-human-readable format and a similarly machine-oriented protocol would be more efficient? Since the Web's inception, there have now been literally trillions of HTTP transactions. Was it really a good idea for them to use (English) words like "GET" and "POST" as part of the protocol?

The answer, as we've all seen, is yes! Whatever humans can read and undertstand, human developers can work with more easily. There is a time and place for a high level of optimization (and obscurity), but when the goal is universal acceptance and cross-platform portability, simplicity and transparency are paramount. This is the first fundamental proposition of XML: simple and nominally human-readable data.

A Universal Parser

Using text to exchange data is not exactly a new idea, either, but historically, for every new document format that came along, a new *parser* would have to be written. A parser is an application that reads a document and understands its formatting conventions, usually enforcing some rules about the content. For example, the Java `Properties` class has a parser for the standard properties file format (Chapter 11). In our simple spreadsheet in Chapter 18, we wrote a parser capable of understanding basic mathematical expressions. As we've seen, depending on complexity, parsing can be quite tricky.

With XML, we can represent data without having to write this kind of custom parser. This isn't to say that it's reasonable to use XML for everything (e.g., typing math expressions into our spreadsheet), but for the common types of information that we exchange on the Net, we shouldn't have to write parsers that deal with basic syntax and string manipulation. In conjunction with document-verifying components (Document Type Definitions [DTDs] or XML Schema), much of the complex error checking is also done automatically. This is the second fundamental proposition of XML: standardized parsing and validation.

The State of XML

The APIs we'll discuss in this chapter are powerful and popular. They are being used around the world to build enterprise-scale systems every day. In recent years, JAXB Java to XML binding has been vastly streamlined and simplified (primarily through the use

1. To read Berners-Lee's original proposal to CERN, go to *http://www.w3.org/History/1989/proposal.html.*

of Java annotations to replace configuration files and support a "code first" methodology). However, as with any popular technology, there has been a recognition of its limitations and some complexity has crept into what began as simple concepts. In the area of browser-based applications, some have turned to JavaScript Object Notation (JSON) as an even lighter-weight approach that maps natively to JavaScript, especially for transient communications between client and server. However, XML tools are still widely used in this area as well. Google's Protocol Buffers-encoding scheme is another example of a system-to-system communication format that has been used in place of XML; in this case, where very high performance trumps flexibility. But XML remains the most powerful general format for document and data exchange with the widest array of tools support.

The XML APIs

All the basic APIs for working with XML are now bundled with the standard release of Java. This included the `javax.xml` standard extension packages for working with Simple API for XML (SAX), Document Object Model (DOM), XML Binding JAXB, and Extensible Stylesheet Language (XSL) transforms, as well as APIs such as XPath, and XInclude. If you are using an older version of Java, you can still use many of these tools but you will have to download these packages separately.

XML and Web Browsers

All modern web browsers support XML explicitly, both in terms of simple rendering of XML content and also client-side transformation of XML into HTML for display. If you load an XML document in you browser it will generally be displayed as a tree with controls to allow you to collapse and expand nodes (like an outline). Displaying XML in this way is used mainly for debugging, but JavaScript can also support client-side XSL transformation directly in the browser. XSL is a language for transforming XML into other documents; we'll talk about it later in this chapter.

When viewed in older browsers or in contexts that do not explicitly format XML for viewing, the browser will generally simply display the text of the document with all the tags (structural information) stripped off. This is the prescribed behavior for working with unknown XML markup in a viewing environment. Remember that you can always use the "view source" option to display the text of a file in your browser if you want to see the original source.

XML Basics

The basic syntax of XML is extremely simple. If you've worked with HTML, you're already halfway there. As with HTML, XML represents information as text using *tags* to add structure. A tag begins with a name sandwiched between less than (<) and greater than (>) characters. Unlike HTML, XML tags must always be *balanced*; in other words, an opening tag must always be followed by a closing tag. A closing tag looks just like the opening tag but starts with a less than sign and a slash (</). An opening tag, closing tag, and any content in between are collectively referred to as an *element* of the XML document. Elements can contain other elements, but they must be properly nested (all tags started within an element must be closed before the element itself is closed). Elements can also contain plain text or a mixture of elements and text (called mixed content). Comments are enclosed between <!– and –> markers. Here are a few examples:

```
<!-- Simple -->
<Sentence>This is text.</Sentence>

<!-- Element -->
<Paragraph><Sentence>This is text.</Sentence></Paragraph>

<!-- Mixed -->
<Paragraph>
        <Sentence>This <verb>is</verb> text.</Sentence>
</Paragraph>

<!-- Empty -->
<PageBreak></PageBreak>
```

An empty tag can be written more compactly in a special form using a single tag ending with a slash and a greater-than sign (/>):

```
<PageBreak/>
```

Attributes

An XML element can contain *attributes*, which are simple name-value pairs supplied inside the start tag.

```
<Document type="LEGAL"id="42">...</Document>
<Image name="truffle.jpg"/>
```

The attribute value must always be enclosed in quotes. You can use double (") or single (') quotes. Single quotes are useful if the value contains double quotes.

Attributes are intended to be used for simple, unstructured properties or compact identifiers associated with the element data. It is always possible to make an attribute into a child element, so, strictly speaking, there is no real need for attributes. But they often make the XML easier to read and more logical. In the case of the `Document` element in our preceding snippet, the attributes `type` and `ID` represent metadata about the document. We might expect that a Java class representing the `Document` would have an enumeration of document types such as `LEGAL`. In the case of the `Image` element, the attribute is simply a more compact way of including the filename. As a rule, attributes should be compact, with little significant internal structure (URLs push the envelope); by contrast, child elements can have arbitrary complexity.

The id attribute in the previous example may have special significance when used with a corresponding idref attribute. Together, these standard attributes are used with document validation to enforce referential integrity in documents. When validated, an id attribute value must be unique within the document and an idref attribute value must refer to a valid id within the document.

XML Documents

An XML document begins with a header like the following and one *root element*:

```
<?xml version="1.0" encoding="UTF-8"?>
<MyDocument>
</MyDocument>
```

The header identifies the version of XML and the character encoding used. The root element is simply the top of the element hierarchy, which can be considered a tree. If you omit this header or have XML text without a single root element (as in our earlier simple examples), technically what you have is called an XML *fragment*.

Encoding

The default encoding for an XML document is UTF-8, the ASCII-friendly 8-bit Unicode encoding. This encoding preserves ASCII values, so English text is unaltered by it. It also allows Unicode values to be stored in a reasonably efficient way. An XML document may specify another encoding using the encoding attribute of the XML header.

Within an XML document, certain characters are necessarily sacrosanct: for example, the < and > characters that indicate element tags. When you need to include these in your text, you must encode them. XML provides an escape mechanism called "entities" that allows for encoding special structures. XML has five predefined entities, as shown in Table 24-1.

Table 24-1. XML entities

Entity	Encodes
&	& (ampersand)
<	< (less than)
>	> (greater than)
"	" (quotation mark)
'	' (apostrophe)

An alternative to encoding text in this way is to use a special "unparsed" section of text called a character data (CDATA) section. A CDATA section starts with the cryptic string <![CDATA[and ends with]]>, like this:

```
<![CDATA[  Learning Java, O'Reilly & Associates ]]>
```

The CDATA section looks a little like a comment, but the data is still part of the document, just opaque to the parser.

There is one more alternative, which is to use a special `<include>` directive to include the contents of a URL or file either as pre-escaped text or optionally parsed as XML. XML includes are very convenient, and we'll talk about them later in this chapter.

Namespaces

You've probably seen that HTML has a `<body>` tag that is used to structure web pages. Suppose for a moment that we are writing XML for a funeral home that also uses the tag `<body>` for some other, more macabre, purpose. This could be a problem if we want to mix HTML with our mortuary information.

If you consider HTML and the funeral home tags to be languages in this case, the elements (tag names) used in a document are really the vocabulary of those languages. An XML *namespace* is a way of saying whose dictionary you are using for a given element, allowing us to mix them freely. (Later, we'll talk about XML Schemas, which enforce the grammar and syntax of the language.)

A namespace is specified with the `xmlns` attribute, whose value is a Uniform Resource Identifier (URI) that uniquely defines the set (and usually the meaning) of tags from that namespace:

```
<element xmlns="namespaceURI">
```

Recall from Chapter 14 that a URI is not necessarily a URL. URIs are more general than URLs. In practical terms, a URI is to be treated as a unique string. Often, the URI is in fact also a URL for a document describing the namespace, but when true it is only by convention.

An `xmlns` namespace attribute can be applied to an element and affects all its (nested) children; this is called a default namespace for the element:

```
<body xmlns="http://funeral-procedures.org/">
```

Often it is desirable to mix and match namespaces on a tag-by-tag basis. To do this, we can use the special `xmlns` attribute to define a special identifier for the namespace and use that identifier as a prefix on the tags in question. For example:

```
<funeral xmlns:fun="http://funeral-procedures.org/">
    <html><head></head><body>
    <fun:body>Corpse #42</fun:body>
</funeral>
```

In the preceding snippet of XML, we've qualified the body tag with the prefix "fun:", which we defined in the `<funeral>` tag. In this case, we should qualify the root tag as well, reflexively:

```
<fun:funeral xmlns:fun="http://funeral-procedures.org/">
```

The XML parser factories supplied with Java have a switch to specify whether you want the parser to interpret namespaces. This switch defaults to off for historical reasons.

```
parserFactory.setNamespaceAware( true );
```

We'll talk more about parsing in the sections on SAX and DOM later in this chapter.

Validation

A document that conforms to the basic rules of XML with proper encoding and balanced tags is called a *well-formed* document. Just because a document is syntactically correct, however, doesn't mean that it makes sense. Two related sets of tools, DTDs and XML Schemas, define ways to provide a grammar for your XML elements. They allow you to create syntactic rules, such as "a `City` element can appear only once inside an `Address` element and comes before a `State` element." XML Schema goes further to provide a flexible language for describing the validity of data content of the tags, including both simple and compound data types made of numbers and strings.

A document that is checked against a DTD or XML Schema description and follows the rules is called a *valid* document. A document can be well formed without being valid, but not vice versa.

HTML to XHTML

To speak very loosely, we could say that the most popular and widely used form of XML in the world today is HTML. The terminology is loose because HTML is not really well-formed XML. HTML tags violate XML's rule forbidding unbalanced elements; the common `<p>` tag is typically used without a closing tag, for example. HTML attributes also don't require quotes. XML tags are also case-sensitive; `<P>` and `<p>` are two different tags in XML. We could generously say that HTML is "forgiving" with respect to details like this, but as a developer, you know that sloppy syntax results in ambiguity. XHTML is an alternate, strict XML version of HTML that is clear and unambiguous. This form of HTML works in modern browsers. Fortunately, if you want to switch, you don't have to manually clean up all your HTML documents; Tidy (*http://tidy.sourceforge.net*) is an open source program that automatically converts HTML to XHTML, validates it, and corrects common mistakes.

SAX

SAX is a low-level, event-style API for parsing XML documents. SAX originated in Java, but has been implemented in many languages. We'll begin our discussion of the Java XML APIs here at this lower level, and work our way up to higher-level (and often more convenient) APIs as we go.

The SAX API

To use SAX, we'll draw on classes from the `org.xml.sax` package, standardized by the W3C. This package holds interfaces common to all implementations of SAX. To perform the actual parsing, we'll need the `javax.xml.parsers` package, which is the standard Java package for accessing XML parsers. The `java.xml.parsers` package is part of the Java API for XML Processing (JAXP), which allows different parser implementations to be used with Java in a portable way.

To read an XML document with SAX, we first register an `org.xml.sax.ContentHandler` class with the parser. The `ContentHandler` has methods that are called in response to parts of the document. For example, the `ContentHandler`'s `startElement()` method is called when an opening tag is encountered, and the `endElement()` method is called when the tag is closed. Attributes are provided with the `startElement()` call. Text content of elements is passed through a separate method called `characters()`. The `characters()` method may be invoked repeatedly to supply more text as it is read, but it often gets the whole string in one bite. The following are the method signatures of these methods of the `ContentHandler` class.

```
public void startElement(
    String namespace, String localname, String qname, Attributes atts );
public void characters(
    char[] ch, int start, int len );
public void endElement(
    String namespace, String localname, String qname );
```

The `qname` parameter is the *qualified name* of the element: this is the element name, prefixed with any namespace that may be applied. When you're working with namespaces, the `namespace` and `localname` parameters are also supplied, providing the namespace and unqualified element name separately.

The `ContentHandler` interface also contains methods called in response to the start and end of the document, `startDocument()` and `endDocument()`, as well as those for handling namespace mapping, special XML instructions, and whitespace that is not part of the text content and may optionally be ignored. We'll confine ourselves to the three previous methods for our examples. As with many other Java interfaces, a simple implementation, `org.xml.sax.helpers.DefaultHandler`, is provided for us that allows us to override only the methods in which we're interested.

JAXP

To perform the parsing, we'll need to get a parser from the `javax.xml.parsers` package. JAXP abstracts the process of getting a parser through a *factory pattern*, allowing different parser implementations to be plugged into the Java platform. The following snippet constructs a `SAXParser` object and then gets an `XMLReader` used to parse a file:

```
import javax.xml.parsers.*;
SAXParserFactory factory = SAXParserFactory.newInstance();
SAXParser saxParser = factory.newSAXParser();
XMLReader reader = saxParser.getXMLReader();

reader.setContentHandler( myContentHandler );
reader.parse( "myfile.xml" );
```

You might expect the `SAXParser` to have the `parse` method. The `XMLReader` intermediary was added to support changes in the SAX API between 1.0 and 2.0. Later, we'll discuss some options that can be set to govern how XML parsers operate. These options are normally set through methods on the parser factory (e.g., `SAXParserFactory`) and not the parser itself. This is because the factory may wish to use different implementations to support different required features.

SAX's strengths and weaknesses

The primary motivation for using SAX instead of the higher-level APIs that we'll discuss later is that it is lightweight and event-driven. SAX doesn't require maintaining the entire document in memory. So if, for example, you need to grab the text of just a few elements from a document, or if you need to extract elements from a large stream of XML, you can do so efficiently with SAX. The event-driven nature of SAX also allows you to take actions as the beginning and end tags are parsed. This can be useful for directly manipulating your own models without first going through another representation. The primary weakness of SAX is that you are operating on a tag-by-tag level with no help from the parser to maintain context. We'll talk about how to overcome this limitation next. Later, we'll also talk about the new XPath API, which combines much of the benefits of both SAX and DOM in a form that is easier to use.

Building a Model Using SAX

The `ContentHandler` mechanism for receiving SAX events is very simple. It should be easy to see how one could use it to capture the value or attributes of a single element in a document. What may be harder to see is how one could use SAX to populate a real Java object model. Creating or pushing data into Java objects from XML is such a common activity that it's worth considering how the SAX API applies to this problem. The following example, `SAXModelBuilder`, does just this, reading an XML description and creating Java objects on command. This example is a bit unusual in that we resort to using some reflection to do the job, but this is a case where we're trying to interact with Java objects dynamically.

In this section, we'll start by creating some XML along with corresponding Java classes that serve as the model for this XML. The focus of the example code here is to create the generic model builder that uses SAX to read the XML and populate the model classes with their data. The idea is that the developer is creating only XML and model classes—no custom code—to do the parsing. You might use code like this to read configuration files for an application or to implement a custom XML "language" for describing workflows. The advantage is that there is no real parsing code in the application at all, only in the generic builder tool. Finally, late in this chapter when we discuss the more powerful JAXB APIs, we'll reuse the Java object model from this example simply by adding a few annotations.

Creating the XML file

The first thing we'll need is a nice XML document to parse. Luckily, it's inventory time at the zoo! The following document, *zooinventory.xml*, describes two of the zoo's residents, including some vital information about their diets:

```
<?xml version="1.0" encoding="UTF-8"?>
    <inventory>
        <animal animalClass="mammal">
            <name>Song Fang</name>
            <species>Giant Panda</species>
            <habitat>China</habitat>
            <food>Bamboo</food>
            <temperament>Friendly</temperament>
            <weight>45.0</weight>
        </animal>
        <animal animalClass="mammal">
            <name>Cocoa</name>
            <species>Gorilla</species>
            <habitat>Central Africa</habitat>
            <foodRecipe>
                <name>Gorilla Chow</name>
                <ingredient>fruit</ingredient>
                <ingredient>shoots</ingredient>
                <ingredient>leaves</ingredient>
            </foodRecipe>
            <temperament>Know-it-all</temperament>
            <weight>45.0</weight>
        </animal>
    </inventory>
```

The document is fairly simple. The root element, `<inventory>`, contains two `<animal>` elements as children. `<animal>` contains several simple text elements for things like name, species, and habitat. It also contains either a simple `<food>` element or a complex `<foodRecipe>` element. Finally, note that the `<animal>` element has one attribute, `animalClass`, that describes the zoological classification of the creature (e.g., Mammal, Bird, Fish, etc.). This gives us a representative set of XML features to play with in our examples.

The model

Now let's make a Java object model for our zoo inventory. This part is very mechanical—we simply create a class for each of the complex element types in our XML; anything other than a simple string or number. Best practices would probably be to use the standard JavaBeans property design pattern here—that is, to use a private field (instance variable) plus a pair of get and set methods for each property. However, because these classes are just simple data holders and we want to keep our example small, we're going to opt to use public fields. Everything we're going to do in this example and, much more importantly, everything we're going to do when we reuse this model in the later JAXB binding example, can be made to work with either field or JavaBeans-style method-based properties equivalently. In this example, it would just be a matter of how we set the values and later in the JAXB case, it would be a matter of where we put the annotations. So here are the classes:

```
public class Inventory {
        public List<Animal> animal = new ArrayList<>();
}

public class Animal
{
    public static enum AnimalClass { mammal, reptile, bird, fish, amphibian,
        invertebrate }

    public AnimalClass animalClass;
    public String name, species, habitat, food, temperament;
    public Double weight;
    public FoodRecipe foodRecipe;

    public String toString() { return name +"("+animalClass+",
        "+species+")"; }
}

public class FoodRecipe
{
    public String name;
    public List<String> ingredient = new ArrayList<String>();

    public String toString() { return name + ": "+ ingredient.toString(); }
}
```

As you can see, for the cases where we need to represent a sequence of elements (e.g., animal in inventory), we have used a `List` collection. Also note that the property that will serve to hold our `animalClass` attribute (e.g., mammal) is represented as an enum type. We've also throw in simple `toString()` methods for later use. One more thing—we've chosen to name our collections in the singular form here (e.g., "animal," as opposed to "animals") just because it is convenient. We'll talk about mapping names more in the JAXB example.

The SAXModelBuilder

Let's get down to business and write our builder tool. Now we could do this by using the SAX API in combination with some "hardcoded" knowledge about the incoming tags and the classes we want to output (imagine a whole bunch of switches or if/then statements); however, we're going do better than that and make a more generic model builder that maps our XML to classes by name. The `SAXModelBuilder` that we create in this section receives SAX events from parsing an XML file and dynamically constructs objects or sets properties corresponding to the names of the element tags. Our model builder is small, but it handles the most common structures: nested elements and elements with simple text or numeric content. We treat attributes as equivalent to element data as far as our model classes go and we support three basic types: `String`, `Double`, and `Enum`.

Here is the code:

```
import org.xml.sax.*;
import org.xml.sax.helpers.*;
import java.util.*;
import java.lang.reflect.*;

public class SAXModelBuilder extends DefaultHandler
{
    Stack<Object> stack = new Stack<>();

    public void startElement( String namespace, String localname, String qname,
        Attributes atts ) throws SAXException
    {
        // Construct the new element and set any attributes on it
        Object element;
        try {
            String className = Character.toUpperCase( qname.charAt( 0 ) ) +
                qname.substring( 1 );
            element = Class.forName( className ).newInstance();
        } catch ( Exception e ) {
            element = new StringBuffer();
        }

        for( int i=0; i<atts.getLength(); i++) {
            try {
                setProperty( atts.getQName( i ), element, atts.getValue( i ) );
            } catch ( Exception e ) { throw new SAXException( "Error: ", e ); }
        }

        stack.push( element );
    }

    public void endElement( String namespace, String localname, String qname )
        throws SAXException
    {
        // Add the element to its parent
        if ( stack.size() > 1) {
            Object element = stack.pop();
            try {
                setProperty( qname, stack.peek(), element );
```

```
            } catch ( Exception e ) { throw new SAXException( "Error: ", e ); }
        }
    }

    public void characters(char[] ch, int start, int len )
    {
        // Receive element content text
        String text = new String( ch, start, len );
        if ( text.trim().length() == 0 ) { return; }
        ((StringBuffer)stack.peek()).append( text );
    }

    void setProperty( String name, Object target, Object value )
        throws SAXException, IllegalAccessException, NoSuchFieldException
    {
        Field field = target.getClass().getField( name );

        // Convert values to field type
        if ( value instanceof StringBuffer ) {
            value = value.toString();
        }
        if ( field.getType() == Double.class ) {
            value = Double.parseDouble( value.toString() );
        }
        if ( Enum.class.isAssignableFrom( field.getType() ) ) {
            value = Enum.valueOf( (Class<Enum>)field.getType(),
                value.toString() );
        }

        // Apply to field
        if ( field.getType() == value.getClass() ) {
            field.set( target, value );
        } else
        if ( Collection.class.isAssignableFrom( field.getType() ) ) {
            Collection collection = (Collection)field.get( target );
            collection.add( value );
        } else {
            throw new RuntimeException( "Unable to set property..." );
        }
    }

    public Object getModel() { return stack.pop(); }
}
```

The code may be a little hard to digest at first: we are using reflection to construct the objects and set the properties on the fields. But the gist of it is really just that the three methods, `startElement()`, `characters()`, and `endElement()`, are called in response to the tags of the input and we store the data as we receive it. Let's take a look.

The `SAXModelBuilder` extends `DefaultHandler` to help us implement the `ContentHandler` interface. Because SAX events follow the hierarchical structure of the XML document, we use a simple stack to keep track of which object we are currently parsing. At the start of each element, the model builder attempts to create an instance of a class with the same name (uppercase) as the element and push it onto the top of the stack. Each nested opening tag creates a new object on the stack until we encounter a closing tag. Upon reaching an end of an element, we pop the current object off the stack and attempt to apply its value to its parent (the enclosing XML element), which is the new top of the stack. For elements with simple content that do not have a corresponding class, we place a `StringBuffer` on the stack as a stand-in to hold the character content until the tag is closed. In this case, the name of the tag indicates the property on the parent that should get the text and upon seeing the closing tag, we apply it in the same way. Attributes are applied to the current object on the stack within the `startElement()` method using the same technique. The final closing tag leaves the top-level element (inventory in this case) on the stack for us to retrieve.

To set values on our objects, we use our `setProperty()` method. It uses reflection to look for a field matching the name of the tag within the specified object. It also handles some simple type conversions based on the type of the field found. If the field is of type `Double`, we parse the text to a number; if it is an `Enum` type, we find the matching enum value represented by the text. Finally, if the field is not a simple field but is a `Collection` representing an XML sequence, then we invoke its `add()` method to add the child to the collection instead of trying to assign to the field itself.

Test drive

Finally, we can test drive the model builder with the following class, `TestSAXModelBuilder`, which calls the SAX parser, setting an instance of our `SAXModelBuilder` as the content handler. The test class then prints some of the information parsed from the *zooinventory.xml* file:

```
import org.xml.sax.*;
import javax.xml.parsers.*;

public class TestSAXModelBuilder
{
    public static void main( String [] args ) throws Exception
    {
        SAXParserFactory factory = SAXParserFactory
            .newInstance();
        SAXParser saxParser = factory.newSAXParser();
        XMLReader parser = saxParser.getXMLReader();
        SAXModelBuilder mb = new SAXModelBuilder();
        parser.setContentHandler( mb );

        parser.parse( new InputSource("zooinventory.xml") );
        Inventory inventory = (Inventory)mb.getModel();
        System.out.println("Animals = "+inventory.animal);
        Animal cocoa = (Animal)(inventory.animal.get(1));
        FoodRecipe recipe = cocoa.foodRecipe;
```

```
            System.out.println( "Recipe = "+recipe );
        }
    }
```

The output should look like this:

```
Animals = [Song Fang(mammal, Giant Panda), Cocoa(mammal, Gorilla)]
Recipe = Gorilla Chow: [fruit, shoots, leaves]
```

In the following sections, we'll generate the equivalent output using different tools.

Limitations and possibilities

To make our model builder more complete, we could use more robust naming conventions for our tags and model classes (taking into account packages and mixed capitalization, etc.). More generally, we might want to introduce arbitrary mappings (bindings) between names and classes or properties. And of course, there is the problem of taking our model and going the other way, using it to generate an XML document. You can see where this is going: JAXB will do all of that for us, coming up later in this chapter.

XMLEncoder/Decoder

Java includes a standard tool for serializing JavaBeans classes to XML. The `java.beans` package `XMLEncoder` and `XMLDecoder` classes are analogous to `java.ioObjectInputStream` and `ObjectOutputStream`. Instead of using the native Java serialization format, they store the object state in a high-level XML format. We say that they are analogous, but the XML encoder is not a general replacement for Java object serialization. Instead, it is specialized to work with objects that follow the JavaBeans design patterns (setter and getter methods for properties), and it can only store and recover the state of the object that is expressed through a bean's public properties in this way.

When you call it, the `XMLEncoder` attempts to construct an in-memory copy of the graph of beans that you are serializing using only public constructors and JavaBean properties. As it works, it writes out the steps required as "instructions" in an XML format. Later, the `XMLDecoder` executes these instructions and reproduces the result. The primary advantage of this process is that it is highly resilient to changes in the class implementation. While standard Java object serialization can accommodate many kinds of "compatible changes" in classes, it requires some help from the developer to get it right. Because the `XMLEncoder` uses only public APIs and writes instructions in simple XML, it is expected that this form of serialization will be the most robust way to store the state of JavaBeans. The process is referred to as *long-term persistence* for JavaBeans.

It might seem at first like this would obviate the need for our `SAXModelBuilder` example. Why not simply write our XML in the format that `XMLDecoder` understands and use it to build our model? Although `XMLEncoder` is very efficient at eliminating redundancy, you would see that its output is still very verbose (about two to three times larger than our original XML) and not very human-friendly. Although it's possible to write it by hand, this XML format wasn't designed for that. Finally, although `XMLEncoder` can be customized for how it handles specific object types, it suffers from the same problem that our model builder does, in that "binding" (the namespace of tags) is determined strictly by our Java class names. As we've said before, what is really needed is a more general tool to map our own classes to XML and back.

DOM

In the last section, we used SAX to parse an XML document and build a Java object model representing it. In that case, we created specific Java types for each of our complex elements. If we were planning to use our model extensively in an application, this technique would give us a great deal of flexibility. But often it is sufficient (and much easier) to use a "generic" model that simply represents the content of the XML in a neutral form. The Document Object Model (DOM) is just that. The DOM API parses an XML document into a generic representation consisting of classes with names such as `Element` and `Attribute` that hold their own values. You could use this to inspect the document structure and pull out the parts you want in a way that is perhaps more convenient than the low-level SAX. The tradeoff is that the entire document is parsed and read into memory—but for most applications, that is fine.

As we saw in our zoo example, once you have an object model, using the data is a breeze. So a generic DOM would seem like an appealing solution, especially when working mainly with text. One catch in this case is that DOM didn't evolve first as a Java API and it doesn't map well to Java. DOM is very complete and provides access to every facet of the original XML document, but it's so generic (and language-neutral) that it's cumbersome to use in Java. Later, we'll also mention a native Java alternative to DOM called JDOM that is more pleasant to use.

The DOM API

The core DOM classes belong to the `org.w3c.dom` package. The result of parsing an XML document with DOM is a `Document` object from this package (see Figure 24-1). The `Document` is both a factory and a container for a hierarchical collection of `Node` objects, representing the document structure. A node has a parent and may have children, which can be traversed using its `getChildNodes()`, `getFirstChild()`, or `getLastChild()` methods. A node may also have "attributes" associated with it, which consist of a named map of nodes.

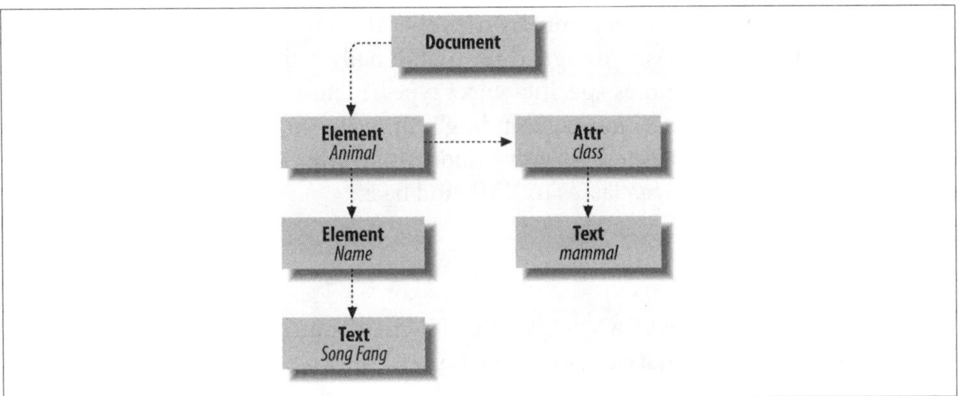

Figure 24-1. The parsed DOM

Subtypes of `Node`—`Element`, `Text`, and `Attr`—represent elements, text, and attributes in XML. Some types of nodes (including these) have a text "value." For example, the value of a `Text` node is the text of the element it represents. The same is true of an `attribute`, `cdata`, or `comment` node. The value of a node can be accessed by the `getNodeValue()` and `setNodeValue()` methods. We'll also make use of `Node`'s `getTextContent()` method, which retrieves the plain-text content of the node and all of its child nodes.

The `Element` node provides "random" access to its child elements through its `getElementsByTagName()` method, which returns a `NodeList` (a simple collection type). You can also fetch an attribute by name from the `Element` using the `getAttribute()` method.

The `javax.xml.parsers` package contains a factory for DOM parsers, just as it does for SAX parsers. An instance of `DocumentBuilderFactory` can be used to create a `DocumentBuilder` object to parse the file and produce a `Document` result.

Test-Driving DOM

Here is our `TestDOM` class:

```
import javax.xml.parsers.*;
import org.w3c.dom.*;

public class TestDOM
{
    public static void main( String [] args ) throws Exception
    {
        DocumentBuilderFactory factory = DocumentBuilderFactory
            .newInstance();
        DocumentBuilder parser = factory.newDocumentBuilder();
        Document document = parser.parse( "zooinventory.xml" );
```

```
            Element inventory = document.getDocumentElement();
            NodeList animals = inventory.getElementsByTagName("animal");
            System.out.println("Animals = ");
            for( int i=0; i<animals.getLength(); i++ ) {
                Element item = (Element)animals.item( i );
                String name = item.getElementsByTagName( "name" ).item( 0 )
                    .getTextContent();
                String species = item.getElementsByTagName( "species" )
                    .item( 0 ).getTextContent();
                String animalClass = item.getAttribute( "animalClass" );
                System.out.println( "  "+ name +" ("+animalClass+",
                    "+species+")" );
            }

            Element cocoa = (Element)animals.item( 1 );
            Element recipe = (Element)cocoa.getElementsByTagName( "foodRecipe" )
                .item( 0 );
            String recipeName = recipe.getElementsByTagName( "name" ).item( 0 )
                .getTextContent();
            System.out.println("Recipe = " + recipeName );
            NodeList ingredients = recipe.getElementsByTagName("ingredient");
            for(int i=0; i<ingredients.getLength(); i++) {
                System.out.println( "  " + ingredients.item( i )
                    .getTextContent() );
            }
        }
    }
```

TestDOM creates an instance of a DocumentBuilder and uses it to parse our *zooinventory.xml* file. We use the DocumentgetDocumentElement() method to get the root element of the document, from which we will begin our traversal. From there, we ask for all the animal child nodes. The getElementbyTagName() method returns a NodeList object, which we then use to iterate through our creatures. For each animal, we use the ElementgetElementsByTagName() method to retrieve the name and species child element information. Each of those queries can potentially return a list of matching elements, but we only allow for one here by taking the first element returned and asking for its text content. We also use the getAttribute() method to retrieve the animalClass attribute from the element.

Next, we use the getElementsByTagName() to retrieve the element called foodRecipe from the second animal. We use it to fetch a NodeList for all of the tags matching ingredient and print them as before. The output should contain the same information as our SAX-based example. But as you can see, the tradeoff in not having to create our own model classes is that we have to suffer through the use of the generic model and produce code that is considerably harder to read and less flexible.

Generating XML with DOM

Thus far, we've used the SAX and DOM APIs to parse XML. But what about generating XML? Sure, it's easy to generate trivial XML documents simply by printing the appropriate strings. But if we plan to create a complex document on the fly, we might want some help with all those quotes and closing tags. We may also want to validate our model against an XML DTD or Schema before writing it out. What we can do is to build a DOM representation of our object in memory and then transform it to text. This is also useful if we want to read a document and then make some alterations to it. To do this, we'll use of the `java.xml.transform` package. This package does a lot more than just printing XML. As its name implies, it's part of a general transformation facility. It includes the XSL/XSLT languages for generating one XML document from another. (We'll talk about XSL later in this chapter.)

We won't discuss the details of constructing a DOM in memory here, but it follows fairly naturally from what you've learned about traversing the tree in our previous example. The following example, `PrintDOM`, simply parses our *zooinventory.xml* file to a DOM and then prints that DOM back to the screen. The same output code would print any DOM whether read from a file or created in memory using the factory methods on the DOM `Document` and `Element`, etc.

```
import javax.xml.parsers.*;
import org.xml.sax.InputSource;
import org.w3c.dom.*;
import javax.xml.transform.*;
import javax.xml.transform.dom.DOMSource;
import javax.xml.transform.stream.StreamResult;

public class PrintDOM {
    public static void main( String [] args ) throws Exception
    {
        DocumentBuilder parser = DocumentBuilderFactory.newInstance()
            .newDocumentBuilder();
        Document document = parser.parse(
            new InputSource("zooinventory.xml") );
        Transformer transformer =  TransformerFactory.newInstance()
            .newTransformer();
        Source source = new DOMSource( document );
        Result output = new StreamResult( System.out );
        transformer.transform( source, output );
    }
}
```

Note that the imports are almost as long as the entire program! Here, we are using an instance of a `Transformer` object in its simplest capacity to copy from a source to an output. We'll return to the `Transformer` later when we discuss XSL, at which point it will be doing a lot more work for us.

JDOM

As we promised earlier, we'll now describe an easier DOM API: JDOM, created by Jason Hunter and Brett McLaughlin, two fellow O'Reilly authors (*Java Servlet Programming* and *Java and XML*, respectively). It is a more natural Java DOM that uses real Java collection types such as `List` for its hierarchy and provides marginally more streamlined methods for building documents. You can get the latest JDOM from *http://www.jdom.org/*. Here's the JDOM version of our standard "test" program:

```
import org.jdom.*;
import org.jdom.input.*;
import org.jdom.output.*;
import java.util.*;

public class TestJDOM {
    public static void main( String[] args ) throws Exception {
        Document doc = new SAXBuilder().build("zooinventory.xml");
        List animals = doc.getRootElement().getChildren("Animal");
        System.out.println("Animals = ");
        for( int i=0; i<animals.size(); i++ ) {
            String name = ((Element)animals.get(i)).getChildText("Name");
            String species = ((Element)animals.get(i))
                .getChildText("Species");
            System.out.println( "  "+ name +" ("+species+")" );
        }
        Element foodRecipe = ((Element)animals.get(1))
            .getChild("FoodRecipe");
        String name = foodRecipe.getChildText("Name");
        System.out.println("Recipe = " + name );
        List ingredients = foodRecipe.getChildren("Ingredient");
        for(int i=0; i<ingredients.size(); i++)
            System.out.println( "  "+((Element)ingredients.get(i))
                .getText() );
    }
}
```

The JDOM `Element` class has some convenient `getChild()` and `getChildren()` methods, as well as a `getChildText()` method for retrieving node text by element name.

Now that we've covered the basics of SAX and DOM, we're going to look at a new API that, in a sense, straddles the two. XPath allows us to target only the parts of a document that we want and gives us the option of getting at those components in DOM form.

XPath

XPath is an expression language for addressing parts of an XML document. You can think of XPath expressions as sort of like regular expressions for XML. They let you pull out parts of an XML document based on patterns. In the case of XPath, the patterns are more concerned with structural information than with character content and the values returned may be either simple text or "live" DOM nodes. With XPath, we can query an XML document for all of the elements with a certain name or in a certain parent-child relationship. We can also apply fairly sophisticated tests or *predicates* to the nodes, which allows us to construct complex queries such as this one: give me all of the `Animals` with a `Weight` greater than the number 400 and a `Temperament` of `irritable` whose `animalClass` attribute is `mammal`.

The full XPath specification has many features and includes both a compact and more verbose syntax. We won't try to cover it all here, but the basics are easy and it's important to know them because XPath expressions are at the core of XSL transformations and other APIs that refer to parts of XML documents. The full specification does not make great bedtime reading, but can be found at *http://www.w3.org/TR/xpath*.

Nodes

An XPath expression addresses a `Node` in an XML document tree. The node may be an element (possibly with children) like `<animal>...</animal>` or it may be a lower-level document node representing an attribute (e.g., `animalClass="mammal"`), a CDATA block, or even a comment. All of the structure of an XML document is accessible through the XPath syntax. Once we've addressed the node, we can either reduce the content to a text string (as we might with a simple text content element like `name`) or we can access it as a proper DOM tree to further read or manipulate it.

Table 24-2 shows the most basic node-related syntax.

Table 24-2. Basic node-related syntax

Syntax	Example	Description
`/Name`	`/inventory/animal`	All animal nodes under `/inventory`.
`//Name`	`//animal`	All animal nodes anywhere in document. A `foodRecipe/animal` would also match.
`Name/*`	`/inventory/*`	All child nodes of inventory (`animals` and any other elements directly under `inventory`).
`@Name`	`//animal/@animalClass`	All `animalClass` attributes of `animals`.
`.`	`/inventory/animal/.`	The current node (all `animals`).
`..`	`/inventory/animal/..`	The parent node (`inventory`).

Nodes are addressed with a slash-separated path based on name. For example, `/Inventory/Animal` refers to the set of all `Animal` nodes under the `Inventory` node. If we want to list the names of all `Animals`, we would use `/Inventory/Animal/Name`. The `//` syntax matches a node anywhere in a document, at any level of nesting, so `//Name` would match the name elements of `Animals`, `FoodRecipes`, and possibly many other elements. We could be more specific, using `//Animal/Name` to match only `Name` elements whose parent is an `Animal` element. The at sign (@) matches attributes. This becomes much more useful with predicates, which we describe next. Finally, the familiar `.` and `..` notation can be used to "move" relative to a node; read on to see how this is used.

Predicates

Predicates let us apply a test to a node. Nodes that pass the test are included in the result set or used to select other nodes (child or parent) relative to them. There are many types of tests available in XPath. Table 24-3 lists a few examples.

Table 24-3. Predicates

Syntax	Example	Description
`[n]`	`/inventory/animal[1]`	Select the *n*th element of a set. (Starts with 1 rather than 0.) For example, select the first `animal` in the `inventory`.
`[@name=value]`	`//animal[@animal Class="mammal"]`	Match nodes with the specified attribute value. For example, `ani mals` with the `animalClass` attribute `"mammal"`.
`[element=val ue]`	`//animal[name="Cocoa"]`	Match nodes with a child node whose text value is specified. For example, match the `animal` with a `name` element containing the simple text `"Cocoa"`.
`=!=><`	`//animal[weight > 400]`	Predicates may also test for inequality and numeric greater-/lesser-than value.
`and, or`	`//animal[@animalClass= "mammal"` or `@class="rep tile"]]`	Predicates may use logical AND and OR to test. For example, `animals` whose `animalClass` is `mammal` or `reptile`.

Predicates can be compounded (AND'ed) using this syntax or simply by adding more predicates, like so:

```
//animal[@animalClass="mammal"][weight > 400]
```

Here, we've asked for `animals` with a class attribute of `"mammal"` and a `weight` element containing a number greater than 400.

We can now also see the usefulness of the `..` operator. Suppose we want to find all of the `animals` with a `foodRecipe` that uses `Fruit` as an ingredient:

```
//animal/foodRecipe[ingredient="Fruit"]/..
```

The `..` means that instead of returning the matching `foodRecipe` node itself, we return its parent—the `animal` element. The `.` (current node) operator is useful in other cases where we use XPath functions to manipulate values in more refined ways. We'll say a few words about functions next.

Functions

The XPath specification includes not only the basic node traversal and predicate syntax we've shown, but also the ability to invoke more open-ended functions that operate on nodes and the node context. These XPath functions cover a wide range of duties and we'll just give a couple of examples here. The functions fall into a few general categories.

Some functions select node types other than an element. For example, there is no special syntax for selecting an XML comment. Instead you invoke a special method called `comment()`, like this:

```
/inventory/comment()
```

This expression returns any XML comment nodes that are children of the `inventory` element. XPath also offers functions that duplicate all of the (compact) syntax we've discussed, including methods like `child()` and `parent()` (corresponding to `.` and `..`).

Other functions look at the context of nodes—for example, `last()` and `count()`.

```
/inventory/animal[last()]
```

This expression selects the last `animal` child element of `inventory` in the same way that `[n]` selects the *n*th.

```
//foodRecipe[count(ingredient)>2]
```

This expression matches all of the `foodRecipe` elements with more than two ingredients. (Cool, eh?)

Finally, there are many string-related functions. Some are useful for simple tests, but others are really useful only in the context of XSL, where they help out the language (in an awkward way) with basic formatting and string manipulation. For example, the `contains()` and `starts-with()` methods can be used to look at the text values inside XML documents:

```
//animal[starts-with(name,"S")]
```

This expression matches `animals` whose `name` starts with the character `S` (e.g., Song Fang). The `contains()` method, similarly, can be used to look for a substring in text.

The XPath API

Now that we've got a taste for the syntax, let's look at how to use the API. The procedure is similar to that of the Java regular expression API for strings. We use a factory to create an XPath object. We can then either evaluate expressions with it or "compile" an expression down to an `XPathExpression` for better performance if we're going to use it more than once.

```
XPath xpath = XPathFactory.newInstance().newXPath();
InputSource source = new InputSource( filename );

String result = xpath.evaluate( "//animal/name", source );
// Song Fang
```

Here we've used the simplest form of the `evaluate()` method, which returns only the first match and takes the value as a string. This method is useful for pulling simple text values from elements. However, if we want the full set of values (e.g., the names of all the `animals` matched by this expression), we need to return the results as a set of `Node` objects instead.

The return type of (the overloaded forms of) `evaluate()` is controlled by identifiers of the `XPathConstants` class. We can get the result as one of the following: `STRING`, `BOOLEAN`, `NUMBER`, `NODE`, or `NODESET`. The default is `STRING`, which strips out child element tags and returns just the text of the matching nodes. `BOOLEAN` and `NUMBER` are conveniences for getting primitive types. `NODE` and `NODESET` return `org.w3c.dom.Node` and `NodeList` objects, respectively. We need the `NodeList` to get all the values.

```
NodeList elements = (NodeList)xpath.evaluate(
    expression, inputSource, XPathConstants.NODESET );
```

Next, let's put this together in a useful example.

XMLGrep

This simple example can be used as a command-line utility, such as *grep*, for testing XPath expressions against a file. It applies an XPath expression and then prints the resulting elements as XML text using the same technique we used in our `PrintDOM` example. Nodes that are not elements (e.g., attributes, comments, and so on) are simply printed with their `toString()` method, which normally serves well enough to identify them, but you can expand the example to your taste. Here it is:

```
import org.w3c.dom.*;
import org.xml.sax.InputSource;
import javax.xml.xpath.*;
import javax.xml.transform.*;
import javax.xml.transform.dom.DOMSource;
import javax.xml.transform.stream.StreamResult;

public class XMLGrep {

    public static void printXML( Element element )
        throws TransformerException {

        Transformer transformer =
            TransformerFactory.newInstance().newTransformer();
        transformer.setOutputProperty( OutputKeys.OMIT_XML_DECLARATION,
            "yes" );
        Source source = new DOMSource( element );
        Result output = new StreamResult( System.out );
        transformer.transform( source, output );
        System.out.println();
    }
```

```
    public static void main( String [] args ) throws Exception {
        if ( args.length != 2 ) {
            System.out.println( "usage: PrintXPath expression file.xml" );
            System.exit(1);
        }
        String expression = args[0], filename = args[1];

        XPath xpath = XPathFactory.newInstance().newXPath();
        InputSource inputSource = new InputSource( filename );

        NodeList elements = (NodeList)xpath.evaluate(
        expression, inputSource, XPathConstants.NODESET );

        for( int i=0; i<elements.getLength(); i++ )
            if ( elements.item(i) instanceof Element ) {
                printXML( (Element)elements.item(i) );
            } else
                System.out.println( elements.item(i) );
    }
}
```

There are again a lot of `imports` in this example. The transform code in our `printXML()` method is drawn from the `PrintDOM` example with one addition. We've set a property on the transformer to omit the standard XML declaration that would normally be output for us at the head of our document. Since we may print more than one (root) element, the output is not well formed XML anyway.

Run the example by passing an XPath expression and the name of an XML file as arguments:

```
% java XMLGrep "//animal[starts-with(name,'C')]" zooinventory.xml
```

This example really is useful for trying out XPath. Please give it a whirl. Mastering these expressions (and learning more) will give you great power over XML documents and, again, form the basis for learning about XSL transformations.

XInclude

XInclude is a very simple "import" facility for XML documents. With the XInclude directive, you can easily include one XML document in another either as XML or as plain (and escaped) text. This means that you can break down your documents into as many files as you see fit and reference the pieces in a simple, standard way. We should note that it is also possible to do this in another way, using XML entity declarations, but they are fraught with problems. XInclude is simpler and does what its name implies, including the specified document at the current location; you just have to declare the proper namespace for the new `<include>` element. Here is an example:

```
<Book xmlns:xi="http://www.w3.org/2001/XInclude">
  <Title>Learning Java</Title>
  <xi:include href="chapter1.xml"/>
  <xi:include href="chapter2.xml"/>
  <xi:include href="chapter3.xml"/>
  ...
</Book>
```

We've used the namespace identifier `xi` to qualify the `<include>` elements that we use to import the chapters of our book. By default, the file is imported as XML content, which means that the parser incorporates the included document as part of our document. The resulting DOM or SAX view will show the merged documents as one. Alternatively, we can use the `parse` attribute to specify that we want the target included as text only. In this case, the text is automatically escaped for us like a CDATA section. For example, we could use it to include an XML example in our book without danger of it being intepreted as part of our file:

```
<Example>
  <Title>The Zoo Inventory Example</Title>
  <xi:include parse="text" href="zooinventory.xml"/>
</Example>
```

Here, the entire *zooinventory.xml* file will be included as nicely escaped text for us (not added to our document as XML).

XInclude also allows for "fallback" content to be specified using a nested `fallback` element. The `fallback` element may point to another file or simply hold XML to be used if the included file can't be found. For example:

```
<xi:include parse="text " href="zooinventory.xml">
    <xi:fallback href="filenotfound.xml"/>
</xi:include>

<xi:include parse="text" href="example.xml">
    <xi:fallback>This example is missing...</xi:fallback>
</xi:include>
```

In the first case, if *zooinventory.xml* is not found, the *filenotfound.xml* file will be included. In the second case, the "missing" text will be included instead of the file. If there is no fallback specified, a parse-time fatal error occurs. An empty `fallback` element can be used to suppress any error. Fallbacks may also be nested within fallbacks to combine these behaviors.

Enabling XInclude

Getting XInclude to work for us requires simply turning on a couple of flags before we begin parsing our file. First, because the XInclude facility uses namespaces, we have to turn on namespace processing in our parser factory. Second, we have to explicitly tell the parser to interpret the include directives. To modify our `PrintDOM` example to perform the includes before printing the result, we turn these flags on the factory before creating a DocumentBuilder instance:

```
DocumentBuilderFactory factory = DocumentBuilderFactory.newInstance();

// enable XInclude processing
factory.setNamespaceAware( true );
factory.setXIncludeAware( true );

DocumentBuilder parser = factory.newDocumentBuilder();
Document document = parser.parse( input );
```

Both of those options should really be the defaults these days. But they have historically come later to XML and so been treated as special features that have to be enabled. We should also mention before we move on that XInclude can make use of XPath expressions (via an API called XPointer) in order to include just selected parts of an XML document.

Validating Documents

Words, words, mere words, no matter from the heart.

—William Shakespeare, *Troilus and Cressida*

In this section, we talk about DTDs and XML Schema, two ways to enforce rules in an XML document. A DTD is a simple grammar guide for an XML document, defining which tags may appear where, in what order, with what attributes, etc. XML Schema is the next generation of DTD. With XML Schema, you can describe the data content of the document as well as the structure. XML Schemas are written in terms of primitives, such as numbers, dates, and simple regular expressions, and also allow the user to define complex types in a grammar-like fashion. The word *schema* means a blueprint or plan for structure, so we'll refer to DTDs and XML Schema collectively as schema where either applies.

DTDs, although much more limited in capability, are still widely used. This may be partly due to the complexity involved in writing XML Schemas by hand. The W3C XML Schema standard is verbose and cumbersome, which may explain why several alternative syntaxes have sprung up. The `javax.xml.validation` API performs XML validation in a pluggable way. Out of the box, it supports only W3C XML Schema, but new schema languages can be added in the future. Validating with a DTD is supported as an older feature directly in the SAX parser. We'll use both in this section.

Using Document Validation

XML's validation of documents is a key piece of what makes it useful as a data format. Using a schema is somewhat analogous to the way Java classes enforce type checking in the language. A schema defines document types. Documents conforming to a given schema are often referred to as *instance documents* of the schema.

This type safety provides a layer of protection that eliminates having to write complex error-checking code. However, validation may not be necessary in every environment. For example, when the same tool generates XML and reads it back in a short time span, validation may not be necessary. It is invaluable, though, during development. Sometimes document validation is used during development and turned off in production environments.

DTDs

The DTD language is fairly simple. A DTD is primarily a set of special tags that define each element in the document and, for complex types, provide a list of the elements it may contain. The DTD `<!ELEMENT>` tag consists of the name of the tag and either a special keyword for the data type or a parenthesized list of elements.

```
<!ELEMENT Name ( #PCDATA )>
<!ELEMENT Document ( Head, Body )>
```

The special identifier `#PCDATA` (parsed character data) indicates a string. When a list is provided, the elements are expected to appear in that order. The list may contain sublists, and items may be made optional using a vertical bar (`|`) as an OR operator. Special notation can also be used to indicate how many of each item may appear; two examples of this notation are shown in Table 24-4.

Table 24-4. DTD notation defining occurrences

Character	Meaning
*	Zero or more occurrences
?	Zero or one occurrences

Attributes of an element are defined with the `<!ATTLIST>` tag. This tag enables the DTD to enforce rules about attributes. It accepts a list of identifiers and a default value:

```
<!ATTLIST Animal animalClass (unknown | mammal | reptile) "unknown">
```

This `ATTLIST` says that the `animal` element has an `animalClass` attribute that can have one of several values (e.g.: `unknown`, `mammal`, `reptile`). The default is `unknown`.

We won't cover everything you can do with DTDs here. But the following example will guarantee *zooinventory.xml* follows the format we've described. Place the following in a file called *zooinventory.dtd* (or grab this file from *http://oreil.ly/Java_4E*):

```
<!ELEMENT inventory ( animal* )>
<!ELEMENT animal ( name, species, habitat, (food | foodRecipe), temperament,
    weight )>
<!ATTLIST animal animalClass ( unknown | mammal | reptile | bird | fish )
    "unknown">
```

```
<!ELEMENT name ( #PCDATA )>
<!ELEMENT species ( #PCDATA )>
<!ELEMENT habitat ( #PCDATA )>
<!ELEMENT food ( #PCDATA )>
<!ELEMENT weight ( #PCDATA )>
<!ELEMENT foodRecipe ( name, ingredient+ )>
<!ELEMENT ingredient ( #PCDATA )>
<!ELEMENT temperament ( #PCDATA )>
```

The DTD says that an `inventory` consists of any number of `animal` elements. An `animal` has a `name`, `species`, and `habitat` tag followed by either a `food` or `foodRecipe`. `foodRecipe`'s structure is further defined later.

To use a DTD, we associate it with the XML document. We can do this by placing a `DOCTYPE` declaration in the XML document itself and allow the XML parser to recognize and enforce it. The Java validation API that we'll talk about in the next section separates the roles of parsing and validation and can be used to validate arbitrary XML against any kind of schema, including DTDs. The problem is that out of the box, the validation API only implements the (newer) XML schema syntax. So we'll have to rely on the parser to validate the DTD for us here.

In this case, when a validating parser encounters the `DOCTYPE`, it attempts to load the DTD and validate the document. There are several forms the `DOCTYPE` can have, but the one we'll use is:

```
<!DOCTYPE Inventory SYSTEM "zooinventory.dtd">
```

Both SAX and DOM parsers can automatically validate documents as they read them, provided that the documents contain a `DOCTYPE` declaration. However, you have to explicitly ask the parser factory to provide a parser that is capable of validation. To do this, just set the validating property of the parser factory to `true` before you ask it for an instance of the parser. For example:

```
...
        SAXParserFactory factory = SAXParserFactory.newInstance();
        factory.setValidating( true );
```

Again, this `setValidating()` method is an older, more simplistic way to enable validation of documents that contain DTD references and it is tied to the parser. The new validation package that we'll discuss later is independent of the parser and more flexible. You should not use the parser-validating method in combination with the new validation API unless you want to validate documents twice for some reason.

Try inserting the `setValidating()` line in our model builder example after the factory is created. Abuse the *zooinventory.xml* file by adding or removing an element or attribute and then see what happens when you run the example. You should get useful error messages from the parser indicating the problems and parsing should fail. To get more information about the validation, we can register an `org.xml.sax.ErrorHandler` object with the parser, but by default, Java installs one that simply prints the errors for us.

XML Schema

Although DTDs can define the basic structure of an XML document, they don't provide a very rich vocabulary for describing the relationships between elements and say very little about their content. For example, there is no reasonable way with DTDs to specify that an element is to contain a numeric type or even to govern the length of string data. The XML Schema standard addresses both the structural and data content of an XML document. It is the next logical step and it (or one of the competing schema languages with similar capabilities) should replace DTDs in the future.

XML Schema brings the equivalent of strong typing to XML by drawing on many predefined primitive element types and allowing users to define new complex types of their own. These schemas even allow for types to be extended and used polymorphically, like types in the Java language. Although we can't cover XML Schema in any detail, we'll present the equivalent W3C XML Schema for our *zooinventory.xml* file here:

```
<?xml version="1.0" encoding="UTF-8"?>
<xs:schema xmlns:xs="http://www.w3.org/2001/XMLSchema">

<xs:element name="inventory">
  <xs:complexType>
    <xs:sequence>
       <xs:element maxOccurs="unbounded" ref="animal"/>
    </xs:sequence>
  </xs:complexType>
</xs:element>

<xs:element name="name" type="xs:string"/>

<xs:element name="animal">
  <xs:complexType>
    <xs:sequence>
      <xs:element ref="name"/>
      <xs:element name="species" type="xs:string"/>
      <xs:element name="habitat" type="xs:string"/>
      <xs:choice>
         <xs:element name="food" type="xs:string"/>
         <xs:element ref="foodRecipe"/>
      </xs:choice>
      <xs:element name="temperament" type="xs:string"/>
      <xs:element name="weight" type="xs:double"/>
    </xs:sequence>
    <xs:attribute name="animalClass" default="unknown">
      <xs:simpleType>
        <xs:restriction base="xs:token">
          <xs:enumeration value="unknown"/>
          <xs:enumeration value="mammal"/>
          <xs:enumeration value="reptile"/>
          <xs:enumeration value="bird"/>
        </xs:restriction>
```

```
      </xs:simpleType>
    </xs:attribute>
  </xs:complexType>
</xs:element>

<xs:element name="foodRecipe">
  <xs:complexType>
    <xs:sequence>
      <xs:element ref="name"/>
      <xs:element maxOccurs="unbounded" name="ingredient" type="xs:string"/>
    </xs:sequence>
  </xs:complexType>
</xs:element>

</xs:schema>
```

This schema would normally be placed into an XML Schema Definition file, which has a *.xsd* extension. The first thing to note is that this schema file is a normal, well-formed XML file that uses elements from the W3C XML Schema namespace. In it, we use nested `element` declarations to define the elements that will appear in our document. As with most languages, there is more than one way to accomplish this task. Here, we have broken out the "complex" `animal` and `foodRecipe` elements into their own separate element declarations and referred to them in their parent elements using the `ref` attribute. In this case, we did it mainly for readability; it would have been legal to have one big, deeply nested element declaration starting at `inventory`. However, referring to elements by reference in this way also allows us to reuse the same element declaration in multiple places in the document, if needed. Our `name` element is a small example of this. Although it didn't do much for us here, we have broken out the `name` element and referred to it for both the `Animal/Name` and the `FoodRecipe/Name`. Breaking out `name` like this would allow us to use more advanced features of schema and write rules for what a `name` can be (e.g., how long, what kind of characters are allowed) in one place and reuse that "type" where needed.

Control directives like `sequence` and `choice` allow us to define the structure of the child elements allowed and attributes like `minOccurs` and `maxOccurs` let us specify cardinality (how many instances). The `sequence` directive says that the enclosed elements should appear in the specified order (if they are required). The `choice` directive allows us to specify alternative child elements like `food` or `foodRecipe`. We declared the legal values for our `animalClass` attribute using a `restriction` declaration and `enumeration` tags.

Simple types

Although we've not really exercised it here, the `type` attribute of our elements touches on the standardization of types in XML Schema. All of our "text" elements specify a type `xs:string`, which is a standard XML Schema string type (kind of equivalent to PCDATA in our DTD). There are many other standard types covering things such as dates, times, periods, numbers, and even URLs. These are called *simple types* (though some of them are not so simple) because they are standardized or "built-in." Table 24-5 lists W3C Schema simple types and their corresponding Java types. The correspondence will become useful later when we talk about JAXB and automated binding of XML to Java classes.

Table 24-5. W3C Schema simple types

Schema element type	Java type	Example
xsd:string	java.lang.String	"This is text"
xsd:boolean	boolean	true, false, 1, 0
xsd:byte	byte	
xsd:unsignedByte	short	
xsd:integer	java.math.BigInteger	
xsd:int	int	
xsd:unsignedInt	long	
xsd.long	long	
xsd:short	short	
xsd:unsignedShort	int	
xsd:decimal	java.math.BigDecimal	
xsd:float	float	
xsd:double	double	
xsd:Qname	javax.xml.namespace.QName	funeral:corpse
xsd:dateTime	java.util.Calendar	2004-12-27T15:39:05.000-06:00
xsd:base64Binary	byte[]	PGZv
xsd:hexBinary	byte[]	FFFF
xsd:time	java.util.Calendar	15:39:05.000-06:00
xsd:date	java.util.Calendar	2004-12-27
xsd:anySimpleType	java.lang.String	

For example, we have a floating-point `weight` element like this in our `animal`:

```
<Weight>400.5</Weight>
```

We can now validate it in our schema by inserting the following entry at the appropriate place:

```
<xs:element name="weight" type="xs:double"/>
```

In addition to enforcing that the content of elements matches these simple types, XML Schema can give us much more control over the text and values of elements in our document using simple rules and patterns analogous to regular expressions.

Complex types

In addition to the predefined simple types listed in Table 24-5, we can define our own, *complex types* in our schema. Complex types are element types that have internal structure and possibly child elements. Our `inventory`, `animal`, and `foodRecipe` elements are all complex types and their content must be declared with the `complexType` tag in our schema. Complex type definitions can be reused, similar to the way that element definitions can be reused in our schema; that is, we can break out a complex type definition and give it a name. We can then refer to that type by name in the `type` attributes of other elements. Because all of our complex types were only used once in their corresponding elements, we didn't give them names. They were considered *anonymous type definitions*, declared and used in the same spot. For example, we could have separated our `animal`'s type from its element declaration, like so:

```
<xs:element name="inventory">
  <xs:complexType>
    <xs:sequence>
       <xs:element name="animal" maxOccurs="unbounded"
           type="AnimalType"/>
    </xs:sequence>
  </xs:complexType>
</xs:element>

<xs:complexType name="AnimalType">
  <xs:sequence>
    <xs:element ref="name"/>
    <xs:element name="species" type="xs:string"/>
    <xs:element name="habitat" type="xs:string"/>
    ...
```

Declaring the `AnimalType` separately from the instance of the `animal` element declaration would allow us to have other, differently named elements with the same structure. For example, our `inventory` element may hold another element, `mainAttraction`, which is a type of `animal` with a different tag name.

There's a lot more to say about W3C XML Schema and they can get quite a bit more complex than our simple example. However, you can do a lot with the few pieces we've previously shown. Some tools are available to help you get started. We'll talk about one called Trang in a moment. For more information about XML Schema, see the W3C's site (*http://www.w3.org/XML/Schema*) or *XML Schema* by Eric van der Vlist (O'Reilly). In the next section, we'll show how to validate a file or DOM model against the XML Schema we've just created, using the new validation API.

Generating Schema from XML samples

Many tools can help you write XML Schema. One helpful tool is called Trang (*http://bit.ly/10PPbTO*). It is part of an alternative schema language project called RELAX NG (which we mention later in this chapter), but Trang is very useful in and of itself. It is an open source tool that can not only convert between DTDs and XML Schema, but also create a rough DTD or XML Schema by reading an "example" XML document. This is a great way to sketch out a basic, starting schema for your documents.

The Validation API

To use our example's XML schema, we need to exercise the new `javax.xml.validation` API. As we said earlier, the validation API is an alternative to the simple, parser-based validation supported through the `setValidating()` method of the parser factories. To use the validation package, we create an instance of a `SchemaFactory`, specifying the schema language. We can then validate a DOM or stream source against the schema.

The following example, `Validate`, is in the form of a simple command-line utility that you can use to test out your XML and schemas. Just give it the XML filename and an XML Schema file (*.xsd* file) as arguments:

```
import javax.xml.XMLConstants;
import javax.xml.validation.*;
import org.xml.sax.*;
import javax.xml.transform.sax.SAXSource;
import javax.xml.transform.Source;
import javax.xml.transform.stream.StreamSource;

public class Validate
{
    public static void main( String [] args ) throws Exception {
        if ( args.length != 2 ) {
            System.err.println("usage: Validate xmlfile.xml xsdfile.xsd");
            System.exit(1);
        }
        String xmlfile = args[0], xsdfile = args[1];

        SchemaFactory factory =
        SchemaFactory.newInstance( XMLConstants.W3C_XML_SCHEMA_NS_URI);
        Schema schema = factory.newSchema( new StreamSource( xsdfile ) );
        Validator validator = schema.newValidator();

        ErrorHandler errHandler = new ErrorHandler() {
            public void error( SAXParseException e ) {
                System.out.println(e);
            }
            public void fatalError( SAXParseException e ) {
                System.out.println(e);
            }
            public void warning( SAXParseException e ) {
                System.out.println(e);
            }
        };
        validator.setErrorHandler( errHandler );
```

```
            try {
                validator.validate( new SAXSource(
                new InputSource("zooinventory.xml") ) );
            } catch ( SAXException e ) {
                // Invalid Document, no error handler
            }
        }
    }
```

The schema types supported initially are listed as constants in the `XMLConstants` class. Right now, only W3C XML Schema is implemented and there is also another intriguing type in there that we'll mention later. Our validation example follows the pattern we've seen before, creating a factory, then a `Schema` instance. The `Schema` represents the grammar and can create `Validator` instances that do the work of checking the document structure. Here, we've called the `validate()` method on a `SAXSource`, which comes from our file, but we could just as well have used a `DOMSource` to check an in-memory DOM representation:

```
validator.validate( new DOMSource(document) );
```

Any errors encountered will cause the validate method to throw a `SAXException`, but this is just a coarse means of detecting errors. More generally, and as we've shown in this example, we'd want to register an `ErrorHandler` object with the `validator`. The error handler can be told about many errors in the document and convey more information. When the error handler is present, the exceptions are given to it and not thrown from the validate method.

The errors generated by these parsers can be a bit cryptic. In some cases, the errors may not be able to report line numbers because the validation is not necessarily being done against a stream.

Alternative schema languages

In addition to DTDs and W3C XML Schema, several other popular schema languages are being used today. One interesting alternative that is tantalizingly referenced in the `XMLConstants` class is called RELAX NG. This schema language offers the most widely used features of XML Schema in a more human-readable format. In fact, it offers both a very compact, non-XML syntax and a regular XML-based syntax. RELAX NG doesn't offer the same text pattern and value validation that W3C XML Schema does. Instead, these aspects of validation are left to other tools (many people consider this to be "business logic," more appropriately implemented outside of the schema anyway). If you are interested in exploring other schema languages, be sure to check out RELAX NG and its useful schema conversion utility, Trang.

JAXB Code Binding and Generation

We've said that our ultimate goal in this chapter is automated binding of XML to Java classes. Now we'll discuss the standard Java API for XML Binding, JAXB. (This should not be confused with JAXP, the parser API.) JAXB is a standard extension that is bundled with Java 6 and later. With JAXB, the developer does not need to create any fragile parsing code. An XML schema or Java code can be used as the starting point for transforming XML to Java and back. ("Schema first" and "code first" are both supported.) With JAXB, you can either mark up your Java classes with simple annotations that map (bind) them to XML or start with an XML schema and generate plain Java classes (POJOs) with the necessary annotations included. You can even derive an XML schema from your Java classes to use as a starting point or contract with non-Java systems.

At runtime, JAXB can read an XML document and parse it into the model that you have defined or you can go the other way, populating your object model and then writing it out to XML. In both cases, JAXB can validate the data to make sure it matches a schema. This may sound like the DOM interface, but in this case we're not using generic classes—we're using our own model. In this section, we'll reuse the class model that we created for the SAX example with our *zooinventory.xml* file. We'll use the familiar `Inventory`, `Animal`, and `FoodRecipe` classes directly, but this time you'll see that we'll be more focused on the schema and names and less on the parsing machinery.

Annotating Our Model

JAXB gives us a great deal of flexibility in mapping our Java classes to XML elements and there are a lot of special cases. But if we accept most of the default behavior for our model, we can get started with very little work. Let's start by taking our zoo inventory classes and adding the necessary annotations to allow JAXB to bind it to XML:

```
@XmlRootElement
public class Inventory {
        public List<Animal> animal = new ArrayList<>();
}
```

Well, that was easy! Yes, in fact as we hinted at the beginning of the chapter, adding just the `@XmlRootElement` annotation to the "top level" or root class of our model will yield nearly the same XML that we used before. To generate the XML, we'll use the following test harness:

```
import javax.xml.bind.JAXBContext;
import javax.xml.bind.JAXBException;
import javax.xml.bind.Marshaller;

public class TestJAXBMarshall
{
    public static void main( String [] args ) throws JAXBException {
        Inventory inventory = new Inventory();
```

```
        FoodRecipe recipe = new FoodRecipe();
        recipe.name = "Gorilla Chow";
        recipe.ingredient.addAll( Arrays.asList( "leaves", "insects",
            "fruit" ) );
        Animal animal = new Animal( Animal.AnimalClass.mammal, "Song Fang",
            "Giant Panda", "China", "Bamboo", "Friendly", 45.0, recipe );
        inventory.animal.add( animal );

        marshall( inventory );
    }

    public static void marshall( Object jaxbObject ) throws JAXBException {
        JAXBContext context = JAXBContext.newInstance(
            jaxbObject.getClass() );
        Marshaller marshaller = context.createMarshaller();
        marshaller.setProperty(Marshaller.JAXB_FORMATTED_OUTPUT,
            Boolean.TRUE);
        marshaller.marshal(jaxbObject, System.out);
    }
}
```

We've taken the liberty of adding some constructors to shorten the code for creating the model, but it doesn't change the behavior here. It's just the four lines of our `marshall()` method that actually use JAXB to write out the XML. We first create a `JAXBContext`, passing in the class type to be marshalled. We've made our `marshall()` method somewhat reusable by getting the class type from the object passed in. However, it's sometimes necessary to pass in additional classes to the `newInstance()` method in order for JAXB to be aware of all of the bound classes that may be needed. In that case, we'd simpy pass more class types to the `newInstance()` method (it accepts a variable argument list with any number of arguments—of class types). We then create a `Marshaller` from the context and, for our purposes, set a flag indicating that we would like nice, human-readable output (the default output is one long line of XML). Finally, we tell the marshaller to send our object to `System.out`.

The output looks like this:

```
<?xml version="1.0" encoding="UTF-8" standalone="yes"?>
<inventory>
    <animal>
        <animalClass>mammal</animalClass>
        <name>Song Fang</name>
        <species>Giant Panda</species>
        <habitat>China</habitat>
        <food>Bamboo</food>
        <temperament>Friendly</temperament>
        <weight>45.0</weight>
    </animal>
    <animal>
        <animalClass>mammal</animalClass>
        <name>Cocoa</name>
```

```
        <species>Gorilla</species>
        <habitat>Ceneral Africa</habitat>
        <temperament>Know-it-all</temperament>
        <weight>45.0</weight>
        <foodRecipe>
            <name>Gorilla Chow</name>
            <ingredient>fruit</ingredient>
            <ingredient>shoots</ingredient>
            <ingredient>leaves</ingredient>
        </foodRecipe>
    </animal>
</inventory>
```

As we said, it's almost identical to the XML we worked with earlier. Admittedly, we chose to create our XML using the same (common) conventions that JAXB uses, so it's not entirely magic. The first thing to notice is that JAXB automatically mapped our class names to lowercase XML element names (e.g., class `Animal` to `<animal>`). If we had used JavaBeans-style getter methods instead of public fields, the same would be true; for example, a `getSpecies()` method would produce a default element name of `species`.

If we wanted to map our class names and property names to completely different XML names, we could easily accomplish that using the name attribute of the `@XmlRootElement` and `@XmlElement` annotations. For example, we can call our `Animal` "creature" and rename `temperament` to "personality" like so:

```
@XmlRootElement(name="creature")
public class Animal
{
    ...
    @XmlElement(name="personality")
    public String temperament;
```

The real difference between our generated XML and our earlier sample is that our `animalClass` attribute is not acting like an attribute. By default, is has been mapped to an element, like the other properties of `Animal`. We can rectify that with another annotation, `@XmlAttribute`:

```
public class Animal
{
    @XmlAttribute
    public AnimalClass animalClass;
    ...

// Produces...

<inventory>
    <animal animalClass="mammal">
        <name>Song Fang</name>
```

Also note that JAXB has shown the `food` element in the first animal and the `foodRecipe` in the second. JAXB will ignore a field or property that is `null` (as is the case here) unless you specify that the property is "nillable" using `@XmlElement(nillable=true)`. That behavior automatically supported the alternation between our two properties.

There are many additional annotations that provide support for mapping Java classes, fields, and properties to other features of XML. Table 24-6 attempts to provide a concise description of what each annotation is used for. Some of the usages get a little complex,so you may want to refer to the Javadoc for more details.

Table 24-6. JAXB Annotations

Annotation	Description
`@XmlAccessorOrder`	Used on a package or class to set alphabetic ordering of marshalled fields and properties. (The default ordering is undefined.) See `@XmlType` to specify the ordering yourself. As a reminder: package-level annotations in Java are placed on a (lonely) package statement in a special file named *package-info.java* within the corresponding package structure. (See "Annotations" on page 219.)
`@XmlAccessorType`	Used on a package or class to specify whether fields and properties are marshalled by default. You can choose: only fields, only properties (getters/setters), none (only those annotated by the user), or all public fields and properties. See `@XmlTransient` to exclude items.
`@XmlAnyAttribute`	Designates a Java `Map` object to receive any unbound XML attribute name-value pairs for an entity (i.e., the `Map` will collect any leftover attributes for which no corresponding property or field can be found).
`@XmlAnyElement`	Designates a Java `List` or `Array` object to receive any unbound XML elements for an entity (i.e., the `List` will accumulate any leftover elements for which no corresponding property or field can be found).
`@XmlAttachmentRef`	Designates a `java.activation.DataHandler` object to handle an XML MIME attachment.
`@XmlAttribute`	Binds a Java field or property to an XML attribute. The `name` attribute can be used to specify an XML attribute name that is different from the name of the field or property. Use the `required` attribute to specify whether the attribute is required.
`@XmlElement`	Binds a a Java field or property to an XML element. The `name` attribute can be used to specify an XML element name different from the name of the field or property. Use the `required` attribute to specify whether the element is required.
`@XmlElements`	Used on a Java collection to specify distinct element names for contained items based on their Java type. Holds a list of `@XmlElement` annotations with `name` and `type` attributes that explicitly map Java types in the collection to XML element names (e.g., in our example, `inventory` contains `animal` elements because our List property is named "animal"). If we chose to have subclasses of `Animal` in our inventory collection, we could map them to XML element names such as `gorilla` and `lemur`. See `@XmlElementRef`.

Annotation	Description
`@XmlElementRef`	Similar to `@XmlElements`, used to generate individualized names for Java types in a collection. However, instead of the names for each type being specified directly, they are determined at runtime by the individual types' Java type bindings (e.g., in our example, `inventory` contains `animal` elements because our List is named "animal"). Using `@XmlElementRef`, we could subclass `Animal` and have our `inventory` contain elements like `gorilla` and `lemur`, with the names determined by `@XmlRootElement` annotations on the respective subclasses. See important class binding info in `@XmlElementRefs`.
`@XmlElementRefs`	Used on a Java collection to provide a list of `@XmlElementRef` annotations with `type` attributes that explicitly specify the Java types that may appear in the collection. The effect is the same as using a simple `@XmlElementRef` on the collection, but we actively tell JAXB the class names that have bindings. If not supplied in this way, we have to provide the full list of bound classes to the `JAXBContextnewInstance()` method in order for them to be recognized.
`@XmlElementWrapper`	Used on a Java collection to cause the sequence of XML elements to be wrapped in the specified element instead of appearing directly inline in the XML (e.g., our `animal` elements appear directly in `inventory`). Using this annotation, we could nest them all within a new `animals` element.
`@XmlEnum`	Binds a Java Enum to XML and allows `@XmlEnum`Values annotations to be used to map the enum values for XML if required.
`@XmlEnumValue`	Binds an individual Java Enum value to a string to be used in the XML (e.g., our `mammal` enum value could be mapped to "mammalia").
`@XmlID`	Supports referential integrity by designating a Java property or field of a class as being the XML `ID` attribute (a unique key) for the XML element within the document.
`@XmlIDREF`	Supports referential integrity by designating a Java property or field as an `idref` attribute pointing to an element with an `@XmlID`. The annotated property or field must contain an instance of a Java type containing an `@XmlID` annotation. When marshalled, the attribute name will be the property name and the value will be the contained XML ID value.
`@XmlInlineBinaryData`	Bind a Java byte array to receive base64 binary data encoded in the XML.
`@XmlList`	Used on a Java collection to map items to a single simple content element with a whitespace-separated list of values instead of a series of elements.
`@XmlMimeType`	Used with a Java Image or Source type to specify a MIME type for XML base64-encoded binary data bound to it.
`@XmlMixed`	Binds a Java object collection to XML "mixed content" (i.e., XML containing both text and element tags within it). Text will be added to the collection as `String` objects interleaved with the usual Java types representing the other elements.
`@XmlRootElement`	Bind a Java class to an XML element optionally provide a name. This is the minimum annotation required on your class to make it possible to marshal it to XML and back.
`@XmlElementDecl`	Used in binding XML schema elements to methods in Java object factories created in some code generation scenarios.
`@XmlRegistry`	Used with `@XmlElementDecl` in designating Java object factories used in some code generation scenarios.
`@XmlSchema`	Binds a Java package to a default XML namespace.

Annotation	Description
`@XmlNs`	Used with `@XmlSchema` to bind a Java package to one or more XML namespace prefixes.
`@XmlSchemaType`	Used on a Java property, field, or package. Specifies a Java type to be used for a standard XML schema built-in types, such as date or a numeric type.
`@XmlSchemaTypes`	Used on a Java package. Holds a list of `@XmlSchemaType` annotations mapping Java types to built-in XML schema types.
`@XmlTransient`	Designates that a Java property or field should not be marshaled to the XML. This can be used in conjunction with defaults that marshal all properties or fields to exclude individual items. See `@XmlAccessorType`.
`@XmlType`	Binds a Java class to an XML schema type. Additionally, the `propOrder` attribute may be used to explicitly list the order in which elements are marshalled to XML.
`@XmlValue`	Designates that a Java property or field contains the "simple" XML content for the Java type; that is, instead of marshalling the class as an XML element containing a nested element for the property, the value of the annotated property will appear directly as the content. The Java type may have only one property designated as `@XmlValue`.

Unmarshalling from XML

Creating our object model from XML just requires a few lines to create an `Unmarshaller` from our `JAXBContext` and a cast to the Java type of our root element:

```
JAXBContext context = JAXBContext.newInstance( Inventory.class );
Unmarshaller unmarshaller = context.createUnmarshaller();
Inventory inventory = (Inventory)unmarshaller.unmarshal(
    new File("zooinventory.xml") );
```

The `Unmarshaller` class has a `setValidating()` method like the `SAXParser`, but it is deprecated. Instead, we could use the `setSchema()` method to set an XML Schema representation if we want validation as part of the parsing process. Alternately, we could just validate the schema separately. See "XML Schema" on page 879.

Generating a Java Model from an XML Schema

If you are starting with an XML Schema (*xsd* file), you can generate annotated Java classes from the schema using the JAXB `xjc` command-line tool that comes with the JDK.

```
xjc zooinventory.xsd

// Output
parsing a schema...
compiling a schema...
generated/Animal.java
generated/FoodRecipe.java
generated/Inventory.java
generated/ObjectFactory.java
```

By default, the output is placed in the default package in a directory named *generated*. You can control the package name with the `-p` switch and the directory with `-d`. See the `xjc` documentation for more options.

Studying the generated classes will give you some hints as to how many annotations are used, although `xjc` is a little more verbose than it has to be. Also note that `xjc` produces a class called `ObjectFactory` that contains factory methods for each type, such as `createInventory()` and `createAnimal()`. If you look at these methods, you'll see that they really just call `new` on the plain Java objects and they seem superfluous. The `ObjectFactory` is mainly there for legacy reasons. In ealier versions of JAXB, before annotations, the generated classes were not as simple to construct. Additionally, the `ObjectFactory` contains a helper method to create a `JAXBElement` type, which may be useful in special situations. For the most part, you can ignore these.

Generating an XML Schema from a Java Model

You can also generate an XML Schema directly from your annotated Java classes using the JAXB XML Schema binding generator: `schemagen`. The `schemagen` command-line tool comes with the JDK. It can generate a schema starting with Java source or class files. Use the `-classpath` argument to specify the location of the classes or source files and then provide the name of the root class in your hierarchy:

```
schemagen -classpath . Inventory
```

Having worked our way through the options for bridging XML to Java, we'll now turn our attention to transformations on XML itself with XSL, the styling language for XML.

Transforming Documents with XSL/XSLT

Earlier in this chapter, we used a `Transformer` object to copy a DOM representation of an example back to XML text. We mentioned that we were not really tapping the potential of the `Transformer`. Now, we'll give you the full story.

The `javax.xml.transform` package is the API for using the XSL/XSLT transformation language. XSL stands for Extensible Stylesheet Language. Like Cascading Stylesheets (CSS) for HTML, XSL allows us to "mark up" XML documents by adding tags that provide presentation information. XSL Transformation (XSLT) takes this further by adding the ability to completely restructure the XML and produce arbitrary output. XSL and XSLT together make up their own programming language for processing an XML document as input and producing another (usually XML) document as output. (From here on in, we'll refer to them collectively as XSL.)

XSL is extremely powerful, and new applications for its use arise every day. For example, consider a website that is frequently updated and that must provide access to a variety of mobile devices and traditional browsers. Rather than recreating the site for these and additional platforms, XSL can transform the content to an appropriate format for each platform. More generally, rendering content from XML is simply a better way to preserve your data and keep it separate from your presentation information. XSL can be used to render an entire website in different styles from files containing "pure data" in XML, much like a database. Multilingual sites also benefit from XSL to lay out text in different ways for different audiences.

You can probably guess the caveat that we're going to issue: XSL is a big topic worthy of its own books (see, for example, O'Reilly's *Java and XSLT* by Eric Burke), and we can only give you a taste of it here. Furthermore, some people find XSL difficult to understand at first glance because it requires thinking in terms of recursively processing document tags. In recent years, much of the impetus behind XSL as a way to produce web-based content has fallen away in favor of using more JavaScript on the client. However, XSL remains a powerful way to transform XML and is widely used in other document-oriented applications.

XSL Basics

XSL is an XML-based standard, so it should come as no surprise that the language is based on XML. An XSL *stylesheet* is an XML document using special tags defined by the XSL namespace to describe the transformation. The most basic XSL operations involve matching parts of the input XML document and generating output based on their contents. One or more XSL *templates* live within the stylesheet and are called in response to tags appearing in the input. XSL is often used in a purely input-driven way, whereas input XML tags trigger output in the order in which they appear, using only the information they contain. But more generally, the output can be constructed from arbitrary parts of the input, drawing from it like a database, composing elements and attributes. The XSLT transformation part of XSL adds things like conditionals and iteration to this mix, which enable any kind of output to be generated based on the input.

An XSL stylesheet contains a stylesheet tag as its root element. By convention, the stylesheet defines a namespace prefix `xsl` for the XSL namespace. Within the stylesheet, are one or more template tags contain a `match` attribute that describes the element upon which they operate.

```
<xsl:stylesheet
   xmlns:xsl="http://www.w3.org/1999/XSL/Transform" version="1.0">

   <xsl:template match="/">
     I found the root of the document!
   </xsl:template>

</xsl:stylesheet>
```

When a template matches an element, it has an opportunity to handle all the children of the element. The simple stylesheet shown here has one template that matches the root of the input document and simply outputs some plain text. By default, input not matched is simply copied to the output with its tags stripped (HTML convention). But here we match the root so we consume the entire input and nothing but our message appears on the output.

The `match` attribute can refer to elements using the XPath notation that we described earlier. This is a hierarchical path starting with the root element. For example, `match="/inventory/animal"` would match only the `animal` elements from our *zooinventory.xml* file. In XSL, the path may be absolute (starting with "/") or relative, in which case, the template detects whenever that element appears in any subcontext (equivalent to "//" in XPath).

Within the template, we can put whatever we want as long as it is well-formed XML (if not, we can use a CDATA section or XInclude). But the real power comes when we use parts of the input to generate output. The XSL `value-of` tag is used to output the content or child of the element. For example, the following template would match an `animal` element and output the value of its `Name` child element:

```
<xsl:template match="animal">
   Name: <xsl:value-of select="name"/>
</xsl:template>
```

The `select` attribute uses an XPath expression relative to the current node. In this case, we tell it to print the value of the `name` element within `animal`. We could have used a relative path to a more deeply nested element within `animal` or even an absolute path to another part of the document. To refer to the "current" element (in this case, the `animal` element itself), a `select` expression can use "`.`" as the path. The `select` expression can also retrieve attributes from the elements that it references.

If we try to add the `animal` template to our simple example, it won't generate any output. What's the problem? If you recall, we said that a template matching an element has the opportunity to process all its children. We already have a template matching the root ("/"), so it is consuming all the input. The answer to our dilemma—and this is where things get a little tricky—is to delegate the matching to other templates using the `apply-templates` tag. The following example correctly prints the names of all the animals in our document:

```
<xsl:stylesheet
   xmlns:xsl="http://www.w3.org/1999/XSL/
   Transform" version="1.0">

   <xsl:template match="/">
      Found the root!
      <xsl:apply-templates/>
   </xsl:template>

   <xsl:template match="animal">
      Name: <xsl:value-of select="name"/>
```

```
    </xsl:template>

</xsl:stylesheet>
```

We still have the opportunity to add output before and after the `apply-templates` tag. But upon invoking it, the template matching continues from the current node. Next, we'll use what we have so far and add a few bells and whistles.

Transforming the Zoo Inventory

Your boss just called, and it's now imperative that your zoo clients have access to the zoo inventory through the Web, today! After reading Chapter 15, you should be thoroughly prepared to build a nice "zoo app." Let's get started by creating an XSL stylesheet to turn our *zooinventory.xml* into HTML:

```
<?xml version="1.0" encoding="UTF-8"?>
<xs:schema xmlns:xs="http://www.w3.org/2001/XMLSchema">

<xs:element name="inventory">
  <xs:complexType>
    <xs:sequence>
       <xs:element maxOccurs="unbounded" ref="animal"/>
    </xs:sequence>
  </xs:complexType>
</xs:element>

<xs:element name="name" type="xs:string"/>

<xs:element name="animal">
  <xs:complexType>
    <xs:sequence>
      <xs:element ref="name"/>
      <xs:element name="species" type="xs:string"/>
      <xs:element name="habitat" type="xs:string"/>
      <xs:choice>
         <xs:element name="food" type="xs:string"/>
         <xs:element ref="foodRecipe"/>
      </xs:choice>
      <xs:element name="temperament" type="xs:string"/>
      <xs:element name="weight" type="xs:double"/>
    </xs:sequence>
    <xs:attribute name="animalClass" default="unknown">
      <xs:simpleType>
        <xs:restriction base="xs:token">
          <xs:enumeration value="unknown"/>
          <xs:enumeration value="mammal"/>
          <xs:enumeration value="reptile"/>
          <xs:enumeration value="bird"/>
        </xs:restriction>
      </xs:simpleType>
    </xs:attribute>
```

```
    </xs:complexType>
  </xs:element>

  <xs:element name="foodRecipe">
    <xs:complexType>
      <xs:sequence>
        <xs:element ref="name"/>
        <xs:element maxOccurs="unbounded" name="ingredient" type="xs:string"/>
      </xs:sequence>
    </xs:complexType>
  </xs:element>

  </xs:schema>
```

The stylesheet contains three templates. The first matches `/inventory` and outputs the beginning of our HTML document (the header) along with the start of a table for the animals. It then delegates using `apply-templates` before closing the table and adding the HTML footer. The next template matches `inventory/animal`, printing one row of an HTML table for each animal. Although there are no other `animal` elements in the document, it still doesn't hurt to specify that we will match an `animal` only in the context of an `inventory`, because, in this case, we are relying on `inventory` to start and end our table. (This template makes sense only in the context of an `inventory`.) Finally, we provide a template that matches `foodRecipe` and prints a small, nested table for that information. `foodRecipe` makes use of the "`for-each`" operation to loop over child nodes with a `select` specifying that we are only interested in `ingredient` children. For each `ingredient`, we output its value in a row.

There is one more thing to note in the `animal` template. Our `apply-templates` element has a `select` attribute that limits the elements affected. In this case, we are using the "`|`" regular expression-like syntax to say that we want to apply templates for only the `food`*or*`foodRecipe` child elements. Why do we do this? Because we didn't match the root of the document (only `inventory`), we still have the default stylesheet behavior of outputting the plain text of nodes that aren't matched anywhere else. We take advantage of this behavior to print the text of the `food` element. But we don't want to output the text of all of the other elements of `animal` that we've already printed explicitly, so we process only the `food` and `foodRecipe` elements. Alternatively, we could have been more verbose, adding a template matching the root and another template just for the `food` element. That would also mean that new tags added to our XML would, by default, be ignored and not change the output. This may or may not be the behavior you want, and there are other options as well. As with all powerful tools, there is usually more than one way to do something.

XSLTransform

Now that we have a stylesheet, let's apply it! The following simple program, `XSLTransform`, uses the `javax.xml.transform` package to apply the stylesheet to an XML document and print the result. You can use it to experiment with XSL and our example code.

```
import javax.xml.transform.*;
import javax.xml.transform.stream.*;

public class XSLTransform
{
    public static void main( String [] args ) throws Exception {
        if ( args.length < 2 || !args[0].endsWith(".xsl") ) {
            System.err.println("usage: XSLTransform file.xsl file.xml");
            System.exit(1);
        }
        String xslFile = args[0], xmlFile = args[1];

        TransformerFactory factory = TransformerFactory.newInstance();
        Transformer transformer =
            factory.newTransformer( new StreamSource( xslFile ) );
        StreamSource xmlsource = new StreamSource( xmlFile );
        StreamResult output = new StreamResult( System.out );
        transformer.transform( xmlsource, output );
    }
}
```

Run `XSLTransform`, passing the XSL stylesheet and XML input, as in the following command:

```
% java XSLTransform zooinventory.xsl zooinventory.xml > zooinventory.html
```

The output should look like Figure 24-2.

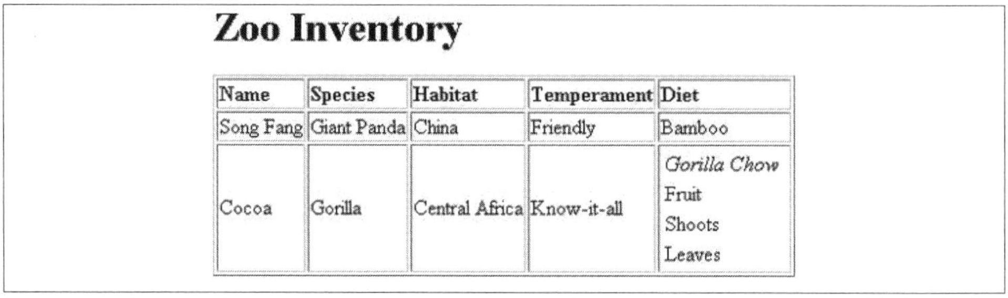

Zoo Inventory

Name	Species	Habitat	Temperament	Diet
Song Fang	Giant Panda	China	Friendly	Bamboo
Cocoa	Gorilla	Central Africa	Know-it-all	*Gorilla Chow* Fruit Shoots Leaves

Figure 24-2. Image of the zoo inventory table

Constructing the transform is a similar process to that of getting a SAX or DOM parser. The difference from our earlier use of the `TransformerFactory` is that this time, we construct the transformer, passing it the XSL stylesheet source. The resulting

Transformer object is then a dedicated machine that knows how to take input XML and generate output according to its rules.

One important thing to note about XSLTransform is that it is not guaranteed thread-safe. In our example, we run the transform only once. If you are planning to run the same transform many times, you should take the additional step of getting a Templates object for the transform first, then using it to create Transformers.

```
Templates templates =
    factory.newTemplates( new StreamSource( args[0] ) );
Transformer transformer = templates.newTransformer();
```

The Templates object holds the parsed representation of the stylesheet in a compiled form and makes the process of getting a new Transformer much faster. The transformers themselves may also be more highly optimized in this case. The XSL transformer actually generates bytecode for very efficient "translets" that implement the transform. This means that instead of the transformer reading a description of what to do with your XML, it actually produces a small compiled program to execute the instructions!

XSL in the Browser

With our XSLTransform example, you can see how you'd go about rendering XML to an HTML document on the server side. But as mentioned in the introduction, modern web browsers support XSL on the client side as well. Browsers can automatically download an XSL stylesheet and use it to transform an XML document. To make this happen, just add a standard XSL stylesheet reference in your XML. You can put the stylesheet directive next to your DOCTYPE declaration in the *zooinventory.xml* file:

```
<?xml-stylesheet type="text/xsl" href="zooinventory.xsl"?>
```

As long as the *zooinventory.xsl* file is available at the same location (base URL) as the *zooinventory.xml* file, the browser will use it to render HTML on the client side.

Web Services

As we saw in our web services examples in Chapters 14 and 15, one of the most interesting uses for XML is web services. A web service is simply an application service supplied over the network, making use of XML to describe the request and response. Normally, web services run over HTTP and use an XML-based protocol called Simple Object Access Protocol (SOAP), a W3C standard. The combination of XML and HTTP provides a widely accessible interface for services.

SOAP and other XML-based remote procedure call mechanisms can be used in place of Java RMI for cross-platform communications. Web services are widely used and it is likely that they will continue to grow in importance in coming years. To learn more about Java APIs related to web services, check out the networking chapters of this book and take a look at *http://java.sun.com/webservices/*.

That's it for our brief introduction to XML. There is a lot more to learn about this exciting area, and many of the APIs are evolving rapidly. We hope we've given you a good start.

The End of the Book

With this chapter, we also wrap up the main part of our book. We hope that you've enjoyed *Learning Java*. This, the fourth edition of *Learning Java*, is really the sixth edition of the series that began seventeen years ago with *Exploring Java*. It's been a long and amazing trip watching Java develop in that time, and we thank those of you who have come along with us over the years. As always, we welcome your feedback to help us keep making this book better in the future. Ready for another decade of Java? We are!

APPENDIX A
The Eclipse IDE

In this book, we have tried to focus on the Java language and APIs without spending too much time talking about specific tools. But Java programming today really requires the use of an Integrated Development Envrionment (IDE). Modern languages and develoment tools are intertwined to such an extent that it's hard to imagine working on large projects without the support of a good IDE. Modern development tools "understand" the language deeply and give you great power to create, search, modify, and fix problems with your code.

A wide array of Java IDEs with varying features are available. Like all power tools, IDEs are constantly changing and improving. Our preferred development environment of many years is Intellij IDEA by JetBrains. However, by far the most widely used IDE for Java is the open source Eclipse project. In the tutorial introduction to this book, we briefly introduced Eclipse. In this appendix, we will go a little farther and use it to load and explore the example code from this book, which have been packaged for you as an Eclipse project.

IDEs offer many benefits as well as a few drawbacks, especially for the new Java programmer. The benefits include an all-in-one view of Java source code with syntax highlighting, navigation help, source control, integrated documentation, building, refactoring, and deployment all at your fingertips. The downside, historically at least, has been that the all-in-one tool tends to become an all-or-nothing tool that locks users into the product and makes them all but helpless without it. IDEs tend to encourage an overly simplistic project layout with no structure or partitioning to help humans understand it. IDEs can also become hairballs of state and information about the project that cannot be easily shared with other developers or across projects. Many of these problems are being addressed by the latest generation of IDEs and for most people, the benefits far outweigh the negatives.

The IDE Wars

Comparing IDEs on features alone is futile because all modern IDEs are based on a plug-in architecture that allows new tools to be added by third parties. Saying that an IDE has feature X is just an invitation for someone to retort that her IDE has plug-ins for X and Y. Still, it is worth taking a moment to draw some comparisons here (if we dare). In this book, we have used both the NetBeans 7.2 and Eclipse 4.2 editors. How do they stack up? The short answer is that, at the time of this writing, Eclipse is more popular and a bit more polished at the expense of being platform-dependent, whereas the latest release of NetBeans offers a few more advanced features out of the box. NetBeans offers a visual application builder and a web application development environment. Of course, you can add those to Eclipse, but you must choose from (possibly pay-ware) alternatives. Another important feature of NetBeans 4.x is that it uses a fully externalized Ant build process. This means that you can build your application inside or outside of the IDE in exactly the same way. With that said, let's move on to Eclipse.

Getting Started with Eclipse

Let's get started. First, you'll need to install Eclipse. Download the latest version of "Eclipse IDE for Java Developers" (*http://eclipse.org/*). Choose the correct version for your platform. Unpack the ZIP file to a location of your choice and then launch the application.

The first time you run Eclipse, you'll be prompted to select a workspace. This is a root directory to hold new projects that you create within Eclipse. The default location may be inside the application's install folder itself, which is probably not what you want. Pick a location and click OK.

Eclipse greets you with the Welcome screen. Close this window by closing the Welcome tab within the application. If you want to come back later and go through the Eclipse tutorials and related help topics, you can get this window back by choosing Help → Welcome.

One last thing before we move on: Eclipse stores all of its configuration information in the *configuration* folder inside the Eclipse installation directory. If, at any point in this introduction, you feel that things are not right and you want to start from scratch, you can quit the application and remove this folder. You may also wish to remove your workspace items as they hold per-project state. Less drastically, if you wish to reset all of the application windows to their default locations, you can choose Window → Reset Perspective. We'll talk more about perspectives later.

Importing the Learning Java Examples

Before we talk about the IDE itself, let's load the examples from this book. You can find a ZIP file containing all of the examples from this book nicely packaged as an Eclipse project at *http://oreil.ly/Java_4E*. The Eclipse version of the examples is called *examples-eclipse.zip*.

Open the Import Wizard with File → Import and select General → Existing Projects Into Workspace as the source and click Next. Choose Select Archive File. Click the Browse button and locate the *examples-eclipse.zip* file. The Import wizard should look like Figure A-1. Click Finish.

Eclipse will now import all of the files from the archive and immediately begin building the source in the background (a small progress bar at the bottom of the screen will show this).

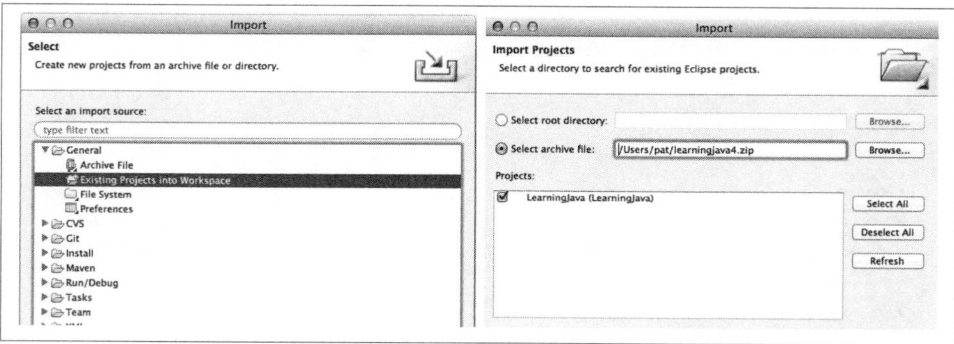

Figure A-1. The import projects dialog box

Using Eclipse

The first thing we need to do is set up the IDE for browsing and editing our Java source code. If you downloaded the standard Java developer version of Eclipse, it should be set up for Java development. If you chose another package, you may need to select Window → Open Perspective → Java to put Eclipse into the Java editing *perspective*. A perspective in Eclipse is an arrangement of different tools, menu bars, and shortcuts geared toward a particular kind of task, such as Java editing or source repository browsing. You can open additional tools and move things around to your liking, but the predefined perspectives give you a good start. Now the *Learning Java* examples appear in Eclipse, as shown in Figure A-2.

On the left is the Package Explorer. It shows a tree view of the Java packages, libraries, and resources of our project. Click the folder handles to expand the tree and see source folders for each chapter in the book.

The bottom area holds tabs related to Java editing. The tab that is open in Figure A-2, Problems, shows errors and warnings associated with our project code. Eclipse has already compiled our code in the background. In general, you don't have to tell it to do so. You'll also notice red Xs on some of the source folders and files. These files have errors. We'll talk about why some of our examples are being flagged in a moment. The other tabs, Javadoc and Declaration, give information about the file we're editing or the source code item selected. The Declaration tab can show a preview of the source for an item selected in the main editor window without requiring you to open it explicitly.

To clear up some of those red Xs, we need to make sure that Eclipse is in Java 7.0-compatible mode. Choose Eclipse (or Window) → Preferences → Java → Compiler and set the Compiler Compliance Level to 7.0. Click OK and select Yes to rebuild the source. (It is also possible to set the compiler level on a per-project basis through the project preferences.)

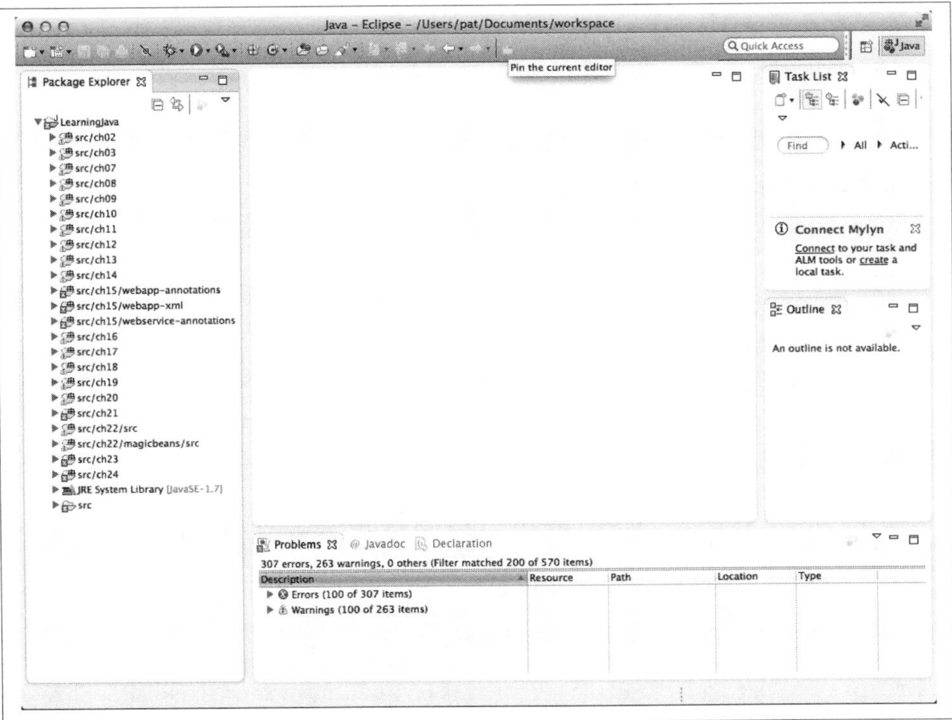

Figure A-2. Learning Java examples in Eclipse's Java editing perspective

If there are still some red Xs left, double-click the *README-Eclipse.txt* file in the project tree to read the latest explanations for these issues. Some of these issues relate to generating source code or installing additional libraries to make the examples work properly.

Getting at the Source

Let's navigate to a source file. Go to the *Calculator.java* file located in the *ch19/default package*. Double-click it to open the source, as shown in Figure A-3.

When you're expanding the source folder tree, you can actually continue "deeper" than the Java source file level, expanding elements of the file itself. By moving into the source file in the explorer, you can expose parts of the Java source like methods, variables, and inner classes. By double-clicking these elements, you can open the file and jump right to the corresponding line. This is similar to the outline view that we'll see in the next section.

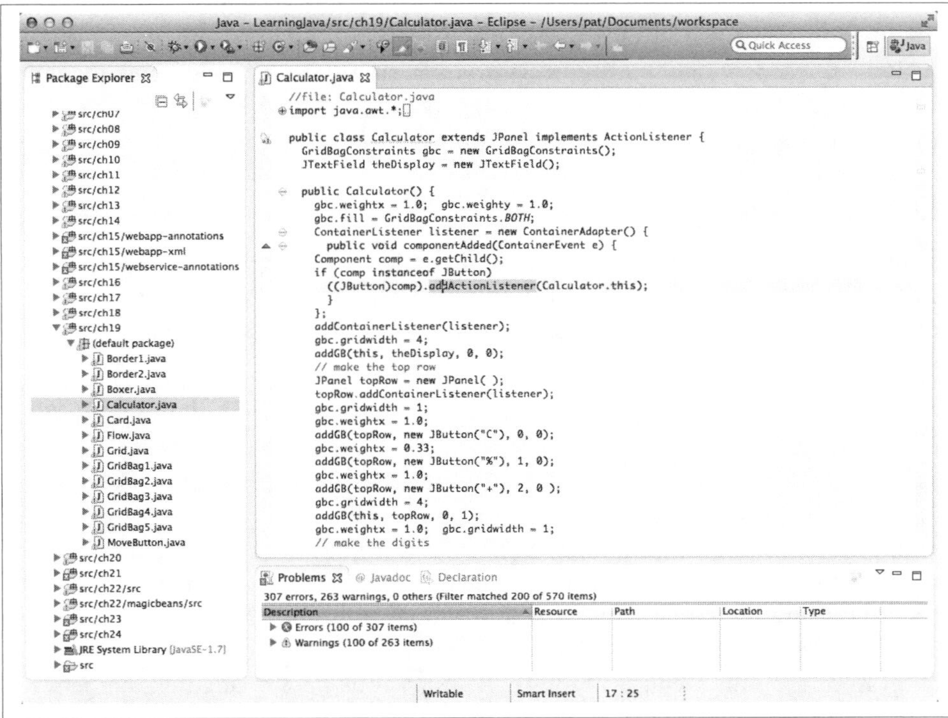

Figure A-3. Opening Calculator.java

The Lay of the Land

In the center of the screen, the open file is displayed in a new editor tab. The editor is, of course, the center of much of the action in a Java IDE. Note the color-coded syntax highlighting. Also, notice the little arrows immediately to the left of the source code. These are *folds*. A fold groups a section of Java code, such as a Java method or comment, and allows you to collapse or expand it like an outline. For example, the `import` statements in the file are folded by default. Click the blue arrow to the left of the import line to expand them and see all of the imports.

Next, warnings and errors are highlighted in the column to the left of the folds column. Try making a small error in the file. For example, try changing the `javax.swing` import to `javax.boofa` and see what happens. Note all the red Xs indicating problems. When you hover over a red X, you get a pop-up report of the problem. The column on the right of the scrollbar provides a view of the location of warnings and errors. Clicking on these areas takes you to the corresponding line of code. The *problems area* in the bottom tab is also linked; clicking on a problem report opens the corresponding file at the correct line.

On the right side of the IDE is the *outline pane* that shows a structured view of the Java code similar to what we saw by expanding the source file tab in the project browser. By clicking on a field, method, or inner class, you jump to the corresponding line in the source editor. Options at the top of the pane let you filter which members are shown for quick access.

Running the Examples

To run the Calculator example, you can simply hit the large green arrow Run button while the source file is open or select the source file in the explorer and choose Run → Run As → Java Application. The Calculator runs, as shown in Figure A-4.

You may use Run As to tell Eclipse that this file actually is a standalone class with a `main()` method. Normally, a project has a lot of code and only one or a few `main()` methods. In that case, the Run menu option (and large green "play" button icon on the toolbar) can be configured to launch the default class for the overall application. An individual file can also be launched from its context menu, which you display by right-clicking on the file (control-click on the Mac). If we had chosen an application that printed output to `System.out`, Eclipse would have opened a Console tab in the bottom panel to capture the output. To see this in action, run the *ch10/PrintfExamples.java* example. To run an example that requires arguments, you choose the more general Run option from the Run menu instead. This option pops up a dialog box that lets you configure, among other things, command-line arguments for the launch. The Run menu also includes a Run History option with recent launches so you can run them again quickly.

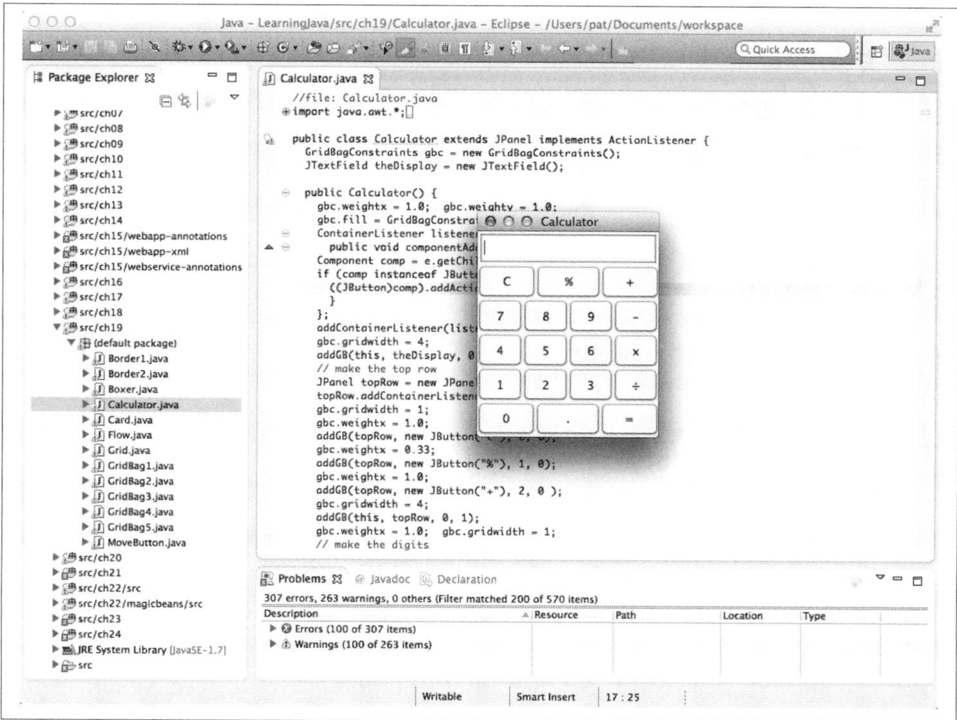

Figure A-4. Running the calculator

Building the Ant-Based Examples

Some of the chapters include components that must be built with the supplied Ant build file. For example, the JavaBeans JAR in Chapter 22 and the Web Application WAR file in Chapter 15 have Ant builds. You can run Ant from within Eclipse simply by right-clicking the *build.xml* file in the folder and selecting Run As → Ant Build. However, in order to see it you'll have to open the Project Explorer using Windows → Show View → Project Explorer. (The Project Explorer shows all files in the project as opposed to the view of the Java class hierarchy shown by the Package Explorer.) There are two Ant Build options. The first runs the default target for the build, while the second lets you choose a target (analogous to Run As and Run in the Run menu). For example, to build the *magicbeans.jar* file from Chapter 22, navigate to *sr/ch22/magicbeans/build.xml*, right-click, and select Run As → Ant Build (the first option). You may have to use the File → Refresh option to see new files generated by the Ant build in the project tree.

Loner Examples

Some of the examples in the book may be a little easier to deal with outside of Eclipse, at least until you become immersed in the IDE. For example, some of the networking examples may be more easily run on the command line. There's no reason to stay in the IDE for everything. Get comfortable in both environments.

Eclipse Features

Eclipse has too many interesting features to really do them justice here, but we'll mention a few to show you why people love this IDE.

Coding Shortcuts

Of course, you've noticed all the color coding and meta-information present when viewing Java source code in Eclipse. You can customize all of this behavior to suit your taste through the Eclipse → Preferences → Java → Editor → Syntax Coloring panel. Many other options can be set through the Eclipse → Preferences → Java → Code Style and Editor panes.

What may not be immediately obvious is that editing is also enhanced. When typing, try pressing Ctrl-Space to attempt autocompletion or have Eclipse present you with relevant options. For example, instead of typing `JButton`, try typing `JBu` plus Ctrl-Space. Eclipse completes the name for you. If the portion of the name you type is ambiguous, a drop-down list appears, similar to that shown in Figure A-5.

Eclipse also provides abbreviations for common items. Try typing `sysout` and pressing Crtl-Space. Eclipse expands this to `System.out.println()` and places the cursor in the parentheses automatically. If you type a quotation mark, Eclipse closes the quotation for you. Note the green bar that it places after the closing quote. Pressing Tab takes you to that point so that you don't have to use the arrow keys. Pressing Tab again takes you to the next green bar spot, which is the end of the line.

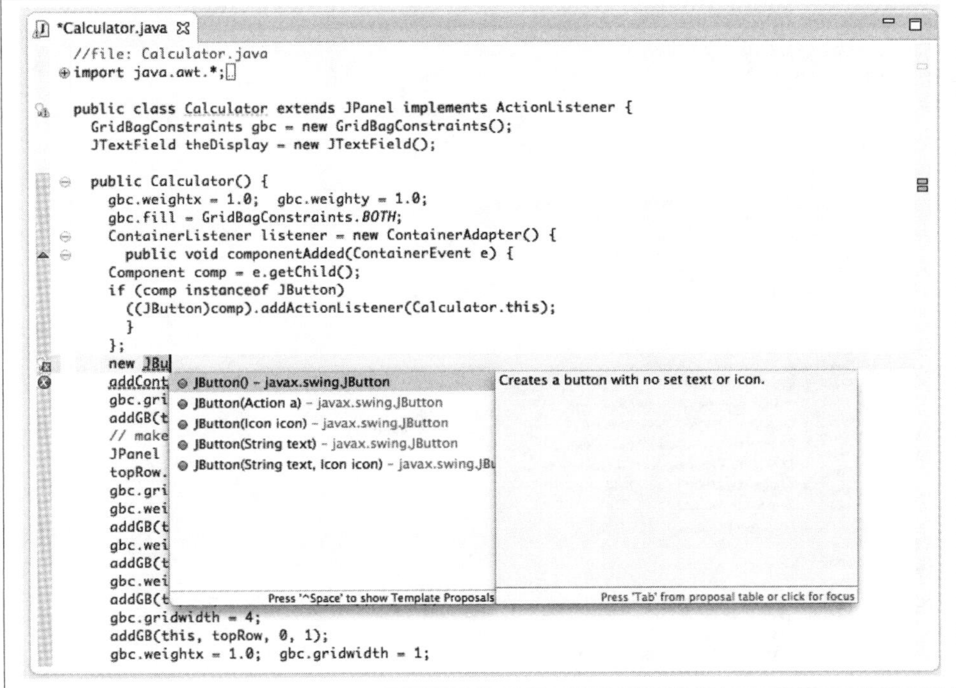

Figure A-5. Using completion in Eclipse

Autocorrection

Eclipse can offer fixes for simple problems in your code when it detects them. To see suggested fixes, click on the red X next to a problem line. Eclipse presents a drop-down menu of possible fixes for the problem. Selecting an option shows you the code changes that Eclipse will make before you choose it.

For example, try changing the name of one of the `JButton`s in our Calculator to `JBButton`. Now, click the red X and a screen similar to Figure A-6 appears. Eclipse offers several possible corrections; the best one is to fix the misspelling and change it back to `JButton`. Of course, if we'd really meant to refer to a new kind of button, we could choose the option to create the new class right there and Eclipse would help us do that by creating a skeleton for us.

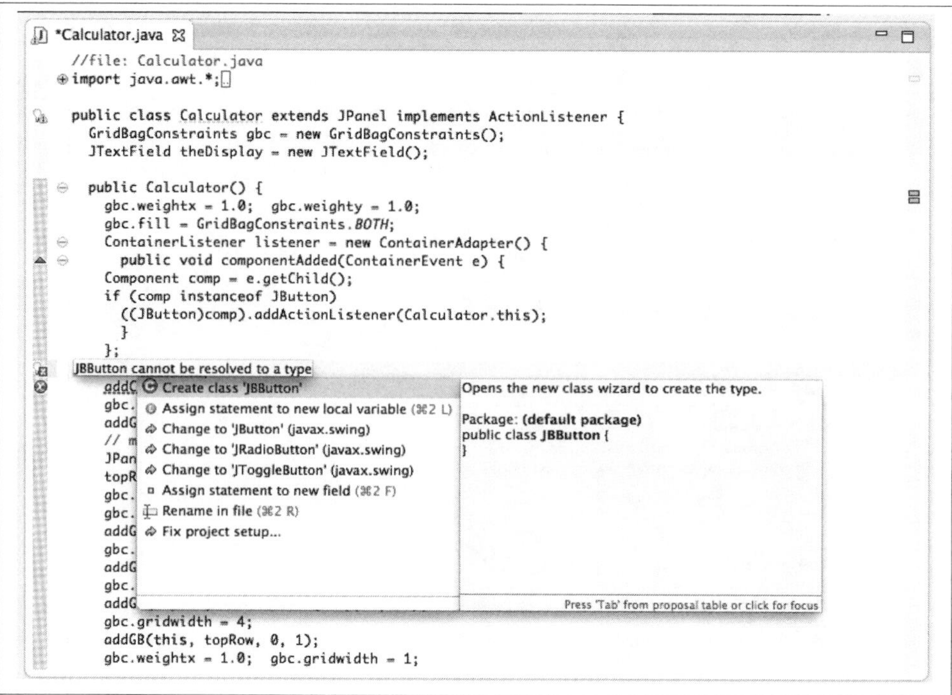

Figure A-6. Autocorrection in Eclipse

Refactoring

Eclipse offers a number of tools under the collective title *refactoring*. These include the ability to rename and move members, automatically tracking down references to them and changing them throughout the project. More advanced options allow you to do things like create an interface for your class by copying all of its public methods or add a factory pattern to your code to encapsulate all object creation for a type. You can even encapsulate access to a variable, changing the code to use an accessor method instead. These tools can save you a lot of typing (or retyping, as the case may be).

As an example, let's look at our Calculator again. Click on the `addGB()` method in the outline or select the method definition yourself. We use this method a lot, so let's give it a better name. Select Refactor → Rename and change the name to `addToGridBag`. If you want to see what it's going to do in advance, press the preview button to get a diff view of the code. By selecting OK, Eclipse changes the name and all references to the method in your project (in this case that would include all of the source directories for all chapters). You can also refactor methods in order to change the method signature and add or remove arguments.

Diffing Files

Eclipse provides the ability to quickly diff two files. Select two files simultaneously in the Package Explorer. Right-click one of the files to display a context menu and select Compare With → Each Other. Eclipse opens a dual-source view editor pane that shows the differences between the files graphically. You can even resolve conflicts by copying differences from one file to the other with the arrows at the top of the pane. For example, open *ch15/webapp-xml/all-web.xml* and *ch15/webapp-xml/filters-web.xml* and view the differences. You can also review changes made to a file using the Compare With → Local History option that lets you compare the current state of the file with previous saves in the project. These are very useful tools.

Organizing Imports

Eclipse can tidy up the `import` statements in your source code. Selecting Source → Organize Imports causes Eclipse to turn package imports into single class imports. Eclipse automatically determines exactly which classes from each package are used and breaks the package imports into individual imports. This makes the code a little more explicit, but some people prefer package imports when too many classes are used.

Formatting Source Code

Eclipse can autoformat your source code using the Source → Format option. This applies standard Java conventions and indentation. The style is highly customizable; choose Window → Preferences → Java → Code Style → Formatter to see the available options.

Conclusion

This appendix provides the briefest of introductions to the sorts of things that you can do in Eclipse and other Java IDEs. Please investigate more on your own to learn about what these tools can do to increase your productivity as a Java developer. You should also compare Eclipse, NetBeans, and others such as Intellij IDEA to see which you prefer. And don't forget to read more about Apache Ant for building Java applications.

APPENDIX B

BeanShell: Java Scripting

In this book, we (in this case, I, Pat) have avoided talking about many third-party tools that aren't part of the standard JDK. I'm going to make an exception here to give a shout out to a nifty, free Java tool called BeanShell. As its name suggests, BeanShell can be used as a Java "shell." It allows you to type standard Java syntax—statements, expressions, and even classes—on the command line or evaluate bits of source code from within your applications. With BeanShell, you can try out bits of code as you work through the book. You can access all Java APIs and even create graphical user interface components and manipulate them "live." BeanShell uses only reflection, so there is no need to compile class files.

I wrote BeanShell while developing the examples for this book, and I think it makes a fun companion to have along on your journey through Java. BeanShell is an open source software project and at the time of this writing is in the process of being adopted by the Apache foundation. You can find the latest updates and more information at its current home (*http://www.beanshell.org*). Over the years, BeanShell has been a popular tool and has been widely used in tools and projects that require scripting. However, today there are probably better options for serious scripting integration with Java. For example, you may wish to look at Jython, an implementation of the Python scripting language, as another option. Many scripting languages can be accessed in a plug-in/ provider fashion using the `java.scripting` API (JSR-223). The JDK 7 is bundled with the Mozilla Rhino implementation of JavaScript, as another option.

Running BeanShell

All you need to run BeanShell is the Java runtime system (version 1.1 or greater) and the *bsh* JAR file. Under Mac OS X and Windows, you can launch a graphical desktop for BeanShell by simply double-clicking the JAR file. More generally, you can add the JAR to your classpath:

```
Unix:     export CLASSPATH=$CLASSPATH:bsh.jar
Windows:  set classpath %classpath%;bsh.jar
```

You can then run BeanShell interactively in either a GUI or command-line mode:

```
java bsh.Console       // run the graphical desktop
java bsh.Interpreter   // run as text-only on the command line
```

Running BeanShell with the GUI console brings up a simple, Swing-based desktop that allows you to open multiple shell windows with basic command history, line editing, and cut-and-paste capability. There are some other GUI tools available as well, including a simple text editor and class browser. Alternately, you can run BeanShell on the command line, in text-only mode.

You can run BeanShell scripts from files, like so:

```
% java bsh.Interpreter myfile.bsh
```

Within some versions of the NetBeans and Sun Java Studio IDEs, you can create BeanShell script files using the New File wizard or run any file with a *.bsh* extension just as you would execute Java code.

Java Statements and Expressions

At the prompt or in a BeanShell script, you can type standard Java statements and expressions. Statements and expressions are all of the normal things that you'd include in a Java method: variable declarations and assignments, method calls, loops, and conditionals. You can declare classes in the usual way if you want to, but BeanShell allows you to write statements outside of a class or method in an unstructured way as well.

You can type statements exactly as they would appear in Java. You also have the option of working in a more scripting-language-like fashion, with "loosely typed" variables and arguments. In other words, you can be lazy and not declare the types of variables that you use (both primitives and objects). BeanShell will still give you an error if you attempt to misuse the actual contents of the variable. If you do declare types of variables or primitives, BeanShell will enforce them.

Here are some examples:

```
foo = "Foo";
four = (2 + 2)*2/2;
print( foo + " = " + four );   // print() is a bsh command
// do a loop
for (i=0; i<5; i++)
    print(i);
// pop up an AWT frame with a button in it
button = new JButton("My Button");
frame = new JFrame("My Frame");
frame.getContentPane().add( button, "Center" );
```

```
frame.pack();
frame.setVisible( true );
```

If you don't like the idea of "loosening" Java syntax at all, you can turn off this feature of BeanShell with the following command:

```
setStrictJava( true );
```

Imports

By default, BeanShell imports all of the core Java packages for you. You can import your own classes using the standard Java import declaration:

```
import mypackage.*;
```

In addition to regular package, class, and static imports, BeanShell can also import the methods and variables of an object instance into the current context using the `importObject()` command. For example:

```
Map map = new HashMap();
importObject( map );
put("foo", "bar");
print( get("foo") ); // "bar"
```

BeanShell Commands

BeanShell comes with a number of useful built-in commands in the form of Java methods. These commands are implemented as BeanShell scripts, and are supplied in the *bsh* JAR file. You can make your own commands by defining methods in your own scripts or adding them to your classpath. See the BeanShell user's manual for more information.

One important BeanShell command is `print()`, which displays values. `print()` does pretty much the same thing as `System.out.println()` except that it ensures the output always goes to the command line (if you have multiple windows open). `print()` also displays some types of objects (such as arrays) more verbosely than Java would. Another very useful command is `show()`, which toggles on and off automatic printing of the result of every line you type. (You can turn this on if you want to see every result value.)

Here are a few other examples of BeanShell commands:

`source()`, `run()`
: Reads a script into this interpreter, or runs it in a new interpreter

`frame()`
: Displays an AWT or Swing component in a frame

`load()`, `save()`
: Loads or saves serializable objects (such as JavaBeans)

`cd()`
`cat()`
`dir()`
`pwd()`
: Unix-like shell commands

`exec()`
: Runs a native application

`addClassPath()`
`reloadClasses()`
: Modifies the classpath or reload classes

`javap()`
: Prints a javap-style class description for the class or object specified

See the BeanShell user's manual for a full list of commands.

Scripted Methods and Objects

You can declare and use methods in BeanShell, just as you would inside a Java class:

```
int addTwoNumbers( int a, int b ) {
    return a + b;
}
sum = addTwoNumbers( 5, 7 );  // 12
```

BeanShell methods may also have dynamic (loose) argument and return types.

```
add( a, b ) {
    return a + b;
}
foo = add(1, 2);                // 3
foo = add("Hello ", "Kitty");   // "Hello Kitty"
```

In BeanShell, as in JavaScript and Perl, method *closures* can take the place of classes for scripting objects (but in BeanShell you can also use the regular class syntax). You can turn the context of a method call into an object reference by having the method return the special value `this`. You can then use the `this` reference to refer to any variables that were set during the method call. To be useful, an object may also need methods; so in BeanShell, methods may also contain methods at any level. Here is a simple example:

```
user( n ) {
    name = n;
    reset() {
        print( "Reset user:"+name );
    }
    return this;  // return user as object
}
bob = user("Bob" );
```

```
print( bob.name ); // "Bob"
bob.reset();      // prints "Reset user: Bob"
```

This example assigns the context of the `user()` method to the variable `bob` and refers to the field `bob.name` and the method `bob.reset()`.

If you find this strange, don't worry. The most common reason you'd want to script an object is to implement a Java interface, and you can do that using the standard Java anonymous inner class syntax, as we'll discuss next, or just use a regular class. BeanShell gives you a lot of options.

Scripting Interfaces and Adapters

One of the most powerful features of BeanShell is that you can "script" any interface type. BeanShell-scripted objects can automatically implement any required interface type. The only thing you need to do is implement the necessary method (or at least the ones that are going to be invoked). You can use this feature either by explicitly referring to a BeanShell script using a `this`-style reference as described earlier, or by using the standard Java anonymous inner class syntax. Here is an example:

```
actionPerformed( event ) { print( event ); }
button = new JButton("Press Me!");
button.addActionListener( this );
frame( button );
```

You can type this code right on the command line and press the button to see the events it generates. In this case, the `this` reference refers to the current context, just as in a method. BeanShell automatically implements the `ActionListener` interface and delegates calls to its `actionPerformed()` method to our scripted method.

Alternately, we could use the anonymous inner class syntax to create an `ActionListener` for our button:

```
button = new JButton("Press Me!");
button.addActionListener( new ActionListener() {
    actionPerformed( event ) { print( event ); }
} );
frame( button );
```

In this case the "anonymous inner class" is actually a BeanShell script that implements the `ActionListener` interface for us in the same way as the previous example.

One more thing: we hinted earlier that you only have to implement those methods of the interface that you want to use. If you don't script a method, it's OK as long as it's not invoked (in which case, you'd get an exception). For convenience in implementing a large interface, you can define the special `invoke()` method, which handles calls to scripted methods that don't exist:

```
invoke( name, args ) { print("Method: "+name+" invoked!"); }
```

This `invoke()` method will handle method calls for methods that are not defined and simply print their names. See the user manual for more details.

Changing the Classpath

Within BeanShell, you can add to your classpath and even reload classes:

```
addClassPath("mystuff.jar");
addClassPath("http://examples.oreilly.com/learnjava3/magicbeans.jar");
```

To reload all classes in the classpath, simply use:

```
reloadClasses();
```

You can do more elaborate things as well, such as reloading individual classes, if you know what you're doing. See the user manual for more details.

Learning More . . .

BeanShell has many more features than I've described here. You can embed BeanShell into your applications as a lightweight scripting engine, passing live Java objects into and out of scripts. You can even run BeanShell in a remote server mode, which lets you work in a shell inside your running application, for debugging and experimentation. There is also a BeanShell servlet that can be used for running scripts inside an application server.

BeanShell is small (only about 200 KB) and it's free, licensed under multiple open source licenses. You can learn more by checking out the full user's manual and FAQ on the website.

Please feel free to send feedback using the book's web page (*http://oreil.ly/Java_4E*). So long until the next edition!

Glossary

abstract

The `abstract` keyword is used to declare abstract methods and classes. An abstract method has no implementation defined; it is declared with arguments and a return type as usual, but the body enclosed in curly braces is replaced with a semicolon. The implementation of an abstract method is provided by a subclass of the class in which it is defined. If an abstract method appears in a class, the class is also abstract.

annotations

Metadata added to Java source code using the @ tag syntax. Annotations can be used by the compiler or at runtime to augment classes, provide data or mappings, or flag additional services.

Ant

A popular, XML-based build tool for Java applications. Ant builds can compile, package, and deploy Java source code as well as generate documentation and perform other activities through pluggable "targets."

API (Application Programming Interface)

An API consists of the methods and variables programmers use to work with a component or tool in their applications. The Java language APIs consist of the classes and methods of the `java.lang`, `java.util`, `java.io`, `java.text`, and `java.net` packages and many others.

applet

An embedded Java application that runs in the context of an applet viewer, such as a web browser.

<applet> tag

An HTML tag that embeds an applet within a web document.

appletviewer

Sun's application that runs and displays Java applets outside of a web browser.

application

A Java program that runs standalone, as compared with an applet.

apt (Annotation Processing Tool)

A frontend for the Java compiler that processes annotations via a pluggable factory architecture, allowing users to implement custom compile-time annotations.

assertion

A language feature used to test for conditions that should be guaranteed by program logic. If a condition checked by an assertion is found to be *false*, a fatal error is thrown. For added performance, assertions can be disabled when an application is deployed.

atomic

Discrete or transactional in the sense that an operation happens as a unit, in an all-or-nothing fashion. Certain operations in the Java virtual machine (VM) and provided by the Java concurrency API are atomic.

AWT (Abstract Window Toolkit)

Java's original platform-independent windowing, graphics, and user interface toolkit.

BeanShell

An open source, lightweight, Java-compatible scripting language that can be used for Java experimentation, teaching, application extension, configuration, and debugging.

Boojum

The mystical, spectral, alter ego of a Snark. From the 1876 Lewis Carroll poem "The Hunting of the Snark."

Boolean

A primitive Java data type that contains a `true` or `false` value.

bounds

In Java generics, a limitation on the type of a type parameter. An upper bound specifies that a type must extend (or is assignable to) a specific Java class. A lower bound is used to indicate that a type must be a supertype of (or is assignable from) the specified type.

boxing

Wrapping of primitive types in Java by their object wrapper types. See also *unboxing*.

byte

A primitive Java data type that's an 8-bit two's-complement signed number.

callback

A behavior that is defined by one object and then later invoked by another object when a particular event occurs. The Java event mechanism is a kind of callback.

cast

The changing of the apparent type of a Java object from one type to another, specified type. Java casts are checked both statically by the Java compiler and at runtime.

catch

The Java `catch` statement introduces an exception-handling block of code following a `try` statement. The `catch` keyword is followed by an exception type and argument name in parentheses and a block of code within curly braces.

certificate

An electronic document using a digital signature to assert the identity of a person, group, or organization. Certificates attest to the identity of a person or group and contain that organization's public key. A certificate is signed by a certificate authority with its digital signature.

certificate authority (CA)

An organization that is entrusted to issue certificates, taking whatever steps are necessary to verify the real-world identity for which it is issuing the certificate.

char

A primitive Java data type; a variable of type `char` holds a single 16-bit Unicode character.

class

1. The fundamental unit that defines an object in most object-oriented programming languages. A class is an encapsulated collection of variables and methods that may have privileged access to one another. Usually a class can be instantiated to produce an object that's an instance of the class, with its own unique set of data.
2. The `class` keyword is used to declare a class, thereby defining a new object type.

classloader

An instance of the class `java.lang.ClassLoader`, which is responsible for loading Java binary classes into the Java VM. Classloaders help partition classes based on their source for both structural and security purposes and can also be chained in a parent-child hierarchy.

class method
: See *static method*.

classpath
: The sequence of path locations specifying directories and archive files containing compiled Java class files and resources, which are searched in order to find components of a Java application.

class variable
: See *static variable*.

client
: The consumer of a resource or the party that initiates a conversation in the case of a networked client/server application. See also *server*.

Collections API
: Classes in the core `java.util` package for working with and sorting structured collections or maps of items. This API includes the `Vector` and `Hashtable` classes as well as newer items such as `List`, `Map`, and `Queue`.

compilation unit
: The unit of source code for a Java class. A compilation unit normally contains a single class definition and in most current development environments is simply a file with a *.java* extension.

compiler
: A program that translates source code into executable code.

component architecture
: A methodology for building parts of an application. It is a way to build reusable objects that can be easily assembled to form applications.

composition
: Combining existing objects to create another, more complex object. When you compose a new object, you create complex behavior by delegating tasks to the internal objects. Composition is different from inheritance, which defines a new object by changing or refining the behavior of an old object. See also *inheritance*.

constructor
: A special method that is invoked automatically when a new instance of a class is created. Constructors are used to initialize the variables of the newly created object. The constructor method has the same name as the class and no explicit return value.

content handler
: A class that is called to parse a particular type of data and that converts it to an appropriate object.

datagram
: A packet of data normally sent using a connectionless protocol such as UDP, which provides no guarantees about delivery or error checking and provides no control information.

data hiding
: See *encapsulation*.

deep copy
: A duplicate of an object along with all of the objects that it references, transitively. A deep copy duplicates the entire "graph" of objects, instead of just duplicating references. See also *shallow copy*.

DOM (Document Object Model)
: An in-memory representation of a fully parsed XML document using objects with names like `Element`, `Attribute`, and `Text`. The Java XML DOM API binding is standardized by the World Wide Web Consortium (W3C).

double
: A Java primitive data type; a `double` value is a 64-bit (double-precision) floating-point number.

DTD (Document Type Definition)
: A document containing specialized language that expresses constraints on the structure of XML tags and tag attributes. DTDs are used to validate an XML document and can constrain the order and

nesting of tags as well as the allowed values of attributes.

EJB (Enterprise JavaBeans)
: A server-side business component architecture named for, but not significantly related to, the JavaBeans component architecture. EJBs represent business services and database components and provide declarative security and transactions.

encapsulation
: The object-oriented programming technique of limiting the exposure of variables and methods to simplify the API of a class or package. Using the private and *protected* keywords, a programmer can limit the exposure of internal ("black box") parts of a class. Encapsulation reduces bugs and promotes reusability and modularity of classes. This technique is also known as *data hiding*.

enum
: The Java keyword for declaring an enumerated type. An enum holds a list of constant object identifiers that can be used as a type-safe alternative to numeric constants that serve as identifiers or labels.

enumeration
: See *enum*.

erasure
: The implementation technique used by Java generics in which generic type information is removed (erased) and distilled to raw Java types at compilation. Erasure provides backward compatibility with non-generic Java code, but introduces some difficulties in the language.

event
: 1. A user's action, such as a mouse-click or keypress.
  2. The Java object delivered to a registered event listener in response to a user action or other activity in the system.

exception
: A signal that some unexpected condition has occurred in the program. In Java, exceptions are objects that are subclasses of `Exception` or `Error`(which themselves are subclasses of `Throwable`). Exceptions in Java are "raised" with the `throw` keyword and handled with the `catch` keyword. See also *catch*, *throw*, and *throws*.

exception chaining
: The design pattern of catching an exception and throwing a new, higher-level, or more appropriate exception that contains the underlying exception as its *cause*. The "cause" exception can be retrieved if necessary.

extends
: A keyword used in a `class` declaration to specify the superclass of the class being defined. The class being defined has access to all the `public` and `protected` variables and methods of the superclass (or, if the class being defined is in the same package, it has access to all `nonprivate` variables and methods). If a class definition omits the `extends` clause, its superclass is taken to be `java.lang.Object`.

final
: A keyword modifier that may be applied to classes, methods, and variables. It has a similar, but not identical, meaning in each case. When `final` is applied to a class, it means that the class may never be subclassed. `java.lang.System` is an example of a `final` class. When `final` is applied to a variable, the variable is a constant—that is, it can't be modified.

finalize
: A reserved method name. The `finalize()` method is called by the Java VM when an object is no longer being used (i.e., when there are no further references to it) but before the object's memory is actually reclaimed by the system. A finalizer should perform cleanup tasks and free system resources before the object is discarded by Java's garbage collection system.

finally
: A keyword that introduces the `finally` block of a `try/catch/finally` construct. `catch` and `finally` blocks provide

exception handling and routine cleanup for code in a `try` block. The `finally` block is optional and appears after the `try` block, and after zero or more `catch` blocks. The code in a `finally` block is executed once, regardless of how the code in the try block executes. In normal execution, control reaches the end of the `try` block and proceeds to the `finally` block, which generally performs any necessary cleanup.

float
: A Java primitive data type; a `float` value is a 32-bit (single-precision) floating-point number represented in IEEE 754 format.

garbage collection
: The process of reclaiming the memory of objects no longer in use. An object is no longer in use when there are no references to it from other objects in the system and no references in any local variables on the method call stack.

generics
: The syntax and implementation of parameterized types in the Java language, added in Java 5.0. Generic types are Java classes that are parameterized by the user on one or more additional Java types to specialize the behavior of the class. Generics are sometimes referred to as *templates* in other languages.

generic class
: A class that uses the Java generics syntax and is parameterized by one or more type variables, which represent class types to be substituted by the user of the class. Generic classes are particularly useful for container objects and collections that can be specialized to operate on a specific type of element.

generic method
: A method that uses the Java generics syntax and has one or more arguments or return types that refer to type variables representing the actual type of data element the method will use. The Java compiler can often infer the types of the type variables from the usage context of the method.

graphics context
: A drawable surface represented by the `java.awt.Graphics` class. A graphics context contains contextual information about the drawing area and provides methods for performing drawing operations in it.

GUI (graphical user interface)
: A traditional, visual user interface consisting of a window containing graphical items such as buttons, text fields, pull-down menus, dialog boxes, and other standard interface components.

hashcode
: A random-looking identifying number, based on the data content of an object, used as a kind of signature for the object. A hashcode is used to store an object in a hash table (or hash map). See also *hash table*.

hash table
: An object that is like a dictionary or an associative array. A hash table stores and retrieves elements using key values called hashcodes. See also *hashcode*.

hostname
: The human-readable name given to an individual computer attached to the Internet.

HotJava
: An early web browser written in Java, capable of downloading and running Java applets.

HTTP (Hypertext Transfer Protocol)
: The protocol used by web browsers or other clients to talk to web servers. The simplest form of the protocol uses the commands `GET` to request a file and POST to send data.

IDE (Integrated Development Environment)
: A GUI tool such as NetBeans or Eclipse that provides source editing, compiling, running, debugging, and deployment functionality for developing Java applications.

implements
: A keyword used in class declarations to indicate that the class implements the named interface or interfaces. The `implements` clause is optional in class declarations; if it

appears, it must follow the `extends` clause (if any). If an implements clause appears in the declaration of a non-`abstract` class, every method from each specified interface must be implemented by the class or by one of its superclasses.

import
: The `import` statement makes Java classes available to the current class under an abbreviated name or disambiguates classes imported in bulk by other `import` statements. (Java classes are always available by their fully qualified name, assuming the appropriate class file can be found relative to the `CLASSPATH` environment variable and that the class file is readable. `import` doesn't make the class available; it just saves typing and makes your code more legible.) Any number of `import` statements may appear in a Java program. They must appear, however, after the optional `package` statement at the top of the file, and before the first class or interface definition in the file.

inheritance
: An important feature of object-oriented programming that involves defining a new object by changing or refining the behavior of an existing object. Through inheritance, an object implicitly contains all of the non-`private` variables and methods of its superclass. Java supports single inheritance of classes and multiple inheritance of interfaces.

inner class
: A class definition that is nested within another class or a method. An inner class functions within the lexical scope of another class.

instance
: An occurrence of something, usually an object. When a class is instantiated to produce an object, we say the object is an *instance* of the class.

instance method
: A non-`static` method of a class. Such a method is passed an implicit `this` reference to the object that invoked it. See also *static*; *static method.*

instanceof
: A Java operator that returns `true` if the object on its left side is an instance of the class (or implements the interface) specified on its right side. `instanceof` returns `false` if the object isn't an instance of the specified class or doesn't implement the specified interface. It also returns `false` if the specified object is `null`.

instance variable
: A non-`static` variable of a class. Each instance of a class has an independent copy of all of the instance variables of the class. See also *class variable*; *static*.

int
: A primitive Java data type that's a 32-bit two's-complement signed number.

interface
: 1. A keyword used to declare an interface.
  2. A collection of abstract methods that collectively define a type in the Java language. Classes implementing the methods may declare that they implement the interface type and instances of them may be treated as that type.

internationalization
: The process of making an application accessible to people who speak a variety of languages. Sometimes abbreviated I18N.

interpreter
: The module that decodes and executes Java bytecode. Most Java bytecode is not, strictly speaking, interpreted any longer but compiled to native code dynamically by the Java VM.

introspection
: The process by which a JavaBean provides additional information about itself, supplementing information learned by reflection.

ISO 8859-1
: An 8-bit character encoding standardized by the ISO. This encoding is also known as Latin-1 and contains characters from the Latin alphabet suitable for English and most languages of western Europe.

JavaBeans
: A component architecture for Java. It is a way to build interoperable Java objects that can be manipulated easily in a visual application builder environment.

Java beans
: Java classes that are built following the JavaBeans design patterns and conventions.

JavaScript
: A language developed early in the history of the Web by Netscape for creating dynamic web pages. From a programmer's point of view, it's unrelated to Java, although some of its syntax is similar.

JAXB (Java API for XML Binding)
: A Java API that allows for generation of Java classes from XML DTD or Schema descriptions and the generation of XML from Java classes.

JAXP (Java API for XML Parsers)
: The Java API that allows for pluggable implementations of XML and XSL engines. This API provides an implementation-neutral way to construct parsers and transforms.

JAX-RPC
: The Java API for XML Remote Procedure Calls, used by web services.

JDBC (Java Database Connectivity)
: The standard Java API for talking to an SQL (Structured Query Language) database.

JDOM
: A native Java XML DOM created by Jason Hunter and Brett McLaughlin. JDOM is easier to use than the standard DOM API for Java. It uses the Java collections API and standard Java conventions. Available at *http://www.jdom.org/*.

JWSDP (Java Web Services Developer Pack)
: A bundle of standard extension APIs packaged as a group with an installer from Sun. The JWSDP includes JAXB, JAX-RPC, and other XML and web services-related packages.

Latin-1
: A nickname for ISO 8859-1.

layout manager
: An object that controls the arrangement of components within the display area of a Swing or AWT container.

lightweight component
: A pure Java GUI component that has no native peer in the AWT.

local variable
: A variable that is declared inside a method. A local variable can be seen only by code within that method.

Logging API
: The Java API for structured logging and reporting of messages from within application components. The Logging API supports logging levels indicating the importance of messages, as well as filtering and output capabilities.

long
: A primitive Java data type that's a 64-bit two's-complement signed number.

message digest
: A cryptographically computed number based on the content of a message, used to determine whether the message's contents have been changed in any way. A change to a message's contents will change its message digest. When implemented properly, it is almost impossible to create two similar messages with the same digest.

method
: The object-oriented programming term for a function or procedure.

method overloading
: Provides definitions of more than one method with the same name but with

different argument lists. When an overloaded method is called, the compiler determines which one is intended by examining the supplied argument types.

method overriding
: Defines a method that matches the name and argument types of a method defined in a superclass. When an overridden method is invoked, the interpreter uses *dynamic method lookup* to determine which method definition is applicable to the current object. Beginning in Java 5.0, overridden methods can have different return types, with restrictions.

Model-View-Controller (MVC) framework
: A user interface design that originated in Smalltalk. In MVC, the data for a display item is called the *model*. A *view* displays a particular representation of the model, and a *controller* provides user interaction with both. Java incorporates many MVC concepts.

modifier
: A keyword placed before a class, variable, or method that alters the item's accessibility, behavior, or semantics. See also *abstract*; *final*; *native method*; *private*; *protected*; *public*; *static*; *synchronized*.

NaN (not-a-number)
: This is a special value of the `double` and `float` data types that represents an undefined result of a mathematical operation, such as zero divided by zero.

native method
: A method that is implemented in a native language on a host platform, rather than being implemented in Java. Native methods provide access to such resources as the network, the windowing system, and the host filesystem.

new
: A unary operator that creates a new object or array (or raises an *OutOfMemoryException* if there is not enough memory available).

NIO
: The Java "new" I/O package. A core package introduced in Java 1.4 to support asynchronous, interruptible, and scalable I/O operations. The NIO API supports nonthreadbound "select" style I/O handling.

null
: `null` is a special value that indicates that a reference-type variable doesn't refer to any object instance. Static and instance variables of classes default to the value `null` if not otherwise assigned.

object
: 1. The fundamental structural unit of an object-oriented programming language, encapsulating a set of data and behavior that operates on that data.
  2. An instance of a class, having the structure of the class but its own copy of data elements. See also *instance*.

<object> tag
: An HTML tag used to embed media objects and applications into web browsers like the `<applet>` tag.

package
: The `package` statement specifies the Java package for a Java class. Java code that is part of a particular package has access to all classes (`public` and non-`public`) in the package, and all non-`private` methods and fields in all those classes. When Java code is part of a named package, the compiled class file must be placed at the appropriate position in the `CLASSPATH` directory hierarchy before it can be accessed by the Java interpreter or other utilities. If the *package* statement is omitted from a file, the code in that file is part of an unnamed default package. This is convenient for small test programs run from the command line, or during development because it means that the code can be interpreted from the current directory.

<param> tag
: An HTML tag used within `<applet> ... </applet>` to specify a named parameter

and string value to an applet within a web page.

parameterized type
: A class, using Java generics syntax, that is dependent on one or more types to be specified by the user. The user-supplied parameter types fill in type values in the class and adapt it for use with the specified types.

plug-in
: A modular application component for a web browser designed to extend the browser's capabilities to handle a specific type of data (MIME type). The Java Plug-in supports Java applets in browsers that do not have up-to-date Java runtime support.

polymorphism
: One of the fundamental principles of an object-oriented language. Polymorphism states that a type that extends another type is a "kind of" the parent type and can be used interchangeably with the original type by augmenting or refining its capabilities.

Preferences API
: The Java API for storing small amounts of information on a per-user or systemwide basis across executions of the Java VM. The Preferences API is analogous to a small database or the Windows registry.

primitive type
: One of the Java data types: `boolean`, `char`, `byte`, `short`, `int`, `long`, `float`, `double`. Primitive types are manipulated, assigned, and passed to methods "by value" (i.e., the actual bytes of the data are copied). See also *reference type*.

printf
: A style of text formatting originating in the C language, relying on an embedded identifier syntax and variable-length argument lists to supply parameters.

private
: The `private` keyword is a visibility modifier that can be applied to method and field variables of classes. A private method or field is not visible outside its class definition and cannot be accessed by subclasses.

protected
: A keyword that is a visibility modifier; it can be applied to method and field variables of classes. A `protected` field is visible only within its class, within subclasses, and within the package of which its class is a part. Note that subclasses in different packages can access only `protected` fields within themselves or within other objects that are subclasses; they cannot access protected fields within instances of the superclass.

protocol handler
: A URL component that implements the network connection required to access a resource for a type of URL scheme (such as HTTP or FTP). A Java protocol handler consists of two classes: a `StreamHandler` and a `URLConnection`.

public
: A keyword that is a visibility modifier; it can be applied to classes and interfaces and to the method and field variables of classes and interfaces. A `public` class or interface is visible everywhere. A non-`public` class or interface is visible only within its package. A `public` method or variable is visible everywhere its class is visible. When none of the `private`, `protected`, or `public` modifiers are specified, a field is visible only within the package of which its class is a part.

public-key cryptography
: A cryptographic system that requires public and private keys. The private key can decrypt messages encrypted with the corresponding public key, and vice versa. The public key can be made available to the public without compromising security and used to verify that messages sent by the holder of the private key must be genuine.

queue
: A list-like data structure normally used in a first in, first out fashion to buffer work items.

raw type
: In Java generics, the plain Java type of a class without any generic type parameter

information. This is the true type of all Java classes after they are compiled. See also *erasure*.

reference type
: Any object or array. Reference types are manipulated, assigned, and passed to methods "by reference." In other words, the underlying value is not copied; only a reference to it is. See also *primitive type*.

reflection
: The ability of a programming language to interact with structures of the language itself at runtime. Reflection in Java allows a Java program to examine class files at runtime to find out about their methods and variables, and to invoke methods or modify variables dynamically.

regular expression
: A compact yet powerful syntax for describing a pattern in text. Regular expressions can be used to recognize and parse most kinds of textual constructs, allowing for wide variation in their form.

Regular Expression API
: The core `java.util.regex` package for using regular expressions. The regex package can be used to search and replace text based on sophisticated patterns.

Remote Method Invocation (RMI)
: RMI is a native Java distributed object system. With RMI, you can pass references to objects on remote hosts and invoke methods in them as if they were local objects.

SAX (Simple API for XML)
: SAX is an event-driven API for parsing XML documents in which the client receives events in response to activities such as the opening of tags, character data, and the closing of tags.

Schema
: XML Schemas are a replacement for DTDs. Introduced by the W3C, XML Schema is an XML-based language for expressing constraints on the structure of XML tags and tag attributes, as well as the structure and type of the data content. Other types of XML schema languages have different syntaxes.

SDK (Software Development Kit)
: A package of software distributed by Sun Microsystems for Java developers. It includes the Java interpreter, Java classes, and Java development tools: compiler, debugger, disassembler, applet viewer, stub file generator, and documentation generator. Also called the JDK.

SecurityManager
: The Java class that defines the methods the system calls to check whether a certain operation is permitted in the current environment.

serialize
: To serialize means to put in order or make sequential. A serialized object is an object that has been packaged so that it can be stored or transmitted over the network. Serialized methods are methods that have been synchronized with respect to threads so that only one may be executing at a given time.

server
: The party that provides a resource or accepts a request for a conversation in the case of a networked client/server application. See also *client*.

servlet
: A Java application component that implements the `javax.servlet.Servlet` API, allowing it to run inside a servlet container or web server. Servlets are widely used in web applications to process user data and generate HTML or other forms of output.

servlet context
: In the Servlet API, this is the web application environment of a servlet that provides server and application resources. The base URL path of the web application is also often referred to as the servlet context.

shadow
: To declare a variable with the same name as a variable defined in a superclass. We say the variable "shadows" the superclass's

variable. Use the `super` keyword to refer to the shadowed variable or refer to it by casting the object to the type of the superclass.

shallow copy
: A copy of an object that duplicates only values contained in the object itself. References to other objects are repeated as references and are not duplicated themselves. See also *deep copy*.

short
: A primitive Java data type that's a 16-bit two's-complement signed number.

signature
: 1. Referring to a digital signature. A combination of a message's message digest, encrypted with the signer's private key, and the signer's certificate, attesting to the signer's identity. Someone receiving a signed message can get the signer's public key from the certificate, decrypt the encrypted message digest, and compare that result with the message digest computed from the signed message. If the two message digests agree, the recipient knows that the message has not been modified and that the signer is who he or she claims to be.
  2. Referring to a Java method. The method name and argument types and possibly return type, collectively uniquely identifying the method in some context.

signed applet
: An applet packaged in a JAR file signed with a digital signature, allowing for authentication of its origin and validation of the integrity of its contents.

signed class
: A Java class (or Java archive) that has a signature attached. The signature allows the recipient to verify the class's origin and that it is unmodified. The recipient can therefore grant the class greater runtime privileges.

sockets
: A networking API originating in BSD Unix. A pair of sockets provide the endpoints for communication between two parties on the network. A server socket listens for connections from clients and creates individual server-side sockets for each conversation.

spinner
: A GUI component that displays a value and a pair of small up and down buttons that increment or decrement the value. The Swing `JSpinner` can work with number ranges and dates as well as arbitrary enumerations.

static
: A keyword that is a modifier applied to method and variable declarations within a class. A `static` variable is also known as a class variable as opposed to nonstatic instance variables. While each instance of a class has a full set of its own instance variables, there is only one copy of each *static* class variable, regardless of the number of instances of the class (perhaps zero) that are created. `static` variables may be accessed by class name or through an instance. Non-`static` variables can be accessed only through an instance.

static import
: A statement, similar to the class and package import, that imports the names of static methods and variables of a class into a class scope. The static import is a convenience that provides the effect of global methods and constants.

static method
: A method declared *static*. Methods of this type are not passed implicit `this` references and may refer only to class variables and invoke other class methods of the current class. A class method may be invoked through the class name, rather than through an instance of the class.

static variable
: A variable declared *static*. Variables of this type are associated with the class, rather than with a particular instance of the class.

There is only one copy of a static variable, regardless of the number of instances of the class that are created.

stream
: A flow of data, or a channel of communication. All fundamental I/O in Java is based on streams. The NIO package uses channels, which are packet oriented.

String
: A sequence of character data and the Java class used to represent this kind of character data. The `String` class includes many methods for operating on string objects.

subclass
: A class that extends another. The subclass inherits the `public` and `protected` methods and variables of its superclass. See also *extends*.

super
: A keyword used by a class to refer to variables and methods of its parent class. The special reference `super` is used in the same way as the special reference `this` is used to qualify references to the current object context.

superclass
: A parent class, extended by some other class. The superclass's `public` and `protected` methods and variables are available to the subclass. See also *extends*.

synchronized
: A keyword used in two related ways in Java: as a modifier and as a statement. First, it is a modifier applied to class or instance methods. It indicates that the method modifies the internal state of the class or the internal state of an instance of the class in a way that is not threadsafe. Before running a `synchronized` class method, Java obtains a lock on the class to ensure that no other threads can modify the class concurrently. Before running a `synchronized` instance method, Java obtains a lock on the instance that invoked the method, ensuring that no other threads can modify the object at the same time.

  Java also supports a `synchronized` statement that serves to specify a "critical section" of code. The `synchronized` keyword is followed by an expression in parentheses and a statement or block of statements. The expression must evaluate to an object or array. Java obtains a lock on the specified object or array before executing the statements.

TCP (Transmission Control Protocol)
: A connection-oriented, reliable protocol. One of the protocols on which the Internet is based.

this
: Within an instance method or constructor of a class, `this` refers to "this object"— the instance currently being operated on. It is useful to refer to an instance variable of the class that has been shadowed by a local variable or method argument. It is also useful to pass the current object as an argument to static methods or methods of other classes. There is one additional use of `this`: when it appears as the first statement in a constructor method, it refers to one of the other constructors of the class.

thread
: An independent stream of execution within a program. Because Java is a multithreaded programming language, more than one thread may be running within the Java interpreter at a time. Threads in Java are represented and controlled through the `Thread` object.

thread pool
: A group of "recyclable" threads used to service work requests. A thread is allocated to handle one item and then returned to the pool.

throw
: The `throw` statement signals that an exceptional condition has occurred by throwing a specified `Throwable` (exception) object. This statement stops program execution and passes it to the nearest containing `catch` statement that can handle the specified exception object.

throws

The `throws` keyword is used in a method declaration to list the exceptions the method can throw. Any exceptions a method can raise that are not subclasses of `Error` or `RuntimeException` must either be caught within the method or declared in the method's `throws` clause.

try

The `try` keyword indicates a guarded block of code to which subsequent catch and `finally` clauses apply. The `try` statement itself performs no special action. See also *catch* and *finally* for more information on the `try/catch/finally` construct.

type instantiation

In Java generics, the point at which a generic type is applied by supplying actual or wildcard types as its type parameters. A generic type is instantiated by the user of the type, effectively creating a new type in the Java language specialized for the parameter types.

type invocation

See *type instantiation*. The term *type invocation* is sometimes used by analogy with the syntax of method invocation.

UDP (User Datagram Protocol)

A connectionless unreliable protocol. UDP describes a network data connection based on datagrams with little packet control.

unboxing

Unwrapping a primitive value that is held in its object wrapper type and retrieving the value as a primitive.

Unicode

A universal standard for text character encoding, accommodating the written forms of almost all languages. Unicode is standardized by the Unicode Consortium. Java uses Unicode for its `char` and `String` types.

UTF-8 (UCS transformation format 8-bit form)

An encoding for Unicode characters (and more generally, UCS characters) commonly used for transmission and storage. It is a multibyte format in which different characters require different numbers of bytes to be represented.

variable-length argument list

A method in Java may indicate that it can accept any number of a specified type of argument after its initial fixed list of arguments. The arguments are handled by packaging them as an array.

varargs

See *variable-length argument list*.

vector

A dynamic array of elements.

verifier

A kind of theorem prover that steps through the Java bytecode before it is run and makes sure that it is well behaved and does not violate the Java security model. The bytecode verifier is the first line of defense in Java's security model.

WAR file (Web Applications Resources file)

A JAR file with additional structure to hold classes and resources for web applications. A WAR file includes a *WEB-INF* directory for classes, libraries, and the *web.xml* deployment file.

web application

An application that runs on a web server or application server, normally using a web browser as a client.

web service

An application-level service that runs on a server and is accessed in a standard way using XML for data marshalling and HTTP as its network transport.

wildcard type

In Java generics, a "*" syntax used in lieu of an actual parameter type for type instantiation to indicate that the generic type represents a set or supertype of many concrete type instantiations.

XInclude

An XML standard and Java API for inclusion of XML documents.

XML (Extensible Markup Language)
: A universal markup language for text and data, using nested *tags* to add structure and meta-information to the content.

XPath
: An XML standard and Java API for matching elements and attributes in XML using a hierarchical, regex-like expression language.

XSL/XSLT (Extensible Stylesheet Language/XSLTransformations)
: An XML-based language for describing styling and transformation of XML documents. Styling involves simple addition of markup, usually for presentation. XSLT allows complete restructuring of documents, in addition to styling.

Index

Symbols

We'd like to hear your suggestions for improving our indexes. Send email to index@oreilly.com.

A

B

C

D

E

F

H

I

J

K

M

N

O

P

Q

R

S

T

U

V

W

Y

Z

About the Authors

Patrick Niemeyer became involved with Oak (Java's predecessor) while working at Southwestern Bell Technology Resources. He is the CTO of Ikayzo, Inc., and an independent consultant and author. Pat is the creator of BeanShell, a popular Java scripting language. He has served as a member of several JCP expert groups that guided features of the Java language and is a contributor to many open source projects. Most recently, Pat has been developing analytics software for the financial industry as well as advanced mobile applications. He currently lives in St. Louis with his family and various creatures.

Dan Leuck is the CEO of Ikayzo, Inc., a Tokyo- and Honolulu-based interactive design and software development firm with customers that include Sony, Oracle, Nomura, PIMCO, and the federal government. He previously served as Senior Vice President of Research and Development for Tokyo-based ValueCommerce, Asia's largest online marketing company; Global Head of Development for London-based LastMinute.com, Europe's largest B2C website; and President of the US division of DML. Dan has extensive experience managing teams of 150-plus developers in five countries. He has served on numerous advisory boards and panels for companies such as Macromedia and Sun Microsystems. Dan is active in the Java community, is a contributor to BeanShell and the project lead for SDL, and sits on numerous Java Community Process expert groups.

Colophon

The animals on the cover of *Learning Java*, Fourth Edition are a Bengal tigress and her cubs. The Bengal tiger (*Panthera tigris*) lives in Southern Asia. It has been hunted practically to extinction, principally for its bone, which is reputed to have medicinal value. It now lives mostly in natural preserves and national parks, where it is strictly protected. It's estimated that there are fewer than 3,000 Bengal tigers left in the wild.

The Bengal tiger is reddish orange with narrow black, gray, or brown stripes, generally in a vertical direction. Males can grow to nine feet long and weigh as much as 500 pounds; they are the largest existing members of the cat family. Preferred habitats include dense thickets, long grass, or tamarisk shrubs along river banks. Maximum longevity can be 26 years but is usually only about 15 years in the wild.

Tigers most commonly conceive after the monsoon rains; the majority of cubs are born between February and May after a gestation of three and a half months. Females bear single litters every two to three years. Cubs weigh under three pounds at birth and are striped. Litters consist of one to four cubs, with occasionally as many as six, but it's unusual for more than two or three to survive. Cubs are weaned at four to six months but depend on their mother for food and protection for another two years. Female tigers are mature at three to four years, males at four to five years.

Their white ear spots may help mothers and cubs to keep track of each other in the dim forests at night.

The cover image is an original engraving from the book *Forest and Jungle: An Illustrated History of the Animal Kingdom* by P.T. Barnum (1899). The cover font is Adobe ITC Garamond. The text font is Adobe Minion Pro; the heading font is Adobe Myriad Condensed; and the code font is Dalton Maag's Ubuntu Mono.